REA

ALLEN COUNTY PUBLIC LIBRARY
3 1833 05283 5706

FRIENDS
OF ACPL

D0087040

AUG 15 2007

Great Lives from History

The 19th Century

1801-1900

Great Lives from History

The 19th Century

1801-1900

Volume 1

Abdelkader - Porfirio Díaz

Editor
John Powell
Oklahoma Baptist University

Editor, First Edition
Frank N. Magill

SALEM PRESS
Pasadena, California Hackensack, New Jersey

Editor in Chief: Dawn P. Dawson
Editorial Director: Christina J. Moose
Acquisitions Editor: Mark Rehn
Research Supervisor: Jeffry Jensen
Research Assistant: Rebecca Kuzins
Manuscript Editor: R. Kent Rasmussen
Indexer: Rowena Wildin Dehanke
Production Editor: Andrea E. Miller
Graphics and Design: James Hutson
Layout: Eddie Murillo
Photo Editor: Cynthia Breslin Beres
Editorial Assistant: Dana Garey

Cover photos: The Granger Collection, New York (Pictured left to right, top to bottom: Sitting Bull, Charles Darwin, Liliuokalani, Louisa May Alcott, Ludwig van Beethoven, Saʿīd ibn Sulṭān, Simón Bolívar, Cixi, Mark Twain)

Copyright © 2007, by Salem Press, Inc.
All rights in this book are reserved. No part of this work may be used or reproduced in any manner whatsoever or transmitted in any form or by any means, electronic or mechanical, including photocopy, recording, or any information storage and retrieval system, without written permission from the copyright owner except in the case of brief quotations embodied in critical articles and reviews. For information address the publisher, Salem Press, Inc., P.O. Box 50062, Pasadena, California 91115.

∞ The paper used in these volumes conforms to the American National Standard for Permanence of Paper for Printed Library Materials, Z39.48-1992 (R1997).

Some of the essays in this work originally appeared in the following Salem Press sets: *Dictionary of World Biography* (© 1998-1999, edited by Frank N. Magill) and *Great Lives from History* (© 1987-1995, edited by Frank N. Magill). New material has been added.

Library of Congress Cataloging-in-Publication Data

Great lives from history. The 19th century, 1801-1900 / editor, John Powell.
p. cm.
"Editor, first edition, Frank N. Magill."
Some of the essays in this work were originally published in Dictionary of world biography and the series of works collectively titled, Great lives from history, both edited by Frank N. Magill; with new material added.
Includes bibliographical references and index.
ISBN-13: 978-1-58765-292-9 (set : alk. paper)
ISBN-10: 1-58765-292-7 (set : alk. paper)
ISBN-13: 978-1-58765-293-6 (v. 1 : alk. paper)
ISBN-10: 1-58765-293-5 (v. 1 : alk. paper)
[etc.]
1. Biography—19th century. I. Powell, John, 1954- II. Magill, Frank Northen, 1907-1997 III. Dictionary of world biography. IV. Great lives from history. V. Title: 19th century, 1801-1900. VI. Title: Nineteenth century, 1801-1900.
CT119.G69 2006
920.009′034—dc22

2006020187

First Printing

PRINTED IN THE UNITED STATES OF AMERICA

Contents

Publisher's Note ix
Contributors. xiii
Key to Pronunciation xxiii
Complete List of Contents xxv
List of Maps and Sidebars xxxv
Maps of the Nineteenth Century xlv

Abdelkader 1
Muḥammad ʿAbduh 4
Abdülhamid II 7
Niels Henrik Abel. 9
Lord Acton. 12
Henry Adams 16
John Quincy Adams 20
Felix Adler 26
Elizabeth Cabot Agassiz 29
Louis Agassiz 31
Sir Sayyid Ahmad Khan. 35
Bronson Alcott 38
Louisa May Alcott. 41
Alexander I 45
Alexander II 48
Horatio Alger 51
Ali Paşa Tepelenë 55
John Peter Altgeld 57
Hans Christian Andersen 61
Susan B. Anthony 65
Johnny Appleseed 68
Matthew Arnold 71
Thomas Arnold 76
Chester A. Arthur 79
Luise Aston 83
John Jacob Astor 86
Hubertine Auclert 89
John James Audubon 91
Jane Austen 94
Stephen Fuller Austin 98
Amedeo Avogadro 101

The Bāb 105
Charles Babbage 107
Sir Robert Stephenson Smyth
Baden-Powell 110
Karl Ernst von Baer 114
Bahāʾullāh 117
Mikhail Bakunin 119
Robert Baldwin 122
Honoré de Balzac 126
George Bancroft 130
Henry Barnard 135
P. T. Barnum 138
Sir Charles Barry 142
Clara Barton 145
Sir Edmund Barton 149
Charles Baudelaire 152
L. Frank Baum 155
Dorothea Beale 159
Aubrey Beardsley 162
The Becquerel Family 165
Catharine Beecher 168
Henry Ward Beecher 172
Ludwig van Beethoven. 175
Emil von Behring 179
Alexander Graham Bell 182
Muḥammad Bello 186
James Gordon Bennett 188
Thomas Hart Benton 192
Carl Benz. 197
Hector Berlioz 200
Claude Bernard. 205
Sarah Bernhardt 208
Annie Besant 211
Friedrich Wilhelm Bessel 215
Sir Henry Bessemer 218
Friedrich von Beust 222
Nicholas Biddle 225
Ambrose Bierce 228
Albert Bierstadt 232
George Caleb Bingham 234
Otto von Bismarck 238
Georges Bizet 241
Black Hawk 244
Elizabeth Blackwell 247
James G. Blaine 251
Louis Blanc 254
Amelia Bloomer 257
Gebhard Leberecht von Blücher 260
Barbara Leigh Smith Bodichon 263
Marie Anne Victorine Boivin 265
Simón Bolívar 267
Edwin Booth 271
William Booth 274

Lizzie Borden 277
Aleksandr Borodin 280
Mary Elizabeth Braddon 284
F. H. Bradley 288
Mathew B. Brady 291
Johannes Brahms 296
Louis Braille 299
John Bright 302
Sir Isaac Brock 306
The Brontë Sisters 308
Henry Brougham 312
George Brown 316
John Brown 319
Olympia Brown 323
Elizabeth Barrett Browning 326
Anton Bruckner 329
Isambard Kingdom Brunel 333
Marc Isambard Brunel 337
William Cullen Bryant 340
James Buchanan 343
Charles Bulfinch 346
Luther Burbank 350
Jacob Burckhardt 354
Frances Hodgson Burnett 357
Daniel Hudson Burnham 360
Aaron Burr 363
Sir Richard Francis Burton 368
Josephine Butler 371
Samuel Butler 374
Sir Thomas Fowell Buxton 376
Lord Byron 379

Frances Xavier Cabrini 383
Calamity Jane 386
Fanny Calderón de la Barca 389
John C. Calhoun 392
Jean-Jacques-Régis de Cambacérès 396
Alexander Campbell 399
George Canning 403
Antonio Canova 406
William Carey 409
Don Carlos 412
Thomas Carlyle 415
Andrew Carnegie 419
Lewis Carroll 423
Kit Carson 426
Mary Ann Shadd Cary 431
Mary Cassatt 433
Viscount Castlereagh 437
George Catlin 441
Count Cavour 444
George Cayley 447
Cetshwayo 450
Paul Cézanne 453
Edwin Chadwick 456
Joseph Chamberlain 460
William Ellery Channing 464
Charles XIV John 468
Salmon P. Chase 470
François-René de Chateaubriand 474
Anton Chekhov 478
Lydia Maria Child 482
Frédéric Chopin 486
Kate Chopin 490
Henri Christophe 494
Cixi 496
Carl von Clausewitz 499
Henry Clay 502
Grover Cleveland 507
DeWitt Clinton 512
William Cobbett 517
Richard Cobden 520
William Cody 524
Ferdinand Julius Cohn 527
Samuel Taylor Coleridge 529
Samuel Colt 533
Auguste Comte 536
John Constable 540
Jay Cooke 544
William Fothergill Cooke and
Charles Wheatstone 547
James Fenimore Cooper 552
Carolina Coronado 556
Gustave Courbet 559
Stephen Crane 562
Crazy Horse 566
David Crockett 571
Samuel Ajayi Crowther 574
Paul Cuffe 576
Caleb Cushing 578
George A. Custer 582
Georges Cuvier 585

Jacques Daguerre 589
Gottlieb Daimler 592
First Marquis of Dalhousie 595
John Dalton 597
Rubén Darío 601
Charles Darwin 603
Jacques-Louis David 607

Jefferson Davis 610
Sir Humphry Davy 616
Ferenc Deák 619
Alfred Deakin 623
Stephen Decatur 626
Richard Dedekind 629
Edgar Degas 632
Eugène Delacroix 635
Léo Delibes 639
Fourteenth Earl of Derby 642
George Dewey 645
Melvil Dewey 649
Porfirio Díaz 652

PUBLISHER'S NOTE

Great Lives from History: The Nineteenth Century, 1801-1900 is the sixth installment in the revised and expanded *Great Lives* series, initiated in 2004 with *The Ancient World, Prehistory-476 C.E.* (2 vols.) and followed in 2005 by *The Middle Ages, 477-1453* (2 vols.) and *The Renaissance and Early Modern Era, 1454-1600* (2 vols.) and in 2006 by *The Seventeenth Century, 1601-1700* (2 vols.) and *The Eighteenth Century, 1701-1800* (2 vols.). It will be joined in 2008 by more than 1,300 additional biographies in *Great Lives from History: The Twentieth Century*. The entire series, when complete, will cover more than 3,300 lives, with 900 essays (27 percent) appearing for the first time.

EXPANDED COVERAGE

This ongoing series is a revision of the 10-volume *Dictionary of World Biography* (*DWB*) series (1998-1999). The expanded *Great Lives* differs in substantial ways from *DWB*:

- The coverage of each set has been increased significantly. In the current four volumes, for example, 617 original essays from *Dictionary of World Biography* (1999) are enhanced by 120 new entries for a total of 737 essays covering 757 major figures, including 123 women.

- 189 sidebars, including many quotations from primary source documents, have been added to enhance and supplement the text throughout.

- A section of maps has been added to the front matter of each volume to allow students and other users of this reference work to locate personages geographically.

- Essays from the original *DWB* on all personages falling into the time frame are reprinted in this new series with updated and annotated bibliographies.

SCOPE OF COVERAGE

Both the geographic and the occupational scope of the individuals covered in *Great Lives from History: The Nineteenth Century, 1801-1900* is intentionally broad, with a view to including influential individuals worldwide. The figures covered in these volumes are identified with one or more of the following countries and regions: Africa (10 essays), Albania (1), Algeria (1), Argentina (2), Australia (8), Austria (11), Belgium (1), Bohemia (1), Brazil (4), Canada (19), Chile (1), China (7), Colombia (1), Cuba (1), Denmark (4), Egypt (2), England (147), Estonia (1), Ethiopia (2), France (77), Germany (65), Greece (3), Haiti (1), Hungary (3), India (9), Iran (4), Ireland (13), Italy (13), Japan (7), Mexico (6), Middle East (5), Netherlands (1), New Zealand (5), Nicaragua (1), Nigeria (3), North Africa (3), Norway (3), Oman (1), Ottoman Empire (5), Peru (2), Poland (2), Portugal (1), Russia (23), Scotland (22), Sierra Leone (1), South Africa (9), South America (10), Spain (5), Sudan (1), Sweden (3), Switzerland (4), Tanzania (2), Thailand (1), United States (282), Venezuela (2), Vietnam (3), Wales (3), West Africa (5), and Zimbabwe (1).

The editors have sought to provide coverage that is broad in areas of achievement as well as geography, while at the same time including the recognized shapers of history essential in any liberal arts curriculum. Major world leaders appear here, as well as the giants of religious faith who were central to the century: monarchs, presidents, popes, philosophers, writers, social reformers, educators, and military leaders who left their imprint on political as well as spiritual institutions. Also, however, the set includes figures who have received little attention in the past, from American educator and science writer Elizabeth Cabot Agassiz to Chinese statesman and military leader Zeng Guofan.

By category, the contents include figures whose achievements fall into one or more of the following areas: agriculture (5 essays), architecture (14), art (43), astronomy (11), biology (18), business (29), chemistry (13), church government (5), communications (5), crime (7), diplomacy (27), economics (8), education (43), engineering (22), entertainment (20), exploration (27), geography and geology (12), government and politics (188), historiography (18), journalism (27), law (23), linguistics (6), literature (114), mathematics (21), medicine (20), military (45), music (38), philanthropy and arts patronage (8), philosophy (32), photography (9), physics (20), psychology (7), religion and theology (42), science and technology (43), social reform (68), sociology (9), sports (5), theater (18), warfare and conquest (20), and women's rights (44).

ESSAY LENGTH AND FORMAT

Each essay ranges from 1,500 to 3,000 words in length (roughly 3 to 5 pages) and displays standard ready-reference top matter offering easy access to biographical information:

- The essay title is the name of the individual; editors have chosen the name as it is most commonly found in Western English-language sources.

- The individual's nationality or ethnicity and occupation or historical role follow on the second line, including reign dates and terms of ofice for rulers and heads of state.

- A summary paragraph highlighting the individual's historical importance indicates why the person is studied today.

- The "Born" and "Died" lines list the most complete dates of birth and death available, followed by the most precise location available, as well as an indication of when these are unknown, only probable, or only approximate; both contemporary and modern place-names (where different) are listed. A question mark (?) is appended to a date or place if the information is considered likely to be the precise date or place but remains in question. A "c." denotes circa and indicates that historians have only enough information to place the date of birth or death in a more general period. When a range of dates is provided for birth or death, historians are relatively certain that it could not have occurred prior to or after the range.

- "Also known as" lists all known versions of the individual's name, including full names, given names, alternative spellings, pseudonyms, and common epithets.

- "Area(s) of achievement" lists all categories of contribution, from Architecture and Art through Social Reform and Theater.

The body of each essay is divided into three parts:

- "Early Life" provides facts about the individual's upbringing and the environment in which he or she was reared, as well as the pronunciation of his or her name, if unfamiliar to English speakers. Pronunciation guidelines are provided for those individuals whose names are difficult to pronounce for an English-speaking audience. Where little is known about the individual's early life, historical context is provided.

- "Life's Work," the heart of the essay, consists of a straightforward, generally chronological, account of the period during which the individual's most significant achievements were accomplished.

- "Significance" is an overview of the individual's place in history.

- "Further Reading" is an annotated bibliography, a starting point for further research.

- "See also" lists cross-references to essays in the set covering related personages.

- "Related articles" lists essays of interest in Salem's companion publication, *Great Events from History: The Nineteenth Century, 1801-1900* (4 vols., 2007).

SPECIAL FEATURES

Several features distinguish this series as a whole from other biographical reference works. The front matter includes the following aids:

- Complete List of Contents: This alphabetical list of contents appears in all volumes.

- Key to Pronunciation: A key to in-text pronunciation appears in all volumes.

- List of Maps and Sidebars.

- Maps: The front matter of each volume contains a section of maps displaying major regions of the world during the nineteenth century.

The back matter to Volume 4 includes several appendixes and indexes:

- Rulers and Heads of State: a geographically arranged set of tables listing major world rulers and leaders, including their regnal dates or terms of office.

- Chronological List of Entries: individuals covered, arranged by birth year.

- Category Index: entries by area of achievement, from Architecture to Women's Rights.

- Geographical Index: entries by country or region, from Albania to Zimbabwe.

3 1833 05283 5706

- Personages Index: an index of all persons, both those covered in the essays and those discussed within the text.

- Subject Index: a comprehensive index including personages, concepts, books, artworks, terms, battles, civilizations, and other topics of discussion, with full cross-references from alternative spellings and to the Category and Geographical Indexes.

USAGE NOTES

The worldwide scope of *Great Lives from History* resulted in the inclusion of names and words transliterated from languages that do not use the modern Roman alphabet. In some cases, there is more than one transliterated form in use. In many cases, transliterated words in this set follow the American Library Association and Library of Congress (ALA-LC) transliteration format for that language. However, if another form of a name or word has been judged to be more familiar to the general audience, it is used instead. The variants for names of essay subjects are listed in ready-reference top matter and are cross-referenced in the subject and personages indexes. The Pinyin transliteration was used for Chinese topics, with Wade-Giles variants provided for major names and dynasties. In a few cases, a common name that is not Pinyin has been used. Sanskrit and other South Asian names generally follow the ALA-LC transliteration rules, although again, the more familiar form of a word is used when deemed appropriate for the general reader.

Titles of books and other literature appear, upon first mention in the essay, with their full publication and translation data as known: an indication of the first date of publication or appearance, followed by the English title in translation and its first date of appearance in English; if no translation has been published in English, and if the context of the discussion does not make the meaning of the title obvious, a "literal translation" appears in roman type.

Throughout, readers will find a limited number of abbreviations used in both top matter and text, including "r." for "reigned," "b." for "born," "d." for "died," and "fl." for flourished. Where a date range appears appended to a name without one of these designators, the reader may assume it signifies birth and death dates.

CONTRIBUTORS

Salem Press would like to extend its appreciation to all who have been involved in the development and production of this work. Special thanks go to John Powell, Associate Professor of History at Oklahoma Baptist University, who developed the contents list and coverage notes for contributing writers to ensure the set's relevance to the high school and undergraduate curricula. The essays were written and signed by historians, political scientists, and scholars of regional studies as well as independent scholars. Without their expert contributions, a project of this nature would not be possible. A full list of their names and affiliations appears in the front matter of this volume.

Contributors

Amy Ackerberg-Hastings
University of Maryland University College

Michael Adams
City University New York, Graduate Center

Richard Adler
University of Michigan—Dearborn

William H. Alexander
Norfolk State University

Jennifer Hudson Allen
Independent Scholar

Beverley Allix
University of Toronto

Arthur L. Alt
Independent Scholar

Eleanor B. Amico
Independent Scholar

Richard J. Amundson
Independent Scholar

Nicole Anae
University of Tasmania

John D. Anderson, Jr.
University of Maryland at College Park

Nancy Fix Anderson
Loyola University

Peggy J. Anderson
Wichita State University

Debra D. Andrist
University of St. Thomas

Andrew J. Angyal
Elon University

Stanley Archer
Texas A&M University

James A. Arieti
Hampden-Sydney College

Stephen M. Ashby
Independent Scholar

Bryan Aubrey
Independent Scholar

Tom L. Auffenberg
Ouachita Baptist University

Ann Marie B. Bahr
South Dakota State University

Brian S. Baigrie
University of Calgary

John W. Bailey
Independent Scholar

Ann Stewart Balakier
University of South Dakota

John W. Barker
University of Wisconsin—Madison

Jeffrey G. Barlow
Lewis & Clark College

Dan Barnett
Butte College

David Barratt
Independent Scholar

Thomas F. Barry
Himeji Dokkyo University

Iraj Bashiri
University of Minnesota

Christopher Bassford
Independent Scholar

Erving E. Beauregard
University of Dayton

Erika Behrisch
Royal Military College of Canada

Alvin K. Benson
Utah Valley State College

S. Carol Berg
College of St. Benedict

Martin Berger
Youngstown State University

Donna Berliner
Southern Methodist University

Milton Berman
University of Rochester

Robert L. Berner
University of Wisconsin—Oshkosh

Robert E. Bieder
Independent Scholar

Terry D. Bilhartz
Sam Houston State University

Cynthia A. Bily
Adrian College

Margaret Boe Birns
New York University

Nicholas Birns
New School University

Carol Bishop
Point Loma Nazarene University

Brian L. Blakeley
Texas Technical University

Wayne M. Bledsoe
University of Missouri—Rolla

Arnold Blumberg
Towson University

Pegge Bochynski
Salem State College

David Warren Bowen
Livingston University

Keith Bowen
Independent Scholar

Newell D. Boyd
Independent Scholar

John Braeman
University of Nebraska

Harold Branam
Independent Scholar

Gerhard Brand
California State University, Los Angeles

Jeff R. Bremer
University of Kansas

Wesley Britton
Harrisburg Area Community College

J. R. Broadus
University of North Carolina

Celeste Williams Brockington
Independent Scholar

Judit Brody
Independent Scholar

Jerry H. Brookshire
Middle Tennessee State University

Keith H. Brower
Salisbury State University

Alan Brown
Independent Scholar

Norman D. Brown
University of Texas

Philip C. Brown
University of North Carolina at Charlotte

Anthony Brundage
California Polytechnic University, Pomona

David D. Buck
University of Wisconsin—Milwaukee

David L. Bullock
Independent Scholar

William H. Burnside
John Brown University

Donald Burrill
Independent Scholar

Larry W. Burt
Southwest Missouri State University

Stephen Burwood
State University of New York, Binghamton

Charles J. Bussey
Western Kentucky University

Andrew J. Butrica
Rutgers University

John R. Bylsma
Augustana College

Joseph P. Byrne
Belmont University

John A. Calabrese
Texas Woman's University

Susanna Calkins
Purdue University

Rosemary M. Canfield-Reisman
Charleston Southern University

Byron D. Cannon
University of Utah

Jack J. Cardoso
Independent Scholar

W. Bernard Carlson
University of Virginia

John Carpenter
University of Michigan

James A. Casada
Independent Scholar

Thomas J. Cassidy
South Carolina State University

Elisabeth A. Cawthon
University of Texas at Arlington

Ranès C. Chakravorty
University of Virginia

Allan D. Charles
University of South Carolina

Deborah Charlie
Independent Scholar

Victor W. Chen
Chabot College

Ellen Clark
Independent Scholar

Walter Aaron Clark
University of California, Los Angeles

William Condon
University of Michigan

Richard G. Cormack
Independent Scholar

Albert B. Costa
Duquesne University

Dennis Costanzo
State University of New York, Plattsburgh

David A. Crain
South Dakota State University

Lee B. Croft
Arizona State University

Tyler T. Crogg
Southern Illinois University—Carbondale

Carol Crowe-Carraco
Western Kentucky University

E. R. Crowther
Adams State College

LouAnn Faris Culley
Kansas State University

Light Townsend Cummins
Austin College

J. D. Daubs
The College Board

Abraham A. Davidson
Independent Scholar

Ronald W. Davis
Western Michigan University

Frank Day
Clemson University

George W. Van Devender
Independent Scholar

Tom Dewey II
University of Mississippi—Oxford

M. Casey Diana
University of Illinois, Urbana-Champaign

Reidar Dittmann
Independent Scholar

Margaret A. Dodson
Independent Scholar

Charles A. Dranguet, Jr.
Independent Scholar

Steven L. Driever
University of Missouri—Kansas City

Thomas Drucker
University of Wisconsin—Whitewater

Ian Duffy
Lehigh University

Frederick Dumin
Independent Scholar

Charles Duncan
Clark-Atlanta University

Kathleen E. Dunlop
Independent Scholar

Natasha Duquette
Royal Military College

Steven I. Dutch
University of Wisconsin—Green Bay

William E. Eagan
Moorhead State University

Wilton Eckley
Colorado School of Mines

Bruce L. Edwards
Independent Scholar

Harry J. Eisenman
University of Missouri—Rolla

Thomas J. Elliott
California Polytechnic University, Pomona

Mark R. Ellis
University of Nebraska at Kearney

Robert P. Ellis
Independent Scholar

Paul H. Elovitz
Independent Scholar

Linda Eikmeier Endersby
The Missouri State Museum

Thomas L. Erskine
Salisbury University

Paul F. Erwin
University of Cincinnati

Kimberly K. Estep
Wesleyan College

Peter R. Faber
United States Air Force Academy

Dean Fafoutis
Salisbury State University

Norman B. Ferris
Middle Tennessee State University

James E. Fickle
Memphis State University

Donald M. Fiene
University of Tennessee

Paul Finkelman
Brooklyn Law School

Roy E. Finkenbine
Hampton University

Edward Fiorelli
St. John's University

David Marc Fischer
Independent Scholar

Michael S. Fitzgerald
Pikeville College

Dale L. Flesher
University of Mississippi

Bonnie L. Ford
Sacramento City College

Kirk Ford, Jr.
Independent Scholar

Margot K. Frank
Randolph-Macon Women's College

Timothy C. Frazer
Western Illinois University

C. E. Frazier
Independent Scholar

C. George Fry
Winebrenner Theological Seminary

Gloria Fulton
Humboldt State University

Jean C. Fulton
Landmark College

William Gahan
University of California, Santa Barbara

John G. Gallaher
Southern Illinois University at Edwardsville

Francesca Gamber
Southern Illinois University at Carbondale

Joy M. Gambill
Appalachian State University

Keith Garebian
Independent Scholar

K. Fred Gillum
Colby College

Juana Goergen
DePaul University

Joseph A. Goldenberg
Independent Scholar

Sheldon Goldfarb
University of British Columbia

Nancy M. Gordon
Independent Scholar

Margaret Bozenna Goscilo
University of Pittsburgh

Lewis L. Gould
University of Texas at Austin

C. L. Grant
Independent Scholar

Lloyd J. Graybar
Eastern Kentucky University

William C. Griffin
Appalachian State University

Christopher E. Guthrie
Tarleton State University

D. Harland Hagler
North Texas State University

Irwin Halfond
McKendree College

Gavin R. G. Hambly
University of Texas at Dallas

William S. Haney II
Maharishi International University

Elizabeth Harris
Eastern Illinois University

Fred R. van Hartesveldt
Fort Valley State College

John Harty
Independent Scholar

Albert A. Hayden
Independent Scholar

David S. Heidler
Salisbury State College

John A. Heitmann
University of Dayton

Terry Heller
Coe College

Michael F. Hembree
Independent Scholar

Carlanna L. Hendrick
Independent Scholar

Erwin Hester
East Carolina University

Anna Dunlap Higgins
Gordon College

Richard L. Hillard
University of Arkansas at Pine Bluff

James R. Hofmann
California State University, Fullerton

Hal Holladay
Simon's Rock College of Bard

Authur B. Holmes
West Virginia Wesleyan College

Ari Hoogenboom
Independent Scholar

Lisa Hopkins
Sheffield Hallam University

Allen Horstman
Albion College

Ronald Howard
Mississippi College

Tonya Huber
Wichita State University

E. D. Huntley
Appalachian State University

Mary Hurd
East Tennessee State University

Raymond Pierre Hylton
Virginia Union University

John Quinn Imholte
University of Minnesota, Morris

Carlton Jackson
Western Kentucky University

Duncan R. Jamieson
Ashland University

George Javor
Independent Scholar

Shakuntala Jayaswal
Independent Scholar

Bruce E. Johansen
University of Nebraska at Omaha

Sheila Golburgh Johnson
Independent Scholar

Eileen T. Johnston
Independent Scholar

Jonathan M. Jones
University of Memphis

Michelle L. Jones
Muskingum College

Philip Dwight Jones
Bradley University

Marcella Joy
Independent Scholar

Charles L. Kammer
The College of Wooster

Paul Kane
Independent Scholar

Anand Karnad
Boston City Hospital

David Kasserman
Independent Scholar

Cynthia Lee Katona
Ohlone College

Anne Kearney
Jefferson Community College

Jeanette Keith
Independent Scholar

Steven G. Kellman
University of Texas at San Antonio

W. P. Kenney
Manhattan College

Karen A. Kildahl
South Dakota State University

Kenneth F. Kiple
Independent Scholar

Kenneth F. Kitchell, Jr.
Louisiana State University

Wm. Laird Kleine-Ahlbrandt
Purdue University

Dwight A. Klett
Rutgers University

Phillip E. Koerper
Independent Scholar

Gayla Koerting
University of South Dakota

Gregory C. Kozlowski
DePaul University

Carl E. Kramer
Independent Scholar

Charles Kraszewski
Independent Scholar

Henry Kratz
University of Tennessee, Knoxville

Marjorie Kratz
Maryville College

Abraham D. Kriegel
Memphis State University

Lynn C. Kronzek
Independent Scholar

David W. Krueger
Arkansas Tech University

Paul E. Kuhl
Winston-Salem State University

Neil Kunze
Northern Arizona University

David Z. Kushner
Independent Scholar

Pavlin Lange
Independent Scholar

Ralph L. Langenheim, Jr.
University of Illinois—Urbana

Karl G. Larew
Towson University

J. C. Larrabee
Case Western Reserve University

Eugene S. Larson
Los Angeles Pierce College

Jack M. Lauber
University of Wisconsin—Eau Claire

Harry Lawton
University of California, Santa Barbara

Linda Ledford-Miller
University of Scranton

Steven Lehman
John Abbott College

Denyse Lemaire
Rowan University

Leon Lewis
Appalachian State University

Victor Lindsey
East Central University

Monroe H. Little, Jr.
Indiana University

James D. Lockett
Independent Scholar

Roger D. Long
Eastern Michigan University

Rey M. Longyear
Independent Scholar

John L. Loos
Louisiana State University

Rita E. Loos
Independent Scholar

Eric v.d. Luft
State University of New York, Upstate Medical University

R. C. Lutz
CII

Marion Sheila McAvey
Becker College

Richard B. McCaslin
Independent Scholar

Sandra C. McClain
James Madison University

Robert McColley
University of Illinois

C. S. McConnell
University of Calgary

Philip McDermott
Independent Scholar

Kathryne S. McDorman
Texas Christian University

Barry McGill
Oberlin College

James E. McGoldrick
Greenville Presbyterian Theological Seminary

William McGucken
University of Akron

Jennifer McLeod
Independent Scholar

Robert J. McNutt
Independent Scholar

Kerrie L. MacPherson
State University of New York, Buffalo

David K. McQuilkin
Independent Scholar

Paul Madden
Hardin-Simmons University

Claudette R. Mainzer
Independent Scholar

Richard L. Mallery
Independent Scholar

E. Deanne Malpass
Independent Scholar

Nancy Farm Mannikko
National Park Service

Jo Manning
Independent Scholar

Carl Henry Marcoux
University of California, Riverside

Marsha Kass Marks
Independent Scholar

Joss Marsh
Stanford University

John F. Marszalek
Xavier University of Louisiana

Paul Marx
University of New Haven

Thomas Matchie
Independent Scholar

Elaine Mathiasen
Independent Scholar

Jeffrey J. Matthews
University of Kentucky

Anne Laura Mattrella
Southeastern University

Charles E. May
California State University, Long Beach

Laurence W. Mazzeno
Alvernia College

Patrick Meanor
State University of New York, College at Oneonta

Deborah T. Meem
University of Cincinnati

Doris H. Meriwether
University of Louisiana—Lafayette

Linda J. Meyers
Independent Scholar

Rose Ethel Althaus Meza
Independent Scholar

Joan E. Meznar
Eastern Connecticut State University

Norton Mezvinsky
Central Connecticut State University

Sara Joan Miles
Wheaton College

Michele L. Mock
University of Pittsburgh at Johnstown

Ronald O. Moore
Independent Scholar

William V. Moore
College of Charleston

Robert A. Morace
Daemen College

Gordon R. Mork
Purdue University

Raymond Lee Muncy
Independent Scholar

B. Keith Murphy
Fort Valley State University

D. Gosselin Nakeeb
Pace University

William Nelles
University of Massachusetts—Dartmouth

Bryan D. Ness
Pacific Union College

Brian J. Nichelson
Independent Scholar

Glenn O. Nichols
Independent Scholar

Michael R. Nichols
Texas Christian University

Roger L. Nichols
Independent Scholar

Frank Nickell
Southeast Missouri State University

Richard L. Niswonger
Independent Scholar

Helen Jean M. Nugent
Independent Scholar

Parker Bradley Nutting
Framingham State College

James W. Oberly
University of Wisconsin—Eau Claire

Maurice R. O'Connell
Fordham University

Robert H. O'Connor
North Dakota State University

Patricia Okker
University of Missouri—Columbia

Paul Michael O'Shea
University of Oregon

Gary B. Ostrower
Alfred University

Adrianna M. Paliyenko
Colby College

Robert J. Paradowski
Rochester Institute of Technology

Harold M. Parker, Jr.
Independent Scholar

Judith A. Parsons
Sul Ross State University

D. G. Paz
University of North Texas

Martha E. Pemberton
Independent Scholar

Jan Pendergrass
University of Georgia

Robert C. Petersen
Middle Tennessee State University

R. Craig Philips
Michigan State University

Hugh J. Phillips
Intertech Associates

John Phillips
University of California, Riverside

Donald K. Pickens
University of North Texas

Evelyne L. Pickett
Independent Scholar

Erika E. Pilver
Westfield State College

Leslie Todd Pitre
Independent Scholar

George R. Plitnik
Frostburg State University

Marjorie J. Podolsky
Penn State Erie, The Behrend College

Clifton W. Potter, Jr.
Lynchburg College

Dorothy T. Potter
Lynchburg College

Annette Potts
Monash University

Tina Powell
Fordham University

William S. Pretzer
Henry Ford Museum

Charles H. Pullen
Queen's University

Edna B. Quinn
Salisbury University

John Ranlett
State University of New York, Potsdam College

Eugene L. Rasor
Emory & Henry College

William G. Ratliff
Georgia Southern University

James A. Rawley
Independent Scholar

John D. Raymer
Holy Cross College

Christel Reges
Grand Valley State University

Rose Reifsnyder
Independent Scholar

Dennis Reinhartz
University of Texas at Arlington

Clark G. Reynolds
College of Charleston

Victoria Reynolds
Mandeville High School

Mary Rice-DeFosse
Bates College

Betty Richardson
Southern Illinois University, Edwardsville

Vivian L. Richardson
Central Missouri State University

Edward A. Riedinger
Ohio State University Libraries

St. John Robinson
Montana State University at Billings

Vicki Robinson
State University of New York, Farmingdale

JoAnne M. Rogers
Southwestern Oklahoma State University

Carl Rollyson
Baruch College, City University New York

Paul Rosefeldt
Delgado Community College

Joseph Rosenblum
Independent Scholar

Robert Ross
Independent Scholar

Marc Rothenberg
Smithsonian Institution

Bruce A. Rubenstein
University of Michigan

Emanuel D. Rudolph
Ohio State University

J. Edmund Rush
Independent Scholar

Wendy Sacket
Independent Scholar

Mary Wilson Sage
Independent Scholar

Hilel B. Salomon
University of South Carolina

Daniel C. Scavone
University of Southern Indiana

Elizabeth D. Schafer
Independent Scholar

William J. Scheick
University of Texas at Austin

Per Schelde
Independent Scholar

Beverly Schneller
Millersville University

Roger Sensenbaugh
Indiana University

Patricia Sharpe
Independent Scholar

David Shayt
Smithsonian Institution

Melvin Shefftz
State University of New York, Binghamton

Martha A. Sherwood
University of Oregon

J. Lee Shneidman
Adelphi University

Steven W. Shrader
Independent Scholar

R. Baird Shuman
University of Illinois, Urbana-Champaign

Anne W. Sienkewicz
Independent Scholar

Narasingha P. Sil
Western Oregon University

Donald C. Simmons, Jr.
South Dakota Humanities Council

L. Moody Simms, Jr.
Illinois State University

Sanford S. Singer
University of Dayton

Shumet Sishagne
Christopher Newport University

David Curtis Skaggs
Bowling Green State University

C. Edward Skeen
Memphis State University

Anna Sloan
Amherst College

Genevieve Slomski
Independent Scholar

Dale Edwyna Smith
Independent Scholar

Harold L. Smith
University of Houston at Victoria

Roger Smith
Independent Scholar

Ira Smolensky
Monmouth College

Valerie Snyder
Independent Scholar

Norbert C. Soldon
Independent Scholar

Katherine R. Sopka
Four Corners Analytic Sciences

James E. Southerland
Brenau College

Richard Francis Spall, Jr.
Ohio Wesleyan University

Robert M. Spector
Worcester State College

Joseph L. Spradley
Wheaton College

Brian Stableford
University College

James Stanlaw
Illinois State University

August W. Staub
University of Georgia

S. J. Stearns
College of Staten Island, City University of New York

David L. Sterling
University of Cincinnati

John Knox Stevens
University of Indiana

James Brewer Stewart
Macallister College

Fred Strickert
Wartburg College

Marian E. Strobel
Furman University

Paul Stuewe
Green Mountain College

Charles R. Sullivan
University of Dallas

James Sullivan
California State University, Los Angeles

Joseph E. Suppiger
Independent Scholar

Roy Arthur Swanson
University of Wisconsin—Milwaukee

Patricia E. Sweeney
Derby Neck Library

Roy Talbert, Jr.
Coastal Carolina College

Alice Taylor
Shorter College

Cassandra Lee Tellier
Capital University

Nicholas C. Thomas
Auburn University at Montgomery

J. A. Thompson
Independent Scholar

Thomas John Thomson
Limestone College

Jonathan L. Thorndike
Belmont University

Kenneth William Townsend
Coastal Carolina University

Paul B. Trescott
Southern Illinois University

Judith Ann Trolander
University of Minnesota

Eileen Tess Tyler
United States Naval Academy

Ronald D. Tyler
Independent Scholar

David Underdown
Yale University

Diane C. Vecchio
University of Wisconsin—Whitewater

Charles L. Vigue
University of New Haven

Mary E. Virginia
Independent Scholar

Vernon L. Volpe
Texas A&M University

LeRoy J. Votto
The Urban School of San Francisco

Paul R. Waibel
Belhaven College

Miriam Wallraven
University of Tübingen, Germany

Harry M. Ward
University of Richmond

Brent Waters
University of Redlands

Duncan Waterson
Macquarie University

Dover C. Watkins
Independent Scholar

Sharon B. Watkins
Western Illinois University

Robert P. Watson
Florida Atlantic University

Donald V. Weatherman
Lyon College

Stewart A. Weaver
University of Rochester

Shawncey Webb
Independent Scholar

Henry Weisser
Colorado State University

Allen Wells
Bowdoin College

Mary B. Wickwire
University of Massachusetts

Barbara Wiedemann
Auburn University at Montgomery

Lance Williams
Independent Scholar

David B. Wilson
Iowa State University

David L. Wilson
Independent Scholar

Jan Doolittle Wilson
Fort Hays State University

John Wilson
University of Hawaii—Manoa

Major L. Wilson
Memphis State University

John D. Windhausen
Saint Anselm College

George Wise
Appalachian State University

Michael Witkoski
University of South Carolina

Ken Wolf
Murray State University

Donald Yacovone
Florida State University

Clifton K. Yearley
State University of New York, Buffalo

Irwin Yellowitz
City University of New York

Kristen L. Zacharias
Albright College

William M. Zanella
Hawaii Loa College

Robert F. Zeidel
Independent Scholar

Key to Pronunciation

Many of the names of personages covered in *Great Lives from History: The Nineteenth Century, 1801-1900* may be unfamiliar to students and general readers. For these unfamiliar names, guides to pronunciation have been provided upon first mention of the names in the text. These guidelines do not purport to achieve the subtleties of the languages in question but will offer readers a rough equivalent of how English speakers may approximate the proper pronunciation.

Vowel Sounds

Symbol	**Spelled (Pronounced)**
a	answer (AN-suhr), laugh (laf), sample (SAM-puhl), that (that)
ah	father (FAH-thur), hospital (HAHS-pih-tuhl)
aw	awful (AW-fuhl), caught (kawt)
ay	blaze (blayz), fade (fayd), waiter (WAYT-ur), weigh (way)
eh	bed (behd), head (hehd), said (sehd)
ee	believe (bee-LEEV), cedar (SEE-dur), leader (LEED-ur), liter (LEE-tur)
ew	boot (bewt), lose (lewz)
i	buy (bi), height (hit), lie (li), surprise (sur-PRIZ)
ih	bitter (BIH-tur), pill (pihl)
o	cotton (KO-tuhn), hot (hot)
oh	below (bee-LOH), coat (koht), note (noht), wholesome (HOHL-suhm)
oo	good (good), look (look)
ow	couch (kowch), how (how)
oy	boy (boy), coin (koyn)
uh	about (uh-BOWT), butter (BUH-tuhr), enough (ee-NUHF), other (UH-thur)

Consonant Sounds

Symbol	**Spelled (Pronounced)**
ch	beach (beech), chimp (chihmp)
g	beg (behg), disguise (dihs-GIZ), get (geht)
j	digit (DIH-juht), edge (ehj), jet (jeht)
k	cat (kat), kitten (KIH-tuhn), hex (hehks)
s	cellar (SEHL-ur), save (sayv), scent (sehnt)
sh	champagne (sham-PAYN), issue (IH-shew), shop (shop)
ur	birth (burth), disturb (dihs-TURB), earth (urth), letter (LEH-tur)
y	useful (YEWS-fuhl), young (yuhng)
z	business (BIHZ-nehs), zest (zehst)
zh	vision (VIH-zhuhn)

Complete List of Contents

Volume I

Contents v
Publisher's Note ix
Contributors xiii
Key to Pronunciation xxiii
List of Maps and Sidebars xxxv
Maps of the Nineteenth Century xlv

Abdelkader 1
Muḥammad ʿAbduh 4
Abdülhamid II 7
Niels Henrik Abel 9
Lord Acton 12
Henry Adams 16
John Quincy Adams 20
Felix Adler 26
Elizabeth Cabot Agassiz 29
Louis Agassiz 31
Sir Sayyid Ahmad Khan 35
Bronson Alcott 38
Louisa May Alcott 41
Alexander I 45
Alexander II 48
Horatio Alger 51
Ali Paşa Tepelenë 55
John Peter Altgeld 57
Hans Christian Andersen 61
Susan B. Anthony 65
Johnny Appleseed 68
Matthew Arnold 71
Thomas Arnold 76
Chester A. Arthur 79
Luise Aston 83
John Jacob Astor 86
Hubertine Auclert 89
John James Audubon 91
Jane Austen 94
Stephen Fuller Austin 98
Amedeo Avogadro 101

The Bāb 105
Charles Babbage 107
Sir Robert Stephenson Smyth Baden-Powell 110
Karl Ernst von Baer 114
Bahāʾullāh 117
Mikhail Bakunin 119
Robert Baldwin 122
Honoré de Balzac 126
George Bancroft 130
Henry Barnard 135
P. T. Barnum 138
Sir Charles Barry 142
Clara Barton 145
Sir Edmund Barton 149
Charles Baudelaire 152
L. Frank Baum 155
Dorothea Beale 159
Aubrey Beardsley 162
The Becquerel Family 165
Catharine Beecher 168
Henry Ward Beecher 172
Ludwig van Beethoven 175
Emil von Behring 179
Alexander Graham Bell 182
Muḥammad Bello 186
James Gordon Bennett 188
Thomas Hart Benton 192
Carl Benz 197
Hector Berlioz 200
Claude Bernard 205
Sarah Bernhardt 208
Annie Besant 211
Friedrich Wilhelm Bessel 215
Sir Henry Bessemer 218
Friedrich von Beust 222
Nicholas Biddle 225
Ambrose Bierce 228
Albert Bierstadt 232
George Caleb Bingham 234
Otto von Bismarck 238
Georges Bizet 241
Black Hawk 244
Elizabeth Blackwell 247
James G. Blaine 251
Louis Blanc 254
Amelia Bloomer 257
Gebhard Leberecht von Blücher 260
Barbara Leigh Smith Bodichon 263

Marie Anne Victorine Boivin 265
Simón Bolívar 267
Edwin Booth 271
William Booth 274
Lizzie Borden 277
Aleksandr Borodin 280
Mary Elizabeth Braddon 284
F. H. Bradley 288
Mathew B. Brady 291
Johannes Brahms 296
Louis Braille 299
John Bright 302
Sir Isaac Brock 306
The Brontë Sisters 308
Henry Brougham 312
George Brown 316
John Brown 319
Olympia Brown 323
Elizabeth Barrett Browning 326
Anton Bruckner 329
Isambard Kingdom Brunel 333
Marc Isambard Brunel 337
William Cullen Bryant 340
James Buchanan 343
Charles Bulfinch 346
Luther Burbank 350
Jacob Burckhardt 354
Frances Hodgson Burnett 357
Daniel Hudson Burnham 360
Aaron Burr 363
Sir Richard Francis Burton 368
Josephine Butler 371
Samuel Butler 374
Sir Thomas Fowell Buxton 376
Lord Byron 379

Frances Xavier Cabrini 383
Calamity Jane 386
Fanny Calderón de la Barca 389
John C. Calhoun 392
Jean-Jacques-Régis de Cambacérès 396
Alexander Campbell 399
George Canning 403
Antonio Canova 406
William Carey 409
Don Carlos 412
Thomas Carlyle 415
Andrew Carnegie 419
Lewis Carroll 423
Kit Carson 426
Mary Ann Shadd Cary 431
Mary Cassatt 433
Viscount Castlereagh 437
George Catlin 441
Count Cavour 444
George Cayley 447
Cetshwayo 450
Paul Cézanne 453
Edwin Chadwick 456
Joseph Chamberlain 460
William Ellery Channing 464
Charles XIV John 468
Salmon P. Chase 470
François-René de Chateaubriand 474
Anton Chekhov 478
Lydia Maria Child 482
Frédéric Chopin 486
Kate Chopin 490
Henri Christophe 494
Cixi 496
Carl von Clausewitz 499
Henry Clay 502
Grover Cleveland 507
DeWitt Clinton 512
William Cobbett 517
Richard Cobden 520
William Cody 524
Ferdinand Julius Cohn 527
Samuel Taylor Coleridge 529
Samuel Colt 533
Auguste Comte 536
John Constable 540
Jay Cooke 544
William Fothergill Cooke and
Charles Wheatstone 547
James Fenimore Cooper 552
Carolina Coronado 556
Gustave Courbet 559
Stephen Crane 562
Crazy Horse 566
David Crockett 571
Samuel Ajayi Crowther 574
Paul Cuffe 576
Caleb Cushing 578
George A. Custer 582
Georges Cuvier 585

Jacques Daguerre 589
Gottlieb Daimler 592
First Marquis of Dalhousie 595

John Dalton 597
Rubén Darío 601
Charles Darwin 603
Jacques-Louis David 607
Jefferson Davis 610
Sir Humphry Davy 616
Ferenc Deák 619
Alfred Deakin 623
Stephen Decatur 626
Richard Dedekind 629
Edgar Degas 632
Eugène Delacroix 635
Léo Delibes 639
Fourteenth Earl of Derby 642
George Dewey 645
Melvil Dewey 649
Porfirio Díaz 652

Volume 2

Contents lvii
Key to Pronunciation lxi
Complete List of Contents lxiii
List of Maps and Sidebars lxxiii
Maps of the Nineteenth Century lxxxiii

Charles Dickens 655
Emily Dickinson 658
Rudolf Diesel 663
Benjamin Disraeli 666
Dorothea Dix 671
Gaetano Donizetti 674
Fyodor Dostoevski 677
Stephen A. Douglas 681
Frederick Douglass 684
Sir Arthur Conan Doyle 688
James Buchanan Duke 692
Alexandre Dumas, *père* 695
Jean-Henri Dunant 699
Paul Laurence Dunbar 701
Eleuthère Irénée du Pont 705
First Earl of Durham 708
Antonín Dvořák 711

James Buchanan Eads 715
Thomas Eakins 717
Wyatt Earp 720
Mary Baker Eddy 723
Maria Edgeworth 728
Thomas Alva Edison 731
Gustave Eiffel 734
Charles William Eliot 737
George Eliot 740
Fanny Elssler 743
Ralph Waldo Emerson 745
Friedrich Engels 750
Sir Arthur Evans 753

Louis Faidherbe 756
Michael Faraday 759
David G. Farragut 762
Dame Millicent Garrett Fawcett 766
Gustav Theodor Fechner 770
Marshall Field 773
Stephen J. Field 777
Millard Fillmore 781
Gustave Flaubert 785
Williamina Paton Stevens Fleming 788
Edwin Forrest 790
William Edward Forster 793
Charlotte Forten 796
Abby Kelley Foster 799
Stephen Collins Foster 802
Charles Fourier 805
Joseph Fourier 809
Lydia Folger Fowler 812
Anatole France 815
Francis Joseph I 818
César Franck 821
Sir John Franklin 825
Gottlob Frege 828
John C. Frémont 831
Friedrich Froebel 835
Elizabeth Fry 839
Margaret Fuller 841
Robert Fulton 845

James Gadsden 849
Matilda Joslyn Gage 852
Albert Gallatin 854
Évariste Galois 857

Francis Galton 860
Léon Gambetta 864
James A. Garfield 867
Giuseppe Garibaldi 871
William Lloyd Garrison 874
Paul Gauguin 879
Carl Friedrich Gauss 883
Joseph-Louis Gay-Lussac 886
George IV 890
Henry George 894
Théodore Géricault 898
Sophie Germain 901
Geronimo 904
Gia Long 907
James Gibbons 910
Josiah Willard Gibbs 913
W. S. Gilbert and Arthur Sullivan 916
Vincenzo Gioberti 921
William Ewart Gladstone 924
August von Gneisenau 928
Vincent van Gogh 932
Nikolai Gogol 937
Sir George Goldie 940
Samuel Gompers 943
Charles Goodyear 946
Charles George Gordon 949
Charles Gounod 952
William Gilbert Grace 955
Ulysses S. Grant 958
Asa Gray 963
Horace Greeley 966
Thomas Hill Green 971
Francis Greenway 974
Charles Grey 977
Sir George Grey 981
Edvard Grieg 984
Sarah and Angelina Grimké 988
Jacob and Wilhelm Grimm 992
Sir William Robert Grove 996

Sir Robert Abbott Hadfield 1000
Ernst Haeckel 1002
H. Rider Haggard 1006
Samuel Hahnemann 1009
Sarah Josepha Hale 1012
Sir William Rowan Hamilton 1015
Marcus A. Hanna 1018
Karl von Hardenberg 1021
Keir Hardie 1025
Thomas Hardy 1028
William Rainey Harper 1031
Joel Chandler Harris 1036
Benjamin Harrison 1040
Frederic Harrison 1044
William Henry Harrison 1048
Nathaniel Hawthorne 1051
John Hay 1054
Ferdinand Vandeveer Hayden 1058
Rutherford B. Hayes 1061
Georg Wilhelm Friedrich Hegel 1065
Heinrich Heine 1069
Hermann von Helmholtz 1073
Felicia Dorothea Hemans 1076
Joseph Henry 1078
O. Henry 1081
Aleksandr Herzen 1085
Theodor Herzl 1088
Wild Bill Hickok 1091
Miguel Hidalgo y Costilla 1094
Thomas Wentworth Higginson 1097
James Jerome Hill 1100
Octavia Hill 1103
Hiroshige 1107
Ho Xuan Huong 1110
John Philip Holland 1113
Oliver Wendell Holmes 1116
Friedrich von Holstein 1119
Winslow Homer 1122
Hong Xiuquan 1127
Sam Houston 1130
Elias Howe 1133
Julia Ward Howe 1137
Samuel Gridley Howe 1141
Margaret Lindsay Huggins 1144
Victor Hugo 1146
Alexander von Humboldt 1151
Engelbert Humperdinck 1154
William Holman Hunt 1157
Thomas Henry Huxley 1161

Henrik Ibsen 1165
Ii Naosuke 1168
Jean-Auguste-Dominique Ingres 1171
Henry Irving 1175
Washington Irving 1180
Isabella II 1183
Itō Hirobumi 1185

Andrew Jackson 1189
Helen Hunt Jackson 1193

Stonewall Jackson 1197
Mary Putnam Jacobi 1200
Jamāl al-Dīn al-Afghānī 1203
Henry James 1206
Jesse and Frank James 1211
William James 1213
Anna Jameson 1217
Jean Jaurès 1220
Lord Jeffrey 1223
Sarah Orne Jewett 1226
Andrew Johnson 1229
Scott Joplin 1235
Chief Joseph 1238
Joséphine 1241
Benito Juárez 1245

Kamehameha I 1249
Kang Youwei 1252
Edmund Kean 1254
John Keats 1259
Baron Kelvin 1264
Fanny Kemble 1267
James Kent 1271
Francis Scott Key 1274
Søren Kierkegaard 1278
Mary Kingsley 1281
Rudyard Kipling 1284
Heinrich von Kleist 1289
Robert Koch 1291
Sofya Kovalevskaya 1295
Paul Kruger 1298
Alfred Krupp 1301

Joseph Lancaster 1304
Helene Lange 1307
Samuel Pierpont Langley 1309
Lillie Langtry 1312
Sir Edwin Ray Lankester 1315
Pierre-Simon Laplace 1317
Ferdinand Lassalle 1321

Volume 3

Contents xcv
Key to Pronunciation xcix
Complete List of Contents ci
List of Maps and Sidebars cxi
Maps of the Nineteenth Century cxxi

Benjamin Henry Latrobe 1325
John Laird Mair Lawrence 1328
Emma Lazarus 1331
Robert E. Lee 1334
Étienne Lenoir 1338
Leo XIII 1342
Anna Leonowens 1346
Leopold II 1349
Mikhail Lermontov 1352
Ferdinand de Lesseps 1356
Meriwether Lewis and William Clark 1359
Li Hongzhang 1363
Justus von Liebig 1366
Wilhelm Liebknecht 1370
Liliuokalani 1373
Lin Zexu 1376
Abraham Lincoln 1380
Mary Todd Lincoln 1385
Jenny Lind 1387
Joseph Lister 1390
Franz Liszt 1393
Second Earl of Liverpool 1397
David Livingstone 1400
Nikolay Ivanovich Lobachevsky 1403
Lobengula 1406
Belva A. Lockwood 1409
Sir Joseph Norman Lockyer 1412
Henry Wadsworth Longfellow 1416
Countess of Lovelace 1420
Sir Charles Lyell 1423
Mary Lyon 1428

John MacArthur 1431
Thomas Babington Macaulay 1433
Cyrus Hall McCormick 1438
Sir John Alexander Macdonald 1441
William Holmes McGuffey 1445
Joaquim Maria Machado de Assis 1449
Alexander Mackenzie 1452
William Lyon Mackenzie 1454
William McKinley 1460
Daniel and Alexander Macmillan 1464

William Charles Macready 1467
Dolley Madison 1470
The Mahdi 1473
Thomas Robert Malthus 1475
Édouard Manet 1479
Meri Te Tai Mangakahia 1483
Horace Mann 1486
Henry Edward Manning 1489
Daniel Mannix 1492
Alessandro Manzoni 1495
John Marshall 1498
José Martí 1503
Harriet Martineau 1505
Karl Marx 1508
Clorinda Matto de Turner 1512
Guy de Maupassant 1515
Frederick Denison Maurice 1518
Matthew Fontaine Maury 1522
Maximilian 1525
James Clerk Maxwell 1528
Giuseppe Mazzini 1531
Second Viscount Melbourne 1534
Herman Melville 1537
Gregor Mendel 1541
Dmitry Ivanovich Mendeleyev 1544
Felix Mendelssohn 1549
Menelik II 1552
Adah Isaacs Menken 1555
Ottmar Mergenthaler 1558
Metternich 1561
Jules Michelet 1564
Albert A. Michelson 1567
James Mill 1571
John Stuart Mill 1574
Maria Mitchell 1580
Theodor Mommsen 1582
James Monroe 1586
Lola Montez 1590
Susanna Moodie 1593
Dwight L. Moody 1596
J. P. Morgan 1599
Lewis Henry Morgan 1603
William Morris 1606
Samuel F. B. Morse 1610
William Thomas Green Morton 1613
Lucretia Mott 1616
Muḥammad ʿAlī Pasha 1620
John Muir 1623
Modest Mussorgsky 1626
Mutsuhito 1631
Dadabhai Naoroji 1634
Napoleon I 1636
Napoleon III 1639
John Nash 1642
James Nasmyth 1646
Thomas Nast 1649
Carry Nation 1652
Lord Nelson 1656
Simon Newcomb 1660
John Henry Newman 1663
Michel Ney 1667
Nicholas I 1670
Barthold Georg Niebuhr 1673
Nicéphore Niépce 1676
Friedrich Nietzsche 1680
Florence Nightingale 1684
Alfred Nobel 1689

Annie Oakley 1692
Daniel O'Connell 1695
Jacques Offenbach 1699
Bernardo O'Higgins 1703
Frederick Law Olmsted 1706
Osceola 1709
Sir William Osler 1711
Nikolaus August Otto 1714
Sir James Outram 1717
Robert Owen 1720

Niccolò Paganini 1724
Alice Freeman Palmer 1727
Lord Palmerston 1731
Theodore Parker 1735
Sir Henry Parkes 1739
Francis Parkman 1742
Charles Stewart Parnell 1747
Louis Pasteur 1751
Walter Pater 1755
A. B. Paterson 1758
Elizabeth Palmer Peabody 1761
Pedro I 1763
Pedro II 1766
Sir Robert Peel 1768
Charles Sanders Peirce 1772
Matthew C. Perry 1776
Oliver Hazard Perry 1779
Johann Heinrich Pestalozzi 1782
Wendell Phillips 1785
Franklin Pierce 1789
Zebulon Pike 1793

Lydia E. Pinkham 1796
Camille Pissarro 1799
Pius IX 1802
Francis Place 1806
Konstantin Petrovich Pobedonostsev 1810
Edgar Allan Poe 1813
Henri Poincaré 1816
James K. Polk 1819
Aleksandr Stepanovich Popov 1824
John Wesley Powell 1827
William Hickling Prescott 1831
Pierre-Joseph Proudhon 1834
Augustus Welby Northmore Pugin 1838
Joseph Pulitzer 1841
E. B. Pusey 1844
Alexander Pushkin 1848

Sir Henry Raeburn 1852
Mahadev Govind Ranade 1855
Ranjit Singh 1857
Leopold von Ranke 1860
Grigori Yefimovich Rasputin 1863
Rammohan Ray 1866
André Rebouças 1869
Red Cloud 1871
Odilon Redon 1875
Walter Reed 1877
Frederic Remington 1881
Ernest Renan 1884
Pierre-Auguste Renoir 1888
Cecil Rhodes 1891
David Ricardo 1896
Ellen Swallow Richards 1899
Abby Sage Richardson 1902
Henry Hobson Richardson 1905
Louis Riel 1908
Arthur Rimbaud 1912
Nikolay Rimsky-Korsakov 1915
Albrecht Ritschl 1918
John D. Rockefeller 1921
Auguste Rodin 1925
John Augustus Roebling 1928
Wilhelm Conrad Röntgen 1931
Sir James Clark Ross 1934
John Ross 1937
Christina Rossetti 1940
Gioacchino Rossini 1944
The Rothschild Family 1947
Henri Rousseau 1951
John Ruskin 1954
John Russell 1958

Sacagawea 1962
Saʿīd ibn Sulṭān 1965
Saigō Takamori 1968
Augustus Saint-Gaudens 1972
Henri de Saint-Simon 1975
Third Marquis of Salisbury 1977
Samory Touré 1981
José de San Martín 1984
George Sand 1987
Antonio López de Santa Anna 1990
La Saragossa 1993
John Singer Sargent 1996
Domingo Faustino Sarmiento 2000

Volume 4

Contents cxxxiii
Key to Pronunciation cxxxv
Complete List of Contents cxxxvii
List of Maps and Sidebars cxlvii
Maps of the Nineteenth Century clvii

Friedrich Karl von Savigny 2003
Gerhard Johann David von Scharnhorst 2006
Friedrich Wilhelm Joseph von Schelling 2009
Friedrich Schleiermacher 2013
Heinrich Schliemann 2016
Arthur Schopenhauer 2019
Olive Schreiner 2023
Franz Schubert 2026
Clara Schumann 2029
Robert Schumann 2031
Carl Schurz 2035
Charlotte Angas Scott 2039
Dred Scott 2041
Sir George Gilbert Scott 2044
Sir Walter Scott 2047
Winfield Scott 2051

Edward Wyllis Scripps 2055
Richard John Seddon 2058
Anaïs Ségalas 2062
Ignaz Philipp Semmelweis 2064
Sequoyah 2067
Saint Elizabeth Seton 2071
Georges Seurat 2074
William H. Seward 2077
Shaka 2081
Anna Howard Shaw 2084
Mary Wollstonecraft Shelley 2088
Percy Bysshe Shelley 2092
William Tecumseh Sherman 2097
Henry Sidgwick 2102
The Siemens Family 2105
Sitting Bull 2108
Samuel Slater 2111
Jedediah Smith 2114
Joseph Smith 2117
Mary Somerville 2121
John Hanning Speke 2123
Herbert Spencer 2126
Mikhail Mikhaylovich Speransky 2129
Leland Stanford 2132
Henry Morton Stanley 2136
Edwin M. Stanton 2142
Elizabeth Cady Stanton 2146
Freiherr vom Stein 2151
Jakob Steiner 2154
Charles Proteus Steinmetz 2156
Stendhal 2160
Alexander H. Stephens 2164
George Stephenson 2167
Thaddeus Stevens 2171
Robert Louis Stevenson 2173
Lucy Stone 2177
Joseph Story 2180
Harriet Beecher Stowe 2184
Johann Strauss 2188
George Edmund Street 2191
Antonio José de Sucre 2195
Louis Sullivan 2198
Charles Sumner 2201
Bertha von Suttner 2205
Joseph Wilson Swan 2209

Tadano Makuzu 2212
Táhirih 2214
Hippolyte Taine 2216
Thomas Talbot 2219
Talleyrand 2221
Roger Brooke Taney 2225
Zachary Taylor 2230
Peter Ilich Tchaikovsky 2233
Tecumseh 2237
Thomas Telford 2240
Alfred, Lord Tennyson 2244
Ellen Terry 2248
Nikola Tesla 2252
Tewodros II 2255
William Makepeace Thackeray 2257
Sylvanus Thayer 2260
Adolphe Thiers 2263
Theodore Thomas 2267
David Thompson 2271
Henry David Thoreau 2274
Tippu Tib 2277
Alexis de Tocqueville 2280
Leo Tolstoy 2283
Henri de Toulouse-Lautrec 2287
Catharine Parr Traill 2291
Richard Trevithick 2294
Flora Tristan 2297
Anthony Trollope 2299
Frances Trollope 2303
Sojourner Truth 2306
Tu Duc 2310
Harriet Tubman 2312
Sir Charles Tupper 2316
Ivan Turgenev 2319
J. M. W. Turner 2322
Nat Turner 2326
Mark Twain 2329
William Marcy Tweed 2333
John Tyler 2337

ʿUthman dan Fodio 2342

Martin Van Buren 2344
Cornelius Vanderbilt 2348
Giuseppe Verdi 2351
Jules Verne 2354
Queen Victoria 2359
Iswar Chandra Vidyasagar 2363
Rudolf Virchow 2365
Vivekananda 2368
Sir Julius Vogel 2371

Richard Wagner 2374
Edward Gibbon Wakefield 2378

John Walter II 2380
Lester Frank Ward 2384
Montgomery Ward 2386
Booker T. Washington 2390
Carl Maria von Weber 2395
Daniel Webster 2398
Noah Webster 2402
August Weismann 2406
Duke of Wellington 2409
W. C. Wentworth 2412
George Westinghouse 2416
James McNeill Whistler 2420
Walt Whitman 2423
John Greenleaf Whittier 2428
Oscar Wilde 2432
Charles Wilkes 2435
Emma Willard 2438
Frances Willard 2442
William IV 2445
George Washington Williams 2449
Isaac Mayer Wise 2453
Friedrich Wöhler 2456
Victoria Woodhull 2459
William Wordsworth 2462
Fanny Bullock Workman 2466
Frances Wright 2469

Charlotte Mary Yonge 2472
Brigham Young 2474
Alexander and Demetrios Ypsilantis 2478

Marie Elizabeth Zakrzewska 2481
Zeng Guofan 2483
Zhang Zhidong 2486
Émile Zola 2489

Rulers and Heads of State 2495
Chronological List of Entries 2550
Category Index 2562
Geographical Index 2571

Personages Index III
Subject Index XXV

List of Maps and Sidebars

Volume I

Adams's Last State of the Union Address (*primary source*) 23
Address, Adams's Last State of the Union (*primary source*) 23
Advice to Young Men (*primary source*) 519
Africa at the End of the Nineteenth Century (*map*) . . . . . *xlvi*
Agassiz's Childhood (*primary source*) 33
Alcott's Major Works (*list*) 43
Alger's Novels About Success (*list*) 53
America at the End of the Nineteenth Century, North (*map*) . . . . . *xlix*
America at the End of the Nineteenth Century, South (*map*). . . . . *l*
Ancient Mariner, The Rime of the (*primary source*) 531
Andersen's Best-Known Fairy Tales (*list*). 63
Argument for Foreign Missions, The (*primary source*) 410
Art of Money Getting, The (*primary source*) 140
Asia and Australasia at the End of the Nineteenth Century (*map*) . . . . . *xlvii*
Austen's Major Works (*list*) 96
Australasia at the End of the Nineteenth Century, Asia and (*map*) . . . . . *xlvii*
Autobiography, Dedication of Black Hawk's (*primary source*) 245
Balzac's *The Human Comedy* (*list*) 127
Bank, Benton on the National (*primary source*) 194
Baum's Oz Novels (*list*) 157
Beethoven the Businessperson (*primary source*) 177
Benton on the National Bank (*primary source*) 194
Benz's Four-Cycle Engine (*sidebar*). 198
Bernhardt's Motion Picture Roles (*list*) 210
Black Hawk's Autobiography, Dedication of (*primary source*) 245
Borden Rhyme, The Lizzie (*primary source*) 278
Boyhood Interests, Darwin's (*primary source*) 605
Braddon's Novels (*list*). 285
British Policy in the Crimea (*primary source*) 303
Brontë Sisters' Major Works, The (*list*) 310
Building the Thames Tunnel (*sidebar*) 338
Businessperson, Beethoven the (*primary source*) 177
Butler on "Unconscious Memory" (*primary source*) 375
Campbell, Mark Twain Remembers (*primary source*) 401
Carlyle's Major Works (*list*) 417
Carroll's Works for Children (*list*). 425
Case for India, The (*primary source*) 213
Chekhov's Maxims (*primary source*) 480
Childe Harold's Pilgrimage (*primary source*) . . . 56
Childhood, Agassiz's (*primary source*) 33
Children, Carroll's Works for (*list*) 425
Chinese Question, The (*primary source*) 509
Chopin's Major Works (*list*) 492
Christian Home, The Proper (*primary source*) 170
Comedy, Balzac's *The Human* (*list*) 127
Compromise of 1850, The (*primary source*). . . . 613
Cooper's Major Works (*list*) 554
Crane's Major Works (*list*). 564
Crimea, British Policy in the (*primary source*) 303
Criticism, The Function of (*primary source*) 73
Culture Movement, Goals of the Ethical (*primary source*) 28
Custer's Last Stand (*primary source*) 526
Darkest England (*primary source*). 275
Darwin's Boyhood Interests (*primary source*) 605
Decimal System, The Dewey (*primary source*) 651
Dedication of Black Hawk's Autobiography (*primary source*) 245
Devil's Dictionary, Extracts from *The* (*primary source*) 230

Dewey Decimal System, The (*primary source*) 651
Dictionary, Extracts from *The Devil's* (*primary source*) 230
Dynamo Metaphor, The (*primary source*) 18
Economies, Tips on Household (*primary source*) 484
1850, The Compromise of (*primary source*) . . . 613
Engine, Benz's Four-Cycle (*sidebar*) 198
England, Darkest (*primary source*) 275
Ethical Culture Movement, Goals of the (*primary source*) 28
Europe at the End of the Nineteenth Century (*map*) . . . . . *xlviii*
Expunging Resolution, The (*primary source*) . . . 505
Extracts from *The Devil's Dictionary* (*primary source*) 230
Fairy Tales, Andersen's Best-Known (*list*) 63
Ferry, Robert E. Lee's Letter from Harpers (*primary source*) 320
Foreign Missions, The Argument for (*primary source*) 410
Four-Cycle Engine, Benz's (*sidebar*) 198
Function of Criticism, The (*primary source*) 73
Goals of the Ethical Culture Movement (*primary source*) 28
Harpers Ferry, Robert E. Lee's Letter from (*primary source*) 320
Hide-and-Seek, The Value of (*primary source*) 112
Home, The Proper Christian (*primary source*) 170
Household Economies, Tips on (*primary source*) 484
Human Comedy, Balzac's *The* (*list*) 127
India, The Case for (*primary source*) 213
Interests, Darwin's Boyhood (*primary source*) 605
Knowledge (*primary source*) 77
Last Stand, Custer's (*primary source*) 526
Lee's Letter from Harpers Ferry, Robert E. (*primary source*) 320
Letter from Harpers Ferry, Robert E. Lee's (*primary source*) 320
Lizzie Borden Rhyme, The (*primary source*) . . . 278
Mariner, The Rime of the Ancient (*primary source*) 531
Mark Twain Remembers Campbell (*primary source*) 401
Maxims, Chekhov's (*primary source*) 480
Memory," Butler on "Unconscious (*primary source*) 375
Men, Advice to Young (*primary source*) 519
Metaphor, The Dynamo (*primary source*) 18
Missions, The Argument for Foreign (*primary source*) 410
Money Getting, The Art of (*primary source*) 140
Motion Picture Roles, Bernhardt's (*list*) 210
Movement, Goals of the Ethical Culture (*primary source*) 28
National Bank, Benton on the (*primary source*) 194
North America at the End of the Nineteenth Century (*map*) . . . . . *xlix*
Novels About Success, Alger's (*list*) 53
Novels, Baum's Oz (*list*) 157
Novels, Braddon's (*list*) 285
On War (*primary source*) 501
Oz Novels, Baum's (*list*) 157
Pilgrimage, Childe Harold's (*primary source*) 56
Policy in the Crimea, British (*primary source*) 303
Proper Christian Home, The (*primary source*) 170
Question, The Chinese (*primary source*) 509
Resolution, The Expunging (*primary source*) 505
Rhyme, The Lizzie Borden (*primary source*) 278
Rime of the Ancient Mariner, The (*primary source*) 531
Robert E. Lee's Letter from Harpers Ferry (*primary source*) 320
Roles, Bernhardt's Motion Picture (*list*) 210
Sisters' Major Works, The Brontë (*list*) 310
South America at the End of the Nineteenth Century (*map*) . . . . . *l*
Stand, Custer's Last (*primary source*) 526
State of the Union Address, Adams's Last (*primary source*) 23
Success, Alger's Novels About (*list*) 53
System, The Dewey Decimal (*primary source*) 651
Tales, Andersen's Best-Known Fairy (*list*) 63
Thames Tunnel, Building the (*sidebar*) 338
Tips on Household Economies (*primary source*) 484
Tunnel, Building the Thames (*sidebar*) 338

"Unconscious Memory," Butler on (*primary source*) 375
Union Address, Adams's Last State of the (*primary source*) 23
Value of Hide-and-Seek, The (*primary source*) 112
Veracruz (*primary source*) 390
War, On (*primary source*) 501
Works for Children, Carroll's (*list*) 425
Works, Alcott's Major (*list*) 43
Works, Austen's Major (*list*) 96
Works, The Brontë Sisters' Major (*list*) 310
Works, Carlyle's Major (*list*) 417
Works, Chopin's Major (*list*) 492
Works, Cooper's Major (*list*) 554
Works, Crane's Major (*list*) 564
World in 1801 (*map*) . . . . . *xlv*
World in 1900 (*map*) . . . . . *xlv*
Young Men, Advice to (*primary source*) 519

Volume 2

Abraham Lincoln, Mourning (*primary source*) 1232
Address, Fillmore's First State of the Union (*primary source*) 783
Address, Harrison's Inaugural (*primary source*) 1041
Address, Hayes's First State of the Union (*primary source*) 1063
Advice to Her Followers, Eddy's (*primary source*) 725
Africa at the End of the Nineteenth Century (*map*) . . . . . *lxxxiv*
Africa, The Decision to Go to West (*primary source*) 1282
Agassiz, Darwin vs. (*primary source*) 965
America at the End of the Nineteenth Century, North (*map*) . . . . . *lxxxvii*
America at the End of the Nineteenth Century, South (*map*) . . . . . *lxxxviii*
"American Negroes, Representative" (*primary source*) 703
Appeal to the Christian Women of the South (*primary source*) 990
Arctic, Hunger in the (*primary source*) 826
Asia and Australasia at the End of the Nineteenth Century (*map*) . . . . . *lxxxv*
Australasia at the End of the Nineteenth Century, Asia and (*map*) . . . . . *lxxxv*
Authors, Holmes on (*primary source*) 1118
"Baby Story, The Wonderful Tar" (*primary source*) 1038
Banner, The Star-Spangled (*primary source*) 1276
"Battle Hymn of the Republic, The" (*primary source*) 1139
"Bean, The Straw, the Coal, and the" (*primary source*) 994
Birth, Douglass's Uncertainty About His (*primary source*) 685
Black Regiment, The First (*primary source*) 1099
"Bludso, of the 'Prairie Belle,' Jim" (*primary source*) 1056
Books, Haggard's (*list*) 1008
Casetaking, Guidelines for a Model Medical (*primary source*) 1010
Christian Women of the South, Appeal to the (*primary source*) 990
Christianity, St. Mael Converts the Penguins to (*primary source*) 817
Christianity and Slavery (*primary source*) 1269
Civil War Memoirs (*primary source*) 961
"Coal, and the Bean, The Straw, the" (*primary source*) 994
Coining the Name "Kindergarten" (*primary source*) 837
Coningsby, Disraeli's (*primary source*) 668
Converts the Penguins to Christianity, St. Mael (*primary source*) 817
Darwin vs. Agassiz (*primary source*) 965
Decision to Go to West Africa, The (*primary source*) 1282
Dickens's Major Works (*list*) 656
Dickinson's "Letter to the World" (*primary source*) 659
Disraeli's *Coningsby* (*primary source*) 668
Donizetti's Operas (*list*) 675

Dostoevski's Major Works (*list*) 679
Douglass's Uncertainty About His Birth (*primary source*) 685
Dumas's Major Works 697
Eddy's Advice to Her Followers (*primary source*) 725
Edgeworth's Major Fictional Works (*list*) 729
Emerson's Major Works (*list*) 747
Engels's Major Works 751
Epitaph to General Gordon (*primary source*) 951
Europe at the End of the Nineteenth Century (*map*) . . . . . *lxxxvi*
Explore, Humboldt's Impulse to (*primary source*) 1152
Fictional Works, Edgeworth's Major (*list*) 729
"Fight No More Forever, I Will" (*primary source*) 1240
Fillmore's First State of the Union Address (*primary source*) 783
First Black Regiment, The (*primary source*) 1099
First State of the Union Address, Hayes's (*primary source*) 1063
Flaubert's Major Works (*list*) 786
Followers, Eddy's Advice to Her (*primary source*) 725
"Forever, I Will Fight No More" (*primary source*) 1240
"General, I Am the Very Model of a Modern Major" (*primary source*) 918
General Gordon, Epitaph to (*primary source*) 951
Gogol's Major Works (*list*) 938
Gordon, Epitaph to General (*primary source*) 951
Guidelines for a Model Medical Casetaking (*primary source*) 1010
Haggard's Books (*list*) 1008
Harrison's Inaugural Address (*primary source*) 1041
Hayes's First State of the Union Address (*primary source*) 1063
History, Irish (*primary source*) 926
Holmes, Introducing Sherlock (*primary source*) 690
Holmes on Authors (*primary source*) 1118
Humboldt's Impulse to Explore (*primary source*) 1152
Hunger in the Arctic (*primary source*) 826
Huxley's Schooldays (*primary source*) 1163
"Hymn of the Republic, The Battle" (*primary source*) 1139
"I Am the Very Model of a Modern Major General" (*primary source*) 918
"I Will Fight No More Forever" (*primary source*) 1240
Ibsen's Major Plays (*list*) 1166
"Imitation of Spenser" (*primary source*) 1261
Inaugural Address, Harrison's (*primary source*) 1041
Indian Removal (*primary source*) 1191
Introducing Sherlock Holmes (*primary source*) 690
Irish History (*primary source*) 926
Irving and Ellen Terry (*primary source*) 1177
Irving's Major Works (*list*) 1181
"Jackfruit, The" (*primary source*) 1111
Jackson's Principal Works (*list*) 1195
James's Major Works (*list*) 1208
"Jim Bludso, of the 'Prairie Belle'" (*primary source*) 1056
John Stuart Mill, Remembering (*primary source*) 768
"Kindergarten," Coining the Name (*primary source*) 837
"Letter to the World," Dickinson's (*primary source*) 659
Lincoln, Mourning Abraham (*primary source*) 1232
"Major General, I Am the Very Model of a Modern" (*primary source*) 918
Medical Casetaking, Guidelines for a Model (*primary source*) 1010
Memoirs, Civil War (*primary source*) 961
Mill, Remembering John Stuart (*primary source*) 768
Model Medical Casetaking, Guidelines for a (*primary source*) 1010
"Model of a Modern Major General, I Am the Very" (*primary source*) 918
"Modern Major General, I Am the Very Model of a" (*primary source*) 918
Monism (*primary source*) 1003
Mourning Abraham Lincoln (*primary source*) 1232
"Negroes, Representative American" (*primary source*) 703
North America at the End of the Nineteenth Century (*map*) . . . . . *lxxxvii*

Operas, Donizetti's (*list*) 675
Penguins to Christianity, St. Mael Converts the (*primary source*) 817
Plays, Ibsen's Major 1166
"'Prairie Belle,' Jim Bludso, of the" (*primary source*) 1056
Psychology, Religion and (*primary source*) . . . 1214
Regiment, The First Black (*primary source*) . . . 1099
Religion and Psychology (*primary source*) . . . 1214
Remembering John Stuart Mill (*primary source*) 768
Removal, Indian (*primary source*) 1191
"Representative American Negroes" (*primary source*) 703
"Republic, The Battle Hymn of the" (*primary source*) 1139
St. Mael Converts the Penguins to Christianity (*primary source*) 817
Schooldays, Huxley's (*primary source*) 1163
Sherlock Holmes, Introducing (*primary source*) 690
Slavery, Christianity and (*primary source*) . . . 1269
South America at the End of the Nineteenth Century (*map*) . . . . . *lxxxviii*
South, Appeal to the Christian Women of the (*primary source*) 990
Spangled Banner, The Star- (*primary source*) 1276
"Spenser, Imitation of" (*primary source*) 1261
Star-Spangled Banner, The (*primary source*) 1276
State of the Union Address, Fillmore's First (*primary source*) 783
State of the Union Address, Hayes's First (*primary source*) 1063
"Story, The Wonderful Tar Baby" (*primary source*) 1038
"Straw, the Coal, and the Bean, The" (*primary source*) 994
"Tar Baby Story, The Wonderful" (*primary source*) 1038
Terry, Irving and Ellen (*primary source*) 1177
Union Address, Fillmore's First State of the (*primary source*) 783
Union Address, Hayes's First State of the (*primary source*) 1063
War Memoirs, Civil (*primary source*) 961
West Africa, The Decision to Go to (*primary source*) 1282
Women of the South, Appeal to the Christian (*primary source*) 990
"Wonderful Tar Baby Story, The" (*primary source*) 1038
Works, Dickens's Major (*list*) 656
Works, Dostoevski's Major (*list*) 679
Works, Dumas's Major 697
Works, Edgeworth's Major Fictional (*list*) 729
Works, Emerson's Major (*list*) 747
Works, Engels's Major 751
Works, Flaubert's Major (*list*) 786
Works, Gogol's Major (*list*) 938
Works, Irving's Major (*list*) 1181
Works, Jackson's Principal (*list*) 1195
Works, James's Major (*list*) 1208
World," Dickinson's "Letter to the (*primary source*) 659
World in 1801 (*map*) . . . . . *lxxxiii*
World in 1900 (*map*) . . . . . *lxxxiii*

VOLUME 3

Acquittal of Richardson's Former Husband, The (*primary source*) 1903
Address, The Gettysburg (*primary source*) . . . 1382
Admirable Properties of Glass and Cork, The (*primary source*) 1367
Africa at the End of the Nineteenth Century (*map*) . . . . . *cxxii*
"Aloha 'Oe" (Farewell to Thee) (*primary source*) 1375
America at the End of the Nineteenth Century, North (*map*) . . . . . *cxxv*
America at the End of the Nineteenth Century, South (*map*) . . . . . *cxxvi*
Ancient Cliff Dwellers, The (*primary source*) 1829
Architecture, On Perfection in Art and (*primary source*) 1956

Arrival on the Pacific Coast (*primary source*) 1361
Art and Architecture, On Perfection in (*primary source*) 1956
Asia and Australasia at the End of the Nineteenth Century (*map*) . . . . . *cxxiii*
Australasia at the End of the Nineteenth Century, Asia and (*map*) . . . . . *cxxiii*
Border Settlement, The Mexican (*primary source*) 1791
Canada's Future Prospects (*primary source*) 1594
Cliff Dwellers, The Ancient (*primary source*) 1829
Coast, Arrival on the Pacific (*primary source*) 1361
College?, Why Go to (*primary source*) 1729
Color Spectrum, The (*primary source*) 1530
"Colossus, The New" (*primary source*) 1333
Communist Manifesto, The (*primary source*) 1510
Compound, Pinkham's Vegetable (*primary source*) 1797
Confederate General, From Union Officer to (*primary source*) 1336
Cork, The Admirable Properties of Glass and (*primary source*) 1367
Daughter, Saʿīd ibn Sulṭān Remembered by His (*primary source*) 1967
Doctrine, The Monroe (*primary source*) 1588
Dwellers, The Ancient Cliff (*primary source*) 1829
1872, Lobengula in (*primary source*) 1407
Emma Hamilton, A Letter to (*primary source*) 1658
England, The History of (*primary source*) 1435
Essay on the Principle of Population (*primary source*) 1477
Europe at the End of the Nineteenth Century (*map*) . . . . . *cxxiv*
Falls, First Visit to Victoria (*primary source*) 1402
First Visit to Victoria Falls (*primary source*) 1402
From Union Officer to Confederate General (*primary source*) 1336
Future Prospects, Canada's (*primary source*) 1594
General, From Union Officer to Confederate (*primary source*) 1336
Gettysburg Address, The (*primary source*) . . . 1382
Glass and Cork, The Admirable Properties of (*primary source*) 1367
"Goblin Market" (*primary source*) 1942
Hamilton, A Letter to Emma (*primary source*) 1658
Hetch Hetchy Valley (*primary source*) 1625
History of England, The (*primary source*) 1435
Husband, The Acquittal of Richardson's Former (*primary source*) 1903
Influences in Mill's Youth, Moral (*primary source*) 1576
Kansas, An Unfriendly Mob in (*primary source*) 1654
"King Leopold's Soliloquy" (*primary source*) 1351
King Mongkut Invites Leonowens to Come to Siam (*primary source*) 1347
Leonowens to Come to Siam, King Mongkut Invites (*primary source*) 1347
"Leopold's Soliloquy, King" (*primary source*) 1351
Letter to Emma Hamilton, A (*primary source*) 1658
Lobengula in 1872 (*primary source*) 1407
"Lost Youth, My" (*primary source*) 1418
Machado d'Assis's Major Works (*list*) 1450
Manifesto, The Communist (*primary source*) 1510
Mark Twain Reviews *Mazeppa* (*primary source*) 1556
"Market, Goblin" (*primary source*) 1942
"Matilda, Waltzing" (*primary source*) 1759
Mazeppa, Mark Twain Reviews (*primary source*) 1556
Medicine, The Origins of (*primary source*) . . . 1712
Melville's Novels (*list*) 1539
Mexican Border Settlement, The (*primary source*) 1791
Mexico, War with (*primary source*) 1821
Mill's Youth, Moral Influences in (*primary source*) 1576
Mob in Kansas, An Unfriendly (*primary source*) 1654
Mongkut Invites Leonowens to Come to Siam, King (*primary source*) 1347
Monroe Doctrine, The (*primary source*) 1588
Moon, The Possibility of Life on the (*primary source*) 1661

Moral Influences in Mill's Youth (*primary source*) 1576
"My Lost Youth" (*primary source*) 1418
"New Colossus, The" (*primary source*) 1333
Nonfiction Works, Parkman's (*list*). 1744
North America at the End of the Nineteenth Century (*map*) . . . . . *cxxv*
Novels, Melville's (*list*). 1539
Novels, Sand's (*list*) 1988
"Observation of the Sick" (*primary source*). 1686
"'Oe, Aloha" (*primary source*) 1375
Officer to Confederate General, From Union (*primary source*) 1336
On Perfection in Art and Architecture (*primary source*). 1956
Organizations That Ranade Founded or Cofounded (*list*) 1856
Origins of Medicine, The (*primary source*) . . . 1712
Pacific Coast, Arrival on the (*primary source*). 1361
Parkman's Nonfiction Works (*list*) 1744
Perfection in Art and Architecture, On (*primary source*). 1956
Pinkham's Vegetable Compound (*primary source*). 1797
Poe's Major Works (*list*) 1815
Population, Essay on the Principle of (*primary source*). 1477
Possibility of Life on the Moon, The (*primary source*). 1661
Principle of Population, Essay on the (*primary source*). 1477
Properties of Glass and Cork, The Admirable (*primary source*). 1367
Prospects, Canada's Future (*primary source*). 1594
Pushkin's Major Works (*list*) 1850
Ranade Founded or Cofounded, Organizations That (*list*) 1856
Recollections of Youth (*primary source*). 1886
Remembered by His Daughter, Saʿīd ibn Sulṭān (*primary source*) 1967
Richardson's Former Husband, The Acquittal of (*primary source*) 1903
Riel's Last Testament (*primary source*) 1910
Saʿīd ibn Sulṭān Remembered by His Daughter (*primary source*) 1967
Sand's Novels (*list*) 1988
Settlement, The Mexican Border (*primary source*). 1791
Siam, King Mongkut Invites Leonowens to Come to (*primary source*) 1347
"Sick, Observation of the" (*primary source*) . . . 1686
"Soliloquy, King Leopold's" (*primary source*). 1351
South America at the End of the Nineteenth Century (*map*). . . . . *cxxvi*
Spectrum, The Color (*primary source*). 1530
Testament, Riel's Last (*primary source*) 1910
Twain Reviews *Mazeppa*, Mark (*primary source*). 1556
Unfriendly Mob in Kansas, An (*primary source*). 1654
Union Officer to Confederate General, From (*primary source*) 1336
Valley, Hetch Hetchy (*primary source*) 1625
Vegetable Compound, Pinkham's (*primary source*). 1797
Victoria Falls, First Visit to (*primary source*). 1402
Visit to Victoria Falls, First (*primary source*). 1402
"Waltzing Matilda" (*primary source*) 1759
War with Mexico (*primary source*) 1821
Why Go to College? (*primary source*) 1729
Works, Machado d'Assis's Major (*list*). 1450
Works, Parkman's Nonfiction (list). 1744
Works, Poe's Major (*list*) 1815
Works, Pushkin's Major (*list*). 1850
World in 1801 (*map*) . . . . . *cxxi*
World in 1900 (*map*) . . . . . *cxxi*
Youth, Moral Influences in Mill's (*primary source*). 1576
"Youth, My Lost" (*primary source*) 1418
Youth, Recollections of (*primary source*) 1886

VOLUME 4

Advice from Authors, Taking (*primary source*) 2250
Africa at the End of the Nineteenth Century (*map*) . . . . . *clviii*
African Farm, The Story of an (*primary source*) 2024
African Race, "Degradation" of the (*primary source*) 2451
America at the End of the Nineteenth Century, North (*map*) . . . . . *clxi*
America at the End of the Nineteenth Century, South (*map*) . . . . . *clxii*
Apology for the French Revolution (*primary source*) 2464
Art Students, Lecture to (*primary source*) 2433
Asia and Australasia at the End of the Nineteenth Century (*map*) . . . . . *clix*
Australasia at the End of the Nineteenth Century, Asia and (*map*) . . . . . *clix*
Australia's Advantages over the United States (*primary source*) 2414
Authors, Taking Advice from (*primary source*) 2250
Autobiography, An Eccentric (*primary source*) 2331
"Beauty, Hymn to Intellectual" (*primary source*) 2094
Blackbirds (*primary source*) 2292
Book of Mormon, Witnesses to the (*primary source*) 2119
Burton on Brigham Young, Richard F. (*primary source*) 2476
"Captain!, O Captain! My" (*primary source*) 2425
Childhood Mystery Woman, A (*primary source*) 2085
Civil Disobedience, On (*primary source*) 2276
Civil War Southerners, Classifying Post- (*primary source*) 2037
Classifying Post-Civil War Southerners (*primary source*) 2037
Constitution, In Defense of the (*primary source*) 2400
Creation, Frankenstein Meets His (*primary source*) 2090
Death of Wagner's Father (*primary source*) . . . 2376
Defense of the Constitution, In (*primary source*) 2400
"Degradation" of the African Race (*primary source*) 2451
Disobedience, On Civil (*primary source*) 2276
Early Exposure to the Law (*primary source*) 2148
Eccentric Autobiography, An (*primary source*) 2331
Europe, U.S. Relations with (*primary source*) 2231
Europe at the End of the Nineteenth Century (*map*) . . . . . *clx*
Exposure to the Law, Early (*primary source*) 2148
Farm, The Story of an African (*primary source*) 2024
Father, Death of Wagner's (*primary source*) 2376
Fiction, Tolstoy's (*list*) 2285
Fiction, Turgenev's Major 2320
Fiction and Poetry, Scott's (*list*) 2049
Finding Livingstone (*primary source*) 2138
Frankenstein Meets His Creation (*primary source*) 2090
French Revolution, Apology for the (*primary source*) 2464
"Heartless Libertine," Thomas Jefferson, the (*primary source*) 2304
"Hymn to Intellectual Beauty" (*primary source*) 2094
In Defense of the Constitution (*primary source*) 2400
"Intellectual Beauty, Hymn to" (*primary source*) 2094
Introducing Uncle Tom (*primary source*) 2186
Jefferson, the "Heartless Libertine," Thomas (*primary source*) 2304
Law, Early Exposure to the (*primary source*) 2148
Lecture to Art Students (*primary source*) 2433
Libertine," Thomas Jefferson, the "Heartless (*primary source*) 2304
Livingstone, Finding (*primary source*) 2138
"Lotos-Eaters, The" (*primary source*) 2246
Mark Twain, Yonge and (*sidebar*) 2473
Mexico's War with Texas (*primary source*) . . . 2339

Mormon, Witnesses to the Book of (*primary source*) 2119
Motives, Turner's (*primary source*) 2327
"My Captain!, O Captain!" (*primary source*) 2425
Mystery Woman, A Childhood (*primary source*) 2085
North America at the End of the Nineteenth Century (*map*) . . . . . *clxi*
Novels, Thackeray's (*list*). 2259
Novels, Trollope's (*list*). 2301
Novels, Verne's (*list*) 2356
Novels, Zola's (*list*) 2491
"O Captain! My Captain!" (*primary source*) . . . 2425
On Civil Disobedience (*primary source*) 2276
Origins, Washington's (*primary source*) 2392
Poetry, Scott's Fiction and (*list*) 2049
Post-Civil War Southerners, Classifying (*primary source*) 2037
Race, "Degradation" of the African (*primary source*) 2451
Revolution, Apology for the French (*primary source*) 2464
Richard F. Burton on Brigham Young (*primary source*) 2476
Scott's Fiction and Poetry (*list*) 2049
"Ships, The Slave" (*primary source*) 2430
"Slave Ships, The" (*primary source*) 2430
Slave Trade, Suppression of the (*primary source*) 2345
Slavery's Impact on the South (*primary source*) 2281
Sojourner Truth's Search for Her Son (*primary source*) 2308
Son, Sojourner Truth's Search for Her (*primary source*) 2308
South, Slavery's Impact on the (*primary source*) 2281
South America at the End of the Nineteenth Century (*map*) . . . . . *clxii*
Southerners, Classifying Post-Civil War (*primary source*) 2037
Stendhal's Major Works (*list*) 2162
Stevenson's Major Works (*list*). 2175
Story of an African Farm, The (*primary source*) 2024
Students, Lecture to Art (*primary source*) 2433
Suppression of the Slave Trade (*primary source*) 2345
Taking Advice from Authors (*primary source*) 2250
Texas, Mexico's War with (*primary source*) . . . 2339
Thackeray's Novels (*list*) 2259
Thomas Jefferson, the "Heartless Libertine" (*primary source*) 2304
Tolstoy's Fiction (*list*) 2285
Tom, Introducing Uncle (*primary source*) 2186
Trade, Suppression of the Slave (*primary source*) 2345
Tristan's Major Works (*list*) 2298
Trollope's Novels (*list*) 2301
Truth's Search for Her Son, Sojourner (*primary source*) 2308
Turgenev's Major Fiction. 2320
Turner's Motives (*primary source*). 2327
Twain, Yonge and Mark (*sidebar*) 2473
Uncle Tom, Introducing (*primary source*) 2186
U.S. Relations with Europe (*primary source*) 2231
United States, Australia's Advantages over the (*primary source*) 2414
Verne's Novels (*list*) 2356
Wagner's Father, Death of (*primary source*) 2376
War Southerners, Classifying Post-Civil (*primary source*) 2037
War with Texas, Mexico's (*primary source*) 2339
Washington's Origins (*primary source*) 2392
Witnesses to the Book of Mormon (*primary source*) 2119
Woman, A Childhood Mystery (*primary source*) 2085
Works, Stendhal's Major (*list*) 2162
Works, Stevenson's Major (*list*) 2175
Works, Tristan's Major (*list*) 2298
World in 1801 (*map*). . . . . *clvii*
World in 1900 (*map*). . . . . *clvii*
Yonge and Mark Twain (*sidebar*) 2473
Young, Richard F. Burton on Brigham (*primary source*) 2476
Zola's Novels (*list*) 2491

The World in 1801

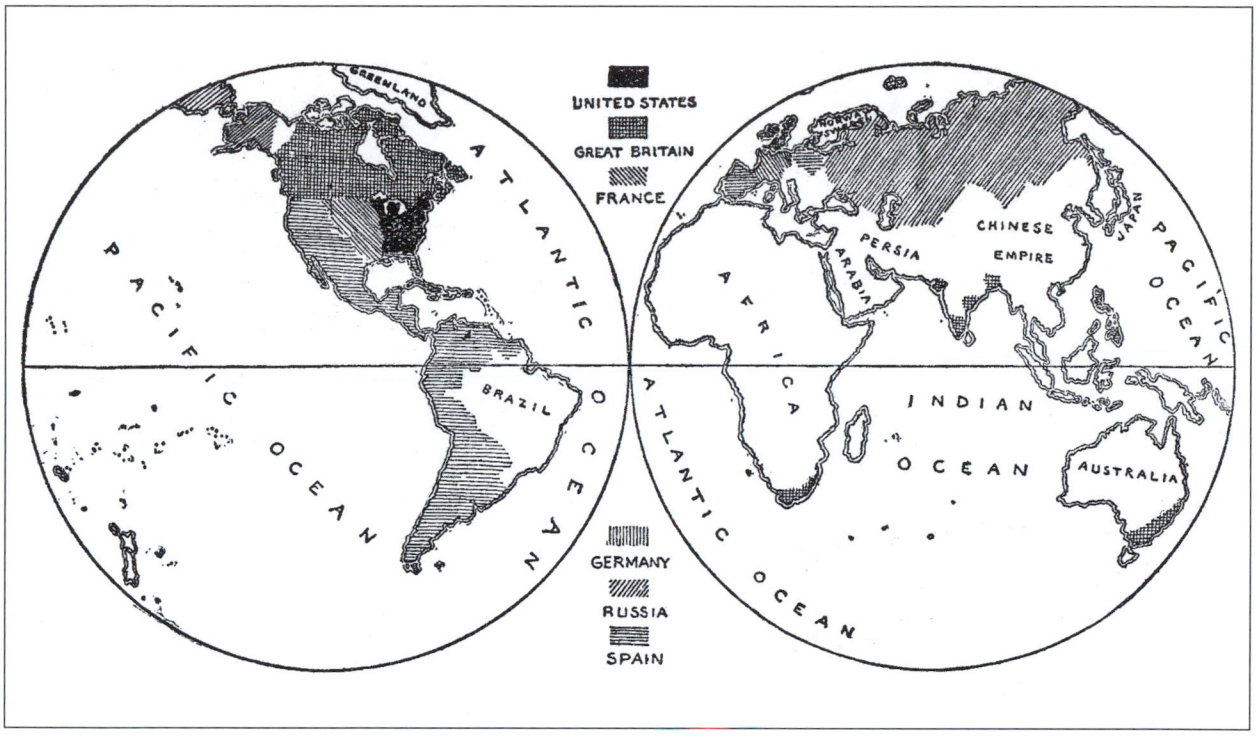

The World in 1900

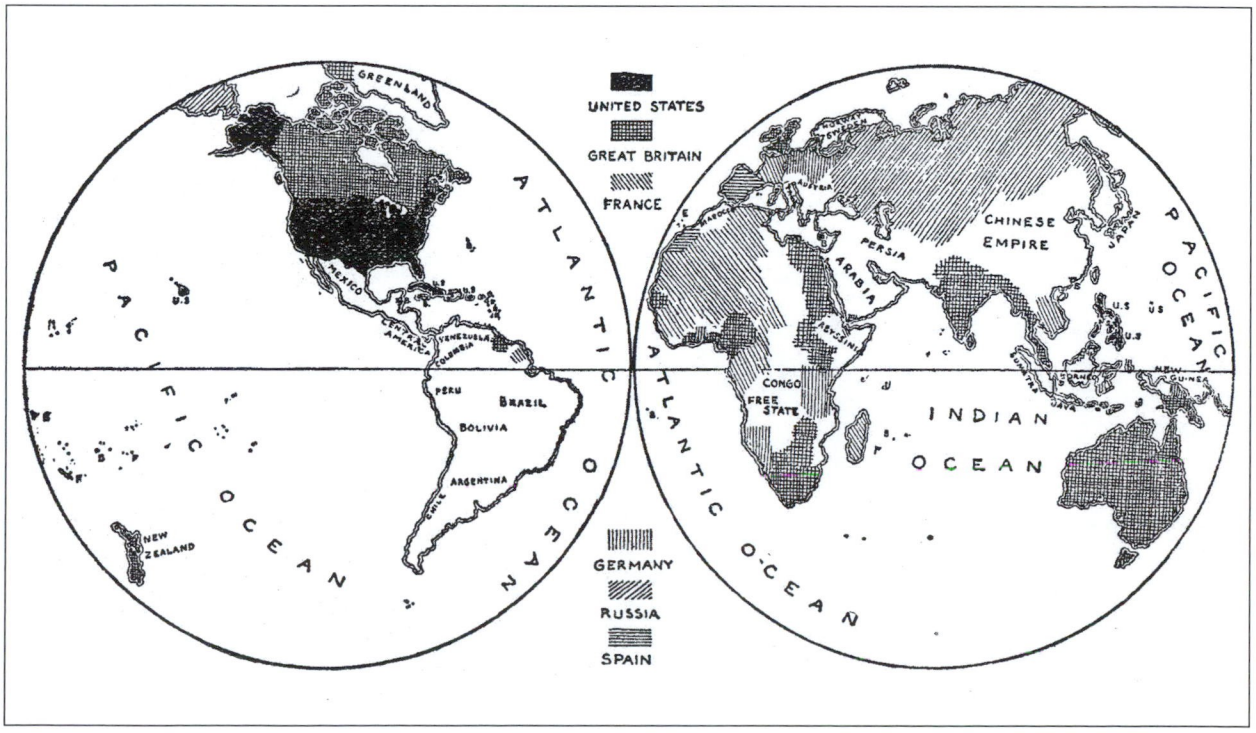

Africa at the End of the Nineteenth Century

Asia and Australasia at the End of the Nineteenth Century

Europe at the End of the Nineteenth Century

North America at the End of the Nineteenth Century

South America at the End of the Nineteenth Century

Great Lives from History

The 19th Century

1801-1900

ABDELKADER
Algerian protonationalist leader

Now remembered as an Algerian national hero, Abdelkader carved a semiautonomous state out of the remnants of the former Turkish possessions after the French landed in Algiers in 1830. He achieved lasting fame for his various campaigns against the French, whom he fought until his surrender in 1847.

BORN: September 6, 1808; Guetna of the Wadi al-Ḥammām, near Mascara, Ottoman Empire (now in Algeria)

DIED: May 25/26, 1883; Damascus, Ottoman Empire (now in Syria)

ALSO KNOWN AS: Abd el-Kader; Adul-Qādir; ʿAbd al-Qādir ibn Muḥyī ad-Dīn ibn Muṣṭafā al-Ḥasanī al-Jazāʿirī (full name)

AREAS OF ACHIEVEMENT: Government and politics, military

EARLY LIFE

The first son of Zurah, the second wife of the Islamic holy man Muhi al-Din, who traced his ancestry as far back as the Prophet Muḥammad, Abdelkader (ahb-dehl-KAH-dehr) was born in a small town near Mascara in what is now Algeria. There his grandfather had founded a religious school of the Sufi Order, and Muhi al-Din had followed him as leader and himself taught his son reading, writing, and the Qurʾān. Abdelkader's mother was learned and venerated by the people as a marabout, or holy person, as well; for a woman to accomplish this was quite extraordinary and could have helped Abdelkader to surpass his half brother, the son of his father's first wife, in the affection of his father.

As a boy, Abdelkader's handsome features and his remarkable intellectual gifts endeared him to his parents and to the people of Guetna. Throughout his life, Abdelkader would be quite aware of the potential impressiveness of his well-made body and keep himself in condition so as to command maximum respect. His dark eyes, together with the clear features of his well-formed face and full beard, conveyed an image of Oriental nobility that would prove to affect friend and foe alike.

A fine horseman and a quick learner, Abdelkader soon developed the qualities of a leader. When his father sent him to the coastal city of Oran as a student of religion in 1821, the boy became a classmate of the scions of the ruling Turks. He observed at first hand how even while the country suffered from famine and plague its Turkish masters continued to levy taxes and luxuriate in a life of debauchery and neglect of Islamic moral principles. In reaction, Arabs gathered around their holy men and led several unsuccessful revolts during the 1820's against the Turks, who repressed upheaval and summarily executed suspicious subjects. As a marabout, Muhi al-din was spared execution and placed under house arrest with his son in Oran for two years, before the two set out on a pilgrimage to Mecca in 1826. Traveling further widened Abdelkader's experience.

Two years after Abdelkader's return to Guetna, the French captured Algiers on July 5, 1830, thus ending three hundred years of Turkish rule. When the neighboring Moroccans tried to assume power in Algeria, Muhi al-Din accepted their mandate and became the leader of a jiḥad, or holy war, against the French, whom they regarded as infidels. The Moroccans withdrew, but Abdelkader commanded a force of ten thousand men for his father and, in the Battle of Oran from May 3 to 8, 1832, fought courageously but was defeated.

LIFE'S WORK

On November 22, 1832, tribes of the Oran Province gathered to witness the proclamation of Abdelkader as emir al-mu'minin, or commander of the believers, on the plain of Eghris. Thus, the twenty-four-year-old man was made leader of a movement to scourge the land of the French. Rather than fighting in open attacks, which his weak forces were sure to lose, Abdelkader began his jiḥad with a boycott against French-held Oran; Arabs who traded with the infidels were mutilated or hanged.

In his dealings with Muslim tribes, Abdelkader soon strove for political recognition as emir and even tried to win the support of the sultan of Morocco. As emir, Abdelkader wielded a power that was legitimated by religion and used it to the fullest. From the believers, he collected both new and traditional taxes to finance the jiḥad and used these monies to build a strong force of his own. Thus, from 1832 to 1834, he was able to subjugate most people in the Oran Province, and the sporadic French attacks were too limited to threaten seriously his nascent power; further, French blunders such as the humiliation of Turks and local leaders played into his hands.

In January, 1834, the French general Louis Alexis Desmichels, whose troops had defeated Abdelkader's without achieving a lasting effect, negotiated a bilingual treaty, complete with a secret codicil. Officially, Abdelkader would rule the Oran Province under the French, with the exception of three coastal cities; however, both Desmichels and Abdelkader told their people that the other had completely submitted to him.

For more than a year, Abdelkader enjoyed the valuable support of Desmichels, who helped him to build an army with which to defeat his indigenous enemies. The replacement of the general brought new fighting with the French, who prevented Abdelkader from forcefully relocating two tribes who had placed themselves under French protection. At the onset of his second jiḥad in June, 1835, Abdelkader ambushed a French force at Macta and killed 210 of their men; however, the French were able to occupy temporarily two of his cities.

While the blockade of Oran continued, General Thomas Robert Bugeaud organized a mobile French force and delivered Abdelkader a stinging blow at the Battle of Sikkak on July 6, 1836. However, Bugeaud knew that he could not occupy the whole country. In the Treaty of Tafna, ratified on June 21, 1837, Bugeaud conceded and placed most of Algeria under Abdelkader's immediate rule. In return, Abdelkader promised peace, free trade, and, secretly, 180,000 gold francs for Bugeaud; however, only 25,000 francs were delivered, as the clause was discovered. Now, Abdelkader could even buy rifles through the French, and he established a firm rule over two-thirds of Algeria. There, he established an Islamic government and consolidated his rule by placing strong emphasis on the one factor that united his subjects against the Europeans: the Muslim religion.

In the summer of 1839, it became clear that France and Abdelkader would soon clash over Algeria. On July 3, Abdelkader declared a conditional jiḥad, which became fully effective November 3, after the French crown prince had marched through Abdelkader's territory. The warriors of the jiḥad scored a first victory when they attacked a European settlement on the Mitidja plains near Algiers on November 20 and succeeded in massacring or chasing away its colonists. Until the return of Bugeaud, Abdelkader maintained the military initiative.

In May, 1841, however, Tagdempt, Abdelkader's capital, fell to Bugeaud, whose forces had razed most of his cities by October 12. In turn, Abdelkader moved to a tent city, the Zmalah, and continued to harass the enemy throughout the next year. However, on May 16, 1843, a surprise attack on the Zmalah led to its destruction, the capture of three thousand of Abdelkader's people, and the loss of his treasury. With the French following on his heels and devastating the land of his tribes after the fashion of local warfare, Abdelkader was forced to flee into Morocco late in 1843.

From his exile, Abdelkader saw Bugeaud's defeat of the Moroccan army at the Battle of Isly in August, 1844, and the French military begin to control Algeria. However, the harshness of their rule led to a popular uprising and agitation for a new jiḥad. Until he returned in September, 1845, Abdelkader had wielded no influence, but now people followed him. However, his renewed campaign culminated in a failed attempt at capturing Algiers in January, 1846; thereafter, Abdelkader was again chased into Morocco. While the war wound down with heavy civilian casualties, Morocco grew hostile to Abdelkader. On December 21, 1847, he surrendered himself to General Christophe de Lamoricière, who had promised that he could stay in Africa. Instead, the French government kept the rebel leader under arrest in France for four years before Napoleon III released him in 1852.

From 1855 on, Abdelkader stayed in Damascus as a philosopher and religious man. During an uprising there in 1860, he saved the lives of thousands of Christians, and, when unrest returned to Algeria in 1871, he disowned one of his sons who took sides with the rebels. Abdelkader died in Damascus on May 25 or 26, 1883. In 1968, his remains were returned to Algeria.

SIGNIFICANCE

As an exile in Damascus, Abdelkader was seen by the French as a prime example of the beneficial effects of their rule, which had transformed a fiery Muslim fanatic and hero of desert warfare into an elder statesman of the French empire; the French government even had plans to establish a throne for him somewhere in the Middle East. With the coming of another bitter war in Algeria after 1945, Algerian interest turned to Abdelkader, who was idolized as an early protagonist of independence; the French quickly discovered that his legend had been kept alive. In 1962, after independence, Abdelkader was declared a national hero, and in Algiers his statue soon replaced the toppled one of Bugeaud.

A final historical assessment can only stress the charisma of Abdelkader and his profound impact on the history of two countries. Abdelkader's qualities as a leader of men who venerated him for his religious conviction enabled him to build an indigenous state in defiance of the French-controlled cities on the coast. When open warfare erupted, Abdelkader achieved lasting fame through his never-ending zeal and military prowess, a combination that led him into battle as long as there was a chance to reverse fortunes and prevent French rule over Algeria.

—R. C. Lutz

FURTHER READING

Abun-Nasr, Jamil N. "The Emergence of French Algeria." In *A History of the Maghrib*. Cambridge, England: Cambridge University Press, 1971. Briefly describes Abdelkader's accomplishments and places him in the context of the overall history of the region. Presents an Arab point of view.

Alby, François Antoine. *The Prisoners of Abd-el-Kader: Or, Five Months' Captivity Among the Arabs in the Autumn of 1836*. Translated by R. F. Porter. London: Smith, Elder, 1838. An account of the ordeal of a French sailor who was captured in Algeria in 1836, delivered to Abdelkader, and released five months later. An intimate description of Abdelkader, his people, and their actions; shows what the common person in Paris or London believed about Arabs.

Blunt, Wilfrid. *Desert Hawk: Abd el Kader and the French Conquest of Algeria*. London: Methuen, 1947. A descriptive account of Abdelkader's life and military campaigns. A readable and interesting work that admires Abdelkader's position against the French.

Churchill, Charles Henry. *The Life of Abdelkader: Ex-Sultan of the Arabs of Algeria*. London: Chapman and Hall, 1867. This is the oldest biography of Abdelkader in English. Invaluable because it exemplifies the popular European reaction to Abdelkader during his lifetime.

Clancy-Smith, Julia A. *Rebel and Saint: Muslim Notables, Populist Protest, Colonial Encounters (Algeria and Tunisia, 1800-1904)*. Berkeley: University of California Press, 1994. Abdelkader is included in this examination of the religious beliefs and political actions of prominent Muslims and their followers. Analyzes Algerian resistance to, and accommodation with, French colonists.

Clayton, Vista. *The Phantom: Or, Abd el Kader, Emir of Algeria, 1808-1883*. Hicksville, N.Y.: Exposition Press, 1975. An analysis of the life and warfare strategies of Abdelkader. Presents Abdelkader's life against the background of his region and gives a detailed account of his military exploits.

Danziger, Raphael. *Abd al-Qadir and the Algerians: Resistance to the French and Internal Consolidation*. New York: Holmes & Meier, 1977. A detailed account of Abdelkader's struggle for power, the consolidation of his rule, and dealings with the French. Deals primarily with the time period before 1839. This is a sympathetic view, written for both a scholarly and a general audience. Sources.

Sullivan, Antony Thrall. *Thomas-Robert Bugeaud, France, and Algeria 1784-1849: Politics, Power, and the Good Society*. Hamden, Conn.: Archon Books, 1983. A fascinating portrait of Abdelkader's great adversary, and a description of the two men's relationship. Illuminates the historical background of the actions of Abdelkader's enemies by providing an explanation for the French interest in Algeria and the methods of warfare employed. For a general audience.

SEE ALSO: Ali Paşa Tepelenë; Muḥammad ʿAlī Pasha.

RELATED ARTICLE in *Great Events from History: The Nineteenth Century, 1801-1900:* June 14-July 5, 1830: France Conquers Algeria.

MUḤAMMAD ʿABDUH

Egyptian writer and nationalist leader

ʿAbduh was a major figure in the articulation of modern political, ethical, and social values in an Islamic context. His writings were a major stimulus to the development of Egyptian nationalism and, in a wider sense, to the elaboration of social and political thought throughout Islam.

BORN: c. 1849; Mahallat Nasr, Gharbiyyah Province, Egypt
DIED: July 11, 1905; Alexandria, Egypt
AREA OF ACHIEVEMENT: Philosophy

EARLY LIFE

Muḥammad ʿAbduh (ahb-dew) was the child of Egyptian peasants of the the great Nile River's delta region. His family life appears to have been serene and his father highly respected in his village. Although without formal education themselves, ʿAbduh's parents went to considerable effort, and no doubt sacrificed much, to ensure his receiving educational opportunities. ʿAbduh was trained in basic literary skills and, when ten years of age, went to learn recitation of the Qurʾān with a professional. Few other educational opportunities were available to Egyptian peasants at the time.

ʿAbduh shortly became restless with Qurʾānic memorization and Arabic grammar. Instead, he became enamored of the teachings of a number of Sufi mystics. From them, ʿAbduh first perceived the relationship between the true practice of and devotion to Islam, and the pursuit of morality and ethical conduct. He gravitated toward Cairo and the great theological center of Al Azhar, where he continued his education and increasingly rigorous Sufi practices.

ʿAbduh's mentor at Al Azhar was the famed Jamāl al-Dīn al-Afghānī, perhaps the most important Muslim intellectual figure in the nineteenth century. Although equally devoted to Sufism, Jamāl, a dynamic reformer and pan-Islamic advocate, turned ʿAbduh from the internal contemplation that had absorbed nearly all of his energies to more worldly avenues of learning and social involvement. With Jamāl's encouragement, many of his students, ʿAbduh included, began writing articles for newspapers on a host of subjects related to the state of Egypt at the time and the challenge of modernization.

Despite his outstanding academic work, ʿAbduh's outspoken opinions on Egyptian society and the suspicion that he meant to revive the skeptical philosophical movements characteristic of earlier periods in Islam drew the wrath of conservative clerics at Al Azhar. It required the intervention of the more liberal rector for ʿAbduh to receive passing marks on his examinations and his teaching certificate in 1877.

LIFE'S WORK

Although he held numerous positions throughout his life in addition to his explicitly educational ones, ʿAbduh always regarded himself as a teacher. The essence of his teachings is first a concern for the state of Egypt. He and fellow intellectuals deplored their country's drift during the 1870's toward financial chaos and foreign intervention. They understood that only internal reforms could change Egypt's fortunes. ʿAbduh's experience at Al Azhar convinced him that the most essential reform must come in education. At a time when European economic and technological forces were closing in on Egypt, its greatest academic institution was still under the control of rigidly conservative theologians who resisted curricular innovation. (ʿAbduh had been obliged to seek instruction in mathematics and natural sciences in the streets, among unofficial, black market classes held outside the walls of Al Azhar.)

However, it was not merely these additions to curriculum that concerned ʿAbduh. He also argued that the study of religion itself must be subject to the same rigor and philosophical scrutiny that attended the sciences and other secular studies. Further, he believed that leading institutions such as Al Azhar must, in their own reforms, assume leadership in rebuilding and expanding the entire Egyptian educational system. ʿAbduh's ideas and teaching methods generated much controversy at Al Azhar but also earned for him support from the reform-minded prime minister Riad Pasha, who in 1878 appointed him to the experimental school Dar al-'Ulum, founded as a pilot institution for educational reform.

In 1879, the Egyptian ruler Khedive Ismāʿīl, who had been intent on modernizing Egypt but went far beyond the country's limited financial means, under European pressure abdicated in favor of his son, Tawfiq. The new khedive expelled Jamāl from the country and fired ʿAbduh, placing him under virtual house arrest. ʿAbduh was rescued from potential oblivion by Riad Pasha, who appointed him to the editorial staff of the official Egyptian government gazette *al-Waqaʿi al-Misriyyah*. ʿAbduh quickly turned this rather stodgy publication into a vibrant, reformist organ, with contributions from many Egyptian intellectuals and government critics. In his own editorials, ʿAbduh continually returned to the need for educational reform and his campaign to cast Egyptian national consciousness in a new Islamic mold. Islam, he argued, should return to its basic simplicity and revive the spirit of inquiry and pursuit of knowledge characteristic of its early history.

In 1881, Egyptian army officers, led by the nationalist firebrand Colonel Ahmed ʿArabi, mutinied. The uprising sparked a general confrontation between the government and its critics. Alarmed at the prospect of violence against Europeans, British troops landed in Egypt in May, 1882. ʿAbduh, though opposed to ʿArabi's methods, spoke out as usual in favor of national revival and reform. In September, a government tribunal ordered him expelled from Egypt.

ʿAbduh went first to Syria and later to Paris, where he was reunited with Jamāl. In exile, he continued to speak and publish actively. The wide venue of his travels led ʿAbduh to perceive the potential vitality of a unified Islam and the cultural renaissance of all Muslims. Increasingly he drew on the early history of Islam as a source of inspiration. On the other hand, his experiences in Syria, a country rife with ethnic and religious factionalism, led him to question whether Islam was a suitable rubric for the expression of modern Arab national aspirations. ʿAbduh's reservations about pan-Islamic agitation caused him to part ways with Jamāl, who was disposed to intrigue and political maneuvering. ʿAbduh insisted that his role should be educational and instructive rather than activist.

In 1886, having received a government pardon, ʿAbduh returned to Egypt a national hero. He was now able to use this influence to implement his earlier ideas of curricular and institutional reform at Al Azhar, in order to make it a model of education in Islam. In 1895, the new khedive, Abbas II, at ʿAbduh's instigation created an administrative committee for Al Azhar, dominated by ʿAbduh and other reformists.

In an effort to enlist faculty support for curriculum changes, the government provided significant new sums for salaries, to be distributed according to a merit system rather than at the discretion of the rector. Students, many of whom lived under appalling conditions, received double their previous board allowance. New dormitories with running water and suitable furniture appeared. The committee significantly lengthened the academic year, organized it according to European standards, and eliminated many disruptive holidays. It also established modern administrative systems for the university's finances and organized its library collections.

Fears that these changes would turn students away from theology and ancient history disappeared when the student success rate on examinations increased by nearly an order of magnitude in the first two years of reform. ʿAbduh himself produced statistics that he claimed proved that students who studied modern subjects along with the traditional ones performed better in both areas on examinations.

The climax of ʿAbduh's career came with his appointment as mufti of Egypt in 1899, from which post he was the final arbiter of questions of shariʿa, or Muslim canon law. In this position ʿAbduh had to confront, more than ever before, his own ambivalence about the relationship between Islam and modern nationalism. His arguments with respect to interpretation of shariʿa generated more controversy than anything else in his career. Like many other Muslim scholars, particularly in Egypt, ʿAbduh regarded shariʿa as possessing a divinely inspired core of behavior and values to which all Muslims are expected to adhere. The community, however, by consensus might accept amendations to shariʿa pertinent to its own experience and circumstances.

ʿAbduh perceived the emerging Egyptian nation as the logical outgrowth of this sense of community in Islam. However, he believed that the nation, because it contained citizens who were Christian or Jewish rather than Muslim, and because it aspired to a role in a secular world not anticipated by shariʿa, should exercise a consensus of its own. Thus ʿAbduh decided that Muslims could eat animal flesh killed by Christians or Jews. Despite the ban on usury, in shariʿa Egyptians could, and should, make use of modern postal savings and banking systems opposed by traditional clergy on the grounds that their strength contributed to the welfare of the nation. These positions ʿAbduh regarded not as a repudiation of Islam but as an act of defense of Islam, in that they reconstituted Islam as an open and tolerant culture capable of meeting the demands of a changing world.

SIGNIFICANCE

When Muḥammad ʿAbduh died in July, 1905, he received the equivalent of a state funeral. The public demonstration of respect and reverence from all political factions and religious communities was unprecedented in Egypt. The country sensed that it had lost a singular patriot and scholar, and one of the most important figures in Egypt's transformation. Later generations have borne out this assessment. Because of ʿAbduh's reforms and the new intellectual environment they created, Al Azhar, and other large Egyptian universities, remain in the forefront of higher education in Islam and are recognized as among the world's major institutions of higher learning.

In all of his teachings, ʿAbduh struggled to articulate an Egyptian sense of identity that reconciled the inconsistencies and often conflicting perceptions of Islam, the Islamic community, the modern nation and its role in a European-dominated world, and the tensions between modernity and tradition.

ʿAbduh is most fairly regarded, perhaps, as one who, rather than answering the multitude of questions arising from these issues, helped to air the issues and suggest ways in which they could be addressed satisfactorily. ʿAbduh is a symbol, rather than a model, for the contemporary, educated Egyptian. His intellectual journey represents what each Egyptian individually—and the nation as a whole—must consider in the process of finding a satisfying and rewarding identity in the modern world.

—*Ronald W. Davis*

FURTHER READING

Adams, Charles C. *Islam and Modernism in Egypt: A Study of the Modern Reform Movement Inaugurated by Muḥammad ʿAbduh*. Reprint. New York: Routledge, 2002. Includes one of the most extensive biographical accounts of ʿAbduh. Attempts to analyze his personality and ideas in the light of his life experience.

Ahmed, Jamal Mohammed. *The Intellectual Origins of Egyptian Nationalism*. New York: Oxford University Press, 1960. A survey of the varied sources of inspiration for Egyptian nationalism. Stresses how this variety contributes to the often conflicting roles of issues such as Egyptian ethnic identity, pan-Arabism, Ottomanism, and Islamic and pan-Islamic values.

Badawi, Muhammad Zaki. *The Reformers of Egypt*. London: Croom Helm, 1978. Treats ʿAbduh as a product of the same circumstances that produced other Egyptian nationalists and intellectuals, and attempts to draw comparisons among the careers of these figures.

Jankowski, James. "Ottomanism and Arabism in Egypt, 1860-1914." *Muslim World* 70 (1980): 226-259. During the late nineteenth century, many Egyptians regarded the Ottoman Empire—to the extent that it stood for Islam as a whole—as a more legitimate outlet than identifying with the Arabs. This article shows how Ottomanism provided a more vigorous environment for the growth of Egyptian ethnic nationalism.

Kedourie, Elie. *Afghani and ʿAbduh: An Essay on Religious Unbelief and Political Activism in Modern Islam*. London: Frank Cass, 1966. Reprint. Portland, Oreg.: Frank Cass, 1997. A brief but controversial essay when it appeared. Argues that ʿAbduh was an atheist and subverter of Islam, and a Machiavellian who behaved as a Muslim only to advance his career.

Kerr, Malcolm. *Islamic Reform: The Political and Legal Theories of Muḥammad ʿAbduh and Rashīd Ridā*. Berkeley: University of California Press, 1966. Considers the many influences that contributed to ʿAbduh's ideas about the nature of the state and the legal system.

SEE ALSO: Jamāl al-Dīn al-Afghānī.

RELATED ARTICLES in *Great Events from History: The Nineteenth Century, 1801-1900:* 19th century: Arabic Literary Renaissance; September 13, 1882: Battle of Tel el Kebir.

ABDÜLHAMID II

Sultan of the Ottoman Empire (r. 1876-1909)

Abdülhamid earned a negative reputation as an autocratic ruler and was widely denounced for his brutal tactics to quell the Armenian nationalist movement. However, other sides of his reign deserve more favorable recognition, especially his contributions to Turkish economic development.

BORN: September 21, 1842; Constantinople, Ottoman Empire (now Istanbul, Turkey)
DIED: February 10, 1918; Constantinople, Ottoman Empire
ALSO KNOWN AS: Abdül Hamid II; ʿAbd al-Hamid
AREA OF ACHIEVEMENT: Government and politics

EARLY LIFE

Abdülhamid II (AHB-dewl-hah-MEED) was the son of the Ottoman sultan Abdülmecid I. Little is known about his early years, but a good part of his youth would have involved survival, within the confines of the harem, in the face of intrigues mounted by factions that championed others—full or half brothers—for possible succession. Following the typical pattern for sultanic succession in the Ottoman Empire, heirs to the imperial throne lived relatively obscure lives prior before they were publicly announced as the choices as new rulers. Although the young Abdülhamid held several posts that were meant to prepare him for sultanic responsibilities, he was catapulted to imperial, and indeed world, attention not because of his particular skills, but because of an unforeseen confluence of circumstances in 1876.

LIFE'S WORK

The events surrounding Abdülhamid II's accession were unique. In 1876, the reform movement known as the Tanzimat that had been attempted between 1839 and 1876 reached what many considered to be its logical conclusion: the expectation that the empire needed a representative parliament and a constitutional monarchy. In particular, the 1860-1876 generation of "Young Ottoman" reformers wished to convince Western observers that the empire known as the "Sick Man of Europe" could cure itself through limitations on absolute sultanic authority. The Young Ottomans also wanted to bring the multinational and multiconfessional groupings—including Turkish, Arab, Kurd, Armenian, and Balkan communities—under a single representative system. They probably hoped to use this new form of government to stave off bankruptcy—an event that would paralyze the imperial government's search for more foreign loans to cover imperial treasury deficits.

While a constitution was being drafted for submission to an as yet to be elected parliament, it was obvious that resistance would come from the reigning sultan, Abdülaziz. A coup deposed Abdülaziz Aziz in May, 1876, only to be followed in December by another coup against his equally resistant successor, Murad V. Recognition of Abdülhamid II, as the next in line, was based on his acceptance of constitutional limits on his authority.

Although Abdülhamid gave the impression of welcoming his new constitutionally limited status, he soon found a way to thwart the efforts of the short-lived first Ottoman parliament. The circumstances involved the looming menace of Russian military advances supposedly to protect Balkan Slavs from harsh Turkish rule. The confrontation grew into the Russo-Turkish War of 1877-1878 and the near-disastrous San Stefano Treaty, which carried the threat of serious dismemberment, particularly of Ottoman Bulgaria. Wartime pressures, plus tensions connected with the terms of San Stefano, served as a pretext for suspension of the 1876 constitution, which would not be reinstituted until 1908, close to the end of Abdülhamid's reign. The paralyzing terms of San Stefano were offset by the actions of Germany's Chancellor Otto von Bismarck, who hosted the famous Berlin Conference of 1884-1885.

The new sultan was apparently determined to show that progress in economic development and military advances would offset visible weakness in the empire's political system. Thus, he devoted considerable effort to investing in infrastructural improvements, especially development of telegraph lines and railways to link key Ottoman provinces. By the end of the nineteenth century, the symbol of railway expansion came to be associated with two internationally famous projects.

The first project involved an announcement by the sultan that he would sponsor, in the name of all Muslims in and beyond Ottoman territory, construction of a "Hijaz Railway" from Damascus to the Islamic holy pilgrimage city of Mecca in the Arabian peninsula. Abdülhamid called for contributions from Muslims everywhere to finance this project, which seemed to be closely linked to what many have called the pan-Islamic direction of his reign.

Abdülhamid's second project, the Berlin-to-Baghdad railway, reflected Abdülhamid's use of his good relations with Germany for both political and economic advantages. German financial participation led several other international sources of capital for this and other railway projects. Increasing German interest in the Ottoman Empire raised British worries that German cooperation would lead to a stronger alliance between Germany and the Ottoman Empire. This impression only grew as Abdülhamid actively encouraged military aid and training exchanges between the Ottoman Empire and Germany. A growing number of Ottoman military officers received training in Germany, and German military missions to Turkey became more evident.

The Berlin-to-Baghdad railroad line, had it been completed, would have provided an alternative route from the interior of Europe to the Arabian Sea and the Indian Ocean, diminishing the obvious importance of the Suez Canal. This was an important consideration behind Great Britain's offer of a protectorate to Kuwait in 1900—a move that risked an open break with Abdülhamid.

The most dramatic event to occur in the last years of Abdülhamid's reign, however, was the beginning of violent outbursts involving nationalists from the empire's minority Armenian community, both in the capital Constantinople (now Istanbul) and in the provinces. A series of clashes begun with terrorist bombings in Constantinople during the late 1890's expanded into wholesale destruction of Armenian villages and enormous loss of life. The conflict continued unresolved into World War I, after Abdülhamid II was out of power.

The growth of internal opposition to Abdülhamid's excesses from what came to be known as the Young Turk Movement, or Committee of Union and Progress (CUP), which ended his reign. The CUP eventually depended on gradually expanding secret participation by army officers to carry off two coups against the sultan, in 1908 and 1909. CUP organizers, however, believed that the empire could survive only by restoring the 1876 constitution and calling elections for a new parliament.

In July, 1908, a flurry of excitement followed a seemingly successful uprising in Salonica that was led by officers of the Third Army Corps in Macedonia who had ties with the Young Turks. They called for the restoration of the 1876 constitution. Giving in, at least on the surface, Abdülhamid convinced the constitutionalists that he could and would adjust his rule to their demands. According to some sources, he even offered to become a candidate for election as president of the CUP. Behind the scenes, however, the sultan devoted himself to fomenting discontent with a newly elected all-Ottoman parliament, with representatives from provinces as distant as Mosul and Basra in Iraq, Syria, and even British-occupied Egypt.

Abdülhamid's efforts, combined with those of other supporters of the system that had evolved between 1876 and 1908, sparked several forms of opposition. There were demonstrations by students training for traditional Islamic religious careers. Many of them feared a secularizing move by the CUP against the traditional prominence of Islamic religious law.

In April, 1909, a dramatic mutiny by select military garrisons in the capital itself tried to unseat Abdülhamid's newly appointed cabinet. This revolt, coupled with its leaders' open support for Abdülhamid, menaced the continuation of CUP-dominated constitutional government. This time the Third Army Corps marched from Macedonia to Constantinople to reverse the "pocket rebellion." Sultan Abdülhamid was identified as the hidden force behind the reactionary movement, and the Sheikh al-Islām, whether willingly or under duress, announced to the parliament that Abdülhamid had given up his throne. Abdülhamid was replaced by Sultan Muhammad V (r. 1909-1918). The CUP's original intention was to exile the former sultan permanently to Salonika, but during the unsettling events that accompanied the Balkan Wars of 1912-1913 and the outbreak of World War I, Abdülhamid was allowed to return to Constantinople, where he died in early 1918.

SIGNIFICANCE

Abdülhamid II was the last historically notable sultan of the Ottoman Empire. Whatever his other, obviously varied contributions might have been, he left a permanent mark on global perceptions of the Turkish sultanate in the last years of its existence before the institution was abolished by the Turkish republic. The fact that his reign began and ended with efforts to install a multinational Ottoman imperial parliament was in itself important, even though those efforts failed. The image that Abdülhamid left of sultanic opposition to parliamentary representation was not a positive one. This, coupled with his involvement in the first stages of violent suppression of nascent Armenian nationalism, served to earn him the notorious label, "The Red Sultan."

—Byron D. Cannon

FURTHER READING

Dadrian, Vahakn. *The History of the Armenian Genocide: Ethnic Conflict from the Balkans to Anatolia to the Caucasus*. New York: Berghahn Books, 2003. A new edition of an Armenian historian's account of the breakdown of Armenian-Turkish relations during and after Abdülhamid's reign.

Deringil, Selim. "Legitimacy Structures in the Ottoman State: The Reign of Abdulhamid II." *International Journal of Middle East Studies* 23 (1991): 345-359. Examination of institutions defining both religious and political authority in the Ottoman Empire.

Swenson, Victor. "The Military Rising in Istanbul in 1909." *Journal of Contemporary History* 5 (1970): 171-184. Describes events leading to Abdülhamid's overthrow one year after the Young Turk coup.

Yasamee, F. A. K. *Ottoman Diplomacy: Abdülhamid II and the Great Powers*. Istanbul: Isis Press, 1996. Traces the delicate balance in Turkish relations with Germany, Russia, France, and Britain from the 1878 Congress of Berlin to 1909.

SEE ALSO: Otto von Bismarck; Theodor Herzl; Jamāl al-Dīn al-Afghānī.

RELATED ARTICLES in *Great Events from History: The Nineteenth Century, 1801-1900:* May, 1876: Bulgarian Revolt Against the Ottoman Empire; 1894-1896: Ottomans Attempt to Exterminate Armenians.

NIELS HENRIK ABEL

Norwegian mathematician

Abel was a central figure in the evolution of modern mathematics, especially in the field of algebra. Regarded as one of the foremost analysts of his time, he insisted that a rigorous approach to mathematical proof was critical for the further development of abstract mathematics.

BORN: August 5, 1802; Finnøy, Norway
DIED: April 6, 1829; Froland, Norway
AREA OF ACHIEVEMENT: Mathematics

EARLY LIFE

Niels Henrik Abel (AH-behl) was the second child of Søren Georg Abel, a second-generation Lutheran minister, and Anne Marie Simonsen, a daughter of a successful merchant and shipowner. Soon after his birth, his father was transferred to the parish of Gjerstad, in southeastern Norway, about 150 miles from Oslo, where Abel spent his childhood with his five brothers and sisters. Abel was an attractive youth, with light ash-brown hair and blue eyes.

Although his father's earnings were never adequate to provide for the large family, the emphasis on educational stimulation in the Abel household was an important formative influence on the young boy. Although his early education was conducted at home, it was sufficient to allow him to attend the Cathedral School at Oslo when he was thirteen years old. It was there that his talent in mathematics was discovered, although his initial efforts were somewhat unpromising.

The Cathedral School had once been quite good, but many positions had been filled by inexperienced or inadequate teachers because their predecessors had been recruited to join the faculty of the newly formed University of Oslo. Indeed, Abel's first mathematics instructor was dismissed abruptly after beating a student to death. The replacement in that position was Bernt Michael Holmboe, who was the first to recognize Abel's talent and who later edited the first edition of his work. Holmboe also assisted Christopher Hansteen, a professor at the university; this connection would prove valuable to Abel.

When Holmboe first arrived at the school, he noticed Abel's ability in mathematics and suggested that the two of them study some of the contemporary mathematics works together. Abel soon outpaced Holmboe and began developing a general solution for the quintic equation, that is, an equation of the fifth degree ($ax^5 + bx^4 + cx^3 + dx^2 + ex + f = 0$). When Abel believed that the work was complete, Holmboe and Hansteen sensed that no one in Norway, including themselves, could review the work capably. They forwarded the paper to Ferdinand Degen of the Danish Academy, who carefully reviewed the work. Before publication, Degen helped Abel discover that his solution was flawed, but he steered Abel into the field of elliptic functions, which Degen believed would be more fruitful.

At about that same time, Abel discovered that several of his predecessors, particularly Leonhard Euler and Joseph-Louis Lagrange, had not completed the reasoning required to prove some of their work. Abel diligently supplied rigorous proofs where they were missing; a noted case is his proof of the general binomial theorem, which had been stated previously in part by Sir Isaac Newton and Euler. The mathematics community later was to find his meticulous treatment of the works he studied invaluable. Unfortunately for his personal life and his financial situation, Abel's father, who had served two terms in the *Storting* (congress), was impeached and disgraced. His father died in 1829, leaving his family in even more desperate financial straits than ever before.

LIFE'S WORK

The nineteen-year-old Abel entered the University of Oslo in 1821. Although this entering age would not normally denote a prodigy, the fact that the university granted him a free room and that several professors donated funds for his support does. Abel completed the preliminary requirements for a degree in a single year. He was then free to study mathematics on his own, as he had no peers among the faculty. He developed a love for the theater at that time that lasted throughout his short life. A modest person, he made many lasting friendships.

In addition to studying all available work, he began writing papers, the first of which were published in the journal *Magazin for Naturvidenskaberne* begun by Hansteen. In 1823, Abel's first important paper, "Opläsning afet Par Opgaver ved bjoelp af bestemte Integraler" ("Solution of Some Problems by Means of Definite Integrals"), was published, containing the first published solutions of integral equations. During 1822 and 1823, he also developed a longer paper discussing the integration of functions. This work is recognized as very significant in the evolution of that field of study.

Niels Henrik Abel. (Library of Congress)

At that time, Abel's work was largely ignored by the international mathematics community because Abel was from Norway and wrote in Norwegian, and the focal point of the mathematics community of the day was Paris, with the language of the learned being French. By applying himself diligently, Abel learned French and began to publish work in that language. The quintic equation still held his attention, and, as he thought of possibilities for its solution, he also considered that there might be no solution that could be found for all such equations. In time, he was able to prove this result. Nevertheless, the mathematicians whose approval he desired so fervently, those in Paris, ignored his work.

Abel began to press for the opportunity to go to Paris, but penniless as he was he was forced to rely on grants. After his first application, it was decided that he needed to study more foreign languages before going abroad. Although it meant delaying his dream for nearly two years, Abel applied himself to learning various languages. Meanwhile, he became engaged to Christine (Krelly) Kemp before he finally received a royal grant to travel abroad in 1825.

This trip was unsuccessful in many ways. When he arrived at Copenhagen, he discovered that Degen had died. Instead of going on to Paris, Abel decided to go to Berlin because several of his friends were there. The time in Berlin was invaluable, for he met and befriended August Leopold Crelle, who became his strongest supporter and mentor. When Abel met him, Crelle was preparing to begin publication of a new journal, *Journal für die reine und angewandte Mathematik* (journal for pure and applied mathematics). Crelle was so taken by Abel's ability that much of the first few issues was devoted to Abel's work in an attempt to win recognition for the young mathematician.

For a variety of reasons, Abel did not proceed to Paris until the spring of 1826. By this time, he had spent most of his grant and was physically tired, and the Parisian mathematicians he had hoped to convince were nearly all on holiday. However, his masterwork, *Mémoire sur une propriété générale d'une classe très-étendue de fonc-*

tions transcendantes (memoir on a general property of a very extensive class of transcendental functions), was presented to the Academy of Sciences on October 30, 1826. The paper was left in the keeping of Augustin-Louis Cauchy, a prominent mathematician, and Cauchy and Adrien-Marie Legendre were to be the referees. Whether the paper was illegible, as Cauchy claimed, or was misplaced, as most historians believe, no judgment was issued until after Abel's death.

Abel felt a great sense of failure, for many young mathematicians had been established by recognition from the academy. He returned first to Berlin and finally to Oslo in May, 1827. His prospects were bleak: He had contracted tuberculosis, there was no prospect for a mathematical position in Norway, and he was in debt. Abel began tutoring and lecturing at the university on a substitute basis in order to support himself.

Another young mathematician, Carl Gustav Jacob Jacobi, soon began publishing work in Abel's foremost field, the theory of elliptic functions and integrals. The rivalry created between them dominated the rest of Abel's life. He worked furiously to prove his ideas, and his efforts were spurred by his correspondence with Legendre. As he finally began to be recognized in Europe, many mathematicians, led by Crelle, attempted to secure a patronage for him. However, he succumbed to tuberculosis on April 6, 1829, two days before Crelle wrote to inform him that such financial support had been found. In June, 1830, he and Jacobi were awarded the Grand Prix of the French Academy of Sciences for their work in elliptic integrals. Abel's original manuscript was found and finally published in 1841.

SIGNIFICANCE

Although Niels Henrik Abel's life was short and his work was unrecognized for most of his life, he has exercised a great influence on modern mathematics. His primary work with elliptic functions and integrals led to interest in what became one of the great research topics of his century. Without his preliminary findings, many of the developments in mathematics and, consequently, science, may not have been made. One example of this is his theory of elliptic functions, much of which was developed very quickly during his race with Jacobi. In addition, his proof that there is no general solution to the quintic equation is quite important, as are his other findings in equation theory.

Abel's theory of solutions using definite integrals, including what is now called Abel's theorem, is also widely used in engineering and the physical sciences and provided a foundation for the later work of others. Abelian (commutative) groups, Abelian functions, and Abelian equations are but three of the ideas that commonly carry his name. Given Abel's short life span and his living in Norway, a definite academic backwater at the time, his prolific achievements are amazing.

Abel is also significant because his writing and mathematical styles, which were easily comprehended, made his discoveries available to his contemporaries and successors. Abel's insistence that ideas should be demonstrated in such a way that the conclusions would be supported by clear and easily comprehended arguments, that is, proved rigorously, is the cornerstone of modern mathematics. It is in this regard that Abel is most often remembered.

—*Celeste Williams Brockington*

FURTHER READING

Abel, Niels Henrik. "From a Memoir on Algebraic Equations, Proving the Impossibility of a Solution of the General Equation of the Fifth Degree." In *Classics of Mathematics*, edited by Ronald Calinger. Oak Park, Ill.: Moore, 1982. This extract of Abel's paper on the general quintic equation demonstrates Abel's style. Although it is too technical for the casual reader, it is of interest to mathematicians and demonstrates Abel's place in the development of mathematics. Also includes a brief biography.

Bell, Eric T. "Genius and Poverty: Abel." In *Men of Mathematics*. New York: Simon & Schuster, 1937. This compilation of brief biographies of famous mathematicians includes a chapter on Abel, focusing more on the subject's life than on his mathematical achievements.

Boyer, Carl B. *A History of Mathematics*. New York: John Wiley & Sons, 1968. This general history of mathematics will help the reader place Abel within the general development of mathematics.

Kline, Morris. *Mathematical Thought from Ancient to Modern Times*. New York: Oxford University Press, 1972. Kline includes both a brief biography of Abel and discussions of his most important work in this history of mathematics.

Ore, Øystein. *Niels Henrik Abel: Mathematician Extraordinary*. Minneapolis: University of Minnesota Press, 1957. This English-language biography gives a detailed account of Abel's life without requiring a specialized knowledge of mathematics.

Pesic, Peter. *Abel's Proof: An Essay on the Sources and Meaning of Mathematical Unsolvability*. Cambridge,

Mass.: MIT Press, 2003. Describes Abel's life, focusing on his proof of the quintic equation. Pesic discusses why and how the proof changed the perception of mathematics. Includes a new annotated translation of Abel's original proof.

Stubhaug, Arild. *Niels Henrik Abel and His Times: Called Too Soon by Flames Afar*. Translated by Richard H. Daly. Berlin: Springer, 2000. Stubhaug, a Norwegian mathematician and historian, recounts Abel's brief life and achievements in this readable biography intended for a general audience. Includes illustrations.

SEE ALSO: Sophie Germain; Jakob Steiner.

RELATED ARTICLES in *Great Events from History: The Nineteenth Century, 1801-1900:* 1819-1833: Babbage Designs a Mechanical Calculator; 1899: Hilbert Publishes *The Foundations of Geometry*; 1900: Lebesgue Develops New Integration Theory.

LORD ACTON

English historian and moralist

Although he never finished his planned monumental "History of Liberty," Acton was one of the most learned scholars and probing intellects of his time. Although a devout Roman Catholic, he was for much of his life at odds with the church hierarchy because of its authoritarian tendencies. He was first and foremost a moralist, and his most passionate commitment was to the defense of individual freedom.

BORN: January 10, 1834; Naples (now in Italy)
DIED: June 19, 1902; Tegernsee, Bavaria, Germany
ALSO KNOWN AS: John Emerich Edward Dalberg Acton (full name)
AREAS OF ACHIEVEMENT: Historiography, scholarship

EARLY LIFE

John Emerich Edward Dalberg Acton, or Lord Acton as he was known after his elevation to the peerage in 1869, was born in southern Italy. He was the only child of Sir Ferdinand Richard Edward Acton, seventh baronet, and the former Marie Louise Pelline de Dalberg. The Actons were an old Shropshire family, the first baronet having received his title (conferred in 1643) in reward for his loyalty to Charles I. Acton's paternal grandfather had been prime minister of the Kingdom of the Two Sicilies; his mother belonged to one of Germany's oldest noble families. His family heritage—on both sides—was staunchly Roman Catholic. Acton attended the Roman Catholic St. Mary's School at Oscott, near Oxford, and then studied under a private tutor.

The turning point in Acton's intellectual development was his study, from 1850 to 1858, with Johann Joseph Ignaz von Döllinger of the University of Munich, the leading Roman Catholic theologian and church historian of the time. The close ties that were forged between the two men had a decisive influence in shaping Acton's most salient values. Döllinger was a champion of the Rankean scientific approach to the study of history, based upon exacting research into the primary sources. He simultaneously aspired to make Roman Catholicism intellectually and theologically respectable by opening the Church to modern philosophical and scientific thought. Most important, Döllinger taught that Christian dogma was not fixed but underwent change and development. The test of any doctrine thus lay in historical evidence. The revolutionary implications of this position first became apparent when Döllinger protested the 1854 proclamation of the Immaculate Conception of Mary because of its lack of historical status.

LIFE'S WORK

Acton's social position gave him the opportunity to travel widely and provided him with access to the leading political and intellectual figures in England and on the Continent. An avid book collector, he built up a personal library of approximately fifty-nine thousand volumes that would, after his death, become part of the University of Cambridge collection. He was a prodigious reader, reputed to read, annotate, and memorize an average of two volumes per day. Fluent in English, German, French, and Italian, he was a brilliant conversationalist. "If the gods granted me the privilege of recalling to life for half an hour's conversation some of the great men of the past I have had the good fortune to know," politician and historian John Morley remarked, "I should say Acton."

Acton's father died when the younger Acton was three, and Acton succeeded to the title as the eighth baronet. His mother in 1840 married Granville George Leveson-Gower (who would become the second earl of Granville), a power in the British Liberal Party. His stepfather arranged for Acton's election to the House of Commons in 1859, but he was not temperamentally cut out for the rough-and-tumble of politics and remained during his six years in the Commons an unimportant backbencher. His personal inclinations and talents lay in journalism and scholarship. In 1858, he became part-owner and an editor of the "liberal" Roman Catholic monthly, the *Rambler*, which in 1862 was converted into a quarterly under the name *Home and Foreign Review*. After worsening conflict with the church hierarchy led to its termination in 1864, Acton became associated with two other short-lived journals of liberal Catholic opinion—the weekly *Chronicle* (1867-1868) and the quarterly *North British Review* (1869-1872).

Acton's difficulties with the Roman Catholic Church hierarchy grew out of his hostility to its ultramontanism. In its narrower meaning, ultramontanism stood for the centralization of power within the Church in the papacy. More broadly, the ultramontanist position—most explicitly summarized by Pope Pius IX in the *Syllabus Errorum* appended to his 1864 encyclical *Quanta Cura*—repudiated "progress, Liberalism, and modern civilization." Among the heresies condemned in the *Syllabus Errorum* were separation of church and state, freedom of worship, and free intellectual inquiry in science, philosophy, and history. On the opposite side, Acton affirmed that faith could be reconciled with reason and science.

Second, Acton called for a free church in a free state. Relying upon the force of the state would inevitably subordinate the Church to mere political expediency; alternately, an absolutist state could not tolerate an independent Church. Most important, Acton regarded individual liberty not as the antithesis of Christianity but as its product. In contrast with the theocracy of the Jews and the ancient Greek states, the Christian distinction between what was due to God and what was due to Caesar introduced the new conception of the individual conscience immune from political interference. When ultramontanists glorified the Inquisition, Acton replied that murder was no less murder because it was sanctioned by the pope. He even published in 1869 a painstakingly researched article, "The Massacre of St. Bartholomew," showing papal complicity in the bloody 1572 attack upon the Huguenots.

The high point of Acton's conflict with the church hierarchy came over the doctrine of papal infallibility that Pius IX pushed through a tightly managed general council in 1870. Acton was in Rome during the meeting of the council, working behind the scenes as an adviser

Lord Acton. (Library of Congress)

to the minority of prelates opposed to the promulgation of the doctrine. He even made an unsuccessful attempt to organize a protest from all the major European powers. In the aftermath of the council, he publicly marshaled the historical evidence in support of the anti-infallibilist position. His old mentor Döllinger was excommunicated because of his refusal to accept the new doctrine.

For a time, it appeared that Acton would suffer the same fate. Such action was not taken, however, partly because Acton was a layman rather than a priest as was Döllinger, partly because of the political difficulties that his excommunication would have raised for the Church in England, and partly because of Acton's tactfulness in keeping his distance from Rome while still avoiding open defiance. Shrinking from a break with the Church, Acton adopted the face-saving formula "I have yielded obedience." He squared this acquiescence with his conscience by personally adopting a minimalist interpretation of the doctrine's meaning. Regarding the Church as a holy body transcending the shortcomings of its official leaders, he took refuge in his faith that time—or what he termed "God's providence in His government of the

Church"—would undo the damage. While upholding the right of others to disbelieve, he never doubted that membership in the Church was the necessary means for his own personal salvation.

Acton appears to have begun working upon what he envisaged as his masterwork, the "History of Liberty," during the 1870's. Although rather sarcastically described as "the greatest book that never was written," its broad outlines can be reconstructed from his essays and manuscript notes. Acton's starting point was his definition of liberty as the freedom of the individual to follow the dictates of his conscience. Liberty, in turn, depended upon the existence of the rule of law; its antithesis was the exercise of arbitrary power untrammeled by any limitation. Although Acton found glimmerings of that conception in antiquity, despotism was the norm: "In religion, morality, and politics there was only one legislator and one authority."

The Middle Ages represented a major advance in the growth of liberty. One reason was its corporatist social organization, whereby each class and interest had defined rights and privileges. Even more important was the belief in the existence of a higher law to which temporal rulers were subject and which the Church in theory, if not always in practice, was charged with upholding. The Renaissance, however, saw the emergence of the absolute state that accepted no law outside itself and followed the Machiavellian principle that the end justified the means. After first paying lip service to liberty, the Protestant reformers ended up in a marriage of convenience with royal absolutism. Meanwhile, the Roman Catholic Church copied the Protestant enemy by joining in an alliance with monarchical power that ended in the monarchies' subjection to church power.

The liberating promise of the English revolution of the seventeenth century was successfully blunted. The result of the 1688 settlement was simply to replace the divine right of kings with the divine right of property. The American Revolution was for Acton the epochal turning point in modern history. He eulogized the revolutionaries' philosophy of natural rights and their denial of the legitimacy of all authority not derived from the people, but what he most admired was how the framers of the U.S. Constitution had built into their plan of government a set of checks and balances to prevent unrestrained majority rule. By contrast, the disastrous flaw in the French Revolution was its acceptance of a doctrine of unlimited popular sovereignty that substituted for monarchical absolutism the despotism of the majority. The result was the most dangerous threat to liberty yet:

> The true democratic principle, that none shall have power over the people, is taken to mean that none shall be able to restrain or to elude its power. The true democratic principle, that the people shall not be made to do what it does not like, is taken to mean that it shall never be required to tolerate what it does not like. The true democratic principle, that every person's free will shall be as unfettered as possible, is taken to mean the free will of the collective people shall be fettered in nothing.

Aggravating the situation was the accompanying rise of nationalism. Domestically, nationalism fostered a centralization of authority that swept away all intermediate institutions between the isolated individual and the omnipotent state; internationally, nationalism meant rule by force of the strong over the weak. Acton summed up his indictment in an epigram: "The nations aim at power, and the world at freedom."

Acton's hero among contemporary political leaders was British Liberal Party leader William Ewart Gladstone. He was attracted partly by Gladstone's own tendency to define issues in moral terms, even more by what he saw as Gladstone's commitment to striking a balance between democracy and liberty. Although the propertied minority had rights that must be respected, the majority simultaneously had a right to social legislation that would improve the lot of the masses. Gladstone's "Little Englandism," his opposition to the imperialism of the national state run amok, was even more attractive. Deep ties of affection and mutual respect joined the two men.

Gladstone submitted for Acton's criticism nearly everything he wrote. Acton, in turn, influenced Gladstone in his politics—most important, his espousal of disestablishment of the Irish (Anglican) church and Irish home rule. Gladstone was responsible for Acton's elevation to the peerage in 1869 as Baron Acton of Aldenham, his election as honorary Fellow of All Souls, Oxford, in 1891, and his appointment as lord-in-waiting to Queen Victoria in 1892. Acton had been one of the founders of the *English Historical Review* in 1886, himself contributing to the first issue an impressively learned survey of nineteenth century German historians and philosophers of history. As early as 1872, the University of Munich awarded him an honorary doctorate of philosophy. Cambridge followed with an honorary LL.D. in 1888; Oxford, with an honorary D.C.L. the year after. In 1895, Acton was named Regius Professor of Modern History at Cambridge. Along with the professorship came election as an honorary Fellow of Trinity College.

Acton's six years at Cambridge were probably the happiest of his life. Although he lectured on the French

Revolution for the historical tripos, the greater part of his energy was devoted to the editorship of the *Cambridge Modern History* (1899-1912). Although only the first volume and half of the second were in type at his death, he was largely responsible for the planning of the full twelve volumes and the selection of most of the individual contributors.

The burden of handling the manifold details of so large an undertaking badly strained Acton's already poor health. In 1901, he suffered a stroke that forced him to leave Cambridge. He died on June 19, 1902, at a villa owned by his wife's family at Tegernsee in Bavaria. He was survived by his wife, Countess Maria von Arco-Valley (whom he had married in 1865), and four children—one son and three daughters.

Acton's publication during his lifetime consisted mostly of periodical contributions and reprinted lectures. After his death, however, his more important writings were collected in four volumes edited by John N. Figgis and Reginald V. Laurence: *Lectures on Modern History* (1906), *The History of Freedom and Other Essays* (1907), *Historical Essays and Studies* (1908), and *Lectures on the French Revolution* (1910). The years since World War II have witnessed a resurgence of interest in Acton's work, resulting in the appearance of such new anthologies as *Essays on Freedom and Power* (1948; edited by Gertrude Himmelfarb), *Essays on Church and State* (1952; edited by Douglas Woodruff), *Essays in the Liberal Interpretation of History* (1967; edited by William H. McNeill), and *Lord Acton on Papal Power* (1973; edited by H. A. MacDougall).

SIGNIFICANCE

Lord Acton's strength as a historian lay in his painstaking research in and analysis of the primary sources. However, his high scholarly standards were simultaneously a weakness. He could not bring himself to stop until he had explored everything remotely pertaining to the subject. His papers in the Cambridge University Library are filled with pages of notes for projects that were never finished. Even his planned opening chapter for the first volume of the *Cambridge Modern History*, "The Legacy of the Middle Ages," was left in too fragmentary shape for inclusion. This weakness was aggravated by the breadth of his interests, which kept him from focusing his energies upon any single period or topic. Moreover, he was not an outstanding literary stylist.

Acton's importance as a historian lies in his broader philosophy of history. For Acton, ideas were the forces that moved the world. Therein lay the source of his conception of the historian's role. The historian's task was not the Rankean ideal of the impartial chronicler of what had actually happened. Even worse was the moral relativism that explained away—even excused—wrongdoing in terms of the values of the time. The historian's duty to the present and to the future was to judge the past by the canons of eternal justice. His judgment that murder is still murder no matter what its ostensible noble justification has a special resonance for the late twentieth century. "If we lower our standard in History," he admonished in his inaugural lecture as Regius Professor, "we cannot uphold it in Church or State."

Part of the reason for the renewed interest in Acton is his championship of what is now called "political pluralism"—his argument that the preservation of individual liberty depends upon the widest possible dispersion of power. Underlying his commitment to pluralism was his awareness of the corruptibility of human nature. "Most assuredly, now as heretofore," he explained to a friend, "the Men of the Time are, in most cases, unprincipled, and act from motives of interest, of passion, of prejudice, cherished and unchecked, of selfish hope or unworthy fear." The most dangerous temptation to which humans succumbed was ambition for power. In that recognition, Acton belonged more to the present age than to his own. Only those generations that have witnessed the horrors of the twentieth century can fully appreciate his prophetic warning:

> Power tends to corrupt and absolute power corrupts absolutely. Great men are almost always bad men, even when they exercise influence and not authority: still more when you superadd the tendency or the certainty of corruption by authority. There is no worse heresy than that the office sanctifies the holder of it. . . . The inflexible authority of the moral code is, to me, the secret of the authority, the dignity, the utility of history. If we may debase the currency for the sake of genius, or success or rank, or reputation, we may debase it for the sake of a man's influence, of his religion, of his party, of the good cause which prospers by his credit and suffers by his disgrace. Then history ceases to be a science, an arbiter of controversy, a guide of the wanderer. . . . It serves where it ought to reign; and it serves the worst cause better than the purest.

—*John Braeman*

FURTHER READING

Altholz, Josef L. *The Liberal Catholic Movement in England: "The Rambler" and Its Contributors, 1848-1864*. London: Burns and Oates, 1962. An excellent account of the controversy over ultramontanism in England.

Butterfield, Herbert. *Lord Acton*. London: G. Philip, 1948. A brief, though astute, sketch of Acton's intellectual development.

Chadwick, Owen. *Acton and History*. New York: Cambridge University Press, 1998. An edited collection of essays by a noted Acton scholar. Examines Acton's ideas and his contributions to the study of history.

Fasnacht, George E. *Acton's Political Philosophy*. London: Hollis and Carter, 1952. A detailed examination of Acton as a political theorist.

Hill, Roland. *Lord Acton*. New Haven, Conn.: Yale University Press, 2000. Comprehensive biography, placing Acton within the context of Catholic politics in Great Britain. Includes a foreword by Owen Chadwick, a leading authority on Acton.

Himmelfarb, Gertrude. *Lord Acton: A Study in Conscience and Politics*. Chicago: University of Chicago Press, 1952. An insightful and perceptive intellectual biography that did much to stimulate renewed interest in Acton.

_____. *Victorian Minds*. New York: Alfred A. Knopf, 1968. Although the chapter on Acton basically summarizes Himmelfarb's 1952 study, the volume's broader scope clarifies Acton's place within the spectrum of Victorian thought.

Schuettinger, Robert L. *Lord Acton: Historian of Liberty*. LaSalle, Ill.: Open Court, 1976. Includes more personal details, but thinner analysis, than Himmelfarb's works.

SEE ALSO: Thomas Carlyle; William Ewart Gladstone; Pius IX; Leopold von Ranke.

RELATED ARTICLES in *Great Events from History: The Nineteenth Century, 1801-1900:* December 8, 1869-October 20, 1870: Vatican I Decrees Papal Infallibility Dogma; 1871-1877: *Kulturkampf* Against the Catholic Church in Germany; May 15, 1891: Papal Encyclical on Labor.

HENRY ADAMS

American historian

A first-rate historian, Adams wrote several biographies and the monumental nine-volume History of the United States of America, *covering the administrations of Thomas Jefferson and James Madison. His two most famous works are interconnected and autobiographical:* Mont-Saint-Michel and Chartres *and* The Education of Henry Adams.

BORN: February 16, 1838; Boston, Massachusetts
DIED: March 27, 1918; Washington, D.C.
ALSO KNOWN AS: Henry Brooks Adams (full name)
AREAS OF ACHIEVEMENT: Historiography, literature

EARLY LIFE

Henry Brooks Adams was the fourth of five children of Charles Francis Adams and Abigail Brown Brooks. His father was a cold and distant figure, and it was to his mother that he looked for affection. It is not surprising that Henry would always feel out of place. His elite Brahmin heritage both paved the way for his future and controlled it. A kinsman, Samuel Adams, had become involved in the American Revolution as a manipulator of mobs. His great-grandfather John Adams helped draft the Declaration of Independence and was the first vice president and the second president. Henry's grandfather John Quincy Adams served as secretary of state and then as president. Henry's father served as ambassador to England during the diplomatically crucial period of the Civil War and was later elected to Congress.

In addition to his distinguished heritage, Henry's immediate family was one of the wealthiest in Boston, based on the mercantile fortune of his mother, Abigail Brooks. Adams's full name appears to sum up his life—"Henry" betokening the scholar rather than the man of action; "Brooks" the moneyed inheritance that was his by birth; and "Adams" the line of blue-blooded forefathers who had taken such an active part in the creation of the United States. Henry's dilemma was to live a successful life in the shadow of such eminence.

Adams attended Harvard from 1854 through 1858. In *The Education of Henry Adams* (1907), he later stated that he had learned nothing while there. Upon graduation, in typical patrician fashion, he set out on a tour of Europe. He studied law and learned to speak German while at the University of Berlin, from 1858 to 1860. While in Europe, he also began his efforts in journalism, which he would continue throughout his life.

Henry Adams. (Harvard University Archives)

In 1861, as the Civil War broke out in the United States, President Abraham Lincoln appointed Adams's father minister to England, a critical position, because the South was attempting to gain recognition from England. At the age of twenty-three, Adams accompanied his father and acted as his private secretary. While in England, Adams continued his journalism, working anonymously for *The New York Times*, and he also began his historical work by writing articles for the *North American Review*.

LIFE'S WORK

In 1868, Adams returned to Washington. He and his brothers decided that politics had done nothing but bring sorrow to the family. Adams's worldview might be broken into two segments: his philosophical speculations about the world, especially the United States, and what he was going to do with the remainder of his life. As it turned out, Adams spent the remainder of his life looking for answers to both questions through an interaction of the two. In a way, Adams became one of the most versatile intellectuals the United States has ever produced.

Adams did not spend his whole life behind a desk. He enjoyed parties, people, and friendships immensely, and his family fame brought him into contact with the celebrities of the time. Although short in stature, he was handsome, and he became known as one of the three best dancers in Washington.

From 1868 until 1870, Adams was a freelance journalist, serving as a correspondent for *The Nation* and other leading journals as he plunged into both the social and the political worlds of Washington. His primary interest was the reconstruction of a war-shattered nation. He fought for civil service reform and the retention of the gold standard. He wrote articles exposing political corruption and warning against economic monopolies, especially within the railroads.

In 1870, Charles W. Eliot, the famous Harvard president, asked Adams to become assistant professor of medieval history. Out of tune with the world for which he was destined, Adams accepted. Despite having one of the best minds in the country, Adams was ill-trained to be a teacher. He threw himself furiously into his new task, often staying only one lecture ahead of his class. Without planning it, Adams was preparing the groundwork for what would become one of his masterpieces, *Mont-Saint-Michel and Chartres* (1904). Adams also became the first American to employ the seminar method in his classes.

Adams's work at Harvard became his first step toward studying the American past. In 1877, he resigned from Harvard to complete two biographies, *The Life of Albert Gallatin* (1879) and *John Randolph* (1882). This research increased his interest in the early American period, and hoping to understand the nature of an evolving American democracy, he began what was to become his nine-volume *History of the United States of America* (1889-1891).

In 1872, Adams married Marian "Clover" Hooper, a woman with impeccable family connections, great intelligence, and a solid income. The two took a yearlong wedding trip that included a tour of Europe and boating up the Nile. Henry and Clover made a complementary couple, and Adams would later speak of their years together as years of happiness. Their union produced no children.

Adams published two novels anonymously, *Democracy: An American Novel* (1880) and *Esther: A Novel* (1884). Neither novel was a success, because Adams did not possess the artistic talents necessary to produce fiction. Of the two, *Democracy* was the more popular and the superior. *Democracy* was a roman à clef, which accounted for its initial demand. Mrs. Lightfoot Lee is the heroine through the eyes of whom Washington is revealed. She becomes a confidant of a midwestern sena-

THE DYNAMO METAPHOR

When Henry Adams visited Paris in the summer of 1900, he spent a great deal of time at the Great Exposition, where much of the advanced technology of the late nineteenth century was on display. He was particularly fascinated by the exhibit of gigantic electrical dynamos. His autobiography—which he wrote in the third person—describes his reaction to the displays.

Then [Langley] showed his scholar [Adams] the great hall of dynamos, and explained how little he knew about electricity or force of any kind, even of his own special sun, which spouted heat in inconceivable volume, but which, as far as he knew, might spout less or more, at any time, for all the certainty he felt in it. To him, the dynamo itself was but an ingenious channel for conveying somewhere the heat latent in a few tons of poor coal hidden in a dirty enginehouse carefully kept out of sight; but to Adams the dynamo became a symbol of infinity. As he grew accustomed to the great gallery of machines, he began to feel the forty-foot dynamos as a moral force, much as the early Christians felt the Cross. The planet itself seemed less impressive, in its old-fashioned, deliberate, annual or daily revolution, than this huge wheel, revolving within arm's length at some vertiginous speed, and barely murmuring—scarcely humming an audible warning to stand a hair's-breadth further for respect of power—while it would not wake the baby lying close against its frame. Before the end, one began to pray to it; inherited instinct taught the natural expression of man before silent and infinite force. Among the thousand symbols of ultimate energy the dynamo was not so human as some, but it was the most expressive.

Yet the dynamo, next to the steam-engine, was the most familiar of exhibits. For Adams's objects its value lay chiefly in its occult mechanism. Between the dynamo in the gallery of machines and the enginehouse outside, the break of continuity amounted to abysmal fracture for a historian's objects. No more relation could he discover between the steam and the electric current than between the Cross and the cathedral. The forces were interchangeable if not reversible, but he could see only an absolute fiat in electricity as in faith. . . .

Source: Henry Adams, *The Education of Henry Adams* (1907), chapter 25, "The Dynamo and the Virgin."

tor, and she is introduced to the processes of democracy. She meets the president and other high-ranking figures, only to find them all to be vacuous. She represents Adams's alter ego; indeed, both came up with much the same summation of Washington: After an initial attraction for the cause, they both reject it in the end because of the emptiness and moral ambiguity they find there. *Democracy* served Adams as a trial run for *The Education of Henry Adams*.

Adams's second novel, *Esther*, is less interesting. It is similar in that it also has a woman as its main character, this one based on Adams's wife. As a novel of ideas, *Esther* investigates the relationship between religion and modern science, a theme that Adams pursued throughout his life. As the novel ends, the heroine, in her quest for meaning, stares at and listens to Niagara Falls, Adams's overpowering symbol for the life force. The roar symbolizes a natural representation of the dynamo Adams was to make so much of and of the eternal law of history.

In 1885, Adams was stunned when his wife of thirteen years took potassium cyanide and killed herself. There was no discernible motive for her suicide except that she feared madness, which existed in her family. Strangely, Adams had a sculpture of a mysterious, cloaked woman placed on her grave. At the time of her death, Adams had been working on his *History of the United States of America*. He set the manuscript aside and began a period of restless traveling that included Japan.

As time passed, Adams narrowed his travel to winters in Washington and summers in Paris. He eventually returned to his *History of the United States of America* and completed it in September, 1888. The work was published in nine volumes between 1889 and 1891. Initially, it was met by apathy, but eventually it would be considered of the highest order, second only to the work of Francis Parkman.

Adams's best-known works, *Mont-Saint-Michel and Chartres* and *The Education of Henry Adams*, were privately printed and distributed to friends and only later were published for general use. The two works are interconnected and are based on thoughts that Adams spent a lifetime trying to untangle.

Mont-Saint-Michel and Chartres is a work of history, aesthetics, philosophy, and theology. The book is like a Symbolist poem, with one event flowing into another and all rules of chronology and reason being defied.

Adams's starting point for *Mont-Saint-Michel and Chartres* can be found in his travels to France and his visits to the thirteenth century cathedrals. Adams was in search of a fixed point from which to measure motion down to his own time, and that point became the medieval worldview as expressed especially in the cathedrals.

Adams believed that their monumental structures expressed the deepest emotions that humans ever felt. For Adams, an entire age could be said to have unity, purpose, mission, and fullness of experience toward an ideological unity represented by the Blessed Virgin Mary.

The Education of Henry Adams was not finished until Adams was sixty-eight years old. It remains his best-known work and one of the most distinguished autobiographies of all time, compared by some to Saint Augustine's *Confessions* (c. 1397). Whereas the Virgin had been the center for *Mont-Saint-Michel and Chartres*, the symbol for the twentieth century became the dynamo, one of which Adams had seen at the Chicago World's Fair. Adams found the twentieth century to be incomprehensible. Under the impact of the alarming growth of science and technology, historical forces had accelerated, leading to what Adams called the "multiverse" of the modern world.

Adams died on March 27, 1918, in Washington, D.C., the city from which he could not separate himself. World War I was still raging, and the breakup of the modern, civilized world, which Adams had predicted, had become reality. Adams was buried next to his wife in the Rock Creek Cemetery. At his direction, the grave was unmarked.

SIGNIFICANCE

Henry Adams's life situation allowed him the freedom to be rebellious. He scornfully accepted the mantle of responsibility that destiny had given him. He became the first modern historian in the United States. He briefly shared his enormous intellect with students and then resigned permanently from teaching, undertaking full time the completion of his research and compiling his magnum opus, the nine-volume *History of the United States of America*.

Adams also made his mark on the historical and literary world with his *Mont-Saint-Michel and Chartres* and his *The Education of Henry Adams*. These two works, especially *The Education of Henry Adams*, are still widely read by students and the general public. One central connection between the two is the juxtaposition Adams proposed between the Virgin of the thirteenth century and the dynamo of the twentieth. Adams was interested in power—religious power, political power, and scientific power.

Adams was almost as good a prophet as he was a historian. He believed that the twentieth century was heading toward chaos; humankind was being swept away by seemingly uncontrollable technology, represented by the dynamo. Ahead of his time and unable to comprehend modern man, Adams foresaw the ultimate possibility of humanity's self-destruction.

—John Harty

FURTHER READING

Adams, Henry Brooks. *The Education of Henry Adams: An Autobiography*. Introduction by Donald Hall. Washington, D.C.: Privately printed, 1907. Reprint. Boston: Houghton Mifflin, 2000. The best starting point for a study of Adams would be his three works listed in this bibliography, especially *The Education of Henry Adams*, one of the most distinguished autobiographies of the twentieth century.

_____. *The Letters of Henry Adams*. 3 vols. Edited by J. C. Levenson et al. Cambridge, Mass.: Belknap Press of Harvard University Press, 1982. Adams's letters are valuable because they reveal his thoughts and reflect the times in which he lived.

_____. *Mont-Saint-Michel and Chartres*. Washington, D.C.: Privately printed, 1904. Reprint. New York: New American Library, 1961. Adams's thoughts on the medieval world, Gothic cathedrals, and thirteenth century Unity.

Byrnes, Joseph F. *The Virgin of Chartres: An Intellectual and Psychological History of the Work of Henry Adams*. Rutherford, N.J.: Fairleigh Dickinson University Press, 1981. Discusses Adams's relationships with women. Concentrates mainly on *Mont-Saint-Michel and Chartres* and Adams's thoughts concerning the Virgin Mary.

Chalfant, Edward. *Both Sides of the Ocean: A Biography of Henry Adams, His First Life, 1838-1862*. Hamden, Conn.: Archon Books, 1982.

_____. *Better in Darkness: A Biography of Henry Adams, His Second Life, 1862-1891*. Hamden, Conn.: Archon Books, 1994.

_____. *Improvement of the World: A Biography of Henry Adams, His Last Life, 1891-1918*. North Haven, Conn.: Archon Books, 2001. Chalfant has compiled an exhaustively detailed three-volume scholarly study of Adams's life based on archival and private material previously unavailable to biographers.

Harbert, Earl N., ed. *Critical Essays on Henry Adams*. Boston: G. K. Hall, 1981. The editor has compiled essays on Adams by R. P. Blackmur, H. S. Commager, Ernest Samuels, Charles Anderson, Howard Mumford, J. C. Levenson, and others. The essays cover various matters, including Adams's fiction and his two autobiographical works.

Levenson, J. C. *The Mind and Art of Henry Adams*. Boston: Houghton Mifflin, 1957. This critical work concentrates on Adams's life and on his enormous distinction as a writer and interpretive scholar. Major concepts associated with Adams, such as modern humankind existing within a "multiverse" and Adams's thesis concerning the Unity found in *Mont-Saint-Michel and Chartres*, are developed and discussed in detail.

Samuels, Ernest. *The Young Henry Adams*. Cambridge, Mass.: Belknap Press of Harvard University Press, 1948.

_____. *Henry Adams: The Middle Years*. Cambridge, Mass.: Belknap Press of Harvard University Press, 1958.

_____. *Henry Adams: The Major Phase*. Cambridge, Mass.: Belknap Press of Harvard University Press, 1964. These three books constitute a comprehensive and distinguished biography of Henry Adams. Samuels examines the pattern of failure and futility that Adams experienced during his attempts at education, his observations of others' efforts, and his perplexities with language itself.

SEE ALSO: Francis Parkman; William Hickling Prescott.

RELATED ARTICLE in *Great Events from History: The Nineteenth Century, 1801-1900:* 1824: Ranke Develops Systematic History.

JOHN QUINCY ADAMS

President of the United States (1825-1829)

As diplomat, secretary of state, president, and member of the House of Representatives, in a career spanning the early national period to nearly the time of the Civil War, John Quincy Adams helped to shape the major foreign and domestic policies of the United States, always in the direction of strengthening the nation as a unified whole.

BORN: July 11, 1767; Braintree (now Quincy), Massachusetts

DIED: February 23, 1848; Washington, D.C.

AREA OF ACHIEVEMENT: Government and politics

EARLY LIFE

John Quincy Adams was the second child and first son of future president John Adams and Abigail (Smith) Adams. At such a time and in such a family, he was a child of both the revolution and the Enlightenment, nurtured as well with a strong Puritan sense of duty and destiny, directed throughout his life toward politics (and its attendant sacrifices), always striving to fulfill the expectations and retain the approbation of his parents, especially the redoubtable Abigail. His unorthodox and irregular education was to produce both a scholar and a nationalist, unswerving in his principles and forever unsatisfied with his performance, always striving to increase his learning and improve his habits, and never able to mingle easily with others or develop satisfying personal relationships.

As a boy, John Quincy imbibed patriotism in the midst of the revolution and then spent a number of years in Europe while his father was engaged in the nation's diplomatic business; in France, Holland, and Russia he learned languages, associated with important men of the time, studied sporadically, and began what was to be a lifelong diary. Returning to the United States in 1785 (while his father remained as minister to England), he became again a schoolboy and was graduated from Harvard in 1787. In his commencement address, he referred to this time as a "critical period." He then studied law in Newburyport with Theophilus Parsons until his admission to the bar in 1790.

Uninterested in the legal profession yet reluctant to be drawn into the hardships of public service, John Quincy entered the newspaper battles with essays on the French Revolution (against Thomas Paine's *Rights of Man*, 1791) and the Genêt affair. His arguments in favor of American neutrality won for him the attention of President George Washington and the post of minister resident at The Hague, in 1794. He took up his position at this excellent listening post during the Napoleonic expansion over Europe, reporting in detail to Washington and to the secretary of state on its course, his ideas influencing Washington's foreign policy statements in the Farewell Address.

John Quincy Adams's appointment as minister to Portugal was changed before he took it up, and he and his wife, Louisa, whom he had married in 1797, traveled to Berlin, where the new minister plenipotentiary to Prussia negotiated a treaty, saw his wife successfully enter court society, and began a volume of descriptive letters about a visit to Silesia. Recalled by his father, John Adams, who had lost reelection to the presidency, Adams brought his wife and son (George Washington Adams, born April 12, 1801) to an America they had never seen in order to renew an interrupted law practice. Drawn inevitably to public service, Adams was elected to the Massachusetts Senate in April, 1802, and to the U.S. Senate in February, 1803. He immediately demonstrated the qualities that were to characterize and frustrate his political career: commitment to the nation rather than to any party, consistency of principle and attention to detail, and the inability to deal effectively with varied personalities and the social demands of the Washington political scene.

The young senator was five feet, seven inches tall, balding, with rather sharp and expressive features; he had always been careless in his dress, and despite his lifelong habit of exercise frequently suffered from dizziness, insomnia, stomach trouble, and attacks of anxiety and depression. Always introspective and self-critical, he was reserved and humorless; formally a Unitarian, he was well versed in the Bible, classical literature, science, and the humanities.

Although Adams opposed the Republican administration's acquisition of Louisiana for constitutional reasons, he soon demonstrated his differences from the Federalists on the important issues of the Aaron Burr intrigue, Judge John Pickering's impeachment, and the *Chesapeake* incident and embargo policy. His nationalism and independence in supporting Republican policies provoked Federalist hostility in both political and personal relations; he resigned his Senate seat before his Federalist replacement took over, and he experienced problems even in his lectures as Boylston Professor of Oratory and Rhetoric at Harvard. Without consulting Louisa, he accepted President James Madison's appointment as minister plenipotentiary to Russia; the two older boys remained with their grandparents in Quincy, and Adams, Louisa, and Charles Francis (born August 18, 1807) arrived in St. Petersburg late in 1809.

Despite inadequate funds, both Adamses established themselves with the diplomatic community and at the extravagant court of Czar Alexander I. John Quincy was able to achieve some diplomatic successes with the Russian government, attend to his youngest son, and maintain a correspondence with his older sons filled with stern expectations for their education and achievements—expectations that neither was ever able to fulfill.

As Alexander and Napoleon Bonaparte fell out over the Continental System and the War of 1812 opened, Adams was an obvious choice for the commission to negotiate peace with Great Britain. When its five members met finally in Ghent in 1814, they achieved a satisfactory treaty based on the prewar status quo. Adams then journeyed to Paris to meet Louisa, who had, by herself, wound up their affairs in Russia and traversed Europe with young Charles in the aftermath of war and during the Hundred Days. The Adamses then spent the next two years happily in London, as John Quincy had been appointed by President James Monroe as minister plenipotentiary to Great Britain. It became apparent that Great Britain was willing to negotiate and arbitrate the points still at issue after the Treaty of Ghent.

Adams's appointment as Monroe's secretary of state brought the family back to the United States late in 1817 and renewed the pattern of separation (the parents in Washington, the boys educated elsewhere) and family

John Quincy Adams. (White House Historical Society)

problems. At the age of fifty, Adams reentered domestic politics by becoming embroiled with the new generation of politicians. He was still and always a nationalist and an independent in a time of growing partisanship and sectional controversy, and reserved and scholarly during the development of popular sovereignty and anti-intellectualism. For the rest of his long life, despite personal tragedy and bitter political disappointments, he was to shape much of American domestic and foreign policy.

LIFE'S WORK

Adams became secretary of state as the Era of Good Feelings began to dissolve in personal and partisan contention for the presidency, and at a time when the State Department conducted both foreign and domestic affairs with one chief clerk and seven assistant clerks. Adams organized the department and its papers, did much of the office work himself during long days and nights (even cutting down on his reading), and attended to the census, congressional printing, extraditions, and commissions. He had, early in his career as a Federalist, demonstrated his political independence; he had received his appointments from Republican administrations; as secretary of state and son of John Adams, he was inevitably a presidential candidate. His foreign policy positions therefore developed as much in response to domestic political concerns as to the international situation. Nevertheless, his early principles dominated: He was a nationalist and an expansionist, cautious but determined to develop a hemispheric role for the United States.

Attempting to defend and expand American trade interests, Adams concentrated on the problem of discriminatory British customs duties in the West Indies trade. British interests and disturbed world conditions, however, meant the retention of those duties. Boundary problems with Great Britain and Russia in the Northwest presented less difficulty than those with Spain in Florida. The Treaty of 1818 settled United States-Canadian boundary and fisheries problems and provided for joint United States-British occupation of Oregon for ten years (the northern boundary fixed with Russia at 54 degrees, 40 minutes in the Convention of 1824). When General Andrew Jackson's sensational raid into Florida threatened an international incident, Adams alone in the cabinet supported the general and used the uncontrolled Florida situation as an effective point in the negotiations that led to the 1819 Adams-Onís (Transcontinental) Treaty.

Acquisition of Florida and the demarcation of a clear southwestern boundary to the Pacific represented major gains for the United States, even though Adams's opponents then and later attacked him on certain details (in which he had been uncharacteristically careless) and charged him with deliberately giving up Texas. Although he was not directly involved in the Missouri Compromise, Adams was against slavery and fearful that the sectional controversy had the potential to dissolve the Union. Even more immediately threatening was the possibility of European powers acting in the Western Hemisphere to regain newly independent colonies. Adams urged a unilateral American statement and greatly influenced the formulation of the basic policies of nonintervention and noncolonization, and American noninvolvement in Europe, points that President Monroe incorporated into his December, 1823, message, later known as the Monroe Doctrine.

A presidential nominating system still in flux made social events crucial for politics: Protocol for formal calls was subject matter for Senate resolutions and cabinet papers; Louisa Adams's entertaining was vital for the cold, unsocial, and ambitious John Quincy, who furthermore refused to pursue the nomination actively, preferring it unsought as recognition of his ability and service. Throughout his political career he was to spurn the idea of active campaigning directed at the mass of voters, seeing public service as properly in the hands of the dedicated and qualified rather than the "popular" politicians.

In the election of 1824, Adams received eighty-four electoral votes to Jackson's ninety-nine, but as there was no majority, the House was to decide between Jackson, Adams, and Henry Clay, the third-place finisher. While Adams actively swayed some Federalists, it was Clay's influence that turned the tide; "Harry of the West" feared the rash general more than a fellow nationalist, and the two rivals realized their basic agreement on major issues. With Clay's influence added, the House chose Adams to be president; Adams's appointment of Clay as secretary of state (and therefore a potential next president) led the Jacksonians to open their presidential campaign almost immediately, based on the charge of "bargain and corruption." The accusation of an Adams-Clay collusion continued to affect American politics for many years.

A U.S. president like his father, and like his father a single-term executive facing the more popular candidate, Adams was a minority president in a period of great partisan pressures, a nationalist in an era of deepening sectionalism, and an executive with a program at a time of legislative dominance. He never really controlled the National Republicans, nor could he prevent the development of the Democratic Republican Party. Determined

ADAMS'S LAST STATE OF THE UNION ADDRESS

John Quincy Adams was often criticized for delivering speeches that were overly scholarly and elaborate. This extract from his last state of the union address helps to illustrate his style. The second sentence alone contains 217 words.

A revolution of the seasons has nearly been completed since the representatives of the people and States of this Union were last assembled at this place to deliberate and to act upon the common important interests of their constituents. In that interval the never slumbering eye of a wise and beneficent Providence has continued its guardian care over the welfare of our beloved country; the blessing of health has continued generally to prevail throughout the land; the blessing of peace with our brethren of the human race has been enjoyed without interruption; internal quiet has left our fellow citizens in the full enjoyment of all their rights and in the free exercise of all their faculties, to pursue the impulse of their nature and the obligation of their duty in the improvement of their own condition; the productions of the soil, the exchanges of commerce, the vivifying labors of human industry, have combined to mingle in our cup a portion of enjoyment as large and liberal as the indulgence of Heaven has perhaps ever granted to the imperfect state of man upon earth; and as the purest of human felicity consists in its participation with others, it is no small addition to the sum of our national happiness at this time that peace and prosperity prevail to a degree seldom experienced over the whole habitable globe, presenting, though as yet with painful exceptions, a foretaste of that blessed period of promise when the lion shall lie down with the lamb and wars shall be no more.

Source: John Quincy Adams, "State of the Union Address," December 5, 1826.

to avoid party considerations in appointments, he kept many in his cabinet and other offices (such as Postmaster General John McLean) who worked actively against him. He proposed large-scale national government action for general improvement in both learning and scientific activity (a national university, national observatories) and in the specifics of the "American System," usually identified as Clay's program, but which Adams claimed as his own.

Not surprisingly, Adams considered foreign affairs very important; he had a Jeffersonian view of developing American world trade, with an emphasis on reciprocity and neutral rights. The administration's diplomatic failures, particularly Great Britain's closure of West Indies trade, were often a result of domestic politics and sectional interests. The same was true of Adams's concept of the democratic mission of the United States vis-à-vis Latin America: Any possibility of United States leadership in the Western Hemisphere was broken on the reefs of partisan opposition. The Panama Congress and the sensitive status of Cuba overshadowed negotiations and consultations that often laid the foundations for later administrations' successes.

Adams delegated much domestic policy to his cabinet and was therefore not deeply involved in the sectional maneuvering that produced the Tariff of Abominations. He strongly supported internal improvements, regarded the public lands as a long-term national resource, and backed off from a confrontation with Georgia over states' rights stemming from the Indian removal policy. Despite his concept of interdependent sectional interests producing national unity, Adams was usually identified with the economic interests of the Northeast.

A large antiadministration majority in Congress after the 1826 midterm elections left Adams a lame-duck president, depressed, ill, and socially isolated in the White House, mourning his father (who had died on July 4, 1826) and attempting to come to terms with his wife's depression and illness and the total disappointment of his hopes for his two elder sons, George, a debt-ridden depressive, and John, something of a rake. A developing interest in botany was a diverting hobby, although the live-oak plantation he established in Florida (to benefit naval construction) was abandoned by the next administration. All of Adams's personal difficulties, combined with his political ineptitude, helped ensure his isolation in the campaign of 1828, one of the most bitter and vicious ever waged.

Adams was politically inept for a variety of reasons. The Adams family considered its members to be different from the general public, more principled and determined and therefore doomed to popular misunderstanding and lack of support. Adams preferred not to respond to public criticism or to explain and justify his actions; he refused to "electioneer," and his public speeches were scholarly, elaborate, and open to ridicule. His handling of the patronage (a difficult field complicated by factions within the parties) alienated his supporters and gave aid and comfort to his political enemies. He had not been able to rally support for a nonpartisan federal government program of wide-ranging improvements for the national benefit; he could not develop an effective party organization or even meld Federalists and nationalistic Republicans into a politically supportive bloc.

Adams's administration ignored the developing labor movement and the broadening popular base of voters and played into Jacksonian egalitarian propaganda. The well-organized Jacksonians easily set the cold Yankee aristocrat against the man of the people, concentrating on Jackson's personal popularity rather than his positions on issues (such as the tariff and internal improvements), which would alienate his disparate supporters.

Like his father before him, Adams felt his defeat deeply, taking it as his country's repudiation, refusing (also like his father) to attend his successor's inauguration and moving into regular routines, exercise, and writing in order to make the transition to private life. On April 30, 1829, George Washington Adams jumped or fell from a steamboat and drowned in Long Island Sound, leaving a mass of debts and an illegitimate child. Adams at sixty-one was a failed president with his eldest son dead; nevertheless, mutual guilt brought him and Louisa closer (they had left George with others to rear; they had pushed him too hard) and helped them to concentrate on their two grandchildren and their youngest and favorite son. The latter soon married a wealthy and passive wife and began to produce a large family (Louisa Catherine II, John Quincy II, Charles Francis, Jr., Henry, Arthur, Mary, and Brooks).

Political ambition (which Adams regarded as his chief character flaw) led him to agree (as usual, without consulting his wife) to represent his district in the House of Representatives. In 1831, he was elected by a large popular majority, a victory he regarded as the most satisfying of his entire political career. He missed politics and needed the salary, and for seventeen years and eight elections he carved out another and even more effective position in the service of the nation.

Still short, stout, and bald except for a fringe, Adams, as he had done all of his life, rose early, read his Bible and classical works regularly, swam, and walked; he developed into a connoisseur of wine and mellowed socially. He accepted anti-Masonic support for a presidential nomination in 1832 (which did not eventuate) and lost the election for governor of Massachusetts in 1833 and for Massachusetts (Whig) senator in 1835; none of this lessened his commitment to his House career. The House chamber had bad acoustics, as a result of which Adams at his desk could hear whispers from everywhere; his own high-pitched voice was to become a feared instrument in the coming House debates. After he spoke against Daniel Webster in connection with the "French Question" (of treaty payments) in 1836, he began to be called "Old Man Eloquent."

In the Nullification Controversy, Adams recognized again the divisive potential of sectionalism, but in the next few years he focused more on the slavery issue as the greatest threat to the Union. He was neither an egalitarian nor an abolitionist per se; while Louisa began to acquaint herself with the problem, associating with the Grimkés and other abolitionists and coming to see the parallels between black slavery and the oppression of women, Adams viewed slavery in terms of principle: as morally reprehensible and politically dangerous to the continued existence of the nation. It was fitting, therefore, that he reacted first to the House's vote, in May of 1836, to table without reading all petitions dealing with slavery.

The long battle against the "gag rule" invigorated Adams; the issue of the rights of petition and free speech gave him a broad ground on which to stand and aided him in debate when he dealt with slavery as a threat to the Union, a possible provocation of war with Mexico, a politically divisive question, and the source of the denial of basic rights of citizens. In this period also he began to examine the question of slavery in a broader context. Reading his mother's papers (Abigail Adams had died on October 28, 1818) and reacting to his wife's growing involvement with feminism, Adams came to support the concept of women's political rights, although without endorsing specific issues or deflecting his emphasis on the slavery question.

Always a political independent, Adams supported many of the Jackson administration's policies, disagreeing, however, on bank policy. As an independent and a skilled parliamentarian, he was able in 1839 to effect the necessary organization of the House committees despite paralyzing partisan divisions. Southern members frequently opposed his actions and called for resolutions of censure. Although his early ponderous and erudite *Report on Weights and Measures* (1821) had never had any direct influence, Adams was able, from 1838 to 1846, to direct the use of the fund that established the Smithsonian Institution.

Despite bitter opposition, Adams maintained his battle in the House on all issues connected with slavery, although he believed that he could only begin what must be a long struggle. He opposed the 1838 attempt to annex Texas for constitutional reasons and because he believed that it would lead to a free-land policy to gain Western political support, thus dissipating a national resource. In

1841, he argued for the defense in the *Amistad* case before the Supreme Court, never submitting a bill for his legal services. In 1842, demonstrating great intellectual resources and physical stamina, he conducted a six-day, successful defense against a House resolution to censure him. He now received and enjoyed public adulation, and in December of 1844, on his resolution, the House rescinded the gag rule.

Feebler and somewhat absentminded, Adams continued to oppose the Mexican War, being reelected as a Conscience Whig in November of 1846. Nearing eighty, he had had to discontinue his daily early morning swims in the Potomac, and on November 20, 1846, he suffered a stroke but was able to resume his seat in early February, 1847. He spoke only once, in opposition to indemnifying the *Amistad* owners, and on February 21, 1848, had another stroke in the House. Carried to the Speaker's room in the Capitol, he died two days later without having regained consciousness. The national mourning ceremonies were like none since Washington's death. John Quincy Adams was buried in the family plot in Quincy. Louisa remained in Washington, keeping in touch with politics, buying and freeing a woman slave, and for much of the time suffering from ill health; she died on May 15, 1852.

SIGNIFICANCE

President of a disintegrating party, politically impotent halfway into his only term, his personal life marred by an unsatisfying relationship with his wife and bitter disappointments with his two elder sons, Adams left—almost fled—the nation's highest political office, the lifelong goal of his great ambition and dynastic sense of duty and destiny. He seemed to be facing a lifetime in the ebb tide of politics and the treacherous shoals of financial insecurity and family disappointment. Even as his personal tragedy deepened with the death of his eldest son, he entered into a new phase, a time nearly as long as his life until then. He experienced a growing satisfaction, a greater harmony in relationships and decision making within his own family: his remaining son, his growing brood of grandchildren, and his wife, finding her way to her own identity and a political role that could afford her a long-delayed satisfaction in contributing to and participating in the real life of the nation, rather than the confined, ornamental, subservient place expected by contemporary society.

During the course of his "two careers," John Quincy Adams contributed mightily to the basic elements of American foreign policy, influenced domestic issues, and stood as a beacon in the sectional controversy which, as he foresaw, was to lead the Union into civil war.

—*Marsha Kass Marks*

FURTHER READING

Bemis, Samuel Flagg. *John Quincy Adams and the Foundations of American Foreign Policy*. New York: Alfred A. Knopf, 1949.

_____. *John Quincy Adams and the Union*. New York: Alfred A. Knopf, 1956. Two-volume detailed, scholarly biography by a major authority on diplomatic history.

Hargreaves, Mary W. M. *The Presidency of John Quincy Adams*. Lawrence: University Press of Kansas, 1985. Detailed and scholarly examination of Adams's presidency, including the political and economic background. Concludes that Adams's term was more positive in goals and action than many historians have judged it.

Hecht, Marie B. *John Quincy Adams: A Personal History of an Independent Man*. New York: Macmillan, 1972. Provides political background, with good attention to various personalities. Admires John Quincy but is rather critical of Louisa.

Morse, John T., Jr. *John Quincy Adams*. Boston: Houghton Mifflin, 1882. Brief, basic narrative written in 1882 by the editor of the American Statesmen series.

Nagel, Paul C. *John Quincy Adams: A Public Life, a Private Life*. New York: Random House, 1997. Nagel draws upon Adams's massive diary to re-create his private life. Challenges the view that Adams was cold and aloof, and concludes Adams was a complex man who struggled to choose his own career despite the expectations of his famous parents.

Remini, Robert V. *John Quincy Adams*. New York: Times Books, 2002. Brief and generally admiring portrait focusing on Adams's fifty-year public career. Portrays Adams as a deficient husband and father but a great secretary of state and an illustrious retired president.

Shepherd, Jack. *Cannibals of the Heart: A Personal Biography of Louisa Catherine and John Quincy Adams*. New York: McGraw-Hill, 1980. An insightful, well-written analysis of the private life of a very public man, with equal attention to the lives of his wife and children. Good blend of political and social background.

Weeks, William Earl. *John Quincy Adams and American Global Empire*. Lexington: University Press of Kentucky, 1992. Unflattering portrait of Quincy as an overly ambitious secretary of state. Focuses on negotiations with Spain for possession of Florida.

SEE ALSO: Henry Adams; Andrew Jackson; James Monroe; Martin Van Buren.

RELATED ARTICLES in *Great Events from History: The Nineteenth Century, 1801-1900:* March 16, 1810: *Fletcher v. Peck*; June 18, 1812-December 24, 1814: War of 1812; February 17, 1815: Treaty of Ghent Takes Effect; December 2, 1823: President Monroe Articulates the Monroe Doctrine; December 1, 1824-February 9, 1825: U.S. Election of 1824; December 3, 1828: U.S. Election of 1828; July 2, 1839: *Amistad* Slave Revolt.

FELIX ADLER

German-born American philosopher and ethicist

Adler founded the Ethical Culture movement, whose goal was to overcome the divisions created by religious creeds and unite all people in ethical deeds.

BORN: August 13, 1851; Alzey, Hesse-Darmstadt (now in Germany)
DIED: April 24, 1933; New York, New York
AREAS OF ACHIEVEMENT: Education, social reform

EARLY LIFE

Born in what is now Germany, Felix Adler came to the United States at the age of six when his father, Rabbi Samuel Adler, accepted the country's most prestigious Jewish Reform pulpit at Temple Emanu-El in New York City. Samuel had been active in Europe in both secular struggles for freedom and religious reform. His passion for social justice was wedded to a love of scholarship. The Adler home was filled with books. Indeed, one of the best collections of Judaica in New York was to be found there. Felix's mother engaged in the works of charity characteristic of the life of the Jewish community. Felix accompanied her as she visited the poor and the sick. She was no doubt one of Felix's earliest examples of the power of the good deed.

The young Adler saw the socioeconomic problems that accompanied industrialization. In the second half of the nineteenth century, immigrants were swelling the populations of U.S. cities and crowding into slum areas, where they were exploited by industrialists and politicians.

Adler's boyhood was punctuated by the sounds of the Civil War. When he was thirteen years old, President Abraham Lincoln was assassinated; Adler later said that this occasion was the first time that he had seen tears in his father's eyes. His adolescence paralleled the post-Civil War era, when the calls to abolish slavery gave way to Jim Crow laws and the Ku Klux Klan.

Adler entered Columbia College at fifteen years of age and graduated in 1870, after which he was sent to Germany to study with Abraham Geiger in preparation for a career in the Reform rabbinate. When a lengthy delay in the school's opening undercut that plan, Adler turned to university studies in Berlin and Heidelberg; he received a doctorate in Semitics from Heidelberg in 1873.

Upon returning to the United States, Adler was expected to succeed his father as chief rabbi at Emanu-El, but his university studies in Germany precipitated a break with Judaism. After being exposed to historical and critical studies of the Bible, evolutionary theory, anthropology, and neo-Kantianism, Adler could no longer maintain his former beliefs. He rejected the idea of a personal God and concentrated instead on a universal moral good, which he saw as a metaphysical reality. Because he had not followed his expected career track, Adler needed a new vocation. He inaugurated a Sunday lecture movement on May 15, 1876. In February of the following year, this movement was incorporated as the New York Society for Ethical Culture.

LIFE'S WORK

After the New York Society for Ethical Culture was incorporated, Adler was employed as its lecturer. In Adler's mind, the society was a religious organization that transcended creeds and united people in ethical deeds. Its philosophic linchpin was a belief in the inherent worth of each individual, a belief that Adler had drawn from German philosopher Immanuel Kant's assertion that all human beings were ends in themselves. Members of the society were to abide by three basic goals: sexual purity for males as well as females, donation of surplus income to the improvement of the working classes, and continued intellectual development.

The society included among its members workers and housewives, businesspeople and teachers, professionals and tradespeople. Among its most influential members were Joseph Seligman, a founder of the banking house of J. and W. Seligman and Company, and one of the wealthiest men in the country; Samuel Gompers, founder of the American Federation of Labor; and Henry Morgenthau, who assisted in establishing the Ethical Culture School and in securing the site for the meetinghouse of the New York Society for Ethical Culture on Central Park Avenue West in New York City at the beginning of the twentieth century.

As important as Adler's weekly lectures were in laying the philosophic bases of the society, they were obviously not sufficient for a movement centered on the importance of performing ethical deeds. Adler and his followers did not shirk the responsibilities of their commitment to such ethical action. During the late 1870's, they founded the first free kindergarten east of the Mississippi River in New York City, established a district nursing program (forerunner of the Visiting Nurse Service), and launched a tenement house building company. The Workingman's School was organized in 1880. In 1882, Adler became a member of the New York State Tenement Housing Commission. In 1883, he and Edmond Kelly founded the Good Government Club to oppose political corruption in the city.

Felix Adler. (Library of Congress)

During the 1880's, Adler and his followers established Ethical Culture Societies in Philadelphia, Chicago, and St. Louis. These societies worked toward the reform of faith through active participation in modern communities, the reconstruction of society through ethical religion, and the moral growth of the individual through interaction with other people in the process of "ethicizing" society.

After 1890, Adler became better known in the international arena. He founded the *International Journal of Ethics* in 1890 (still published today as *Ethics: An International Journal of Social, Political and Legal Philosophy* by the University of Chicago). The Ethical Culture movement also became international with the founding of societies in most of the countries of Western Europe as well as in Japan. In 1896, an International Ethical Union was established through which Adler helped to develop the International Moral Education Congresses in 1908. In 1911, he and Gustave Spiller established the first International Races Congress. In 1923, he gave the Hibbert Lectures at Oxford, which were published as *The Reconstruction of the Spiritual Ideal* in 1924. He also gave another series of talks at Oxford on the reconstruction of education.

Even as the European setting was pushing Adler toward new endeavors, events in the United States were raising troubling questions in his mind. Adler moved to the forefront of those who, in the name of American ideals, were increasingly critical of U.S. imperialism. From 1898 onward, he began to raise the issue of what he came to call the "national crisis." Adler saw Central and Latin American adventurism as the beginning of the crisis and World War I as the climax. The problem lay in the incompatibility of two American myths: manifest destiny and spiritual democracy. If the United States was to become an ethical model, the nation had to first set itself right. Illusions of American self-righteousness had to be revealed for what they were, and a clear commitment needed to be made to spiritual democracy and against the imperialism of manifest destiny.

As the twentieth century dawned, increasing attention to minority rights began to characterize Adler's thought. Labor and child labor in particular had interested him for a long time. The influence of the Civil War and Lincoln reappeared in his concern with the question of racial justice. Although he opposed the popular movement for equal rights for women, he did so on the grounds that the problem could not be dealt with merely by a superficial adjustment of social forms such as voting. He did support the rights of women to have careers but also saw in motherhood a vocation equal in its claims to other vocations.

From about 1890 until the end of his life in 1933, Adler developed a philosophy of industrial culture. The struggle for the rights of labor was meeting with violent repression. Economic depression was joined with political unwillingness to deal with the problems. In this setting, Adler, together with Crawford Howell Toy of Harvard University and Henry Carter Adams of Michigan, founded the Summer School of Applied Ethics at Plymouth, Massachusetts, in 1891. William James, Josiah Royce, and Jane Addams taught courses there, among others. In 1894, Adler gave a series of twelve lectures on the labor question. The clue to the reconstruction of industrial society, Adler believed, was the development of vocational opportunities for every member of society. Vocation, the commitment of a person to meaningful work, was the way in which the attribute of inalienable human worth gained realistic content in an industrial society.

GOALS OF THE ETHICAL CULTURE MOVEMENT

Felix Adler once summed up the purpose of the Ethical Culture movement in this statement:

Now the daring thought that we had, in the beginning of the Ethical Movement, was to unite in one group, in one bond, those who had this religious feeling and those who simply cared for the moral betterment. . . . In the broader sense religion means zealousness and devotion to something supreme, in the special sense it means cosmic outreaching. Now I myself have always been a religious person in the second sense, and never a mere moralist. But I founded this Society with the express purpose and intent that it should not consist only of those who stood as I did, who had the same religious feeling and needs, but that it should be open to all those who believed in moral betterment, because that is the point on which we all agree. Our ethical religion has its basis in the effort to improve the world and ourselves morally.

Source: American Ethical Union. http://www.aeu.org/. Accessed June, 2005.

As Adler thought through his philosophy of industrial democracy, he was led inevitably to a reconsideration of schooling. His interest in education had manifested itself as early as the founding of the Workingman's School in 1880. During the 1890's, a concept of "organic" education was germinating in his mind, which led to a curriculum that integrated classical studies, modern science, industrial arts, and ethics. During the 1920's, Adler began to dream more dramatically about a major new step in education, and in 1926 he formulated his ideals for the new school as one in which values were preeminent and specifically brought into the realm of commerce and business. The result was the Fieldston School, launched in 1928. On April 24, 1933, Adler died in New York City after a long struggle with cancer.

SIGNIFICANCE

The potential relevance of Felix Adler for modern times is great. In his own life, he overcame the perennial tension between the life of thought and the life of action, and his struggle to point out an ethical path in a world that was becoming increasingly pluralistic and increasingly secular is, if anything, even more timely now than it was during his lifetime. Sadly, however, Adler has been largely ignored by history. Although the Ethical Culture Societies still exist, the knowledge that most members have of Adler is limited to the bare fact that he was their founder. His penetrating and original philosophy has seldom been studied or even referenced by more recent philosophers. The reforms in social welfare, politics, and labor relations in which he played such an important role continue, but their benefactors are largely unaware of Adler's part in their development.

Perhaps his life was simply too well rounded for specialists to notice him. Philosophers considered him suspicious because he did not hold himself aloof from social reform efforts or religion. Activists, on the other hand, thought he was too much of a thinker. Perhaps he has suffered the fate of being considered irrelevant to later time periods because he was so immersed in the issues of his own historical period. For example, even his relatively well known work in the field of education is perceived as being too unattuned to modern psychologized education to be totally acceptable. Among religionists, he has suffered a similar fate, being neither absolute enough for the neoorthodox nor sufficiently disdainful of absolutes to find a place among situation ethicists. However, this man who was known as an exceptionally gifted pedagogue while he was alive still has much to teach later generations. Both his life and his thought deserve to be resurrected.

—Ann Marie B. Bahr

FURTHER READING

Beard, Annie E. S. *Our Foreign-Born Citizens*. 6th ed. New York: Thomas Y. Crowell, 1968. The chapter on

Adler gives a very simple introduction to his thought. The narrative is peppered with some excellent quotations from Adler's works, but the sources of the citations are not given, frustrating any serious scholar of Adler.

Ericson, Edward L. *The Humanist Way: An Introduction to Ethical Humanist Religion*. Foreword by Isaac Asimov. New York: Continuum, 1988. A discussion of the Ethical Culture movement and the older tradition of humanism from which the movement evolved. Recounts the history of the movement from its birth in 1876 through its subsequent growth, and explains the basic tenets of Ethical Culture.

Friess, Horace L. *Felix Adler and Ethical Culture*. New York: Columbia University Press, 1981. This book, written by Adler's son-in-law, provides personal memories of Adler in addition to more objective biographical information. Also offers an insightful analysis of Adler's intellectual evolution.

Guttchen, Robert S. *Felix Adler*. New York: Twayne, 1974. Guttchen analyzes Adler's ethical and educational ideas, with Adler's concept of human worth presented as the linchpin of his philosophy. The philosophical analysis is preceded by a very useful chronology and a fine biographical sketch.

Kraut, Benny. *From Reform Judaism to Ethical Culture: The Religious Evolution of Felix Adler*. Cincinnati: Hebrew Union College Press, 1979. Kraut analyzes Adler's religious evolution and the Jewish reaction to Adler and the Ethical Culture movement. This very useful study focuses on the early evolution of Adler's thought up until about 1880.

Neumann, Henry. *Spokesmen for Ethical Religion*. Boston: Beacon Press, 1951. Provides a simple introduction to Adler as the founder of Ethical Culture and to the leaders who followed him. Neumann attempts to present both a history of the movement through the lives of its leaders and a sympathetic (if not evangelistic) explanation of the movement's purpose and worth.

Radest, Howard B. *Felix B. Adler: An Ethical Culture*. New York: P. Lang, 1998. Describes Adler's proposals for a more democratic moral ideal and how this ideal could reform work, education, and politics.

SEE ALSO: Samuel Gompers; Isaac Mayer Wise.

RELATED ARTICLES in *Great Events from History: The Nineteenth Century, 1801-1900:* April, 1807: Hegel Publishes *The Phenomenology of Spirit*; 1851-1854: Comte Advances His Theory of Positivism; 1859: Mill Publishes *On Liberty*.

ELIZABETH CABOT AGASSIZ

American educator and science writer

One of the founders and the first president of Radcliffe College, Agassiz was an influential pioneer in higher education for women and was also noted for her writings on natural history and her work with her husband, naturalist Louis Agassiz.

BORN: December 5, 1822; Boston, Massachusetts

DIED: June 27, 1907; Arlington Heights, Massachusetts

ALSO KNOWN AS: Elizabeth Cabot Cary (birth name); Elizabeth Cabot Cary Agassiz

AREAS OF ACHIEVEMENT: Education, science and technology

EARLY LIFE

Born Elizabeth Cabot Cary, Elizabeth Cabot Agassiz (ah-gah-see) was a member of a well-connected Massachusetts family. The second of the seven children of Thomas and Mary Cushing Perkins Cary, she received no formal education because of her physical weakness and fragile health as a child. Instead, she was taught at home by a governess who tutored her in languages, music, and art. However, the overall scope of her schooling was somewhat haphazard. During her youth, she exhibited no particular interest in science, which would become one of her keenest interests later in life.

At the age of twenty-eight, Elizabeth met Louis Agassiz, a Swiss professor of natural history employed at Switzerland's University of Neuchâtel. Agassiz had recently been widowed and left with his three children. When he met Elizabeth, he was on his first trip to the United States on a speaking engagement at Harvard. Shortly after returning home, he decided to emigrate to the United States to accept a position at the prestigious Harvard University as chair of natural history in the Lawrence Scientific School. Elizabeth married him in April, 1850, and became mother to his children. They had no children together.

To help support her family and to promote education among girls, Elizabeth opened the Agassiz School for Girls in her Cambridge, Massachusetts, home in 1856. During the seven years that she operated her school, she never taught in it herself but oversaw its management and day-to-day operations. Her husband, however, taught natural history to her students, in addition to his work at the university. Elizabeth often attended his classes and developed a keen interest in natural sciences. Her notes from her husband's lectures became the basis for much of his published work in later years. After the school closed in 1863, Elizabeth devoted herself to supporting her husband's field expeditions. She organized and traveled with him on his field trips and collaborated with him on the documentation of the marine and biological life that he observed.

Louis Agassiz was not only a naturalist but also a man who left his mark as an innovator in educational methods. Scholars remember him as a brilliant educator as well as a famed naturalist because he used an innovative approach to learning natural history by interacting with nature rather than studying it only in books. In Europe, he was recognized as one of the foremost ichthyologists of his time. He also put forth the idea of the ice age. Elizabeth contributed significantly to his success in both areas.

LIFE'S WORK

Elizabeth Agassiz organized, managed, and accompanied her husband on the Thayer expedition to Brazil in 1865-1866 and the Hassler expedition to the Strait of Magellan in 1871-1872. She and her husband founded the Anderson School of Natural History, a marine laboratory on Penikese Island in Buzzards Bay, Massachusetts. She attempted to write in a way that made scientific inquiry accessible and interesting to nonscientists. Multiple printings of her books attested to her success in achieving this goal. Her own writings included *A First Lesson in Natural History* (1859), *Geological Studies* (1886), and an article in the *Atlantic Monthly* recounting her husband's expedition to the Pacific Ocean. She also coauthored, with her stepson Alexander Agassiz, the popular textbook and field guide *Seaside Studies in Natural History* (1865). With her husband, she coauthored *A Journey in Brazil* (1867).

In 1873, soon after her husband's death, Agassiz began writing an insightful biography of her famed partner, *Louis Agassiz: His Life and Correspondence*, that was was published in 1885. The "correspondence" to which the book's title alludes involved insights selected from a large collection of mostly personal letters Louis Agassiz had written over time to a friend and fellow naturalist, Arnold Guyot, as well as letters to his wife and son.

With her husband gone, Elizabeth Agassiz devoted herself to the care and nurturing of her grandchildren, as well as the book about her husband. Through this initial writing effort, she became recognized as a gifted author. Her work proved to be invaluable to her husband's career. About four years after completing her husband's memoirs, she took up a dream she had had since her husband's death: founding a college for women taught by the faculty of Harvard University. She believed that this would open up extensive resources and opportunities for women that up to that time had been accessible only to men.

Agassiz worked with Arthur Gilman and Alice Longfellow to help develop the "Harvard Annex," which was incorporated as the Society for the Collegiate Instruction of Women in 1879. Agassiz herself was appointed its first president. In 1894, the new institution was renamed Radcliffe College in honor of Ann Radcliffe Mowison, who had founded the first Harvard scholarship in 1643. Agassiz remained president until 1899, when she was seventy-six years old. On her retirement, she was given the title of honorary president.

SIGNIFICANCE

Agassiz was mostly self-taught—an incredible accomplishment—in a society where this was not encouraged. Her academic achievements gave credence to the importance of educating women, and the potential value of women's contributions in the field of science. Her unique ability to make scientific notions accessible, interesting, and animated to the nonscientific reader was an important contribution to scientific education.

During World War II, four decades after Agassiz retired, Harvard and Radcliffe signed an agreement allowing women to attend classes at Harvard for the first time. The implementation of the joint instruction began in 1943. This agreement legitimized the education of women both at Harvard and, later, other institutions of higher education, and was, perhaps, the ultimate achievement of Elizabeth Cabot Agassiz.

—Peggy J. Anderson

FURTHER READING

Agassiz, Elizabeth Cabot Cary, ed. *Louis Agassiz: His Life and Correspondence*. 2 vols. Bristol, England: Thoemmes Continuum, 2002-2003. Originally published in 1885, this book contains a biography of Elizabeth's husband and copies of his correspondence with many of the leading scientists of his day.

Agassiz, Elizabeth Cabot, and Alexander Agassiz. *Seaside Studies in Natural History*. New York: Arno, 1865. Reprint 1970. A textbook and field guide for zoologists.

Howells, Dorothy Elia. *A Century to Celebrate: Radcliffe College, 1979-1979*. Cambridge, Mass.: Radcliffe College, 1978. A history of the college, describing how its founding aimed to increase educational opportunities for nineteenth century women.

Lurie, Edward. *Louis Agassiz: A Life in Science*. Chicago: University of Chicago Press, 1960. A persuasive interpretation of the life of the husband of Elizabeth Agassiz, Louis Agassiz, and an exhaustive study of his papers. Lurie acknowledges Agassiz's weaknesses and pictures a genius with faults.

Paton, Lucy A. *Elizabeth Cary Agassiz: A Biography*. 1919. Reprint. New York: Arno Press, 1974. Still the only full-length biography of Elizabeth Cabot Agassiz, this book provides that details on her collaborative writing efforts with her husband and stepson and her role as a pioneer in the education of women.

Tharp, Louis Hall. *Adventurous Alliance: The Story of the Agassiz Family of Boston*. Boston: Little, Brown, 1959. Describes the lives and work of Elizabeth and Louis Agassiz, Elizabeth's family's connections in Boston, and her contributions to women's education.

SEE ALSO: Louis Agassiz; Charles William Eliot; Alice Freeman Palmer.

RELATED ARTICLE in *Great Events from History: The Nineteenth Century, 1801-1900:* September 26, 1865: Vassar College Opens.

LOUIS AGASSIZ

American naturalist

Agassiz created an awareness of the importance of the study of natural history in the United States with his founding of the Museum of Comparative Zoology at Harvard University. He was a pioneer in making science an integral part of the curriculum in American higher education and is particularly known for his work on glaciers.

BORN: May 28, 1807; Motier-en-Vuly, Switzerland
DIED: December 14, 1873; Cambridge, Massachusetts
ALSO KNOWN AS: Jean Louis Rodolphe Agassiz (full name)
AREAS OF ACHIEVEMENT: Biology, education

EARLY LIFE

Jean Louis Rodolphe Agassiz (ah-gah-see) was one of four children of a Protestant Swiss clergyman. At the age of ten, he was sent to school at Bienne, where he spent much of his time observing freshwater fish, which fascinated him. In 1822, he entered the Academy of Lausanne. Out of deference to his parents, after he graduated, he enrolled in the school of medicine at the University of Zurich. After two years of studies in medicine, he enrolled in the University of Heidelberg, where he developed a special interest in natural history. The following year, he transferred to the University of Munich to study under Ignaz von Döllinger, a pioneer embryologist whom Agassiz credited as the source of his scientific training.

In 1829, he received a doctorate in philosophy at Erlanger and returned to Munich to complete his studies in medicine. The following year, he received a doctorate in medicine and thereafter never examined a patient; his mind was set on pursuing studies in ichthyology, paleontology, and glacial geology.

While Agassiz was enrolled in Munich, Lorenz Oken, one of his professors, presented a paper on Agassiz's discovery of a new species of carp. In 1829, Agassiz published his first book on this species of Brazilian fish based on his study of a collection of specimens from the Amazon brought to Munich in 1821 by J. B. Spix and K. F. Philip von Martius. The book was written with such beauty and clarity that it was soon evident that Agassiz would become not only a man of science but also a man of letters.

Agassiz married Cecile Braun, sister of the eminent botanist Alexander Braun. There were three children born to the union, a son and two daughters. Cecile was a natural history artist whose drawings of fossil and freshwater fish forms appeared in several of Agassiz's books. She died of tuberculosis in 1848.

Agassiz was a large, robust man, slightly above medium height, who had keen brown eyes that could light up with enthusiasm. He had chestnut brown hair that

Louis Agassiz. (Library of Congress)

gradually thinned with age but retained its color into his declining years.

LIFE'S WORK

The professional life of Agassiz is clearly divided into two chapters: his work as a research scientist in Europe, in the course of which he made significant advances in the fields of ichthyology and glacial geology, and his teaching career in the United States, during which he dedicated himself to making science an integral and respected part of the curriculum of higher education in his adopted country.

Upon completion of his formal schooling, Agassiz went to Paris to continue his studies in medicine. While there, he spent much of his time at the museum of natural history at the Jardin des Plantes, where he met Georges Cuvier, the master of comparative anatomy. The aging Cuvier willingly turned over much of his unfinished work to the young naturalist to complete. Agassiz also met the naturalist Alexander von Humboldt, who in 1832 secured for him an appointment as professor in natural history at the University of Neuchâtel.

While at Neuchâtel, Agassiz formed a natural history society and took scientists on excursions into the Alps to study and observe flora and fauna. Agassiz turned Neuchâtel into a research center, and over the course of fifteen years he published more than two hundred works, including twenty substantial volumes illustrated with more than two thousand plates. Before Agassiz began his research, only eight generic types of fossil fish had been named in formal publications. Agassiz identified 340 new genera, many of them in his books *History of the Fresh Water Fishes of Central Europe* (1839-1842) and *Monograph on the Fossil Fishes of the Old Red or Devonian of the British Isles and Russia* (1844-1845).

While at Neuchâtel, Agassiz's attention was drawn to the nearby glacier of the great median moraine of the lower Aar valley, and this sent his scientific investigations in a new direction, that of glacial geology. He concluded from his observations that gravity controls glacial movements and that glaciers travel faster in the middle and at the surface, disproving the commonly held theory that glaciers are pushed along by water freezing underneath. He published his findings in *Études sur les glaciers* (1840; studies on glaciers) and *Systèmes glaciaires* (1846; glacial systems). Agassiz came to accept Karl Schimper's "ice age" thesis and added that Europe had been subjected once to a period of extreme cold from the North Pole to the Mediterranean and Caspian Seas in a widespread Pleistocene ice age. He studied earth surfaces all over Europe and concluded that drift material and polished and striated boulders gave evidence of earlier glacial movements.

A gift from the king of Prussia in 1846 enabled Agassiz to pursue his work in the United States. Sir Charles Lyell had arranged for him to participate in a course of lectures at the Lowell Institute in Boston. Agassiz's life took another turn. His intense research gave way to teaching and campaigning on behalf of natural history as a legitimate academic endeavor.

Agassiz continued to write of his discoveries with verbal precision and lucid description. He could devote fifty pages of unmatched prose describing the interior of an egg. He set about to produce a twelve-volume series entitled *Contributions to the Natural History of the United States*. More than twenty-five hundred advance subscriptions were taken, but only four volumes were ever produced (1857-1862). These four volumes represented a triumph of thought and scholarship and contributed to the nature-consciousness of the American public.

In 1848, Agassiz accepted the chair of natural history of the new Lawrence Scientific School at Harvard University, and the same year he published his popular *Principles of Zoology*. When he visited Washington, D.C., he was disappointed to find so little scientific activity in the nation's capital. At the time, the Smithsonian Institution had not begun to function. Agassiz was later made a member of the Smithsonian Board of Regents, and the institution's natural history division was developed.

In 1850, Agassiz married Elizabeth Cary, and the following year he accepted a teaching appointment at the Medical College of Charleston, South Carolina. After two years, he resigned because he found the climate unsuitable and returned to Harvard. He and his wife opened a school for young women in Cambridge that became the precursor of Radcliffe College.

Agassiz was quite disappointed with Harvard's science department and claimed that the chemistry laboratory at Cambridge High School was better equipped; he often did his work there. In 1859, Agassiz founded the Museum of Comparative Zoology at Harvard and helped to create a new era in American higher education. He emphasized advanced and original works as factors in mental training and stressed the direct, hands-on study of nature. Ralph Waldo Emerson complained that something ought to be done to check this rush toward natural history at Harvard. Agassiz countered that the rest of the curriculum should be brought up to the standards he had set for the zoology laboratories. Agassiz found a kindred soul in Henry David Thoreau and often visited Walden Pond. At a dinner hosted by Emerson, Thoreau and Agassiz once talked of mating turtles, to the disgust of Emerson. From Walden, Thoreau sent Agassiz varieties of fish, turtles, and snakes, and was paid handsomely for them.

The same year that Agassiz opened the museum at Harvard, Charles Darwin published his *On the Origin of Species by Means of Natural Selection* (1859). The theory of evolution did not begin with Darwin, and Agassiz was thoroughly acquainted with the works of Georges-Louis Leclerc Buffon, Jean-Baptiste Lamarck, and Charles Darwin's own grandfather, Erasmus Darwin, and their ideas of the gradual, continuous progress of species that contributed to the theory of evolution.

Much of the knowledge of embryology that is integral to Darwin's theory was originally discovered by Agassiz. Agassiz once admitted that he had been on the verge of anticipating Darwinism when he found that the highest fishes were those that came first, and therefore he rejected the theory. Sharks, one of the most primitive species, had the largest brains and the most specialized teeth and muscular systems. Two years before Darwin's theory was published, Agassiz wrote "An Essay on Classification," in which he asserted that the plan of creation was the "free conception" of an all-powerful intelligence in accordance with a predetermined pattern for each of the species, which, he argued, were destined to remain changeless.

AGASSIZ'S CHILDHOOD

After Louis Agassiz died, his wife, Elizabeth Cabot Agassiz, published a collection of his correspondence to which she added a biography. This extract discusses Agassiz's early interest in science.

It does not appear that he had any precocious predilection for study, and his parents, who for the first ten years of his life were his only teachers, were too wise to stimulate his mind beyond the ordinary attainments of his age. Having lost her first four children in infancy, his mother watched with trembling solicitude over his early years. It was perhaps for this reason that she was drawn so closely to her boy, and understood that his love of nature, and especially of all living things, was an intellectual tendency, and not simply a child's disposition to find friends and playmates in the animals about him. In later years her sympathy gave her the key to the work of his manhood, as it had done to the sports of his childhood. She remained his most intimate friend to the last hour of her life, and he survived her but six years.

Louis's love of natural history showed itself almost from infancy. When a very little fellow he had, beside his collection of fishes, all sorts of pets: birds, field-mice, hares, rabbits, guinea-pigs, etc., whose families he reared with the greatest care. Guided by his knowledge of the haunts and habits of fishes, he and his brother Auguste became the most adroit of young fishermen—using processes all their own and quite independent of hook, line, or net. Their hunting grounds were the holes and crevices beneath the stones or in the waterwashed walls of the lake shore. No such shelter was safe from their curious fingers, and they acquired such dexterity that when bathing they could seize the fish even in the open water, attracting them by little arts to which the fish submitted as to a kind of fascination. Such amusements are no doubt the delight of many a lad living in the country, nor would they be worth recording except as illustrating the unity of Agassiz's intellectual development from beginning to end. His pet animals suggested questions, to answer which was the task of his life; and his intimate study of the freshwater fishes of Europe, later the subject of one of his important works, began with his first collection from the Lake of Morat.

Source: Elizabeth Cabot Agassiz, ed., *Louis Agassiz: His Life and Correspondence* (New York: Houghton, Mifflin, 1885), chapter 1.

Agassiz became Darwin's most formidable opponent in the United States. His studies of fossils led him to conclude that the changes that animals undergo during their embryonic growth coincide with the order of succession of the fossils of the same type in past geological ages. He believed that all species had been immutable since their creation. From time to time, the Creator may have annihilated old species and created new ones. His exhibits at the Harvard museum were intended to reflect the permanence of the species.

Agassiz regarded himself as the "librarian of the works of God," but he was not a theologian and gave no support to those ministers who parroted his responses to Darwin. He claimed that in Europe he was accused of deriving his scientific ideas from the church and in the United States he was regarded as an infidel because he would not let churchmen pat him on the head. Agassiz believed that there was a creator and even went so far as to posit a multiple creation theory. He claimed that black people were created separately and were a different species from whites, an argument that gave great comfort to the defenders of slavery in the South.

Only a few American scientists, such as his Harvard colleague Asa Gray, dared to take open issue with the erudite and popular Agassiz before his death. Gray argued that the species had originated in a single creative act and that their variations were the result of causes such as climate, geographical isolation, and the phenomena described by the same glacial theory that Agassiz had done so much to establish.

Agassiz became an American citizen in 1861 and continued his opposition to Darwinism. He fought a losing battle for fifteen years with the Darwinists and went to his grave denying the reality of evolution. His last article, published posthumously in the *Atlantic Monthly* (1874), was entitled "Evolution and the Permanence of Type."

Agassiz was appointed a visiting professor at Cornell in 1868, but the following year he suffered a stroke. Although this slowed him considerably, he continued his strenuous schedule of speaking and writing. In 1872, he sailed on board a coastal survey ship from Boston around the horn to San Francisco. The trip was disappointing, because Agassiz was unable to make the scientific progress he had hoped on the voyage. In 1873, John Anderson of New York deeded the island of Penikese in Buzzards Bay off the coast of Massachusetts and gave fifty thousand dollars to help Agassiz create a summer school for science teachers. The Anderson School of Natural History became the forerunner of the Woods Hole Biological Institute.

SIGNIFICANCE

Louis Agassiz was the man who made the United States nature-conscious. He was a major figure in American nineteenth century culture, in the fields of both literature and science. He assumed that the organization of nature was everyone's concern and that each community should collect and identify the elements of its own zoology and botany.

Agassiz would appear to have been the most likely to champion the theory of evolution, particularly with his vast knowledge of paleontology and embryology. Instead, he chose to do battle with the evolutionists and to maintain stoutly his belief in the unchanging forms of created species. In his *Methods of Study in Natural History* (1863), Agassiz wrote:

> I have devoted my whole life to the study of Nature, and yet a single sentence may express all that I have done. I have shown that there is a correspondence between the succession of Fishes in geological times and the different stages of their growth in the egg,—this is all.

Agassiz had done much more than he modestly claimed. In the age of Chautauqua speakers, he was a spellbinder. Above all, he was a teacher who was not only a dedicated scholar but also a friend to his students. With all of his talents as lecturer and author, he might have been a wealthy man, but he remained in debt all of his life and even mortgaged his house to support the museum at Harvard.

Agassiz wished above all to be remembered as a teacher. After he died in Cambridge in December, 1873, an unshaped boulder brought from the glacier of the Aar marked his grave at Boston's Mount Auburn Cemetery. On it were carved the words he had requested: "Agassiz the Teacher."

—Raymond Lee Muncy

FURTHER READING

Agassiz, Louis. *Studies on Glaciers: Preceded by the Discourses of Neuchatel.* Translated and edited by Albert V. Carozzi. New York: Hafner Press, 1967. Carozzi's introduction is excellent. Included is a reprint of the atlas that Agassiz used.

Baird, Spencer Fullerton. *Correspondence Between Spencer Fullerton Baird and Louis Agassiz: Two Pioneer American Naturalists.* Edited by Elmer Charles Herber. Washington, D.C.: Smithsonian, 1964. Baird was the editor of the papers of the Smithsonian Institution and carried on extensive correspondence with

Agassiz. The letters contained the latest news on discoveries in natural history.

Bolles, Edmund Blair. *The Ice Finders: How a Poet, a Professor, and a Politician Discovered the Ice Age.* Washington, D.C.: Counterpoint, 1999. Describes how interactions between Agassiz, geologist Sir Charles Lyell, and poet Elisha Kent Kane created public acceptance for the idea of an ice age.

Davenport, Guy, ed. *The Intelligence of Agassiz: A Specimen Book of Scientific Writings.* Boston: Beacon Press, 1963. The foreword by Alfred Romer is an excellent overview of the work of Agassiz. Davenport has selected Agassiz's most incisive works and introduces each with a skill that makes this slim volume invaluable.

Fry, C. George, and Jon Paul Fry. *Congregationalists and Evolution: Asa Gray and Louis Agassiz.* Lanham, Md.: University Press of America, 1989. Compares the lives and philosophies of Agassiz and his Harvard colleague, botanist Asa Gray, focusing on their dispute over Darwin's theory of evolution and their membership in the Congregationalist Church.

Lurie, Edward. *Louis Agassiz: A Life in Science.* Chicago: University of Chicago Press, 1960. A persuasive interpretation of Agassiz and an exhaustive study of his papers. Lurie acknowledges Agassiz's weaknesses and pictures a genius with faults.

Marcou, Jules. *Life, Letters, and Works of Louis Agassiz.* 2 vols. New York: Macmillan, 1896. Valuable for range and accuracy of details, including an annotated list of American and European publications concerning Agassiz. Also included is a complete catalog of his 425 scientific papers.

Tharp, Louise Hall. *Adventurous Alliance: The Story of the Agassiz Family of Boston.* Boston: Little, Brown, 1960. An account of the personal lives of Agassiz and his second wife, Elizabeth. An interesting story that relates something of the background of late nineteenth century Boston society.

Winsor, Mary P. *Reading the Shape of Nature: Comparative Zoology at the Agassiz Museum.* Chicago: University of Chicago Press, 1991. Recounts the early history of Harvard's Museum of Comparative Zoology, focusing on the dispute between Agassiz and his son, Alexander, over Darwin's theory of evolution.

SEE ALSO: Elizabeth Cabot Agassiz; Charles Darwin; Charles William Eliot; Lewis Henry Morgan; August Weismann.

RELATED ARTICLES in *Great Events from History: The Nineteenth Century, 1801-1900:* 1809: Lamarck Publishes *Zoological Philosophy*; August 10, 1846: Smithsonian Institution Is Founded; 1854-1862: Wallace's Expeditions Give Rise to Biogeography; November 24, 1859: Darwin Publishes *On the Origin of Species*; 1871: Darwin Publishes *The Descent of Man.*

SIR SAYYID AHMAD KHAN

Indian Islamic scholar, educator, and writer

Sayyid Ahmad's theological writings summarized a number of important trends within Islamic thought and attempted to redirect religious thinking to meet the challenges of the modern European-dominated world. His religious views were too controversial to be widely influential, but in the field of education he founded the Muhammadan Anglo-Oriental College, and in literature he created modern Urdu prose.

BORN: October 17, 1817; Delhi, India

DIED: March 27, 1898; Alīgarh, India

ALSO KNOWN AS: Saiyid Ahmad Khan; Sayyid Ahmed Khan

AREAS OF ACHIEVEMENT: Education, literature, religion and theology

EARLY LIFE

Sir Sayyid Ahmad Khan was an exceptional man born into an exceptional family. Although custom in well-to-do Indian families required brides to move in with their husbands' parents, Sayyid Ahmad's mother was the favorite daughter of a wealthy and distinguished man who wanted her to remain in his home. Sayyid Ahmad's father enjoyed high status as a descendant of the Prophet Muḥammad, a sayyid, but he was relatively poor. Moving into his wife's home gave him the leisure to pursue his interest in archery and swimming. In that way Sayyid Ahmad came to be reared in his maternal grandfather's house.

The careers of grandfather and grandson resembled each other in many ways. The grandfather, Khwajah

Farid ud-din Ahmad, not only held the post of chief minister in the much reduced Mughal court but also had the trust of the British, who sent him on a number of diplomatic missions. During an extended stay in Calcutta, he acted as superintendent of that city's premier Muslim educational establishment, the Calcutta Madrasah. He enjoyed a reputation as a mathematician and astronomer.

Sayyid Ahmad's early education took place in Khwajah Farid's home. It involved learning the Qur'ān and the rudiments of Persian grammar. One of his maternal uncles instructed him in mathematics. He then went to study Greek medicine (*Yunani Tibb*) with one of Delhi's prominent physicians. Apart from this training, Sayyid Ahmad educated himself prodigiously in theology and history, while retaining a lifelong interest in the sciences. In addition to that small amount of formal learning, Sayyid Ahmad absorbed a deep religious seriousness. Both his mother's and his father's families were connected to the noted spiritual reformers of the seventeenth and eighteenth centuries: Ahmad Sirhindī and Shah Walliullah. These men and their disciples stressed a rational approach to Islam that avoided miracle-mongering and criticized the lax behavior of the Muslim masses. They also emphasized a moral earnestness that especially affected Sayyid Ahmad's mother. He saw dedication to high moral values as her chief legacy to him.

LIFE'S WORK

In 1838, the year of his father's death, Sayyid Ahmad began attending the office of an uncle who worked as a subordinate judge for the British. Before the latter instituted examinations and educational qualifications for government employees, this was the most common way of securing appointment as an official. Sayyid Ahmad soon began ascending through the ranks of the East India Company's judiciary. He served as a magistrate in a number of north Indian district towns before retiring in 1876.

Sayyid Ahmad's literary career began during the 1840's. He wrote a number of religious tracts encouraging the reform of Muslim social customs. He contributed to a newspaper published by his brother and edited a number of Persian works, such as the memoirs of the Mughal emperor Jahāngīr. In 1846, he published a unique book, *Āthār assanadīd* (*Asar-oos-sunnadeed: A History of Old and New Rules, or Governments and of Old and New Buildings, in the District of Delhi*, 1854), which described some of the famous buildings and personalities of Old Delhi. Though his early style of Urdu imitated the flowery diction and indirect discourse of Persian, throughout his life his writing became more vigorous and straightforward. Later writers considered him a model of clarity and acknowledged him as the creator of Urdu political rhetoric. His collected writings and speeches occupied nineteen volumes.

The Mutiny of 1857 had a lasting impact on Sayyid Ahmad's activity and thought. During the conflict, he remained loyal to the British, even risking his own life to save a number of Englishmen as well as the Bijnor district's cash box. After the uprising, a number of British officials blamed Muslims for fomenting the rebellion. Sayyid Ahmad spent the rest of his life refuting that notion, constantly reminding the government that many of India's Muslims stood firmly for the empire. To his fellow Muslims, he repeated the message that the failure of the revolt proved that England's way was the way of the future and that Muslims need not abandon their religion in order to adapt to the new order. He argued that in following the "new light," they were being faithful to Islam's highest ideals. After all, Islam's advanced civilization had influenced that of Europe and made the Renaissance possible. The decline of his own day Sayyid Ahmad attributed to superstitions that had become commonplace only in the century or so before. Until then, Islam had been in the vanguard of human progress.

Sayyid Ahmad's loyalty to the British and his liberal opinions about Islam brought him honors from the imperial government. In 1869, he became a commander in the Order of the Star of India, and in 1888 he received a knighthood in that fraternity. He became a member of the viceroy's legislative council in 1878 and sat on this largely advisory body until 1883. When he visited England in 1869-1870, he was presented to Queen Victoria and the Prince of Wales while mixing with London's literary notables.

More tangible support came from a number of Sayyid Ahmad's British friends. They encouraged his educational projects both in spirit and in various forms of government aid. When he founded a translation society to render English books, especially mathematics and science texts, into Urdu, the provincial education bureau supported the effort by buying most of the books published. At this stage of his career, Sayyid Ahmad's efforts were not solely devoted to India's Muslims. The Mughal gentry of his youth had many non-Muslim members. Hindus counted in their number masters of Persian and Urdu whose talents were equal or even superior to those of Muslims. Sayyid Ahmad was concerned that this entire class, the north Indian Urdu-speaking elite, was in danger of annihilation.

With the founding of the Muhammadan Anglo-Oriental College at Aligarh in 1875, Sayyid Ahmad labored increasingly for Muslims. He envisioned the Muhammadan Anglo-Oriental College to be a residential school on the model of Eton. He thought it essential that young boys be removed from the easy discipline of their homes and taught the virtues of diligence. In place of the intensely personal, but seemingly slipshod, educational methods of his own youth, Sayyid Ahmad installed the classroom and the fixed daily schedule of study, prayer, and sport, and regular academic examinations.

Many of the school's first students came from families that combined landowning and government service. By the 1870's, posts in the imperial bureaucracy increasingly required modern educational qualifications. The Muhammadan Anglo-Oriental College provided the training in English, history, and the sciences that helped in obtaining those appointments. The majority of the school's earliest graduates became officials or lawyers.

Throughout the latter years of his life, Sayyid Ahmad spent countless hours requesting contributions to the Muhammadan Anglo-Oriental College. Often his political stands were influenced by his belief that he should utter the sentiments most likely to ensure continued government support for the college. On the surface at least, his thinking became increasingly communal, urging Muslims to develop a separate political agenda. At the same time, Sayyid Ahmad was responding to an ever more assertive Hindu nationalism. When these groups demanded democracy, Sayyid Ahmad became fearful because the Muslim minority was bound to be overwhelmed by the majority community in any strictly representative system.

While pursuing his educational and political work, Sayyid Ahmad remained a social critic and theological controversialist. As publisher of the Urdu journal *Tahzib ul-Akhlaq* (moral reform), he had a forum in which to publicize his views on religious and moral subjects. Many religious scholars hotly opposed him, finding his thought dangerously close to pure rationalism. Many of the gentry attached to the accustomed ways in religion considered him too rational. Sayyid Ahmad held on tenaciously to his approach, but his opinions did not receive a hearing even in his own college. Many of his financial backers insisted that Sayyid Ahmad have no influence over religious instruction at the Muhammadan Anglo-Oriental College. Less controversial men took charge of introducing the young to their faith.

The affairs of the college on which he lavished such great care made the last years of Sayyid Ahmad's life miserable. In 1895, his chief clerk was caught embezzling considerable sums from the college's funds. This led to confrontations between Sayyid Ahmad and one of his sons, who wanted to acquire more control over the college. On two occasions, the son ordered Sayyid Ahmad out of his own home. For a short period, he stayed in a dormitory but finally moved to the house of a longtime friend, where he died a discouraged and embittered man in March, 1898.

SIGNIFICANCE

Within Sir Sayyid Ahmad Khan's lifetime, the last shadows of Mughal glory disappeared and India became the brightest diamond in Great Britain's imperial diadem. Although his family had been attached to the Mughal court, Sayyid Ahmad's achievements depended, in part, on his close association with the British. Although his early education had been conducted along traditional lines, he founded a college with a curriculum and discipline modeled on Great Britain's public schools. He somehow found time to write extensively on religious and social matters, presenting a bold theological program that incorporated elements from Islam's classical tradition and European sources. In the realm of politics, he encouraged Muslims to develop a renewed self-confidence. The Muhammadan Anglo-Oriental College went on to become a university that would attract thousands of students not only from India but also from Africa and the Middle East. This university, with its many buildings clustered around Sayyid Ahmad's grave, is his most obvious and fitting memorial.

—Gregory C. Kozlowski

FURTHER READING

Ahmad, Aziz. *Islamic Modernism in India and Pakistan, 1857-1964*. New York: Oxford University Press, 1967. This work provides an important discussion of Sayyid Ahmad and his critics. Tends to concentrate on Sayyid Ahmad's political thought and work to the exclusion of his theology.

Ahmad, Aziz, and G. E. von Grunebaum, eds. *Muslim Self-Statement in India and Pakistan*. Weisbaden, Germany: Otto Harrassowitz, 1970. Because very little of the writings of India's Muslims has been translated into English, this is a valuable anthology of their work. It contains selections from the writings of Sayyid Ahmad and a number of his contemporaries.

Hardy, Peter. *The Muslims of British India*. Cambridge, England: Cambridge University Press, 1972. This is a fine overview of the political, social, and religious history of Muslims in the British period. Readers will find all the basic interpretive themes employed by contemporary scholars—both Euro-Americans and South Asians—introduced here. The chapter "The Medieval Legacy" is a good summary of the governmental style of the Mughals.

Lelyveld, David. *Aligarh's First Generation: Muslim Solidarity in British India*. Princeton, N.J.: Princeton University Press, 1977. This brilliantly written book evokes the lives of Muslims from the period of Sayyid Ahmad's birth to the early years of the college. Not only is its scholarship first rate, but it also is written with a literary flair that makes it easily accessible to the nonspecialist.

Metcalf, Barbara D. *Islamic Revival in British India*. Princeton, N.J.: Princeton University Press, 1982. While focusing on the school of theology founded at the town of Deoband during the 1860's, Metcalf does a masterful job of describing the various groups of Muslim scholars and their divergent opinions. Covers the intellectual atmosphere of the period of Sayyid Ahmad's maturity and provides accounts of a number of debates between him and theologians connected with the Deoband movement.

Ridgeon, Lloyd V. J. *Crescents on the Cross: Islamic Visions of Christianity*. Oxford, England: Oxford University Press, 2001. Examines Sayyid Ahmad's views on Christianity.

Robinson, Francis. *Separatism Among Indian Muslims: The Politics of the United Provinces' Muslims, 1860-1923*. Cambridge, England: Cambridge University Press, 1974. An encyclopedic treatment of individual Muslims, including Sayyid Ahmad, and the issues that concerned them in the nineteenth and twentieth centuries. Contains a good description of the interplay between British imperial policy and Muslim politics.

Troll, Christian. *Sayyid Ahmad Khan: A Reinterpretation of Muslim Theology*. Atlantic Highlands, N.J.: Humanities Press, 1978. Written by a trained theologian, this book reemphasizes the importance of Sayyid Ahmad's theology. The author has a fund of knowledge of classical Islamic thought, and he connects Sayyid Ahmad's views with it. He frequently refers to Sayyid Ahmad's writings and provides in an appendix a translation of one of his most important works.

SEE ALSO: Dadabhai Naoroji; Ranjit Singh; Iswar Chandra Vidyasagar; Vivekananda.

RELATED ARTICLES in *Great Events from History: The Nineteenth Century, 1801-1900:* May 10, 1857-July 8, 1858: Sepoy Mutiny Against British Rule; 1885: Indian National Congress Is Founded.

BRONSON ALCOTT

American educator and social reformer

Alcott was a teacher and a prominent member of New England's Transcendental community. His educational methods focused on moral, spiritual, and imaginative development and encouraged independent thought. He also founded a short-lived utopian community called Fruitlands. However, he is perhaps most famous as the father of author Louisa May Alcott.

BORN: November 29, 1799; Wolcott, Connecticut
DIED: March 4, 1888; Concord, Massachusetts
ALSO KNOWN AS: Amos Bronson Alcott (full name)
AREAS OF ACHIEVEMENT: Education, philosophy

EARLY LIFE

Amos Bronson Alcott was the eldest of eight children in a Connecticut farming family. He attended Wolcott's local district school and displayed, from the start, a fondness for literature and elegant rhetoric. When he reached the age of thirteen, his father sent him to study with his mother's brother, the Reverend Tillotson Bronson, who was principal of the Cheshire Academy. It was hoped that Alcott might enter the academy and eventually become a clergyman, but, overcome by homesickness, he returned home within a month.

The following year, Alcott was sent to nearby Plymouth, Massachusetts, to learn clock making. Again he was unhappy, this time depressed by the monotony of the work, and again he returned home. A few months' study with the local pastor completed his formal education, but his trade was still unsettled. The idea of teaching appealed to him, and he received a license to teach. However, he was not hired by any of the local schools, so he became a peddler. Alcott enjoyed the life of an itinerant salesperson, which allowed him to set his own hours.

Furthermore, the changing landscapes and the people he met both stimulated and educated him. Alcott stated years later that peddling had been his university.

After initially working the New England countryside, Alcott embarked on a southerly trek. In Virginia, the planters who gave him lodging were charmed by his good looks and civilized speech. Alcott was likewise taken by the southerners' elegance and easygoing warmth, which was a far cry from the austerity of New England. They opened their homes and libraries to the intellectual young peddler, and it was from them that Alcott (who, around this time, began going by the name Bronson Alcott) acquired one of his most remarked-upon characteristics: an elegant, royal manner that some would later refer to as his princely air. On a more substantial level, he also gained the vision of a way of life that valued ideas and pleasures as much as pious hard work.

Further south, in North Carolina, Alcott found himself trading among Quakers. These people were certainly less pleasure-loving and flashy than the Virginia planters, but their ideas—at least as contrasted with New England Calvinism—were radical. The Quakers emphasized the essential goodness of the human soul and the primacy of a personal relationship to God. Their libraries yielded William Penn, Robert Barclay, and George Fox, whose ideas would form the basis of Alcott's budding Transcendentalism. The Quakers also gave Alcott his first brief taste of school teaching. At the age of twenty-four, Alcott returned out of this "university" to Connecticut. He was transformed not only in name but also in philosophy and was determined to be a teacher.

Bronson Alcott. (Library of Congress)

LIFE'S WORK

Over the next five years, Alcott taught in the areas around his native Wolcott. His cousin William was already an established teacher in the region and served as a mentor to the younger Alcott. William was intelligent and hard-working and was known for the absolute discipline he maintained in his classrooms. Alcott also insisted on complete silence and attention in his classroom (this was by no means the norm in rural nineteenth century schools), but the two young men, although congenial, had very different emphases. Although William had a reputation as a "smart" teacher, Alcott was emerging as a visionary—and a heretic.

Alcott's aims were lofty: an education that addressed not only the intellectual but also the physical, emotional, and moral aspects of each child. Believing that a child learned better in a beautiful environment than in a plain one, he decorated his classrooms with fine art and busts of great thinkers and philosophers. His curriculums incorporated organized games and calisthenics, singing, and group discussions; they were contrived to make learning fun, not arduous. He rarely resorted to corporal punishment, as he did not want any of his students to associate learning with pain. His classes operated largely on an honor system. Such radical restructurings were enough in themselves to create distrust. To exacerbate matters, Alcott's spiritual beliefs were also suspect.

To his earlier philosophic pastiche Alcott had added the ideas of English poet Samuel Taylor Coleridge and Plato. His Transcendental beliefs were becoming more pronounced. Alcott believed, as did most Transcendentalists, that physical reality—including human souls—was an emanation of the mind of God and that physical, intellectual, and spiritual principles operated by congruent laws. He also espoused a belief in the preexistence of the soul. Although he declared himself a staunch admirer of the tenets of Christianity, he stopped short of calling himself a Christian. This amounted, in nineteenth century New England, to a declaration of moral war. Despite his talents, he repeatedly lost teaching posts—he was either let go or simply not rehired.

On May 23, 1830, Alcott married Abigail May, a clergyman's sister. The union produced four daughters (the second-born was Louisa May Alcott, who would become a well-known children's author) and complicated the young philosopher-teacher's lot: He was the sole and inadequate support of a growing family.

These mounting responsibilities drove Alcott to try teaching once again, and, in 1834, he leased a room in the Masonic Temple in Boston and opened the Temple School. Its form and philosophy—a strong emphasis on moral and religious inquiry—were even more radical than anything Alcott had tried before. Sharp public censure ensued. When two books—*The Record of a School, Exemplifying the General Principles of Spiritual Culture* (1835) and *Conversations with Children on the Gospels* (two volumes, 1836 and 1837)—published by Alcott revealed that the topics under discussion included religion and human reproduction, he was declared a public menace in more than one respected newspaper. Alcott still garnered praise for his visionary methods (from James Freeman Clark and Ralph Waldo Emerson, among others), and the school struggled on in one location or another and in the face of falling enrollments and mounting debts for several more years. It closed in 1839 when Alcott's attempt to racially integrate the school met with overpowering resistance.

In 1842, Alcott, in search of direction and inspiration, decamped from his struggling family and sailed to England, where a group of fellow Transcendentalists had opened a school founded on his principles and named after him: Alcott House. He stayed in England for six months; when he returned to the United States, he brought three of the British mystics with him: Henry Wright, Charles Lane, and Lane's son, William.

Cooperative agrarian communities were not uncommon during the mid-nineteenth century. Many of these were fueled by a revulsion against the increasing industrialization that was quickly transforming social and economic landscapes. Alcott combined his slim resources with those of his compatriots, and together they acquired a one-hundred-acre farm near the village of Harvard. They named their enterprise Fruitlands and, in June, 1844, moved themselves, Alcott's wife and children, and several followers onto the land.

Most of the communal experiments of Alcott's time failed, but the failure of Fruitlands was on a scale comparable to the genius of its founders. Fruitlands' heroic principles clashed with the pragmatics of survival: No animals were used for either food or labor, and the Fruitlanders subsisted on a diet of fruit, grain, vegetables, and water. Alcott and his friends were well meaning but dilatory. They loved talk more than labor, and theory more than action. A disproportionate part of the actual running of the place devolved upon the capable but increasingly Protestant Abigail Alcott and her daughters. Winter came, starvation threatened, and by January of 1845, Fruitlands was abandoned.

Thereafter, from 1845 until 1868, when Louisa May's literary success improved her family's fortunes, the Alcotts were supported by the women of the family, who variously taught, mended, and went out as servants. Alcott eventually developed a series of lectures that he plied with some popular (as opposed to monetary) success throughout the Northeast. In 1859, he was appointed superintendent of the dozen schools in Concord, Massachusetts, where he was at last able to apply many of his earlier innovations on a larger scale, albeit in diluted form. In 1879, he founded the Concord Summer School of Philosophy and Literature, which was dedicated to the furthering of Transcendental thought. Alcott was directly involved with this school until 1882, when he was stricken with paralysis while writing. He never fully recovered and died in March, 1888.

SIGNIFICANCE

The central puzzle of Bronson Alcott's career is how, with such talent, intelligence, and capability at his command, he managed to make so much trouble for himself and so little money: He was usually in debt and was often the object of public censure. The trouble seems to have lain in his idealistic inflexibility. His educational philosophies were radical, and he was seemingly unable to temper them no matter how much they upset the parents of his pupils. Thus, although talented and capable, he was often unemployed. Alcott's imprint upon educational theory and practice, however, is considerable. Most of his reforms that were rejected by his contemporaries—physical education, sex education, flexible classroom design, free discussion, and racial integration—are now standard practice.

Ironically, even Alcott's impracticality and improvidence may have proved, in the end, unexpectedly influential. It was in good part the want of money and a fierce determination to lighten her mother's burdens that fueled Louisa May Alcott's literary ambitions and may have helped ensure her success.

—*Christel Reges*

FURTHER READING

Baker, Carlos. *Emerson Among the Eccentrics: A Group Portrait*. London: Viking Press, 1996. Baker provides an indispensable overview of the complex and shifting intellectual community in which Alcott moved, with individual portraits of Alcott, Ralph Waldo Emerson, Henry David Thoreau, and others.

Barton, Cynthia H. *Transcendental Wife: The Life of Abigail May Alcott*. Lanham, Md.: University Press of America, 1996. Biography of Bronson's wife, and Louisa May's mother, describing how her life with Bronson led her to advance the cause of women's rights.

Brooks, Geraldine. *Orpheus at the Plough: The Father of "Little Women." The New Yorker* 80, no. 42 (January 20, 2005): 58-65. Biography of Alcott, focusing on his experiences at Fruitlands.

Dahlstrand, Frederick C. *Amos Bronson Alcott: An Intellectual Biography*. Rutherford, N.J.: Fairleigh Dickinson University Press, 1982. A full-length biography of Alcott, written by a history professor at Ohio State University at Mansfield.

McCluskey, Dorothy. *Bronson Alcott: Teacher*. New York: Arno Press, 1969. Sympathetic and subjective look at Alcott, focusing on his teaching career. Contains numerous excerpts from his journals and notebooks.

Sears, Clara Endicott. *Bronson Alcott's Fruitlands*. Philadelphia: Porcupine Press, 1975. A fascinating account of Alcott's short-lived utopian community. Includes journal accounts by Louisa May Alcott and many others associated with Fruitlands, correspondence, photographs, and a fictionalized account of Fruitlands by Louisa May called "Transcendental Wild Oats."

Shepard, Odell. *Pedlar's Progress: The Life of Bronson Alcott*. Boston: Little, Brown, 1937. A comprehensive biography of Alcott, providing a detailed look at the man and his times.

Stoehr, Taylor. *Nay-Saying in Concord: Emerson, Alcott, and Thoreau*. Hamden, Conn.: Archon Books, 1979. Focuses on the political, philosophical, and personal relationships between the three Transcendentalists and the impact they had on their times. The author compares the Transcendental movement and the counterculture movements of the 1960's.

SEE ALSO: Louisa May Alcott; Ralph Waldo Emerson; Margaret Fuller; Theodore Parker; Elizabeth Palmer Peabody; Henry David Thoreau.

RELATED ARTICLES in *Great Events from History: The Nineteenth Century, 1801-1900:* May 4, 1805-1830: Exploration of West Africa; 1836: Transcendental Movement Arises in New England.

LOUISA MAY ALCOTT

American novelist

After assuming financial responsibility for the support of her family, Alcott enjoyed a literary career as a prolific writer of works for both adult and juvenile audiences. Her writing reveals the vitality of everyday life, with the family being her most frequent subject.

BORN: November 29, 1832; Germantown, Pennsylvania
DIED: March 6, 1888; Boston, Massachusetts
AREA OF ACHIEVEMENT: Literature

EARLY LIFE

Louisa May Alcott was devoted to her family throughout her life. Her father, Bronson Alcott, was an educator who struggled to earn a decent living for his family. Soon after Louisa's birth, he moved the family to Boston. During the years preceding Louisa's success at writing, her family lived in poverty. This poverty forced the young Alcott daughters to work in order to contribute to the family funds. The family moved frequently, covering the areas from Boston to Concord. The four sisters, Anna, Louisa, Elizabeth, and Abba May, were reared by their father and their mother, Abigail (Abba) May.

As a result of their frequent relocations, the Alcotts came into contact with a variety of people. Through contact with Quaker neighbors, Louisa was exposed to Quaker notions of simplicity, which emphasized family relationships, rather than materialistic acquisitions. The Alcott family's admiration for this ideal of simplicity made their poverty more bearable. Louisa was also exposed to Transcendentalism by her father, a serious philosopher who believed that honesty, sincerity, unselfishness, and other spiritual characteristics were more important to acquire and practice than the material pursuit of wealth and comfort. Bronson Alcott launched a utopian communal experiment on a farm known as Fruitlands in Harvard, Massachusetts, where the girls maintained the family garden and worked in the barley fields. During this time, the family was influenced by their close proximity to the Shakers, who owned property in common and who worked together to complete tasks.

Because her father was interested in philosophy and education, Louisa and her family were acquainted with many of the great minds of the time. Bronson Alcott was a close friend of Ralph Waldo Emerson and Henry David Thoreau, and these men greatly influenced Louisa, who had little formal education. After Thoreau's death, Louisa wrote a poem, entitled "Thoreau's Flute," which was published in *Atlantic* in May, 1863.

In Concord, at the age of thirteen, Louisa began to write and produce little dramatic plays in the barn. At the age of sixteen, she decided to accept a job as teacher to Emerson's children so that she could contribute to her family's earnings. During these years of teaching, Louisa wrote stories for Ellen Emerson. These stories were later compiled into a book, entitled *Flower Fables*, published by George W. Briggs in 1855.

Louisa May Alcott. (The Granger Collection, New York)

As a child, Louisa was deeply affected by contrabands, runaway slaves who had escaped from the South and fled to northern towns for protection. She was filled with compassion for the slaves and later wrote a poem for John Brown, the radical abolitionist who led the raid on Harpers Ferry. When the Civil War broke out, Louisa volunteered as a nurse and went to Georgetown Hospital in Washington, D.C. During her experiences in the hospital, she wrote a series of "Hospital Sketches" that were printed serially in *Commonwealth* and later published as a book in 1863. Her volunteer service as a nurse was terminated after only a month because Louisa came down with typhoid and had to return to Concord.

In 1865, Louisa sailed to Europe as a nurse and companion to a family friend's invalid daughter. During this year-long trip, Louisa met Ladislas Wisniewski, who became a close friend. Ladislas would later serve as the model for the character Laurie in *Little Women*.

LIFE'S WORK

A wide range of experiences gave Louisa May Alcott the opportunity to observe many different people. She knew farmers, Quakers, Shakers, and people of Boston society. She knew poverty, but she was also exposed to a rich intellectual world by her father, and by Emerson and Thoreau. Her travels to Europe gave her further perspectives on people, but when it came time to write, she wrote of what she knew best—her family.

Little Women, Alcott's most popular book, was published by Roberts Brothers in Boston. The book was published in two parts: part 1 (1868) and part 2 (1869). *Little Women* was Alcott's story of her life as one of four sisters. Family members and family friends were at the core of her writing. Daughters, mothers, and grandmothers across the country loved this book written by a female author who understood their experiences. With the success of *Little Women*, Alcott's works were in demand, and she wasted no time in producing more books.

In 1870, Alcott began work on *An Old-Fashioned Girl*, which was published in March of the same year. Many readers praised the story for offering an accurate picture of life in Boston society during that time period. Alcott's observations of life in Boston were particularly keen because she drew upon her own rural background to offer a point of comparison.

Alcott's next book, *Little Men*, was published in June, 1871. Although it was a fictional work, the book drew upon the real-life experiences of Alcott's sister Anna, who reared two sons alone following her husband's

ALCOTT'S MAJOR WORKS

1864 *Moods* (revised 1881)
1868 *Little Women*
1869 *Little Women*, part 2 (also known as *Good Wives*, 1953)
1870 *An Old-Fashioned Girl*
1871 *Little Men*
1873 *Work: A Study of Experience*
1875 *Eight Cousins*
1876 *Rose in Bloom*
1877 *A Modern Mephistopheles*
1878 *Under the Lilacs*
1880 *Jack and Jill*
1886 *Jo's Boys and How They Turned Out*

death. Louisa May Alcott wrote *Little Men* in three weeks while staying at an apartment in Rome. Her description of the death of the character based on her brother-in-law John Pratt is a fine illustration of how she translated intimate personal experiences into literature.

Eight Cousins was written within six to eight weeks and was published in 1875. By this time, Alcott had been labeled as a writer for children, so when Henry James read a copy of this book, he was puzzled by its content. The satirical tone used in describing elders and social mysteries seemed out of place. Nevertheless, Alcott's many juvenile readers seemed eager to accept *Eight Cousins* as a mirror of reality.

The book's sequel, *Rose in Bloom* (1876), was written in three weeks while Alcott stayed at Orchard House in Concord. Just as *Eight Cousins* revealed something of Alcott's social theory, *Rose in Bloom* reflected her views on love and morality. In *Rose in Bloom*, Alcott combines reason with emotion in warning readers to look closely at potential marriage partners before commitment. She advises that no person is completely perfect; all humans have their flaws. The story of Rose and Mac is a rational approach to love and was written for a public that used common sense to control the extremes of romance.

Alcott abandoned her customary juvenile subject matter in 1877, when she wrote *A Modern Mephistopheles*, a story inspired by Johann Wolfgang von Goethe's Faust. Critics claimed that this novel of emotion was similar to the romances Alcott had written at the age of fifteen, but this story lacked the vitality of her earlier material. The book met with an indifferent reception and was called by some "her middle-aged folly."

Louisa May Alcott went on to write additional stories, but they came out of a life that was increasingly more difficult. In her 1938 biography on Alcott, Katharine Anthony aptly described how Alcott translated her life into writing: "Out of such flights into loneliness, restlessness, and emptiness she made her rich, breathing, ardent stories of home." When Alcott's life was touched by the tragedy of losing family members and close family friends, she concealed her grief over their deaths and wrote cheerful, lively tales. Although she enjoyed literary celebrity and financial security as a result of her publications, Alcott suffered from a variety of illnesses during her later years. After visiting her dying father in Boston on March 4, 1888, she herself fell unconscious and died in her sleep there two days later, at the age of fifty-five.

SIGNIFICANCE

Louisa May Alcott was a born storyteller who could deliver realistic plots and maintain a compelling point of view. She wrote of the life she saw in Boston and Concord and also offered simple reforms to improve American society. Honing her writing skills in her early sentimental stories and Gothic thrillers for magazine readers, she was most popular as a children's writer who captured family life during a particular time in history. Although many critics admired her skill in portraying affectionate and intelligent American families, some questioned her literary art. Some claimed she wrote of a simplicity that was common rather than intelligent; others claimed that her stories were too coldly rational, mercenary, and didactic. Nevertheless, admirers praised Alcott's importance as a writer of childhood tragedy and melodrama whose popularity with young readers stemmed from her ability to depict the ups and downs of childhood from a sympathetic point of view. Her stories were read widely by daughters, mothers, and grandmothers who admired Alcott's writing because they perceived themselves in her stories.

Alcott's concern for women went beyond her stories of family and relationships. With her interests in philanthropy, abolitionism, and other aspects of the reform movements that flourished during her era, Alcott was concerned with social issues. She was particularly interested in the right of women to work to support themselves economically. Having grown up in a family of poverty, she recognized the need for women to be respected in the workplace. During the early years, Alcott concentrated her efforts in gaining recognition for women workers and in striving for economic equality for women.

Later, however, she became more active in her support of political rights for women. She edited a suffrage magazine and led a procession to gain delegates for woman suffrage. She also persuaded her chief publisher, Thomas Niles, to publish a history of the suffrage movement. In addition, Alcott was interested in other reforms concerning education, temperance, housing, and prisons. Realizing that because she paid a poll tax, she was entitled to vote, Alcott encouraged several other women to follow her example. Although she took a stance on these issues, her primary interest in life was storytelling. While instructing her readers on the nature of democracy, simplicity, and affection, Alcott also created stories that convey a strong and picturesque image of life in the United States during the late nineteenth century.

—*Linda J. Meyers*

FURTHER READING

Alcott, Louisa May. *A Double Life: Newly Discovered Thrillers of Louisa May Alcott.* Edited by Madeleine B. Stern. Boston: Little, Brown, 1988. This book contains tales of mystery and melodrama that were published anonymously in weeklies before Alcott wrote her tales of social realism. These stories reveal a side of Alcott that is little known by the general public.

_____. *Louisa May Alcott: Selected Fiction.* Edited by Daniel Shealy, Madeleine B. Stern, and Joel Myerson. Boston: Little, Brown, 1990. A collection of stories covering the romances Alcott wrote during her teens and the thrillers and gothic novels she wrote before turning to realism. In these stories, Alcott's rebellious spirit is reflected as a supporter of abolition and women's rights.

_____. *The Selected Letters of Louisa May Alcott.* Edited by Joel Myerson and Daniel Shealy. Boston: Little, Brown, 1987. Offers a personal look at the experiences and responses Alcott wrote in letters to family members and friends throughout her life.

Anthony, Katharine S. *Louisa May Alcott.* New York: Alfred A. Knopf, 1938. Reprint. Westport, Conn.: Greenwood Press, 1977. Reveals the social influence of Alcott's writing as she kept alive the ideals of the Victorian period. Discusses the misrepresentation of Alcott by the literary world, which consistently categorizes her as a children's writer. Includes an excellent bibliography on Alcott and her family.

Clark, Beverly Lynn, ed. *Louisa May Alcott: The Contemporary Reviews.* Cambridge, England: Cambridge University Press, 2004. A collection of contemporary reviews of Alcott's work, demonstrating nineteenth century attitudes toward popular fiction and women writers.

Elbert, Sarah. *A Hunger for Home: Louisa May Alcott and "Little Women."* Philadelphia: Temple University Press, 1984. A feminist study of Alcott, this critical biography analyzes the connections between Alcott's family life and her work. Places Alcott squarely within the reform tradition of the nineteenth century and the debate over the proper role of women.

Meigs, Cornelia. *Invincible Louisa.* Boston: Little, Brown, 1933. Emphasizes Alcott's work with young people and her belief that children must have the opportunity to earn independence. Meigs also discusses Alcott's assistance to soldiers during the Civil War and her trip to Europe. Contains a fine chronology of Alcott's life.

Stern, Madeleine B. *Louisa May Alcott.* Boston: Northeastern University Press, 1999. First published in 1950, this is considered by many to be the standard biography of Alcott.

Strickland, Charles. *Victorian Domesticity: Families in the Life and Art of Louisa May Alcott.* University: University of Alabama Press, 1985. Strickland's study surveys the range of Alcott's ideas about domestic life. Considers Alcott's literary treatment of women, families, and children within the various fictional forms in which she worked.

SEE ALSO: Bronson Alcott; Ralph Waldo Emerson; Henry David Thoreau; Mark Twain; Charlotte Mary Yonge.

RELATED ARTICLE in *Great Events from History: The Nineteenth Century, 1801-1900:* December, 1884-February, 1885: Twain Publishes *Adventures of Huckleberry Finn.*

ALEXANDER I

Emperor of Russia (r. 1801-1825)

As the autocratic ruler of Russia, Czar Alexander I initiated a series of educational, social, and political reforms early in his reign. He was instrumental in forming the coalition that defeated Napoleon I, and he personally played a major role in the Congress of Vienna following the Napoleonic Wars.

BORN: December 23, 1777; St. Petersburg, Russia
DIED: December 1, 1825; Taganrog, Russia
ALSO KNOWN AS: Aleksandr Pavlovich (birth name)
AREA OF ACHIEVEMENT: Government and politics

EARLY LIFE

Czar Alexander's birth in the Winter Palace of St. Petersburg marked his destiny to occupy the Russian throne. He was the first child of Grand Duke Pavel Petrovich (later Czar Paul I) and Grand Duchess Maria Fyodorovna. Shortly after his birth, he was taken from his parents by his grandmother, Empress Catherine II (Catherine the Great), to be reared under her careful supervision. It was Catherine's intent to disinherit her son, Pavel, because she believed that he was mentally unstable and unfit to inherit her throne. Alexander would be trained to succeed her directly.

A number of outstanding tutors were brought to the imperial court by Catherine to provide an education that would prepare her grandson to be czar. The most notable tutor was Frédéric-César de La Harpe, a Swiss republican, who used classical and Enlightenment texts to inspire many of the future czar's liberal ideals. In his adolescence, Alexander was also allowed an extended visit with his father at Gatchina, where he received his military training. Alexander's formal education ended at the age of sixteen, when his grandmother arranged his marriage to Princess Louise of Baden-Durlach (later Grand Duchess and Empress Elizabeth) in 1793.

Three years later, Catherine died suddenly on November 17. She had written a manifesto disinheriting her son and naming Alexander her heir. Because the document had not been released, however, her son assumed the title of Czar Paul I. His reign was characterized by a fanatical tyranny and an irrational foreign policy. A small group of nobles and military officers formed a conspiracy to remove Paul from the throne. Alexander reluctantly agreed to the plot on the condition that his father's life be spared. Paul, however, was assassinated on the night of March 23, 1801. The next day, Alexander was proclaimed the new czar.

At the age of twenty-three, Alexander became the leader of the most populous as well as one of the most backward and troubled nations of Europe. He was a handsome young man known for his intelligence and charm, but some worried that he did not have the necessary courage to fulfill his new duties. On the night that his father was murdered, he reportedly sobbed: "I cannot go on with it. I have no strength to reign. Let someone else take my place." To this, Count Peter von der Pahlen, the chief conspirator, replied: "You have played the child long enough; go reign."

LIFE'S WORK

Upon assuming his new responsibilities, Alexander I rescinded Paul's tyrannical laws. He also formed a private committee composed of four liberal friends from noble families to advise him on a variety of domestic issues. They urged him to pursue a series of educational, social, and political reforms. A comprehensive educational system was proposed by Alexander's private committee. Public and parish schools were opened to all Russians. In addition, a number of specialized and college preparatory schools were established. Existing universities received increased support, and three new ones were built during Alexander's reign.

The social institution of serfdom had long been a problem. Nearly three-quarters of the population was owned by the nobility. Alexander detested this widespread slavery among his subjects, but he moved cautiously to avoid alienating the nobility whose wealth and support depended upon this slave labor. In 1803, however, the Free Cultivator's Law was enacted that permitted the nobility to free their serfs under certain highly restricted conditions. Although its success was extremely limited—only thirty-seven thousand serfs out of ten million were freed during Alexander's reign—the new law did prompt a national debate on serfdom leading to its abolition in 1861.

Alexander also reformed the corrupt and inept bureaucracy he inherited from Catherine and Paul. The senate and state council were relieved of administrative duties, and their role was limited to offering advice and comment on proposed legislation. Administration of the czar's laws would be the responsibility of a "collegium," or cabinet, of eight ministers who reported directly to Alexander. Measures to ensure greater control over the imperial treasury and to limit expenditures by the court

Alexander I. (Library of Congress)

were also implemented. The most ambitious proposal was for a constitution that would limit the czar's autocracy. Although Alexander supported a constitution in principle—he granted constitutions to the Ionian Islands in 1803, to Finland in 1809, and to Poland in 1815—the document was never made public for fear that such rapid change would be opposed by reactionary elements in the nobility.

At the height of his reforming zeal, however, Alexander suddenly and unexpectedly turned his attention to foreign affairs. Initially his foreign policy was based on his hope for a peaceful and unified Europe. He reestablished an alliance with England that had been broken by his father, while at the same time he pursued good relations with France. A treaty of friendship was signed with Prussia, and relations with Austria were improved. Alexander believed that these alliances and overtures not only would moderate Napoleon I's aggressive ambitions but also would eventually lead to a European federation of nations.

Alexander's idealistic hopes were shattered with Napoleon's conquests and with his coronation as emperor of France, forcing Russia to declare war in 1804. The czar assumed the role of field commander, and, along with the Austrians, suffered a bitter defeat at the Battle of Austerlitz in 1805. The following year, Napoleon invaded Prussia. Against the advice of his ministers, Alexander again intervened against the French, losing a series of battles in eastern Prussia.

Following these defeats, Alexander and Napoleon met at the village of Tilsit (now Sovetsk) on June 25, 1807. The czar used his charm to flatter the French emperor and to gain a favorable peace treaty. Russia agreed to break all relations with England and to recognize the newly created Grand Duchy of Warsaw. In exchange, Alexander would be allowed to expand his empire at the expense of Persia, Sweden, and Turkey. Napoleon left Tilsit believing that in Alexander he had a new friend and ally, and that they would conquer and divide Europe between them. The czar, however, was deceptive; his flattery and acceptance of the peace treaty were designed to buy time.

When Alexander returned to St. Petersburg, his popularity quickly declined. The Tilsit Alliance was perceived as a humiliation, and the trade restrictions with England hurt the economy. Partly in response to this criticism, Alexander backed away from any of his earlier reforms and increasingly aligned himself with reactionary forces among the nobility. He imposed his autocratic prerogatives to ensure domestic stability in order to reorganize the army and to devise a strategy that once again would challenge the French emperor.

Alexander's public break with Napoleon came slowly. Trade with England was secretly resumed, and Russia failed to aid France in its war with Austria in 1809. Napoleon retaliated by annexing the Grand Duchy of Oldenburg (territory controlled by the czar's brother-in-law) and threatened to establish an independent kingdom of Poland. Relations between the two nations steadily deteriorated as both sides prepared for war.

On June 24, 1812, Napoleon's grand army invaded Russia. Although Alexander had been rebuilding his army for a number of years, the Russians were still outnumbered by nearly three to one. Given these odds, the Russian army quickly retreated until it faced the French at the Battle of Borodino. The two armies fought to a stalemate, but, as a result of their inferior strength, the Russians were again forced to retreat. Napoleon entered a burning Moscow that had already been torched by its citizens. The French pitched their winter camp in a burned-out city. Disease and lack of supplies took their toll, forcing a retreat. Constant raids by Russian soldiers and partisans during the retreat inflicted heavy casualties. Napoleon escaped from Russia with a devastated army.

Throughout the invasion Alexander provided forceful and inspirational leadership. Even in the darkest days of the campaign, the Russian people rallied behind their czar and vowed never to surrender. The burning of Moscow had reportedly "illuminated his soul," and Alexander swore that he would defeat Napoleon. Alexander's resolve was contagious. He rallied the leaders of Europe to join his crusade against Napoleon. Along with the Prussians and Austrians, he won the decisive Battle of Nations, near Leipzig, in October, 1813. Five months later, Alexander triumphantly entered Paris, forcing Napoleon's abdication and restoring Louis XVIII to the French throne.

Alexander was now the most powerful monarch in Europe. He annexed Poland over the objections of other leaders, but none could challenge his strength. He helped convene and was a dominant figure at the Congress of Vienna, which restored European political stability following the unrest of the Napoleonic era. Even with Napoleon's brief return from exile in 1815, Alexander was still the premier monarch until his death in 1825, and he established a new era of European peace that lasted until 1871. With the defeat of his archenemy, Alexander had achieved his dream of becoming the arbiter of Europe.

SIGNIFICANCE

Alexander I never exploited his position of power. During the last ten years of his life, after 1815, he largely withdrew from public life both in terms of foreign affairs and in terms of domestic reforms. His last foray into international politics was an unsuccessful attempt to form the Holy Alliance. The purpose of this alliance was to unite European leaders by using the principles of Christian love, peace, and justice as a common basis for their political activities. In practice, it was used to justify reactionary policies against revolutionaries. Alexander's domestic policies became increasingly autocratic and repressive because of his fear of conspiracies and revolts. The czar retreated into a private religious mysticism and piety, and, shortly before his death, he indicated a desire to abdicate.

Alexander displayed contradictory attitudes that helped shape the future of Russia and Europe. He was deeply influenced by liberal ideals, yet at crucial moments he backed away from specific reforms. Had he resolved the serfdom issue and enacted a constitution, the numerous Russian revolts of the nineteenth century and the Russian Revolution of 1917 perhaps could have been avoided. With the defeat of Napoleon, Alexander reached the pinnacle of political power, only to retreat into a private world of religious devotion, leaving the future of Europe primarily in the hands of Austria's Prince Metternich. Despite this inconsistent behavior, Alexander was both a progressive, though paternalistic, reformer and the driving force that rid Europe of Napoleon's tyranny.

—Brent Waters

FURTHER READING

Almedingen, Edith M. *The Emperor Alexander I.* New York: Vanguard Press, 1964. A sympathetic biography of Alexander and his court. Provides much personal information about the czar and his relations with family, friends, and colleagues.

Evreinov, Ludmila. *Alexander I, Emperor of Russia: A Reappraisal.* 2 vols. New York: Xlibris, 2001. The author maintains her book differs from previous biographies because she has based her conclusions on diplomatic correspondence, Russian laws, and other previously untapped primary sources of information.

Glover, Michael. *The Napoleonic Wars: An Illustrated History, 1792-1815.* New York: Hippocrene Books, 1978. A general summary of the major military battles and campaigns during the Napoleonic era. Primarily useful for its reproductions of numerous nineteenth century illustrations.

Grimstead, Patricia Kennedy. *The Foreign Ministers of Alexander I: Political Attitudes and the Conduct of Russian Diplomacy, 1801-1825.* Berkeley: University of California Press, 1969. A penetrating study of the foreign ministers who served during Alexander's reign. Provides some insight into the development of Russia's foreign policy and the influence of liberal and reactionary ideas on Alexander's thinking.

Hartley, Janet M. *Alexander I.* London: Longman, 1994. One in a series of interpretive essays analyzing major historical figures within the context of their times. Hartley surveys Alexander's career within the context of Russian and European history and finds him to be a more consistent ruler than circumstances, and posterity, have deemed him to be.

Holt, Lucius Hudson, and Alexander Wheeler Chilton. *A Brief History of Europe from 1789 to 1815.* New York: Macmillan, 1919. This text offers a general historical summary of major European events during this period. Provides good background material for placing Alexander in a larger context during the time of his greatest achievements.

Klimenko, Michael. *Alexander I, Emperor of Russia: A Reappraisal.* Tenafly, N.J.: Hermitage, 2002. A full-length account of Alexander's life written by a professor of Russian history.

McConnell, Allen. *Tsar Alexander I: Paternalistic Reformer.* New York: Thomas Y. Crowell, 1970. Provides a critical review of Alexander's foreign and domestic policies. The author's intent is primarily to evaluate the czar's political career and to influence rather than to provide biographical information.

Nicolson, Harold. *The Congress of Vienna: A Study in Allied Unity, 1812-1822.* New York: Harcourt Brace Jovanovich, 1946. Beginning with Napoleon's retreat from Moscow, this book offers a detailed overview of European politics from 1812 to 1822.

Tarle, Eugene. *Napoleon's Invasion of Russia, 1812.* New York: Oxford University Press, 1942. A detailed account of Napoleon's invasion, campaign, and retreat from Russia.

SEE ALSO: Alexander II; Napoleon I; Nicholas I; Mikhail Mikhaylovich Speransky.

RELATED ARTICLES in *Great Events from History: The Nineteenth Century, 1801-1900:* June 23-December 14, 1812: Napoleon Invades Russia; September 15, 1814-June 11, 1815: Congress of Vienna; February 17, 1815: Treaty of Ghent Takes Effect; June 8-9, 1815: Organization of the German Confederation; November 20, 1815: Second Peace of Paris; December 26, 1825: Decembrist Revolt.

ALEXANDER II

Emperor of Russia (r. 1855-1881)

Called the czar liberator, Alexander emancipated the serfs in 1861 in the first of a series of political and legal reforms designed to quicken the pace of modernization in Russia. Despite his reforms, rising expectations caused dissidents to become radicalized. Hence, Alexander's life was ended by political assassins, and his reforms were suspended by his successor.

BORN: April 29, 1818; Moscow, Russia
DIED: March 13, 1881; St. Petersburg, Russia
ALSO KNOWN AS: Aleksandr Nikolayevich Romanov (birth name)
AREA OF ACHIEVEMENT: Government and politics

EARLY LIFE

Born in the Chudov Monastery within Moscow's Kremlin during an Easter week, Aleksandr Nikolayevich Romanov (nih-koh-LAY-vihch roh-MAHN-awf) was the oldest son of Czar Nicholas I (r. 1825-1855), then grand duke, and Charlotte, daughter of King Frederick William III of Prussia and sister of future German emperor Wilhelm I. Alexander had five siblings: Nicholas, Michael, Maria, Olga, and Alexandra. After their father became czar in 1825 they lived in the royal Russian residence, the Winter Palace, and in a royal palace at Tsarskoe Selo.

The heir to the throne was given two tutors: Captain Karl Karlovich Merder and the poet Vasily Zhukovsky. The former was hired when Alexander was six years old, and he stressed martial values and discipline; the latter emphasized history, letters, and the cultivation of humane sentiments. Both teachers believed in autocracy. A model soldier, throughout his life Alexander expressed excitement at watching and participating in military drills and parades.

In 1837, after completing his formal education, Alexander was sent on a seven-month tour through thirty provinces of the empire. Accompanied by Zhukovsky, he received his first acquaintance with poverty. A year later Alexander took his grand tour of western Europe, where he fell in love with fourteen-year-old Princess Wilhelmina of Hesse-Darmstadt. His father reluctantly accepted the proposed match, and the girl arrived in Russia in 1840 to be rebaptized in the Orthodox Church as Maria Alexandrovna. They were married on April 16, 1841. Among their eight children the first two, Alexandra and Nicholas, died in 1849 and 1865, respectively;

the third child, the future Alexander III, was born in 1845.

Czar Nicholas I carefully prepared his son for governance by appointing him to numerous positions such as chancellor of Alexander University in Finland, member of the Holy Synod and several imperial councils, and, in his father's absence, chairman of the state council. Several times Alexander participated in diplomatic missions, including one to Vienna in 1849 to persuade the Austrian emperor Franz Joseph to pardon the Hungarian rebel generals. Although frightened by the European revolutions in 1849 and reminded by Zhukovsky about the irresponsibility of rapid reforms, Alexander would launch a movement for widespread changes after his accession.

LIFE'S WORK

Alexander came to power on February 19, 1855, during the Crimean War before the fall of Sebastopol to the French and English. Although he reminded his generals of the victory after the fall of Moscow in 1812, he was soon persuaded to negotiate for peace. The czar was compelled to accept defeat and sign the Treaty of Paris on March 30, 1856. His coronation did not occur until August 26. It is unclear to what extent Russia's weak performance in the war led him to embark upon reforms. Because his background did not portend such a reign, historians are divided as to what occurred. Furthermore, because his policies were not uniformly progressive, his goals are difficult to assess. Less dictatorial than his predecessors, he freely accepted advice.

In matters of foreign affairs, he relied upon his chief aide, General Aleksandr Mikhailovich Gorchakov, who agreed with the czar that foreign affairs must be subordinated to domestic developments. Together they forged a rapprochement with Napoleon III of France, only to see it fail when the French extended sympathy to the Polish rebels in 1863. Thereafter, Alexander II drew closer to his German relatives, whom he supported during the creation of the German Empire in 1871. By that year Alexander dared to violate the terms of the Treaty of Paris by sailing warships on the Black Sea. Russia also joined with Germany and Austria-Hungary in the Three Emperors' League, but it fell apart when Alexander succumbed to pan-Slavic pressures and to a war with the Ottoman Empire on April 24, 1877.

Victorious Russian armies forced the sultan to sign a peace at San Stephano the following year, allowing Russia significant gains in Bessarabia and the lower Caucasus. Western powers compelled the Russians to scale

Alexander II. (Library of Congress)

back their gains at a congress in Berlin later that year. That event damaged Russian-German ties, but Otto von Bismarck managed to assuage the czar's feelings somewhat. The end of German-Russian cooperation came in the following reign.

Meanwhile, Russian expansion in the Far East and Central Asia was impressive. Although Alaska was sold to the United States in 1867, and Gorchakov tried to restrain commanders from conquests in Asia, the czar was pleased with their acquisitions. From 1859 to 1861 China ceded territory to Russia in the Amur-Ussuri district, and Japan yielded Sakhalin Island for the remaining Kurile Islands in 1875. Between 1865 and 1876, Alexander's empire reached Kokand, Bokhara, and Khiva in Central Asia; in 1881, other lands east of the Caspian Sea were added. Such gains in the East, however, were little appreciated.

The centerpiece of the reign was the emancipation of about twenty-five million serfs on February 19, 1861. Not only did this measure fulfill a goal that had baffled previous rulers such as Alexander I, it also made possible free labor that was so indispensable for later industrial programs and a free citizenry that was a precondition for further reforms. Alexander opened discussions for serf reform in his state council after the Crimean War and urged that the deliberations of the matter be removed from secret negotiations. He indicated that he wanted the obstacles to solution of this question overcome. Hence, the gentry accepted its inevitability and joined the czar in realizing the edict. The decree gave peasants immediate legal freedoms with lands to buy from the state. Although the terms allowed concessions to the gentry, many people agreed with Aleksandr Ivanovich Herzen that official society had moved in a progressive direction. Much of the credit was attributed to Alexander. Peasants, however, were bewildered by the requirement to purchase their lands.

Despite the uprising in Poland in 1863, Alexander forged ahead with decrees in 1864 to reform the legal administration. Reforms that were introduced were trial by jury in civil cases, equal access to the courts for all, life tenure for judges, and measures to protect due process. Also that year, local government was reorganized and newly elected assemblies called *zemstvos* were given wide control over local education, fire fighting, veterinary medicine, road and bridge construction, hospital care, and other matters in the thirty-four provinces of the empire.

Members were elected on the all-class principle, removing the monopoly of local authority from the gentry. Alexander eased censorship in 1865 and disbanded the secret police. Similar elective bodies were introduced in 1870 in urban administration. During the 1870's, military reforms drawn up by D. A. Miliutin incorporated many principles of civil law into military law, and the penal environment of the soldier was changed to a dignified profession for national defense. Hence the brutality of military training was largely eliminated, and terms of active service were reduced from fifteen to six years.

Alexander's reforming zeal was tempered by firm measures to protect his regime. In 1862 he ordered the arrest of radical journalist Nikolay Chernyshevsky for inciting violence, and he ordered Russification of the Poles after 1863. On April 4, 1866, while Alexander was walking through the Summer Gardens, an inept attempt on his life was made by a deranged nihilist, Dmitry V. Karakazov. Although the attempt failed, Alexander was shaken by the incident and appointed reactionary minister Dmitry Andreyevich Tolstoy to preside over the ministry of education. When the populist intelligentsia failed to arouse the peasantry by talking about socialism in the early 1870's, some turned to violence. Alexander responded with strong measures of his own, and the nation witnessed several treason trials that gave exposure to the radical cause and undermined respect for the czar. Eventually, a faction of radicals decided upon the ultimate act of terrorism—the killing of the czar.

Members of the People's Will Party believed that the assassination of the czar would bring peasants to the point of national rebellion. Their single-minded devotion to this end was realized on the morning of March 13, 1881, as Alexander was riding a coach through the streets of his capital after addressing a meeting. When a bomb was thrown at this coach, wounding his coachmen, the czar alighted from the carriage to help attend to the victims; a second bomb then killed him. On that spot was constructed the Church of the Spilt Blood.

SIGNIFICANCE

Despite relapses into conservative policies, Alexander II authored the most significant reforms in czarist history. Designed to modernize Russian life so that the nation could better compete internationally, the reforms also fulfilled Alexander's own desires for the improvement of the commonwealth. However, they were not effective in stemming the tide of radical politics. Some regard the reforms as too little, too late; others believe that they were meant simply to strengthen the old structures in order to make additional reforms unnecessary; and yet others believe that they were too much, too soon. The most radical intelligentsia feared that the reforms might defuse the public's desire for revolution.

The czar's popularity waned in his last years, partly through his own doing. The moving of his second family into the Winter Palace under the same roof as the empress, his hasty marriage to Princess Catherine E. Dolgoruka on the fortieth day after his wife died in 1880, and his replacement of progressive ministers with conservative ministers obscured the fact that he was, at the end, considering a major step toward representative government, having commissioned Count Mikhail Tariyelovich Loris-Melikov to draw up a plan for a national consultative assembly. Alexander's assassination came just before the plan was unveiled; the new czar dismissed the proposal and began measures to undo the work of his father.

—*John D. Windhausen*

FURTHER READING

Almedingen, E. M. *The Emperor Alexander II*. London: Bodley Head, 1962. This work, by a writer who specializes in biographies of Russian figures, contains the most extensive account of Alexander's personal life. Despite Alexander's vacillations, the author la-ments that Alexander's successors failed to continue his work.

Billington, James H. *The Icon and the Axe: An Interpretive History of Russian Culture*. New York: Vintage Books, 1970. The author divides Alexander's reign into a period of reform followed by a period of reaction, while brilliantly exploring the sociopolitical dimensions of art and literature in this era.

Kornilov, Alexander. *Modern Russian History from the Age of Catherine the Great to the End of the Nineteenth Century*. New York: Alfred A. Knopf, 1952. This classic view of the age demonstrates with keen insight the political machinations of the czar and his court.

Moss, Walter G. *A History of Russia*. 2d ed. 2 vols. London: Anthem Press, 2002. The second volume describes Alexander's reforms and foreign policies.

_____. *Russia in the Age of Alexander II, Tolstoy, and Dostoevsky*. London: Anthem Press, 2002. Examines the personal and public lives of Alexander, incorporating this information with details about Tolstoy, Dostoevsky, and other nineteenth century Russian writers and thinkers.

Mosse, W. E. *Alexander II and the Modernization of Russia*. London: English Universities Press, 1958. A short but scholarly synopsis of the reign that traces much of the czar's troubles to his alienation of society and even of the police during the 1870's.

Pereira, N. G. O. *Tsar-Liberator: Alexander II of Russia, 1818-1881*. Newtonville, Mass.: Oriental Research Partners, 1983. Despite the author's modest claim to the contrary, this is the best biographical study of the czar's reign. Pereira, an academic historian, clearly lauds Alexander's imperial policies in the East.

Pushkarev, Sergei. *The Emergence of Modern Russia, 1801-1917*. Translated by Robert H. McNeal and Tova Yedlin. New York: Holt, Rinehart and Winston, 1963. Pushkarev, a modern liberal historian, maximizes the changes at the beginning of the century and minimizes those during the 1860's.

Seton-Watson, Hugh. *The Decline of Imperial Russia, 1855-1914*. New York: Praeger, 1952. In part 1, "The Tsar Liberator 1855-1881," the author discovers the roots of the collapse of the old regime.

Van der Kiste, John. *The Romanovs, 1818-1959: Alexander II of Russia and His Family*. Stroud, England: Sutton, 1998. A history of the Romanov family, focusing on Alexander II's life, reign, and children.

SEE ALSO: Alexander I; Nicholas I.

RELATED ARTICLES in *Great Events from History: The Nineteenth Century, 1801-1900:* March 23, 1858: Fraser River Gold Rush Begins; March 3, 1861: Emancipation of Russian Serfs; March 30, 1867: Russia Sells Alaska to the United States; May 6-October 22, 1873: Three Emperors' League Is Formed.

HORATIO ALGER

American novelist

Alger was a writer of books for juveniles that popularized business as a career for young boys, while at the same time motivating the poor to work hard in the hope of eventual success. Because of the popularity of his books, real-life tales of poor people who became successful life became known as "Horatio Alger stories."

BORN: January 13, 1832; Chelsea, Massachusetts
DIED: July 18, 1899; Natick, Massachusetts
ALSO KNOWN AS: Horatio Alger, Jr. (full name)
AREA OF ACHIEVEMENT: Literature

EARLY LIFE

Horatio Alger, Jr. (AL-jihr) spent most of his life in Massachusetts and traced his ancestry to Puritans who came to Plymouth, Massachusetts, in 1621. His father, Horatio Alger, Sr., was a graduate of the Harvard Theological School and the minister at the First Congregational Church in Chelsea, Massachusetts. His mother, Olive Augusta Fenno, had married his father just ten months before the birth of Horatio, Jr. The ministerial stipend was not large; thus, the family was usually in debt. In 1844, when Horatio, Jr., was twelve, his father went bankrupt. For a time his father turned to farming, but he eventually went back into the ministry and later served in the Massachusetts state legislature.

Alger was a sickly child; he was nearsighted and had asthma. In 1848, at the age of sixteen, he was admitted to Harvard College. The first publication for which he received payment came in 1849 when a Boston magazine bought a poem he had penned. During his senior year, he

Horatio Alger.

was elected to Phi Beta Kappa, and he graduated in 1852. Although he immediately planned to enter the Harvard Divinity School, a writing job arose, and he decided to become a journalist—a career he was to follow for five years. In the fall of 1857, he entered the Harvard Divinity School, from which he graduated in 1860. Alger was soon named to the pulpit of the Unitarian Church in Brewster, Massachusetts. Because his church duties were often light, he spent a great deal of time writing stories for children, which was not a praiseworthy sideline in the eyes of his parishioners.

Alger apparently had a homosexual relationship with one or more of the young boys in his church. Once this came to light in 1866, he was forced not only to resign his church but also to resign the ministry. The Unitarians agreed to keep the situation quiet if Alger agreed to never again serve as a minister. He then moved to New York, where he became a full-time writer. His personal relations with boys never again came into question. Many authors, however, have speculated that Alger's love for boys was a vicarious motivation that surfaced in his writing. From the event, Alger learned discretion and was never again accused of a homosexual relationship, but he also never allowed himself to be in the public eye. His books and short stories were all that people ever really knew about the man during the remainder of his lifetime.

LIFE'S WORK

In middle age, at a time when he had been relatively unsuccessful in other endeavors, Alger began writing books for juveniles. He was best known as a writer of books in which the heroes started out poor and ended up wealthy. Among his more popular titles were *Ragged Dick: Or, Street Life in New York with the Bootblacks* (1868), *Luck and Pluck: Or, John Oakley's Inheritance* (1869), and *Tattered Tom: Or, The Story of a Street Arab* (1871). His heroes were typically newsboys, shoe shiners, match sellers, farmers, or luggage carriers who rose to fame and fortune via their own efforts, bravery, and courage. His young entrepreneurs earned and spent their wealth honestly. His books were particularly popular during the Progressive Era because they satisfied the Progressives' desire to reform business and government through a return to morality.

Alger's adult life was ostensibly dull, as he did almost nothing but write. In addition to writing more than 120 books, he published hundreds of short stories and over one hundred poems. Many of his short stories were written under pseudonyms. His writing was not particularly difficult in that it was formulaic fiction that required little research. Short stories were turned into serials, and serials were turned into books. In one sense, Alger was a self-plagiarizer because he used the same work over and over. His first book, *Bertha's Christmas Vision*, was published in 1856. His fourth book, and first financially successful volume, was *Paul Prescott's Charge* in 1865.

Alger's writings captured the spirit of the United States. In his books, the reader could hear the turmoil of the city streets and the rattle of the milk pails on the farms. He portrayed the ambitious soul of the nation. Manly forbearance was an important part of Alger's writings; it was okay to fight or even shoot someone, but only after Alger had made it clear that there was no other possibility. Money, contracts, and instruments such as mortgages were often discussed in detail—usually with the hero eventually paying off the mortgage for his widowed mother.

Alger has been criticized at times because the event that moves the hero from destitution to wealth is often somewhat fortuitous, such as a gift arriving in the mail from a long-lost aunt, an inheritance from a little-known relative, or a payment received for an invention that had not been discussed previously in the book. Despite these criticisms, the message was that hard work and pluck on the part of the hero was the key to prosperity.

Alger's books, although popular, were not huge sellers during his lifetime. He had few assets at the time of his death in July, 1899. It was only after his death, when the books were reissued in inexpensive editions, that he became a household name. His books remained popular until about 1920. A total of at least seventy different publishers issued Alger's books, some of which were first editions and some of which were reprints. Alger was so prolific that one or two publishers could not handle all of his work. Approximately forty different publishers issued reprints of his books during the first two decades of the twentieth century. The reprints sold, in hardcover, for as little as ten cents each—a price that allowed almost every child to have access to Alger's work. It has been estimated that more than 400 million copies of his novels have been sold.

It was not until 1926 that the term "Horatio Alger hero" first appeared in print as a synonym for someone who had gone from rags to riches. During the Great Depression of the 1930's, Alger's plots were again hailed as the way out of hard times. Alger's thesis was that virtue and hard work were always rewarded, and newspapers often published articles to the effect that if Americans would work harder, the Depression would cease to exist. In 1939, on the fortieth anniversary of Alger's death, New York governor Herbert Lehman essentially prescribed Alger as a home remedy for the economic ills afflicting the nation.

In 1947, a *New York Times* editorial attributed the American disdain for communism and socialism to Alger; because so many Americans believed that every poor boy had a chance to succeed, they would not fall for the rantings of the anarchists and socialists who saw nothing but evil in capitalism. Readers of Alger, however, knew better; every newsboy had the potential to become rich

ALGER'S NOVELS ABOUT SUCCESS

Alger wrote more than 120 novels, mostly about boys rising from poverty and hardship to great success through pluck and fortitude. This selection of his titles reveals his favorite themes.

1868 *Ragged Dick: Or, Street Life in New York with the Bootblacks*
1868 *Fame and Fortune: Or, The Progress of Richard Hunter*
1869 *Luck and Pluck: Or, John Oakley's Inheritance*
1869 *Mark the Match Boy: Or, Richard Hunter's Ward*
1869 *Rough and Ready: Or, Life Among the New York Newsboys*
1870 *Ben the Luggage Boy: Or, Among the Wharves*
1870 *Rufus and Rose: Or, The Fortunes of Rough and Ready*
1870 *Sink or Swim: Or, Harry Raymond's Resolve*
1871 *Paul the Peddler: Or, The Adventures of a Young Street Merchant*
1871 *Tattered Tom: Or, The Story of a Street Arab*
1872 *Phil the Fiddler: Or, The Story of a Young Street Musician*
1872 *Slow and Sure: Or, From the Street to the Shop*
1872 *Strive and Succeed: Or, The Progress of Walter Conrad*
1873 *Bound to Rise: Or, Harry Walton's Motto*
1873 *Try and Trust: Or, The Story of a Bound Boy*
1874 *Brave and Bold: Or, The Fortunes of a Factory Boy*
1874 *Risen from the Ranks: Or, Harry Walton's Success*
1875 *The Young Outlaw: Or, Adrift in the Streets*
1876 *Shifting for Himself: Or, Gilbert Greyson's Fortunes*
1878 *The Western Boy: Or, The Road to Success*
1884 *Do and Dare: Or, A Brave Boy's Fight for Fortune*
1887 *The Store Boy: Or, The Fortunes of Ben Barclay*
1888 *The Errand Boy: Or, How Phil Brent Won Success*
1890 *Ned Newton: Or, The Fortunes of a New York Bootblack*
1890 *Struggling Upward: Or, Luke Larkin's Luck*
1895 *Adrift in the City: Or, Oliver Conrad's Plucky Fight*
1897 *Frank and Fearless: Or, The Fortunes of Jasper Kent*
1899 *Jed the Poorhouse Boy*
1899 *Silas Snobden's Office Boy*
1901 *Ben Bruce: Scenes in the Life of a Bowery Newsboy*
1901 *Nelson the Newsboy: Or, Afloat in New York*
1905 *From Farm to Fortune: Or, Nat Nason's Strange Experience*
1905 *Mark Manning's Mission: The Story of a Shoe Factory Boy*
1905 *The Young Book Agent: Or, Frank Hardy's Road to Success*
1906 *Joe the Hotel Boy: Or, Winning Out by Pluck*
1908 *Wait and Win: The Story of Jack Drummond's Pluck*

and famous. Perhaps the following review from *Publishers Weekly* is an overstatement, but it indicates the mind-set with which Alger is remembered: "To Call Horatio Alger, Jr., America's most influential writer may seem like an overstatement . . . but . . . only Benjamin Franklin meant as much to the formation of the American popular mind."

SIGNIFICANCE

Horatio Alger was a private person who shunned publicity throughout his life, perhaps fearing that his reputation would be harmed if an unsavory incident from his early adulthood were to be exposed. Thus, he was one of the most widely read writers in the United States during his lifetime, yet he was unknown. To deter future biographers, he even ordered his sister to destroy all of his personal papers following his death, which she did. Even some documents in the hands of others mysteriously disappeared in the years following his death.

Other writers adapted Alger's fiction formula for their own uses. Edward Stratemeyer, who dominated the juvenile fiction market between 1910 and 1930 (and who completed eleven of Alger's book manuscripts that were left unfinished at Alger's death), also used moral heroism and economic success in his books. Owen Wister, the author of *The Virginian* (1902), applied the technique to Western stories.

More than a century after his death, Alger's name stands as a symbol for central American values. It is not because his books are still widely known and read but because his name has entered the language as a synonym for a success story. His books have been lampooned and maligned, but as symbols they are so pervasive in American culture that they have far outlived a man who was undoubtedly nothing more than a hack writer.

In 1940, authors Nathanael West and Boris Ingster summarized Alger's life by writing, "only fools laugh at Horatio Alger, and his poor boys who make good. The wiser man who thinks twice about that sterling author will realize that Alger is to America what Homer was to the Greeks." Indeed, Alger's stories may not have been based on fact, but they told about the way Americans wanted life to be. Today, Alger would probably be a motivational speaker or writer of some sort who would encourage people to be the best that they could be and promising that success would follow. He has been called one of the great mythmakers of the modern world. There is even an award for successful individuals named the Horatio Alger Award. Historian Henry Steele Commager stated that Alger probably exerted more influence on the national character than any other writer except perhaps Mark Twain.

—Dale L. Flesher

FURTHER READING

Klein, Marcus. *Easterns, Westerns, and Private Eyes: American Matters, 1870-1900*. Madison: University of Wisconsin Press, 1994. Examines late nineteenth century popular fiction, focusing on Alger's rags-to-riches tales, Westerns, and detective stories.

Mayes, Herbert R. *A Biography Without a Hero*. New York: Macy-Masius, 1928. This work is a complete fabrication. When Mayes discovered there was insufficient information to write a true biography, he decided, with the approval of his publisher, to write a parody of Alger's life based on nonexistent diaries and letters. Surprisingly, his parody was not recognized as such and was viewed as a legitimate biography for several decades. Reviews were generally favorable. Alger's surviving friends and relatives apparently did not reveal the truth, probably because they were happy that the truth had not been revealed. Many subsequent biographers unwittingly used this book as a source of factual information on Alger's life.

Nackenoff, Carol. *The Fictional Republic: Horatio Alger and American Political Discourse*. New York: Oxford University Press, 1994. Examines how Alger's formulaic success stories have shaped political discourse in Ronald Reagan's America and beyond. Nackenoff maintains that Alger responded to the increasing industrialization and division in the nineteenth century by devising a set of symbols to address Americans' anxieties about power and identity.

Scharnhorst, Gary, and Jack Bales. *The Lost Life of Horatio Alger, Jr.* Bloomington: Indiana University Press, 1985. The best work on the life of Alger, and the first to fully unmask the faulty, fictionalized biography of Herbert R. Mayes.

Tebbel, John. *From Rags to Riches: Horatio Alger and the American Dream*. New York: Macmillan, 1963. Although based on the fictional work of Mayes, this volume does contain a complete bibliography of Alger's works.

Weiss, Richard. *The American Myth of Success: From Horatio Alger to Norman Vincent Peale*. New York: Basic Books, 1969. Analyzes the work of popular writers who portray the ease with which Americans can become successful.

SEE ALSO: Louisa May Alcott; Frances Hodgson Burnett; Robert Louis Stevenson; Mark Twain.

RELATED ARTICLES in *Great Events from History: The Nineteenth Century, 1801-1900:* July, 1881-1883: Stevenson Publishes *Treasure Island*; December, 1884-February, 1885: Twain Publishes *Adventures of Huckleberry Finn.*

ALI PAŞA TEPELENË

Albanian ruler under the Ottoman Empire

Ali Paşa Tepelenë's Albanian revolt against the Ottoman Empire helped set off the Greek War of Independence, and he himself achieved literary fame in Lord Byron's epic poem Childe Harold's Pilgrimage.

BORN: c. 1744; Tepelenë, Ottoman Empire (now in Albania)

DIED: February 5, 1822; Janina, Ottoman Empire (now Ioánnina, Greece)

ALSO KNOWN AS: Ali Paşa; Ali Pasha Tepelenë; Ali Pasha; Lion of Janina

AREAS OF ACHIEVEMENT: Government and politics, warfare and conquest

EARLY LIFE

The year in which Ali Paşa Tepelenë (AH-lee pah-SHAH teh-peh-leh-NEE) was born is uncertain but historians estimate it to have been between 1740 and 1750. His father, Veli, the governor (*bey*) of Tepelenë, a town in southern Albania and a province of the Ottoman Empire, was murdered when Ali was fourteen years old. With his mother, Khamco, the young Ali was forced to flee into the mountains, where he and his mother formed a bandit group that roamed the countryside. Intent on restoring the political prestige and fortunes of the family, young Ali became notorious as the band's leader. After providing military support to the provincial governor, or pasha, of Negroponte (Euboea), he married the daughter of the pasha of Delvino in 1768. His next step up the ladder included his service to the pasha of Rumelia.

While continuing to enrich himself, Ali kept the roads of his region free of other bandits. His many gifts to the Ottoman government in Constantinople gained favored attention with the ruling Turkish government, and in 1787, the Turks rewarded him by making him provincial governor (pasha) over the territory of Trikkala. As an Ottoman representative, Ali gained even more attention and governmental merit when he defeated the rebellious governor at Scutari, Albania. During the following year, through murder and intrigue, he took control of Janina (also known as Yannina and Ioánnina) in what is now northern Greece.

LIFE'S WORK

In his attempt to create the largest province, or pashalik, within the Ottoman Empire, Ali came to be known as the ruthless and infinitely clever Muslim "Arslan" or "Lion" of Janina. However, he eventually became dissatisfied with being merely another provincial governor at a time when the Ottoman Empire was declining. His new ambition was to rule all of Albania and northern Greece. Through mass deception and continued acts of murder, he brutally extended his power. Eventually, he ruled a region that included much of Albania, Macedonia, Epirus, Thessaly, and the Morea.

As his power and territories expanded, Ali Paşa placed his son Veli in Trikkala and later the Morea, and made another son, Mukhtar, the pasha of Lepanto. All this time, through continued murder and extortion, he expanded his authority and increased his wealth until he ruled most of Greece. In 1803, Ali Paşa got control of the Gulf of Arta; the ports of Butrinto, Preveza, and Vonitsa; and the provinces of Elbasan, Delvino, Berat, and Valona (Vlore).

As Ali's power increased, his attention to the Ottoman sultan in Constantinople diminished. Although he was officially the imperial viceroy of Rumelia, he failed to carry out orders and attempted instead to appease Sultan Mahmud II with extravagant gifts. Eventually, he set himself up as an independent sovereign and courted the sultan's enemies, the British and French, in an effort to establish a profitable seaport in Janina. Ever self-serving, he also tried to manipulate diplomatic relations among Great Britain's Lord Nelson, the Russian czar, and even Napoleon I in France.

The European rulers realized the strategic position of Ali's dominions in the eastern Adriatic. Foreign governments trained Ali Paşa's troops and favored him with gifts of modern artillery. In 1814, Ali declared war on the French, as Napoleon's power was fading, and entered into an alliance with Great Britain. Meanwhile, Ali Paşa's reputation as both a despot and a romanticized "Oriental" sovereign grew throughout Europe. Indeed, during the early nineteenth century, Ali Paşa lived vividly in the European imagination. His harem contained more than six hundred women.

In 1809, Lord Byron, who called Ali Paşa the "Muslim Bonaparte," traveled with John Cam Hobhouse to Janina in Greece and then to Ali Paşa's birthplace in the remote and mountainous Tepelenë, Albania. At that time, Janina was considered the center of Greek culture. Although Ali himself was illiterate, he made an attempt at erudition by founding many Greek schools. A Romantic poet, Byron wrote of his travel experience in his epic poem *Childe Harold's Pilgrimage* (1816), which describes Ali at once as both a gracious, brave, and learned man and a despot capable of "most horrible cruelties."

Ali Paşa, who stood at only five feet, five inches, thought nothing of murder as a means of eliminating his enemies. Hobhouse described arriving at Janina, where he and his traveling companions spied the dismembered body of a Greek bandit who had been tortured to death on Ali's command. In 1812, Ali Paşa came to believe that through alchemy he could find immortality; to achieve that goal, he bought a laboratory and hired scientists to staff it. Five years later, when it became clear that the scientists had achieved nothing, he hanged them.

Ali Paşa went to extremes in his seizures of territory. Before long, his enemies, especially those rival feudal lords who had lost land to him, appealed to Sultan Mahmud in Constantinople to remove Ali from power. Continually exasperated by Ali's repeated attempts to achieve independence, the sultan stripped him of his titles in 1820 and declared him an enemy of the Ottoman Empire. A Turkish army of 20,000 men then attacked Janina. Afterward, Ali Paşa's allies and even his sons abandoned him. He was promised a pardon if he would surrender, but while he was waiting for the pardon, he was killed in February, 1822, by a Turkish spy. His assassin decapitated him and placed his head on a silver tray for all to view. After three days, his head was sent to Constantinople, where it was put on public display so that Sultan Mahmud and the people of Constantinople could see that their old enemy was indeed finally dead.

CHILDE HAROLD'S PILGRIMAGE

The English poet Lord Byron met Ali Paşa Tepelenë in 1809 and later mentioned him in two verses of the second canto of his epic poem Childe Harold's Pilgrimage *(1812-1818, 1819).*

In marble-paved pavilion, where a spring
Of living water from the centre rose,
Whose bubbling did a genial freshness fling,
And soft voluptuous couches breathed repose,
Ali reclined, a man of war and woes:
Yet in his lineaments ye cannot trace,
While Gentleness her milder radiance throws
Along that aged venerable face,
The deeds that lurk beneath, and stain him with disgrace
. . . . . .
I talk not of mercy, I talk not of fear;
He neither must know who would serve the Vizier;
Since the days of our prophet, the crescent ne'er saw
A chief ever glorious like Ali Pasha.

Source: Lord Byron, *Childe Harold's Pilgrimage*, canto 2, stanzas 62 and 72.

SIGNIFICANCE

Some historians argue about whether Ali Paşa's death was a decisive precursor to the outbreak of the Greek War of Independence. All agree, however, that he played a significant role in bringing about the war. During the sixteenth and seventeenth centuries the Greeks had merely survived as a people. During the eighteenth century, especially in the light of the siege of Vienna in 1683, hope emerged that the Greeks might actually succeed in revolting against the Ottoman Empire. By 1819, Sultan Mahmud II attempted to centralize the government of his declining empire. In both European and Asiatic Turkey, provincial pashas appropriated the authority of the sultan. Knowing full well that the Ottoman Empire was no longer indomitable, Ali Paşa supported the Greek struggle for liberation from Turkish rule by encouraging the uprising of the Greek nationalists.

Throughout most of Ali Paşa's career, the Turkish sultan allowed him great autonomy because he relied on his services. However, in 1820, after Ali ordered the assassination of an enemy in Constantinople, the sultan sent Turkish troops to Janina to remove Ali from power. Ali's refusal to comply kept Turkish troops engaged while they were needed against the Greeks, who had begun their fight for independence. Ali Paşa's actions thus split the military and artillery power of the Turks and enabled the Greeks to win their war of independence—in which, incidentally, Ali's old friend Lord Byron lost his life in 1826. Meanwhile, Ali Paşa won lasting literary fame in Byron's epic poem *Childe Harold's Pilgrimage*.

—*M. Casey Diana*

FURTHER READING

Christowe, Stoyan. *The Lion of Yanina: A Narrative Based on the Life of Ali Pasha, Despot of Epirus*. London: Modern Age Books, 1941. Comprehensive biography detailing the legendary life of Ali Paşa Tepelenë.

Fleming, K. E. *The Muslim Bonaparte*. Princeton, N.J.: Princeton University Press, 2000. Scholarly work addressing how modern Greece, in the context of European history, came under a surrogate form of colonial control—in which Greek history and culture became colonized.

McGann, Jerome J. *Lord Byron: The Major Works*. Oxford, England: Oxford University Press, 2000. Includes Byron's 1816 Romantic epic poem *Childe Harold's Pilgrimage*, which portrays Ali Paşa as an enlightened despot.

Marmullaku, Ramadan. *Albania and the Albanians*. London: C. Hurst, 1975. Discusses the roles of Ali Paşa Tepelenë and the Albanian people in overcoming the Ottoman Empire after hundreds of years of subjection.

Roesse, David E. *In Byron's Shadow: Modern Greece in English and American Literature from 1770 to 1967*. Oxford, England: Oxford University Press, 2001. Discusses the beginnings of the Greek War of Independence against Ottoman rule and includes the important role of Ali Paşa Tepelenë in its successful outcome.

SEE ALSO: Lord Byron; Napoleon I; Lord Nelson.

RELATED ARTICLE in *Great Events from History: The Nineteenth Century, 1801-1900:* 1863-1913: Greece Unifies Under the Glücksburg Dynasty.

JOHN PETER ALTGELD

German-born governor of Illinois (1893-1897)

A German immigrant who rose to become one of the most influential Democratic politicians in the United States, Altgeld furnished American political life with a high standard of moral courage and helped to establish the principle that maintenance of the welfare society is an obligation of government during a crucial period of political change.

BORN: December 30, 1847; Niederselters, Prussia (now in Germany)

DIED: March 12, 1902; Joliet, Illinois

AREAS OF ACHIEVEMENT: Government and politics, social reform

EARLY LIFE

John Peter Altgeld (awlt-gehld) was born in the Prussian province of Nassau, the eldest son of a wagon maker, also named John Peter Altgeld, and his wife, Mary Lanehart. The family came to the United States in the spring of the following year, and Altgeld grew up on farms near Mansfield, Ohio. Because his father was against the idea of education for his children, Altgeld attended country schools for only three terms. When he was sixteen, he enlisted in an Ohio militia regiment and was sent to Virginia. There, he contracted a fever that permanently damaged his health, but he refused to be sent home and finished out the hundred days for which the regiment had been mustered.

When he returned to Ohio, Altgeld, much against his father's wishes, attended high school in Mansfield and a teacher-training school in Lexington, Ohio, and taught school for a time. Until he was twenty-one, he turned over all of his wages to his father, but in the spring of 1869, perhaps because the parents of Emma Ford would not permit her to marry him, he headed west on foot, working on farms as he went.

Altgeld arrived finally in St. Louis with only fifteen cents, worked there for a time in a chemical plant, and later worked on a railroad that was being built in southern Kansas. When a recurrence of his fever forced him to quit, he went to northwestern Missouri, most of the way on foot. Dressed in rags, he collapsed at a farm near Savannah, Missouri, and was taken in by a farmer who restored him to health and gave him work. Later, he taught school and read law, and in April, 1871, was admitted to the bar and began legal practice in Savannah. He had not revealed any interest in politics until this time, beyond a devotion to the ideals of Thomas Jefferson, but he served as city attorney for Savannah for a year and ran successfully as the Populist candidate for prosecuting attorney of Andrew County in 1874.

For reasons that remain obscure, Altgeld resigned this office after a year and, with only one hundred dollars, moved to Chicago. There he established a law practice, and in 1877, on a visit to his parents in Ohio, he married Emma Ford. During the next years, Altgeld achieved great success investing in Chicago real estate and in 1890 held property valued at a million dollars.

LIFE'S WORK

In 1884, Altgeld was the unsuccessful Democratic candidate for Congress in Illinois's traditionally Republican Fourth District. At this time, he was an apparent conservative in politics and part of the Chicago economic establishment. In the same year, however, he published *Our Penal Machinery and Its Victims*, which revealed many of the ideas for reform that he sought to implement later in his political career. The book pleaded for the elimination of the causes of crime and the rehabilitation of criminals, and it condemned police brutality against vagrants. In 1886, in the immediate wake of the Haymarket Riot, he wrote a newspaper article in which he argued for the compulsory arbitration of strikes.

John Peter Altgeld. (Library of Congress)

That year, he ran successfully for judge of the Cook County Superior Court, serving for five years. Apparently Altgeld regarded the judgeship as the first step toward his ultimate goal—a seat in the U.S. Senate, the highest national office open to citizens of foreign birth. When he resigned his judgeship and failed to win election to the Senate, he embarked on his greatest project in real estate—the construction of the sixteen-story Unity Block, at that time one of Chicago's greatest buildings.

In 1892, Altgeld was nominated by the Democrats for the Illinois governorship, probably more for his success as a businessperson than for any stand he had taken on social issues. In this campaign, he revealed the strict ethics and liberal instincts for which his followers admired him, mixed with a real hunger for power and an occasional tendency to political chicanery. As the first Democratic governor of Illinois in forty years, Altgeld cleared out all the Republicans in state government, and though many of his replacements were brilliant, he fired some able Republicans and appointed some incompetent Democrats.

In the aftermath of the Haymarket Riot, when a bomb killed several policemen, eight anarchists had been sentenced to death; one of them committed suicide in prison, and four others were hanged. The sentences of the other three—Samuel Fielden, Michael Schwab, and Oscar Neebe—had been commuted to life imprisonment. Altgeld's supporters expected him to pardon these three men and assumed that he would be motivated only by feelings of mercy. Nevertheless, when the pardons were issued on June 26, 1893, it was clear that though he detested anarchism, he was convinced that the eight men had been convicted not for their deeds but for their opinions, that the jury had been impaneled improperly, that the judge was prejudiced, and that five of the accused were, in effect, the victims of judicial murder.

Altgeld issued a pamphlet of eighteen thousand words in which he presented his arguments with great clarity and logic, but this explanation could not allay the storm of abuse that fell upon him for his act. Those who had favored the sentences now raged at him in virtually every newspaper in the country, and those who had favored a pardon were angered that he had issued an absolute pardon and that the pamphlet exposed the errors of the judicial system itself. Altgeld was accused of being an anarchist; this was said by many editorialists to be the result of his foreign birth.

The charge that he was an anarchist seems absurd when one considers his use of the Illinois militia during the labor troubles of his term as governor. Only two weeks before he issued the pardons, he sent the militia to Lemont in response to a plea from local authorities that they could not maintain order in a labor dispute. In June, 1894, he sent the militia to Mount Olive, where striking miners were interfering with mail trains. These affirmations of the power of the state did not satisfy his enemies, because, unlike his predecessors, Altgeld used the militia only to maintain order, not to break the strikes.

This was one of several issues that led to Altgeld's break with President Grover Cleveland. In July, 1894, when the Pullman Company had locked out its employees, and federal troops had been dispatched by Cleveland to break the "strike," Altgeld, in a letter to the president, condemned his action on the grounds that sufficient Illinois militia were available on the scene to preserve order. The Chicago newspapers, still harping on Altgeld's supposed anarchism, wildly denounced him for this protest, but in fact violence did not occur until the federal troops arrived, and then Chicago police and the state militia put it down. In fact, the disorder actually ended when a company of Altgeld's militia killed seven men by firing point-blank into a mob.

This dispute was only one of Altgeld's quarrels with the president. Altgeld saw Cleveland as an unquestioning supporter of "government by injunction," the use of the courts to rule strikes illegal, and he condemned the Supreme Court when it struck down the federal income tax in 1894, in an opinion written by Cleveland's appointee, Chief Justice Melville Fuller. Altgeld saw little difference between Republicans and Cleveland Democrats on the tariff question or on the silver issue. By thorough study, he made himself the outstanding authority on the latter question in American public life, and he embraced the silver issue in 1895, calling for the coinage of silver to increase the money supply.

By this time, in spite of the campaign of vilification against Altgeld in the press for the Haymarket pardons and his stand on the Pullman dispute, Altgeld was the most influential Democrat in the country. With the laboring class throughout the country, he enjoyed an affection that verged on idolatry, and his stand on silver gave him a large following in the West and South. As a result, there is little reason to doubt that, had it not been for his foreign birth, he would have been the Democratic nominee for president in 1896.

As it was, he was clearly the master of the Democratic convention of that year. The platform reflected his views—free coinage of silver and gold at a ratio of sixteen to one, opposition to government by injunction, arbitration of labor disputes involving interstate commerce, protection of the rights of labor, and an income tax. Although he did not favor the nomination of William Jennings Bryan, Altgeld worked mightily for his election, even at the expense of his own reelection campaign. He did not want another term as governor—his finances had suffered from the economic depression of the time, and his health was bad—but he bowed to the party's wishes.

The Republican strategy, in the face of a national trend away from the gold standard, was to depict Bryan as the tool of the "anarchist" and communist Altgeld. Not for the last time in the nation's history, political profit was made from calling an opponent a communist. On October 17, 1896, in a great speech at Cooper Union, Altgeld took the fight to the enemy, arguing against government by injunction and against federal interference in the rights of states to maintain order within their own borders. Throughout the campaign, he literally rose from a sickbed to speak, sometimes seven or eight times a day.

In the Bryan debacle, Altgeld's defeat for reelection was probably inevitable, and he was defeated in the legislature as a candidate for the U.S. Senate. He returned to Chicago to attempt to rebuild his shattered finances, but he lost control of the Unity Building and returned to the practice of law. As governor, he had rejected a bribe of a half-million dollars from the Chicago traction magnate Charles Yerkes, and he had always favored public ownership of monopolies. On this platform, he ran unsuccessfully as an independent for mayor in 1899.

During the 1900 presidential campaign, Altgeld was still a powerful influence, as was evident in the Democratic Party's repetition of its 1896 stand on the silver issue, and he campaigned with great energy for Bryan. At this time, he was also condemning American policy in the Philippines. He died suddenly on March 12, 1902, a few hours after making a speech in Joliet, Illinois, that condemned Great Britain's treatment of captured Afrikaner (Boer) women and children in concentration during the South African War.

SIGNIFICANCE

During his governorship, John Peter Altgeld achieved much for Illinois in the improvement of existing state institutions and the building of others, and his use of the state's police power to preserve order reflected a deep conservative respect for the rights of property, contrary to the charge of anarchism leveled against him by journalistic hacks and by politicians who must have known better.

Altgeld's pardoning of Samuel Fielden, Michael Schwab, and Oscar Neebe, an act of courage with few parallels in American political life, was consistent with his stands on social and economic issues—stands that have been vindicated by history. In 1896, he forced the Democratic Party to commit itself for the first time to social reform, and the achievements of the Progressive Era and the New Deal were the fruits of the seeds he planted. Indeed, it is an irony of history that Altgeld is forgotten by most Americans, while Theodore Roosevelt, who once in a foolish speech called him an apologist for wholesale murder, is a hero of American Progressivism because he enacted much of Altgeld's program. Altgeld remains what the poet Vachel Lindsay called the "wise man, that kindled the flame."

—*Robert L. Berner*

FURTHER READING

Barnard, Harry. *Eagle Forgotten: The Life of John Peter Altgeld.* Indianapolis: Bobbs-Merrill, 1938. The definitive biography of Altgeld, not likely to be superseded, and the basic source for information on his early years.

Browne, Waldo R. *Altgeld of Illinois.* New York: B. W. Huebsch, 1924. The first biography of Altgeld, written out of profound respect for its subject and informed by a deep sense of social justice. Lacks a thorough account of Altgeld's pre-Chicago years. Valuable, though superseded by Barnard's biography.

Christman, Henry M., ed. *The Mind and Spirit of John Peter Altgeld.* Urbana: University of Illinois Press, 1960. Includes a useful though brief biographical account and a representative selection of Altgeld's writings, including the Cooper Union speech of 1896 and "Reasons for Pardoning Fielden, Neebe, and Schwab."

Ginger, Ray. *Altgeld's America.* New York: Funk & Wagnalls, 1958. A thorough study of Altgeld's achievements in developing a progressivism that would adapt American political idealism to modern industrial conditions.

Pegram, Thomas R. *Partisans and Progressives: Private Interests and Public Policy in Illinois, 1870-1922.* Urbana: University of Illinois Press, 1992. Pegram describes how Progressives in Chicago and other parts of Illinois sought to implement reforms and create a more efficient government. Includes information about Altgeld's governorship.

Whitlock, Brand. *Forty Years of It.* New York: D. Appleton, 1925. Whitlock served in the Illinois government during Altgeld's governorship and was his close associate. This autobiography provides a firsthand account of events surrounding the Haymarket pardons and the Pullman dispute.

Wish, Harvey. "Altgeld and the Progressive Tradition." *American Historical Review* 46 (July, 1941): 813-831. Emphasizes the progressivism of Altgeld's social and economic beliefs. Puts his career in a perspective that is frequently lacking in accounts that concentrate on his role in the Haymarket case.

SEE ALSO: Grover Cleveland.

RELATED ARTICLES in *Great Events from History: The Nineteenth Century, 1801-1900:* December 8, 1886: American Federation of Labor Is Founded; May 11-July 11, 1894: Pullman Strike; November 3, 1896: McKinley Is Elected President.

HANS CHRISTIAN ANDERSEN
Danish writer

Andersen is the best-known Danish writer. His greatest achievement was as the author of universally beloved fairy tales, such as "The Princess and the Pea," "Thumbelina," "The Little Mermaid," and "The Emperor's New Clothes."

BORN: April 2, 1805; Odense, Denmark
DIED: August 4, 1875; Rolighed, near Copenhagen, Denmark
AREA OF ACHIEVEMENT: Literature

EARLY LIFE

Hans Christian Andersen was the first notable Danish writer of proletarian origins. He grew up with little education and in extreme poverty, and his great personal charm and exceptional talent earned him the affection and regard of both the common people and the artistic and social aristocracies of his time. Andersen's father was a shoemaker but was well read; he took his son to the theater, introduced him to books, and even built a little puppet theater for him. Andersen's mother, who eventually became a washerwoman, came from a world of hardship and penury. Illiterate and superstitious, she was one of three illegitimate daughters raised in an atmosphere of poverty and promiscuity; she turned to drink in her old age.

Although he received little formal education, Andersen developed performing skills that brought him to the attention of Prince Christian at Odense Castle. In spite of this distinction, he received little encouragement and was pressured to enter a conventional trade. Reluctant to give up his dream of becoming an actor and living a life of adventure, Andersen left for Copenhagen in 1819 with the blessings of his mother, who had been told by a fortune-teller that the entire town would one day be illuminated to celebrate her son's great achievements.

In Copenhagen, Andersen found little success in the theater but made friends among the most prominent members of society as well as among poets and scientists. Particularly important was his friendship with Jonas Collin, a senior civil servant and principal adviser to the king who supervised Andersen's return to school to acquire a passable education and who acted as a second father. Andersen demonstrated that in spite of his strange appearance—a lanky body, loosely swinging arms, enormous feet, and a face with a long nose and broad cheekbones—he possessed a charismatic personality that led many important people to help him succeed as an artist. By the early 1830's, he had won favor with the public, critics, and fellow poets with his poetry and, despite his unpromising origins, had been welcomed into the upper echelons of Danish society. It was in 1830 that he also fell in love for the first time, with Riborg Voigt, the sister of an old school friend. His despondency over her rejection of him, combined with his restless nature, led him to begin a lifetime of almost incessant travel.

LIFE'S WORK

By 1831, Andersen had realized his dream of world fame, having made a name for himself as a lyric poet, dramatist, and travel writer. His greatest achievements came, however, in 1835 with the publication of his first fairy tales and his first novel, *Improvisatoren* (1835; *The Improvisatore*, 1845), the somewhat autobiographical story of a Danish boy who goes from rags to riches. Succeeding novels, *O. T.* (1836; English translation, 1845) and *Kun en Spillemand* (1837; *Only a Fiddler*, 1845), were also based on his own life, depicting the bleak conditions of the poor and warning that Danish society was failing to recognize underprivileged artists. Favorably compared with the works of Sir Walter Scott and Victor Hugo, Andersen's novels were at the forefront of contemporary European fiction.

Although his novels were important and successful, Andersen's literary reputation has come to rest largely on his fairy tales, a short and unassuming form of fiction in which Andersen demonstrated his true genius. His first collection, *Eventyr* (1835; wonder tales), included stories of his own invention along with stories from his childhood and from the folklore of other countries. Unlike the scholarly collections of the folklorists Jacob and Wilhelm Grimm, however, Andersen's fairy tales were essentially creative and of high literary quality.

Like the tales of the Brothers Grimm, however, Andersen's tales were the product of the romantic movement, which inspired a new interest in the world of the common people and the child. In this regard, Andersen had the advantage of being from the common people himself. Never disguising the fact that he was the son of a poor shoemaker and a washerwoman, Andersen was perfectly capable of calling attention to the shortcomings of the upper classes. Andersen also retained a childlike quality that made it easy for him to speak to children on their level. At the same time, however, his stylistically sophisticated and even philosophical approach to his stories also drew an adult readership.

Andersen's stories include such well-known favorites as "The Princess and the Pea," "Thumbelina," "The Little Mermaid," "The Tinder-Box," and "The Emperor's New Clothes." These stories are notable for their strong romantic feeling and open sentimentality, for which Andersen is sometimes brought to task. His stories are also witty and playful, with a refreshing absence of obvious moralizing. Andersen continued to publish collections of fairy tales over the years, and the 1840's were an especially productive decade during which he perfected a style that discarded conventional literary diction in favor of everyday, colloquial speech.

Of special note is "The Ugly Duckling," in which a gawky and peculiar duckling turns into a beautiful swan, a tale that is very much the story of Andersen's own life. Another important story from this period, "The Nightingale," is a tribute to the celebrated singer Jenny Lind, known as the Swedish Nightingale, with whom Andersen fell in love in 1840; he unsuccessfully courted her in the years to come. Other notable stories of this period include "The Fir Tree," "The Snow Queen," "The Red Shoes," and "The Little Match Girl." In 1850 Andersen rounded off this rich decade with stories such as "The Shadow," "The Ice Maiden," "Auntie Toothache," and "Clod-Hans."

All in all, Andersen published 156 tales, which were eventually collected under the title *Eventyr og Historier* (1874; *The Complete Andersen*, 1949; also, *Fairy Tales*, 1950-1958; also, *The Complete Fairy Tales and Stories*, 1974). These stories were translated into more languages than almost any book except the Bible. Although humorous and entertaining, Andersen's stories have become classics because they also treat serious issues such as the struggle for love and recognition as well as the realities of loss, deprivation, and death. In addition, his stories affirmed the liberal and social humanism of the European Enlightenment and had a strong spiritual component, reflective of Andersen's belief that he was always under the protection of higher powers.

Andersen's gift for writing for children was the product of his own character, which remained childlike. Andersen was also emotionally fragile, with a thin skin and a nervous, irritable temperament. At times he could be a trying companion. Of particular note in this regard was his friendship with English novelist Charles Dickens, which began amid mutual admiration and affection but ended abruptly in 1856 when the eccentric Andersen overstayed his welcome as Dickens's houseguest. On the whole, however, Andersen had a remarkable gift for friendship. Poets and men of letters flocked around him wherever he went, and among his friends were an impressive number of outstanding European writers such as Heinrich Heine, Honoré de Balzac, and Victor Hugo; composers such as Felix Mendelssohn, Robert Schumann, and Franz Liszt; and numerous painters and performers. In addition, one of his closest friends was the Grand Duke Carl Alexander of Weimar. In fact, his universal fame led Andersen to be favored by the ruling classes all over Europe, a prerogative Andersen sought and felt he not only deserved but also desperately needed.

Although given accolades and surrounded by friends, Andersen was often a sad and lonely man. He never married, even though he fell in love at least twice, once with Riborg Voigt and later with Jenny Lind. In each case, his love was ultimately unrequited. To some extent, however, Andersen seems to have made a calculated renunciation of women in order to devote himself tirelessly to his creative life and to protect his sensitive temperament from the pressures of love and marriage. In spite of his gift for friendship, Andersen was always something of an outsider, and his travels were in part an escape from a lonely life.

Andersen's nomadic wanderings served also as voyages of self-discovery that fed his artistic temperament. As Andersen said in his autobiography *Mit Livs Eventyr* (1855; *The Story of My Life*, 1871), to travel was to live. In spite of his notorious phobias and general hypochondria, Andersen's strong sense of curiosity and need to explore led him on many intrepid journeys. By the end of his life, Andersen had gone abroad thirty times in all, traveling all over Europe, especially to Italy, France, and Germany, and by all means available, including carriage, horseback, stagecoach, steamship, and railroad. He even ventured into North Africa and Asia Minor and wrote many books about his travels, the best of which is *En digters bazar* (1842; *The Poet's Bazaar*, 1846). By the end of his life, Andersen had become Denmark's greatest storyteller and greatest travel writer.

SIGNIFICANCE

In his later years, Hans Christian Andersen continued to write novels, plays, stories, and travelogues. It was the great achievement of his fairy tales, however, that gave Andersen literary immortality. As the product of both Andersen's genius and the romantic movement that welcomed the fairy tale as a source of wisdom and aesthetic merit, his tales have spread throughout the world. It is important to note that by 1843, Andersen had removed the phrase "told for children" from his tales even though various poor and spurious English translations of his tales in the nineteenth century consigned him to the nursery. In fact, it is likely that only adults may really understand his tales, especially his later ones.

With his impoverished origins and his strange personality, it seemed highly unlikely that Andersen would one day be found dining at the table of Danish king Christian VIII or receiving a knighthood from the king of Prussia. There were those who felt that his guiding motive as a writer was to be admired and loved by the upper crust of society. Be that as it may, his literary merit is unquestionable. He spent his old age not merely as a celebrated bohemian but also as a national institution. In 1867, he was made an honorary citizen of Odense, and, taking its cue from the fortune-teller's prediction that Andersen had recorded in his autobiography, the entire town was illumi-

ANDERSEN'S BEST-KNOWN FAIRY TALES

1835 "The Tinder-Box"
1835 "Little Claus and Big Claus"
1835 "The Princess and the Pea"
1835 "Little Ida's Flowers"
1835 "Thumbelina"
1836 "The Talisman"
1836 "The Little Mermaid"
1837 "The Emperor's New Clothes"
1838 "The Goloshes of Fortune"
1838 "The Daisy"
1838 "The Brave Tin Soldier"
1838 "The Wild Swans"
1838 "The Garden of Paradise"
1838 "The Flying Trunk"
1838 "The Storks"
1839 "The Elf of the Rose"
1840 "What the Moon Saw"
1840 "The Wicked Prince"
1842 "The Metal Pig"
1842 "The Swineherd"
1844 "The Angel"
1844 "The Nightingale"
1844 "The Ugly Duckling"
1845 "The Snow Queen"
1845 "The Elfin Hill"
1845 "The Red Shoes"
1845 "The Jumper"
1845 "The Bell"
1846 "The Little Match Girl"
1847 "The Sunbeam and the Captive"
1847 "By the Almshouse Window"
1848 "The Happy Family"
1850 "The Phoenix Bird"
1851 "The Pigs"
1851 "The Dumb Book"
1852 "In a Thousand Years"
1852 "The Story of the Year"
1853 "The Goblin and the Huckster"
1853 "The Pea Blossom"
1854 "Two Maidens"
1855 "The Money-Box"
1855 "A Leaf from Heaven"
1856 "The Thorny Road of Honor"
1857 "A String of Pearls"
1858 "Something"
1858 "The Marsh King's Daughter"
1859 "The Philosopher's Stone"
1859 "The Story of the Wind"
1859 "Ole the Tower-Keeper"
1860 "The Farm-Yard Cock and the Weather-Cock"
1861 "The Butterfly"
1861 "The Snow Man"
1861 "The Portuguese Duck"
1861 "The New Century's Goddess"
1863 "The Snowdrop"
1865 "The Windmill"
1865 "The Golden Treasure"
1866 "Our Aunt"
1868 "The Goblin and the Woman"
1868 "Peiter, Peter, and Peer"
1868 "Godfather's Picture Book"
1869 "The Court Cards"
1869 "Luck May Lie in a Pin"
1869 "Sunshine Stories"
1869 "The Thistle's Experiences"
1869 "Poultry Meg's Family"
1870 "The Candles"
1870 "Lucky Peer"
1871 "Dance, Dance, Doll of Mine!"
1871 "The Great Sea-Serpent"
1871 "The Gardener and the Manor"
1872 "What Old Johanne Told"
1872 "Auntie Toothache"
1873 "The Flea and the Professor"

nated in his honor. After he died in August, 1875, his funeral service in the cathedral in Copenhagen was crowded with mourners, including members of the Danish royal family.

—*Margaret Boe Birns*

FURTHER READING

Andersen, Hans Christian. *The Fairy Tale of My Life*. Translated by W. Glyn Jones. New York: British Book Centre, 1954. Andersen's autobiography depicts his life as a beautiful fairy tale that affirmed the existence of a loving God who directed all things for the best. This translation features color illustrations.

Andersen, Jens. *Hans Christian Andersen: A New Life*. Translated from the Danish by Tina Nunnally. Woodstock, N.Y.: Overlook Press, 2005. Comprehensive biography. The author (no relation to his subject) concludes that Andersen "never grew up," and describes how this quality was an asset in his tales, but a tragic detriment in his life.

Bloom, Harold, ed. *Hans Christian Andersen*. Philadelphia: Chelsea House, 2004. Collection of essays by Bloom, Elias Bredsdorff, Jackie Wullschläger, and others about Andersen's life and work. The fairy tale of Andersen's life, his heroes and heroines, and his place within the European literary tradition are among the subjects discussed.

Bredsdorff, Elias. *Hans Christian Andersen: The Story of His Life and Work, 1805-75*. New York: Charles Scribner's Sons, 1975. This is an indispensable, highly readable, and well-researched biography by a major Andersen scholar. A special section examines the fairy tales as works of great artistic merit that contribute to the mainstream of European literature. Among the photographs and drawings are some of Andersen's own illustrations.

Grobech, Bo. *Hans Christian Andersen*. Boston: Twayne, 1980. Grobech provides a solid introduction to Andersen's life told in an entertaining narrative style. The book includes studies of Andersen's fairy tales, his international influence, and his influence in the twentieth century. It can be read by the general reader as well as literary specialists.

Rossel, Sven Hakon, ed. *Hans Christian Andersen: Danish Writer and Citizen of the World*. Amsterdam: Rodopi, 1996. This scholarly collection of essays establishes Andersen as a major European writer of the nineteenth century. Special attention is given to his biography as well as his travel writing and fairy tales.

Spink, Reginald. *Hans Christian Andersen and His World*. London: Thames and Hudson, 1972. This basic introduction to Andersen's life and times is written in a simple readable style and with considerable psychological acumen. The book contains many charming photographs and drawings, including some of Andersen's own artwork.

Wullschläger, Jackie. *Hans Christian Andersen: The Life of a Storyteller*. New York: A. A. Knopf, 2001. In this English-language biography, Andersen emerges as a dissatisfied, lonely man, sexually confused, vain, anxious, and hypochondriacal. Wullschläger demonstrates how Andersen drew upon the complexity of his life to create his stories.

SEE ALSO: L. Frank Baum; Lewis Carroll; Jacob and Wilhelm Grimm; Engelbert Humperdinck; Oscar Wilde.

RELATED ARTICLES in *Great Events from History: The Nineteenth Century, 1801-1900:* 1812-1815: Brothers Grimm Publish Fairy Tales; May 8, 1835: Andersen Publishes His First Fairy Tales.

SUSAN B. ANTHONY

American feminist and social reformer

A gifted and tireless worker for feminist causes, Anthony was for five decades the preeminent voice and inspiration of the woman suffrage movement.

BORN: February 15, 1820; Adams, Massachusetts
DIED: March 13, 1906; Rochester, New York
ALSO KNOWN AS: Susan Brownell Anthony (full name)
AREAS OF ACHIEVEMENT: Women's rights, social reform

EARLY LIFE

Susan Brownell Anthony was the second child of Daniel and Lucy Read Anthony. Her mother, a sullen, withdrawn woman, grudgingly accepted her domestic role as housewife and mother of six. Susan loved but pitied her mother and learned from her more what to avoid than what to emulate. Her father, in contrast, always loomed large in his daughter's eyes. A radical Quaker, Daniel Anthony was liberal in creed and illiberal toward those who tolerated the social evils that he so adamantly despised. Strong-willed and independent of mind, Daniel Anthony taught his children to be firm in their convictions and to demonstrate their love for God by working for human betterment.

As an owner of a small cotton mill, Daniel Anthony had the means to provide for his daughter's education. A precocious child, Anthony took full advantage of her opportunities, first attending the village school and later receiving private instruction from a tutor hired by her father. At the age of seventeen, Anthony left with her older sister Guelma for a Quaker boarding school in Philadelphia. Anthony's seminary training, however, was cut short by the Panic of 1837. With mounting business debts, Daniel Anthony was forced to auction his cotton mill, homestead, furniture, and even personal belongings, and to relocate as a dirt farmer on a small tract of land outside Rochester, New York.

In response to the family crisis, Susan Anthony left boarding school, secured a teaching position, and began sending half of her two-dollar weekly salary home to the family. For the next decade, Anthony remained in the classroom, instructing her pupils in the three R's, even as she augmented her own education with extensive reading and study. Intelligent yet unpretentious, Anthony matured into an athletic, tall, and slender woman with thick brown hair and warm blue eyes. Hardly the ugly, unsexed "battle-ax" her future enemies portrayed her to be, Anthony was courted by several suitors and remained single largely because none of her admirers, in her opinion, equaled her father in character or conviction.

Like her father, Anthony was a reformer who yearned for a society free from the evils of slavery and alcoholism. An idealist but not a dreamer, Anthony worked actively in these reform efforts, serving during her twenties as president of the Canajoharie Daughters of Temperance. In 1849, at her father's request, Anthony resigned from teaching to take over management of the family farm near Rochester. This relocation enabled Daniel Anthony to devote his full attention to a new business venture (an insurance agency that eventually made him prosperous again). The move also allowed Anthony to commit herself more fully to reform activity.

LIFE'S WORK

While still a teacher in Canajoharie, Anthony read a newspaper account of a meeting in nearby Seneca Falls, where a group of sixty-eight women and thirty-two men issued a Declaration of Women's Rights. This declaration demanded free education, equality of economic opportunity, free speech, the right to participate in public affairs, and the right to vote. As a schoolteacher making only one-third the salary of her male colleagues, Anthony sympathized with many of these demands for equal rights. Her Quaker upbringing, however, had convinced her that no person should participate in a government that waged war or condoned slavery, and she was thus not yet ready to take up the cause of woman suffrage.

In 1851, while attending an antislavery lecture in Seneca Falls, Anthony met the renowned Elizabeth Cady Stanton. The two women developed an instant friendship that led to a strong partnership in reform work. Together they organized the Woman's State Temperance Society of New York and petitioned the state legislature for a prohibition law. On numerous occasions during the 1850's, Anthony left Rochester for Seneca Falls to care for Stanton's children while their mother was away on speaking tours.

Although agreeing with Stanton on most issues, Anthony for several years refrained from embracing Stanton's call for woman suffrage. Gradually, however, the arrogance and disregard of many male reformers for the rights of women altered Anthony's view. Finally, in 1853, after the male delegates of the New York Woman's Temperance Society monopolized the annual convention and rudely ousted Stanton as president, Anthony declared her full allegiance to the women's crusade for equal rights and political equality.

Anthony's political conversion brought new life to the fledgling woman movement. An experienced worker willing to assume the time-consuming chores that no one else wanted, Anthony labored around the clock for feminist causes, organizing women into local associations, scheduling conventions and arranging speakers, seeking contributions, and paying administrative expenses. During the winter of 1854-1855, Anthony personally visited fifty-four of the sixty New York counties, collecting signatures in support of legal rights for married women.

When the legislature failed to act, Anthony promised to return with petitions every year until the inequities were rectified. For five years the tireless Anthony kept her promise, and in 1860, following a stirring address by coworker Stanton, the New York legislature granted property and guardian rights to married women. Much to Anthony's and Stanton's dismay, however, two years later the same body repealed portions of the marriage reform bill. This setback confirmed what Anthony had been saying for a decade: Benevolent legislation alone was insufficient; women would be fully protected only when they enjoyed full political powers.

Susan B. Anthony. (Library of Congress)

For Anthony and her associates, the decade of the 1860's was eventful but largely disappointing. Before the Civil War, Anthony campaigned hard for the American Anti-Slavery Society, and during the war she helped establish the Women's Loyalty League to lobby for a constitutional amendment that would abolish slavery and guarantee civil and political rights for all Americans. Nevertheless, despite her lifelong commitment to black rights, after the war Anthony opposed both the wording of the Fourteenth Amendment, because it inserted the word "male" in reference to citizen's rights, and the Fifteenth Amendment, for its failure to include the word "sex" in protecting voting rights for all citizens.

Berated by her former allies, who insisted that women must not endanger the long-awaited liberation of slaves with additional demands for women's rights, Anthony countered the accusations by asserting that if reformers linked these two great causes, then the moment in history called by some "the Negro's hour" could be the woman's hour as well. This controversy ultimately split the women's movement. Following an explosive Equal Rights Association convention in 1869, Anthony and Stanton organized the National Woman Suffrage Association (NWSA), a "for women only" organization committed to the passage of a national woman suffrage amendment. The more conservative reformers established the American Woman Suffrage Association (AWSA), a rival body that focused its efforts at the state rather than the national level.

At this time, Anthony's commitment to feminist goals did not deter her from other reform activities. In 1868, Anthony organized the Working Woman's Association in a futile attempt to unionize woman workers and build female solidarity across class lines. In the same year, Anthony and Stanton allied themselves with the eccentric millionaire George Francis Train and began publishing a radical newspaper entitled *The Revolution*. On its masthead was the motto: Principle, not policy; justice, not favors. Men, their rights, and nothing more: Women, their rights and nothing less. This paper, which opened its columns to editorials on greenback currency, divorce laws, prostitution, and a variety of other controversial issues, survived only two years and left Anthony with a debt of ten thousand dollars. It took six years, but Anthony ultimately repaid the entire debt from income she earned delivering suffrage lectures on the Lyceum circuit. Following this experience, Anthony determined to disassociate herself from other controversial reforms and focus all of her energy on the crusade for woman suffrage.

In 1872, Anthony gained national media attention when she registered and voted in the presidential election. Several weeks later, a federal marshal issued her an arrest warrant for illegal voting. While awaiting trial, Anthony went on a whirlwind tour delivering the lecture "Is It a Crime for a U.S. Citizen to Vote?" Her defense was that the Fourteenth Amendment made her a citizen, and citizenship carried with it the right to vote. During her trial, the judge refused to allow her to testify on her own behalf, demanded that the jury render a guilty verdict, and fined her one hundred dollars. Outraged by this travesty of justice, thousands sent contributions to the NWSA treasury. Although she lost the trial, Anthony (who never paid the fine) won added respect for herself and her cause.

Anthony spent the last three decades of her life recruiting and training a new generation of suffragist leaders, including, among many others, Anna Howard Shaw and Carrie Chapman Catt. In 1889, at the age of sixty-nine, Anthony worked to secure a merger of the rival NWSA and AWSA. Three years later, she accepted the presidency of the unified National American Woman Suffrage Association, and she served in this capacity until 1900, when she passed her mantle of leadership onto her handpicked successors. As honorary president emeritus, Anthony remained the dominant figure in the movement until the time of her death in March, 1906.

SIGNIFICANCE

When Anthony joined the women's rights movement, women had little social, professional, or educational standing. They were denied the right to vote, to hold office, or to be tried by their peers. As wives, they lost their legal individuality, having no rights to inherit property, keep earnings, sign contracts, or claim more than one-third of their husbands' estates. As mothers, they lacked legal custody or control over their own children. By the time of Anthony's death, however, 80 percent of American colleges, universities, and professional schools admitted women. In many states women had legal control over their own earnings and property and, in case of divorce, generally were awarded custody of their children. Although much discrimination remained, reform legislation along with advances in the medical treatment of women had increased the life expectancy of women from forty to fifty-one years. In four states, women enjoyed full suffrage rights, and in the majority of the remaining states, women voted in school or municipal elections.

Many of these changes were in part a consequence of the Industrial Revolution, which freed many women from a portion of their domestic chores, created new opportunities for employment, and provided increasing numbers with the wealth and leisure to sponsor reform work. The improved status of American women, however, was also a result of the heroic efforts of individuals who endured decades of hardship and ridicule in their quest for equal rights. For more than half a century, Anthony campaigned tirelessly for feminist goals. A radical visionary, the "Napoleon of Feminism" was also a shrewd, practical politician who did more than any other reformer to change the minds of men toward women, and of women toward themselves. Although vilified throughout much of her career, by the time of her death Anthony was the heroine of a second generation of suffragists, who in 1920 would win the victory she had fought so hard to achieve.

—*Terry D. Bilhartz*

FURTHER READING

Barry, Kathleen. *Susan B. Anthony: A Biography of a Singular Feminist*. New York: New York University Press, 1988. Scholarly but readable biography, explaining how Anthony's family background, education, and Quaker upbringing, and the early temperance movement, produced a woman with a striving for social justice. Outlines Anthony's involvement in the abolition and suffrage movements.

Buhle, Mary Jo, and Paul Bulhe. *A Concise History of Woman Suffrage: Selections from the Classic Works of Stanton, Anthony, Gage, and Harper*. Urbana: University of Illinois Press, 1978. An abridged volume of the basic sources of the woman suffrage movement. Provides useful selections from the writings of Anthony and other eminent suffrage leaders.

DuBois, Ellen Carol, ed. *The Elizabeth Cady Stanton-Susan B. Anthony Reader: Correspondence, Writings, Speeches*. Boston: Northeastern University Press, 1992. Collection of letters, speeches, and other written works tracing the relationship and political development of the two women. DuBois provides critical commentary to illuminate the women's writings and experiences.

Edwards, G. Thomas. *Sowing Good Seeds: The Northwest Suffrage Campaigns of Susan B. Anthony*. Portland: Oregon Historical Society, 1990. Anthony traveled to Oregon in 1871, 1896, and 1905 to campaign for woman suffrage. Edwards uses newspaper accounts of her trips to describe how Anthony organized her campaign and obtained publicity and support for women's right to vote.

Flexner, Eleanor. *Century of Struggle: The Woman's Rights Movement in the United States*. Cambridge, Mass.: Harvard University Press, 1959. An overview of the women's rights movement that offers insights into the intellectual origins of American feminism. It remains the standard history of the suffrage crusade.

Harper, Ida H. *The Life and Work of Susan B. Anthony*. 3 vols. Indianapolis: Bowen-Merrill, 1898-1908. The authoritative biography, written with Anthony's assistance. The only source for numerous Anthony papers that were destroyed after its publication.

Lutz, Alma. *Susan B. Anthony: Rebel, Crusader, Humanitarian*. Boston: Beacon Press, 1959. A well-documented, straightforward biography. Informative, but like the other dated biographies, it makes no attempt to penetrate beyond the surface record of events.

Sherr, Lynn. *Failure Is Impossible: Susan B. Anthony in Her Own Words*. New York: Times Books, 1995. Excerpts from Anthony's speeches and letters. Sherr provides commentary about Anthony's life and career.

Truman, Margaret. *Women of Courage*. New York: William Morrow, 1976. A popular collection of biographical sketches of noted American women. The Anthony essay concentrates on her arrest, trial, and conviction for illegal voting in the 1872 presidential election.

SEE ALSO: Lucretia Mott; Anna Howard Shaw; Elizabeth Cady Stanton; Lucy Stone; Victoria Woodhull.

RELATED ARTICLES in *Great Events from History: The Nineteenth Century, 1801-1900:* May 10, 1866: Suffragists Protest the Fourteenth Amendment; May, 1869: Woman Suffrage Associations Begin Forming; December, 1869: Wyoming Gives Women the Vote; June 17-18, 1873: Anthony Is Tried for Voting; March 9, 1875: *Minor v. Happersett*; July 4, 1876: Declaration of the Rights of Women; February 17-18, 1890: Women's Rights Associations Unite.

JOHNNY APPLESEED

American pioneer and agriculturalist

A legendary figure in American frontier history, Johnny Appleseed introduced apple trees to the Ohio Valley, where the seeds he planted helped to make apple orchards an important part of midwestern agricultural development.

BORN: September 26, 1774; Leominster, Massachusetts

DIED: March 18?, 1845; near Fort Wayne, Allen County, Indiana

ALSO KNOWN AS: John Chapman (birth name)

AREAS OF ACHIEVEMENT: Agriculture, exploration

EARLY LIFE

John Chapman, who would become famous as Johnny Appleseed, was the son of Nathaniel and Elizabeth Chapman, modest inhabitants of the Worcester County, Massachusetts, town of Leominster. His mother died when he was two, and his father served in the American Revolution and remarried when he returned home from military service. The father then moved his family to the vicinity of Springfield, Massachusetts. As soon as he was grown, John Chapman yielded to a deep-seated urge to wander, on foot, through the frontier regions of the new republic. He headed first for western Pennsylvania, where he was listed in the 1801 census as a resident of Venango County.

After the conflict with American Indians in the Ohio territory was resolved by the victory of General Anthony Wayne at the Battle of Fallen Timbers in 1794 and the Greenville Treaty of 1795, settlers began to pour into the area. Chapman was far from the first to settle there, but he had made forays into Ohio—mostly to the valley of the Muskingum River—during the early years of the nineteenth century. By 1809 he had already moved his base to Ohio, where he bought two town lots in the town of Mount Vernon, which was to be his base for the next twenty years.

LIFE'S WORK

Around the beginning of the nineteenth century, Chapman had the notion of gathering apple seeds from the cider presses that were ubiquitous in every frontier community and planting them on uninhabited land along the banks of a stream or a river. Wherever he found a productive plot, he planted apple seeds and created nurseries from which he later offered seedlings to the surrounding settlers. Most of his nurseries were located on the floodplains of the many streams that flowed southward toward the Muskingum River, which, in turn, flowed farther southward until it reached the Ohio River. Chapman's methodology consisted of locating a suitable planting site during the early spring and planting the seeds that he carried with him in a sack. Before moving on, he would locate a nearby settler and arrange for that individual to keep an eye on his new nursery and to arrange for the subsequent transplantation of seedlings to the clearings of the new settlements.

It has often been objected that because apples do not "grow true" from seed but can only be properly propagated by grafting scions or new twigs from an existing tree onto the "root stock" of a smaller tree, Chapman's efforts were those of an itinerant rustic. There were, however, both practical and ideological reasons for Chapman's methodology. According to legend, when someone tried to convince Chapman of the superiority of grafting, he replied, "They can improve the apple in that way but that is only a device of man, and it is wicked to cut up trees that way. The correct method is to select good seeds and plant them in good ground and God only can improve the apples." For Chapman, then, grafting was artificial, and planting seeds was the natural way to expand orchards.

On the practical level, securing and carrying scions from established orchards on the East Coast over frontier roads posed real problems. Keeping the scions moist and viable over the long periods needed to make the trek was difficult, and they required far more space than seeds. It had, however, been done. In the first years of the nineteenth century, General Rufus Putnam had brought scions from the famous Putnam Orchards of Connecticut and developed a substantial quantity of grafted trees at the mouth of the Muskingum River near Marietta, Ohio.

Johnny Appleseed. (Library of Congress)

By 1808 the area boasted 774 acres of apple orchards composed largely of grafted trees.

Despite the criticism, there was still practical merit in Chapman's technique. Most apples in the frontier settlements wound up as cider, and the apples produced by ordinary seedlings were perfectly adequate for this purpose. Cider was drunk in huge quantities by the early settlers. Some of it went on to become hard cider, or apple brandy, which also enjoyed widespread popularity. For such purposes, wild apples—the kind produced by trees grown from seed—were fully adequate, and occasionally the throw of the genetic dice would produce a tree bearing outstanding apples.

The result of Chapman's efforts was that an apple orchard existed on virtually every new farm created in the Ohio wilderness. The apples were used for cider, dried to make fruit that could last through the winter, or turned into apple butter. Those who had cold cellars could keep some apples fresh through the winter. The part of the crop that wound up as apple brandy was drunk throughout the region, and some even found its way down the Ohio River to New Orleans, Louisiana, where it had commercial value.

After the War of 1812, Chapman became an itinerant peddler of his seedlings, for he had nurseries throughout central Ohio. He had also become a convert to the religious philosophy of Emanuel Swedenborg, who stressed the reality of the spirit as opposed to its bodily incarnation. This philosophy appealed to such a fervent lover of nature as Chapman, and he combined peddling his seedlings with pushing Swedenborg's ideas. Thanks in large part to his missionary efforts, a number of Swedenborgian communities arose in the area, and Chapman occasionally preached at such gatherings. He distributed tracts at every isolated farmhouse and often discussed the ideas they contained with the inhabitants.

Also after the war, when settlement of Ohio resumed, Chapman began buying land in sizable pieces rather than just the town lots of Mount Vernon. He began leasing school lots for ninety-nine years, with no rent due for the first three, during which the lessee had to clear three acres and build a cabin. The rent that became due, annually, after the first three years was supposed to provide funding for schools. At one time or another, Chapman had leases on at least five parcels of 160 acres each. Although he eventually lost all these leases through failure to pay the annual rent, he did clear the necessary three acres and build a cabin on several, and he planted a nursery on at least one. A major reason that Chapman was unable to retain ownership of the school-lot leases was the depression that hit the country during the early 1820's. The experience caused him to scale back his acquisitions and occasionally lease a small, one-half-acre plot from a settler in order to plant a nursery on the site.

At the same time, sensing that the frontier had moved westward, Chapman began to explore the section of northwestern Ohio that had previously been reserved for American Indians. In this region, the Maumee River flows northward, while across the border in Indiana the Wabash River flows southward; the watersheds of the two rivers are separated by only a small ridge of land. By 1834 Chapman had again begun to purchase land in large blocks in the Fort Wayne, Indiana, area. In that year he purchased one forty-two-acre plot and one ninety-nine-acre plot. In 1836 he was back at the Fort Wayne Land Office to purchase two more parcels, one of eighteen acres and another of seventy-four. In 1838 he bought forty acres northwest of Fort Wayne. Much of the remainder of his life was spent developing these Indiana holdings with the assistance of his brother-in-law, William Broom, who, with his wife Persis, had followed Chapman first to Ohio and then to Indiana.

Chapman first ventured into Indiana only in the spring and summer. In the fall he would return to Ohio, often staying with his sister and brother-in-law, the Brooms, over the winter. By the late 1830's, however, he had transferred his activities almost wholly to Indiana, returning only occasionally and briefly to Ohio. It was near Fort Wayne that he died on or near March 18, 1845.

SIGNIFICANCE

The legend of Johnny Appleseed began during Chapman's lifetime but ballooned after his death. A major boost to the legend, hitherto largely an oral tradition, was the publication, in 1871, of an article in *Harper's Magazine*. After the article, many people came forward to add anecdotes to the legend. Prior to that time, Chapman had been largely remembered in horticultural circles. T. S. Humerickhouse published an article praising Chapman as a nurseryman in *Hovey's Magazine of Horticulture* in 1846. In the same year, Henry Howe, an author of local histories, began producing a history of Ohio's counties in which Chapman figured. In 1858 the first fictional account of Chapman appeared in James F. McGaw's novel *Philip Seymour*. In 1904 a novel entitled *The Quest of John Chapman* by Newell Dwight Hillis ascribed Chapman's itinerant lifestyle to blighted love. Johnny Appleseed has also appeared in a number of poems, the most famous of which is Vachel Lindsay's "In Praise of Johnny Appleseed."

Various memorials to Johnny Appleseed have been erected over the years. Fort Wayne created a Johnny Appleseed Commission, and its secretary, Robert C. Harris, researched some of the historical details of his life. In 1935 the Optimist Club of Fort Wayne erected a monument at the site where Chapman is believed to have been buried. His career in Ohio is memorialized by monuments in Ashland, Mansfield, and the vicinity of Mifflin. The city of Leominster, whose public librarian, Florence Wheeler, uncovered the details of Chapman's birth there, set up a monument (later taken down to prevent vandalism) and now has a large sign proclaiming Leominster as the "birthplace of Johnny Appleseed." Commemorative celebrations have been held in both Fort Wayne and Leominster.

—Nancy M. Gordon

FURTHER READING

Hensley, Tim. "Apples of Your Eye." *Smithsonian* 33, no. 8 (November, 2002): 110. Examines efforts to save America's apple heritage, surveys the history of apple growing in the United States, and recounts Chapman's story.

Hurt, Douglas. *The Ohio Frontier: Crucible of the Old Northwest, 1726-1830.* Bloomington: Indiana University Press, 1996. Hurt, author of other scholarly books on American agriculture, provides a comprehensive account of the early days of settlement in Ohio. The book provides the setting for Chapman's early nurseries and gives some account of Chapman's career.

Jones, Robert Leslie. *History of Agriculture in Ohio.* Kent, Ohio: Kent State University Press, 1983. Jones places Chapman's work in the context of agricultural development in Ohio.

Jones, William Ellery, ed. *Johnny Appleseed, a Voice in the Wilderness: The Story of Pioneer John Chapman, a Tribute.* 7th ed. West Chester, Pa.: Chrysalis Books, 2000. Jones, founder of the Johnny Appleseed Heritage Center in Ohio, edited this collection of essays about Chapman's life and legend. Includes an essay by Robert Price about Appleseed's depiction in folklore and literature, and an essay about Chapman's religion.

Lindsay, Vachel. *Johnny Appleseed and Other Poems.* New York: Macmillan, 1928. Contains Lindsay's poetic tribute to Johnny Appleseed.

Price, Robert. *Johnny Appleseed: Man and Myth.* Bloomington: Indiana University Press, 1954. Price devoted many years to searching out the historical truth about Johnny Appleseed, and it is reported in this book. Price separates truth from myth and reviews the documentary records of Chapman's life, notably his numerous land purchases. Indispensable for a historical appreciation of Johnny Appleseed.

Thoreau, Henry David. *Wild Apples.* Boston: Houghton Mifflin, 1923. Another lover of the wilderness explains the potential of the wild apple trees that still dot the landscape.

SEE ALSO: Luther Burbank; Washington Irving; Cyrus Hall McCormick.

RELATED ARTICLES in *Great Events from History: The Nineteenth Century, 1801-1900:* Summer, 1831: McCormick Invents the Reaper; July 14, 1833: Oxford Movement Begins; October 14, 1834: Blair Patents His First Seed Planter; November 24, 1874: Glidden Patents Barbed Wire; 1890: U.S. Census Bureau Announces Closing of the Frontier.

MATTHEW ARNOLD

English poet and literary critic

One of the finest elegiac poets in the English language, Arnold was also considered the greatest British literary and cultural critic of the Victorian era.

BORN: December 24, 1822; Laleham, England
DIED: April 15, 1888; Dingle Bank, Liverpool, England
AREA OF ACHIEVEMENT: Literature

EARLY LIFE

Matthew Arnold was born in a small English town on the River Thames near London. His father, Thomas Arnold, conducted a school there; his mother, Mary Penrose Arnold, was an Anglican clergyman's daughter. The Arnolds were a closely knit family; Matthew, the second of nine children, was especially devoted to his older sister, Jane. He had a close relationship with his mother until her death in 1873, and his father's influence on him was crucial. In 1828, the Arnold family moved to Rugby, and in the years that followed, Thomas Arnold became famous as an educational and religious leader.

As headmaster of Rugby School, Thomas Arnold instituted reforms designed to regenerate his students' moral, spiritual, and intellectual lives and to prepare them to become responsible leaders in a rapidly changing society. A notable writer on the religious and political issues of the day, Thomas Arnold was a proponent of a broadly Christian and unified national church. Throughout his career, Thomas Arnold also devoted himself to the study and teaching of history. This devotion, along with his ethical seriousness, his activity as an educational reformer, and his engagement in religious controversies, helped to shape his son Matthew's interests and thinking throughout his adult life.

In his boyhood and youth, however, Matthew Arnold did not prove to be a particularly devoted or distinguished student. Because he failed to progress under private tutorship at home, he was sent away for two years (1831-1832) to his uncle's strict school at Laleham. There, he felt exiled from his family. When he returned home to study with a private tutor, he became a somewhat more conscientious—though certainly not brilliant—student, and he began to develop a love of poetry. His family and his environment helped this love to grow.

In 1831, the Arnolds had begun to make summer trips to the Lake District, where the poets Robert Southey and William Wordsworth lived, and in 1833-1834, they built a summer residence at Fox How, near Wordsworth's home. Thus the Wordsworths and the Arnolds became friends. Wordsworth's poetry eventually was to influence Arnold's at least as much as any other English poet's; many of Arnold's poems directly echo or respond to Wordsworth. A significant part of the drama of Arnold's career as a poet and critic, in fact, arises from his sad realization that, whether for personal or cultural reasons, he was unable to speak to the Victorian age as Wordsworth had to the Romantic: "But where will Europe's latter hour/ Again find Wordsworth's healing power?"

After spending a year at Winchester, the public school his father had attended, Arnold came back to Rugby School, where he studied from 1837 to 1841. There, in 1840, he met Arthur Hugh Clough (1819-1861), a brilliant scholar and accomplished poet who was to become his close friend at Oxford. This important friendship continued until Clough's death. In his conversations and correspondence with Clough, Arnold began to develop and articulate many of his ideas, feelings, and values relating to poetry and modern life. In his letters, Arnold criticized Clough's poetry as overly topical and intellectual, but he also found fault with his own poems. His chief target, however, was his age: "Reflect too, as I cannot but do here more and more, in spite of all the nonsense some people talk, how deeply *unpoetical* the age and all one's surroundings are. Not unprofound, not ungrand, not unmoving:—but *unpoetical*." Arnold wrote these words in 1849, and in much of his later work as a critic, he would proceed from that point of view.

A decade earlier, however, when he was still a student at Rugby, no one would have predicted such concern on his part, least of all his father, who worried constantly about Arnold's apparent carelessness about his studies. A normal adolescent, Arnold chose to react against his father's high seriousness by devoting much time to fishing, hunting, enjoying himself with casual acquaintances, and dressing in elegant clothes. He adopted the insouciant air of a dandy at Rugby, but his mask of sophistication slipped occasionally. Beneath the mask one could find, on one hand, a prankster: During his final year at Rugby, having been asked to stand behind his father's chair, he decided to take advantage of the occasion by making faces at the other students. On the other hand, he managed to write a fair amount of poetry at Rugby, to win a prize for his long poem "Alaric at Rome" in 1840, and, ultimately, to win a scholarship to Balliol College at Oxford, where he began his studies on October 15, 1841.

During his university years, Arnold continued much in the same pattern he had set at Rugby. Elegant and lively, he enjoyed himself immensely and took a casual attitude toward his studies: "The life of Oxford," he wrote in 1851, was "the *freest* and most delightful part, perhaps, of my life, when . . . I shook off all the bonds and formality of the place." At this time, however, several people and events helped move him toward a steadier, more purposeful course in life. He was influenced by the thinking of John Henry Newman and by his father's opposition to the Oxford Movement, through which Newman and his intellectual party seemed to be leading the Church of England toward Roman Catholicism.

Thomas Arnold was appointed to a professorship of history at Oxford in 1841 but died suddenly in June, 1842. Matthew Arnold felt the loss deeply. His friendship with Clough strengthened after his father's death, and together they read and were impressed by the social thought of Thomas Carlyle. In 1843, Arnold won the prestigious Newdigate Prize for his poem "Cromwell," which reflected his feelings about his father's death. This award led him to decide that he wanted seriously to be a poet. He began writing the poems that would eventually appear in 1849 in his first volume of verse, *The Strayed Reveller, and Other Poems*.

Arnold's intensified focus on writing poetry did not lead him to amend his careless study habits. He left Oxford in 1844 with a second-class degree after a mediocre performance on his final examinations. His second-class degree embarrassed him and disappointed his family; he redeemed himself after a year of teaching and study at Rugby by winning, as his father had done years before, a fellowship at Oriel College, Oxford. There, he read widely in philosophy and literature and developed broad intellectual interests: He read extensively in German literature and philosophy; admired the novels of George Sand, whom he called upon during a trip to France and

THE FUNCTION OF CRITICISM

Many objections have been made to a proposition which, in some remarks of mine on translating Homer, I ventured to put forth; a proposition about criticism, and its importance at the present day. I said: "Of the literature of France and Germany, as of the intellect of Europe in general, the main effort, for now many years, has been a critical effort; the endeavor, in all branches of knowledge, theology, philosophy, history, art, science, to see the object as in itself it really is." I added, that owing to the operation in English literature of certain causes, "almost the last thing for which one would come to English literature is just that very thing which now Europe most desires,—criticism"; and that the power and value of English literature was thereby impaired. More than one rejoinder declared that the importance I here assigned to criticism was excessive, and asserted the inherent superiority of the creative effort of the human spirit over its critical effort. And the other day, having been led by a Mr. Shairp's excellent notice of Wordsworth to turn again to his biography, I found, in the words of this great man, whom I, for one, must always listen to with the profoundest respect, a sentence passed on the critic's business, which seems to justify every possible disparagement of it.

Source: Selections from the Prose Works of Matthew Arnold, edited by William Savage Johnson (Boston: Houghton Mifflin, 1913).

Switzerland in the summer of 1846; and read the *Bhagavadgita* and other Asian writings.

In April, 1847, Arnold moved to London to become the private secretary to Lord Landsdowne, then president of council in the Liberal government. In 1848 and 1849, he was devoted to the beautiful and gifted Mary Claude, whom he fictionalized as "Marguerite" in "Switzerland," a sequence of lyrics tracing the course of a failed love affair.

LIFE'S WORK

The twenty-seven poems in Arnold's first published collection, *The Strayed Reveller, and Other Poems*, strike a note that is predominantly melancholy, lonely, and introspective. Arnold's family and friends were very surprised, because they had heretofore known him as a debonair, lighthearted, worldly young man. Revealing through these poems a radical split between his outward behavior and inner feelings, Arnold himself exemplified one of the major themes of his poetry: the divided self.

In most of his major works, whether in poetry or prose, in fact, Arnold addresses questions of separation and division. His poems tend to define breaches; his critical prose defines, analyzes, and attempts to heal them. His poems articulate the loneliness, the confusion, the sense of disintegration that occurs when individuals feel alienated from nature, from their personal or cultural pasts, from God, or from other people—whether through conflicting aims and values, failed attempts at love, or death.

Neither Arnold's poems nor his prose were written in a vacuum. In 1851, Arnold became an inspector of schools, and for the next thirty-five years, he was intensely occupied with his travels in England and on the Continent, visiting schools and teacher-training colleges, administering oral and written examinations, and writing reports for the government on school conditions. This work was very demanding: In a single year (1855), for example, he visited 280 schools and institutions and examined 465 teachers and twenty thousand students. At the same time, he was building a family, to which he was deeply devoted: His appointment as inspector of schools made it economically feasible for him to marry Frances Lucy Wightman, a judge's daughter, in 1851; they had four sons and two daughters between 1852 and 1866.

Arnold wrote most of his major poetry between 1847 and 1853. His most important volume of poetry, *Empedocles on Etna*, appeared in 1852. Its title poem is now regarded by many as his major poetic achievement, although "Dover Beach" is his best-known poem. *Empedocles on Etna* dramatizes a Greek philosopher of the fifth century B.C.E. who chose to take his own life rather than face depression and spiritual death as a result of the split between his skeptical intellect and his feelings. Arnold decided to exclude this work from the new edition of his poems published in 1853, and in his famous preface to that volume, he explained his reasons for doing so.

Arnold asserted that poetry must not only interest but also "inspirit and rejoice the reader"; it must "convey a charm, and infuse delight." By depicting "suffering that finds no vent in action," *Empedocles on Etna*, he found, produced not joy but pain. Arnold went on in his preface to theorize about the nature of poetry, to discuss the shortcomings of the poetry of his day, and to recommend ways of addressing these defects—most notably through the study of classical Greek literature and the adoption of its principles.

The 1853 preface marks a watershed in Arnold's career as a writer. From this point onward, most of his major work was in the form of critical prose on literary, cultural, and religious topics. "Poetry," he wrote, "is a criticism of life"; it expresses what is best in human beings and helps to civilize them. Crucial to poetry's important office is the cultivation of the critical spirit, which Arnold defined as "a disinterested endeavor to learn and propagate the best that is known and thought in the world, and thus to establish a current of fresh and true ideas." Arnold himself became his century's finest exemplar of that spirit.

In works such as *On Translating Homer* (1861) and the two series of *Essays in Criticism* (1865 and 1888), Arnold attempted, in witty and lucid prose, to persuade his readers to combat their British insularity and contemporary narrowness by reading the literature of other places and times. He opposed the contemporary tendencies toward transitory topicality, subjectivity, vulgar shallowness, and concern with decorative fragments and instead advocated the classical values of universality, objectivity, moral depth, wholeness, and stylistic restraint. He was a great comparative critic and was aware, as his father before him had been, of the need to reevaluate constantly the present in the light of the past, and the past in the light of the present.

A number of Arnold's essays on literary topics were first delivered as lectures at Oxford University, where he was appointed for two five-year terms as professor of poetry. Among these works, "On the Modern Element in Literature" is of special note. He was required to deliver three lectures a year, and he was the first to give the lectures in English rather than Latin.

At the same time, Arnold continued his grueling career as a school inspector, and this work lent experiential authority to his criticism on educational, social, and political topics. His central achievement in that area is *Culture and Anarchy* (1869), a series of lectures on British political, social, and cultural life. In these lectures, he presented his idea of culture as "Sweetness and Light," a classical ideal of human perfection balancing beauty and intelligence; he criticized the British upper, middle, and lower classes ("Barbarians, Philistines and Populace"); he contrasted and called for a proper balance of the two human tendencies of "Hebraism" (moral awareness and strictness of conscience) and "Hellenism" (the critical urge to "see things as they really are"); and he attacked the idea that freedom consists merely in "Doing as One Likes." Although a number of his contemporaries chafed at Arnold's strictures in his cultural criticism (one reviewer called him an "elegant Jeremiah"), he became increasingly influential in his day. *Culture and Anarchy* has also had an important influence on twentieth century social thinkers.

Arnold turned next to writing and lecturing about religion. He published his thoughts in four books: *St. Paul and Protestantism* (1870), *Literature and Dogma* (1873), *God and the Bible* (1875), and *Last Essays on Church and Religion* (1877). The inquiries of nineteenth century biologists and geologists, rationalist philosophers, and biblical scholars had helped create a crisis of religious faith in the minds of many Christians. The Bible no longer appeared to be literally true, and much religious dogma had been called into question. In the light of these developments, Arnold's effort in his writings on religion was to define an intellectually honest approach to Christian faith, to preserve the spirit, if not adhere strictly to the letter (codified dogma and biblical fundamentalism), of Christianity, and to reassert the vital connection between faith and morality: "Religion is that which binds and holds us to the practice of righteousness."

During the late 1870's and early 1880's, Arnold wrote more essays about politics and literature; "The Study of Poetry," one of his most famous essays on literature, appeared in 1880. He made two visits to the United States: a lecture tour in 1883-1884 and a visit to his daughter, who had married an American, in the summer of 1886, just after he retired from school inspecting. Of all of his prose writings, the one he wanted most to be remembered for was *Discourses in America* (1885), three lectures from his tour: "Numbers: Or, The Majority and the Remnant," "Literature and Science," and "Emerson."

Arnold died of a heart attack in a suburb of Liverpool on April 15, 1888, at the age of sixty-five. He was buried at Laleham, the town where he was born, next to the graves of three sons who had died early. He was survived by his wife, Fanny Lucy, who died in 1901, and by two daughters and a son.

SIGNIFICANCE

In an 1859 letter, Matthew Arnold wrote:

> My poems represent . . . the main movement of mind of the last quarter of a century. . . . It might be fairly urged that I have less poetical sentiment than Tennyson, and less intellectual vigour and abundance than Browning; yet, because I have perhaps more of a fusion of the two than either of them, and have more regularly applied that

> fusion to the main line of modern development, I am likely enough to have my turn, as they have had theirs.

Arnold's self-estimate was prescient. His poetry articulates the problems and feelings of an age that is modern, and much of it is remarkably relevant to twentieth century society. Among Victorian poets, his importance is surpassed only by that of Alfred, Lord Tennyson and Robert Browning.

Arnold's legacy as a critic is even more significant. More than anyone else in the nineteenth century, he helped shape the course of literary studies and values in the modern university. His cultural and religious criticism has also been very influential. It continues to foster intellectual curiosity, a humanistic outlook, and deep moral awareness. His lucid and urbane style and tone have established him as one of the great masters of English prose.

—*Eileen T. Johnston*

FURTHER READING

Arnold, Matthew. *The Complete Prose Works of Matthew Arnold*. Edited by R. H. Super. 11 vols. Ann Arbor: University of Michigan Press, 1960-1977. The standard edition of Arnold's prose. Includes comprehensive critical and explanatory notes.

_____. *Letters of Matthew Arnold, 1848-1888*. Edited by G. W. E. Russell. 2 vols. New York: Macmillan, 1895. The standard edition of Arnold's letters. It is not complete, however, and many of the letters are abridged.

_____. *The Letters of Matthew Arnold to Arthur Hugh Clough*. Edited by Howard F. Lowry. London: Oxford University Press, 1932. These letters are an important record of Arnold's friendship with Clough; in them Arnold develops many of his ideas about poetry and life in the nineteenth century.

_____. *The Poems of Matthew Arnold*. Edited by Kenneth Allott. 2d ed. London: Longman, 1979. The second edition is the first fully annotated edition of Arnold's poems, including previously unpublished material. The poems are arranged by order of composition, and the editor includes informative headnotes about the composition, publication, and historical and biographical backgrounds of each poem.

Culler, A. Dwight. *Imaginative Reason: The Poetry of Matthew Arnold*. New Haven, Conn.: Yale University Press, 1966. The best study of Arnold's poetry.

Hamilton, Ian. *A Gift Imprisoned: The Poetic Life of Matthew Arnold*. London: Bloomsbury, 1998. Although he was a gifted poet, Arnold stopped writing poetry and focused on prose criticism in his later years. Hamilton explores the reasons for Arnold's decision and demonstrates the tension between passion and repression in his poetry.

Honan, Park. *Matthew Arnold: A Life*. New York: McGraw-Hill, 1981. The most comprehensive biography of Arnold to date. Includes much previously unpublished information about Arnold and his family drawn from unpublished letters, journals, and diaries.

Machann, Clinton. *Matthew Arnold: A Literary Life*. New York: St. Martin's Press, 1998. Explains how Arnold's poetry and prose grew out of his life experiences.

Murray, Nicholas. *A Life of Matthew Arnold*. New York: St. Martin's Press, 1997. Uses information from Arnold's letters to paint a portrait of a social critic and masterful writer.

Trilling, Lionel. *Matthew Arnold*. New York: Columbia University Press, 1939. Rev. ed. Cleveland: World, 1955. Trilling calls his study "a biography of Arnold's mind." It is the best account of Arnold's ideas and career.

SEE ALSO: Thomas Arnold; John Henry Newman; Alfred, Lord Tennyson; William Wordsworth.

RELATED ARTICLES in *Great Events from History: The Nineteenth Century, 1801-1900:* 1828-1842: Arnold Reforms Rugby School; 1843: Carlyle Publishes *Past and Present*; November 5, 1850: Tennyson Becomes England's Poet Laureate.

THOMAS ARNOLD

English educator and social reformer

As the headmaster of England's Rugby School, Arnold professionalized the teaching profession and introduced reforms that helped to transform education in English public schools.

BORN: June 13, 1795; Cowes, Isle of Wight, England
DIED: June 12, 1842; Rugby, Warwickshire, England
AREAS OF ACHIEVEMENT: Education, social reform

EARLY LIFE

Born on the Isle of Wight, off the southern coast of England, Thomas Arnold began his education at home and later attended a school in Warminster, Wiltshire, and the great public school at Winchester. He did well in these schools, although he did display a youthful rebelliousness. In 1810, he began his university education at Corpus Christi College, Oxford. Arnold was enchanted by Oxford, and after three years of intense study, he received a first-class degree in humane letters in 1814 at the age of nineteen. His success at Oxford was followed by a fellowship at Oriel College, Oxford, and he looked forward to a teaching career as a don. At twenty-four, however, he fell in love, and with a professorship many years away, he had to resign himself to becoming a schoolmaster, taking in private pupils at Laleham. The school was a success, and Arnold was happy with the school and the large family surrounding him.

In 1827, Arnold's great opportunity came when he was elected headmaster at Rugby School. His application for the position was supported by Edward Hawkins, the provost of Oriel, who predicted in a letter that Arnold would "change the face of education all through the public schools of England." The public schools (the equivalent of private schools in the United States) at that time were notorious for floggings by the masters and the lawlessness of the pupils; they were described by the Reverend Bowlder as "the very seats and nurseries of vice." As Hawkins suggested, Arnold was to change all that.

Arnold was a young man, only thirty-two, when he became headmaster at Rugby. However, he was a man who had boundless energy and the assurance that he could transform the former nurseries of vice into places where a "really Christian education" was the aim. Arnold experienced moments of doubt about Christianity in his early years, just as he had been a rebel earlier, but those doubts and that rebelliousness were put aside as he confidently began to take charge at Rugby. Lytton Strachey describes the Arnold of this period as a man whose "outward appearance was the index of his inward character: everything about him denoted energy, earnestness, and the best intentions."

LIFE'S WORK

Rugby School had declined from a high of 381 pupils to a low of 123 when Arnold became headmaster. He planned to reverse that trend and put his educational ideas into practice. The first thing that he did was to make the whole sixth form (seniors) praepositors (prefects). The school became a republic, and the boys were to be responsible for their own government. In addition, Arnold cultivated the boys in the sixth form and through them changed the tone of the school. The former rowdiness was replaced by a mood of piety and respectability. In addition, Arnold's sermons and presence made the boys both fear and respect him, and they tried to live up to the ideal he set for them. Nothing less than total commitment would do.

Arnold's next major reform was to raise the status and salary of the undermasters. By this move, he turned them into a professional corps and replaced the earlier brutality and carelessness with dedication. The annual salaries of the undermasters rose from about 125 to 500 pounds, so Arnold attracted some of the most skilled and effective teachers to Rugby. As a result, Rugby boys began impressing others by their serious demeanor and their success in the Schools exams at Oxford and Cambridge. In turn, Rugby became more popular, and the decline in the number of students was reversed.

Arnold did not, however, make major reforms in the curriculum of the school. He maintained the emphasis on Latin and Greek texts and resisted any attempt to add science to the curriculum. He stated his educational ideal succinctly: "Surely, the one thing needful for a Christian and an Englishman to study is Christian and moral and political philosophy." That aim was achieved by the study of the Greek and Roman classics, not science or modern languages; Arnold even taught English history through those Greek and Roman texts. The study of science might be suitable, even useful, for the masses, but Greek and Latin remained the one thing needful for the future governors of the country and its far-flung empire. Arnold did, however, help to standardize the teaching of Latin and Greek by proposing a headmasters' conference and uniform textbooks.

Arnold did not approve of the incessant flogging that took place in the public schools of the time. He believed that it degraded both pupil and master, and he preferred to expel a boy rather than flog him. He did not, however, eliminate flogging altogether at Rugby. In a letter, he was proud to announce that he had flogged only seven boys during half of one school year. Arnold had few illusions about young boys, and he did not believe that they were "innocent." They were victims of Original Sin, and the evil within them had to be exorcized in order to make them display "a more manly and Christian standard of duty." This sense of duty was extended from the classroom to the playing fields, as can be seen in a novel written by a Rugby "old boy," Thomas Hughes: *Tom Brown's School Days* (1857).

Arnold had a strong belief in social reform and progress, and these views led to some conflicts with the more conservative parents of the boys at Rugby. Although Arnold's belief in the necessity of an established church and an aristocracy was hardly radical, his approval of the Reform Bill of 1832 and his essays and sermons disturbed many of the parents. As T. W. Bamford has noted: "Inevitably, one of them was moved to write a letter of protest to the local paper claiming that Arnold, as a Headmaster, ought to be non-political." That letter was followed by many others, and a campaign against Arnold began to gather supporters. Arnold survived this campaign but continued to have strong opposition to his rule at Rugby.

The next controversy in which Arnold became involved was the Oxford Movement. The movement began with the writings of John Keble, who wished to challenge the right of the state to appoint bishops in the Anglican Church. Keble saw the church as an Apostolic institution rather than one controlled by the secular arm. E. B. Pusey and John Henry Newman joined the Oxford Movement and published a number of tracts supporting this position. Arnold's Christianity was rooted in the life and example of Jesus Christ, and the Oxford Movement struck at his first principles. As he said in a letter to one of his pupils, "The moral fault . . . is in the

KNOWLEDGE

During his years as headmaster of England's Rugby School, Thomas Arnold developed a theory of teaching that balanced wisdom and knowledge. This extract from one of his lectures articulates some of his views on that subject.

Yet it is true that I described the change from childhood to manhood, as a change from ignorance to wisdom. I did so, certainly; but yet, rare as knowledge is, wisdom is rarer; and knowledge, unhappily, can exist without wisdom, as wisdom can exist with a very inferior degree of knowledge. We shall see this, if we consider what we mean by knowledge; and, without going into a more general definition of it, let us see what we mean by it here. We mean by it, either a knowledge of points of scholarship, of grammar, and matters connected with grammar; or a knowledge of history and geography; or a knowledge of mathematics: or, it may be, of natural history; or, if we use the term, "knowledge of the world," then we mean, I think, a knowledge of points of manner and fashion; such a knowledge as may save us from exposing ourselves in trifling things, by awkwardness or inexperience. Now the knowledge of none of these things brings us of necessity any nearer to real thoughtfulness, such as alone gives wisdom, than the knowledge of a well-contrived game. Some of you, probably, well know that there are games from which chance is wholly excluded, and skill in which is only the result of much thought and calculation. There is no doubt that the game of chess may properly be called an intellectual study; but why does it not, and cannot, make any man wise? Because, in the first place, the calculations do but respect the movements of little pieces of wood or ivory, and not those of our own minds and hearts; and, again, they are calculations which have nothing to do whatever with our being better men, or worse, with our pleasing God or displeasing him. And what is true of this game, is true no less of the highest calculations of Astronomy, of the profoundest researches into language; nay, what may seem stranger still, it is often true no less of the deepest study even of the actions and principles of man's nature; and, strangest of all, it may be, and is often true, also, of the study of the very Scripture itself; and that, not only of the incidental points of Scripture, its antiquities, chronology, and history, but of its very most divine truths, of man's justification and of God's nature. Here, indeed, we are considering about things where wisdom, so to speak, sits enshrined. We are very near her, we see the place where she abides; but her very self we obtain not. And why?—but because, in the most solemn study, no less than in the lightest, our own moral state may be set apart from our consideration; we may be unconscious all the while of our great want; and forgetting our great business, to be reconciled to God, and to do his will: for wisdom, to speak properly, is to us nothing else than the true answer to the Philippian jailor's question, "What must I do to be saved?"

Source: Thomas Arnold, *The Christian Life: Its Course, Its Hindrances, and Its Helps* (5th ed. London, 1856), Lecture 3.

idolatry—the setting up of some idea . . . and then putting it in place of Christ."

Arnold felt compelled to oppose the movement in print, and he published "The Oxford Malignants" in the *Edinburgh Review*. In that essay, he described those in the Oxford Movement as "malignant fanatics" and accused them of "moral wickedness." Because of Arnold's tone as much as his content, he was attacked by the conservative press; one newspaper asked if the trustees would appoint a headmaster who wrote "in such a style as this." One of the trustees did ask Arnold if he were the author of such an article, but Arnold refused to answer and said that his private life and opinions were his own business. There was even a vote by the trustees on retaining Arnold, but the tie vote was not enough to oust him, and he remained headmaster. He did lose a bishopric, however, because of this incident; he was the top man on the list, but after the prime minister read Arnold's essay, he believed that Arnold was too controversial a figure to be appointed a bishop.

Arnold found relief from the burdens of his position as headmaster in the Lake Country of northern England, which has been celebrated by William Wordsworth. In fact, Arnold's summer home, Fox How, was close to Wordsworth's home, and they often met and talked. Arnold often invited his sixth-form students to visit him at Fox How, and while they were there, they saw not the stern headmaster but the nature-loving human being. Arnold's teaching function did not stop in the Lake Country. He spoke of showing his students "the mountains and dales, a great point in education . . . to those who only know the central or southern counties of England."

Arnold was also involved in scholarly work while he was headmaster. He published a three-volume edition of Thucydides and a three-volume (the third volume, however, was left unfinished) *History of Rome* (1838-1843). Arnold wanted to write a Roman history that would oppose the anti-Christian attitude in Edward Gibbon's great *History of the Decline and Fall of the Roman Empire* (1776-1788). For these scholarly achievements and his Liberal politics, Arnold was appointed Regius Professor of Modern History in 1841. He continued as headmaster of Rugby and lectured at Oxford when he could arrange it.

Arnold returned to Rugby full time in 1842 and was pleased to see that the school had continued to increase in reputation and enrollment. He fell ill, however, in June of that year and died on June 12, 1842, at the early age of forty-six. His reputation did not decline as a result of his early death; his pupils and disciples continued and enhanced the Arnold legend. Essays in the *Quarterly Review* and Arthur Penrhyn Stanley's *Life and Correspondence of Dr. Arnold* (1844) gave support to the earlier claim of Hawkins, and it became clear to all that Arnold had reformed not only Rugby School but also the whole public school system.

SIGNIFICANCE

Thomas Arnold's specific reforms did change and improve the public schools in England. However, Arnold's insistence that a Rugby education be Christian and emphasize a sense of duty was, perhaps, even more important. The whole tone of the school was altered, as was the relationship of student and master. After Arnold's death, new public schools such as Marlborough and Wellington were founded on Arnoldian principles. Older schools such as Repton and Winchester also changed their tone and became more like Rugby. In addition, several of Arnold's old praepositors became headmasters at such prestigious public schools as Harrow. The Arnold model became the model for nearly all the public schools in England and for many of the most important preparatory schools and universities in the United States.

Arnold was very much a man of his age. He believed, as many Victorians did, in progress. All that was needed to create progress was to reform certain institutions in the society. Arnold died too young to see his concept of reform and an ideal Christian state be dashed by the discoveries of Charles Darwin and the doubt and cynicism that plagued many Victorians, including his famous son, Matthew. What Arnold attempted and partially achieved, however, remains impressive. Matthew Arnold's poem on the death of his father, "Rugby Chapel," says it best:

> But thou would'st not *alone*
> Be saved, my father! *alone*
> Conquer and come to thy goal,
> Leaving the rest in the wild.
> We were weary, and we
> Fearful, and we in our march
> Fain to drop down and die.
> Still thou turnedst, and still
> Beckonedst the trembler, and still
> Gavest the weary thy hand.

—*James Sullivan*

FURTHER READING

Arnold, Thomas. *Thomas Arnold on Education*. Edited by T. W. Bamford. Cambridge, England: Cambridge

University Press, 1970. A very good brief introduction to Arnold's religious, social, and educational views, with a fine selection of Arnold's writings on education.

Bamford, T. W. *The Rise of the Public Schools*. London: Thomas Nelson and Sons, 1967. A detailed study of public schools since 1837; especially good on Rugby and Arnold.

_____. *Thomas Arnold*. London: Cresset Press, 1960. The best available intellectual biography of Arnold. Critically surveys his ideas and the controversies in which he engaged.

Copley, Terence. *Black Tom: Arnold of Rugby, the Myth and the Man*. London: Continuum, 2002. Examines Arnold's life and his influence as an educator, theologian, and churchman. Provides a more balanced view than previous uncritical biographies and Strachey's cynical perspective.

McCrum, Michael. *Thomas Arnold, Headmaster: A Reassessment*. New York: Oxford University Press, 1989. Focuses on Arnold's life and achievements as headmaster of Rugby School.

Strachey, Lytton. *Eminent Victorians*. New York: G. P. Putnam's Sons, 1918. An amusing if somewhat inaccurate study of Arnold's life; the insights are marred by sarcasm.

Wiley, Basil. "Thomas Arnold." In *Nineteenth Century Studies*. New York: Columbia University Press, 1949. A sensitive essay on various aspects of Arnold, including his love for the Lake Country.

Wymer, Norman. *Dr. Arnold of Rugby*. London: Robert Hale, 1953. An uncritical examination of Arnold's life and influence; the best book on Arnold the man.

SEE ALSO: Matthew Arnold; William Edward Forster; Henry Sidgwick; William Wordsworth.

RELATED ARTICLES in *Great Events from History: The Nineteenth Century, 1801-1900:* 1828-1842: Arnold Reforms Rugby School; December 3, 1868-February 20, 1874: Gladstone Becomes Prime Minister of Britain.

CHESTER A. ARTHUR

President of the United States (1881-1885)

Arthur's presidency, virtually free of corruption, comforted a nation grieving over the assassination of President James A. Garfield, maintained peace and order, promoted economic growth, and demonstrated the stability and adaptability of the American political system in crises.

BORN: October 5, 1829; Fairfield, Vermont
DIED: November 18, 1886; New York, New York
ALSO KNOWN AS: Chester Alan Arthur (full name)
AREAS OF ACHIEVEMENT: Government and politics, law

EARLY LIFE

Chester Alan Arthur was the oldest of seven children in a Vermont family. His mother, Malvina Stone, was a Canadian whose Baptist ancestors had immigrated from England. His father, William Arthur, was an Irish immigrant turned Baptist minister as well as a respectable scholar. Under the tutorship of his father, Arthur showed an intense interest in learning and a high aptitude in the subjects he studied, matriculating at Union College in Schenectady, New York (at that time, one of the best-known colleges in the East), on September 5, 1845, at the age of fifteen. He became a member of the Psi Upsilon Society, taught in the local schools to help defray the cost of his education, and in July, 1848, at the age of eighteen, was graduated with high honors, including membership in the Phi Beta Kappa honor society.

After his graduation from college, Arthur pursued his ambition to become a lawyer by enrolling in the law school at Ballston Springs, New York, where he studied for a few months, continuing his studies at home and teaching. In 1851, he became principal and teacher at the North Pownal Academy in Bennington County, Vermont, ten miles from his family across the border in Hoosick, New York. During Arthur's tenure as principal there, James A. Garfield served for a time as a faculty member, teaching business and penmanship—a circumstance that was to be fully exploited in the presidential campaign of 1880. In 1852, Arthur became principal of an academy at Cohoes, New York; in 1853, he continued his legal studies in the office of the prestigious firm of Erastus D. Culver.

On May 4, 1854, after having been certified to the Supreme Court of New York by the Culver firm that he had satisfactorily completed his studies, Arthur was admitted to the bar. He joined Culver's firm and began practicing law. In 1856, upon becoming a judge of the Civil Court of Brooklyn, Arthur formed a partnership with an old friend, Henry D. Gardiner. For three months, Arthur and his friend tried to establish a practice out West but returned to New York City after becoming disillusioned by widespread lawlessness. Two of Arthur's first and most celebrated cases involved the Fugitive Slave Law and discrimination against black people on New York City streetcars. As a staunch abolitionist, Arthur found in these two cases an opportunity to make a significant contribution to the antislavery movement.

As a Whig delegate from Brooklyn, dedicated to the abolitionist movement, Arthur participated in the convention that met at Saratoga in August of 1854, for the purpose of developing methods for combating the Kansas-Nebraska Act, which repealed the Missouri Compromise of 1820. The action of the convention led to the birth of the Republican Party. In the party's first campaign for the presidency, Arthur wholeheartedly supported and campaigned for the first presidential nominee of the Republican Party, John C. Frémont. During the campaign, Arthur served on an executive committee that worked for the election of Frémont. On election day, Arthur served as an inspector of elections at the polls.

In October, 1859, Arthur married Ellen Lewis Herndon, a member of a distinguished Virginia family and sister of a good friend, Dabney Herndon. Their union produced two sons (one son died at the age of four) and one daughter. Arthur's wife died in January, 1881.

Chester A. Arthur. (Library of Congress)

LIFE'S WORK

After joining the state's militia, Arthur gained extensive knowledge of military science, especially concerning strategy and logistics. His highly rated performance led to his appointment as judge advocate-general of the Second Brigade of the New York Militia. Having fully assisted him in his bid for reelection, the governor of New York appointed Arthur as engineer-in-chief and charged him with the responsibility of drawing plans to protect the state.

After the Civil War began, the governor promoted Arthur to the position of inspector general of New York troops in the field. Later, he was appointed assistant quartermaster general, then quartermaster general of New York, responsible for raising regiments to fight on the battlefields and maintaining the troops. While serving in the post of quartermaster general, Arthur got his long-awaited chance to participate in direct combat on the battlefields. He was elected first by the Ninth Regiment of the New York Militia and, second, by the Metropolitan Brigade of New York City to lead them in battle. Both times, the governor successfully dissuaded Arthur, persuading him to remain in his post as quartermaster general, wherein he ably carried out his responsibilities for the cause of the Union.

After he resigned his position following the election of a Democrat as governor of New York, Arthur spent much time in Albany and Washington working on war claims and drafting important bills that required quick action, soon becoming one of the best lawyers in New York. In 1866, Arthur helped Roscoe Conkling get elected to the U.S. Senate, then became his chief henchman until he became president.

In 1867, Arthur was elected to the Century Club, a prestigious intellectual and social organization, and was elected chairman of the executive committee of the New York Republican Party. In 1871, Arthur established one of the most outstanding law firms in New York; in the same year, President Ulysses S. Grant appointed him collector of the Port of New York—the most important political position outside Washington, D.C. Impressed with

Arthur's management of the Port of New York, Grant reappointed him to the collectorship, and the Senate confirmed the reappointment unanimously.

In 1878, however, President Rutherford B. Hayes dismissed Arthur from the collectorship on the grounds that his positions in the government and the Republican Party were incompatible with respect to civil service reforms. The outrageous scandals of Grant's two administrations had convinced Hayes of the dire need for an appreciable reform program in government designed to take politics out of the bureaucracy. The removal of Arthur was therefore not based on his competence but on the fact that, as a consummate politician, he had manipulated his position in a way that made him the undisputed "boss" of the Republican Party of New York City as well as chairman of the Central Committee of the Republican Party of the state. Upon his removal, a petition signed by some of the most reputable persons of the time, asking that Arthur be retained, was suppressed by Arthur. Like Garfield, Arthur never sought a position; he wished to retain the collectorship on his own merit, but as a result of a bitter struggle between the Hayes administration and the Conkling machine, he chose to return to practicing law.

In 1879, as chairman of the Republican Central Committee, Arthur worked hard to strengthen the Republican Party of his state—particularly the Stalwarts (1869-1880), the "regular" or machine wing of his party, who were opposed to the reform program of Hayes's administration—and, disregarding the two-term tradition honored by all the presidents since George Washington, strongly advocated and worked to secure a third term for Grant. In Chicago in June, 1880, at the Republican National Convention, destiny brought Garfield and Arthur together again as it had twenty-six years earlier at the North Pownal Academy in Vermont. This time their relationship was reversed: Arthur worked under Garfield. The nomination of Garfield and Arthur as candidates for president and vice president of the Republican Party startled the nation, including the candidates themselves.

Both men went to Chicago to do everything within their power to help get the leader of their wing nominated. A bitter struggle was expected between the Stalwarts and the Half-Breeds (a wing of the Republican Party, 1876-1884, that supported Hayes's conciliatory policy toward the South, opposed a third term for Grant, and supported the nomination of Garfield), but there were those who believed that the leaders would find a way to resolve the struggle with some kind of compromise. Finally, in order to end the deadlocked convention, the Half-Breeds turned to Garfield on the thirty-sixth ballot and nominated him to lead the Republican Party to victory in 1880. Because they knew that they had no chance of winning the presidency without the support of the Stalwarts, they offered the nomination for vice president to the second most powerful boss of the New York political machine, Chester A. Arthur.

Arthur's nomination was based on political strategy designed to produce some semblance of unity within the Republican Party. On the basis of the experiences of all the candidates available in 1880, Arthur was one of the least qualified to serve as vice president and had no qualifications that would have justified his nomination for the office of the president. Arthur was chosen because he was Conkling's right-hand man. Without the support of the New York political machine, the Republican Party could not win the election. At the outset, Conkling squawked at Arthur's decision to join the Garfield forces, but before the campaign ended, he gave some support.

As the campaign got under way in 1880, the jockeying by the various factions for control left the Republican Party in a state of disarray, and consequently, the opposing forces expediently closed ranks. One of the most thrilling national political conventions in American history produced one of the most unusual tickets in the history of presidential nominating conventions: The presidential candidate thoroughly qualified, with seventeen years of yeoman's service in the House of Representatives on behalf of the people of his district and the nation; the vice presidential candidate a skilled politician deeply tied to a powerful political machine, with all of his work experience limited to his home state, and with no experience that equipped him to serve as president. The ticket that had surprised the party, the nation, and the candidates themselves succeeded in achieving a narrow victory at the polls in November.

Only a few months after his inauguration, however—on July 2, 1881—Garfield was shot by a deranged office-seeker, Charles J. Guiteau, in a Washington railroad station. Eighty days later, Garfield died, and the agonizing wait of the people who had prayed so hard for his recovery came to an end. Arthur remained extremely apprehensive throughout the lingering death struggle, hoping that somehow Garfield would survive, recover, and resume his duties as president. When Arthur accepted the invitation to run on the ticket with Garfield, he did so on the basis that it would give him the opportunity to escape the continual and perplexing problems associated with his management of the political machine. After his removal from his position as collector of the New York

Customhouse by the outgoing President Hayes, Arthur regarded his selection as vice presidential candidate as a vindication of his integrity.

Garfield's tragic death cast the nation into a state of shock that for a while quelled the political discord that to an appreciable degree remained constant in the wake of the presidential campaign of the previous year. As the shock gradually subsided, however, consternation gripped the nation, for the office and power of the president had devolved on the second most powerful political boss in the country, who himself was the chief lieutenant of the most powerful boss in America. To allay such fears, Arthur gradually dissolved his relationship with Conkling and his machine.

During his term as president, Arthur fought hard for a canal in Nicaragua, owned and operated by the United States; advocated a program of reciprocal trade agreements; developed the first modern American steel navy; prosecuted those who defrauded the Post Office Department; and vetoed the Chinese Exclusion Act, changing the suspension of Chinese immigration from twenty to ten years. Possibly Arthur's greatest achievement was his strong support of the act that became the foundation of civil service reform—the Pendleton Act of 1883.

In addition, Arthur recognized the significance of issues that, although not resolved during his presidency, were later to confirm the soundness of his judgment. Among the recommendations Arthur proposed were statehood for Alaska, a building for the Library of Congress, a law determining who should count the electoral votes in order to avoid the type of dispute that occurred in 1876, and the regulation of interstate commerce. In order to avoid another presidential succession crisis, Arthur strongly recommended a constitutional amendment that would provide for the expedient resolution of questions pertaining to presidential succession. Arthur's proposal concerning presidential succession was ultimately realized with the ratification of the Twenty-fifth Amendment to the Constitution on February 10, 1967.

Arthur's long bout with Bright's disease (he had it at the time he assumed the presidency) failed to affect his administration significantly; it did, however, to a large extent prevent him from succeeding himself, which was an eventuality he very much desired. After his unsuccessful efforts to obtain the nomination of his party in 1884, his supporters in the Republican Party of New York tried to urge him for a seat in the U.S. Senate in their efforts to repair their badly damaged "machine." Because of his infirmity and lack of interest (after having been president, he considered campaigning for the Senate to be improper), he rejected the idea. He attended ceremonies opening the Brooklyn Bridge in May, 1883. Just before his term expired, Arthur dedicated the Washington Monument, on February 22, 1885.

After Arthur left office, he was elected president of his fraternity, Psi Upsilon, and elected head of the forerunner of the subway system of New York City, the New York Arcade Railway. Arthur died on November 18, 1886, at his home in New York City.

SIGNIFICANCE

Arthur showed that the aura of the office and power of the presidency can transform a politician wedded to a political machine into a president who dissociates himself from the machine and bases his policies and programs on what he deems best for the people and the nation. Under the leadership of President Arthur, the intense perturbation of the American people caused by the assassination of Garfield was greatly alleviated. Arthur demonstrated that a man of limited experience could be inspired by the prestige, office, and authority of the presidency to exploit his talents and experience to the fullest extent possible, to become an effective president.

When the leading historians in the United States were polled to rate the presidents, they evaluated their subjects as great, near great, above average, average, or below average, with a final slot reserved for outright failures. The historians assigned Arthur to the average class, along with seven other presidents: William McKinley, William Howard Taft, Martin Van Buren, Rutherford B. Hayes, Benjamin Harrison, Zachary Taylor, and Jimmy Carter. Arthur's rating indicates that he overcame his political handicaps and commendably performed his responsibilities as president.

—James D. Lockett

FURTHER READING

Brisbin, James S. *From the Tow-Path to the White House: The Early Life and Public Career of James A. Garfield, Including Also a Sketch of the Life of Honorable Chester A. Arthur.* Philadelphia: Hubbard Brothers, 1880. Classic work containing a readable story of Arthur's life.

Doenecke, Justus D. *The Presidencies of James A. Garfield and Chester A. Arthur.* Lawrence: University Press of Kansas, 1981. Revisionist work inspired by the renewed examination occurring during the centennial of the Gilded Age (1870-1896). Includes brilliant notes and bibliographical essays.

Howe, George Frederick. *Chester A. Arthur: A Quarter-Century of Machine Politics.* New York: Dodd,

Mead, 1934. One of the most significant biographical studies of Arthur. This was the only major scholarly biography of Arthur until the publication of Thomas C. Reeves's study in 1975 (see below). Howe's major thesis is that Arthur filled a place of power and responsibility far above his aspirations, bravely and adequately, if not with greatness.

Karabell, Zachary. *Chester Alan Arthur*. New York: Times Books, 2004. Brief biography, one in a series of books on American presidents, providing an overview of Arthur's life and career. Although Arthur enacted civil service reform, Karabell argues he was not a true reformer but a president who "conducted himself with honor when politics was venal and petty."

Levin, Peter R. *Seven by Chance: Accidental Presidents*. New York: Farrar, Straus, 1948. Study of the seven men who became president because of the death of a president. The most valuable section of the book is Levin's assessment of the method for choosing a vice presidential candidate and his suggestions for improving the vice presidency. An erudite work that provides an excellent source for studying the vice presidency.

Reeves, Thomas C. *Gentleman Boss: The Life of Chester Alan Arthur*. New York: Alfred A. Knopf, 1975. Covers Arthur's career in New York politics before he became president, demonstrating that he was a more skillful political organizer and manager than previous accounts indicate. Reeves's work provides a fresh view of Arthur and has become the standard biography.

Sievers, Harry J., ed. *Six Presidents from the Empire State*. Tarrytown, N.Y.: Sleepy Hollow Restorations, 1974. Scholarly study of the impact on the presidency of the six presidents from New York. They are divided into three pairs whose terms in office correspond broadly to three major historical eras, including Arthur and Grover Cleveland in the Gilded Age. Contains the Schlesinger polls on presidential greatness, a selected bibliography of New York's presidents and their contemporaries, and splendid illustrations of the six presidents.

SEE ALSO: James G. Blaine; James A. Garfield; Rutherford B. Hayes.

RELATED ARTICLES in *Great Events from History: The Nineteenth Century, 1801-1900:* May 9, 1882: Arthur Signs the Chinese Exclusion Act; January 16, 1883: Pendleton Act Reforms the Federal Civil Service; November 4, 1884: U.S. Election of 1884.

LUISE ASTON

German author and feminist

Aston was one of the pioneers of the modern feminist movement. Through her writings, she advocated emancipation and equal rights for women. She was also a prominent figure in the failed German revolution of 1848.

BORN: November 26, 1814; Gröningen an der Bode (now in Germany)

DIED: December 21, 1871; Wangen im Allgäu, Germany

ALSO KNOWN AS: Luise Hoche (birth name); Louise Aston

AREA OF ACHIEVEMENT: Women's rights

EARLY LIFE

Born Luise Hoche, Luise Aston (loo-EE-sur AHS-tahn) was the youngest daughter of Dr. Johann Gottfried Hoche, a conservative Lutheran minister and adviser to the church, and his wife, Luise Charlotte Berning Hoche, a disinherited German duchess. Aston received private schooling and was well educated, especially in music and literature. Many of her ideas were shaped in response to growing up during a period of harsh political and intellectual repression. At the time of her childhood, Germany was a collection of mostly small states governed by a quasi-feudal system that favored the rulers and oppressed the working class and peasants. Aston's concern over the social injustices and inequalities that she observed as a child became her lifelong motivation for seeking changes in society and government. She was attracted to radical ideas such as liberalism, nationalism, and equality for women.

LIFE'S WORK

In 1835, Luise Hoche married Samuel Aston, an English industrialist from Magdeburg who was twenty-four years her senior. Although the details surrounding the marriage are debated, it is generally believed that it was an unhappy union, which ended in divorce in 1838. Some time later, the couple reconciled at their daughter's sickbed, and they remarried in 1841. Once again, however, the marriage failed, and the couple again divorced in April, 1844.

After her second divorce, Aston's life changed radically. She moved with her daughter to Berlin, the capital of the powerful Prussian state. There she began to live as a writer, working for social and political change. She socialized with a group of young intellectuals known for their all-night merrymaking and liberal ideas. Her unconventional behavior gained her notoriety among the Berlin bourgeoisie. In addition to being known for her outspoken opinions, she developed a reputation for smoking cigars, drinking beer, wearing trousers, and practicing free love. Berliners often referred to her as the "German George Sand," comparing her to the androgynous French writer.

Aston's behavior and beliefs were seen as a threat to society by Prussian authorities. The accusations against her included contact with extremist writers, founding a club for emancipated women, and atheism. On March 21, 1846, she was ordered to leave Berlin or face imprisonment, so she retreated to nearby Köpenick. The ensuing period between 1846 and 1850 was Aston's most productive. All of her published works appeared for the first time during these years. Her activities were documented through police and newspaper reports as well as through her writings. There is clear evidence that during this time, she fought for the democratization of society, relief for the oppressed working class, and emancipation of women.

Aston began her literary career in 1846 with a collection of twelve poems in a publication called *Wilde Rosen* (wild roses). These poems all focused on women's issues. The first five poems compared marriage to something like a prison or a funeral; the remaining seven were more optimistic and celebrated the image of a free woman. Also in 1846, Aston published *Meine Emancipation, Verweisung, und Rechtfertigung* (my emancipation, expulsion, and vindication). In this autobiographic commentary, she expressed her views on her expulsion from Berlin. A believer in the power of the press, she used this document to develop a public forum. She defended and justified her views and called for the liberation of women.

In 1847, Aston published her first novel, *Aus dem Leben einer Frau* (from a woman's life). In this partly autobiographical work, the main character undergoes an awakening process from traditional values to more liberal ideas. Although the main character is forced into an arranged marriage, she remains faithful to her husband until he tries to offer her as a prostitute to an aristocrat in exchange for a business loan.

In the spring of 1848, Aston returned to Berlin as the city erupted into revolutionary violence. Through much of the year, she participated as a nurse in the military campaign against Denmark in the disputed provinces of Schleswig-Holstein. For a few months in 1848, she edited a weekly journal, *Der Freischärler* (the volunteer) and wrote most of its articles. By the end of 1848, the revolution collapsed, and Aston was once again expelled from Berlin by the police. Her dream for a democratic and united Germany was defeated.

Aston wrote two other novels: *Lydia*, published in 1848, and *Revolution und Conterrevolution* (revolution and counterrevolution), published in 1849. *Lydia* is the story of two female characters with diametrically opposed models of femininity. One lives and thinks much as Aston does. The novel deals this new model of the emancipated woman and the problems encountered by men trying to cope with this new model. *Revolution und Conterrevolution* sets the same characters in the 1848 revolution. Its main character is a leader and fighter. Representatives of the church and aristocracy are seen as traitors who aid the counterrevolutionary forces. Working-class people are seen as the heroes of the story.

Aston's last work, published in 1850, is a collection of poems titled *Freischärler-Reminiscenzen* (reminiscences of the volunteers). These poems deal with the 1848 revolutionary events, as well as women's issues and the need for change.

Little is known about the last twenty years of Aston's life. After being expelled from Berlin in 1848, she traveled a good deal and finally settled in Bremen in 1849. There she married a physician named Daniel Eduard Meier. She had met him during the fighting in Schleswig-Holstein and shared his political beliefs. Aston accompanied her husband on assignments to Austria, Russia, the Ukraine, and Hungary, after which they returned to Germany in 1871. Aston died on December 21 of that year in Wangen im Allgäu. By the time of her death, she was mostly forgotten by her contemporaries and was unknown to the younger generation of feminists and intellectuals.

SIGNIFICANCE

In many ways, Luise Aston's life serves as an inspiration for modern activists and liberals. Her deeply held convictions regarding the inequalities of society led her to live an unconventional lifestyle while carrying the torch for democracy and equal rights for women in the face of societal rejection and the threat of imprisonment.

The greatest gift that Aston shared with the world was her writings. Through her firsthand accounts, she offered a glimpse of what life was like in nineteenth century Germany for a radical female intellectual. She broke the literary mold by creating politically engaged women characters who acted on their own initiative, and she introduced the literary theme of social consciousness. She left behind a clear record of her convictions. Although her efforts were not always viewed favorably in her day, her words can be used to inspire other radical thinkers for years to come.

—Joy M. Gambill

FURTHER READING

Adler, Hans. "On a Feminist Controversy: Louise Otto vs. Louise Aston." In *German Women in the Eighteenth and Nineteenth Centuries*, edited by Ruth-Ellen B. Joeres and Mary Jo Maynes. Bloomington: Indiana University Press, 1986. This author examines the writings of Louise Otto and Louise Aston in regard to the emancipation movement. Religious belief in relation to the feminist movement is examined. Extensive notes.

Goodman, Katherine. "The Cases of Aston and Meysenbug." *Dis/Closures: Women's Autobiography in Germany Between 1790 and 1914*. New York: Peter Lang, 1986. Goodman examines Aston's partly autobiographical work *Aus dem Leben einer Frau*. Bibliography.

Joeres, Ruth-Ellen Boetcher. "Radicality, Gender and the Ambiguity of Representation." In *Respectability and Deviance: Nineteenth-Century German Women Writers and the Ambiguity of Representation*. Chicago: University of Chicago Press, 1998. Joeres focuses on the ambiguity in Aston's writings. Includes an illustration of Aston.

Jones, Michael. "Emancipation and Louise: Female Perspectives on the Events of 1848." In *Das schwierige neunzehnte Jahrhundert*, edited by Jürgen Barkhoff, Gilbert Carr, and Roger Paulin. Tübingen, Germany: Max Neimeyer Verlag, 2000. Compares Luise Aston's novel *Revolution und Conterrevolution* with *Drei verhängnissvolle Jahre* (1867) by Louise Otto (1819-1895). Extensive footnotes.

Kontje, Todd. "Feminists in the 'Vormärz.'" In *Women, the Novel, and the German Nation 1771-1871: Domestic Fiction in the Fatherland*. New York: Cambridge University Press, 1998. Gives an excellent overview of the life and writings of Luise Aston and offers a historic framework for better understanding her works.

Peterson, Uta. "Louise Aston (1814-1871) Germany." In *Women Writers in German-Speaking Countries: a Bio-Bibliographical Critical Sourcebook*, edited by Elke P. Frederiksen and Elizabeth G. Ametsbichler. Westport, Conn.: Greenwood Press, 1998. Sections include a brief biography, major themes and narrative/poetic strategies, and a survey of criticism. Extensive bibliography.

SEE ALSO: Helene Lange; George Sand; Marie Elizabeth Zakrzewska.

RELATED ARTICLE in *Great Events from History: The Nineteenth Century, 1801-1900:* March 3-November 3, 1848: Prussian Revolution of 1848.

JOHN JACOB ASTOR

German-born American fur trader and financier

Combining a shrewd eye for profits with relentless determination, Astor was, in turn, the first American monopolist, the country's leading fur trader, its leading trader to China, and "landlord of New York." By the end of his life, he was by far the richest man in the United States.

BORN: July 17, 1763; Waldorf, near Heidelberg, Baden (now in Germany)
DIED: March 29, 1848; New York, New York
ALSO KNOWN AS: Johann Jakob Astor (birth name)
AREA OF ACHIEVEMENT: Business

EARLY LIFE

It is known that John Jacob Astor was born near the ancient German city of Heidelberg, but information concerning the origins of his family is incomplete. It seems certain that the Astors (or Ashdoers) were not originally German. The first Astor in Germany arrived in either the sixteenth or the eighteenth century, was either Italian or Spanish, and was either a religious refugee or a soldier, depending on which story is preferred. In any case, the Astor family was not a wealthy one. Astor's father was a butcher who had very little aptitude for business. His mother, fortunately, was methodical and frugal, qualities she passed on to her four sons. John Jacob was the youngest.

With the death of his mother and the arrival of a stepmother, John Jacob became very unhappy and discontented. He left home at the age of sixteen or seventeen and worked his passage down the River Rhine to join an older brother in London. For two or three years, John Jacob worked in his brother's piano manufacturing company, learning English and saving money to travel to America, where a second brother was established as a butcher in New York.

In November, 1783, Astor set sail bound for Baltimore with money enough to tide him over, a stock of German flutes to trade, and a berth in steerage for the trip. The ship arrived in the Chesapeake in January but remained icebound for two months, unable to reach its destination. During that time, Astor became acquainted with a young German returning to America, where he had previously been a fur trapper and trader. Once aroused to the potential for fabulous profits, Astor inquired into the minutest details of the trade and determined to enter the fur business himself. In March, 1784, Astor arrived in New York and soon obtained a job with an old Quaker fur trader. His marriage to Sarah Todd in 1785 brought him a handsome dowry of three hundred dollars, connections with the upper classes of New York City and with various sea captains, and a wife with great business ability of her own. The following year, Astor was able to set up business on his own account as a fur trader and agent for the sale of imported musical instruments.

LIFE'S WORK

John Jacob Astor quickly became affluent. To be truly successful as a fur trader, Astor had to compete with the giant Hudson's Bay Company and the Northwest Company, both based in Montreal, and which, between them, dominated much of the trade. With a secure financial base from the music shop run by his wife, Sarah, he was able to spend the time to gain the confidence of trappers and Indians in upstate New York through personal contact and by offering a better price than his enormous rivals.

In 1789, Astor was invited to attend the annual meeting of the Northwest Company at Fort William on Lake Superior. What he saw convinced him that if he was ever to compete seriously, he had to develop trade in volume. Consequently, Astor began to develop a regular trade in furs between Montreal and London, and between London and New York (direct trade between Canada and the newly independent United States was illegal until 1796). At the same time, he continued to develop his contacts and agents in the woods in anticipation of the day when he could replace the two great Canadian fur companies.

As his income soared, Astor took his brother's advice and began to invest in real estate. To further his financial interests, John Jacob began to frequent the meeting places of powerful city merchants and became a member of the Masons. By the time of Jay's Treaty in 1796, by which Great Britain agreed to leave the rich hunting grounds south of the Great Lakes and to end the trade ban on goods from Canada to the United States, Astor was in a good position to attempt to rival the great fur companies. He was, by then, one of the leading merchants of New York, estimated to be worth fifty thousand dollars.

In 1800, Astor invested in a cargo of furs bound for China. His share of the profit from this one voyage was estimated at fifty-five thousand dollars and was reinvested in the China trade. By 1803, he had ships of his own built and was becoming the leading American merchant in the China trade. All the while, Astor continued to invest several thousand dollars per year in Manhattan real estate, trading in anything that would bring a good profit from the return journeys of his fur ships, and extending his contacts among fur trappers in the woods.

In 1808, Astor was ready to exploit the possibilities opened up by the Louisiana Purchase. He founded the American Fur Company to monopolize the fur trade west of the Mississippi. The company was capitalized at one million dollars, all of it supplied by Astor himself, and was blessed by the American government, which was full of Astor's business acquaintances and clients. The key to Astor's scheme was to establish a settlement at the mouth of the Columbia River on the Pacific coast—to be called Astoria—as a clearinghouse for furs from animals caught in the region; they could then be sent directly to China, the world's best market. Never before had the merchant taken such a big gamble.

The venture was accompanied by great suspicion between Americans hired to run the settlement and the Scots-Canadians hired for their expertise. It was a suspicion shared by Astor himself and was compounded by his assignment of responsibilities. The result was the complete failure of an overland expedition sent to set up trading posts on its way to Astoria and the subsequent loss of the ship that Astor sent out to build the settlement. Worse yet, the War of 1812 allowed the Northwest Company to send an armed ship to Astoria to claim it for Great Britain. Astor's Scots-Canadians sold the settlement to their former employers, the Northwest Company, for a fraction of its real value. It was Astor's greatest setback, one of remarkably few. The nearly one-million-dollar loss sustained by Astor was subsequently made up from profits derived from his investment in American war bonds.

John Jacob Astor. (Library of Congress)

After the war, Astor was in a strong position. He had been able to buy several ships at cheap rates and had invested in real estate and mortgages, both at low prices as a result of wartime depression and a British blockade. Also, despite the Astoria catastrophe, the American Fur Company after 1815 was able to drive out or take over all rivals in the rich Missouri country and around the Great Lakes. It achieved a complete monopoly by 1822.

During the decade of the 1820's, Astor wound down his interests in the China trade as commodities such as tea glutted the market. He shifted his investments to transportation, insurance companies, banks, federal and state securities, and, most heavily, to real estate. During the 1830's, returns from land and property in Manhattan were so great that Astor decided to liquidate all of his interests in commerce and concentrate instead on his investments, particularly real estate. By this time, the fur trade was in decline and so was Astor, now in his seventies.

To perpetuate his name, Astor built the finest hotel in New York, Astor House, and commissioned the writing of a book defending his actions in the Pacific Northwest. Both Astor House and the book *Astoria*, by Washington Irving, were completed in 1836. Both were immediate and conspicuous successes.

The Panic of 1837 drove many businesspeople to ruin, but not Astor. His great wealth cushioned him and, indeed, he took advantage of the economic depression to extend his investments in Manhattan real estate. With recovery came a huge influx of immigrants, all desperately in need of housing. The value of Astor's investments soared as New York expanded as never before.

John Jacob Astor died on March 29, 1848, after suffering for several years from palsy, extremely poor circulation, and painful stomach disorders. To his son, William Backhouse Astor, he left the bulk of his fortune.

SIGNIFICANCE

John Jacob Astor's career spanned the period from the infancy of the young American republic to the early years of its industrial revolution. It was a time of great commercial opportunity. No other single individual was able to capitalize on the possibilities with such singular success. His drive and determination to make money dominated all those with whom he did business. It mattered little to Astor in what branch of commerce or finance he made money; profit margins were all that counted. Astor is principally remembered, however, for his achievement in building the first private monopoly in United States history. It was his American Fur Company that, over the course of fifteen years, attained almost total control over the fur trade in the United States. His purchase of large tracts of Manhattan and the dispersal of investments in banking, insurance, and government stocks secured Astor's fortune for his family and ensured that it would thrive.

—*Stephen Burwood*

FURTHER READING

Chittenden, Hiram M. *The American Fur Trade of the Far West*. New York: Press of the Pioneers, 1935. Reprint. Stanford, Calif.: Academic Reprints, 1985. A comprehensive examination of the complex structure and pattern that existed before and during the establishment of the American Fur Company. It follows the policies and actions by which independent trappers and companies were driven out of business or incorporated into Astor's company, and the ways in which the Native Americans were dealt with, employees kept in line, and the trade rationalized.

Gebhard, Elizabeth L. *The Life and Ventures of the Original John Jacob Astor*. Hudson, N.Y.: Bryan Printing, 1915. A highly colored and favorable account of the great man, written by a descendant of Astor's friend and fellow German immigrant, John Gabriel Gebhard. Full of detail.

Haeger, John Denis. *John Jacob Astor: Business and Finance in the Early Republic*. Detroit: Wayne State University Press, 1991. Describes Astor's life and career as a merchant, fur trader, and speculator to examine American economic development between 1790 and 1860.

Irving, Pierre M. *The Life and Letters of Washington Irving*. 4 vols. New York: G. P. Putnam's Sons, 1863. An account of the great literary figure by his nephew. Washington Irving was a longtime friend of Astor, which was why he was commissioned to write *Astoria*. Pierre and his uncle lived in Astor's house for two years preparing materials for the novel. There are a number of revealing letters and episodes concerning Astor.

Irving, Washington. *Astoria*. Philadelphia: Carey, Lea, and Blanchard, 1836. Reprint. Edited by Richard Dilworth Rust. Boston: Twayne, 1976. This is the authorized version of Astor's astounding career, written by a longtime friend and literary client. It is the most detailed version of Astor's early career and serves as the main reference point for all later accounts. However, some of its facts have been questioned, because Irving seems to have accepted many of the myths propagated about, and by, Astor. The book was a best-seller when it appeared.

Madsen, Axel. *John Jacob Astor: America's First Multimillionaire*. New York: John Wiley & Sons 2001. Straightforward recounting of Astor's life and business enterprises.

Minnigerode, Meade. *Certain Rich Men*. New York: G. P. Putnam's Sons, 1927. Of the seven men studied, Astor merits the second chapter, following his friend Stephen Girard, the banker. This is a balanced account that stresses Astor's ruthless business practice and his love of family.

Porter, Kenneth Wiggins. *John Jacob Astor: Business Man*. 2 vols. Cambridge, Mass.: Harvard University Press, 1931. Easily the most detailed and informative account of Astor's career, questioning some of Irving's assumptions. Porter concentrates largely on Astor's financial interests but does not neglect the personal aspects of his subject.

Sinclair, David. *Dynasty: The Astors and Their Times*.

London: J. M. Dent & Sons, 1983. A book primarily about the fortune bequeathed by John Jacob Astor. It offers an iconoclastic view that subjects Astor to biting criticism in places and that is informed throughout by a skepticism about business practices and "great men." A good corrective to some of the favorable accounts cited above.

SEE ALSO: Albert Gallatin.

RELATED ARTICLES in *Great Events from History: The Nineteenth Century, 1801-1900:* April 6, 1808: American Fur Company Is Chartered; September 8, 1810-May, 1812: Astorian Expeditions Explore the Pacific Northwest Coast; April, 1816: Second Bank of the United States Is Chartered.

HUBERTINE AUCLERT
French journalist and feminist

Auclert was a prominent figure in the struggle for women's political and civil equality in France through the last four decades of her life. As a journalist, she published more than seven hundred signed articles in leading periodicals and lent currency to the terms "feminist" and "feminism."

BORN: April 10, 1848; Tilly, France
DIED: April 4, 1914; Paris, France
ALSO KNOWN AS: Marie-Anne-Hubertine Auclert (full name); Hubertine Auclert-Lévrier; Liberata (pseudonym); Jeanne Voitout (pseudonym)
AREAS OF ACHIEVEMENT: Women's rights, communications

EARLY LIFE

The fifth in a family of seven children, Marie-Anne-Hubertine Auclert (mah-ree ahn ew-bur-teen oh-klehr) grew up in the department of Allier in central France. Her father, Jean-Baptiste Auclert, a republican landowner of Jacobin heritage, held appointments as mayor and adjunct mayor in the small communities of Tilly and Saint-Priest-en-Murat. Her mother, Marie Chanudet, married her father during the late spring of 1835. From 1857 to 1864, Hubertine was educated at a local convent, probably the Dames de l'Enfant Jésus (Ladies of the Child Jesus) in nearby Montmirail, where her father died in 1861.

In 1864, when Hubertine was sixteen, she sought admission into Saint Vincent de Paul's Sisters of Charity, but her application was rejected. When her mother died in 1866, she was placed—against her will—in a convent in Monluçon. Her experience there, although brief, seems to have kindled anticlerical feelings and reinforced in her a strong desire for independence. Financial independence came to her at the age of twenty-one, when she gained access to her portion of the family estate.

Hubertine's inheritance, assessed at about sixty thousand francs, did not make her wealthy but was enough to ensure a comfortable annual revenue that freed her from the need to work for a living. This freedom allowed her to volunteer service to the victims of a smallpox epidemic during the Franco-Prussian war (1870-1871) before she turned her attention—almost exclusively—to the cause of women's rights.

In June, 1872, the feminist paper *L'Avenir des femmes* (the future of women) published a letter by French poet and playwright Victor Hugo equating the treatment of women in French society with slavery and calling for an end to government's discriminatory policies against women. It was that letter, as Auclert later recalled, that determined her to go to Paris to lend support to the growing feminist movement.

LIFE'S WORK

Hubertine Auclert arrived in Paris in the first half of 1873, during what appeared to be a revival of political activism in France. In the latter years of the country's Second Empire, most notably during the late 1860's, a liberalization of governmental policies had given new impetus to the formation of women's organizations in Paris. In 1866, the left-wing journalist André Léo—born Léodile Bera—founded the Society for the Concession of Women's Rights. Three years later, activists Maria Deraismes and Léon Richer created a long-lived weekly journal, *Le Droit des femmes* (rights of women), which was known as *L'Avenir des femmes* from 1871 to 1879. They also announced the formation of the Association for the Rights of Women. In 1871, the first woman to receive a secondary school diploma in France, Julie Daubié, established the Association for the Emancipation of Women. These activists represented the vanguard of the French feminist movement.

Within months of her arrival in Paris, Auclert became a regular participant in Richer and Deraismes's circle, occupying a chair in the association's central committee of eighteen members until her election to a full three-year term in January, 1874. She also accepted an appointment as an editorial assistant and published occasional letters in *L'Avenir des femmes*. By early 1875, the local police had recognized in Auclert one of the capital's leading feminists and began keeping a file on her activities. Later that same year, Richer and Deraismes's association was officially prohibited. Auclert then founded a new society, Droit des femmes, an organization that sought full civil and political rights for women. It was later renamed Suffrage des femmes (woman suffrage) to reflect its primary objective more accurately. The society first met in March, 1877, and acquired legal status on September 28, 1879.

Historians have described Richer's and Deraismes's *politique de la brèche* (tactic of the breach) as a moderate and cautious program of sociopolitical reform aimed at achieving minor victories by avoiding divisive political issues such as woman suffrage and full equality. Auclert, who was more radical in her approach, refused to sacrifice major goals in exchange for minor concessions, preferring instead an offensive strategy (*stratégie de l'assaut*) that was more aggressive. Her militant approach to social reform was inspired in part by left-wing activists. Auclert argued that women must obtain the right to vote before they could exert any real influence in the political arena. The philosophical rift between her and her cautious mentors became evident when Richer and Deraismes opposed her attempts to introduce the issue of woman suffrage into the program of the International Woman's Rights Congress of 1878. As a result of their refusal, Auclert withdrew from the congress's planning committees so she could seek other venues for her feminist agenda.

In 1881, Auclert founded the newspaper *La Citoyenne* (the citizeness) as a platform for her ideas, using it to coordinate and publicize the various aspects of her "assaultist" program over the next decade. In addition to the publication of more than 250 articles and editorials for *La Citoyenne* during its ten-year existence, her activities included participation in public demonstrations, protest actions, promotional campaigns, numerous petitions to governmental agencies, and acts of civil disobedience.

In 1888, Auclert married her long-standing companion, the journalist Antonin Lévrier. She then spent four years with him in Algeria, until he succumbed to chronic illness, leaving her a widow. During her stay in that North African French colony, she observed with horror the abuses of polygamy, the common practices of prepubescent marriage and divorce by repudiation, and the racism inherent in colonial rule, denouncing them in a collection of essays titled *Les Femmes arabes en Algérie* (1900; Arab women of Algeria).

When Auclert returned to Paris in 1892, *La Citoyenne* had ceased to exist. During her absence, new activists had gained prominence in the women's movement. In 1896, after placing a small number of articles in various newspapers, including the right-wing *La Libre parole* (free speech), she began writing a weekly column titled "Le Féminisme" for a well-funded newspaper, *Le Radical*. Between October, 1896, and November, 1909, she wrote more than four hundred weekly columns on a wide range of women's issues, helping promote public awareness of her movement's worthy goals.

In addition to earlier pamphlets and her book on Algerian women, Auclert also published collected articles in *Le Vote des femmes* (the women's vote) and *Les Femmes au gouvernail* (women at the helm). A copy of her diary survives among the "Auclert Papers" housed at the City of Paris Historical Library.

SIGNIFICANCE

Hubertine Auclert played a crucial role in social politics during the formative phase of the French feminist movement. A determined advocate for women's rights, she helped educate her contemporaries on the myriad hues of discrimination endured by women under the nominally democratic regime of France's Third Republic. Between the early days of her militant activism and the years immediately preceding World War I—which began four months after she died—feminism became a household word and participation in women's rights organizations rose dramatically.

Auclert's many militant actions, including tax and census boycotts (1880-1881, 1885), suffragist petition campaigns (1880-1887), mock campaigns for public office (1881, 1885, 1910), and the defiant burning of the Napoleonic Code (1904), attracted considerable media attention to the women's movement, promoted discussion of issues important to women, and helped establish foundations for the movement's future success. One of Auclert's last militant actions, the willful destruction of a ballot box in 1908, earned her the derisive soubriquet "the French suffragette." A fitting tribute to her lifelong struggle, it was a title that she bore with pride.

—*Jan Pendergrass*

FURTHER READING

Bidelman, Patrick Kay. *Pariahs Stand Up! The Founding of the Liberal Feminist Movement in France, 1858-1889*. Westport, Conn.: Greenwood Press, 1982.

Chapter 4 concentrates on Auclert's "strategy of assault" and provides an overview of her major achievements. Includes insights based on Auclert's personal diary.

Hause, Steven C. *Hubertine Auclert, the French Suffragette*. New Haven, Conn.: Yale University Press, 1987. This comprehensive biography has ample discussion of the social and political context and includes a list of Auclert's newspaper articles (1876-1911) and petitions (1898-1912), descriptions of programs and statutes (1877-1910), and an extensive bibliography.

Ozouf, Mona. *Women's Words: Essay on French Singularity*. Chicago: University of Chicago Press, 1997. A chapter devoted to Auclert underscores the suffragist's intransigent idealism and austere morality.

Rochefort, Florence. "The French Feminist Movement and Republicanism, 1868-1914." In *Emancipation Movements in the Nineteenth Century: A European Perspective*, edited by Sylvia Paletschek and Bianka Pietrow-Ennker. Stanford, Calif.: Stanford University Press, 2004. Examines the history of nineteenth century feminist journalism, from the Saint-Simonian *La Femme libre* (the free woman) to Auclert's *La Citoyenne* and Marguerite Durand's *La Fronde* (the sling).

Scott, Joan Wallach. *Only Paradoxes to Offer: French Feminists and the Rights of Man*. Cambridge, Mass.: Harvard University Press, 1996. Chapter 4 discusses Auclert's activism within the political framework of the Third Republic.

Taïeb, Edith. "Abuses of 'Masculinism' in Hubertine Auclert's *La Citoyenne*." In *Women Seeking Expression*, edited by Rosemary Lloyd and Brian Nelson. Melbourne: Monash University, 2000. Focuses on the journalist's critique of a "masculinist" social order.

SEE ALSO: Victor Hugo; Pierre-Joseph Proudhon; Anaïs Ségalas.

RELATED ARTICLE in *Great Events from History: The Nineteenth Century, 1801-1900:* February 17-18, 1890: Women's Rights Associations Unite.

JOHN JAMES AUDUBON

American naturalist and painter

A gifted artist with a love of nature and a passion for discovery, Audubon became the greatest painter of birds of his time, an important natural scientist, and an inspiration to conservationists.

BORN: April 26, 1785; Les Cayes, Saint-Domingue (now Haiti)
DIED: January 27, 1851; New York, New York
AREAS OF ACHIEVEMENT: Biology, art

EARLY LIFE

John James Audubon (AH-dew-bahn) was born in Haiti on April 26, 1785, the illegitimate son of Jean Audubon, a French naval officer, and Jeanne Rabin, a French servant girl from Brittany. After his mother's death, Audubon's father took him and a younger half sister to France, where he legally adopted his children in 1794. In school, Audubon early revealed his talents for drawing and music. He learned to play the violin and flute and by age fifteen had begun drawing birds and collecting birds' eggs. After he proved unfit for a naval career, the elder Audubon sent him to Mill Grove, his farm near Valley Forge, Pennsylvania. In 1808, following a four-year engagement, Audubon married Lucy Bakewell, a girl of English descent who lived on a neighboring estate. Of their four children, two sons—Victor Gifford and John Woodhouse—survived to adulthood and provided significant help to their father in his painting and publishing projects.

In the United States, Audubon formed a partnership with Ferdinand Rozier, an older Frenchman whom his father had sent to look after him. They became frontier merchants, with stores in Kentucky, first in Louisville, then in Henderson, and finally in Ste. Genevieve, Missouri. However, Audubon preferred to trek the forests, observing and painting birds and other wildlife. Finding business irksome, he dissolved the partnership and entered into an ill-fated trade arrangement with his brother-in-law, Thomas Bakewell. In 1813, Audubon and a group of associates built a combination sawmill and gristmill in Henderson, Kentucky. It proved far too ambitious a project to be sustained by the local economy, and its failure left him bankrupt. After being imprisoned for debt, he worked as a taxidermist for the Western Museum in Cincinnati, receiving additional income from portrait painting. In 1820, he set out for New Orleans to continue work as an artist, but, more important, to add to his portfolio of bird paintings. His wife worked as a tutor to support the family, and the two endured many months apart before she joined him in Louisiana.

LIFE'S WORK

For Audubon, an avocation developed into a vocation, though it is not known precisely when the change occurred. In 1810, while he and Rozier were in their Louisville store, Alexander Wilson, the pioneer American ornithologist, showed them his bird paintings and sought a subscription to support publication of his nine-volume *American Ornithology* (1808-1814). After seeing Wilson's work, Rozier remarked that his partner's paintings were better. By allowing Audubon to realize that his amateur work surpassed the work of a professional, this incident probably served as a catalyst to his fertile imagination.

Audubon gradually developed the idea for *The Birds of America* (1827-1838), an ambitious portfolio of all American species, life-size, in their natural habitats. In its scope, scale, and fidelity to nature, Audubon's work would eclipse that of his predecessors. In order to include all the known species, he would rely upon the discoveries and observations of others for some of his paintings, not limiting the work to his own observations as Wilson had done. By the time he left for New Orleans in late 1820, the outlines of the work, which would require almost two decades to complete, were formed.

John James Audubon. (Library of Congress)

An experienced hunter and skilled woodsman, Audubon combined an intense interest in nature with a sharp eye and essential survival skills. He was equally comfortable alone or in company, and equally ingratiating to Native Americans or European noblemen. At five feet, ten and a half inches tall, he was a man of almost regal appearance, with smooth facial lines, long brown hair, and blue eyes. A contemporary, Mrs. Nathaniel Wells Pope, described him as "one of the handsomest men I ever saw . . . tall and slender. . . . His bearing was courteous and refined, simple and unassuming."

In Audubon's time, a naturalist needed to collect specimens (usually by shooting), to record his observations in a journal, and to sketch or paint all that he found interesting. To collect specimens, he shot thousands of birds on his expeditions. The collecting, however, did not stop there: He obtained insects, reptiles, and mammals for many other scientists throughout the world. In his lengthy journals, often romantic and even grandiloquent in tone, he made detailed notes about bird sightings and behavior. An almost compulsive painter, he sometimes began sketching a bird by placing its body on a sheet of paper and drawing an outline. Although Audubon occasionally painted live birds, his normal mode was to paint dead ones, which he wired into positions that suited him.

After his efforts to interest New York and Philadelphia publishers in his work failed, Audubon embarked in 1826 for England, where he attempted to attract wealthy patrons for his project by exhibiting his paintings. There, where he was regarded as a natural untaught genius, he became something of a celebrity, being named a fellow of the Royal Society. For *The Birds of America* he sought two hundred subscribers willing to pay one thousand dollars each; he eventually obtained 161, about half of them from the United States. Subscribers paid for a set of five prints at a time, with eighty sets, or four hundred prints, projected.

The publication, requiring eleven years, began in 1827, in Edinburgh, under the engraver William Lizars. Audubon quickly changed to Robert Havell and Company in London, after Havell impressed the painter with his ability to reproduce color tones. The images were etched on copper plates using aquatint, producing shades of gray and black on a light background. They were engraved on sheets measuring thirty-nine and a half by twenty-six and a half inches, forming the Double Elephant Folio, one of the largest books ever printed. After the engraving, artists colored the prints professionally by hand to match Audubon's original paintings.

When completed, the work included life-size color prints of 489 species on 435 pages. The total number of bird paintings was 1,065, for Audubon attempted to illustrate different color phases of each species, and for birds of varied coloration he often produced several poses to reveal the colors more effectively. One of his own favorite paintings, that of the wood duck, includes four birds so positioned as to reveal the rich coloration of the species. His painting of the little blue heron shows a full-size adult in the foreground and, at a distance, standing in a marsh, the white immature representative of the species.

During the production of his major work, Audubon returned to the United States three times to collect more specimens and to complete his paintings, leaving publication in the hands of his son Victor and Havell. In the United States, he mounted extended expeditions into the interior of the country, along the Gulf of Mexico, and to Labrador. Meanwhile, with the assistance of the gifted Scottish ornithologist William MacGillivray, he prepared and issued five volumes of commentaries as companion volumes to the paintings, *Ornithological Biography* (1831-1839). The work names and describes each species, provides an account of its behavior and habitats, and often includes vivid narration of Audubon's experience with the species, the primary source being his unpublished journals.

After completing *The Birds of America*, Audubon issued the work in a smaller and less expensive edition. He then turned to a new project, this time concerning North American mammals, *Viviparous Quadrupeds of North America* (1846-1854; plates, 1842-1845), in collaboration with his friend John Bachman. Seeking specimens to paint, he organized his last great expedition in 1843, traveling up the Missouri River to the mouth of the Yellowstone in North Dakota. After age sixty, he suffered a rapid decline in health, marked by a loss of mental powers. He died quietly at his New York City home, Minnie's Land, on January 27, 1851, leaving completion of his work on the mammals to his sons and to Bachman.

SIGNIFICANCE

In ornithology, art, and conservation, Audubon's fame and influence have endured. During his time, taxonomy was in its early stages, and science developed largely through observation and compilation. Vast areas of the world lay unexplored and unstudied. To discover new species of flora or fauna was an obvious route to achievement, possibly even to fame. Never a theorist and little inclined toward experimentation, Audubon possessed intense curiosity about nature, keen eyes, and a questing, somewhat romantic nature. He discovered a dozen subspecies, more than twenty species, and one genus of American birds. The list, though impressive, is shorter than he believed, because he mistook several variant color phases for new species and unwittingly claimed some prior discoveries of others.

The artistic quality of *The Birds of America* surpassed that of its predecessors, and the work has not been equaled since in its scale, scope, and aesthetic appeal. Although he occasionally painted with oils, Audubon achieved his best effects using watercolors with an overlay of pastels to enhance color and sharpen detail. Critics, however, have called attention to his limitations as an artist. He sometimes posed his subjects in unnatural positions and uncharacteristic settings, gave some birds human expressions, and could not sustain a uniformly high aesthetic level throughout the long project. However, he succeeded in arousing widespread interest in ornithology and made the birds of the New World familiar to the Old.

In the twentieth century, his name has become synonymous with conservation of wildlife, a legacy not without irony considering the number of birds he felled with his gun. Still, toward the end of his life, he spoke out against egg collecting as a threat to bird populations. During his final Western expedition, he was troubled by the indiscriminate slaughter of bison. He genuinely loved the primitive frontier and feared that it might disappear under the pressure of civilization. In 1886, his protégé and admirer, George Bird Grinnell, organized the first Audubon Society to preserve some of the natural beauty and living creatures of the land Audubon loved.

—*Stanley Archer*

FURTHER READING

Audubon, John James. *Audubon's Birds of America: The Audubon Society Baby Elephant Portfolio*. New York: Abbeville, 2003. An affordable volume of Audubon's lifework, endorsed by the Audubon Society and edited by Roger Tory Peterson, a renowned ornithologist. Contains reproductions of 435 hand-colored engravings from the Double Elephant portfolio.

_____. *The 1826 Journal of John James Audubon*. Edited by Alice Ford. Norman: University of Oklahoma Press, 1967. Careful editing and extensive commentary supplement this important surviving Audubon journal. It reveals Audubon as a careful observer of birds from shipboard during his journey to England.

Chancellor, John. *Audubon: A Biography*. London: Weidenfeld & Nicholson, 1978. A readable brief biography of Audubon, with a judicious assessment of his achievement. Rich in illustrations.

Ford, Alice. *John James Audubon*. Norman: University of Oklahoma Press, 1964. Now the standard biography, it gives a carefully researched account of Audubon's origins and early life, adding extensive details about his early life in France.

Hart-Davis, Duff. *Audubon's Elephant: America's Greatest Naturalist and the Making of "The Birds of America."* New York: Henry Holt, 2004. Describes Audubon's unlikely success in Europe, where he lived for twelve years and obtained the money needed to publish his greatest work.

Harwood, Michael. "Mr. Audubon's Last Hurrah." *Audubon* 87 (November, 1985): 80-117. A lengthy account of Audubon's journey to North Dakota in 1843, the article provides numerous excerpts from his journals and those of contemporaries.

Harwood, Michael, and Mary Durant. "In Search of the Real Mr. Audubon." *Audubon* 87 (May, 1985): 58-119. This article traces Audubon's career in detail, assesses the many myths that surround him, and provides a critique of his biographers. Generously and judiciously illustrated, with numerous reproductions.

Herrick, Francis Hobart. *Audubon the Naturalist: A History of His Life and Time*. 2 vols. New York: D. Appleton, 1917, 1938. Although somewhat dated in its research, the biography remains a valuable resource for its comprehensive treatment and its inclusion of many original letters, papers, official records, and documents.

Lindsey, Alton A., ed. *The Bicentennial of John James Audubon*. Bloomington: Indiana University Press, 1985. A collection of essays by various writers, the book assesses Audubon's character, his contributions to science and art, and his influence on conservation.

Rhodes, Richard. *John James Audubon: The Making of an American*. New York: Alfred A. Knopf, 2004. Extensively researched and comprehensive biography. Aimed at general readers, the book vividly recounts episodes in Audubon's life, including his relationship with his wife, his move to Kentucky, and his explorations to discover and draw birds.

SEE ALSO: Louis Agassiz; Albert Bierstadt; Charles Darwin.

RELATED ARTICLE in *Great Events from History: The Nineteenth Century, 1801-1900:* August 10, 1846: Smithsonian Institution Is Founded.

JANE AUSTEN
English novelist

Austen's realistic rendering of dialogue and her satirical accuracy make her novels a matchless recreation of upper-class English society during the late eighteenth and early nineteenth centuries. Her novels owe their lasting popularity, however, to Austen's understanding of human nature as it operates in everyday life.

BORN: December 16, 1775; Steventon, Hampshire, England
DIED: July 18, 1817; Winchester, Hampshire, England
AREA OF ACHIEVEMENT: Literature

EARLY LIFE

Jane Austen was born December 16, 1775, in Steventon, Hampshire, England, the seventh child and second daughter of George Austen and Cassandra Leigh Austen. Her father was the rector of Steventon and nearby Deane. A member of an old but poor family, he had been reared by a wealthy uncle, who educated him at St. John's College, Oxford, where he was later a fellow. Austen's mother was the daughter of a clergyman of noble ancestry, also an Oxford graduate and also a former fellow.

Although Jane and her older sister, Cassandra Austen, spent several years in schools in Southampton and Reading, their real education took place at home. The Austens loved words and books. The children could roam at will through George Austen's impressive library. As they grew older, they staged amateur theatricals. The environment stimulated their curiosity, whether they were observing their mother's experiments in farming or hearing their aristocratic French cousin talk about life in prerevolutionary France. With an ever-increasing family and a wide circle of friends, the Austen children had ample opportunity to analyze human motivations and relationships; it is not surprising that two of Jane's brothers and her sister Cassandra all did some writing at one time or another.

The Austens also shared in remarkable good looks; Jane and Cassandra were sometimes called the best-looking girls in England. However flattering such comments may have been, it is true that Jane was a tall, slender brunette with brown, curly hair, hazel eyes, a good complexion, and a sweet voice. Although neither Jane nor Cassandra was ever married, it was not for lack of prospects. Indeed, both were engaged, Cassandra for some time, to a young clergyman who died in the West Indies, and Jane only overnight, to a family friend whom she rejected in the morning. There was evidently at least one other serious relationship for Jane, a holiday romance that was not pursued and that terminated when that young man, too, died.

Because Jane never left the family circle, her life has often been called uneventful. In fact, it was so busy that Jane had to snatch time to write. In addition to the normal social activities of her class, there were frequent visits to and from the brothers and their families, including lengthy stays by their children, several of whom were very close to their Aunt Jane. There were births, deaths, marriages, and remarriages; there was anxiety about Jane's cousin, whose husband was executed in the French Revolution, and about two brothers, who were British naval officers. Thus, Jane was immersed in life, grieving and rejoicing with family members and friends, mothering nieces and nephews, and worrying about the effect of her unstable times on those she loved. As one may note from her letters, she was also a perceptive observer of human behavior, unimpressed by pomposity, unfooled by pretense, and always alert to the comic dimension of human relationships.

It was this comic sense that first led Austen to writing. Her three notebooks collect jokes, skits, and rudimentary character sketches dating from the time she was eleven or twelve, along with a later comic history of England and a brief, unfinished novel named "Catherine." By 1795, when she was twenty, Austen had produced "Elinor and Marianne" (which was later revised and published in 1811 as *Sense and Sensibility*). By 1797, she had completed "First Impressions," which the publisher Cadell refused even to read but which, revised, became her most famous novel, *Pride and Prejudice* (1813). Although none of her novels was to be published until 1811 (six years before her death, when *Sense and Sensibility* made its public appearance), Austen was thus involved in her mature work before her twenty-first birthday. No longer a superficially amusing girl, she had become a serious woman of letters.

Jane Austen. (Library of Congress)

LIFE'S WORK

Austen's literary reputation rests on six novels, four of which were published during the last years of her life and two posthumously. Because she revised and retitled her early works before she was able to find a publisher for them, it is difficult to trace her development. Evidently, after a work was rejected, she would put it aside, begin another work, and then later revise the earlier one. Her most famous work, *Pride and Prejudice*, for example, was the product of twelve or fourteen years; *Sense and Sensibility* took at least sixteen years and two revisions between conception and publication.

Austen's creative maturity can be divided into two major periods. During the first, she wrote three novels and vainly attempted to get them published. During the second, she revised, completed, and published two of her early novels and wrote three more, two of which were

AUSTEN'S MAJOR WORKS

1811 *Sense and Sensibility*
1813 *Pride and Prejudice*
1814 *Mansfield Park*
1815 *Emma*
1818 *Northanger Abbey*
1818 *Persuasion*
1871 *Lady Susan* (novella)
1871 *The Watsons* (unfinished fragment)
1925 *Sanditon* (unfinished fragment)

published before her death. It was only during the last half dozen years of her life, then, that she received the recognition which her genius merited.

During her years at Steventon, Austen wrote the first version of what was to be her first published work. "Elinor and Marianne" was the story of two sisters whose lives were governed by two different principles. In every crisis, one tried to be sensible, while the other gave way to uncontrolled emotion. The theme was reflected in Austen's revision a year or two later, when she changed the title to *Sense and Sensibility*. It was under the second title that the novel, again revised, was finally published in 1811.

During 1797, Austen completed "First Impressions," which pointed out how foolish rash assessments of other people may be. Like *Sense and Sensibility*, this work told the love stories of two sisters; in this case, however, the prejudiced sister, with all of her faults, captures the reader, who can hardly wait for her to capture the proud nobleman. Tentatively, Austen's father offered the manuscript to a publisher, but the publisher refused even to read it. Austen put it away. In 1809, she revised it, and in 1813, it was published as *Pride and Prejudice*, which is still one of England's best-known and best-loved novels.

The third novel of the Steventon period, *Northanger Abbey* (1818; originally titled "Susan"), began as a satire of the gothic and sentimental novels that were so popular during the late eighteenth century. Like a gothic heroine, the central character is determined to find a murderer in the country house that she visits; her curiosity is interpreted as bad manners, however, and she very nearly loses the eligible man who had invited her. However, Austen's genius could not be confined in a mere literary satire, and like her other works, *Northanger Abbey* is a full-fledged commentary on morals and manners.

Northanger Abbey is also interesting because it was the first novel actually sold for publication. The publisher who bought it in 1803, however, evidently changed his plans, and six years later Austen paid him for its return. It was published the year after her death.

In 1801, George Austen suddenly decided to retire and to move his household to Bath, where he and his family lived until his death in 1805. Despite her reluctance to leave Steventon, Austen was fascinated with the famous watering place, which was the setting both for *Northanger Abbey* and for *Persuasion* (1818). Whether her inability to publish discouraged her or she continued to work on her earlier manuscripts is a matter of conjecture; at any rate, *The Watsons*, begun in 1804, was never completed (although its fragment was published in 1871 in J. E. Austen-Leigh's *Memoir of Jane Austen*). In 1809, Jane, Cassandra, and their mother moved back to Hampshire, to a house in the village of Chawton, which had been made available to them by Jane's brother Edward Knight. There Jane spent the remaining years of her life, years that at last brought her success. In 1809, Jane revised *Sense and Sensibility* and *Pride and Prejudice*. Probably with the encouragement and help of her brother Henry Austen, who lived in London, in 1811 she found a publisher for *Sense and Sensibility*. Like all of her novels printed during her lifetime, it was anonymous. It was also highly successful. In 1813, it was followed by *Pride and Prejudice*.

Henry was too proud of his sister to keep her secret any longer, and in 1813 Jane had to acknowledge that she was known to be the author. By that moment, she had written another novel, *Mansfield Park* (1814), a serious work that deals with religious and ethical issues, particularly as they relate to clerical life. After its publication, she wrote *Emma* (1815), thought by many to be her best novel, even though Jane worried that her readers might dislike the spoiled, snobbish heroine. Drawing from the world of her naval officer brothers, Jane then wrote her final completed novel, *Persuasion*, whose noble but misled heroine had once rejected her true love, a navy captain. Tragicomic in tone, *Persuasion* has often been considered to be Austen's most moving book.

Happy in her Chawton home, surrounded by family and friends, admired by the public and critics alike, and inspired with her ideas for another novel, at the end of 1816 Austen seemed destined for years of happiness. She was struck down, however, with a debilitating and crippling illness. By March, 1817, she put aside her novel; by May, she had moved to nearby Winchester, where her physician lived; on July 18, she died. She was buried in Winchester Cathedral.

SIGNIFICANCE

Jane Austen has often been praised because of what she did not do: She did not write about characters or scenes with which she was unfamiliar; she did not attempt a scope that might have been above her powers; she did not indulge in self-conscious digressions, as did Henry Fielding and his imitator William Makepeace Thackeray, which displayed the author and delayed the novel; and she did not permit herself errors in plotting.

The genius of this restraint has become even more fully appreciated with time. A child of the neoclassical period, she was determined to point out the virtues of moderation in a period that was increasingly infatuated with excess, the need for reason at a time when emotion was increasingly enthroned. She had observed life; she had found that only the classical standards, combined with Christian virtues, could direct one toward happiness. She also had observed that the real dramas of life were played out in the everyday world of ordinary people. People were annihilated as hopelessly at Bath as in battle; families were destroyed as suddenly by foolish marriages as by the guillotine. Therefore, her themes were as profound as human life itself.

That restraint that Austen counseled was exemplified in her work. Every character she introduced was essential to her plot and theme. Every scene and every authorial comment were so carefully pruned that no word could be omitted. Thus, perhaps more than any previous novelist, she understood the artistic heights to which the novel could rise, and while in theme she reflected the age of Samuel Johnson, in technique she anticipated the twentieth century.

—Rosemary M. Canfield-Reisman

FURTHER READING

Austen-Leigh, William, and Richard Arthur Austen-Leigh. *Jane Austen: Her Life and Letters—A Family Record*. London: Smith, Elder, 1913. 2d ed. New York: Russell & Russell, 1965. This work by family members has been considerably augmented as later materials have become available. The seminal work of Austen biography, it includes a useful appendix with textual comments and a detailed genealogical chart.

Cecil, David. *A Portrait of Jane Austen*. New York: Hill & Wang, 1979. One of the most readable introductions to Jane Austen's life and work. Cecil integrates biographical data, Austen's own letters, and historical details in an attempt to place Austen within the society about which she is writing. Contains numerous color illustrations, including watercolors by Jane's sister Cassandra.

Galperin, William H. *The Historical Austen*. Philadelphia: University of Pennsylvania Press, 2003. This study provides a fresh explication of Austen's work. Galperin examines how Austen used her fiction to as a "social and political" tool.

Gill, Richard. *Happy Rural Seat: The English Country House and the Literary Imagination*. New Haven, Conn.: Yale University Press, 1972. Although specifically a study of the English country house in early twentieth century fiction, Gill's book includes an appendix on earlier literature that deals extensively with the works of Austen, particularly *Mansfield Park*. An essential work for anyone who wishes to understand the viewpoint of Austen and later English writers of her class.

Le Faye, Dierdre. *Jane Austen: A Family Record*. 2d ed. New York: Cambridge University Press, 2004. Detailed account of Austen's life and literary career. The author explains how Austen made her life in Hampshire and her brothers' military careers the material for six novels.

Menon, Patricia. *Austen, Eliot, Charlotte Brontë, and the Mentor-Lover*. New York: Palgrave Macmillan, 2003. An examination of how Austen, Eliot, and Brontë handled matters of gender, sexuality, family, behavior, and freedom in their work.

Pinion, F. B. *A Jane Austen Companion: Critical Survey and Reference Book*. London: Macmillan, 1973. Useful brief biography and separate analyses of the six completed novels, along with a commentary on *Sanditon*. Contains an alphabetical listing of characters and places in the novels, a glossary of unusual words, appendixes, maps, and a number of black-and-white illustrations. A thorough, careful book.

Sherry, Norman. *Jane Austen*. New York: Arno Press, 1969. A brief, simple study for the nonacademic reader, Sherry's book includes a short biography and critical generalizations on Austen's work as a whole and specifically on each of the six completed novels. Although the comments on her work are fairly standard, Sherry provides helpful illustrations drawn from the novels to support his points. Convenient for a beginning student of the novel form.

Shields, Carol. *Jane Austen*. New York: Viking Press, 2001. Shields, the Pulitzer Prize-winning author of *The Stone Diaries*, provides a brief account of Austen's life and how her personal experiences influenced her writing.

Spence, Jon. *Becoming Jane Austen: A Life*. London: Hambledon and London, 2003. Spence focuses on Austen's personal experiences to examine how these experiences are reflected in her work.

SEE ALSO: Mary Elizabeth Braddon; The Brontë Sisters; George Eliot; Emma Lazarus.

RELATED ARTICLE in *Great Events from History: The Nineteenth Century, 1801-1900:* 1814: Scott Publishes *Waverley*.

STEPHEN FULLER AUSTIN

American military leader and politician

Austin established the first Anglo-American colony in Texas and played a significant role in the Texas Revolution, which resulted in that province's securing its independence from Mexico and later joining the United States.

BORN: November 3, 1793; Wythe County, Virginia
DIED: December 27, 1836; Columbia, Texas
AREAS OF ACHIEVEMENT: Military, government and politics

EARLY LIFE

Stephen Fuller Austin was born on November 3, 1793, in Wythe County, Virginia. His father, Moses Austin, was a mine owner who came from a family of Connecticut merchants. His mother, née Maria Brown, had a New Jersey Quaker heritage. The Austin family moved to the province of Spanish Louisiana in 1798 to seek better lead deposits for mining. Moses established and operated a lead mine south of St. Louis. There young Stephen passed his childhood until the age of eleven years. In 1804, his family sent him to Connecticut to begin his formal education. He spent several years as a pupil at Bacon Academy and then entered Transylvania University in Kentucky. In 1810, the youth returned to Missouri, which had become part of the United States because of the Louisiana Purchase. The young man worked at a bank in St. Louis and, for a time, engaged in storekeeping. In 1814, his neighbors elected him as a delegate to the Missouri Territorial Legislature, a post he held until 1820.

In 1817, Austin took charge of the financially troubled family mining operation at Potosi. He was, however, unable to make it a profitable business. In 1820, he therefore followed his brother-in-law James Perry to the Arkansas Territory. There he established a farm near Long Prairie on the Red River. The governor of Arkansas appointed him a district judge in July of 1820.

By early adulthood, it had become obvious that Austin had natural leadership ability. He had a pleasing personality along with a mature outlook. He was a physically small person of slight build, only five feet, six inches in height. Dark haired and fine featured, Stephen was no doubt a handsome youth who inspired confidence in all whom he met. His greatest strengths, however, were his moderate personal habits. A well-educated man, he was charitable, tolerant, and loyal in his relationships with others. Also, although he never married, he seldom lacked companionship from the many friends he made throughout his life. It is not surprising, therefore, that Austin decided upon the practice of law as his career. In 1821, he went to New Orleans to study for the bar.

Events set in motion about this time by his father, however, changed forever the course of Austin's life. Moses Austin decided to found a colony in the Spanish province of Texas. The fertile and unsettled land there had rich agricultural potential. Many Anglo-Americans from the United States, especially cotton farmers from the South, would probably be glad to immigrate to Texas. They would exploit the land, something the Spanish had never done. Moses went to San Antonio, where he secured a colonization grant from the Spanish governor in 1821. This grant permitted him to settle three hundred families in the province. These immigrants would agree to become Spanish subjects in return for grants of land. Moses Austin, however, died in 1821, before he could begin his colonization venture. With his dying breath, he asked that Austin carry through this enterprise and bring it to successful conclusion. This his son agreed to do.

LIFE'S WORK

The summer of 1821 found Austin in San Antonio. There he secured a reconfirmation of his father's colonization grant from the Spanish authorities. Unfortunately, however, Mexico became independent from Spain in early 1822, and, consequently, the grant was no longer valid. Austin, who could not secure a renewal from the incoming Mexican authorities in Texas, decided to travel to Mexico City to speak about his grant directly with the newly independent government. He arrived there on April 29, 1822, in the hope that meeting with the Mexican leaders would restore his concession. In the meantime, various Anglo-American farmers began moving to Texas in anticipation of Austin's success in Mexico City.

Austin remained in Mexico for a year while he witnessed the turmoil and instabilities of the new Mexican government. Because of problems related to establishing a workable form of government, Austin could not immediately secure a confirmation of his Texas concession. He did use this time in Mexico City to personal advantage, however, learning to speak and write Spanish with marked fluency. He also made many friends among the Mexican leaders, including Miguel Ramos Arispe, who authored the Mexican Constitution of 1824. Austin furnished Arispe with a translated copy of the U.S. Constitution and made recommendations concerning the contents of the Mexican document.

The Mexican government confirmed the Austin grant in early 1823. Austin returned to Texas and assumed direction of the colony, which grew rapidly. By the end of 1824, almost all three hundred colonists permitted by the colonization charter had received grants. The Austin colony centered along the rich land of the Brazos River. Most colonists settled in a region called "the bottom," several leagues inland from the Gulf coast. The small town of San Felipe became its chief settlement. A formal census of the colony taken in 1825 showed eighteen hundred residents, of whom 443 were slaves.

During the summer of 1824, the Mexican government approved the establishment of additional Anglo colonies in Texas. Any prospective colonizer could apply for an *empresario* contract, the Spanish term used to describe these concessions. In all, Mexico issued several dozen such contracts to various individuals during the following decade. Most of them did not enjoy success, although Austin continued to do so. His original contract fulfilled, he applied for additional colonial grants under the *empresario* provisions. The additional settlements that he sponsored brought hundreds of families into Texas. By 1830, Austin had attracted some five thousand people into Texas. This influx, added to the families who came under the leadership of the other *empresarios*, resulted in a considerable Anglo population in the province by the end of the 1820's.

Austin became involved in Mexican politics that, during this period, were chaotic and complicated by factions. The Anglo-Texans increasingly came to identify with the Federalists, a Mexican political group whose beliefs seemed similar to their own. The Centralists, the opposing faction, thus began to identify Austin and the Anglo-Texans as members of the Federalists by the early 1830's. Therein lay one of the causes of the Texas Revolution.

In addition, the Mexican government was concerned that too many Anglo-Americans had immigrated to Texas. As a result, it passed the law of April 6, 1830, which (among other restrictions) ended all future immigration into Texas from the United States. Austin worked hard to secure a repeal of this law. He once again went to Mexico City to lobby for measures favorable to Texas.

Stephen Fuller Austin. (Library of Congress)

Although he failed to secure all the concessions he wanted, he did persuade the government to repeal some of the most objectionable aspects of the law. By the time he returned to Texas in late 1831, events during his absence had made it increasingly difficult for Anglo-Texans to reconcile themselves to continued Mexican rule.

The actions of the post commander at Anahuac on the Texas coast had caused great dissatisfaction among Anglo residents. During the summer of 1832, the colonists took to arms to force his removal. The military commander in Texas eventually removed the offensive garrison commander at Anahuac. For a time, this forestalled additional armed confrontations with the increasingly unhappy Anglo population. By then, however, the crisis had begun. The town council of San Felipe issued a call for a convention of Anglo colonists to discuss common problems and desires. The fifty-eight delegates who composed this group assembled in October, 1832, and elected Austin the presiding officer.

This Convention of 1832, as it subsequently came to be called, drafted a long list of concessions that the Anglo-Texans wanted from the Mexican government. It also created a standing committee of correspondence in each area of Texas for the purpose of monitoring additional problems with Mexico. The delegates also agreed that another convention would be held the following year. This second convention met in 1833 and drafted a provincial constitution for Texas as a separate state within the Mexican government. The Convention of 1833 delegated Austin to deliver this document to the central government. Austin left Texas in May, 1833, on a journey that would result in a two-year absence from Texas. He spent much of this time in a Mexican prison.

Austin arrived in Mexico City, where he presented the proposed constitution to government officials. He also wrote a letter to the town council in San Antonio that complained about the political situation in Mexico. A government official intercepted this letter en route to Texas and believed that it contained treason. Austin, arrested for this in early January of 1834, remained in prison until December of that year. He did not return to Texas until July 11, 1835. Austin's confinement in Mexico City, much of it in the harsh Prison of the Inquisition, permanently ruined his health. During his absence from Texas, dissatisfaction there with Mexico continued. By late 1835, many Anglo-Texans, including Austin, had come to favor a break with Mexico.

The Texas Revolution began on October 2, 1835, with a skirmish between Anglo and Mexican troops near Gonzales, Texas. A committee of colonists issued a call for a provincial convention that appointed Austin commander of the revolutionary army. He held this position for only a few months. The Texas government then appointed him as an agent to the United States, charged with finding materials and supplies for the revolt. Austin spent much of the Texas Revolution in the United States, visiting Washington, D.C., Richmond, Philadelphia, and other cities. He returned to Texas during the summer of 1836 after the Texas Revolution had ended in an Anglo-American victory. Austin permitted his supporters to place his name in candidacy as president of the Republic of Texas. When Sam Houston won election to this office, Austin looked forward to retiring to private life. Houston, however, prevailed upon him to become secretary of state in the new government, which Austin reluctantly agreed to do. He served only a few months. His health broken by the imprisonment in Mexico, Austin died on December 27, 1836.

SIGNIFICANCE

Stephen Fuller Austin played a significant role in the westward expansion of the United States. Although credit for the Anglo colonization of Hispanic Texas belongs to his father, Austin carried out the dream, and its success belongs to him. He approached the colonization of Texas with a single-minded determination that consumed all of his efforts. In fact, he had time for little else from 1821 until the events of the Texas Revolution. Although he initially believed that Texas should remain a part of Mexico, Austin had become a vocal advocate of independence by 1835. His activities during the revolt materially assisted the Texan victory. It had been his intention to retire from public life after the success of the revolt. He had earlier selected a picturesque, unsettled location—on the lower Colorado River in Texas—as the site for his home. It is fitting that the modern city of Austin, the state capital, occupies that location. It is there Stephen Fuller Austin rests, in the State Cemetery.

—Light Townsend Cummins

FURTHER READING

Barker, Eugene C. *The Life of Stephen F. Austin, Founder of Texas, 1793-1836: A Chapter in the Westward Movement of the Anglo-American People.* Nashville, Tenn.: Cokesbury Press, 1925. Standard scholarly biography from original sources, mainly the Austin family papers. Until the publication of Cantrell's book (see below), this was the only full-length biography and study of Austin's life, his Texas colony, and his impact on American history.

_____. "Stephen F. Austin." In *Handbook of Texas*. Vol. 1, edited by Walter P. Webb. Austin: University of Texas Press, 1952. Provides highlights of Austin's career in a short biography. It offers a concise, short treatment of Austin's life in a factual manner.

_____, ed. *The Austin Papers*. 3 vols. Washington, D.C.: American Historical Association, 1919-1926. Collection of personal papers and letters of Moses and Stephen F. Austin. Covers the early years of the Austin family in Missouri, with the major part of the collection dealing with the period from 1822 to 1836.

Cantrell, Gregg. *Stephen F. Austin: Empresario of Texas*. New Haven, Conn.: Yale University Press, 1999. The only significant biography since Barker's (see above). Cantrell describes how Austin transcended his self-interest in Texas land speculation to become a believer in the idea of an independent Texas. Accessible book for general readers as well as history buffs.

Glascock, Sallie. *Dreams of Empire: The Story of Stephen Fuller Austin and His Colony in Texas*. San Antonio, Tex.: Naylor, 1951. Well-written biography designed for the general reader or for young readers. Good starting place for those unfamiliar with Austin's life.

Holley, Mary Austin. *Texas: Observations, Historical, Geographical, and Descriptive*. Baltimore: Armstrong and Plaskett, 1833. Holley was Austin's cousin. Provides a firsthand account of life and events in the colony and useful insights into the Austin settlement.

Tracy, Milton, and Richard Havelock-Bailie. *The Colonizer: A Saga of Stephen F. Austin*. El Paso, Tex.: Guynes Printing, 1941. Concentrates on the *empresario* career. Makes few improvements on the Barker biography of Austin but is a solid, general assessment of Austin's life, placing him in historical perspective.

SEE ALSO: David Crockett; Sam Houston.

RELATED ARTICLE in *Great Events from History: The Nineteenth Century, 1801-1900:* October 2, 1835-April 21, 1836: Texas Revolution.

AMEDEO AVOGADRO

Italian physicist

A pioneer in atomic theory, Avogadro was the first scientist to distinguish between atoms and molecules. Avogadro's law, a hypothesis that relates the volume of a gas to the number of particles present, greatly advanced the understanding of chemical reactions and resolved many chemical problems.

BORN: August 9, 1776; Turin, Kingdom of Sardinia (now in Italy)
DIED: July 9, 1856; Turin, Kingdom of Sardinia
AREAS OF ACHIEVEMENT: Chemistry, physics

EARLY LIFE

Amedeo Avogadro (AH-vah-GAH-droh) was born in Turin in the Kingdom of Sardinia about 60 miles southwest of Milan in what is now Italy. He was one of four sons born to Count Filippo Avogadro and Anna Maria Vercellone. Count Avogadro was a distinguished lawyer and civil servant who came from a prominent family in the region that had produced many generations of Italian military and civil administrative leaders. The name Avogadro possibly is derived from the Italian word *avvocato* (barrister).

As a young child, Avogadro likely received his first education at home from the local priests; he later attended secondary schools in Turin. Between 1792 and 1796 he studied law at the University of Turin with the intention of following his father in a legal career. For some years after graduating from law school, he held several government positions. Around 1800 he began to show an interest in natural philosophy, undertook private study of physics and mathematics, and attended physics lectures at the university. His interest in science seems likely to have been stimulated by the recent research on electricity by fellow Italian Alessandro Volta, who came from neighboring Lombardy.

After 1806, Avogadro abandoned his interest in a legal career to concentrate on science and, with one of his brothers, began working on electricity experiments. He was soon appointed as a demonstrator at the Academy of Turin. In 1809 he became professor of natural philosophy at the Royal College of Vercelli. Within one decade, Avogadro was elected as a full member of the Turin Academy of Sciences and one year later was appointed to the first Italian chair of mathematical physics at Turin. His salary was six hundred lire per year.

LIFE'S WORK

Avogadro was a prolific writer and published articles in many areas of the physical sciences throughout his life. His name appears in most modern chemistry and physics textbooks, although he has often been misrepresented as being a chemist because his work had a profound influence on the development of chemical theories. His name is usually associated with two important aspects of chemistry: Avogadro's law, which describes the relationship between the volume and number of particles of a gas, and the Avogadro number, which represents the number of particles in one mole of a substance. The concept of the mole as a unit for the measurement of atomic particles was unknown in Avogadro's time, and the term was not introduced until the twentieth century.

In many ways it is remarkable that Avogadro had a successful scientific career. He received no formal training in science and made a dramatic career change when he was thirty years old. The former was not particularly unusual in the eighteenth and nineteenth centuries, as some of the greatest scientists of the period were self-educated, including Humphry Davy and Michael Faraday. Others (for example, Nicolas Lémery and Jakob Berzelius) had received their early training in a related field such as pharmacy or medicine before concentrating on a career in the physical sciences.

It was surprising that Avogadro made the transition from law to science so effortlessly, and it was an obvious testament to his good mind and dedicated spirit of discovery. However, Avogadro was not a good experimentalist and had a poor reputation as such among his colleagues. He preferred to interpret the experimental results of others using a mathematical approach. Much of his work was translated and published, but it generally appeared in obscure journals. In addition, Turin was geographically isolated from the world centers of scientific research, which were generally considered to be in Germany and France. Finally Avogadro was, by nature, modest and reserved, and he never actively sought fame. He never traveled to other countries and rarely corresponded or met with other scientists outside his region. It was not until after his death that the world really comprehended and recognized his contributions to science.

During the early nineteenth century, chemists began serious attempts to understand the nature of matter and chemical reactions. John Dalton measured the mass ratios of elements in compounds and found these ratios to always be simple whole numbers. For the first time, he demonstrated that the elements must exist as discrete units, or atoms. The nature of one particular form of matter, gases, had always been difficult for early scientists to understand. In 1808, Joseph-Louis Gay-Lussac published studies on the combining volumes of gases. He showed that gases always combined in simple whole number ratios. For example, 200 cubic centimeters of hydrogen always combined with 100 cubic centimeters of oxygen to form 200 cubic centimeters of water vapor (a 2:1:2 ratio).

Amedeo Avogadro. (Library of Congress)

Although such observations suggested that equal volumes of gases contained equal numbers of atoms, Dalton rejected this hypothesis, believing that Gay-Lussac's experiments were inaccurate. Dalton and others argued that one volume of oxygen gas contained a specific number of oxygen atoms and therefore must produce the same volume of water vapor with an equivalent number of water atoms. It should be remembered that at the time, it was still generally believed that water had a chemical formula of HO and was composed of HO atoms.

Like Dalton, most chemists of the day believed that common gaseous elements such as hydrogen, oxygen, nitrogen, and chlorine existed as individual atoms. Avogadro's explanation appeared in his 1811 article *Essai d'une manière de déterminer les masses relatives des molécules élémentaires des corps et les proportions selon lesquelles elles entrent dans ces combinaisons* (essay on a manner of determining the relative masses of the elementary molecules of bodies and the proportions in which they enter into combinations), in which he attempted to explain the inconsistencies with existing theories by assuming that equal volumes of all gases contained equal numbers of molecules rather than atoms, provided conditions of temperature and pressure were kept constant. Avogadro's hypothesis (also known as the molecular hypothesis) would later become known as Avogadro's law. During a chemical reaction, therefore, Avogadro proposed that molecules could split into half-molecules (atoms) and combine with other half-molecules to form the observed product compounds.

By contrast, Dalton viewed the combination of two gases such as hydrogen and oxygen as involving individual atoms. It is now known, thanks to Avogadro's insight, that this reaction involves molecules that are composed of two atoms each (diatomic molecules), which is consistent with Gay-Lussac's experimental results on combining volumes in which two volumes of hydrogen react with one volume of oxygen to generate two volumes of water vapor. According to Avogadro, each molecule of water must contain one molecule of hydrogen (H_2) and one half-molecule of oxygen (one O atom). It followed from this that the correct chemical formula for water was H_2O and not HO as Dalton and others believed. It should be noted that Avogadro never used the modern system of chemical formulas that are shown in the previous equations. If he had, his theory may have been more understandable and therefore readily accepted sooner.

Avogadro's hypothesis also explained discrepancies in the measured densities of gases and resulted in more accurate determinations of atomic weights. Water vapor was known to have a lower density than oxygen, but this fact was difficult to explain if the latter existed as single atoms. The occurrence of diatomic oxygen molecules easily explained why oxygen had a greater density than water vapor. In Dalton's early table of atomic weights, which were a measurement of the relative weights of atoms, hydrogen was assigned a value of 1 and oxygen a value of 7.5. When viewed as diatomic molecules, the value of hydrogen became 2 and oxygen 15. In other words, Dalton's atomic weights had to be doubled for diatomic molecules. This eventually led to a more accurate table of atomic weights.

Avogadro's molecular hypothesis was largely ignored during his lifetime. His theory did have the support of a fellow Italian chemist, Stanislao Cannizzaro, who was one of the few who seemed to grasp the significance of Avogadro's idea, but only after Avogadro's death. Most scientists, however, failed to distinguish between atoms and molecules, and Avogadro, isolated in Turin and largely unknown in Europe, never witnessed the universal acceptance of his theory. Cannizzaro showed that Avogadro's theory could be used for determining molecular size and accurate chemical formulas. His enthusiasm for the molecular hypothesis had a profound influence on the German chemist Lothar Meyer. In his 1864 textbook, Meyer employed Avogadro's hypothesis to develop his ideas on theoretical chemistry. This book had considerable influence on other chemists, who applied Avogadro's ideas to many other aspects of physical chemistry.

Avogadro held his position as the chair of mathematical physics at Turin from 1820 until 1822, when it was abolished because of regional political turmoil. The position was reestablished in 1832, and Avogadro was reappointed in 1834. He held this post until his retirement in 1850 at the age of seventy-four. He spent the last six years of his life continuing with his scientific studies and died in Turin on July 9, 1856.

SIGNIFICANCE

It was not until around 1870 that the term "Avogadro's law" first appeared in print; by the 1880's it had received universal recognition. The realization that common elemental gases existed as diatomic units had an enormous influence on obliterating chemical inconsistencies and linking the chemical and physical properties of substances. Accurate density determinations and atomic and molecular weight measurements for gases also became possible, which aided the rapidly developing area of organic chemistry in the nineteenth century.

Once Avogadro's law was understood, a new era in the development of chemical theories and molecular composition became possible. The Dutch chemist Jacobus van't Hoff showed that Avogadro's law could be applied to solutions as well as gases, for which he was awarded the first Nobel Prize in Chemistry in 1901. For chemists, a significant consequence of Avogadro's law was the realization that one mole of all substances (that is, the atomic or molecular weight of a substance expressed in grams) contains the same number of particles. This quantity, equal to 6.02252×10^{23}, is now known as the Avogadro number in honor of a great scientist who was not recognized in his own lifetime.

—*Nicholas C. Thomas*

FURTHER READING

Causey, Robert J. "Avogadro's Hypothesis and the Duhemian Pitfall." *Journal of Chemical Education* 48 (June, 1971): 365-367. This short article looks at the role of certain chemists in the history of the delayed acceptance of Avogadro's hypothesis.

Fisher, Nicholas. "Avogadro's Hypothesis: Why Did the Chemists Ignore It?" Parts 1 and 2. *History of Science* 20, nos. 2 and 3 (1982): 77-102, 212-231. Fisher examines the reasons why it took so long for Avogadro's ideas to become widely accepted.

Holmyard, E. J. *Makers of Chemistry*. London: Oxford University Press, 1962. Section 52 discusses Avogadro's work in the context of its historical importance. Contains a sample of his handwriting.

Ihde, Aaron J. *The Development of Modern Chemistry*. New York: Harper & Row, 1964. Ihde gives a good account of the Avogadro story in one of the classic texts on chemical history.

Jaffe, Bernard. *Crucibles: The Story of Chemistry*. New York: Dover, 1976. This is one of the most delightful and easy to read accounts of the history of chemistry. Chapter 9 is devoted to Avogadro.

Lavere, Trevor H. *Transforming Matter: A History of Chemistry from Alchemy to Buckyball*. Baltimore: Johns Hopkins University Press, 2001. Chapter 8, "The Rise of Organic Chemistry," contains information about Avogadro and Avogadro's hypothesis.

Morselli, Mario. *Amedeo Avogadro*. Dordrecht, Netherlands: Reidel, 1984. This is the most thorough account of Avogadro's life. Morselli describes most of his major contributions to science, not just the molecular hypothesis. Includes bibliographies for each chapter.

SEE ALSO: John Dalton; Joseph-Louis Gay-Lussac; Dmitry Ivanovich Mendeleyev.

RELATED ARTICLES in *Great Events from History: The Nineteenth Century, 1801-1900:* 1803-1808: Dalton Formulates the Atomic Theory of Matter; 1814: Fraunhofer Invents the Spectroscope; 1869-1871: Mendeleyev Develops the Periodic Table of Elements.

THE BĀB

Persian religious leader

The charismatic religious leader known as the Bāb encouraged revolt against the Persian state and traditional Islamic religious scholars and founded Bābīism, which became the basis for the modern Bahāʾī and Azali faiths.

BORN: October 20, 1819; Shīrāz, Persia (now in Iran)
DIED: July 9, 1850; Tabriz, Persia (now in Iran)
ALSO KNOWN AS: Sayyid ʿAlī Muḥammad Shīrāzi (birth name); Mīrzā ʿalī; Muḥammad; ʿAlī Muḥammad Mīrzā; ʿAlī Muḥammad
AREA OF ACHIEVEMENT: Religion and theology

EARLY LIFE

Born Sayyid ʿAlī Muḥammad Shīrāzi (SAY-yid a-li mu-HAH-mahd shih-RAHZ-ee), the man who would later become known as the Bāb was orphaned as a boy and raised by a maternal uncle. The family believed itself to have been descended from the Prophet Muḥammad. After he received a few years of schooling, his uncle brought him into the family's mercantile business. This experience exposed him to new regions of Iran and to Bushehr in Iraq. During this period, ʿAlī Muḥammad began to study religious literature and to compose prayers and sermons. His lack of institutional religious education and his idiosyncratic use of Arabic language positioned him outside the formalized ranks of religious scholars, or *ulama*. At the same time, the originality of thinking that he demonstrated in his early writings foreshadowed the unique and powerful character of his later work.

In 1840-1841, ʿAlī Muḥammad visited the renowned Shīʿi shrines at Karbala in Iraq, where he came into contact with the leader of the Shaykhī Movement, Sayyid Kazim Rashtī. Although his relationship to Shaykhīʿism during his stay there is poorly documented, it is clear that the visit allowed him to meet many of Rashti's younger disciples, some of whom would later become his own followers. During the following year, ʿAlī Muḥammad was called home to Shīrāz by his family. In August of 1842, he married Kadija Begum, the daughter of his mother's paternal uncle. The following year, his wife bore a child, who died not long afterward.

LIFE'S WORK

After Rashti's death in 1843, his disciples were expecting the appearance of a messiah, the Hidden (twelfth or occulted) Imam of Shīʿi Islam. One of the disciples, Mullā Ḥūsayn of Bushruyah, met with ʿAlī Muḥammad in Shīrāz on May 22, 1844. During their encounter, ʿAlī Muḥammad presented himself as Rashti's successor and as the channel of communication, or "Bāb" (meaning "gate" in Persian), between the Hidden Imam and the Muslim community. When Mullā Husayn accepted the young man's claim that evening, he became the first of many followers to recognize the Bāb as a new spiritual leader. During that same long night, the Bāb began a long commentary in Arabic on the Qurʾān's Yusuf chapter (sura). Bābīs and Bahāʾīism consider that commentary the first of their faith's revealed works, and both communities mark it as the beginning of a new era.

The Bāb's followers were made up principally of Shaykhīs and Shīʿi Muslims, from whom he selected eighteen persons whom he designated the "Letters of the Living." Foremost among them were Mullā Ḥūsayn and a radical female follower Qurrat al-ʿAyn, who would afterward be known as Táhirih. The Bāb instructed his new disciples and sent them out as missionaries on his behalf to the provinces of Iran and Iraq.

In September of 1844, the Bāb made the traditional Islamic pilgrimage to Mecca. He hoped that he might reform mainstream Muslims. However, his journey was a disappointment, because he discovered that the majority of Muslims did not accept his views.

In 1845, while the Bāb was returning home from Mecca, an incident in Shīrāz involving some Bābīs led the governor there to seek the Bāb's arrest. He was taken into custody and placed under house arrest in his uncle's home. There he continued to write and meet with visitors, many of whom were followers arriving from Karbala. Even while under arrest, he continued to direct his growing movement, which by that time had taken its name, Bābīism, from his title. Although successive imprisonments over the next five years prevented the Bāb from active participation in the affairs of his movement, his writings were copied and disseminated, and many pilgrims were able to interview him personally.

During an outbreak of cholera in Shīrāz in September of 1846, the Bāb managed to escape from his imprisonment and make his way to Iṣfahān, where he had sent ahead several of his disciples. Soon, however, growing opposition to his views from the clergy in Iṣfahān resulted in the issue of a holy order (*fatwa*) for his execution. After finding brief refuge at the governor's residence, he was taken to the town of Maku in Azerbaijan, where he arrived in the summer of 1847. Meanwhile, his continued popularity in Persia was a source of consternation for the Persian prime minister. The Persian government feared that a new messianic movement would cause agitation on Russia's Azerbaijani border. In May 1848, the Bāb was transferred to Chiriq near Urmia and placed under strict confinement.

In letters written to his followers during his stay at Maku, the Bāb began to make startling claims, including a proclamation that he was not merely the Gate to the Hidden Imam, but also the messiah himself. In those letters he called for the abolition of Islamic law. These pronouncements led to his being taken to Tabriz, where he was examined by a tribunal of religious and civil dignitaries. Before the tribunal, he made public his claims and was unofficially sentenced to death by several of the religious scholars present.

The Bāb's execution was delayed. However, after Bābī groups rose up against the government in Māzandarān, Neyrīz, and Zanjān, Mirza Taqi Khan Amir Nezam ordered that he be put to death by firing squad. Some sources record the date of his execution as July 8, 1850, but Bahāʾīs commemorate the event on July 9. According to contemporary sources, the Bāb survived the first round of his executioners' shots after bullets broke the rope suspending him. However, a second round of bullets finished the task. The Bāb's body was then apparently thrown into a ditch, along with that of a disciple, where, according to some sources, they were eaten by dogs. Bābī sources, however, maintain that their leader was buried in secret at the Emamzada Ḥasan and later moved from one hiding place to another until put to a final rest in Palestine in 1899. Today, a marble superstructure topped by a gold dome stands over the shrine to the Bāb at Mount Carmel in Haifa, Israel.

The Bāb left a number of writings, the foremost of which is the Bayan (declaration), the repository of laws announced formally by the leader in Azerbaijan. The Bayan provides the main source of Bābī doctrine, replacing the Islamic Shariʾa. It dictates a new direction for prayer, a new ritual calendar, and new eschatological ideas.

In nineteenth century Europe, the Bāb was recognized less for his spiritual doctrines than for his fine features, charismatic presence, and highly developed aesthetic temperament. During the years following his death, however, the Bāb's doctrines were fixed by the two religious figures who succeeded him, Bahāʾullāh and Subh-i Azal. During the 1860's, Bābīs who followed Baha Allah became known as the Bahāʾī, while the minority group that views Subh-i Azal as the successor of the Bāb were known as the Azali.

SIGNIFICANCE

During the era of the Qajar Dynasty (1794-1925), Iran witnessed a proliferation of Shīʿi beliefs and practices, which included both learned and popular expressions of piety. Bābīism and its successors, Azalism and Bahāʾīism, reflect the focus on messianic return that fueled the development of other heterodox doctrines during the nineteenth century. By reinterpreting Shīʿi traditions concerning the Hidden Imam and proclaiming the coming of a new age, the Bāb challenged one of the bases for Iran's religious and political order. Unlike many other messianic movements of the period, Bābīism broke with Islam in significant ways, and it established its own system of administration and ritual practice.

The significance of the Bāb as a charismatic authority figure has endured primarily for members of the Bahāʾī faith, for which he remains not only a founder but also the herald of their messiah, Baha Allah. Though the Bāb and many of his followers were persecuted during the middle of the century, their fierce methods brought them considerable success in propagating their new faith under significant state resistance. At the turn of the twenty-first century, Bahāʾīs constituted the largest religious minority in Iran.

—*Anna Sloan*

FURTHER READING

ʿAbbas Effendi ʿAbd al-Baha. *A Traveller's Narrative Written to Illustrate the Episode of the Bab*. Edited and translated by Edward G. Browne. 2 vols. Cambridge, England: Cambridge University Press, 1891. A firsthand account of the Bāb by the founder of the Bahāʾī faith.

Amanat, Abbas. *Resurrection and Renewal: The Making of the Babi Movement in Iran, 1844-1850*. Ithaca, N.Y.: Cornell University Press, 1989. Study of the historical and sociological background of the early Bābī period.

Browne, Edward G. *Materials for the Study of Babi Religion*. Cambridge, England: Cambridge University Press, 1918. Seminal collection of primary sources on the Bābī faith.

MacEoin, Denis M. "Bab, Sayyed ʿAli Mohammad Sirazi." In *Encyclopaedia Iranica*, edited by Ehsan Yarshater. Vol. 3. New York: Bibliotheca Persia, 2001. Concise article on the Bāb's life and ideas, with a complete bibliography.

_____. *The Sources for the Early Babi Doctrine and History: A Survey*. Leiden, Netherlands: E. J. Brill, 1992. Important study of partly unpublished manuscripts for Bābī history; supplements Edward Browne's earlier collection of documents.

Momen, Mohsen, ed. *The Babi and Baha'i Religions, 1844-1944: Some Contemporary Western Accounts*. Oxford, England: G. Ronald, 1981. A collection of important contemporary European sources on the Bāb.

Nabil Zarandi, Mulla Muhammad. *The Dawn Breakers: Nabil's Narrative of the Early Days of the Baha'i Revelation*. Reprint. Wilmette, Ill.: Baha'i Public Trust, 1999. The primary historical source for the Bāb's life. Written between 1888 and 1890, and first published in English translation by the Bahā'ī leader Shoghi Effendi in 1932.

SEE ALSO: Bahā'ullāh; Jamāl al-Dīn al-Afghānī; Táhirih.

RELATED ARTICLE in *Great Events from History: The Nineteenth Century, 1801-1900:* 1863: Bahā'īism Takes Form.

CHARLES BABBAGE

English mathematician and inventor

While contributing significantly to the mathematics of his time and inventing several practical devices, Babbage conceptually anticipated many of the developments that would later be realized in twentieth century computation science.

BORN: December 26, 1791; London(?), England
DIED: October 18, 1871; London, England
AREAS OF ACHIEVEMENT: Mathematics, science and technology

EARLY LIFE

Charles Babbage, the first child of Benjamin and Elizabeth (Teape) Babbage, was born on December 26, 1791. The exact location of his birth is not known, but it was in the vicinity of London, where his father was a well-to-do banker. The family, on both sides, had been comfortably established in the nearby countryside for several generations. Two more sons were born but died in early childhood. A daughter, Mary Anne, outlived her brother Charles, with whom she had a lifelong close relationship.

As a young child, Charles was subject to fevers, which were naturally of great concern to his parents; when it came time for some formal education, he was placed under the tutelage of a clergyman with the admonition "to attend to his health, but not to press too much knowledge upon him." He later attended school in Enfield, where he was instructed in the classics. Charles's natural aptitude for mathematics in particular, and logical, systematic thinking in general, manifested itself early. As a schoolboy he discovered algebra and, for several months, arose at 3:00 A.M. for self-instruction along with a similarly precocious classmate.

As he grew older, Charles became more robust, and as an adult he was full-figured and rather handsome. When he was twelve years old his parents moved back to Totnes, where they had lived before going to London. That was Charles's home until he entered Cambridge University in 1810. By that time his mathematical self-instruction had progressed into differential and integral calculus. He was very disappointed to find himself far in advance of the mathematical instruction available at the university.

At Cambridge Babbage's social nature developed. He had many friends and joined in numerous nonacademic activities. In addition, Babbage's liberal political consciousness emerged, curiously manifesting itself, in part, by his espousal of Gottfried Wilhelm Leibniz's calculus notation over that of England's Isaac Newton. With a group of like-minded fellow undergraduates, he formed the Analytical Society to study the mathematical developments being made on the Continent.

Babbage was graduated from Cambridge University in 1814. Soon thereafter, against his father's wishes, he was married to Georgiana Whitmore. The young newlyweds settled in London, but Charles continued his studies, receiving his master's degree in 1817. He had no income-producing position at that time, but family moneys allowed the couple to live quite comfortably in London society. Charles was accepted in scientific circles and was elected to the Royal Society in 1816.

LIFE'S WORK

The only professional appointment that Babbage ever held was to the Lucasian Chair of Mathematics at Cam-

Charles Babbage. (Library of Congress)

bridge University (1828-1839), an appointment that had few formal duties. Consequently, and by virtue of his private wealth, he was free to pursue his own interests from his home in London.

For a dozen years after he and Georgiana settled there, he thoroughly enjoyed the social and intellectual atmosphere of the city. Eight children were born to them. Only four survived infancy, and Georgiana died in childbirth with the eighth in 1827. Babbage, devastated by the loss, became an increasingly bitter and sharply critical man. He spent the year following his wife's death traveling on the Continent. He never remarried or had a normal home life again. His surviving children were reared by relatives living outside London. Of the four, the only daughter, also named Georgiana, died as a young girl. Only after they had reached adulthood did Babbage get to know his sons well.

Nevertheless, Babbage, a gregarious man of great vitality, traveled widely and associated with a broad circle of contemporaries such as Charles Darwin and Charles Dickens as well as with fellow scientists at home and abroad. He was a great admirer of the scientific developments in Germany and France and of their associated educational institutions and professional societies. He was a significant force in establishing in England the Cambridge Philosophical Society, the Astronomical Society, the Statistical Society of London, and the British Association for the Advancement of Science. In 1830, he wrote *Reflections on the Decline of Science in England and on Some of Its Causes*, deploring the sad state of the Royal Society in England at the time.

Babbage continued to pursue his mathematical interests beyond his university days, publishing a number of significant papers in the areas of the calculus of functions, algebraic analysis, probability, and geometry. Because this was at a time when British mathematics had reached a dismally low level, Babbage's mathematical work was held in especially high regard on the Continent.

One of the important mathematical needs of that time was for tables of trigonometric, logarithmic, and other functions. Those in existence had been laboriously generated by human calculators and were not without error. About 1821, Babbage, impressed by the potential of machines to carry out fixed operations and recognizing that successive entries in such tables could be expressed in terms of finite differences, conceived of an infallible calculating machine to replace fallible human calculators. The calculated results would be automatically printed out to eliminate transcribing errors.

In constructing his first mechanical calculator, the "difference engine," Babbage was assisted by sizable funding from the British government, which recognized the importance of accurate tables for use in navigation, for example. He designed the engine and personally supervised its construction by a skilled, hired engineer. In connection with this activity Babbage devised some new machine tooling techniques and an unambiguous method of mechanical notation for parts drawings to aid in communication between designer and engineer. A working model was built that may be seen in the British Museum of South Kensington.

The upset associated with his wife's death interrupted further developments for the machine planned by Babbage. After his return to England he faced difficulties with his engineer and with obtaining further government funding. No more work was done on the difference engine after 1832. By that time, however, Babbage had conceived of a much more sophisticated and versatile "analytical engine," one that embodied many ideas now familiar in the world of electronic computers.

The analytical engine had a storage unit for holding numerical input data, a mill for working on them, and a separate operations control section, and he used punched-card systems for input and operation. The rest of Babbage's life—and much of his private fortune—was devoted to improving and refining these basic ideas. Only a modified version of the analytical engine was ever built, but detailed plans for several versions of it were carefully drawn up that show the soundness of Babbage's ideas.

In England, Babbage was widely regarded as an eccentric, irascible genius, but he was much respected abroad. In 1840, he traveled to Italy, where he gave a series of lectures on his analytical engine that was especially well received. A member of the audience, L. F. Menabrea, wrote up those lectures and published them in French. Subsequently, they were translated into English and provided with a lengthy commentary by Countess Ada Lovelace, the daughter of the poet Lord Byron. She was a mathematically precocious teenager when she first met Charles Babbage in 1833. He was pleased with her interest in and appreciation of his calculating machines, and the warm friendship that developed between them lasted throughout her sadly short lifetime.

Babbage was a prolific writer on social, political, economic, and religious, as well as technical, topics. He was the outstanding cryptologist of his time, using mathematical techniques to decipher the codes devised by others. In addition, he invented many practical devices, such as an occulting light that could be used to send messages and an ophthalmoscope for studying the eye. The American scientist Joseph Henry, who visited Babbage on two occasions, wrote of him:

> Hundreds of mechanical appliances in the factories and workshops of Europe and America, scores of ingenious expedients in mining and architecture, the construction of bridges and boring of tunnels, and a world of tools by which labor benefited and the arts improved—all the overflowings of a mind so rich that its very waste became valuable—came from Charles Babbage. He more, perhaps, than any man who ever lived, narrowed the chasm separating science and practical mechanics.

SIGNIFICANCE

Charles Babbage enjoys higher and more widespread esteem today than he ever did during his lifetime. Many of his ideas regarding computing machines were realized only during the late twentieth century, with the advent of modern electronic devices. In his time he was the leading advocate of the systematic application of science to industry and commerce and of statistical methods to economic and social problems—what would today be called "operations research."

Babbage was a man born ahead of his time. Disappointed with the current state of affairs in England, unappreciated, even snubbed at times in his home country, he nevertheless looked forward with optimism to the future that could be made by the application of scientific principles. He has been quoted as saying that he would willingly give up the rest of his life to be able to return five hundred years hence with a guide to explain the intervening advances that he believed were sure to come.

—Katherine R. Sopka

FURTHER READING

Babbage, Charles. *Passages from the Life of a Philosopher.* London: Longman, Green, Longman, Roberts and Green, 1864. Thirty-six autobiographical fragments of very uneven quality and style.

Babbage, Henry P., ed. *Babbage's Calculating Engines: A Collection of Papers Relating to Them—Their History, and Construction.* Los Angeles: Tomash, 1982. Facsimile reprint of 1889 edition published in London, with a new introduction by Allan G. Bromley. Contains thirty-three items, most of them assembled by Charles Babbage before his death. Additions and editing provided by his youngest son.

Collier, Bruce. *The Little Engines That Could've: The Calculating Machines of Charles Babbage.* New York: Garland, 1990. Detailed technical exposition of Babbage's "difference engines," originally written as the author's Harvard University Ph.D. thesis.

Dubbey, J. M. *The Mathematical Work of Charles Babbage.* Cambridge, England: Cambridge University Press, 1978. A critique of the mathematical work of Babbage with extended commentary on the calculus of functions, mathematical notation, and the mathematical basis for the operation of his calculating engines. Includes a list of all of Babbage's mathematical books and papers.

Goldstine, Herman H. *The Computer from Pascal to Von Neumann.* Princeton, N.J.: Princeton University Press, 1972. Chapter 2, "Charles Babbage and His Analytical Engine," describes the concepts developed by Babbage that are inherent in modern computing. Shows how Babbage built upon what previously had been accomplished by others and introduced significant conceptual advances.

Hyman, Anthony. *Charles Babbage: Pioneer of the Modern Computer.* Princeton, N.J.: Princeton University Press, 1982. Full-length biography based on the author's extended research on published works and archival materials. Analyzes the social and political climate of Babbage's time and his involvement aside from his technical achievement. Mathematical discussion of Babbage's engines is contained in the appendixes.

Merz, John Theodore. *A History of European Scientific Thought in the Nineteenth Century*. 2 vols. New York: Dover, 1965. Republication of a work originally published between 1904 and 1912. Chapters 1-3 of volume 1 compare and contrast the scientific spirit in France, Germany, and England during the lifetime of Charles Babbage, with several references to Babbage.

Moseley, Maboth. *Irascible Genius: A Life of Charles Babbage, Inventor*. London: Hutchinson, 1964. Focuses on personal details of Babbage's life. Quotes extensively from correspondence deposited in archives.

Stein, Dorothy. *Ada: A Life and a Legacy*. Cambridge, Mass.: MIT Press, 1985. Biography of Augusta Ada Byron, later countess of Lovelace, with extensive discussion of her relationship with Charles Babbage.

Swade, Doron. *The Difference Engine: Charles Babbage and the Quest to Build the First Computer*. New York: Viking Press, 2001. Technical examination of Babbage's career, focusing on the difficulties he encountered when he tried to build his first "difference engine." Includes sixteen illustrations and photographs.

SEE ALSO: Countess of Lovelace; Mary Somerville.

RELATED ARTICLE in *Great Events from History: The Nineteenth Century, 1801-1900:* 1819-1833: Babbage Designs a Mechanical Calculator.

SIR ROBERT STEPHENSON SMYTH BADEN-POWELL

British military leader

A celebrated military hero of the South African (Boer) War, Baden-Powell gained universal and lasting fame as the founder of the Boy Scouts and the Girl Guides. He was revered as the "chief scout" of the movement, shaped its ideals, and provided its essential literature.

BORN: February 22, 1857; London, England
DIED: January 8, 1941; Nyeri, Kenya
AREAS OF ACHIEVEMENT: Military, social reform

EARLY LIFE

Robert Stephenson Smyth Baden-Powell was the sixth son of an ordained professor of geometry at Oxford University. His mother, his father's third wife, was the daughter of an admiral. Because Baden-Powell's father died when he was three, his mother, whom he always admired greatly, had to raise a family of ten children with extremely limited financial resources. She encouraged the study of natural history and took her children on holidays that featured camping and boating. Nevertheless, Baden-Powell was sent to a famous private school, Charterhouse, where he was very happy.

Baden-Powell participated intensely in school activities, and while he did not make a mark as a scholar or as an athlete, he excelled in theatrical performances and cartooning. He also spent much time learning woodcraft. Later he would borrow much from the principles and practices of his exclusive education for the mass movement that scouting became. Denied admission to Oxford because of his scholarly weaknesses, Baden-Powell took the open examination for direct commission in the army and scored so high that he did not have to attend Sandhurst, the British equivalent of West Point.

Baden-Powell was commissioned as an officer in the Thirteenth Hussars, a cavalry regiment that was stationed in India at the time. He proved to be particularly skillful on reconnaissance missions, which enabled him to develop various scouting techniques. In the military sense, scouting meant sneaking up to spy in order to find out where the enemy was, where they stationed their forces, what their regular routines were, how many men they had, and what kind of equipment they used. The first of his many books were on scouting and boar hunting. He was also a noted polo player.

Baden-Powell's skills were augmented as he fulfilled various military assignments in the empire. He scouted the lesser-known passes of the Drakensberg Mountains of Natal in South Africa disguised as a reporter. He took part in the Southern African campaigns in Zululand and Matabeleland, later to become part of Zimbabwe. He also took part in the West African campaign against the Ashanti in the area that later became Ghana. Adroit scouting of enemy positions, particularly at night, became one of his special talents. While stationed once again in India, he sought to institute training in scouting as a regular feature of soldiers' preparation.

LIFE'S WORK

Baden-Powell was slender and of medium height for his day. He was sandy haired, mustached, and freckled and liked to wear American Western-style hats. He was a warm, friendly, and modest person who nonetheless had a gift for advertising his activities. Before the South African War, commonly known as the Boer War, Baden-Powell was a colonel with a good reputation but no particular fame. He emerged from that war as the youngest major general in the British army and famous throughout the world as a legendary hero. The queen of England honored him, and the public revered him.

Baden-Powell was sent to South Africa as war threatened to break out between the British and the descendants of Dutch settlers, the Afrikaners, who were strongest in the Afrikaner republics of the Transvaal and the Orange Free State. His mission was to organize two regiments of local forces to defend the British colonies of Bechuanaland (which became Botswana) and Matabeleland. He became the commander in charge during the siege of the small but strategic Southern African town of Mafeking for 217 days in 1899 and 1900.

Throughout the early stages of the war, while the British suffered a string of defeats, Mafeking held out and would not surrender despite the constant bombardment, the horde of enemies surrounding it, and dwindling supplies. Baden-Powell distinguished himself by holding up the morale of his troops and the inhabitants. He did so by keeping everybody busy and providing entertainment designed to promote cheerfulness. The defenders enjoyed theatrical productions and cricket games in between bouts of fending off attacks by the numerically superior enemy, often by cleverly outsmarting them. Throughout the siege, Baden-Powell was brave, resourceful, and optimistic and expressed himself in the style of confident understatement so loved by the British public. Because mail could get out, the siege was followed very closely in Great Britain, and its importance was exaggerated in the press. Therefore, there were massive celebrations when the siege was lifted, and Baden-Powell found that he had been made into a hero.

One particular aspect of the siege of Mafeking led to the creation of the scouting movement and thereby determined Baden-Powell's whole future. Baden-Powell organized the young cadets in the town to carry on routine work and thereby free older men for defense. They were so useful that they inspired Baden-Powell to try to organize youth for peaceful pursuits after the war. Another significant accomplishment at this time was the publication of *Aids to Scouting for N.C.O.s and Men* (1899). Noncommissioned officers (NCOs) were subordinate officers, while the "men" in the title were ordinary enlisted soldiers. Baden-Powell was surprised to learn that the book was widely used by teachers and read by boys in Britain.

Sir Robert Stephenson Smyth Baden-Powell. (Library of Congress)

Baden-Powell's military career continued after Mafeking. He was selected to raise and train a police force, called a constabulary, for South Africa. After that he became inspector general of the cavalry. He established a cavalry school and a journal to aid training. He also commanded a division of the Territorial Army, which was similar to a division of the National Guard in the United States. Lieutenant General Baden-Powell retired from the army in 1910 at the age of fifty-three so that he could devote himself full time to the scouting movement.

Baden-Powell was impressed by the religiously oriented Boy's Brigade movement and sought to create a program that would involve masses of boys from all backgrounds and creeds. To this end he rewrote his popular *Aids to Scouting for N.C.O.s and Men* to create the enormously popular *Scouting for Boys* (1908), a book that changed through many editions published over decades. The book led to the sprouting of Boy Scout troops all over Britain and then in Canada, New Zealand, Australia, the United States, and, finally, throughout the world. Rallies, called jamborees, brought together scouts from all over the world. Girls demanded a similar organization; with the help of his sister, Agnes, Baden-Powell established the Girl Guides (called the Girl Scouts in the United States). Several other variations of the movement appeared to satisfy different age groups and interest areas.

As with any large organization, there were dissensions about strong leadership at the center, public recriminations, and forced resignations over various issues. Baden-Powell's reputation survived all of the confrontations. One contentious issue for modern scholars about Baden-Powell's leadership of the Boy Scouts centers on the question of militarism. Because he was a military man, critics perceived militaristic indoctrination as one of the goals of the movement and thought its aim was to strengthen the pool of able-bodied and obedient young men available for British forces. On the other hand, other writers cite the helpfulness, kindness, and generosity advocated in *Scouting for Boys* as well as the clear emphasis on peacetime pursuits. Baden-Powell himself brushed aside the matter by saying that the movement was aimed at developing qualities that served the nation best in peace or war.

Baden-Powell married at the age of fifty-five and had one son and two daughters. His wife, Olave, came to preside over the Girl Guide movement in place of Agnes. Baden-Powell always enjoyed sketching and was able to illustrate many of the books he wrote. He was a prolific and accomplished writer who produced thirty-five books from 1883 to 1940. Some were histories of his campaigns, some were accounts of his travel adventures, and the most widely circulated were about scouting. *Scouting for Boys* was his most famous work.

Baden-Powell was named chief scout of the whole world at one international jamboree. This was perhaps

THE VALUE OF HIDE-AND-SEEK

One of Sir Robert Stephenson Smyth Baden-Powell's goals in creating the Boy Scout movement was to develop skills and moral character in boys that they could put to the service of their country as adults. This passage on the children's game of hide-and-go-seek is an example of how Baden-Powell looked for ways in which to connect children's play with serious adult pursuits.

The game of Hide-and-Seek is really one of the best games for a boy, and can be elaborated until it becomes scouting in the field. It teaches you a lot.

I was strongly addicted to it as a child, and the craft learned in that innocent field of sport has stood me in good stead in many a critical time since. To lie flat in a furrow among the currant bushes when I had not time to reach the neighbouring box bushes before the pursuer came in sight taught me the value of not using the most obvious cover, since it would at once be searched. The hunters went at once to the box bushes as the likely spot, while I could watch their doings from among the stems of the currant bushes.

Often I have seen hostile scouts searching the obvious bits of cover, but they did not find *me* there; and, like the elephant hunter among the fern trees, or a boar in a cotton crop, so a boy in the currant bushes is invisible to the enemy, while he can watch every move of the enemy's legs.

This I found of value when I came to be pursued by mounted military police, who suspected me of being a spy at some manoeuvres abroad. After a rare chase I scrambled over a wall and dropped into an orchard of low fruit trees. Here squatting in a ditch, I watched the legs of the gendarmes' horses while they quartered the plantation, and when they drew away from me I crept to the bank of a deep water channel which formed one of the boundaries of the enclosure. Here I found a small plank bridge by which I could cross, but before doing so I loosened the near end, and passed over, dragging the plank after me.

On the far side the country was open, and before I had gone far the gendarmes spied me, and after a hurried consultation, dashed off at a gallop for the nearest bridge, half a mile away. I promptly turned back, replaced my bridge and recrossed the stream, throwing the plank into the river, and made my way past the village to the next station down the line while the horsemen were still hunting for me in the wrong place.

Source: Robert Baden-Powell, *My Adventures as a Spy* (London: C. A. Pearson, 1915).

one of the greatest of the many honors of his life. Baden-Powell received nearly forty significant medals, the freedom of eleven cities in the United Kingdom, and six honorary doctorates. Nevertheless, he was a man who shied away from the hero worship he inspired and enjoyed the solitude that the hobby of fishing provided.

SIGNIFICANCE

Since it began, the scouting movement has attracted approximately 500 million members and become the most successful and most enduring scheme for training youth ever known. It has had an enormously positive influence on youth through the organized practice of its ideals of loyalty, duty, honesty, kindness, helpfulness, self-reliance, and love of adventure and the outdoors. It was intended to be an inclusive movement, indifferent to class, creed, or ethnic background. It sought to incorporate boys who suffered from bad environments and excite them with adventures in the outdoors and romantic, noble ideals from knights and American Indians. Baden-Powell was the person who started this movement, sustained it, and provided its attractive ideology. From the creation of the scouts in 1908 until his death in East Africa in 1941, it absorbed all of his energies. The movement is his enduring legacy. He was also one of the most prolific and popular writers of the twentieth century. He wrote more than fifty books and pamphlets, gave countless addresses, and wrote countless articles.

Baden-Powell was a kind and cheerful person who shunned the hero worship he inspired. Nevertheless, he was a military man and an imperialist who fought in several colonial wars and made a name for himself by his very heroic and very colorful defense of Mafeking. In the first half of the twentieth century, he was usually revered as a selfless, secular saint. Some recent writers have been quite critical, pointing out how he naturally reflected some of the less pleasant ideas and assumptions of his background and time, such as militarism, racism, nationalism, and self-advertising. However, even the sharpest critics cannot deny the complexity of his character, his charisma, and his enduring influence throughout the world.

—Henry Weisser

FURTHER READING

Baden-Powell of Gilwell, Robert Stephenson Smyth Baden-Powell, Baron. *Scouting for Boys*. London: Pearson, 1967. First published in 1908 by the same publisher, this book has gone through many editions and gives good insight into the ideology of the scouting movement and how it evolved over the years. One author claimed that this book made Baden-Powell the most read of all British authors, with the single exception of William Shakespeare.

Brendon, Piers. *Eminent Edwardians*. Boston: Houghton Mifflin, 1980. An essay on Baden-Powell concludes this book, which examines several of the revered figures of the age with a critical eye. Brendon raises questions about Baden-Powell's treatment of African peoples at Mafeking and unsubstantiated questions about his sexual orientation.

Churchill, Winston S. *Great Contemporaries*. New York: Macmillan, 1942. First published in 1937, this is a collection of Churchill's sharp and witty character sketches that appeared in various magazines and newspapers. Churchill included a sketch of Baden-Powell in this collection. Always an admirer of men of action who upheld the British Empire, Churchill uses his considerable literary skills to present a kind and heroic depiction of Baden-Powell.

Hopkins, Pat, and Heather Dugmore. *The Boy: Baden-Powell and the Siege of Mafeking*. Rivonia, South Africa: Zebra Press, 1999. Revisionist history, maintaining Baden-Powell was a genocidal tyrant, responsible for untold suffering, during his command of the siege.

Jeal, Tim. *The Boy-Man: The Life of Lord Baden-Powell*. New York: William Morrow, 1990. This modern biography is well written and sympathetic toward Baden-Powell. With a total of 670 pages, it chronicles every known episode of the subject's life in considerable detail. Provides both sides of controversies.

MacDonald, Robert H. *Sons of the Empire: The First Frontier and the Boy Scout Movement, 1890-1918*. Toronto: University of Toronto Press, 1993. Explores how the popular mythology of Edwardian Britain influenced Baden-Powell's conception of the scouting movement. Places particular emphasis on the myth of the frontiersman/adventurer, a model of masculinity and preparedness.

Reynolds, Ernest Edwin. *Baden-Powell: A Biography of Lord Baden-Powell of Gilwell, O.M., G.C.M.G., G.C.V.O., K.C.B.* New York: Oxford University Press, 1943. This early biography was written shortly after Baden-Powell's death and tends toward hero worship and an uncritical view of Baden-Powell's shortcomings. Nevertheless, it gives a good idea of the tremendously high esteem in which Baden-Powell was held by nearly all contemporaries.

Rosenthal, Michael. *The Character Factory: Baden-Powell and the Origins of the Boy Scout Movement.* New York: Pantheon Books, 1986. This is a work of sharp revisionism that seeks to knock the hero from his pedestal. The very worst things Baden-Powell said and did are highlighted, particularly his hypocrisy on racial matters. The book is more about the origins of the scouting movement than a biography, and it puts emphasis on the usefulness of the scouting movement for British military ends.

SEE ALSO: Paul Kruger; Cecil Rhodes.

RELATED ARTICLE in *Great Events from History: The Nineteenth Century, 1801-1900:* October 11, 1899-May 31, 1902: South African War.

KARL ERNST VON BAER

German embryologist

Baer gained his greatest fame early in his career through his discovery of the mammalian egg and his contributions to the understanding of embryological development. In his later years, Baer would turn his attention to anthropological investigations, including the state of primitiveness of various races, and to geological studies, especially in Russia.

BORN: February 29, 1792; Piep, near Jerwen, Estonia
DIED: November 28, 1876; Dorpat, Estonia
AREAS OF ACHIEVEMENT: Biology, science and technology

EARLY LIFE

During the mid-sixteenth century, an ancestor of Karl Ernst von Baer (behr) emigrated from Prussia to Livonia, and one of that ancestor's descendants bought an estate in Estonia during the mid-seventeenth century. He was made a member of the Prussian nobility, and by the time of Karl's father, Magnus Johann von Baer, the estate at Piep was of modest size. Karl's father was trained in law and served as a public official. Karl's parents were first cousins, and they had seven daughters and three sons. Because of the large size of the family, Karl was sent to live with his father's childless brother and wife on a nearby estate. It was there that Karl began to cultivate his love of botany and natural history.

Baer entered medical school at the University of Dorpat in 1810 but apparently never planned on a medical career. Instead, upon graduation, he continued his studies in Berlin, Vienna, and finally Würzburg. There he studied under the anatomist Ignaz von Döllinger, a disciple of the German Romantic Friedrich Schelling, and was inspired to devote himself to the study of comparative embryology. In 1819, Baer finally received an appointment as an anatomy professor at Königsberg, where he stayed until 1834. That allowed him to marry Auguste von Medem, a resident of Königsberg, on January 1, 1820. They had five sons, of whom one died in childhood and a second of typhus at the age of twenty-one, and one daughter.

During Baer's tenure at Königsberg, he established himself as a brilliant embryologist and made his initial discoveries of the mammalian egg. His initial contributions are found in the first two volumes of Karl Friedrich Burdach's *Die Physiologie als Erfahrungswissenschaft* (1826-1828; physiology as empirical science). A small brochure entitled *De ovi mammalium et hominis genesis epistola* (1827; *The Discovery of the Mammalian Egg*, 1956) appeared at about the same time. In 1834, he left Königsberg for the Academy of Sciences in St. Petersburg, and in 1837 the still-unfinished second volume of his animal embryology was published, with the two volumes now entitled *Über Entwickelungsgeschichte der Thiere* (1828-1837; on the developmental history of animals). A portion of the missing material for this volume was published posthumously in 1888.

LIFE'S WORK

While at the University of Würzburg, Baer was encouraged by Döllinger and Christian Heinrich Pander to continue the largely unknown work of Caspar Friedrich Wolff concerning the detailed development of the hen's egg. Baer expanded that research to include a wide range of organisms, and the results of his studies virtually assured the epigeneticists of victory in their battle with the preformationists. He was the first to discover and describe the mammalian egg (first found in Burdach's house dog), and he concluded that "every animal which springs from the coition of male and female is developed from an ovum, and none from a simple formative liquid." This important theoretical statement, although based on German *Naturphilosophie* and rejected by later embryologists in the vitalistic terms understood by Baer, allowed for reproductive and embryological studies to continue on a doctrinally unified basis and hence permitted the development of comparative embryology as a discipline.

In addition to describing mammalian and other vertebrate ova, Baer described the developing embryo. One of his major conceptual innovations was that he could see the individual organism as a historical entity that underwent a developmental process. He thus examined organisms at various stages of development, and he was one of the first to describe the process in terms of the formation of germ layers and the gradual production of organs and body parts. Conducting research for the second volume of his monumental work, he examined and compared the developmental processes of different organisms.

In the process, Baer discovered the notochord (the flexible supportive rod ventral to the nerve chord, which is characteristic of all chordates) in the chicken embryo; explained the significance of the gill slits and gill arches, which Martin Rathke had earlier discovered in the embryo; and then explained the cause of the amnion formation. Finally, he described the development of the urogenital system, the formation of the lungs, the development of the digestive canal, and the formation of the nervous system. These findings are detailed and commented on in his pioneering *Über Entwickelungsgeschichte der Thiere*.

Baer is best known for his remarks in the fifth scholium of this work, in which he argued against a single scala naturae (chain of being); presented a parody of Jean-Baptiste de Monet, chevalier de Lamarck; rejected evolution in any form as well as the idea that embryos of higher animals pass through the adult forms of the lower animals; and proposed his own laws of individual development. His comparative embryology had led him to the same conclusions that Georges Cuvier's comparative anatomy had produced, that is, that instead of a single chain of being, there were essentially four animal types. He further argued that comparative embryology actually provided better data than did comparative anatomy for classifying animals. Baer's method for classifying organisms was based on the fact that all animal embryos begin as a single fertilized egg. According to Baer, they diverged immediately into one of four types of development. Vertebrate embryos can be distinguished from the annulate embryos (essentially worms), which in turn are different from the embryos of the mollusks, and all of which differ from the radiata (echinoderms).

In addition, Baer argued that the more general traits of the group of animals to which an embryo belongs appear earlier in individual development than the specialized characteristics; that the more general form always precedes a more specialized form; that every embryo of a given form, rather than passing through the stages of other forms, instead diverges more and more from them; and that, as a result, the embryo of a higher form never resembles the adult of lower animals but only the embryonic form of those animals. He concluded that development takes place from homogeneous and general to heterogeneous and special and that ontological development reflects divergence from other forms rather than parallelism or recapitulation. With this latter conclusion, he thus argued against Johann Meckel's law of parallel development and against Ernst Haeckel's biogenetic law of ontogeny recapitulating phylogeny.

With the publication of the second volume of *Über Entwickelungsgeschichte der Thiere* in 1837, Baer had transformed embryology into a modern laboratory science. Moreover, he had produced a theoretical framework that would greatly influence evolutionary thought even though he would strongly maintain a lifelong anti-evolutionary position. Charles Darwin, for example, used embryological evidence to support his theory and noted that he agreed with Baer's view of divergence rather than the competing doctrine of recapitulation. Darwin also used Baer's standard for judging an organism to be "higher" than another as being related to the degree of differentiation of parts and specialization of function.

By the time the second volume of his great embryological work was published, Baer had left Königsberg for reasons that are not well understood and had settled in St. Petersburg, working at the Academy of Sciences. In 1846, he took a position with the academy in comparative anatomy and physiology, a decision that was related to his long-term interest in anthropology. Under the academy's auspices, he made a number of expeditions to such places as Novaya Zemlya, Lapland, the North Cape, and other regions of Russia as well as England and continental Europe. He collected specimens and made a number of geological discoveries. Although none of his work in these areas was as significant as his embryological achievements, he was instrumental in the founding of the Society of Geography and Ethnology of St. Petersburg and became a cofounder of the German Anthropological Society.

Baer retired from the academy in St. Petersburg in 1862 because of increasing problems with his vision and hearing. In 1867, he went to Dorpat, where he continued his studies and writing until November, 1876, when he died at the age of eighty-four.

SIGNIFICANCE

Karl Ernst von Baer's contributions to the fledgling science of embryology in the nineteenth century were immeasurable. Methodologically and conceptually he provided the basis for further research. However, apart from his empirical findings, little remains in modern biology of Baer's embryology. His adherence to German Idealism and *Naturphilosophie*, including the use of vitalistic explanations in embryological development, and his fervent antievolutionary position caused many scientists in the latter part of the century to ignore him. Nevertheless, his contributions were viewed as monumental during his time. He published more than three hundred papers on topics ranging from embryology and entomology to anthropology, Russian fisheries, and the routes of Odysseus's voyage. He was honored and respected by scientists throughout the world, and admired and loved for his loyalty and wit by his Estonian neighbors.

—*Sara Joan Miles*

FURTHER READING

Baer, Karl Ernst von. *Autobiography of Karl Ernst von Baer*. Edited by Jane Oppenheimer. Translated by H. Schneider. Canton, Mass.: Science History, 1986. This relatively long autobiography was first published by the Estonian Knights in 1864 on the golden jubilee of Baer's doctorate. Oppenheimer provides a very helpful preface.

_____. *Correspondence: Karl Ernst von Baer (1792-1876), Anton Dohrn (1840-1909)*. Edited by Christiane Groeben, translated by Christiane Groeben and Jane M. Oppenheimer. Philadelphia: American Philosophical Society, 1993. A translation of the German correspondence between Baer and Dohrn, a zoologist who was influenced by Baer and Darwin. Includes an introduction by Oppenheimer, a Baer scholar.

Coleman, William. *Biology in the Nineteenth Century: Problems of Form, Function, and Transformation*. New York: Cambridge University Press, 1977. Chapter 3 provides an excellent context for Baer's embryological work as it details the advances in cytology, explains the arguments between preformationists and epigeneticists, and describes the contributions Baer made to the understanding of ontogeny.

Gilbert, Scott F. *A Conceptual History of Modern Embryology*. Baltimore: Johns Hopkins University Press, 1994. Collection of essays exploring the concepts underlying modern embryology and evolutionary biology. Includes an essay about theories by Baer and other embryologists regarding induction, or the processes that determine the fate of embryonic cells and the development of tissues and organs.

Gould, Stephen Jay. "Abscheulich! (Atrocious!)" *Natural History* 109, no. 2 (March, 2000): 42. Describes the lives of Baer and two other scientists—Louis Agassiz and Ernst Haeckel—who became involved in the debate over Darwin's theory of evolution. Explains the trio's contributions to the debate.

Lovejoy, Arthur O. "Recent Criticism of the Darwinian Theory of Recapitulation: Its Grounds and Its Initiator." In *Forerunners of Darwin, 1745-1859*, edited by Bentley Glass et al. Baltimore: Johns Hopkins University Press, 1968. Lovejoy explains why so many misread Baer. Describes Baer's four embryological laws; examines Darwin's misreading of Baer and Baer's fallacies in his criticism of Darwin's theory.

Oppenheimer, Jane M. "An Embryological Enigma in the *Origin of Species*." In *Forerunners of Darwin, 1745-1859*, edited by Bentley Glass et al. Baltimore: Johns Hopkins University Press, 1968. Oppenheimer explores the professional relationship between Darwin and Baer. She examines the various ideas that each developed independently of the other and the diverse ways in which each incorporated these ideas into a total system. Provides an understanding of why Darwin used many of Baer's findings while rejecting his conclusion, and why Baer was unable to support Darwin's evolutionary position.

Ospovat, Dov. "The Influence of Karl Ernst von Baer's Embryology, 1828-1859." *Journal of the History of Biology* 9 (Spring, 1976): 1-28. Discusses the degree of influence that Baer's embryological explanations had during his life, especially in terms of their ability to dislodge the earlier theory of recapitulation. Clarifies the content of Baer's theories and shows the similarities and differences to other theories then available. Ospovat also explains why he disagrees with some of the Baerean scholarship, including the articles by Oppenheimer and Lovejoy cited above.

Winsor, Mary P. *Starfish, Jellyfish, and the Order of Life: Issues in Nineteenth Century Science*. New Haven, Conn.: Yale University Press, 1976. Although this book is not specifically about Baer, it is concerned with the issues and debates that surrounded his work and the work of other embryologists, comparative anatomists, taxonomists, and proponents of evolution. For that reason, it provides the scientific and philosophical context for understanding Baer.

SEE ALSO: Louis Agassiz; Charles Darwin; Sir Edwin Ray Lankester.

RELATED ARTICLES in *Great Events from History: The Nineteenth Century, 1801-1900:* 1854-1862: Wallace's Expeditions Give Rise to Biogeography; November 24, 1859: Darwin Publishes *On the Origin of Species*; 1871: Darwin Publishes *The Descent of Man.*

BAHĀʾULLĀH

Persian religious leader

A leader of a Persian messianic group, Bahāʾullāh founded an Islamic cult known as Bahāʾī that developed into a world religion during the twentieth century. Through his writings, his beliefs in radical social justice and pacifism spread, and Bahāʾī remains a moral force in the modern world.

BORN: November 12, 1817; Tehran, Persia (now in Iran)

DIED: May 29, 1892; Acre, Ottoman Empire (now ʿAkko, Israel)

ALSO KNOWN AS: Mīrzā Ḥoseynʿalī Nūrī (birth name); Mīrzā Ḥusaynʿalī Nūrī; Bahāʾ Allāh; Bahāʾ Ullāh

AREA OF ACHIEVEMENT: Religion and theology

EARLY LIFE

Bahāʾullāh (bah-HAH-oo-LAH) was born Mīrzā Ḥoseynʿalī Nūrī, the son of Mīrzā Abbas Nūrī, a highly placed member of the court of Fath-Ali Shah Qajar. He served as the vizier to the twelfth son of the shah of Persia and was rewarded for his service with the positions of governor and tax-farmer of the provinces of Borojerd and Luristan. Young Mīrzā and his brothers were educated in the best fashion of the day, basking in the expectation that they would one day serve at the royal court.

In 1835, the situation of Mīrzā's family was upset when the father's patron at court, the first minister, fell into disfavor with the new monarch, Muḥammad Shah, and was executed. Having been reduced from courtier to refugee, Mīrzā and his family retired to family estates near Takor. The disillusionment with worldly power and wealth that followed his father's fall helped shape young Mīrzā into an antimaterialist, and one who distrusted power in all of its forms.

Said to have been a sensitive child, Mīrzā also developed a radical pacifism that would deny to political powers the right to use force in enforcing their arbitrary wills. As part of his reaction against the Persian power structure he at first flirted with and then joined, in 1844, a newly developing sect of Shīʿites known as Bābīism. Members of this group believed that one of their number, an imam known as the Bāb, or "gate," had received special post-Islamic revelations from Allah, and that his teachings constituted a new layer of authority atop Islam. Despite the family's fall from grace, young Mīrzā retained friends and some influence at the Persian court and soon emerged as a kind of protector for other Bābīists, whose messianic ideas conflicted with Muslim tradition and teaching.

LIFE'S WORK

At a meeting of Bābīists in Khorasan in 1848, Mīrzā adopted a new name: Bahāʾullāh, which means Glory of Allah. Other Bābīists adopted similar names, as the group's members decided that changing their names was a fine means to give glory to God. At the same meeting, they also decided to reject shariʾa law—the Muslim code of correct conduct—completely in favor of following the revelations of the Bāb, Sayyid ʿAlī-Muḥammad Shīrāzi. However, the Bāb had been arrested and imprisoned in 1847, and at the 1848 meeting a majority of the group chose Bahāʾullāh's brother Azal to serve as its leader in the Bāb's absence. The minority split off in several factions, all harboring some degree of resentment toward to the government for having seized their leader. By 1850, some of these people had directly threatened the government, which executed the Bāb himself and generally attempted to suppress the movement.

Amid this chaos, Bahāʾullāh abandoned Tehran for Karbala in neighboring Iraq in June, 1851. There he served as a missionary for Bābīism and treated his brother as the sect's leader. At the same time, however, he began to sense his own divinely appointed role, though he kept it to himself. Soon, a new first minister in Tehran called Bahāʾullāh back in order to gain Bābīist support for the throne and generally mend fences. An attack on the shah's life by a fringe Bābīist forced Bahāʾullāh to seek safety at the quarters of the Russian ambassador. However, Anti-Bābīist riots forced the Russians to turn Bahāʾullāh over to the authorities, and he spent an agonizing time in a dark, dank Tehran prison. However, this experience among the most downtrodden had its impact on him, too. Although found innocent at his trial, Bahāʾullāh was exiled to Baghdad on January 12, 1853. Many of his followers, including Azal, accompanied him there. However, the group again fractured, and Bahāʾullāh left for Kurdistan in 1854 to live the life of a Sufi dervish in one of Islam's oldest mystical sects.

The two years that Bahāʾullāh spent among the mystics adjusted his vision of the religious life from worldly concerns for religious power to an emphasis on inner spiritual transformation. After returning to Baghdad at his followers' insistence, Bahāʾullāh began writing some of his key texts, which he composed in both Persian and Arabic. These included the Book of Certitude, Hidden Words, and Seven Valleys. Meanwhile, his own influence among the Bābīists grew and spread, as did his reputation as their leader. Persian authorities blamed him for fringe Bābīist violence and insisted that the Ottoman rulers of Baghdad move him farther away from Persian soil. Before leaving Baghdad, however, he decided to share with a few of his closest followers his slowly dawning revelation that he was the promised one promised by the Bāb himself. Indeed, Shīrāzi had prophesied the coming of one greater than he, and Bahāʾullāh was convinced that he was that person. His followers agreed.

Along with twenty family members and Bābīists, Bahāʾullāh trekked westward to the Ottoman capital of Constantinople, where he began laying the groundwork for a new worldwide ministry of personal and social reform. As part of this plan, he called for the development and use of a universal language that would unite all people and began writing letters to world leaders. When he wrote to Christian leaders, he referred to himself as the returned Messiah, Jesus Christ himself. To others he made it clear that he was a special divine manifestation, a prophet whose message trumped the Qurʾān and all other holy books. Indeed, Bahāʾullāh called his letters "suras"—a term normally used by Muslims for chapters of the Qurʾān.

Once again, the Persian government asked the Ottomans to relocate the troublesome Bahāʾullāh, and the latter complied by sending him to Edirne in Rumelia. There Bahāʾullāh's small colony lived from December, 1863, until August, 1868. Meanwhile, Azal and Bābīism were slowly eclipsed as Bahāʾullāh developed his new message, role, and persona. His followers slowly abandoned the label "Bābīist" and adopted a new one, derived from Bahāʾullāh's name: Bahāʾī, the people of glory.

In August, 1868, Bahāʾullāh and his followers were again exiled, this time to the prison colony of Acre on the Mediterranean coast of Palestine. Bahāʾullāh spent two years there, locked in the citadel, but continued to write to such world leaders as the Roman Catholic pope, the Russian czar, and Queen Victoria of Great Britain. Azal and his followers were sent to Famagusta on the island of Cyprus in a parting that embodied the end of Bābīism. In Persia and elsewhere, many Bābīists became Bahāʾīs, while Bahāʾullāh created new rituals and codes to replace the Qurʾān and Shariʾa, and all other such works. These were laid out in his *Kitab-i-aqdas* (most holy book).

Following Bābīist custom, Bahāʾullāh had two wives (some authorities claim that he had three), who bore him a total of fourteen children. From 1877 to 1879 he lived in a fine mansion in Acre. He died in 1892. Before he died he appointed his oldest son, ʿAbd ol-Bahā, to lead the new faith.

SIGNIFICANCE

Bahāʾullāh's significance is bound up with the success and influence of the religion he founded. During the 1990's it was estimated that about five million Bahāʾī followers were living in nearly two hundred countries. Their belief in ultimately a single, universal world religion to which all current ones are related directly reflects Bahāʾullāh's understanding of God's presence in the world and the imperfection of humanity's relation to it. Many followers are drawn by the Bahāʾī emphasis on social justice and pacifism.

Remarkably, the exiled and imprisoned prophet Bahāʾullāh was able not only to establish a new world religion but also to exert a powerful and independent moral voice in the modern world. On the other hand, he was not able to fulfill the mission he believed that he had been called to undertake. His letters to world leaders had little effect, and the century that followed him was history's most violent and, in many ways, least just.

—Joseph P. Byrne

FURTHER READING

Bahaʾuʾllah. *The Kitab-i-Aqdas*. Haifa, Israel: Bahai Publishing Trust, 1994. English translation of the key Bahāʾī text on ritual and conduct.

Balyuzi, H. M. *Bahaʾuʾllah*. New York: Oxford University Press, 1980. Although written more than one-quarter century ago, this book remains the only scholarly monograph on the life of Bahāʾullāh.

Esslemont, J. E. *Bahāʾullāh and the New Era: An Introduction to the Bahaʾi Faith*. Includes a biographical sketch of Bahāʾullāh and material on the development of his ideas, as well as detailed coverage of the later history of the Bahāʾī faith.

Momen, Moojan. *The Bábí and Bahá'í Religions, 1844-*

1944: Some Contemporary Western Accounts. Oxford, England: G. Ronald, 1981. Contains original sources that reveal the impact of Bahāʾullāh's thought on non-Muslims in Europe and America.

Smith, Peter. *The Babi and Bahaʾi Religions: From Messianic Shīʿism to a World Religion*. New York: Cambridge University Press, 1987. A study of the emergence of Bahāʾī out of Bābīism. It places Bahāʾullāh's role in reshaping the Muslim cult in the context of the development of a truly universal moral system.

SEE ALSO: The Bāb; Jamāl al-Dīn al-Afghānī; Táhirih; Queen Victoria.

RELATED ARTICLE in *Great Events from History: The Nineteenth Century, 1801-1900:* 1863: Bahāʾīism Takes Form.

MIKHAIL BAKUNIN

Russian revolutionary leader

The foremost anarchist of his time, Bakunin was a relentless revolutionary agitator who wrote prolifically and inspired a political movement that survived well into the twentieth century.

BORN: May 30, 1814; Premukhino, Russia
DIED: July 1, 1876; Bern, Switzerland
ALSO KNOWN AS: Mikhail Aleksandrovich Bakunin (full name)
AREAS OF ACHIEVEMENT: Philosophy, social reform

EARLY LIFE

Mikhail Aleksandrovich Bakunin (bah-KEW-nihn) was born into a noble Russian family in 1814. The oldest male child in a large family, Bakunin enjoyed an especially close relationship with his four sisters, born between 1811 and 1816. His parents' marriage seems to have been a good one, and Bakunin's childhood, by all accounts, was outwardly happy. A small landowner, Bakunin's father had become a doctor of philosophy at the University of Padua in Italy. He instilled in Bakunin an appreciation of the encyclopedists and the ideas of Jean-Jacques Rousseau. Ultimately, Bakunin would retain traces of both of these influences, elevating reason over faith and advocating a social philosophy that carried Rousseau's emphasis on individual consent to radical lengths.

Bakunin was sent to artillery school in St. Petersburg at the age of fourteen. He eventually was granted a commission and was posted to a military unit on the Polish frontier. The military life was not for Bakunin, and in 1835, he bolted from his unit, narrowly avoiding arrest and certain disgrace for desertion. His disdain for authority now established, Bakunin began the study of German philosophers such as Johann Gottlieb Fichte and Georg Wilhelm Friedrich Hegel and spent time in Moscow, where he became acquainted with Vissarion Grigoryevich Belinsky, advocate of the poor, and Aleksandr Herzen, a reform-minded journalist. In 1840, Bakunin journeyed to Berlin to continue his education. There, he was further influenced toward political radicalism by his contact with some of the Young Hegelians.

This atmosphere of unlimited potential for change fastened Bakunin into a career of revolutionary activism. In 1842, having moved to Dresden, Bakunin published his first theoretical work in a radical journal, concluding it with what remains his most famous aphorism: "The passion for destruction is also a creative passion." A vigorous young man with a charismatic presence, Bakunin had come of age. His education continued as he journeyed to Paris, where he met Pierre-Joseph Proudhon and Karl Marx. Bakunin's concerns would expand to include everything from national liberation for the Slavic peoples to social revolution on a global scale.

LIFE'S WORK

Bakunin began his revolutionary career in earnest during the revolutions of 1848, a series of uprisings by workers that took place in a number of European cities. Bakunin took part in street fighting during the Paris uprising, which began in February. He then traveled to Germany and Poland in an effort to aid the revolutions' spread. In June of 1848, he was present at the Slav congress in Prague, which was brought to an unceremonious end by Austrian troops. Later that year, Bakunin produced his first major manifesto, *An Appeal to the Slavs*. In it, Bakunin cited the tradition of peasant insurrections in Russia as the model for more far-reaching social revolution throughout Europe.

In May, 1849, Bakunin took part in the Dresden insurrection. He was arrested by German authorities and imprisoned until 1851, when he was sent back to Russia. There, after six more years of imprisonment, Bakunin was released to live in Siberia. Prison life had weakened his health and perhaps even dampened his revolutionary spirit temporarily. In 1857, Bakunin married Antonia Kwiatkowski, the daughter of a Polish merchant. The marriage was curious in a number of ways. Antonia was in her teens, Bakunin in his mid-forties at the time of the marriage. Troubled by impotence, Bakunin reportedly never consummated the marriage. Antonia displayed no interest in politics and disliked Bakunin's revolutionary associates. She also appears to have been unfaithful to Bakunin. However, the marriage lasted nearly twenty years. During that time, Antonia endured embarrassing financial straits, dislocation, and a variety of other disappointments, apparently serving as a comfort to her husband until his death.

In 1861, Bakunin managed to escape from his exile in Siberia and traveled to London via Japan and the United States. In London, he renewed his acquaintance with Herzen. Herzen, however, was alienated both by Bakunin's political extremism and by his nearly complete disregard for the dictates of financial responsibility. In 1863, Bakunin tried to take part in the Polish insurrection but got only as far as Sweden. The next year, Bakunin established himself in Italy, surrounding himself with a band of disciples and organizing a largely illusory network of secret revolutionary societies across Europe.

In 1868, Bakunin relocated to Geneva, where he joined the First International, a federation of various working-class parties for world socialism. It was during this period that Bakunin quarreled with Marx, also a powerful member of the International. Though ideological disparities were undoubtedly a factor, much of the conflict was personal, with neither Marx nor Bakunin inclined to share power or the spotlight. In 1872, Marx managed to have Bakunin and his followers expelled from the International. The move ultimately destroyed the International and divided the revolutionary movement in Europe for decades.

Prior to this split, the Paris Commune was formed as a result of the revolution of 1870. Bakunin played no direct role in bringing the Commune into existence, and its success was brief. Nevertheless, the Paris Commune constituted the peak of revolutionary achievement during the nineteenth century. In its rejection of conventional political organization, the Commune lent credibility to Bakunin's ideal of an anarchistic order based on voluntary compliance rather than obedience to laws, no matter how democratically they might be derived.

The last years of Bakunin's life, spent in Switzerland, were marred by his brief association with Sergey Gennadiyevich Nechayev, an unscrupulous opportunist and nihilist who gained Bakunin's favor. This association did little to improve the image of anarchists, and common usage often finds the words anarchist and nihilist treated as synonyms. Otherwise, Bakunin continued to work on a variety of projects, attracted disciples, and wrote. His health and financial situation grew worse, but Bakunin continued working, convinced that the revolution, though it must wait a decade or two, would triumph eventually.

By the time of his death in 1876, Bakunin had written enough to fill volumes, but he never finished a single major work. The fragments that he left behind were ill organized and often unfocused. Thus, where Bakunin far surpassed his rival Marx in terms of direct political action, Marx clearly won the battle of theory, leaving an unfinished but nevertheless impressive body of written work that would inspire successful revolutionary movements as well as a broad array of scholars. Bakuninism also survived but was based more on legend than on the written word.

For Bakunin, the very essence of humanity lay in thought and rebellion. Thought, or science, allowed human beings to understand the world around them in a way that other animals could never approach. Rebellion, or freedom, allowed human beings to exercise thought rather than blindly follow external authorities. To accept religious or political authority was, for Bakunin, to be less than fully human. The full development of humanity, in turn, demanded thoroughgoing social revolution, which would erase all manner of legal tyranny, class domination, and privilege, opening the way for true community.

This mandated not only exposing the bogus foundations of religion and the state but also using mass violence to overthrow established governments once they had been discredited. Bakunin disagreed with Marx on the use of political power to consolidate the gains of revolution. Marx believed that a dictatorship of the proletariat would be needed temporarily (though just how temporarily he did not say) in order to avoid counterrevolution. Bakunin's principled anarchism would not allow this compromise: All political power was tyrannical in Bakunin's eyes, even that exercised in the name of the working class. Bakunin's was a social or communitarian anarchism: Freedom and authority would no longer be at odds with each other. The result, according to Bakunin, would be a splendid harmony, featuring spontaneous cooperation rather than coercion.

SIGNIFICANCE

During his lifetime, Mikhail Bakunin established himself as a charismatic and energetic figure, one who can truly be said to have devoted himself to social revolution. This involved extraordinary hardships. Bakunin risked his life repeatedly, spent years in prison, and, except for his highly sporadic efforts to please Antonia, disregarded material possessions. He was thoroughly impoverished at the end of his life, dependent on friends for his survival. In addition to this life of direct revolutionary action and the sacrifices it entailed, Bakunin wrote tirelessly, producing thousands of pages of treatises, polemics, and letters.

Despite all of this, Bakunin has left behind a rather small footprint. Though anarchist movements remained a force in Italy and Spain through the 1930's, they rarely achieved major status and never achieved victory. Bakuninism never came to rival Marxism. Both have been overshadowed by nationalism, the greatest anathema of all to Bakunin's prescriptions regarding political authority.

Why has Bakunin's influence faded so completely? One reason is that he never achieved the theoretical depth or clarity that Marx did. Marx raised questions, in a systematic way, about history, economics, sociology, and politics that have remained vitally interesting to ideologues as well as to scholars. Bakunin's fragmentary and undisciplined writings could not do the same.

Still, Bakunin's accomplishments were considerable. He transformed a polite, drawing-room philosophy into a notable historical movement, raised pertinent questions about the unlimited power of revolutionary parties and regimes that have come to haunt twentieth century Marxists, and produced written work rich in imagery and ideas. Though they may strike many people as bizarre, these images and ideas reflect commonly held values extrapolated to uncommon lengths. Bakunin valued personal freedom, and he carried this value to a logical extreme. He also tried to honor his beliefs with a life devoted to unflinching action. In this respect, too, Bakunin was uncommon.

—Ira Smolensky

FURTHER READING

Avrich, Paul. *The Russian Anarchists*. Princeton, N.J.: Princeton University Press, 1967. Focuses on the fate of the Russian anarchists, Bakunin's closest political heirs, from the revolution of 1905 to the movement's dissolution shortly after the triumph of Bolshevism in 1917.

Bakunin, Mikhail A. *The Political Philosophy of Bakunin: Scientific Anarchism*. Edited by G. P. Maximoff. New York: Free Press, 1953. Maximoff has carefully assembled a selection of Bakunin's written work, organizing sections according to topic. The result is more coherent and comprehensive than anything produced by Bakunin during his lifetime. Includes a helpful preface, an introduction, and a biographical sketch by three different Bakunin scholars.

Carr, E. H. *Michael Bakunin*. London: Macmillan, 1937. A straightforward biography, innocent of any discernible ideological agenda. Provides a balanced account of the conflict between Bakunin and Marx. Carr does not examine Bakunin's political philosophy in any detail.

Kelly, Aileen. *Mikhail Bakunin: A Study in the Psychology and Politics of Utopianism*. Oxford, England: Clarendon Press, 1982. Kelly tries to reconcile the polar images of Bakunin as champion of liberty, on one hand, and dictatorial confederate of the cynical and despotic Nechayev, on the other. She does so by showing the psychological link between absolute liberty and absolute dictatorship.

McLaughlin, Paul. *Mikhail Bakunin: The Philosophical Basis of His Theory of Anarchism*. New York: Algora, 2002. Challenges Marxist and liberal interpretations of Bakunin's philosophy and criticizes Aileen Kelly's analysis of his ideas (see above).

Masters, Anthony. *Bakunin: The Father of Anarchism*. New York: Saturday Review Press, 1974. A sympathetic view of Bakunin's life and work. Includes a chapter on the fate of Bakuninism in the hundred years or so following Bakunin's death.

Mendel, Arthur P. *Michael Bakunin: Roots of Apocalypse*. New York: Praeger, 1981. A haunting psychohistory which reveals the dark side of Bakunin's revolutionary zeal, linking it to some very personal details in his life as well as the notion of Christian Apocalypse. Impassioned and controversial.

Morland, David. *Demanding the Impossible? Human Nature and Politics in Nineteenth-Century Anarchism*. London: Cassell, 1997. Examines the philosophies of Bakunin, Pierre-Joseph Proudhon, and Pyotr Alekseyevich Kropotkin to explore the relationship between anarchism's notion of human nature and its vision of a stateless society.

Morris, Brian. *Bakunin: The Philosophy of Freedom*. Montreal, Que.: Black Rose Books, 1993. Describes how Bakunin's philosophy combined Enlightenment ideas of freedom with nineteenth century concepts of socialism.

Pyziur, Eugene. *The Doctrine of Anarchism of Michael A. Bakunin*. Milwaukee: Gateway Press, 1955. Provides a clear and undogmatic exposition of Bakunin's political and social philosophy.

Wolff, Robert Paul. *In Defense of Anarchism*. New York: Harper & Row, 1970. Coming from a perspective far different from that of Bakunin, Wolff contends that, philosophically speaking, anarchism is defensible, because the authority of even a democratic state must come at the expense of individual autonomy. Most critics have considered the book subversively clever rather than profound, partly because Wolff lacks Bakunin's commitment to action.

SEE ALSO: Friedrich von Beust; Aleksandr Herzen; Karl Marx; Pierre-Joseph Proudhon.

RELATED ARTICLE in *Great Events from History: The Nineteenth Century, 1801-1900:* September 28, 1864: First International Is Founded.

ROBERT BALDWIN

Canadian politician

Baldwin worked for reform policies that led to responsible government in Upper Canada and, as part of the mid-century "Great Ministry," with Louis Hippolyte La Fontaine, upheld the idea of biculturalism in forging the eventual responsible government established in Canada.

BORN: May 12, 1804; York, Upper Canada (now Toronto, Canada)
DIED: December 9, 1858; Toronto, Canada
AREA OF ACHIEVEMENT: Government and politics

EARLY LIFE

Robert Baldwin's family was of English origin, but its members were established members of the Church of Ireland in Cork before emigrating to Upper Canada in 1799. Robert Baldwin's grandfather was a widower; two sons and four daughters arrived in Canada with him, while one daughter and two sons remained in Ireland.

The eldest son, William Warren Baldwin, earned a degree in medicine from the University of Edinburgh and opted to relocate in the capital, York, rather than remain on his father's sizable acreage. When his medical practice did not prove sufficiently absorbing, Baldwin pursued the study of law. In 1803, he received his license to practice law, and that same year he opened a school and married Margaret Phoebe Willcocks, daughter of an old family friend who had also emigrated from Cork. In 1804, the couple gave birth to their first child, Robert. All told, four Baldwin sons were born to William and Phoebe, but only Robert and William Augustus lived to adulthood.

Through the next several years, William Baldwin acquired considerable wealth and acreage through his legal practice, several fortuitous bequests, and even some architectural undertakings. Following the War of 1812, he continued to prosper in all of his endeavors; in 1818, he built an elegant country home, Spadina House.

William's son Robert was educated by the noted Anglican rector John Strachan, and, in 1820, Robert became a clerk in his father's law office. Soon, he was assuming considerable responsibility during William's frequent absences, and when he was admitted to the bar in 1825, he became a full partner; the firm became W. W. Baldwin and Son. All this success, however, was secondary to Robert's deep and abiding love for his cousin, Augusta Elizabeth Sullivan, daughter of William's sister, Barbara, who had remained in Ireland until after the War of 1812. During a two-year separation, Robert wrote passionate and emotional letters to Eliza, revealing an affection that would remain undimmed to the end of his life.

Although the Baldwin family had the wealth, property, and connections to be a secure part of the Family Compact of Upper Canada, an oligarchical body that cooperated with the British governor, William Baldwin thoroughly rejected that association. By 1824, partly because of his Irish heritage, which excluded him from the largely Scottish clique that dominated the Family Compact, and partly because of the influence of Robert the Emigrant, an Irish Whig supporter of parliamentary reform, William had become influential in the reform movement. Young Robert was also active in the movement, although not as active as two of his friends, Marshall Bidwell and John Rolph.

Robert's personal life took a blissful turn when he married his beloved Eliza in 1827. The following year political controversies made his professional life more adventurous. Libel charges against Francis Collins, publisher of the radical *Canadian Freeman*, and the subsequent dismissal of Judge John Walpole Willis brought Baldwin and Rolph into the midst of the reform agitation which was raging against Lieutenant Governor Sir Peregrine Maitland.

LIFE'S WORK

The increased interest in the reform movement led both William and Robert to seek seats in the parliament of Upper Canada in the general election of 1828. Although William gained the seat in Norfolk County, Robert lost the riding of York, where two other, more avid reformers, William Lyon Mackenzie and Jesse Ketchum, were elected. Robert remained active in the reform movement, however, and gained the riding of the town of York in 1829, in an election held when John Beverly Robinson resigned to become chief justice. His incumbency was brief, because Parliament was dissolved when George IV died in June of 1830, and both Baldwins fell victim, in the next election, to a lessening of reform interest.

For the next few years both Baldwins were preoccupied with their law practices, property management, and architectural concerns. When the large home at Spadina burned in 1834, William built a new mansion in Toronto and rebuilt Spadina as a country home, completing both by 1836. Meanwhile, Robert was engaged in estate planning and legal activities, and was occupied with a growing family. Two sons and two daughters were born during a six-year period: Phoebe Maria (1828), William Willcocks (1830), Augusta Elizabeth (1831), and Robert (1834). The last birth was difficult for Eliza and left her in a weakened condition.

Robert Baldwin. (Library of Congress)

Although the reform movement had regained favor, neither of the Baldwins sought election in 1834. The radical element of the party, led by Mackenzie, seemed to have embraced a republican philosophy more compatible with American interests than with British. This was entirely unsatisfactory to the Baldwins, who still sought a system of responsible cabinet government.

In January of 1836, just before a new lieutenant governor, Sir Francis Bond Head, arrived in Upper Canada, Eliza Baldwin died. Robert was emotionally devastated by her death; always reserved and introspective, he suffered from severe depression for the rest of his life.

Less than two weeks after Eliza's death, Bond Head recognized the need to extend the Executive Council beyond the Family Compact and offered seats to John Rolph and to Robert. Although his personal desire was to decline, Robert heeded the advice of his father, Rolph, and Bidwell, and accepted the position in February of 1836. The appointment was short-lived, as differences between Bond Head and the Council led to the resignation of all six councillors on March 12. The action was significant, however, because they were functioning according to the Baldwin idea—performing in unison as a responsible cabinet.

Neither Robert nor William stood for election in 1836, and in the hope that a change of scene might lessen his deep depression, Robert left, in June, for an extended stay in England and Ireland. The trip had some political ramifications, as he spent time in London trying to persuade the Colonial Office that responsible government, with the Executive Council functioning as a parliamentary cabinet, was feasible for Upper Canada. He found little knowledge of, or interest in, Canada at the Colonial Ministry, although some Whig sympathies did exist. After a sentimental sojourn in Ireland, he returned home in February to find Tory control being angrily challenged by the radical Mackenzie, who was perceived to hold Yankee-type republican tendencies. Moderate voices went unheeded as economic depression and a bank crisis brought on calls for forceful rebellions in both Upper and Lower Canada. The Mackenzie Rebellion rose out of this unrest in 1837 but was suppressed by the British militia.

The crisis prompted Lord Durham's arrival in Upper Canada from England. William Baldwin outlined for him Upper Canada's problems while Robert had drawn up a succinct plan for responsible government. This information formed the core of Durham's 1839 report, which enumerated the wrongs in Canada and recommended responsible government and a union of the two Canadas.

Union took precedence under Durham's successor, Governor Sydenham, and was implemented by imperial authority in 1840. The underlying intent was to demonstrate to the French Canadians the benefits of their assimilation into Anglo-Canadian society. The bait was the possibility that the French could share in controlling public affairs if and when responsible government became a reality.

William Baldwin expected that responsible government would be immediately forthcoming, but major emphasis was put upon realigning the Executive Council. Reluctantly, Robert accepted the position of solicitor general in the new government without a council seat.

After the union became effective in 1841, reformers began to question the wisdom of Robert Baldwin remaining as solicitor general. The March, 1841, election demonstrated that corruption and intimidation could still return a nonreformist majority to Upper Canada. Only Baldwin and five other dedicated reformers were elected. After refusing the oath of supremacy because he denied the position of a foreign prelate, Baldwin demanded from Sydenham that French Canadians be given four cabinet posts. Thoroughly irritated with Baldwin, Sydenham accepted a resignation which Baldwin had offered only as a threat.

In the ensuing session of Parliament, which met in Kingston, Baldwin continued to insist upon the rights of the French Canadians. His popularity in Upper Canada was threatened as even Francis Hincks became sympathetic to the Sydenham ministry. Even though Baldwin assisted Louis Hippolyte La Fontaine, the French party leader, in gaining the seat from fourth York, he was unsuccessful in attempting to push total bicultural institutions. The sincerity of his endeavors was illustrated by the fact that all Robert Baldwin's children were sent to French schools in order that they never be embarrassed, as he was, by the handicap of monolingualism.

Baldwin continued his relentless drive for responsible government against Sydenham's adamant opposition. When Sydenham died in September of 1841, the new governor, Sir Charles Bagot, was persuaded by his advisers that the French Canadian leaders and Robert Baldwin must be brought into the ministry. In September of 1842, both La Fontaine and Baldwin entered the ministry. In November, Bagot became ill and Baldwin and La Fontaine functioned as copremiers of the province. Relations with Bagot's successor, Sir Charles Metcalfe, deteriorated steadily. In November of 1843, the Executive Council resigned and the reformers carried only twelve seats, including Baldwin's, in Upper Canada.

For Robert, the party's defeat followed a period of depression that had come with the death of his father. Having rejected the idea of permanently retiring from politics, Robert rallied for a strong session in the 1844-1845 parliament. The tendencies toward depression, which had been evident since his wife's death in 1836, were growing increasingly troublesome and eventually became incapacitating. His frequent mentions of resignation were not idle threats, but honestly expressed doubts of his own capabilities.

Baldwin dedicated himself during the 1844-1845 session, however, to the cause of responsible government as a constitutional system that would allow Canadians to manage their own affairs. The reform party was too divided to challenge effectively the weak Tory leadership, even though Metcalfe was terminally ill and his replacement, Charles Murray Cathcart, was far less partisan than Metcalfe had been. Not until after the general election of 1848 could the reformers summon the strength to challenge the Tories on a confidence vote. In March of 1848, a vote of nonconfidence brought down the government, and Lord Elgin (who had succeeded Cathcart in January of 1847) called on La Fontaine, whose alliance with Baldwin created the so-called Great Ministry of 1848-1851.

The ministry was plagued by difficulties within the reform party, as well as by questions over provincial finances, brutality in Kingston Penitentiary, compensation for losses during the 1837 rebellions, and trade relations with both the Maritimes and the United States. Nevertheless, the reputation of the Great Ministry was well earned when responsible government was confirmed, when the Municipal Corporations Act passed, and when Canadian nationalism affirmed both actions by rejecting discussions of annexation with the United States, and by recognition of the bicultural aspect of Canadian society. In addition, Baldwin himself can be credited with the creation of the University of Toronto as a government-controlled, rather than church-controlled, institution.

In January of 1851, while Baldwin was under attack from both the Tories and the Clear Grits from within his own party, his mother died. Once more he was overwhelmed with deep depression, becoming seriously ill during the late spring of that year. On June 30, he announced his resignation. La Fontaine did the same, and the Great Ministry was ended. In the ensuing general election, Baldwin stood for reelection in North York but was soundly defeated.

Never again was Robert Baldwin an active participant in political affairs, although he remained important as a perennial potential candidate. Gradually he withdrew into a very private existence, obsessed by the memory of his wife and troubled with the problems of his children. In December of 1858, his wearied body finally gave out, and Robert Baldwin died, leaving a puzzling personal legacy but a solid, secure foundation for responsible government and French rights in Canada.

SIGNIFICANCE

Throughout his life, Robert Baldwin was devoted to family responsibility, dedicated to Christian duty, and consumed by self-doubt. In his own view, he always came up short when he compared his accomplishments to those of his father—when he considered what he himself should have done, and what needed to be done for God and country. Early in life he thought he had found perfect happiness in marrying his cousin, Elizabeth. Her death, after only nine years of marriage, heightened his sense of failure and contributed to the melancholy bouts of depression which often left him dysfunctional.

Despite his self-perceived inadequacies, Baldwin persevered in obtaining a foothold for Dominion status for Canada and a degree of recognition for biculturalism that have since matured into the reality of Canadian identity.

—Helen Jean M. Nugent

FURTHER READING

Baldwin, Robert Macqueen, and Joyce Baldwin. *The Baldwins and the Great Experiment*. Don Mills, Ont.: Longmans, Green, 1969. Helpful work detailing the work of Robert and his father William toward responsible government for Upper Canada.

Baskerville, Peter A. *Ontario: Image, Identity, and Power*. Don Mills, Ont.: Oxford University Press, 2002. Illustrated survey of Ontario history includes information about Baldwin and La Fontaine.

Careless, J. M. S. "Robert Baldwin." In *The Pre-Confederation Premiers: Ontario Government Leaders, 1841-1867*. Toronto: University of Toronto Press, 1980. Well-researched and well-written account utilizing Careless's extensive familiarity with manuscript collections, personal papers, and histories of the period. The complex personality of Baldwin and inter-family relationships are well treated.

Cross, Michael, and Robert L. Fraser. "'The Waste That Lies Before Me': The Public and Private Worlds of Robert Baldwin." In *Canadian Historical Association Historical Papers*, 1983. Sensitive and insightful comparison of Baldwin the politician and Baldwin the family man. The title is taken from Baldwin's own view of his remaining years after the death of his wife. Cross and Fraser relate Baldwin's personal tragedy to his public difficulties.

Leacock, Stephen Butler. *Baldwin, LaFontaine, Hincks: Responsible Government*. Toronto: Morang, 1907, 1910.

Wilson, George E. *The Life of Robert Baldwin: A Study in the Struggle for Responsible Government*. Toronto: Ryerson Press, 1933. Both of the above are interesting earlier works that focus on the role of Baldwin during the years following the Union Act.

SEE ALSO: William Lyon Mackenzie; Susanna Moodie.

RELATED ARTICLES in *Great Events from History: The Nineteenth Century, 1801-1900:* October 23-December 16, 1837: Rebellions Rock British Canada; February 10, 1841: Upper and Lower Canada Unite.

HONORÉ DE BALZAC
French novelist

Balzac's novels, assembled under the collective title The Human Comedy, *form a literary monument comprising some ninety-five works, with more than two thousand characters, that provide a comprehensive survey and analysis of French society and culture at all levels during the first half of the nineteenth century.*

BORN: May 20, 1799; Tours, France
DIED: August 18, 1850; Paris, France
ALSO KNOWN AS: Honoré Balzac (birth name)
AREA OF ACHIEVEMENT: Literature

EARLY LIFE

Honoré Balzac (ahn-noh-ray bahl-zahk) was the son of a peasant, Bernard-François Balzac, who had risen in society to become the head of the hospital administration and deputy mayor of the town of Tours. His mother, Anne Laure Sallambier, was the daughter of an affluent merchant. At the time of his parents' arranged marriage, his father was fifty-one and his mother was nineteen. Perhaps understandably, the eccentric elderly husband and romantic (but soon bitter) young wife both engaged in extramarital affairs and were not always devoted parents. After Balzac was born, he was sent to a wet nurse and was joined two years later by his sister Laure.

After spending the first four years of his life away from his mother, Balzac lived at home until he was seven (though even during this period he attended boarding school and was brought home only on Sundays). At the age of eight, he was sent to the Collège de Vendôme for five years, partly to get him out of the way while his mother had a child by another man, during which time he later claimed never to have been visited by his parents. Many of his biographers see his perception of this early neglect, especially on the part of his mother, as one of the reasons that several of his early love affairs were with older women. These relationships, many of which developed into friendships that lasted for decades, may in turn account for the many portraits of strong, intelligent women in his novels.

Balzac studied law for three years, a knowledge of which later became useful to him as a novelist, but after passing his law examinations in 1819 he announced to his family his determination to become a writer. Despite their apparent coldness, his parents generously agreed to support him for a two-year trial period, during which he lived in a fifth-floor attic in Paris and wrote a five-act verse tragedy on Oliver Cromwell. The experiment was a failure, never produced or even published during his lifetime, but Balzac was committed to his new vocation and merely resolved to turn from the theater to journalism and novel writing to support himself.

Balzac produced a series of novels under various pseudonyms over the next several years, all written in haste and many in collaboration with other hack writers. During this time he also borrowed large sums of money, much of it from his mother and mistress, to establish himself in business, first as a printer, then as a publisher, and eventually as a typefounder, the beginning of a lifelong series of business failures. As a result of these speculative ventures as well as of an always extravagant lifestyle, he was heavily in debt throughout his life, despite a considerable income from his writing in later years.

LIFE'S WORK

In 1829, Balzac published *Les Chouans* (English translation, 1890), the first of his novels to have lasting merit and, significantly, the first published under his own name. Indeed, for his next novel, *La Peau de chagrin* (1831; *The Magic Skin*, 1888), the first of his masterpieces, he even embellished his name by the addition, before his surname, of the particle "de," a sign of nobility to which he was not entitled by law or birth. It is a sign of the esteem of posterity that his name has since been written invariably, if technically inaccurately, as "Honoré de Balzac."

As a result of the pressure to earn money created by his constant condition of indebtedness, Balzac's literary output reached staggering proportions. In the twenty years between 1830 and his death in 1850, the period of his maturity as a writer, he produced some ninety-five novels, featuring more than two thousand characters, as well as several hundred short stories, essays, reviews, and plays. Even more remarkable than the sheer quantity of his work is its remarkably high quality. All but a handful of his novels are of the first rank. Balzac was able to produce so much good work only by virtue of his tremendous physical and mental vitality.

Balzac would begin a typical working day at midnight, when his servant would knock on his door to wake him. He always worked in a long white robe, similar to a monk's, at a table with candles, blank paper (of a slightly blue tinge—so as to tire his eyes less rapidly—and with an especially smooth surface that would allow him to write as quickly and effortlessly as possible), an inkwell, and several raven's quill pens. He never used any notes or books, having already fixed everything in his mind before writing. Balzac would then write for eight hours with no interruptions except for preparing and drinking large quantities of strong black coffee. At eight, he would have a light breakfast and a bath and send the night's work to the printer.

The composition of a novel had only just begun for Balzac at this stage. At about nine o'clock he would begin revising the proofs of the pages he had written the night before. His emendations and additions were often much longer than the text he was correcting, and he therefore required that his galleys be printed on large sheets, with the text occupying only a small square in the middle. After he had completely filled all the margins with scribbled changes, he would send them back to be

BALZAC'S *THE HUMAN COMEDY*

1829	*Les Chouans* (*The Chouans*)
1829	*Physiologie du mariage* (*The Physiology of Marriage*)
1830	*Gobseck* (English translation)
1830, 1869	*La Maison du chat-qui-pelote* (*At the Sign of the Cat and Racket*)
1831	*Le Chef-d'oeuvre inconnu* (*The Unknown Masterpiece*)
1831	*La Peau de chagrin* (*The Wild Ass's Skin*; also as *The Magic Skin*)
1831	*Sarrasine* (English translation)
1832	*Le Curé de Tours* (*The Vicar of Tours*)
1832	*Louis Lambert* (English translation)
1832	*Maître Cornélius* (English translation)
1832-1842	*La Femme de trente ans* (includes *Premières fautes*, 1832, 1842; *Souffrances inconnues*, 1834-1835; *À trente ans*, 1832, 1842; *Le Doigt de dieu*, 1832, 1834-1835, 1842; *Les Deux rencontres*, 1832, 1834-1835, 1842; *and La Vieillesse d'une mère coupable*, 1832, 1842)
1833	*Eugénie Grandet* (English translation, 1859)
1834	*La Recherche de l'absolut* (*Balthazar: Or, Science and Love*, 1859; also as *The Quest of the Absolute*)
1834-1835	*Histoire des treize* (*History of the Thirteen*; also as *The Thirteen*; includes *Ferragus, chef des dévorants, 1834* [*Ferragus, Chief of the Devorants*; also as *The Mystery of the Rue Solymane*]; *La Duchesse de Langeais*, 1834 [*The Duchesse de Langeais*]; and *La Fille aus yeux d'or*, 1834-1835 [*The Girl with the Golden Eyes*])
1834-1835	*Le Père Goriot* (*Daddy Goriot*, 1860; also as *Père Goriot*)
1835	*Melmoth réconcilié* (*Melmoth Converted*)
1836	*Le Lys dans la vallée* (*The Lily in the Valley*)
1837	*Histoire de la grandeur et de la décadence de César Birotteau* (*History of the Grandeur and Downfall of César Birotteau*, 1860; also as *The Rise and Fall of César Birotteau*)
1837-1843	*Illusions perdues* (*Lost Illusions*)
1838-1847, 1869	*Splendeurs et misères des courtisanes* (*The Splendors and Miseries of Courtesans*; includes *Comment aiment les filles*, 1838, 1844 [*The Way That Girls Love*]; *À combien l'amour revient aux viellards*, 1844 [*How Much Love Costs Old Men*] *Où mènent les mauvais chemins*, 1846 [*The End of Bad Roads*]; and *La Dernière incarnation de Vautrin*, 1847 [*The Last Incarnation of Vautrin*])
1840	*Pierrette* (English translation)
1841	*Le Curé de village* (*The Country Parson*)
1842	*Mémoires de deux jeunes mariées* (*The Two Young Brides*)
1842	*Une Ténébreuse affaire* (*The Gondreville Mystery*)
1842	*Ursule Mirouët* (English translation)
1846	*La Cousine Bette* (*Cousin Bette*, 1888)
1847	*Le Cousin Pons* (*Cousin Pons*, 1880)

reset. Even experienced compositors had difficulty deciphering these corrections, and even at double wages they would refuse to work more than an hour at a time on his proof sheets.

When Balzac received the second revised galleys he would repeat the process, sometimes entirely rewriting a book in this manner fifteen or twenty times. Often the exorbitant cost of these typesetting charges would come out of his own fees, but his effort to make all of his work as nearly perfect as possible could never be compromised. He kept a copy of each of his books together with all the successive revisions, and these would often total two thousand pages for a two-hundred-page novel. Finally, toward five in the afternoon, he would finish the day's writing. He would then eat, perhaps see a friend, and plan the next night's writing. At eight he would go to bed, to be awakened again at midnight for another sixteen to eighteen hours of continuous labor.

Only a powerful constitution allowed him to carry out such a demanding work schedule, and Balzac was not the stereotypical delicate poet. Though only five feet, two or three inches tall, he was very strongly built, with a thick, muscular neck, broad shoulders, and a huge chest. His bulk made him an easy target for caricaturists, and most of the likenesses of Balzac that remain are caricatures, not only because of his build but also because he always insisted on attempting to dress in the latest, and invariably the least flattering, fashions, frequently carrying one of his famous gem-studded walking sticks. Despite his lack of what would normally be thought good looks and his absurd manner of dressing, Balzac was quite attractive to women because of his depth of understanding and the intensity of his personality, which immediately dominated any gathering at which he was present, an intensity that even his enemies admitted.

Balzac's workload certainly played a part in shortening his life—he died at the age of fifty-one—but in any given year or two he produced more lasting work than many of his contemporaries did in their entire careers. The huge scale of his achievement makes it impossible to represent or judge his work on the basis of one or two, or even a dozen, examples. Although *Le Père Goriot* (1834-1835; *Father Goriot*, 1844) and *Eugénie Grandet* (1833; English translation, 1859) might be singled out as his best-known works, there are literally dozens of others of the same caliber.

It is doubtful that any other writer has produced so much work of such consistent quality, a consistency that extends over the full twenty years of his maturity. Early novels such as *La Peau de chagrin* and late novels such as *La Cousine Bette* (1846; *Cousin Bette*, 1888) are equally likely to be chosen as examples of his best work. Whereas some critics have noticed certain types of development over this period, for example a tendency toward greater realism, exceptions can be found to every rule. Balzac seems to have reached his full development almost at one stroke, at the age of thirty, and to have continued at full power until a year or two before his death, with few pauses between masterpieces.

When Balzac began the program for *La Comédie humaine* (1829-1848; *The Comedy of Human Life*, 1885-1893, 1896; also known as *The Human Comedy*), he set himself the task of writing the gigantic work in three sections: the "Studies of Manners," which would depict every kind of character and every way of living for every stratum of society; the "Philosophical Studies," which would analyze the motivating causes behind all of this social behavior; and the "Analytical Studies," which would outline the principles behind these various effects and causes. While his project was never to be finished (at his death he left some fifty titles of works to be written in order to complete the structure of the whole), the novels he did write are usually grouped according to these categories, with the "Studies of Manners" further subdivided into scenes of private, provincial, Parisian, political, military, and country life.

In 1842, Balzac signed a contract to issue a collected edition of his works, a massive undertaking requiring the collaboration of three publishers. Believing that "Collected Works" was too commonplace a title for the edition, they asked Balzac to find another title. He chose *The Human Comedy* by way of contrasting his work with Dante's *La divina commedia* (c. 1320; *The Divine Comedy*, 1802) and also to suggest its comprehensive scope, announcing in his preface to the edition his intention to present a history and criticism of the whole of society.

SIGNIFICANCE

Although Honoré de Balzac lived to write "only" 95 of the 144 novels he had planned for the structure of *The Human Comedy*, the completed sections constitute one of the greatest achievements ever produced by the literary imagination, a series of explorations not only of French society of the first half of the nineteenth century but also of an unparalleled range of human types. Balzac was, in his time, France's most popular writer and, internationally, France's most respected author. Since that time, his prestige has steadily grown. As André Maurois has asserted:

> It has been said that the works of Balzac, of William Shakespeare, and of [Leo] Tolstoy constitute the three great monuments raised by humanity to humanity. That is true and moreover *The Human Comedy* is the vastest and most complete of the three.
>
> —*William Nelles*

FURTHER READING

Bertault, Philippe. *Balzac and the Human Comedy*. Translated by Richard Monges. New York: New York University Press, 1963. Primarily a study of *The Human Comedy* rather than of its author, but it does include analysis of the effects of Balzac's life on his work. Features a convenient ten-page biographical sketch at the beginning of the text.

Gerson, Noel B. *The Prodigal Genius: The Life and Times of Honoré de Balzac*. Garden City, N.Y.: Doubleday, 1972. Written by a best-selling author for a general audience. Despite occasional sensationalism, an absorbing and well-researched account and a very good introduction for the nonspecialist.

Hunt, Herbert J. *Honoré de Balzac: A Biography*. London: Athlone Press, 1957. A straightforward historical narration of the major events of Balzac's life, competent and concise, though superseded by more recent works. Hunt's running commentary on the literary works is often still interesting. Many passages quoted in French are not translated.

Marceau, Félicien. *Balzac and His World*. Translated by Derek Coltman. New York: Orion Press, 1966. More a study of Balzac's characters than of his life, but interspersed with much relevant biographical information.

Maurois, André. *Prometheus: The Life of Balzac*. Translated by Norman Denny. New York: Harper & Row, 1965. The definitive biography by France's premier literary biographer. Primarily aimed at an audience already knowledgeable about the subject. A thorough and usually objective account of the facts of Balzac's life, clarifying many previously obscure details. Despite its close attention to specifics, however, Maurois's book is also a highly readable and entertaining narrative.

Oliver, E. J. *Balzac: The European*. London: Sheed & Ward, 1959. An overview of both the life and the novels, organized around a variety of thematic emphases such as "Women of Letters," "Religion," and "The Absolute." Provides a usefully condensed survey.

Pritchett, V. S. *Balzac*. New York: Alfred A. Knopf, 1973. Reprint. London: Hogarth Press, 1992. Includes more than two hundred valuable illustrations of Balzac, his contemporaries, and his environment, among them forty high-quality color plates. Extremely valuable for orienting the reader unfamiliar with Balzac and his time and place.

Robb, Graham. *Balzac: A Life*. New York: W. W. Norton, 1994. Robb's biography portrays Balzac as a man whose powers of creation were equaled by his self-destructive tendencies.

Zweig, Stefan. *Balzac*. Edited by Richard Friedenthal, translated by William Rose and Dorothy Rose. New York: Viking Press, 1946. After Maurois, Zweig is the best biographer of Balzac. Although slightly dated, this fascinating book reads almost like a novel about his life. Zweig's tendency to offer his own interpretations of events makes his work more subjective than Maurois's, and perhaps less reliable in some particulars, but it remains the best introduction for the nonspecialist.

SEE ALSO: Auguste Rodin; Stendhal; Hippolyte Taine.

RELATED ARTICLES in *Great Events from History: The Nineteenth Century, 1801-1900:* October 1-December 15, 1856: Flaubert Publishes *Madame Bovary*; c. 1865: Naturalist Movement Begins.

GEORGE BANCROFT
American historian

Contributing greatly to both scholarly and popular thought in the nineteenth century United States, George Bancroft explained the transformation of the British colonies into the United States in terms of the growth and development of liberty, democracy, and nationalism.

BORN: October 3, 1800; Worcester, Massachusetts
DIED: January 17, 1891; Washington, D.C.
AREAS OF ACHIEVEMENT: Historiography, scholarship

EARLY LIFE

George Bancroft was born on October 3, 1800, in Worcester, Massachusetts. He was the eighth of thirteen children produced by the union of Aaron Bancroft and Lucretia Chandler, both of whom came from old-stock New England families. Lucretia Chandler, the daughter of Judge John Chandler, known as "Tory John" because he had opposed independence, was a good-natured and spirited woman, unlettered, but devoted to her husband and children. Aaron Bancroft was a struggling Congregational minister who played a leading role in the early Unitarian movement. Devoted to education as the basis for personal and social reform, he introduced young George to the classics, emphasized the virtues of self-discipline and obedience, and passed on to his offspring the conviction that humankind is essentially good, but not without sin, and flawed by ignorance and misunderstanding.

Bancroft attended Phillips Exeter Academy, entered Harvard College at thirteen, and became a favorite of President John Thornton Kirkland. Moral philosophy dominated the Harvard curriculum at that time, and like his father before him, Bancroft found that particular mixture of Lockean rationalism and Scottish common sense captivating. It clearly categorized knowledge, stressed the importance of faith as well as reason, and acknowledged divine law as the driving force of the universe. In fact, moral philosophy provided the intellectual and theological perspective that would stay with Bancroft all of his life.

After taking his A.B. degree in 1817, Bancroft continued at Harvard for another year as a graduate student in divinity before continuing his education at the University of Göttingen in Germany. He was encouraged to go to Göttingen by Edward Everett, Joseph Green Cogswell, and George Ticknor, three young Harvard teachers who had done graduate work there and confirmed its reputation as the leading university in Europe. Thanks to President Kirkland, Bancroft got financial support from Harvard and began his studies at Göttingen in the fall of 1818.

Over the next two years, Bancroft rose early and studied late, immersed himself in German literature, and took courses in philosophy, biblical criticism, and history from some of the leading scholars in Europe. His hard work allowed him to take the grueling doctoral examinations early. In September, 1820, he successfully defended his thesis and was awarded the degree of Doctor of Philosophy and Master of Arts. After six more months of study at the University of Berlin, Bancroft traveled Europe and the British Isles for the next year. He met and talked with Johann Wolfgang von Goethe, George Gordon, Lord Byron, the Marquis de Lafayette, and Alexander von Humboldt, to mention the most prominent personages whom he sought out. Bancroft grew up, both intellectually and psychologically, during his four years in Europe.

When he returned to the United States in 1822, Bancroft was still considering either teaching or preaching. He was an engaging young man, known for his social grace and dignified bearing. He was shorter than average and slight in build, rather handsome, and distinguished by clear-cut facial features that included a prominent nose, strikingly alert eyes, and carefully trimmed hair and beard. Some of his former Harvard teachers were put off by his foreign manners, his suggested reforms for the college, and his pompous request that he be given a professorship. President Kirkland remained a faithful ally, however, and secured for him an appointment as tutor in Greek. Though the opportunity hardly offered him the status he had had in mind, Bancroft decided to make the most of it. He added new rigor to his Greek courses and drove his students to the brink of rebellion, though they reportedly were far ahead of other Greek students.

During the year of his rather unsuccessful tutorship, Bancroft also tried his hand at preaching in various churches on several occasions. He seems to have pleased few people with his sermons, not even his father, and certainly not himself. In early 1823, disheartened by his failure to reform Harvard and by the resistance of the students, Bancroft joined with Joseph Cogswell to set up the Round Hill School for Boys at Northampton. For the next eight years, he labored to adapt the educational methods of the German gymnasium to the United States. Round Hill was ahead of its time and widely praised, but it had financial problems, and Bancroft, the primary teacher, contributed to them with his demanding academic standards and less than cordial relations with students. In 1831, he sold his interest in Round Hill to Cogswell and put classroom teaching behind him.

Bancroft married Sarah Dwight in 1827. Her family was involved in various business enterprises in Springfield, Massachusetts, and Bancroft became an agent for the Dwight banking interests. To the chagrin of his young wife, who stayed home and often felt neglected, he traveled much of the time on business. He also embarked upon a literary career.

Bancroft's first published work had been a pedestrian volume of poetry (*Poems*, 1823), whose existence he later found embarrassing. While teaching at Round Hill, he translated several German works on Latin and Greek grammar and three volumes of history by Arnold H. L. Heeren, one of the distinguished professors who had taught him at Göttingen. Under the encouragement of editor Jared Sparks, he became a regular contributor of book reviews and essays on finance, politics, and scholarly topics to the *North American Review*. Sparks was much involved in collecting documents and writing history and may well have influenced Bancroft to embark upon his own work in American history.

George Bancroft. (Library of Congress)

Bancroft was ambitious—so much so that Lillian Handlin, one of his biographers, maintains that he was rather insensitive toward his first wife and never very sympathetic toward his children. Sickly and morose, Sarah Bancroft died in 1837, shortly after the death of an infant daughter. Thereafter, relations between Bancroft and his three surviving children—Louise, John, and George—were seldom harmonious and often very strained.

LIFE'S WORK

While achieving a measure of success in business, Bancroft became even more committed to the notion that a man of letters could and should play an important part in improving society. That conviction increasingly shaped his political involvement and scholarly ambitions. In an oration that he delivered on July 4, 1826, at Northampton, Bancroft had made it clear that he was a Jeffersonian Democrat, favoring the dispersion of property and the removal of voting restrictions. His views were in sympathy with the emerging Jacksonian Party.

Writing in the *North American Review* in 1831, Bancroft analyzed the National Bank in terms that pleased Jacksonians and shocked his Whig associates. His Harvard friends as well as the Dwights were almost solidly against Andrew Jackson, and Massachusetts itself was completely dominated by the Whigs. The Jacksonians in the state were badly divided, as Bancroft himself found out when the Northampton Workingmen nominated him for the General Court but failed to line up the other elements of the fragmented Democratic coalition in the election of 1834. Viciously attacked by the Whigs in the press and distrusted by many Jacksonians, Bancroft got few votes. Nevertheless, he was attracted to politics, and Jacksonian leaders recognized his talents and cultivated him.

Rebuffed politically, Bancroft experienced considerable scholarly acclaim in 1834 with the publication of the first volume of his history of the United States. He may have acquired an interest in history from his father, who had written a modestly successful popular biography of George Washington years before. At Göttingen, he studied history under Hereen. While at Round Hill, he had worked up an outline of American history for a proposed world history course at Round Hill.

By the early 1830's, Bancroft had decided that there was a real need for a "critical history" of the United States and believed himself superbly equipped to write it. The first volume, which carried development of the American colonies to 1650, was popular with both the literary critics and the general public. "You have written a work that will last while the memory of America lasts," wrote Edward Everett, still a good friend despite diverging politics. It was a classic, Everett continued, "full of learning, information, common sense, and philosophy; full of taste and eloquence; full of life and power." Ralph Waldo Emerson was equally complimentary, writing that the grandeur of the work made him weep. Emerson proclaimed it "the most valuable and splendid piece of historical composition, not only in English, but in any tongue."

Heady praise indeed, calculated to encourage the masterful young scholar, and it did. Two other volumes, the second published in 1837 and the third in 1840, followed the development of the colonies to 1748. The central theme was clear enough. From the beginning of English settlement, the United States had progressively expanded the twin realms of economic and political liberty. Indeed, political and economic monopoly gave way to the rise of representative politics and free enterprise economics in colonial America. According to Bancroft, this burgeoning freedom nurtured an emerging American nationality. It was a grand and inspiring story, and Bancroft told it with an eloquence and appreciation for drama that appealed not only to Emerson but also to thousands of his countrymen disturbed by growing sectional tensions that threatened national unity during the 1830's. By 1841, his annual income from sales of the three volumes reached $4,350. Bancroft was almost unique among scholars; he made scholarship pay, and pay handsomely.

Political success came upon the heels of scholarly recognition. In 1837, as a reward for Bancroft's efforts on behalf of the Democratic Party in Massachusetts, President Martin Van Buren appointed the budding historian collector of the Port of Boston, a most important patronage position. Over the next few years, Bancroft emerged as the leader of the Democratic Party in Massachusetts and edited its leading newspaper. He was the Democratic nominee for governor in 1844, and though he lost that election, his efforts on behalf of James K. Polk secured for him a place in the new president's cabinet as secretary of the Navy (1845-1846).

While serving in that position, Bancroft endorsed Polk's expansionist plans and the Mexican War, tied promotion in the Navy more to merit than to seniority, and founded the Naval Academy at Annapolis. What he wanted most, however, was a diplomatic assignment, and Polk obligingly appointed him ambassador to England in 1846, where he served for the next two years and relished every minute. He moved in the highest political and literary circles, gained access to collections of documents in both England and France, and made friends with the English historians Thomas Macaulay, Henry Milman, and Henry Hallam and the French historians François Guizot and Louis Adolphe Thiers. He hired clerks to copy significant documents and undoubtedly had more information available to him than any previous American historian. His tenure as minister to the Court of St. James certainly enriched subsequent volumes of his history of the United States.

Returning to the United States in 1849, Bancroft decided to make his home in cosmopolitan New York. In 1838, a year after his first wife died, he had remarried, taking as his second wife Mrs. Elizabeth (Davis) Bliss, a Boston widow with two sons of her own. Her first husband had been a law partner of Daniel Webster. She was bright, witty, and urbane; Bancroft found her the perfect mate and reveled in their marriage. He and his three children, however, remained on less than cordial terms, despite the efforts of Elizabeth to heal the breach.

From 1849 to 1867, Bancroft devoted himself to writing his history and participating in the intellectual and social life of New York City and Newport, Rhode Island, where he maintained a summer home. He wrote six more volumes that brought his *History of the United States* to the year 1782. These volumes recounted American nationalism being forged by the fires of protest and revolution. They were quite popular and sold well, though the critics were less laudatory than before. Bancroft provoked a minor storm when he dared to question the military decisions of certain American generals in the revolution; the descendants of the generals responded with vehemence in what became known as the War of the Grandfathers.

Much more troubling to him was the talk of nullification and secession that increasingly threatened the nation by the late 1840's. Bancroft took refuge in his work as the nation drifted toward civil war. As a politician and as a historian, he showed little concern regarding slavery, though he privately deplored the peculiar institution and the threat it posed to the Union. Once the war began, though still a states' rights Democrat, Bancroft came to appreciate Abraham Lincoln's leadership, subsequently advised President Andrew Johnson during Reconstruction, and was rewarded by appointment as ambassador to Prussia, where he served from 1867 to 1874. Once again, he took advantage of diplomatic service to search for American materials in European archives. He became an ardent supporter of Prince Otto von Bismarck and German unification and made friends with Leopold von Ranke and other German scholars. His public statement praising the Germans during the Franco-Prussian War enraged the French, but President Ulysses S. Grant retained him as ambassador to Germany because of his intimacy with Bismarck and the Prussian elite.

Returning to the United States in 1874, Bancroft lived the remainder of his life in Washington, D.C., usually spending the summers in Newport. That same year, he finished the tenth volume of his history, focusing on the closing years of the American Revolution. Two years later, he published the "Centenary Edition" of his *History of the United States* in six volumes. In 1882, he brought out two volumes entitled *History of the Formation of the Constitution of the United States of America*, apparently inspired by recent Supreme Court decisions that, in his opinion, violated the principles of the nation's Founders. Interestingly, he portrayed the Constitution as enshrining democratic ideas that ought not to be tampered with either by the Supreme Court or by legislative majorities.

Bancroft's last published work was a biography, *Martin Van Buren to the End of His Political Career* (1889), which he had begun during the early 1840's but put aside when Van Buren did not run in 1844. During his last years, Bancroft, still as charming and urbane as ever and wearing a flowing white beard, was the acknowledged patriarch of Washington literary and social circles. After his wife died in 1886, a daughter of his eldest son, George, stayed with him for a few years, and he then lived with his youngest son, John Chandler Bancroft. He died in Washington, D.C., in January, 1891.

SIGNIFICANCE

Upon his death, George Bancroft was eulogized as the "Father of American History." His contribution was truly profound. It is sometimes forgotten that Bancroft pioneered the collection of American documents from foreign archives. He joined Jared Sparks and Peter Force in collecting and encouraging others to preserve early American documents scattered throughout the United States. In 1869, Bancroft estimated that he had spent between $50,000 and $75,000 in paying copyists, collecting, and researching. By the time of his death, that figure was well over $100,000. As a diplomat in England and later Germany, he had unparalleled access to both public and private archives in Europe and exploited his privileges to the fullest; his several hundred volumes of collected documents, located now in the New York Public Library, bear eloquent testimony to his industry. Whatever his shortcomings as a historian, Bancroft recognized that the sources were all important, and he must be credited with doing much to make sure that subsequent generations would have access to them.

Bancroft believed that his writing of American history accurately reflected the sources. He was not a little offended when the great von Ranke told him that "his history" was the best ever written from the democratic point of view. The fact is, though, that Bancroft projected his own patriotism and politics into his interpretation of American history. As J. Franklin Jameson put it, Bancroft voted for Jackson throughout his historical writing. He also had a tendency to quote material rather loosely, leaving himself open to the charge of manipulating the sources. By the time of his death, academic historians were dismissing his work as simply not adequate in terms of the canons of critical scholarship.

Bancroft was zealous, not dishonest, and his shortcomings were no worse than those of most other gentlemanly scholars of his day. Like his peers, he slighted economics and social factors, emphasizing instead politics, military affairs, and religion. Despite his knowledge of the English sources, he virtually neglected the British point of view of the American Revolution and constantly equated Catholicism with corruption and tyranny.

During the late twentieth century, Bancroft's writings have not been widely read because of his unabashed nationalism. Much of his basic interpretation has been retained, however, by scholars of the so-called Consensus School of American history, and that interpretation, though considerably more complex than Bancroft's limited point of view, still dominates American historiography.

Bancroft did more than simply write history. He explained American nationalism in terms of heroic deeds, economic and political freedom, and the inevitable triumph of goodness and justice over abusive tyranny. His popular history reinforced a national mythology that brought comfort to nineteenth century Americans stunned by civil war, the Industrial Revolution, and political turmoil. He found a unity of purpose and experience in early American history that continues to appeal to the pluralistic United States. George Bancroft's legacy has proven to be a lasting one. He shaped the past in terms of the dreams and aspirations of his generation. If any historian deserves to be called the Herodotus of the American people, Bancroft is surely the one.

—*Ronald Howard*

FURTHER READING

Bassett, John Spencer. *The Middle Group of American Historians*. New York: Macmillan. Reprint. Freeport, N.Y.: Books for Libraries Press, 1966. A fine study of the nineteenth century historians known loosely as the Patriotic School, with special emphasis on leading figures such as Jeremy Belknap, George Bancroft, Jared Sparks, William Hickling Prescott, John Lothrop Motley, and Peter Force. Critical of Bancroft's methods and political bias, it is excellent for placing his life and work in its cultural context. Credits Bancroft for his literary style and ability to reflect the nationalistic aspirations of his generation of Americans.

Bush, Harold K., Jr. "Re-inventing the Puritan Fathers: George Bancroft, Nathaniel Hawthorne, and the Birth of Endicott's Ghost." *ATQ* 9, no. 2 (June, 1995): 31. Describes Bancroft's attempts to establish historical opinion about the Puritans.

Handlin, Lilian. *George Bancroft: The Intellectual as Democrat*. New York: Harper & Row, 1984. The most recent and perhaps best biography of Bancroft in terms of integrating his personality, scholarship, and politics. Emphasis is given to the influence of moral philosophy in his thinking and writing. Challenges the notion that either German Romanticism or egalitarian politics primarily influenced his work.

Hoffer, Peter Charles. *Liberty or Order: Two Views of American History from the Revolutionary Crisis to the Early Works of George Bancroft and Wendell Phillips*. New York: Garland, 1988. Analyzes the consistent theme of liberty versus order in the work of eighteenth and nineteenth century historians, including Bancroft.

Howe, M. A. DeWolf. *The Life and Letters of George Bancroft*. 2 vols. New York: Charles Scribner's Sons, 1908. The authorized biography of Bancroft, this work is exceptionally detailed, filled with extensive quotations from his correspondence. Bancroft literally speaks for himself here. Not analytical, but tells much about the man and his time.

Kraus, Michael. *The Writing of American History*. Norman: University of Oklahoma Press, 1953. Dated for historical trends after the 1950's, this remains one of the best historiographical works ever written. It judiciously evaluates Bancroft as a historian and places him in relationship to other nineteenth century historians. Very good for the broad perspective.

Leeman, William P. "George Bancroft's Great Legacy." *Naval History* 14, no. 5 (October, 2001): 48. Recounts Bancroft's successful attempt to create the U.S. Naval Academy.

Nye, Russel B. *George Bancroft: Brahmin Rebel*. New York: Alfred A. Knopf, 1945. Beautifully written biography that focuses on the intellectual forces that shaped Bancroft as a historian. It portrays him as a political rebel yet part of the mainstream of New England thought, very much in the Emersonian tradition and significantly influenced by German Romanticism. Although modified by Handlin's research, this is in many ways the most insightful biography of Bancroft.

Vitzthum, Richard C. *The American Compromise: Theme and Method in the Histories of Bancroft, Parkman, and Adams*. Norman: University of Oklahoma Press, 1974. A fascinating study that relates Bancroft and his work to the efforts of two other popular nineteenth century historians. Vitzthum claims the three were guided by the belief that Americans were driven by the struggle between separatist forces and unifying forces; very nationalistic, they viewed progress in terms of union and a strong central government.

Wood, Kirk. "George Bancroft." In *American Historians, 1607-1865*. Vol. 30 in *Dictionary of Literary Biography*, edited by Clyde Wilson. Detroit: Gale Research, 1984. A concise but analytical study of Bancroft as a historian and the differing views scholars have taken of him. Wood summarizes Bancroft's history and explains it in terms of the quest for American nationality and union before the Civil War.

SEE ALSO: Francis Parkman; James K. Polk; William Hickling Prescott.

RELATED ARTICLE in *Great Events from History: The Nineteenth Century, 1801-1900:* 1820's-1830's: Free Public School Movement.

HENRY BARNARD
American educator

Combining a high regard for learning and a strong sense of civic responsibility, Barnard stimulated and directed the development of American public education during its formative years.

BORN: January 24, 1811; Hartford, Connecticut
DIED: July 5, 1900; Hartford, Connecticut
AREA OF ACHIEVEMENT: Education

EARLY LIFE

Henry Barnard was born January 24, 1811, in Hartford, Connecticut. Barnard's mother, Elizabeth Andrus, died when Henry was four years old; his father, Chauncey Barnard, was a former sailor and prosperous farmer-businessperson. Hartford was little more than a small country town during Barnard's childhood, but its status as one of Connecticut's capitals meant that he grew up in an atmosphere of politics and public service.

Ironically, the man who would later be hailed as a founder of the public school so hated his first encounter with that institution that he conspired with a classmate to run away to sea. His father overheard them and the following day offered Henry a choice of leaving the district school and going to either sea or boarding school. Barnard chose the latter alternative and enrolled in Monson Academy, Monson, Massachusetts. Barnard was no bookworm, but he enjoyed his studies at Monson and developed an interest in literature and debating. Returning to Hartford, he received private tutoring and attended the Hopkins Grammar School in preparation for college. In 1826, Barnard entered Yale University, where he not only enhanced his writing and speaking skills but also was suspended briefly for participating in a student food protest.

Having been graduated with distinction from Yale in 1830, Barnard resolved to devote his life to public service. He taught for a year but appears at first to have given little thought of devoting himself exclusively to the field of education. Instead, he became involved in Whig politics and studied law. Barnard was admitted to the bar in 1835, but before beginning his legal practice he spent a year in Europe, where he met and talked with prominent European intellectuals and educators.

A year after Barnard's return to the United States, Hartford voters elected him to the Connecticut legislature, where he served from 1837 to 1840. He was active in promoting a broad range of social reform legislation, his most notable legislative achievement occurring in 1838, when he wrote and secured passage of a bill creating a state board of school commissioners and a secretary to supervise public education. This event proved to have a decisive influence on his life.

LIFE'S WORK

In 1838, Barnard was appointed one of the board's eight commissioners. He campaigned for his friend Thomas Gallaudet, a pioneering advocate of education for the deaf, to become secretary of the board. Gallaudet declined the position, however, and Barnard himself was urged to take it. At first he hesitated, partly because the office had been created through his efforts, and partly because he had been offered a partnership in a prestigious law firm. However, in the end, he accepted the position.

As Connecticut's first secretary of education, Barnard attempted to develop widespread support for school and library reform. He wrote a letter to the people outlining the plans of the new board, distributed questionnaires, and personally visited hundreds of school districts. He presented data on schools to the legislature and the public, founded and edited the *Connecticut Common School Journal*, and lobbied for changes in school laws. Barnard also emphasized the need for trained teachers and established teachers' institutes that were among the first, if not the first, in the nation.

Events in Connecticut did not go well for Barnard. His campaign to improve public education awakened public opposition in the state to school reform and disturbed local politicians. In 1842, the Democrats came to power in the state and, in a move aimed at gaining support among voters, called for an end to direct state supervision of schools. Furthermore, Barnard's past affiliation with the opposition Whig Party did not help matters. After only four years of operation, the State Board of School Commissioners was abolished.

Barnard's Connecticut experience soured him on politics, but it did not dampen his enthusiasm for school reform. In 1843, he was appointed state school commissioner in Rhode Island. Predictably, Barnard engaged in a whirlwind of activity and in a relatively short time had developed popular support for public education in that state. At his urging, the Rhode Island Institute of Instruction was established in 1845. In that same year, he also secured passage of legislation to support a public education system in the state; when he resigned in 1849 for

Henry Barnard. (Library of Congress)

health reasons, he had already put it into successful operation. Barnard arranged for educational supplements to appear in state almanacs and caused the proceedings of school meetings to be reported in the press. In addition, he edited the state's school journal, published a book on teachers' colleges, and completed a volume on school architecture.

By the time of his marriage in 1847, Barnard was widely known and in great demand as a speaker. He was offered at least two professorships and four city school superintendencies, all of which he declined. When his home state of Connecticut again sought his leadership, however, he could not refuse. During his term of service as Connecticut's superintendent of common schools, Barnard drew up a revised code of school legislation, prepared a history of public school legislation in the state, and served as delegate to the International Exposition of Educational Methods in London, England. Still plagued by ill health, Barnard resigned as superintendent in 1855 to edit and publish the *American Journal of Education*, a monumental work that eventually comprised thirty-two volumes of more than eight hundred pages each.

Although the journal received most of Barnard's attention during the remainder of his life, he briefly held three additional administrative posts. From 1858 to 1860, he was chancellor of the University of Wisconsin and agent of the board of regents of the normal school fund. In 1866, Barnard was named president of St. John's College, resigning the following year to become the first commissioner of the newly created United States Department of Education. From the outset, Barnard's tenure as commissioner was plagued with problems. In 1868, growing criticism of the Department of Education and Barnard led Congress to downgrade it to a bureau (later, office) within the Department of the Interior. Two years later, he was unceremoniously removed from office by President Ulysses S. Grant.

Photographs of Barnard in the latter years of his life reveal a man perfectly suited for the role of reformer. His long white beard, white hair, and benign facial features gave him a patriarchal appearance. Deeply humiliated at his dismissal by Grant, he left Washington and returned to Hartford, where he continued to edit the *American Journal of Education* until 1881. Barnard lectured frequently, continued a voluminous correspondence, and in countless other ways attempted to keep busy until his death in the same house where he was born on July 5, 1900. Such activities, however, belied his true feelings. Despite the accolades he received from citizens and friends for his contribution to school reform, Barnard died doubting that his labors were sufficiently appreciated.

SIGNIFICANCE

Barnard's contribution to the development of American education was manifold. The changes he introduced to public education in Connecticut and Rhode Island were of lasting importance and, in some degree, served as models for school reform in other states. He was always willing to offer advice and encouragement to fellow school reformers. His chief service, however, was rendered as a publicist and propagandist for education. As editor and publisher of the *American Journal of Education*, he not only furthered educational scholarship but also helped create the necessary preconditions for the emergence of the modern teaching profession.

Undeniably, Barnard exemplified the best and the worst in nineteenth century American reform. A genuine idealist, he believed in the ability of people properly informed to make the right decision. At the same time, however, confidence in his own moral excellence could deteriorate into a brass-bolted certitude that denied any sense of rightness in others. Indeed, at times Barnard's methods suggest that he thought the average citizen deserved little voice in school reform, except to rubber-stamp his own ideas.

The transformation which Barnard helped bring to American education is evident everywhere. It is most visible in older school-building architecture, public school systems, and schools of education throughout the United States. Less obvious, but equally important, is his role in supplying a professional literature and raising professional standards for the whole field of education.

—*Monroe H. Little, Jr.*

FURTHER READING

Barnard, Henry. *Henry Barnard: American Educator.* Edited and introduced by Vincent P. Lannie. New York: Teacher's College Press, 1974. This collection of Barnard's writings contains excerpts from his personal correspondence, from an annual report of 1841 on public education in Connecticut, and from the *American Journal of Education.* Of particular note is the introduction by Lannie, which provides a concise biographical sketch of Barnard.

_____. *Henry Barnard on Education.* Edited by John S. Brubacher. New York: McGraw-Hill, 1931. Comprising some of Barnard's most important writings, this book presents his thoughts on a variety of educational issues ranging from public interest in education to educational administration. It includes an introductory chapter that discusses Barnard's life and work.

Brickman, William W. "Early Development of Research and Writing of Educational History in the United States." *Paedagogica Historica* 19 (June, 1979): 41-76. Traces early nineteenth century developments in educational historiography and discusses the work of Barnard and others in this area. Includes an examination of European influences and the impact of teachers' college curricula on writing about the history of American education.

MacMullen, Edith Nye. *In the Cause of True Education: Henry Barnard and Nineteenth Century School Reform.* New Haven, Conn.: Yale University Press, 1991. Scholarly study of Barnard's life and work, including his role in the common school reform movement and his adaptation of European educational philosophy to the United States.

Rothfork, John. "Transcendentalism and Henry Barnard's School Architecture." *Journal of General Education* 29 (Fall, 1977): 173-187. Discusses the intellectual and social climate that led Barnard to advocate Greek Revival architecture for school buildings. Examines the reasons for which this style and its implicit values were popular in the nineteenth century.

Thursfield, Richard Emmons. *Henry Barnard's American Journal of Education.* Baltimore: Johns Hopkins University Press, 1945. Somewhat dated, this book nevertheless remains indispensable. It not only presents information on the journal's founding and financing but also attempts to assess the significance of its content and its influence on readers.

Tyack, David B. *The One Best System: A History of American Urban Education.* Cambridge, Mass.: Harvard University Press, 1974. This well-documented study mentions Barnard only in passing but provides a detailed account of the social milieu in which he worked and the ideology that guided him and other educational reformers.

Warren, Donald R. *To Enforce Education: A History of the Founding Years of the United States Office of Education.* Detroit: Wayne State University Press, 1974. Examines issues surrounding the founding of the Department of Education. Discusses the attempt by Barnard and other reformers to establish a federal bureau of education.

SEE ALSO: Horace Mann; Emma Willard.

RELATED ARTICLES in *Great Events from History: The Nineteenth Century, 1801-1900:* 1820's-1830's: Free Public School Movement; March 2, 1867: U.S. Department of Education Is Created.

P. T. BARNUM
American showman

With a strong business sense and the ability to take huge risks, Barnum invented the modern museum and the musical concert, and converted the tent carnival into the three-ring circus. He also ran for a variety of political offices, serving for two terms on the Connecticut legislature and for one as a mayor of his hometown.

BORN: July 5, 1810; Bethel, Connecticut
DIED: April 7, 1891; Bridgeport, Connecticut
ALSO KNOWN AS: Phineas Taylor Barnum (full name)
AREAS OF ACHIEVEMENT: Entertainment, government and politics

EARLY LIFE

Phineas Taylor Barnum was born on July 5, 1810, in Bethel, Connecticut. Throughout his life, Barnum always regretted that he had not been born on the Fourth of July, the perfect birth date for the man who would become one of the first American showmen. He was the sixth child of Philo and Irene Barnum, Philo's second wife. Barnum was named for his maternal grandfather, Phineas (a biblical name meaning "brazen mouth") Taylor. As Barnum's life progressed, it turned out that the name fit him and that the ancestor he was named for would influence Barnum unlike anyone else in his life.

As a boy, Barnum looked to his grandfather Phineas for amusement. Phineas Taylor, a great practical joker whose antics helped liven up the harsh New England winters, would go further than most to create his little jokes and hoaxes that he concocted to weather the stern Calvinism of his day. When Barnum was christened, grandfather Phineas deeded to him five acres of land called Ivy Island. Phineas liked to brag to others in Barnum's presence that, because of that land, Barnum would one day be wealthy, and Barnum believed this throughout his childhood. At the age of four, he began begging his father to see his inheritance; finally, when Barnum was ten, his father acquiesced. The boy was led to an ivy-infested swamp, and even at that young age he knew that he had been the butt of a long-running hoax and that his inheritance was worthless. (Ironically, later in life Barnum put Ivy Island up for collateral.) P. T. Barnum, who loved his grandfather Phineas, ended up getting the last laugh by naming his illegitimate son Phineas Taylor.

The young P. T. Barnum, who would one day prudently know when to cut his losses, excelled in mathematics. While in grammar school (high school), Barnum helped his father out on the family farm; like thinkers down through the ages, however, he detested menial work and began planning for a different life. Philo's farm was a disappointment, and so, with a partner, he bought a general store and put Barnum in charge. In that position Barnum learned much about people, about bartering, and about business. By chance, he was being trained and goaded toward his future.

When Barnum was only fifteen, his father died. Suddenly finding himself the head of the family, he liquidated the store only to discover that the family was bankrupt. Quickly he obtained a similar job in another store. Tiring of that, he moved to Brooklyn to clerk at a better store. His influential grandfather, Phineas, wanted him to return to Bethel and offered to set him up in business if he would come home. That was all the encouragement Barnum needed, and he returned to set up a profitable business in half of his grandfather's carriage house.

On November 8, 1829, at the age of nineteen, Barnum eloped with Charity Hallett, a twenty-one-year-old Bethel woman. One of Barnum's daughters, Frances, died before her second birthday; his surviving daughters were Caroline, Helen, and Pauline. Like King Lear, Barnum suffered much from the actions of his daughters, who let their father down innumerable times, disappointing him by their various divorce scandals and their eagerness to divide up their father's estates while he was still alive.

Barnum, disappointed that his wife never had sons, left twenty-five thousand dollars and a yearly 3 percent of his enterprises to his eldest grandson, Clinton H. Seeley. To receive the inheritance, Seeley was required to change his middle name to Barnum in order to perpetuate Barnum's name. Clinton Barnum Seeley accepted the bequest but dishonored Barnum by conducting licentious parties, one of which included a nude Little Egypt in the center ring.

LIFE'S WORK

P. T. Barnum's life is almost inseparable from the freaks, the oddities, the hoaxes, the hokum, the sheer entertainment that he presented to the world, from the "sucker" on the street to Queen Victoria and the president. This six-foot-two man with curly, receding hair, blue eyes, a cleft chin, a bulbous nose, and a high voice was a pitchman par excellence and might almost be said to have invented the art of mass publicity.

After an apprenticeship spent selling hats, working in grocery stores, running lotteries, and maintaining a boardinghouse, Barnum found his métier. The catalyst was his discovery and purchase of Joice Heth, a black woman with legal documents that proved she was 161 years old and had served as George Washington's nurse. Barnum quit his grocery job and gambled both borrowed money and his life savings to make his break from convention.

In 1835, a Mr. Lindsay showed Barnum documents on the old woman and sold her to him for one thousand dollars. Barnum hired a hall by promising the owner half the gross, and he employed several people to help him launch a publicity campaign. At her shows, Joice Heth sang hymns and told her story of rearing Washington. The newspaper helped to spread the story, and eventually the show was a success, with Barnum splitting the weekly gross of fifteen hundred dollars with his partner.

Finally the dreaded event occurred: Joice Heth died. Barnum had given Dr. David Rogers permission to perform an autopsy, which in the end proved that Joice Heth was not more than eighty years old. Thus, the hoax was exposed and the newspapers made Barnum even more famous.

P. T. Barnum. (Library of Congress)

Barnum continued to collect and display oddities, both human and otherwise. He needed a central stage for his show and in 1841 acquired a dilapidated museum at Broadway and Ann Street in New York City that became known as Barnum's American Museum. For the admission fee, one could see the Feejee Mermaid (which was nothing more than a female monkey torso joined to a large stuffed fish tail), midgets, beauty contests, a bearded lady (she went to court to prove she was not a man), a tattooed man, the world's tallest woman, the Woolly Horse, the authentic "Siamese twins" Chang and Eng, and countless other abnormalities.

Barnum was always in search of another main attraction, and one materialized for him in 1842 when he discovered a five-year-old midget named Charles Stratton. Barnum taught him to sing and dance, to tell jokes, and to perform other stunts, all while wearing several different military uniforms. Stratton was thus converted into General Tom Thumb, one of Barnum's biggest entertainment successes.

To gain greater fame, Barnum took Tom Thumb on tour in Europe. There he was a huge success before five million people (according to Barnum's own count), and Barnum connived to make headlines when the General performed for Queen Victoria, who presented Tom with a court uniform. When Barnum and Tom Thumb returned to the United States, the clamor was great, and even President James K. Polk requested and got a private show at the White House.

Barnum's next big success was the signing of the famous Swedish singer Jenny Lind, whom he had neither seen nor heard, to perform on a concert tour. To finance the tour, he was forced to mortgage both his $150,000 home and his museum, as well as borrow heavily from friends. The risk paid off; Jenny Lind's tour was both a critical and a financial success. The Swedish Nightingale opened in New York City on September 11, 1850, and after ninety-five concerts in nineteen cities, Barnum had cleared profits in excess of $500,000.

In 1855, however, Barnum's time for high-risk profits had run out. As he had in the past, he became obsessed with an investment, this one with the Jerome Clock Company. Through his own bad management, Barnum carelessly invested more than $500,000 in the company, only to watch it go bankrupt. Barnum contemplated suicide, but instead, this religious man concluded that the Almighty Himself wished to teach him that there was something higher in life than money. Except for Charity's nineteen thousand dollars a year from the museum lease, all was lost. "Without Charity," he quipped, "I am nothing." This may have simply been a clever pun, however, because his financial recovery had begun immediately after the losses.

At forty-six, Barnum began his long climb toward repaying his debts. He turned to his standby, General Tom Thumb; he also realized that he himself was a marketable commodity and began lecturing to packed houses. Capitalizing, as always, on a good thing, he turned his lecture notes into a best-selling pamphlet, *The Art of Money Getting*, and reused the notes a second time in his autobiography.

Fire seemed to follow Barnum around like a demon. His home, Iranistan, was lost in a fire. The Barnum American Museum burned to the ground (miraculously, the freaks with their immobile bodies all escaped). The museum loss was calculated at $400,000, with insurance covering only $40,000. Many precious objects, including irreplaceable relics of the Revolutionary War, were lost. Barnum, with his typical verve, rebuilt the museum.

One of Barnum's greatest claims to fame began when he was sixty. He joined forces with James Anthony Bailey to created "The Greatest Show on Earth." Barnum's London Zoo purchase of Jumbo the Elephant (who had given rides to some five million British children, including Winston Churchill) became one of his most famous and most disputed purchases. Queen Victoria and others in England wanted the famous elephant back. By the time Jumbo reached the American shores, the elephant was an international cause célèbre and had generated much free publicity. The elephant act was an instant success: The purchase price of thirty thousand dollars was recouped in six weeks, with a box office of $336,000.

In 1873, Charity died, and in the following year Barnum married Nancy Fish, an Englishwoman forty years his junior. Barnum and his second wife had no children.

In 1891, Barnum was almost eighty-one and in poor health. After a lifetime of financial reversals, he was surrounded by wealth. He remarked to a friend that he wondered how his obituary would read. Word of this got back to the New York *Evening Sun*, and the newspaper asked for and got permission to print

THE ART OF MONEY GETTING

P. T. Barnum is famous for his flamboyant showmanship, but one of the reasons for his fabulous success as a businessman was no doubt his levelheaded practicality in handling money. After climbing out of debt at the age of forty-six, he turned what he had learned about money into a profitable tour, then he turned his lectures into a profitable pamphlet, The Art of Money Getting or Golden Rules for Making Money, *from which this extract is taken.*

In the United States, where we have more land than people, it is not at all difficult for persons in good health to make money. In this comparatively new field there are so many avenues of success open, so many vocations which are not crowded, that any person of either sex who is willing, at least for the time being, to engage in any respectable occupation that offers, may find lucrative employment.

Those who really desire to attain an independence, have only to set their minds upon it, and adopt the proper means, as they do in regard to any other object which they wish to accomplish, and the thing is easily done. But however easy it may be found to make money, I have no doubt many of my hearers will agree it is the most difficult thing in the world to keep it. The road to wealth is, as Dr. [Benjamin] Franklin truly says, "as plain as the road to the mill." It consists simply in expending less than we earn; that seems to be a very simple problem. Mr. Micawber, one of those happy creations of the genial [Charles] Dickens, puts the case in a strong light when he says that to have annual income of twenty pounds per annum, and spend twenty pounds and sixpence, is to be the most miserable of men; whereas, to have an income of only twenty pounds, and spend but nineteen pounds and sixpence is to be the happiest of mortals. Many of my readers may say, "we understand this: this is economy, and we know economy is wealth; we know we can't eat our cake and keep it also." Yet I beg to say that perhaps more cases of failure arise from mistakes on this point than almost any other. The fact is, many people think they understand economy when they really do not.

True economy is misapprehended, and people go through life without properly comprehending what that principle is. One says, "I have an income of so much, and here is my neighbor who has the same; yet every year he gets something ahead and I fall short; why is it? I know all about economy." He thinks he does, but he does not. . . .

Source: P. T. Barnum, *The Art of Money Getting or Golden Rules for Making Money* (New York, 1882).

Barnum's obituary before he died. On April 7, 1891, this American folk hero died at his home in Bridgeport.

SIGNIFICANCE

According to Bartlett's *Familiar Quotations*, the expression "There's a sucker born every minute" is attributed to P. T. Barnum. Researchers have stated repeatedly that Barnum never said this. Indeed, in his own life he was often a "sucker." He assumed as a child that Ivy Island would make him wealthy, and as an adult he thought that he could get rich quick through his Jerome Clock investment.

Barnum knew many secrets about human nature, one of which was that although no one enjoys being duped, if the game is all in good fun, people do enjoy becoming "suckers" to an extent—so much so that they are willing to pay for the honor. Another secret Barnum learned was that of the publicist: In his pre-"global village" age, Barnum might be said to have invented the high-pressure sales campaign, creating the "hype" that sold his wares.

Barnum himself became a household name and an original American folk hero. His life was filled with contradictions. He was a good family man, yet he fathered an illegitimate son, the only son he was ever to have. He was reared in an anti-entertainment age yet believed devoutly that each person deserved to be entertained. He made a great amount of money; he lost all of his money; he made more money. He sustained spectacular triumphs unmatched by rivals. Living a long life, he experienced many personal tragedies, including the death of a daughter, the death of his wife, Charity, the loss of property and money, and the divisiveness and greed of his surviving three daughters.

Barnum became an archetype of American Dream merchants such as Walt Disney, Samuel Goldwyn, Oscar Hammerstein I, John Ringling, Mike Todd, Cecil B. DeMille, Billy Rose, the brothers Shubert, Florenz Ziegfeld, Steven Spielberg, George Lucas, and hundreds of others. A lively musical, *Barnum*, and the circus that bears his name reintroduces Barnum to thousands each year.

"To the Egress," a sign in the Barnum's American Museum once read. Expecting to find another oddity, people entered and found themselves outside the museum, on the street.

—*John Harty*

FURTHER READING

Adams, Bluford. *E Pluribus Barnum: The Great Showman and the Making of U.S. Popular Culture*. Minneapolis: University of Minnesota Press, 1997. Written for readers who have a basic knowledge of Barnum's life, this book examines the cultural context of his mass entertainment. Adams maintains Barnum's productions appealed to low- and middle-class audiences' desire for "high" culture.

Barnum, Phineas T. *The Life of P. T. Barnum*. Introduction by Terence Whalen. Urbana: University of Illinois Press, 2000. A recent reprint of Barnum's autobiography.

_____. *Selected Letters of P. T. Barnum*. Edited by A. H. Saxon. New York: Columbia University Press, 1983. The only published collection of Barnum's letters.

_____. *Struggles and Triumphs: Or, Forty Years' Recollections of P. T. Barnum*. Edited by Carl Bode. New York: Penguin Books, 1981. Good starting point for research. Barnum wrote three versions of this book, which Bode condenses into one readable volume. Bode has written an excellent introduction and has included a short, annotated bibliography.

Benton, Joel. *Life of Honorable Phineas T. Barnum*. Philadelphia: Edgewood, 1891. This book largely paraphrases (in the third person) Barnum's own autobiography. Benton knew Barnum, and he includes some of his own recollections.

Cook, James W. *The Arts of Deception: Playing with Fraud in the Age of Barnum*. Cambridge, Mass.: Harvard University Press, 2001. An analysis of mass entertainment in nineteenth century America, focusing on Barnum.

Dennett, Andrea Stulman. *Weird and Wonderful: The Dime Museum in America*. New York: New York University Press, 1997. History of Barnum's American Museum.

Desmond, Alice Curtis. *Barnum Presents: General Tom Thumb*. New York: Macmillan, 1954. The story of one of the most famous midgets in the world and how he became a gigantic drawing card for Barnum.

Harding, Less. *Elephant Story: Jumbo and P. T. Barnum Under the Big Top*. Jefferson, N.C.: McFarland, 2000. History of the famed elephant, a star attraction in Barnum's circus.

Harris, Neil. *Humbug: The Art of P. T. Barnum*. Boston: Little, Brown, 1973. The most reliable biography. Sound scholarship is used to place Barnum in his own cultural setting.

Sutton, Felix. *Master of Ballyhoo: The Story of P. T. Barnum*. New York: G. P. Putnam's Sons, 1968. A Literary Guild edition with large print for juveniles.

Wallace, Irving. *The Fabulous Showman: The Life and Times of P. T. Barnum.* New York: Alfred A. Knopf, 1959. One of the best introductions available on Barnum, covering all the major events. Well researched with an excellent bibliography and sixteen pages of photographs.

SEE ALSO: Sarah Bernhardt; Mathew B. Brady; William Cody; Jenny Lind.

RELATED ARTICLES in *Great Events from History: The Nineteenth Century, 1801-1900:* August 10, 1846: Smithsonian Institution Is Founded; 1850's-1880's: Rise of Burlesque and Vaudeville; April 10, 1871: Barnum Creates the First Modern American Circus.

SIR CHARLES BARRY

British architect

The chief architect of some of the most famous buildings in England, Barry designed London's Houses of Parliament, one of the finest examples of the Victorian Gothic Revival.

BORN: May 23, 1795; London, England
DIED: May 12, 1860; London, England
AREA OF ACHIEVEMENT: Architecture

EARLY LIFE

Charles Barry's father was a successful merchant in the city of London, the owner of a stationery business. At the age of fifteen, Barry was articled to a London firm of architects and surveyors, and he remained with them until his father died six years later. At the age of twenty-one, he used his inheritance to finance a Grand Tour of the Continent, intent on studying the architecture. Over a three-year period, he traveled through France, Italy, Greece, and the Near East, accumulating the firsthand knowledge of the architectural styles that he was to use with such facility in his professional life.

A personable, genial young man of considerable confidence, he set himself up as a practicing architect upon his return to England. Shortly after settling into business, he entered a government competition that was to provide churches in newly developed suburbs in cities throughout England. Barry, despite his modest experience, was awarded contracts for churches in the Islington district of London, in Manchester, and in Brighton. The neo-Gothic style in public buildings (particularly church buildings) was popular at the time, and Barry was able to adapt his skills to it easily, if not with any particular brilliance. He showed himself able to work within modest budgets and to deal sensibly with the complications of government contracts. The churches were aesthetically interesting, built of brick with Gothic detail added in stone, but they showed little depth of artistic power.

The fact is that Barry was not a fully committed adherent to the Gothic revival. He could, and often did, work in other styles, providing his clients with what they wanted. He seemed most at home, and most engaging, in designing nineteenth century British versions of the Italian Renaissance palazzo. In Rome or Florence such buildings were combinations of the town house and the palace of the great family. Barry put them to use in the first instance as havens for the English clubmen. His first important commission for such a building was the Travellers' Club in Pall Mall, which he began in 1829 (finishing it in 1832) and which is one of the best examples of how he could adopt models from another culture and time, without self-consciousness, to the needs of Victorian London. The Travellers' Club still possesses the dignity and charm that make it one of the handsomest buildings on that famous street. Its success established Barry as a designer of distinction.

LIFE'S WORK

Barry's ability to manipulate different styles, to adapt himself to the taste and enthusiasms of his patrons, made him a popular architect not only in the city but also in the country, where he gained commissions to reproduce a version of the Italianized country house. He was also willing and able to renovate and add to houses that in one way or another had become boring or unsuitable to their owners, and there are several great houses throughout England that have additions by Barry, sometimes in his Italian style, sometimes in his Gothic style, occasionally in Tudor imitation.

Architecture, perhaps of all the arts, is the one most inclined to allow imitation, and it was not considered invalid for owners to request the renovation of buildings that had come down through the family and through several centuries. Often, such renovations, such demands for additions from other historical styles, could make for the unfortunate destruction of original masterpieces. Occasionally, such messing about with the buildings not only made them more civilized but also added to their aesthetic value. At Harewood House in Yorkshire, Barry's facade, grand outer staircase, and some interior work in the library seem to have been successful, but his addition of an Italianate tower to Georgian Bowood in Wiltshire is, in the eyes of Nikolaus Pevsner, the architectural historian, "incongruous."

Such imitations seemed to work best if they were all of a piece, and Barry's Reform Club, a return to the Renaissance Italian urban palace, was set immediately west of his former success, the Travellers' Club. There is some considerable opinion that the Reform Club (begun in 1837) is not only a finer building but also his greatest work in the Renaissance style. Weightier, somewhat grander than the Travellers', both inside and out, it displays the growing maturity of his work and his ability to go back to the same model with sufficient variation and imagination to allow it to be put side by side with his older building without fear of cloying the appetite, despite the basic similarity of the two structures. It was the mark of an architect of breadth and some considerable courage.

Barry's greatest fame, however, was not to come from tour de force juxtapositions of buildings in the same style. Indeed, it was not to come from his practice in the neo-Renaissance Italian mode at all, but from that style with which his career had begun, with the city church commissions—from answering, once again, the English allegiance to the Gothic, the style that was always before their eyes in the great cathedrals. The English Baroque architects of the late seventeenth century and the early eighteenth century, Christopher Wren, Sir John Vanbrugh, and Nicholas Hawksmoor, in their sometimes eccentric eclecticism, had managed to use Gothic motifs in a mix with classical and Renaissance ideas, but the Palladians, who came into vogue in the period after 1715, deprecated such barbarism for the high, fastidious purity of neoclassicism. The result was some of the finest architecture in the history of Great Britain, but it was not to last out the century unchallenged.

If the Gothic was unfashionable at the higher levels of aesthetic decision, it retained its hold on the affection of less sophisticated provincials, and the local church was often constructed with Gothic models in mind. Aside from these residual traces, however, Gothic came to mean, first, in the literary arts, a world of imagination, of teasing fantasy, of escape from the high rationality of the eighteenth century into the mysterious, into personal feeling. Horace Walpole not only invented the horror story (*The Castle of Otranto*, 1764) but also shared in the antiquarian enthusiasm about which he wrote; he assiduously collected examples of Gothic design and built himself a Gothic play-palace, Strawberry Hill. The pointed arch, the delicate tracery, the machicolated profile that reeked of fortified castles, the rich plethora of motif caught the late eighteenth century imagination in letters and was to lead to the Romantic movement, but architecture was also to be gradually influenced. If some wanted to live in the grandeur of Renaissance Italy, others wanted the frisson of an idealized medievalism.

Barry's early churches had been exercises in satisfying that desire to link the new, industrialized England with its roots in antiquity. The opportunity for a project on an entirely different scale came in 1834, when the House of Parliament burned down. It was decided that the new buildings should be either "Gothic" or "Elizabethan"; Barry chose to enter the competition with a plan that was basically classical in form, but dressed from head to toe (right down to the inkwells) in Gothic detail. To achieve this, he brought in as his assistant Augustus Pugin, who, despite his youth, was already a master of the Gothic mode. Barry provided the overall plan, and Pugin did the drawings, adding the details that were to turn the buildings into the best example of the Gothic Revival in Britain.

Although the overall conception of the project was Barry's, Pugin's contribution was central to their success in winning the commission. Years later, after both men were dead, their children were to engage in a public quarrel over who really was the major contributor. It is true that Barry was somewhat less generous than he might have been in sharing the praise, but Pugin admitted that he could not have led the project. He believed that he had nothing like Barry's organizing ability or stubbornness in fighting back the onslaughts of the bureaucrats, the public, and the envious architectural community, all of whom threw themselves singly and collectively into thwarting Barry, who exhausted himself in making the buildings such a success.

Whether the Parliament complex is a major work of art is questionable—Pugin himself considered it somewhat fraudulent, a classic shape decked out in Gothic trappings—but there is no doubt that it is the most famous seat of government in the world, and that its Thames-side profile, punctuated by the Big Ben Tower, has appeared on more labels for English products than perhaps any other object in the history of art.

The success of this massive project fully established Barry's reputation and was to do the same for Pugin in later years when the extent of his contribution was fully known. So ambitious was this undertaking that Barry was not to be free of it during his lifetime, and the project was finally completed by his son. Meanwhile, however, Barry worked on other contracts as well. The Reform Club was designed after he had begun the Parliament project; in Birmingham, he designed the King Edward Grammar School in the Tudor style; in Manchester, he used his Italian palazzo plan for the Atheneum. He provided the ground plan for Parliament Square in London, and he also had a hand in laying out Trafalgar Square. Both have been altered since, but his terrace on the north side of Trafalgar Square is extant.

Perhaps the finest example of Barry's use of the Italian palazzo for a residence (although it is now a corporate head office) is Bridgewater House in Cleveland Row, facing onto Green Park. Built quite late in his career (1847-1849), it is a longer, lower, richer variation on the model that he used just down the street in the Reform Club. The long side is to the park, a quite splendidly arrogant display of architectural sonority, floating slightly above the park level, crowned by a richly detailed cornice topped by his favorite device, the ornamental urn.

SIGNIFICANCE

If it is understood that art need not necessarily be original, that it can just as well be memory of that which has preceded it, the history of architecture and of some architects can be better appreciated. Sir Charles Barry was an imitator in the best sense of the word, just as Palladio was, and as Burlington was of Palladio. It is probably true that Barry was not quite as great an architect as either of these men, but he produced individual buildings of some considerable merit, whose aesthetic worth lies not in their originality but in the way in which the style of established merit has been made to work again, in another place at another time.

Barry also showed that it was possible to satisfy the public, to give them what they wanted, without necessarily destroying artistic integrity or merit. On several occasions, it must be admitted, Barry's additions to already established buildings did not quite work, but he was often able to solve problems of mixed styles in ways that showed how technically ingenious he was, how able to manipulate the highly difficult art of design and execution in order to make architecture that had some lasting value. He never forgot the obligation of the architect to make art that was also useful. He was not a great artist, but he was often close to being so, even when he was obliged to give his patrons what were, in fact, copies of something long ago and far away.

—*Charles H. Pullen*

FURTHER READING

Barry, Alfred. *The Life and Works of Sir Charles Barry*. London: John Murray, 1867. A family bias, aggravated by the fight between the Pugins and the Barrys, should be remembered in reading this work, but it does give a strong sense of the Victorian sensibility.

Cannadine, David, et al. *The Houses of Parliament: History, Art, Architecture*. London: Merrell, 2000. An illustrated history of Barry's most famous work, placing the buildings in a historical, political, and cultural context.

Clark, Kenneth. *The Gothic Revival: An Essay in the History of Taste*. Harmondsworth, England: Penguin Books, 1964. The most popular, readily available essay on the peculiar zest for making everything old that seized the Victorians and turned their architectural landscape and all its trappings into the new Middle Ages. Enormously readable and scholarly; the ramifications of the movement are fully explored, not only in architecture but also in literature and life.

Dixon, Roger, and Stefan Muthesius. *Victorian Architecture*. London: Thames and Hudson, 1978. One of those handsome, easily read, popular books on the period. Generous illustration. Some care taken to avoid technical mystery. Barry turns up quite often but is most carefully discussed in the chapters on public and religious architecture.

Ferriday, Peter, ed. *Victorian Architecture*. London: Jonathan Cape, 1963. Barry is best understood in the full context of Victorian architecture in general. This book is a collection of essays by leading experts. Peter Fleetwood-Hesketh, one of the best commentators on Barry, contributes an essay; there is also an essay on Pugin that provides some sense of the collaboration between Barry and Pugin.

Goodhart-Rendel, H. S. *English Architecture Since the Regency*. London: Constable, 1953. This author provides the essay on the country house in Ferriday's *Victorian Architecture* (see above). In this book, he meets the problem of the originality of nineteenth century English architecture, given its dependence upon prior models. It is densely argued and deeply attached to the idea that architecture is part of the social history of ideas and must be judged in context.

Little, Bryan. *English Historic Architecture*. New York: Hastings House, 1964. Puts the great public buildings into the context of English history. The last five chapters, beginning with the eighteenth century, are very good for setting the Gothic movement clearly in the mind as something more than a fad.

Pevsner, Nikolaus. *London: The Cities of London and Westminster.* Harmondsworth, England: Penguin Books, 1981. The best and most detailed examination of Parliament, the Pall Mall clubs, and Bridgewater House. An education in how to look at, and talk about, a building.

Service, Alastair. *The Architects of London.* London: Architectural Press, 1979. For all his roaming around in the country, Barry's best work is to be found in the city of London. The short, informed chapter on him in this book, putting him in the context of his contemporaries, is very good.

SEE ALSO: Daniel Hudson Burnham; Augustus Welby Northmore Pugin; Sir George Gilbert Scott; George Edmund Street.

RELATED ARTICLE in *Great Events from History: The Nineteenth Century, 1801-1900:* April 27, 1840-February, 1852: British Houses of Parliament Are Rebuilt.

CLARA BARTON

American nursing pioneer

After devoting half of her life to humanitarian pursuits, Barton became the key figure in establishing the American Red Cross.

BORN: December 25, 1821; North Oxford, Massachusetts
DIED: April 12, 1912; Glen Echo, Maryland
ALSO KNOWN AS: Clara Harlowe Barton (full name)
AREAS OF ACHIEVEMENT: Medicine, social reform

EARLY LIFE

Clarissa Harlowe Barton (known as Clara) was influenced by her parents' liberal political attitudes. The youngest child, Clara had identity problems that worsened when she showed interests in academic and other pursuits considered masculine. Farmwork and nursing relatives who were ill, however, led her increasingly to connect approval and praise to helping others.

In 1836, Barton began teaching school. She was a gifted teacher who chose to enforce discipline through kindness and persuasion at a time when physical force was the standard. During the next decade, Barton developed quite a reputation as she moved from town to town, taming obstreperous students and leaving for another challenge. As she gained self-confidence, she began to have an active social life, though she never married. Tired of teaching and concerned that her own education was inadequate, she enrolled at the Clinton Liberal Institute in Clinton, New York, at the end of 1850. She studied for a year, but as an older student, she felt out of place and made few friends.

Unable to afford more school and unwilling to be dependent on her family, Barton went to live with friends in New Jersey. In 1852, she persuaded authorities to offer free public education by allowing her to open a free school. Although she was initially unpaid, Barton eventually made the school such a success that she was offered a salary and the opportunity to expand her program. As the school grew, however, the school board decided that a man should be placed in charge and paid more than any women involved. Frustrated and angry, Barton moved to Washington, D.C., in search of new opportunities in 1854.

Barton found work as a clerk in the Patent Office, where the commissioner was willing to give women positions. For several years Barton made good money and earned respect for her efficiency despite the resentment of her male colleagues. Shifting political fortunes forced Barton to leave her post in 1857. For three years, she lived at home in Massachusetts before returning to the Patent Office in 1860.

LIFE'S WORK

With the outbreak of the Civil War in 1861, Clara Barton began the humanitarian work that would occupy the rest of her life. Federal troops were arriving in Washington without baggage or food. She began to gather and distribute supplies to ease their distress. Her efforts quickly grew to include battlefield assistance in helping the wounded at the beginning of the war. Because the military had badly underestimated medical needs, Barton's individual effort gathering supplies and caring for the wounded at battles such as Fredericksburg proved immensely valuable. By the end of 1862, however, the Army was becoming better organized and the work of amateurs was no longer significant. Barton also had problems getting official support and recognition because, unlike Barton, most volunteers were more harm than help. The Army could not accept one volunteer while denying others. Barton, as she often did, became defensive, taking every rebuke, regardless of the source, personally.

After the war, Barton undertook a project to identify missing soldiers and inform their families of their fates. Her efforts included a trip to Andersonville prison where, with the help of a former inmate who had kept the death roll, Barton supervised the identification and marking of some 13,000 graves. Despite some success, Barton's work in tracing missing soldiers resulted in identification of less than 10 percent of the missing.

During her pursuit of these activities, Barton confronted two difficulties of a sort typical of her career. One problem arose because the Army was also attempting to find missing soldiers. Barton sought sole control of the whole effort, but this control was not granted and she feuded with the officer in charge. Barton possessed a zeal for efficiency that made her reluctant to share responsibility or credit. This attitude prevented her from delegating authority and provoked hostility among many people who actually wanted to help her. The second problem was a result of poor accounting. She could not provide details of expenses, leaving herself open to charges of malfeasance.

Although she was always more interested in field work than administration, Barton was unwilling to share power with someone who would handle paperwork. She paid little attention to tracking the disbursement of donated funds and poured her own limited resources into her projects even though she could produce no receipts. There is no evidence that she sought personal gain. Nevertheless, her poor accounting resulted in repeated complaints that ultimately came back to haunt her during her work with the Red Cross.

Barton's involvement with the Red Cross began in Europe, where she met some of the organization's leaders and learned that the United States had not ratified the Treaty of Geneva (1864) that had created the organization. Barton was invited to assist in the work of the International Red Cross during the Franco-Prussian War of 1870-1871. Her experiences gave her a new perspective on the suffering of civilians during war—she had worked almost entirely on behalf of soldiers in the Civil War. Friendship with Grand Duchess Louise of Baden, a Red Cross leader, resulted in Barton working six months in Strasbourg. She was convinced of the value of the Red Cross and determined that supporting self-help was better than handouts. She held these convictions the rest of her life.

Clara Barton. (Library of Congress)

In 1872, Barton returned to the United States, after suffering a nervous breakdown that some regarded as partially psychosomatic. Retiring from public life to stay in a sanatorium eventually improved her health. In 1877, she decided to form an American Red Cross society to gather funds to help victims of the Russo-Turkish War. She received permission from the International Red Cross, and began a campaign to secure American ratification of the Treaty of Geneva. U.S. government officials, however, insisted that because the country observed the tenets of the treaty, there was no reason for a formal alliance.

Barton lobbied diligently for ratification. She sought help from friends in Washington, D.C., cultivated the press, and relied upon her friendship with members of the Grand Army of the Republic, a Civil War veterans group that had honored her. To increase awareness of the work of the Red Cross, Barton made peacetime disaster relief a priority. Progress was slow, but the treaty was ratified in 1882. Her group was officially recognized by the government, paving the way for it to be associated with the International Red Cross. This recognition helped Barton launch her next campaign: to make the American Association of the Red Cross the central relief agency in the United States.

The 1880's and 1890's were times of heroic effort for Barton. Her labor was certainly greatly increased by her refusal to yield any share of control, and, during the decades of her presidency, she and the Red Cross were essentially synonymous. She wanted the national agency to be the center of a network of state groups, but she was frequently drawn away from organizing to oversee field work and was hampered by continual shortages of funds. She also spent much of 1883 running a women's prison at the request of Benjamin Butler, the former Union general who had become governor of Massachusetts. Assisting Butler with his political problems concerning the funding of the progressive prison, Barton established that the costs were mostly appropriate, despite sloppy administrative work. Unfortunately, her efforts on Butler's behalf diverted Barton's attention from the urgent demands of Red Cross work.

For the rest of her life, however, Barton devoted herself almost exclusively to Red Cross work. She traveled, seeking funds and public support—sometimes for herself as well as her cause—and attended annual meetings of the International Red Cross, where she was accepted as a delegate when no other woman was even allowed on the convention floor. She was a hero to feminists, whose cause she supported, although never so vigorously as to cause hostility toward the Red Cross. Field work continued to beckon, including relief efforts in the wake of floods in the Ohio and Mississippi River valleys in 1884 and an earthquake in Charleston, South Carolina, in 1886. She allowed the head of the New Orleans chapter to lead an effort in a yellow fever epidemic around Jacksonville, Florida, only to find that the nurses he took resembled camp followers more than caregivers. This incident confirmed her determination to do everything herself.

Barton received praise from the press for relief efforts in the wake of the 1889 Johnstown flood, but she was later greatly criticized for not keeping track of expenditures. Some of the expenses appear to have been inappropriate, though not fraudulent, but her lack of receipts made defense against such criticism almost impossible. Barton hoped to parlay the Johnstown success into government funding for the Red Cross as the official agency for coordinating wartime relief. This effort stalled, however, and she turned her attention to efforts to alleviate a Russian famine.

By the mid-1890's, relief funds were at a low ebb and criticism of her poor accounting hampered the activities of both the American and international organizations. Although Barton was in her seventies and her energy was beginning to decline, she repudiated every criticism, attacked critics, and continued. In 1896, she went to Turkey to aid Armenians suffering from Turkish atrocities. She secured permission from the Turkish sultan to send Dr. Julian Hubbell, one of her most loyal collaborators, into Armenia, where he had significant success.

Back in the United States, she found appeals from Cuban civilians suffering in the struggle against Spain. Because the U.S. government wanted to keep out of the situation, little was being done to provide relief. Eventually, Barton went to survey the situation with a committee of relief agencies. When the head of another agency criticized her work and tried to supplant her, Barton returned to the United States and got her rival discredited. By the time she returned to Cuba, however, the Spanish-American War had begun. The New York Red Cross chapter, which, along with several others, had been acting almost autonomously, provided necessary assistance to stateside military hospitals, and the California chapter sent aid to the Pacific front in the Philippines. Barton headed for Cuba, eventually leaving without official sanction. Although intending to help civilians, her team stumbled into a battle fought by the Rough Riders. To her delight, Barton found herself nursing soldiers again. Important work with civilians followed, and the Red Cross proved its value.

The organization's efforts during the Spanish-American War and its aftermath did lead to legislation granting a federal charter to the American Red Cross in 1900. In the end, however, this success was also Barton's downfall. Concerned that donations were in decline, some members of the Red Cross organized independent efforts during Barton's absence and were reluctant to relinquish control to her. The crisis came after a hurricane in Galveston, Texas, in September of 1900.

Barton launched relief efforts without consulting the organization's new board of directors, and her bookkeeping was so lackadaisical that the national treasurer resigned rather than defend her expenditures. The struggle went on for several years, becoming more acrimonious because Barton came to regard her critics as personal foes. Finally, Barton was forced to resign all ties to the Red Cross in 1904. She did retain quarters at a house in

Maryland that had been built largely with her own money and had served as Red Cross headquarters during the final years of her presidency. Continuing to support public health efforts and the woman's rights movement, Barton alternated living in Maryland and in North Oxford, Massachusetts, until her death in April, 1912.

SIGNIFICANCE

Clara Barton established the American Red Cross almost singlehandedly. Earlier efforts to do so had failed, and the nation lacked a major disaster relief agency. Rival organizations did arise, but most were launched later in imitation of Barton's efforts. Barton's prodigious labor and self-sacrifice on behalf of establishing the American Red Cross ultimately earned for her the recognition she desired, yet she never allowed her ego to prevent her from giving unstintingly of her work and wealth to those who needed help.

That ego did, however, cause problems. The combination of childhood insecurity and individual success in the Civil War rendered Barton incapable of working equally with others. She preferred to work with trusted aides who deferred to her authority, and she seemed to interpret any initiative outside her control as a personal affront. This caused Barton much disquiet and slowed the growth of the Red Cross. Although most if not all the charges made against her personally were without merit, it cannot be denied that had she shared leadership with someone who was willing to do the vital paperwork much more progress could have been made. Furthermore, Barton's reputation would not have been sullied. Nevertheless, her crusading spirit on behalf of nursing reform created for Barton an impressive legacy.

—*Fred R. van Hartesveldt*

FURTHER READING

Barton, Clara. *The Story of My Childhood*. Reprint. New York: Arno Press, 1980. Although it was intended to be the first chapter of an autobiography and hence covers only Barton's first years, this work is a valuable source given the influence of her childhood on her character.

Barton, William E. *The Life of Clara Barton*. 2 vols. Boston: Houghton Mifflin, 1922. An old-fashioned and uncritical biography, but filled with details and information often missing in modern studies.

Burton, David H. *Clara Barton: In the Service of Humanity*. Westport, Conn.: Greenwood Press, 1995. Sympathetic yet critical biography, which suggests that Barton's dedication to helping people in need was not entirely selfless. While he recounts the many examples of Barton's heroism and generosity, the author also portrays his subject as a self-centered and thin-skinned personality.

Dulles, Foster Rhea. *The American Red Cross*. New York: Harper & Brothers, 1950. Written by an excellent historian, this valuable work provides background on Barton and her work with the Red Cross.

Oates, Stephen B. *A Woman of Valor: Clara Barton and the Civil War*. New York: Free Press, 1994. Best known for his biographies of Abraham Lincoln, Oates provides a vivid account of Clara Barton's early career during the Civil War years. While revealing Barton's drive to succeed and her skill in generating public support for her relief efforts, Oates's detailed narrative also illuminates her difficult personality and strained emotional life, thus providing a welcome corrective to older, less critical accounts.

Pryor, Elizabeth B. *Clara Barton: Professional Angel*. Philadelphia: University of Pennsylvania Press, 1987. Although informed by the author's research into numerous primary sources, this biography suffers somewhat from a lack of critical distance in its approach, as suggested by its subtitle.

Ross, Ishbel. *Angel of the Battlefield: The Life of Clara Barton*. New York: Harper & Brothers, 1956. A reasonable biography, though somewhat dated. Like most of the work on Barton, this volume is adulatory in its approach.

SEE ALSO: Jean-Henri Dunant; Florence Nightingale.

RELATED ARTICLES in *Great Events from History: The Nineteenth Century, 1801-1900:* November 4, 1854: Nightingale Takes Charge of Nursing in the Crimea; May 12, 1857: New York Infirmary for Indigent Women and Children Opens; February 25, 1863-June 3, 1864: Congress Passes the National Bank Acts; May 31, 1889: Johnstown Flood; September 8, 1900: Galveston Hurricane.

SIR EDMUND BARTON

Australian politician

Barton was the leader of the movement to form a federated Australian Commonwealth and was one of the authors of the new nation's constitution. During the twentieth century, he served as Australia's first prime minister and also served as a judge on the first High Court of Australia.

BORN: January 18, 1849; Sydney, New South Wales (now in Australia)
DIED: January 7, 1920; Medlow Bath, Australia
AREAS OF ACHIEVEMENT: Government and politics, law

EARLY LIFE

Edmund Barton was born in Sydney, Australia, on January 18, 1849. He was the second youngest of eleven children born to William and Mary Louisa Barton. William Barton was the younger son of a London merchant who had come to the colony of New South Wales as an agent for an agricultural company. Although a notable figure in the commercial life of Sydney—he was its first stockbroker—William Barton did not become a wealthy man. At one stage, his wife conducted a girls' school to assist in supporting the family.

Edmund, who was often known as "Ted" or "Toby," was a healthy young man, in many ways typical of the new breed of Australian-born youth. The Sydney of his time was a bustling colonial community, still somewhat wild, and very aware of itself as one of several coastal toeholds on a vast continent waiting to be developed. The young Barton was first sent to the government school at Fort Street, often known as the "Model School." He then went to Sydney Grammar School. There he met Richard O'Connor, with whom he was to form a lifelong friendship and who was to be his partner in later political life. Twice school captain of Sydney Grammar School, Barton took the classics prize and went on to Sydney University.

At the university, Barton took several prizes and scholarships, culminating in first-class honors in classics. He also fell under the influence of the noted English classical scholar and humanist Dr. Charles Badham, who brought Barton to a wide appreciation of culture. In 1870, he completed his university education with a master of arts degree. There were few opportunities in commercially minded Sydney for a classical scholar, even one of Barton's ability, and he took to the law. He started out as an articled clerk in the firm of Burton Bradely, a Sydney solicitor (a lawyer in the lower courts), and later studied under G. C. Davis, a barrister. He was called to the New South Wales bar in 1872.

As a young man, Barton was large, more than six feet tall, and in his middle age he became quite stout. His features were always handsome, and he was described as dignified and well dressed. Throughout his life he was criticized for indolence, a charge difficult to support in the light of his achievements. There is no doubt that he loved the pleasures of the cultured gentleman: good company, intelligent conversation, fine wine and food. These he often found in the Athenaeum Club in Sydney, which from 1880 to 1920 was frequented by many of Australia's most prominent lawyers, politicians, and men of letters. Although once described as Australia's greatest orator, the power of his speeches came not from thundering tones or emotional rhetoric, but rather from carefully chosen phrases, which slowly and methodically established his position.

In 1876, Barton was visiting Newcastle with the Sydney cricket team, of which he was a member. There he met Jean Mason Ross, the daughter of a Scottish engineer who had emigrated to New South Wales. Their courtship lasted a year, and they were married on December 28, 1877. Together they had six children.

LIFE'S WORK

Barton was first elected to the New South Wales legislative assembly in 1879, as the representative of the graduates of the University of Sydney. Within a year his somewhat unusual constituency was abolished, and he ran for the Sydney seat of Wellington and was returned to office without opposition. He was described as a moderate free trader and supporter of the government of Sir Henry Parkes. He spoke to all the issues of the day, particularly the questions of public instruction and the laws governing the opening up of the lands in the interior. The period 1879-1883 was marked by instability in the governments of New South Wales. No less than seven ministries were formed and dissolved, and, not surprisingly, little legislative progress was made. Barton's equanimity and grasp of parliamentary procedure were recognized early, and on January 3, 1883, he was elected as the youngest speaker of the legislative assembly.

Barton's four-year tenure as speaker brought him to great prominence in colonial affairs, helping to establish his reputation as a leader of deliberative assemblies.

Shortly after he resigned as Speaker, he was appointed to the upper house, the Legislative Council, where he was to serve until 1894. He was attorney general in Sir George Richard Dibbs's government, which included his friend Richard O'Connor. This government saw New South Wales through some of its stormiest times, including the great strikes of 1890 and 1891 and the constant controversy over protectionism.

New South Wales was the most densely populated and most commercial of the Australian colonies. The other colonies, particularly Victoria, favored intercolonial tariffs, for the protection of their local industries. One of the arguments for federating the Australian states was the removal of such tariffs and their replacement with national customs and excise. Barton first became interested in the issue when, as acting premier of New South Wales, he attended a conference on Asian immigration, in 1888. After a conference to consider the problems of colonial defense, Sir Henry Parkes stopped at Tenterfield in northern New South Wales to deliver what became known as the "Tenterfield Oration," one of the earliest calls for a federated Australia by a prominent figure. Barton, who by this time was in the camp opposite Parkes in New South Wales politics, wrote to him and pledged his support for the federal cause.

A few days later, on November 3, 1889, Barton made his first public speech in support of federation, at a meeting of the Australian Natives Association at Sydney's town hall. As a member of the protectionist party led by Dibbs, Barton's support for the free trader Parkes brought much criticism. Barton worked hard with Parkes, O'Connor, and others to secure support for a National Australasian Convention, the first meeting of which was held in Sydney in March of 1891. At this gathering of the most prominent men in the colonies, Barton distinguished himself as a speaker and member of the Drafting Committee. He, Sir Samuel Griffith of Queensland, and Sir Charles Kingston of South Australia are noted for having retired to the Queensland government yacht, called the *Lucinda*, cruising the Hawkesbury River, on March 27. On March 29, they emerged with a finished constitution, which formed the basis for all further debate.

The draft bill passed by the convention had then to be accepted by the colonial parliaments. This process and the accompanying referenda were to take until 1900 and involved Barton in his greatest work. He was embarrassed, after the defeat of Parkes in 1892, by having served in the protectionist Dibbs ministry, whose leader was opposed to federation. During these difficult times, he was faced with a parliament concerned with local issues and, at best, indifferent to the cause to which Barton had devoted himself.

Eventually Barton's position in the Dibbs government became untenable, and he resigned in 1894. Having been instrumental in the founding of the populist group the Federation League, he now became a missionary for the federalist cause. During the next three years, it is recorded that he addressed three hundred meetings in New South Wales alone and, despite the difficulties of intercolonial travel, visited the other colonies and spoke at a total of a thousand meetings. Whether speaking to the profederation Australian Natives Association or the Federation League, or addressing hostile antifederalist businesspeople or trade unionists, Barton stated his case simply and forcefully.

Other colonial politicians responded to the growing popularity of federation, and a second Australasian National Convention met in Adelaide on March 22, 1897. Barton, despite holding no political office, was elected first to represent New South Wales, ahead of the premier, George Reid. Barton was almost unanimously elected to the leadership of the convention and faced his greatest test within the first week, when the issue of representation and powers for the Senate, the state's house, was hotly contested. His speech on the morning of April 14, 1897, is said to have been his greatest, and the division shortly afterward approved the draft for the Senate, which has remained as the compromise between the smaller and larger states in the Australian Commonwealth.

Once again, a draft bill was passed and Barton worked tirelessly for its acceptance by all the colonies. On June 3, 1898, the bill was put to a referendum in four of the six colonies and failed by eight thousand votes to achieve the requisite majority. There are tales of Barton traveling through the bush to address a small meeting and of taking fresh horses for the drive through the night to the next town. When the bill was again put to a vote, this time in all six colonies, in 1899 (1900 in Western Australia), it passed in each colony.

Barton now faced the task of leading the colonial delegation to the imperial parliament at Westminster. Although not opposed to federating the Australian colonies, the powerful colonial secretary, Joseph Chamberlain, insisted that the Privy Council in London remain as the highest court of appeal. Barton realized that the Constitution Bill must be passed in its original form if it was to retain support in Australia. After much negotiation, he secured a compromise amendment, retaining the right of appeal to the Privy Council but making such an appeal dependent on a certificate of the High Court of Australia. The bill was passed and given royal assent on July 9, 1900.

Despite his acknowledged leadership of the movement for federation, Barton almost did not become the first prime minister of the Commonwealth he did so much to create. Lord Hopetoun, the first governor-general, was so much impressed by the premier of New South Wales, Sir William Lyne, that on December 19, 1900, he commissioned him to form the first Commonwealth government. Lyne, who had been an active opponent of federation, failed to attract men of sufficient standing to form a successful government. On December 24, therefore, he returned his commission, and the next day Barton was asked to form a ministry that was sworn in when the new parliament was opened in 1901 by the duke of York. The elections held three months later confirmed Barton's place as prime minister.

As the leader of the new Commonwealth, Barton's principal task was the establishment of the organs of government, particularly the High Court. He attended the coronation of Edward VII in 1902 and was knighted by the new king. Upon his return, after the Imperial Conference, Barton's government addressed itself to the questions of immigration, defense, and the setting up of seven new departments. After thirty-three months in office, Barton resigned to take a seat on the first bench of the High Court of Australia.

Although Barton was himself a successful lawyer—he had been a King's Counsel since 1889—he recommended the chief justice of Queensland, Sir Samuel Griffith, rather than himself, to be the first chief justice of the Commonwealth of Australia. Critics have commented on the number of times he concurred with Griffith rather than publish his own judgment. It may be pointed out that on these occasions he had often written his own reasons, but concurred in order to clarify judicial precedent. His years on the Court were marked by appreciation of his wisdom and courtesy from the bench. On the morning of January 7, 1920, he collapsed after a bath and died immediately. Barton was given a state funeral and was buried at South Head Cemetery, Sydney.

SIGNIFICANCE

To attribute the creation of the Commonwealth of Australia solely to Sir Edmund Barton is unrealistic. There were many others who worked for federation. Barton's role was, however, pivotal. A man not normally known for passionate commitment, he threw himself into what he considered the great cause of his time. His parliamentary skills, urbanity, and capacity for advantageous compromise were essential to the success of the constitutional conventions, made up, as they were, of strong-minded, colonially interested politicians. The respect he commanded as prime minister was important for a smooth start for the fledgling Commonwealth. In his own words, the establishment of the Commonwealth of Australia saw for the first time in history "a continent for a nation and a nation for a continent."

—Paul Michael O'Shea

FURTHER READING

Bolton, Geoffrey. *Edmund Barton*. St. Leonards, N.S.W.: Allen & Unwin, 2000. The first full-length biography of Barton in more than 50 years. Bolton is the general editor of the *Oxford History of Australia* and the author of numerous books about Australian history.

Headon, David, and John Williams, eds. *Makers of Miracles: The Cast of the Federation Story*. Carlton, Victoria: Melbourne University Press, 2000. One of several books commemorating the centenary of Australian federation, this book focuses on the people who were instrumental in creating a unified Australian nation.

Irving, Helen, ed. *The Centenary Companion to Australian Federation*. New York: Cambridge University Press, 1999. Information about Barton is included in this reference book. The book features essays on each colony that eventually joined the federation and alphabetical entries on key people in the federation movement.

Martin, A. W. *Essays in Australian Federation*. Melbourne, Vic.: Melbourne University Press, 1969. Barton's role is discussed extensively in the chapters on the Australian Natives Association and the New South Wales referendum.

Norris, R. *The Emergent Commonwealth*. Melbourne, Vic.: Melbourne University Press, 1975. Gives a detailed account of the proceedings at the constitutional conventions and of Barton's tenure as prime minster.

Quick, John, and Robert Garran. *The Annotated Constitution of the Australian Commonwealth*. Sydney: Angus and Robertson, 1901. Written by two convention participants, this is the most authoritative work on the Australian constitution. The chapter "Historical Introduction" deals, not uncritically, with Barton's role.

Reynolds, John. *Edmund Barton.* Sydney: Angus and Robertson, 1948. One of the few detailed accounts of Barton's life. Scholarly, though dated, it treats him well. The forewords in the 1979 edition are worth reading.

SEE ALSO: Alfred Deakin; Sir Henry Parkes.

RELATED ARTICLE in *Great Events from History: The Nineteenth Century, 1801-1900:* 1868: Last Convicts Land in Western Australia.

CHARLES BAUDELAIRE

French poet

Baudelaire was instrumental in the transformation from a classical conception of poetry, which concentrated on the subject, to the Romantic focus on the self and presented in his own poetry a heightened sensitivity to the dark dimensions of the beautiful, which served as a consolation for his own awareness of the human inclination toward self-destruction.

BORN: April 9, 1821; Paris, France
DIED: August 31, 1867; Paris, France
ALSO KNOWN AS: Charles Pierre Baudelaire (full name)
AREA OF ACHIEVEMENT: Literature

EARLY LIFE

Charles Baudelaire (bohd-lehr) was born in Paris in 1821. His father, a member of the senate during the reign of Napoleon I, died in 1827 at the age of sixty-eight, and his mother was married to a successful career officer twenty months later. In 1830, Baudelaire entered the Collège Royal, a boarding school in Lyons, where his stepfather was stationed, and remained there until his family returned to Paris in 1836. He loathed the routine and the excessively strict code of discipline at the Collège Louis-le-Grand and was expelled in 1839. To satisfy his stepfather, who hoped that he would follow a career in law, Baudelaire continued his studies at the Collège Saint-Louis and passed the examination for his baccalaureate later that year.

Between 1839 and 1841, Baudelaire lived as a sort of idle protodandy in the Latin Quarter while he tried to pursue a literary career. One of his closest friends, Ernest Praround, described him:

> coming down a staircase in the Baily house, slim, a low collar, an extremely long waistcoat, detached cuffs, carrying a light cane with a small gold head, walking with a supple, almost rhythmic step . . . Baudelaire had a somewhat yellow and even complexion, which had a little color on the cheekbones, a delicate beard which he didn't clip, and which did not smother his face. His expression, sharpened sometimes by genuine malice, sometimes by irony, would relax when he stopped talking or listening to withdraw into himself.

Théodore de Banville remarked on his "long, dense, and silk-black hair," while others noted that he presented himself with a painterly regard for appearance, a reflection of his growing commitment to art as a means of enhancing every aspect of life. His stepfather believed that he could find "better sources of inspiration" than "the sewers of Paris," and, to separate him from his "abominable friends," persuaded him to sail to India. The trip lasted eight months, giving Baudelaire a taste for the exotic.

In 1842, having returned to France, Baudelaire took possession of his inheritance, a small fortune equivalent to $100,000. He settled in the expensive Quai de Bethune area, the first of fourteen addresses he maintained in Paris during the next fourteen years, and with the resources to cultivate his public presentation of himself, he moved with a crowd that valued the shocking remark and the outrageous gesture. His experiments with hashish began at about this time, as did his liaison with Jeanne Duval, a beautiful actress of mixed racial descent—the "Black Venus" of *Les Fleurs du Mal* (1857, 1861, 1868; *Flowers of Evil*, 1909). His stepfather was so alarmed by Baudelaire's style of living that he appointed a guardian to handle his monetary affairs, an act that irritated Baudelaire for the remainder of his life and may have contributed to a halfhearted attempt at suicide in 1845.

Baudelaire's spirits were revived by his first real success as a writer, his review of the 1845 exhibition at the Louvre, which blended the emotional responsiveness of the poet with the critical acuity of the trained art critic. His "Salon de 1846" ("Salon of 1846," 1964) was similarly successful, and on its last pages there was an announcement for a book of poems to be titled "Les Lesbiennes"—a title designed for its effect. This was the first public reference to *Flowers of Evil*, which in fact would not be published for another decade. In 1847, Baudelaire published *La Fanfarlo*, an extended short story with a protagonist who served as a semisatiric reflection on his inclinations toward the sensational, and began to suffer from the periodic onslaughts of syphilis, which eventually led to his death. His gradually declining health caused a radical change in his appearance, the dandy now transposed into a prematurely aged flaneur with an almost-grim visage, high forehead, and piercing eyes.

LIFE'S WORK

In 1846 or 1847, Baudelaire read Edgar Allan Poe and remarked, "The first time I opened a book of his, I saw, with horror and delight, not just subjects I had dreamt of, but *sentences* I had thought of." He began to publish translations of Poe in 1848 and was also placing some poetry in *Revue de Paris*, a journal edited by Théophile Gautier and other friends. In 1857, the first edition of *Flowers of Evil* appeared. The title was proposed by Hippolyte Babou; Baudelaire liked its suggestion that beauty could be born of evil and that the seemingly perverse could be recast into poetic grace.

Charles Baudelaire. (Library of Congress)

Baudelaire knew that the book might be considered obscene, but a critic in *Le Figaro* may have exceeded his expectations by saying, "The book is a hospital open to all forms of mental derangements and emotional putrefaction." The government agreed and brought an indictment that compelled the confiscation of the book on July 17, three weeks after it had gone on sale. Baudelaire was found not guilty of blasphemy at the resulting hearing, but the charge of offending public morality stood, and six poems were banned. When asked if he expected to be acquitted, Baudelaire replied, "Acquitted! I was hoping for a public apology."

The prosecution of his masterwork diminished whatever remained of an optimistic outlook, and in 1860 Baudelaire published *Les Paradis artificiels: Opium et haschisch* (partial translation as *Artificial Paradises: On Hashish and Wine as a Means of Expanding Individuality*, 1971). The book condemned hallucinogenic agents as providers of an illusion of the paradisiacal and described opium as a sapper of the will, which made it impossible to work. The essay, however, was misread as a celebration of decadence. Baudelaire knew that this was likely, but his imp of the perverse compelled him to continue.

In 1861, Baudelaire completed his definitive edition of *Flowers of Evil* (although an uncensored version did not appear in France until the twentieth century) and briefly considered applying for election to the French Academy. From 1862 to 1864, the twin plagues of poor health and poverty continued to unsettle him, but he was able to focus his mood into his final collection of poetry, *Le Spleen de Paris* (1869; *Paris Spleen*, 1869, 1905), a volume that dealt with the unreal city of T. S. Eliot's vision. He attempted to capitalize on his notoriety by scheduling a lecture tour of Belgium, and when this failed he remained in Europe until July, 1866, suffering from the effects of a stroke. His health worsened steadily, and he died in Paris in August, 1867.

SIGNIFICANCE

Along with his transoceanic double, his brother in letters Edgar Allan Poe, Charles Baudelaire was the model for the nineteenth century archetype of the doomed artist, driven by an implacable destiny while struggling against his own self-destructive tendencies, an ignorant public, and a reactionary literary establishment. Underrated and misunderstood in his own time, Baudelaire—like Poe—had mythic aspects of his life that have a perverse allure that captures the imagination; but—like Poe—the perfected originality of his art, and the intensity and seriousness of his approach to his profession (which he listed as "lyric poet" on a passport application), have ultimately been recognized as the real attributes of his genius.

Baudelaire was one of the inventors of the Romantic attitude that has shaped and influenced the manner in which artists see themselves in relation to their work to this day. As Victor Brombert notes, Baudelaire's poetry defined Romantic sensibility in some of its most crucial aspects. The obsessive fascination with "erotic exoticism"; the urge to escape from the world while, in turn, being lured into its debauchery; the urge to follow the imagination to the furthest ranges of the conceivable; the sense of the artist as simultaneous victim and tyrant; the inclination toward prophetic affirmation of poetic destiny; a pervasive sense of sadness leading to strange beauty and an expression of the artist's awareness that he is damned by a kind of hyperconsciousness are some of the elements of the Romantic vision which Baudelaire fashioned.

On the other hand, as T. S. Eliot's well-known essay "Tradition and the Individual Talent" argues, Baudelaire had other attributes that are ordinarily included under the rubric of classical constraint. Baudelaire's background and early formal education enabled him to use the French language with subtlety, elegance, and precision. His command of traditional poetic technique permitted him to employ a philosophy of composition that called for the accumulation of effect through a mastery of poetic means that would overcome or transform the ugly into the beautiful, the evil into the potentially divine.

Even as Baudelaire's life and work projected a counterstrain to classical aesthetics that has become a permanent part of modern artistic thinking, his ability to use the resources of language with a meticulous awareness of linguistic traditions demonstrates that placing the self at the center of experience does not mean that a refinement of craft is obsolete. The power of art, he believed, could enable humankind to transcend the limits of an inherently evil world and a fundamentally sinful human condition. This belief was based on his Catholic background, but Baudelaire's real religion was poetry, and his own work was its truest sacrament.

As Peter Quennel observes, Baudelaire was "the chief accuser of the modern world, yet he is also its most patriotic citizen." Baudelaire never felt really comfortable in his world, but he knew how to make the most of his life there. "One must always be drunk," he advised. "To escape being the martyred slaves of time, be continually drunk. On wine, poetry, or virtue, whatever you fancy." For Baudelaire himself, an intoxication with art was the only form of addiction that provided true satisfaction.

—*Leon Lewis*

FURTHER READING

Baudelaire, Charles. *The Flowers of Evil*. New York: New Directions, 1955. A complete bilingual edition which includes the work of many translators. The best single source for Baudelaire's poetry in English.

_____. *Selected Poems of Charles Baudelaire*. New York: Grove Press, 1974. A collection of translations by Geoffrey Wagner that concentrate chiefly on the erotic poetry, including some of the poems banned from the 1857 edition of *Flowers of Evil*. Includes an excellent introduction by Enid Starkie, which covers Baudelaire's life and work.

Brombert, Victor. *The Hidden Reader*. Cambridge, Mass.: Harvard University Press, 1988. Described as "a close reading of a high order," Brombert places Baudelaire within the context of Romanticism.

Butor, Michel. *Histoire Extraordinaire: Essay on a Dream of Baudelaire*. Translated by Richard Howard. London: Jonathan Cape, 1969. An approach to Baudelaire from the underside. Written in a very contemporary, somewhat fragmented style, this is a most perceptive psychoanalytic study. Speculative, daring, and sympathetic, it covers Baudelaire's life and his relationship with Poe, and captures the spirit of Baudelaire's work.

de Jonge, Alex. *Baudelaire: Prince of Clouds*. New York: Paddington Press, 1976. Probably the best biography of Baudelaire in English. De Jonge is an intelligent and understanding biographer and translator, who has utilized the best biographical work prior to his own book and included many of Baudelaire's letters to substantiate his observations.

Hilton, Frank. *Baudelaire in Chains: Portrait of the Artist as a Drug Addict*. London: Peter Owen, 2004. Biography focusing on Baudelaire's opium addiction. Hilton maintains Baudelaire's drug use was the root of all of his problems, particularly his inability to concentrate on prolonged creative work.

Lloyd, Rosemary. *Baudelaire's World*. Ithaca, N.Y.: Cornell University Press, 2002. Lloyd uses the major themes in Baudelaire's writing—childhood, women, reading, the city, dreams, art, nature, and death—to offer a biographical, cultural, and historical analysis of his work.

Poulet, Georges. *Exploding Poetry: Baudelaire/Rimbaud*. Translated by Françoise Meltzer. Chicago: University of Chicago Press, 1984. A study of the affinities between two poets from the perspective of a critic who is firmly located in the cerebral realm of contemporary French literary criticism. Much arcane terminology combined with much critical insight. Tends toward the philosophical but offers some quite worthwhile conjectures for the advanced student.

Richardson, Joanna. *Baudelaire*. New York: St. Martin's Press, 1994. Biography of Baudelaire, focusing on his complex and tortured relationship with his mother.

Ruff, Marcel A. *Baudelaire*. Translated by Agnes Kertesz. New York: New York University Press, 1966. An extremely thorough but very readable biography, based on sound scholarship, sympathetic understanding, and an appealing basic decency. A good companion to de Jonge's more dramatic presentation, with a list of all Baudelaire's publications, including dates and other important annotations.

Sartre, Jean-Paul. *Baudelaire*. Translated by Martin Turnell. London: Horizon, 1949. One brilliant, quirky, singular genius regarding another. Sometimes incisive, sometimes wrongheaded, almost always fascinating if not always reliable.

Starkie, Enid. *Baudelaire*. New York: G. P. Putnam's Sons, 1933. Accurately described as the "foremost modern English authority on Baudelaire's life and work," Starkie writes a groundbreaking work that has provided an essential foundation for all Baudelaire studies in the United States and the United Kingdom. Still unsurpassed for breadth of coverage and intelligent commentary on the poetry and its sources in Baudelaire's life.

SEE ALSO: François-René de Chateaubriand; Odilon Redon; Arthur Rimbaud; Anaïs Ségalas.

RELATED ARTICLES in *Great Events from History: The Nineteenth Century, 1801-1900:* 1819: Schopenhauer Publishes *The World as Will and Idea*; c. 1865: Naturalist Movement Begins; c. 1884-1924: Decadent Movement Flourishes.

L. FRANK BAUM

American writer

Baum is best known for creating the marvelous land of Oz, a utopian fantasy world chronicled in a series of children's books that began with The Wonderful Wizard of Oz. *Through his Oz series, Baum created a uniquely American version of the standard fairy tale.*

BORN: May 15, 1856; Chittenango, New York
DIED: May 6, 1919; Hollywood, California
ALSO KNOWN AS: Lyman Frank Baum (full name)
AREA OF ACHIEVEMENT: Literature

EARLY LIFE

Lyman Frank Baum was the seventh of nine children born to German immigrants Cynthia and Benjamin Baum. The Baum family immigrated to the United States seeking religious freedom. Frank's grandfather was a Methodist circuit rider. His father was a cooper who later became wealthy in the oil skimming business. Born with a weak heart, Frank is said to have suffered from bouts of angina throughout his entire life and was tutored at home until age twelve, when his parents decided he was healthy enough to attend the prestigious Peerskill Academy, a military boarding school in Peerskill, New York. Baum left Peerskill after two years and finished his education at home.

Baum's writing career began when his father bought him a small, foot-powered printing press for his fourteenth birthday. Within a year, in May of 1871, Frank and his younger brother Harry were publishing *The Rose Lawn Home Journal*, a neighborhood newspaper. In 1872 Baum began publishing *The Stamp Collector*, a monthly magazine for philatelists. In 1873, Baum purchased a new press and, along with Thomas G. Alford, founded *The Empire*.

When Baum turned nineteen, he put his writing and publishing career on hold to become an actor and a breeder of Hamburg chickens. After winning awards from several poultry associations, Baum started a new magazine, *The Poultry Record*. Poultry was to remain one of Baum's preoccupations. In 1886 he wrote his first book, *The Book of the Hamburgs*, a complete guide to Hamburg husbandry.

Through his late teens, Baum wandered through numerous jobs ranging from salesperson to oil worker.

Born with good looks, a strong stage presence, and a strong baritone voice, Baum seemed to be a natural for the stage. He attempted to fulfill his desire to act by joining up with traveling theater troupes. After being fleeced by a number of troupes, he turned to theater management when his father purchased a small chain of opera houses in New York and Pennsylvania. In 1881 Baum published the successful musical melodrama *The Maid of Arran*, which was based on the Scottish novel *A Princess of Thule* by William Black. One year later, Baum married Maude Gage, daughter of Matilda Joslyn Gage, a prominent figure in the woman suffrage movement.

In 1887, after the death of his father and the loss of most of the family fortune, Baum followed members of the Gage family to Aberdeen in the Dakota Territory. Baum opened a store called Baum's Bazaar. It was on the bazaar's sidewalks that Baum spent hours telling stories to his own children and children from the neighborhood. The bazaar failed in 1890, forcing Baum to return to journalism as he took the job of running the *Aberdeen Saturday Pioneer*, a weekly newspaper. While in this position, Baum published editorials that ranged from vehement support for the woman suffragist movement to advocating the "extermination of the [Sioux] Indians." By March, 1891, the *Aberdeen Saturday Pioneer* had gone bankrupt, and the Baum family, which now included four sons, headed to Chicago, Illinois.

Once in Chicago, Baum quickly landed a job as a reporter for the *Evening Post*. To make ends meet, Baum also became a traveling salesperson for Pitkin and Brooks, a company that sold china. Baum used the traveling time as an opportunity to devise characters and story lines for the tales he told his sons. Baum's china sales were remarkably high because he took the time to teach his customers how to construct effective window displays for the products. Baum turned these lessons into a successful magazine called *The Window Dresser*, a professional organization of window trimmers, and a book, *The Art of Decorating Dry Good Windows and Interiors* (1900).

Baum continued to spend a great deal of his free time telling stories to children. When his sons had difficulty understanding the Mother Goose verses, Baum developed prose explanations of the stories. Baum's mother-in-law, Matilda Gage, urged him to submit these explanations to a publisher. Way and Williams publishers teamed Baum with artist Maxfield Parrish to produce *Mother Goose in Prose* (1897). The modest sales of *Mother Goose* led to *Father Goose, His Book* (1899), with color illustrations (a radical idea for the day) by William Wallace Denslow. *Father Goose, His Book* was an instant success and became the best-selling children's book of 1899.

LIFE'S WORK

Denslow and Baum soon began work on their second book, tentatively titled *The Emerald City*. Because of a publishing superstition about using jewels as part of titles, the name was changed to *The Wonderful Wizard of Oz* (1900). Denslow and Baum again insisted on color illustrations. In this case, the color of the plates referred to Oz geography: For example, blue was used for color illustrations of Munchkin Country. At first, publishers rejected the book because of the expense of reproducing color plates. Eventually George M. Hill published the book in the fall of 1900.

In the introduction to *The Wonderful Wizard of Oz*, Baum wrote,

L. Frank Baum. (Library of Congress)

> The time has come for a series of newer 'wonder tales' in which the stereotyped genie, dwarf and fairy are eliminated, together with all the horrible and blood-curdling incidents devised by their authors to point a fearsome moral to each tale.

With Oz, Baum created a utopia that, for the first time, urged American children to see the wonder of the world around them. For the first time, a fairyland was constructed from American ideals and materials. *The Wonderful Wizard of Oz* became the best-selling children's book for 1900. Its cast of characters began their journey toward becoming an integral part of the American consciousness.

Baum did not want to write sequels to *The Wonderful Wizard of Oz*, but he continued to produce a variety of children's books. In 1902, a non-Oz work, *Dot and Tot of Merryland*, also illustrated by Denslow, failed to match the commercial success of the previous two releases. During the early twentieth century, Baum wrote numerous non-Oz books under his own name and under pseudonyms. As Edith Van Dyne, Baum penned *Aunt Jane's Nieces*, a highly successful series of books that targeted teenage girls and was as commercially successful as the Oz books.

Baum's love for the theater led to a collaboration with Denslow and composer Paul Tietjens to produce a musical stage play of *The Wonderful Wizard of Oz*. The production was an enormous hit and ran for 293 nights on Broadway between 1902 and 1911.

In 1904, publisher Reilly and Britton persuaded Baum to continue the Oz series. Refusing to return Dorothy to Oz, Baum created the gender-changing character "Tip/Ozma" as the protagonist for *The Marvelous Land of Oz*. Tip starts as a young boy, but readers eventually discover that the witch Mombi had turned Ozma, the rightful ruler of Oz, into Tip to hide her from the wizard.

Baum attempted to capture the same theatrical success with *The Marvelous Land of Oz* that he had garnered with his musical adaptation of *The Wonderful Wizard of Oz*. *The Woggle-Bug*, Baum's adaptation of *The Marvelous Land of Oz*, opened in Chicago in 1905. While critics liked Frederic Chapman's score for the play, the show was a financial disaster and closed in one month.

Baum's readers and publisher continued to request more adventures in Oz. In 1907 Baum relented to the pressure and, in *Ozma of Oz*, Dorothy returned to Oz. *Ozma of Oz* proved to be a critical and commercial success. One of the book's characters was a mechanical being who could talk and think called Tik-Tok, one of the first artificially intelligent robots to appear in fiction. *Ozma of Oz* was quickly followed with the fourth Oz book, *Dorothy and the Wizard of Oz*, in 1908. The success of the third and fourth Oz books persuaded Baum to take his Oz stories back to the stage. He financed the creation of *Fairylogue and Radio-Plays* in 1908. The show was a travelogue narrated by Baum. Hand-colored silent films displayed the action, and child actors portraying Oz characters stepped from a huge book onto the stage. The work was a critical and popular success, but it was prohibitively expensive to produce and closed after only three months, leading, in part, to Baum's bankruptcy in 1911.

Baum continued to write Oz books. In 1909, *The Road to Oz* was released to commercial success, but sales were not enough to pay the bills left by *Fairylogue and Radio-Plays*. In the sixth Oz book, *The Emerald City of Oz* (1910), Baum tried to end the series by claiming that the coming of airships led the residents of Oz to fear that they would be overrun by tourists. Glinda the Good cast a spell to render Oz invisible. The spell lasted only three years. In the introduction to the seventh Oz book, *The Patchwork Girl of Oz* (1913), Baum explained that a child wrote him to suggest that he communicate with Oz using wireless telegraphy. With that, Baum, who now

BAUM'S OZ NOVELS

L. Frank Baum wrote fifteen Oz books himself. After he died, his widow authorized a writer named Ruth Plumly Thompson to continue the series, and Thompson eventually wrote an additional eighteen Oz books.

1900	*The Wonderful Wizard of Oz*
1904	*The Marvelous Land of Oz*
1907	*Ozma of Oz*
1908	*Dorothy and the Wizard in Oz*
1909	*The Road to Oz*
1910	*The Emerald City of Oz*
1913	*The Patchwork Girl of Oz*
1914	*Little Wizard Stories of Oz*
1914	*Tik-Tok of Oz*
1915	*The Scarecrow of Oz*
1916	*Rinkitink in Oz*
1917	*The Lost Princess of Oz*
1918	*The Tin Woodman of Oz*
1919	*The Magic of Oz*
1920	*Glinda of Oz*

called himself the Royal Historian of Oz, continued his chronicles. Baum tried the stage again with *The Tik-Tok Man* in 1913. He formed the Oz Film Company in 1914 and produced a number of Oz-related films. Distribution problems plagued the Oz Film Company, and the company was sold to Universal in 1914.

In 1915, Baum released *The Scarecrow of Oz*. Although his health was becoming increasingly worse, he continued to write, releasing at least one additional Oz book each year from 1915 to 1919. On May 5, 1919, Baum suffered a stroke. He died in Hollywood, California, the next day. His last words were reported to have been in reference to Oz: "Now we can cross the Shifting Sands."

The final Baum-authored Oz book, *Glinda of Oz*, was released in 1920. Maud Baum, after she was promised royalties from any future Oz books, allowed publisher Reilly and Britton to find a new Royal Historian. They chose established children's writer Ruth Plumly Thompson. Thompson would write eighteen Oz books (five more than Baum) before retiring in 1939.

SIGNIFICANCE

Oz remained a part of the American consciousness thanks to radio shows, silent film adaptations, and a steady string of new Oz books. In 1939 Metro-Goldwyn-Mayer released its film adaptation of *The Wonderful Wizard of Oz*, starring Judy Garland as Dorothy. Yearly showings of the film have made it an American classic. The film was named a national treasure under the National Film Preservation Act of 1988.

Despite the fact that Baum's work was considered "hack" work by many librarians and scholars until the 1960's, Baum established a truly American form of fairy tale. During the last nineteen years of his life, he wrote and published sixty-two books, yet it was the thirteen Oz books that created an iconic cast of characters and an archetypal story that became a permanent part of American mythology.

The marvelous land of Oz and its inhabitants are known worldwide. The concepts Baum created have become such an integral part of the growing global culture that the characters and ideas created in the books and perpetuated by the film appear in advertisements, editorial cartoons, and political speeches around the world.

—*B. Keith Murphy*

FURTHER READING

Baum, Frank Joslyn, and Russell P. MacFall. *To Please a Child: A Biography of L. Frank Baum, Royal Historian of Oz*. Chicago: Reilly & Lee, 1961. Co-written by L. Frank Baum's son, Frank Joslyn, this work, while continuing to perpetuate some of the more mythic aspects of the Baum legend, provides unique insights into the more private histories of Baum and Oz.

Baum, L. Frank. *The Wonderful Wizard of Oz*. New York: Oxford University Press, 1997. This edition of Baum's most significant work is prefaced with a history of the author as well as cultural and literary analysis of Baum and Oz.

Carpenter, Angelica Shirley, and Jean Shirley. *L. Frank Baum: Royal Historian of Oz*. Minneapolis, Minn.: Lerner, 1991. A detailed history of Baum's life and works and their continuing impact.

Gardner, Martin, and Russell B. Nye. *The Wizard of Oz and Who He Was*. East Lansing, Mich.: Michigan State University Press, 1957. Provides a scholarly and literary approach to understanding the history and impact of Baum's works.

Harmetz, Aljean. *The Making of the Wizard of Oz*. New York: Alfred A. Knopf, 1977. Provides insight into the making of the film that placed Oz firmly in the American consciousness.

Riley, Michael O. *Oz and Beyond: The Fantasy World of L. Frank Baum*. Lawrence: University Press of Kansas, 1997. An analysis of all of Baum's written works within the context of his childhood and adult experiences. Riley describes how Baum expanded and altered Oz throughout the course of his books, and created a host of characters who are united in a single "other world."

Rogers, Katherine M. *L. Frank Baum: Creator of Oz*. New York: St. Martin's Press, 2002. A good companion to the Oz series that demonstrates how Baum animated his progressive ideals in the persons of Dorothy and company.

SEE ALSO: Horatio Alger; Hans Christian Andersen; Frances Hodgson Burnett; Lewis Carroll.

RELATED ARTICLES in *Great Events from History: The Nineteenth Century, 1801-1900:* 1812-1815: Brothers Grimm Publish Fairy Tales; May 8, 1835: Andersen Publishes His First Fairy Tales; July, 1881-1883: Stevenson Publishes *Treasure Island*.

DOROTHEA BEALE
British educator

Combining business acumen, enthusiasm for reform, and mystical idealism, Beale shaped an educational breakthrough with her advocacy of intellectual training for girls.

BORN: March 21, 1831; Bishopsgate, London, England
DIED: November 9, 1906; Cheltenham, England
AREAS OF ACHIEVEMENT: Education, women's rights

EARLY LIFE

Born on March 21, 1831, in Bishopsgate, London, England, one of eleven children, Dorothea Beale owed some of her success as a pioneer in the field of women's education to familial tradition. Her mother, Dorothea Margaret Complin, came from a family of literary women who included feminist writer Caroline Francis Cornwallis. Her father, Miles Beale, a surgeon, displayed a keen interest in contemporary social and educational issues and believed that his daughters should have every opportunity to cultivate their minds and to pursue whatever vocation they chose. In addition, Dorothea Beale possessed the traits of severe self-discipline, a driving desire to succeed, and a sense of divinely directed destiny. Religion was a potent factor in the Beale household, and Dorothea felt the pull of mysticism, expressing a strong affinity with St. Hilda of Whitby, an erudite seventh century abbess.

From early childhood, Beale wanted to be an educator, and while still small, she often created an imaginary world in which she would preside over a girls' school. Grave, quiet, and slight of stature, she did not care for outdoor activities and spent her leisure hours studying, believing that teaching carried a sacred trust. Despite this dedication, her early education was disjointed and incomplete, a result of a succession of incompetent governesses and brief stays at an English boarding school and at a Parisian finishing school. Nurturing an aptitude for mathematics, she attended lectures at London's Gresham College and Crosby Hall Institution.

In 1848, Beale and her sisters began classes at the newly established Queen's College, Harley Street. The institution's roster also included another student, Frances Mary Buss, although the two women did not meet at this time. Subsequently Beale and Buss became warm personal and professional friends, and their names and unmarried status were frozen together in time because of the rhyme, "Miss Buss and Miss Beale/ Cupid's darts do not feel;/ How different from us,/ Miss Beale and Miss Buss."

In 1849, Queen's College awarded eighteen-year-old Dorothea Beale certificates in six subjects—mathematics, geography, English, Latin, French, and German—and offered her a position on the staff. She accepted and became the college's first woman faculty member. Appointed mathematics tutor, then Latin tutor, and finally head teacher in the school connected to the college, she remained on the staff for seven years. Long chafing at the limited authority given to women faculty and the lowering of standards for student admission, Beale resigned in 1856.

In January, 1857, Beale accepted the position of head teacher in the Clergy Daughters School at Casterton. This institution, immortalized as Lowood by Charlotte Brontë's *Jane Eyre* (1847), proved to be ugly and rigid in architecture as well as philosophy and demanded that Beale teach Scripture; ancient, modern, and Church history; physical and political geography; English literature; grammar and composition; and Latin, French, German, and Italian. Beale disliked the school and requested reforms, suggesting that unless changes occurred she would resign. The school authorities accepted the challenge and dismissed her. After this humiliating blow to her pride, she returned home, did some part-time teaching, and wrote two books, *The Student's Text-Book of English and General History from B.C. 100 to the Present Time* (1858) and *Self-Examination* (1858). This period also offered Beale time for introspection. She had failed in her chosen profession not once but twice. Never again, she determined, would she accept a post that did not provide her the measure of authority she desired.

LIFE'S WORK

In the summer of 1858, after the series of unhappy teaching interludes, the twenty-seven-year-old Beale, attired in a borrowed blue silk dress instead of her usual black wool, sought a position at England's oldest proprietary girls' school. Defeating fifty other candidates, she became the principal of Cheltenham Ladies' College, where she reigned for nearly fifty years. Her initial task was to ensure the school's survival, for students numbered only sixty-nine and total capital came to a mere four hundred pounds. Within four years she reversed the decline, almost doubled enrollment, and placed the institution on firm financial footing.

Equally important she began a slow but steady crusade for public acceptance of intellectual training for young ladies from upper- and upper-middle-class homes. Guided by what she thought female students needed, she curtailed the emphasis on needlework and piano exercises and encouraged greater attention to English history and the German language. Because contemporaries considered even simple arithmetic useless for women, Beale ignored her personal preference for geometry and introduced scientific reasoning in the guise of physical geography. The inclusion of an earth science in the curriculum of a girls' school did not attract attention as few males studied geography. Beale also experimented with the school day and introduced a nine to one o'clock schedule, keeping afternoons free for individual music, drawing, and needlework lessons.

At the national level, the status of girls' education gained attention when the government's School Inquiry Commission included it as part of a mid-1860's investigation. Asked to testify, Beale provided a vivid picture of the abysmal ignorance of England's upper- and middle-class young women. An examination of the entrance tests of one hundred fifteen-year-olds revealed that not one of the students understood fractions, only four could conjugate the French verb "to be," and one girl insisted that Geoffrey Chaucer lived during the reign of George III. Beale refused to make any comparisons between the mental abilities of boys and girls and insisted that she desired to educate young marriageable ladies for their subordinate role in society. She argued that well-educated women became better wives and mothers than those who were poorly educated. Her testimony, along with that of other female educators, gave impetus to much-needed improvements in education. In 1869, Beale published, with a personal introduction, an edited version of the Commission's findings, entitled *Reports on the Education of Girls, with Extracts from the Evidence* (1869).

The next three decades saw Beale's Ladies' College make great strides. Curriculum offerings expanded and the school's physical plant grew. By the turn of the century, there were more than one thousand students, fourteen boardinghouses, a secondary and kindergarten department called St. Hilda's College, a library of seven thousand volumes, and fifteen acres of grounds. In order to provide a link between alumni and students, Beale founded *The Cheltenham Ladies' College Magazine* in 1882 and the Guild of the Cheltenham Ladies' College in 1884.

In addition to her administrative and teaching duties at Ladies' College, Beale maintained an active professional career with close ties to other female educators, especially Frances Mary Buss of the North London Collegiate School. She held life membership in the Head Mistress Association and served as president from 1895 to 1897, she testified frequently on educational issues to various royal commissions, and she introduced the concept of an annual teachers' retreat, Quiet Days. She also wrote a number of educational treatises: *Home-Life in Relation to Day Schools* (1879); *A Few Words to Those Who Are Leaving* (1881); *Work and Play in Girls Schools* (1898; with Lucy H. M. Soulsby and Jane F. Dove); *Literary Studies of Poems, New and Old* (1902); *Addresses to Teachers* (1909); and her labor of love, *History of the Cheltenham Ladies' College, 1853-1901* (1904).

With the advent of the new century more accolades came Beale's way. In 1901, the freedom of the borough of Cheltenham was conferred upon her and in 1902 she received an honorary doctorate from the University of Edinburgh. Despite deafness and infirmity, she continued to work until a few weeks before her death from cancer on November 9, 1906. After cremation, her ashes were placed in Gloucester Cathedral's Lady Chapel. A week later in memorial services at St. Paul's Cathedral, an honor accorded to very few women, the future archbishop of Canterbury Cosmo Lang detailed her successes and piety, calling her "great."

SIGNIFICANCE

For most of her seventy-five years, Dorothea Beale devoted her energy to the cause of girls' education. In maturity the robust spinster, dressed always in black with a white fichu, appeared aloof and unapproachable, yet she had a disarming sense of humor and often teased visitors by referring to Cheltenham Ladies' College as her husband. As a teacher, she tried to instill a hunger for knowledge rather than simply to impart information, and she proved equally adept at providing instruction in the humanities and the sciences. She also believed that a teacher's personality and mental outlook, including religious devotion, contribute greatly to the overall education process. As a school administrator, her innovations included direct supervision of the institution's boardinghouses, the inception of a rule of silence among pupils, the absence of competition and prizes, and the weekly evaluation of every student by the principal. Open-minded and willing to experiment, Beale successfully combined business acumen, reform enthusiasm, and mystical idealism.

Beale ruled Cheltenham Ladies' College as a benevolent despot and expected her own energy and sense of duty to be mirrored in her staff and students. Her associates accepted and propagated her intense belief that the education of women was a holy gift. However, Beale was a product of her times, and her educational horizons, unlike those of Buss and other contemporary female educators, were bound by conventional notions concerning gender roles. She did not insist that girls' and boys' education programs be the same but accepted the prevailing view of alternate preparation for different roles. Very much an elitist, she had no interest in universal education for all girls.

Although England's evolving system of girls' public schools did not model itself after Cheltenham Ladies' College, the staffs of the various institutions were often graduates of the Cheltenham establishment, and thus the influence continued. Through her dedication, insight, and hard work, Dorothea Beale opened the portals of education to future generations of women.

—*Carol Crowe-Carraco*

FURTHER READING

Digby, Anne, and Peter Searby. *Children, School, and Society in Nineteenth Century England*. London: Macmillan, 1981. A pertinent analysis of the problems and perspectives of schools and schooling in nineteenth century England. Contains approximately two hundred pages of contemporary documents and includes an extract of Beale's "Girls' Schools Past and Present," which appeared in the journal *Nineteenth Century* (1888).

Gathorne-Hardy, Jonathan. *The Old School Tie: The Phenomenon of the English Public School*. New York: Viking Press, 1978. A comprehensive yet readable account of all facets of the English public school system. Author acknowledges limits of materials on girls' schools, but work contains a sparkling examination of Beale's character and work. Follows the development of Cheltenham Ladies' College from its founding to the 1970's.

Gorham, Deborah. *The Victorian Girl and the Feminine Ideal*. Bloomington: Indiana University Press, 1982. A thoughtful and thought-provoking examination of the place of women and girls in Victorian England. Uses biographical evidence to examine the childhood and adolescence of a number of Victorian women. Although there are few references to Beale, the milieu in which she lived and worked is thoroughly explored.

Kamm, Josephine. *Hope Deferred: Girls' Education in English History*. London: Methuen, 1965. A general survey of the status of girls' education in England from the Anglo-Saxon period to the reign of Queen Elizabeth II. Contains a comprehensive overview of Beale's career and a critical evaluation of her impact upon nineteenth century educational reforms. Title indicates author's viewpoint.

_____. *How Different from Us: A Biography of Miss Buss and Miss Beale*. London: Bodley Head, 1958. Definitive biography of two of England's most noted female education pioneers. Cleverly written and objective in analysis of motivations, successes, and failures of both Beale and Buss. For Beale study, Kamm relies heavily upon source material found in Raikes (see below).

_____. *Indicative Past: A Hundred Years of the Girls' Public School Trust*. London: Allen & Unwin, 1971. Seminal study of the growth of educational opportunities for English girls, set against a background of changing social attitudes and ideas; contains photographs of Trust's founders and cooperating institutions. Comprehensive, balanced material on Beale is well researched and drawn from author's biographical study.

Raikes, Elizabeth. *Dorothea Beale of Cheltenham*. London: Archibald Constable, 1909. Official biography and intimate portrait by a colleague, with extracts from correspondence, manuscript autobiography, and private diary. Stilted in style, not objective, long out of print and difficult to find, the work remains an indispensable source because primary materials have been destroyed. All subsequent biographies draw upon it.

Sanderson, Michael. *Education, Economic Change, and Society in England, 1780-1870*. 2d ed. New York: Cambridge University Press, 1995. A more recent overview of the history of education in nineteenth century England and the debates surrounding it. Beale is briefly mentioned in the chapter about feminism and the education of women. The short (92-page) book is good for understanding Beale's place within the educational system of her day.

Steadham, Florence Cecily. *Miss Beale: A Study of Her Work and Influence*. London: E. J. Burrow, 1931. Greatly dependent upon Raikes (see above). Pedantic in style and far from objective, it should be used with caution and only if Raikes's work cannot be obtained.

SEE ALSO: Susan B. Anthony; Henry Barnard; Catharine Beecher; Charles William Eliot; Alice Freeman Palmer.

RELATED ARTICLES in *Great Events from History: The Nineteenth Century, 1801-1900:* September 26, 1865: Vassar College Opens; March 2, 1867: U.S. Department of Education Is Created.

AUBREY BEARDSLEY
English artist

One of the best-remembered illustrators of his time, Beardsley assimilated diverse artistic influences to produce black-and-white illustrations for magazines and books that epitomize the achievement of the English aesthetic movement of the 1890's.

BORN: August 21, 1872; Brighton, England
DIED: March 16, 1898; Menton, France
AREA OF ACHIEVEMENT: Art

EARLY LIFE

Born in Brighton, England, on August 21, 1872, Aubrey Beardsley was the son of Vincent Paul Beardsley, himself the son of a London goldsmith, and Ellen Agnus Pitt. He was educated in Brighton, the home of his maternal grandfather, Surgeon-Major William Pitt, but left Brighton Grammar School in 1888 to work in the District Surveyor's Office, Clerkenwell and Islington, London. In January, 1889, Beardsley started as a clerk at the Guardian Life and Fire Insurance office in London, where he was employed until late 1892. He left the firm when the publisher J. M. Dent gave him a commission to produce illustrations for an edition of Sir Thomas Malory's *Le Morte d'Arthur* (1485). For the rest of his short life, Beardsley worked as an illustrator and as art editor for various periodicals.

Beardsley's career was brief but meteoric, especially for an artist without much formal training. He had drawn since childhood, copying the work of the illustrator Kate Greenaway at first and then developing a style reflecting the various influences of William Morris, Edward Burne-Jones, and the Pre-Raphaelite Brotherhood. Beardsley and his older sister, Mabel, soon to begin her career as an actress, called upon Burne-Jones in 1891. The older artist encouraged Beardsley to take classes, so for a time he studied with the painter Frederick Brown at the Westminster School of Art. That, however, was the extent of his academic training as an artist. Beardsley's real education came from his observation of the work of others. He spent time with Mabel in the National Gallery and saw exhibitions in various London and Paris galleries, and he adapted for his own work motifs and techniques from the work he saw.

In filling his commission from J. M. Dent for illustrations, chapter headings, and page borders for an edition of *Le Morte d'Arthur*, Beardsley drew upon stylistic elements from the work of Burne-Jones and Morris. It took him eighteen months to produce the nearly six hundred individual designs that went into the edition Dent began publishing serially in 1893; from the first installment, however, it was clear that Beardsley had met Dent's expectation that his pseudomedieval designs would recall work printed by hand at Morris's Kelmscott Press. While working on these drawings, Beardsley was also producing sixty "grotesques" for Dent's three-volume series of *Bon-Mots* (1893, 1894) by various English writers. These pieces are not in the style derived from Burne-Jones and Morris; rather, they reflect the graphic styles of Walter Crane and James McNeill Whistler: In them Beardsley allowed himself to explore a vein of fantasy not found in the drawings for *Le Morte d'Arthur*.

One of the motifs unique to Beardsley in the *Bon-Mots* series is the figure of a fetus, perhaps a miscarried or an aborted child but treated humorously. While Beardsley's biographers disagree concerning the psychological significance of this figure, one inference drawn is that it represents the artist himself and reflects his reaction to the tuberculosis that eventually killed him. Beardsley was seven when his lungs first became a problem, and he lost time to illness while employed by the insurance company. His physical appearance signaled the presence of his disease. Tall and almost skeletally thin, as shown in a portrait done by Walter Sickert in 1894, Beardsley had piercing eyes and a shock of reddish-brown hair worn in a bang over his forehead. He kept his feelings about his illness largely to himself, frequently casting himself in the role expected by his associates. Even his letters are not very revealing of his emotions. The two people to whom Beardsley was closest throughout his life were his mother Ellen and sister Mabel.

LIFE'S WORK

Beardsley began to do drawings for periodicals as well as the books to be published by J. M. Dent, and he prepared the cover and ten pictures for the first issue of *The Studio* in April, 1893. For this issue, the editor C. Lewis Hind commissioned from Joseph Pennell, an American graphic artist, an essay entitled "A New Illustrator: Aubrey Beardsley," and the combination of article and illustrations gave Beardsley his first taste of fame.

One of the drawings for *The Studio* is of the climax of Oscar Wilde's play *Salomé*, published in Paris (and in French) in 1893, the scene in which Salomé kisses the severed head of John the Baptist. Given public reaction to this startling drawing, John Lane and Elkin Mathews

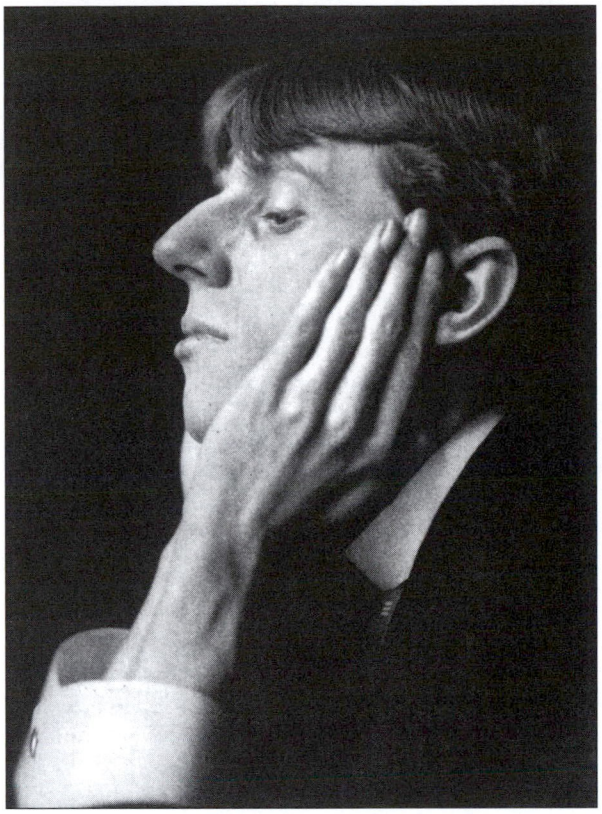

Aubrey Beardsley. (Library of Congress)

(of the Bodley Head publishers) asked Beardsley to do the illustrations for the English edition of the play, translated by Wilde's male lover Lord Alfred Douglas and published in 1894. The *Salomé* illustrations contain motifs from Japanese prints and the etchings of Whistler, but they are not derivative at all. In their use of black and white and in their reliance on elongated forms and sinuous lines, Beardsley's drawings prefigure the Art Nouveau style they helped to create.

Publication of the Bodley Head's *Salomé* (1894) by Lane and Mathews preceded by two months the April appearance of the first volume of *The Yellow Book*, a magazine of literature and art conceived and edited by Henry Harland and Beardsley. It, too, was printed at the Bodley Head in the form of a hardback volume. Beardsley served as art editor for the first four quarterly issues (those published in April, July, and October, 1894, and in January, 1895), designing covers, bindings, and title pages for each volume, selecting graphic materials from other artists, and providing additional illustrations himself. The hardbound quarterly magazine was a novelty, and Beardsley's contributions, given his recently published work in *Le Morte d'Arthur*, *Bon-Mots*, and *Salomé*, attracted both praise and negative criticism.

Those who saw Beardsley's work as eccentric, too frankly sexual in focus, and even morally corrupt cited his association with Wilde as proof of his decadence. When Wilde was arrested in April, 1895, after losing his libel suit against the marquis of Queensberry, the father of Lord Alfred Douglas, he was carrying a yellow volume widely reported to be *The Yellow Book*. It was not, and indeed one of the conditions Beardsley had given Lane when he assumed the art editorship was that Wilde not be accepted as a contributor. Nevertheless, the damage to Beardsley's reputation was done, and Lane, by this time the sole publisher of *The Yellow Book*, bowed to pressure from various authors, removed Beardsley's work from volume 5 of the magazine, and terminated his service as art editor. Wilde was tried and sentenced to two years' hard labor for sexual offenses involving other men.

Beardsley's biographers agree that he was not actively homosexual, but in the public mind the association with Wilde made him suspect. For many people, he became the artist who drew the sexually suggestive illustrations for Wilde's *Salomé*, and that was evidence enough to persuade some critics that Beardsley had an unhealthy interest in sexuality. This assessment ignores the work he did between 1895 and 1898, which matured in style and moved beyond Beardsley's earlier need to shock the bourgeoisie.

When Beardsley's arrangements with Lane ended, Beardsley turned to the publisher Leonard Smithers for backing for a new magazine called *The Savoy*. The first issue was published in January, 1896, with Beardsley as art editor and Arthur Symons, a friend of the poet William Butler Yeats, as literary editor. A quarterly for its January, April, and July issues, the magazine became a monthly in August, 1896, and ended publication with the eighth issue in December. Part of the problem was financial. Smithers did not have the capital to back a monthly printing schedule. Another part of the difficulty was Beardsley's health. By the middle of 1896, he was experiencing symptoms of advanced tuberculosis, and he started the series of moves from one supposedly healthy location in England and France to another that ended with his death in Menton on March 16, 1898.

The quality of the work Beardsley was able to do, and the amount of it, given the state of his health, is remarkable. It includes the beautifully crafted set of illustrations he produced for Smithers's edition in 1896 of Alexander Pope's mock-heroic poem *The Rape of the Lock* (1712).

The use of close-laid and dotted lines, for example, to achieve the effects of the textures of fabrics is remarkable, and while the Baroque and Rococo style of the drawings is not historically appropriate for Pope's poem, Beardsley manages to make each convey a single dramatic and satiric moment in the text.

The tone of the illustrations that Beardsley produced for an edition (also in 1896) of Aristophanes' *Lysistrata* (411 B.C.E.), which was also for Smithers, is more broadly satiric than that of the drawings for *The Rape of the Lock*. Prompted by the play's fifth century B.C.E. origins, Beardsley turned to the style of figure drawing found on classical Greek vases, but he exaggerated the distortion of the figures to reflect the satire of Aristophanes' text. The lines are heavy and definite. In style, the *Lysistrata* illustrations have little in common with those for *The Rape of the Lock* or for an edition of Ben Jonson's *Volpone: Or, The Fox* (1606), on which Beardsley was at work at the time of his death. In these drawings, he sought to recapture the effects of seventeenth century engraving. They rely less on outline than Beardsley's earlier work and more on highlighting to give them a three-dimensional effect.

SIGNIFICANCE

Because Aubrey Beardsley died so young, and had a career as a professional artist that lasted only seven years, it is hard to say how his work might have developed if he had lived longer. The variety of styles he used, the rapidity with which one gave way to another, and the fact that he sought to match his style to that of the text he was illustrating all suggest that Beardsley might have continued to mature as an artist. His actual accomplishment was so singular, however, that contemporary artists William Rothenstein and Max Beerbohm both saw him as the chief artist in the black-and-white medium of the 1890's. A generation later, Osbert Burdett suggested in *The Beardsley Period: An Essay in Perspective* (1925) that he epitomized the sense of identity and the accomplishment of his generation. While later commentators do not make so large a claim, they do see Beardsley as influencing the development of Art Nouveau in Europe. They claim, further, that his graphic work continues to appeal to each new viewing generation.

In various ways, Beardsley's work reflects both the end of nineteenth century European Romanticism and the development of modernism in the twentieth century. His unfinished *The Story of Venus and Tannhäuser: A Romantic Novel* (1967), for which he produced both text and illustrations, is a case in point. Like so much of Beardsley's work, it satirizes the conventions of romantic love. The mixture of cloying sentimentality and overt sexuality, however, in his description of the encounter of his central characters, drawn from the opera by Richard Wagner, becomes something close to a case study in sexual obsession. It invites psychoanalytic analysis, and Beardsley's biographers have mined *The Story of Venus and Tannhäuser* for evidence of the artist's real sexual nature. They are equally interested in Beardsley's conversion to Roman Catholicism in 1897, debating the genuineness of his faith in the light of his financial dependence on André Raffalovich, whose influence led to Beardsley's decision.

While Aubrey Beardsley's art can be examined in this light, stressing its affinities with so much late nineteenth century literature and art in its obsession with the irrational elements of human personality, such an emphasis obscures the grace of so much of his accomplishment. In drawings, playbills, bookplates, and bindings, there is so much vital experimentation in design that Beardsley sparked a revolution in the way fine editions are printed and illustrated. That some of this work was overtly, even morbidly, sexual in emphasis does not detract from this accomplishment. Beardsley's imagination was sparked by literary subject matter, both the texts he read and the men and women who, as authors and performers, brought the words on the page to life. His finest drawings also serve to bring words to life and to comment, at times sardonically, on them. Beardsley delighted in paradox. Appropriately, therefore, he is buried, a Roman Catholic convert, in the Protestant section of a cemetery in Menton.

—Robert C. Petersen

FURTHER READING

Beardsley, Aubrey. *The Letters of Aubrey Beardsley*. Edited by Henry Maas, J. L. Duncan, and W. G. Good. Rutherford, N.J.: Fairleigh Dickinson University Press, 1970. The most complete edition of Beardsley's letters.

Benkovitz, Miriam J. *Aubrey Beardsley: An Account of His Life*. New York: G. P. Putnam's Sons, 1981. This book benefits from later research into Beardsley's life and artistic output.

Brophy, Brigid. *Beardsley and His World*. London: Thames and Hudson, 1976. While this book is essentially a pictorial introduction to Beardsley, it is reliable and easy to read.

Burdett, Osbert. *The Beardsley Period: An Essay in Perspective*. New York: Boni and Liveright, 1925. Reprint. New York: Cooper Square, 1969. A useful introduction to art movements of the 1890's.

Calloway, Stephen. *Aubrey Beardsley*. New York: Harry N. Abrams, 1998. This book accompanied a centenary exhibit of Beardsley's drawings organized by Calloway, a curator at the Victoria and Albert Museum in London. The book contains reproductions of Beardsley's drawings and an essay by Calloway, analyzing the artist's life within the context of his work.

Easton, Malcolm. *Aubrey and the Dying Lady: A Beardsley Riddle*. Boston: David R. Godine, 1972. Challenging accepted interpretations, Easton provides analysis of the psychosexual elements in Beardsley's life and art.

MacFall, Haldane. *Aubrey Beardsley: The Man and His Work*. London: Bodley Head, 1928. The first biography of the artist, MacFall's book contains plenty of anecdotal evidence collected from contemporaries.

Reade, Brian. *Aubrey Beardsley*. New York: Viking Press, 1967. The most complete catalog of Beardsley's work; Reade's annotations are invaluable. Includes an introduction by John Rothenstein.

Sturgis, Matthew. *Aubrey Beardsley: A Biography*. Woodstock, N.Y.: Overlook Press, 1998. Biography of Beardsley, examining his life and the artistic influences that shaped him. The author describes Beardsley's connections to both the Pre-Raphaelite and the aesthetic movements.

Weintraub, Stanley. *Aubrey Beardsley: Imp of the Perverse*. University Park: Pennsylvania State University Press, 1976. This is the most complete, and easily the most readable, of the Beardsley biographies.

SEE ALSO: Thomas Nast; Henri de Toulouse-Lautrec; Oscar Wilde.

RELATED ARTICLES in *Great Events from History: The Nineteenth Century, 1801-1900:* Fall, 1848: Pre-Raphaelite Brotherhood Begins; 1870's: Aesthetic Movement Arises.

THE BECQUEREL FAMILY

French physicists and chemists

The remarkable Becquerel family spans four generations of science, with several of its members making important discoveries in physics and chemistry, particularly in the realms of electrochemistry, electromagnetic radiation, and radioactive decay physics.

ANTOINE-CÉSAR BECQUEREL

BORN: March 8, 1788; Châtillon-Coligny, France
DIED: January 18, 1878; Paris, France

ALEXANDRE-EDMOND BECQUEREL

BORN: March 24, 1820; Paris, France
DIED: May 11, 1891; Paris, France

ANTOINE-HENRI BECQUEREL

BORN: December 15, 1852; Paris, France
DIED: August 25, 1908; Le Croisic, France
AREAS OF ACHIEVEMENT: Physics, chemistry

EARLY LIVES

Little is known of Antoine-César Becquerel's (behkrehl) early life. He is known to have served in the French army as an officer in the engineering corps until 1815. In 1837, he was appointed a professor at the Museum of National History in Paris, where he began work on numerous projects in physics and chemistry.

Alexandre-Edmond Becquerel was the second son of Antoine, the family's founder. He did not attend a university but instead became assistant to his father at the Museum of Natural History at the age of eighteen. He later collaborated with his distinguished father on several important treatises. On the basis of his work, he received the doctor's degree in 1840 from the University of Paris.

Antoine-Henri Becquerel spent his early years at the Lycée-Louis-le-Grand. Already showing his brilliance, in 1872 he entered l'École Polytechnique, transferring two years later to l'École des Ponts et Chaussées, where he would later work for ten years as chief engineer. From 1875 onward, he researched various aspects of optics and engineering, obtaining his doctorate in 1888. Appointed under his father at the museum, he became professor of physics there in 1892, gaining the chair both his father and grandfather had held. In 1895, he also earned the physics professorship at l'École Polytechnique, where he had started. In 1899, he was elected to the French Academy of Sciences, continuing in the family tradition.

LIVES' WORK

Antoine spent his life at the Museum of Natural History in Paris. His works, during the early nineteenth century, were devoted to research on phosphorescence, fluorescence, thermoelectricity, the magnetic properties of materials, crystal optics, the theory of primary cells, and the electrical conductivity of matter. He is best known for his work in 1829, when he invented a primary cell with weak polarization.

After receiving his doctorate in 1840, Alexandre-Edmond became professor of physics at the Agronomy Institute of Versailles. While there, he became deeply involved in investigations of electricity and magnetism. His most significant discovery was the magnetic property of liquid oxygen. He was able to show that light, through the action of inducing chemical reactions, could cause the flow of an electric current. He invented an instrument that measured light intensity by determining the electric current intensity produced. As a by-product, he determined a means of measuring the heat radiated by objects hot enough to be emitting visible light by establishing the intensity of that light. He also originated the platinum-palladium thermocouple, which is used for high-temperature measurements.

Henri Becquerel. (Library of Congress)

Alexandre-Edmond's interests became centered on fluorescence and phosphorescence phenomena. He was the first to discriminate between these ideas and used them for the study of ultraviolet and infrared radiation from 1857 to 1878. The problems where certain chemical materials absorbed light of one wavelength and then reemitted light of another wavelength fascinated him, particularly the circumstances in which substances were seen to glow in the dark. In 1859, he invented the phosphoroscope for doing detailed studies of light-emission intensity. As a side interest, he made the first complete solar spectrum photograph. His 1872 studies of the phosphorescence spectra or uranium compounds are considered the beginning of the path that led his son, Henri, to discover radioactivity.

Henri was involved, for most of his researches, with the phenomena of light. He had coauthored a series of memoirs with his father, Alexandre-Edmond, on the temperature of Earth, but his real interest was in light interactions in materials. Henri was the first physicist to observe rotatory magnetic polarization in gases. Expanding the experiment, he discovered the magnetic rotation of the plane of polarized light by Earth's magnetic field. From 1886 to 1890, he performed experiments on the absorption of light by crystals, particularly investigating the anomalies of light passage along different axes within the crystal body. He then utilized that work to devise a new method of spectral analysis.

Fascinated by phosphorescence, Henri continued his father's research. By determined and careful investigations, he discovered the laws relating to the emission of radiation by materials being bombarded by light waves. He also showed how the emitted phosphorescence decreased with time, and why it did so. The work for which Henri is best known involved his discovery in 1896 that uranium compounds emitted some type of invisible but highly penetrating radiation, a type of light wave that would contaminate photographic plates and greatly influence the electrical conductivity in gases. He had been researching the idea that fluorescing materials might be emitting X rays (which had recently been discovered by Wilhelm Conrad Röntgen).

With the aid of potassium uranyl sulfate, a fluorescent material, wrapped photographic negatives, and a fortuitous series of cloudy days, Henri discovered that the fogging of plates by the chemical did not depend on sunlight or phosphorescence but instead was a result of something's being emitted by the compound itself. Ignoring the sun and the fluorescence process, he studied the radiation and showed that it was quite like X rays, particularly in causing air to ionize. The radiation was emitted continuously in an unending, uninterrupted stream, heading in all directions. At his suggestion, Madame Marie Curie undertook the study of those radiations for a large number of minerals. For a brief period, the radiation was called "Becquerel rays," but in 1898, at Curie's suggestion, the phenomenon was renamed "radioactivity."

Henri's observations were announced at the French Academy of Sciences meeting on February 24, 1896, in his article entitled "Émission de radiations nouvelles par l'uranium métallique." He confirmed his studies with detailed work on the materials emitting the rays and on the properties of the rays themselves in "Sur diverses propriétés des rayons uraniques" (1896). By 1899, he had discovered that the radiation could be deflected by a magnetic field, so that at least some part of it had to be tiny charged particles: "Sur le rayonnement des corps radio-actifs" (1899). On the basis of further investigations, in 1900 he was able to announce that the part that was influenced by the field was negatively charged speeding electrons, identical to those identified in cathode-ray tubes by Sir Joseph John Thomson.

After identifying the uranium atoms as the radioactive portion of the compound in 1901, Henri concluded that the electrons radiated had to be coming from within the uranium atoms themselves. This was, in the physics world, the first real indication that the atom was not a featureless sphere, that it had an internal structure. For all of his illustrious work, but particularly for the discovery of radioactivity, Henri Becquerel was awarded, along with Pierre and Marie Curie, the 1903 Nobel Prize in Physics.

Members of the family continued achievements into the twentieth century. Henri's son, Jean-Antoine-Édouard-Marie, also a member of the Paris Academy of Sciences, concentrated his work on the interactions of electromagnetic energy with solid materials. Notably, he studied the propagation of circularly polarized waves in various magnetic media. In addition, he did work on the anomalous dispersion of light by sodium vapors, the Zeeman effect in pleochroic crystals, and (with Heike Kamerlingh Onnes) the phenomena occurring in a substance placed in a magnetic field at the temperatures of liquid air and liquid hydrogen.

SIGNIFICANCE

The Becquerels are outstanding examples of a family whose members distinguished themselves in science. Of its members, Alexandre-Edmond and Antoine-Henri played the grandest roles in the history of physics. Antoine-César, a pioneer in the development of electrochemistry, set a precedent by gaining the professorship of physics at the Paris Museum of Natural History—a position that was passed on through succeeding generations. Alexandre-Edmond's discoveries on light, particularly its transmission in materials and its interactions with magnetic fields in minerals, laid the foundation for modern optical mineralogy and crystallography, vastly important in the fields of geophysical exploration and ore identification.

Alexandre-Edmond's works, along with his father's, on phosphorescence and fluorescence, paved the way for modern chemical studies on reaction rates, mechanisms, and complex formations. Henri, the best known of the family members, founded the field of radioactivity and furthered the use of light-magnetic-field interactions, particularly important in geology, optics, and electromagnetism. Moreover, his experiments helped to refute the belief, widely held during the late nineteenth century, that physics had produced all that it ever would. The idea of radioactivity, coupled with X rays, new elements, and quantum and relativity ideas, heralded the new age of modern physics.

—Arthur L. Alt

FURTHER READING

Abro, A. d'. *The Rise of the New Physics: Its Mathematical and Physical Theories*. New York: Dover, 1951. This work covers all the major ideas and experiments that have led to modern quantum physics. Besides the topic of radioactivity, it deals with the people who worked with the Becquerels to extend the realms of physics. Contains chapters for readers with mathematical background, which can be skipped. Best suited for advanced students of physics.

Badash, Lawrence. "Marie Curie: In the Laboratory and on the Battlefield." *Physics Today* 57, no. 7 (July, 2003): 37. Describes Becquerel's experiments in radioactivity, and how Marie Curie continued his research to further the use of X rays.

Curie, Marie. *Radioactive Substances*. New York: Philosophical Library, 1961. This work deals with the research conducted by Marie Curie and her husband, Pierre Curie, based on Henri Becquerel's discovery of radioactivity. Details their experiments, their hardships, and the discoveries they made. Tedious in spots, but presents a true picture of science at work.

Franklin, Allen. "The Road to the Neutrino." *Physics Today* 53, no. 2 (February, 2003): 22. Information on experiments that scientists have conducted regarding the decay of beta rays, including Henri Becquerel's discovery of radioactivity.

Holmyard, Eric. *Makers of Chemistry*. Oxford, England: Clarendon Press, 1931. A history of chemistry from its obscure beginnings to the modern science of the twentieth century. Details the explosion of chemistry programs in the nineteenth and twentieth centuries. Extensive pictures help describe important scientific contributions.

Ihde, Aaron. *The Development of Modern Chemistry*. New York: Harper & Row, 1964. This book covers the history of chemistry from ancient concepts of matter to present technology. Chapters on electrochemistry and radioactivity deal with the materials on which the Becquerels worked, including discoveries and interrelationships between physics and chemistry. Extensive references and pictures of the proponents of many theories.

Magie, William. *A Source Book in Physics*. New York: McGraw-Hill, 1935. This is a collection of the most important abstracts from physics in the last three centuries, from Galileo to Max Planck. Henri Becquerel's discovery of radioactivity from uranium is presented, along with numerous articles on his predecessors. Allows the reader to see the high points of physics.

Ronan, Colin A. *The Atlas of Scientific Discovery*. New York: Crescent Books, 1983. Surveys the march of science, tracing the development of new fields of study and the new techniques they demanded. Excellent pictures; accurate and easy to read.

Taton, René. *Science to the Twentieth Century*. Vol. 4 in *History of Science*. New York: Basic Books, 1964. This work covers science from the Renaissance to the present, including astronomy, physics, chemistry, biology, and mathematics. All the major finds and their discoverers are included from Europe and North America. Numerous illustrations are provided, as are some asides on other areas of the world. Detailed and complicated reading.

Toulmin, Stephen, and June Goodfield. *The Architecture of Matter*. New York: Harper & Row, 1962. This reference work deals with the evolution of the scientific ideas of animate and inanimate matter in terms of chemistry and physics. Various theories of matter are presented to illustrate turning points and breakthroughs. Covers significant experiments and ideas through time. Good references and lively exposition.

SEE ALSO: Sir Humphry Davy; Michael Faraday; Sir William Robert Grove; James Clerk Maxwell.

RELATED ARTICLE in *Great Events from History: The Nineteenth Century, 1801-1900:* October, 1831: Faraday Converts Magnetic Force into Electricity.

CATHARINE BEECHER

American educator

While she pursued higher status and influence for women in the domestic arena, Beecher promoted women's education, urging professionalization and appreciation of women's traditional roles.

BORN: September 6, 1800; East Hampton, Long Island, New York

DIED: May 12, 1878; Elmira, New York

ALSO KNOWN AS: Catharine Esther Beecher (full name)

AREAS OF ACHIEVEMENT: Education, women's rights

EARLY LIFE

The eldest of nine children, Catharine Esther Beecher was influenced most deeply by her father, Lyman Beecher, a Presbyterian minister descended from a long line of Calvinist colonial ancestors. Her mother, Roxana Ward Beecher, also from a prominent family, was reared traditionally and passed many of her domestic skills to her children. Catharine resisted these domestic tasks initially, preferring intellectual and outdoor activities.

Lyman Beecher played a major role in the Second Great Awakening, an evangelical movement that spread throughout the United States during the early nineteenth century. He used revivals to seek conversion and social cohesion in his communities. As a child, Catharine was enveloped by her father's dominant personality and religious zeal, and all of her life she struggled with her faith, never completely embracing it or completely deserting it.

In 1809, the Beecher family moved to Litchfield, Connecticut, a conservative town and site of a renowned law school as well as a celebrated school for young ladies. Catharine entered Miss Pierce's school in 1810, keeping a journal that reveals not only the school's emphasis on the social graces but also on the development of a social consciousness. She flourished in those years, exercising leadership and other social skills.

After Roxana died in 1816, Catharine left school to take on domestic duties, supervising her younger siblings, cooking, and sewing. Her father remarried in late 1817, but Catharine lived at home for a while longer, the ties between father and daughter remaining very strong. At the age of eighteen, she left Litchfield to teach in New London, Connecticut.

In 1822, Catharine became engaged to Alexander Fisher, a Yale professor in natural philosophy. Her father approved of Fisher wholeheartedly, but Catharine was uncertain about his potential as a husband, finding him somewhat lacking in affection. In April of 1822, Fisher died at sea when his ship crashed into cliffs on the west coast of Ireland. Catharine remained single throughout her life, devoting herself to the education of women.

LIFE'S WORK

In 1823, Catharine Beecher opened a school in Hartford, Connecticut; it flourished, allowing her to exert social, religious, and intellectual leadership. The Hartford Female Seminary offered courses in rhetoric, logic, chemistry, history, philosophy, Latin, and algebra. As principal, Beecher's status rose, and she socialized with Hartford's most respected citizens of both genders. Her self-confidence grew along with her competence as an educator. She began expanding and expounding her ideas of good pedagogy.

Beecher placed great emphasis on molding the moral character of her students. In 1829, she published an essay entitled "Suggestions Respecting Improvements in Education." In it, she stated that the most important objective of education was "the foundation of the conscience, and the direction of the moral character and habits." To accomplish such training, Beecher tried to hire an associate principal to direct the religious teaching but she was unsuccessful. Suffering a nervous collapse, she took several months rest away from Hartford while her sister, Harriet Beecher, filled in for her at the school. Upon her return to Hartford, Catharine herself gave moral instruction.

During the 1830's, Beecher became focused on women's roles and the need for more professionalism. She clearly expected women to exercise power in the home as mothers and outside it as schoolteachers. The means for enhancing this power would be a better-crafted education. Beecher viewed teaching as a noble profession, enabling women to have influence, respectability, and independence while maintaining themselves within the accepted boundaries of femininity. The time was ripe for such thinking.

The 1830's and 1840's were decades of dramatic population growth in the United States. This growing population called for more teachers. Although men had dominated the profession, fewer males were available to teach, because many of them chose to go into industrial or commercial careers. Tax-supported schools, a leisured female middle class, and the emphasis on women's nurturing qualities all aided Beecher as she began to focus on teacher training.

Resigning her position in September of 1831, Beecher left Hartford to be with her father, who had accepted the presidency of Cincinnati's Lane Theological Seminary. They arrived in Cincinnati in the spring of 1832. Within a year, Catharine Beecher founded the Western Female Institute, dedicated to both the acquisition of knowledge and moral development.

Choosing not to be fully employed in the school, Beecher busied herself with social activities and some writing. She spoke to a group of women in New York in 1835, and her lecture, "An Essay on the Education of Female Teachers," was published in New York and Cincinnati. She presented a plan for women to educate the children of immigrants and working-class families in the West.

Beecher noted that one-third of Ohio's children were without schools and that thousands of teachers would be needed to staff new schools. She envisioned her Western Female Institute as the model seminary for a national system whereby women would be trained and, in turn, would train others to educate American children and youth. She began a fund-raising campaign, appealing to Cincinnati's wealthy citizens to endow the seminary and others like it. The Cincinnati elite did not contribute, however, in part because Catharine Beecher and her father were regarded as troublemakers. Some members of Cincinnati society were angered by what they believed was a certain cultural snobbery expressed by Catharine Beecher. Further antagonism was generated by the Beechers' strong support for abolition in a city much divided over the issue even before their arrival.

The Western Female Institute closed in 1837 because of low enrollment and Beecher's alienation of her constituency. Some of Cincinnati's aristocratic families saw her as an "intellectual and social upstart." That same year, Beecher began developing a new constituency as she urged a broader image of women's role in American society. Her "Essay on Slavery and Abolition with Reference to the Duty of American Females" attempted to shape a unified consciousness in American women.

Unlike social reformers such as Sarah and Angelina Grimké, Beecher believed that female influence could best be utilized within the traditional family hierarchy and that this influence was at the core of national morals. Women would exemplify domestic virtues and by their superior moral sensibility would be a stabilizing force in the nation. The foundation of her future work was laid in this essay and Beecher turned to what she hoped would be a lucrative literary career.

Beecher wrote copiously, but only one book, published in Boston in 1841, gave her the financial base she craved. By 1843, her *Treatise on Domestic Economy* was in its fourth printing and it gave her access to a national audience. Her book intended to give women a sense of purpose, of mission: the formation of the moral and intellectual character of the young. Beecher saw that women needed specialized training for this mission. She stressed that, because of their service to others, women needed more education that would be specially tailored to prepare them for this responsibility.

Glorifying domesticity, Beecher assured women that they were engaged in "the greatest work that was ever committed to human responsibility." Women's subordinate status, Beecher stated, was not imposed by nature; rather, it was necessary to promote the general welfare. Domesticity knew no boundaries and therefore could be a focus for a new, unified national identity. Beecher intended to transcend divisions between women of different social classes by emphasizing the universality of domestic values as she built on traditional distinctions between the sex roles.

Women were uniquely able to be constructive agents of social change. The home, therefore, was not a place of isolation but rather a base from which to influence all of society. Beecher's reasoning was particularly comforting to a nation undergoing dramatic changes, as it did not require elimination of the traditional male prerogatives.

THE PROPER CHRISTIAN HOME

Catharine Beecher, with her more famous sister, Harriet Beecher Stowe, wrote The American Woman's Home: Or, Principles of Domestic Science—Being a Guide to the Formation and Maintenance of Economical, Healthful, Beautiful, and Christian Homes *as their contribution to the uplift of American women. This extract from Catharine Beecher's introduction to the book reveals a great deal about the sisters' philosophy and goals.*

The authors of this volume, while they sympathize with every honest effort to relieve the disabilities and sufferings of their sex, are confident that the chief cause of these evils is the fact that the honor and duties of the family state are not duly appreciated, that women are not trained for these duties as men are trained for their trades and professions, and that, as the consequence, family labor is poorly done, poorly paid, and regarded as menial and disgraceful.

To be the nurse of young children, a cook, or a housemaid, is regarded as the lowest and last resort of poverty, and one which no woman of culture and position can assume without loss of caste and respectability.

It is the aim of this volume to elevate both the honor and the remuneration of all the employments that sustain the many difficult and sacred duties of the family state, and thus to render each department of woman's true profession as much desired and respected as are the most honored professions of men.

When the other sex are to be instructed in law, medicine, or divinity, they are favored with numerous institutions richly endowed, with teachers of the highest talents and acquirements, with extensive libraries, and abundant and costly apparatus. With such advantages they devote nearly ten of the best years of life to preparing themselves for their profession; and to secure the public from unqualified members of these professions, none can enter them until examined by a competent body, who certify to their due preparation for their duties.

Woman's profession embraces the care and nursing of the body in the critical periods of infancy and sickness, the training of the human mind in the most impressible period of childhood, the instruction and control of servants, and most of the government and economies of the family state. These duties of woman are as sacred and important as any ordained to man; and yet no such advantages for preparation have been accorded to her, nor is there any qualified body to certify the public that a woman is duly prepared to give proper instruction in her profession. . . .

Source: Catharine E. Beecher and Harriet Beecher Stowe, *The American Woman's Home* (Boston: H. A. Brown, 1869), Introduction.

Beecher's treatise was published by Harper and Brothers after 1842, ensuring it national distribution. Reprinted almost every year from 1841 to 1856, it became Beecher's best-selling work. Previously, women had to read separate books on health, childcare, cooking, and general well-being. The treatise pulled together all the domestic arts, giving simple rules for resolving the contradictions and ambiguities of daily life.

With the continuing popularity of the treatise, Beecher's career entered a second phase in which she founded and directed the American Woman's Education Association, which was to aid in the establishment of numerous women's schools. Traveling widely during the 1840's and 1850's, she helped define women's potential both within and outside the home, though primarily the former.

The last two decades of Beecher's life were given to extensive travel, fund-raising, promotion of her books, and publicizing women's education. A major focus was the founding of colleges in the West to train women for professions as teachers and homemakers. The American Woman's Education Association (founded in New York in 1852) was a source of educational funding; although it helped raise respectable sums of money, the association did not meet all of Beecher's needs or expectations. For this she relied on private help, especially from well-to-do relatives and longtime friends. Beecher continued her efforts on behalf of women's education until her death in May, 1878.

SIGNIFICANCE

Catharine Beecher's last years were active ones, attending teachers' conventions, keeping up a wide correspondence, and giving public lectures. Based in the East again, Beecher lived with her siblings' families on and off, becoming closest to Harriet Beecher Stowe. She continued to travel and write on behalf of women teachers, even after the disbanding of the American Woman's Education Association in 1862.

With Harriet, Catharine coauthored *The American Woman's Home* in 1869, a sequel to the *Treatise on Domestic Economy*. It repeated much of that first book while emphasizing the family as a model of how society should function: in harmonious social interdependence. The post-Civil War years saw an urgent need for such a model because society was experiencing much change at a rapid pace. Catharine Beecher argued that an expanding democracy needed the stability provided by families supporting one another—parents and children sacrificing themselves for the good of all. In her schema, men were also tied into domesticity, although women were to be the chief ministers.

Above all, the *Treatise on Domestic Economy* assured Beecher's reputation and place in history. In it she asserted women's active role in society, according them a greater degree of dignity and respect than had been theirs. The keystone of her programs and policies was the promotion of a superior education for all females. She helped enlarge the world and role of women, offering strategies for autonomous growth. Catharine Beecher's vision of strong womanhood added much to the expansion of nineteenth century feminism.

—*S. Carol Berg*

FURTHER READING

Barker-Benfield, Graham J., and Catherine Clinton. *Portraits of American Women*. New York: St. Martin's Press, 1991. A history of gender roles and relations from the period of early settlement to the 1980's. Gives a broad scope of social history. One succinct chapter on Catharine Beecher.

Flexner, Eleanor. *Century of Struggle: The Woman's Rights Movement in the United States*. Rev. ed. Cambridge, Mass.: Belknap Press of Harvard University Press, 1975. An excellent overview of the women's rights movement. Chapter 11, "Early Stages Toward Equal Education," is very helpful.

Kerber, Linda K., and Jane S. DeHart, eds. *Women's America*. 3d ed. New York: Oxford University Press, 1991. A collection of essays on women and their roles from 1600-1990. Selections in part 2 provide excellent background for Beecher's thinking and experiences. Includes one essay on Beecher's educational efforts in the West.

Parker, Gail T., ed. *The Oven Birds: American Women on Womanhood, 1820-1920*. Garden City, N.Y.: Anchor Books, 1972. An anthology of women's writings. A lengthy excellent introduction, situating each woman in her era, relating themes and experiences. Two excerpts are included from Beecher's *Woman Suffrage* and *Woman's Profession*, published in 1871.

Sklar, Kathryn Kish. *Catharine Beecher: A Study in American Domesticity*. New York: W. W. Norton, 1976. An analytical study of Beecher and her times. Very thorough on her writings. Detailed chapter notes, a bibliography, and an index.

Tonkovich, Nicole. *Domesticity with a Difference: The Nonfiction of Catharine Beecher, Sarah J. Hale, Fanny Fern, and Margaret Fuller*. Jackson: University Press of Mississippi, 1997. Examines the work of four nineteenth century women writers, including Beecher. Tonkovich points out the conflict between the women's nonfiction, in which they preached a life of ideal domesticity for women, and their lives, which were lived outside the traditional domestic world.

Tyler, Alice Felt. *Freedom's Ferment: Phases of American Social History to 1860.* Minneapolis: University of Minnesota Press, 1944. Reprint. New York: Books for Libraries Press, 1970. Traces the crusades, reforms, and reformers in U.S. society from colonial times to the Civil War. Especially helpful are chapter 2 on "Evangelical Religion" and chapter 10 on "Education and the American Faith." Bibliography, chapter notes, and index.

White, Barbara A. *The Beecher Sisters.* New Haven, Conn.: Yale University Press, 2003. Joint biography of Catharine, her sisters, Harriet Beecher Stowe, author of *Uncle Tom's Cabin*, and Isabel, an outspoken liberal and leader in the women's movement.

Woloch, Nancy. *Women and the American Experience.* New York: Alfred A. Knopf, 1984. Examines main themes of women's history in given eras by reference to particular lives. Connects public and private spheres and women's strategies, individual and collective, as agents of change. Chapter 6, "Promoting Women's Sphere, 1800-1860," is particularly useful.

SEE ALSO: Susan B. Anthony; Henry Barnard; Dorothea Beale; Charles William Eliot; Sarah and Angelina Grimké; Alice Freeman Palmer.

RELATED ARTICLES in *Great Events from History: The Nineteenth Century, 1801-1900:* May, 1823: Hartford Female Seminary Is Founded; September 26, 1865: Vassar College Opens; March 2, 1867: U.S. Department of Education Is Created.

HENRY WARD BEECHER

American Protestant cleric

The best-known American Protestant cleric of his time, Beecher was pastor of Brooklyn's Plymouth Church for forty years. He became one of the most articulate ministers in the United States and broke with traditional methods of preaching in both style and content, while ushering in a new era of homiletic expertise that reached far beyond his podium.

BORN: June 24, 1813; Litchfield, Connecticut
DIED: March 8, 1887; Brooklyn, New York
AREA OF ACHIEVEMENT: Religion and theology

EARLY LIFE

Henry Ward Beecher was born June 24, 1813, in Litchfield, Connecticut, one of thirteen children. His father, the Reverend Lyman Beecher, was descended from colonial settlers dating back to the 1630's. The elder Beecher was one of the leading lights in the American pulpit, as well as an outstanding theologian and educator. His mother, Roxana Foote, whose lineage could be traced back to seventeenth century England, died of consumption when Henry was three years old. Many of the elder Beecher's children later became preachers, and one of his daughters, Harriet Beecher Stowe, became a writer, philanthropist, and abolitionist.

Because there were so many children, there was little time for each one to receive personal attention. Henry's stepmother, Harriett Porter, however, engendered in them at least a sense of awe, if not affection. However, for the most part, Henry was a loner, growing up somewhat aloof in disposition and self-centered in outlook.

At the age of ten, he was sent away to school but had little success in his studies. Later, he went to a school conducted by his sister Catharine in Hartford—the only boy among some forty girls. He then enrolled in Mount Pleasant Classical Institute in Amherst, Massachusetts, where, for the first time, he had contact with boys his own age. There, Beecher attained some measure of popularity and encountered teachers who taught him to study and to express himself.

In 1830, Beecher entered Amherst College, where he read English classics and began writing for one of the college publications. However, his spiritual life languished. Because his father expected all of his sons to follow him into the ministry, Beecher, following his graduation from Amherst, matriculated at Lane Theological Seminary, Cincinnati, where his father was president. Beecher's time was about equally divided between his studies and extracurricular activities, particularly writing. Theology held no charm for him, and his father's

Calvinism repelled him. One May morning, alone in the Ohio woods, however, Beecher underwent a religious experience that shaped his ideas about God and provided the structure for his spiritual life, providing a broad area for preaching that conformed to his own temperament and lifestyle.

LIFE'S WORK

After his graduation from Lane Seminary in 1837, Beecher became minister at the Presbyterian Church at Lawrenceburg, Indiana. There, he married Eunice White Bullard, with whom he would have ten children. On November 9, 1838, Beecher was ordained by the New School Presbytery of Cincinnati. The following July, he moved to the Second Presbyterian Church in Indianapolis, where he remained until October, 1848, when he went to Plymouth Church, Brooklyn, a Congregational church.

In appearance, Beecher was imposing. It has been said that he was one of the most striking figures in Brooklyn. A man of medium height and large girth, his broad shoulders accorded a resting place for his hair and a foundation for his lionesque head. His voice was responsive to every shade of emotion.

During the decade of his first two pastorates, Beecher had gradually developed his principles and his style of preaching, which was intended to bring about a moral change in his listeners. His sermons began to be published—sermons that dealt with moral renewal. Certain of these were gathered into a book, *Seven Lectures to Young Men*, published in 1844.

Like all the Beechers, he was opposed to slavery, but his thoughts on the subject were complicated and perhaps contradictory. In 1860, he announced a six-point creed on slavery: First a man may hold a slave and do no wrong; second, immediate emancipation is impossible; third, a slaveholder may still be considered a good Christian; fourth, the influence of slavery is not always evil; fifth, some slaveholders are doing more for the cause of freedom than some violent reformers; finally, anti-slavery bigotry is worse than the Papacy. His position on this issue probably evolved from his desire to present the Gospel to as many and as varied a group of people as possible.

Plymouth Church had only recently been organized and built when Beecher arrived. Soon afterward, the edifice burned. A new structure was then built, a large auditorium that could accommodate more than three thousand people. From his platform—he did not desire a pulpit—he gained fame as a man of eloquence and high

Henry Ward Beecher. (Library of Congress)

ideals and was widely considered to be the best preacher of the age. Even after 1874, when he was accused of committing adultery with one of his parishioners, he continued to be seen almost as a national saint. This veneration was a measure of the degree to which his message had captured the spirit of popular Protestantism of the time.

Beecher's messages were frequently directed at relieving the anxieties of his affluent Brooklyn suburban audience, who sensed a conflict between their new wealth and the stern Puritan morality in which they had been reared. He preached a gospel of "virtuous wealth" as a commendable moral example to the poor, providing relief from traditional Calvinistic theological anxieties with a general liberalism that gradually unfolded as his sensibilities developed along with those of his national audience.

Beecher urged that American preaching strive for unassailable goals that would "inspire men with an idea of manhood" and kindle the "nobility of a heart opened when God has touched it." The Brooklyn preacher had discovered a formula that would, for many years, allay the apprehensions of the respectable, evangelical Americans concerning the new science and learning. He commented,

> While we are taught by the scientists in truths that belong to sensual nature, while we are taught by the economists of things that belong to the social nature, we need the Christian ministry to teach us those things which are invisible.

Beecher was among the first American preachers to accept Charles Darwin's theory of evolution, by which he sought to reinterpret essential Christian convictions "in terms congenial with the assured convictions of the latest scientific theories." Beecher's acceptance of evolution had a tremendous impact on the American Protestant community. The theory of evolution, coupled with biblical criticism coming out of Germany, produced the dominant Protestant theology of the late nineteenth century, a position that was in ascendance until the rise of neoorthodoxy during the 1930's.

In 1861, Beecher became editor of the *Independent*, a Congregational journal; from 1870 to 1881, he was editor of the nondenominational *Christian Union*, which he founded. In this latter position he wrote what were considered some of the strongest editorials in the American press. His sermons were reproduced in weekly columns; others were published as pamphlets.

Beecher launched attacks against slavery, but he was not an abolitionist. He opposed the Fugitive Slave Law and the Compromise of 1850. He urged northerners to emigrate to Kansas, using force to make it free soil. At the same time, he decried bitterness toward the South. When the Civil War erupted, he pushed for a strong prosecution by the North. In his orations, Beecher skillfully equated Christian redemptive meaning with the spirit of the Union. In 1863, he visited England, where he boldly presented the position of the North.

It is questionable whether Beecher's speeches accomplished much, but they did no harm to his popularity. When hostilities ceased, Beecher went to Fort Sumter to give the oration celebrating the fourth anniversary of that fort's fall. Beecher favored Andrew Johnson's position regarding Reconstruction; he longed to see the Union reunited and the military government in the South brought to a speedy end. Indeed, he was so sympathetic to Reconstruction that he brought down upon himself the wrath of his congregation and was forced to recant.

Neither a scholar nor an original thinker, Beecher was often very impetuous in enunciating his position on various topics before thoroughly considering the logical ramifications of such pronouncements. Uninterested in theory so much as in practical application, he abhorred theological controversy, probably because his father had so delighted in it.

SIGNIFICANCE

Beecher possessed the ability to present the most advanced thought of his generation in easily understood language and to stamp it indelibly, by means of word pictures, upon the minds of his listeners. Those who heard him were mesmerized by his delivery; those who read him were tantalized by his clarity. Many twentieth century Protestant preachers employ the same approach in their preaching, unaware that, a century earlier, Beecher was in the vanguard of those who employed such a method. Similarly, his *Yale Lectures on Preaching* (1872-1874) still rank as the apogee of instruction in the entire field of the ministry.

Henry Ward Beecher continued to be, as long as he lived, the most prominent preacher in the United States. Through a continuous stream of published sermons, in pamphlets as well as collected volumes, he preached to a whole country as completely as had any man before the coming of the radio. Beecher strongly influenced the style of delivery, worship, music, and content that has become the standard in the modern pulpit. Further, his social conscience and oratorical skill made him a spiritual and moral force in his time.

—*Harold M. Parker, Jr.*

FURTHER READING

Abbott, Lyman. *Henry Ward Beecher*. Boston: Houghton Mifflin, 1903. A sympathetic biography of Beecher, written by one who was converted by his preaching and who succeeded him at Plymouth Church. Contains Beecher's 1882 theological statement, which resulted in his leaving the Congregational Church.

Beecher, Henry Ward. *Yale Lectures on Preaching*. New York: J. B. Ford, 1872-1874. Probably the best material on Beecher's art of preaching and pastoral work.

Clark, Clifford E., Jr. *Henry Ward Beecher: Spokesman for Middle-Class America*. Urbana: University of Illinois Press, 1978. Interprets Beecher as one who defended the middle-class ethics and ethos of Plymouth Church, particularly during the Panic of 1873.

Fox, Richard Wrightman. *Trials of Intimacy: Love and Loss in the Beecher-Tilton Scandal*. Chicago: University of Chicago Press, 1999. Chronicles Beecher's adultery trial, in which author Theodore Tilton, a Beecher confidant, accused Beecher of having an affair with his wife, Elizabeth Tilton. Beecher was not convicted, but Fox contends the nation was shocked by the allegations of immorality and the trial forever tainted Beecher's reputation.

Garrison, Winfred Ernest. *The March of Faith: The Story of Religion in America Since 1865*. New York: Harper & Brothers, 1933. This survey includes a sympathetic account of Beecher, placing him in the context of his times.

Hibben, Paxton. *Henry Ward Beecher: An American Portrait*. New York: George H. Doran, 1927. This essentially negative biographical study asserts that Beecher was not a pioneer in the great work of liberalizing American theology and religion, but rather was able to present modern ideas in a form that the masses could grasp. Hibben argues that Beecher's personal development, moving from a rejection of his father's Calvinism to embrace religious liberalism, mirrored a transformation in American society.

McLoughlin, William G. *The Meaning of Henry Ward Beecher: An Essay on the Shifting Values of Mid-Victorian America, 1840-1870*. New York: Alfred A. Knopf, 1970. Claims that the meaning of Beecher's life lies in the story of the great shift between the Age of Jackson and the Gilded Age. Like Hibben (see above), it points out how the development of Beecher's theological views corresponded to the major social, economic, political, and religious shifts in American society between 1840 and 1875.

Marsden, George M. *Fundamentalism and American Culture: The Shaping of Twentieth-Century Evangelicalism, 1870-1925*. New York: Oxford University Press, 1980. Places Beecher in the forefront of those who viewed progress in science and morality as the coming of the Kingdom of God.

Rugoff, Milton. *The Beechers: An American Family in the Nineteenth Century*. New York: Harper & Row, 1981. Places Henry Ward Beecher in the family context of the Beechers, beginning with Lyman, and extending to Henry's brothers and sisters. Four chapters give a fairly objective biography of Beecher, including a succinct presentation and appraisal of Beecher's trial for adultery. Based on extensive documents.

Ryan, Halford R. *Henry Ward Beecher: Peripatetic Preacher*. New York: Greenwood Press, 1990. Although Beecher's career was the ministry, Ryan argues his true calling was public speaking. The book contains reprints of Beecher's public speeches and sermons, with an analysis of his rhetorical style.

SEE ALSO: Charles Darwin; Harriet Beecher Stowe; Mark Twain; Victoria Woodhull.

RELATED ARTICLES in *Great Events from History: The Nineteenth Century, 1801-1900:* May 12, 1857: New York Infirmary for Indigent Women and Children Opens; February 17-18, 1890: Women's Rights Associations Unite.

LUDWIG VAN BEETHOVEN

German composer

One of the giants of classical music, Beethoven contributed greatly to Western music. Clearly reflecting the transition from the classical tradition in music to the Romantic, he made numerous innovations in the piano sonata, the string quartet, and the symphony.

BORN: December 17, 1770 (baptized); Bonn, archbishopric of Cologne (now in Germany)
DIED: March 26, 1827; Vienna, Austria
AREA OF ACHIEVEMENT: Music

EARLY LIFE

Born in Bonn in 1770, Ludwig van Beethoven (BAY-toh-vahn) did not enjoy the happiest of childhoods. His father, a minor musician in the court of the archbishop-elector of Cologne, was generally more interested in drinking than in making music and was often a trial to his family. He knew well enough, however, that his son had a talent for music. Hoping that the boy might be a wunderkind, another Wolfgang Amadeus Mozart, he pushed him into a severe musical training that left little time for the pleasures of childhood. Beethoven's playmates were the piano, the organ, and the viola.

Not another Mozart, the young Beethoven nevertheless began to develop his musical abilities slowly but surely. By his thirteenth year, he was composing and was serving as an assistant to his teacher Christian Gottlob Neefe, the court organist, with the result that he began to gain notice from members of the aristocracy, people who, throughout the rest of his life, were to be patrons and friends. The family of Emanuel Joseph Breuning, for example, welcomed the boy, and he spent much time with them.

With the help of Neefe, the Breunings, and the archbishop-elector, Beethoven, at the age of seventeen, journeyed to Vienna, the preeminent musical city of Europe. It was for him a dream come true. There, he met Mozart, then at the peak of his career, and impressed him, moreover, with his own extemporaneous pieces on the piano. His stay in Vienna, however, was to be cut short. Upon hearing of his mother's illness, he hurried back to Bonn to find that she had died. He lost not only a mother but also, in his words, his "best and most faithful friend."

Shortly after his return to Bonn, Beethoven suffered another blow—the death of his younger sister. His father's drinking, moreover, had reached the point at which he could no longer support the family, and that task now fell to Beethoven. With the same indomitable spirit that marked his whole life, he accepted the challenge and cared for his two younger brothers. He also met the challenge of his musical talent and continued to increase his social and intellectual contacts among both young and old in Bonn.

When Joseph Haydn passed through Bonn in 1790, he encouraged Beethoven to come to Vienna to study with him. It took two years for Beethoven to complete the arrangements, but in 1792, he journeyed once again to Vienna, the city that was to be his permanent home. Although his relationship with Haydn lasted only two years, Beethoven began building a reputation that was to become only stronger as the years passed.

Ludwig van Beethoven. (The Granger Collection, New York)

LIFE'S WORK

In Vienna, Beethoven studied counterpoint with Haydn, but the relationship between them was not a positive one. Beethoven thought that Haydn's teaching was perfunctory, and Haydn was displeased by his student's slow development—particularly in contrast to the genius of Mozart—and by his personal mannerisms and his audacious compositions. The result was that Beethoven found a new teacher of counterpoint. The young composer was, however, in the right place at the right time, because Vienna was a city rich in musical tradition and alive with the spirit of revolution.

Like so many artists and intellectuals, Beethoven was caught up in the fervor of the political changes sweeping the United States and Europe, and he no doubt saw a clear relationship between such changes and those occurring in the world of music. Although composers still found their main employment in the Church, the court, and the opera house, new possibilities of support were being introduced. Public concert halls, for example, offered sources of income, as did increased patronage from an aristocracy that was becoming more interested in the arts. Not content with the somewhat demeaning position to which artists and composers were relegated in relationships with their patrons, Beethoven, through his own strength of personality, worked to define a new kind of relationship that enabled him to be the careful creator and craftsperson he was. Indeed, the Viennese aristocrats were eager not only to give Beethoven the support he demanded but also to gain his friendship.

While it is a general custom to approach the works of a composer, writer, or painter in terms of periods such as style and chronology, one must remember that the works themselves do not necessarily fall neatly into such divisions. As for Beethoven, most musicologists see his work falling into three distinct periods. The first period ends at 1802 or 1803 and includes the Op. 18 string quartets, the early piano sonatas, and the first two symphonies. The compositions of this period show the singular influences of Mozart and Haydn. The second period covers approximately the next ten years and may well be considered Beethoven's most productive, with 1814 being his peak year. This second period includes the Third Symphony (*Eroica*) through the Eighth Symphony, the opera *Fidelio*, the Op. 59 string quartets, some piano sonatas, and two piano concertos. The last period includes the last piano sonatas and quartets and the powerful Ninth Symphony (*Choral*).

While Beethoven was fulfilling his early promise as a composer, he discovered in his late twenties that his hearing was gradually getting weaker. With the devastating realization that he was going deaf, he contemplated suicide. "But how humbled I feel when someone near me hears the distant sound of a flute, and I hear *nothing*; when someone hears a shepherd singing, and I hear nothing!" he wrote to his brother. His faith in his art, however, was stronger than his desire for death, and, despite this cruel blow, he prepared to go on with his life and his music.

Stone-deaf at thirty-two, Beethoven became more depressed and eccentric in his daily living; in his music, however, he sought hope amid despair. His Third Symphony, the *Eroica*, was dedicated to Napoleon I and was meant to celebrate the heroic ideals of revolutionary leaders. The symphony itself was revolutionary, representing a distinct break with the classical past. Its length and complexity caused consternation among some critics, but through the years it has become one of the most widely performed of Beethoven's works.

Following the *Eroica* and the opera *Fidelio*, Beethoven concentrated primarily on the symphony, and between 1806 and 1808 he completed his Fourth, Fifth, and Sixth Symphonies. The Fourth Symphony is light and jovial and seems to be an effort on Beethoven's part to capture in music the joy that he was unable to realize in life. The powerful Fifth Symphony, on the other hand, is generally seen as symbolic of Beethoven's struggle against, and victory over, fate. The Sixth Symphony (*Pastoral*) expresses the romantic feelings and moods aroused by a walk through the Vienna woods.

Having accepted his silent world, one in which he could hear music only in his mind,

BEETHOVEN THE BUSINESSPERSON

This 1801 letter from Ludwig van Beethoven to his music publisher reveals something about Beethoven's attitude toward business at an early stage in his career. The letter's request for payment also gives an indication of how much income he was receiving.

TO KAPELLMEISTER HOFMEISTER.

Vienna, Jan. 15 (or thereabouts), 1801.

I read your letter, dear brother and friend, with much pleasure, and I thank you for your good opinion of me and of my works, and hope I may continue to deserve it. I also beg you to present all due thanks to Herr K. [Kühnel] for his politeness and friendship towards me. I, on my part, rejoice in your undertakings, and am glad that when works of art do turn out profitable, they fall to the share of true artists, rather than to that of mere tradesmen.

Your intention to publish Sebastian Bach's works really gladdens my heart, which beats with devotion for the lofty and grand productions of this our father of the science of harmony, and I trust I shall soon see them appear. I hope when golden peace is proclaimed, and your subscription list opened, to procure you many subscribers here.

With regard to our own transactions, as you wish to know my proposals, they are as follows. I offer you at present the following works:—The Septet (which I already wrote to you about), 20 ducats; Symphony, 20 ducats; Concerto, 10 ducats; Grand Solo Sonata, allegro, adagio, minuetto, rondo, 20 ducats. This Sonata [Op. 22] is well up to the mark, my dear brother!

Now for explanations. You may perhaps be surprised that I make no difference of price between the sonata, septet, and symphony. I do so because I find that a septet or a symphony has not so great a sale as a sonata, though a symphony ought unquestionably to be of the most value. (N.B. The septet consists of a short introductory adagio, an allegro, adagio, minuetto, andante, with variations, minuetto, and another short adagio preceding a presto.) I only ask ten ducats for the concerto, for, as I already wrote to you, I do not consider it one of my best. I cannot think that, taken as a whole, you will consider these prices exorbitant; at least, I have endeavored to make them as moderate as possible for you.

With regard to the banker's draft, as you give me my choice, I beg you will make it payable by Germüller or Schüller. The entire sum for the four works will amount to 70 ducats; I understand no currency but Vienna ducats, so how many dollars in gold they make in your money is no affair of mine, for really I am a very bad man of business and accountant. Now this troublesome business is concluded;—I call it so, heartily wishing that it could be otherwise here below! There ought to be only one grand dépôt of art in the world, to which the artist might repair with his works, and on presenting them receive what he required; but as it now is, one must be half a tradesman besides—and how is this to be endured? Good heavens! I may well call it troublesome. . . .

L. V. BEETHOVEN!

Source: Ludwig van Beethoven, *Beethoven's Letters, 1790-1826*, translated by Grace Wallace (London: Longmans, Green, 1866), vol. 1.

Beethoven turned meditative in his later work. Two works dominate this third period—the Mass in D (*Missa Solemnis*) and the *Choral*. The former, which Beethoven himself believed to be his greatest work, is a complex vocal and instrumental piece that owes much to George Frideric Handel. More a symphony than a mass, it is considered both a personal and a universal confession of faith. The *Choral*, whose outlines developed over eight years, was first performed on May 7, 1824, with Beethoven sharing in the conducting. The occasion was Beethoven's public farewell, and a tumultuous one it was as the audience applauded and waved handkerchiefs in appreciation not only for the *Choral* but also for a glorious career of musical creativity.

SIGNIFICANCE

Each lover of classical music has his own favorite or favorites among the many great composers who have made the music of the Western world what it is. No one, however, can dismiss the tremendous contributions to that music made by Ludwig van Beethoven. A bridge between the classical tradition and the Romantic in music, he did much to transform a number of musical forms. His innovations included expanding the length of the symphony and of the piano concerto and increasing the number of movements in the string quartet from four to seven. His experiments in harmony and rhythm brought a new dimension to the symphony, as did his expansion of the orchestra itself. Introducing the trombone, the contrabassoon, and the piccolo, he sought to give the orchestra a broader range through which to reflect the breadth and depth of his compositions. In regard to his own instrument, the piano, he did much to bring it from its status as a relatively new invention (1710) to one in which it was seen to become the dominant and versatile instrument it is today.

Surely the greatest testament to Beethoven's power of creativity and to his overall contribution to the world of music is the universal and lasting popularity of so many of his works. His symphonies—particularly the Third, Fifth, Sixth, and Ninth—are performed regularly by virtually all orchestras. The same is true for the Fourth and Fifth Piano Concertos and the Violin Concerto in D. The opera *Fidelio* is also widely performed, as are the *Missa Solemnis* and the piano sonatas and string quartets.

Beethoven had his arrogance and his uncompromising character. He also had pain and tragedy in his life. Most of all, however, he had genius—and the strength of spirit to bring that genius to the highest level of accomplishment. Some twenty thousand admirers attended his funeral. They were saying goodbye to the man. The genius, however, lives on in the music.

—*Wilton Eckley*

FURTHER READING

Burnham, Scott, and Michael P. Steinberg, eds. *Beethoven and His World*. Princeton, N.J.: Princeton University Press, 2000. Collection of essays, describing Beethoven's compositions, creative process, use of instruments, and other aspects of his music and life.

Comini, Alessandra. *The Changing Image of Beethoven: A Study in Mythmaking*. New York: Rizzoli, 1987. Examines the image of Beethoven and the mythmaking process that began during his lifetime. Attempts to analyze the interior image of Beethoven held by those who contributed to the mythmaking process. A solid study that places Beethoven very clearly in his time.

Cooper, Barry. *Beethoven*. New York: Oxford University Press, 2000. More recent biography, examining Beethoven's life and music.

Landon, H. C. Robbins. *Beethoven: A Documentary Study*. New York: Macmillan, 1970. Provides a good picture of many members of the aristocracy and ruling class who were close to Beethoven. Includes excerpts from diaries and letters that provide an insight into Beethoven and those who knew him well.

Lockwood, Lewis. *Beethoven: The Music and the Life*. New York: W. W. Norton, 2003. Aimed at the general reader, this biography focuses on Beethoven's compositions, placing them within a musical and historical context.

Matthews, Denis. *Beethoven*. London: J. M. Dent & Sons, 1985. One of a series of books on great musicians. A revision of an earlier number and a reassessment of Beethoven. Covers his life in the first five chapters and his music in the next eight, attempting to place Beethoven in the world of music.

Solomon, Maynard. *Beethoven*. New York: Schirmer Books, 1977. A standard biography that divides Beethoven's life into four phases—the Bonn years, the early Vienna years, the period of heightened creativity, and the declining years. Good introduction to Beethoven. A good essay on his music closes the book.

Stanley, Glenn, ed. *The Cambridge Companion to Beethoven*. New York: Cambridge University Press, 2000. Series of essays analyzing Beethoven's personality and musical compositions.

Thayer, Alexander Wheelock. *Thayer's Life of Beethoven*. Princeton, N.J.: Princeton University Press, 1964, rev. ed. 1967. Revised and edited by Elliot Forbes. One of the basic studies of Beethoven that attempts to correct errors and add new material. Good treatment of the facts of Beethoven's life, but no analytical interpretation of his music.

Valentin, Erich. *Beethoven and His World*. New York: Viking Press, 1958. Focuses more on Beethoven's life than on the music. Presents an excellent picture of Vienna during the early nineteenth century and of the politics of the period. Good introductory work.

SEE ALSO: Johannes Brahms; Franz Liszt; Franz Schubert; Robert Schumann; Peter Ilich Tchaikovsky.

RELATED ARTICLES in *Great Events from History: The Nineteenth Century, 1801-1900:* April 7, 1805: Beethoven's *Eroica* Symphony Introduces the Romantic Age; May 7, 1824: First Performance of Beethoven's Ninth Symphony.

EMIL VON BEHRING

German physiologist

Behring's development of effective vaccinations against tetanus and diphtheria saved great numbers of lives, and Behring also did important work in bacteriology that led to the modern understanding of infectious disease.

BORN: March 15, 1854; Hansdorf, West Prussia (now Jankowa Zagńska, Poland)
DIED: March 31, 1917; Marburg, Germany
ALSO KNOWN AS: Emil Adolf von Behring (full name)
AREA OF ACHIEVEMENT: Medicine

EARLY LIFE

August George Behring (BAHR-ihng) had four children from his first marriage. Emil Adolf von Behring was the eldest of the nine additional children he had from his second marriage to Augustine Zech, the daughter of a teacher. Teaching was a family tradition on both sides of Emil's family. His great-grandfather had been appointed as a teacher by Frederick the Great, and his grandfather and father had followed the same profession. Emil stood out as the best student among the village children in Hansdorf, prompting his father to seek a better education for him than was locally available. Emil attended the City School of Eylau (now in Poland), and a local minister tutored him for free in preparation for his admission to the gymnasium in Hohenstein, which was later renamed in his honor.

Behring's parents ran out of money before he completed his course of instruction at the gymnasium, but the faculty members were so impressed with his abilities as a science student that they insisted he continue, although he could not pay the tuition. Financial difficulties continued to be an obstacle, and he determined that he could not pursue the career in medicine that he had hoped for. He was on the point of leaving for the University of Königsberg to begin a course as a prospective minister when one of his teachers sent for him to come and discuss another option. The teacher's nephew, a military doctor, was visiting and had become interested in the story of the poor but brilliant student. He helped Behring receive an appointment at the Friedrich Wilhelms Institute in Berlin as a medical student in 1874. The appointment meant that Behring was committing himself to ten years of service as a military doctor after he received his degree, but it was the only way he could achieve his ambition.

Behring received his medical doctorate in 1878 and was licensed in 1880. After a brief period as an intern at the Charité hospital in Berlin, he began service with the Fifty-ninth Fusilier Battalion in Wohlau in June, 1880. In 1881 he was transferred to the Second Hussars in Posen. During the same year, he wrote his first paper on sepsis and antisepsis in theory and practice, but it was not published. His next paper was on the use of iodoform, which had been adopted as a disinfectant for wounds in 1880. He had the idea that taking iodoform internally might be more effective as a disinfectant than applying it externally. However, he was forced to conclude that the poisonous effect produced by taking iodoform internally was too great to make any disinfecting it might do worthwhile. This line of inquiry seemed to be a dead end, but it was to bear significant results, as it led to his interest in antitoxins and subsequent successes.

LIFE'S WORK

In 1887 Behring was promoted to captain and sent to the Pharmacological Institute in Bonn, but his military career was nearing an end. He was already studying for the civil service medical exam because he intended to apply

Emil von Behring. (The Nobel Foundation)

to the Prussian Public Health Service as soon as his ten-year military obligation was over. His duties at the Pharmacological Institute changed the direction of his life, and he turned from the life of a practicing physician with an interest in research to that of a full-time researcher. While at the institute, Behring acquired the necessary skills for a life in research and continued his work on the disinfecting effects of iodoform and acetylene. In 1888 he served at the Academy for Military Medicine in Berlin and established a working relationship with Robert Koch at the Institute of Hygiene at the Berlin University. When his term of military service was over in 1889, he went to work as Koch's assistant.

Behring's first serious research as a civilian was in partnership with Japanese scientist Kitasato Shibasaburo. They were trying to discover what made serum extracted from white rats that were immune to tetanus neutralize anthrax toxins. Their work finally led to the publication of a paper in late 1890 in which they suggested that antitoxins formed in the blood against particular diseases and that these antitoxins could be transferred to other organisms to fight the same disease. This led to some controversy with other scientists who proposed different mechanisms and explanations for the way bacteria cause disease.

The basic argument centered on the question of whether all disease-producing bacteria produce the same harmful substance, which is more or less virulent depending on the quantity present, or whether each type of bacteria produces a unique toxin. Paul Ehrlich, who was a colleague of Behring at the Institute of Hygiene, showed in 1891 that Behring and Kitasato were correct by proving that organisms could form antitoxins to vegetable poisons in addition to bacteria. The vegetable poisons could not have the protein produced by bacteria that Behring's opponents believed caused disease.

Behring seems to have had a rather irritating personality. He was constantly involved in controversy about his theories and attacked others who claimed to have made some of his discoveries before he did. Many of his addresses and papers contained harsh words for his opponents. One of the pamphlets he published was titled "Streitschrift und Verteidigungsschrift gegenuber meinen medizinischen Gegnem" (attack and defense in response to my medical opponents). He made few friends and did not warm up to people very readily. His reputation for arrogance and coldness is illustrated by an encounter with a young assistant on his staff who saw him in a café and approached to ask if he could sit at his table. Behring's response was a harsh "No!" The assistant recalled the incident with bitterness for the rest of his life.

When some of Behring's claims appeared to be exaggerated, his lack of personal charm probably increased the number of his critics. By 1894, he was not getting along very well with his employer, Koch, and he accepted a position on the faculty of the University of Halle. He was not well received there and obtained a professorship at the Marburg University with the help of a friend in the Prussian Ministry of Education, despite the objections of the faculty at Marburg.

Behring is best known for his work on diphtheria. He was a significant, if not the most important, developer of the serum used to treat the disease and later produced the vaccine to prevent it. Popular accounts suggested that he first used the serum on Christmas Eve of 1891 in the surgical clinic of Berlin University, but there is some doubt that he had enough serum to use that early. He collected serum from guinea pigs and, later, from sheep, which he then used to treat the disease in other animals. His friends Andre Martin and Émile Roux successfully immunized horses against diphtheria in 1894, and Behring extended their work to humans. Many others were involved in the development of the serum. Albrecht Kossel reported that serum therapy had reduced the mortality rate in diphtheria cases from 52 to 25 percent. In both England and the United States, further experiments were under way when Behring published two books on infectious disease; his work brought him international attention.

Behring had less success with his attempt to apply the methods used to develop a diphtheria serum to finding a serum that would be effective against tuberculosis. From 1899 to 1900, he devoted much of his time to the effort. Although he was unsuccessful, his work had important results when he showed that milk was a major vehicle for the transmission of the disease to infants. He suggested several ways to kill the tuberculosis bacillus in milk, but none proved practical. A major obstacle in his work on tuberculosis was his mistaken belief that the same bacillus produced the disease in both humans and cattle. This led him down so many dead-end lines of investigation that finally, in 1900, he announced he was giving up on the project.

Behring ultimately achieved success and lasting fame with a diphtheria preventative vaccination in 1913. His view of "serum therapy" was that low levels of a toxin could lead to the production of antitoxins in an organism, and this led him to the diphtheria vaccination. During World War I, he applied the theory to tetanus and developed a successful tetanus vaccine. Even before these accomplishments, he had received a number of honors and awards for his work. This vaccine was almost as important in saving the lives of German soldiers during World War I as the diphtheria vaccine had been in saving the lives of children.

All of his work brought him a considerable amount of recognition. The French awarded him the Legion of Honor in 1895 as well as 100,000 francs, which he shared with Roux. In 1901 he received the first Nobel Prize in Physiology or Medicine. Within his own country, he was made a German hereditary noble. He used his wealth and position to lead a comfortable life. In 1896 he married Else Spinola, the daughter of a physician. They had six sons, and their house in Marburg became a center for local society. Behring enjoyed visiting his other house on the island of Capri, but he suffered from bouts of depression that required him to be institutionalized in Switzerland from time to time. A broken thigh led to complications that weakened him, and he died of pneumonia in Marburg in March, 1917.

SIGNIFICANCE

Together with Louis Pasteur, Robert Koch, and Paul Ehrlich, Emil Behring was one of the most important people in the story of human success against infectious disease during the late nineteenth and twentieth centuries. Even more important than their development of treatments for use against individual diseases were their discoveries about the mechanism of bacterial disease. Often working against the conventional wisdom of the day, they established ways of thinking about and dealing with microorganisms that continue to form the basis of the understanding of disease and its causes.

In addition to his fundamental theoretical and laboratory scientific work, Behring saved millions of lives and showed the way to save millions more with his vaccines and serum therapy. His difficult and contentious personality notwithstanding, his contributions to humanity and medical science are indisputable. The knowledge of the way antitoxins work and are formed is one of the most valuable discoveries in all of medical science, and Behring played an important role in that discovery. Toward the end of his life, he was described as "The Children's Savior." If he had accomplished nothing else, his development of the diphtheria vaccine was enough to assure him of a place among the most honored of medical researchers.

—Philip Dwight Jones

FURTHER READING

Behring, Emil. *Gesammelte Abhandlungen zur ätiologischen Therapie von ansteckenden Krankenheiten.* Leipzig, Germany: Thieme, 1893. This book contains most of Behring's scientific papers to 1893. In German.

Behring, Emil. *Gesammelte Abhandlungen. Neue Folge.* Bonn, Germany: A. Marcus & E. Webers, 1915. This volume contains the scientific papers that Behring wrote between 1893 and 1915. In German.

De Kruif, Paul. *Microbe Hunters.* New York: Harcourt, Brace & World, 1953. In a very enthusiastic and easy-to-read manner, De Kruif describes the scientific adventures of twelve men who played significant roles in the war on disease. One chapter deals specifically with diphtheria (Roux and Behring), and others give important supporting information.

Lagerkvist, Ulf. *Pioneers of Microbiology and the Nobel Prize.* River Edge, N.J.: World Scientific, 2003. Behring is one of the scientists prominently featured in this book about Nobel Prize-winning microbiologists. The book contains a section about Behring's life and his scientific discoveries. One of the few books about Behring written in English.

Satter, Heinrich. *Emil von Behring*. Bad Godesberg, Germany: Inter Nationes, 1967. Written fifty years after Behring's death, this short (fifty-page), very readable biography provides a wealth of detail about his life and work. The author clearly had access to a considerable amount of original material. In German.

Unger, Hellmuth. *Emil von Behring: Sein Lebenswerk als unvergangliches Erbe*. Hamburg: Hoffman und Campe, 1948. This is an interesting biographical novel. In German.

Waller, John. *The Discovery of the Germ: Twenty Years That Transformed the Way We Think About Disease*. New York: Columbia University Press, 2002. Waller examines the breakthroughs in microbiology that occurred between 1879 and 1900, including the discoveries of Koch and Pasteur. Places Behring in a larger medical and historical context.

Zeiss, Heinz, and Richard Bieling. *Behring: Gestalt und Werk*. Berlin: B. Schultz, 1940. Other accounts of Behring depend on this standard biography, although the style is a bit dated and flowery. In German.

SEE ALSO: Robert Koch; Louis Pasteur.

RELATED ARTICLES in *Great Events from History: The Nineteenth Century, 1801-1900:* March 24, 1882: Koch Announces His Discovery of the Tuberculosis Bacillus; December 11, 1890: Behring Discovers the Diphtheria Antitoxin; 1898: Beijerinck Discovers Viruses.

ALEXANDER GRAHAM BELL

Scottish American inventor

One of the major inventive geniuses of modern times, Bell created and perfected the telephone and greatly advanced the teaching of the deaf.

BORN: March 3, 1847; Edinburgh, Scotland
DIED: August 2, 1922; Baddeck, Nova Scotia
AREA OF ACHIEVEMENT: Science and technology

EARLY LIFE

The second of three boys, Alexander Graham Bell was born into a Scottish family prominent in the field of elocution. Both his grandfather Alexander Bell and his father, Alexander Melville Bell, taught the subject. The former invented a technique to check stammering, while the latter became a major innovator and author in corrective speech. His mother, Eliza Grace Symonds Bell, a portrait painter and musician, educated her son until his tenth year. After three years of formal schooling, he spent a year in London with his grandfather, who inspired the young Bell with his deep commitment to the study of the science of sound. Bell then taught music and elocution as a student teacher in Elgin, in the midst of which he spent a year at the University of Edinburgh. During 1866-1867, he taught at a college in Bath, England. Thus, he was largely family-taught and self-taught; his black, penetrating eyes and intense, though modest, manner attested his inquiring mind.

LIFE'S WORK

Bell's genius had begun to reveal itself in 1864, when, at the age of seventeen, he undertook his first experiments in the science of sound, followed the next year by initial work in the application of electricity to transmitting speech via sound waves. Upon the death of his grandfather, Bell's father replaced the former in London and published his major tract *Visible Speech: The Science of Universal Alphabetics* in 1867, the year that young Alexander became his assistant. From his father, Bell had inherited the notion of visible speech—that is, a visual-symbolic alphabet for use in producing spoken sounds—and therefore also his father's dedication to improving methods for teaching the deaf to talk. During 1868-1870, father and son established an equal partnership, even as Bell studied anatomy and physiology at University College, London, and applied his father's techniques of visible speech at a school for the deaf at Kensington.

Such a heavy work load began to undermine Bell's health, alarming his parents, inasmuch as they had recently lost both their other sons to tuberculosis. In 1870, they emigrated to Canada, settling in the countryside near Brantford, Ontario. There, Bell's health was quickly restored, and he resumed his work in Boston, tutoring and teaching at schools for the deaf, opening his own school for other teachers, continuing his experiments in sound, and making an improvement in the system of visible speech that has remained a standard technique ever since. He also invented an audiometer. Formal recognition came early in 1873 when Boston University made him professor of vocal physiology and the mechanics of speech, a post he held for four years.

During 1873-1876, Bell brought together his disparate studies of the science of sound and its electrical telegraphic transmission. Ever since his first experiments with the latter in 1865, Bell spent whatever spare time he had in attempting to invent a device by which oral sounds could be transmitted via electrical wires: the telephone. Concurrently, he studied the human ear to discover the importance of the membrane for such a device, and he learned to transmit multiple electrical messages over a single wire. In applying the key element of acoustics to telegraphy, Bell sought and received the counsel and encouragement of the venerable experimental physicist Joseph Henry, who had worked along similar lines.

Basically a scientist, Bell was fortunate to hire as his technical assistant Thomas A. Watson, an adept mechanic who shared his long nights of experiments on electrical sound transmission. Unable to fund this work himself, Bell found two patrons in the fathers of deaf children he was teaching. These men were Thomas Sanders and Gardiner G. Hubbard. Only rest, however, could restore Bell's physical strength from occasional fatigue resulting from these considerable labors, and Bell obtained it at his parents' home in Canada.

The first, though unintelligible, human sounds, Bell's to Watson, came through their wire in June, 1875, but it was not until the following March 10 that a twenty-foot-long wire carried the monumental, though unanticipated, first message: "Mr. Watson, come here; I want to see you." The two men rapidly improved their invention, and Bell astounded the scientific world with his first public demonstration of the telephone at the International Centennial Exposition at Philadelphia in June, 1876. The following spring, he demonstrated the first long-distance telephone conversation, between Boston and New York.

In July, 1877, Bell, Hubbard, and Sanders created the Bell Telephone Company. Having patented all the related inventions, Bell finally began to enjoy the resulting financial rewards, although some six hundred lawsuits ensued, with rivals claiming credit—until 1888, when the Supreme Court ruled in Bell's favor as sole inventor of the telephone.

Though his fame was assured through his epic creation, Bell remained equally dedicated to the education of the deaf, especially after he married Hubbard's daughter Mabel, one of his deaf students, in July, 1877. She became an important source of encouragement and inspiration for the rest of his life and gave him two daughters. During their subsequent trip to Europe, where he introduced the telephone, Bell lectured on the teaching of the deaf at Oxford University. After settling in Washington in 1878, Bell enlarged his study of the physical nature of deafness and in 1880 founded the Volta Laboratory upon receiving the French Volta Prize of fifty thousands francs (about ten thousand dollars).

Alexander Graham Bell. (Library of Congress)

Bell used the Volta Laboratory in the spirit of scientific philanthropy; instead of patenting new discoveries made there, he allowed their general use for the public good. Most important were the photophone to send words by light ray and an induction balance or electric probe to locate metal objects in the human body, the latter first used to find the assassin's bullet that mortally wounded President James A. Garfield.

Bell became an American citizen in 1882 and soon thereafter built a summer home and research laboratory at Baddeck, Cape Breton Island, Nova Scotia. Among many honors he received from European countries was a Ph.D., awarded by the University of Würzburg in Bavaria.

Bell's restless, inquisitive mind seemed to accelerate as he grew older, and his black hair, beard, and sideburns turned a striking, billowy white. At the Volta Laboratory, he improved upon Thomas Alva Edison's phonograph during the mid-1880's; proceeds from the sale of some of the patents were used to transform the Laboratory into the Volta Bureau for the Increase and Diffusion of Knowledge Relating to the Deaf. His prize pupil the next decade became Helen Keller.

In 1890, Bell founded and became first president of the American Association to Promote Teaching of Speech to the Deaf (renamed the Alexander Graham Bell Association for the Deaf in 1956). An early study of marriage among the deaf led into eugenics and the problems of longevity, research that emerged as a major book in 1918. He also supported Albert A. Michelson's first measurements of the speed of light. Bell continued to improve upon the telephone, and he and Watson inaugurated the first transcontinental phone call when, in 1915, they conversed between San Francisco and New York.

The possibilities of manned powered flight held the greatest fascination for Bell from before 1891, when he supported the pioneering work of Samuel P. Langley, until the end of his life. Bell believed that tetrahedron-shaped cells could be joined for lift, and experimented with them in immense kites. During 1907-1909, he teamed up with aviation pioneer Glenn H. Curtiss and three other young men in the Aerial Experiment Association (AEA), the brainstorm of his wife, who also funded its work. Among the aircraft the five men created at Bell's Nova Scotia laboratory and Curtiss's facility at Hammondsport, New York, was Bell's own tetrahedral plane. Though it finally flew in 1912, it proved too unwieldy, but where the tetrahedron failed as an aeronautical device, it eventually proved highly successful in architecture (as, for example, in R. Buckminster Fuller's geodesic dome).

In 1916, Bell advocated American preparedness in military air power, and inasmuch as the AEA operated their craft from the water and the ice, Bell during and after World War I developed a high-speed hydrofoil motorboat for riding above the water at speeds of up to seventy miles per hour.

At his Nova Scotia laboratory and in Washington, Bell carried on his manifold experiments, which also included a home air-cooling unit, an artificial respirator, the breeding of sheep, improved methods of lithography and sonar detection, and a vertical-propelled, aircraft-type engine that anticipated the helicopter and jet propulsion. His extensive notebooks were filled with other ideas that he never had time to develop; he was working on a means to distill saltwater when he died. His chief fame, however, rests on the invention of the telephone, of which thirteen million existed worldwide at the time of his death on August 2, 1922. Two days later, on the day of his funeral, all telephones in the United States and Canada fell silent for one minute in tribute to him.

SIGNIFICANCE

Alexander Graham Bell typified the remarkable generation of American inventor-scientists of the late nineteenth century whose ability to apply scientific discoveries to everyday practical technological uses played a major part in the rise of contemporary urban civilization. Driven by an insatiable curiosity and endowed with sheer experimental (though not theoretical) genius—and perfect pitch—Bell was able to focus his many interests on two or three projects simultaneously, often complementing one another. Thus, his humanitarian work on helping the deaf to learn to speak was wedded early to his efforts to invent the practical telephone. He never lost interest in either project, although aviation commanded equal attention the second half of his life. This was a fascination shared by many prominent peers in the scientific and technological worlds, among them, for example, explorer Robert Edwin Peary, yacht designer W. Starling Burgess, and naval inventor Bradley A. Fiske.

An immensely generous person, Bell was completely selfless in his devotion to the deaf, to whose improvement he committed many of the profits from the telephone. Because he championed the diffusion of scientific knowledge, he became a major catalyst in the cause of popular science. With Hubbard, in 1883, he founded and operated for eleven years *Science* magazine, subsequently taken over by the American Association for the Advancement of Science.

In 1888, Bell was a founder of the National Geographic Society, ten years later succeeding Hubbard as its president, until 1904. Under his presidency, in 1899, the *National Geographic* magazine began publication. One of his daughters married the editor Gilbert H. Grosvenor; Bell's grandson, Melville Bell Grosvenor, succeeded to the editorship half a century later. In 1891, Bell funded the creation of the Astrophysical Observatory of the Smithsonian Institution and seven years after that became a regent of the Smithsonian, a post he held the rest of his life. Largely through Bell's efforts, the remains of James Smithson were returned from Genoa, Italy, to Washington, D.C., in 1904.

Like other major inventors of his day, Bell had to protect his patents from challengers, and did so by keeping copious notes and having numerous photographs taken. His love of nature was embodied in his summer home and laboratory, named Beinn Bhreagh, the commanding view of the Bras d'Or Lakes in this "New Scotland" (Nova Scotia) reminding him of his native land. Such an idyllic environment proved especially conducive to his experiments over the last thirty-five years of his life. There he died, and there—in a mountainside—he was buried. He had shared the wonders of nature with the world at large through the pages of the *National Geographic*. The full legacy of Alexander Graham Bell is beyond measure.

—*Clark G. Reynolds*

FURTHER READING

Bruce, Robert V. *Bell: Alexander Graham Bell and the Conquest of Solitude*. Boston: Little, Brown, 1973. The standard biography, this heavily annotated work focuses on the development of the telephone but offers a good general treatment of Bell's life before and after its invention.

Casey, Louis S. *Curtiss: The Hammondsport Era, 1907-1915*. New York: Crown, 1981. Though a biography of pioneer aviator and manufacturer Glenn H. Curtiss in his early years of aviation, the book discusses Bell's role in the AEA, utilizing among its sources the AEA *Bulletin*.

Costain, Thomas B. *Chord of Steel*. Garden City, N.Y.: Doubleday, 1960. A popular account of the invention of the telephone.

Grosvenor, Edwin S., and Morgan Wesson. *Alexander Graham Bell: The Life and Times of the Man Who Invented the Telephone*. New York: Harry N. Abrams, 1997. A biography of Bell, focusing on the early history of the telephone, enlivened by more than four hundred color and black-and-white illustrations.

Mackay, James. *Alexander Graham Bell: A Life*. New York: John Wiley & Sons, 1997. Mackay depicts Bell as a man of great intelligence and curiosity, and describes his varied interests and inventions. Provides new information on Bell's early years and how these years influenced his later life.

Mackenzie, Catherine Dunlap. *Alexander Graham Bell: The Man Who Contracted Space*. Boston: Houghton Mifflin, 1928. This early biography is a sound though dated work.

Parkin, J. H. *Bell and Baldwin*. Toronto: University of Toronto Press, 1964. Centers on the association of Bell with the Canadian F. W. "Casey" Baldwin during the AEA period with Glenn Curtiss.

Waite, Helen E. *Make a Joyful Sound: The Romance of Mabel Hubbard and Alexander Graham Bell*. Philadelphia: MacRae Smith, 1961. A moving account of the relationship between Bell and his wife, who, though twelve years his junior, emerges as a key figure in her own right and proof positive of Bell's success in overcoming the disability of deafness. She died in 1923.

Watson, Thomas A. *Exploring Life*. New York: D. Appleton, 1926. This autobiography by Bell's main assistant (1854-1934) illuminates the great inventor's character and methods.

SEE ALSO: Thomas Alva Edison; Joseph Henry; Pedro II.

RELATED ARTICLES in *Great Events from History: The Nineteenth Century, 1801-1900:* May 10-November 10, 1876: Philadelphia Hosts the Centennial Exposition; June 25, 1876: Bell Demonstrates the Telephone; December 24, 1877: Edison Patents the Cylinder Phonograph; March 11, 1891: Strowger Patents Automatic Dial Telephone System.

MUḤAMMAD BELLO

Ruler of Nigeria's Sokoto caliphate (r. 1817-1837)

As the son and successor to ʿUthman dan Fodio, the head of the first Fulani-led Islamic jiḥad in West Africa, Muḥammad Bello served as both sultan and caliph in Sokoto. He continued his father's campaign to bring about a religious and political confederation of Hausa states, within which ethnic Hausas and Fulanis would live as equals.

BORN: 1781; Hausaland, West Africa (now in Nigeria)

DIED: October 26, 1837; Sokoto (now in Nigeria)

ALSO KNOWN AS: Muḥammad Bello ibn Uthman (full name); Bello; Muhammad Ballo

AREAS OF ACHIEVEMENT: Government and politics, religion and theology

EARLY LIFE

Muḥammad Bello was one of several sons of ʿUthman dan Fodio and was the best-known early successor to head the Fulani-led jiḥad movement created by his father. However, the actions of his father after launching his jiḥad movement in 1804 so dominate the sparse historical records of the period that little is known about Bello prior to his accession. One thing that is known is that from an early age, he was expected to develop military skills that would help strengthen his father's reform mission. In that respect, he differed from his father and his father's generation in not being expected to follow either of the occupations traditionally open to Fulani men, pastoralism and trading.

Although recorded details are lacking, he probably contributed much to the success of the Sokoto sultanate before he became its official head. Moreover, not only did he learn the importance of military discipline in the ranks of his father's armed forces, he must also have learned a great deal about the various Hausa city-states and other peoples whom he would eventually rule.

LIFE'S WORK

What Muḥammad Bello inherited shortly after his father's death in 1817 represented the initial stages of the caliphate, and eventually, the sultanate of Sokoto. The polity founded by his father held hegemony only over a part of the Hausa city-states in the northern region of what is now Nigeria. With time, and particularly under Bello's leadership, the Sokoto sultanate would eventually extend its control over peoples of different ethnic and religious origins to the south of the traditional Hausaland region. In addition to groups that came under Sokoto's sway during his father's reign—including the main Hausa city-states of Katsina, Kano, and Zaria—Bello extended indirect control southward to Nupe and zones associated with Ilorin, thus penetrating the limits of Yoruba territory near the confluence of the Benue and Niger Rivers.

In his efforts to extend Sokoto power, Bello had to contend not only with traditional religious issues connected with jiḥad, but also with the problem of creating a polity that could accept the principles of Fulani/Hausa social and political integration that his father had begun to preach. The initial aim of the Fulani jiḥad, which had started around 1804 in Gobir, was to call for a purging of questionable practices followed by different, presumably Islamic rulers of the Hausa city-states. Beyond such issues, the jiḥad aimed at correcting perceived injustices and discrimination in relations between "native" Hausas and the traditionally pastoral Fulani population, who had previously occupied a subordinate status vis-à-vis the Hausas.

A confrontation with Sarkin Yunfa, the ruler of Gobir, had been delayed when Yunfa promised to recognize ʿUthman dan Fodio's right to organize his own religiously based Fulani community away from Gobir, in the settlement of Degel. ʿUthman's local followers urged him to widen the bases of his support, and ʿUthman then called upon both Fulani and Hausa Muslim supporters from several Hausa states to join in a jiḥad. His forces won their first victory against conservative supporters—including some Fulanis—of Yunfa. The next step, which definitely affected Muḥammad Bello's future tenure as ʿUthman dan Fodio's successor, involved "temporary" acts of submission by other Hausa city-states that feared advances by the jiḥadists against them.

Leadership responsibilities for jiḥad were divided between elaborating and announcing its religiously based principles and carrying on military activities more directly designed to bring different Hausa states under jiḥadist control. ʿUthman first delegated the latter task tovhis sons Abdullahi and Muḥammad Bello. Successful military operations headed by Abdullahi and Bello produced results. By 1809, the major Hausa state at Kano was under the control of the jiḥadists. It appears that by that date, Muḥammad Bello had already distinguished himself, not only as a military commander, but also as someone with effective writing skills. He put the latter skill to work by composing letters for distribution to potential supporters of his father's cause.

Muḥammad Bello's success in ruling the Sokoto sultanate should be seen in the context of the ethnically mixed polity's religious and political characteristics. Instead of assuming a single center for rule from Sokoto, Bello retained the pattern of divided responsibilities that had been established by his father. He himself governed the western part of the sultanate, while his brother Abdullahi administered areas in the east from a second political base at Gwandu.

This system did guarantee that the component parts of Bello's largely symbolic regime would remain continuously loyal to Sokoto. However, the boundaries of the sultanate expanded, reaching their fullest extent around 1831, when fourteen Fulani emirates held sway over both Hausa and non-Hausa states in the northern and central regions of what eventually became Nigeria. However, Bello found that after that date he could maintain his authority only with force in the face of multiple revolts. By the time he died in 1837, he had organized at least fifty different military campaigns. Ironically, he even had difficulty controlling Gobir, where his father's jiḥad had begun but which lost its preeminence after Sokoto was founded.

Even during the reign of his immediate successor, Abubakar Atiku, between 1837 and 1842, and then the ascendancy of his son ʿAli ibn Bello, who was caliph from 1842 to 1859, multiple military campaigns had to be undertaken to try to maintain the effective allegiance of territories that had accepted Bello's leadership.

It appears that Europeans took no serious interest in establishing communications or ties with Bello's capital during his lifetime. Western involvement would grow after the 1860's, culminating in a late nineteenth century British military campaign against Sokoto under Sir Frederick Lugard. Although Lugard occupied Kano and Sokoto in 1903, he left the symbolic structure of the Sokoto sultanate in place.

It was during Muḥammad Bello's period of rule, however, that prominent visitors from other areas of West and East Africa, especially those who were interested in carrying the impetus of the original Fulani jiḥad to their lands, came to Sokoto for guidance in both religious and political matters. The most outstanding example of this involved a five-year sojourn in Sokoto by Sheikh ʿUmar (Fall), originally from the Senegal Tukulor region, and the future founder of a major jiḥadist state in what became modern Mali. Sheikh ʿUmar forged bonds with Muḥammad Bello by marrying the latter's daughter during the 1830's. Many years later, ʿUmar's son by Bello's daughter, Ahmadu, became ʿUmar's successor. When Ahmadu himself was later forced out of the remaining core of his father's jiḥadist empire by advancing French forces, he became an exile in Sokoto under the protection of his grandfather's successors.

SIGNIFICANCE

Two historically important developments are associated with Muḥammad Bello's tenure as sultan of Sokoto. The most obvious is the fact that he was able to forge sufficient political continuity to enable West Africa's first jiḥadist state to survive—symbolically, at least—into the colonial era of the twentieth century.

Muḥammad Bello also stands out as one of the few nineteenth century West African political and religious leaders to leave behind an extensive corpus of personal writings. Not only did he write a near contemporary account of his father, ʿUthman dan Fodio's, life, he also left a number of didactic tracts that have drawn the attention of Nigerian translators into English.

—Byron D. Cannon

FURTHER READING

Ballo, Muhammad. *Ballo's Fatwa on Urbanization of Nomads*. Edited and translated by Omar Bello. Sokoto, Nigeria: Islamic Academy, 2000.

_____. *Embellishment of the Minds with the Necessary Provisions to the Wayfarer*. Sokoto, Nigeria: Milestone Publishing House, 2000. These modern translations of Bello's writings illustrate his interest in a variety of subjects. *Ballo's Fatwa* is political and social in nature, while *Embellishment of the Minds* is more spiritual in nature.

Bello, Muhammad. *Infaku'l Maisuri*. Translated by C. E. J. Whitting. London: Luzac, 1957. An important source for the life and teachings of ʿUthman written by his son Bello.

Fuglestad, Finn. "A Reconsideration of Hausa History Before the Jihad." *Journal of African History* 19 (1978): 319-339. This article provides insights into the type of society, as well as the religious setting prevailing in Hausaland before Bello's father declared his religious and political cause.

Kanya-Forstner, A. S., and Paul E. Lovejoy. "Editing Nineteenth Century Intelligence Reports on the Sokoto Caliphate and Borno." *History in Africa* 24 (1997): 195-204. Analysis of rare primary source documents dealing with relations between the Sokoto caliphate and its primary political rival to the east.

SEE ALSO: Jamāl al-Dīn al-Afghānī; The Mahdi; ʿUthman dan Fodio.

RELATED ARTICLE in *Great Events from History: The Nineteenth Century, 1801-1900:* May 4, 1805-1830: Exploration of West Africa.

JAMES GORDON BENNETT

American newspaper publisher

Bennett made American newspapers independent enterprises and established the foundations of the profession of journalism.

BORN: September 1, 1795; Newmill, Keith, Banffshire, Scotland
DIED: June 1, 1872; New York, New York
AREA OF ACHIEVEMENT: Journalism

EARLY LIFE

James Gordon Bennett was the first son of landholding Roman Catholic parents who abided by the teachings of the Church. At the time of Bennett's birth, there were perhaps fewer than forty thousand Catholics in all of Scotland, but his parents were steadfast in the faith and in their determination to have a son join the priesthood. Two sisters and a close younger brother named Cosmo completed the Bennett family. James Gordon in later life became embittered by the Church, blaming it for mistreatment of his brother, who died in seminary.

In the strict, Presbyterian-dominated public school system of the time, the Bible was regarded as central to education and to the development of good manners and industry. Latin, Greek, some English, mathematics, history, and a large dosage of the doctrines of John Knox constituted the curriculum, which continued until the child reached the early teens. Bennett's formal education was reinforced at home by his parents, who read the Scriptures regularly and discussed the colloquial history of the family, the region, and Scotland. Bennett attributed his later success as a newspaperman to this early training. At fifteen, he was taken to the Catholic Seminary at Aberdeen, which was some sixty miles from his home. He attended Blair's College, the smallest of three schools that would eventually combine to form the University of Aberdeen. There, he was steeped in the study of classical literature and philosophy and the criticism of the great journal the *Edinburgh Review*.

Rejecting the priesthood, training for which was to follow college, Bennett spent the years from 1814 to 1819 traveling extensively in Scotland and living for a time in Glasgow, which had replaced Edinburgh in size and economic importance. Glasgow was also the embarkation port for emigrants to the West, and literature about America was in great demand. Bennett read Benjamin Franklin's autobiography (recently reprinted in Glasgow), with which he was much impressed; twenty-five years old and at a crossroads in his life, Bennett set his sights on America.

In 1819, Bennett set sail for Halifax, Nova Scotia, with only twenty-five dollars and a classical education to his name. Halifax was little more than an English loyalist outpost, and Bennett—having inherited a Scot's hatred and fear of the English—taught bookkeeping for a time in that town and then moved on to Portland, Maine. Looking for the America he had read about in Scotland, Bennett found more of it in Maine, where he was impressed with the self-confidence of the people and saw in them something of the children of equality and liberty.

Bennett took a teaching job in the village of Addison and then continued on to Boston, where he discovered the reasons for which the people of Maine had expressed dislike of that city: Boston was a snob's town, and Bennett was quickly reminded of Edinburgh, with its arrogance and presumption as a center of learning and culture. In Boston, he did, however, find a position as a clerk with a well-known bookseller and printer. He was made a proofreader in the print shop, where he learned something more of the rudiments of the trade that was to make him famous. He took what he could from Boston before moving farther south to New York.

In New York, Bennett was once again a new arrival with little money and even smaller prospects. The city excited him, however, as it seemed to be a microcosm of America: It was more representative of the nation about which he had read. He did some bookkeeping and proofreading, and fortune smiled on him in the person of Aaron Willington, the owner of the *Charleston Courier*, who eventually hired him to translate Spanish and French news and dispatches for his paper.

In Charleston, South Carolina, Bennett enjoyed the experience of working with well-educated and intelligent associates, men who enjoyed all that Charleston and its culture offered. The shy and withdrawn Bennett mixed only on the job, however, and then sparingly. He was aware early that appearances rather than ideas and wit counted the most in social gatherings, and in the former he was always lacking.

After ten months in Charleston, Bennett returned to New York. Bennett set about determining which were the best newspapers in New York, but he found that none of them was interested in a still-uncouth immigrant. He finally gained a job with the *National Advocate*, a moribund publication underwritten by the New York General Republican Committee, which was connected to the Tammany Hall political machine. The original editor was Mordecai Noah, who had large political aspirations for himself and even larger aspirations for creation of a Jewish colony on Grant (modern Grand) Island in the Niagara River, some fifteen miles west of Niagara Falls.

James Gordon Bennett. (Library of Congress)

The agitation provoked by the Grant Island scheme led to Noah's dismissal, but he was soon brought back. Bennett, meanwhile, became known in the newspaper world as a bright and industrious young man with a flair for writing. He was soon getting freelance work with other papers, and in 1825 he took over ownership of a struggling weekly called the *New York Courier*, the first Sunday paper in the United States. It was a doomed project, and Bennett soon found himself working for Noah, who had changed his paper's name to the *New York Enquirer*.

When Bennett offered to write some light and humorous sketches for the *New York Enquirer*, Noah accepted, and on April 27, 1827, an article entitled "Shaking Hands" appeared. It dealt with alternatives to shaking hands as a form of greeting, with examples ranging from the Philippines to Africa. Noah was amazed at the increase in the paper's circulation following the publication of this article. Bennett followed up the piece with one called "Intemperance," which was a portent of his later tactic of using a subject to take a competing newspaper to task by making fun of it. In this case, it was *The New York Times* and its claim that New York was a very moral city that came in for a spoofing. As a result, a new excitement took hold over journalism in New York, despite the fact that disgruntled competing editors were already complaining that Bennett's work was degrading the profession.

Bennett was promoted to the position of assistant editor on the death of the incumbent in a duel. Bennett asked to go to Washington to report on Congress and the Adams administration. In a short time, he became the first full-fledged Washington correspondent in American journalism. For four years, he was everywhere politicians traveled, submitting comment on legislation, on speeches and idiosyncrasies, on merchants, bankers, and stock hustlers. He listened for tips and rumors and followed up leads to confirm information and otherwise mastered the techniques of journalism, techniques that seemed to be lost on his contemporaries.

In the meantime, Bennett's paper combined with James Watson Webb's *Morning Courier* under Webb's control as publisher of the new *Morning Courier and New York Enquirer*. Bennett contributed greatly to the success of the paper, but Webb never granted him recognition by name. Like Noah, Webb took credit for Bennett's pieces or attributed them to the rewriting of others. This experience later encouraged Bennett to allow reporters their own bylines when writing for his papers.

During Bennett's stay with the *Morning Courier and New York Enquirer*, the paper became perhaps the most influential in New York, though it printed only thirty-five hundred copies daily and took in an average of less than fifty dollars per issue. In 1832, the paper joined the side of the National Bank and Nicholas Biddle in its fight against the Jacksonians (though the paper had been an organ of the Democratic Party), and Bennett resigned rather than work for the opposition. The compromising of the paper's independence grated on Bennett, who now turned again to starting his own daily.

Bennett started the *Globe*, which failed to gain political support. He then went to Philadelphia, where he published the *Pennsylvanian*, which also failed. Needing capital, he appealed to Martin Van Buren and the Democrats for financing, only to be rejected. Returning to New York, he visited Horace Greeley with the hope of starting a partnership. Greeley referred Bennett to two printers with whom he had worked. The penny daily was enjoying marked success via Benjamin Day's New York *Sun*, from which spun the Philadelphia *Public Ledger* and the Baltimore *Sun*, both of which were begun by former associates of Day. With the barest of capital and a promise to print, Bennett grabbed the opportunity to create an independent newspaper.

LIFE'S WORK

Bennett started his newspaper in a basement New York City room at 20 Wall Street with only planks and barrels for furniture. He called it the *New York Herald*. It was the traditional size for such papers—four pages with four columns to the page—and sold for one penny. The first issue appeared on May 6, 1835. Bennett worked sixteen-hour days, carefully structuring his time for each facet of publication. He spent three hours writing editorials before arriving at his office at eight o'clock and continued until he retired to his single room on Nassau Street at 10:00 P.M. Originality was his byword.

Unlike his competition, Bennett used few reprinted stories. Fresh news flowed constantly. He sought to provide a view of the city and its people by creating scenarios, reporting conversations, relating anecdotes with a social point of view, and delivering humorous accounts of manners, fashion, and the foibles of people generally. He brought to public view the *demi-monde*; often he relegated politicians to this realm, all to the delight of his supporters and to the rage of his growing list of enemies and competitors. Women, religion, abolitionists, bankers, speculators, and merchant hustlers all came in for a fair share of Bennett's gibes. Reformers were left to rail against his ridiculing columns. He cultivated rumor and gossip, and his coy exposition of events often of his own invention but attributable to unnamed sources foreshadowed the use of the "informed source."

Bennett took to the street to gain information firsthand and then to exploit it to its fullest. He covered an infamous murder case involving a fashionable house of prostitution to the point of questioning the guilt of the prime suspect, thereby influencing the jury's decision to acquit. He viewed the body of the dead woman, describing her in intimate detail. He also interviewed the keeper of the house in the first use of the didactic question-answer interview by a newspaper. The financial panic of 1836 and the huge fire of the same period encouraged Bennett to print the first financial news, which became an instant hit among a new business readership. He visited the fire area as well, talked to owners of properties that were burned, and interviewed displaced tenants. He printed a sketch of the burned-over area and again outdistanced his rivals.

Because the public generally bought one paper only, the one with the latest news was the one in demand, and the *New York Herald* was the paper of choice. Bennett, encouraged, hired a police reporter and expanded the size of his publication, moving the paper's offices to Broadway and Ann streets. He found more time for leisure, though he was still irascible in print. Threatened with lawsuits for libel and slander, pummeled and horsewhipped for his writings, he never wavered in his attacks. His pen was his sword. Over six feet in height and sturdy in build, he was uncoordinated in his movement and hopelessly cross-eyed; although he was always courteous and polite, he was reserved and shy.

In 1838, his wealth allowed him time to go to Europe, where he was crushed to learn of his brother Cosmo's death. Two years later, he announced his marriage to Henrietta Agnes Crean in St. Peter's Roman Catholic Church, after which they went on to Niagara Falls on their honeymoon. His declaration of his love and the description of his bride in the *New York Herald* enraged his competitors, who attacked him unmercifully. When their son, James Gordon, Jr., was born on May 10, 1841, whispers abounded as to the true father. His former associate Mordecai Noah printed the rumors, which caused Bennett to bring suit; it was successful and cost Noah a $250 fine. The Bennetts had three other children: a girl who died at eight months; a boy, Cosmo Gordon, who died within a year; and Jeanette, who married Isaac Bell and lived a long life.

Bennett enjoyed all the luxuries money could buy, but because of the harassment by his enemies, his wife spent much of her time traveling abroad or sailing. The children were taught by private tutor, and James, Jr., was especially pampered. Bennett even traded a family sailing sloop complete with cannon in return for a lieutenancy for his son in the Union navy in 1862. When the ship was put out of service in 1864, the youth promptly resigned his commission. In 1866, he was installed as managing editor of the *New York Herald* and, within two years, his father gave him ownership of the enterprise, which had grown to five hundred employees.

Bennett always put profits back into the paper by keeping a battery of reporters in Washington and as many as sixty-five in the field during the Civil War. His people were in all parts of the world. His paper was the only one Abraham Lincoln read daily because of its influence. Lincoln tried to co-opt Bennett by offering him an ambassadorship to France, but to no avail. Independence had come too hard for Bennett for him to give it up so easily. Even after his retirement in 1867, he continued to visit the offices and make suggestions. His wife visited briefly in May, 1872, and he promised to join her in Europe, but he was overcome by a stroke that paralyzed his lower body and caused his death in New York City on June 1, 1872. No family members were present, though he had asked the Catholic archbishop John McCloskey to take his confession and administer the Sacraments. His son attended his funeral, accompanied by Bennett's lifelong friends and adversaries.

The *New York Herald* did not print a lengthy obituary of its own, choosing instead to reprint those of other New York papers. Every significant editor in the city had served as a pallbearer. The service was held at Bennett's home on Fifth Avenue, and he was buried in the nonsectarian Greenwood Cemetery in Brooklyn. His will left the paper to his son and his properties to his wife. His daughter's wherewithal was guaranteed in the estate. His wife did not live long after. Dying of cancer, she prevented her children from seeing her. She died in the company of strangers in Sachsen, Germany, on March 28, 1873. The *New York Tribune* was first to carry news of her death.

SIGNIFICANCE

Along with Horace Greeley and Charles Dana, James Gordon Bennett was one of the three giants of journalism and publishing in the United States during the nineteenth century. Of the three, Bennett alone mastered every facet of journalism, from getting stories to editing to proofreading to printing to total management of advertising, distribution, and marketing. His public was his power. His ideas—for example, that advertisers and distributors pay cash for copy and papers—flourished and multiplied as sound practice. The byline and feature articles on styles, theater, books, business, and so on all became part of the *New York Herald* style. Bennett's organization was a model of efficiency, with meetings of the key staff held each day to plan the day's production and assign future stories and leads. As a result of these innovations, many consider Bennett to be the founder of the modern newspaper.

Bennett had to survive a vicious, competitive struggle for success, and he was not above using his paper to pull down his competition. Neither money nor institutional power frightened him when he believed in a principle. His sardonic wit and sophisticated interplay of scenes and anecdotes sorely tried his enemies, and he was not reluctant to exploit the frailties inherent in the pompous and the fatuous. He instinctively knew the power he could wield with his readers, who were legion.

—*Jack J. Cardoso*

FURTHER READING

Carlson, Oliver. *The Man Who Made the News: James Gordon Bennett*. New York: Duell, Sloan and Pearce, 1942. This is the only complete biography of James Gordon Bennett. Though impressionistic and containing no illustrations, it is nevertheless very useful.

Croffut, William A. *An American Procession: A Personal Chronicle of Famous Men*. Boston: Little, Brown, 1931. Reprint. Freeport, N.Y.: Books for Libraries, 1968. This is a collection of personal views and portraits of famous Americans and puts the work of Isaac Pray (see below) in perspective, showing that Pray actually tried to get Bennett to authorize his biography, which came out the same year as James Parton's biography of Horace Greeley.

Crouthamel, James L. *Bennett's "New York Herald" and the Rise of the Popular Press*. Syracuse, N.Y.: Syracuse University Press, 1989. Focuses on the journalistic methods Bennett employed between 1835 and 1872 to make the *New York Herald* the country's largest and most prosperous newspaper. Crouthamel attributes the newspaper's success to its middle-class readers, and not to its working-class populism.

Fermer, Douglas. *James Gordon Bennett and the "New York Herald": A Study of Editorial Opinion in the*

Civil War Era, 1854-1867. New York: St. Martin's Press, 1986. Analyzes the newspaper's editorial columns to explore its opinions during the Civil War and to examine the power of the press upon politics and politicians.

Herd, Harold. *Seven Editors*. Westport, Conn.: Greenwood Press, 1977. Reprint. London: George Allen & Unwin, 1955. This work recognizes Bennett's journalistic achievements and puts them in context.

Hudson, Frederic. *History of Journalism in the United States from 1690 to 1872*. New York: Harper & Brothers, 1873. This is a very useful book by Bennett's confidant and last managing editor of the *New York Herald* during his tenure, which ended in 1867. It contains great amounts of detail about newspaper development and the personalities surrounding it.

Mott, Frank Luther. *American Journalism: 1690-1960*. 3d ed. New York: Macmillan, 1962. Any overview of the growth of journalism in the United States owes something to this work.

Pray, Isaac Clark. *Memoirs of James Gordon Bennett and His Times*. Westport, Conn.: Greenwood Press, 1855. Reprint. New York: Arno Press, 1970. This work was written without the cooperation of Bennett and is taken largely from the columns of the *New York Herald* and from hearsay gathered by a man who had once worked for the Bennett paper as a theater critic. Pray was also a successful playwright and managed several theaters.

Seitz, Don C. *The James Gordon Bennetts: Father and Son, Proprietors of the "New York Herald."* Indianapolis: Bobbs-Merrill, 1928. This is a useful introduction to Bennett, written in a breezy, journalistic style. It shows a heavy relationship to Pray (see above), but contains some useful illustrations and photographic material.

Tebbell, John, and Sarah Miles Watts. *The Press and the Presidency*. New York: Oxford University Press, 1985. This has some interesting material relating to Bennett's considerable influence, most notably on Abraham Lincoln, who was always a reader of the *New York Herald* and ever-concerned with that paper's lukewarm editorial attitude toward the Republican Party.

Turner, Hy B. *When Giants Ruled: The Story of Park Row, New York's Great Newspaper Street*. New York: Fordham University Press, 1999. A history of New York City journalism, focusing on the 100-year period when the *Herald* and other newspapers were located on Park Row. Contains information on Bennett, his newspaper, and his rivalry with Horace Greeley.

SEE ALSO: Nicholas Biddle; Horace Greeley; Joseph Pulitzer; Henry Morton Stanley.

RELATED ARTICLES in *Great Events from History: The Nineteenth Century, 1801-1900:* September 3, 1833: Birth of the Penny Press; 1895: Rise of Yellow Journalism.

THOMAS HART BENTON
American politician

A prominent United States senator from Missouri through three decades of the early nineteenth century, Benton championed Western expansion, public land distribution, and "hard money." He was also a leading supporter of President Andrew Jackson and his policies.

BORN: March 14, 1782; Harts Mill, near Hillsboro, North Carolina
DIED: April 10, 1858; Washington, D.C.
AREA OF ACHIEVEMENT: Government and politics

EARLY LIFE

Thomas Hart Benton was the son of Jesse and Ann Gooch Benton. His father was a lawyer who had been a secretary to the British governor of colonial North Carolina, a member of that state's legislature, and a speculator in Western lands. His mother was reared by her uncle, Thomas Hart, a prominent Virginia political and military leader with extensive wealth in land. Another uncle of Ann Gooch had been a British governor of Virginia.

Although Benton's father died when he was eight, his mother was able to keep the large family together. Benton attended local grammar schools and in 1798 enrolled at the recently established University of North Carolina, but was forced to leave in disgrace after one year when he was expelled for having stolen money from his three roommates. When he was nineteen, his mother moved the family of eight children and several slaves to a large tract of land south of Nashville, Tennessee, which had been claimed by Jesse Benton prior to his death.

After three years on the family farm, young Benton left to teach school and study law. In 1806, he was admitted to the Tennessee bar and rather quickly became a successful attorney whose philosophy and practice reflected the rural frontier environment. Benton specialized in land cases, and he began to pursue the reform of the Tennessee judicial system, an issue that helped him to a seat in the state senate and wide recognition.

During the War of 1812, Benton joined Andrew Jackson in raising volunteers for the military effort against England. For this work he received an appointment as a colonel of a regiment, but Jackson apparently did not trust him enough to place him in a field command, and Benton therefore saw no action in the war. In 1813, Benton's relationship with Jackson was interrupted by a wild tavern fight in which his brother, Jesse Benton, was severely stabbed, Jackson was shot, and Thomas Benton was cut with a knife and either pushed or thrown down a flight of stairs.

In the fall of 1815, when Benton was thirty-three years of age, he moved to Missouri Territory, settling in the small riverfront village of St. Louis. He rapidly involved himself in the affairs of the city. Between 1815 and 1820, he established an active law practice, ran for local political offices, bought a house and property to which he relocated his mother and family, killed another St. Louis attorney in a duel, and for two years served as the editor of the *St. Louis Enquirer*. At this point in his life, he was clearly an imposing figure who seldom backed away from a quarrel or a fight. He was a large and physically powerful person with a wide and muscular upper body, a large head, a short, thick neck, and wide shoulders. He possessed a long nose, high forehead, and dark, wavy hair that was often worn long in the back and at the temples.

Benton used the pages of the *St. Louis Enquirer* to address current political issues. He concentrated upon the development of the West, banking and currency, and national land distribution policies, and he vigorously advanced Missouri statehood. By 1820, he was clearly established as a leader in Missouri politics. When Missouri entered the Union as a result of the great compromise of 1820, David Barton and Thomas Hart Benton were selected to represent the new state in the U.S. Senate.

LIFE'S WORK

After a four-week horseback ride from St. Louis, Benton reached Washington, D.C., in mid-November of 1820 to begin a celebrated thirty-year career in the Senate. En route to the capital, he stopped at the Cherry Grove Plantation, near Lexington, Virginia, and proposed marriage to Elizabeth McDowell, whom he had met in 1815. She accepted the offer and the marriage took place in March of 1821.

Once he was in the Senate, Benton moved quickly to an active involvement in national issues. He first pressed forward those items with a Missouri base and about which he had written in the *St. Louis Enquirer:* the opening of government mineral lands, the development of the Oregon country, federal support of the Western fur trade, and the revision of the national land distribution policy. During the early months of 1824, he introduced two proposals that became closely identified with him and that he would continue to promote throughout his senatorial career: the elimination of the electoral college and the graduated land distribution system. In the former, his goal was to amend the Constitution so that the president and vice president could be directly elected by the people; in the latter, he pursued legislation to reduce the price of public lands by twenty-five cents per acre per year until the land was available at no cost. This practice, he argued, not only would broaden the base of the new democratic system but also would effectively serve to increase the prosperity of the entire nation.

As a result of the controversies surrounding the presidential election of 1824, Benton and Jackson established a close personal and political relationship as a result of which the Missouri senator was elevated to a leadership position in the Democratic Party. When Jacksonian Democracy carried Jackson into the presidency in 1828, Benton became the leading Jacksonian in the Senate and one of the most powerful men in American government in the first half of the nineteenth century. He was often mentioned as a possible candidate for the presidency himself, but he quickly rejected such promotion.

As a member of Jackson's famous Kitchen Cabinet, Benton led the fight to oppose the rechartering of the Bank of the United States and successfully expunged from the record the Senate resolution censuring Jackson for his role in the famous bank struggle. Benton also became the most ardent champion of hard-money policies—that is, those favoring a money system based upon the circulation of gold and silver only. It was his view that such a policy would best serve the common people, as paper currency was too easily manipulated by people of privilege. To this end, he prepared Jackson's famous 1836 Specie Circular, which required that public land purchases be made only with gold or silver coin. Because of his dedication to this issue, he received the nickname "Old Bullion."

Benton also played a key role in the Texas and Oregon annexation controversies. Although he was an ardent expansionist and westerner, he opposed the acquisition of Texas in 1845 out of concern that it was unfair to Mexico and would lead to war between the two new nations. He was successful in his efforts to establish the northern boundary of Oregon at the forty-ninth latitude rather than the 54-40 line favored by many Americans in 1844 and 1845. His position on these two issues lost him much support in his home state, and he only narrowly won reelection to the Senate in 1844.

In spite of his opposition to the Texas annexation and resulting war with Mexico, Benton supported the American war effort and served as chairman of the Senate Military Affairs Committee and as an important military adviser to President James K. Polk. In fact, Polk, who was suspicious of the leading field generals who were members of the Whig Party, extended to Benton the unprecedented position of joint military-diplomatic leader of the American war effort with a rank of major general. Benton considered the offer but rejected it when he could not receive from Polk the pledge of authority that he believed should cohere to such a position.

The American victory in the Mexican War and the subsequent annexation of vast new territories raised the issue of slavery to the forefront of the national political scene in 1848-1850. Although Benton was a slaveholder all of his adult life, he opposed slavery's expansion and expressed contempt for both secessionists and abolitionists. He reacted vigorously to John C. Calhoun's resolutions for noninterference with slavery in the new territories and was angered by the Missouri legislature's 1849 endorsement of the action.

The Missouri resolutions assumed a strong proslavery position and directed the two Missouri senators to act accordingly. Benton spent most of 1849 in Missouri campaigning against this legislative policy and directive, and conducted a statewide speaking tour in an effort to reverse

BENTON ON THE NATIONAL BANK

As one of President Andrew Jackson's strongest supporters, Senator Thomas Hart Benton opposed the rechartering of the Bank of the United States and deeply resented a Senate resolution formally censuring Jackson for his opposition to the bank. On January 12, 1837, Benton asked the Senate to expunge from its official record its resolution censuring Jackson. This extract is from the opening of Benton's speech.

It is now three years since the resolve was adopted by the Senate, which it is my present motion to expunge from the journal. At the moment that this resolve was adopted, I gave notice of my intention to move to expunge it; and then expressed my confident belief that the motion would eventually prevail. That expression of confidence was not an ebullition of vanity, or a presumptuous calculation, intended to accelerate the event it affected to foretell. It was not a vain boast, or an idle assumption, but was the result of a deep conviction of the injustice done President Jackson, and a thorough reliance upon the justice of the American people. I felt that the President had been wronged; and my heart told me that this wrong would be redressed! The event proves that I was not mistaken. The question of expunging this resolution has been carried to the people, and their decision has been had upon it. They decide in favor of the expurgation; and their decision has been both made and manifested, and communicated to us in a great variety of ways. A great number of States have expressly instructed their Senators to vote for this expurgation. A very great majority of the States have elected Senators and Representatives to Congress, upon the express ground of favoring this expurgation. The Bank of the United States, which took the initiative in the accusation against the President, and furnished the material, and worked the machinery which was used against him, and which was then so powerful on this floor, has become more and more odious to the public mind, and musters now but a slender phalanx of friends in the two Houses of Congress. The late Presidential election furnishes additional evidence of public sentiment. The candidate who was the friend of President Jackson, the supporter of his administration, and the avowed advocate for the expurgation, has received a large majority of the suffrages of the whole Union, and that after an express declaration of his sentiments on this precise point. The evidence of the public will, exhibited in all these forms, is too manifest to be mistaken, too explicit to require illustration, and too imperative to be disregarded. Omitting details and specific enumeration of proofs, I refer to our own files for the instructions to expunge—to the complexion of the two Houses for the temper of the people—to the denationalized condition of the Bank of the United States for the fate of the imperious accuser—and to the issue of the Presidential election for the answer of the Union.

Source: Thomas Hart Benton, "Remarks to the United States Senate on the Expunging Resolution."

the action. This was a turbulent affair marked by name-calling, charges, countercharges, and threats of violence.

The 1850 session of the U.S. Senate was one of the most famous in its history. For Thomas Hart Benton, it was one of the most crucial. He was a vigorous opponent of the slavery sections of the great compromise of that year as he believed there was too much sympathy for proslavery interests and secessionist threats. His rhetoric of opposition to Henry Clay's resolutions was direct and critical and elicited a strong response from southern senators. On one occasion, Senator Henry S. Foote of Mississippi drew and aimed a loaded revolver at the Missouri senator on the Senate floor. Benton's strong and highly publicized opposition to sections of the 1850 compromise left him with a severely weakened political base at home, and when the Missouri legislature in January of 1851 moved to the senatorial election, Benton lost to the Whig and anti-Benton candidate Henry S. Geyer, bringing his thirty-year Senate career to a close.

Frustrated by his defeat in the Missouri legislature for reelection to the Senate, the sixty-nine-year-old Benton launched a campaign for election to the House of Representatives. Few people have ever pursued a House of Representatives seat with as much to prove as Benton did in 1852—and, for the moment, victory was his. From 1853 to 1854, he returned to Congress as a member of the House of Representatives, where he took the lead in opposing the Kansas-Nebraska Act as well as all other attempts to extend slavery into the territories. Because of his determined position on this issue, he lost further support in his home state, and his effort to win reelection to the House seat failed in 1854.

Undaunted by this reversal, Benton developed an unsuccessful campaign for the governorship of Missouri in 1856 and worked nationally for the election of James Buchanan and the Democratic Party, refusing to vote for John C. Frémont, who headed the newly formed and sectional Republican Party, even though Frémont was his son-in-law, having married his daughter, Jessie.

With his political defeats in 1854 and 1856 and the death of his wife in 1854, Benton retired to his Washington, D.C., home to work on a number of writing projects. He continued an active schedule of appearances at political rallies and public speeches. He published a large two-volume summary of his thirty-year Senate career in 1854-1856, a sixteen-volume *Abridgement of the Debates of Congress from 1789 to 1856* (1857-1861), and a historical and legal examination of the *Dred Scott* decision, *Examination of the Dred Scott Case* (1857). His work in this direction was hampered by the increasing pain and complications of cancer and a fire that destroyed his home and personal records. The final page of his collection of the debates in Congress was completed on April 9, 1858. He died early the next morning, April 10, 1858, at the age of seventy-six. His wife and two sons had preceded him in death; four daughters survived.

SIGNIFICANCE

Thomas Hart Benton reflects, in many ways, the character and nature of the United States in the first half of the nineteenth century. An easterner who became a westerner, he was tough, bold, aggressive, egotistical, talkative, shrewd, self-educated, and fiercely independent. He found his career and gained a reputation on the frontier. He moved easily into law, banking, land investment, newspapers, the military, and politics. He extolled the strength and virtues of the common person in a society struggling with the issue of whether the elite or the common person should govern. As a leading proponent of Jacksonian democracy, Benton became the voice of union, a supporter of nationalism in an age of nationalism, and a builder of the nation in an era of change.

Benton believed that the great American West held the promise of the American future. He pressed for the development of the area from Missouri to Oregon and California and believed this region would provide unparalleled opportunity for the common person and unparalleled prosperity for the nation. To this end, more than anyone in American history, Benton stands as the champion of cheap land, developing policies and procedures that anticipated the great homestead movement later in the century.

To remove the benefits of privilege in a democratic society, he fought vigorously against the use of paper currency. It was his view that a financial system based upon the use of specie would protect "the people" from exploitation by people of influence. He was, thus, the leader of Jackson's war against the Bank of the United States and was the author of Jackson's famous and controversial Specie Circular.

In order to advance the cause of union and American nationalism, Benton sought to suppress the issue of slavery on the national political scene. He believed that this could best be accomplished by preventing the extension of slavery into the territories. His great emphasis upon this may have had much to do with keeping Missouri in the Union when the great crisis of nationalism came in 1861.

—Frank Nickell

FURTHER READING

Benton, Thomas Hart. *Thirty Years' View: Or, A History of the Working of the American Government for Thirty Years, from 1820 to 1850.* 2 vols. New York: D. Appleton, 1854-1856. An autobiographical summary of Benton's senatorial career. A valuable political commentary for insight into Benton and American politics of the era.

Chambers, William Nisbet. *Old Bullion Benton: Senator from the New West.* Boston: Little, Brown, 1956. A well-researched biography of Benton based upon extensive manuscript material. Follows Benton's life in chronological order and provides numerous quotations from his speeches and writings. This is the most widely used biography of Benton.

Kennedy, John F. *Profiles in Courage.* New York: Harper & Brothers, 1955. This well-known book contains a laudatory chapter on Benton, clearly emphasizing his great individualism and political independence. Kennedy finds Benton's opposition to the extension of slavery in the face of Missouri's perspective to be a courageous act of principle.

Meigs, William M. *The Life of Thomas Hart Benton.* Philadelphia: J. B. Lippincott, 1904. An early biography of Benton that depends much upon Benton's autobiography and the memoirs of his brilliant daughter Jessie and her husband John C. Frémont. Now outdated by the research of Chambers and Smith.

Oliver, Robert T. *History of Public Speaking in America.* Boston: Allyn & Bacon, 1965. A good analysis of Benton's oratorical skills with several examples of his most striking comments and most famous speeches. Incorporates the observations from several doctoral and masters' analyses of Benton's speaking methods.

Roosevelt, Theodore. *Thomas Hart Benton.* Boston: Houghton Mifflin, 1900. A biography in the American Statesmen series by President Theodore Roosevelt. Badly dated but reflects the interpretation of Benton held at the end of the nineteenth century. Roosevelt viewed Benton not as a great intellect but as a person unique for his hard work, determination, and speaking abilities.

Sandweiss, Eric. *St. Louis in the Century of Henry Shaw: A View Beyond the Garden Wall.* Columbia: University of Missouri Press, 2003. Collection of essays commemorating the two-hundredth anniversary of the birth of Shaw, a St. Louis entrepreneur and philanthropist. The essays describe life in nineteenth century St. Louis, including information about Benton and other prominent residents of the city.

Smith, Elbert B. *Francis Preston Blair.* New York: Macmillan, 1980. An excellent biography of Francis Blair, who was a Jacksonian editor and close personal friend of Benton. Provides good insight into Benton from the perspective of his closest friend and friendly biographer.

_____. *Magnificent Missourian: The Life of Thomas Hart Benton.* Philadelphia: J. B. Lippincott, 1958. A very well-written biography of Benton based exclusively upon manuscript and original sources. Provides excellent coverage of Benton's senatorial career and his role on the national political scene. Especially good coverage of Benton's role in the bank war.

SEE ALSO: John C. Calhoun; Andrew Jackson; James K. Polk.

RELATED ARTICLES in *Great Events from History: The Nineteenth Century, 1801-1900:* April 24, 1820: Congress Passes Land Act of 1820; January 19-27, 1830: Webster and Hayne Debate Slavery and Westward Expansion; July 10, 1832: Jackson Vetoes Rechartering of the Bank of the United States; September 4, 1841: Congress Passes Preemption Act of 1841; March 2, 1853-1857: Pacific Railroad Surveys; May 20, 1862: Lincoln Signs the Homestead Act.

CARL BENZ
German inventor

As one of the earliest inventors of a practical automobile, Benz made contributions of great importance to the modern way of life. He developed several features essential to automobile design and function.

BORN: November 25, 1844; Karlsruhe, Baden (now in Germany)
DIED: April 4, 1929; Ladenburg, Germany
ALSO KNOWN AS: Carl Friedrich Benz (full name)
AREA OF ACHIEVEMENT: Engineering

EARLY LIFE

When Carl Benz was only two years old, his father, a railroad engineer, died of pneumonia. His widowed mother was left with only a small income for the support of her family. Benz was able to contribute to the family finances by profiting from his interest in technical matters. While still a child, he repaired clocks and watches for the neighbors and had his own darkroom. He used the darkroom to develop pictures he took for the visitors to the area of the Black Forest around Karlsruhe, where he lived.

At secondary school he remained interested in technical subjects and became an assistant to the physics instructor. After attending Karlsruhe Polytechnic, he gained valuable experience by working for a manufacturer of engines. Even at this time, he had in mind the construction of a horseless carriage and spent evenings drawing plans for it. In 1871, he went to Mannheim to work for a firm that made wagons, pumps, and cranes. Soon thereafter, in 1872, he opened his own shop to produce engines. He was apparently confident of success, as he was married to Berta Ringer, whom he had met on a job in Pforzheim, just before starting out on his own.

Benz's confidence was not misplaced. His engines sold well, and he found investors who provided funds for him to establish the Mannheim Gas Engine Manufacturing Company. The new company employed forty people and was profitable. The venture lasted only a short time, however, as his shareholders were more interested in profits than in experimentation. They refused to allow him to use any of the profits for work on a horseless carriage, and he withdrew from the company, losing his investment after only three months of operations.

A man with Benz's experience, ability, and money-making record could not fail to attract sympathetic investors for long, and on October 1, 1883, Benz and Company was founded. Two Mannheim businesspeople, Max Caspar Rose and Friedrich Wilhelm Esslinger, were the investors in the new company for the production of "internal combustion engines after the plans of Carl Benz." While his new partners were not enthusiastic about his experiments with horseless carriages, they were willing to tolerate them as long as he attended to the primary business of the company—the production of stationary gas engines. They were not to regret their indulgence.

LIFE'S WORK

It is difficult to maintain that Benz was the first to invent the automobile because of the difficulty in establishing the definition of an automobile. Self-propelled, steam-driven vehicles had been in operation since the early nineteenth century. An Austrian, Siegfried Marcus, designed handcarts propelled by internal combustion engines during the 1860's, and French experimenters constructed similar vehicles. In these circumstances it cannot be maintained that Benz was the first to produce an automobile, but his vehicles were the earliest practical, marketable horseless carriages.

The plans that Benz had been developing for nearly two decades quickly bore fruit once he had the necessary resources at his disposal. Probably the most important feature of the motorized tricycle he produced in 1885 was the engine. This is not surprising given his years of experience in designing and building engines. It was a four-cycle, or Otto-cycle, engine that burned gasoline.

The innovation that made the Benz engine particularly important was the ignition system. For the most part, previous engines had used a heated tube for ignition. This system left much to be desired. Benz used an electrical ignition system consisting of a four-volt battery connected to an induction coil wrapped around an iron core. In the circuit was a flat spring that was magnetically attracted to the iron core when current flowed through the coil. The attraction of the spring, known as a trembler, broke the circuit, allowing the spring to return to its original position and to reestablish the circuit.

The result was a rapid vibration of the trembler and the production of a series of charges to the spark plug, which sparked and ignited the gas in the combustion chamber. The spark had to be produced at the correct time. To achieve the correct timing, a rotor made of insulating material with a metal chip in its circumference was introduced into the circuit. The rotor was connected mechanically to the piston-driven shaft in such a way that the metal chip closed the circuit to the spark plug when the piston was at the top of the compression stroke. A switch allowed the circuit to be opened to stop the engine. This ignition system was the basis for all others from that time to the present.

Other features of his motorized tricycle included elliptical rear springs, rack-and-pinion steering, and water cooling. Belts and chains transmitted power from the engine to the solid rear axle. Benz later claimed that he had driven the tricycle in the spring of 1885, and many consider this to have been the first automobile powered by an internal combustion engine. In the autumn of 1885, he tested the vehicle before witnesses. The test was a short one. In fact, Benz never made it to the road outside his workshop yard: He ran into a brick wall, but he and his passenger—his wife—escaped injury. There were other tests as he developed his design, but his first public notice came on June 4, 1886, when the *Neue Badische Landeszeitung* printed a description of the vehicle, followed on July 3, 1886, by a favorable report of a test-drive.

Benz continued to improve his invention by adding a sun and planet gear that provided a second gear. He applied for a patent for this feature in April, 1887. Further improvements included a larger engine (three horsepower instead of one horsepower), better springs, and more effective brakes. By 1887, the vehicle had reached such a stage of development that it was possible to market it.

The first customer for a Benz automobile was a Frenchman named Émile Roger, who saw one demonstrated at the Paris Exhibition of 1887. In the following year, Benz won a gold medal at the Imperial Exhibition in Munich. The publicity from these exhibitions apparently stimulated a number of orders. In 1889, the Benz Company employed fifty workers. Business was so brisk that Benz was able to find new partners who financed a move to a larger factory where the company began producing vehicles with four wheels in 1890.

BENZ'S FOUR-CYCLE ENGINE

The Otto-cycle engine had existed since the late 1870's, and its principle of operation had been established in the 1860's. It is called a four-cycle engine because the explosion of gasoline in the combustion chamber occurs only on every fourth stroke of the piston. During the first stroke, as the piston moves downward, atmospheric pressure forces the gaseous fuel into the piston cylinder through a valve. When the piston reaches the end of its downward movement, a spring closes the valve to prevent the gas from escaping as the piston makes its return, or second stroke. At the top of the second stroke the gas is compressed in the combustion chamber above the piston to about one-third of its normal volume. The gas is then ignited, and its expansion as it burns forces the piston down in its third, or power, stroke. When the power rises on its fourth stroke, it forces the burned gas out through an exhaust valve that is opened mechanically.

In order to convert the liquid gasoline to a gaseous state, a carburetor is necessary. The carburetor used by Benz was very simple. He routed the hot exhaust gases through a pipe that passed through a chamber containing liquid gasoline, thus warming it. Air admitted through holes in an outer container flowed over the evaporating gasoline, and the mixture of air and gasoline proceeded on to the combustion chamber. The mixture could be left rich in gasoline or leaned by the addition of air as required by means of a pipe with holes between the carburetor and combustion chamber. A sliding cover allowed more, or less, air to enter the holes.

The addition of a fourth wheel was one of the few concessions Benz was to make to those who wanted him to maintain an up-to-date design. He appears to have regarded the design of 1890 as final and refused to make changes in it. Even when he consented to the addition of a hood to the front of the car, it was only an empty shell added for the sake of appearance. He insisted on keeping the engine at the rear. In 1905, he finally bowed to pressure from his colleagues and allowed sweeping design changes, but he and his wife continued to drive their older models.

Photographs of Benz posing as driver of his automobiles show a man of medium stature, dark hair, and constantly changing facial hair. He always wore a large mustache, but his goatees came and went presumably in accord with fashions of the day. Pictures of him in later life indicate that he became thinner and the hair and mustache turned white. The later photographs are of a man with a prominent, sharp nose and deep-set eyes.

Benz was not alone in the attempt to build a horseless carriage. His most significant German rival was Gottlieb Daimler. Many argue that Daimler should be regarded as the inventor of a practical, engine-driven vehicle with internal combustion. His engine was better in many respects, and his patent of August, 1885, predates Benz's by five months. Benz's adherents concede these points but note that Daimler's work involved a motorcycle rather than a three- or four-wheeled vehicle. Competition between the two involved more than mere claims to priority. The two companies vied for sales, especially in France and Germany. It was for the sake of the French market that the Daimler product became known as the Mercedes. The French distributor suggested the name of his daughter, Mercedes, as sounding more French than Daimler and, therefore, more acceptable to the French buying public. Rivalry between Benz and Daimler was strictly on a commercial basis; they had never met when Daimler died in 1900.

During the economic depression that followed World War I in Germany, both the Daimler and Benz companies faltered. That led to their merger to form Mercedes-Benz in 1926. By that time Benz had little to do with the active management of the company that he had founded nearly forty years before.

SIGNIFICANCE

The inventive genius of Carl Benz was considerable. Working independently, he managed to invent the necessary components for an automobile and combine them in a practical machine. The fact that Daimler and others produced better engines and made wider use of them in boats and for other applications does not detract from his accomplishments. Whether a motorized tricycle actually qualifies as the first automobile and whether it deserves such a title more than a motorcycle are less important concerns in assessing Benz's career than his status as a pioneer in the marketing of automobiles. His contributions were certainly recognized as significant during his lifetime. Early examples of his cars were in museums, and two days before his death, on April 4, 1929, a procession of several hundred automobiles drove from Heidelberg to his house in Ladenburg, where dignitaries delivered a number of speeches acclaiming him as the inventor of the automobile.

As shown by the earlier inventions of Siegfried Marcus, it is one thing to produce a self-propelled vehicle but quite another to turn it into something that people will buy in significant numbers. It was to take the mass production techniques of Henry Ford and others to make the automobile into more than a plaything of the rich, but Benz and his rivals brought the idea of automobile ownership and its practicality into the minds of the buying public.

—*Philip Dwight Jones*

FURTHER READING

Auer, Greg. "Inventor of the Three-Wheeler Was Never Whiz Kid at Business." *Automotive News* 75, no. 5908 (December 18, 2000): 20E. Tribute to Benz and his invention. Focuses on Benz's wife, Bertha Ringer, who publicized her husband's invention by taking the first automobile trip.

Kames, Beverly Rae. *The Star and the Laurel: The Centennial History of Daimler, Mercedes, and Benz, 1886-1986*. Montvale, N.J.: Mercedes-Benz of North America, 1986. The history of Daimler-Benz's first hundred years, including information on Benz's and Daimler's inventions before and after they joined forces.

Karwatka, Dennis. "Technology's Past." *Tech Directions* 56, no. 6 (January, 1997): 10. Biography of Benz, credited as the inventor of the first car powered by an internal combustion engine. Includes information about Benz's machine shop and the products he manufactured.

Nevins, Allan. *Ford: The Times, the Man, and the Company*. New York: Charles Scribner's Sons, 1954. Although devoted to Henry Ford, the first volume of this work contains considerable discussion of the development of the early automobile in general and of the contributions of Benz in particular. It also contains a useful bibliography for use in further research on the early development of the automobile.

Nixon, St. John C. *The Invention of the Automobile*. London: Country Life, 1936. This book is the story of Benz and Daimler and the creation of their company. Most of it is devoted to Benz, and it gives him the lion's share of credit for the invention of the automobile, proclaiming him as its inventor. Contains helpful illustrations and photographs of several Daimler cars as well as a comparative chronology of Daimler's and Benz's lives.

Nye, Doug. *Carl Benz and the Motor Car*. London: Priory Press, 1973. Brief (96-page) discussion of Benz's life and invention.

Poole, Lynn, and Gray Poole. *Men Who Pioneered Inventions*. New York: Dodd, Mead, 1969. A book intended for juvenile readers. Gives considerable credit to Benz and boldly recognizes him as the inventor of the automobile.

Roberts, Peter. *Veteran and Vintage Cars*. London: Paul Hamlyn, 1963. One of the more readily available picture books dealing with early automobiles. Contains a descriptive text as well as color photographs and reproductions of advertisements. Covers the period to 1914 and has illustrations of the Benz products.

Singer, Charles, et al., eds. *The Late Nineteenth Century, c. 1850 to c. 1900.* Vol. 5 in *A History of Technology.* New York: Oxford University Press, 1958. A useful book for more detailed explanations of the technical aspects of the work of Benz and the other early designers of internal combustion engines. The authors do not enter into the discussion of priority in the invention of the automobile.

SEE ALSO: Gottlieb Daimler; Rudolf Diesel; Étienne Lenoir; Nikolaus August Otto.

RELATED ARTICLE in *Great Events from History: The Nineteenth Century, 1801-1900:* January 29, 1886: Benz Patents the First Practical Automobile.

HECTOR BERLIOZ

French composer

One of the foremost exponents of Romanticism, Berlioz extended the art of orchestration in compositions of striking originality. His writings—which include a treatise on orchestration and a colorful memoir of his life—made contributions to both musical craft and cultural history. During his lifetime Berlioz's music attained more popularity outside France than within it, where the eccentric notoriety of the man often overshadowed his genius.

BORN: December 11, 1803; La Côte-Saint-André, France
DIED: March 8, 1869; Paris, France
ALSO KNOWN AS: Louis-Hector Berlioz (full name)
AREA OF ACHIEVEMENT: Music

EARLY LIFE

Louis-Hector Berlioz (behr-lee-ohs) was born on the morning of December 11, 1803, in the town of La Côte-Saint-André, about fifty-five kilometers northwest of Grenoble, France. Hector was the first of six children born to Louis-Joseph and Marie Antoinette Berlioz; his family, which had prospered over generations from tanning and other enterprises, could be traced on his father's side to the beginning of the seventeenth century. Louis Berlioz was a kindly but serious man, who had received his medical degree in Paris only months after Hector's birth; though culturally and intellectually refined far beyond the custom of his provincial locale, he came to be loved by the peasants he served. Hector's mother figures in his life much less prominently than her husband. As a devout Roman Catholic, she provided him with a religious upbringing, but it seems not to have had a lasting impact.

After briefly attending school in La Côte, Berlioz's education was directed with great success by his father at home. His studies included mathematics, history, and French literature, but geography became his favorite topic. At an early age, he also came to love Vergil's *Aeneid* (c. 29-19 B.C.E.), learning to read the Roman author in the original Latin. At the age of twelve, on a family holiday in nearby Meylan, he experienced his first feelings of romantic love, a passion for a young woman of eighteen named Estelle Deboeuf. This brief, one-sided experience only slowly lost its hold upon his imagination.

Part of Berlioz's education at home consisted of lessons in practical music making; Hector had learned to play the flageolet, a form of recorder, after finding one in a bureau drawer at home; in his teens, he was given a flute, which he soon learned to play capably. Later, he learned the guitar, but there was no piano in his home, and he never learned the instrument aside from picking out harmonies on its keys. Hector was not a child prodigy, but his natural musical gifts soon led him to compose short instrumental and vocal works, which he would play with family and friends. At the age of fifteen, he was naïvely offering his pieces to a well-known publisher.

Louis Berlioz had determined that his son should follow a medical career and set about preparing Hector and a young friend for medical studies, which commenced in Paris in 1821. Hector's intellectual interest in his subjects was sincere, and he later praised some of the lecturers, but, when the course of study turned to the dissection of human cadavers, he recoiled violently from the work.

By 1824, Berlioz no longer pretended that he was studying medicine. Since the previous year, he had been a student in the classes of the composer Jean-François Le Sueur, who took a warm interest in him, and much of his time was devoted to attending opera performances, reading scores in the library of the music conservatory, and composing. This development was viewed with dismay by Berlioz's parents, who had hoped that a few disappointments with music would persuade him to abandon his plans for a musical career. Despite occasional modest successes in the performance of his works, his failure to pass a music examination in 1826 caused his father to demand his return to La Côte. Louis persuaded his son to attempt once more to pass the examination; if he failed, he would choose a different profession.

By living extremely frugally and giving lessons in singing, flute, and guitar, Belioz was repaying a loan given by an acquaintance to finance a concert, when the thoughtless creditor requested the balance owing from Berlioz's father. Enraged by Hector's improvidence, Louis paid the debt but terminated Hector's allowance, and the twenty-three-year-old composer was thrown into virtual poverty, surviving only by taking a job in a theater chorus. Disciplining mind and body, however, he continued his studies. After a period of months, he passed the examination qualifying him to compete for the Prix de Rome, a lucrative award of the Academy of Fine Arts of the Institute of France. Soon after, his father restored his allowance, and Berlioz was able to continue his operagoing on a grand scale. His favorite composers at the time were Christoph Gluck and Gaspare Spontini, but he despised the popular Gioacchino Rossini.

Hector Berlioz. (Library of Congress)

Like many of his contemporaries who regarded themselves as Romantic artists, Berlioz embraced the experience and display of emotion. In 1827, a company of actors arrived from England to present a season of performances of plays by William Shakespeare. This was Berlioz's overwhelming introduction to Shakespeare on the stage, and it was also the beginning of his love for the actress Harriet Smithson, who played Ophelia on opening night. Berlioz's involved and somewhat ostentatious passion for Henriette (as she is called in his memoirs) was to play a large part in the inspiration for his *Symphonie fantastique* (1830) and its sequel, *Le Retour à la vie* (1831), or *Lélio*, as it was later known. Unsuccessful attempts to get Henriette's attention, including public concerts of his own work, were finally abandoned, but the beautiful and talented Henriette had already left her mark on Hector's imagination.

Berlioz continued his musical studies at the conservatoire and began, around 1829, to write articles on music for the Paris press. Literary work, which he generally undertook to relieve his strained finances, often seemed to Berlioz to be a curse, but he had a natural capacity for writing and his contributions to music criticism are substantial. His literary experience also led him to compose music to poems by Victor Hugo and others, and the first composition to which Berlioz gave an opus number, *Huit Scènes de Faust* (1828), was based upon Johann Wolfgang von Goethe's *Faust: Eine Tragödie* (1808). In 1830, *The Death of Sardanapalus* was the subject of a composition that won for him the Prix de Rome on his fourth attempt. The fictional but grotesque story of *Sardanapalus* had been broached only three years before by the painter Eugène Delacroix, partly relieving Berlioz of the reputation for excess that had dogged his previous competition efforts.

In the spring of 1830, Berlioz again fell in love, this time with a nineteen-year-old pianist, Marie Moke. They were soon engaged, despite the prospect of being separated by Berlioz's impending year-long stay in Rome, a condition of the Prix de Rome stipend. Sensing that his absence would be a kind of spiritual imprisonment, he tried to gain an exemption from the requirement, but the authorities would not agree to it. His fiancé's family was similarly unyielding, making the engagement conditional both upon his absence and upon the success of a pending performance of his *Symphonie fantastique*. After the work was successfully presented in December, Berlioz left for Rome, stopping to visit his family at La Côte early in the new year.

In residence at the French Academy in Rome for only a few weeks, growing fears about his engagement drove him to abandon the academy. Soon he learned in a letter from Marie's mother that his fiancé was to marry a prosperous man of fifty-eight. Berlioz, enraged, became intent upon murder and suicide, and got as far as Nice before thinking better of his plan. Berlioz was allowed to return to the academy, but he was often moody, bored, and distracted in Rome, which was to him little more than a museum. Preferring nature to city life, he toured the surrounding countryside on foot, gathering impressions of its landscape and inhabitants that later inspired the symphonic work *Harold in Italy* (1834), a musical essay evoking the atmosphere of Lord Byron's poem *Childe Harold's Pilgrimage* (1812-1818, 1819). After more than a year in Italy, Berlioz returned to Paris, arriving in the capital on November 6, 1832. On the eve of his thirtieth year, he had been well seasoned by artistic struggles and by painful episodes in his personal life.

LIFE'S WORK

The professional difficulties of Berlioz's career were often concerned with finances or with the quality of performances that could be extracted from the French orchestras of the day. Sometimes these circumstances met to produce concerts that were financial as well as artistic failures, but more often Berlioz, an excellent conductor, fared well with Parisian audiences. A concert of December 9, 1832, designed to reintroduce himself to the public, featured the *Symphonie fantastique* and *Lélio*. Harriet Smithson, his unrequited love of four years past, was in the audience, doubtless uneasily aware that the two works had grown out of Berlioz's passion for her in 1827-1828. The following day they met for the first time, and after months of fervent but strained courtship they were married. In August, 1834, their only child, Louis, was born.

The two works of that fateful December concert were conceived as a spiritual autobiography in music. From the moment Berlioz discovered his tragic muse in Henriette's portrayals of Ophelia and Juliet, he had been immersed in a painful rapture that for a time had made creative activity almost impossible, and *Symphonie fantastique* was both a fulfillment and an exorcism of Berlioz's torment. It is a "program symphony," evoking "an episode in the life of an artist," and follows a novelistic scenario including a ball, a march to execution, and a witches' Sabbath. For all of its eccentricities and weaknesses, it is an influential landmark in music. *Lélio*, however, is generally regarded as a gratuitous, provocatively egotistic, and somewhat incoherent sequel. The true artistic sequel to the *Symphonie fantastique* is Berlioz's *Harold in Italy*, featuring a solo viola part that gives the symphony something of the nature of a concerto.

The German poet Heinrich Heine, who was a friend of Berlioz, described the latter as "an immense nightingale, or a lark the size of an eagle," whose music "causes me to dream of fabulous empires with fabulous sins." This characterization encompasses something of the spirit of the man as well as his appearance: Berlioz's artistic soul was both lyric and violent, as his appearance could seem either wistful or dramatic in turn. He was of medium height and angular, with a pronounced beaklike nose framed by intense, deep-set eyes and a great mass of hair.

The decade of 1835 through 1845 brought Berlioz fame both as composer and as conductor, but his successes were punctuated by the same kind of difficulties he had faced in previous years. He seems to have been a difficult man and was rarely at peace with the official cultural apparatus or with his colleagues. Financial problems continued and were intensified by the failure of Henriette's career following a leg injury (by 1842, Berlioz had separated from her, though his affection survived to her death in 1854). His journalistic work and his need continually to promote his own compositions strained his health, which was not robust. Nevertheless, these were the years in which he composed some of his greatest works, including the *Messe de morts*, or *Requiem* (1837), the opera *Benvenuto Cellini* (1834-1838), the symphony *Roméo et Juliette* (1839), and the dramatic cantata *La Damnation de Faust* (1846), derived in part from his early *Huit Scènes de Faust*.

The *Requiem*, commissioned by the government for a civic funeral, shows Berlioz in full command both of his musical materials and of his sense of public occasion.

Berlioz specified for the work 190 instruments and 210 voices, not including timpani and brass choirs to be heard at a distance. Certain passages achieve a great acoustical and emotional effect, but other parts of the mass are models of delicacy. Berlioz's reputation for colossal effect is only partly justified, for he knew how to use large musical forces with restraint.

In 1842, Berlioz began a series of trips abroad that were to bring him many artistic triumphs and, not incidentally, a further source of income. He was in demand both as composer and conductor, and the accounts he gives in his memoirs of his travels in England, Germany, Austria, Hungary, and Russia show him directing his own works as well as those of Gluck, Ludwig van Beethoven, and others. His journeys also gave him an opportunity to meet many of the leading performers and composers of Europe, including Franz Liszt, Robert Schumann, and Richard Wagner, with whom he had a long-standing but ambivalent relationship.

When Berlioz was in his forties, his musical style began to show signs of retreat from the adventurous Romanticism of his youth. Official honors had already come his way: In 1839, he was made a member of the Legion of Honor and was given a modest salary as an official of the conservatory library. His treatise on orchestration and his *Voyage musical en Allemagne et en Italie* (a musical voyage in Germany and Italy) were published in 1844. Beyond these signs of increasing acceptance, however, the subtle moderation of his artistic outlook can be traced to other circumstances.

Berlioz was drained by work undertaken for the sake of paying for two households—Henriette's and his own; his son, Louis, who had become a sailor, was often troublesome. More important, though, the melancholy streak in his character came to overrule his penchant for ostentation and experimentation. Berlioz turned more and more to the poetry of Vergil, which had stirred him as a child; a current of classicism emerged in his musical thought, expressing a conception of beauty that had perhaps lain dormant in him since youth. From this sensibility emerged much of Berlioz's late work: *L'Enfance du Christ*, first performed in December, 1854, belongs to this late phase of his career; *Les Troyens* (1856-1858), with a libretto by Berlioz, is its culmination.

Berlioz's musical work might well have ended with the staging of *Les Troyens*—he was suffering increasingly from an ill-defined internal malady—but a final commission, the two-act opera *Béatrice et Bénédict*, occupied him during 1860-1862. Based upon Shakespeare's *Much Ado About Nothing* (1598-1599), it is a gracious comedy that Berlioz found to be a relaxation after the immense labors of *Les Troyens*.

Berlioz's last years brought him personal loss; in 1862, his second wife, Marie Recio, died suddenly. Her mother selflessly continued to look after Berlioz. In 1867, he was shattered by the news of his son's death in Havana from a fever. Their relationship had been a close one, marked on the father's side by patience and on the son's by intense devotion. In his grief and physical suffering, Berlioz told a close friend that he hardly knew how he managed to continue living. However, in the winter of 1867-1868, he made a successful last tour to Russia on the invitation of the Grand Duchess Helena. To this evidence of his undiminished artistic renown, he is said to have exclaimed "Why am I so old and feeble?" In fact, he was to survive only one more year. In March, 1868, he suffered a serious fall while visiting the rocky coast near Nice; although by August he had recovered enough to attend a musical festival in Grenoble, he was unwell and began to experience loss of memory. After returning to Paris, he died on March 8, 1869.

SIGNIFICANCE

Hector Berlioz was an artist whose career was formed to a great extent by the era into which he was born, the extraordinary period of upheaval when Napoleon I sought to subjugate Europe. The military conflicts of the period from 1805 to 1815 were followed in France by a reactionary politics that robbed the nation of economic and cultural vitality. Although Berlioz was, by most standards, not a political person, he was obliged to struggle against the cultural environment produced by politics. The soil on which his artistic genius had to take root was shallow and impoverished, and throughout his life—even discounting his contrary personality and his own exaggerations of his trials—he had to struggle against many odds, though they were perhaps more persistent than they were overwhelming.

The factor of temperament in Berlioz was undoubtedly strong. His precocious affinity for Vergil's poetry is shown in an anecdote from his memoirs, where he recalls bursting into tears while reciting to his father the episode of the death of Dido in the *Aeneid*. Sensitivity to landscape—a legacy both of his formative environment and early literary experiences—become bonded, in the encounter with Estelle, to an enduring conception of ideal love. Around all of these circumstances lingers an echo of classical myth with a primitive accent, which the young provincial carried with him to Paris. Berlioz's innate depth of sensibility was to be both a strength and a burden: It was a source of creative vitality that made him steadfast in the face of mediocre convention, but it also caused conflict in his professional relationships and probably narrowed his musical sympathies beyond necessity.

In his early years in Paris, Berlioz became a leading figure of the Romantic movement, acquiring a reputation as a somewhat rebellious genius. His unquestioned originality in certain spheres of musical composition was countered by a frequent lack of judgment in others. As an orchestrator he charted new territory, but his harmony and rhythm have often been criticized. Berlioz's sense of melody has also had many detractors, but in fact he was a fine and original melodist at times and was capable of great delicacy of feeling. His reputation as a seeker after effects is not unjustified, but many of the effects are astonishingly impressive—as in the offstage brass choirs of the *Requiem*, for example.

Berlioz's defiance of authority, his artistic daring, and the vigor of his journalistic rhetoric closely harmonize with the modern image of the Romantic artist, but the view of life he evoked in many of his major works exceeds the usual bounds of Romantic darkness. His capacity for despair, as man and artist, contrasts with more resilient figures such as Victor Hugo and Eugène Delacroix, who were his contemporaries. Though he gravitated toward classical ideals in his later music, clarity and harmony were never his secure possessions, either in art or in life.

—C. S. McConnell

FURTHER READING

Barzun, Jacques. *Berlioz and the Romantic Century*. 3d ed. 2 vols. New York: Columbia University Press, 1969. First published in 1950, Barzun's massive study was conceived in the spirit of the poet W. H. Auden's remark that "whoever wants to know about the nineteenth century must know about Berlioz." The author succeeds in being charming as well as thorough, and he provides an unmatched bibliography.

_____. *Berlioz and His Century: An Introduction to the Age of Romanticism*. Chicago: University of Chicago Press, 1982. This condensation of Barzun's two-volume work on Berlioz concentrates on the composer's life rather than his music. It has no sense of being a mere editing of the earlier books, but it is an introduction to Romanticism only in the most oblique way; as such, it cannot be substituted for a true survey of the period of Berlioz's life.

Berlioz, Hector. *The Memoirs of Hector Berlioz: Member of the French Institute, Including His Travels in Italy, Germany, Russia, and England, 1803-1865*. Edited and translated by David Cairns. London: Gollancz, 1969. One of the great documents of nineteenth century European culture, but one that has to be read skeptically. Apart from some portions of the book that provide details of Berlioz's concerts abroad, it is highly entertaining. Berlioz declined to write an autobiography in the manner of Jean-Jacques Rousseau, but there is a quantity of intense self-revelation nevertheless.

Bloom, Peter. *The Life of Berlioz*. New York: Cambridge University Press, 1998. Biography, placing Berlioz's life within the context of nineteenth century French history. Does not provide musical examples or analysis.

Cairns, David. *Berlioz*. 2 vols. Berkeley: University of California Press, 1999. Detailed narrative of Berlioz's life, based in part on previously unused material. Does not provide an analysis of Berlioz's music or musical examples.

Elliot, J. H. *Berlioz*. London: J. M. Dent & Sons, 1938. A volume in the Master Musicians series, it efficiently fulfills all the standard requirements of biography, description, and analysis. Its perspective, though intelligently critical, appears inordinately fastidious. Excellent appendixes—a calendar, list of works, and the like—redeem the author's somewhat limited enthusiasm for his subject.

Macdonald, Hugh. *Berlioz*. New York: Oxford University Press, 2000. A comprehensive work that offers a biography, analysis of Berlioz's character, and an examination of his compositions, tracing his musical influences and describing his compositions.

Rose, Michael. *Berlioz Remembered*. London: Faber & Faber, 2001. Rose seeks to supplement Berlioz's memoirs by focusing on the effect the producer had on other people, including his friends, enemies, supporters, and critics.

Rushton, Julian. *The Musical Language of Berlioz*. Cambridge, England: Cambridge University Press, 1983. A work of critical scholarship rather than biography, this book may be consulted by the general reader for its introductory and concluding chapters and for its more recent bibliography.

Wotton, Tom S. *Berlioz*. New York: Johnson Reprint, 1969. Barzun honored Wotton as the foremost Berlioz scholar of his time, but the style and diction of the book are rather antiquated.

SEE ALSO: Lord Byron; Léo Delibes; César Franck; Charles Gounod; Modest Mussorgsky.

RELATED ARTICLES in *Great Events from History: The Nineteenth Century, 1801-1900:* April 7, 1805: Beethoven's *Eroica* Symphony Introduces the Romantic Age; December 22, 1894: Debussy's *Prelude to the Afternoon of a Faun* Premieres.

CLAUDE BERNARD
French physiologist

Bernard has been dubbed the "Father of Physiology," for developing the experimental methods and conceptual framework needed to change physiology from a primarily deductive science based on statistics to one that can discover empirical data using procedures borrowed from chemistry.

BORN: July 12, 1813; Saint-Julien, France
DIED: February 10, 1878; Paris, France
AREAS OF ACHIEVEMENT: Medicine, science and technology

EARLY LIFE

The parents of Claude Bernard (behr-nar) were vineyard workers, and Bernard retained a lifelong attachment to the vineyards, returning there each fall to relax and help with the grape harvest and, later, to make his own wine. In the fields of his boyhood, he learned to observe nature and developed the manual dexterity and precision necessary for both wine making and scientific research. His father apparently died while Bernard was still a youth, though little is known concerning him. It is known, however, that Bernard adored his pious mother.

Bernard's early schooling was in the Jesuit school at Villefranche and later at the Collège de Thoissey, where he studied the humanities but little science or philosophy. When he finished this education, he became a pharmacy apprentice and during his evenings attended the theater and wrote a light comedy, *La Rose du Rhône*, and a five-act drama, *Arthur de Bretagne* (1887). His goal of becoming a playwright was shattered when the well-known literary critic Saint-Marc Girardin judged his drama as lacking merit and the author as without literary promise. The critic urged him to study medicine instead.

Bernard entered medical school in 1834 but divided his time between attending lectures and studying and giving lessons at a girls' school to help his mother pay the bills. His grades were only average, and when he took the internship examination in 1839, he ranked twenty-sixth out of twenty-nine. He began his internship, which was split between two hospitals.

At one of the hospitals, the Hôtel Dieu, Bernard became an unpaid assistant to a clinician and professor of physiology at the Collège de France, François Magendie. This experience had a life-changing effect on Bernard, for Magendie was an outspoken devotee of both experimentation and skepticism. Magendie recognized Bernard's talents in the laboratory and in 1841 hired him as an assistant on several projects. Bernard was granted his medical degree on December 7, 1843, on the basis of his thesis, *Du suc gastrique et de son rôle dans la nutrition* (1843; gastric juice and its role in metabolism). Earlier the same year, his first publication had appeared, *Recherches anatomiques et physiologiques sur la corde du tympan, pour servir à l'histoire de l'hémiplegie faciale* (1843; anatomical and physiological research on the chorda tympani).

In 1844, Bernard failed the examination for a teaching position with the faculty of medicine. Disheartened, he resigned his position with Magendie and considered becoming a country doctor in his home village. A colleague suggested that he find a wife with a good dowry instead, and in July, 1845, he married the daughter of a Parisian doctor. His marriage to Marie Françoise Martin was a matter of financial convenience, allowing him to continue his research, but it was also to be the source of much unhappiness in the years ahead. His wife obtained a legal separation from him in 1870, partly because of her opposition to his vivisectionist experiments. Both sons born to the marriage died in infancy, and the two daughters, like their mother, renounced him and apparently refused to be reconciled with him even on his deathbed.

Between 1843 and 1845, he made discoveries on the chemical and nerve control of the gastric juices and on the role of bile and began experiments with curare and on the innervation of the vocal cords and the functions of the cranial nerves. With the money from the dowry, he was able to continue this research as well as initiate others, and he published a number of papers on various subjects through the mid-1840's.

LIFE'S WORK

The year 1848 is generally taken to be the year from which Bernard's mature work dates. In December, 1847, he became an assistant to Magendie at the Collège de France, and the following year began teaching the course on experimental medicine during the winter terms. He also became a charter member and the first vice president of the Société de Biologie, which indicates his growing stature within the scientific community.

In 1848, Bernard's research led him to two discoveries that were to provide not only new facts but also new ways of conceptualizing bodily functions. First, in his observations on the differences between the urine of carnivores and herbivores, he discovered the part played by the pancreas in the digestion of fats. He published the results of this discovery in *Du suc pancréatique, et de son rôle dans les phénomènes de la digestion* (1848; pancreatic juice and its role in the phenomena of digestion). Second, he discovered the glycogenous function of the liver. Formerly it was believed that the body could not produce sugars and was therefore dependent upon plants for their source. Bernard's discovery explained the constancy of sugar in the body and was instrumental in leading Bernard to a concept, which he first articulated during the late 1850's, of *milieu intérieur*, or internal environment.

Between the time that he first described this condition of a constant interior environment and his death, Bernard developed and extended the idea until it became the generalized and widely accepted biological notion of homeostasis. In his last comments about it, published in 1878, he explained that the organism does not exist in the *milieu extérieur* (the external environment of air or water) but rather in a liquid *milieu intérieur*, which is made of all the intracellular liquids of the organism. These liquids are the bases of all forms of cellular metabolism and the common factor of all simple chemical or physiological exchanges. The body's task is to maintain the stability of the *milieu intérieur*; hence, the task of the physiologist is to discover how this regulation occurs.

Bernard's work during the 1850's and 1860's was directed precisely to this task. In 1851, he discovered the control of local skin temperature by sympathetic nerves, and later he showed the importance of the nervous system in regulating the vascular system. In 1856, he demonstrated that curare blocks motor nerve endings, and the following year he reported that the toxic effect of carbon monoxide resulted from blocked respiration in the erythrocytes. He was finally able to isolate glycogen in a pure form in 1857.

Bernard started teaching during the early 1850's, and in his lectures he argued against vitalism in favor of what he called experimental determinism. He contended that the laws governing the functioning of the organism were precise and rigorous, with the laws of physics and chemistry being fundamental for understanding living phenomena. By varying conditions, the experimental biologists could make the organism respond in a strictly determined manner.

In 1865, Bernard had more time to work on his philosophical ideas, for he became too ill to teach or to conduct research. He retired to the vineyards and wrote his most famous work, *Introduction à l'étude de la médecine expérimentale* (1865; *An Introduction to the Study of Experimental Medicine*, 1927), which for many years was his only work translated into English. In this work, he showed his indebtedness to his mentor, Magendie, and to Auguste Comte's positivism; both stressed the necessity of making observations and determining facts from the evidence. Bernard was unwilling to be shackled by their strict Baconianism, and, against current opinion, he argued that the forming of hypotheses was an essential and necessary part of the scientific process.

The following year, the minister of public education asked Bernard to prepare a report on the state of physiology in France to be published on the occasion of the World Exposition of 1867. Instead of the objective, factual, historical report that was commissioned, Bernard wrote an ideological tract that continued his philosophical thinking. In his *Rapport sur les progrès et la marche de la physiologie générale en France* (1867; report on the progress and course of general physiology in France), he described his vision of a new brand of physiology founded on the concept of the *milieu intérieur* and the elucidation of regulatory functions. This report demonstrated what Bernard hoped physiology would become—not what it was.

In later years, Bernard continued to pursue his interests in the phenomena characteristic of all living organisms. He had begun to explore this issue in his lessons at the Sorbonne in 1864, and, when offered the chair of comparative physiology at the Musée d'Histoire Naturelle in 1868, he insisted that the chair be renamed "general physiology." This willingness to treat general biological problems instead of strictly medical ones not only restructured the way in which questions about living material, life processes, and the properties of living beings were framed and studied but also freed physiology from its subservience to medicine and established it as an independent discipline.

In 1869, Bernard returned to his teaching duties at the Collège de France. He attracted a large and diverse audience, including, at times, Louis Pasteur, and entertained them with demonstrations to support both his physiological and philosophical views. Bernard's ideas were publicized through ten works, the best known being *Leçons sur les propriétés des tissus vivants* (1866; lessons on the properties of living tissues) and *Leçons sur les phénomènes de la vie communs aux animaux et aux végétaux* (1878-1879; lessons on the phenomena of life common to animals and plants).

SIGNIFICANCE

The painting *Claude Bernard's Lesson in the Laboratory* by Léon Lhermitte delineates one of the most important aspects of Claude Bernard's work—his teaching and mentoring of younger scientists. In this picture, Bernard, with dark hair and eyes, is dressed in a white gardener's apron and wears a metal pince-nez around his neck. Near him are several of his disciples, including the electrophysiologist Arsène d'Arsonval; Bernard's most famous student, Paul Bert; and Louis Ranvier, the founder of histophysiology. Not all of Bernard's students agreed with him, but the discussions furthered the understanding of science in general and physiology in particular. As a teacher, Bernard ensured the continuation and independence of the new discipline of physiology.

During his lifetime, Bernard showed that general biological laws could be derived from specific experimental data; incorporated the latest techniques and findings of physics and chemistry into biology; developed the concepts of homeostasis, internal secretions, and organismic self-regulation; demonstrated the unity between physiology and medicine; and provided a philosophical basis for experimental biology. These contributions defined modern physiology, and current work in regulatory biology and much neurophysiology is the outgrowth of Bernard's scientific and philosophical initiatives.

In recognition of his work and status, he was given a chair in physiology at the University of Paris in 1854 and elected to the Academy of Medicine in 1861. In 1867, he was made a commander of the Legion of Honor and served as president of the Société de Biologie. In 1868, he was elected to the Académie Française and served as its president in 1869. In 1870, he was appointed to the senate by Napoleon III and barely escaped from Paris before the Prussian army arrived.

After his illness-enforced retirement in 1865, Bernard never fully recovered his health, although he was able to do some teaching and research. His mind was ever active, and it is reported in many sources that as he grew older, he repeated more and more often, "My mind abounds with things I want to finish." He became seriously ill in early January, 1878, and died on February 10, 1878, probably of kidney disease. He was the first scientist upon whom France bestowed the honor of a public funeral.

—*Sara Joan Miles*

FURTHER READING

Bernard, Claude. *An Introduction to the Study of Experimental Medicine*. Translated by Henry Copley Green. New York: Dover, 1957. This classic by Bernard has been widely read. Bernard's purpose in writing it was to describe the basic principles of scientific research and to outline and explain his philosophy of science. For a philosophical treatise, this book is remarkably clear and easy to follow.

Coleman, William, and Frederic L. Holmes, eds. *The Investigative Enterprise: Experimental Physiology in Nineteenth-Century Medicine*. Berkeley: University of California Press, 1988. Collection of essays about the development of experimental physiology, including an essay about discoveries in nineteenth century France.

Hall, Thomas S. *Ideas of Life and Matter, 600 B.C. to A.D. 1900*. Vol 2. Chicago: University of Chicago Press, 1969. Hall succinctly describes Bernard's answer to four questions: How is the organism constituted? What part or parts of it appear to be alive? By what sign does one recognize "living"? and What does "life" mean?

Holmes, Frederic L. *Claude Bernard and Animal Chemistry: The Emergence of a Scientist*. Cambridge, Mass.: Harvard University Press, 1974. This work focuses on Bernard's early research period (1842-1848), when he began to develop his views on experimentation, which would lead him to discover the role and function of the liver. Holmes also describes the scientific environment within which Bernard worked to provide a context for his thought and activities.

_____. "Claude Bernard, the *Milieu Intérieur*, and Regulatory Physiology." *History and Philosophy of the Life Sciences* 8 (1986): 3-25. Holmes explains the intellectual context in which Bernard developed the concept of *milieu intérieur* and shows how twentieth century physiologists have reinterpreted Bernard's original ideas to fit the concept of homeostasis. This article demonstrates the problems involved in understanding a scientist-philosopher in his own period instead of trying to make him say what is currently believed to be true.

Lesch, John E. *Science and Medicine in France: The Emergence of Experimental Physiology, 1790-1955.* Cambridge, Mass.: Harvard University Press, 1984. Surveys the development of experimental physiology and its impact on science and medicine in France.

Olmsted, J. M. D. *Claude Bernard: Physiologist.* New York: Harper & Row, 1938. This is probably the best-known biography of Bernard and is very good despite the pre-World War II date of publication.

Roll-Hansen, Nils. "Critical Teleology: Immanuel Kant and Claude Bernard on the Limitations of Experimental Biology." *Journal of the History of Biology* 9 (Spring, 1979): 55-91. Kant and Bernard proposed similar methodologies for biology. This article examines those methodologies, compares them, and shows how Kant's program had ethical and moral implications, while Bernard's approach was related to questions of science policy. The article describes the similarities and differences between Bernard and many of the natural historians and physicians of his period.

SEE ALSO: Karl Ernst von Baer; Ferdinand Julius Cohn; Lydia Folger Fowler; Hermann von Helmholtz; Émile Zola.

RELATED ARTICLE in *Great Events from History: The Nineteenth Century, 1801-1900:* c. 1865: Naturalist Movement Begins.

SARAH BERNHARDT

French actor

Bernhardt is generally regarded as the greatest female actor of the nineteenth century. She not only appeared in stage productions throughout Europe and America during the late nineteenth and early twentieth centuries but also made sound recordings and films during the twentieth century. She was also a painter and sculptor of some accomplishment, a theater manager, and an author of books, poetry, and plays.

BORN: October 22, 1844; Paris, France
DIED: March 26, 1923; Paris, France
ALSO KNOWN AS: Henrietta-Rosine Bernard (birth name); Divine Sarah; Golden Voice; Sarah Barnum
AREAS OF ACHIEVEMENT: Theater, art, literature

EARLY LIFE

Sarah Bernhardt's mother was Jewish and her father was Roman Catholic. Her parents did not live together, and her mother earned her living as a courtesan, so young Sarah was placed in a boarding house (*pensione*). Soon, however, her father moved her to a Catholic convent. She remained there until she was thirteen and became a student at the Conservatoire de Musique et Declamation in Paris. Although she won second prize for tragedy in 1861 and second prize for comedy in 1862, she regarded the conservatory's methods as antiquated. She left the conservatory in 1862 and accepted a contract with the national theater of France, the famed Comedie Francaise. However, her contract was canceled the following year because she could not get along with the more senior women actors. She then found work in burlesque at the Theatre Porte St-Martin and the Gymnase. During this period she became involved with the Belgium prince de Ligne and in 1864 had a child by him whom she named Maurice.

In 1867, when Bernhardt was twenty-two years old, she became a member of the company at the Odeon, where she found definite successes in roles such as Cordelia in a French translation of William Shakespeare's play *King Lear* (pr. c. 1605-1606), as Zanetto in François Coppée's verse play, *La Passant* (1869), and as the queen in Victor Hugo's *Ruy Blas* (1838). Indeed, it was Hugo himself who called Bernhardt the girl with the Golden Voice (*vox d'or*)—a name that stayed with her throughout her life. Meanwhile, Bernhardt's success was so immediate that she even gave a command performance for France's Emperor Napoleon III. However, the Franco-Prussian War interrupted her rising career with the closing of the Paris theaters in 1870.

LIFE'S WORK

Bernhardt's major life's work began in 1871, when peace was restored, and she left the Odeon to rejoin the Comedie Francaise, where her reputation steadily grew with each performance, including her especially praised lead performances in Jean Racine's 1677 play *Phèdre* (1874) and as Dona Sol in Victor Hugo's 1830 play *Hernani* (1877). Bernhardt's powerful emotional acting, the

Sarah Bernhardt. (Library of Congress)

beauty of her voice, and the realistic pathos of her death scenes brought her praise as France's leading woman actor. In 1879, she began winning an international reputation when she took London by storm with a triumphal season at the Gaiety Theater. Her artistic endeavors in other fields were also becoming noticed, and in 1876 she exhibited her sculpting work at the Paris Salon, where she won an honorable mention. In 1880, she exhibited paintings at the Salon.

Bernhardt's success on stage seemed to increase her already strained relationships with other members of the Comedie Francaise, and in 1880 she paid a large forfeit to break her contract with that theater. To pay that debt she gave a series of performances in London, followed by tours of Russia, Denmark, and the United States, where she became extremely popular. For her performances on this grand tour, she relied principally on the role of Camille in *La Dame aux camélias*, an 1852 dramatization of the 1848 novel by Alexander Dumas, *fils*. In 1882, she married Jacques Damala in London. The marriage lasted only a year.

Now a world-famous actor, Bernhardt returned to Paris for a triumphal production of Victorien Sardou's new play *Fedora* at the Vaudeville Theatre. In 1883, she took over management of the Theatre Porte St-Martin, where she produced, among other important works, several of Sardou's plays. She also wrote a play of her own, *L'Aveu*, a comedy that received only mildly favorable response. She managed the Theatre Porte St-Martin through a ten-year period during which she starred in several new productions and repeated many of her already famous roles. Her most celebrated role may have been that of the tragic title character in Victorien Sardou's play *Cleopatra*, but she also received high praise for her sensitive performance as Joan of Arc in Jules Barbier's 1873 opera *Jeanne d'Arc*. In 1893, she gave up her management of Porte St-Martin to become the proprietor of the Renaissance Theatre.

In addition to managing Paris theaters, Bernhardt made several foreign tours. In 1891 and 1893, she toured both North and South America, Australia, and most of the chief European cities. By then, she was, without doubt, the toast of the Western world. In November, 1893, she opened the season at the Renaissance Theatre with Jules Lemaitre's *Les Rois*. During the next few years she divided her time between Paris and London and in 1896 again toured the United States.

In December of 1896, a great celebration was organized in her honor in Paris, and she received greetings from important people from all over the world. Among her far-flung admirers were D. H. Lawrence, Oscar Wilde, and even Sigmund Freud. Oscar Wilde wrote *Salomé* for her, but the Paris authorities banned its production. There was no doubt that Bernhardt was at the pinnacle of her profession, having created 112 different roles during her career.

In 1899, Bernhardt gave up the Renaissance Theatre and acquired a much larger house, the Theatre des Nations, which she renamed the Theatre Sarah Bernhardt.

BERNHARDT'S MOTION PICTURE ROLES

Year	*Film (alternative title)*	*Role*
1900	*Le Duel d'Hamlet (Hamlet)*	Hamlet
1909	*La Tosca*	Tosca
1912	*La Dame aux camélias (Camille)*	Marguerite Gauthier
1912	*Les Amours de la reine Élisabeth (Queen Elizabeth)*	Queen Elizabeth I
1913	*Adrienne Lecouvreur*	Adrienne Lecouvreur
1915	*Jeanne Dore*	Jeanne Dore
1917	*Mères françaises (Mothers of France)*	
1923	*La Voyante*	

There she first played her famous Hamlet in a French translation of Shakespeare's play. She soon repeated her performance as Hamlet in London, where she also received great acclaim.

Bernhardt did not limit her acting to the stage, but enthusiastically embraced the new media that were then being invented. During the 1880's, she made a sound recording of Racine's *Phèdre* at the home of the American inventor Thomas Edison. Other recordings followed and then, commencing in 1900, she began to appear in films. In her eight feature films she played some of her most famous stage parts, including Hamlet, Camille, and Queen Elizabeth.

Bernhardt also turned to extensive writing during the twentieth century. In addition to plays and poetry, she published three books: *The Idol of Paris* (1921), a novel based on her own life; *Ma double vie: Mémoires de Sarah Bernhardt* (1907; *My Double Life*, 1907), an autobiography; and *L'Art du théâtre: La voix, le geste, la prononciation* (1923; *The Art of Theatre*, 1924), a textbook on acting.

In 1914, Bernhardt was inducted into the French Legion of Honor. The following year she had to have a leg amputated, but that did not prevent her being carried on a litter chair to visit French troops during World War I. Wearing a wooden leg, she continued to act until she died in 1923.

SIGNIFICANCE

The greatest woman actor of the nineteenth century, Sarah Bernhardt was also a sculptor and painter of some accomplishment. In addition she wrote poetry and plays and published three books. Moreover, she also proved a successful businesswoman by managing several theaters in Paris. Most important of all, she became a symbol not only of what a woman could accomplish, but also of women's rights to live and practice life with as much freedom as their male counterparts.

Bernhardt was also a good mother, dearly loved by her son, in whose arms she died. She married and divorced and had romantic affairs with both men and women. She wore men's pants in the face of scandalous reaction, and played both male and female parts on the stage. Her male parts included the bearded role of Shylock in Shakespeare's *The Merchant of Venice* (pr. c. 1596-1597). She was also the first modern performer to play the roles of both Ophelia and Hamlet in Shakespeare's *Hamlet* (pr. c. 1600-1601), and she became famous for playing the latter role both on stage and in film. To enhance her rebellious image, she even had a photograph taken of herself sleeping in a coffin.

—August W. Staub

FURTHER READING

Aston, Elaine. *Sarah Bernhardt: French Actress on the English Stage*. Oxford, England: Berg Publishers, 1989. A thorough treatment of Bernhardt's many appearances in England and the British reaction to her.

Bernhardt, Sarah. *My Double Life*. Translated by Victoria Tietze Larson. Albany: State University of New York Press, 1999. New translation of Bernhardt's own tell-it-all biography, which was first published in 1907. Not all of this book is verifiable fact, but it is useful in understanding Bernhardt as both an artist and a nineteenth century woman.

Brockett, Oscar, and Franklin J. Hildy. *History of the Theatre*. 9th ed. Boston: Allyn and Bacon, 2002. This basic general resource on theatrical history offers excellent information on Bernhardt and her impact throughout the world.

Duerr, Edwin. *The Length and Depth of Acting*. New York: Holt, Rinehart and Winston, 1963. Detailed study of actors from the time of the ancient Greeks through the mid-twentieth century. Good entries on the work and theory of Sarah Bernhardt.

Gold, Arthur, and Robert Fitzdale. *The Divine Sarah: A Life of Sarah Bernhardt*. New York: Alfred A. Knopf, 1991. A thorough study of the life, times, and contributions of the great actor.

SEE ALSO: Thomas Alva Edison; Victor Hugo; Lola Montez; Napoleon III; Ellen Terry; Henri de Toulouse-Lautrec; Oscar Wilde.

RELATED ARTICLES in *Great Events from History: The Nineteenth Century, 1801-1900:* 1878-1899: Irving Manages London's Lyceum Theatre; January 14, 1900: Puccini's *Tosca* Premieres in Rome.

ANNIE BESANT

English social reformer

After her early work promoting radical reform in England, Besant became leader of the Theosophical Society and was active in the nationalist movement in India.

BORN: October 1, 1847; London, England
DIED: September 20, 1933; Adyar, India
ALSO KNOWN AS: Annie Wood (birth name)
AREAS OF ACHIEVEMENT: Social reform, religion and theology

EARLY LIFE

Annie Wood Besant was born on October 1, 1847, in London, England, the second of three children of William and Emily Morris Wood. Despite her English birth, Besant had a strong sense of Irish heritage, because her mother was Irish and her father half Irish. William Wood, although trained as a physician, engaged in commerce in London. He died when Besant was five, a loss the trauma of which was compounded by the death several months later of her baby brother.

When Besant was eight, her impoverished widowed mother moved the family to Harrow so that her ten-year-old son Henry could more cheaply attend that prestigious public school. Shortly after the move, Miss Ellen Marryat, youngest sister of the novelist Frederick Marryat, offered to take Annie into her home in Devon to educate her. Although heartsick to be separated from her adored mother for the eight years she spent with Miss Marryat, Besant received excellent training, especially in literary skills, which enabled her to produce throughout her life a prodigious volume of writings for her many causes.

During her adolescent years, Besant was intensely religious. Reading stories of early Christian martyrs, she longed to follow in their steps. She fasted regularly, tortured herself with self-flagellation, and engaged in other extremist behavior, a pattern that became characteristic of her personality. A person of deep if changing beliefs, she would always commit herself enthusiastically and wholeheartedly to her convictions, with the ever-present, self-proclaimed wish for martyrdom.

At the age of sixteen, Besant returned to her mother's home. She was a beautiful young woman, of small stature, with brown hair and eyes. She had, however, no romantic fantasies, for her emotional life was absorbed by her passionate love for Jesus Christ and for her mother. She nevertheless married, in 1867, the Reverend Frank Besant, younger brother of the essayist Walter Besant, because she believed that she could best serve God as a clergyman's wife.

The marriage was a disaster. Annie, who married with no knowledge of sex, was shocked by her wedding night. Self-willed and rebellious, she also resented submitting to her domineering husband's authority. Her unhappiness was only somewhat alleviated by her success in selling several stories to the *Family Herald* and by the births of her son Digby, in 1869, and daughter Mabel, in 1870. She also found satisfaction in parish work when Frank Besant became vicar at Sibsey, a village in Lincolnshire. The marriage ended when Annie lost her religious faith after the grave illness of her children, whose sufferings made her doubt her belief in a loving and merciful God. The Besants were legally separated in 1873. She moved to London to make her way on her own with her daughter, while her son remained in the custody of the Reverend Besant.

LIFE'S WORK

Annie Besant's public career went through many distinct stages. After her loss of Christian faith and separation from her husband, she came under the influence of England's leading freethinker, Charles Bradlaugh. In 1874, she joined the National Secular Society and soon became one of its vice presidents. She edited with Bradlaugh the freethinking *National Reformer*, and, from 1883 to 1889, she also edited the magazine *Our Corner*. In these journals, she wrote in support of atheism, women's rights, Irish home rule, and land-tenure reform, and against British imperialism. Besant propagated her beliefs not only in written form but also as a public speaker, an activity not considered respectable for women at that time. Her rich, vibrant voice made her a great success, and she took

Annie Besant. (Library of Congress)

intense pleasure in the power she had over her audiences. Ever eager to absorb new knowledge, the energetic Besant also found time to enroll in courses in science at London University.

Besant's most controversial work with Bradlaugh was their republication in 1877 of Charles Knowlton's 1832 treatise on birth control, *Fruits of Philosophy*. They were arrested, and, in a sensational trial, they were convicted of publishing obscene literature, although their conviction was dismissed on appeal on a technicality. The defiant Besant then published her own birth control pamphlet, *Law of Population: Its Consequence and Its Bearing upon Human Conduct and Morals* (1881). She was the first Englishwoman to advocate publicly the use of birth control methods. Even though she was not prosecuted for her pamphlet, the controversy did cause her to lose custody of her daughter.

Besant's humanitarian concerns led her in 1885 to become a socialist. Joining the moderate Fabian Society, she contributed an article to the influential 1889 *Fabian Essays in Socialism*, edited by her close friend George Bernard Shaw. She later also joined the revolutionary Marxist Social Democratic Federation. Ever concerned with theatrical display, she began to dress in proletarian garb and always wore a piece of red clothing to show her socialist affiliation. This latest cause separated her from Bradlaugh, who was a strong antisocialist individualist. They remained personal friends, but she resigned as coeditor of the *National Reformer*.

As a socialist, Besant fought tirelessly to help working people, especially in trade union activity. Her most significant achievement was her organization of matchgirl workers into a union, after helping them in a successful strike against the Bryant and May Match Company in 1888. The Matchmaker's Union, considered the beginning of the new unionism of unskilled labor, was moreover the first successful effort to organize women workers, who had been ignored by the Trades Union Council. Besant also worked for socialist causes as a member of the London school board, to which she was elected in 1889.

Despite her advocacy of atheism, Besant felt increasingly unsatisfied by it and later spoke of her desperate hunger for spiritual ideals. This need was fulfilled by Theosophy, to which she, to the shock of her friends and associates, converted in 1889 after reading Mme Helena Blavatsky's *The Secret Doctrine* (1888). A charismatic Russian émigrée, Mme Blavatsky founded the Theosophical Society in 1875 along with the American lawyer Colonel Henry Olcott. The society, which remains active, aims at fostering bonds among all humanity; studying comparative religions and philosophies, especially those from ancient Eastern civilizations; and investigating and communicating with the world of the occult. Although not identified with any specific religion, Theosophists accept the Hindu and Buddhist belief in karma and reincarnation.

Committing herself fully to her new faith, Besant withdrew from the National Secular Society and the socialist organizations. She became editor of the Theosophist publication *Lucifer* and the leader of the Theosophical Society in England after Mme Blavatsky's death in 1891. In 1907, she was elected President of the Theosophical Society worldwide, a position she held for the rest of her life. As a Theosophist, in 1891 she renounced Malthusianism and withdrew her *Law of Population* from circulation. Although anguished at the effect this might have on the lives of poor women, she accepted Mme Blavatsky's view that humans must rise above animal passion through self-control and ascetic self-denial. Besant later returned to a qualified endorsement of birth control.

Besant traveled extensively throughout the world, organizing and lecturing for the Theosophical Society. After her first trip to India in 1893, she thought of that country as her home and believed that in earlier incarnations she had been Indian. She adopted Indian dress and in public always wore a white sari, which matched her now-white hair. Strongly drawn toward Hinduism, she learned Sanskrit and in 1895 translated the Bhagavadgītā (first or second century C.E.).

Always the reformer, Besant was concerned to revitalize Indian civilization, to restore pride and self-respect in a people who had been made to feel inferior by British imperialists. She condemned child marriage, the seclusion of women, and eventually the caste system, but otherwise opposed efforts to westernize India. Disavowing at first political activity, Besant worked primarily for educational reform. Her major accomplishment was the establishment of the Central Hindu College in Benares in 1898, a college for Hindu boys based on ancient Indian religion and culture as well as modern Western science. In 1904, she established the Central Hindu Girls' School, an important step in the emancipation of Indian women. The Hindu University, which absorbed the Central Hindu College in 1916, granted Besant an honorary degree in 1921, and thereafter she always styled herself Dr. Besant.

Besant eventually came to believe that efforts to strengthen Indian cultural pride were impossible as long as India was under British domination. In 1913, therefore, she entered the political arena by working actively for Indian home rule. As a vehicle for her campaign, she bought a Madras newspaper and renamed it *New India*. Founding the Home Rule for India League in 1916, she campaigned for self-government within the British Empire, which she envisioned as a partnership among equal nations. Her agitation against the British caused the government to intern her briefly during World War I, which only increased her popularity among Indians. In 1917, after her release, she was elected President of the Indian National Congress. She did not, however, remain long as leader of the Indian nationalists. She was soon eclipsed by the rise of the Mahatma Gandhi, with whose tactic of civil disobedience she disagreed, for fear that it would lead to violence. Considered too conservative in her insistence on law and order, she lost much of her political following in India.

Besant continued working for Indian home rule, and in 1925 she had an abortive Commonwealth of India Bill introduced into the English House of Commons. Her primary focus in the last part of her life, however, was in the promotion of her

THE CASE FOR INDIA

On December 26, 1917, Annie Besant delivered the Presidential Address at the Indian National Congress meeting at Calcutta. The theme of her address was the case for Indian home rule—a cause for which she campaigned tirelessly. These brief extracts from her speech outline her basic arguments.

India demands Home Rule for two reasons, one essential and vital, the other less important but necessary: Firstly, because Freedom is the birthright of every Nation; secondly, because her most important interests are now made subservient to the interests of the British Empire without her consent, and her resources are not utilised for her greatest needs. It is enough only to mention the money spent on her Army, not for local defence but for Imperial purposes, as compared with that spent on primary education. . . .

Self-Government is necessary to the self-respect and dignity of a People; Other-Government emasculates a Nation, lowers its character, and lessens its capacity. The wrong done by the Arms Act, which Raja Rampal Singh voiced in the Second Congress as a wrong which outweighed all the benefits of British Rule, was its weakening and debasing effect on Indian manhood. "We cannot," he declared, "be grateful to it for degrading our natures, for systematically crushing out all martial spirit, for converting a race of soldiers and heroes into a timid flock of quill-driving sheep." This was done not by the fact that a man did not carry arms—few carry them in England—but that men were deprived of the *right* to carry them. A Nation, an individual, cannot develop his capacities to the utmost without liberty. And this is recognised everywhere except in India. . . .

Hence the cry of a Nation for Freedom, for Self-Rule, is not a cry of mere selfishness demanding more Rights that it may enjoy more happiness. Even in that there is nothing wrong, for happiness means fulness of life, and to enjoy such fulness is a righteous claim. But the demand for Self-Rule is a demand for the evolution of its own nature for the Service of Humanity. It is a demand of the deepest Spirituality, an expression of the longing to give its very best to the world. . . .

Source: Annie Besant, *The Case for India* (1917).

Hindu protégé, Jiddu Krishnamurti, as the new Messiah. Believing that in times of world crisis the Divine Spirit enters a human body to help humankind toward higher spiritual consciousness, she was convinced that Krishnamurti was the chosen vehicle. He ultimately disappointed her by renouncing his role in the divine plan. Besant nevertheless continued working for her beliefs almost until her death on September 20, 1933, in Adyar, India, the international headquarters of the Theosophical Society. A portion of her ashes was sprinkled in the holy Ganges River, the rest deposited in a Garden of Remembrance at Adyar.

SIGNIFICANCE

An enthusiast for many causes, the leader of diverse movements, Annie Besant remained throughout her life committed to the principles of compassion, freedom, tolerance, and human equality. As a young woman, she had the courage to challenge such icons of Victorian respectability as the Church, patriarchy, propriety, capitalism, and imperialism. Although ultimately unsuccessful in her later years as a leader of the Indian home rule movement, she nevertheless made a significant contribution to Indian nationalism in helping to restore the pride of Indians in their own cultural heritage and in sensitizing the British to the narrowness and bigotry of their attitude of superiority toward India.

In her work as a Theosophist, to which she gave her most loyal and lasting allegiance, she incorporated the humanitarian concerns that had informed her other campaigns. Through her leadership she enabled the society to survive scandals, power struggles, and schisms. Although professing beliefs that the conventional world considered bizarre, she remained a personage of influence and respect and left as her legacy the vision of one world, seen and unseen, undivided by race, class, or sex, and bound together by love.

—Nancy Fix Anderson

FURTHER READING

Besant, Annie. *An Autobiography*. London: T. Fisher Unwin, 1893. A passionate, frank account of her life up to 1891. A revision of her 1885 *Autobiographical Sketches*.

_____. *A Selection of the Social and Political Pamphlets of Annie Besant*. New York: Augustus M. Kelley, 1970. A collection of twenty-seven of Besant's pamphlets on English radical reform, published from 1874 to 1889, with a preface and bibliographical notes by John Saville.

Besant, Annie, and Charles Knowlton. *"A Dirty, Filthy Book": The Writings of Charles Knowlton and Annie Besant on Reproductive Physiology and Birth Control and an Account of the Bradlaugh-Besant Trial*. Edited by Sripati Chandrasekhar. Berkeley: University of California Press, 1981. Includes Besant's *Law of Population* and her recantation *Theosophy and the Law of Population* (1891), as well as Knowlton's *Fruits of Philosophy*. The texts are prefaced by a useful introduction.

Nethercot, Arthur H. *The First Five Lives of Annie Besant*. London: Rupert Hart-Davis, 1960. A balanced, detailed life of Besant up to 1893. Although it sometimes relies uncritically on Besant's autobiographical writings, this book and the second volume (below), is the most complete and reliable biography.

_____. *The Last Four Lives of Annie Besant*. London: Rupert Hart-Davis, 1963. Besant's life and work in India from 1893 to her death. Based on extensive research in archives of the Theosophical Society and on interviews with Besant's family members and associates. An indispensable source.

Taylor, Anne. *Annie Besant: A Biography*. New York: Oxford University Press, 1992. Recent biography based in part on Besant's previously unpublished letters. Includes information on Besant's love affairs and her bid for religious and political power in India.

Washington, Peter. *Madame Blavatsky's Baboon: Theosophy and the Emergence of the Western Guru*. London: Secker & Warburg, 1993. Skeptical, yet fair and accurate history of Theosophy from the eighteenth century to the current new age movement. Includes information about Besant's life and career.

West, Geoffrey. *The Life of Annie Besant*. London: Gerald Howe, 1929. A lively, opinionated biography, written by a contemporary who admired Besant's achievements but was skeptical of Theosophy.

Williams, Gertrude Marvin. *The Passionate Pilgrim: A Life of Annie Besant*. New York: Coward-McCann, 1931. A readable popular biography. No footnotes, but a good bibliography.

SEE ALSO: Harriet Martineau; Dadabhai Naoroji.

RELATED ARTICLES in *Great Events from History: The Nineteenth Century, 1801-1900:* September, 1875: Theosophical Society Is Founded; 1882: First Birth Control Clinic Opens in Amsterdam; 1885: Indian National Congress Is Founded.

FRIEDRICH WILHELM BESSEL

German astronomer

Bessel's contribution to astronomy was to increase greatly the accuracy of measuring the positions of stars by using more advanced instruments and developing methods to account for instrument and observer error. The most famous discovery resulting from these observations was the first accurate determination of the distance to a star.

BORN: July 22, 1784; Minden, Brandenburg (now in Germany)

DIED: March 17, 1846; Königsberg, Prussia (now Kaliningrad, Russia)

AREAS OF ACHIEVEMENT: Astronomy, mathematics

EARLY LIFE

Friedrich Wilhelm Bessel (BEHS-ehl) was born to a civil servant and a minister's daughter. One of nine children, he went to the local gymnasium but left after only four years to become a merchant's apprentice. He showed no particular talent at school. At the age of fifteen, he began his unpaid seven-year apprenticeship to a merchant firm in Bremen. He excelled at his accounting job and received a small salary after one year. He spent his spare time teaching himself geography and languages because of his interest in foreign trade. He also learned about ships and practical navigation through self-study. Determining the position of a ship at sea—a long-standing problem in navigation—intrigued him. He therefore began to study astronomy and mathematics to understand the theory behind the existing methods.

Bessel began to make observations of stars on his own, which he was able to compare to observations reported in numerous professional journals of astronomy. One of his earliest tasks was to determine the orbit of Halley's Comet based on several observations of its position. He studied existing methods to determine the easiest way to do this, and he used observations made in 1607 to supplement his own. The precision of his observations and the scrupulous care given to minimizing or correcting for observational errors would characterize his professional work throughout his life. He made the observations, adjusted (or reduced) the 1607 data to make them directly comparable to his own, and submitted the results to Wilhelm Olbers in 1804.

Olbers, a physician and highly esteemed amateur astronomer, was impressed with the agreement between Bessel's observations and Edmond Halley's calculation of the orbit. He urged Bessel to improve it further with more observations. Olbers was impressed enough to recommend Bessel in 1806 for a position as assistant at a private observatory near Bremen. Bessel made further observations of the comet and published the results in 1807 to wide acclaim.

LIFE'S WORK

In 1809, Bessel was appointed director of the new observatory at Königsberg, where he remained for the rest of his life. His early fame came from his reduction of the earlier observations of James Bradley. Bradley's measurement of the apparent position of stars had to be corrected for the motion of Earth, the bending of starlight as it passes through the air, and instrument errors. With sufficient care, any observation can be reduced to a universal coordinate system.

While waiting for the construction of the observatory, Bessel worked on reducing Bradley's observations of more than thirty-two hundred stars with the goal of producing a reference system for measuring the positions of other stars. Bessel received the Lalande Prize of the Institute of France for his production of tables of refraction based on these observations. In 1818, he completed the reduction and published the results in his work *Fundamenta astronomiae* (1818; fundamental astronomy). This work provided the most accurate positions of a chosen set of stars. Accurate positions of a few stars are required to form the basis for extremely accurate measurements of positions for all other stars. This work has been said to mark the birth of modern astrometry. Bessel also provided accurate proper motions of many stars. (The so-called fixed stars actually move a very small amount over the centuries. When all perturbing effects are removed, the motion that is left to the star is called its proper motion.)

Bessel's next important contribution was to increase the accuracy of the measurement of stellar positions and motions. In 1820, he determined the position of the vernal equinox with great accuracy. The equinox is employed as the origin of the coordinate system used to record a star's position. He further improved accuracy in his work *Tabulae regiomontanae* (1830; *Refraction Tables*, 1855), in which he published the mean positions for thirty-eight stars for the period 1750-1850. In 1821, he noticed a systematic error in observation that was peculiar to each observer and called it the personal equation. This systematic error was reduced as each observer became more experienced, but it never disappeared. Bessel devised a method to remove the error.

Identifying and measuring the proper motion of stars was crucial in producing an important contribution to astronomy. The slight but periodic variation in proper motion of a few stars was not accountable by considering the motion of Earth or instrumental factors. In making the observations that later appeared in the *Refraction Tables*, Bessel suggested that the variations in proper motion of the stars Sirius and Procyon could be explained by the existence of an as-yet-unseen companion star. More than a century later, the companions to these stars were observed, as well as companions to many others.

Bessel also made important contributions to mathematics. Prior to Bessel, it was common for observers of the heavens to record their data and only later, if ever, reduce that data. Bradley, whose observations Bessel used extensively, carefully noted any possible perturbing effects in his observations. Nevertheless, reduction of the data for the positions of the stars was put aside in favor of recording lunar data. Bessel emphasized the need for the data reduction to be done immediately by the observer. Such reduction required extensive manipulation of complicated equations. In the process of developing ways to remove errors, Bessel noticed that he could use a class of functions that solved problems involving the perturbing influence of one planet on the orbit of another. He systematically investigated and described this class of functions in 1824. These functions, which bear Bessel's name, are not restricted to astronomy: They are used in the solution of a wide variety of problems in physics, mathematics, and engineering.

Another direct benefit of increased accuracy in stellar positions was Bessel's determination of the distance to a star, which is his most important contribution to astronomy. Although many astronomers had earlier claimed to have measured stellar distance using methods based on questionable assumptions, and although two of Bessel's contemporaries also correctly determined such distances, Bessel's comprehensive treatment of the data and his high accuracy of observations were convincing to his contemporaries.

As Earth moves in its annual orbit around the sun, the stars appear to move across the dome of the sky. By determining the location of a star at opposite ends of Earth's orbit and using some simple trigonometry, the distance to a star can be measured. However, this so-called parallax (the apparent motion of an object caused by the motion of the observer) was small because the stars are very far away. The parallax had therefore never been measured. Indeed, some opponents of the heliocentric theory, according to which Earth revolves around the sun, used this failure to measure parallax as an argument against the theory. Astronomers had a rough figure for the radius of Earth's orbit and some idea of the extent of the solar system, but there did not seem to be a way to determine stellar distances that did not require the assumption that all stars had the same intrinsic brightness.

Earlier attempts at measuring parallax involved circumventing the problem of the immeasurably small parallax by looking at two stars that appeared to be very near to each other but were of different brightness. It was thought that the dimmer star would be farther away and that observing the relative change of position could lead to a determination of stellar distances. This method did not work, because not all stars are of the same intrinsic brightness. Most stars that appear near to each other are in fact binary stars and really are near each other.

Bessel used a different approach: He assumed that stars with large proper motions are closer than stars with small proper motions. He chose the star known as 61 Cygni, because it had the largest proper motion known. He used a new measuring device called the Fraunhofer heliometer (after Joseph von Fraunhofer, a nineteenth century optician), which was designed to measure the angular diameter of the sun and the planets. Its manner of comparing the images from two objects to determine angular diameter was more accurate than earlier instruments. Using nearby stars for comparison and observing for eighteen months, Bessel was able to measure a parallax of slightly under one-third of a second of arc, which is equal to the width of a dime viewed from twenty miles. From this amount of parallax, Bessel calculated that 61 Cygni was 10.9 light years or seventy trillion miles away. He completed his calculations and published the results in 1838.

The last six years of Bessel's life were marked by deteriorating health, but he managed to complete a number of works before his death from cancer in March, 1846.

SIGNIFICANCE

Friedrich Wilhelm Bessel made important contributions to astronomy, mathematics, and geodesy. His work marks the turning point from a concern with planetary, solar, and lunar observations to investigations of the stars. His measurement of the distance to a star is noteworthy because it settled the centuries-old question of whether stars exhibited parallax. The care he took in his observations set much higher standards for the science of astronomy. Bessel's goal was to observe the stars accurately enough to predict their motion and to establish a reference system for their positions. As part of that plan, he developed methods for the careful determination of instrument and observer error, conducted years of observations himself, and developed the mathematical techniques to reduce the data. Bessel's lasting achievement was to raise the science of observing, reducing, and correcting astronomical data to an art.

—*Roger Sensenbaugh*

FURTHER READING

Clerke, Agnes. *A Popular History of Astronomy During the Nineteenth Century*. New York: Macmillan, 1887. Although written during the period it was supposed to cover, this work has several redeeming qualities. Expressly written for a general audience, the book's language is clear and precise. A valuable record of what near-contemporaries thought of Bessel.

"The Deep Sky." *Astronomy* 31, no. 8 (August, 2003): 65. Describes the special place the star system Cygnus holds in the history of astronomy because of Bessel's measurements of 61 Cygni.

Herrmann, Dieter B. *The History of Astronomy from Herschel to Hertzsprung*. Translated by Kevin Krisciunos. Rev. ed. New York: Cambridge University Press, 1984. Traces the history of astronomy from 1780 to 1930. Written from a Marxist perspective.

Hirshfeld, Alan. *Parallax: The Race to Measure the Cosmos*. New York: W. H. Freeman, 2001. Bessel's measurement of 61 Cygni is recounted in this history of astronomers' attempts to measure the distances to stars and plants by parallax observation.

Hoskin, Michael A. *Stellar Astronomy: Historical Studies*. Chalfont, England: Science History, 1982. A collection of material published in *Journal for the History of Astronomy*, with the addition of some new material. Attempts a synthesis of existing scholarship on the history of stellar (as opposed to planetary) astronomy as of the early 1980's.

Pannekoek, Anton. *A History of Astronomy*. New York: Interscience, 1961. Traces the history of astronomy from antiquity to the present. Part 3, "Astronomy Surveying the Universe," contains information on Bessel and places him in the historical context of nineteenth century astronomy.

Williams, Henry Smith. *The Great Astronomers*. Westport, Conn.: Greenwood Press, 1930. Reprint. New York: Newton, 1932. Book 5 deals with Bessel, among other subjects. Concerns parallax and Bessel's contributions to measuring the distance to 61 Cygni. Describes the work of Bessel's contemporaries who measured the parallax of other stars at about the same time.

SEE ALSO: Williamina Paton Stevens Fleming; Margaret Lindsay Huggins; Pierre-Simon Laplace; Simon Newcomb.

RELATED ARTICLES in *Great Events from History: The Nineteenth Century, 1801-1900:* January 1, 1801: First Asteroid Is Discovered; 1814: Fraunhofer Invents the Spectroscope.

SIR HENRY BESSEMER
English inventor and metallurgist

Bessemer advanced the field of metallurgy by developing the Bessemer process for purifying molten iron. This process cut in half the cost of steel, made possible a great increase in production, and ushered in the "Age of Steel."

BORN: January 19, 1813; Charlton, Hertfordshire, England
DIED: March 15, 1898; London, England
AREA OF ACHIEVEMENT: Science and technology

EARLY LIFE

Henry Bessemer was born on January 19, 1813, in Charlton in Hertfordshire, just north of London, where his father, Anthony Bessemer, was an engineer and typefounder. Young Bessemer grew up in his father's shops and, aside from an elementary education in local schools, soon demonstrated the initiative, inventiveness, and artistic talent that had characterized his parent. Anthony had moved to Holland from London as a young engineer, helping to erect the first steam pumping engine there, and went on to Paris to become a member of the French Academy of Sciences because of his skills, including engraving, die-sinking, and the invention of a copying machine. The French Revolution forced the family to flee to England, where the elder Bessemer started a firm making gold chains and then with William Caslon turned to manufacturing in the more profitable line of typefounding. Until the age of seventeen, Henry labored in his father's workshop in Charlton; in 1830, his family moved to London, where he began his own trade in artwork of white metal.

At the age of twenty, in 1833, Bessemer married Anne Allen, daughter of Richard Allen of Amersham, in London; their marriage proved to be a long and happy one; she lived until June, 1897, less than a year before he died. They had two sons and a daughter who lived into the twentieth century. Anne's three brothers joined her husband in his bronze and steel enterprises: John and Richard Allen managed the secret operations of the bronze works that Henry eventually turned over to Richard; William D. Allen aided in the steel experiments and then ran the steelworks at Sheffield. The Bessemers spent most of their lives in three homes: first the Baxter House, at St. Pancras, to which were added large buildings for Bessemer's experimental work and the bronze factory; then Charlton, a country house and grounds; and finally, Denmark Hill, a home he enlarged with spacious grounds and gardens.

Photographs of Bessemer depict a man with a stern countenance, a short neck, and heavy eyebrows and side whiskers beneath a balding crown.

LIFE'S WORK

Three major inventions occupied most of Bessemer's active life. His first activities in artwork in white metal led him into copper-coating castings and then embossing metals, cards, and fabrics. He showed some of his work at exhibitions of the Royal Academy at Somerset House. There, Sir Charles Presley accepted his suggestion that forging and reusing old stamps on deeds and documents could be permanently halted by use of a perforated die with a date so that each parchment or paper would be pierced by the application of the government stamp. Bessemer was promised a government job in return for his invention, which was to save the British government an estimated 100,000 pounds annually. Months passed, however, and Bessemer was never rewarded for the new government stamp, which was installed by an act of Parliament on August 29, 1833. Years later, when the British ambassador refused him permission to accept the Grand Cross of the French Legion of Honor, Bessemer sought and received recognition for his invention. He was granted a knighthood in 1879.

During the 1830's, Bessemer also worked successfully on compressing plumbago dust into marking material for cheaper black-lead pencils. He then designed a machine to make type for printers and later created a type-composing machine with a pianolike keyboard for James Young, who patented the device. He also created a device and method for stamping or embossing on Utrecht velvet.

Bessemer's second great invention he dared not patent, but kept as a family secret for more than thirty-five years at great profit to himself and his brothers-in-law, who ran a plant for making bronze powder from solid brass. Replacing the secret pounding process of the German and Oriental suppliers of these "gold" powders—used to tint paints of all kinds—Bessemer devised a way of cutting tiny flakes from a solid bar of brass on a lathe, polishing and tinting them, and finally blowing them into graded sizes.

What was most impressive about Bessemer's bronze-powder project was the extreme secrecy essential to designing the entire series of shop machines and equipment for the bronze manufacturing process. To prevent anyone from learning about the secret process, Bessemer had to design each part of each machine personally, then send each part to be manufactured to different firms in four different cities. Later, he and his relatives assembled the entire lot in the closed buildings erected behind his Baxter House. With only a few modifications, the entire plant was started without trouble, and the tiny bottles of various colored bronze powder were sold for high profits by the family. Bessemer's income alone was large enough to finance his experiments for the rest of his career.

In 1849, the British inventor met a Jamaican sugar-planter who told him of the problems involved in crushing sugar juices from the stocks of cane. When the Society of Arts and Prince Albert offered a gold medal for the person who could effect the greatest improvement in sugarcane production, Bessemer began a serious effort to solve those problems. Instead of the traditional rolling action of sugar mills, he developed a lightweight, movable press with hydraulic pressure that compressed six-inch lengths of cane, producing a higher percentage of sugar than any other sugar mill. He patented the first of thirteen sugar-related inventions in 1849 and won the Gold Medal the next year.

Sir Henry Bessemer. (Library of Congress)

At the London Crystal Palace International Exhibition in 1851, Bessemer exhibited his version of an early centrifugal pump, which he had patented two years earlier. He spent many hours each week as a consultant to other inventors and manufacturers who came to his office for advice.

The famous Bessemer process for making steel was his most important invention, for which the Patent Office of Great Britain granted him patent number 356, dated February 12, 1856. Between 1853 and 1883, Bessemer won more than seventy-five patents in England for making iron and steel, for construction of the Bessemer converter, and for numerous soft steel products that evolved from his extensive experimentation.

During the 1850's, Bernard was already a well-established inventor. He turned his attention to finding a cheaper way to make malleable iron. Cast-iron (twelve-pounder) cannon used in the Crimean War were not strong enough to fire the twenty-four-pound and thirty-pound revolving projectiles that Bessemer had presented to the French government. Nevertheless, Bessemer's projectile had proven itself; he came home with a burning desire to develop metal to build stronger cannon. While testing his small open-hearth furnace (some ten years before the Siemens-Martin patent on the open-hearth method of steelmaking), Bessemer accidentally discovered what he thought were two unmelted pieces of pig iron at the mouth of the furnace. Examination of them indicated that "they were merely thin shells of decarburized iron . . . showing that atmospheric air alone was capable of wholly decarburizing grey pig iron, and converting it into malleable iron without puddling or any other manipulation."

Further trials led Bessemer to create a new style "Bessemer Converter," with a movable furnace that tipped on its side while loading hot pig iron or pouring molten steel but that turned upright during the thirty-minute heating process. Air was forced into the furnace from the bottom below the melted pig iron, gradually consuming the silicon. As the carbon in the iron was burned, it created a much-intensified heat that purified the iron into steel. That first successful melting of pig iron into steel was exciting to the British inventor, and he reflected the wonderment of that event in his autobiography: "All this was a revelation to me, as I had in no way anticipated such violent results."

Bernard invited his friend George Rennie, an engineer, to see the process and Rennie persuaded Bessemer to present his discovery to the British Association for the Advancement of Science, meeting at Cheltenham, Gloucestershire, on August 13, 1856. The complete address, titled "The Manufacture of Iron Without Fuel," was published in *The Times* of London on August 14, and within a few weeks Bessemer sold licenses to British ironmasters worth more than twenty-seven thousand pounds. This money repaid much of his costs and contributed to further research that gradually made the process commercially successful.

Within the next several years, Bessemer overcame many serious problems still plaguing his steelmaking process. Obtaining quantities of phosphorous-free iron for British steel manufacturers forced him to import Swedish ore until he could get pig iron from British mines refined sufficiently to make mild steel. He learned to add ferromanganese or spiegeleisen to remove excess oxygen, a technique patented by Robert Forester Mushet in 1856 in England (Bessemer claimed that he had previously developed the process but later granted Mushet an annual allowance as partial settlement of his claims). Eventually, Bessemer furnaces were lined with a special fire brick that aided in the removal of phosphorous; after 1878, the more widely available phosphorous iron ores expanded the tonnage of Bessemer steel production.

Much like Thomas Edison, Bessemer quickly turned many of his inventions into commercial enterprises, thereby accumulating a small fortune. In 1858, he founded his own steel plant at Sheffield. There, he designed all the supplementary equipment to support the Bessemer furnaces; in 1860, he was granted a patent on his movable converter with hydraulic controls. The five partners, including Bessemer and his brother-in-law William D. Allen, who ran the works, eventually sold the plant after fourteen years "for exactly twenty-four times the amount of the whole subscribed capital of the firm, notwithstanding that we had divided in profits during the partnership a sum equal to fifty-seven times the gross capital." As production increased during the 1860's and 1870's, the price of Bessemer steel dropped rapidly. The transportation industries were the first to benefit.

The first steel rail, laid down as a test between two iron rails, was installed on May 9, 1862, at the busy Camden Goods Station of the London and North-Western Railway; it outlasted iron rails by seven times in two years and was only slightly worn when exhibited at a trade show. The railroad industry of Europe and the United States soon adopted the new steel rails at great savings and with added safety.

While boiler plate made from steel soon became an important use of the more durable metal in steam locomotives and steamships, the development of steel for shipbuilding, particularly for the rise of new naval vessels with protective armor plate, consumed millions of tons of steel. In 1863, at the age of fifty, Bessemer saw the first Bessemer steel used in the construction of a steel steamship.

At the end of the Civil War, the first Bessemer works built in the United States were opened by A. L. Holley at Troy, New York, in 1865. He had gone to England in 1864 and purchased the license to make steel under the Bessemer process and the right to use the Bessemer converter and machinery. A Michigan firm, however, had obtained the Mushet patent rights for the United States to use along with the Kelly Pneumatic Process, patented by the American inventor of a similar steel process. Consolidation of the two firms led to the construction of the Wyandotte Iron Works near Detroit, which made the steel rolled into rails by the North Chicago Rolling Mill on November 24, 1865, for track of the Chicago and Northwestern Railroad.

William Kelly in Eddyville, Kentucky, had worked seven or more years near the Ohio River making malleable iron for sugar kettles for farmers and boiler plate for Cincinnati steamboat builders. After 1851, he erected a series of converters and learned that the carbon in pig iron could be burned out by air alone, because the carbon itself acted as a fuel if heated enough. When he learned that Bessemer had been granted a United States patent on November 11, 1856, Kelly quickly filed his own claim and on July 23, 1857, he was awarded a patent and an interference that placed his claim ahead of Bessemer. Unfortunately, in the Panic of 1857, Kelly went bankrupt and eventually lost all chance of income from his pioneering work.

SIGNIFICANCE

At the age of fifty-nine, Sir Henry Bessemer retired from all business enterprises and devoted nearly a quarter of a century to four new pursuits: construction of an observatory and telescope, experiments with a solar furnace, installation of a diamond-polishing factory for his grandson, and his autobiography.

Many honors and awards were presented to Bessemer in his lifetime. Perhaps the highest was also the longest in coming, for on June 26, 1879, he was knighted by Queen Victoria at Windsor Castle for his unpatented invention of a stamp for dating government documents and deeds. The French government offered Bessemer the Legion of

Honor award in 1856, but he was not allowed to accept it by his own nation. The Society of Arts conferred upon him its Albert Gold Medal in 1872 for his achievements in steel manufacturing. He was one of the founders of the Iron and Steel Institute and served for a time as its president; he established the Bessemer Gold Medal of that body to be granted to distinguished metallurgists of the world thereafter. In 1877, Bessemer was elected to the Institution of Civil Engineers; in 1879, he was made a Fellow in the Royal Society of London. Many other societies made him an honorary member for his inventions; at least six steelmaking towns and counties in the United States were named for him.

Within fifty-six years he was awarded 114 patents by the British Patent office, a record of achievement that reflects the ingenuity of the man and the spirit of inquiry that motivated him far beyond any monetary rewards.

—Paul F. Erwin

FURTHER READING

Bessemer, Sir Henry. *Sir Henry Bessemer, F.R.S.: An Autobiography*. London: Offices of "Engineering," 1905. This autobiography, with a concluding chapter by Bessemer's son, is a rambling collection of the inventor's reminiscences and letters about his unique experiments, discoveries, patents, and manufacturing ventures. Development of the Bessemer process for making steel is related in two hundred of the 380 pages of text; numerous illustrations and fifty plates help make this volume the major source of all that has been written about the process and the inventor.

Bodsworth, C., ed. *Sir Henry Bessemer: Father of the Steel Industry*. London: IOM Communications, 1998. Collection of essays commemorating the centenary of Bessemer's death. The essays discuss the significance of Bessemer's achievements. Illustrated with photographs and drawings.

Boucher, John N. *William Kelly: A True History of the So-called Bessemer Process*. Greensburg, Pa.: Private printing, 1924. This biography presents an American counterclaim that William Kelly of Eddyville, Kentucky, a native of Pittsburgh, discovered and used the "pneumatic process" successfully in converting molten pig iron into malleable iron (steel) at least seven years before Bessemer patented his process. The United States Patent Office upheld Kelly's claim and granted him a patent in 1857, but the British exports of Bessemer rails and Bessemer converters swamped the American market and Kelly's bankruptcy prevented him from gaining any financial rewards for his achievements in the Ohio Valley.

Boyns, T., ed. *The Steel Industry*. 4 vols. New York: I. B. Tauris, 1997. Comprehensive history contains information in volumes 1 and 2 about the steel industry in nineteenth century England.

Derry, T. K., and Trevor I. Williams. *A Short History of Technology: From the Earliest Times to A.D. 1900*. Oxford, England: Oxford University Press, 1961. This text is a sequel to the five-volume *A History of Technology* (see below). Good coverage of the Industrial Revolution and a chapter on "Coal and the Metals" includes developments in the making of inexpensive steel. Comparative tables showing chronological events of technological achievements in Great Britain, the Continent, and the United States, along with a selected bibliography for each chapter, enhance this introductory study.

Singer, Charles, ed. *A History of Technology*. 5 vols. Oxford, England: Clarendon Press, 1954-1958. Volume 5 covers the late nineteenth century, 1850 to 1900; chapter 3, on the steel industry, is especially useful. The impact of Bessemer's inventions in the steel industry is best seen in histories of the railroads, steamshipping, and structural steel industries, which burgeoned as a result of the manufacture of low-priced steel. The Bessemer process dominated the production of steel until the turn of the century; after 1900, the Siemens-Martin open-hearth process outstripped both the tonnage and cost of Bessemer process steel.

SEE ALSO: Andrew Carnegie; James Buchanan Eads; Sir Robert Abbott Hadfield; The Siemens Family.

RELATED ARTICLE in *Great Events from History: The Nineteenth Century, 1801-1900:* 1855: Bessemer Patents Improved Steel-Processing Method.

FRIEDRICH VON BEUST

Austrian politician

Beust played a leading role from his position in the Saxon government in suppressing the revolutions of 1848 in the German states and in formulating reactionary policies adopted by the governments of those states over the following two decades. First in the Saxon government, then in the Austrian, he was Otto von Bismarck's most formidable opponent during the Prussian chancellor's attempt to unify the small German states under the leadership of Prussia. Beust was also the architect of the 1868 political settlement that created the Austro-Hungarian Empire.

BORN: January 13, 1809; Dresden, Saxony (now in Germany)

DIED: October 24, 1886; Altenberg Castle, Austro-Hungarian Empire (now in Austria)

ALSO KNOWN AS: Friedrich Ferdinand von Beust (full name)

AREAS OF ACHIEVEMENT: Government and politics, diplomacy

EARLY LIFE

Friedrich Ferdinand von Beust (bewst) was the scion of an aristocratic Saxon family whose members had served the Saxon monarchy for more than three centuries by the time he was born in Dresden on January 13, 1809. His father, an officer in the Saxon court, married the daughter of a Saxon government official just prior to the Napoleonic Wars, which formed the backdrop to Beust's early life.

When the Napoleonic Wars ended in 1815, the diplomats representing all the nations of Europe gathered in Vienna to establish a new political order in Europe, or, more accurately, to restore insofar as possible the old order that had been destroyed by the French Revolution and Napoleon I. Although there was widespread popular support in the German states for the creation of a nation that would include all German-speaking people, nationalist hopes were frustrated through the machinations of the Austrian representative at the Congress of Vienna, Metternich. The German universities remained hotbeds of support for the unification of the small German states under a liberal, constitutional government until 1819, when Metternich persuaded the leaders of all the German states to suppress the *Burchenschaften*, the student fraternities in the universities that had been among the most enthusiastic and sometimes violent organizations calling for the unification of Germany. By the time Beust entered the University of Leipzig, the voices of liberalism and nationalism had been legally silenced on German campuses.

Beust's parents determined that he should pursue the traditional career of his family and sent him to the Universities of Leipzig and Göttingen to study law and government. Accordingly, he entered the University of Leipzig in 1826, when the repressive policies imposed on the German states by Metternich in 1819 were effectively stifling liberal and nationalist ideas. The professors who lectured in Beust's classes were largely champions of the status quo and critical of liberalism and nationalism. His own opposition to those two powerful forces of the nineteenth century formed during his university years and determined the course of his life.

After completing his studies, Beust entered the Saxon bureaucracy in 1830 and married a Bavarian heiress chosen for him by his parents. He served in various diplomatic capacities in Berlin, Paris, Munich, and London, where he gained a reputation as a capable spokesman for conservatism before assuming the post of Saxon foreign minister in 1849.

LIFE'S WORK

Beust immediately became the most influential member of the Saxon ministry and was primarily responsible for its reactionary policies in 1849. On Beust's advice, the Saxon king rejected the constitution proclaimed by the Frankfurt Parliament. The parliament, comprising elected representatives from all the German states, came into being as a result of the revolutions of 1848, which convulsed most of Europe. In 1849, it attempted to promulgate a constitution that would have established a union of all the German states. The government of the new nation would have been a constitutional monarchy with a parliament elected by universal manhood suffrage.

The rejection of the Frankfurt constitution in Saxony led to the outbreak of revolution in the capital city of Dresden. Beust's first act as foreign minister was to request military assistance from Prussia to suppress the revolutionaries, who included among their numbers Mikhail Bakunin and Richard Wagner. Both men gained considerable prominence in later years and were among Beust's most outspoken critics. The assistance was quickly forthcoming. Consequently, Beust fell into disrepute with German liberals and nationalists but became the hero of conservatives and reactionaries throughout the German states.

Upon the successful suppression of the revolt, Beust assumed the ministry of education and public worship in addition to his duties as foreign minister. For the next decade and a half, he was the dominant force in the Saxon government. He reorganized the police and used them to crush resistance to the monarchy, including especially student demonstrations at the university. The next year, he overthrew the liberal constitution adopted in Saxony in 1848 and restored the full powers and prerogatives of the monarchy. In 1851, he sided with Austria in that country's successful effort diplomatically to defeat an effort by Frederick William IV of Prussia to unify the small German states under Prussian leadership. In 1853, Beust assumed the Ministry of Internal Affairs and the post of Minister-President of Saxony in addition to his other duties, making him by far the most powerful individual in the country.

With the domestic situation well in hand, Beust devoted most of his attention to foreign affairs after 1853. He became the leader of the aristocratic faction in the German states that opposed a political or economic unification of Germany. He took the lead in proposing at the Bamberg Conference in 1854 that the small German states should form a closer union among themselves to make them better able to resist pressure from the two great monarchies, Austria and Prussia. Largely through Beust's efforts, the unification of Germany was delayed for yet another decade.

In 1864, Beust's policies led him into a direct conflict with the chancellor of Prussia, Otto von Bismarck, who was intent on territorially aggrandizing the state of Prussia at the expense of the small German states. At Bismarck's urging, the Prussian press began vitriolic denunciations of Beust in that year, condemning him as a "particularist" (one who wished to preserve the independence of the small states within the Germanic Confederation). When Bismarck's policies of expansion led to war with Austria in 1866, Beust persuaded the Saxon king to side with the Austrians. Beust tried to rescue a disastrous situation after the Austrian defeat at Hradec Kralové by traveling to France and seeking aid from Napoleon III, but his mission failed. He then resigned his post when Bismarck refused to negotiate with him at the ensuing peace conference. It appeared that Beust's public career was over, but events proved otherwise.

Unexpectedly, Austrian emperor Francis Joseph asked Beust to assume the duties of Austrian foreign minister in December, 1866 (he became minister-president of Austria the following year). The Hungarians had used the opportunity presented by Austria's defeat at the hands of Prussia to pursue their ancient dream of independence. Beust's primary responsibility when he assumed his new post was somehow to pacify the Hungarians and preserve the empire intact. The result of Beust's efforts was the creation of the so-called dual monarchy of Austria-Hungary that in effect granted the Hungarians control of their own domestic affairs but left their foreign policy in the hands of the Habsburg monarchy.

In 1868, Beust was appointed chancellor of the empire and awarded the title of count. He continued to direct the foreign policy of his adopted empire. Initially, he remained adamantly opposed to Bismarck's ambitions and consequently sought close relations with France. Even after the defeat of the French at the hands of Prussia in 1870-1871 and the proclamation by Bismarck of the German Empire, Beust was unwilling to accept the idea of a unified Germany. When it became obvious that there was nothing he could do to reverse the decision of the war, Beust reluctantly sought a détente with Bismarck, who accepted eagerly, because it meant Austrian recognition of the new German Empire. In July, 1871, Beust announced the agreement to his governments and consummated it with a personal meeting with Bismarck at Gastein the next month.

Later that year, Beust managed to dissuade Franz Joseph from instating a plan to grant greater local autonomy to the various ethnic groups within the empire. Very shortly thereafter, he was relieved of his post as chancellor without explanation. He requested and received appointment as Austrian ambassador to England, in which capacity he served for seven years. In 1878, he was transferred to Paris, where he retired from public life four years later. Beust died at his Altenberg villa, near Vienna, on October 24, 1886.

SIGNIFICANCE

Friedrich von Beust was a leading spokesperson for those aristocratic elements in the Germanic Confederation that successfully prevented the democratic unification of the German states in 1848-1849. He was also instrumental in preventing a more authoritarian but still peaceful unification in 1851. Taken together, his successes prepared the way for the creation of the German Empire by force of arms completed under Bismarck's leadership and the distinctly Prussian and militarist nature of the new state that resulted. In addition, the delaying tactics adopted by Beust and those he represented against the installation of representative, constitutional government exacerbated the class conflicts that convulsed the German states throughout the latter half of the nineteenth century and contributed both to the coming of World War I and to the eventual triumph of National Socialism in the first half of the twentieth century.

The opposition of Beust and those he represented to pluralism in the Austrian Empire also had disastrous consequences long after Beust died. The struggle of the various ethnic groups within and without the empire for autonomy or self-determination led directly to the events at Sarajevo in June of 1914 that sparked the outbreak of World War I, with calamitous results for all nations involved. Beust alone did not bring about the apocalyptic events of the first half of the twentieth century. He was, however, a clever and effective champion of the policies that led directly to the catastrophic events that befell the generations of Germans that came after him.

An ancient proverb holds that the road to Hell is paved with good intentions. Beust's intentions from his own perspective were good. He intended to preserve intact the institutions of pre-1848 Europe and to crush the twin threats of liberalism and nationalism that would destroy those institutions. His very success paved the road to the modern hell of total war.

—*Paul Madden*

FURTHER READING

Beust, Friedrich von. *Memoirs of Friedrich Ferdinand, Count von Beust*. Translated by Henry de Worms. 2 vols. London: Remington, 1887. Beust's memoirs offer a wealth of information about the man and his policies but must be used with great caution because of Beust's tendencies toward self-glorification and magnification of his own importance in the unfolding of historical events.

Ellis, William Ashton. *1849*. London: Remington, 1892. This is the only book-length treatment of the Saxon revolution available in English. Ellis is very critical of Beust's role in the events of 1849, describing him as the chief culprit in the crushing of liberal democracy in Saxony.

Greenville, J. A. S. *Europe Reshaped, 1848-1878*. 2d ed. Malden, Mass.: Blackwell, 2000. Beust is mentioned several times in this book, and receives special attention in chapter 17, which examines the unification of Germany.

Kann, Robert A. *The Multinational Empire: Nationalism and National Reform in the Habsburg Monarchy 1848-1918*. 2 vols. New York: Columbia University Press, 1950. Kann's book is the most complete account of Beust's career in the Austrian government. Kann treats Beust kindly and is especially complimentary concerning Beust's role in the formation of the dual monarchy.

May, Arthur J. *The Hapsburg Monarchy, 1867-1914*. Cambridge, Mass.: Harvard University Press, 1951. May offers a balanced account of Beust's career in the Austrian government. Beust emerges from May's pages as an egotistical but competent statesman.

Palmer, Alan. *Twilight of the Habsburgs: The Life and Times of Emperor Francis Joseph*. New York: Grove Press, 1995. This biography of Francis Joseph contains information about the emperor's relationship with Beust and Beust's career in the Austrian government.

Taylor, A. J. P. *The Habsburg Monarchy, 1809-1918: A History of the Austrian Empire and Austria-Hungary*. Rev. ed. London: Hamish Hamilton, 1948. An outstanding account of Beust's foreign and domestic policies during his career in the Austrian government, including his duel with Bismarck.

SEE ALSO: Otto von Bismarck; Francis Joseph I; Metternich.

RELATED ARTICLES in *Great Events from History: The Nineteenth Century, 1801-1900:* May 29, 1867: Austrian Ausgleich; January 18, 1871: German States Unite Within German Empire.

NICHOLAS BIDDLE
American financier

Biddle was the outstanding figure in American banking during the early nineteenth century. By combining superb managerial skills and a keen understanding of finance and banking, he made the Bank of the United States a prototype for modern central banking systems.

BORN: January 8, 1786; Philadelphia, Pennsylvania
DIED: February 27, 1844; Philadelphia, Pennsylvania
AREA OF ACHIEVEMENT: Government and politics

EARLY LIFE

Nicholas Biddle was descended from one of the most distinguished families in Pennsylvania. His father, Charles Biddle, was a successful merchant and had become vice president of the Supreme Executive Council of Pennsylvania. His mother, Hannah Shepard Biddle, was the daughter of a North Carolina merchant. Nicholas was extremely precocious and was admitted at the age of ten to the University of Pennsylvania. His parents transferred him before he was graduated, and he was entered in Princeton as a sophomore at the age of thirteen. Nicholas was graduated in September, 1801, at the age of fifteen, as the valedictorian.

Biddle began the study of law, but his personal interests seemed to mark him for a literary career. He contributed two pieces to Joseph Dennie's literary magazine, *The Port Folio*, which showed considerable talent. Then, in the fall of 1804, Biddle went with General John Armstrong, Jr., who had been appointed minister to France, as his secretary. He assisted ably in the duties of handling claims authorized in the Louisiana Purchase, gaining valuable insights into the problems and techniques of international finance. After a year, he departed on a grand tour of Europe, including a visit to Greece. He served briefly as secretary for James Monroe in London, and he finally returned to the United States in September, 1807.

Biddle had reached his adult height of five feet, seven inches. He had a handsome oval face, a high forehead, and chestnut eyes and hair. He had a serious and dignified demeanor and an aristocratic bearing. He decided to practice law, but he also found time to make contributions to Dennie's *The Port Folio*. In 1810, he was persuaded by William Clark to edit the journals of the Lewis and Clark expedition. Biddle did most of the work, but the journals were eventually published under another editor's name.

In October, 1810, Biddle was elected to the Pennsylvania legislature. The highlight of his service was his eloquent defense of the first Bank of the United States. He displayed a knowledge of finance that impressed all listeners. Biddle declined renomination. One reason was that he had met and later married Jane Craig, whose father's estate was one of the largest in Philadelphia. During the War of 1812, he returned to the Pennsylvania legislature and vigorously supported the war effort, parting company with his fellow Federalists.

Secure financially, Biddle spent the next few years managing his country estate, "Andalusia," and engaging in civic and philanthropic activities. In 1818, he was defeated in a race for Congress, in part because his republicanism was still suspect and because of internal splits in Pennsylvania. President Monroe, although a good friend, hesitated to appoint Biddle to office. When mismanagement occurred in the operation of the second Bank of the United States, however, and the president of the bank, William Jones, was removed early in 1819, Biddle was one of the directors chosen by the government. For the next twenty years, his life revolved around the bank.

LIFE'S WORK

Langdon Cheves of South Carolina, who replaced Jones as president of the bank, followed a policy of retrenchment. "The bank was saved," as they said in the southwestern part of the United States, "but the people were ruined." When Cheves resigned in 1822, Biddle was chosen as the bank's third president. The position he assumed was one of the most important in the United States. The bank was in sound financial condition, but Cheves's policies had alienated many. Biddle gradually dropped many of the restrictions imposed upon the operations of the branch banks. Enlargement of the credit operations stimulated the economy, which was still suffering from the effects of the Panic of 1819. He also increased the profits of the bank and gradually gained complete control over its operations.

From his splendid Greek Revival building on Chestnut Street in Philadelphia, Biddle controlled the operations of eventually twenty-nine branches, from New Hampshire to New Orleans. He used the power of the bank to expand and contract the credit and money supply according to the fluctuations in business activity. He was a superb administrator: The result was a sound banking system and a stable currency that greatly benefited the country.

Biddle's success won for him many friends and growing support for the bank. He sought to avoid involving the bank in politics and tried to remain neutral in the presidential race between President John Quincy Adams and Andrew Jackson in 1828. Biddle was well aware that there were still many powerful people who were hostile toward the bank, and that one was Jackson himself.

After Jackson's election, some members of his party attempted to gain control of the bank. Allegations were made that some branches had exercised an improper influence in the past election by refusing loans to Jacksonians. Biddle was overly sensitive about bank operations. He tended to be defensive rather than to investigate fully charges of mismanagement. At first, Biddle did not appreciate the depth of President Jackson's hostility to the Bank of the United States. Jackson had a prejudice against all banks based on little more than economic ignorance and some bad personal experiences with bank notes.

A large number of voters also believed that the bank, with one-fifth of the country's loans and bank notes in circulation, and one-third of the total bank deposits and specie (gold and silver), had too much money and power for the safety of the republic. The bank was further opposed by a group who believed that it unfairly restricted loans and denied them economic opportunities, and by yet another group of state bankers and their stockholders who resented the size, wealth, and controlling influence of the bank. Despite this opposition, a substantial majority of the American people supported the bank and favored its recharter.

Jackson's attitude and the hostility of many of the advisers around him toward the bank made Biddle uncertain about the prospect of rechartering the bank. Despite conflicting advice, he chose to ask for the rechartering in 1832, four years early, basically because it was an election year and Biddle believed that Jackson would not oppose the bank for fear of losing popularity.

The recharter bill passed both houses in the summer of 1832 by comfortable margins. Biddle had miscalculated: Jackson was not easily intimidated. He responded with a veto and denounced the Bank of the United States as a monopoly, under too much foreign influence, and unconstitutional, and he asserted that it was an institution of the rich and powerful. The message was blatantly misleading, but it was undeniably a powerful and cleverly written polemic, well calculated to appeal to the prejudices of the mass of American people. Despite the goodwill that Biddle had built up for the bank, Jackson successfully changed the debate from the utility of the bank to whether it was a bastion of aristocratic privilege.

Nicholas Biddle. (Library of Congress)

He portrayed himself as saving the republic from the "monster."

Although his victory was more a personal triumph than approval of his stand against the bank, Jackson resolved to destroy the bank. He directed the removal of government deposits, which would be placed in state banks, dubbed "pet banks" by opponents. Biddle responded by curtailing loans. While this action may have been necessary to protect the bank from a reduction of funds (and almost ten million dollars in government deposits were withdrawn), the effect of this restriction on credit staggered commercial and manufacturing interests. Business failures and bankruptcies multiplied, and wages and prices declined. Biddle was not entirely to blame; in fact, he thought that it would ultimately force Jackson to restore the deposits. Neither man was willing to budge. Public opinion, initially anti-Jackson, slowly turned against Biddle. Jackson was unrelenting. He administered a final blow to the Bank of the United States, declaring that the government would no longer accept branch drafts for the payment of taxes.

In 1836, with the death of the bank imminent, Biddle secured a charter from the Pennsylvania legislature to operate it as a state bank. There was no longer a central bank to keep the state banks in order by calling upon them for specie or refusing to receive their bills. Moreover, the American economy was overheating as a result of speculation in large measure stimulated by government deposits in pet banks, which then numbered approximately ninety. The country was inundated with paper money.

The frenzy of speculation was brought to an abrupt end by the Panic of 1837. The Bank of the United States was forced in May, 1837, to suspend payment of specie for the redemption of notes, as did all other banks in the country. Biddle was still the most prominent banker in the country, and he played an important role in trying to shore up the nation's banking system and restore specie payments. Biddle also intervened massively in the cotton market exchange, thus preventing the collapse of that important part of the American economy. He also turned a profit for his bank.

Resumption of specie payments began again in August, 1838. The economy seemed to be recovering, and Biddle, in March, 1839, intending to devote his remaining years to leisure, resigned. In the summer of 1839, however, largely because of the operations of the Bank of England, the United States and the remainder of the world was plunged again into depression. Biddle may have had the grim satisfaction of knowing that the lack of a national bank only made the situation worse, but it was small consolation, because it was also the source of the bank's and Biddle's ruin. Falling cotton prices and mismanagement by the bank's directors led to a second suspension of specie payments in October, 1839. The bank continued to operate, but its situation grew steadily worse, and the bank closed its doors forever in February, 1841.

Biddle's personal fortune, as well as the bank's, collapsed. In his last years, he was harassed by lawsuits, and at one point in 1842, he was arrested on charges of criminal conspiracy, but he was exonerated. Other litigation followed and were only brought to an end by his death on February 27, 1844, from complications arising from bronchitis accompanied by dropsy.

SIGNIFICANCE

Despite his failures, Biddle was an imposing figure in American history. He had the qualities of a statesman who saw the potential of the American economy and formulated the means for realizing it. He wanted to establish American prosperity and to make the country stronger and more secure. His views were guided by a considerable intelligence, but by inclination he displayed more the traits of the idealist and the romantic than the hard-headed, pragmatic businessperson. He showed a preference more for what ought to be than the situation as it was. His naïveté, even arrogance, that reason and truth would prevail in his battle with Jackson proved disastrous for the bank.

Biddle was a brilliant administrator who maintained complete control over the Bank of the United States; yet he also gave an aristocratic tone to the bank and lent credibility to the charge of its having excessive power. Because he saw the value of the bank to the nation's economy, he believed that all men of reason must see it as well. Jackson, he assumed, could not possibly destroy an institution that was in the best interest of the country. Even at the end, his actions were still guided by a larger view of the good of the country rather than the practicalities of sound business.

Perhaps, in retrospect, the country needed the laissez-faire economics that dominated the United States for the next three quarters of a century. The exuberant economic growth, however, was characterized by wild speculation and the persistence of monetary evils. The Bank of the United States offered a more "managed" economic growth and a more stable currency, but it might have dampened the enterprising spirit of American business. When the abuses of the "robber barons" brought on a reform movement during the early twentieth century, one reform was to reestablish a central banking system very similar to Biddle's bank.

—C. Edward Skeen

FURTHER READING

Brown, Marion A. *The Second Bank of the United States and Ohio, 1803-1860: A Collision of Interests*. Lewiston, N.Y.: Edwin Mellen Press, 1998. A more recent study of the bank, not as good as Catterall's book (see below).

Catterall, Ralph C. H. *The Second Bank of the United States*. Chicago: University of Chicago Press, 1903. Although dated both in content and interpretation, this classic work is still the most comprehensive study of the bank.

Govan, Thomas Payne. *Nicholas Biddle: Nationalist and Public Banker, 1786-1844*. Chicago: University of Chicago Press, 1959. The only satisfactory biography of Biddle. The author is partial to his subject and presents a sensitive portrayal of Biddle's role in running the bank. The book is well researched and well written.

Hammond, Bray. *Banks and Politics in America from the Revolution to the Civil War*. Princeton, N.J.: Princeton University Press, 1957. A Pulitzer Prize-winning book that is not simply about banking. Hammond pays particular attention to Biddle and gives a fair appraisal of him. Hammond's interpretation of the Bank War, while controversial, broke new ground.

Kaplan, Edward S. *The Bank of the United States and the American Economy*. Westport, Conn.: Greenwood Press, 1999. Chapter 6 focuses on Biddle and the Second Bank of the United States.

McFaul, John M. *The Politics of Jacksonian Finance*. Ithaca, N.Y.: Cornell University Press, 1972. A good general study of the issues involved in the Bank War. The positions of probank and antibank forces are carefully analyzed.

Remini, Robert V. *Andrew Jackson and the Bank War*. New York: W. W. Norton, 1968. A good, short introduction to the Bank War. Remini is partial to Jackson, but his account is generally a fair, succinct exposition of the issues.

Temin, Peter. *The Jacksonian Economy*. New York: W. W. Norton, 1969. Temin presents a provocative, revisionary interpretation of the sources of the Panic of 1837. While his analysis is not entirely convincing, he adds a new dimension to the study of the Bank War.

Wilburn, Jean Alexander. *Biddle's Bank: The Crucial Years*. New York: Columbia University Press, 1967. Wilburn refutes the Jacksonian allegation of the unpopularity of the bank. She shows support for the bank's services from the people, their congressional representatives, and many local bankers.

SEE ALSO: James Gordon Bennett; Jay Cooke; Andrew Jackson.

RELATED ARTICLES in *Great Events from History: The Nineteenth Century, 1801-1900:* April, 1816: Second Bank of the United States Is Chartered; July 10, 1832: Jackson Vetoes Rechartering of the Bank of the United States; March 17, 1837: Panic of 1837 Begins; August 1, 1846: Establishment of Independent U.S. Treasury; February 25, 1863-June 3, 1864: Congress Passes the National Bank Acts.

AMBROSE BIERCE

American writer

A legendary cynic and social satirist, Bierce won local fame in San Francisco, California, as a newspaper and magazine columnist and secured a place in American literature with his nonrealist short stories, many of which are set against the backdrop of the American Civil War.

BORN: June 24, 1842; Horse Cave Creek, Ohio
DIED: January, 1914?; Mexico?
ALSO KNOWN AS: Ambrose Gwinett Bierce (full name)
AREAS OF ACHIEVEMENT: Literature, journalism

EARLY LIFE

Ambrose Gwinett Bierce was the tenth of thirteen children born to Laura and Marcus Aurelius Bierce. When he was four, his family moved to Indiana, where he was raised among books and religion. At the age of fifteen, Bierce began work as a printer's devil for a local newspaper, and at seventeen he entered the Kentucky Military Institute. Soon after he left the institute, the Civil War broke out, and Bierce enlisted in the Ninth Regiment of the Indiana Volunteers. During his three years with the volunteers, Bierce was wounded in the head, won numerous citations for bravery, and rose to the rank of lieutenant.

After the war, Bierce recovered confiscated Confederate cotton for the federal government and then participated in a mapping expedition in the far West. This trip took Bierce to San Francisco, California, where he would make his home for most of his adult life and earn his name as a writer. Bierce worked as a columnist for a newspaper called the *News-Letter*, where, as the "Town Crier," he used biting satire and blatant sarcasm, as well as a strong dose of tall-tale humor, to attack public figures and institutions he considered guilty of hypocrisy. As he would throughout his career, Bierce angered many of those about whom he wrote and made numerous enemies, but his column quickly won a loyal following among readers. Bierce was not content with his local reputation in journalism, however. He sought literary respectability and national fame and began publishing poems, short stories, and essays in various publications. Literary success, however, was still far in the future.

Bierce married Molly Day in 1871, and a honeymoon trip took the couple to London, England, where Bierce wrote for the publications *Fun* and *Figaro* under the pen name Dod Grile. He also published three collections of columns, sketches, and fiction while in London: *The Fiend's Delight* (1873), *Nuggets and Dust Panned in California* (1873), and *Cobwebs from an Empty Skull* (1874). The cynicism expressed in these collections, as well as in the articles he wrote for London papers, earned him the nickname "Bitter Bierce."

Bierce reluctantly returned to San Francisco in 1875, thinking that his literary future lay in England. His career, both as a social satirist and as a short-story writer, however, was just about to flourish. Soon working again as a columnist, he became a mentor for several aspiring writers, and he appears to have loved the attention. He lived apart from his wife and family, frequently hosting literary discussions with his followers and writing through the night. His marriage would eventually fail, but Bierce the writer and man of letters was just hitting his stride.

LIFE'S WORK

Bierce won local fame—some might even say infamy—as a newspaper and magazine columnist, and the egotistical and cynical personality expressed through this writing has helped make Bierce a legendary figure in American letters. Bierce's most enduring legacy as a writer, however, is found in his short stories, two of which are among the most anthologized stories in American literature.

Between 1877, two years after his return from England, and 1913, when he would attach himself to Pancho Villa's army in the Mexican Revolution and never be heard from again (also part of his legend), Bierce continued his work as a columnist almost nonstop, even after his career as a short-story writer took off. He loved journalistic writing, particularly his brand of it, and he relished the attention, both good and bad, that it brought him. He was also never satisfied with the level of national attention he received for his fiction; thus Bierce the acid-tongued columnist never fully gave way to Bierce the fiction writer.

The most enduring work from Bierce's newspaper and magazine writing is a book entitled *The Devil's Dictionary* (1906), a collection of definitions published by Bierce in his columns over the years. It is Bierce the cynic at his very best, or worst, depending on one's point of view. Although *The Devil's Dictionary* has not proved as popular as his short stories over the years, Bierce's cynical definitions continue to delight many readers.

Bierce's career as a short-story writer blossomed in 1891 with the publication of *Tales of Soldiers and Civilians*, better known as *In the Midst of Life* (the title of the London edition). The stories of this one collection, with their bizarre, frequently supernatural, violent, and ironic nature, are what has earned Bierce his place in American literature. They are stories that clearly do not fit in with the realist, local-color literature of their time.

This last point is key to understanding why Bierce did not earn great fame with his fiction during his lifetime. Though he wrote almost all of his fiction during the realist movement in American literature, Bierce was blatantly nonrealist. Bierce believed that fiction should be *fiction*, that it should make use of the author's imagination and engage the reader's imagination. It should take the improbable, perhaps even the impossible, and make it seem real, rather than simply document the social reality of the time. It was this belief, which Bierce stubbornly held, that placed Bierce clearly outside the mainstream of American literature during his lifetime. It was also this belief, however, that made many of the stories of *In the Midst of Life* seem ahead of their time and therefore more appealing to later readers than to readers of Bierce's own time.

In the Midst of Life contains Bierce's most popular stories, two of which, "An Occurrence at Owl Creek Bridge" and "Chickamauga," rank among the most anthologized stories in American literature. Set against the backdrop of the American Civil War, as are so many of Bierce's stories, "An Occurrence at Owl Creek Bridge" relates the apparently bungled execution of a Southern conspirator who escapes the hangman's noose, flees downriver, and eventually makes it home to his waiting wife. Just as he is about to reach her, he feels a blow to the back of his neck. He is not home, but instead hangs dead below the Owl Creek bridge. His escape has been nothing more than an illusion played out in the mind of the about-to-be executed spy.

Another Bierce story set during the Civil War, "Chickamauga" tells of a small boy playing soldier with a wooden sword by himself in the woods. He gets lost and falls asleep on the ground for several hours. When he awakens, he sees the macabre sight of hundreds of wounded and dying soldiers retreating, almost zombie-like, over where he lies. Rather than be frightened, he attempts to play with them. Eventually they reach the

EXTRACTS FROM *THE DEVIL'S DICTIONARY*

bore	A person who talks when you wish him to listen.
Congress	A body of men who meet to repeal laws.
consult	To seek another's disapproval of a course already decided on.
contempt	The feeling of a prudent man for an enemy who is too formidable safely to be opposed.
corporation	An ingenious device for obtaining individual profit without individual responsibility.
cynic	A blackguard whose faulty vision sees things as they are, not as they ought to be. Hence the custom among the Scythians of plucking out a cynic's eyes to improve his vision.
diary	A daily record of that part of one's life, which he can relate to himself without blushing.
dentist	A prestidigitator who, putting metal into your mouth, pulls coins out of your pocket.
happiness	An agreeable sensation arising from contemplating the misery of another.
historian	A broad-gauge gossip.
lawyer	One skilled in circumvention of the law.
once	Enough.

Source: Ambrose Bierce, *The Devil's Dictionary* (1906).

boy's plantation, which is immersed in flames. The boy finds his mother, who is mortally and grotesquely wounded about the head. He tries to scream out in horror, but he is a deaf mute, which explains how so much has happened around him as he slept. The chief irony of the story may be the one played on the reader, who, perhaps having read other Bierce stories or because of the dreamlike quality of the story once the boy wakes up, expects the graphic war scenes to be only a dream; they are, however, reality, which Bierce has presented in a most nonrealistic manner.

Other stories in *In the Midst of Life* that show Bierce's flare for everything from cruel irony to improbable reality to supernatural events include "The Affair at Coulter's Notch," in which a Civil War artillery officer fires on his own plantation; "The Man and the Snake," in which a man literally dies of fright of what turns out to be a stuffed snake with shoe buttons for eyes; and "The Suitable Surroundings," in which a man dies after reading a ghost story in a haunted house.

More collections of creative writing followed *In the Midst of Life*. Bierce published *Black Beetles in Amber*, a book of satirical poems, in 1892, and *Can Such Things Be?*, a collection of stories, in 1893, but his career as a fiction writer had clearly peaked with *In the Midst of Life*. His fame, though more limited at the time than he had hoped, had been made as well. He moved to Washington, D.C., in 1896, and between 1896 and 1913 he continued to write for the *San Francisco Examiner* and later for the magazine *Cosmopolitan*, all the while assembling his complete works for publication. His *Devil's Dictionary* came out in 1906 under the title *The Cynic's Word Book*.

In 1913, Bierce left Washington and headed to Mexico to observe the Mexican Revolution. Except for a letter he wrote in December of 1913 regarding his experiences with Pancho Villa, he was never heard from again. It is not certain when, where, or how Bierce died.

SIGNIFICANCE

Ambrose Bierce is one of the true rogue characters of American letters, as well as one of the most enigmatic ones. As a journalist, he was loved by his readers and despised in many cases by those who became the targets of his bitter wit, from railroad executives and political leaders to literary contemporaries. As cruel as he was in his newspaper column, he was also the mentor to many fledgling writers in his beloved San Francisco. Still, his cynical view of the world went so far as to manifest itself in an alternative lexicon—*The Devil's Dictionary*—for the language he manipulated first as a teenage typesetter and then later as an acclaimed fiction writer. That acclaim was less than he had hoped for, however, and it made "Bitter Bierce" clearly envious of the likes of Stephen Crane, whom he considered an inferior writer, and other more mainstream authors of his time.

Writing *when* he did rather than *what* he did was precisely Bierce's problem as a fiction writer hoping for wide critical and popular acceptance. As he did in so many areas of his life, Bierce the short-story writer chose to go against the grain, and this cost him; however, he was, as always, true to himself. Though he did not live to know it, the short-story writer who disappeared into revolutionary Mexico in 1913 actually would have been right at home in the nonrealist, psychological, post-Freudian fiction of the twentieth century as practiced by writers ranging from Franz Kafka to Jorge Luis Borges. It would be with the readers of this generation and beyond that Bierce would find a more accepting reading public for his stories.

—*Keith H. Brower*

FURTHER READING

Bierce, Ambrose. *A Sole Survivor: Bits of Autobiography*. Edited by S. T. Joshi and David E. Schultz. Knoxville: University of Tennessee Press, 1998. *Bits of Autobiography*, Bierce's brief account of his life, is included in this book, along with some autobiographical pieces published in the *San Francisco Examiner*, *New York Journal*, and *Cosmopolitan*. Also contains some of Bierce's letters and reports from Civil War battlegrounds.

Davidson, Cathy N. *The Experimental Fictions of Ambrose Bierce: Structuring the Ineffable*. Lincoln: University of Nebraska Press, 1984. Contends that Bierce served as a direct influence for three twentieth century writers, among them Argentines Jorge Luis Borges and Julio Cortázar. Advanced literary analysis for serious readers.

Grenander, M. E. *Ambrose Bierce*. New York: Twayne, 1971. Excellent and highly readable overview of Bierce's life and career with literary analysis. Includes chronology, annotated bibliography, and index. Part of Twayne's United States Authors Series.

Lindley, Daniel. *Ambrose Bierce Takes on the Railroad: The Journalist as Muckraker and Cynic*. Westport, Conn.: Praeger, 1999. Focuses on Bierce's thirty-year journalistic battle with the Central Pacific Railroad and its undue influence over California's politics and economy.

Morris, Roy, Jr. *Ambrose Bierce: Alone in Bad Company*. New York: Crown, 1995. The definitive biography of Bierce. Includes some literary commentary, but it is not intended as a critical study of Bierce's works. Contains an extensive, though unannotated, secondary bibliography and a comprehensive index.

Saunders, Richard. *Ambrose Bierce: The Making of a Misanthrope*. San Francisco: Chronicle Books, 1985. Another insightful biography, though not as exhaustive as Morris. Includes a brief, unannotated bibliography and an index. Part of the Literary West Series.

Wiggins, Robert A. *Ambrose Bierce*. University of Minnesota Pamphlets on American Writers 37. Minneapolis: University of Minnesota Press, 1964. An excellent thumbnail sketch of Bierce's life and career that provides a good starting point for student readers. Includes some literary commentary.

SEE ALSO: Stephen Crane; Guy de Maupassant; Mark Twain.

RELATED ARTICLE in *Great Events from History: The Nineteenth Century, 1801-1900:* c. 1865: Naturalist Movement Begins.

ALBERT BIERSTADT
American painter

Using an exaggerated, romantic style, Bierstadt painted giant landscapes of spectacular Western vistas that helped to shape the myth of the American West, establish the Rocky Mountain school of art, and interest easterners in preservation of Western scenic areas as national parks.

BORN: January 7, 1830; Solingen, Westphalia (now in Germany)
DIED: February 18, 1902; New York, New York
AREA OF ACHIEVEMENT: Art

EARLY LIFE

Albert Bierstadt (BIHR-staht) was born in 1830 at Solingen, Germany, near the city of Düsseldorf, which was a mecca for émigré American artists. He migrated to the United States with his parents at the age of two and was reared amid the maritime atmosphere in the whaling town of New Bedford, Massachusetts. He exhibited his first painting in Boston at the age of twenty-one but returned to Europe for further training at Düsseldorf and in Rome. On the Continent, he was attracted to pastoral scenes, sketching castles along the Rhine and taking hiking expeditions among the Alps. Bierstadt returned to the United States in 1857 and painted in New England. The following year the bearded, sharp-featured artist seized the opportunity to see the trans-Mississippi regions for the first time, when he joined Colonel Frederick W. Lander on a survey party that set out for the West from St. Louis. This expedition literally opened new vistas for Bierstadt and shaped the rest of his artistic career, establishing his place in the history of both the American West and American art.

The explorer, scientist, and artist traveled hand in hand and contributed jointly to the opening of the trans-Mississippi West and in the shaping of its image in the national consciousness. Prior to the exploration of the region, most American painters had slavishly imitated the themes and styles of their European counterparts and mentors. It was almost inevitable, however, that the rising tide of nationalism would find artistic expression, as the United States sought to establish its own and unique cultural identity. Two traditions, the scientific and the artistic, were eventually conjoined in that search.

The artistic tradition established its roots in the eastern part of the country during the 1820's and 1830's as several artists, including Thomas Cole and Asher B. Durand, honed the vision and produced the work that established the Hudson River school. They grappled with the balance between civilization and wilderness and focused upon the vistas of the Hudson River, the White Mountains, Niagara Falls, and other northeastern features as expressions of truth, beauty, and eternal laws and values. Their appreciation of and emphasis upon landscape and nature would shape the perceptions of later artists, including Bierstadt, who spent time at the emerging artists' colony at North Conway, New Hampshire, on the Saco River in the White Mountain region.

In the meantime, following the historic expedition of Meriwether Lewis and William Clark, explorers and scientists were beginning to penetrate the great unknown of the trans-Mississippi West. Their expeditions often enlisted artists who traveled along and sketched the plants, animals, people, and lands they encountered both for artistic purposes and to document visually the information acquired. They traveled and worked under primitive conditions foreign to the overwhelming majority of their artistic colleagues past and present, and they were virtually to a man overwhelmed and deeply impressed by what they saw and recorded.

First were two Philadelphians, Samuel Seymour and Titian Ramsay Peale, who accompanied the Stephen Long expedition to the Rockies in 1820. They were soon followed by George Catlin, who made several trips up the Missouri River during the 1830's and produced pictorial records of the Plains Indians prior to extensive contact with white civilization. Later came the Swiss artist Karl Bodmer, who produced extremely accurate depictions of the Indians and painted landscapes of the American interior as well. During the late 1830's, Baltimore artist Alfred Jacob Miller traveled the Oregon Trail and depicted the world of the mountain man, and within a few more years John James Audubon was at work painting the animals along the Missouri River. These and other artists created the scientific-artistic tradition which was part of Albert Bierstadt's milieu.

LIFE'S WORK

After his return from Europe, Bierstadt learned of Colonel Frederick W. Lander's proposed expedition to prepare a survey for a railroad route from the Mississippi River, across the north fork of the Platte, through Nebraska Territory, across South Pass, and connecting with San Francisco and Puget Sound. Bierstadt and photographer F. S. Frost joined the party and in 1858-1859 journeyed as far as the Wasatch range on the western slope of the Rockies. They then returned on their own, traveling through the Wind River range and the land of the Shoshone, producing sketches and photographic images of the scenery and people they encountered. Bierstadt was thus the first artist to utilize photography to supplement his own sketches and watercolors while on a journey of Western exploration. Bierstadt and Frost paid their own way and none of their work from this expedition survives, but the artist had been captivated by what he had seen.

Upon returning to the East, Bierstadt relocated his studio from New Bedford to New York City, where in 1860 the first of his paintings went on public display. Among them was *The Base of the Rocky Mountains, Laramie Peak* that measured some four and a half by nine feet. This canvas was prototypical of the Bierstadt style, which the public enthusiastically applauded. It was characterized by a seeming realism, which in fact presented a romanticized and even falsified depiction of a Western scene on a grandiose scale. It reflected both the romanticization of nature and the cultural nationalism that were to be representative of the Rocky Mountain school.

Bierstadt was soon getting higher prices in Europe for his paintings than any other American artist had ever received, and with his new wealth he built a large house on the Hudson River at Irvington and a second studio in San Francisco, which served as a base for further excursions into the Western regions. He traveled through the Colorado Rockies, the Great Salt Lake region, the Pacific Northwest, and in 1863 into California's Yosemite and Hetch Hetchy valleys, sketching the vistas that became the subjects for some of his most commercially successful paintings. A series of paintings of grandiose dimension, produced during the mid-1860's, sold for the highest sums ever earned by an American artist. Featuring towering mountains, shimmering waters, and dark forests, these canvases carried the romantic concepts of nature to their apex of grandeur. While some critics scoffed, the public loved the huge size and detail of the Bierstadt canvases.

The giant paintings were done in Bierstadt's studio, based on his field sketches, photographs, stereoscopic views, and watercolors. The artist rearranged the features, gave names to nonexistent locales, and generally falsified his portrayals, even as the public praised his "realism." It is not accidental that the growing interest of the American people in the spectacular land features of the West and their preservation coincided chronologically with the popularity of Bierstadt and Thomas Moran, whose paintings of Yellowstone would contribute to the creation of the national park in 1872.

Ironically, at the height of Bierstadt's popularity two trends were developing that would relegate his large canvases to relative obscurity and general critical disdain by the turn of the century. First, with the rise of the Impressionist style in Europe, realistic painters of the Romantic school fell out of fashion. Second, those who were interested in literal depictions of the West could now examine the striking photographs of William Henry Jackson and others who were elevating photography to the status of an art form.

Bierstadt continued to paint, and his elevated reputation secured large commissions, as during the late 1870's, when he received fifteen thousand dollars from the earl of Dunraven to paint a large landscape of Estes Park, Colorado, and Long's Peak. Bierstadt's sales and commissions steadily diminished, however, even as his critical reputation continued to decline. By the time he died in February, 1902, fashion and popularity had passed him by.

SIGNIFICANCE

Although not considered a great artist by most critics, Albert Bierstadt remains a major figure in the history of both American art and the trans-Mississippi West. A founder of the Rocky Mountain school, Bierstadt's giant landscapes of the American West—its mountains, forests, waterfalls, and spectacular landforms—brought romantic appreciation of nature to a new artistic peak in nineteenth century America. Although he took numerous liberties with fact in his larger works, the general public regarded Bierstadt's paintings as quite realistic, and he thus helped to generate the mythic perception of the American West and its landscapes that contributed to the movement for preservation of spectacular landforms in national parks. Ironically, although not as well known as his large canvases, Bierstadt's smaller pieces and sketches, done during or immediately following journeys in the field, have retained a much higher critical standing. Bierstadt's works are found in major collections across the United States and have enjoyed constant popularity among those interested in the West and its history.

—*James E. Fickle*

FURTHER READING

Anderson, Nancy K., and Linda S. Ferber. *Albert Bierstadt: Art and Enterprise*. New York: Hidden Hills Press, 1990. This catalog accompanied an exhibit of Bierstadt's work and includes essays about his life and art. Also contains reproductions of some of the 79 paintings, prints, and drawings on display.

Hassrick, Peter. *The Way West: Art of Frontier America*. New York: Harry N. Abrams, 1977. A profusely illustrated introduction to the work of major artists of the nineteenth century West, including Bierstadt.

Hendricks, Gordon. *Albert Bierstadt: Painter of the American West*. New York: Harry N. Abrams, 1974. The standard biography. Makes extensive use of Bierstadt's letters. Includes 63 color and 365 black-and-white illustrations, a catalog of Bierstadt's paintings, and a bibliography.

Hine, Robert V. *The American West: An Interpretive History*. Boston: Little, Brown, 1973. An excellent survey of Western history, with a first-rate chapter, "The Image of the West in Art."

Huth, Hans. *Nature and the American: Three Centuries of Changing Attitudes*. Berkeley: University of California Press, 1957. Evaluates the developments and factors that shaped the conservation movement in the United States. The contributions of artists, including Bierstadt, are an important part of the story.

Kornhauser, Elizabeth Mankin, Amy Ellis, and Maureen Miesmer. *Hudson River School: Masterworks from the Wadsworth Atheneum Museum of Art*. New Haven, Conn.: Yale University Press, 2003. A catalog accompanying an exhibit of paintings by Bierstadt and other Hudson River school artists. A good source for understanding the school's influence on Bierstadt.

McCracken, Harold. *Portrait of the Old West*. New York: McGraw-Hill, 1952. A scholarly account with material on Bierstadt's early career.

Nash, Roderick. *Wilderness and the American Mind*. 4th ed. New Haven, Conn.: Yale University Press, 2001. While Bierstadt is mentioned only in passing, this is the standard work on the evolution of American attitudes toward wilderness.

Runte, Alfred. *National Parks: The American Experience*. Lincoln: University of Nebraska Press, 1979. As part of his discussion of cultural nationalism, Runte describes Bierstadt as a significant influence in the establishment of national parks.

SEE ALSO: George Caleb Bingham; Mathew B. Brady; John Constable; Ferdinand Vandeveer Hayden; J. M. W. Turner.

RELATED ARTICLE in *Great Events from History: The Nineteenth Century, 1801-1900:* February 20, 1872: Metropolitan Museum of Art Opens.

GEORGE CALEB BINGHAM

American painter

Bingham was the first American artist to record life on the mid-nineteenth century frontier in paintings of sensitive social commentary and high aesthetic quality.

BORN: March 20, 1811; Augusta County, Virginia
DIED: July 7, 1879; Kansas City, Missouri
AREA OF ACHIEVEMENT: Art

EARLY LIFE

Known throughout his career as "the Missouri Artist," Bingham was, in fact, born into a long-established southern family. Henry Vest Bingham, his father, whose ancestors probably came from England in the latter half of the seventeenth century, married Mary Amend, of German and French Huguenot descent, and they started their married life farming tobacco in Virginia. George, born on the farm, which was just west of Charlottesville, Virginia, was one of eight children. In 1819, Bingham's father got into financial difficulties, lost his business, and went west with his family to Franklin, Missouri. In 1820, he opened an inn and dealt in tobacco as a sideline. On his death in 1823, the family moved to a farm outside town, where Mrs. Bingham ran a small school.

There is some biographical evidence that Bingham was interested in drawing, but there is no proof that he ever had any formal training. Apprenticed to a cabinetmaker at sixteen, he may have worked as such, and perhaps as a sign painter, and there is some suggestion that he planned to study law. In 1833, he was a professional portrait painter. His early work is awkward and somewhat primitive, and seems to indicate that he was self-taught. Nevertheless, he was able to make a living at it, moving around the Columbia, Missouri, area, and in 1836, he was sufficiently confident to offer his services in St. Louis. In that year, he married Sarah Elizabeth Hutchinson of Boonville.

During the late spring of 1838, Bingham went to Philadelphia, evidently to study. There is no record of his entering any art school, but he did buy a collection of old master engravings and some antique sculpture casts, both of which were commonly used for art instruction at the time. The city itself was rich in examples of international art, and Bingham must have seen some of it. He may have gone on to New York also, because a painting of his, one of his first genre pieces, *Western Boatmen Ashore*, was shown at the Apollo Gallery in New York in the autumn.

In 1840, Bingham exhibited six paintings at the National Academy of Design in New York. By that time he was technically much more accomplished; already evident in these works is the flair for genre subjects, simple incidents of everyday life, which was to become his distinctive mark as an artist. He also decided to move to Washington, D.C., ambitious to try his skills painting federal politicians. He spent four years, off and on, in the capital, during which he painted portraits of important figures including John Quincy Adams and Daniel Webster. By this time, he was a painter of some modest reputation, but he had not produced any works of serious moment. Looking at his *Self-Portrait of the Artist*, which he had painted a few years earlier, it would be hard to guess that this square-jawed young man with the wide brow and the slight curl in his forelock, rather tentatively painted, would suddenly during the mid-1840's produce paintings of considerable importance.

LIFE'S WORK

It is, in the main, the painting that Bingham did roughly in the ten years between 1845 and 1855 that has given him his reputation as one of the foremost American artists. After that time, for several reasons, the quality of his art fell back into competent professionalism, with occasional paintings reminding the art world of his heights in what is called his "great genre period." During this period, he continued to paint portraits, but his best work was in studies of simple life in Missouri, with special emphasis placed upon the world of the flatboatmen plying their hard trade on the Missouri River. He had anticipated the theme in his *Western Boatmen Ashore* during the late 1830's, and during the 1840's he found a market for the theme, rather surprisingly in New York.

The celebration of the simple life of the American plainsman, trapper, and boatman had already been prepared for in literature in the writing of Washington Irving, James Fenimore Cooper, John Greenleaf Whittier, and Henry Wadsworth Longfellow. Bingham, in a sense, was following the eastern painter William Sidney Mount in putting that growing admiration for the muscle and sweat of American frontier life into pictorial terms, but in his own way.

The American Art-Union in New York City was dedicated to supporting American artists through purchase, sale, and reproduction of their paintings, and in a seven-year period it purchased twenty paintings by Bingham, all of them examples of his genre themes.

Fur Traders Descending the Missouri was one of the first paintings so purchased, and it stunningly reveals the power of Bingham as a painter, which had never been revealed in his portrait work. It is, at one and the same time, his most powerful painting and the most representative of his studies of those singular men who, in working the river, seem to exemplify an admirable truth about American life. Variations on the theme were to occupy Bingham through the next ten years, and occasionally the theme was to catch the popular imagination in ways that Bingham could hardly have imagined.

If *Fur Traders Descending the Missouri* has a focused intensity that reminds viewers of Le Nain and slightly awes on sight, Bingham also had the ability to use the theme charmingly. *The Jolly Flatboatmen*, showing its simple subjects in a moment of dance and song, was engraved by the Art-Union and eighteen thousand copies were sent out to American homes. Part of the secret lay, undoubtedly, in Bingham's fastidious choice of how he saw the humble boatmen. He eschewed the real vulgarity of their lives, the hard toil, the danger, for gentle, often humorous scenes of cardplaying or quiet moments of rest. He did not patronize them, but he did not tell all the story. The paintings of lively, unsentimental masculinity framed by the beauty of the western riverscapes brought out the best in Bingham, both as an artist and as a recorder of an aspect of American frontier life.

During the early 1850's, he carried the taste for paintings of Missouri life a step further in his "Election" series. These were quite as popular as his studies of the working Westerners, and he spent considerable time not only in painting them but also in promoting the sales of the originals and of engravings of the same. As in his first series, he avoided adverse comment. William Hogarth's famous election works may be seen as an influence, but while Hogarth was intent on satire, Bingham never was. Although the characters in these technically complicated paintings of speech-making, polling, and post-voting celebration may sometimes be less than proper, they are never savaged. A cheerful, sensitive appreciation of the democratic process in action, however makeshift it might be in the rural fastness of Missouri, was the dominant tone in these works, which brought Bingham praise for his appreciation of the American way of choosing their legislators.

However modest the topics of this period were, Bingham's use of them was not unsophisticated. He displayed a strong sense of composition, a considerable talent for marshaling large groups of people, and a use of light and shadow that complemented the mood succinctly. His drawing was confident, and his settings appropriate and sometimes charming. He was no longer merely a journeyman painter.

Despite the support of the Art-Union, he was never as popular in the East as he was out West. There was constant sniping at his rude subjects and at his use of color. He quarreled with the Art-Union administrators over criticism of his work printed in their house journal and became dissatisfied with the prices they paid him for his paintings.

By the mid-1850's, Bingham, dissatisfied with his career, was determined to move on to more important work. He had painted a Daniel Boone subject a few years earlier, and he saw the historical painting as the kind of theme that he wanted to pursue. He hoped to convince the federal government of the appropriateness of having a Boone painting, of major proportions, commissioned for the Capitol. A step in that direction came in the form of a commission from the state of Missouri to provide paintings of George Washington and Thomas Jefferson, and in 1856, Bingham went to Europe to work on those paintings. He visited Paris but settled in Düsseldorf, then a center for painters and sculptors, and he completed his Washington and Jefferson there. Unfortunately, in the eyes of some critics, Düsseldorf, with its emphasis on high technical polish in painting, influenced Bingham adversely, and there is some informed opinion which sees a decline in the quality of his work dating from the Düsseldorf experience.

Bingham returned to Missouri with his commissions and was asked to provide two further paintings, one of Henry Clay and one of Andrew Jackson. Nevertheless, the hoped-for major commission from the government did not come, and he kept busy doing portraits until the Civil War broke out. Always interested and sometimes involved in politics as a Whig (Republican) supporter, he served from 1862 until 1865 as the state treasurer, painting as time permitted. Although an active supporter of the war against the South, he split with the party after the war over the excessive zeal with which Republicans conducted themselves; his painting *Order 11*, not a particularly good example of his talents, got him into a continuing battle, because it illustrated the arrogance of the military during the war. It was one of the few occasions on which he used his talent to make political comment, and it did him little good.

Bingham continued to paint portraits, landscapes (which had always been least interesting to him), and genre topics, and to take a hand in Missouri politics. There was some desultory talk at one time of standing for governor, and he served as adjutant general during the 1870's. In 1877, the University of Missouri made him its first professor of art, a post that seems to have been largely honorary; he had a studio on the campus but spent little time there. When he died in July, 1879, he was almost totally forgotten in the East but honored in Missouri as the state's own painter, the "Missouri Artist."

SIGNIFICANCE

Despite the length of Bingham's career, the amount of work he produced, his constant comings and goings between Missouri and the East, and the sales of his engravings and paintings, Bingham's reputation in the main was confined principally to the Midwest, and he was patronized as a competent portraitist and a sometime regional genre artist.

After Bingham's death he remained relatively unknown until 1917, when an article in *Art World* suggested that he was more than a simple hack. The first important confirmation of that idea came in 1933, when the Metropolitan Museum of Art purchased *Fur Traders Descending the Missouri*. In 1934, the City Art Museum in St. Louis mounted the first major show of his works, and in 1935, the Museum of Modern Art in New York exhibited his work. Since then his reputation has been secure, but it is based, in the main, not upon his entire life's work as a painter but on the output of that ten-year period between 1845 and 1855 when he was principally concerned with recording the working, social, and political lives of the native Missourians. He is recognized as the first master painter of the American West, and his political paintings are a vivid record of the brash, lively vitality of a world that he knew so well—not only as an artist but also as a participant.

Bingham's reputation as a painter of serious quality, however, is centered on those brilliantly evocative paintings of trappers, flatboatmen, river people, and other simple citizens of the West, whom he sees with a stunningly poetic clarity that transcends the particularity of detail that he was so determined to record. Some critics have seen in this aesthetic aura touches of an American "luminism," that quality that gives great paintings a universal ideality and connection with the "oneness" of all things. In those paintings, the truth of Bingham's record of simple life goes beyond its factuality.

—*Charles H. Pullen*

FURTHER READING

Baigell, Matthew. *A History of American Painting*. New York: Praeger, 1971. This book is theoretically less adventurous than the Novak work (see below), but it does, in a genial way, put Bingham into the American tradition, and that is where it is easiest to understand and appreciate him.

Bingham, George Caleb. *An Address to the Public, Vindicating a Work of Art Illustrative of the Federal Military Policy in Missouri During the Late Civil War*. Kansas City, Mo., 1871. Expresses Bingham's conviction that it is the duty of the artist to make political use of his gift.

_____. "Art, the Ideal of Art and the Utility of Art." In *Public Lectures Delivered in the Chapel of the University of the State of Missouri, Columbia, Missouri, by Members of the Faculty, 1878-79*, course 2, vol. 1, 311-324. Columbia, Mo.: Statesman Book and Job Print, 1879. One of Bingham's rare statements about art and the role of the artist.

Bloch, E. Maurice. *George Caleb Bingham*. 2 vols. Berkeley: University of California Press, 1967. The major study of Bingham's work. Excellent illustration. Very careful discussion of his major paintings.

Larkin, Lew. *Bingham, Fighting Artist: The Story of Missouri's Immortal Painter, Patriot, Soldier, and Statesman*. St. Louis: State Publishing, 1955. The title of the book may seem a bit fulsome, but Bingham was much more than simply a painter, and something less than a statesman. This book tries to bring the multiple lives of the man into context.

McDermott, John Francis. *George Caleb Bingham: River Portraitist*. Norman: University of Oklahoma Press, 1959. The title of this full-scale critical biography is misleading. It does, in fact, cover Bingham's entire career, using specific paintings or groups of paintings as a critical focus, interspersed with details of his career and life. Good illustrations.

Novak, Barbara. *American Painting of the Nineteenth Century: Realism, Idealism, and the American Experience*. New York: Praeger, 1969. This book is helpful in putting Bingham in the tradition of American painting in interesting ways. He has a chapter to himself, and his connections, implicit and explicit, to other painters are explored with much grace.

Rash, Nancy. *The Painting and Politics of George Caleb Bingham*. New Haven, Conn.: Yale University Press, 1991. Rash describes Bingham's painting within the context of his political career to demonstrate how his art influenced and recorded the political and cultural life of his time.

Shapiro, Michael Edward, et al. *George Caleb Bingham*. New York: Harry N. Abrams, 1993. Five art historians analyze Bingham's personality and art works, refuting the opinion that his simple and democratic paintings directly reflect his personality. Includes color plates and other illustrations.

SEE ALSO: Albert Bierstadt; John Constable; Ferdinand Vandeveer Hayden; J. M. W. Turner.

RELATED ARTICLE in *Great Events from History: The Nineteenth Century, 1801-1900:* February 20, 1872: Metropolitan Museum of Art Opens.

OTTO VON BISMARCK

Chancellor of the German Empire (1871-1890)

Known as the "blood and iron chancellor," Bismarck occasioned the unification of the several German states into the German Empire of 1871-1918. Though his image is that of an aristocrat in a spiked helmet, he was above all a diplomat and a politician, skillfully manipulating the forces at work within Germany and among the European states to achieve his goals.

BORN: April 1, 1815; Schönhausen, Prussia (now in Germany)

DIED: July 30, 1898; Friedrichsruh, Germany

ALSO KNOWN AS: Otto Eduard Leopold von Bismarck-Schönhausen (full name); Iron Chancellor

AREAS OF ACHIEVEMENT: Government and politics, diplomacy

EARLY LIFE

Young Otto von Bismarck (bihz-MARK) was influenced both by his father's and his mother's heritages. His father was a Prussian Junker, an aristocrat of proud lineage but modest financial means. The family estates were not particularly large or productive, but provided a setting of paternalistic rule over peasants long accustomed to serve. From his mother and her family, Bismarck learned the sophistication of the upper bourgeoisie, the cosmopolitanism of city life and foreign languages, and something of the ideals of the Enlightenment. Both sides of the family took pride in service to the Prussian state and its ruling dynasty, the Hohenzollern. The Junker aristocrats often served in the military, while the upper bourgeoisie chose the civil service.

Bismarck received a rigorous classical education and attended Göttingen and Berlin universities. He tried his hand at a career in the Prussian diplomatic and civil service. Though his excellent family connections and quick mind should have assured his success, his early career was a disaster. He was temperamentally unsuited to the discipline of a subordinate position, and he alienated his supervisors time after time. "I want to play the tune the way it sounds good to me," he commented, "or not at all. . . . My pride bids me command rather than obey." Like all young men of his class, Bismarck served a few months in the army and remained a reserve officer throughout his life, but he never considered a military career. At the age of twenty-four, he resigned from the Prussian bureaucracy and took charge of one of the family's estates. Then his life changed under the influence of pietist Lutheran families; he married Johanna von Puttkamer, a woman from one such family, in 1847, and settled down to the domesticity of country life.

The revolutions of 1848 roused him from the country and brought Bismarck into politics. He quickly made a name for himself as a champion of the Hohenzollern monarchy against the liberal and democratic revolutionaries, and, after the failure of the revolution, the grateful King Frederick William IV appointed him to a choice position in the diplomatic corps. He represented Prussia at the German Diet at Frankfurt am Main and then at the courts of Czar Alexander II of Russia and Emperor Napoleon III of France, making a name for himself as a shrewd negotiator and a vigorous advocate of Prussian interests.

LIFE'S WORK

Bismarck was recalled to Berlin by King William I of Prussia in 1862 to solve a political and constitutional crisis. The Prussian Diet was refusing to pass the royal budget, because it disagreed with military reforms instituted by the king and his government. To break the deadlock, Bismarck told parliament that "great questions will not be settled by speeches and majority decisions—that was the great mistake of 1848 and 1849—but by blood and iron," and he went ahead with the royal policies in spite of parliamentary opposition. In spite of his reputation as an old-fashioned Prussian monarchist, Bismarck was making an attempt to attract middle-class German nationalists to the support of the Prussian monarchy and its military establishment. When the newly reformed Prussian armies proved their effectiveness by defeating Denmark in 1864 and Austria in 1866 and by setting Prussia on the pathway toward a united Germany, Bismarck was a hero.

Now only France could block German unity. Through a masterful (if rather deceitful) set of diplomatic maneuvers, Bismarck forced the hand of Napoleon III, causing him to declare war on Prussia. Faced by the apparent aggression of a new Napoleon, the southern German states (except for Austria) joined with Prussian-dominated northern Germany. In the Franco-Prussian War that followed, France was defeated and the German Empire was proclaimed. Its capital was Berlin, and its reigning monarch was simultaneously the king of Prussia, William I; but the triumph was Bismarck's.

Even his old enemies among the German liberals were forced to recognize Bismarck's genius. Nevertheless, under the leadership of the Prussian-Jewish National Liberal politician Eduard Lasker, they pressured Bismarck to create a constitutional government for the newly formed empire. Bismarck's constitution was a masterful manipulation of the political power structure of the age. It contained a popularly elected parliament to represent the people (the *Reichstag*), an aristocratic upper house to represent the princely German states (the *Bundesrat*), and a chancellor as the chief executive—himself. Only the emperor could appoint or dismiss the chancellor, and as long as Bismarck held the ear of William I, his position was secure. As a further means of controlling power, Bismarck retained the positions of Prussian prime minister and Prussian foreign minister throughout most of the period.

Bismarck was a man of great physical stature, who enjoyed the outdoor life of the country squire, riding horses and hunting game. He indulged himself in eating, drinking, and smoking, and, though he fell ill from time to time, he revived again and again with great vigor. He was an eloquent speaker, though with an amazingly high-pitched voice, and he was a master of the German language. He loved the domestic haven of his family life, and he was capable of bitter hatred of his political opponents, at home and abroad. For a statesman famed for his cool exploitation of realistic politics, he showed surprisingly irrational passion when faced with determined opposition.

Otto von Bismarck. (Library of Congress)

Bismarck continued to face both domestic and foreign challenges throughout his tenure as chancellor. He opposed the power of the Catholic Center Party in the so-called *Kulturkampf*, the German version of the struggle between the Roman Catholic Church and the modern state. He sought to limit the growth of the Social Democratic Party by a combination of social legislation and limits on the political freedoms of left-wing parties. He exploited the forces of anti-Semitism and economic nationalism to undermine the German liberal and progressive parties. He made many political enemies, but he was able to retain power by balancing forces against one another and shifting coalitions among political groups.

In foreign affairs, Bismarck used the talents he had once displayed in causing three wars to keep the peace once he had achieved his major goal of German unity. He caused great bitterness in France by taking Alsace-Lorraine in 1871. However, he simultaneously wooed Austria and Russia, establishing a "Three Emperors' League" among the three conservative states to preserve the status quo. Bismarck organized the Congress of Berlin of 1878 to settle conflicts in the Balkans, and when it was successful he chose for himself the title of the "honest broker." As nationalism in eastern Europe and colonial rivalries overseas continued to threaten the peace of the world, Bismarck skillfully sailed the German ship of state on the safest course he could.

In 1890, however, the seventy-five-year-old Bismarck clashed with his new sovereign, the thirty-one-year-old Emperor William II. When the young man wanted to do things his own way and forced Bismarck to resign, the British magazine *Punch* published one of the most famous cartoons in history, entitled "Dropping the Pilot." Bismarck retired to his estates, where he was the object of honors from the great and powerful and much adulation from the public. However, he loved the reality of power, not mere applause, and he died in 1898, a frustrated and embittered man in his eighty-third year.

SIGNIFICANCE

Otto von Bismarck is known to history as the "blood and iron chancellor" and the practitioner of realpolitik. He was no sentimental humanitarian, and military power always figured strongly in his calculations. However, he was not a single-minded dictator or heavy-handed militarist as he is sometimes portrayed.

Above all, Bismarck was a diplomat and a politician. He kept open several options as long as possible before choosing a final course of action. His shift from a parliamentary alliance with the liberals during the 1870's to an alliance with the Catholics and the conservatives during the 1880's was designed to achieve a single goal: the perpetuation of the power of the traditional elites of feudal and monarchical Germany and the emerging elites of business and industry. Prior to Bismarck, liberalism and nationalism seemed inevitably linked, and those movements were opposed by the aristocratic establishment; Bismarck broke that link and attached German nationalism to the Prussian conservatism that he valued.

For all of his skill, walking the tightropes of domestic and foreign policy as Prussian prime minister and German chancellor for twenty-eight years, he could not create a system that would endure. The forces of liberalism and socialism continued to grow, pushing Germany toward either democracy or revolution, and the Hohenzollern monarchs were swept away in 1918. The forces of radical nationalism and pan-German racism were not checked by the new republic, and Adolf Hitler's Nazism led Germany to disaster between 1933 and 1945. The German unity that Bismarck created lasted only twenty years after his death, and the map of the German-speaking states of Europe after 1945 bears little resemblance to that of Bismarckian Germany. Nevertheless, in a country that saw so much political instability and military defeat in the twentieth century, the figure of Bismarck still looms large and continues to fascinate practitioners of statecraft and writers of history.

—*Gordon R. Mork*

FURTHER READING

Crankshaw, Edward. *Bismarck*. New York: Viking Press, 1981. A standard volume for the general reader, colorfully written by an Englishman with a flair for political biography. Crankshaw is critical of Bismarck but does not see in him the roots of Nazism.

Feuchtwanger, Edgar. *Bismarck*. London: Routledge, 2002. Concise biography, reassessing Bismarck's historical significance.

Gall, Lothar. *Bismarck: The White Revolutionary*. Translated by J. A. Underwood. 2 vols. London: Allen & Unwin, 1986. Though no biography of so controversial a figure as Bismarck will ever be accepted as definitive, this one by a West German historian comes close. Gall argues that Bismarck was a conservative who revolutionized German politics and European international affairs.

Hamerow, Theodore S., ed. *Otto von Bismarck: A Historical Assessment*. 2d ed. Lexington, Mass.: D. C. Heath, 1972. An anthology on Bismarck drawn from German, English, and American authors, introduced and edited by a knowledgeable American professor. Several of the pieces are unavailable in English except in this volume.

Kent, George O. *Bismarck and His Times*. Carbondale: Southern Illinois University Press, 1978. A brief and lucid account of Bismarck and his age, suitable for American college students and the general reader. Kent is familiar with the primary and secondary sources, and his excellent notes provide a springboard for further reading.

Lerman, Katharine Anne. *Bismarck*. New York: Pearson Longman, 2004. One of the titles in the Profiles in Power series, this book focuses on Bismarck's exercise of power as a crucial means of understanding his personality and statecraft.

Pflanze, Otto. *Bismarck and the Development of Germany*. Princeton, N.J.: Princeton University Press, 1962. The first volume of a life's work on Bismarck by the acknowledged American scholarly master of the subject. It takes the story through German unification in 1871.

Stern, Fritz. *Gold and Iron: Bismarck, Bleichroeder, and the Building of the German Empire*. New York: Alfred A. Knopf, 1977. A study of Bismarck and his Jewish banker Gerson von Bleichroeder that sheds important light on both the personal and the economic aspects of the men and their time.

Taylor, A. J. P. *Bismarck: The Man and the Statesman*. New York: Alfred A. Knopf, 1955. A cleverly written portrait of Bismarck by an Oxford don famous for his acid commentaries on German history. He sees the chancellor as a man interested only in his personal power, who simply used the persons and institutions around him for his own aggrandizement.

Wehler, Hans-Ulrich. *The German Empire, 1871-1918*. Translated by Kim Traynor. Dover, N.H.: Berg, 1985. A leading West German historian, who emphasizes the social and economic aspects of the Bismarck era, summarizes his argument in this useful book. Wehler sees Bismarck as representing the traditional elites of Prussia, whose "fatal successes" contributed to the German disasters of the twentieth century.

SEE ALSO: Friedrich von Beust; Friedrich von Holstein; Ferdinand Lassalle; Wilhelm Liebknecht; Theodor Mommsen.

RELATED ARTICLES in *Great Events from History: The Nineteenth Century, 1801-1900:* March 3-November 3, 1848: Prussian Revolution of 1848; September 24, 1862: Bismarck Becomes Prussia's Minister-President; February 1-October 30, 1864: Danish-Prussian War; 1866-1867: North German Confederation Is Formed; June 15-August 23, 1866: Austria and Prussia's Seven Weeks' War; July 19, 1870-January 28, 1871: Franco-Prussian War; 1871-1877: *Kulturkampf* Against the Catholic Church in Germany; January 18, 1871: German States Unite Within German Empire; May 6-October 22, 1873: Three Emperors' League Is Formed; May 20, 1882: Triple Alliance Is Formed; January 4, 1894: Franco-Russian Alliance.

GEORGES BIZET

French composer

Bizet was one of the foremost French composers of the nineteenth century and the author of one of the most popular operas of all time, Carmen. *His influence on later generations is difficult to measure, but it is clear that he was one of the greatest musical geniuses of nineteenth century Europe.*

BORN: October 25, 1838; Paris, France
DIED: June 3, 1875; Bougival, near Paris, France
ALSO KNOWN AS: Alexandre César Léopold Bizet (birth name)
AREA OF ACHIEVEMENT: Music

EARLY LIFE

Georges Bizet (bee-zay) was an only child of musically inclined parents. His father, Adolphe Arnaud Bizet, was a teacher of voice and a composer. His mother, Aimée Marie Louise Léopoldine Joséphine Delsarte, was a gifted pianist. Bizet began informal music studies with his mother at the age of four. Groomed for a musical career, at the age of eight he began piano lessons with the celebrated teacher Antoine François Marmontel and was admitted to the Paris Conservatoire shortly before his tenth birthday. A brilliant student, Bizet excelled in his courses, winning the Premier Prix in *solfège* (sight-singing) and in Marmontel's piano class. His virtuosity was such that he could easily have launched a concert career in his late teens, had he wished to do so. The young Bizet, however, had his heart set on becoming a composer.

Bizet's first attempts in composition date from 1850, when he was twelve years old. His early works consist of virtuosic piano pieces, choruses, and a one-act comic opera. Bizet's first major work, the Symphony in C, was composed when he was seventeen. Aside from an abundance of charming themes, this work displays a mastery of orchestration unusual in a composer at any age.

In 1857, Bizet won the prestigious Prix de Rome for his cantata *Clovis et Clotilde*. That enabled him to travel to Rome, where he remained for three years, imbibing Italian culture and refining his skills as a composer. During this time, his attitude toward composition changed drastically. Always a composer of immense natural gifts, he decided to adopt a more rational approach to writing music. This, however, produced an identity crisis that resulted in a creeping paralysis of his creative powers and a series of projected and abandoned works.

Bizet's problems in Rome were compounded when the Académie des Beaux-Arts, under whose aegis the Prix de Rome was offered, refused to accept his opera *Don Procopio* (1859) in place of the mass he had originally been obliged to write according to the stipulations of the prize. Bizet, for whom the Christian faith held little appeal, was reluctant to write religious music. An ode-symphony, *Vasco de Gama* (1860), was brought to completion and accepted by the Académie.

LIFE'S WORK

In 1860, Bizet returned to Paris, where he persisted in his desire to forge a career as a composer, even in the face of tempting offers to teach and make concert appearances. In 1861, he presented his third submission to the Académie in the form of the *Scherzo et marche funèbre* and an overture entitled *La Chasse d'Ossian*, both of which were well received. His final submission, in 1862, was a one-act comic opera, *La Guzla de l'émir*. Though the music for this opera has disappeared, much of it was incorporated into Bizet's first important stage work, *Les Pêcheurs de perles*. Premiered in 1863, it was received coolly by the critics, who criticized its apparent imitation of Richard Wagner and Giuseppe Verdi in orchestration, harmony, and dynamics.

By 1863, Bizet's Rome pension had run out, and he was compelled to earn a living making transcriptions and arrangements for the publishers Choudens and Heugel. The sixteen-hour days he often worked affected his health, which had never been good. Since childhood, he had suffered from a chronic ulceration of the throat that continued to bother him and that would eventually prove fatal. He was also afflicted with articular rheumatism. Nevertheless, he found the time to begin a new operatic endeavor, *Ivan IV*, which, though finished in 1865, was never produced.

Bizet's next opera, composed in 1866, was *La Jolie Fille de Perth*, based on the 1828 novel *The Fair Maid of Perth* by Sir Walter Scott. It premiered in December of the following year and was reviewed enthusiastically by the press, the only one of his operas to be so received. During the period 1865-1868, Bizet wrote a considerable amount of piano music, most of which, though published, remains obscure. Full of effects in imitation of the orchestra, these pieces also reveal Bizet's ongoing fascination with Lisztian virtuosity as well as with the works of Ludwig van Beethoven and Robert Schumann. He also composed a number of songs, the finest of which is "Adieux de l'hôtesse arabe" (1866).

Georges Bizet. (Library of Congress)

In 1868, Bizet underwent another period of soul-searching as a composer, resulting again in a series of aborted projects. He also endured a severe bout of quinsy. Adding to his despair was the rejection of a new opera, *La Coupe du roi de Thulé*, which he had submitted in a competition sponsored by the Paris Opéra. In the following year, at the age of thirty-one, Bizet married Geneviève Halévy, the daughter of his former composition teacher at the Paris Conservatoire. Their union was not a harmonious one, as she came from a family with a history of mental illness and was herself emotionally unstable. Their only child, Jacques, born in 1872, inherited this trait and committed suicide when he was fifty.

At the outbreak of the Franco-Prussian War, Bizet enlisted in the National Guard and remained with his wife in Paris. After the war, Bizet resumed work on two operas, *Clarissa Harlowe* and *Grisélidis*, neither of which reached completion. These were followed, however, by his opera *Djamileh*, a one-act work with a libretto by Louis Gallet, which premiered in May, 1872. Bizet's highly original harmonies bewildered audiences and annoyed the critics. As a result, the opera was a complete failure.

Among Bizet's most engaging works for orchestra is the incidental music to Alphonse Daudet's *L'Arlésienne*, a melodrama produced at the Théâtre du Vaudeville in October, 1872. Once again, the production was ill-fated, and Bizet's music was not well received. Nevertheless, the individual numbers, twenty-seven in all, are brilliant studies in orchestration. Four of them were arranged by Bizet for full orchestra (the original scoring having been for a small ensemble of twenty-six performers), and the resulting suite, premiered the following month, was greeted with approval by audiences and critics alike.

It was in the year 1872 as well that Bizet began work on his most important opera, one that would elevate him, though posthumously, to greatness. He was offered the services of Henri Meilhac and Ludovic Halévy as librettists and chose Prosper Mérimée's novel *Carmen* (1845; English translation, 1878) as his subject. Already by 1873 the first act was completed, and in the summer of 1874 the score was finished. Some aspects of the opera were controversial from the outset, especially its conclusion with a murder, which was unprecedented at the Opéra-Comique.

Bizet's realistic portrayal of the seamier aspects of Merimée's *Carmen*, as well as his highly original and difficult music, caused considerable consternation among the proprietors of the theater. The opera's initial reception in the spring of 1875 seemed to confirm their worst fears. It was dismissed as obscene and Wagnerian, though it ran for forty-eight performances in its first year. It was successfully staged in Vienna in October, 1875, and this led directly to its worldwide popularity.

Bizet's brilliant musical characterization of the principal characters, José and Carmen, his exploitation of exotic musical material and colorful orchestration, and his depiction of violent human emotion imbue the opera with a sensual vitality and pathos that continue to enthrall modern audiences. It is worth noting, however, that Bizet never set foot in Spain and did not utilize Spanish musical folklore extensively, though he did resort to quoting a few popular songs of the day.

Bizet, dejected at the poor reception of *Carmen* and suffering from a bout of quinsy, became seriously ill in May, 1875. His condition worsened when he contracted rheumatism and a high fever. That was followed by a heart attack on June 1, and he died two days later, during the early morning of his wedding anniversary. In a funeral ceremony attended by four thousand people, he was buried in Père Lachaise cemetery in Paris.

SIGNIFICANCE

Although he lived for the relatively short span of thirty-seven years, Georges Bizet produced a sizable body of work. His output—encompassing some twenty-seven operas, ten orchestral works, more than fifteen choral works, and dozens of songs and pieces for piano—was prodigious but uneven. He showed scant interest in writing chamber music, solos for instruments other than piano, or concerti. The love for literature that he displayed early in life probably dictated his preference for writing music that had some dramatic or literary connection. Bizet is an example of a composer who has suffered from his own success. The enormous popularity of a few of his works, such as *Carmen* and *L'Arléssienne*, has tended to overshadow the rest of his oeuvre. Though not all of his music is of the same quality and many pieces were left unfinished, much beautiful music awaits discovery by anyone willing to probe beneath the surface of his accomplishments.

Posterity's judgment of Bizet has fluctuated between extremes of adulation and disdain. Only in the latter half of the twentieth century did a clearer image of his achievements begin to emerge. Though he was receptive to forward-looking trends in the music of his own time, his style was highly original and not easily imitated. As a result, his influence on succeeding generations is difficult to gauge and is not necessarily commensurate with his intrinsic stature as a composer. Nevertheless, he must be counted among the greatest musical geniuses of nineteenth century Europe.

—*Walter Aaron Clark*

FURTHER READING

Curtiss, Mina. *Bizet and His World*. New York: Alfred A. Knopf, 1958. A singular biography that sheds much light on Bizet's personal life. Little emphasis is placed on analysis and critique of Bizet's music, and the text includes no musical examples. In addition to a selected bibliography and an index, the appendixes include translations of Bizet's unpublished correspondence, a list of the contents of Bizet's music library, a catalog of his works, and accounts of their posthumous presentations.

Dean, Winton. *Bizet*. London: J. M. Dent & Sons, 1948. A standard biography by the preeminent English-language Bizet scholar. In addition to a carefully researched biographical discussion interspersed with musical examples, the author includes valuable appendixes: a catalog of Bizet's works, a calendar of Bizet's life, and a list of individuals associated with Bizet and short biographies of them. Includes an extensive bibliography and an index.

_____. "Bizet's *Ivan IV*." In *Fanfare for Ernest Newman*, edited by Herbert Van Thal. London: A. Barker, 1955. Documents the history of Bizet's opera *Ivan IV*, which was never performed in his lifetime. Discusses the probable chronology of its composition and treats the problems involved in its posthumous productions. Presents an act-by-act critical examination of the music and the drama and establishes Bizet's use of ideas from *Ivan IV* in his later operas, especially *Carmen*.

_____. *Carmen*. London: Folio Society, 1949. For devotees of the opera, an invaluable work that is divided into three parts. Part 1 presents an English translation (by Lady Mary Lloyd) of Mérimée's *Carmen*. Part 2 discusses the genesis of the libretto by Halévy and Meilhac. Part 3 treats the music of the opera and emphasizes the relationship of the music to the dramatic action.

Lacombe, Hervé. *The Keys to French Opera in the Nineteenth Century*. Translated by Edward Schneider. Berkeley: University of California Press, 2001. Lacombe, who has written a French-language biography of Bizet, provides an overview of French opera and its place within nineteenth century society. He focuses on Bizet's opera *Les Pêcheurs de Perles (The Pearl Fishers)* as an example of the style and aesthetics common to operas of that period. Includes seven appendixes about *Les Pêcheurs de Perles*, listing Bizet's sources, the opera's staging and evolution during rehearsal and performance, and daily box office receipts for an 1830 performance.

Shanet, Howard. "Bizet's Suppressed Symphony." *The Musical Quarterly* 54 (October, 1958): 461-476. Seeks to explain the mystery of Bizet's Symphony in C, a masterpiece written when Bizet was only seventeen years old but that waited eighty years for its first performance. Why did Bizet never have it performed, and why did his widow forbid its performance or publication? An engaging article that appeals to layperson and scholar alike.

SEE ALSO: Léo Delibes; Charles Gounod.

RELATED ARTICLES in *Great Events from History: The Nineteenth Century, 1801-1900:* July 19, 1870-January 28, 1871: Franco-Prussian War; March 3, 1875: Bizet's *Carmen* Premieres in Paris; October 22, 1883: Metropolitan Opera House Opens in New York.

BLACK HAWK

Native American leader

Black Hawk was a leader in the last Indian war of the old Northwest, and he dictated one of the most revealing and enduring Native American autobiographies of his time.

BORN: 1767; Saukenak, Virginia Colony (now near Rock River, Illinois)

DIED: October 3, 1838; near the Des Moines River, Iowa

ALSO KNOWN AS: Ma-ka-tai-me-she-kia-kiak

AREAS OF ACHIEVEMENT: Government and politics, warfare and conquest

EARLY LIFE

Known as Ma-ka-tai-me-she-kia-kiak in his native language, Black Hawk was the adopted brother of a chief of the Foxes and was brought up by the Sauk (Sacs)—"Sac" was the original French spelling. The Sauk and Foxes were small tribes that formed an alliance, sometimes including the Potawatomi and Winnebago, to defend themselves against larger neighboring nations. Black Hawk was already a warrior and a leader among his people at the age of fifteen.

In his autobiography, *Life of Ma-ka-tai-me-she-kia-kiak: Or, Black Hawk* (1834), Black Hawk described how he became chief at the death of his father when they were fighting together against the Cherokee near the Meramec River, a short distance below modern St. Louis. Black Hawk fell heir to the chieftainship but was obliged to mourn, pray, and fast for five years in what he called a "civil capacity," hunting and fishing. When he was twenty-one he became head chief of the Sauk and Foxes. The two tribes were united and lived together as a single group.

Black Hawk's early years were spent in warfare against neighbors, primarily the Osage, Kaskaskia (a member of the Illinois Confederacy), and Chippewa. According to Black Hawk, there were two major reasons for warfare among the Indians: the preservation of hunting grounds and revenge for the deaths of relatives. Despite Black Hawk's renown as a warrior, there was a highly developed ethical and spiritual side of his character, and he tried to do what the Supreme Spirit directed.

LIFE'S WORK

Black Hawk's personality was complex, and it would be a mistake to oversimplify the main events in his life. Probably he should not be considered a great leader. He was highly individualistic, often impulsive, colorful, and emotional. His policies did not significantly help his nation, and other Indian leaders such as Pontiac and Crazy Horse were greater than he. It could be argued that his leadership was shortsighted and brought disaster on his people. The Black Hawk War could have been avoided.

Black Hawk never liked the American settlers, and for this he may be easily forgiven—during his lifetime the Sauk continually suffered from white armies, white officials, white traders, and white settlers. His adopted son was murdered by white American settlers. He liked the British. He was on good terms with a British trader and with Robert Dixon, British agent in the War of 1812, during which Black Hawk took an active role against the Americans. Most of Black Hawk's life prior to his capture in 1832 was marked by his dislike of Americans. The experience that contributed to this attitude more than any other was the St. Louis treaty of 1804, which Black Hawk rejected. In his own words, "It has been the origin of all our difficulties."

Napoleon sold Louisiana to the United States in 1803; soon after, American officials arrived in St. Louis to claim control and sign treaties with Indian tribes in the area. According to Black Hawk, the treaty with the Sauk was fraudulent. The Sauk had sent four representatives to St. Louis to obtain the release of a Sauk imprisoned there for killing an American—these were negotiators with a specific mission, not diplomats or chiefs. Much later they returned dressed in fine coats and wearing medals, and they could not remember much of what had happened. They were drunk most of the time they were in St. Louis. They also signed a treaty ceding all the Sauk lands east of the Mississippi to the United States.

Black Hawk and the rest of the Sauk were indignant. Not long after, a United States Army detachment came to erect Fort Madison near the Sauk villages. Black Hawk was scandalized by the treaty, asserting that the Sauk and Fox signers of the treaty had no authority from their nations. Twentieth century historian Milo Quaife, however, claims that "no more than the usual cajolery of the Indians was indulged in by the white representatives in securing the cession." The rejection of this treaty by the Indians, and the acceptance of its legality by the United States, says much about the quality of American law during this period.

The second major event in Black Hawk's life prior to his battles during the 1830's against the Illinois militia and the United States Army was his rivalry with another Sauk chief, Keokuk. Although not a chief by birth, Keokuk rose by the exercise of political talents to a position of leadership in his tribe. He was more of a realist than Black Hawk, and although he may not have liked the Americans any more than Black Hawk did, he tried not to antagonize them. As a nation the Sauk were divided, some favoring Black Hawk and others, Keokuk. In 1819, Keokuk and other members of the nation were persuaded by American authorities to leave the Sauk home on Rock Island and go to the western side of the Mississippi. Keokuk ultimately triumphed over Black Hawk after the war of 1832, which placed Black Hawk under the governance of Keokuk.

The rivalry between Black Hawk and Keokuk had a long history. Throughout the 1820's, Black Hawk resisted the encroachments of white settlers, and he tried to hold on to the Sauk's ancestral home on Rock Island. At first Black Hawk favored negotiation with the white Americans no less than Keokuk. Eventually, however, having exhausted all means of peaceful resistance, Black Hawk took up arms and tried to recruit allies among the Potawatomi. He led his entire nation—warriors, women, and children—on a long anabasis from Rock Island to Bad Axe River, winning some battles and losing others, culminating in the final attempt to reach the safety of the western bank of the Mississippi. The most pitiful aspect of the tragedy was the fate of the Sauk women and children. In the words of historian Reuben Thwaites,

DEDICATION OF BLACK HAWK'S AUTOBIOGRAPHY

To Brigadier General H[enry] Atkinson:

SIR—The changes of fortune and vicissitudes of war made you my conqueror. When my last resources were exhausted, my warriors worn down with long and toilsome marches, we yielded, and I became your prisoner.

The story of my life is told in the following pages: it is intimately connected, and in some measure, identified, with a part of the history of your own: I have, therefore, dedicated it to you.

The changes of many summers have brought old age upon me, and I can not expect to survive many moons. Before I set out on my journey to the land of my fathers, I have determined to give my motives and reasons for my former hostilities to the whites, and to vindicate my character from misrepresentation. The kindness I received from you whilst a prisoner of war assures me that you will vouch for the facts contained in my narrative, so far as they came under your observation.

I am now an obscure member of a nation that formerly honored and respected my opinions. The pathway to glory is rough, and many gloomy hours obscure it. May the Great Spirit shed light on yours, and that you may never experience the humility that the power of the American government has reduced me to, is the wish of him, who, in his native forests, was once as proud and bold as yourself.

BLACK HAWK
10th Moon, 1833.

> Some of the fugitives succeeded in swimming to the west bank of the Mississippi, but many were drowned on the way, or cooly picked off by sharpshooters, who exercised no more mercy towards squaws and children than they did towards braves—treating them all as though they were rats instead of human beings.

Black Hawk led the last great war between Indians and whites on the eastern side of the Mississippi; if it terrified numerous white settlers in the frontier regions of the old Northwest—what is now Illinois and Wisconsin—it should be stressed that the Indian civilian populations living on ancestral lands had been terrorized by whites for a far longer period of time. Although Black Hawk initiated the battle, the final tragedy was not his doing. The deliberate killing of noncombatants was an act of the United States, not an Indian act. A few Sauk managed to reach the western bank only to be attacked by a war party of Lakota (Sioux) Indians under the orders of General Atkinson.

Black Hawk would have been the first to condemn these military practices, and he fully expressed his indignation in his autobiography. These massacres went far beyond his conception of the conduct of war. Some historians have been hasty to blame him, failing to consider the requirements of defensive warfare at the time. Although the Indians received few favorable settlements in their negotiations with the whites, those who suffered the most were perhaps the most pacific—those who, because they never fought the whites, never signed treaties with them either, and consequently never received rights or privileges. Most of these nations have completely disappeared, leaving no survivors. In one of Black Hawk's most telling critiques of Keokuk, he said: "I conceived that the *peaceable disposition* of Keokuk and his people had been, in a great measure, the cause of our having been driven from our village."

Black Hawk had a quixotic, romantic temperament. He could be impulsively emotional and also ethical, courageous, even idealistic and chivalrous in battle. Some of these traits might surprise a modern reader accustomed to clichés about Indians. Repeatedly Black Hawk complimented the braver of his adversaries, whether enemy Indians or whites. If he encountered an enemy group that had less than half his number, he declined to do battle. He admired both determination and heroism in war, and the traits he came to admire in his white conquerors after 1832 were largely military virtues.

It was probably not a coincidence that Black Hawk struck up a spontaneous friendship with Lieutenant Jefferson Davis in 1832; these two leaders of rebellion had traits in common. Jefferson Davis was to repeat Black Hawk's act of defiance against superior military forces twenty-five years later as president of the Confederate States, and the results would be comparable.

Black Hawk's autobiography was dictated and translated on the spot in 1833; there is no extant text in the Sauk language. The book has a seemingly childish quality that is probably more attributable to the interpreter and editor than to Black Hawk himself. There are many exclamation points, underlinings, and expressions of delight, and much reveling in the good fight. Nevertheless, the document gives an ample, three-dimensional portrait of a man spontaneously describing his thoughts and feelings, trying to account for what he has done and what has happened to him.

Black Hawk died a broken man on an Indian reservation in Iowa in 1838. A decade later, his rival Keokuk died a wealthy man in Kansas, where he had moved after selling the Sauk and Fox lands in Iowa.

SIGNIFICANCE

After the Black Hawk War, the combined population of the Sauk and Foxes was greatly diminished. They were finally resettled in an area west of the Mississippi in a segment of what was known as "the Permanent Indian Frontier of 1840." It adjoined the Potawatomi to the west, the Lakota to the north, and the Winnebago to the northeast. The Sauk and Foxes would still need military virtues as well as diplomacy when they jostled with these Indians and, later, with whites in their new habitat. Military abilities did not immediately become obsolete—far from it. Soon, however, the Indians' greatest adversaries were to become alcoholism, diseases such as cholera, and starvation.

Black Hawk's major weakness was probably diplomacy. In his war against the whites he did not secure the adherence of a significant number of other Indian nations, nor did he spend much time or effort in attempting it. Seventy years earlier, Pontiac had been more successful in forging an antiwhite alliance. Whether Black Hawk could have been more successful if he had put more effort into negotiations, especially with other Indian nations, is a matter of speculation. Black Hawk thought in broad ethical categories. He believed the Great Spirit would reward him if he fought for justice. Patient diplomacy, with its concomitant drudgery and uncertainty, was not for him.

—John Carpenter

FURTHER READING

Black Hawk. *Life of Ma-ka-tai-me-she-kia-kiak: Or, Black Hawk*. Edited by Milo Milton Quaife. New York: Dover, 1994. Originally published during the 1830's, Black Hawk's autobiography is a fascinating document. However, it has many inaccuracies and biases, and should be read with critical skepticism. His account of the British is naïve, as well as his description of the "prophet" White Cloud. Black Hawk grossly understates his own losses in the battles of 1832. Still, a vivid picture of an admirable human being emerges from the pages of his autobiography.

Drake, Benjamin. *The Life and Adventures of Black Hawk*. Cincinnati: G. Conclin, 1844. Half history and half fiction, written shortly after the events described.

Eby, Cecil. *"That Disgraceful Affair": The Black Hawk War*. New York: W. W. Norton., 1973. Perhaps the best book about the Black Hawk War. Very thoroughly documented and at the same time a readable narrative, as well as incisive critique of the major actors in the war.

Nichols, Roger L. *Black Hawk and the Warrior's Path*. Arlington Heights, Ill.: H. Davidson, 1992. Biography of Black Hawk, focusing on the wars he waged against rival tribes, white pioneers, and others. Nichols seeks the reasons for Black Hawk's actions, particularly his involvement in the war that bears his name.

Quaife, Milo Milton. *Chicago and the Old Northwest, 1673-1833*. Chicago: University of Chicago Press, 1913. Well-documented and thorough general history that draws somewhat specious conclusions.

Slotkin, Richard. *Regeneration Through Violence: The Mythology of the American Frontier, 1600-1860*. Middletown, Conn.: Wesleyan University Press, 1973. A critical or "revisionist" account of the frontier. A welcome antidote to earlier sentimental accounts of the frontier wars, but obsessively overstated.

Stevens, Frank E. *The Black Hawk War*. Chicago: F. E. Stevens, 1903. A thorough account, still useful.

Thwaites, Reuben G. *Story of the Black Hawk War*. Madison: Wisconsin State Historical Society, 1892. A narrative by one of the best American historians of the period; Thwaites combined great erudition with a keen critical spirit.

SEE ALSO: Jefferson Davis; Abraham Lincoln; Winfield Scott; Zachary Taylor.

RELATED ARTICLE in *Great Events from History: The Nineteenth Century, 1801-1900:* November 7, 1811: Battle of Tippecanoe.

ELIZABETH BLACKWELL

American physician

As the first woman to receive a degree from an American medical school, Elizabeth Blackwell became a leading figure in the drive to open the field of medicine to women.

BORN: February 3, 1821; Counterslip, England
DIED: May 31, 1910; Hastings, England
AREAS OF ACHIEVEMENT: Medicine, women's rights

EARLY LIFE

Elizabeth Blackwell was born on February 3, 1821, in a small town near Bristol, England. The third of nine surviving children of Samuel and Hannah Blackwell, Elizabeth joined a family heavily influenced by the progressive and reformist values held by her father. In addition to being a successful sugar refiner, Samuel Blackwell was an outspoken member of his community, having wedded the practice of his Puritan faith with the support of various liberal causes, such as women's rights, temperance, and the abolition of slavery.

The destruction of his refinery by fire in 1832 led Samuel Blackwell to move his family to America. After a few years spent in New York and New Jersey, the Blackwells came to settle in Cincinnati, Ohio, in May, 1838. Pursued to the end by his monetary troubles, Samuel Blackwell died in August of that year, leaving Hannah, her two eldest daughters, and Elizabeth responsible for providing for the family. They were able to do so by opening what would become a successful boarding school, where Elizabeth spent the first four of her seven years as a teacher.

It was during these seven years, which also included one year in Kentucky and two more in North and South Carolina, that Elizabeth Blackwell began to grow frustrated at the limits of the teaching profession, both in its poor remuneration and its low social status. She also became aware of her growing aversion to the idea of marriage, an institution which, at the time, imposed even greater restrictions than did teaching on the women who entered into it. These realizations became important factors in Blackwell's decision to pursue a career in the highly respected field of medicine, a field so utterly dominated by men that no woman had ever before received a diploma from an American medical school.

LIFE'S WORK

It was during her final two years teaching in the Carolinas that Elizabeth Blackwell, within the personal libraries of the distinguished physicians John and Samuel Dickson, began her study of medicine. These years of self-education served to prepare Blackwell for her move, in May of 1847, to Philadelphia, the home of several well-respected medical schools to which she would subsequently apply. This application process forced Blackwell to confront the institutional prejudices of the day. Although they were often supported by sympathetic faculty members, her applications were rejected by every medical school in Philadelphia and New York as well as by several rural colleges of much less stellar reputations. It was only when the administration of Geneva Medical College in upstate New York put her application up for review by the all-male student body that Blackwell's determination won her a chance for a legitimate education. Presented with a woman's name, the students had thought the submission was a joke and passed it unanimously.

Immediately upon beginning her studies, Blackwell experienced the scorn of both townspeople and fellow students alike. Even the women within the community were taken aback by what they perceived as brash and unfeminine behavior by Blackwell in her pursuit of medical training, and she was often made aware that the idea of a woman physician upset many of those who would one day benefit from the course of action she was endeavoring to take. Gradually, however, Blackwell's intelligence and doggedness won her great measures of respect from important faculty members and the other students with whom she worked.

After completing an internship in 1848 at the Philadelphia Hospital and writing a thesis based on her experiences there, Blackwell emerged from her course work with a focus that would last throughout her professional career: the importance of preventative care in the form of improved personal hygiene. With this focus established and her studies complete, Blackwell received her medical degree from Geneva Medical College on January 23, 1849. She became the first woman in the United States to ever earn such an honor and was ranked first in her graduating class.

Before she was to begin her career in earnest in New York in August of 1851, Blackwell spent a year and a half abroad, in both England and France, with the intention of enhancing her education. Though received graciously by the medical community in England and invited by prominent staff members of several hospitals to tour their grounds, Blackwell found that in France the only kind of advanced training available to her was as a midwife.

This period in Blackwell's life is most notable for the eye disease she contracted from a patient during her midwives' course at La Maternité in Paris, the resulting loss of sight in one eye dashed her hopes of ever becoming a surgeon. Through these trials, Blackwell's strength of character enabled her to overcome adversity. Toward the end of her stay in Europe, she returned to England and gained valuable clinical experience under the supervi-

Elizabeth Blackwell. (The Granger Collection, New York)

sion of Dr. James Paget at St. Bartholomew's Hospital. In retrospect, the setbacks she experienced in this interlude abroad helped steel Blackwell for the resistance she encountered in her attempts to establish herself as a practicing physician in New York.

For a woman doctor during the 1850's, merely finding a place in which to practice proved a near impossibility. Blackwell's applications to city dispensaries for positions in the pediatric wards were flatly rejected, as were her requests to visit the female wards of a city hospital. These rejections were handed down despite her rather impressive array of degrees and recommendations. Even more indicative of this era's prejudice was Blackwell's inability even to rent a space of her own for private practice. No landlord would lease a space for such a disreputable practice, knowing that every other tenant who might be sharing a building with a "female physician" (the contemporary euphemism for "abortionist") would be forced to move or be shamed.

While overcoming these obstacles and patiently awaiting the growth of her practice, Blackwell succeeded in publishing a series of lectures on hygiene in 1852. Later, in 1853, Blackwell opened a dispensary for the poor, supported by funds she raised herself. Four years later, her dispensary became the New York Infirmary for Women and Children, the first hospital completely organized and operated by women. Outside her professional life, Blackwell in 1853 took on the responsibility of adopting a seven-year-old orphan named Katherine Barry who would remain her closest relation for the rest of her days.

In her battle to open the infirmary in 1857, Elizabeth Blackwell was joined by two other women doctors: her younger sister, Emily, who had followed Elizabeth into the profession, and Marie Zakrzewska, a Polish émigré who had been educated at Western Reserve College (later Case Western Reserve University) and who would become the resident physician at the infirmary until 1859. Once this hospital was established, Blackwell's next major goal was to create a medical college for women with a commitment to rigorous preparation and to the cause of good hygiene. Before this goal was to materialize, however, Blackwell departed in August of 1858 for a one-year stay in Great Britain, where she both practiced medicine and lectured, and also made the acquaintance of such admirers as Dr. Elizabeth Garrett and Florence Nightingale.

Upon Blackwell's return to the United States, her plans were interrupted by the outbreak of the Civil War, during which she became involved in a committee concerned with the status of care for soldiers and also helped to select and train nurses going out into the field. Finally, in 1868, Blackwell brought her quest to fruition as she founded the Woman's Medical College of the New York Infirmary and served as the first chair of hygiene at the college. (The college eventually became part of Cornell's medical school in 1899, after the university decided to grant admission to women.)

In 1869, Elizabeth Blackwell left the United States to live and work in Great Britain. At first, she took up residence in London, where she practiced privately until she accepted a position at the New Hospital and London School of Medicine for Women in 1875. As a result of her ill health, Blackwell was forced to retire after just one year. Leaving London, she moved with Katherine Barry to Hastings, where Blackwell spent most of her last thirty years. Never one to remain idle for long, Blackwell spent these days writing books, essays, and articles addressing a wide variety of topics, but especially focusing on the issues of medicine and morality. She also visited the continent and traveled to the United States in 1906. In 1907, she suffered injuries as a result of falling down some stairs at her summer house in the Scottish highlands. Blackwell died at her seaside home in Hastings in 1910 and was buried in Scotland.

SIGNIFICANCE

It would not be difficult to present Elizabeth Blackwell's achievements as a list of breakthroughs in the process of opening the field of medicine to women. As the first woman to ever receive a degree from an American medical school, the founder of the first hospital run solely by women, and the founder of one of the earliest medical colleges for women, Blackwell stands as a distinguished pioneer in the fight for a woman's right to become a practicing physician.

To focus on her breakthroughs alone, however, would unfairly limit the scope of Blackwell's contribution. From the moment she decided to pursue her degree, Blackwell committed herself to more than mere medicine. Desiring a greater status than was afforded by traditional feminine pursuits and seeking a level of freedom that she could find nowhere else, Blackwell chose to challenge the various obstacles that hindered women from pursuing professional careers. Medicine was the avenue she selected in order to accomplish her ultimate goal of advancing the opportunities available to women. Immersed in her era's atmosphere of social activism, Blackwell dedicated her work and her writings to causes of morality and equality. The breadth of Elizabeth

Blackwell's influence is amply illustrated by the names of those individuals—people as various as Herbert Spencer and Florence Nightingale, as Dante Gabriel Rossetti and George Eliot—who came to admire and respect Blackwell's ideas and accomplishments.

—*Bonnie L. Ford*

FURTHER READING

Abram, Ruth J., ed. *"Send Us a Lady Physician": Women Doctors in America, 1835-1920.* New York: W. W. Norton, 1986. Compiled to accompany a museum exhibit, this collection of essays celebrates the pioneering spirit of early women physicians and describes the experience of women in the health professions during the nineteenth and early twentieth centuries.

Blackwell, Elizabeth. *Pioneer Work in Opening the Medical Profession to Women.* Reprint. Amherst, N.Y.: Humanity Books, 2004. Originally published in 1895, this work consists of autobiographical sketches that delineate the enormous struggle Blackwell had to endure in order to enter and graduate from medical school. It is clear that she was fully conscious of her historical role.

Brown, Jordan. *Elizabeth Blackwell.* New York: Chelsea House, 1989. This biography is part of the publisher's American Women of Achievement series. Although primarily intended for young adult readers, the book provides an excellent introduction to Blackwell's life and examines the various issues that confronted her in her quest to provide opportunities for women in the medical profession.

Buckmaster, Henrietta. *Women Who Shaped History.* New York: Collier Books, 1966. Six remarkable women of the nineteenth century are the subject of this group biography. Elizabeth Blackwell's life is included with those of Prudence Crandall, Dorothea Dix, Mary Baker Eddy, Elizabeth Cady Stanton, and Harriet Tubman.

Hume, Ruth Fox. *Great Women of Medicine.* New York: Random House, 1964. Hume devotes her first chapter to Blackwell and offers the reader a compact biography that emphasizes Blackwell's early life and career in the United States until her retirement in England.

Morantz-Sanchez, Regina. "Feminist Theory and Historical Practice: Rereading Elizabeth Blackwell." *History and Theory* 31 (December, 1992): 51-69. A scholar analyzes Blackwell's writings to demonstrate how the discussion of scientific topics in these works reflected Blackwell's feminist concerns. Morantz-Sanchez also notes that the growing predominance of laboratory-based treatment of disease and the rigorous application of scientific methodology moved the practice of medicine away from many of the nurturing, feminine aspects of health care championed by Blackwell and her colleagues.

_____. *Sympathy and Science: Women Physicians in American Medicine.* Chapel Hill: University of North Carolina Press, 2000. Originally published in 1985, this book is a history of women physicians from colonial times to the present. Chapter 7 focuses on Blackwell. The 2000 edition includes a preface by the author, surveying recent scholarship and describing women's changing role in medicine during the 1980's and 1990's.

More, Ellen S. *Restoring the Balance: Women Physicians and the Profession of Medicine, 1850-1995.* Cambridge, Mass.: Harvard University Press, 1999. Blackwell's career is included in this history examining how women physicians work to balance the demands of their profession with society's expectations for women.

Ross, Ishbel. *Child of Destiny: The Life Story of the First Woman Doctor.* New York: Harper & Row, 1949. Ross wrote a full-length biography of Blackwell with the aid of interviews with family members. Full of fascinating detail, the book chronicles Blackwell's work as well as her personal life and her many associations with major figures of the nineteenth century. It places her within the reform movement of the era.

Wilson, Dorothy Clarke. *Lone Woman: The Story of Elizabeth Blackwell, the First Woman Doctor.* Boston: Little, Brown, 1970. Novelist, dramatist, and biographer, Dorothy Clarke Wilson brings her dramatic skills to enliven this solid biography that is based on family reminiscences and papers as well as extensive research in primary sources.

SEE ALSO: Lydia Folger Fowler; Thomas Wentworth Higginson; Mary Putnam Jacobi; Marie Elizabeth Zakrzewska.

RELATED ARTICLE in *Great Events from History: The Nineteenth Century, 1801-1900:* May 12, 1857: New York Infirmary for Indigent Women and Children Opens.

JAMES G. BLAINE
American politician

Blaine was the most popular Republican politician of the late nineteenth century. Although he lost in his bid for the presidency, through his personal appeal and his advocacy of the protective tariff, he laid the basis for the emergence of the Republican Party as the majority party during the 1890's.

BORN: January 31, 1830; West Brownsville, Pennsylvania
DIED: January 27, 1893; Washington, D.C.
ALSO KNOWN AS: James Gillespie Blaine (full name)
AREA OF ACHIEVEMENT: Government and politics

EARLY LIFE

James Gillespie Blaine was born January 31, 1830, in West Brownsville, Pennsylvania. His father, Ephraim Lyon Blaine, came from a Scotch-Irish and Scotch-Presbyterian background. Blaine's mother, Maria Louise Gillespie, was an Irish Catholic. Blaine was reared a Presbyterian, as were his brothers, while his sisters followed their mother's faith. In later life, Blaine became a Congregationalist but was tolerant of all creeds and avoided the religious issue in politics. Blaine's maternal background gave him an electoral appeal to Irish-Catholic voters.

Ephraim Blaine was a lawyer who was elected to a county clerk position in Washington County, Pennsylvania, in 1842. His son entered Washington and Jefferson College, a small school in the area, and was graduated in 1847. Blaine then taught at the Western Military Institute in Georgetown, Kentucky, from 1848 to 1851. He admired the policies of Henry Clay, the Whig leader, during his stay in the state. He also found time to court and then marry a teacher at a woman's seminary, Harriet Stanwood, on June 30, 1850. Leaving Kentucky in late 1851, Blaine taught at the Pennsylvania Institute for the Blind from 1852 to 1854. He also pursued legal studies while in Philadelphia.

Harriet Blaine's family had connections in Maine. When a vacancy occurred for editor of the *Kennebec Journal* in 1853, her husband was asked to take over the management of this Whig newspaper. Money from his brothers-in-law helped this arrangement succeed. By November, 1854, Blaine was at work in Augusta, Maine, as a newspaperman, not a lawyer. His growing family eventually reached seven children, four of whom outlived their father. From this point onward, he became known as Blaine of Maine.

Over the next decade, Blaine became identified with the young Republican Party in his adopted state. He was elected to the Maine legislature in 1858, was reelected three times, and became Speaker of the House of Representatives during his last two terms. He was named chairman of the Republican State Committee in 1859, a post he held for two decades. Blaine attended the Republican National Convention in 1860 as a delegate. In 1862, he was elected to the U.S. Congress and took his seat in the House of Representatives in 1863.

As he entered the national scene at the age of thirty-three, Blaine had already shown himself to be a gifted politician. He had a charismatic quality that caused some who knew him to be loyal to him for life, becoming "Blainiacs." His speeches were received enthusiastically in an age that admired oratory. Blaine knew American politics intimately and could remember faces and election results with uncanny accuracy. However, there was another side to him. His health and temperament were uncertain, and his illnesses often came at moments of crisis. In his private affairs, Blaine gained wealth without having a secure income, and he would not reveal information about his finances to the public. Enemies said that he was corrupt. That went too far, but he lacked, as did many of his contemporaries, a clear sense of what constituted a conflict of interest. In fact, James G. Blaine was a diverse blend of good and bad qualities—a truth reflected in the Gilded Age quip that men went insane about him in pairs, one for, and one against.

LIFE'S WORK

Blaine spent thirteen years in the House of Representatives, serving as its Speaker between 1869 and 1875. He was a moderate on the issues of the Civil War and Reconstruction, endorsing black suffrage and a strong policy toward the South without being labeled as a "radical." He became known as a "Half-Breed" in contrast to such "Stalwarts" as New York's Roscoe Conkling. Blaine and Conkling clashed on the House floor in April, 1866. His description of Conkling as having a "majestic, supereminent turkey-gobbler strut" opened a personal and political wound that never healed for the egotistic Conkling. His opposition proved disastrous to Blaine's presidential chances in 1876 and 1880.

By 1876, Blaine had left the House of Representatives to serve in the Senate. He was a leading candidate for the

Republican presidential nomination in that year. Then a public controversy arose over whether Blaine had acted corruptly in helping to save a land grant for an Arkansas railroad in 1869. The facts about favors done and favors repaid were allegedly contained in a packet of documents known as the Mulligan Letters, named for the man who possessed them. The letters came into Blaine's hands, he read from them to the House, and his friends said that he had vindicated himself. Enemies charged that the papers proved his guilt, and the reform element of the time never forgave him.

Shortly before the Republican convention, Blaine fell ill. Nevertheless, his name was placed in nomination as Robert G. Ingersoll called him the "Plumed Knight" of American politics. The Republican delegates decided that Blaine was too controversial to win, and they turned instead to Rutherford B. Hayes of Ohio. Four years later, after Hayes's single term, Blaine led the opposition to a third term for Ulysses S. Grant and again was seen as a contender for the nomination. Blaine was more interested in his party's success than in his own advancement in 1880, and he was pleased when James A. Garfield of Ohio became the compromise nominee. In the fall campaign, Blaine stumped widely for the national ticket and developed the arguments for the protective tariff that he would advance during the 1880's.

After Garfield's narrow victory, he asked Blaine to be his secretary of state. In his first brief tenure at the State Department, Blaine pursued his concern for a canal across Central America, the fostering of Pan-American sentiment, and greater trade for the nation. Garfield's assassination in the summer of 1881 ended his presidency and led to Blaine's resignation at the end of the year. The administration of Chester A. Arthur that followed did not cut into Blaine's popularity with the Republican rank and file. He received the Republican nomination on the first ballot in 1884. John A. Logan of Illinois was his running mate.

Blaine wanted to make the protective tariff the central theme of his race against the nominee of the Democrats, Grover Cleveland, the governor of New York. Instead the campaign turned on the personal character of the two candidates. Republicans stressed Cleveland's admission that he had had an affair with a woman who had given birth to an illegitimate son. Democrats attacked the legal validity of Blaine's marriage and revived the charges of the Mulligan Letters. These sensational aspects overshadowed Blaine's campaign tour, one of the first by a presidential aspirant. The election was close as the voting neared.

All accounts of the election of 1884 note that on October 29, Blaine heard the Reverend Samuel Burchard say in New York that the Democrats were the party of "rum, Romanism, and rebellion." These words supposedly alienated Catholic voters, swung New York to the Democrats, and thus cost Blaine the victory. This episode, however, has been given too much importance. In fact, Blaine improved on Garfield's vote in the state and ran stronger than his party. The significance of 1884 was not that Blaine lost in a Democratic year but that he revived the Republicans and laid the groundwork for the party's victory in 1888.

Over the next four years, Blaine continued to speak out for the tariff. He set the keynote for the 1888 campaign when he responded publicly to Cleveland's attacks on tariff protection in his 1887 annual message to Congress. "The Democratic Party in power is a standing menace to the prosperity of the country," he told an interviewer. Blaine stayed out of the presidential race and supported strongly the party's nominee, Benjamin Harrison of Indiana. After Harrison defeated Cleveland, it was logical that Blaine should again serve as secretary of state.

Blaine faced a variety of diplomatic issues, including Canadian fisheries and a running argument with Great Britain over fur seals in Alaska. He summoned the initial Pan-American Conference to Washington in October, 1889, sought to achieve the annexation of Hawaii, and was instrumental in obtaining reciprocal trade authority in the McKinley Tariff of 1890. In many ways Blaine foreshadowed the overseas expansion of the United States that occurred later in the decade. His working relationship with President Harrison deteriorated as the administration progressed and Blaine's own health faltered. The death of two children in 1890 added to his personal troubles.

Shortly before the Republican convention, on June 4, 1892, Blaine resigned as secretary of state. It is not clear whether Blaine was actually a candidate for the presidency this last time. He received some support when the Republican delegates met, but the incumbent Harrison easily controlled the convention and was renominated on the first ballot. Blaine made one speech for the Republicans in the 1892 race as Harrison lost to Grover Cleveland. In the last months of his life, Blaine gradually wasted away. He died of Bright's disease and a weakened heart on January 27, 1893.

SIGNIFICANCE

When Blaine died, a fellow Republican said, "His is a fame that will grow with time." In fact, he is now largely a forgotten historical figure who is remembered only for a vague connection with "rum, Romanism, and rebellion." That impression does an injustice to one of the most popular and charismatic political leaders of the Gilded Age. Blaine embodied the diverse tendencies of the Republican Party in the formative stages of its development. In his advocacy of economic nationalism and growth, he spoke for a generation that wanted both to preserve the achievements of the Civil War and to move on to the fresh issues of industrial development. He was an important participant in the affairs of the House of Representatives during the early 1870's, and his tenure as Speaker contributed to the growing professionalism of that branch of government.

Blaine also symbolized the popular unease about the ethical standards that public servants should observe. In the Mulligan Letters episode and in his own affairs, he raised issues about conflict of interest and propriety that clouded his historical reputation. He became the epitome of the "spoilsman" who lived on patronage and influence. Blaine correctly understood these attacks as being to some degree partisan, but he failed to recognize the legitimacy of the questions that they posed.

Despite these failings, Blaine was a central figure in the evolution of the Republican Party during the 1870's and 1880's. His conviction that tariff protection offered both the hope of party success and an answer to the issue of economic growth laid the foundation for the emergence of the Republican Party as the majority party during the 1890's. During the 1884 presidential race, he improved the Republican performance and prepared the party for later success. As secretary of state, he was a constructive spokesperson for the national interest. He educated his party on the tariff issue and, in so doing, fulfilled the essential function of a national political leader. For a generation of Republican leaders and voters, James G. Blaine came to stand for inspiration and commitment in politics. Although he failed to reach the presidency, Blaine was the most significant American politician of his era.

—Lewis L. Gould

FURTHER READING

Blaine, James G. *Twenty Years of Congress: From Lincoln to Garfield*. 2 vols. Norwich, Conn.: Henry Bill, 1884-1886. Blaine's memoir of his service in Congress does not contain any striking personal revelations.

Crapol, Edward P. *James G. Blaine: Architect of Empire*. Wilmington, Del.: Scholarly Resources, 2000. Focuses on Blaine's tenure as secretary of state, including his relations with Latin America and his attempts to upgrade the merchant marine and U.S. Navy. Crapol maintains that Blaine's policies aimed to establish U.S. hegemony in the Western Hemisphere.

Dodge, Mary Abigail. *The Biography of James G. Blaine*. Norwich, Conn.: Henry Bill, 1895. The inclusion of Blaine's private letters is the most useful feature of this family biography.

Healy, David. *James G. Blaine and Latin America*. Columbia: University of Missouri Press, 2001. Examines U.S. relations with Latin America during Blaine's tenure as secretary of state. Healy contends that Latin America was crucial to Blaine's foreign policy and his vision of America as a world leader.

Morgan, H. Wayne. *From Hayes to McKinley: National Party Politics, 1877-1896*. Syracuse, N.Y.: Syracuse University Press, 1969. The best analytic treatment of American politics during the heyday of Blaine's career. Morgan is sympathetic and perceptive about Blaine's role as a Republican leader.

Muzzey, David S. *James G. Blaine: A Political Idol of Other Days*. New York: Dodd, Mead, 1934. The best and most objective biography of Blaine. Argues that he was not consumed with the desire to be president.

Stanwood, Edward. *James Gillespie Blaine*. Boston: Houghton Mifflin, 1905. A short biography by a scholar who was related to Blaine.

Thompson, Margaret Susan. *The "Spider Web": Congress and Lobbying in the Age of Grant*. Ithaca, N.Y.: Cornell University Press, 1985. An innovative and interesting treatment of the House of Representatives and the Senate in the years when Blaine was Speaker. Reveals much about the political system in which he operated.

Tyler, Alice Felt. *The Foreign Policy of James G. Blaine*. Minneapolis: University of Minnesota Press, 1927. An older but still helpful examination of Blaine as a diplomat and architect of American foreign policy.

SEE ALSO: Grover Cleveland; Benjamin Harrison; Thomas Nast.

RELATED ARTICLES in *Great Events from History: The Nineteenth Century, 1801-1900:* November 4, 1884: U.S. Election of 1884; October, 1889-April, 1890: First Pan-American Congress.

LOUIS BLANC
French political theorist

Now regarded as the founder of humanitarian socialism, Blanc converted his dissatisfaction with the misery of the French people into an imperative to transform the basic governmental and economic system to end forever the capitalist exploitation of the working class.

BORN: October 29, 1811; Madrid, Spain
DIED: December 6, 1882; Cannes, France
ALSO KNOWN AS: Jean Joseph Charles Louis Blanc (full name)
AREA OF ACHIEVEMENT: Philosophy

EARLY LIFE

A Frenchman, Louis Blanc was born in Spain during the closing, turbulent days of the Napoleonic Empire. His father served King Joseph Bonaparte as an inspector general of Spanish finances. The French hold over Spain, however, was never secure. Joseph, already forced out of his capital several times by the successes of the British army under Sir Arthur Wellesley, finally left the country in 1813. The French bureaucrats, officials, and advisers departed with him. This exodus split the Blanc family. The father abandoned his wife after the birth of a second son, and Louis, the elder, was sent to live with his maternal grandmother in Corsica. Only after 1815, with the establishment of the Restoration Monarchy, did life become more settled. The father returned, managing to secure a royal pension, and Louis was reunited with his family.

In 1821, Blanc and his younger brother, Charles, were enrolled in the Royal College at Rodez, which they attended on scholarship. The school was run by the Catholic clergy, who instructed their pupils in the truth of Bourbon Legitimism and Scholastic theology. The Enlightenment and the revolution were denigrated, if mentioned at all. Louis was a dedicated student. He won prizes in philosophy and rhetoric and excelled at biblical study, from which he derived a sense of obligation to work for the betterment of society. He completed his formal education in 1830 when he was nineteen years of age.

Blanc left Rodez to find work in Paris and arrived there in August, soon after the revolution which had replaced the Bourbon Dynasty with the Orleanist monarchy of Louis-Philippe. Trained as a gentleman, Blanc had difficulty finding work, especially with the new government, which looked with suspicion on all of those associated with the previous regime. To support himself, therefore, Blanc took a variety of part-time jobs such as tutoring, house cleaning, and clerking. He received some money from an uncle but spent much time visiting museums, palaces, and public monuments. In 1832, the prospect of more steady employment led him to leave the capital to accept a post as a tutor with a family in Arras.

While he was in Arras, Blanc met Frédéric Degeorge, a newspaper editor and champion of democratic republicanism, who introduced him to political journalism and prompted his admiration of one of Arras's most famous native sons, Robespierre. The association with Degeorge heightened Blanc's desire to return to Paris and to begin a real career as a writer. He returned in 1834, armed with a letter of introduction, and began work on *Bon Sense* (common sense), a paper founded two years earlier by a group of men who feared the growing power of Louis-Philippe. In 1836, Blanc became the journal's editor in chief. He was only twenty-four years of age.

Journalism had become Blanc's way to right wrongs and to pave the way for the establishment of a more just society. He wanted to inspire men of goodwill to cooperate in a common program to safeguard individual freedom and to exact reform through evolutionary, but decisive, change. He became involved in election politics and, in 1837, was instrumental in forming a committee to present qualified voters with a slate of progressive candidates in the forthcoming elections.

This group failed to form an effective coalition out of the various opposition groups, however, and had little practical effect on the results. The government list was returned with a large majority. The failure did not shake Blanc's faith that government power could be made responsive to the general need. Therefore, he believed it should not be limited but used as the instrument of progress. Such active *étatism* put Blanc at odds with his newspaper's conservative ownership. He insisted, however, that a man should follow his convictions rather than his position and, in 1838, resigned. His entire editorial staff quit with him.

Blanc wanted to create a new kind of newspaper, one committed to the transformation of society, and one that would become a rallying point for all of those who were dedicated to democratic change and who believed in the need for the reorganization of work. This newspaper, *Revue de progrès politique, social et litéraire* (review of political, social, and literary progress), began publication in January, 1839. In the following year, its pages contained a series of Blanc's articles that formed the key to his own thought and the basis on which his subsequent political and intellectual career rested.

LIFE'S WORK

Blanc believed that society was divided into two classes, the bourgeois and the people, or the oppressors and the oppressed, and that only through political action could the oppressed achieve liberation and the ability to develop their true nature. Blanc asserted that exploitation was endemic to the system of his time where not only the rich exploit the poor but also the poor exploit one another and the father exploits his family. Daughters, to earn money for survival, are often driven to prostitution. Thus, capitalist society leads to the breakdown of the family, to the enslavement of women, to the increase of crime, and to moral decay. Only if the forces of the people succeed in capturing the state can the state be used to liberate humankind from the horrors of poverty.

This new government must be popularly elected and run by energetic deputies who will serve the interests of the mass of the voters, not the special interests of the capitalists whose oppression will end only after they are absorbed fraternally into a classless society. Blanc hoped that this process of fraternalization could be accomplished peacefully. He suggested that this could be done through the manipulation of the credit system, controlled by the state, which would force the capitalists to transfer money into state banks to be directed toward investments in public enterprises.

In Blanc's process, the capitalists would be induced to participate in their own destruction. The economic sector would then be organized into ateliers, or social workshops, a production unit of men of the same craft or profession working together at the local level. The bosses would be elected by the workers and would oversee the distribution of earnings. Each man would produce according to his aptitude and strength and would be awarded wages according to his need. The production from the local ateliers would be adjusted to overall production through central organizations that would establish general principles and policies.

The heart of Blanc's concern for human welfare lay in his early religious training that taught him the value of charity. Blanc's God, however, was hardly Roman Catholic. Blanc believed in a pantheistic deity that existed in all beings and bound them together in a sacred spirit of fraternity. The perfect society was one with collective ownership of property and complete unity of objective. People would live communally with competition being replaced by cooperation. Blanc envisaged this transformation as being accomplished peacefully through proper education.

Blanc's utopian vision, however, stood in stark contrast to the society in which he lived. The July Monarchy preserved the Napoleonic laws forbidding workers to engage in common action to establish wages and conditions of work. The government, dominated by a strict laissez-faire ideology, made no attempt to improve the standard of living of the working class; nor did many individual employers concern themselves with bettering the lot of their workers. Indeed, many capitalists believed that, because poverty was inevitable, it would not help to call attention to it. Strikes almost never succeeded because the authorities called out the soldiers and the police to suppress the malcontents and jail their leaders.

Thus, the revolutions of 1848, which overthrew the regime of Louis-Philippe, became an opportunity for deliverance. Blanc and other social reformers viewed the advent of the Second Republic as the beginning of the economic transformation of society. Blanc, however, had developed no clear idea of how to put his concepts into practice, nor did there exist any organized political party to support him. The moderate republicans viewed the revolution as essentially political and were not interested in an economic agenda. Nevertheless, some deference had to be made to the demands of the workers, whose power had formed the backbone of the rebellion. Consequently, the provisional government recognized the socialist principle that the workers could demand government intervention in the industrial life of the nation, and it proclaimed the principle of the right to work. It also established a system of national workshops to guarantee each citizen a job.

Blanc was made president of a special commission to study the improvement of the status of workers. He intended to use his power to enact legislation in accord with his socialist principles. He wanted the people to produce according to their ability and to consume according to their need. Competition would be replaced with workers' associations. Workers would unite like brothers and receive comparable wages. He wanted the state to provide medical insurance and old-age pensions. His commission, he hoped, would assume an active role in the settling of wage disputes. Finally, he wanted to pave the way for the nationalization of the railroads, the factories, the insurance companies, and the banks. His success, however, was limited.

The Luxembourg Commission managed to push the government into passing a law that reduced the workday from eleven hours to ten hours in Paris, and from twelve hours to eleven hours in the provinces. It also had some success in wage disputes. Blanc's schemes, however, for the most part, received a cool reception by the provisional government, whose leadership viewed them as a threat to society. While these social reforms antagonized the middle class, they raised the hopes of the workers and added to the growing class tension. The national workshops scheme ended badly. Blanc had hoped for a plan to help workers become established in a particular profession, but the scheme had never been more than a program of unemployment relief—workers being thrown together without any distinction for their trade and receiving the wages of indigents. Blanc disavowed all connection with it.

The workshops had been established only as a temporary expedient to stall the dangerous masses, and, when the situation in Paris was deemed less volatile, the government began disbanding the groups. In June, a decree was issued that drafted all unwed workers into the army and sent all others connected with the program into the provinces, where they would become less threatening. This outrage sparked six days of street fighting, which left Paris in ruins and the army in control. Blanc's dream of a new France lay in the smoldering wreckage.

Blanc fled to England, where he remained until 1871. During the early days of the Third Republic, he served as a representative to the Chamber of Deputies from Marseilles, but his years of exile had put him out of touch with the new generation of leftist leaders. The Marxists scorned his nonrevolutionary approach. His last days were lonely. He had outlived most of his friends. His wife had died in 1876, and his younger brother, Charles, died in January, 1882. Blanc himself died in December, 1882. France gave him a state funeral, and the city of Paris named a street after him. One hundred and fifty thousand people were present for his interment at Père Lachaise cemetery. Suddenly in death, he received the recognition that he had once enjoyed in his days of power.

SIGNIFICANCE

Like many of his countrymen, Louis Blanc tried to give definition to the revolutionary slogans of Liberty, Equality, and Fraternity. He began his attempt with two main assumptions, both of them drawn from Jean-Jacques Rousseau—that humankind is basically good, and that this goodness can emerge in a proper society. The conclusion was, therefore, inescapable: Injustice exists because of a bad environment, and the fault lies in institutions, not in human nature. Upon such Cartesian assumptions, Blanc built his entire system. His basic dedication to social justice, however, flowed more naturally from a belief that human concern was a logical extension of the teachings of Christ.

Though Blanc's ideas formed the basis of modern French humanitarian socialism (as well as influencing the writings of Karl Marx), their application during his lifetime was nonexistent. The Luxembourg Commission was a practical failure. Nevertheless, it furnished an important precedent for state involvement in regulating conditions of work and in collective bargaining mediation. Blanc's system was hopelessly utopian, but he had made it clear that political liberty is closely related to a society's standard of living and that without significant popular enjoyment of the nation's wealth, real democracy is impossible.

—Wm. Laird Kleine-Ahlbrandt

FURTHER READING

Berenson, Edward. *Populist Religion and Left-Wing Politics in France, 1830-1852*. Princeton, N.J.: Princeton University Press, 1984. The first detailed study of the coalition of democrats and republicans who tried to build social reform on political democracy. Focuses on the interaction of politics and ideology at the national and local levels. Particularly valuable discussion of the diversity of the Montagnard coalition of the Second Republic, of which Blanc was one of the main leaders.

Blanc, Louis. *The History of Ten Years, 1830-1840*. London: Chapman and Hall, 1845. A survey of the first crucial decade of the reign of Louis-Philippe, focusing largely on political events. Valuable for Blanc's partisan descriptions, complete with appropriate moralizing.

Duveau, Georges. *1848: The Making of a Revolution*. Translated by Anne Carter. New York: Pantheon Books, 1966. Disdains formal analysis in favor of a narrative re-creating events through vivid episodes and colorful portraits of the main participants. Contains a lengthy portrait of Blanc, as well as other leaders, in the book's concluding chapters. Blanc's role as head of the Luxembourg Commission is presented side by side with the deliberations of the provisional government. Limited almost exclusively to Paris.

Loubère, Leo A. *Louis Blanc: His Life and His Contribution to the Rise of French Jacobin-Socialism*. Evanston, Ill.: Northwestern University Press, 1961. A descriptive approach to the thought of Blanc, relating it to the circumstances of the times. Main thrust is on Blanc's intellectual development as fashioned by public experience. Shows how principal events were responsible for the change and growth of Blanc's socialist philosophy.

Price, Roger. *The French Second Republic: A Social History*. Ithaca, N.Y.: Cornell University Press, 1972. A graphic re-creation of the wretched working-class conditions and the structure of French society that led to the collapse of the July Monarchy.

Soltau, Roger Henry. *French Political Thought in the Nineteenth Century*. Reprint. New York: Russell & Russell, 1959. A competent survey of the leading political thinkers of the age. Blanc's social ideas are all the more extraordinary when placed in the context of his more conservative contemporaries.

SEE ALSO: Jean Jaurès; Karl Marx.

RELATED ARTICLES in *Great Events from History: The Nineteenth Century, 1801-1900:* 1839: Blanc Publishes *The Organization of Labour*; February 22-June, 1848: Paris Revolution of 1848.

AMELIA BLOOMER

American suffragist

Best known for lending her name to a notorious costume designed for women and an article of women's underwear, Bloomer was also the publisher of the first American women's newspaper, The Lily. *However, her greatest contribution to women's rights may have been to bring together Elizabeth Cady Stanton and Susan B. Anthony, who worked together for women's rights for nearly fifty years.*

BORN: May 27, 1818; Homer, New York
DIED: December 30, 1894; Council Bluffs, Iowa
ALSO KNOWN AS: Amelia Jenks (birth name)
AREAS OF ACHIEVEMENT: Women's rights, communications

EARLY LIFE

Amelia Bloomer was born Amelia Jenks, the youngest daughter of the six children born to Ananias Jenks, clothier, and Lucy Webb of Rhode Island. Both her parents came from New England Puritan stock. Her mother was a devout member of the Presbyterian Church. Amelia's earliest recollections were of the family's pleasant Homer, New York, home, to which "Indians" occasionally came to trade.

Amelia attended the local school and at the age of seventeen was hired as a teacher in Clyde in New York's Wayne County. She taught there for only one term, however, and then went to live with her older married sister, Elvira, in Waterloo. At the age of nineteen, she was employed as a governess to the three children of Oren Chamberlain. During three years at that post, she met a young Quaker law student and former teacher, Dexter C. Bloomer. On April 15, 1840, they were married by the Reverend Samuel H. Gridley, the Presbyterian clergyman of the village. Amelia often noted that the word "obey" had been deleted from her marriage vows. At the time of the marriage, Bloomer was a partner of Isaac Fuller in a Seneca Falls printing business.

LIFE'S WORK

Amelia and her husband settled in Seneca Falls. As editor of the only Whig newspaper in the county, Dexter Bloomer was active in the 1840 presidential campaign that pitted General William Henry Harrison and Martin Van Buren against each other. His political activism gradually influenced Amelia to develop an interest in politics as well as activity in the temperance movement. Under her husband's urging, Amelia wrote regular columns in his newspaper and other publications, using a series of pseudonyms rather than her own name. Both Amelia and her husband joined the Episcopal Church, in which Amelia was not hesitant about speaking out against certain biblical passages that she believed were strained and unnatural about women.

Although Amelia attended the Seneca Falls Convention that was sponsored by Elizabeth Cady Stanton, Lucretia Mott, and several other women of the village in 1848, she signed neither the resolutions nor the declaration of independence of the women's rights convention. Up until that point, her interests centered on the temperance movement; when the Daughters of Temperance formed in 1848, she became an officer in the new organization.

In 1849, Amelia launched *The Lily*, a newspaper that she intended to be about temperance. The Women's Rights Historical Park credits Amelia Bloomer as the ed-

Amelia Bloomer. (The Granger Collection, New York)

itor and publisher of the first American women's newspaper. One of Bloomer's earliest supporters was Susan B. Anthony, a Rochester school teacher, and an early contributor of articles was Elizabeth Cady Stanton.

In the spring of 1850, an important antislavery meeting was held in Seneca Falls whose speakers included the abolitionist newspaper editor William Lloyd Garrison and the English orator George Thompson. Also active in that movement was Susan B. Anthony, who attended the antislavery meeting as the guest of Amelia, who introduced her to Stanton. That fortuitous meeting started a lifelong friendship between Anthony and Stanton that led to their working together for women's rights for nearly half a century. Married and the mother of a growing family, Stanton was the writer; Anthony, who was single by choice, was the traveler and orator. Both gave credit to Bloomer for their life's work.

Over time, Bloomer became increasingly interested in the fight for women's rights and used *The Lily* to support women's property rights, along with the temperance movement, and gradually increased her support of the woman suffrage movement. She also traveled to several states to speak on those two issues. However, the incident that was to bring Bloomer lasting fame occurred early in 1851. No one is sure exactly who invented the "Bloomer costume," but the design has been attributed by some historians to Elizabeth Smith Miller, who wore the costume while visiting the Stantons. The outfit consisted of a skirt that came either a little above or below the knees, over full "Turkish" trousers cuffed at the ankle. Both Stanton and Bloomer abandoned their tight corsets and heavy petticoats and adopted the new, loose and comfortable dress. Bloomer was pictured wearing it in *The Lily*, and she and the outfit were featured in *The New York Times* and other publications in America and England as she traveled to the World Temperance Convention in New York City and to meetings in Chicago, Detroit, Milwaukee, and other cities. Afterward, her name became synonymous with the distinctive costume.

In 1853, the Bloomers moved to Mount Vernon, Ohio, where Dexter bought the weekly family newspaper *Western Home Visitor*, of which Amelia became assistant editor. The paper was devoted to morality, temperance, reform and women's rights. In addition to editing her husband's newspaper, Amelia continued to write, speak publicly, and edit *The Lily*. Putting into practice what she believed, she hired a woman typesetter. When the male typesetter refused to work in the same place with the women, the Bloomers gave them an ultimatum. After the men walked out, Amelia hired more female typesetters—all of whom were teetotalers.

In July, 1854, Dexter sold his interest in his newspaper. When he decided to settle in Council Bluffs, Iowa, where no printing facilities existed, Amelia sold *The Lily* to Mary A. Birdsall of Richmond, Indiana, where it lasted only a few years longer. While the Bloomers waited in St. Joseph, Missouri, for a steamboat to take them up the Missouri River, Amelia was spotted wearing the "Bloomer costume" and was carried off to make a speech, which was well reported in the local paper. Shortly after arriving in Council Bluffs, however, she abandoned the comfortable costume for the fashionable new whaleboned hoop skirt. In the East, the Bloomer costume had become discredited. Amusement turned to ridicule and then to viperous attacks in legislatures and newspapers, associating wearers with socialists and revolutionaries, and calling them "unsexed women," "semi-men," and "hermaphrodites." Women activists decided their cause was more important than their comfort, and went back to traditional dress.

Meanwhile, Dexter Bloomer opened a law office specializing in farm issues. The childless couple then adopted two children, a brother and sister. There was no Episcopal Church in Council Bluffs, so Amelia spoke at the Methodist and Congregational churches on women's rights and was asked by a member of the Nebraska Territory legislature to speak to that body, which she did in

January, 1856. She received loud applause and favorable reporting in Omaha newspapers. Afterward, she often traveled to Omaha and other cities to speak, urging Nebraska women to take advantage of their legal right in that territory to own property. At the same time, she also remained active in the temperance movement and joined the Woman's Christian Temperance Union (WCTU). When Anthony, abolitionist Frederick Douglass, and other activists visited Council Bluffs, they were guests in the Bloomer home. In 1870, she was a charter member and the first president of the Council Bluffs woman suffrage society, and was named first vice president of the newly formed Iowa Woman's State Suffrage Society in 1871. In 1887, she was asked by Stanton and Anthony to write the chapter on Iowa suffrage activity for their history of woman suffrage.

In 1890, the Bloomers celebrated their fiftieth wedding anniversary. In addition to the more than one hundred guests who attended the celebration, letters and telegrams came from prominent people all over the country. Four years later, when Amelia Bloomer died at the age of seventy-six after a brief illness, messages again came to her family from all over. On her tombstone is the inscription, "A pioneer in woman's enfranchisement."

SIGNIFICANCE

Besides her own active work for more than fifty years in temperance, women's rights, and church work, and the epitaph on her tombstone, Amelia Bloomer is memorialized on a plaque explaining the three-statue sculpture that stands on East Bayard Street overlooking Van Cleef Lake in Seneca Falls. Two of the women are dressed in the Bloomer costumes, and the plaque explains

> In May 1851, there was a chance encounter on the streets of Seneca Falls which forever altered the struggle for women's rights. Amelia Jenks Bloomer introduced Susan B. Anthony to Elizabeth Cady Stanton. The friendship that was forged between Stanton and Anthony gave direction and momentum to the seventy-two year struggle for women's suffrage which culminated on August 26, 1920 in the passage of the 19th Amendment to the United States Constitution. Neither woman lived to see this happen.

Bloomer herself also did not live long enough to see the passage of the Nineteenth Amendment. However, her work was far more significant than giving her name to a liberating but short-lived costume for nineteenth century women, and to the style of women's underwear and gym shorts that still bears her name.

—Erika E. Pilver

FURTHER READING

Beale, Irene A. *Genesee Valley Women 1743-1985.* Geneseo, N.Y.: Chestnut Hill Press, 1985. The table of contents names Elizabeth Miller, dress reformer, but information about Bloomer is contained in the short selection.

Bloomer, Amelia Jenks. *Hear Me Patiently: The Reform Speeches of Amelia Jenks Bloomer.* Edited by Anne C. Coon. Westport, Conn.: Greenwood Press, 1994. Collection of Bloomer's speeches, exploring women's lives and issues from 1850 to 1880. Coon portrays Bloomer as a shy women who was thrust into public life by her commitment to reform and endorsement of a new style of dress.

Bloomer, D. C. *Life and Writings of Amelia Bloomer.* 1895. New York: Shocken Books, 1975. Written by Amelia's husband, this extensive biography is the source from which many of the selections in women's history books are taken.

Whitton, Mary Ormsbee. *These Were the Women: The Story of Women Who Helped Make American Culture, 1776-1860.* New York: Hastings House, 1954. Contains three pages with a great deal of information about Bloomer that is based on Dexter Bloomer's biography.

SEE ALSO: Susan B. Anthony; Olympia Brown; Frederick Douglass; William Lloyd Garrison; William Henry Harrison; Lucretia Mott; Elizabeth Cady Stanton; Martin Van Buren.

RELATED ARTICLES in *Great Events from History: The Nineteenth Century, 1801-1900:* May 28-29, 1851: Akron Woman's Rights Convention; February 17-18, 1890: Women's Rights Associations Unite.

GEBHARD LEBERECHT VON BLÜCHER

Prussian military leader

As a military commander, Blücher served the cause of Prussia well throughout his life, especially during the French revolutionary and Napoleonic periods. He was not a great military strategist, but his undisputed ability as a leader of men and his strong support for military reforms following a defeat at Jena in 1806 enabled Prussia to play a major role in the final victory over France, thereby contributing to Prussia's subsequent rise as a major power.

BORN: December 16, 1742; Rostock, Mecklenburg-Schwerin (now in Germany)
DIED: September 12, 1819; Krieblowitz, Silesia, Prussia (now Katy Wrocławskie, Poland)
ALSO KNOWN AS: Alte Vorwärts; Old Forward
AREA OF ACHIEVEMENT: Military

EARLY LIFE

Gebhard Leberecht von Blücher (BLEW-ker) was born the son of a former cavalry officer who had served in the armies of the duke of Mecklenburg-Schwerin and the *Landgraf* of Hesse-Cassell. The family was of old but poor East Elbian nobility and, at the time of Blücher's birth, was nearly penniless. The young Blücher entered Swedish military service at the age of fifteen. He had been sent to live with his married sister on the island of Rügen, then a part of Sweden.

Early during the Seven Years' War, Blücher joined a Swedish regiment of hussars as a cadet. Cavalry service was a well-established tradition in the family. In 1760, Blücher was captured by the Prussians, and, when he was offered a commission in the Prussian army, he joined the regiment that had captured him, after obtaining a formal release from Swedish service. Such shifts of allegiance were neither uncommon nor dishonorable prior to the age of nationalism.

In 1773, when Blücher was passed over for promotion in favor of a person of higher nobility, he resigned his commission. He was in part passed over because of his so-called wild life, primarily gambling, drinking, and reckless displays of horsemanship. For Blücher, gambling was a substitute for the excitement of war, and he frequently compared the skills of gambling to the skills of war. For the next fifteen years, Blücher pursued the life of a noble landlord, first in Prussian Poland and then on his own estate in Pomerania. He married and became the father of five children by his first wife. After her death, he married a second time. At heart, however, he continued to long for the life of a soldier and repeatedly requested reinstatement.

LIFE'S WORK

Blücher's efforts to return to military life finally succeeded in 1787, when King Frederick William II commissioned him as a major in his old regiment. In 1790, Blücher was promoted to colonel of his regiment. He saw action after the Battle of Valmy (September, 1792) and distinguished himself repeatedly during the 1793 and 1794 campaigns against revolutionary France. In 1795, he was promoted to major general (one star), and in 1801, to lieutenant general (two stars).

During the period of peace, Blücher, though primarily a soldier, served successfully as administrator of Münster, which had been annexed to Prussia in 1802. In this capacity, he worked together with Freiherr vom Stein, and the two developed respect for each other. Blücher was among those who advocated war against Napoleon I in 1805 and 1806, despite the fact that he recognized serious shortcomings in the Prussian army. "The army is good," he told a friend, "but the leaders are not well chosen. They include too many princes and old wigs who have outlived their usefulness." Blücher was also motivated by an ever-growing dislike for the French in general (he referred to them as "parlez-vous") and Napoleon in particular.

When Prussia finally joined the war, though belatedly, Blücher participated in the disastrous Battle of Auerstedt (October, 1806). During the inglorious retreat following the humiliating defeat at Jena and Auerstedt, Blücher distinguished himself as commander of the rear guard, covering the flight of the army. While the bulk of the Prussian forces was captured by the pursuing French, Blücher's troops finally retreated northward toward Lübeck, where he was forced to surrender, having run out of ammunition and provisions. Following the disastrous defeat of 1806 and the institution of military reforms, all Prussian officers who had been captured had to justify their action before a commission of inquiry. Blücher was the only one of the field commanders who had surrendered to pass that scrutiny. The commission concluded that "this surrender belongs to the very few which were justified."

Blücher was soon exchanged and appointed governor general of Pomerania, a position in which he again held civil as well as military duties. The king was forced to dismiss him, however, in 1811, under French pressure. Napoleon had become fearful of Blücher's proven ability and undisguised hatred for the French. As early as 1805, having come under the influence of the Prussian military reformers, Blücher advocated the establishment of a national army based on conscription according to the French revolutionary model, in place of the moribund army of unpatriotic mercenaries and impressed peasant boys. He also advocated more humane treatment of the soldiers, better pay, the establishment of self-contained divisions consisting of infantry, cavalry, and artillery, and other military reforms that the French had introduced early in the revolution.

In 1809, Blücher and other progressive officers attempted to persuade Frederick William III to join Austria's anti-French uprising, but they were unable to persuade the cautious and timid king to give the order. The king not only feared defeat but also was extremely distrustful of his subjects, and he did not like the idea of arming the masses. Blücher even considered leaving Prussian service and offering his sword to the Austrians. He spoke of forming a Prussian legion under Austrian command. As Napoleon's empire began to weaken, Blücher and General August von Gneisenau, though not the Prussian military establishment, again advocated a popular uprising and guerrilla war, taking their inspiration from the successful Spanish uprising. In 1808, Blücher wrote to a friend, "I don't know why we cannot display as much respect for ourselves as the Spanish do."

In 1812, Blücher was forced into temporary hiding because Napoleon, preparing his Russian campaign, wanted to arrest him. During this period, Blücher suffered from a serious mental illness, which was a recurring problem, though it usually found expression only in depression and hypochondria. In 1813, Blücher was recalled to active duty, only one of two generals of the 142 in the Prussian army in 1806 who retained troop command. He commanded the joint Prussian-Russian "Army of Silesia" as a three-star general. In the summer of 1813, his army invaded Saxony and defeated the French in a series of engagements, including the Battle of Wahlstatt, and played a major role in the decisive allied victory in the Battle of the Nations (Leipzig), in October, 1813. For his part in this significant victory, he was promoted to field marshal. His impetuous and aggressive leadership earned for him the title "Marshal Forward" (*Vorwärts*), bestowed upon him by the Russians.

Blücher, in keeping with the new concepts of warfare, urged a continuous and unorthodox winter pursuit of Napoleon and with his forces crossed the Rhine River during New Year's night of 1814. The Austrians, on the other hand, wanted to negotiate with Napoleon, their emperor's son-in-law, and retain him on the throne of a reduced and chastened France as a counterweight to growing Russian power. Blücher, however, had no understanding of political considerations, seeing all matters solely from the military viewpoint.

Although the allies still suffered some defeats, Blücher urged them to maintain the pressure until the final capture of Paris and Napoleon's abdication in March, 1814. Throughout this period, Gneisenau served as Blücher's capable chief of staff, complementing Blücher's daring and courage with competent staff work, the value of which Blücher fully and publicly recognized. Blücher, celebrated, decorated, and rewarded for his services, was always quick to praise others and give them credit. While accompanying the victorious monarchs during a visit to Great Britain, he received an honorary doctorate from the University of Oxford and later accepted a similar honor from the University of Berlin.

Ill health and his strong disagreement with the victorious coalition's lenient treatment of defeated France caused Blücher to retire from military service. He was, however, immediately recalled as Prussia's field commander when Napoleon returned from Elba in 1815. Blücher joined forces with the British under the duke of Wellington in the southern Netherlands (modern Belgium), moving his forces dangerously close to the French frontier. On June 16, 1815, the Prussian forces, on Wellington's left flank at Ligny, were defeated by Napoleon's surprise attack, which was designed to separate the two allied forces. Napoleon then turned northward against Wellington, hoping to force him to retire to England.

Although severely injured when he was pinned under his horse when it was killed during a French charge, Blücher managed to rally most of his disheveled army. However, instead of retreating along his line of communication toward Germany as conventional military doctrine would have dictated and as Napoleon expected him to do, Blücher retreated northward, slipped away from the pursuing Marshal Michel Ney, and joined Wellington at Waterloo on the evening of June 18.

Blücher's timely arrival to assist the exhausted British turned a stalemate, or possibly a French victory, into a total French rout. For this victory, Blücher received a unique award, the "Blücher Star"—the Iron Cross superimposed on a golden star. Blücher had already received the Grand Cross of the Iron Cross in 1813 (awarded only seven times during the war). Following this final contribution to the allied cause, Blücher retired again and returned to his Silesian estates, where he devoted much time to his passion for gambling. He died in September, 1819, after a short illness, and his funeral became an occasion for great praise and more honors.

SIGNIFICANCE

Gebhard Leberecht von Blücher was a man of limited formal education, a fact he clearly recognized and often lamented. Although he did not understand the essence of the French Revolution—the emphasis on democratic reforms—he recognized the benefits that a national, patriotic army offered. Though he is not considered to have been a military genius or even a capable strategist, he did join others in promoting reforms that led to the creation of the *Landwehr* (Prussian militia) and a national conscript army, so important in subsequent German history. Blücher is frequently described as being impatient with maps but able and willing to delegate authority, accept advice, and make quick and sound decisions under the pressure of battle. "Gneisenau stirs and I move forward," he said in reference to his chief of staff.

Blücher was one of the few German officers of the old order to make the transition from the organizational and strategic concepts of classical (limited) warfare to the new concepts of revolutionary-national warfare. His most important contributions to victory over Napoleon were his insistence on aggressive action, close pursuit, and, above all, his folksy manner and sincere feeling for his troops. His soldiers in turn repaid him with steadfast loyalty, devotion, and obedience, even when his demands were excessive. He saw matters only from the military viewpoint and was greatly opposed to the lenient postwar diplomatic settlement.

Blücher was also firmly convinced that the army, as well as the Prussian nobility, should occupy privileged positions within the state, though he demonstrated none of the arrogance so common among his fellow aristocrats. At no time did he accept military subordination to civilian authority. His forthright, honest, and earthy character and his physical attractiveness made him a natural, charismatic leader and war hero, much admired by the German population; he is probably the most popular hero in German military history. Blücher, along with Gneisenau, is considered by Marxists to have been among the progressive Prussian officers of the War of Liberation. Karl Marx described him as "the model of a soldier."

—Frederick Dumin

FURTHER READING

Craig, Gordon A. *The Politics of the Prussian Army, 1640-1945*. Oxford, England: Clarendon Press, 1955. A general history, placing Prussian reforms into a broader context. Includes an index and a general bibliography.

Gneisenau, August Wilhelm Anton, Graf Neidhardt von. *The Life and Campaigns of Field Marshal Prince Blücher of Whalstaff: From the Period of His Birth and First Appointment in the Prussian Service Down to His Second Entry into Paris in 1815*. Translated by General Count Gneisenau and J. E. Marston. London: Constable, 1996. A reprint of a biography written by Gneisenau, Blücher's chief of staff.

Henderson, Ernest F. *Blücher and the Uprising of Prussia Against Napoleon, 1806-1815*. New York: Knickerbocker Press, 1911. A critical and balanced history of the period with primary emphasis on Blücher's contributions to the allied victory. Some original sources are listed in the text. Very little is included on his early life and career.

Paret, Peter. *Clausewitz and the State*. New York: Oxford University Press, 1976. Emphasizes military and civil reforms in Prussia with numerous references to Blücher. Includes a very comprehensive listing of primary sources and an extensive index.

_____. *Yorck and the Era of Prussian Reforms, 1807-1815*. Princeton, N.J.: Princeton University Press, 1966. After an introduction to warfare under the old order, this work concentrates on reforms and reorganization in state and army after Jena. Includes several appendixes pertaining to the reform movement, an index, and an extensive bibliography.

Parkinson, Roger. *Clausewitz: A Biography*. London: Wayland, 1970. A balanced treatment of Clausewitz's life and work with detailed description of the battles and frequent references to Blücher as a military leader and a supporter of reforms. Includes a bibliography, an index, and illustrations.

Uffindell, Andrew. *The Eagle's Last Triumph: Napoleon's Victory at Ligny, June 1815*. London: Greenhill Books, 1994. Blücher is prominently featured in this military history of the battle at Ligny.

SEE ALSO: Charles XIV John; August von Gneisenau; Napoleon I.

RELATED ARTICLES in *Great Events from History: The Nineteenth Century, 1801-1900:* October 16-19, 1813: Battle of Leipzig; June 18, 1815: Battle of Waterloo.

BARBARA LEIGH SMITH BODICHON

English artist and social activist

Bodichon was a landscape artist who exhibited widely in England, but she is better known as a leader among early feminists in Great Britain. She lobbied to change British marriage laws and obtain suffrage for women and promoted higher education for women, helping to establish Girton College at Cambridge University.

BORN: April 8, 1827; Whatlingen, Sussex, England
DIED: June 11, 1891; Scalands Gate, Hastings, East Sussex, England
ALSO KNOWN AS: Barbara Leigh Smith (birth name)
AREAS OF ACHIEVEMENT: Art, education, women's rights

EARLY LIFE

Barbara Leigh Smith Bodichon (BAH-dih-kawn) was born Barbara Leigh Smith, the oldest daughter of a highly successful merchant and social iconoclast, Benjamin Smith, and his common-law wife Anne Longden. Annie had four other children by Smith before she died in 1834, but the couple never married, possibly because Smith did not agree with the legal restrictions placed on wives and children by formal marriage.

Barbara inherited her father's reformist spirit. As a child she was educated in a fashion more common for male children and was given exceptional freedom in her home. When she turned twenty-one, her father gave her a bequest that provided an annual income of three hundred pounds, making her financially independent and allowing her to launch a career that would see her distinguish herself in both art and politics. In 1848, she began writing articles for various periodicals, and during the following year she enrolled at the newly formed Bedford College for Ladies, where she studied art under Francis Cory. Her work was first exhibited at the Royal Academy in London in 1850, and during the following year one of her paintings was included in the Society of British Artists exhibition. She would continue to exhibit in both venues over the next two decades.

At Bedford College Barbara also took courses in economics and law, preparing herself for leadership in a movement that influenced her own and future generations. In 1850, she traveled, unchaperoned, to Europe with her friend Bessie Raynor Parkes; it was the first of many times that she flaunted convention and generated mild scandal. Her visit in Munich with fellow women artists Anna Mary Howitt and Jane Benham led her to decide on her life's work outside her artist's studio: promoting women's causes in a patriarchal society in which women were decidedly objects of legal as well as social discrimination.

LIFE'S WORK

When Barbara set up residence in London during the early 1850's, she began working with a number of women whose interests coincided with her own. Although not yet married and financially independent, Barbara believed that current laws making women legally subservient to their husbands were inherently immoral. Urged on by friends such as Parkes, Howitt, Benham, and her new friend Marian Evans—better known as novelist George Eliot—she began agitating for change in laws governing property. Her initial contribution to this cause was a pamphlet, *A Brief Summary of the Most Important Laws of England Concerning Women*. The 1854 publication caused a minor scandal, although most men and women in polite society dismissed it simply as the work of an unconventional bohemian. The Law Amendment Society, however, took Barbara's views seriously enough to appoint a committee to look into the concerns that she raised.

The publication of her pamphlet brought Barbara into contact with her publisher John Chapman, editor of the *Westminster Review*, with whom she had a brief but dispiriting affair. In 1856, she traveled to Algeria to get away from Chapman, and there met Dr. Eugène Bodichon, whom she married the following year. The newly married couple then took a seven-month honeymoon to the United States, where Barbara met leading feminists in Boston, New York, and other cities. From 1858 until her husband's death in 1885, Barbara divided her time between England and Algiers.

Before she left England in 1856, Barbara had been the catalyst in organizing a group to petition Parliament to change laws governing women's rights—especially the rights of women to possess property in their own names and to earn independent livings. The informal committee that she organized in 1856 managed to collect seventy thousand signatures on a petition presented to Parliament the following year. In Parliament, the Married Women's Property Bill passed two readings, but eventually failed to become law.

Bodichon expressed her lobbying efforts on behalf of working women in another pamphlet that she published in 1857: *Women and Work*. The following year she purchased *The English Woman's Journal*, a periodical with a national circulation. She and others in her circle used that publication to promote women's causes through much of the following decade.

During this period of significant political activity, Bodichon still found time to paint and to work on other projects. She continued exhibiting in London, with both the Royal Society and the Society of British Artists, and at the Dudley Gallery and the French Gallery. Her work was included in a traveling exhibition to New York in 1857, and paintings appeared in later years in Birmingham and Liverpool exhibitions. Her artistic circle included many of the Pre-Raphaelite Brotherhood. Dante Gabriel Rossetti and his sister, Christina Georgina Rossetti, claimed her as a friend and spoke highly of her ability as a landscape painter. In 1858, Bodichon worked with her husband as editor of his book *Algeria Considered as a Winter Residence for the English*. Her own winter residences in Algeria over the next twenty years provided her inspiration for some of her best-known paintings.

Bodichon's political activism was not slowed by her art. During the late 1850's, she turned her attention to the issue of suffrage and for several years was active in groups committed to obtaining the vote for women. This activity brought her into contact with the philosopher John Stuart Mill and his wife, Harriet Taylor, who had also been pursuing feminist causes for more than a decade. In 1865, Bodichon helped to circulate another petition, this one demanding suffrage, and asked Mill, a member of Parliament, for assistance. Mill presented her petition to Parliament in 1866 but was not successful in seeing its proposal adopted.

Meanwhile, Bodichon contributed to the public debate on woman suffrage, first in 1866 with a pamphlet, *Objections to the Enfranchisement of Women Considered*, and three years later with a longer, more cogently argued defense of woman suffrage, *Reasons for and Against the Enfranchisement of Women*. It is a small irony of history that Bodichon's spirited argument appeared during the same year as John Stuart Mill's *On the Subjection of Women*, as the latter received much wider circulation and eventually proved more influential in keeping alive interest in many of the issues on which Bodichon and her circle were working.

Throughout her career, Bodichon never abandoned her interest in education for women. During the late 1860's, she began a project that would eventually lead to the acceptance of women in England's great universities. With her associate Emily Davies, Bodichon began drafting plans for a college for women that was to be located at either Oxford or Cambridge. Her proposed college was to have the same admissions standards, curricula, and examinations as those applied to men at the great English universities. Although Bodichon was not officially associated with the new college's establishment because the notoriety she had gained while supporting women's causes was considered a liability by Davies and others, she contributed one thousand pounds to the cause and allowed the college to use her London residence as a site for examining the first applicants. In 1873, Bodichon saw her dream come true when Girton College opened in Cambridge.

After Bodichon suffered a stroke in 1877, she continued to work but at a reduced pace. In 1885, a second stroke followed from which she never fully recovered. She died in 1891, bequeathing Girton College a legacy of ten thousand pounds.

SIGNIFICANCE

Through her writing, political activism, and patronage, Bodichon advanced the cause of women's equality on a number of fronts during her lifetime. Although it is true that her gradualist approach was repudiated by the feminists whose efforts resulted in woman suffrage after World War I, her identification and public statements on issues such as property rights, education, and voting set the agenda for feminists over the next half-century in England.

Bodichon's encouragement of other feminists and her willingness to work with men such as John Stuart Mill broadened the reach of the feminist movement and ensured that issues she and her circle had brought to the forefront of public consciousness would not be forgotten when she retreated from the public eye near the end of her life. Similarly, although women were not officially admitted to Cambridge University until 1945, the presence of Girton College remained a visible symbol of what women could accomplish in higher education when afforded the opportunity to participate as equals to men.

—Laurence W. Mazzeno

FURTHER READING

Burton, Hester. *Barbara Bodichon, 1827-1891*. London: Murray, 1949. Full-length biography that assesses Bodichon's career and helps place her in the culture that concurrently supported and resisted efforts to improve women's status.

Herstein, Sheila R. *A Mid-Victorian Feminist: Barbara Leigh Smith Bodichon*. New Haven, Conn.: Yale University Press, 1985. While covering the major events in Bodichon's life, this biography concentrates on her contributions to the feminist movement and feminist thought.

Hirsch, Pam. *Barbara Leigh Smith Bodichon, 1827-1891: Feminist, Artist and Rebel.* London: Chatto & Windus, 1998. Based not only on published accounts but also on many manuscripts and records, this study provides a measured assessment of Bodichon's life, highlighting her accomplishments in many fields and noting her contributions to the women's movement.

Levine, Philippa. *Victorian Feminism, 1850-1900.* Tallahassee: Florida State University Press, 1987. Sketches Bodichon's role in promoting feminist causes by placing her in relation to others with whom she worked to bring about equal treatment for women in England.

Orr, Clarissa Campbell. *Women in the Victorian World.* Manchester, England: Manchester University Press, 1995. Includes an essay evaluating Bodichon's work as a political activist; other essays suggest how leaders of the feminist movement influenced the advancement of women's causes in Victorian England.

SEE ALSO: John Constable; George Eliot; John Stuart Mill; Christina Rossetti; J. M. W. Turner; Queen Victoria; Duke of Wellington.

RELATED ARTICLE in *Great Events from History: The Nineteenth Century, 1801-1900:* August 28, 1857: British Parliament Passes the Matrimonial Causes Act.

MARIE ANNE VICTORINE BOIVIN

French midwife and medical pioneer

The inventor of the vaginal speculum, Boivin also pioneered in using stethoscopes to listen to fetal heartbeats. She helped improve training for midwives, and her research—especially on female anatomy and causes of uterine hemorrhage and abortion—improved the care of childbearing women and facilitated deliveries of babies. Her textbook on uterus diseases was used in medical schools in Europe and the Americas.

BORN: April 9, 1773; Montreuil, France

DIED: May 16, 1841; Paris, France

ALSO KNOWN AS: Marie Anne Victorine Gillain (birth name); Marie Anne Victoire Boivin; Marie Anne Victorine Boivin Gillain; Madame Boivin; Veuve Boivin

AREA OF ACHIEVEMENT: Medicine

EARLY LIFE

Marie Anne Victorine Boivin (mah-ree ahn veek-tawreen boy-vehn) was born Marie Anne Victorine Gillain in the Paris suburb of Montreuil. She received her education from the nuns at Estampes and showed an aptitude for medical studies during her childhood. In 1797, at the age of twenty-four, Marie Anne married Louis Boivin, who was employed as an assistant in the Bureau of National Domains. Shortly after they had a daughter together, Marie Anne was widowed and moved to Versailles. Tragedy continued to plague her as her daughter was killed in an accident.

After losing both her husband and her daughter, Boivin returned to Paris to continue her medical studies. Around the turn of the nineteenth century, in France, as in many other countries, admission to medical school and careers as physicians were not open to women. However, the field of midwifery was open to them. A long tradition dating back to the Middle Ages recognized women's expertise in the art of midwifery and many of the treatises written on childbearing and its complications were the work of women. Midwifery was the area of medicine in which Boivin was to excel. She pursued her studies at the hospital school of Hôtel-Dieu with Marie-Louise Lachapelle, midwife-in-chief of the hospital and director of practical training, and with Jean-Louis Auguste Baudelocque, who served as lecturer on theory. After receiving a diploma in midwifery, she became an assistant to Lachapelle.

LIFE'S WORK

Boivin's professional life was multifaceted. She not only practiced her profession of midwifery but also taught, wrote, and did research that led to the development of instruments essential to her craft. At the Hôtel-Dieu, Boivin and Lachapelle attended more than forty thousand deliveries of babies, almost all of which were successfully completed. Some deliveries were uncomplicated and required minimal assistance; others were beset by complications and called upon all the exceptional expertise of the two women. Boivin's skill was so respected that the renowned surgeon Guillaume Dupuytren, expecting his only daughter's delivery to be difficult, placed her in the care of Boivin.

In addition to her work in the delivery rooms of the maternity facility of the Hôtel-Dieu, Boivin served as a teacher in the institution's school for midwives. There she taught the practical skills to her students and also lectured on theoretical aspects of midwifery. Both she and Lachapelle emphasized the necessity of thorough training for midwives and for improvement of their training.

Boivin's practical experience in assisting in childbirth provided the material for her first book, *Memorial de l'art d'accouchements* (memoir of the art of birthing), which she published in 1812. Its text was based on her observations of 20,517 births that she attended. By 1824, her book was in its fourth French edition and had been translated into German and Italian. In 1818, she published another book, *Nouveau traité des hemmoragies de l'uterus* (new treatise on uterine hemorrhage), in which she recounted her findings on certain previously undetected causes of uterine hemorrhage.

In 1833, Boivin published a treatise on diseases of the uterus, *Traité des maladies de l'uterus et des annexes*, which she wrote with Lachapelle's nephew Antoine Dugès, then a member of the medical faculty at the University of Montpellier. That book contained forty-one plates and 116 drawings that Boivin is said to have colored herself. During the following year, the book was translated into English as *A Practical Treatise on the Diseases of the Uterus and Its Appendages*. Her most important work, this book became the standard textbook on the uterus used in medical schools throughout Europe and the United States for many years. Boivin also wrote on abortion and diseases of the placenta. In addition to writing books on gynecology, she translated several English works on the subject into French.

Boivin also discovered procedures and invented instruments that improved the examination and care of childbearing women. She was one of the first to listen to fetal heartbeats with stethoscopes. She is credited with invention of the vaginal speculum for examination of the womb. Speculums used in the twenty-first century are based on her original designs.

Throughout her career, Boivin was highly respected and praised and received numerous honors for her work. She was an honorary member of many medical societies, including the Royal Society of the Medical Sciences of Bordeaux, which honored her with a commendation for her thesis on the causes of abortion. The king of Prussia awarded her the Order of Merit. On June 23, 1828, the University of Marburg awarded her an honorary doctorate of medicine. The degree was given to her at the request of Dietrich William Shrubs, professor of gynecology at the university, based upon his assessment of her as the best midwife of the time.

Despite her successes, misfortune followed Boivin. The medical school of the University of Paris continued to oppose the admission of women to the medical profession and refused to recognize Boivin's achievements, even though she did most of her work there. For reasons that are not entirely clear, she quarreled with Lachapelle and resigned from the Hôtel-Dieu. Although she received many offers of excellent positions, even one from the king of Prussia, she eventually took a position at a hospital for prostitutes and accepted a low wage. After thirty-five years of service she retired with a small pension. In May, 1841, she died in Paris at the age of sixty-eight, a victim of paralysis and want.

SIGNIFICANCE

Through her research, teaching and writing, Marie Anne Victorine Boivin made significant changes in the practice of midwifery and contributed important information to the medical sciences, particularly in obstetrics. She was one of the most respected and influential women researchers of the nineteenth century. She rose to be an authority in her field in spite of not being able to attend a medical school and earn a professional degree. Profiting from the education that she received at the Hôtel-Dieu and studying and working independently, she established herself as the foremost authority in her field and became a role model for midwives of her time. Doctors with whom she worked praised her expertise; some actually credited her with knowledge and skill in obstetrics superior to that of male physicians.

—*Shawncey Webb*

FURTHER READING

Alec, Margaret. *Hypatia's Heritage: A History of Women in Science from Antiquity Through the Nineteenth Century*. Boston: Beacon Press, 1986. Discusses Boivin's work with Marie Lachapelle, awards and honors received by Boivin.

Bonner, Thomas Neville. *Medical Education in Britain, France, Germany and the United States, 1750-1945*. Baltimore: Johns Hopkins University Press, 2000. Treats the problems faced by women such as Boivin who sought a university degree and a career in medicine.

Cule, John. *The Timetables of Medicine: An Illustrated Chronology of the History of Medicine from Prehis-*

tory to Present Times. New York: Black Dog and Leventhal, 2000. Ten parallel timetables, country by country treatment of medical history, and traces development of medicine in context of other significant events. Chapter on women in medicine. Good general background information on medical profession.

Golemba, Beverly E. *Lesser-Known Women: A Biographical Dictionary*. Boulder, Colo.: Lynne Rienner, 1992. Organized chronologically, this reference work lists women who made important contributions in diverse areas and gives brief biographical sketches.

Lovejoy, Esther Pohl. *Women Doctors of the World*. New York: Macmillan, 1957. Lovejoy gives a brief but detailed account of Boivin's life and accomplishments.

Marks, Geoffrey, and William K. Beatty. *Women in White*. New York: Charles Scribner's Sons, 1972. Describes Boivin's life and work and includes the comments of eminent physicians of the time on the value of her work.

Mead, Kate Campbell Hurd. *A History of Women in Medicine from the Earliest Times to the Beginning of the Nineteenth Century*. 2 vols. Haddam, Conn.: Haddam Press, 1938. Treats Boivin's life and work in context of developments in midwifery and also contains biographical information.

Ramsey, Matthew. *Professional and Popular Medicine in France, 1770-1830: The Social World of Medical Practice*. New York: Cambridge University Press, 2002. Does not mention Boivin specifically, but gives general information on attitudes toward the medical professions and access to careers at the time of her work.

SEE ALSO: Elizabeth Blackwell; Dorothea Dix; Marie Elizabeth Zakrzewska.

RELATED ARTICLES in *Great Events from History: The Nineteenth Century, 1801-1900:* May, 1847: Semmelweis Develops Antiseptic Procedures; May 12, 1857: New York Infirmary for Indigent Women and Children Opens; 1882: First Birth Control Clinic Opens in Amsterdam.

SIMÓN BOLÍVAR

South American revolutionary leader

The liberator of the northern portion of Spanish South America, Bolívar epitomized the struggle against Spanish colonial rule. His most lasting contributions include his aid in the liberation of Bolivia, Colombia, Ecuador, Peru, and Venezuela, and his farsighted proposals for hemispheric solidarity among Latin American nations.

BORN: July 24, 1783; Caracas, New Granada (now in Venezuela)

DIED: December 17, 1830; Villa of San Pedro Alejandrino, near Santa Marta, Colombia

ALSO KNOWN AS: Simón José Antonio de la Santisima Trinidad Bolívar (full name)

AREAS OF ACHIEVEMENT: Government and politics, military

EARLY LIFE

Simón José Antonio de la Santisima Trinidad Bolívar (BOH-leh-var) was born the son of wealthy Creole parents in 1783. Orphaned at the age of nine (his father had died when Simón was three), the young aristocrat, who was to inherit one of the largest fortunes in the West Indies, was cared for by his maternal uncle, who managed the extensive Bolívar urban properties, agricultural estates, cattle herds, and copper mines. Appropriate to his class, Bolívar had a number of private tutors, including an eccentric disciple of the French philosophe Jean-Jacques Rousseau, Simón Rodríguez. The tutor schooled the impressionable Bolívar in Enlightenment ideas that would later indelibly mark his political thinking.

When Bolívar was sixteen, he went to Spain, ostensibly to further his education, although his actions suggested that he was much more interested in ingratiating himself with the Spanish royal court. While at the court, he met, fell in love with, and married María Teresa Rodríguez, the daughter of a Caracas-born nobleman. During his three-year stay in Madrid, Bolívar came to see the Spanish monarchy as weak and corrupt; moreover, he felt slighted because of his Creole status. He returned home at the age of nineteen. His wife died six months after they returned to Caracas, and Bolívar, although he enjoyed female companionship, never remarried.

Bolívar returned to Europe. In Paris, he read the works of the Enlightenment feverishly and watched with disillusionment the increasingly dictatorial rule of Napoleon I. He also met one of the most prominent scientists of his day, Alexander von Humboldt, who had recently returned from an extended visit to the New World. Humboldt was convinced that independence was imminent for the Spanish colonies. While in Paris, the five-foot, six-inch, slender, dark-haired Bolívar also joined a freemasonry lodge. There he met radicals who espoused similar views. After Paris, Bolívar went to Italy, where he vowed to liberate his native land from Spanish rule. This second trip to Europe, which culminated in 1807, would play a pivotal role in shaping the transformation of this young aristocrat into a firebrand revolutionary.

LIFE'S WORK

After he returned from the Old World, Bolívar spent the better part of the next twenty years in various military campaigns until in 1825, after many defeats, hardships, and bouts of self-imposed exile, Bolívar and his patriot army drove the Spanish royal forces from the continent. During the early years of the conflict against Spain, he vied for leadership of the revolutionary movement with Francisco de Miranda, an expatriate Venezuelan who viewed with suspicion Bolívar's enormous ego and his insatiable lust for glory. After a bitter dispute between the two, Bolívar, believing that Miranda had absconded with the patriot treasury, turned Miranda over to Spanish authorities. Miranda was subsequently taken to Spain in chains and died in a Spanish prison several years later.

Simón Bolívar. (The Granger Collection, New York)

As a commander of the patriot forces, Bolívar demonstrated an uncanny ability to adapt his strategy to the particular circumstances. Faced with poorly trained and poorly equipped troops, Bolívar compensated by using the mountainous terrain of the Andes to his advantage, by delegating responsibility to exceptional field commanders, and by using his persuasive powers to attract new troops. Bolívar endured all the hardships and privations of the military campaigns alongside his soldiers. Moreover, the sheer force of his personality and his single-minded dedication to the goal of a liberated continent inspired his troops.

Despite his military prowess, Bolívar suffered a number of difficult defeats from 1810 to 1818. On two separate occasions during this early phase of the struggle, Royalist forces dealt the rebels serious setbacks and Bolívar was forced to flee South America. He used those occasions to raise funds, secure arms and soldiers, and make alliances with other states that might provide aid for the upcoming campaigns.

Bolívar also demonstrated the ability to unite conflicting ethnic groups and classes of Venezuelans and Colombians into an improvised army. He co-opted as many different sectors of South American society as possible during the seemingly interminable war years. A perfect illustration of this penchant for compromise was his visit to Haiti during one of his exiles. There Bolívar extracted much-needed aid from Haitian president Alexandre Pétion. The Haitian president, the leader of a nation where a successful rebellion had liberated the slaves, insisted that Bolívar abolish slavery when he returned to Venezuela. Bolívar, who had set his own slaves free in 1811, agreed to do so, knowing that the Creole elite's economic life was dependent on slave labor.

Another ethnic group that Bolívar courted were the *llaneros*. Led by their fierce regional chieftain (caudillo), José Antonio Páez, these mobile horsemen dominated the Orinoco River basin and initially supported the Royalist cause. Páez derived his power from control of local resources, especially nearby haciendas, which gave him access to men and provisions. Caudillos such as Páez formed patron-client relationships with their followers, who pledged their loyalty to their commander in return for a share of the spoils. As the abolition of slavery infuriated the Creole elite, the inclusion of Páez and other caudillos in the patriot army also upset members of the upper class, because their property often was ravaged by overzealous guerrilla bands. Bolívar's charisma enabled him to hold this fragile coalition together. After victory was achieved, however, that consensus would be lost, the fissures and fault lines of class and ethnicity would reassert themselves, and the edifice of unity would come tumbling down.

Because of Bolívar's ability to bring together people of diverse ethnic and class interests into a formidable army, the tide of the war changed. Bolívar's army was helped in its efforts to end colonial rule by South America's other liberator, José de San Martín, who began his campaign in the viceroyalty of Rio de la Plata (modern Argentina) and defeated Royalist forces in what is modern Chile and Peru. The two liberators met at an epochal meeting in Guayaquil, Ecuador, in 1822 to plan the final campaign against the Spanish forces in Peru. By 1825, five new nations were created from the Spanish colonial viceroyalties of Peru and New Granada: Venezuela, Colombia, Ecuador, Peru, and Bolivia.

The liberation of the continent was only one of Bolívar's many objectives. A human dynamo who thrived on constant activity, Bolívar also wanted to ensure that the fledgling republics of South America made a successful transition from colonies to nations. A man of words as well as action, Bolívar wrote prolifically amid his grueling military campaigns on almost every conceivable topic of his day. His main political writings—*La Carta de Jamaica* (1815; *The Jamaica Letter*, c. 1888), *Discurso pronunciado por el general Bolívar al congreso general de Venezuela en el aeto de su instalacion* (1819; *Speech of His Excellency, General Bolívar at the Installation of the Congress of Venezuela*, 1819), and his constitution for the new nation of Bolivia (1825)—demonstrate the evolution of his political thinking (and its growing conservatism) over time.

Although Bolívar fervently believed in democracy, he understood that Latin Americans lacked the political experience to adopt the model of democracy found in the United States. The colonial legacy of three centuries of autocratic rule would not be eclipsed overnight, and a transitional period was needed, during which the people had to be educated for democracy. His primary model, roughly sketched in *The Jamaica Letter*, was along the lines of the British constitutional monarchy.

Bolívar's first well-developed theory of government was presented to the Colombian Congress of Angostura in 1819. There, his eclectic mixture of individual rights and centralized government was described in detail. Many of the basic rights and freedoms articulated in the French Declaration of the Rights of Man and Citizen and the United States Bill of Rights were contained in his Angostura Address. Faithful to his promise to Pétion of Haiti, he asked that the congress of Great Colombia abolish slavery. To diminish the popular voice, he limited suffrage and asked for indirect elections. Moreover, the heart of Bolívar's political system was a hereditary senate, selected by a military aristocracy, the Order of Liberators. A strong executive would oversee the government, but his power was checked by his ministers, the senate, and a lower house that oversaw financial matters. Bolívar was elected the new nation's first president in 1821.

Bolívar preferred ideas to administration, opting to delegate responsibility for the day-to-day management of government to his vice president. Bolívar grew increasingly skeptical that a workable democracy could be implemented. His last political treatise, the constitution he wrote for the new nation of Bolivia (named for Bolívar) demonstrates this skepticism. This document included a three-house congress and a president elected for a life term with the power to choose a successor. This latest political creation was nothing more than a poorly disguised monarchy. The constitution pleased no one. When Bolívar tried to persuade Great Colombia—a nation that Bolívar himself had fashioned, comprising what are now Venezuela, Colombia, and Ecuador—to adopt the new constitution, his plea fell on deaf ears. To enact the goals of his administration, Bolívar then did in practice what his constitution permitted on paper: He ruled as a dictator.

Not only did Bolívar meet resistance in implementing his political agenda but he also was frustrated with his farsighted proposals for hemispheric cooperation and solidarity. Convinced that the newly formed Latin American states individually were powerless to withstand outside attack by a European power, he advocated a defensive alliance of Hispanic American states, which would provide military cooperation to defend the hemisphere from invasion. Bolívar invited all the Hispanic American countries, as well as the United States, Great Britain, and other European nations, to send delegates to a congress in Panama in 1826. It was hoped that the Panama Congress would create a league of Hispanic American states, provide for military cooperation, negotiate an alliance with Great Britain, and settle disputes among the nations. Bolívar even articulated the hope for the creation of an international peace-keeping organization. Unfortunately, few nations sent official delegates and Bolívar's visionary internationalist ideas remained dreams for more than a century.

Bolívar's last years were difficult. The new nations he had helped create were racked with internal dissension and violence. After a serious dispute with his vice president Francisco Santander in 1827, a weary Bolívar, suffering from tuberculosis, ruled as a dictator. A year later, an attempt on his life was narrowly averted. Finally, Bolívar was driven from office, when it was discovered that his cabinet had concocted a plan to search for a European monarch to rule after he stepped down. Although he knew nothing of the scheme, he suffered the political consequences. Bolívar resigned from office in 1830, almost penniless. He died on the coast near Santa Marta, Colombia, in December, 1830. He had asked to be buried in his home city of Caracas, but Bolívar had so many political enemies that his family feared for the safety of his remains. In 1842, his body was finally taken home.

SIGNIFICANCE

Not until the wounds of the independence period were healed by time were the accomplishments of Simón Bolívar put in their proper perspective. In retrospect, his successes and his visionary ideas more than compensated for his egocentrism and the defeats he suffered. As a committed revolutionary and a military general, he had few peers. By sheer force of his dynamic persona and his tireless efforts, he ended colonialism and ushered in a new era of nationhood for South America.

On the political front, his successes were tempered by the political realities of the times. Bolívar knew that the new nations were not ready for independence and a long period of political maturation was needed before democracy could be achieved. His dictatorial actions in his last few years betrayed his own republican ideals, but Bolívar, ever the pragmatist, was convinced that the end justified the means. What Bolívar could not foresee was how elusive democracy would be for South America.

Similarly, his ideas for hemispheric solidarity were not accepted. Not until the creation of the Organization of American States and the signing of the Rio Pact in 1947 would the first halting steps toward pan-Americanism be taken. Bolívar's fears of the growing power of the United States and its potentially damaging effects on Hispanic America proved prophetic. One hundred fifty years after his death, Bolívar is lionized throughout Latin America not only for what he accomplished but also for what he dreamed.

—Allen Wells

FURTHER READING

Bolívar, Simón. *Selected Writings*. Edited by Harold A. Bierck, Jr. Translated by Lewis Bertrand. Compiled by Vicente Lecuna. 2 vols. New York: Colonial Press, 1951. A brief, complimentary biographical essay by Bierck introduces this solid collection of Bolívar's most significant political writings.

Bushnell, David. *The Santander Regime in Gran Colombia*. Newark: University of Delaware Press, 1954. A thorough academic monograph on the Santander regime, examining Bolívar's increasingly despotic measures in his last years.

_____. *Símon Bolívar: Liberation and Disappointment*. Edited by Peter Stearns. New York: Longman, 2003. Biography aimed at history students and other readers who want a concise overview of Bolívar's life.

Hispanic American Historical Review 63 (February, 1983). To celebrate the bicentennial of Bolívar's birth, editor John J. Johnson dedicated an entire issue of the preeminent journal in the field to a reappraisal of Bolívar. Four essays by independence period specialists reexamine and reassess both the man and his place in history. Includes John Lynch's "Bolívar and the Caudillos," Simon Collier's "Nationality, Nationalism, and Supranationalism in the Writings of Simón Bolívar," David Bushnell's "The Last Dictatorship: Betrayal or Consummation?" and Germán Carrera Damas's "Simón Bolívar, El Culto Heroico y la Nación."

Johnson, John J. *Simón Bolívar and Spanish American Independence, 1783-1830*. New York: Van Nostrand Reinhold, 1968. An excellent analytical overview of Bolívar's life and times. This book includes an abbreviated sample of some of Bolívar's most important political writings.

Lynch, John. *The Spanish American Revolutions, 1808-1862*. New York: W. W. Norton, 1973. One of the best one-volume syntheses of the revolutionary era. Lynch's adroit analysis provides an overview of the internal and external factors that impinged on the struggle for independence. Includes a good examination of the personalities involved in the fighting.

Masur, Gerhard. *Simón Bolívar*. 2d ed. Albuquerque: University of New Mexico Press, 1969. One of the best English-language biographies of Bolívar. Masur's even-handed narrative is generally sympathetic and conveys an appreciation for the difficulties that Bolívar faced in reconciling the divergent factions that threatened to divide the movement for independence.

Slatta, Richard W., and Jane Lucas De Grummond. *Símon Bolívar's Quest for Glory*. College Station: Texas A&M University Press, 2003. The authors of this biography suggest Bolívar suffered from bipolar disorder, which may have affected his decisions and actions. In examining the battle for independence from Spain, the authors maintain the struggles that Bolívar and his colleagues faced after winning independence set a pattern for Latin American politics for the next century.

SEE ALSO: Bernardo O'Higgins; José de San Martín; Antonio José de Sucre; Flora Tristan.

RELATED ARTICLE in *Great Events from History: The Nineteenth Century, 1801-1900:* March, 1813-December 9, 1824: Bolívar's Military Campaigns.

EDWIN BOOTH

American actor

The most talented member of a family of actors, Edwin Booth suffered greatly from the association of his name with that of his younger brother, the assassin John Wilkes Booth, but nevertheless came to be admired for his art and his role in advancing the profession of acting in the United States.

BORN: November 13, 1833; near Bel Air, Maryland
DIED: June 7, 1893; New York, New York
ALSO KNOWN AS: Edwin Thomas Booth (full name)
AREA OF ACHIEVEMENT: Theater

EARLY LIFE

Edwin Thomas Booth's mother and father immigrated to the United States from London, England. His mother was the former Mary Ann Holmes, and he was the celebrated but temperamental actor Junius Brutus Booth. Ten children were born to the Booths, but only six of these survived early childhood. Edwin's older brother was Junius Brutus, Jr., and his older sister was Rosalie; his younger sister was Asia, and his younger brothers were John Wilkes and Joseph Adrian. Most of them, like Edwin, were short, slim, dark, and sensitive.

Edwin's formal education was cursory, but he was highly intelligent and a quick learner. Traveling with his alcoholic and unstable father as a boy, he determined to become an actor. He made his formal debut in Boston in a minor role in William Shakespeare's *Richard III* (pr. c. 1592-1593); two years later, in 1851, he played the lead for the first time in the same play in New York when his father refused to go on. In 1852, Edwin played the California gold camps. Junius Brutus Booth died later that year, and "Booth the Younger" was heralded in San Francisco as a worthy successor; still, it took several more years before Edwin equaled, and then exceeded, the reputation of his father.

In 1854, Booth joined a troupe headed for Australia, headlined by the distinguished actress Laura Keene; they performed in Sydney and Melbourne. Booth parted company with the troupe in Hawaii, following an argument, but while in Honolulu he was able to perform *Richard III* before King Kamehameha IV, using the king's throne for a prop. Then, in Sacramento, California, Booth proved that he could play romantic as well as tragic roles with remarkable skill when he played Raphael in a new melodrama by Charles Selby, *The Marble Heart: Or, The Sculptor's Dream* (1854). By the time he returned to his family at last in 1856, he had the wide experience of a versatile actor.

LIFE'S WORK

Between 1857 and 1859, Booth triumphed upon the stage in Boston and New York, and became so celebrated in these and other cities for his portrayal of Richard III that both his father's version and that of his namesake, Edwin Forrest, were almost forgotten. Booth's voice was resonant and beautiful, and his gestures and looks were expressive and penetrating. No Shakespearean character was beyond him, but his Richard, Iago, Mark Anthony, Macbeth, and Hamlet were especially well received.

Admired by many, the young Edwin Booth had few close friends, among them journalist Adam Badeau and actor David Anderson. They knew better than most of his independent nature and penchant for drinking, and were surprised when he married an actress on July 7, 1860. This was the charming young Mary Devlin, daughter of a bankrupt Troy Devlin, a New York merchant. The Reverend Mr. Samuel Osgood, an Episcopalian clergyman, officiated at the ceremony in his home in New York City. On December 9, 1861, Mary gave birth to their only child, Edwina, but the mother grew ill and died on February 21, 1863. In 1869, Booth married Mary McVicker, stepdaughter of the proprietor of McVicker's Theater in Chicago; the only child of his second marriage, Edgar, died shortly after birth, and his second Mary became insane before her death in 1881.

Making his home in New York during the 1860's, Edwin played opposite Charlotte Cushman in a Philadelphia run of *Macbeth* (pr. 1606) and starred in *The Merchant of Venice* (pr. c. 1596-1597) and several other plays in London. In England, however, he was not as satisfied with his performances and their reception as he was in New York. The outbreak of the Civil War in the spring of 1861 also persuaded him to stay close to home. Edwin, like most of the Booths, but certainly unlike John Wilkes, was supportive of the Union.

After becoming comanager of New York's Winter Garden Theatre, Edwin was able to produce his favorite Shakespearean plays and star in them as well. Obviously one of these favorites was singularly popular, as his production of *Hamlet, Prince of Denmark* (pr. c. 1600-1601) ran for one hundred consecutive performances. Then, too, his production of *Julius Caesar* (pr. c. 1599-1600) with Edwin as Brutus and his brothers Junius as Cassius and John Wilkes as Mark Anthony, was very well received. The assassination of President Abraham Lincoln, however, by the latter brother five months later, in April, 1865, disgraced the family and forced Edwin to suffer an almost nine-month retirement from the public view.

Having been performing in Boston, Edwin returned to New York for his self-confinement. There he received several death threats, and the *New York Herald* treated him savagely. At first he expected never to perform again, but debts mounted and the *New York Tribune* appealed to him in print that he not waste his considerable talent. At last, on January 3, 1866, a nervous Booth appeared at New York's Winter Garden as Hamlet. The theater was packed, and the audience rose as one to applaud him at the opening curtain.

On January 22, 1867, Booth received a much-delayed gold medal for his unparalleled achievement two years before in the first hundred-night run of *Hamlet*. His popularity was such now that theatergoers in almost every major city in North America asked to see him. A renewed *Hamlet* was followed by a production of Lord Lytton's *Richelieu: Or, The Conspiracy* (1839), then *The Merchant of Venice*, and then *Brutus: Or, The Fall of Tarquin* (pr., pb. 1818), by John Howard Payne. All were well received, but in *Brutus* fire was used to portray the burning of Rome, and it burned out of control one day in March to engulf the theater. With the destruction of the Winter Garden, Booth lost his finest costumes and was compelled to play benefit performances in Chicago and Baltimore.

Edwin Booth. (Library of Congress)

Upon the advice of friends such as William Bispham, Booth built his own, superior, theater at the corner of Twenty-third Street and Sixth Avenue. Richard A. Robertson, a Boston businessperson, was taken in as a partner. The Booth Theatre opened February 3, 1869, with a lackluster performance of *Romeo and Juliet* (pr. c. 1595-1596). The critics felt that Booth and Mary McVicker were unconvincing in their romantic, title roles, yet they were married soon thereafter.

The excellent building, new costumes, props, and actors made the Booth Theatre the outstanding showplace for Shakespearean drama in America. Charlotte Cushman and others were coaxed out of retirement when given the opportunity to perform there. The great Edwin Forrest, however, refused to play in Booth's theater.

Booth's productions followed the Shakespearean texts rather than later adaptations, and historians were consulted to gain authenticity for the sets. Still, Booth was a poor businessperson, and when he quarreled with Robertson the latter sold out to Booth, leaving the actor-manager heavily in debt. Booth's brother Junius tried to straighten out his affairs, but the Panic of 1873 destroyed their hopes. Early in 1874, Edwin Booth filed for bankruptcy, owing almost $200,000.

Repayment came, however, after Booth made a comeback in New York in October, 1875, when he played his unassailable Hamlet at Augustin Daly's Fifth Avenue Theater. A budding star in his own right also in the cast then was Maurice Barrymore, father of Ethel, Lionel, and John. In desperation, Booth now dared even to play Richard II and King Lear, although the former was new to him and the latter role had long been thought the special property of Edwin Forrest. These performances too won him much credit. He also played to packed houses in the South, although he had formerly refused to go there. In 1876, Booth performed with distinction at the California Theater in San Francisco.

Although his debts were paid off within two years of his bankruptcy and he was becoming more popular than ever, he still received threats on his life. On April 23, 1879, a madman named Mark Gray shot at him, twice, from the audience while Booth was acting the role of Richard II at McVicker's Theater in Chicago. Both shots went wild, and a composed Booth strode to the footlights so that he might point out the culprit to the police.

During the 1880's, Booth performed in Europe: in London (with Henry Irving) and elsewhere in the British Isles, in Berlin and other German cities, and in Vienna. Everywhere, but especially in Berlin, he was lauded for his Shakespearean roles, and invitations were extended from France, Spain, Italy, and Russia. Booth declined these offers; his dream was semiretirement in New England, and he returned to build a cottage called "Boothden" on the Rhode Island coast near Newport. He also acquired a larger house in Boston.

In 1888, Booth founded and served as first president of New York's club, The Players. When he performed in his later years, he liked to costar with accomplished younger actors such as Tommaso Salvini, Helena Modjeska, and Otis Skinner, and especially with another "old trouper," Lawrence Barrett. After Barrett's death in 1891, Booth, in ill health, gave fewer and less inspired performances. His last effort was as Hamlet on April 4, 1891, at the Brooklyn Academy of Music. He weakened, suffered a brain hemorrhage, and died in New York City on June 7, 1893, at the age of fifty-nine.

SIGNIFICANCE

Booth, in his prime, was probably the world's preeminent tragedian. His performance as Hamlet moved even Germans unfamiliar with English to tears. His apt movements and the quiet but perfect modulation of his voice, its timbre and clarity, seemed to late nineteenth century audiences much more natural and refined than the loud, forced theatrics of a previous generation. Like Forrest's, Booth's King Lear was considered exquisite, but almost all the other tragic characters in Shakespeare's plays were also his meat.

Unfortunately, Booth's private life echoed the tragedy he played out upon the stage. His actor-brother's assassination of Lincoln, his father's and his own bouts with alcoholism, the failure of the Booth Theatre, the early deaths of his two Marys, and his own rapid aging were truly components of a tragic life. At last he lost heart and almost seemed to will his own death.

While the solid structure of the Booth Theatre was torn down in his lifetime, the subtle delicacy of his acting technique remains in the better theatrical performances of today. In his lifetime, he was forever compared, usually unfavorably, to his father, but Edwin Booth is universally recognized today as the greater actor of the two, and by far superior to Junius, Jr., and John Wilkes. However, it is the continuing tragedy of the Booths that the best known of their number is the one who killed Abraham Lincoln.

—*Joseph E. Suppiger*

FURTHER READING

Goodale, Katherine. *Behind the Scenes with Edwin Booth.* Boston: Houghton Mifflin, 1931. This is a charming and lively account of Booth's professional life during the years when the author knew him (after 1870). Goodale, who performed under the stage name Kitty Molony, makes excellent observations relating to Booth's mastery of his craft and is one of several authors to suggest that, despite his personal tragedies, he led a "charmed life."

Grossman, Edwina Booth. *Edwin Booth: Recollections by His Daughter.* New York: Century, 1894. Booth's sole surviving child was especially close to him during the years of his greatest success. His letters to her and some of his letters to friends such as David Anderson and William Bispham give this eulogy added strength and research value.

Kimmel, Stanley. *The Mad Booths of Maryland.* Indianapolis: Bobbs-Merrill, 1940. One of the best and most readable books ever written about the Booth family. The book deals with all of the Booth family members, treating them with balance and fairness, and does much to explain the strained relationship between Edwin Booth and his brother, John Wilkes.

Lockridge, Richard. *Darling of Misfortune*. New York: Century, 1932. This is a sound enough biography, but it was superseded by Ruggles's work (see below). It is, perhaps, most valuable on the brief life span of the Booth Theatre.

Ruggles, Eleanor. *Prince of Players: Edwin Booth*. New York: W. W. Norton, 1953. At this writing still the definitive biography of Booth, reflecting the author's exhaustive research. While sympathetic toward her tragic subject, Ruggles does not hesitate to reveal the extent of his early struggle with alcoholism, which she believes to have been quieted only by the shock of his first wife's death.

Skinner, Otis. *The Last Tragedian*. New York: Dodd, Mead, 1939. Skinner, the father of the renowned actress Cornelia Otis Skinner, based this insider's account of Booth on their performances together, also making effective use of selected Booth letters.

Smith, Gene. *American Gothic: The Story of America's Legendary Theatrical Family, Junius, Edwin, and John Wilkes Booth*. New York: Simon & Schuster, 1992. Well-written and researched history of the Booth family, focusing on the personalities and careers of Junius and his two sons, Edwin and John Wilkes. Examines how the assassination of Lincoln affected the family.

Tebbell, John. *A Certain Club: One Hundred Years of the Players*. New York: Wieser & Wieser, 1988. History of the Players, including information about Booth's founding and involvement with the club.

Winter, William. *Life and Art of Edwin Booth*. New York: Macmillan, 1893. The celebrated drama critic of the *New York Tribune* was a longtime friend and confidant of Booth; he was also a prolific author, many of whose other works refer to the celebrated actor. This book contains much of value on the ups and downs of a remarkable career.

SEE ALSO: Edwin Forrest; Henry Irving; Edmund Kean; Adah Isaacs Menken; Abby Sage Richardson.

RELATED ARTICLES in *Great Events from History: The Nineteenth Century, 1801-1900:* April 9 and 14, 1865: Surrender at Appomattox and Assassination of Lincoln; 1878-1899: Irving Manages London's Lyceum Theatre.

WILLIAM BOOTH

English religious leader and social reformer

Compelled by his deep Christian faith to seek ways of serving his fellow man, Booth founded the international religious service organization called the Salvation Army, which became established in the United States fifteen years after the Civil War.

BORN: April 10, 1829; Nottingham, Nottinghamshire, England

DIED: August 20, 1912; London, England

AREAS OF ACHIEVEMENT: Religion and theology, social reform

EARLY LIFE

The son of a humble builder, William Booth was left fatherless at the age of thirteen. Determined to help support his family after his father's death, he served as an apprentice to a pawnbroker. At the age of fifteen, he underwent a dramatic Christian conversion, at which time he began his career as a preacher, eventually pursuing formal theological education through private tutors.

In 1849, Booth moved to London, where he worked on the side at a pawnbroker's shop, disliking the work but needing the income. It was during this time that he met the person who would become perhaps the single most important influence on his life and on his view of Christian service: Catherine Mumford, whom he would marry six years later and who would encourage him in his dream of becoming a full-time Christian minister.

By 1852, Booth had become entrenched in a respectable and established Methodist Church, dutifully pastoring the congregation but vaguely yearning for a ministry that would bring him into contact with those who needed the assurance of God's care the most, the "street people" of Victorian London: the alcoholics, the orphans and widows, those abandoned by society. Increasingly uncomfortable with the isolation inherent in the life of a located minister, Booth left this pastorate after nine years. The Booths launched careers as independent revivalists; unattached to any particular denomination, they were free to speak their consciences.

The key event in their lives occurred in July, 1865, when they established a mission outpost at Whitechapel in London, an outreach of the "East London Revival Society," which came to be known as the Christian Mission. In typical revivalist rhetoric, Booth preached salvation from eternal punishment through belief in Christ, but he also offered a different, more immediate salvation from drunkenness, hunger, lack of clothing, and lack of shelter. By 1878, this mission was called the Salvation Army and had become a controversial yet effective means of taking Christianity out of the churches and into the streets; the Booths and their coworkers embraced the words of Jesus to the effect that "the healthy have no need of a physician; therefore, we must go to those who are sick."

LIFE'S WORK

Booth's genius was to employ a central military metaphor in organizing and conceptualizing his missionary work. Many historians of religion would argue that Booth was the first to recognize the need for and value of "packaging" religion in symbols and contexts that would arrest the attention of the public and associate his faith in the minds of adherents with something memorable and concrete. In founding the Salvation Army, Booth took the role of general and created ranks, uniforms, flags, rules of order, and even a military band.

The years between 1878 and 1890 saw the Salvation Army grow astoundingly successful in attracting other Christian workers and in assisting delinquents and lifelong ne'er-do-wells in reforming their lives and becoming respectable citizens within Victorian society. Booth's increasingly rigid, authoritarian manner, however, alienated many within Salvation Army ranks during this period, and his growing public power alarmed many outside the Salvation Army. These fears and objections came to a climax in 1890, when Booth published what was to be the most celebrated and defamed manifesto of his stormy career. Booth's *In Darkest England and the Way Out* proclaimed an elaborate plan for reforming Victorian society so that the poor would no longer be exploited and victimized by the cruelty of industrialized England.

At this time, the Victorian intelligentsia were buoyantly trumpeting the "survival-of-the-fittest" mentality arising from Charles Darwin's work on evolution and equally busily exploring and reporting upon the exotic lifestyles in "Darkest Africa." Their morbid fascination with the sordid tales of slavery and primitive worldviews

DARKEST ENGLAND

In 1890, William Booth published In Darkest England and the Way Out*—a scathing indictment of the degradation of England's poorest classes. He took the title of his book from the recently published book by the explorer Henry Morton Stanley,* In Darkest Africa *(1890). Booth opened his book with a lengthy comparison between equatorial Africa and England to make his case for the need to improve the lives of his fellow citizens. These extracts from Booth's preface indicate the direction he intended to take his book.*

The progress of The Salvation Army in its work amongst the poor and lost of many lands has compelled me to face the problems which are more or less hopefully considered in the following pages. The grim necessities of a huge Campaign carried on for many years against the evils which lie at the root of all the miseries of modern life, attacked in a thousand and one forms by a thousand and one lieutenants, have led me step by step to contemplate as a possible solution of at least some of those problems the Scheme of social Selection and Salvation which I have here set forth.

When but a mere child the degradation and helpless misery of the poor Stockingers of my native town, wandering gaunt and hunger-stricken through the streets droning out their melancholy ditties, crowding the Union or toiling like galley slaves on relief works for a bare subsistence kindled in my heart yearnings to help the poor which have continued to this day and which have had a powerful influence on my whole life. At last I may be going to see my longings to help the workless realised. I think I am. . . .

Alas, what multitudes there are around us everywhere, many known to my readers personally, and any number who may be known to them by a very short walk from their own dwellings, who are in this very plight! Their vicious habits and destitute circumstances make it certain that without some kind of extraordinary help, they must hunger and sin, and sin and hunger, until, having multiplied their kind, and filled up the measure of their miseries, the gaunt fingers of death will close upon them and terminate their wretchedness. And all this will happen this very winter in the midst of the unparalleled wealth, and civilisation, and philanthropy of this professedly most Christian land.

Now, I propose to go straight for these sinking classes, and in doing so shall continue to aim at the heart. . . .

Source: William Booth, *In Darkest England and the Way Out* (London: International Headquarters of the Salvation Army, 1890).

angered Booth, whose book mocked their affluence and offered a ten-point plan for ridding society of poverty, including the creation of employment bureaus, farm colonies, state-provided legal assistance, and a missing-persons' agency. Progressive as it may seem to a twentieth century readership, the book outraged Victorian society and was denounced by churchgoers and social critics as a form of reckless socialism; biologist Thomas Henry Huxley, champion of Darwinism and opponent of religion, felt compelled to launch an unprecedented public attack on Booth and his social agenda.

Essentially, Booth's public image was never rehabilitated after the book's publication, and he lived out the remainder of his years in fervent but quiet service to the Salvation Army, assisting its formation and growth around the world until his final days in August, 1912. Only after his death did the prescience of his work and vision begin to receive the acclaim and respect it warranted.

SIGNIFICANCE

In his time, William Booth was feared by some, loathed by others, but respected by all for his fierce determination to help the less fortunate, to prove that religion had application in this world as well as in the world to come. He succeeded admirably where others had failed in focusing the attention of the upper and middle classes on the plight of the indigent and destitute in an industrialized, capitalist culture.

Directly in England and indirectly in the United States, Booth appealed to the conscience of a wide range of church members, moving them to recognize their duty to reach the souls of men and women by first feeding and clothing them. While not the first to articulate the social dimensions of the Christian gospel, Booth as much as anyone during the early twentieth century was responsible for linking belief with action, faith with social responsibility.

The Salvation Army he started in the British Isles probably has its strongest presence in North America and is one of the most respected and responsible religious service organizations in operation. Indeed, in the minds of many, Booth's Salvation Army is more associated with relief efforts and noble self-sacrifice than it is with any specifically religious orientation or dogma. The Salvation Army's survival and health—more than a century removed from its origins and in a time more than skeptical about service institutions—is a greater tribute to General Booth's tenacity, faith, and love of humankind than any physical monument could be.

—Bruce L. Edwards

FURTHER READING

Begbie, Harold. *The Life of General William Booth.* 2 vols. New York: Macmillan, 1920. The standard, nearly exhaustive biography of Booth, written unabashedly as a tribute to a man whom the author regards as a hero. While this quaintness wears thin very early, the two volumes contain the basic facts about the Booth family and their formation of the Salvation Army. Contains especially valuable excerpts from journals and letters that Booth wrote to his wife, Catherine, and others that illuminate the motivations of this driven man.

Bishop, Edward. *Blood and Fire! The Story of General William Booth and the Salvation Army.* London: Longmans, Green, 1964. A succinct narrative of the life and times of the Booth family and the Salvation Army. Helpful as it is as a brief overview of the main outlines of Booth's life and his program for reforming Victorian England, overall it is quite derivative of the earlier biographies of Booth and the Salvation Army.

Chesham, Sallie. *Born to Battle: The Salvation Army in America.* Chicago: Rand McNally, 1965. Though written primarily as a history of the Salvation Army in the United States, the early chapters of this volume provide a useful summary of Booth's life and the impact of the Salvation Army in the United States in the twenty years before the turn of the century.

Collier, Richard. *General Next to God: The Story of William Booth and the Salvation Army.* New York: E. P. Dutton, 1965. A biography that updates and presents more concisely the information available in Begbie's sprawling two-volume work. Much less hagiographical than Begbie's biography, but still disarming in its undisguised admiration for Booth and his work. The reader will not find a critical assessment of Booth's life or social agenda here.

Hattersley, Roy. *Blood & Fire: William and Catherine Booth and Their Salvation Army.* New York: Doubleday, 2000. Hattersley, a member of the British Labour Party, describes the political and social context in which the Salvation Army operated in Victorian England. He portrays the personalities and peccadillos of the Booths with more honesty than some previous biographers.

Huxley, Thomas H. *Evolution and Ethics.* New York: AMS Press, 1970. Huxley, the Victorian social critic and popularizer of evolution, wrote a series of scathing attacks on Booth that are collected in this volume under the chapter "Social Diseases and Worse Remedies." Huxley's remarks provide an interesting secularist counterpoint within Victorian England to Booth's ambitious social reform programs.

McKinley, E. H. *Somebody's Brother: A History of the Salvation Army Men's Social Services Department, 1891-1985.* Lewiston, N.Y.: Edwin Mellen Press, 1986. This volume examines in great detail the social activism of Booth that motivated him to link evangelism uniquely with feeding, clothing, and housing the poor and destitute.

Spence, Clark. *The Salvation Army Farm Colonies.* Tucson: University of Arizona Press, 1985. An interesting examination of the controversy surrounding Booth's initial call for state donation of farmland to be used for raising food for the poor. Spence chronicles Victorian opposition to what appeared to many as "mere autocratic socialism."

Walker, Pamela J. *Pulling the Devil's Kingdom Down: The Salvation Army in Victorian Britain.* Berkeley: University of California Press, 2001. Walker focuses on the religious origins of the Salvation Army, describing how it was primarily an evangelical religious group, not a charity. She also describes how the Salvation Army adapted secular working-class culture to accomplish its mission and enter into nineteenth century city life.

Winston, Diane. *Red-hot and Righteous: The Urban Religion of the Salvation Army.* Cambridge, Mass.: Harvard University Press, 1999. A history of the Salvation Army in America, from its origins in New York City in 1880 through its work during World War II. Winston examines the mission, methods, and growth of the Salvation Army and its influence on American life.

SEE ALSO: Charles Darwin.

RELATED ARTICLES in *Great Events from History: The Nineteenth Century, 1801-1900:* July, 1865: Booth Establishes the Salvation Army; 1870-1871: Watch Tower Bible and Tract Society Is Founded.

LIZZIE BORDEN

American woman accused of murdering her parents

The legend holding that Lizzie Borden was an axe murderer has endured despite the fact that Borden was acquitted of the August 4, 1892, murder of her father, Andrew Jackson Borden, and stepmother, Abby Durfee Gray Borden.

BORN: July 19, 1860; Fall River, Massachusetts
DIED: June 1, 1927; Fall River, Massachusetts
ALSO KNOWN AS: Lizzie Andrew Borden (full name); Lizbeth Andrews Borden; Lizbeth of Maplecroft
AREA OF ACHIEVEMENT: Crime

EARLY LIFE

Born on July 19, 1860, Lizzie Andrew Borden and her older sister, Emma Lenora, were raised by their stepmother, Abby, and their father, Andrew. Lizzie's mother, Sarah Morse, died when Lizzie was an infant; two years later, Andrew married Abby Durfee Gray, who cared for the Borden girls for thirty years. By 1892, Lizzie was thirty-two and Emma was forty-two years of age. Unmarried, both sisters continued to live in the Borden house on 92 Second Street, one of the busiest streets in Fall River, Massachusetts.

The Borden name was influential in Fall River. The eighth generation of Bordens in the town, Andrew owned numerous properties, served as bank president, sat on the board of directors of three other banks, and was the director of several businesses. He was worth a half-million dollars (a multimillionaire by contemporary standards) and was a man of high social standing, known for his considerable wealth as well as for his penurious nature.

Lizzie was an active member of her church, a Sunday school teacher, a participant in a variety of women's groups, a leader of the town's Christian Endeavor Society, and a member of the Woman's Christian Temperance Union (WCTU). At only twenty years of age, Lizzie was named to the board of the Fall River Hospital. She devoted herself to community work and was recognized for her efforts.

LIFE'S WORK

On Thursday, August 4, 1892, there were five people in the Borden's small house on Second Street: Andrew, Abby, Lizzie, Bridget Sullivan (the family servant), and John Vinnicum Morse (Lizzie and Emma's maternal uncle). Morse had unexpectedly arrived the prior evening; he brought no valise but intended to spend several nights. Emma had been staying in Fairhaven, Massachusetts, visiting friends.

Members of the Borden household had been ill, supposedly from eating spoiled meat. Abby seldom left the house but had visited family physician Seabury Bowen on Wednesday, August 3, with a story about an anonymous note; she believed someone was poisoning the family. Lizzie also told friend Alice Russell that she thought that the family's milk was being poisoned. During the inquest that followed the murders of Abby and Andrew, the prosecution brought forth Eli Bence, a druggist who claimed that Lizzie unsuccessfully attempted to purchase prussic acid in his pharmacy the day before the murders. Lizzie denied Bence's claims, stating that she remained home all day Wednesday, leaving only briefly that evening to visit Russell, who would later testify that on Wednesday night a distraught Lizzie predicted that an ominous event would soon transpire in the Borden house.

By 9:30 or 10:00 Thursday morning, Abby lay face down on the floor of the upstairs guest bedroom, mortally wounded by nineteen axe or hatchet wounds delivered to the back of the scalp. By all accounts, Lizzie was the only individual in the house between 9:30 and 10:45. Lizzie testified that she saw no one and heard nothing. Sullivan indicated that she was outside the home, washing windows at Abby's request. Morse told authorities that he left the house that morning around 8:45 to visit another niece in town and returned approximately forty-five minutes after the murders were discovered.

Lizzie alleged that early that morning Abby claimed to receive a note asking her to visit a sick friend; however, no note was ever discovered, nor did anyone come forward with information about the note despite a $5,000 reward posted by the Borden sisters.

Andrew reportedly returned home around 10:45 that morning. He greeted his daughter and reclined on a sofa in the sitting room. Shortly before 11:00 A.M., Sullivan retired to her third-floor room to rest. Lizzie testified that, supposing her stepmother had left the house, she wandered to the barn and searched the second story of the building for lead for a sinker for Monday's possible fishing excursion. She also ate some pears in the barn, remaining there for a span of fifteen or twenty minutes. Upon her return to the house, she discovered her father's prone body in the sitting room. He had been struck by eleven axe or hatchet wounds and was so disfigured by the blows that he was virtually unrecognizable to Bowen, the family physician. The time was approximately 11:00 or 11:15 A.M. Lizzie cried for Bridget, asking her to find Bowen. Attracted by the commotion, neighbor Adelaide B. Churchill ran to the house at Lizzie's request and stayed with her until the doctor arrived. Shortly after Bowen's arrival, Abby's bludgeoned body was discovered upstairs.

THE LIZZIE BORDEN RHYME

One of the primary reasons that Lizzie Borden's name has lived on in infamy is the enduring popularity of a catchy children's playground rhyme that celebrated her alleged crime. The origins of the rhyme are uncertain, but when it is repeated, it always takes a form similar to this:

Lizzie Borden took an axe
And gave her mother forty whacks;
When she saw what she had done
She gave her father forty-one!

Four legal hearings ensued: the inquest (the only proceeding in which Borden testified), the grand jury hearing, a preliminary hearing, and the murder trial itself. Denied counsel, Lizzie testified without representation at the inquest and, at the conclusion of this testimony, was arrested and held without bail in Taunton Jail for ten months awaiting trial. George D. Robinson and Andrew J. Jennings, friends of the Bordens, represented her. Robinson, former governor of Massachusetts, was hired for a fee of $25,000.

The trial began on June 7, 1893. Charged with first-degree murder, Lizzie, if found guilty, faced death by hanging. William H. Moody and Hosea M. Knowlton prosecuted for the state. (Moody would later be appointed by President Theodore Roosevelt to serve on the U.S. Supreme Court in 1906.) Three justices of the Massachusetts Supreme Court presided at the trial, one of whom faced criticism for his charge to the jurors in what many suggest was a prodefense bias. The jury comprised white, middle- to upper-class men. (Working-class men, many of them foreign-born immigrants who worked in Fall River factories, were excluded from serving on the jury despite the fact that they were naturalized citizens. Women were also excluded.) Lizzie did not testify in her defense, and her inquest testimony was excluded from the trial's proceedings.

The prosecution claimed that Lizzie's motive had been both avarice and hatred, arguing that she had committed parricide not only out of loathing for her stepmother but also to prevent Andrew from changing his will to Abby's favor. The prosecution pointed to one event as representative of the tension between Lizzie and

Abby. Five years prior to the murder, Andrew bought half of a two-dwelling home in Abby's name for her sister. Lizzie's own testimony at the inquest indicated that both daughters took umbrage at their father's generosity, particularly as it was directed toward his wife's family rather than his daughters. Lizzie testified that she ceased calling Abby "mother" about that time but noted that their relationship was cordial.

The defense referred to Lizzie's stellar reputation in Fall River society to refute the prosecution's claims. The defense also noted that the Borden home had been burglarized twelve months before the murders and that the barn had been broken into twice, thus introducing the possibility of an anonymous assailant. The defense continued to stress that Lizzie was not capable of such a fiendish deed.

The prosecution argued that Lizzie, alone in the house with the victims, had ample opportunity to commit parricide. The defense refuted the prosecution's claims, pointing to the lack of blood on the accused. Churchill testified that when she arrived at the Borden house, no blood spotted Borden's dress nor was her hair disheveled. However, contradicting testimonies surfaced regarding Lizzie's attire during the time of the murder as well as which articles of clothing were turned over to the police. Russell complicated matters by testifying for the prosecution that three days after the murders, Lizzie burned a skirt in Emma and Russell's presence, complaining of irremovable paint stains. Lizzie denied that the burned skirt was the one worn during the murders.

The defense refuted the claim that Lizzie had the opportunity to commit the murders by questioning the actions of the police who interviewed her after the crimes. The defense also questioned the lack of a murder weapon, which was never found but was believed to be a handleless hatchet smeared with dust or ash that was found in the Borden basement. However, a microscopic examination of the blade revealed no traces of blood. The handle was never recovered.

After only one hour of deliberation, the jury declared Lizzie "not guilty." Newspaper reports claimed that jurors needed only ten or fifteen minutes to decide but waited another forty-five minutes to inform the court out of respect to the prosecution. Accounts also reported that prosecutor Knowlton, a reluctant litigator, clapped at the verdict.

Because Andrew died intestate, Lizzie and Emma inherited nearly a half-million dollars in cash and real estate. With this considerable wealth, the Borden sisters bought a large new house in a fashionable section of Fall River. Lizzie called the house Maplecroft and renamed herself Lizbeth. She traveled widely, associated with popular actor Nance O'Neal, and continued to live in Fall River until her death on June 1, 1927. The murders of Andrew and Abby Borden remain unsolved.

SIGNIFICANCE

Lizzie Borden has become a part of American legend. For over a century, verses, songs, stories, dramas, and a ballet have been devoted to her. There is an enduring interest in Lizzie and the Fall River murders because she was such an unlikely murderer. The story of a dutiful daughter and Sunday school teacher brutally murdering her wealthy parents with an axe commanded much attention in the press during her legal proceedings.

Lizzie has retained legendary status perhaps in part because of widespread media coverage. The murder of Fall River's socially prominent Bordens was startling, and the arrest of their daughter was even more shocking. The advent of yellow journalism encouraged media attention. Over forty newspapers exploited the case; all of them devoted their attention to the gruesome details of the brutal double murder, and all of them questioned jurisprudence in the United States. Many, including the *Boston Herald*, *The New York Times*, and the *New York Herald*, portrayed Lizzie as a defenseless woman victimized by an inept police department. Only the Fall River *Globe*, condemning the Bordens as elite oppressors, consistently depicted Lizzie as guilty.

After her acquittal, Lizzie's image as a helpless woman maltreated by Fall River police was countered to such a degree that the name of Lizzie Borden eventually became synonymous with a female axe murderer. Children, blissfully unaware of Lizzie's acquittal, continue to sing the famous rhyme about her taking an axe to her parents.

—Michele L. Mock

FURTHER READING

Brown, Arnold R. *Lizzie Borden: The Legend, The Truth, The Final Chapter*. Nashville, Tenn.: Rutledge Hill Press, 1991. Brown argues that the Bordens were murdered by Andrew's illegitimate son. The appendix contains Lizzie's testimony at the inquest.

Hoffman, Paul Dennis. *Yesterday in Old Fall River: A Lizzie Borden Companion*. Durham, N.C.: Carolina Academic Press, 2000. In this book aimed at afficionados of the Lizzie Borden saga, Hoffman aims to alleviate confusion about the many people involved in her case. He has compiled an alphabetical listing of more than 650 people, with information about their lives and connections to the murders.

Kent, David. *Forty Whacks: New Evidence in the Life and Legend of Lizzie Borden*. Emmaus, Pa.: Yankee Books, 1992. Kent demystifies myths surrounding Borden and attempts to provide a balanced treatment of the Borden case.

_____, ed. *Lizzie Borden Sourcebook*. Boston: Branden, 1992. This book contains clippings from forty-three newspapers and shows the images of Lizzie generated by the media.

Lincoln, Victoria. *A Private Disgrace: Lizzie Borden by Daylight*. New York: International Polygonics, 1986. The author suggests that Lizzie committed the murders during an epileptic seizure initiated by her menstrual period.

Pearson, Edmund. *Trial of Lizzie Borden*. New York: Doubleday, 1937. Pearson argues that Borden was guilty of the murders.

Porter, Edwin H. *The Fall River Tragedy: A History of the Borden Murders*. Portland, Maine: King Philip, 1985. This book, initially published in 1893, was the first book about the Lizzie Borden case. Porter was a reporter for the *Globe* and was present at the trial.

Radin, Edward D. *Lizzie Borden: The Untold Story*. New York: Simon & Schuster, 1961. Radin theorizes that Bridget Sullivan committed the murders.

Schuetz, Janice. *The Logic of Women on Trial: Case Studies of Popular American Trials*. Carbondale: Southern Illinois University Press, 1994. This book contains a chapter on the Borden trial and argues that class and gender informed Borden's acquittal despite compelling evidence against her.

Spiering, Frank. *Lizzie*. New York: Dorset Press, 1984. Spiering claims that Emma committed the murders in order to avoid being disinherited and that Lizzie stood trial for her sister.

SEE ALSO: Jesse and Frank James; Abby Sage Richardson.

ALEKSANDR BORODIN

Russian composer

A remarkable creative artist, a respected scientist, and a person of exceptional sensibility and refinement, Borodin made a significant contribution to the repertory of Russian national music, with particular excellence in the domains of opera, symphonic music, chamber music, and song.

BORN: November 12, 1833; St. Petersburg, Russia
DIED: February 27, 1887; St. Petersburg, Russia
ALSO KNOWN AS: Aleksandr Porfiryevich Borodin (full name)
AREA OF ACHIEVEMENT: Music

EARLY LIFE

Aleksandr Porfiryevich Borodin (BORH-ah-deen) was born out of wedlock to Prince Luka Stepanovitch Gedianov and Avdotya Konstantinova Antinova. Following Aleksandr's birth, his father had him registered as the legal son of Porfiry Borodin, one of his servants, in accordance with a custom of the time and arranged for his mistress to marry Christian Ivanovitch Kleinecke, a retired army medical practitioner. Aleksandr was educated by private tutors, with emphasis placed on foreign languages (German, French, and English). Prior to his death, Luka granted freedom to his son. Avdotya, after her husband's death, bore another son, Dmitry, through another liaison, and bought a house near the Semyonov Parade Ground, which is where Aleksandr spent his youth and adolescence.

Borodin composed a Polka in D Minor that he entitled "Hélène." Piano study, attendance at symphonic concerts at the university during the winter and at Joseph Gungl's concerts at Pavlovsk in the summer, and self-instruction on the cello moved the youth toward serious creativity; indeed, in 1847, he composed a Trio in G Major on a theme from Giacomo Meyerbeer's *Robert le diable*, and a concert for flute and piano. There followed, in quick succession, two piano compositions, a fantasy on a theme by Johann Nepomuk Hummel, and a study, *Le Courant*. While developing his emerging musical talent, Borodin evinced an equally strong interest in chemistry.

In the fall of 1850, Borodin was an external student at the Academy of Physicians. By 1855, he completed his course of study with distinction. Borodin moved up the ladder of academic success with alacrity. He gained experience as a surgeon but came to realize that he was ill-suited for this calling. On May 5, 1858, he was awarded the doctor of medicine degree. After travels to western Europe connected with his scientific career, he corresponded in the fall of 1859 with Modest Mussorgsky, from whom he acquired an appreciation for the music of Robert Schumann. Later that year, his teacher Nikolai Zinin arranged for Borodin to work in Heidelberg so as to gain the kind of experience that would enable him to assume a professorial position in chemistry upon his return.

LIFE'S WORK

The Heidelberg period, which extended to 1862, proved to be a turning point in Borodin's life. It was here that he developed a friendship with the Russian chemist Dmitry Mendeleyev and attended lectures by such luminaries as Hermann Helmholtz and Gustav Robert Kirchhoff, the latter a pioneer with Robert Wilhelm Bunsen in the field of spectrum analysis. Travel to Freiburg (where he heard the famed organ there), Italy, and the Netherlands turned the once-sheltered Borodin into a cosmopolite.

In May, 1861, Borodin met his future wife, the twenty-nine-year-old Ekaterina Sergeyevna Protopopova. He traveled with her to Mannheim to hear such Wagnerian epics as *Tannhäuser* (1845) and *Lohengrin* (1848), and settled with her in Pisa. In terms of composition, he produced in this period a Sonata in C Minor for cello and piano (a three-movement work based on the fugue theme from Johann Sebastian Bach's Sonata in G Minor for violin), a Scherzo in E Major for piano duet, several incomplete chamber works, and, most significantly, a Sextet in D Minor for strings.

This last composition was written, according to its creator, to please the Germans. Its two movements reflect Mendelssohnian traits, as, for example, in the lively sonata-allegro first movement with its "feminine" second subject and in the theme and variation second movement based on the song "How Did I Grieve Thee?" employed previously by Borodin. Particularly interesting is the pizzicato variation, a technique that came to be identified with the Russian as it had been with Felix Mendelssohn.

The four-movement Quintet in F Minor for strings establishes Borodin as a master of the early Romantic style associated with the German school, notably in the use of classical forms, lyrical and evocative melodic lines, excellence in part-writing, and elfinlike scherzo movements. In addition, there is present a nostalgic yearning for the homeland, an awareness of the contributions of Mikhail Glinka in particular, and a Russian imprint on the Germanic fabric.

Borodin returned to St. Petersburg in September, 1862, and by December he was actively engaged in the world of academia. Apart from lecturing and translating scientific books, he gravitated again toward musical creativity, especially after meeting Mily Alekseyevich Balakirev, mentor of the so-called Russian Five. After hearing the incipient works by this quintet of nationalists, the groundwork was laid for a shift from mainstream German Romanticism to Russian nationalism. Despite a fitful approach to large-scale composition, necessitated by his vocation, Borodin, under Balakirev's guidance, produced his First Symphony in 1867; it was premiered under Balakirev's direction on March 7, 1868, before the Russian Musical Society's directorate and, on January 16, 1869, it received its first public hearing.

Aleksandr Borodin. (Library of Congress)

Encouraged by Balakirev, Borodin acquired the confidence to pursue his creative avocation on a surer footing. Although the opera-farce *Bogatiri* was a dismal failure at its premiere on November 18, 1867, the songs, which include "Pesnya tyomnovo lesa" (song of the dark forest) and "Falshivaya nota" (the false note) were more successful.

Borodin's personal life was solidified with his marriage to Ekaterina on April 17, 1863, in St. Petersburg. That fall, the couple moved to an apartment in a building owned by the Academy of Military Medicine, and, except for occasional travel, it was Borodin's abode until his death. Throughout his life, Borodin was found attractive by adoring young women; however, with the adoption of seven-year-old Liza Bolaneva, his marriage was established on solid footing.

In April, 1869, the critic Vladimir Stasov suggested that Borodin begin the opera that would be named *Prince Igor*, which was based on a twelfth century epic. By March, 1870, however, when his original interest in the project waned, he adopted some of the music he had already committed to paper for use in his Symphony No. 2 in B Minor. During the early 1870's, professional responsibilities created continuing impediments to uninterrupted musical achievement.

In addition to lecturing on chemistry and supervising student work, Borodin became a leading advocate for medical courses for women. During 1874-1875, the "Polovtsian Dances" and other segments of *Prince Igor* were completed, and between 1874 and 1879 he finished the String Quartet in A Major. On March 10, 1877, Eduard Napravnik conducted the completed Second Symphony with limited success. After some revision, the work was accorded a more favorable response when it was conducted on March 4, 1879, by Nikolay Rimsky-Korsakov. The four-movement work is notable for its coloristic treatment of the orchestra, particularly for the passages for winds and harp, for its rhythmic drive and meter changes, and for its juxtaposition of long-breathed, folkloric melody and exciting, Tartarlike abandon.

Having achieved the succor that comes after so arduous an experience as seeing his Second Symphony through to a public performance, Borodin visited various German universities with a view toward gaining a better understanding of their laboratories. On one such trip, he called on Franz Liszt at Weimar (July, 1877) and met with the Hungarian master on five different occasions over a three-week period. A few more numbers were added to *Prince Igor*, but a streak of procrastination prevented the opera from moving forward to completion; it was left to Rimsky-Korsakov and Aleksandr Glazunov to orchestrate much of it after Borodin's death.

Ironically, Borodin squandered much of the little time he had dallying with musical jokes, such as a polka contrived to be performed with "Chopsticks" as the accompaniment. While other composers contributed their talents to compositions on this motif, among them Rimsky-Korsakov and Anatoly Lyadov, and saw the entire set published in 1880 under the title *Paraphrases*, Balakirev rebuked the perpetrators of this farce for wasting time and effort on such trifles. Meanwhile, through Liszt's influence, Borodin's music obtained a hearing in western Europe. The Symphony No. 1 was performed in Baden-Baden, Germany, on May 20, 1880, the year in which Borodin wrote his symphonic poem, *In the Steppes of Central Asia* (dedicated to Liszt).

A setting of Alexander Pushkin's poem "Dlya beregov otchizni dalnoy" (for the shores of thy far native land) was prompted by the death from alcoholism of Mussorgsky on March 28, 1881. The String Quartet No. 2 in D Major, dedicated to Borodin's wife, suggests an evocation of the idyllic period in Heidelberg. It is best known today for its third movement, the *Nocturne*, in which the cello is given a soaring melodic line of incomparable beauty. Although Ekaterina's health was always precarious, it was Borodin who suffered an attack of cholera in June, 1885, leading, eventually, to the heart disease that took his life.

The European taste for Borodin's music spread to France and Belgium, and, in appreciation of her efforts on his behalf, Borodin dedicated to the Belgian Countess of Mercy-Argenteau his six-movement *Petite Suite* for piano (1885). With César Cui, he enjoyed huge successes in Liège and Brussels. In 1886, despite the illnesses of his wife and mother-in-law, Borodin collaborated with Rimsky-Korsakov, Lyadov, and Glazunov on a string quartet in honor of the publisher M. P. Balaiev. Two movements of his Third Symphony were completed, the second of which is a scherzo whose material is drawn from *Prince Igor*. Although interest in the opera was revived in 1887, only an overture and several additional numbers were actually completed. On the evening of February 27, 1887, at a lavish ball for the families and friends of the faculty of the Medical Academy, Borodin, attired in red shirt and high boots, and in apparent good spirits, succumbed suddenly to heart failure and died instantly. His beloved Ekaterina survived him by five months.

SIGNIFICANCE

Of Aleksandr Borodin, Sir William Hadow said: "No musician has ever claimed immortality with so slender an offering. Yet, if there be, indeed, immortalities in music, his claim is incontestable." It is assuredly a phenomenal achievement when an individual rises to a position of eminence in fields as diverse as music and science, the one so intuitive and subjective but requiring the utmost discipline, the other so measured and objective. Borodin was somehow able to bring his analytical mind to bear on his creative impulses.

Borodin was a remarkable creative artist, a respected scientist, and a human being of the utmost sensibility and refinement. That he found the time and the inclination to cofound the School of Medicine for Women in St. Petersburg and to teach chemistry there from 1872 until his death bespeaks a man well ahead of his time. Borodin's compassion for humankind, his life of industry, and his zeal in the pursuit of excellence serve as reminders to a skeptical world that a job worth doing is a job worth doing well. When his music was adapted for use in the box-office triumph *Kismet*, which opened at New York's Ziegfeld Theatre on December 3, 1953, American audiences were introduced to Borodin's art in popularized format, and they were touched. Since that time, these treasures, in the original versions and touchups, have earned an honored place in the concert halls of the world. Borodin's is a music that contains a civility that transcends national boundaries.

—David Z. Kushner

FURTHER READING

Abraham, Gerald. *Borodin: The Composer and His Music*. London: William Reeves, 1927. A very thorough traversal of Borodin's life and works. Contains musical analyses.

_____. *On Russian Music*. Freeport, N.Y.: Books for Libraries Press, 1970. Two of the book's chapters deal expressly with Borodin and his music. One is devoted to "The History of Prince Igor," while the other deals with "Borodin's Songs."

Abraham, Gerald, and David Lloyd-Jones. "Alexander Borodin." In *The New Grove Russian Masters*, edited by David Brown, et al. Vol. 1. London: Macmillan, 1986. An outstanding encyclopedia entry covering the salient biographical data and providing a clear-cut overview of Borodin's music according to genre. Contains a catalog of works and a fine bibliography.

Asafiev, B. V. *Russian Music from the Beginning of the Nineteenth Century*. Translated by Alfred J. Swan. Ann Arbor, Mich.: J. W. Edwards for the American Council of Learned Societies, 1953. This influential work treats Borodin's music in the context of broad categories of subject matter. The approach allows the reader to see the composer's contributions via-à-vis those of his principal contemporaries and in the light of the aesthetic trends then prevalent in Russia.

Calvocoressi, Michel D., and Gerald Abraham. *Masters of Russian Music*. New York: Alfred A. Knopf, 1936. Presents a fine traversal of the major events in the composer's life and touches on the high points of representative compositions.

Dianin, Sergei. *Borodin*. Translated by Robert Lord. New York: Oxford University Press, 1963. This is a major life and works study of Borodin, with very important coverage of his ancestry, his childhood, and his adolescence. The music is discussed according to genre. Includes a chronological catalog of works and a genealogical table. A first-rate piece of scholarship.

Habets, Alfred. *Borodin and Liszt*. Translated by Rosa Newmarch. London: Digby, Long, 1895. Reprint. New York: AMS Press, 1977. Part 1 covers Borodin's life and works, touching on significant biographical details. A chapter entitled "The Scientist" presents insight into this major aspect of the artist's dual allegiances.

Lloyd-Jones, David. "Borodin in Heidelberg." *Musical Quarterly* 46 (1960): 500. A thorough account of Borodin's stay in Heidelberg. Emphasizes his development as a composer, offers succinct comments and insights into specific compositions, and places the musical contributions in the context of his personal life and his scientific career.

Maes, Francis. *A History of Russian Music: From Kamarinskaya to Babi Yar*. Translated by Arnold J. Pomerans and Erica Pomerans. Berkeley: University of California Press, 2002. A discussion of Borodin's music is included in this overview of Russian music in the nineteenth and twentieth centuries. Maes rejects the traditional belief that nineteenth century Russian nationalism and interest in folklore was synonymous with political and social progressivism.

SEE ALSO: Modest Mussorgsky; Nikolay Rimsky-Korsakov; Robert Schumann; Peter Ilich Tchaikovsky; Richard Wagner.

RELATED ARTICLE in *Great Events from History: The Nineteenth Century, 1801-1900:* August 13-17, 1876: First Performance of Wagner's Ring Cycle.

MARY ELIZABETH BRADDON
English novelist

Although Braddon outraged reviewers and moralists with her sensational plots and her unconventional lifestyle, she wrote some of the best-selling novels of the Victorian period, most notably Lady Audley's Secret. *She attempted serious fiction with less success and advised other novelists, including Henry James.*

BORN: October 4, 1835; London, England
DIED: February 4, 1915; Richmond, Surrey, England
ALSO KNOWN AS: Mary Elizabeth Maxwell; Mary Seyton; Aunt Belinda (pseudonym); Caroline Lascelles (pseudonym); Babbington White (pseudonym)
AREA OF ACHIEVEMENT: Literature

EARLY LIFE

Mary Elizabeth Braddon was the younger of the two daughters of Henry Braddon, a ne'er-do-well English solicitor originally from Cornwall, and his wife Fanny, née White, who was Irish by birth. Her gravestone and memorial tablet both give 1837 as her date of birth, but the 1835 date of her parish register entry is incontestable. When she was about five years old, her parents separated, something extremely unusual at the time, after her mother discovered her father's infidelity. Mary Elizabeth then lived with her mother and went through several moves, including a brief spell at St. Leonards on Sea in East Sussex and time at various London addresses. She and her mother also experienced considerable financial hardship.

When Mary Elizabeth reached her late teens, she became an actor and took the stage name of Mary Seyton, though she seems to have been more dependent on her looks than her talent. Many of her later novels use theatrical allusions or metaphors, but women actors were not considered respectable, and her time on the stage was one of many things for which reviewers of her novels later criticized her. At the same time, she was also writing poetry and plays. Through her poems, she came to the attention of John Gilby, an eccentric Yorkshire squire who established her in Beverley, near Hull, and paid her to write a verse epic on on the Italian nationalist leader Giuseppe Garibaldi; he apparently intended to propose marriage to her after he had helped preserve her delicacy by ensuring her financial independence. However, Mary Elizabeth actually used the time to complete a novel, *Three Times Dead*. It was printed by a Hull publisher in 1860, and her literary career was launched.

LIFE'S WORK

The successful publication of her first novel took Braddon back to London, where she soon met the Irish-born publisher John Maxwell. They fell in love, but Maxwell already had a wife. Like the mother of Braddon's most famous heroine, Lady Audley, Maxwell's wife had been stricken with insanity (presumably puerperal psychosis) after the birth of her sixth child and was permanently incarcerated in a mental asylum in Dublin, Ireland. Nevertheless Braddon and Maxwell became lovers and their first child, Gerald Maxwelll—who later became a novelist himself—was born in March, 1862. He was followed by five more children, of whom four survived infancy. Braddon eventually married Maxwell and seems to have been an affectionate and valued stepmother to his five surviving children by his first wife. She also continued to write at a furious pace.

After 1862, Braddon regularly produced serials for Maxwell's two magazines and also for others, which then went on to be separately published as novels, as well as short stories, essays, and plays. In 1866, she became editor of the magazine *Belgravia*, which was published by Maxwell. Her most notable work during this period was the three-volume novel *Lady Audley's Secret* (1862), which she first published in serial form in one of her husband's magazines. This powerful and gripping book cleverly and teasingly inverts both the story of Charlotte Brontë's novel *Jane Eyre* (1847) and the ideal of the "angel in the house."

Lady Audley's Secret tells a tale of bigamy, but bigamy committed not by a Byronic hero but by a blond, seemingly innocent governess, who also twice attempts murder and—like Bertha in *Jane Eyre*—succeeds in committing arson. The novel scandalized reviewers, who objected both to the sensuality and selfishness of its heroine and her ability to act alone, something considered entirely beyond the capacity of a woman. Reviewers were also shocked that the book appealed to women of all classes and thus seemed to work toward the obliteration of class distinctions. According to the magazine *The Living Age*, it was "one of the most noxious books of the modern times."

While Braddon was buoyed by the success of *Lady Audley's Secret*, she was also distressed by the vitriolic

BRADDON'S NOVELS

1860	*Three Times Dead: Or, The Secret of the Heath* (revised as *The Trail of the Serpent*, 1861)
1861-1862	*The Black Band: Or, The Mysteries of Midnight* (also as *What Is This Mystery?*)
1862	*The Captain of the Vulture* (also as *Darrell Markham: Or, The Captain of the Vulture*)
1862	*Lady Audley's Secret*
1862	*The Lady Lisle*
1863-1864	*The Outcast: Or, The Brand of Society* (also as *Henry Dunbar: The Story of an Outcast*)
1863	*Aurora Floyd*
1863	*Eleanor's Victory*
1863	*John Marchmont's Legacy*
1864	*The Doctor's Wife*
1864	*The Lawyer's Secret*
1865	*Only a Clod*
1865	*Sir Jasper's Tenant*
1866-1867	*Diavola: Or, The Woman's Battle* (also as *Run to Earth and Nobody's Daughter: Or, The Ballad-Singer of Wapping*)
1866	*The Lady's Mile*
1867	*Birds of Prey*
1867	*Circe: Or, Three Acts in the Life of an Artist*
1867	*Rupert Godwin*
1868	*Charlotte's Inheritance*
1868	*Dead Sea Fruit*
1868	*The White Phantom*
1869	*The Factory Girl: Or, All Is Not Gold That Glitters*
1869	*The Octoroon: Or, The Lily of Louisiana*
1869	*Oscar Bertrand: Or, The Idiot of the Mountain*
187?	*The Blue Hand: Or, The Story of a Woman's Vengeance*
187?	*Leighton Grange: Or, Who Killed Edith Woodville* (also as *The Mystery of Leighton Grange*)
1871	*Fenton's Quest*
1871	*The Lovels of Arden*
1872	*Robert Ainsleigh* (also as *Bound to John Company: Or, The Adventures and Misadventures of Robert Ainsleigh*)
1872	*To the Bitter End*
1873	*Lucius Davoren: Or, Publicans and Sinners* (also as *Publicans and Sinners*)
1873	*Strangers and Pilgrims*
1874	*Taken at the Flood*
1874	*Lost for Love*
1875	*Hostages to Fortune*
1875	*A Strange World*
1876	*Dead Men's Shoes*
1876	*Joshua Haggard's Daughter*
1876	*Only a Woman*
1878	*An Open Verdict*
1879	*The Cloven Foot*
1879	*George Caulfield's Journey*
1879	*Vixen*
1880	*Just As I Am*

(continued)

BRADDON'S NOVELS (continued)	
1880	*The Story of Barbara, Her Splendid Misery and Her Gilded Cage* (also as *Her Splendid Misery*)
1881	*Asphodel*
1881	*His Secret*
1881	*Le Pasteur de Marston*
1881	*Wages of Sin*
1882	*Flower and Weed*
1882	*Mount Royal*
1883	*The Golden Calf*
1883	*Married in Haste*
1883	*Phantom Fortune*
1883	*Under the Red Flag*
1884	*Ishmael* (also as *The Ishmaelite*)
1885	*The Fatal Marriage: Or, The Shadow in the Corner*
1885	*Wyllard's Weird*
1886	*The Little Woman in Black*
1886	*Mohawks*
1886	*One Thing Needful, and Cut By the County* (also as *Penalty of Fate: Or, The One Thing Needful*)
1887	*Like and Unlike*
1888	*The Fatal Three*
1889	*The Day Will Come*
1889	*Rough Justice*
1889	*Whose Was the Hand?*
1890	*One Life, One Love*
1891	*Gerard: Or, The World, the Flesh, and the Devil* (also as *The World, the Flesh, and the Devil*)
1892	*The Venetians*
1893	*All Along the River*
1894	*Thou Art the Man*
1895	*Sons of Fire*
1896	*London Pride: Or, When the World Was Younger* (also as *When the World Was Younger*)
1897	*Under Love's Rule*
1898	*In High Places*
1899	*His Darling Sin*
1900	*The Infidel*
1903	*The Conflict*
1904	*A Lost Eden*
1905	*The Rose of Life*
1906	*The White House*
1907	*Dead Love Has Chains*
1907	*Her Convict*
1908	*During Her Majesty's Pleasure*
1909	*Our Adversary*
1910	*Beyond These Voices*
1911	*The Green Curtain*
1913	*Miranda*
1916	*Mary*

nature of many of the reviews of it and of her other works, several of which darkly referred to her own status of "living in sin" with a man already married. In 1867, the much more respectable novelist Margaret Oliphant discussed *Lady Audley's Secret* in *Blackwood's Magazine* and scathingly charged that it

> brought in the reign of bigamy as an interesting and fashionable crime, which no doubt shows a certain deference to the British relish for law and order. It goes against the seventh commandment, no doubt, but it does it in a legitimate sort of way, and is an invention which could only have been possible to an Englishwoman knowing the attraction of impropriety, and yet loving the shelter of law.

Braddon's response to such criticism was to seek respectability wherever she could find it. In 1874, Maxwell's first wife died, and Maxwell was finally able to marry Braddon. Even before her marriage helped make her more respectable, Braddon took care in her writing to ensure that none of her new novels would offend reviewers by not creating heroines who acted independently. Even in "sensation novels" that were otherwise similar in style to *Lady Audley's Secret*—such as *Eleanor's Victory* (1863) and *The Fatal Three* (1888)—she used heroines who rely on male friends or relatives to act for them. The heroine in *The Doctor's Wife* (1864) is too innocent even to understand when the man she loves is suggesting adultery to her.

The Doctor's Wife is also an example of a style of novel that Braddon sought increasingly to develop: clearly a response to Gustave Flaubert's *Madame Bovary* (1857), and apparently an influence on George Eliot's *Middlemarch* (1871-1872), it is obviously an attempt at serious writing. Indeed, one of its characters, Sigismund Smith, is a parodic version of a sensation novelist. Braddon's aim was to produce one such serious novel each year to sit alongside her more commercially successful and more easily written sensation novels; however, it is the latter that offer the most interesting examples of her work.

Braddon never stopped writing, and *Mary*, the last of her ninety-plus novels, was published in 1916, the year after her death. She did, however, gain undoubted respectability. Her many literary visitors at Richmond during the last decades of her life included the novelists Henry James and Bram Stoker. A handsome brass tablet to her memory in the parish church in Richmond, Surrey speaks fulsomely, if not entirely convincingly, of her "rare and refined scholarship." Indeed throughout her life she was always careful to advertise in her novels her knowledge of the fashionable world and of exotic locations such as Paris.

SIGNIFICANCE

Mary Elizabeth Braddon challenged contemporary ideologies of both the nature of women and the purpose and value of prose fiction. In a post-Darwinian world, she represented seemingly respectable society as a jungle in which women must struggle to survive, and the ostensibly happy Victorian household as a bitter battlefield. She tackled previously taboo subjects such as postnatal depression and women's sexuality, as well as more topical issues such as Great Britain's Deceased Wife's Sister's Act and the Victorian crisis of faith, the subjects of her novel *The Fatal Three*.

Braddon's focus on the domestic helped sensation fiction break entirely away from the Gothic to become securely established as a genre in its own right. She also exerted a considerable influence on a number of younger novelists, including two of her own sons, Gerald Maxwell and W. B. Maxwell, Robert Louis Stevenson, Henry James, and George Eliot.

—Lisa Hopkins

FURTHER READING

Carnell, Jennifer. *The Literary Lives of Mary Elizabeth Braddon: A Study of her Life and Work*. Hastings, England: The Sensation Press, 2000. Uses new evidence to update previous accounts of Braddon's biography and explore the full range of her literary activity.

Hopkins, Lisa. "Monsters Under Domestication: Mary Elizabeth Braddon." In *Giants of the Past: Popular Fictions and the Idea of Evolution*. Cranbury, N.J.: Associated University Presses, 2004. This chapter in Hopkins's book examines Braddon's novels as part of a wider investigation into the impact of Darwinian theory on literature.

Tromp, Marlene, Pamela K. Gilbert, and Aeron Haynie, eds. *Beyond Sensation: Mary Elizabeth Braddon in Context*. New York: State University of New York Press, 2000. Collection of recent essays that range widely across Braddon's work.

Wolff, Robert Lee. *Sensational Victorian: The Life and Fiction of Mary Elizabeth Braddon*. New York: Garland, 1979. Now obtainable only from libraries or secondhand, this book still deserves attention as the first serious study of Braddon.

SEE ALSO: The Brontë Sisters; Maria Edgeworth; George Eliot; Gustave Flaubert; Giuseppe Garibaldi; Henry James; Mary Wollstonecraft Shelley; Robert Louis Stevenson.

RELATED ARTICLES in *Great Events from History: The Nineteenth Century, 1801-1900:* March, 1852-September, 1853: Dickens Publishes *Bleak House*; July, 1881-1883: Stevenson Publishes *Treasure Island.*

F. H. BRADLEY
English philosopher

Bradley stands out in the distinguished history of British philosophy as a thinker who represented a point of view that was fundamentally Idealist. He was a vigorous, gifted, brooding critic of England's empirical philosophers.

BORN: January 30, 1846; Clapham, Surrey, England
DIED: September 18, 1924; Oxford, England
ALSO KNOWN AS: Francis Herbert Bradley (full name)
AREA OF ACHIEVEMENT: Philosophy

EARLY LIFE

Francis Herbert Bradley was the fourth child of the Reverend Charles Bradley, an Evangelical minister, and Emma Linton Bradley. Little is known about his early life. He was educated at Cheltenham (1856-1861) and Marlborough (1861-1863), and in 1865 he attended University College, Oxford. In 1870, at the age of twenty-four, he became a Fellow at Merton College, Oxford, where he remained until his death in 1924. A year after arriving at Oxford, he contracted a kidney disease that disabled him and left him sick and suffering, sardonic and sometimes bitter. Fortunately, his fellowship allowed him to pursue scholarships without the added burden of teaching or lecturing, tasks that his disability would never permit. His illness made him something of a recluse, and, in some measure, this accounts for his biting, often cruel prose.

LIFE'S WORK

Bradley's frail constitution frequently forced him to take shelter from Oxford's severe winters on the southern coast of England or on the French Riviera. On one sojourn to Saint-Raphael in the winter of 1911, he became friends with Elinor Glyn, who was later to depict him as "the sage of Cheiron," in her book *Halcyone* (1912).

In appearance Bradley was erect, with a thin face, fine eyes, and a long nose. Fastidious in his habits, he was affable, courteous, and a good conversationalist, although it was said that he did not suffer fools gladly. He is said to have had a small shooting gallery constructed above his living quarters where he practiced routinely. By his own claim he was a good marksman, known to employ his skill on cats.

Bradley had strong political opinions. He was a conservative, perhaps even reactionary, with a lifelong dislike for the English Liberal Party and a specific disgust for its famous leader Prime Minister William Ewart Gladstone. In particular, he was angry at Gladstone for, as he said, betraying General Charles Gordon at Khartoum in the Egyptian Sudan in 1885. For Bradley, Gladstone represented what Bradley characterized as a degrading social sentimentality, an inviolate pacifism, and a false humanitarian notion of the natural equality of persons.

Almost nothing is known about Bradley's private life, except that he dedicated all of his books to "E. R.," an American woman named Mrs. Radcliffe who lived in France. Bradley met her while on holiday in Egypt, and although she had absolutely no literary or philosophical interests, he laid out for her, voluminously, his complete metaphysical system in a series of letters, which she later destroyed.

Although his philosophical system had its roots in German soil (specifically in the ideas of G. W. F. Hegel, Johann Friedrich Herbart, and Arthur Schopenhauer), he had little time or sympathy for the greatest of all German philosophers, Immanuel Kant.

Bradley died of blood poisoning on September 18, 1924, the same year that he was recipient of England's highest literary award, the Order of Merit. Little can be marked of the external events in Bradley's life—primarily because as a philosopher the events of moment were internal and mental—yet there can be no understanding of Bradley the man apart from Bradley the philosopher.

Richard Wollheim has called Bradley a man of caustic epigrams and poetic metaphors. Nevertheless, he was also Great Britain's finest philosopher of metaphysics in the nineteenth century. He wrote numerous articles and reviews but only four book-length pieces are of major importance: *Ethical Studies* (1876), *The Principles of Logic* (1883), *Appearance and Reality* (1893), and *Essays on Truth and Reality* (1914). His *Aphorisms* appeared posthumously in 1930, and his *Collected Essays* was published in 1935. Throughout these volumes there is an obsessive criticism of empiricism, or what he refers to as that English philosophy's devotion to "sense experience."

Empiricism is, Bradley argues, a shallow, surface view of the world with two rather "contemptible" qualities: first, a naïve devotion to the idea that raw sense data is philosophically significant, and second, a pedestrian attachment to the doctrine of Utilitarianism. Utilitarianism, he insists, is the inevitable philosophical result of the ill-conceived dogmas of empiricism. When Bradley was at the height of his powers, his two most illustrious adversaries were the Englishman Bertrand Russell and the American William James. Both men were empiricists and Utilitarians.

Here, too, one runs into difficulty, for an analysis of Bradley's thought is difficult because so much of what he writes is enigmatic and obscure. A primary question for Bradley was that of how one obtains knowledge. Bradley rejected as contradictory the notion that knowledge can be obtained from the senses, as was claimed by the empiricist philosophers John Locke and David Hume. For Bradley, knowledge should begin and end with an analysis of meaning. The proper role of philosophical investigation is understanding the use and meaning of the language. This powerful redirection of philosophy from an analysis of sensate ideas in the mind to an analysis of the structure and meaning of language has become the dominant theme in Anglo-American philosophy and owes much to Bradley's initial critical assessment of empiricism.

For Bradley, proper philosophical study is the examination of rationality; that is, it is understanding the "internal connection" that mental ideas have to one another, the internal relations of species, kind, and class (in more contemporary terminology, the investigation into conceptual elements of signs, symbols, and semantics). In other words, the primary interest of philosophy should be in the laws of intelligibility, rather than in particular physical facts or specific sensations as the empiricists had believed. Universal understanding transcends empirical sensations; it requires absolute knowledge. Such knowledge should embrace the logical possibilities of past, present, and future, the real and the imagined. Further, all conceptual worlds are internal and theoretically complete.

Thus, rather than identifying information about an object, such as a lemon, by collecting sense data, Bradley would begin with the proposition that the lemon exists—in particular, that it possesses qualities. More important, the object, for Bradley, is more than the sum of these qualities. John Locke had recognized that there is more to things than the sum of their parts, and he called this nonsensed element underlying the sensory ideas "substance." However, for Locke, substance is unknowable precisely because it is not sensed, a conclusion that leaves those who sense in a state of skepticism about the reality of substance—a position that was acceptable to almost no one except Locke's philosophical heir, David Hume.

Bradley argues that the confusion fostered by this notion of substance ends in a rational contradiction. Ostensibly, when one says that a lemon is yellow, one never means that "lemon" and "yellow" mean the same thing, that they are equivalent terms, as (2 + 3) and (4 + 1) are equivalent sets. Yellow is a quality of lemon, but lemon is more than the color yellow. The empiricists would add that the lemon is also ellipsoid in shape. However, this, for Bradley, leads to confusion, for to say that being an ellipsoid is identical with being a lemon is contradictory, because it means that a lemon is identical with that which is yellow, which it is not, and with that which is ellipsoid, which it is not; finally, it means that that which is yellow is identical with that which is ellipsoid, which it is not. Thus, the empiricist must argue that a lemon is the sum of all its sensed qualities, not merely one of them in contradiction to some others. Hence, the "substance" of a lemon, for the empiricist, must be the collection of all of these discrete qualities taken together: yellow, elliptical, sour, and so forth. A collective relationship of these qualities constitutes the lemon's substance.

It is at this point that Bradley declares empiricism worthless. Suppose, for example, that a lemon is defined as a yellow object that is elliptical and sour. Then yellow is the subject of the proposition declaring it so, and elliptical and sour are predicates of this proposition. However, it is as possible to define a lemon with sour as the subject and yellow and elliptical as its predicates. These combinations are, in other words, interchangeable. What this demonstrates, Bradley argues, is that these qualities are interchangeable as subjects and predicates, and hence, it is the relationship in which people think and talk about these qualities that properly establishes the meaning of "lemon." Thus, a lemon is something more than the sum of its sensed qualities; it is a cognitive entity. However, one should not assume that there is a kind of Lockean substance underlying the sensed qualities, because this only sustains the contradictions that the limits of sense perceptions produce.

For Bradley, there is an Archimedean point on which any definition of reality is to be balanced: That point is freedom from contradiction. In order to escape contradiction, all qualities must be internally related to all other elements of experience in a single conceptual system. This "transcendent" view of reality, however, requires Bradley to employ the language of the European Idealists, most particularly the discourse of the post-Hegelians. Therefore, reality, the "substance behind" appearances, is not material, it is mental.

In Bradley's words, it is a conceptual "unity of all multiplicity." Human knowledge is filled with contradictions; nevertheless, it is also a part of a wider and higher relation: It is part of "absolute experience." Thus, appearances (sense data) are manifestations in lesser degree of something conceptually truer, morally higher, and aesthetically more beautiful. Collectively for society, idealized experience is nearer to the heart of things. Higher idealized experience draws society closer to ideals of perfection, closer to its historical myths about God. Reality, thus, is idealized experience, not sensible experience. Bradley thus changed the focus in philosophy from observation of phenomena to an examination of pure reality, which is mental.

SIGNIFICANCE

Oxford philosopher Gilbert Ryle has observed that when F. H. Bradley began his career the burning issues in philosophy were between theologians and antitheologians. They were issues of faith and doubt. When he died in 1924, philosophical energies had turned to ratiocinative technique and rigor. Transcendental dicta had lost their influence, and the technicalities of logical theory, linguistic meaning, and the investigation of scientific methodology had changed the tone and temperament of philosophers.

Theologians had withdrawn from the battle with scientists, claiming that their endeavors were conducted in different domains: Religion spoke to the needs, aspirations, and hopes of supplicants, while science was searching for explanations of the world's operations. Theology thus maintained a certain immunity from the restrictive, austere propositions of science, enabling theological language to become more subjective and introspective. It became the language of feeling and aspirations, a verbal instrument of communal persuasion and solidarity. Within these limits, only the most literal believers would fear the quantitative onslaught of science.

Bradley, however, had no sympathy with this verbal compromise. He believed it to be a futile, crippling solution. Scientific knowledge is not in another domain; it is, rather, an attempt to understand reality—theology and metaphysics should do no less, according to Bradley. Transcendental philosophy had been abandoned because it was unable to withstand the inexorable successes of science.

For more than two centuries, English philosophy had attempted to imitate the method of science with a philosophy of "mental science," a science of sense experience. This method failed. In fact, it produced only circumlocutions and contradictions. Bradley led philosophy into the realm of logical and semantical discourse, where its primary task was a search for meaning and understanding. Thought and judgment became the primary function of conceptual inquiry. Bradley's philosophical method begins and ends with the premise that truth is the systematic application of self-consistent coherent propositions that are derivatively appropriate, in a rationally unifying fashion, to all aspects of human experience. He envisioned a rationally coherent metaphysics that would replace an antiquated theology and supplant the spiritually bereft notions of science.

—*Donald Burrill*

FURTHER READING

Bradley, F. H. *Appearance and Reality*. Rev. ed. Oxford, England: Clarendon Press, 1897. This is Bradley's account of metaphysics, his most famous and enduring work. He explains why the world is monistic and not pluralistic, and why logic is necessary for a theory of metaphysics. His principal theme is that a sensory view of things, persons, and qualities is a surface of appearances, while the proper view of reality is embodied in coherent conceptual propositions generated by logical thought.

_____. *Essays on Truth and Reality*. Oxford, England: Oxford University Press, 1914. Bradley demonstrates that the theory of truth goes together with the theory of reality; answering questions about truth entails answering questions about the nature of things. Explanations of reality must be free from conceptual contradictions, which means that truth is neither derivable nor doubtable; it is self-confirming.

_____. *Ethical Studies*. Oxford, England: Oxford University Press, 1962. Bradley produced four major books. This was the first, published originally in 1876; a revised version, published in 1927, contains additional, important material. This volume includes the essay "My Station and Its Duties," perhaps the single most widely read piece he wrote.

_____. *The Principles of Logic*. Rev. ed. Oxford, England: Oxford University Press, 1922. Bradley's text on the meaning of logical arguments. For him, logic includes both judgments and inferences. Much of this volume is devoted to refuting John Stuart Mill's claim that logic is a derivative of sense experience.

Bradley, James, ed. *Philosophy After F. H. Bradley: A Collection of Essays*. Bristol, England: Thoemmes Press, 1996. The essays trace Bradley's influence upon twentieth century philosophy, analyzing his relationship to Alfred North Whitehead, John Dewey, and other thinkers, and explaining how his concept of Absolute Idealism affected modern logic, pragmatics, and idealistic philosophy.

Manser, A., and Guy Stock, eds. *The Philosophy of F. H. Bradley*. Oxford, England: Clarendon Press, 1984. An attempt to show the relation of Bradley's thought to contemporary philosophy. The editors aim to demonstrate the greatness of Bradley, even though he has not been the center of philosophical discussion for more than half a century. They have succeeded; this is a collection of first-rate papers, by first-rate philosophical writers.

Muirhead, John. *The Platonic Tradition in Anglo-Saxon Philosophy*. London: Allen & Unwin, 1931. This is a good, although brief, account of Bradley's philosophical development. Detailed analysis of Bradley's thought is difficult to find or understand. Some of the blame is Bradley's, but much of the reason for his obscurity stems from the fact that he was a speculative philosopher writing in an analytic tradition. Muirhead's work is somewhat informal but still accurate and worthwhile.

Stock, Guy, ed. *Appearance Versus Reality: New Essays on Bradley's Metaphysics*. New York: Oxford University Press, 1998. A collection of papers delivered at a conference to mark the centenary of *Appearance and Reality*. Among the topics examined are Bradley's theory of truth and doctrine of absolutism, and Bertram Russell's criticisms of Bradley's philosophy.

Wollheim, Richard. *F. H. Bradley*. London: Penguin Books, 1959. This excellent book is the most accessible today. Wollheim discusses Bradley's theory of logic and rejection of empiricism, contradiction in the notion of "facts," the relation of thought to truth, and his view of morality and God. He makes it clear why Bradley nearly dominated British philosophy in the latter part of the nineteenth century and why he has little influence today.

SEE ALSO: William Ewart Gladstone; Georg Wilhelm Friedrich Hegel; John Stuart Mill.

RELATED ARTICLE in *Great Events from History: The Nineteenth Century, 1801-1900:* 1836: Transcendental Movement Arises in New England.

MATHEW B. BRADY

American photographer

The most famous American photographer of the nineteenth century, Brady brought to the public eye a panorama of personalities and scenes through the photographic medium and was especially instrumental in creating a poignant pictorial record of the Civil War.

BORN: c. 1823; Warren County, near Lake George, New York
DIED: January 15, 1896; New York, New York
AREA OF ACHIEVEMENT: Photography

EARLY LIFE

Little is known about Mathew B. Brady's birth beyond the fact that he said he was born around 1823 in Warren County, New York. Little is known about his parents, though his father was probably an Irish immigrant. The death certificate for Brady, which was completed in 1896, lists his father's name as Andrew and his mother's name as Julia. Brady's wife had preceded him in death, and he was therefore listed as a widower, with no name given for his spouse. This contributes to a problem surrounding Brady, because his wife, Juliet Elizabeth Handy, was apparently called "Julia," too. The literature about Brady does not deal with this matter of his parents' names, perhaps because there are so many unknowns about the man.

Even the odd spelling of Brady's first name, with a single "t," has no explanation, and as for the middle initial, Brady said it meant nothing. What is known of him comes from the sparest materials. There are no letters, notebooks, diaries, or other written matter. Despite his large enterprise, there are no wills, real estate transactions with his personal signature, or anything that is written by him. He was probably illiterate, though it has been suggested that he could read if not write. However, this is improbable, as there is no evidence to support the claim; indeed, some historians even doubt that the signatures on his photographs are by his hand.

There is no record or account of Brady's education. Considering that all of his life seemed to be spent promoting himself in society and cultivating the prominent and the wealthy, he may have chosen to be mysterious about his humble background. His basic education was practical, beginning when he spent time in Saratoga, New York, where he met a painter named William Page. Saratoga, located just south of Lake George, has a long history as a popular resort and vacation area for prominent Americans. Because of its natural hot springs and attractive setting, as well as its location close to Albany and New York City, it was already an important health spa when Brady arrived.

Page became Brady's first mentor, encouraging the young man from the lake country to sketch and draw. The lifestyles of the wealthy on their summer vacations and perhaps the work ethic of the artist Page, who, like most artists, placed himself in close proximity to potential clients, must have affected Brady. He moved with Page to New York City, where he did odd jobs and came in contact with Samuel F. B. Morse, a professor at the University of New York, which later became New York University. Morse, who later became famous for the invention of the telegraph, was experimenting with the daguerreotype reproduction process. He and a colleague, John William Draper, taught some young men the process; Brady was among them. Brady also learned the rudiments of photography from Morse and Draper.

As early as 1843, Brady was listed in the New York *Doggett's* directory as a manufacturer of jewelry cases specializing in making miniature boxes with embossed tops. He also made cases for surgical instruments and storage and presentation boxes for daguerreotypes. It was shortly thereafter that Brady combined case-making with the production of daguerreotypes, setting up a gallery in a building just off Fulton Street and Broadway, directly across from P. T. Barnum's popular American Museum and a block from the famed Astor House. This location was in the center of potential commercial traffic and in close proximity to the people of power who frequented the Astor House. Brady was quite successful, charging between three and five dollars for a sitting, with posing hours from ten o'clock to three o'clock. During those early years, he maintained his association with Page, Draper, Morse, and other men who were experimenting with new technology.

Brady had adopted the costume and style of his artistic and academic associates. A quick, nervous man of five feet, seven inches in height, he allowed his hair to grow long and frame his face. He later grew a mustache and goatee and took a fancy to bright scarves and a flat-topped, broad-brimmed hat. Sometimes he wore a cape and a cavalier-type hat graced with a feather. By 1855, his eyes were failing him, and he wore increasingly thick-lensed wire-framed glasses. In the prime of life, he was virtually blind.

The United States of the 1840's rewarded technology and industry more than anything else, and Brady quickly prospered, expanded his operations, gave up his case-making business, and increasingly concentrated on a grand project: to photograph and publish pictures of every distinguished American. The newly formed American Institute of Photography held contests, and Brady won medals each year from 1844 to 1850. "Brady of

Mathew B. Brady. (Library of Congress)

Broadway" was what he was called, and in 1849 he received the first gold medal awarded for a picture taken using the daguerreotype process. He worked with reproductions on porcelain and ivory, with tinting and various exposures and light diffusion. Competition in the business was intense, all shops offering something unique to gain customers' attention.

Brady pursued the great and the wealthy to complete his grand plan. It was not unusual for him to pick up the work of others and simply attach his name to it. He began to take on and quickly train a number of "operators" to take the pictures, as he could no longer focus the camera himself. He also branched out, establishing an office in Washington, D.C. There the Anthonys, Edward and Henry, had already set up a gallery and were attracting public officials and foreign dignitaries as subjects. They also set up a prosperous photography supply business on Broadway, which became the foundation for the Ansco company. Many of their pictures were sent to be put on display in their Broadway studio. It is believed that Brady, when frustrated in attempts to attract subjects for his great project, simply purchased the photographs he wanted from men such as the Anthonys.

LIFE'S WORK

Brady's ambitious project was designed to meet the growing competition from studios that stood side by side along Broadway. Camera operators rushed to open their own shops once they learned the rudiments of the craft. Physically unable to operate the equipment alone, Brady sought the grand idea that would sustain him. His master volume, *Gallery of Illustrious Americans* (1850), was a critical success but a financial failure at thirty dollars a copy. Undaunted, Brady hoped to bring out another volume and purchased the lithographic stones at one hundred dollars each. The project had caused him to neglect the paying part of his business. Brady also contributed to his own losses by mimicking the lifestyle of the rich in his choice of colognes, brandy, clothes, hats and scarves, and restaurants. Many of his prestigious clients he photographed free, ignoring the ordinary public that had sustained him. At twenty-eight, he was already well known, but still not financially secure.

During this period, Brady married Juliet Elizabeth Handy, a woman from Maryland whom he seems to have met when he was in Washington soliciting sittings. Though there is considerable speculation about her family's status and wealth as well as her ostensible beauty, there is no support for the former, and Brady's pictures of his wife do not flatter her. The date of the wedding is not known, but it had to be prior to his planning for a trip to London in 1851. Brady's new idea was to enter a collection of forty-eight pictures in the London exposition that was being sponsored by Prince Albert. He won a prize for his entry, traveled through parts of Europe, again attaching himself to influential people, and supposedly took their pictures and purchased others for sale in his New York studio.

Returning home, Brady immediately embarked on the revitalization of his business. He won a prize in the New York World's Fair competition in 1853, but he was never accepted into the community of craftspeople who were moving ahead in technology. He planned a bold move at this time—establishing a permanent Washington studio and hiring Alexander Gardner to manage it. Located on Pennsylvania Avenue between Sixth and Seventh streets, his studio was ideally situated to attract important people. Brady had also moved his New York studio farther uptown, to 359 Broadway. He experimented with skylights to bring greater illumination to his work, as well as blue glass. The future really lay with the collodion wet plate method of photography, but Brady was still infatuated with the primitive daguerreotype. Photography had come of age and Brady rushed to catch up, but the technical skills that would make him famous in history belonged to others.

Stock companies to promote various new techniques and products—Crystalotype, Ambrotype, Melaintype, and tintype—were formed with the most creative inventors as principals. Brady was not among them. A development of which Brady took advantage to his profit, however, was the creation of life-size portraits that, when touched up and tinted with colors, rivaled oil paintings and commanded a high price. They consumed great amounts of time for exposure, however, and tied up studio facilities that were needed for other works.

In 1857, the new rage, *cartes de visite*, captivated the nation and the world. The small portrait-bearing calling cards, printed on thin cardboard, were cheaply produced and very profitable. Brady and others saw the demand increase as immigrants wanted pictures to send abroad, easterners wanted pictures for relatives moving to the West, and the newly married wanted pictures for family and friends. The collecting of cards was another demand that had to be satisfied, and Brady leaped into the competition, offering fees to actors, statesmen, outlaws, and others to sit for the cards, which were then peddled throughout the country. Despite a lull in sales after a few years, the Civil War revived the market for the cards as servicemen rushed to the studios.

Brady was never close to those who were on the cutting edge of photographic innovation. He was more a promoter than an operator-photographer, and the fact that he was known to appropriate the work of others and attach his own name to it did not sit well with his competitors. He picked competitive shows very selectively, such as the 1854 New York Crystal Palace show, in which he drew top honors for his daguerreotypes. Brady was concentrating on his new gallery and studio, the most ornate in New York.

In Washington, Brady placed Alexander Gardner in charge. Gardner was exactly what he needed, as the man had mastered the Archer wet-glass process in England before coming to the United States in 1856. Gardner later was to break from Brady and go on to film the history of the American West, but his experience as Brady's photographer of the Civil War projected them both to early prominence. Business was booming, and Brady again moved his New York studio further uptown in 1860, a location where his name became indelibly linked with that of Abraham Lincoln, who had come to give his celebrated Cooper Institute address.

The election of Lincoln and the advent of the Civil War encouraged all serious photographers to plan the filming of the dramatic times. Brady's early mentor, John W. Draper, formed a committee to approach the secretary of war with a project to photograph events. They were put off, however, and it was now Brady who seized the initiative. Lincoln again sat for a formal picture, this time with beard (he had previously been photographed clean-shaven), and Brady's Washington contingent also took pictures of both the inauguration and the Tyler Peace Commission. Two more photographers were sent to Washington to join Gardner as Brady gained presidential clearance to underwrite privately the photographing of the impending crisis.

More than three hundred photographers were involved in covering the Union during the Civil War, many in the direct employ of the War Department, who were not commercial people such as Brady's men. Countless others, most unknown, filmed Confederate exploits as well. Few, however, had the elaborate laboratories on wheels that Brady put in the field. His black wagons, called "what's its" by the troops, were at Bull Run to catch the first disaster of the long war.

After that debacle, Brady had seen enough of the war to realize that New York was the place for him. Keeping eighteen people in the field demanded money, and the studio in New York had to cover expenses that included his own high-toned lifestyle. The burdens of salaries, rent, transport, chemicals, and the like soon overwhelmed him, precipitating his collapse. His practice of filming dignitaries at no charge eroded his resources, and after Appomattox he drifted into virtual seclusion. He closed down his field operations and missed such events as the huge fire at P. T. Barnum's American Museum, in the same neighborhood as his studio. It was Gardner who persevered in capturing dramatic events in Washington.

Brady soon found that the market was saturated with war pictures. He stored thousands of plates and turned others over to satisfy debts that caused him to go bankrupt in 1873. The United States was exhausted by war and the bloody-shirt politics that followed it. The new excitement lay in the promise of the West, but Brady stayed home while a new army of photographers followed the sun. He sought to interest the government in his collections, to no avail. Ironically, the government was a successful bidder for thousands of wartime plates when he could not pay a storage bill of $2,840. Brady got nothing, and many pictures were destroyed in moving. A petition on his behalf was drawn up by General Benjamin Butler and James A. Garfield in 1875 to reward Brady with $25,000 for full title to his collection. The money was appropriated too late; the collection passed to the Anthony supply firm in lieu of payment on his debts. Although Brady had fallen on hard times, he won a bronze medal for his entry in a competition of photographs at the Centennial Exposition in Philadelphia. Still, he desperately needed money.

Sporadic interest continued during the 1880's, as aging veterans' groups made inquiries about Brady's pictures. The government called in Albert Bierstadt, the famous painter and photographer, to make an assessment of their holdings. The pieces held by the Anthony firm changed hands several times until some seven thousand glass negatives were recovered and turned over to the government by John C. Taylor of Connecticut. The prohibitive cost of making prints meant that the negatives would remain in storage. Brady nevertheless persevered in the Washington gallery at 627 Pennsylvania Avenue, working with his wife's nephew, Levin Handy. His wife, Juliet, had died of a heart condition on May 20, 1887, leaving him childless. In 1891, a newspaperman was startled to find Brady alive, wiry, and vigorous, with white hair and white mustache and goatee and wearing blue-tinted spectacles. In a revealing comment at that time, Brady suggested that he might have better spent his time becoming a craftsperson instead of seeking out personalities to photograph.

Brady continued to struggle to keep his studio going.

On April 16, 1895, however, he was struck by a carriage and suffered a broken leg. This came when he was planning a new exhibition of his personal war slides: 128 pieces to be shown in New York on January 30, 1896. Still ailing, Brady went to the city alone to confirm details with officials of the Seventh Regiment organization. He stayed in a rooming house on East Tenth Street but soon took ill with a kidney ailment. A friend took him to New York City's Presbyterian Hospital, where he died in the indigent ward on January 15, 1896. His remains were shipped to Washington, where he was buried, most probably at Congressional Cemetery.

SIGNIFICANCE

Mathew Brady was a man possessed of vision and a passion for greatness. He was an indefatigable worker and promoter, as well as a believer in the dream of success. He believed in himself and committed his resources to photographing history. The horror and carnage of the war recorded by Brady's men will forever haunt American history. Brady was not a historian with a camera; he was the entrepreneur who put cameramen in the field to make as much of a record as they could. His pictures do not interpret events as history does; rather, they present scenes, many of which would be indescribable in words.

As with many great figures in history, there is much that was not admirable in Brady. He might have been more humble and less self-serving. He might have done a better job keeping up with new technology. He might have been less enamored of great men and women and more conscious of that large constituency that he ignored to the detriment of history. He might have been kinder to those who did the photography, which is the only durable vestige of his glory. He might have been a better businessperson. Nevertheless, Brady's initiative in the use of the craft of photography has provided an irreplaceable record of critical times in the history of the United States.

—*Jack J. Cardoso*

FURTHER READING

Hood, Robert E. *Twelve at War: Great Photographers Under Fire*. New York: G. P. Putnam's Sons, 1967. This volume has a short essay that establishes Brady as the first of the leading war photographers.

Horan, James D. *Mathew Brady: Historian with a Camera*. New York: Crown, 1955. This is a confounding but necessary book, which must be read very carefully as the author plays loose with dates and historical evidence and often passes off conjecture as reality. With regard to Brady, it is adulatory to a fault.

Kunhardt, Dorothy Meserve, and Philip B. Kunhardt, Jr. *Mathew Brady and His World*. New York: Time-Life Books, 1977. This work grew from the collections of Frederick Meserve and, though published as a picture book for popular consumption, is clear, well developed, and more historically correct than most works on Brady. The book also provides what has been a universal weakness in books dealing with Brady: a critique of the photographs and real effort into determining who actually took the picture.

Kunhardt, Philip B., Jr. "Mathew Brady," Parts 1, 2. *Smithsonian* 8 (July, August, 1977): 24-35, 58-67. Some of this material can be found in the book by Dorothy and Philip Kunhardt, which developed from the research done for these articles.

Meredith, Roy. *Mathew Brady's Portrait of an Era*. New York: W. W. Norton, 1982.

_____. *Mr. Lincoln's Camera Man*. New York: Charles Scribner's Sons, 1946. These are large-format picture books much like that of James Horan, though they weave a narrative around the illustrations. *Mathew Brady's Portrait of an Era* has considerable information concerning the activities of Brady at various times in his career, although much of the book seems to cry out for reexamination, especially because the object of the work is to tell a good story.

Panzer, Mary. *Mathew Brady*. London: Phaidon Press, 2001. One in a series of brief biographies of photographers published by Phaidon. This biography of Brady is written by the curator of photographs at the National Portrait Gallery in Washington, D.C.

Sullivan, George. *In the Wake of Battle: The Civil War Images of Mathew Brady*. New York: Prestel, 2004. Contains more than 350 photographs of the war taken by Brady and his cameramen. The photos are arranged by battle site and event, with introductory essays about the battles, and archival information about the images and photographers.

Townsend, G. A. "Still Taking Pictures." *World* (New York). April 12, 1891: 23. This is a newspaper reporter's interview with the elderly Brady that, because of the dearth of material directly relating to the man, is exploited in many accounts of his life.

SEE ALSO: Lewis Carroll; Jacques Daguerre.

RELATED ARTICLES in *Great Events from History: The Nineteenth Century, 1801-1900:* January, 1839: Invention of Daguerreotype Photography Is Announced; 1878: Muybridge Photographs a Galloping Horse; January 14, 1900.

JOHANNES BRAHMS
German composer

One of the greatest composers of his century, Brahms left an enduring body of work, which demonstrated that the forms and genres of Viennese classicism would continue to have artistic validity during the late nineteenth century and that they were not incompatible with the ethos of Romanticism.

BORN: May 7, 1833; Hamburg (now in Germany)
DIED: April 3, 1897; Vienna, Austro-Hungarian Empire (now in Austria)
AREA OF ACHIEVEMENT: Music

EARLY LIFE

Johannes Brahms (brahmz) was the son of Johann Jakob Brahms, a double bassist in the municipal orchestra of Hamburg, and Johanna Henrika Christiane Nissen, a small, disabled woman who was seventeen years her husband's senior. Though romantic biographers often exaggerated the humble origins of their subjects, accounts of Brahms's childhood in a Dickensian tenement in Hamburg are largely accurate, and it appears true that Brahms was required at an early age to play the piano in dockside taverns and dance halls in order to augment the family income. Certainly Brahms's childhood was not altogether wretched: It seems clear that his parents offered considerable affection (Brahms worshiped his mother throughout her life) and did what could be done, given their straitened circumstances, to develop their son's gifts.

Brahms's remarkable musical talent was discovered at an early age by his father. He was given competent instruction at the piano by Otto F. W. Cossel and distinguished, if conservative, instruction in composition by Eduard Marxsen. Though Brahms was not a prodigy on the order of Wolfgang Amadeus Mozart or Felix Mendelssohn, his talent developed rapidly. During the 1848-1849 season, he gave two public piano recitals, performing works as formidable as Ludwig van Beethoven's *Waldstein* Sonata, Op. 53. He was also composing prolifically, though the works from this period are no longer extant; Brahms, ever self-critical, later destroyed these "youthful indiscretions" by the trunkful.

In 1853, Brahms seized an opportunity to participate in a concert tour with the flamboyant Hungarian violinist Eduard Reményi. The tour proved to be a turning point in Brahms's life. Through Reményi's offices, Brahms was introduced first to Franz Liszt in Weimar and then to Robert and Clara Schumann in Düsseldorf. The initial meeting with the Schumanns—he the leading spirit in the German Romantic musical movement and she the greatest female pianist of the century—took place on September 30, 1853.

The three immediately experienced a remarkable personal and musical communion, and Brahms became virtually a member of the Schumann household. At this time, Brahms was twenty years old, small, slightly built, blond, unbearded, and androgynously fair of face (not the bearded, well-fleshed, cigar-smoking doyen of later photographs), and he seems to have exercised a complex fascination on both the Schumanns. So impressed by Brahms's playing and compositions was Robert Schumann that he was moved to issue a review in the prestigious *New Journal for Music* declaring Brahms to be a "young eagle" who had sprung forth "fully armed." Schumann had, in effect, anointed Brahms as his musical heir; the younger man's public career had begun.

LIFE'S WORK

The first works that Brahms allowed posterity to see date from the period of the first meeting with the Schumanns. It is easy to see why Robert Schumann admired the three piano sonatas (Opp. 1, 2, and 5) that Brahms presented to him. Though the shadow of Beethoven looms over these works, they display an emerging individuality, a formal mastery, and a seriousness of purpose that justify Schumann's description of Brahms as already "fully armed." The Sonata in F Minor, Op. 5 is particularly impressive: It is a big-boned work in five movements whose carefully organized ideas are alternately fiery and lyrical. Brahms's unique, thick-textured, robust, and occasionally awkward keyboard idiom, doubtless deriving from his own idiosyncratic piano technique, is already fully present.

The years from 1854 to 1856 were years of personal turmoil for Brahms. Early in 1854, Robert Schumann suffered a nervous collapse that required his institutionalization and that led ultimately to his death in 1856. Brahms devoted much of his energy during this time of trial to the emotional support of Clara. There is no doubt that Brahms believed himself to be in love with Clara at this time. The degree of intimacy to which Brahms and Clara progressed is not known. Shortly after Robert's death, the two evidently agreed to maintain their friendship on a purely platonic basis.

The years of Schumann's illness had not been productive ones for Brahms. Shortly before Schumann's collapse, Brahms had completed his first major chamber work: the Piano Trio in B Major, Op. 8. It was an auspicious beginning. The next large works date from the end of the decade. In 1857, Brahms accepted a post as pianist and choral conductor at the small court of Detmold. There he had an opportunity to work with the court's forty-piece orchestra. In 1859, Brahms completed his first work employing full orchestra, the Concerto No. 1 in D Minor, Op. 15. The work had a complicated genesis: Brahms had first intended to write a symphony, and the work lacks the surface brilliance of most Romantic concertos. Though it was not well received at first, it is a great, if somewhat austere, work. The piano part is in some respects ungracefully written, and the work was long considered unplayable.

Though Brahms was by no means a reactionary, he found himself increasingly allied during the 1850's and 1860's with musical conservatives such as the Schumanns and violinist Joseph Joachim in opposition to radical Romantics such as Franz Liszt and Richard Wagner. Brahms himself had little interest in critical polemics of any sort, but in 1860 he allowed his name to be placed on a manifesto decrying the so-called music of the future of Liszt and his cohorts. Ultimately, Brahms was made to suffer for this gesture: He became the bête noire of radical critics and was the victim of critical vituperation for the remainder of his life. To these thrusts, Brahms appeared stoically indifferent; on later occasions, he expressed admiration for the works of Wagner, the leader of the opposing camp.

Johannes Brahms. (Library of Congress)

In 1863, Brahms accepted a post as director of the Vienna *Singakademie* (choral society) and for the remainder of his life resided chiefly in Vienna. The city of the Habsburgs, with its *Gemütlichkeit* and its memories of Franz Schubert, Mozart, and Beethoven, thus became the backdrop for Brahms's supreme achievements as a composer. The move was probably a healthy one for Brahms: The sunniness of the Viennese doubtless helped to mitigate Brahms's North German dourness and enabled Brahms to show on occasion a more genial and charming face. As Brahms aged, he seemed in some respects to personify the aging of the century itself; his works increasingly assumed that cast that generations of critics have called "autumnal." Brahms's late works are indeed the Indian summer of Romanticism, warmed by a low sun whose rays shine obliquely.

Brahms's great work of the 1860's, and the work that firmly established his international reputation, was the *German Requiem*, Op. 45, for chorus, soloists, and orchestra. Despite its title, this is not a liturgical mass. Brahms assembled his own text from the German Bible, and as Karl Geiringer has observed, Brahms's requiem is not so much a prayer for the dead as an attempt to comfort and reassure the living who mourn. The occasion that gave rise to this work was the death of Brahms's mother in 1865; the great seven-movement edifice that he constructed in her memory was completed in 1868. Brahms's compositional technique was by this time completely assured in both choral and orchestral idioms, and the *German Requiem* shows Brahms working at a sustained level of inspiration throughout.

Among numerous other works that Brahms composed in his fourth decade, mention should be made of the Piano Quintet in F Minor, Op. 34 (1864); the Horn Trio in E-flat Major, Op. 40 (1865); and the orchestral *Variations on a Theme by Haydn*, Op. 56a (1873). The quintet for piano and strings began life as a duet for two pianos but is heard to greatest effect as a quintet. The trio was written for the unusual combination of violin, French horn, and piano; in its euphony and elegiac quality, it is purest Brahms. The Haydn variations show Brahms in his highest spirits; although the theme was not original with Haydn, a measure of his good humor pervades the work.

As Brahms entered his forties, he had not yet completed a symphony. It is part of his lore that he shrank from comparison with Beethoven in this genre. It is ironic, then, that his Symphony No. 1 in C Minor, Op. 68 (1876) was promptly dubbed "Beethoven's Tenth," and it is revealing that Brahms was not displeased by the nickname. The work borrows the key of Beethoven's Fifth Symphony and appropriates some of the emotional world of the Ninth as well, but these borrowings are not the result of a nullity on the part of Brahms; rather, they reveal Brahms emboldened by the sureness of his own voice. Brahms was to write three more symphonies in 1877, 1883, and 1885; each is the product of consummate craftsmanship, and each has become a repertory staple.

Brahms's productivity did not diminish in his later years. Among the notable works of his last two decades are the Violin Concerto in D, Op. 77 (1878), the Piano Concerto No. 2 in B-flat, Op. 83 (perhaps his greatest utterance in concerto form), the second and third piano trios (1882 and 1886), the *Four Serious Songs*, Op. 121 (1896), and the miniatures for piano entitled variously *Intermezzo*, *Capriccio*, and *Ballade*, Opp. 116-119 (1892). These works for piano are an anthology of gems and have a valedictory quality; in some cases, they are an exquisite sort of sublimated café music.

The event that hastened Brahms's end shortly before his sixty-fourth birthday was the death of his great friend and artistic companion Clara Schumann in 1896. Shortly thereafter, Brahms was found to be suffering from cancer of the liver, to which he succumbed in April of 1897.

SIGNIFICANCE

It was fashionable in progressive circles at the turn of the century to disparage Johannes Brahms. Hugo Wolf railed against Brahms's vacuousness and "hypocrisy"; George Bernard Shaw declared his style to be "euphuistic," and quipped that "his *Requiem* is patiently borne only by the corpse." These views seem today to be quaint at best and monuments to critical vanity at worst. A remarkable percentage of Brahms's works have remained in the active repertory, and they seem to appeal equally to the learned and the casual listener. Though the formulation may be simplistic, it can be said that Brahms—like Beethoven—speaks both to the intellect and to the heart. As a builder, Brahms was masterful both in design and in execution, and admirers of craftsmanship will not fail to respond to this. Brahms kindly supplied enough recondite features in his works to subsidize a large corps of scholars. At the same time, Brahms had the courage to speak directly and ingenuously to his listeners on an emotional level. This combination of sophistication and directness is the stamp of a great artist.

—*Steven W. Shrader*

FURTHER READING

Gál, Hans. *Johannes Brahms: His Work and Personality*. Translated by Joseph Stein. Reprint. Westport, Conn.: Greenwood Press, 1977. Gál, a composer as well as a musicologist, was coeditor of the collected works of Brahms; his study is informed by an exhaustive knowledge of Brahms's works.

Geiringer, Karl. *Brahms: His Life and Work*. 2d rev. ed. London: Allen & Unwin, 1948. Geiringer's work remains the standard study in English of Brahms's life and creative achievement. The book is divided into two parts: a chronological account of Brahms's life and a critique of his works organized by genre. Includes an appendix containing an interesting sampling of Brahms's correspondence.

Latham, Peter. *Brahms*. London: J. M. Dent & Sons, 1948. Rev. ed. 1966. A valuable shorter appraisal of Brahms in a two-part life-and-works format. Contains vivid, epigrammatic descriptions of major works.

MacDonald, Malcolm. *Brahms*. New York: Oxford University Press, 2001. A thorough biography aimed at readers who are familiar with Brahms's works and can read music. MacDonald carefully analyzes Brahms's compositions, providing sixty-eight musical examples.

Newman, William S. *The Sonata Since Beethoven*. Chapel Hill: University of North Carolina Press, 1969. Newman's study of the sonata principle contains a section of generous dimensions discussing Brahms's affinity for the sonata form, in general, and his sonatas for violin, piano, and clarinet, in particular.

Ostwald, Peter. *Schumann: The Inner Voices of a Musical Genius*. Boston: Northeastern University Press, 1985. Contains a well-documented and thoughtful account of the relationship between Brahms and Schumann. Ostwald, a practicing psychiatrist, bases much of his presentation on previously inaccessible documents. Essential for the student who would understand the Johannes Brahms-Robert Schumann-Clara Schumann triangle.

Schauffler, Robert H. *The Unknown Brahms: His Life, Character, and Works*. New York: Dodd, Mead, 1933. An anecdotal account of Brahms's personal life,

Schauffler's work is based in large part on interviews with actual acquaintances of Brahms, and herein lies its chief value. In his attempt to unravel the enigma of Brahms's sexuality, Schauffler provides an early specimen of the so-called psychobiography. Schauffler's discussion of the works is old-fashioned and flowery but not altogether useless.

Schönberg, Arnold. "Brahms the Progressive." In *Style and Idea*. New York: Philosophical Library, 1950. An essay by the influential atonal composer demonstrating the progressive aspects (rhythmic complexity and subtlety of motivic manipulation) of Brahms's art. A useful counterpoint to the prevailing view of Brahms as an autumnal composer.

Swafford, Jan. *Johannes Brahms: A Biography*. New York: Alfred A. Knopf, 1997. Swafford, a musician and biographer, has produced a comprehensive biography of Brahms that combines biographical material with musical scholarship. Includes illustrations, extensive notes, and a bibliography.

SEE ALSO: Antonín Dvořák; Clara Schumann; Robert Schumann; Johann Strauss.

RELATED ARTICLE in *Great Events from History: The Nineteenth Century, 1801-1900:* April 7, 1805: Beethoven's *Eroica* Symphony Introduces the Romantic Age.

LOUIS BRAILLE

French inventor and social reformer

Braille invented what became a worldwide system for teaching the blind to read and write and thereby made an enduring contribution to the education and lives of the visually impaired.

BORN: January 4, 1809; Coupvray, near Paris, France
DIED: January 6, 1852; Paris, France
AREAS OF ACHIEVEMENT: Science and technology, social reform

EARLY LIFE

Louis Braille's mother, Constance Braille, was the daughter of a farming family in the countryside near Coupvray. His father, who also bore the name Louis, was a harness-maker. While playing in his father's workshop, the three-year-old Louis suffered an accident that would lead first to sympathetic ophthalmia and then to total blindness. Because there were no special educational facilities for the blind in the provincial areas of France at that time, the child spent the next seven years of his life in a state of relative solitude.

In 1819, when Braille was ten years old, he received a scholarship that enabled him to go to the Royal Institute for the Blind in Paris. It was there that, at the age of fifteen, Braille helped develop a new system of tactile coded impressions that could be used by the blind both to read and to write. This work represented a vast improvement over earlier methods. Although some time passed before this invention gained widespread acceptance, Braille was such a model student at the institute that, once he earned his completion certificate, when he was seventeen, he was appointed as a teacher in the Institute for the Blind.

LIFE'S WORK

As his career as a teacher progressed, Braille played a role in several of the changes that affected not only the organization but also the philosophy of education for the blind in France and other countries. Before 1784, when Valentin Haüy founded what would eventually become the National Institute for the Blind in Paris, few, if any, institutional provisions had existed for special assistance to the blind either in France or elsewhere in Europe or in the United States. This is not to say that the blind had not been the focus of considerable popular attention during prior generations. Indeed, Haüy and others associated with the new institute tried immediately to address some of the most important public-image questions that both he and, ultimately, Braille would face throughout their careers as educators of the blind.

One of these was the task of counteracting traditional prejudices, ranging from innocent pity or emotional compassion to open fear, visibly present among the majority of the population in their attitudes toward the blind. In Haüy's generation, the methods used to achieve this end were not always effective. In some cases, for example, arguments were introduced that underlined special characteristics of the blind. When these had to do with presumed extraordinary talents possessed by the blind by dint of one missing sense (heightened capacities of sense perception through touch or hearing), educators of the blind could emphasize certain positive points. To a certain extent, this was being done at the institute when Braille began there as a student: Many blind children were given training in music, so they could "prove" to society that they had talents worthy of recognition and praise.

On the other hand, there was another stream of literature, supported in part by Haüy, that suggested that the blind possessed a distinct inner nature that touched the realm of the mysterious. Anyone with a tendency to react negatively to obvious differences between the blind and persons with normal vision might also have been tempted to interpret suggestions of this special characteristic more in negative than in positive terms.

Even before Braille came to the Institute for the Blind in Paris, a debate had already challenged the Société Philanthropique (the founding inspiration behind the institute) for offering only charitable assistance to the blind children who came under its care. Some argued that more practical attention needed to be given to preparing blind children for life as participating members of society. In Haüy's generation, such pressures tended to focus on a list of so-called suitable occupations for which the blind could be trained. Most of these were simple manual trades that could be learned through the sense of touch.

In practical terms, the members of the institute knew that, in order for the transmission of intellectual knowledge to occur, some technical method needed to be found to enable the blind both to read the same texts that were available to the literate majority population and to write without assistance. The most obvious method—one that was already in use by the time Braille became a student at the institute—was to print texts with raised letters. Although the blind could thus follow any printed text by tactile progression, there were two disadvantages in this early system. First, the method was rather slow, because the full form of each letter was fairly complicated and difficult to feel. Second, because of the relative complexity of the forms of the letters, the likelihood of errors in reading, particularly if one tried to move rapidly, was fairly high.

On the other hand, those who insisted that fuller integration into so-called normal society would be a desirable by-product of educating the blind to read had also to keep other, less practical, considerations in mind. Prejudices against presumed special inner moral and psychological characteristics of the blind might rise if a communications system were devised for or by them that was not as immediately accessible to the "normal" majority as simple raised letters were. Haüy himself discovered,

Louis Braille. (Library of Congress)

well before Braille made his contribution, that controversy would rise over any form of innovation that went further than the simple method of raised letters: Representation of sounds by raised symbols rather than letters (the Haüy method), for example, never became an established technique for teaching the blind to read.

There are several reasons why the work of Braille—which was technologically rather commonplace—needs to be placed in the wider context of the time and society in which he lived. Braille's system of printing writing by means of a "code" of dots rather than actual letters was obviously meant to simplify the reading process for the blind. Because knowledge of what eventually came to be known as Braille involved mastery of a "secret" code, however, some of Braille's contemporaries believed that the new system ran counter to the normal integrationist objectives that education for the blind was meant to serve. As a consequence, Braille techniques did not spread as rapidly or as widely as the modern observer, more accustomed to practical criteria for judging the effectiveness of technological innovations, might imagine.

Despite its rather slow start (Braille was not used, even in the institute where Braille taught, until 1829), progress toward the official adoption of the six-dot reading code was made gradually. By the mid- to late 1830's, Braille's insistence on the fact of increased teaching efficiency through the use of his system gained important recognition. A special school was founded on the outskirts of Paris (at Maisons Alfort), in which Braille was used exclusively. Later, as the success of the Maisons Alfort program became obvious, the school moved to the center of Paris, on the rue Bagnolet.

By the late 1840's, the use of Braille was enhanced considerably by two new developments. First, in 1847 the first Braille printing press was invented and used in France, soon to be exported for use throughout Europe and the United States. Second, the French government decided to establish a series of branch schools for the blind that would use the same Braille methods as the Paris Institute to provide elementary levels of instruction through reading, as well as manual trade training at the departmental level. From the mid-nineteenth century onward, the most qualified graduates of these provincial elementary schools would qualify to continue their education in full academic subjects at the National Institute for the Blind in Paris.

Braille himself did not live to see the full effects of the application of his reading code for the blind. Because of health complications caused by tuberculosis, he was forced to retire from teaching at the institute in 1837. At the time of his death in January, 1852, Braille lived in seclusion and was a nearly forgotten man. His reputation as an important contributor to modern education came only in stages. In 1887, the town of Coupvray, Braille's birthplace and the site of his grave, erected a monument to his memory in the center of the town square. In 1952, one century after his death, and at a time when the techniques he had pioneered were in use throughout the world, Braille's remains were transferred from Coupvray to a place of national prestige in the Panthéon in Paris.

SIGNIFICANCE

The life of Louis Braille is more representative in many respects of the history of an issue than the history of an individual personality. Before Braille's time, both in France and elsewhere in Europe or the United States, institutions that cared for the blind functioned more as asylums than as places where useful trades could be taught. Intellectual stimuli, and even basic educational instruction, remained even more remote than possibilities for simple vocational training. Until an effective means of communication had been found, learning was restricted to areas concentrating on the senses of touch and/or hearing.

The importance of the contribution of Braille, therefore, should be considered not only in practical terms (development of a simplified system of representing the letters of the alphabet by means of a code of raised dots) but also for its effect on attitudes toward the types of schooling that have since become possible for the blind. Even though the use of Braille to teach reading was initially limited to special schools for the blind, an important difference was in the making: Those who had formerly had no access to normal texts, be they in literature or the sciences, were now able to prepare themselves for interaction with society. Eventually, as Braille became more common and less expensive as a system of printing, this movement in the direction of fuller social and intellectual integration of the blind went further. By the early stages of the twentieth century, the blind were able to attend regular schools and follow the same academic curricula as their fellow classmates, using the same books, printed in Braille for their special use.

—Byron D. Cannon

FURTHER READING

Bickel, Lennard. *Triumph over Darkness: The Life of Louis Braille*. Sydney, Australia: Allen & Unwin Australia, 1988. A brief review of Braille's life, one of the few Braille biographies written for adults, not children.

Davidson, Margaret. *Louis Braille*. New York: Scholastic Book Services, 1971. A work of historical fiction, designed mainly for young readers, recounting the life of Braille. In addition to Braille himself, the author portrays the people who influenced him as a youth in Coupvray and during his adult years.

Dixon, Judith, ed. *Braille Into the Next Millennium*. Washington, D.C.: National Library Service for the Blind and Physically Handicapped, and Friends of Libraries for Blind and Physically Handicapped Individuals in North America, 2000. This 600-page anthology of articles examines the past and present uses of Braille and speculates about how the Braille system might be used in the twenty-first century. The discussion of the Braille system's past uses includes information about Louis Braille's birthplace and the system's origins.

Hampshire, Barry. *Working with Braille*. Lausanne, Switzerland: UNESCO, 1981. This book updates the 1954 United Nations Educational, Scientific, and Cultural Organization (UNESCO) analysis of methods of adapting Braille for international use. It is particularly important for its discussion of the impact of technological changes that have facilitated rapid communication beyond the imagination of the original inventors of the Braille system.

Kugelmass, J. Alvin. *Louis Braille: Windows for the Blind.* New York: Julian Messner, 1951. Although this biography was designed for a popular reading audience, it is the result of fairly extensive research into relevant resources in French and other languages. These lend an impression of historical accuracy, as well as some sense of the technical details of Braille's system, to what is otherwise a simple account of Braille's life.

Mackenzie, Sir Clutha. *World Braille Usage.* Paris: UNESCO, 1953. Provides a historical review of the processes that were followed over a century's time to alter the original Braille system to meet the needs of blind readers and writers of Asian and African languages. It includes a brief review of Braille's life and work as well as a history of the World Braille Council.

Paulson, William R. *Enlightenment, Romanticism, and the Blind in France.* Princeton, N.J.: Princeton University Press, 1987. A scholarly historical study of changing cultural values that affected French attitudes toward the blind from the mid-eighteenth through the mid-nineteenth centuries. Paulson's book fully develops the question of prejudices, particularly toward the presumed mystical inner nature of the blind.

SEE ALSO: Samuel Gridley Howe.

RELATED ARTICLE in *Great Events from History: The Nineteenth Century, 1801-1900:* 1820's-1850's: Social Reform Movement.

JOHN BRIGHT

English politician and social reformer

Dedicated to improving the conditions of life in Great Britain and its dependencies, Bright combined moral courage and personal integrity and was instrumental in bringing about many liberal reforms in nineteenth century Great Britain.

BORN: November 16, 1811; Rochdale, Lancashire, England

DIED: March 27, 1889; Rochdale, Lancashire, England

AREA OF ACHIEVEMENT: Government and politics

EARLY LIFE

John Bright was the second, but oldest-surviving, of eleven children born to Jacob and Martha Wood Bright. Both of his parents came from old, established Society of Friends (Quaker) families. As a boy, Bright attended several Friends schools, until the age of fifteen, when he entered his father's business. Although his formal education ended, he continued his education through reading and travel. He traveled throughout the British Isles, the Continent, and the Mediterranean before he was thirty, and he continued traveling throughout his life. At the age of twenty-two, he and a number of friends organized the Rochdale Literary and Philosophical Society.

Jacob Bright, along with two friends, had founded a cotton mill in 1809. By 1823, he was the sole owner of the mill. Eventually, the firm had six mills, and during the 1850's it added a carpet manufacturing business. Jacob took his sons into the business and it provided a comfortable living for John throughout his life.

John Bright entered public life in 1830, when he began making temperance speeches in Rochdale. In 1834, he joined the Rochdale resistance to paying church rates. His involvement in these public causes led to difficulties when he proposed marriage to Elizabeth Priestman, also a member of the Society of Friends. Before she would marry him, she wanted his assurance that he would not become overly involved in politics. They were married in November, 1839. One daughter, Helen was born to them. Bright was devastated when his wife died in September, 1841. In June, 1847, he married another Friend, Margaret Leatham. They had four sons and three daughters. She died in May, 1878.

LIFE'S WORK

The issue that thrust Bright onto the national stage was his involvement in the Anti-Corn Law League. The Corn Law imposed a duty on imported corn and, according to the league, kept the cost of food artificially high to the advantage of the landed class and to the detriment of the rest of society. Bright had joined the local branch of the league in 1838. Through the league, he became associated with one of its founders, Richard Cobden. Cobden visited Bright three days after Bright's first wife died and persuaded him to forget his melancholy through work.

The two men pledged not to rest until the Corn Law was repealed.

Bright and Cobden became the two most visible agitators for the repeal of the Corn Law. Bright brought to the league his marvelous oratorical ability. He had a voice with a bell-like tone that could be heard with clarity at the large outdoor meetings. He used few gestures while speaking but could portray a variety of emotions solely through the use of his voice. His self-assured speaking style was reinforced by his impressive head and stocky body.

In 1842, the Rochdale voters chose Bright to represent them in the House of Commons. Bright now gave speeches opposing the Corn Law both in the House and in the country. His speeches earned for him the enmity of the landed class: He accused them of being an oligarchy of the worst sort, one that legislated only for its own good. Not only did it maintain the Corn Law, but the landed class also maintained an established church, opposed electoral reform, and kept the poor from having enough to eat through the game laws.

In 1846, the Conservative prime minister Sir Robert Peel pressured both by the league and by famine in Ireland, repealed the Corn Law. Bright and Cobden hoped that other countries would follow Great Britain's lead and move toward free trade. Free trade, they believed, would lead to international harmony among the European nations as they became economically interdependent. As a result of the repeal, both Bright and Cobden were very popular among the middle and lower classes. Bright, much to his delight, was chosen to represent Manchester in the 1847 election.

Although the working class supported Bright's position on the Corn Law, they did not support his position on factory legislation. Bright opposed the 1847 Ten Hours' Act on the principle that the proper role of government did not include regulating conditions of work or wages. Even though Bright recognized that some working conditions needed improvement, he thought that they should be the subject of negotiation between the owners and workers, not government regulation.

The proper role of government intervention concerned Bright not only in domestic affairs but also in foreign affairs. He opposed an interventionist foreign policy throughout his life. The reason for intervention was generally the concept of balance of power. Because the balance of power was always shifting, Bright argued that it was fruitless to intervene and that intervention wasted resources that could much better be used to solve domestic problems. Therefore, when the Aberdeen government became embroiled in the Crimean War in 1854, Bright, along with Cobden, was one of the leading critics of the war.

The immediate cause of the Crimean War was the quarrel between Russia and Turkey over Russia's de-

BRITISH POLICY IN THE CRIMEA

Always a quick critic of government stupidity, John Bright was especially incensed by what he regarded as British folly in becoming involved in the Crimean War. In this extract from a long letter that he wrote to Absalom Watkin in October, 1853, he vents his anger on that subject.

The whole policy of our Government in this matter is marked with an imbecility perhaps without example. I will not say they intended a war from the first, though there are not wanting many evidences that war was the object of at least a section of the Cabinet. A distinguished Member of the House of Commons said to a friend of mine, immediately after the accession of the present Government to office, "You have a war Ministry, and you will have a war." But I leave this question to point out the disgraceful feebleness of the Cabinet, if I am to absolve them from the guilt of having sought occasion for war. They promised the Turk armed assistance on conditions, or without conditions. They, in concert with France, Austria, and Prussia, took the original dispute out of the hands of Russia and Turkey, and formed themselves into a court of arbitration in the interests of Turkey; they made an award, which they declared to be safe and honourable for both parties; this award was accepted by Russia and rejected by Turkey; and they then turned round upon their own award, declared it to be "totally inadmissible," and made war upon the very country whose Government, at their suggestion and urgent recommendation, had frankly accepted it. At this moment England is engaged in a murderous warfare with Russia, although the Russian Government accepted her own terms of peace, and has been willing to accept them in the sense of England's own interpretation of them ever since they were offered; and at the same time England is allied with Turkey, whose Government rejected the award of England, and who entered into the war in opposition to the advice of England. Surely, when the Vienna note was accepted by Russia, the Turks should have been prevented from going to war, or should have been allowed to go to war at their own risk.

Source: John Bright, *Speeches on Questions of Public Policy*, edited by James E. Thorold Rogers (2d ed. London: Macmillan, 1868), vol. 2.

mands that Turkey recognize its proprietary role as protector of the Greek Orthodox subjects in the Turkish Empire. Turkey refused, and war broke out between Turkey and Russia. Great Britain and France came to Turkey's defense. Bright argued that British interests were not involved in the dispute and that the aim of preserving Turkish integrity or preventing Russian expansion was beyond Great Britain's ability to accomplish. Because the war was very popular in the beginning, those such as Bright and Cobden who opposed the war were vilified on all sides. Nevertheless, Bright's speeches in the House of Commons always drew large audiences. In his most famous speech against the war, he stated that "the angel of death has been abroad throughout the land; you may almost hear the beating of his wings."

Bright's exertions during the war contributed to his physical breakdown early in 1856. When the prescribed rest did not seem to help much, a change of scenery was advised. Bright traveled in England, Scotland, and Wales and then to North Africa, France, and Italy. His loneliness was reduced when his daughter Helen joined him. He was still traveling when Manchester rejected him in March, 1857. He returned to England in June, however, and was elected to represent Birmingham in August. He continued to represent Birmingham until his death in 1889. In February, 1858, he was sufficiently recovered to resume his parliamentary activity.

During the controversy over the Crimean War, Bright was often viewed as someone who believed in peace at any price. This view was not true during the Crimean War, and Bright's position during the American Civil War clearly demonstrated that it was not. Many of the British, including William Ewart Gladstone, were sympathetic toward the American South because of the protectionism of the North and the reliance of the textile industry upon cotton from the South. Bright thought that the key issue was a moral one, slavery, and he therefore approved of the war and championed the cause of the North. His many speeches were instrumental in keeping Great Britain neutral during the conflict. At the end of the war, many Americans, including President Abraham Lincoln, expressed their gratitude for the role that Bright had played.

The reform of the electoral system was a major concern throughout Bright's life. He advocated franchise extension, the secret ballot, and the redistribution of parliamentary seats. During the 1850's and most of the 1860's, he had little success, but he did keep the reform issue alive. His agitation contributed to the 1867 and 1884 reform bills and the Ballot Act of 1872.

Bright's positions on the American Civil War and reform having restored his popularity, Bright joined the Gladstone cabinet as the president of the Board of Trade in 1868. He was not to enjoy his position in the cabinet for long, because in 1870 he had another breakdown. He resigned from the cabinet in November, 1870, partially because of his health and partially because he disagreed with Gladstone's resistance to Russia's desire to be a Black Sea power. He remained on the sidelines recovering until February, 1873, when he returned to Commons and the cabinet as chancellor of the Duchy of Lancaster.

The electoral victory of the Conservatives under Benjamin Disraeli in 1874 horrified Bright, because he believed that their primary goal was to block necessary reforms. During the six years of the Disraeli government, he spent a great amount of time with his family in Rochdale and often protested the more aggressive Disraeli foreign policy. The death of his wife in 1878 was a loss from which Bright never completely recovered.

When the Liberals regained the majority in 1880, Bright again joined the Gladstone cabinet as the chancellor of the Duchy of Lancaster. He remained in the cabinet until 1882, when he resigned over the British shelling of Alexandria. Bright thought that Great Britain had no more business meddling in the affairs of Egypt than it had had in meddling in the affairs of Turkey nearly thirty years earlier.

During Bright's last years, the public issue upon which he spent most of his time and energy was opposing Gladstone's attempt to grant home rule to Ireland. Bright had long urged reform rather than repression as the way to treat Ireland. He had supported Gladstone's disestablishment of the Irish Church (1869) and the Irish Land Acts of 1870 and 1881, which recognized that tenants as well as landlords had rights. Bright thought, however, that home rule would be a step toward Irish independence, which he thought unacceptable because it would threaten the security of Great Britain—the only justification for meddling in the affairs of another country. His opposition to home rule lost the popularity in Ireland that his previous support of reform had gained for him.

SIGNIFICANCE

The dominant political creed during the nineteenth century was liberalism. Liberalism supported free trade, reforms that eroded the power of the landed class, and the freedom of the individual. Liberalism found its support primarily among the middle class, and for some Liberals, liberalism did not extend beyond those reforms that benefited the middle class. John Bright personified nineteenth century liberalism but applied its principles beyond middle-class advantage. He wanted to extend the right to vote to include most of the working class. His belief in the freedom of the individual led him to oppose factory legislation, which appears to be very self-serving, but he also supported freedom of the individual when it was in his interest to oppose it. For example, he was a temperance advocate, but he opposed attempts to legislate temperance because of his conviction that the government had no right to curtail the freedom to choose or to reject temperance.

The growing influence of the middle class fundamentally changed Great Britain during the nineteenth century. Bright, a middle-class manufacturer, was a proud representative of his class, even though he was not always comfortable with all elements of it. He detested those parts of the middle class that practiced conspicuous consumption or were deferential toward the landed class.

Bright's position on foreign affairs was not shared by any large segment of nineteenth century British society. He advocated nonintervention and arbitration when most politicians and the public favored intervention and force. He regarded his inability to change the British foreign policy as a major failure on his part.

In 1883, when celebrations were held to recognize Bright's twenty-five years as Birmingham's representative, praise came from all segments of British society, from both friends and foes, and from the United States and Latin America. Bright was praised for his humanity, earnestness, consistency, trustworthiness, courage, independence, fidelity to principle, love of freedom and justice, and trust in the people. Although he acknowledged his role in accomplishing many reforms, he thought that there was much reform yet to be accomplished. He advocated the curtailment of the power of the House of Lords, disestablishment of the Church, economic and political reform in India to prepare for its eventual independence, tax and military cuts, and educational reform.

Despite Bright's many successes and the general approbation in which he was held, Bright remained a modest person. When he died, he requested that he be buried in the graveyard of the Friends Meeting House in Rochdale. The legacy he left was the model of a principled and moral individual who had, at great personal cost, spent his life working to improve the conditions of life in Great Britain and its dependencies.

—*John R. Bylsma*

FURTHER READING

Ausubel, Herman. *John Bright: Victorian Reformer*. New York: John Wiley & Sons, 1966. A well-written, relatively short biography that concentrates almost exclusively on Bright's public life. Ausubel argues that Bright was less self-confident than his public image portrayed. Illustrated by several cartoons from *Punch*.

Briggs, Asa. *Victorian People: A Reassessment of Persons and Themes, 1851-1867*. Chicago: University of Chicago Press, 1955. Rev. ed., 1972. Chapter 8, "John Bright and the Creed of Reform," discusses Bright's reform activity between the 1840's and the 1867 Reform Bill. It places Bright within the context of the "Manchester School" (liberal advocates of free trade) and middle-class politics.

Bright, John. *Diaries of John Bright*. Edited by R. A. J. Walling. New York: William Morrow, 1931. Bright's entries were intended as an aid to his memory, not publication. This edited volume provides valuable insights into Bright's character and his evaluation of contemporaries.

Joyce, Patrick. *Democratic Subjects: The Self and the Social in Nineteenth-Century England*. New York: Cambridge University Press, 1994. An examination of class and identity in nineteenth century English society, focusing on the lives of John Bright, whom the author portrays as a typical member of the emerging middle class, and Lancashire poet Edwin Waugh, who typifies the working class.

McCord, Norman. *The Anti-Corn Law League*. London: Allen & Unwin, 1958. An excellent analysis of the origin, development, and activities of the League as a political pressure group. Bright's role in the League is evaluated.

Pickering, Paul A., and Alex Tyrell. *The People's Bread: A History of the Anti-Corn Law League*. London: Leicester University Press, 2000. Supplements McCord's book (see above) with new information and a detailed analysis of the League's members and activities.

Read, Donald. *Cobden and Bright: A Victorian Political Partnership*. New York: St. Martin's Press, 1968. A good discussion of both the similarities and the differences between the two men. Argues that Cobden was the more important and more radical—an assessment that other historians dispute.

Robbins, Keith. *John Bright*. London: Routledge & Kegan Paul, 1979. A good chronological discussion of Bright's life that provides an analysis of his intellectual and personal characteristics and his contributions. Robbins regards Bright as "the most successful political figure of the Victorian Age."

_____. *Politicians, Diplomacy, and War in Modern British History*. London: Hambledon Press, 1994. Bright is included in this study of modern British politicians who sought the "high moral ground" in domestic or international politics. Robbins offers an appreciation of Bright's political career.

Sturgis, James L. *John Bright and the British Empire*. London: Athlone Press, 1969. A topical discussion of Bright's attitude toward Ireland, India, and the colonies. There is almost no discussion of foreign affairs.

Trevelyan, George Macaulay. *The Life of John Bright*. 2d ed. Boston: Houghton Mifflin, 1925. Reprint. London: Routledge/Thoemmes Press, 1993. A descriptive biography with many quotations from Bright's journals, letters, and speeches. Despite Trevelyan's tendency to overpraise his father's friend, this is still a very readable and interesting biography.

SEE ALSO: Richard Cobden; William Edward Forster; Sir Robert Peel.

RELATED ARTICLES in *Great Events from History: The Nineteenth Century, 1801-1900:* June 15, 1846: British Parliament Repeals the Corn Laws; August, 1867: British Parliament Passes the Reform Act of 1867.

SIR ISAAC BROCK

British military leader and colonial administrator

A career officer in the British army, Brock saw relatively little combat action. However, his victories during the early months of the War of 1812 may have preserved Upper Canada from being conquered by the United States, and he is consequently remembered as the "man who saved Canada."

BORN: October 6, 1769; St. Peter Port, Guernsey, Channel Islands

DIED: October 13, 1812; Queenston, Upper Canada (now in Ontario, Canada)

AREAS OF ACHIEVEMENT: Military, warfare and conquest

EARLY LIFE

Sir Isaac Brock was born on Guernsey, one of Great Britain's Channel Islands off the coast of France, in the year 1769—the same year in which both Napoleon Bonaparte and the duke of Wellington were born. His parents, John and Elizabeth Brock, were moderately wealthy, in part the result of his maternal grandfather's service as lieutenant bailiff on Guernsey. Brock's own father was a midshipman in the Royal Navy when he was born. He was the eighth son of the family's fourteen children, ten of whom lived to maturity. His family was, to a significant degree, a military one. In addition to Isaac and his father, several brothers also served in Britain's army and navy.

As a youth, Isaac demonstrated both a military bearing and significant athletic skills. As an adult, he was a large man, estimated at well over six feet in height, and one who became significantly overweight with time. Considered to have a forceful personality, he could also exhibit significant sociability and loyalty. Though he never married, Brock was also impressive in his gentlemanly interactions with women.

Brock's early schooling took place first on the island and then in Southampton, England. He also spent a year studying French in Rotterdam on the Continent. Brock was proud to own a large collection of books, from which he continued his studies, and was considered significantly self-educated by his friends and peers.

In March, 1785, Brock entered the army at the age of fifteen, purchasing an ensignsy in the Eighth Regiment of Foot. Six years later, he joined the Forty-ninth Regiment of Foot with the rank of captain. He remained with that regiment through the rest of his military career. During those early years, his regiment was posted at Barbados and Jamaica in the Caribbean. After he survived a near-fatal fever and was challenged to a duel, he resigned from the regiment and returned to England.

LIFE'S WORK

In October, 1797, Brock purchased a commission as a lieutenant colonel in the Forty-ninth Regiment, When he rejoined his former regiment, he became its lieutenant colonel. By that time, poor leadership had reduced his regiment to what the duke of York considered one of the worst in the British army. Exhibiting the discipline for which he would become known, as well as showing clear concern for the health and welfare of the troops, Brock restored both pride and quality to the regiment.

At the end of the eighteenth century, Great Britain was engaged in what would develop into a long series of wars with the French under Napoleon I. Between August and October of 1799, the British army and navy, under the command of the duke of York, began a campaign in the Netherlands to wrest that region from France and its Dutch allies. In a series of indecisive actions at Egmont-op-Zee on the coast on October 2, Brock received his first battle wound when he was struck in the neck. The only additional action he saw during that period was in 1801, when his regiment participated in Admiral Lord Horatio Nelson's attack on Copenhagen, Denmark.

In August, 1802, Brock and his men were sent to Quebec City in Canada. A portion of his regiment at Fort George was serving under Lieutenant Colonel Roger Sheaffe, an unusually tough disciplinarian whose attitude angered the men to the point at which a mutiny became imminent. Brock became aware of the threat, and upon his arrival at Fort George, he arrested the ringleaders, seven of whom were subsequently executed. Upon assuming command, Brock immediately relaxed some of his predecessor's harsher regulations.

In 1805, Brock was promoted to full colonel. He remained at Quebec until 1810, by which time relations between Britain's Canadian territories and the United States were deteriorating. During the following year, he was promoted to major general and placed in command of British troops stationed in Upper Canada. In June, 1812, war broke out between the United States and Great Britain. Brock had some 1,200 troops serving directly under him, as well as approximately 11,000 Canadian militiamen. One month later, an American army of 600 regulars and 1,600 militia under General William Hull, the governor of Michigan Territory, entered Canada from Detroit and occupied the town of Sandwich (later known as Windsor). Brock set out from York (later known as Toronto) to meet Hull's threat.

While these events transpired, the American fort at Michilimackinac on the northern tip of the Michigan peninsula fell to the British. Fearing he could not defend his position, Hull retreated to his base at Fort Detroit. Brock shortly afterward reached Amherstburg, immediately east of Sandwich, and there met with the Shawnee chief Tecumseh, with whom he formed an alliance.

The contrast between Tecumseh and Brock was startling: Brock towered over Tecumseh, who was dressed in deerskin and moccasins. However, they were united in their desire to remove the Americans from what was then a frontier region. Brock held council with his aides, and despite warnings of caution, decided that nothing was gained by delay and decided to attack Hull's position. With 300 regular troops, 400 militiamen, and some 800 Indians, Brock and Tecumseh crossed the Thames River and laid siege to the fort. Although his troops held a relatively strong position and outnumbered his opponents, Hull surrendered to Brock on August 16. Hull's surrender dealt a significant blow to American morale, while simultaneously boosting that of the British and Canadians. Hull was later convicted of cowardice in a celebrated court-martial and was sentenced to be executed, but President James Madison set aside his execution.

Meanwhile, three thousand American troops under the command of General Stephen Van Rensselaer crossed the Niagara River from New York in October and attempted to occupy the Canadian village of Queenston. Driven back by a small British force, they instead captured a battery on the heights overlooking the town. On October 13, 1812, cannon fire awakened Brock, who had been sleeping at Fort George. Upon arriving at the scene of the battle, Brock attempted to rally his troops—particularly the York Volunteers, his favorite unit—to charge the battery atop the hill. Before the men could become organized, however, their position was overrun and Brock was forced to retreat, while suffering a hand wound in the process.

While trying to rally his troops in the heroic tradition of British officers, Brock attempted to lead his men a second time against the American position. However, the fact that he was wearing a bright red uniform with an officer's plumed hat made him a clear target, and he was instantly killed when he was shot in the chest by a sharpshooter's bullet. Shortly afterward, his body was temporarily interred at Fort George. Some years later, he was permanently interred near the spot where he had been killed.

SIGNIFICANCE

Controversy has long surrounded the question of Brock's place in history. His own perspective is ironic, as he considered the War of 1812 as a minor conflict in a backwater colony of the growing British Empire. His own goal was to serve with the duke of Wellington in Europe. His major military accomplishment—for which he was knighted—was his capture of Fort Detroit and its inept commander. His death was the result of an ill-conceived charge. Although his major military actions were not stellar, there is no question about his imagination in planning the strategy for war, his courage, and his ability to command.

Brock's death, though a blow to the morale of his men, nevertheless provided inspiration both to the British and Canadian forces and created a legend for the future of the nascent country. Arguably, his leadership was instrumental in preventing the United States from overrunning Upper Canada. If such a campaign had been successful, it might have resulted in the incorporation of the region into the United States. Brock's monument, placed near the site of his death on Queenston Heights, stands nearly two hundred feet high and continues to reflect the admiration still felt by Canadians for the man who died in their service.

—*Richard Adler*

FURTHER READING

Berton, Pierre. *The Invasion of Canada. 1812-1813.* 2 vols. Boston: Little, Brown, 1980. Popular account of the War of 1812 by a major Canadian writer, who is known for his emphasis on nationalism and the Canadian character.

Borneman, Walter. *1812: The War That Forged a Nation.* New York: HarperCollins, 2004. The author's thesis is that despite the internal controversy over the necessity of the war, its prosecution ultimately united the American states into a national entity. Emphasis is placed on the diplomatic background for the conflict.

Fryer, Mary. *Bold, Brave and Born to Lead: Major General Isaac Brock and the Canadas.* Toronto: Dundurn Press, 2004. A biographical account of the general, his ambitions and military prowess.

Hitsman, J. Mackay, and Donald Graves, eds. *The Incredible War of 1812: A Military History.* Toronto: Robin Brass Studio, 2000. Updated version of Hitsman's work on the subject, with emphasis on military aspects of the War of 1812.

Malcomson, Robert. *A Very Brilliant Affair: The Battle of Queenstown Heights, 1812.* Annapolis, Md.: Naval Institute Press, 2003. A detailed account of the battle in which Brock lost his life.

Turner, Wesley. *British Generals in the War of 1812: High Command in the Canadas.* Montreal: McGill-Queens University Press, 1999. Analysis of the five British generals, including Brock, who participated in the war. Addresses the question of why Brock remains the best-known British officer of the war, despite his death in battle.

SEE ALSO: Napoleon I; Oliver Hazard Perry; Tecumseh; Duke of Wellington.

RELATED ARTICLES in *Great Events from History: The Nineteenth Century, 1801-1900:* June 18, 1812-December 24, 1814: War of 1812; October 5, 1813: Battle of the Thames.

THE BRONTË SISTERS

English novelists

The three Brontë sisters rank among the major English novelists of the Victorian era. Charlotte Brontë wrote four novels, the first of which, Jane Eyre, *made her instantly famous. Emily was both a poet and a novelist; her novel* Wuthering Heights *remains a modern favorite of both readers and filmmakers. Anne Brontë published two novels,* Agnes Grey *and* The Tenant of Wildfell Hall, *during her short life and died before she reached her full potential as a writer.*

CHARLOTTE BRONTË

BORN: April 21, 1816; Thornton, Yorkshire, England
DIED: March 31, 1855; Haworth, Yorkshire, England

EMILY BRONTË

BORN: July 30, 1818; Thornton, Yorkshire, England
DIED: December 19, 1848; Haworth, Yorkshire, England

ANNE BRONTË

BORN: January 17, 1820; Thornton, Yorkshire, England
DIED: May 28, 1849; Scarborough, England
AREA OF ACHIEVEMENT: Literature

EARLY LIVES

The father of the Brontë sisters, Patrick Brontë (BRAHN-tee) was a powerful force in his family's personal and creative life. He was born in Ireland in 1777 and overcame poverty to attend Cambridge University in England. The self-disciplined, hard-working young man became a minister in the Church of England and married Maria Branwell in 1812. In seven years, they had six children: Maria, Elizabeth, Charlotte, Patrick Branwell, Emily Jane, and Anne. In 1820 Patrick moved his family to Haworth, England, where he was appointed minister for life. Maria died of cancer in 1821 at the age of thirty-eight, leaving Patrick with six small children.

Even after they became adults, the Brontë sisters seldom ventured far from Haworth, the center of their creative lives. The Brontë home was cold and damp, and the town suffered from the effects of open sewers and industrial pollution. Cholera and tuberculosis were common, and the average life expectancy in Haworth was only twenty-six years. It was a rough provincial town, and the family, while respected and well liked, had little social contact with townsfolk. The Brontë children turned to each other for companionship and entertainment. Although early Brontë scholarship portrayed Patrick as a tyrannical father, later research presented him more favorably. Defying the patriarchal values of his day, he educated his daughters and encouraged them in their creative efforts.

After Maria died, Patrick sent his four oldest daughters to the Clergy Daughters' School at Cowan Bridge, probably the model for Charlotte's vivid portrayal of the harsh conditions in the fictional Jane Eyre's boarding school. After the two oldest girls became ill, Patrick brought his daughters home. Within a five-week period in 1825, Maria and Elizabeth died from tuberculosis. During the next six years Patrick educated the children himself.

The children found the outside world intimidating. In 1831 Charlotte went to Roe Head, a private school that she first attended as a student and then later returned to briefly as a teacher. Emily and Anne attended Roe Head for a short time but were unhappy away from home. In 1842 Charlotte and Emily attended a private school in Belgium, where Charlotte remained until 1844. The three sisters sometimes worked as governesses, which enriched their writing by exposing them to diverse social situations and giving them insights into aspects of human nature from which they were sheltered in Haworth.

LIVES' WORK

While the young Brontë women found their ventures out into the world emotionally trying, their intellectual and creative lives blossomed in Haworth. In 1826 Patrick gave Branwell twelve toy soldiers. Each child chose a soldier and named it after a personal hero and then wrote and performed plays about the character. They set their stories in an imaginary African kingdom called Angria; later Emily and Anne created their own realm, which they named Gondal, and located it on an island in the Pacific Ocean.

Charlotte Brontë. (Library of Congress)

The sisters' fantasy worlds satisfied their emotional needs more than their bleak surroundings did. Charlotte did not free herself from her obsession with Angria until 1839, and Anne and Emily were still writing about Gondal in 1845. Angria and Gondal served as a deep well for the Brontës' creative lives. They populated their kingdoms with people from history and from contemporary society pages. They laid out cities, devised geographies and drew maps, wrote their kingdoms' histories, and incorporated the social and political controversies of their own day into Angria and Gondal. They painted and wrote poetry, drama, prose, and historical narrative.

Charlotte had a wider audience in mind. In 1845, she persuaded Emily and Anne to join her in publishing a collection of their poetry, entitled *Poems by Currer, Ellis, and Acton Bell* (1846). Because the patriarchal Victorian society seldom took female writers seriously, they published their book under male-sounding pseudonyms: Currer (Charlotte), Ellis (Emily), and Acton (Anne) Bell. Even before the poems appeared, the three sisters decided that each, using their pseudonyms, would publish a novel, to be published jointly in a three-volume work. Anne wrote *Agnes Grey* (1847), which drew on her experiences as a governess. Emily contributed *Wuthering Heights* (1847), whose dramatic characters and emotionally charged plot derived from her Gondal writings. Charlotte's *The Professor* (1857) was enriched by her work as a teacher, especially from her years in Belgium.

Publisher Thomas Cautley Newby refused *The Professor* but published Anne's and Emily's novels. Anne's book was warmly accepted by the public. She was concerned with incorporating morality and religion into daily life. *Agnes Grey* provided trenchant criticism of a society that allowed mediocrity to triumph over excellence and that tolerated an ignorant and insensitive upper class that had little understanding of the hard-working, decent people that surrounded and served them.

The first reaction to *Wuthering Heights* was that it was powerful but coarse and disturbing. In the novel, Heathcliff, a wild, abandoned child, is brought into the home—Wuthering Heights—of Mr. Earnshaw, a member of the local gentry, who has two children, Hindley and Cathy. Heathcliff and Cathy form a deep bond, but Hindley and other members of the local gentry scorn and abuse Heathcliff. Through a misunderstanding he thinks Cathy has turned against him as well; he flees, promising to avenge himself on his tormenters. He returns as a rich man and carries out his vow of revenge, destroying his own happiness and the lives of the people around him. In images that disturbed many conventional Christians, Heathcliff and Cathy find peace after their deaths, reunited as spirits wandering the moors they had loved.

Charlotte put *The Professor* aside (it was not published until after her death) and began work on *Jane Eyre* (1847). Jane Eyre, intelligent and self-reliant but poor, becomes the governess at Thornfield, the home of Edward Rochester. Her courage and intelligence attracts the aggressive, restless Rochester, who defies class distinctions by asking Eyre to marry him. At the altar Jane learns the secret of Thornfield's mysterious locked tower. As a young man Rochester had been tricked into marrying a hopelessly insane woman, now locked in the tower and cared for by a companion. Eyre, despite her love for Rochester, refuses to compromise her morality and flees. She later returns, summoned mysteriously by Rochester's voice. She finds him blinded after trying in vain to save his wife when she set fire to Thornfield. Eyre marries Rochester and both find peace and love.

THE BRONTË SISTERS' MAJOR WORKS

ANNE BRONTË
1847 *Agnes Grey*
1848 *The Tenant of Wildfell Hall*

CHARLOTTE BRONTË
1847 *Jane Eyre*
1849 *Shirley*
1853 *Villette*
1857 *The Professor*

EMILY BRONTË
1847 *Wuthering Heights*

Jane Eyre went into its third printing within months of its publication, and Charlotte's remarkable success as Currer Bell fueled interest in Acton and Ellis Bell. When critics began to speculate that all three books were written by one person, Charlotte and Anne went to London to prove to their publisher that they had separate identities. Emily's name became known to the outside world after her death.

People wanted more books from the young writers, but tragedy struck, leaving readers to wonder what the Brontës could have accomplished if they had lived into maturity. Branwell, a dissipated youth weakened from drinking and drugs, died in September, 1848. At his funeral, Emily, probably suffering from tuberculosis, caught a cold and died suddenly on December 19, 1848. In January, 1849, Anne, after finishing *The Tenant of Wildfell Hall* (1848), was diagnosed with tuberculosis and died on May 28, 1849.

Charlotte was devastated by these deaths, but she found relief in writing. Some critics believed that Charlotte intended *Shirley* (1849) as a tribute to Emily as she might have been had she lived. The novel deals with industrial conflict and advocates giving women the opportunity to develop their potential and exercise some control over their lives. Charlotte also wrote *Villette* (1853), which explored some of the themes she dealt with in *The Professor*.

On June 29, 1854, Charlotte married her father's curate, Arthur Bell Nicholls. She became pregnant, and, already physically frail, her health quickly deteriorated.

She died on March 31, 1855. Arthur stayed on to care for Patrick until Patrick's death in 1861 and then returned to his native Ireland and remarried in 1864.

SIGNIFICANCE

The Brontës achieved their place in literary history by overcoming the obstacles of genteel poverty, a rough provincial community, and the bleak landscape of the Yorkshire moors. The artistic and intelligent children lost themselves in fantasy realms that seemed richer and more vivid than the reality of their surroundings. Although the sisters found the outside world intimidating, they were bold and challenging in their creative lives. They believed in moral courage and, like Jane Eyre, in confronting and surmounting all obstacles, including patriarchal restraints on women. Their novels provided exemplary models of strong women confronting emotionally charged situations and dealing successfully with the pains and pleasures of everyday life.

A twentieth century critic called Anne Brontë's *Agnes Grey* English literature's most perfect prose narrative and believed that Anne would have ranked with Jane Austen had she lived another ten years. She died at the age of thirty, however, and has continued to be overshadowed by her famous sisters.

For many years Charlotte Brontë's critical and popular success outshone Emily, whose *Wuthering Heights* troubled many readers. Emily's book challenged conventional morality and religious beliefs. Its twisted hero, Heathcliff, a moral monster, has disturbing appeal and turns a story of cruelty and revenge into a passionate love story. Its gothic overtones provided lasting images of ghostly lovers wandering the moors, images with great appeal to twentieth century readers and filmmakers.

Since its publication, Charlotte Brontë's *Jane Eyre* has retained its important place in the British literary canon and has stood as an inspiring story of a plain woman's moral courage, as one of the great tragic love stories of literary history, and as an early and powerful plea for women's liberation. It was a major source for the literary realism that became dominant later in the nineteenth century.

—*Martha E. Pemberton*

FURTHER READING

Barker, Juliet. *The Brontës*. New York: St. Martin's Press, 1994. This well-researched and clearly written book covers the entire Brontë family and carefully dispels the many myths and misunderstandings that have grown up around them.

_____, ed. *The Brontës: A Life in Letters*. Woodstock, N.Y.: Overlook Press, 1998. This collection of newly discovered letters and manuscripts written by the Brontë sisters re-creates a sense of their life and personalities.

Benvenuto, Richard. *Emily Brontë*. Boston: Twayne, 1982. A brief biography of the Brontë sister whose life remains most obscure. Only three of her letters survive, but Benvenuto stayed within the documentary record to provide a convincing portrait of her life and personality.

Bloom, Harold, ed. *The Brontë Sisters*. Philadelphia: Chelsea House, 2000. One of a series of "Biocritiques" by Bloom, professor of humanities at Yale University and professor of English at New York University. This volume includes biographies of the three sisters and critical analysis of their work by nineteenth- and twentieth century critics.

Chitham, Edward. *A Life of Anne Brontë*. Oxford, England: Blackwell, 1991. This book covers Anne's short life and shows that although she continues to be overshadowed by her famous sisters, she was developing her own voice when she died.

Gaskell, Elizabeth Cleghorn. *The Life of Charlotte Brontë*. London: Smith, Elder, 1857. An invaluable source because Gaskell, a friend of Charlotte Brontë, interviewed the author's father, husband, and friends and had access to Charlotte's correspondence. Despite its importance, it has also been the source of some of the misconceptions of Patrick's role in the family.

Hopkins, Annette B. *The Father of the Brontës*. New York: Greenwood Press, 1968. A good description of Patrick Brontë's life and personality as he changed from an outgoing young man to a reclusive elder. He strikes people today as a stern, authoritarian figure, but he gave his daughters remarkable freedom to develop as artists.

Miller, Lucasta. *The Brontë Myth*. New York: Alfred A. Knopf, 2003. Miller traces the careers of the Brontës to show how they became cultural icons, with each generation creating a new mythology about them to reflect changing social values. She aims to strip away the myths and replace them with the facts of the three sisters' lives.

SEE ALSO: Jane Austen; Elizabeth Barrett Browning; George Eliot; Christina Rossetti.

RELATED ARTICLES in *Great Events from History: The Nineteenth Century, 1801-1900:* 1814: Scott Publishes *Waverley*; October 1-December 15, 1856: Flaubert Publishes *Madame Bovary*.

HENRY BROUGHAM
Scottish politician

Known as a reform politician during his British parliamentary career, Brougham helped in the reformation of the law and began the spread of universal education.

BORN: September 19, 1778; Edinburgh, Scotland
DIED: May 7, 1868; Cannes, France
ALSO KNOWN AS: Henry Peter Brougham (full name); First Baron Brougham and Vaux
AREAS OF ACHIEVEMENT: Law, government and politics

EARLY LIFE

The father of Henry Peter Brougham (brewm), also named Henry Brougham, was a squire from Westmoreland in England. He married Eleanor Syme, the widow of a Scottish minister and niece of the noted historian William Robertson. Her connections led the young Henry—a boy of tremendous talent who spoke clearly in his eighth month and read by the age of two years—to be reared and educated in Edinburgh, which was then still basking in the glow of the Scottish Enlightenment of the eighteenth century. Brougham remained a man of that background all of his life.

Brougham left Edinburgh High School at the head of his class in 1791, and while attending the University of Edinburgh, the best in Great Britain at the time, displayed an interest and ability in mathematics and the natural sciences; throughout his life he studied mathematics for relaxation. While at university and for the decade after he left in 1795, he and a group of talented and like-minded friends explored all topics and discussed new ideas.

In the Scotland of the day, young men of talent and ambition who lacked connections with the dominant Tory Party had few chances, and Brougham, an excellent speaker, chose law as the career least affected by this problem, though his heart was never fully in it. Though he passed the bar in 1800, he did not prosper. With his friends and during the time his languishing legal career gave him, he founded the *Edinburgh Review*, a quarterly periodical devoted to the topics of the day and reviews of books.

As a result of Brougham's connection, which lasted his lifetime, and an article he later contributed in 1808, the *Edinburgh Review* became the leading Whig journal of the nineteenth century. His wide-ranging interests led him to be a cofounder of the Edinburgh Academy of Physics and a leading member of the Speculative Society, a debating group. He also wrote *An Inquiry into the Colonial Policy of the European Powers* (1803), which, because of the section condemning slavery, brought him to the attention of British politicians.

Lacking progress in his legal career, Brougham joined his friends and, as had many Scots both before and since, made the journey to London to seek his fortune. Though enrolled at Lincoln's Inn to study English law and later working in the office of a future judge, Brougham still could not put his heart into the law and never was well versed in it. Rather, his interests turned to politics. The two political parties of his day—Whigs and Tories—often resembled separate connections of aristocratic and gentry families more than groups pursuing policies flowing from principles, though the Whigs had a tradition of defending various liberties that could be traced back to the troubles of the seventeenth century and progressives could be found in the generally conservative Tory Party.

Brougham spent his first few years in London working with William Wilberforce's Tory circle in the campaign for the abolition of slavery, and it appeared that Brougham, the radical and future lord chancellor of a reforming government, was headed for the ranks of the Tories. Nevertheless, by 1806 Brougham was more often found in Whig circles and received the first tangible sign of Whig favor when he was appointed secretary to a special mission to Portugal.

Back in England, Brougham represented certain Liverpool merchants before the House of Commons in an effort to change the government's policy interfering with trade with neutral nations as part of the Napoleonic Wars; though unsuccessful, he displayed his brilliant oratory, making him known to the political nation. This event cemented his connection with the commercial and industrial classes in England, a connection that provided the backbone of the reform movements in politics for the rest of his life. Brougham became the point at which the Whig defense of ancient liberties joined with these increasingly powerful groups. Brougham, unfortunately, threw his lot in with the Whigs at just the moment they were losing power, finding themselves out of office from 1807 to 1830. Nevertheless, as an opposition, the Whigs badly needed to have an effective speaker in the House of Commons, and in 1810 Brougham was found a seat at Camelford through the patronage of the duke of Bedford.

Upon entering Parliament, Brougham, a tall, thin man with long limbs, prominent cheekbones, and dark hair, was not impressive in appearance. Two characteristics stood out to contemporaries: his piercing eyes, which he used to good effect in his speeches, and his turned-up nose, which *Punch* used to good effect in its caricatures of him. In conversation, as opposed to public orations, friends found his sharp tongue bearable because of his amiable nature and obvious goodwill. Of his personal life little is known. He married Mary Ann Spalding, a rich widow, in 1819, and they had two daughters, neither of whom survived to adulthood; she predeceased him in 1865.

LIFE'S WORK

With his election to the House of Commons, Brougham entered into the arena where his talents as a knowledgeable orator could best be displayed, but his parliamentary life, legal career, and reforming interests were all of a piece. As a lawyer, Brougham had several moments of brilliance and fame. In 1811, with the events of the French Revolution and the Napoleonic Wars in mind, the Tory government determined to suppress any efforts within England that smacked of reform or revolution and prosecuted for seditious libel Leigh and John Hunt for a publication attacking military discipline.

Henry Brougham. (Library of Congress)

Brougham's successful defense brought the support of various radicals to the Whigs, as well as enhancing the Whig tradition of defending traditional liberties. His reputation was firmly established by his relationship with Queen Caroline. Caroline, partner in a disastrous and broken marriage with the Prince Regent, the future George IV, took advice from Brougham as well as naming him her attorney general when she became queen in 1820. When George tried to divorce her, Brougham's defense before the House of Lords brought him enormous popularity in the kingdom for opposing the "corruption" of an extravagant king with notorious morals and helped the Whigs in their pose as the party of reform.

As the spokesperson for reform and the defender of liberties, Brougham was perhaps the most popular politician in England, a popularity culminating in 1830. Since his entrance into the House of Commons, he had represented first Camelford, next Winchelsea, then Knaresborough—all small boroughs under the control of Whig magnates. In 1829, his reputation as a reformer led to an electoral victory in Yorkshire, the largest and least controlled constituency in England. Brougham's victory justified him in his belief that he was the spokesperson for all reformers.

As a parliamentarian Brougham brought his Scottish background, utilitarian perspectives, and critical eye to bear on the confused and confusing jungle of English law, and reforming that jungle occupied much of his life. During a famous six-hour speech in the House of Commons in 1828, he rehearsed an enormous litany of problems, most of which were eliminated within the next generation.

Universal education, another of Brougham's goals, he pursued both within and without Parliament. In 1816, he succeeded in getting the House of Commons to appoint a committee to examine education of the poor, and, during the investigations, Brougham uncovered that endowments were often misused. Brougham helped establish mechanics' institutes for the education of working people, a scheme he furthered by forming the Society for the Diffusion of Useful Knowledge to produce inexpensive pamphlets. Brougham also helped set up London University during the late 1820's. He submitted several bills to Parliament during the 1830's to establish a system of national education, something not accomplished until the twentieth century.

Though a brilliant and effective speaker in the House of Commons, Brougham came to have a reputation which prevented colleagues from trusting him. He made speeches in which he claimed his party's support when no such support existed. He changed positions, intrigued for power (and sometimes profit), and always sought to garner all the limelight. As a critic of Tory government, he was without equal, but the Whigs, either in or out of government, could not give him their full confidence. Within six months of his great triumph in the election for Yorkshire, the "tribune of the people" had accepted a patent of nobility and abandoned any realistic claim to be able to speak for the people. Contemporaries saw him as unsteady and untrustworthy, too argumentative and superficial, an intriguer without moral fiber, a man whose character had fatal flaws.

In 1830, the long period of Tory government ended and the Whigs, under Lord Grey, prepared to assume office, but what should have been Brougham's greatest moment never occurred. First offered the office of attorney general in the new government, he declined and threatened to ruin the Whigs' opportunity to govern. The Whig leadership knew that Brougham was too unsteady in his party loyalty to be their spokesperson in the House of Commons and too vain to serve under another there, so, after a tense week of discussions, Brougham was made Lord Chancellor and raised to the peerage as Baron Brougham and Vaux, which meant that he sat in the House of Lords and could cause no trouble to the government in the more important House of Commons. With this decision to accept a peerage, Brougham removed himself from his natural arena, the House of Commons, and never, then or later, could play the role in government that he had long imagined and anticipated.

During his four years in government, Brougham worked diligently to clean up the backlog of cases in the Chancery and to streamline its procedures, a task he largely accomplished. In matters of law reform, he established the Judicial Committee of the Privy Council—his major reform accomplishment—which heard appeals from throughout the vast British Empire.

Following the end of the Whig ministry in 1834 (Brougham's intriguing helped to bring about that end), Brougham continued in public life for nearly three decades but without the influence he had enjoyed earlier. For several years he sought greater power within Whig circles, but his reputation for ambition and intrigue dogged him in all of his parliamentary efforts at organization or leadership. He was not, however, as one of his enemies stated, "a political Ishmael." As a member of the House of Lords he lacked a constituency and, though he often opposed the Whigs during the 1830's, by the 1840's he settled into the role of an active and informed lord taking an interest in selected parliamentary business.

Brougham was active as a judge in the House of Lords and especially in the Judicial Committee of the Privy Council. He maintained an interest in other legal reforms, as, for example, divorce, where in the House of Lords he continually brought in evidence and asked for statistics, activities that kept the issue alive until Lord Palmerston's government passed the Matrimonial Causes Act in 1857. He served as president of the Law Amendment Association, founded in 1844, and as first president from 1857 until 1865 of the National Association for Promotion of Social Science, an organization of reformers interested in all aspects of English life. Articles and reviews on the wide range of topics that had always interested him continued to pour forth, though nothing of lasting value materialized. He spent increasing amounts of time at his house in Cannes, and there he died and was buried in 1868.

SIGNIFICANCE

Henry Brougham was one of many reformers disgusted with an England that had progressed little in a century and a half despite the growth of its world power and industrial life. His criticisms helped end that England. Being a critic and almost always out of political power meant that many accomplishments were negative—bad laws not enacted, administrative decisions abandoned—but Brougham also brought about significant change. The structure of politics being fluid, ministers often adopted his proposals in order to stop his criticisms.

Brougham's work for the abolition of slavery well represents the moral tone of the nineteenth century, and he spoke for the desires of the growing business classes for a society based on merit, restricted government, and respect for the individual. By uniting this moral tone and these classes to the aristocratic Whigs, he contributed to what would become the Liberal Party. Neither law nor education was a glamorous area in which to make a reputation, but Brougham, nevertheless, ridiculed the abuses and suggested alternatives, laying a foundation in both subjects upon which others could build.

As a result of Brougham's efforts, formal education was no longer limited to the Anglican landowning class, and the way to universal education was charted, certainly his most lasting contribution to British life. On a different level, a small carriage designed for him became very popular, and his name became attached to it. All of this contributed to making him the most popular man in England during the 1820's, a popularity he used well. As a founder of the *Edinburgh Review* and as a master of parliamentary debate in a century that valued such, Brougham stands in that select circle that made public life, and Parliament in particular, the focus of attention by most of the kingdom and led the British to seek change through peaceful politics, not violent revolution.

—Allen Horstman

FURTHER READING

Aspinall, Arthur. *Lord Brougham and the Whig Party*. New York: Longmans, Green, 1927. Reprint. Hamden, Conn.: Archon Books, 1972. A political study of Brougham that assumes much knowledge of the period and places less emphasis on reforms of law and education. Brougham's relationship with the Whigs is seen as erratic.

Bagehot, Walter. "The Character of Lord Brougham." In *The English Constitution and Other Political Essays*. New York: D. Appleton, 1884. Written late in Brougham's life by a leading political commentator, who does a fine job of catching the spirit of the times and Brougham's challenges to that spirit.

Ford, Trowbridge H. *Henry Brougham and His World: A Biography*. 2 vols. Chichester, England: B. Rose, 1995-2001. A more recent biography, written by an author who has published several articles on Brougham. The biography focuses on Brougham's legal reforms as well as his political career.

Hawes, Frances. *Henry Brougham*. London: Jonathan Cape, 1957. Well-written popular biography covering important events but little detail of political struggles. Good in overall interpretation.

Huch, Ronald K. *Henry, Lord Brougham: The Later Years, 1830-1868—The "Great Actor."* Lewiston, N.Y.: Edward Mellen Press, 1993. Picks up where New's book (see below) left off. After a chapter summarizing Brougham's life through 1829, the book focuses on the later years of his life and career.

New, Chester W. *The Life of Henry Brougham to 1830*. Oxford, England: Clarendon Press, 1961. Stops at 1830 because of author's death. Detailed, factual study of major events but fails to catch Brougham's personality or reputation. A list of Brougham's contributions to the *Edinburgh Review* is included.

Sockwell, W. D. *Popularizing Classical Economics: Henry Brougham and William Ellis*. New York: St. Martin's Press, 1994. Recounts how Brougham and Ellis disseminated economic ideas to middle- and lower-class people at a time when these ideas were not well developed or widely understood. Describes how Brougham used the mechanics' institutes and the Society for the Diffusion of Useful Knowledge to provide adult education.

Stewart, Robert. *Henry Brougham, 1778-1868: His Public Career*. London: Bodley Head, 1986. A well-written and full-scale life of Brougham that also uses political background well. Discusses all major and many minor events of Brougham's life and does an excellent job of describing Brougham's energy and reputation.

Swinfen, D. B. "Henry Brougham and the Judicial Committee of the Privy Council." *Law Quarterly Review* 90 (1974): 396-411. A detailed study of Brougham's greatest achievement, the court that brought uniform justice to the empire. Brougham's role in the creation of the court as well as its early development is given good treatment.

SEE ALSO: First Earl of Durham; Lord Jeffrey; Second Viscount Melbourne; James Mill; Mary Somerville.

RELATED ARTICLES in *Great Events from History: The Nineteenth Century, 1801-1900:* October 20-30, 1822: Great Britain Withdraws from the Concert of Europe; August 28, 1833: Slavery Is Abolished Throughout the British Empire; August 28, 1857: British Parliament Passes the Matrimonial Causes Act.

GEORGE BROWN

Canadian journalist and politician

One of the most influential Canadian journalists of his time, Brown transformed the Toronto Globe *into a leading Canadian newspaper that backed political reform and was himself elected to the Canadian parliament. Through the last three decades of his life, he continued to be active in both publishing and politics.*

BORN: November 29, 1818; Alloa, Scotland
DIED: May 9, 1880; Toronto, Canada
AREAS OF ACHIEVEMENT: Journalism, government and politics

EARLY LIFE

George Brown was the third of Peter and Marianne Mackenzie Brown's nine children, three of whom died in infancy. The Browns were a closely knit family that had grown prosperous with the increasing success of Peter Brown's draper's business. The family's country home was near the Firth of Forth in Alloa, twenty miles west of Edinburgh, Scotland. It was there that George was born. The family also occupied a succession of increasingly impressive homes in Edinburgh's Hope End Park, Buccleuch Place, and Nicholson Square as George grew up. The genealogy on Marianne Brown's side of the family included such luminaries as John Baliol, John of Gaunt, and King Edward I of England.

After 1825, Brown spent most of his early life in Edinburgh. When he was old enough, he attended Edinburgh's renowned high school, where he had classmates who figured prominently in his later life in the New World, among them William and Thomas Nelson, sons of a prominent publisher, who were to become his brothers-in-law. Daniel Wilson, who later became president of the University of Toronto and a political supporter of Brown, and David Christie, who was politically active as a senator in Canada, were also among his classmates in the Edinburgh High School.

George, however, was not happy in the high school, and using the persuasive powers for which he was noted throughout his lifetime, he convinced his father that he should transfer to the Southern Academy of Edinburgh, a new school that he thought would suit him better than the more traditional high school. He became the top student in his class at Southern Academy and was designated to make the farewell speech for his graduating class. His mentor, Dr. William Gunn, introduced him on this occasion by saying that Brown not only had great enthusiasm himself but also possessed the ability to inspire enthusiasm in others.

Brown's father envisioned a professional career for his son and presumed that he would attend university. Brown, however, had different ideas. He was quick at mathematics, and he reveled in the excitement of the business world, so he persuaded his father to employ him in his draper's business, which was prospering. This turn in his career allowed Brown to go to London for a time to work with his father's agents there.

The red-headed and blue-eyed youth had just turned eighteen and was already more than six feet tall. Brown quickly became indispensable to his father, becoming a virtual partner with him in the business. Peter Brown was a man of refined sensibilities and enjoyed the company of numerous literary friends, including J. A. Lockhart (Sir Walter Scott's son-in-law), who became editor of the *Quarterly Review*.

George Brown had barely begun to make his mark in the family business when disaster struck. Shortly after the Reform Act of 1832, which Peter Brown had been active in supporting, the elder Brown was appointed Collector of Assessments for the reformed municipal administration of Edinburgh. In 1836, he was involved in the loss of twenty-eight hundred pounds of public funds, a huge amount of money in its day. The loss was attributed to bad management rather than dishonesty, but the elder Brown faced financial ruin. Friends and relatives came to his aid and enabled him to cover the loss, but he then was in their debt. When the financial Panic of 1837 followed hot on the heels of this first calamity, Brown believed that his only choice was to leave Edinburgh and try to make his fortune in the New World.

The closeness that Peter Brown and his son shared made it logical for George to accompany his father to the New World, and on April 30, 1837, they set sail aboard the *Eliza Warwick* for New York, arriving on June 10, after nearly six harrowing weeks at sea. It was a year before Peter Brown could establish in New York a residence sufficient to accommodate his wife and five other children. By that time, he and George had opened a modest draper's shop on Broadway. Peter had assiduously saved his money to bring his family to New York and to repay those who had helped him meet his obligations before he left Scotland.

As Peter's business grew, George became its representative in outlying districts and managed to get as far as

Canada on some of his business trips north of New York City. Peter Brown had by now begun to write political articles for the *Albion*, a weekly aimed at British emigrants. He soon wrote regularly for the paper and published a book, *The Fame and Glory of England Vindicated* (1842), which gained for him considerable celebrity. This literary success led directly to his decision to give up his draper's shop and begin the *British Chronicle*, an enterprise in which George was to share fully and enthusiastically. The success of this newspaper encouraged the family to emigrate from the United States to Canada in 1843 to begin publication of the *Banner*. The following year, Peter and George Brown began the Toronto *Globe*, a reform party newspaper published weekly. The *Globe* became a daily in 1853, and George Brown spent the rest of his life as the publisher of this important and widely influential newspaper, a career that catapulted him into politics.

LIFE'S WORK

The *Globe* reached a ready audience. It advocated separation of church and state and opposed the French separatist movement that was then current. By 1845, Brown was able to launch a second newspaper, the *Western Globe*, which would reach people in the remote areas of Ontario north and west of Toronto.

Because both of Brown's newspapers were unequivocal in their political stands, it was inevitable that Brown himself would be drawn into politics. Finally, in 1851, he stood for election as an independent liberal candidate from the county of Kent to the Canadian Parliament, which did not meet until August of the following year. Brown, who had served reform causes well, was elected handily and was to be a force in Canadian politics from that time forth.

Brown's attempts to curtail the political power of the Roman Catholic Church in Canada won for him considerable support from Canada West (modern Ontario), which was largely Protestant. Canada East (modern Quebec), however, opposed his attempts to weaken the hold the Church was gaining in the country. Although Brown succeeded in bringing about the secularization of the land that the Crown had granted as preserves for Protestant clergymen in Canada, he was unable to put into effect his plan to have Parliament secularize all Canadian schools, largely because of concerted opposition from the Roman Catholic forces that would be affected by such legislation.

Brown sought to overturn the provisions of the 1840 Act of Union that gave each province an equal number of representatives. He supported proportional representation and, on that platform, rebuilt the Liberal Party of Canada's sprawling West. Lack of consolidation and general political upheaval led to considerable political instability in Canada during the late 1850's. In 1858, Brown served as prime minister for two days. The French separatists were strong enough to force him from office almost immediately.

Brown did not marry until he was in his forty-fifth year. Anne, his bride, was the accomplished daughter of Thomas Nelson, the London publisher. She returned from Great Britain to Canada with him in 1862 following their wedding on November 27, at Abden House, Edinburgh, where her family lived.

Brown continued his efforts on behalf of the federal union of Canada as an active participant in the important Charlottestown and Quebec conferences of 1864. When a deadlock seemed imminent, Brown had no choice but to form a coalition with his old political rival, Prime Minister John Macdonald. Brown was willing now to bury old political grievances in order to secure the dream, original with him, of a unified Canada. Although his dream of unification was achieved, Brown disliked the terms of a renewed reciprocity treaty with the United States and, in 1865, resigned from government service to devote himself full-time to his newspaper interests, through which he could continue to be an effective and influential spokesman for the views he espoused.

Brown was never to sit in the House of Commons again. He stood for election in 1867 and was defeated. He worked tirelessly to bring about Canada's acquisition of the valuable Northwest Territories. In 1873, he became a senator. His chief contribution as a senator was in his renegotiation of a reciprocity treaty with the United States to replace the one to which he had so strenuously objected in 1865.

In his later years, Brown declined to serve as governor of Ontario and twice declined knighthood. He continued to be active in newspaper work until March 25, 1880, when a disgruntled former employee, George Bennett, whom Brown had never met, barged into his office and, obviously drunk, pulled a gun on Brown. In the ensuing struggle, the gun discharged, wounding Brown in the leg. The wound appeared superficial. After it was treated, Brown was able to walk to his carriage and go home, where he remained in seclusion, visiting with his family and doing newspaper work.

The wound, however, turned gangrenous, and after lingering for six weeks, George Brown ultimately died of gangrene on May 9, 1880. His assailant was tried and found guilty of premeditated murder. He was eventually hanged. Anne Nelson Brown returned permanently to Edinburgh after her husband's death.

SIGNIFICANCE

George Brown will long be remembered as a pioneer in the Canadian newspaper business. He was influential through both his newspaper work and his political career in bringing about the unification of Canada, a country of vast distances and far-flung outposts. Brown also fought a strenuous battle to assure the separation of church and state in Canada, a difficult task given the factionalism that was rife in the country at the time of his greatest political activity.

A polished debater from his high school days, Brown was to use this skill with astonishing effectiveness throughout his lifetime to win opposing elements to his side and to help those at opposite ends of the political spectrum to work together for the greater good of Canada through confederation.

During his lifetime, Brown came to represent the voice of reform and of liberal politics in Canada. Never one to refuse compromise if it was for the good of his country, Brown was a major force in Canadian politics for nearly forty years. His political opponents as well as his political supporters mourned his passing because they realized that the good Brown worked for was one that transcended party politics.

—*R. Baird Shuman*

FURTHER READING

Brebner, John Barlett. *Canada: A Modern History*. Rev. ed. Ann Arbor: University of Michigan Press, 1970. Although this broad history offers only slight coverage of Brown directly, it is valuable for the background it provides for the political stands that Brown took throughout his public life.

Careless, J. M. S. *Brown of "The Globe."* 2 vols. Toronto: Macmillan, 1959. The only thoroughgoing biography of Brown, this two-volume work is exhaustively and accurately researched and is the definitive biography of its subject.

_____. *Canada: A Story of Challenge*. 3d ed. Toronto: Macmillan, 1974. This history of the development of Canada as a nation presents pertinent information about Brown as a publisher and as a politician who crusaded for a united Canada.

Creighton, Donald. *The Road to Confederation: The Emergence of Canada*. Boston: Houghton Mifflin, 1965. This book focuses on the movement that Brown spearheaded and presents extensive material about Brown's continued leadership of that movement both as a newspaper publisher and as a politician.

McInnis, Edgar. *Canada: A Political and Social History*. 4th ed. Toronto: Holt, Rinehart and Winston, 1982. McInnis provides extensive direct coverage of Brown and a thorough discussion of the political arena of which he was a part.

McNaught, Kenneth. *The History of Canada*. New York: Praeger, 1970. Chapter 8 of this book, "Problems of Destiny," presents extensive coverage of Brown, whom McNaught also mentions in salient ways elsewhere in the volume.

Morton, Desmond. *A Short History of Canada*. 3d rev. ed. Toronto: McClelland & Stewart, 1997. This book provides extensive treatment of Brown and of the reform movement in Canada with which he was so crucially affiliated.

SEE ALSO: Sir John Alexander Macdonald; Alexander Mackenzie; William Lyon Mackenzie.

RELATED ARTICLES in *Great Events from History: The Nineteenth Century, 1801-1900:* June 4, 1832: British Parliament Passes the Reform Act of 1832; November 5, 1873-October 9, 1878: Canada's Mackenzie Era.

JOHN BROWN
American abolitionist

Thanks to the notoriety that Brown received from a single dramatic act of rebellion, his name has come to symbolize the struggle over the abolition of slavery in the United States. His action was the catalyst for change from polite debate and parliamentary maneuvering aimed at modification of the institution to physical violence and a direct onslaught on southern territory and the supporters of slavery.

BORN: May 9, 1800; Torrington, Connecticut
DIED: December 2, 1859; Charles Town, Virginia (now in West Virginia)
AREA OF ACHIEVEMENT: Social reform

EARLY LIFE

A native of Connecticut, John Brown was born in a state that, like many others in New England in 1800, was agriculturally exhausted and in religious turmoil. His parents, Owen and Ruth (Mills) Brown, were affected by both problems at his birth. Economically, the Brown family was barely at the subsistence level. John's father moved from job to job: farmer, carpenter, handyman. Though the family descended from the early Mayflower settlers, they were never able to capitalize on their ancestry. Religiously, Owen Brown was a harsh practitioner of the piety of his Puritan forebears, and he instilled in his son a lifelong fear and adoration of a militant and volatile God.

The elder Brown had been married twice and fathered sixteen children. His first wife, John's mother, suffered from mental disease as did others in her family. According to some accounts, John did not take well to his stepmother, but there is little evidence to support this conjecture. The peripatetic life of the family was probably more disturbing to him. When John was five, his father moved to Hudson, Ohio, following the line of the moving frontier. Again, the family was without the necessary capital to take advantage of the opportunities available in the rich Ohio Valley. His father became a herdsman and then a tanner, a vocation that the son quickly mastered. His father had some plans for his son which included sending him to Plainsfield, Massachusetts, to study for the ministry. John did not stay long, however, either because of poor preparation or because of his poor eyesight.

John Brown returned to Hudson to help his father with the cattle and the tanning shop. At the age of twenty, he married Dianthe Lusk, who bore him seven children in twelve years of married life. She, like his mother, had mental problems. Dianthe Brown died in 1831, and within a year of her passing, Brown married Mary Anne Day, then sixteen, who bore him thirteen more children in twenty-one years. Brown, possessing a modicum of education in a frontier region, became a surveyor as well as a tanner like his father. Also like his father, Brown was a mover. In 1825, he moved to Pennsylvania, cleared land, and set up what was to become a successful farm and tannery. He also became a postmaster, but still he was unsatisfied. Quick fortunes were being made in land and business speculation, and Brown sold off his holdings and moved back to Ohio. There he hoped to take advantage of land speculation and canal building contracts. He lost heavily and began pyramiding debt while turning to cattle and sheep selling. His creditors moved in on him and he was compelled to declare bankruptcy.

LIFE'S WORK

Brown's work in the woolen business brought him a partnership with another man, Simon Perkins, to establish a wool brokerage in Springfield, Massachusetts. Fluctuating prices and market instability, however, confounded his efforts to make a success of the business. He was also accused of "weighting" the packs of hides, which were sold by weight to English markets. The collapse of this last business venture was followed by numerous lawsuits, one involving sixty thousand dollars for breach of contract. Brown settled his affairs as best he could. He was fifty years old and virtually penniless, with a large family to support.

Even as a young man, Brown had learned from his father the biblical precept that it was sinful to earn one's living from the sweat of others and that slavery was wrong. In Ohio both he and his father had lent their resources to aiding the underground movement of runaway slaves. John Brown's barn at his farm in Pennsylvania was a station in that movement, and he formed a League of Gileadites among black people in Springfield to encourage them to defend both themselves and fugitive slaves.

Brown's activity in New England brought him in touch with men whose lives would never be the same after meeting him. Gerrit Smith, a New York benefactor of abolitionism who owned much of the Adirondack Mountains, was attracted to Brown. He had given land for use by runaway slaves in a small community known as North Elba. He gave Brown a farm from which he could train and educate the former slaves. Given the severe climate, short growing season, and lack of arable land in the region, not to mention Brown's spotty record as a farmer, problems developed. Brown himself declared that he felt "omnipotent" in his new role as guide and exemplar to the black people in his charge.

Within two years, however, he was in Akron, Ohio. His mind was turned to developing a grand plan for an attack on slavery. As early as 1847, he had talked about gathering a band of men from the free states to make forays into slave territory to rescue black slaves from bondage. He talked of setting up a mountain stronghold as a base of terrorist activity, but the ideas did not take coherent form until the Fugitive Slave Act, part of the Compromise of 1850, was passed. The Kansas-Nebraska Act, four years later, further agitated him and his sons, five of whom moved to the territory to help make Kansas a free state. In May, 1855, John Brown, Jr., wrote a mournful letter to his father explaining the conditions and imploring him to send arms to battle proslavery forces. Brown dispatched his family to North Elba again and set out for Kansas with a wagonload of guns and ammunition.

Brown found his sons impoverished and ill when he arrived at Osawatomie. Though he was to join the colony as a surveyor, he quickly assumed leadership of the local militia and made Free Soil a vengeance-wreaking crusade. His group fought in the ineffectual Wakarusa War and then, after the sacking of Lawrence by proslavery forces, he and his party, which included four sons and two others, ritually slaughtered five settlers at Pottawatomie. He had reached a personal turning point, viewing himself as an instrument in the hands of an angry God.

Brown's own colony was overrun and burned and one of his boys killed in retaliation. Brown now was gray in hair and features, with a bent back and glittering gray-blue eyes; he had grown a full beard that was streaked with gray, which made him appear older than his fifty-six years. His fervent attitude toward slavery fired his listeners, many of whom, such as Franklin Sanborn, Thomas W. Higginson, Theodore Parker, Gerrit Smith, G. L. Stearns, and Samuel Gridley Howe, were ripe for the leadership that Brown promised. He met with these members of the Massachusetts State Kansas Committee, and they responded with some arms and ammunition and money to take with him to Kansas again.

Kansas had no stomach for bloodshed in 1857 as it moved closer to voting the issue of free or slave, and Brown now thought of a daring plan to liberate slaves in the South itself. In the spring of 1858, he visited the colony of runaway slaves in Catham, Canada, to gain volunteers. His money gone, he turned again to Smith and the Massachusetts group. They argued for a delay, gave him some money and supplies, and Brown again headed for Kansas, this time under the name of Shubel Morgan. There he led a raid on some plantations in Missouri in which one planter was killed and some slaves liberated. Brown was now a wanted man with a bounty on his head. He headed for Canada with the slaves in tow and then proceeded east, making speeches in Cleveland and Rochester to solicit funds. Again the old

ROBERT E. LEE'S LETTER FROM HARPERS FERRY

U.S. Army colonel Robert E. Lee—the future commander of the Confederate army—led the Marine detachment that captured John Brown and ended his brief rebellion. In this letter to his wife of December 1, 1859, Lee comments on Brown's capture and Brown's wife.

I arrived here [Harpers Ferry], dearest Mary, yesterday about noon, with four companies from Fort Monroe, and was busy all the evening and night getting accommodation for the men, etc., and posting sentinels and piquets to insure timely notice of the approach of the enemy. The night has passed off quietly. The feelings of the community seem to be calmed down, and I have been received with every kindness. Mr. Fry is among the officers from Old Point. There are several young men, former acquaintances of ours, as cadets, Mr. Bingham of Custis's class, Sam Cooper, etc., but the senior officers I never met before, except Captain Howe, the friend of our Cousin Harriet R—.

I presume we are fixed here till after the 16th. To-morrow will probably be the last of Captain Brown. There will be less interest for the others, but still I think the troops will not be withdrawn till they are similarly disposed of.

Custis will have informed you that I had to go to Baltimore the evening I left you, to make arrangements for the transportation of the troops. . . . This morning I was introduced to Mrs. Brown, who, with a Mrs. Tyndall and a Mr. and Mrs. McKim, all from Philadelphia, had come on to have a last interview with her husband. As it is a matter over which I have no control I referred them to General [William B.] Taliaferro. . . .

Source: Robert E. Lee [Jr.], *Recollections and Letters of General Robert E. Lee* (New York: Doubleday, Page, 1904).

group came through with thirty-eight hundred dollars, knowing full well that Brown was bent on violence.

It was Harpers Ferry that became fixed in Brown's mind; to the commander in chief of a provisional army for liberation it was an ideal objective. The federal arsenal in the town was noted for the quality of arms and its technology since its creation in 1798. The complex of forges, shops, tool and die works, and assembly areas turned out rifles and handguns in an assembly line process that foretold mass production. John Hall of Maine had gained a contract in 1819 to turn out breech-loading rifles using his idea of interchangeable parts, and his contract was renewed yearly until 1844, when a totally new rifle plant was built to produce the Standard United States Model military rifle. The skilled workers were mostly transplanted northerners who were regarded as "foreigners" by local southerners. A canal and a railroad as well as a macadam road led to the town of three thousand, which included 1,250 free blacks and some eighty-eight slaves.

The Brown contingent of fourteen white and five black people established themselves in a farm five miles from the Ferry to lay plans for their attack. On Sunday, October 16, 1859, they marched by night down the dirt road leading to the town. By mid-morning, the men had taken both the town and its leading citizens.

Brown did not know what to do with his victory. He had control of the engine house, the federal armory, the railroad, and the town of Harpers Ferry, and the very magnitude of his success overwhelmed and confused him. He let a train continue, certainly with the knowledge that the passengers would alarm state and federal officials. He did nothing about searching out possible followers from the town population or the countryside. He had guns, powder and shells, and a well-situated natural fortress, as well as a small though very devout band of followers. Brown lost his revolutionary compass at this critical moment. His willingness to fight was not in question. Shots were fired and lives were taken until Lee's troops stormed the engine house and cut Brown down. Though he was not severely wounded, there was little recourse for his men but to surrender.

The military quickly restored order and moved Brown to prison while dispatching squads to investigate the farm that had been the band's headquarters. There they found letters and documentation that implicated Brown's northern associates in the Harpers Ferry venture. Why Brown had kept, let alone brought with him, these damning materials is uncertain. He certainly treasured his association with successful and influential men, and given his life on the margin of society, this connection was important enough to be sustained with physical evidence. Furthermore, Brown was concerned about the shifting commitment of antislavery reformers and therefore by keeping documentation he could hold them to the course. The discovery of these materials, however, proved the conspiracy case against Brown and his men and threw fear into those who had aided them.

Of the twenty-one men who had followed Brown to Harpers Ferry on October 16, only eleven remained alive. Brown had seen two of his sons killed in the melee that followed the arrival of the militia from Charlestown (modern Charles Town, West Virginia) and Lee's marines. On October 18, he was jailed in Charlestown to await indictment, which came a week later.

Brown, Aaron Stevens, Edwin Coppoc, Shields Green (the black man who had chosen to go with Brown despite the admonition and concerns of Frederick Douglass), and John Copeland were all indicted on October 25 for treason against Virginia, for conspiring with slaves to rebel, and for murder. All of them pleaded not guilty and requested separate trials. The court agreed and determined that Brown would be tried first.

The prosecution was headed by Charles Harding, state attorney for Jefferson County, and Andrew Hunter, a seasoned Charlestown attorney. The court was presided over by Judge Richard Parker, who had just begun the semiannual term of his circuit court and already had a grand jury seated. Turner had just gaveled the court to order when Brown's defense attorney read a telegram from one A. H. Lewis of Akron, Ohio, declaring that Brown's family was suffering from hereditary insanity. It proceeded to list the people on his mother's side who were known to have severe mental problems. The inference was that Brown himself was insane and therefore not fit for trial. His attorney had shown Brown the telegram and Brown admitted to his mother's death by insanity and the fact that his first wife and two of his sons were afflicted. Brown, however, rejected the plea of insanity on his behalf, though he apparently gave his attorney permission to use the document. The judge ruled out the plea on the basis that the evidence was in unreliable form. He also rejected a delay to enable Brown to get a new attorney.

Brown's trial began on October 27, 1859, and lasted less than four days. He was carried to the court each day in a litter, and with each day, he became more irritated with his court-appointed attorneys. They had been joined by a twenty-one-year-old Boston attorney, George Hoyt, who had been retained by some Brown supporters who hoped to learn more about the case on behalf of the group of backers who were facing possible indictment as coconspirators. Botts and Green gratefully withdrew from the defense team, leaving the inexperienced Hoyt alone. Legal help soon came in the form of Samuel Chilton of Washington and Hiram Griswold of Cleveland, who were persuaded to take up what Brown himself realized was a lost cause.

The prosecution's case was devastating. Brown's request that he be tried as commander in chief of a provisional army, according to the laws governing warfare, was rejected. Brown's vision of himself as a messianic leader of a noble crusade against slavery was ignored. On October 31, at 1:45 P.M., the case went to the jury, which, after only forty-five minutes, declared Brown guilty on all counts. The verdict cast a pall on the audience, which days before had been vociferous in its rage against Brown. Brown himself said nothing as he lay quietly on his cot. The sentence of death by hanging was passed on November 2, with the date for execution set for December 2.

The coconspirators captured with Brown were tried as well and all sentenced to the same fate. Brown had visited with them in jail, calling on them to be firm and resolute and to implicate no one. Friends of Brown had sought to bring his wife from North Elba, but Brown insisted that she remain at home. Only on the afternoon before his execution did she visit with him and then stand by to claim his body.

Governor Henry Wise was besieged with demands for clemency, threats, and warnings of plots to free Brown. Martial law was proclaimed in Charlestown, and fifteen hundred soldiers, including a company of cadets from Virginia Military Institute commanded by Stonewall Jackson, ringed the gallows on December 2.

John Brown's death on a rope in Charlestown was but the end of a beginning. The larger crisis that Brown had foreshadowed soon came with a character of violence and death that would have perhaps given even Osawatomie pause. The South, by insisting on dealing with Brown's case, had arrogated to itself police authority over what was a crime against federal property. It thereby threw down a gauntlet of defiant sectionalism and states' rights.

None of this was lost on Brown's supporters in the North, who, after suffering gag rules in Congress blocking their petitions against slavery, after almost thirty years of relentless electioneering, pamphleteering, lecturing, haranguing, debating, and propagandizing against slavery, and after suffering dismaying defeats at the hands of every branch of government and in virtually every attempt to work within the system, were ready to exploit John Brown's fateful end.

Antislavery reformers took charge of the body, and by wagon, train, and steamer they took it to the hills where Brown had felt "omnipotent." It was a cortege that would be duplicated six years later on the death of Abraham Lincoln—a slow, somber taking of martyred remains home. Through Lake Placid and on to the little village of North Elba they took Brown, and near his little home they buried him. Gerrit Smith, the man who had given him the land, was not with him at the burial. Smith had become mentally deranged after Brown's capture and was institutionalized. Others who were closely involved with Brown, such as Frederick Douglass, found it convenient to flee to Canada or travel abroad. Brown, the guerrilla fighter and terrorist who had taken the struggle against slavery beyond rhetoric, had made clear that the approaching confrontation would be violent.

SIGNIFICANCE

John Brown was a tragic figure central to the great tragedy of Civil War America. Whether he was a hero in that era is, at best, controversial. There seems little doubt that had his earlier ventures been successful, he would have melded with other entrepreneurs of the moving frontier and probably been lost as another subject representing an enterprising nation. A failure as a businessperson, he turned all of his energies to what became for him a holy mission: rooting out the evil of slavery. Social, economic, and political displacement encouraged many in his region to seek redress. Brown, however, personalized these conflicts to an extreme degree and placed himself at a point from which there was no turning back.

—*Jack J. Cardoso*

FURTHER READING

Boyer, Richard O. *The Legend of John Brown: A Biography and a History*. New York: Alfred A. Knopf, 1972. This is a fine piece of biography that takes the story of Brown up to his arrival in Kansas in 1855. Boyer died before he could complete the second volume.

Malin, James C. *John Brown and the Legend of Fifty-six*. Philadelphia: American Philosophical Society, 1942. Malin's work is highly critical of Brown's activities in Kansas and of Brown personally. It is useful, however, for its detail of that period of Brown's life.

National Park Service. *John Brown's Raid*. Washington, D.C.: Superintendent of Documents, 1974. Here is an outstanding piece of work based on reports by William C. Everhart and Arthur L. Sullivan that gives sweep and substance to Brown and his men at Harpers Ferry in the space of sixty-eight pages.

Oates, Stephen B. *To Purge This Land with Blood: A Biography of John Brown*. New York: Harper & Row, 1970. Oates's book is a full biography of Brown and establishes the point of view that Brown's puritanical heritage was at the base of his thought and action. He also has something to say in a bibliographical essay. See also his article "John Brown and His Judges: A Critique of the Historical Literature" in *Civil War History* vol. 17, 1971, pp. 5-24.

Reynolds, David S. *John Brown, Abolitionist: The Man Who Killed Slavery, Sparked the Civil War, and Seeded Civil Rights*. New York: Alfred A. Knopf, 2005. Reynolds's biography is generally sympathetic toward Brown. He portrays Brown as a Puritan in the tradition of Oliver Cromwell and Jonathan Edwards—a man who saw the world as a battle of good versus evil, and who sought to avenge the evil of slavery.

Sanborn, Franklin B., ed. *The Life and Letters of John Brown*. New York: Negro Universities Press, 1891. This is a book to be used carefully as it is biased toward Brown. However, the gathering of Brown's letters makes this a valuable resource.

Stauffer, John. *The Black Hearts of Men: Radical Abolitionists and the Transformation of Race*. Cambridge, Mass.: Harvard University Press, 2002. During the 1850's, Brown, Gerrit Smith, and two African Americans, Frederick Douglass and doctor/scholar James McCune Smith, formed an interracial alliance to abolish slavery. Stauffer describes how the men worked to promote abolition and other social issues, and how their revolutionary zeal waned after Brown's 1859 raid on Harpers Ferry.

Villard, Oswald Garrison. *John Brown, 1800-1859: A Biography Fifty Years After*. Gloucester, Mass.: Peter Smith, 1910. Villard's biography is still a standard work on Brown and his time. It cannot be ignored in any study.

SEE ALSO: Frederick Douglass; Abby Kelley Foster; Stonewall Jackson; Robert E. Lee; Harriet Tubman.

RELATED ARTICLES in *Great Events from History: The Nineteenth Century, 1801-1900:* c. 1830-1865: Southerners Advance Proslavery Arguments; c. 1850-1860: Underground Railroad Flourishes; 1852: Stowe Publishes *Uncle Tom's Cabin*; October 16-18, 1859: Brown's Raid on Harpers Ferry; December 6, 1865: Thirteenth Amendment Is Ratified.

OLYMPIA BROWN

American Protestant cleric and social reformer

Among the first Americans to demand that higher education be opened to women, Brown managed to graduate from college and become one of the first women ordained a minister. She was also prominent in the woman suffrage movement.

BORN: January 5, 1835; Prairie Ronde, Kalamazoo County, Michigan Territory
DIED: October 23, 1926; Baltimore, Maryland
ALSO KNOWN AS: Olympia Brown Willis
AREAS OF ACHIEVEMENT: Religion and theology, women's rights

EARLY LIFE

Olympia Brown was the first of four children born to Asa and Lephia Brown. Her parents were pioneers who made the eight-hundred-mile trip from their native Vermont to live on the frontier in Michigan Territory during the year before she was born. In contrast to many of their neighbors, the Brown family was one in which education played a vital role. When the children were young, they were taught by their mother, a woman passionate about education, who pasted together articles from newspapers and journals to make books for her children.

Lephia and Asa Brown were also strong in their religious faith, Universalism. They taught their children the main tenants of this religion—a detail that would greatly influence Olympia's later life. In 1837, when Michigan attained statehood and began a state-wide public school system, the Browns built a one-room schoolhouse on their property and took the necessary steps to secure pupils and teachers. After attending Cedar Park Seminary in nearby Schoolcraft, Michigan, the fifteen-year-old Olympia taught at the family schoolhouse. At this time in her life, she experienced sexual discrimination for the first time: She wanted to continue her education, but few colleges admitted women.

After many debates with her father, Olympia and her younger sister left home in 1854 to attend Mount Holyoke Female Seminary in South Hadley, Massachusetts. Although the courses she took deepened her hunger for learning, she left Mount Holyoke after only one year because of its rigid Calvinistic atmosphere and the sexual discrimination she perceived behind the facade of female education. Once again, she struggled to find an institution that would admit women, and she suffered many rejections. Finally, when she was twenty years old, she was accepted at Antioch College in Yellow Springs, Ohio. Antioch was an institution that imposed no religious conversion on its students.

LIFE'S WORK

As had been the case in Brown's education up to that moment, Antioch's educational system was discriminatory, as male and female students were given different assignments. Brown's religious background told her that all humans were created equal, so she refused to accept the system and became the only female student to complete the men's assignments, orations on various topics, a discipline taboo at that time for American women. Brown also was responsible for bringing to the school other women speakers. It was, in fact, while listening to one of the few women ministers in America that Brown sensed her own destiny.

After graduating from Antioch in 1860, Brown struggled for entrance into a theological college. Once admitted, she again endured sexual harassment. She also struggled to perfect her speaking voice and had to fight for ordination. She finally was ordained at the Universalist Divinity School of St. Lawrence University in 1863. Within a year, she received the call to her first full-time parish in Weymouth Landing, Massachusetts. This assignment began a series of assignments to parishes struggling so hard that male ministers turned them down or gave up on them.

Although Brown's first official work for the women's movement began while she was attending Antioch College, it was not until her tenure at Weymouth Landing that she began winning national prominence for her role in the movement's 1867 Kansas campaign, which sought to secure the vote for women in that newly settled territory. Although she had been given many promises concerning arrangements and accommodations that would be in place during the campaign, Brown faced disorganization, a collapsing support base in the Republican Party, and sweltering heat. She also worked almost entirely on her own, as the promised arrangements for a traveling companion also fell through. In Kansas, she was alone, an unmarried woman, hundreds of miles from home and within fifty miles of deadly wars between settlers and Native Americans. She was completely dependent on pioneer farmers for her conveyance, housing, support, and, at times, the means of escape in the face of sometimes hostile crowds. Although the Kansas campaign ultimately failed to achieve its objective, Elizabeth Cady Stanton was so impressed with the fear that the ninety-pound Olympia Brown aroused among opposition speakers that she began trying to persuade Brown to work full-time in the suffrage movement.

Brown chose to remain in her field for the time being, accepting her next religious call to the Universalist Church in Bridgeport, Connecticut, in 1870. Three years later, she married John Henry Willis. Although those around her had feared that marriage would distract her from both the ministry and the women's cause, Brown discovered in her husband one who supported her on every front. He changed his own job to meet the demands of hers and relocated when her work made it necessary. He also supported her then radical decision to keep her maiden name, Brown.

In 1874, Brown gave birth to her first child, John Parker Willis, and then discovered that while she had been on maternity leave some members of her congregation had begun lobbying for a male minister. Although the majority of the congregation supported Brown, she resigned. By 1876, Brown had given birth to a second child, Gwendolen Brown Willis. In 1878, she was appointed to a struggling church in Racine, Wisconsin. In her hands, the Racine parish not only survived, it flourished as an educational and cultural center. The Racine church would prove, however, to be Brown's last full-time ministerial position.

Although Brown never completely quit the ministry, she dedicated her final decades to full-time work within the fight for women's equality. She was active in many organizations, including the Wisconsin Suffrage Association, the Wisconsin Federation of Women's Clubs, the Federal Suffrage Association, the National Woman Suffrage Association, and the Woman's Party.

During the winter of 1917, when she was more than seventy years old, Brown participated in a march on Washington, D.C., in support of woman suffrage. She was among the people who witnessed several men attacking the marchers and then saw President Woodrow Wilson have the women arrested, instead of their attackers. The following year, she again marched in Washington, this time personally burning some of the president's speeches before the crowds. Finally, in 1920, when she was eighty-five years old, she was able to vote in her first election. She then dedicated her remaining six years to worldwide equality by active participation in the Women's League for Peace and Freedom, the League of Nations, the League of Women Voters, and the American Civil Liberties Union.

SIGNIFICANCE

Although Olympia Brown had relatives who ran an Underground Railroad station in their home, she herself never knew the plight of American slaves at first hand. She also had no firsthand knowledge of the abuses of factory workers or of the hardships of immigrants. Nevertheless, hers is an important story in American history. She lived on the American frontier; she shocked college administrators by wearing the costume named after Amelia Bloomer and refusing chaperones; she was ordained into the ministry at a time when the mere idea of such a thing was heresy to many; she knew and was respected by some of the most important leaders in the woman suffrage movement; and she was one of the few prominent figures of the movement still alive in 1920 when the Nineteenth Amendment was passed.

Olympia Brown experienced sexual discrimination both within the educational system and within churches. During her lifetime, she argued against prevailing notions of womanhood, accused novelists of portraying women as insipid, and railed against the notion that young girls should be taught to be "little ladies." At a time in American history when women of her class were expected to be "quiet angels" in their homes, she was politically astute and vocal, taking on the weaknesses in the political positions of prominent figures such as Ralph Waldo Emerson and Frederick Douglass, in their presence. Through it all, she refused to let go of her personal doctrine that all people are created equal and that women are people, too.

—Anna Dunlap Higgins

FURTHER READING

Baker, Jean H., ed. *Votes for Women: The Struggle for Suffrage Revisited.* Oxford, England: Oxford University Press, 2002. A solidly researched work that places Brown in the national struggle for woman suffrage.

Brown, Olympia. *Suffrage and Religious Principle: Speeches and Writings of Olympia Brown.* Edited by Dana Greene. Metuchen, N.J.: Scarecrow Press, 1983. Collection of some of Brown's major writings and speeches.

Buhle, Mari Jo, and Paul Buhle, eds. *The Concise History of Woman Suffrage: Selections from the Classic Work of Stanton, Gage, and Harper.* Urbana: University of Illinois Press, 1978. Like Baker's book, this is an important work that helps place Brown in the larger picture of woman suffrage. Many readers should find this updated version more reader-friendly than the original source, which was published in 1868.

Coté, Charlotte. *Olympia Brown: The Battle for Equality.* Racine, Wis.: Mother Courage Press, 1988. A full-length biography, this book also includes two of Brown's best-remembered addresses and lists the whereabouts of most of the other documents by and about Brown, most of which are located at Radcliffe College in Cambridge, Massachusetts.

Emerson, Dorothy May, ed. *Standing Before Us: Unitarian Universalist Women and Social Reform, 1776-1936.* Boston: Skinner House Books, 2000. This work contains a biographical sketch of Brown and Brown's own "The Higher Education of Women." The book also confirms Brown's status as the first woman ordained to the Universalist ministry.

SEE ALSO: Susan B. Anthony; Amelia Bloomer; Frederick Douglass; Ralph Waldo Emerson; Elizabeth Cady Stanton; Lucy Stone.

RELATED ARTICLE in *Great Events from History: The Nineteenth Century, 1801-1900:* May, 1869: Woman Suffrage Associations Begin Forming.

ELIZABETH BARRETT BROWNING

English poet

Browning was one of the most respected woman poets of the Victorian age. Her work is known for its formal iconoclasm, impetuosity of tone, and political content.

BORN: March 6, 1806; Coxhoe Hall, County Durham, England

DIED: June 29, 1861; Florence, Italy

ALSO KNOWN AS: Elizabeth Barrett Moulton (birth name)

AREA OF ACHIEVEMENT: Literature

EARLY LIFE

Elizabeth Barrett was the eldest of the eleven children of Edward Moulton Barrett and Mary Graham Clarke. She grew up at Hope End, a large country house in Herefordshire. Both parents, but especially her father, encouraged her to read widely; unlike most privileged girls of her time, she was allowed free use of her father's library and shared her brothers' classical tuition. Her father arranged for her epic poem *The Battle of Marathon* (1820) to be privately published when she was fourteen.

In 1821 Elizabeth suffered a severe but unexplained illness that affected her spine and lungs and left her a semi-invalid for the rest of her life. During the 1830's, she produced her first successful poetry: *The Seraphim and Other Poems* (1838) was well received and gained its author considerable notice. At about the same time, her health broke down, and she traveled from London to the milder climate of Torquay to recover. During her convalescence, she begged her favorite brother Edward ("Bro") to visit her in Torquay; while there, he drowned on a sailing excursion. Elizabeth's grief and guilt were so overwhelming that for the rest of her life she could never speak or write of the event.

Somewhat recovered but still very much an invalid, Elizabeth returned to London in 1841 and plunged into literary work. In 1844 her popular two-volume *Poems* appeared. One poem in this collection, "Lady Geraldine's Courtship," referred favorably to the work of then little-known poet Robert Browning. He wrote to thank her, and they began a correspondence that led to their first meeting four months later. For over a year they wrote to each other daily (sometimes twice daily). Elizabeth's father had forbidden any of his children to marry, so Elizabeth and Robert married secretly and left for Italy in 1846. They settled in Florence, in Casa Guidi, where their son Pen was born in 1849 and where they lived for the rest of Elizabeth's life.

LIFE'S WORK

During the 1840's and 1850's, Elizabeth Barrett Browning's major works appeared, and her poetic reputation reached its height. Her 1844 *Poems* contain multiple voices, styles, and subjects. She experiments boldly with form, especially half-rhymes, metrical irregularities, neologisms, compound words, and lacunae. These experiments at once pleased, intrigued, infuriated, and disturbed her contemporary readers. More recently, they have been seen (by Virginia Woolf and others) as formative influences on later poets and harbingers of literary modernism.

In 1850 Browning published a collection of her poetry, including the 1844 poems plus some new material such as the famous *Sonnets from the Portuguese*, written secretly to her husband during their courtship. These poems are by far her best known, less for any intrinsic artistic excellence than for their abiding romantic and psychological portrait of developing love. They trace the emotional state of the poet—a thirty-nine-year-old invalid wooed by a younger man—from surprise, reluctance, and confusion to passion, trust, and hope for the future.

In addition to the sonnets, the 1850 *Poems* includes two poems focused on social issues. "The Runaway Slave at Pilgrim's Point" is an impassioned first-person poem in which a slave murders her own child, who was conceived as a result of rape by her white master. "The Cry of the Children" protests the inhumane conditions for child laborers in British coal mines and factories. Not only did these poems provoke a powerful response from socially conscious readers, but they also anticipated the overtly political concerns of Browning's next book of poetry.

Browning's next book, *Casa Guidi Windows* (1851), revealed her interest in the politics of the Italian Risorgimento. *Casa Guidi Windows* is "A Poem, in Two Parts," the first written in 1848 and filled with the optimism attendant upon the abortive Italian revolution of that year. Part 2 was written in 1851 after the crushing defeat of the patriots at Novara in 1849 and is decidedly more pessimistic. The poem's confident approach is noteworthy, particularly because it was unusual in Browning's time for a woman poet to venture onto political terrain, which was considered reserved for men. *Casa Guidi Windows* is written in a modified terza rima, and some of its vivid ironic characterizations are reminiscent of Robert Browning's poetry and have led critics to assume that Elizabeth was influenced by her husband.

Throughout the 1850's, Elizabeth and Robert traveled widely in Europe and visited England three times, in 1851, 1855, and 1856. Upon their return to Italy after the last trip, Browning, after ten years of work, published what she and generations of readers after her have considered to be her masterpiece, *Aurora Leigh* (1857). *Aurora Leigh* is a novel in verse, an epic poem in nine books inspired in part by the novels of George Sand and Charlotte Brontë but also by the long, reflective *Prelude* (1850) of William Wordsworth. It tells the story of the eponymous poet-heroine Aurora Leigh, her lover-cousin Romney Leigh, and their turbulent and finally successful romance.

Aurora Leigh is described as a successful but lonely and dissatisfied poet. Early in the poem she rejects the marriage proposal of her cousin Romney, a dedicated philanthropist. At that point in the story, Romney is simply too overbearing for the self-consciously feminist Aurora, who believes that human betterment must come through individual inspiration; Romney, by contrast, believes in organized progress by and for large groups of people. Aurora secludes herself and writes, while Romney embarks on several idealistic but hare-brained schemes (such as building a phalanstery on his ancestral estate and proposing marriage to a poor seamstress). After Romney's plans fail—the poor people he has installed in the phalanstery burn it down, he is blinded in the fire, and his intended wife is tricked into prostitution—he and Aurora can finally get together. The poem ends with their marriage, as Romney realizes that social betterment must involve the soul as well as the body and Aurora realizes that a true artist must not separate herself utterly from the world she hopes to influence. Ironically, for all its stated concern for the poor, *Aurora Leigh*'s "moral" is a conservative one: The "mob" is to be feared, and poetry makes a greater impact on society than philanthropic activities.

Elizabeth Barrett Browning. (Library of Congress)

Aurora Leigh contains Browning's highest convictions on life and art, particularly the responsibilities of the poet. She believed fervently that a poet must bear truthful witness to the values of her society, must "represent the age" and never "flinch from modern varnish, coat, or flounce." Thus her most poignant critique of both Aurora and Romney is that they are overly theoretical. Aurora chides Romney that his "social theory" is a better wife to him than she could ever be; she little realizes how greatly she herself is "wedded" to poetic theories.

In *Aurora Leigh*, Browning comes closest to integrating the idea "woman" with the idea "poet." In an important sense, it is about being or becoming a poet in a world that imagines the poet as male. By positioning herself at the center of her own story, the poet Aurora disrupts objectifying male discourse about women; she transforms herself from the object of Romney's gaze to the subject of her own vision and thereby enacts her liberation. Browning has taken a quintessentially male form, the extended blank-verse epic poem, and put it to the service of women's concerns. At the age of twenty, Aurora is aware of herself as "Woman and artist, —either incomplete." By the end of the epic, ten years have passed, and Aurora has learned that true fulfillment comes from finding completion as both woman *and* artist.

Browning's father had not seen or spoken to his daughter since she had left England in 1846. At one point, he sent her a package returning all the unread letters that she had written to him over the years. In 1857, he died unreconciled. In 1860 Browning published *Poems Before Congress*, the last volume to appear in her lifetime. Most English readers found this book to be a disappointment, too imbued with its author's often faulty judgments on contemporary French and Italian politics. Browning herself described it as "a very thin and wicked brochure" and fully expected that its pro-Italian, anti-English tone would lead to a negative public reaction.

In 1861, after a long struggle with failing health and weak lungs, Browning died in her husband's arms on the night of June 29. The following year, Browning's *Last*

Poems were published. This volume included a variety of poems left uncollected at the time of her death: several on the Italian political scene, one ("De Profundis") written after Bro's drowning in 1840 but never published, and several passionate and lyrical poems in the author's rich mature voice.

SIGNIFICANCE

After the death of William Wordsworth, Elizabeth Barrett Browning was seriously considered to replace him as England's poet laureate. Though she was not finally chosen—Alfred, Lord Tennyson was—the mere suggestion that she might fill that position and speak with that "national" voice was extraordinary in 1850. It reveals how well known and well respected Browning was among her peers.

In the decades following her death, her poetry was nearly forgotten. By 1932, Virginia Woolf was complaining that in the "mansion of literature" Browning had been relegated to the "servants' quarters." The revival of interest in her work that Woolf had called for did not take place until the advent of feminist literary criticism during the 1960's and 1970's. Since that time, readers have focused on Browning not simply as a poet but as a woman poet. The very characteristics of her work that were seen as most problematic by earlier generations—intense passion, interest in politics, feminist concerns—are now seen as the greatest strengths of her poetry.

Browning's work is critical to understanding the ways in which a woman poet empowers herself to speak. Browning's career provides a model for the relationship of a woman poet to a poetic tradition that privileges the male voice. Moreover, she has represented a poetic "foremother" for generations of women poets after her—a figure she herself lacked and for whom she longed. Browning has typically been envisioned as a ringleted Victorian invalid living out an unlikely romantic legend. It is important to remember that she was first and foremost a technician devoted to the craft of poetry.

—Deborah T. Meem

FURTHER READING

Cooper, Helen. *Elizabeth Barrett Browning: Woman and Artist*. Chapel Hill: North Carolina University Press, 1988. Cooper discusses Browning's career as an extended effort to bring about a felicitous union of her femaleness with her art. The book deals cogently with all the major work.

Dennis, Barbara. *Elizabeth Barrett Browning: The Hope End Years*. Brigend, Mid Glamorgan, Wales: Seren Books, 1996. Focuses on the first twenty-five years of Browning's life, describing her relationships with her family and her love for her blind tutor, Hugh Boyd. Dennis, a Welsh professor of Victorian studies, credits Browning's later poems to her formative experiences at Hope End.

Forster, Margaret. *Elizabeth Barrett Browning: A Biography*. New York: Doubleday, 1988. This is the best critical biography of the poet. It includes generous selections from the letters as well as discussion of the poet's life and work.

Garrett, Martin, ed. *Elizabeth Barrett Browning and Robert Browning: Interviews and Recollections*. New York: St. Martin's Press, 2000. A collection of comments about the two poets, including observations by Nathaniel Hawthorne, Tennyson, and Henry James, as well as the poets themselves.

Hayter, Alethea. "Elizabeth Barrett Browning (1806-1861)." In *British Writers*. Vol. 4. New York: Charles Scribner's Sons, 1981. This useful overview of the life of the poet includes an excellent six-page discussion of Browning's poetic imagery and style.

Markus, Julia. *Dared and Done: The Marriage of Elizabeth Barrett and Robert Browning*. Athens: Ohio University Press, 1998. A dual biography of the couple, focusing on their marriage and subsequent careers.

Mermin, Dorothy. *Elizabeth Barrett Browning: The Origins of a New Poetry*. Chicago: University of Chicago Press, 1989. This book is a frequently cited extended discussion of Browning's poetics.

Tucker, Herbert F. "*Aurora Leigh:* Epic Solutions to Novel Ends." In *Famous Last Words: Changes in Gender and Narrative Closure*, edited by Alison Booth. Charlottesville: University of Virginia Press, 1993. Tucker analyzes *Aurora Leigh* in light of traditional epic form, stressing its relationship to conventional Victorian fiction and poetry.

Zonana, Joyce. "The Embodied Muse: Elizabeth Barrett Browning's *Aurora Leigh* and Feminist Poetics." *Tulsa Studies in Women's Literature* 8 (Fall, 1989): 240-262. In this interesting essay, Zonana considers the problematic subject-object issue surrounding the idea of the poetic muse in Browning's epic novel. The author explores this idea in relation to previous feminist criticism.

SEE ALSO: Dame Millicent Garrett Fawcett; Anna Jameson; Christina Rossetti; Alfred, Lord Tennyson.

RELATED ARTICLE in *Great Events from History: The Nineteenth Century, 1801-1900:* November 5, 1850: Tennyson Becomes England's Poet Laureate.

ANTON BRUCKNER

Austrian musician and composer

After rising from modest rural origins, Bruckner first established himself as one of the leading organists of his time, then persevered in his creative work to produce a great series of choral and symphonic works. Musically eloquent and possessing a unique sense of spiritual aspiration, the finest of Bruckner's large-scale compositions belong to the essential repertoire of nineteenth century music.

BORN: September 4, 1824; Ansfelden, Austro-Hungarian Empire (now in Austria)
DIED: October 11, 1896; Vienna, Austro-Hungarian Empire (now in Austria)
ALSO KNOWN AS: Josef Anton Bruckner (full name)
AREA OF ACHIEVEMENT: Music

EARLY LIFE

Anton Bruckner (BROOK-nehr) was the son of Anton and Theresa Bruckner. For generations, his family had engaged in modest occupations such as broom-making and innkeeping, but both Bruckner's father and his grandfather had become schoolteachers, a position of modest status but substantial responsibilities. One of the tasks of a schoolteacher in those days was to oversee the basic musical education of his students. Thus, it was Bruckner's father who first instructed him in singing and in the playing of various instruments. Though young Anton seems to have played a child's violin as early as age four, he showed no special talent until the age of ten, when his godfather and cousin, Johann Weiss, took him into his own home in the nearby town of Hörsching to instruct him in the playing of the organ. One likely cause for Anton's move may have been the crowded Bruckner household; he was the first of eleven children, though only five survived to maturity.

Under his cousin's guidance, Anton studied the rudiments of music theory and continued his organ studies. In 1836, he composed his first organ work, a prelude that suggests that Bruckner knew some of the music of Franz Joseph Haydn and Wolfgang Amadeus Mozart, the foremost Austrian composers of the late eighteenth century. Later, Bruckner was to be influenced by the music of Johann Sebastian Bach and the Counter-Reformation master Giovanni Palestrina, but his months of study in his cousin's home were cut short when Anton was needed at home to deputize for his ailing father in the schoolroom. In 1837, the elder Bruckner died, leaving Anton nominally the head of the family.

With surprising resourcefulness, Anton's mother immediately arranged for him to become a student and choirboy at the Augustinian monastery of St. Florian, which boasted a splendid Baroque church containing one of the finest organs of the time. The young student flourished in the environment of the monastery and was able to continue his musical studies with the church organist. His progress as an instrumentalist was rapid, and although little is known of his intellectual growth it is likely that Bruckner was a diligent student, for in October, 1840, he left St. Florian to enter the preparatory course for public school teachers in Linz and was graduated from it the following year without having to repeat the course, as was usually necessary. In Linz, Bruckner was exposed to an increasing range of musical influences. It was there that he heard for the first time a symphony by Ludwig van Beethoven, but he did not record the impression it made upon him.

Upon completing the preparatory course for teachers, Bruckner was assigned as an assistant teacher to the small town of Windhaag, where he endured appalling conditions of employment. Living in the teacher's house, he had to eat his meals with the servant girl. In addition to classroom duties, he was required to ring the church bells at 4:00 A.M., help the village priest dress for services, and work in the fields during the harvest. After fifteen months in Windhaag, an understanding school inspector transferred Bruckner to nearby Kronstorf.

At that time, Bruckner's only stated ambition was to become a schoolteacher, despite evidence that he was capable of either a religious or a musical vocation. Bruckner's need for financial security and his sense of responsibility toward his needy family were undoubtedly factors in his reluctance to declare an interest in a career as a performing musician; even his appointment as assistant organist at St. Florian in 1849 did not quell his insecurity about abandoning a steady, if ill-paying, job as public school teacher. After assuming the permanent post of organist at St. Florian in 1851, Bruckner was still reluctant to entrust his future to music, and he continued to enroll in preparatory courses in order to be qualified for high school teaching. He even applied, unsuccessfully, for a routine clerical position in 1853.

Despite Bruckner's insecurity about finances, his growth as a musician was steady. In 1856, while living in Linz, where he had recently been appointed cathedral organist, Bruckner began studying with the noted Viennese musician Simon Sechter. This elderly organist and conservatory professor was the author of a treatise on musical composition that codified rigorous rules of harmony and counterpoint based upon the musical practices of past centuries.

In accepting private students, Sechter requested that they set aside creative work in composition during their period of study with him, and Bruckner largely complied with this condition for the six years of Sechter's rigid but benevolent instruction. Bruckner's sacrifice was perhaps less significant than it was for other musicians, because he continued improvising at the organ, in itself a creative experience akin to composition. Music historians have regretted that Bruckner seems always to have been indifferent to writing down even the outlines of his acclaimed organ improvisations, and Bruckner himself once remarked upon this fact by saying "One does not write as one plays."

LIFE'S WORK

After completing his study with Sechter—which was carried on by mail and in occasional vists to Vienna—Bruckner's creative output increased remarkably, but at the age of thirty-nine he continued to seek instruction from established musicians. His next teacher was an opera conductor, Otto Kitzler, who introduced Bruckner to the work of Richard Wagner, the German composer of monumental "music-dramas" such as *Tristan und Isolde* (1859) and *Der Ring des Nibelungen* (1874). The influence of Wagner's music and personality upon Bruckner is as unquestionable as it is difficult to assess. Wagner's music released powerful forces in Bruckner's creative personality, but it is clear that the younger composer did not comprehend the literary and ideological content of Wagner's work, even after making Wagner's acquaintance in 1865. Wagner was a sophisticated, cosmopolitan personality, while Bruckner was a man with country schooling and manners; it is a testimony to the unique genius of each that they were able to appreciate each other. Bruckner's formal, even obsequious manner may well have been a source of concealed amusement to the self-possessed Wagner.

Bruckner's career as a composer had blossomed during the early 1860's with the composition of a Mass in D Minor and two symphonies. The second of these symphonies, long forgotten by Bruckner, was later acknowledged by him as "only an attempt," and numbered as "Symphony 0." The composition of Bruckner's great chain of nine symphonies began in 1865 with the Symphony No. 1 in C Minor. Two more masses followed in the years 1866-1868 before the completion of the Symphony No. 2 in C Minor in 1872. This work begins the first of two great creative waves in Bruckner's mature career, encompassing work on the second, third, fourth, and fifth symphonies between 1871 and 1876.

By all standards, this first period of mastery occurred very late in Bruckner's life. At the time of the completion of Symphony No. 4 in E-flat Major, he had just passed his fiftieth birthday, and although he was enjoying professional success as an organist, choral composer, and, to a lesser extent, choral director, his life was a lonely one. In 1867, he had suffered a nervous breakdown and spent three months recovering at a hydropathic establishment in Bad Kreuzen, where he was assailed by thoughts of suicide and a mania for numbers. It is reported that he would count the stars or the leaves on a tree and was possessed by the idea that he had to bail out the Danube River.

Though simple overwork contributed to Bruckner's depression, his inherently solitary and often-melancholy disposition magnified his sense of his life's disappointments. On the personal side, his utter inability to find a partner in marriage weighed unusually heavily upon him. Bruckner was a very religious man, even by the standards of his time, and he would not countenance a sexual relationship outside marriage. Because his romantic interests were rather ineffectually aimed at young women aged sixteen to nineteen, Bruckner's search for a mate seemed almost designed to fail.

Later, Bruckner was unable to take professional disappointments in stride. While the opposition to his music by powerful critics such as Eduard Hanslick was often malicious, the occasional incomprehension of his scores by conductors and orchestral players was essentially a transitory problem, and much of his music was well received. The episode of mental collapse he experienced in 1867-1868 was fortunately not to be repeated, but Bruckner continued to be plagued by doubts about his work, which he sought to resolve by repeated and often ill-advised revision of his scores. The creative period of the early 1870's was followed by a period of revision in 1876 through 1879. He regained his confidence and composed a series of masterpieces in the years 1879 through 1887, including his *Te Deum* (1883-1884) and the magisterial Symphony No. 8 (1884-1886), but another period of revisions ensued in 1887, lasting until 1891.

The most frequently reproduced photographs of Bruckner show him in later life as a dignified and remote man, posing rather formally in his studio—often seated next to the great Bösendorfer grand piano that was left to him by a friend of earlier years. With close-cropped hair and baggy trousers (said to aid an organist's foot-pedaling), Bruckner had nothing of the appearance of a typical artist of his era. He seemed to his friends almost completely unaware of the effect of his awkward appearance and manners, and he was once admonished to take care in dressing so as not to disadvantage himself in his professional life.

Bruckner's formative years occurred during the reign of the Austrian emperor Franz Josef, a period of unrelieved political conservatism and social rigidity; reflecting this background, Bruckner approached most relationships in an archaic and servile manner that irritated many of his acquaintances. Nevertheless, as a professor of music theory at the University of Vienna and as a private teacher, he gained the love and respect of his students not only by his competence but also by his humanity, which must have been all but invisible to the public.

The growing recognition given to Bruckner's music during the 1880's was a partial consolation for the relative neglect he had suffered, which can be measured by reference to the fact that his main rival in the field of symphonic composition, Johannes Brahms, received enormous sums for the publication of his four symphonies, while few of Bruckner's works were published in his lifetime, and then only with subsidies from friends and admirers.

The burden of Bruckner's many professional responsibilities seems to have had little effect on his ability to complete massive compositions. By 1890, however, in declining health, he gave up the last of his teaching positions to devote his full efforts to the completion of his Ninth Symphony. This work was intended to bear the dedication, *Dem lieben Gott . . .* , "To the dear Lord, if he will accept it," revealing a faith that is perhaps as naïve as it is profound. The first three movements of the Ninth Symphony were composed during the period 1891 through 1894, and the fourth was begun in late 1894. By that time, Bruckner had accepted the emperor's offer of accommodation in an annex of the Belvedere Palace, where he labored on the finale of the symphony until days before his death on October 11, 1896. Although speculative completions of the finale have been recorded, the symphony has been performed for generations as a complex but unified work of three movements, concluding with an adagio that embodies, in its final passages, a profound and valedictory innocence.

SIGNIFICANCE

Anton Bruckner's great works were composed after a long musical apprenticeship, and they display a technical and expressive consistency that makes possible a degree of generalization about them. A Bruckner symphony tends to be expansive, developing on a scale where the formal logic of late eighteenth and early nineteenth century music is of limited use as an organizing principle. The grandeur of Bruckner's musical thought was often expressed in compositions of demanding length that some listeners perceive as formless. In reality, Bruckner's music is highly organized, but it is unusually complex and polymorphous, and seldom adheres to familiar forms. Many of Bruckner's obvious structural ideas, such as periodicity within movements, dramatic contrast of blocks of thematic material, and complete rests within movements (which Bruckner compared, perhaps only half seriously, to pausing to take a deep breath before saying something important), were novel in their time and were often remarked upon disparagingly.

Bruckner's harmony became increasingly daring in his mature compositions, but in this he was not out of step with contemporary trends. His harmonic practice has been often attributed to the influence of Wagner's music, but it might also be regarded as Bruckner's inevitable victory over the rigidity of Sechter's rules. Similarly, Bruckner was able to turn a conventional mastery of contrapuntal technique into a creative resource, achieving remarkable powers of thematic metamorphosis and large-scale integration. In all areas of endeavor, Bruckner blended orthodoxy with inspired inventiveness. Many of his contemporaries, acknowledging his idiosyncrasies but not his inspiration, thought him to be a naïve musician, but the more discerning of his colleagues, such as Gustav Mahler, knew the stature of the man from their earliest experience of his music. The public was soon to follow in its appreciation of Bruckner's singular genius. He is recognized as the composer of a magisterial body of music that stands somewhat outside its time, looking as much to the past as to the future, but that forms part of the great continuity of European music.

—C. S. McConnell

FURTHER READING

Barford, Philip. *Bruckner Symphonies*. London: British Broadcasting Corporation, 1978. One of the BBC Music Guides, this slim volume discusses the symphonies in terms understandable to the layperson and with a minimum of musical examples. A brief concluding section, "Understanding Bruckner: A Personal View," is excellent.

Doernberg, Erwin. *The Life and Symphonies of Anton Bruckner*. London: Barrie & Rockliff, 1960. This solid study, divided into independent sections dealing first with Bruckner's life and then with his symphonies, frees Bruckner from many of the character stereotypes that for so long created an almost unbridgeable gap between perceptions of the man and his music. Excerpts from Bruckner's letters are provided in sufficient quantity for the reader to imagine something of his personal trials and his musical triumphs.

Howie, Crawford. *Anton Bruckner: A Documentary Biography*. 2 vols. Lewiston, N.Y.: Edwin Mellen Press, 2002. More recent and comprehensive biography. Volume one, *From Ansfelden to Vienna*, examines Bruckner's early life until 1877, and volume two, *Trial, Tribulation, and Triumph in Vienna*, details his life in Vienna from 1878 until his death.

Johnson, Stephen. *Bruckner Remembered*. London: Faber & Faber, 1998. Part of Composers Remembered, a series of personal recollections about prominent composers. The Bruckner book includes reminiscences by students and colleagues who recall how he composed and recorded, and accounts of his organ improvisations.

Schönzeler, Hans-Hubert. *Bruckner*. London: Calder and Boyars, 1970. The author is a musicologist as well as a conductor who has been an advocate of Bruckner's music, and his account of the composer is notably sympathetic to Bruckner's cause. The book stands apart from others in its quantity of useful illustrations. There is no bibliography, but a chronological list of works is provided.

Simpson, Robert. *The Essence of Bruckner*. 2d ed. London: Gollancz, 1977. This book is the product of twenty-five years of reflection upon Bruckner's symphonies by a noted British composer. Each work is examined in detail, satisfying the most exacting analytical standard. A concluding chapter, "Reflections," is essential for the nonspecialist reader.

Watson, Derek. *Bruckner*. London: J. M. Dent & Sons, 1975. The growth of interest in Bruckner's music in the English-speaking world brought about the publication of this new account of the composer in the Master Musicians series. Readable. The many appendixes are very useful.

Wolff, Werner. *Anton Bruckner: Rustic Genius*. New York: Cooper Square, 1973. The author, whose father was the founder of the Berlin Philharmonic Orchestra, met Bruckner during the early 1890's, when the composer was invited to dinner. As conductor, author, and lecturer, Wolff later championed Bruckner's cause. The bibliography dates from the original edition (1942) and consists almost exclusively of German-language entries.

SEE ALSO: Franz Schubert; Robert Shumann; Richard Wagner.

RELATED ARTICLES in *Great Events from History: The Nineteenth Century, 1801-1900:* January 2, 1843: Wagner's *Flying Dutchman* Debuts; August 13-17, 1876: First Performance of Wagner's Ring Cycle.

ISAMBARD KINGDOM BRUNEL
English engineer

Brunel was the most important developer of iron and steamship construction and the guiding force in the building of the Great Western Railway. Even more importantly, he continued the tradition begun by his father, Marc Isambard Brunel, of capturing the imagination of the public with great engineering projects and thus symbolized the budding age of modern technology.

BORN: April 9, 1806; Portsmouth, Hampshire, England
DIED: September 15, 1859; London, England
AREA OF ACHIEVEMENT: Engineering

EARLY LIFE

Perhaps the most famous English engineer, Isambard Kingdom Brunel (brew-NEHL) was the son of Sophie Kingdom, the daughter of a Plymouth naval contractor. His father, Marc Isambard Brunel, was a French engineer who had fled the Terror for the United States in 1793. After considerable success as an engineer in New York, the elder Brunel went to England in 1799 and married Sophie Kingdom, whom he had met earlier in France. Isambard was the youngest of their three children and their only son.

In 1823, after attending private schools in England and the Henri Quatre College in Paris, the young Brunel entered his father's business to serve his apprenticeship as an engineer. By that time, Marc Brunel was on the verge of beginning the project that would establish him and his son as the most famous engineers of their day: the Thames Tunnel.

LIFE'S WORK

The tunnel was intended to relieve the pressure of traffic on London Bridge. It was obviously desirable, but also a difficult and dangerous undertaking. The younger Brunel, although only nineteen years old when the work began, soon became the superintendent in fact and finally in name. He was involved in two serious accidents that were fully reported in the press. On the first occasion, he was aboveground when the river broke into the tunnel. He had himself lowered by rope into the tunnel to rescue a drowning man. No one was killed then, but eighteen months later, in January, 1828, a second breakthrough resulted in the deaths of three men. Two of them and Brunel were actually at the face of the tunnel when the water burst through. He managed to survive but with internal injuries severe enough to prevent him from returning to the project. After several other accidents and financial crises, Marc Brunel saw the tunnel to completion in 1843 but without the active assistance of his son.

The younger Brunel's fame rested on his accomplishments in three areas: ship construction, the building of the Great Western Railway, and bridge construction. His involvement with shipping began in Bristol, where he designed dock improvements. In later years, he continued the design of docks at other places, but the immediate consequence of the Bristol contract was to bring him into contact with railway promoters and investors interested in building a line between London and Bristol. From this association, there developed a scheme to build the most advanced ship of the day, and the results were the most important basis of his fame.

Steam engines had been used before as auxiliary power, but no ship had crossed the Atlantic solely under steam power. The problem was that a ship could not carry enough coal to make the crossing and leave enough room for freight to make the crossing profitable. Conventional wisdom held that bigger ships would not solve the problem, because they would require bigger engines using more coal. Brunel reasoned that bigger ships would work. As water resistance would be proportional to the cross section of the ship, greater length would not cause greater resistance.

In 1836, the largest ship then in existence was 208 feet long. Brunel's backers in the Great Western Railway Company formed the Great Western Steam Ship Company to build a ship 236 feet long, displacing twenty-three hundred tons—the biggest ship of the time. After one year, the *Great Western* was afloat, and one year later it was ready to depart for New York. In the meantime, competitors had entered the race. In fact, a modified sailing vessel steamed into New York harbor a few hours before the *Great Western* arrived in the afternoon of April 23, 1838. The *Great Western* was twice the size of its rival, had two hundred tons of coal left rather than the fifteen tons of the other ship, and made the voyage three days faster.

The *Great Britain* was an even greater innovation. As soon as the *Great Western* had completed its voyage, Brunel proposed a much larger ship, but size was not as important as its other features. It was the first ship constructed entirely of iron, and it was the first ship intended

Isambard Kingdom Brunel.

for commercial use to employ a screw propeller instead of side-mounted paddle wheels. After its maiden voyage in July, 1845, it continued in service until it was damaged in a storm in 1886 and stopped in the Falkland Islands, where it remained until rescued in 1970 and returned to Bristol.

In 1854, work began on the *Great Eastern*—the last of Brunel's great ships. None of these ships enjoyed commercial success, and the Great Western Steam Ship Company had already failed, but another company was formed to execute the new design. At 680 feet long, this ship was gigantic for its day, but again, its significance lay not so much in its size as in its innovative features. The double-hull design with watertight compartments is still a standard feature in shipbuilding.

Brunel claimed that the ship could break in two and both halves would float independently. No openings were allowed in the hull below the waterline, and the design included a modern-style bridge with a variety of instruments. Construction took five years to complete because of problems with contractors, workers, and critics. The problems did not end even after construction was complete. No one knew how to launch such a huge ship, and men were killed in the attempt, but it finally entered the water in January, 1858. It was used in laying the transatlantic cable and in other notable enterprises, but it, too, failed commercially and was broken up during the 1890's.

As engineer for the Great Western Railway, Brunel surveyed its route in 1833 and determined its technical aspects for as long as he lived. He specified the type of rolling stock, engines, rails, and stations it was to have. His name became associated with a number of remarkable tunnels and other engineering feats along the line, but his railway activities were best known in connection with two controversies rather than those successes. The first was the debate over narrow versus broad-gauge rails.

No one knows how the rail gauge of four feet, eight and one-half inches became standard, but Brunel disapproved of it. He wanted wider spacing of the tracks so that rolling stock would be carried inside the wheels rather than hanging over them. Much larger wheels could then be used, as they no longer had to stay under the vehicles they were carrying. These large wheels meant a reduction in loss of power attributable to friction. From the beginning, the Great Western tracks were seven feet apart, and Brunel remained the most influential champion of the "broad" gauge throughout his life.

Whatever the advantages of the broad gauge, the system caused great difficulty where the lines that served the southwest of England met those in the rest of the country. Brunel devised a variety of plans to accommodate the difference and insisted on maintaining the broad gauge on any extension of the Great Western lines. Interestingly, he did not use the broad gauge on the two Italian railways he designed. The controversy reached a climax during the late 1840's as a parliamentary gauge commission held hearings on the issue. The "Gauge War," as it came to be known, ended with no standard being set, but the broad-gauge lines were converted soon after Brunel's death.

Somewhat less controversial was the "atmospheric" railway that operated for about six months in 1848 from

Exeter to Newton Abbot. Trains operated on this line without benefit of locomotives. A tube fifteen inches in diameter ran between the tracks, and stationary steam engines located along the tracks maintained a partial vacuum in it. Pistons on the underside of the railway carriages fit into the tube by means of a leather flap valve, and atmospheric pressure drove the trains. The system failed for several technical reasons. Most of the controversy involved Brunel's failure to forecast accurately the cost of the project. He grossly underestimated construction costs, and the cost of maintenance proved astronomical. Detractors accused him of being impractical, the ultimate insult for an engineer, and too fanciful in his designs.

Brunel's reputation as a builder of bridges is closely related to his activities in constructing the Great Western Railway, but he was interested in bridge design before the railway. In fact, his first important independent contract was in 1829 for the Clifton Bridge, near Bristol. Lack of funds prevented completion of the bridge until after his death, but the project brought him into contact with the Bristolians who were so important to the rest of his career. There were numerous others, but the Saltash Bridge crossing the Tamar on the Great Western line probably did the most to enhance his reputation with fellow engineers and the public.

The pier footings for this bridge had to be sunk eighty feet through water and mud. The task was accomplished by pumping and digging out the material inside an iron casing thirty-five feet in diameter that had been placed in the river. The two central spans of the bridge, each 455 feet long, were floated to the piers when they had reached above water level. As the stonework extended upward, the spans went up with them by means of two of three jacks located on each pier. Each span was in the form of a truss made with tubular arches, from which were suspended bridge chains, resulting in a shape resembling an oval on its side. It was complete in 1858.

Brunel seemed to attract attention even when he was not involved with such grand projects. He received press coverage for building a prefabricated hospital used in the Crimean War, improvements on large guns, a floating gun carriage also used in the Crimean War, his membership on the building committee of the Great Exhibition of 1851, and his testimony before numerous parliamentary committees. His testimony was nearly always the subject of debate in the press, both because of the importance of the issues involved and because of the force of his convictions. For example, he was a staunch opponent of patent laws, which he believed hindered progress.

Brunel was so well known that an accident that befell him became the subject of a story in R. H. Barham's *The Ingoldsby Legends: Or, Mirth and Marvels, by Thomas Ingoldsby, Esquire* (1855). On April 3, 1843, he was playing with his children by pretending to make a coin go from his ear to his mouth. In the course of performing the trick he swallowed the coin, which lodged in one of his bronchial tubes. The efforts of the surgeons failed, and Brunel constructed a device to invert and shake him. Forty days after the mishap, the inverter finally worked. Brunel was so famous and the incident so well known that when word spread that "it was out," Londoners knew what was out of whom without having to be told.

Brunel seemed to be accident-prone. As mentioned, he suffered severe internal injuries in the flooding of the Thames Tunnel, and one might speculate that these injuries contributed to the kidney failure that killed him at a relatively early age. During the trials of the *Great Western*, a fire broke out, and he tried to climb down a ladder to investigate. A fall of eighteen feet knocked him unconscious, and it took him some time to recover from his injuries.

In July, 1836, Brunel married Mary Horsley. They had two sons and a daughter. The Brunels combined office and home in a rather lavish London residence. Mary kept separate carriages for morning and afternoon use, and the servants, clerks, and apprentices, who paid for the privilege of observing Brunel at work, gave the impression of an important establishment. Brunel seems to have had little time for anything but his work. He was traveling much of the time in order to attend to his many projects. Photographs and descriptions depict him as a rather small, energetic man with a dark complexion. He had several bouts with kidney disease in the last years of his life and finally succumbed to it on September 15, 1859.

SIGNIFICANCE

The Brunels were not the only famous father and son team of engineers during the early nineteenth century. George and Robert Stephenson were much in the public view. There were also other famous individual engineers, such as Thomas Telford and Richard Trevithick, but the Brunels, more than any others, established the professional engineer as a hero of the Industrial Revolution.

Isambard Kingdom Brunel used his tremendous engineering abilities to improve communications both within England and between England and North America. He oversaw construction of more than one thousand miles of railway tracks in central and western England, in Ireland, and in Wales, and he built two railroads in Italy as well. His innovations in shipbuilding made the transatlantic passage both cheaper and less time-consuming, and his ship the *Great Eastern* laid the first transatlantic cable. Finally, both directly and indirectly, Brunel increased the number of bridges linking England's roadways.

—*Philip Dwight Jones*

FURTHER READING

Brunel, Isambard Kingdom. *The Life of Isambard Kingdom Brunel, Civil Engineer*. London: Longmans, Green, 1870. Reprint. Madison, N.J.: Fairleigh Dickinson University Press, 1972. This biography was written by Brunel's son. It is not an intimate family portrait, but rather a traditional nineteenth century formal biography, containing information available nowhere else.

Buchanan, R. Angus. *Brunel: The Life and Times of Isambard Kingdom Brunel*. London: Hambledon and London, 2002. A recent biography, featuring information on some of the neglected areas of Brunel's life, such as his training and connections to Bristol.

Fox, Stephen. *Transatlantic: Isambard Kingdom Brunel, Samuel Cunard, and the Great Atlantic Steamships*. London: HarperCollins, 2003. Narrative history of the transatlantic steamship, describing how Atlantic Ocean travel dramatically changed between 1820 and 1910. Fox traces the evolution of the steamship from Brunel's *Great Western* in 1838 to Cunard's *Mauretania* of 1907.

Gooch, Sir Daniel. *The Diaries of Sir Daniel Gooch*. London: K. Paul, Trench, Trubner, 1892. Reprint. Newton Abbot, England: David and Charles, 1972. Gooch was one of Brunel's colleagues in the construction of the Great Western Railway. His memoir provides information about Brunel's involvement with the railway project.

Hadfield, Charles. *Atmospheric Railways*. Newton Abbot, England: David and Charles, 1967. This history of atmospheric railways includes a fairly extensive treatment of Brunel's involvement with them.

Hay, Peter. *Brunel, Engineering Giant*. London: B. T. Batesford, 1985. A short paperback giving the essential details of its subject's life. It has thirty-three useful black-and-white illustrations and is probably the best choice for someone desiring a brief account. No notes or other scholarly apparatus.

Hearn, Chester G. *Circuits in the Sea: The Men, the Ships, and the Atlantic Cable*. Westport, Conn.: Praeger, 2004. A history of the eleven-year effort to successfully lay a transatlantic telegraph cable, including Brunel's participation in the process. Describes the ships used, technology involved, and the initial failures of the venture.

Pudney, John. *Brunel and His World*. Albuquerque, N.Mex.: Transatlantic Arts, 1974. Another popular account without footnotes. Pudney's work relies mainly on its 140 illustrations. It maintains that Brunel surpassed contemporary engineers because of his ability to gain public attention through grand projects.

Rolt, L. T. C. *Isambard Kingdom Brunel*. London: Longmans, Green, 1957. The closest thing to a standard account. Rolt is the best-known modern scholar dealing with Brunel.

Rowland, K. T. *The Great Britain*. Newton Abbot, England: David and Charles, 1971. An account of the construction and career of the ship that was one of Brunel's best-known creations.

SEE ALSO: Marc Isambard Brunel; George Stephenson; Thomas Telford; Richard Trevithick.

RELATED ARTICLES in *Great Events from History: The Nineteenth Century, 1801-1900:* May 22-June 20, 1819: *Savannah* Is the First Steamship to Cross the Atlantic; January 31, 1858: Brunel Launches the SS *Great Eastern*; July 27, 1866: First Transatlantic Cable Is Completed; December 28, 1895: First Commercial Projection of Motion Pictures.

MARC ISAMBARD BRUNEL

British engineer and inventor

The most famous civil engineer of his day, Brunel was one of the leaders in mechanizing production during the early nineteenth century. He and his son have come to be seen as symbols for the technical achievements of the Industrial Revolution.

BORN: April 25, 1769; Hacqueville, France
DIED: December 12, 1849; London, England
ALSO KNOWN AS: Sir Marc Isambard Brunel
AREA OF ACHIEVEMENT: Engineering

EARLY LIFE

Marc Isambard Brunel (brew-NEHL) was born into a family whose members had been tenant farmers in Normandy for generations. As a younger son, he was intended for the Church by his family. Consequently, he entered the seminary of St. Nicaise at Rouen in 1780. Even at the age of eleven, Brunel showed a strong interest in drawing and mathematics. For the classics, however, he had no interest whatsoever. The Superior of the seminary advised the elder Brunel against forcing the boy into a profession for which he was obviously unsuited.

In 1782, the Brunel family decided on a naval career for young Marc, and he went to live with the Carpentier family in Rouen to prepare for entrance into the navy. There, he studied mathematics, drawing, and other technical subjects. This academic regimen must have suited him, as he was appointed a cadet on a corvette headed for the West Indies in 1786. Little is known of his naval career, which ended in 1792 when his ship returned to France.

The French Revolution occurred during Brunel's absence abroad, and by 1793, Paris was a dangerous place for royalist officers. Brunel must have been particularly outspoken or politically active, because he soon fled from Paris to Rouen in some danger. While visiting the Carpentier family in Rouen, he met his future wife, Sophie Kingdom, an English girl who was staying with the Carpentiers for a few months in order to learn French. The danger for Brunel was considerable. Not even love could detain him, and he managed to obtain a passport from the American vice consul at Le Havre. He arrived in New York on September 6, 1793.

LIFE'S WORK

In America, Brunel first began to practice his profession. He obtained an appointment to survey a tract of land near Ontario, and subsequently he surveyed the route for a canal to connect the Hudson River with Lake Champlain. During these operations, he showed so much ability that he became director of the canal construction. His success in that position won numerous commissions for him. He designed several buildings and finally became chief engineer of New York in 1796. This appointment gave him an opportunity to display his skills as a mechanical engineer, because his duties included construction of an arsenal including an arms manufactory. During the construction, Brunel introduced a number of devices to improve both the boring and casting of cannon.

Brunel became an American citizen in 1796. This fact in combination with such promising prospects for a young man of twenty-nine make it rather surprising that he should have left the United States for England in January, 1799. There were, however, two compelling reasons for his departure. The first was Sophie Kingdom, who had returned to England from France in 1795 after several months of detention by French authorities. The second was his hopes for selling plans for block-making machinery to the Royal Navy.

Britain's Royal Navy required 100,000 blocks every year for sets of blocks and tackles. On shipboard and in the shipyards, the block and tackle was the main source of motive power. Brunel believed that his machines could make better blocks with great savings in labor costs. He intended to convince the firm that had the contract for blocks, Fox and Taylor of Southampton, by means of models made for him by the London toolmaker Henry Maudslay—virtually the founder of the machine-tool industry. The block contractors were not convinced either by his plans or by his models, but their contract was soon due to expire. Brunel made use of letters of introduction from no less a personage than Alexander Hamilton to gain access to the authorities at the Admiralty. He found them easier to convince, and the government agreed to begin its own production in May, 1803, using machines of his design.

During this period of selling and negotiations, Brunel invented several machines for use in textile mills and a writing machine. He had also wasted little time in his pursuit of Sophie Kingdom. They were married in November, 1799. She was six years younger than he. Over the next six years, they had three children—two daughters and, in 1806, a son who was himself to become a great engineer, Isambard Kingdom Brunel.

The block-making machinery was eminently successful. As Brunel had predicted, his blocks not only were much better made but also reduced the number of workers required to produce them to less than one-tenth the number formerly employed. Brunel had been so confident in his invention that his contract with the government stipulated that his fee would be the amount of money saved in one full year of production. Although the saving in the first year amounted to twenty-four thousand pounds, he actually received seventeen thousand pounds, and that only after considerable delay.

Brunel continued to patent various machines, but his interests were increasingly entrepreneurial. Between 1805 and 1812, he built a sawmill and supplied wood to the Royal Navy. In conjunction with this activity, he designed a number of woodworking machines. As his business contacts and interests expanded, he became involved in the manufacture of boots for the army, and by 1810 he had built machinery for producing boots.

All these enterprises came to a bad end. Brunel had chosen partners to run the business side of his affairs so that he could concentrate on invention. His choices were poor. Their lack of ability in combination with a series of disasters led to his financial ruin. The sawmill burned down in 1814. Soon thereafter, in 1815, the war with France came to an end, and he was left holding a large quantity of boots, which the government refused to buy. He still managed to survive financially, until his bankers failed in 1821. That was the final blow.

Unable to pay his creditors, Brunel and Sophie were imprisoned for debt between May and August, 1821. Their release apparently came about through the czar of Russia, who was interested in Brunel's plan for building a tunnel under the river at St. Petersburg so that communication could be maintained when the river was frozen. The influence of the czar and other prominent people led the British government to award Brunel five thousand pounds for the payment of his debts. This period was referred to as "the Misfortune" by the family, and it had the effect of spoiling his taste for independent business ventures. Thereafter Brunel remained strictly an engineer.

As usual for Brunel, he was busily turning out inventions and schemes even during this time of trouble. He invented a knitting machine and two types of tinfoil, and he made improvements in printing machinery. If his business acumen had been greater, he might have solved his financial problems with these inventions, but they brought him little profit. He also designed several bridges. In fact, his proposed solution to the ice problem at St. Petersburg was ultimately a bridge design. Only a few of his bridges were built—all by the French government on the Island of Bourbon.

After his release from jail, Brunel spent the next three years working on plans for floating piers and swing bridges that were built at the Liverpool docks. He also made improvements in paddle wheels and marine steam engines. This interest in steam engines may have led him to the design of a new engine called the gas engine. It was based on the principle that increasing the temperature of liquified gas in a confined space will increase the pressure. He hoped to operate the engine by alternately raising and lowering the temperature of such a gas, but the design never succeeded, despite the expenditure of much time and money.

In 1824, Brunel began his best-known project, the Thames Tunnel. No one had ever built a tunnel large enough for traffic to use that ran under a river, though it had been attempted under the Thames around the turn of the century. A small one could be built but not a large one, because the timbers normally used in mines could not support the great weight of a large expanse of roof

BUILDING THE THAMES TUNNEL

In order to keep water out and prevent caving-in, Marc Isambard Brunel built an iron casing for the shaft, about thirty-five feet high, aboveground. As digging proceeded inside the casing, it sank into the ground, forming the walls of the shaft. He added the rest of the casing as it continued to sink. The shield was then lowered and the tunnel begun.

As completed, the tunnel was thirty-seven and one-half feet wide by twenty-two and one-quarter feet high. It was rectangular in cross section with two arches inside containing the two roadways. The shield was a grid of cells stacked three high and twelve wide. Inside each of the thirty-six cells thus formed were fourteen horizontal planks pressed against the face of the tunnel by means of large screws bracing each against the sides of the cell. Workmen removed the planks one at a time and dug nine inches from the face of the tunnel. After all the planks had been removed and replaced in this fashion, hydraulic rams forced the entire shield forward. Masons then extended the walls to cover the gap between the rim of the shield and the finished wall. The gap was the weak point in the operation. Even such a small exposure of unsupported earth and water could and did result in disaster.

with the even greater weight of water above it. Brunel's solution to the problem came to him in 1818 as he watched a beetle boring through a rotten timber. The creature ate the wood and then excreted waste to form a lining for its tunnel. It occurred to Brunel that an iron shield pressed against the face of a tunnel by hydraulic rams could keep the water from bursting through. The shield would have a wide rim extending back into the tunnel to support the walls and ceiling. As it moved forward, workers would construct brick or masonry walls behind it. He patented the idea in 1818.

Traffic congestion at London Bridge made the desirability of a tunnel under the Thames obvious, and by 1824, Brunel had persuaded a number of investors to form a company, endorsed by the duke of Wellington, for the purpose of digging a tunnel from Rotherhithe to Wapping. This time, Brunel was an employee with a salary of one thousand pounds per year. Digging began at Rotherhithe on February 16, 1825. A shaft fifty feet in diameter and seventy feet deep had to be dug before the tunnel could begin.

The tunnel drew enormous attention from the public. Over Brunel's objections, the directors of the company allowed sightseers into the work area for a fee. Parliament, the press, the public, and friends of the directors all had ideas about how the project should be completed, but Brunel managed to retain control despite numerous battles among the directors. By 1826, his son, Isambard Kingdom Brunel, had become his second in command and actually oversaw the work. On May 18, 1827, the river broke into the tunnel. No one was killed and workmen managed to stop the flow of water by pouring clay into the hole from the river bed. After the tunnel was pumped dry, the Coldstream Guards played at a celebration dinner for fifty held inside the tunnel. On January 12, 1828, a second breakthrough occurred. This time, three men were killed and Isambard Brunel was severely injured. Such disasters in combination with strikes, panics, and strife within the company finally led to the abandonment of the undertaking for seven years in August, 1828. The public simply would not invest any more money in the company.

The company wanted a loan from the government to continue the work, but no loan was possible until the directors could end their quarrels. Finally, in 1832, the directors who questioned Brunel's management were defeated and resigned. A government loan allowed the work to begin again in 1835. Despite the incursion of the river on three more occasions, the tunnel reached completion in November, 1841. Brunel was knighted in March, 1841, and appeared as a hero at the official opening ceremony on March 25, 1843. Contemporaries suggested that the strain of building the tunnel had ruined his health. The portrait of him in the National Portrait Gallery shows a bald, bespectacled man of slight build with a serene expression. Appropriately, if incongruously, he is shown seated at a desk located inside the Thames Tunnel. He obviously considered it the great work of his life, and it may indeed have taken its toll on his health.

Brunel had already suffered his first stroke shortly before the opening ceremony. His productive life was over. He had another stroke in 1845 and died four years later, on December 12, 1849.

SIGNIFICANCE

Marc Isambard Brunel was one of the first to popularize the notion of professional civil engineering. The Thames Tunnel and the story of his block machinery captured the public imagination to an unparalleled extent. He and, to an even greater extent, his son, Isambard Brunel, came to stand almost as symbols for technical achievement in the Industrial Revolution. The fact that he was knighted for his accomplishments as an engineer not only indicated the importance of his activities to his contemporaries but also emphasized the changing spirit of the age. When he was born, in 1769, the idea of knighting someone for engineering accomplishments would hardly have been countenanced.

—Philip Dwight Jones

FURTHER READING

Beamish, Richard. *Memoir of the Life of Sir Marc Isambard Brunel.* London: Longmans, Green and Roberts, 1862. Most later accounts are based on this one. It is still probably the most useful source of information about Brunel's professional life.

Clements, Paul. *Marc Isambard Brunel.* London: Longmans, Green, 1970. Most of this book is devoted to a discussion of the Thames Tunnel construction.

Lampe, David. *The Tunnel.* London: Harrap, 1963. As the title indicates, this book is devoted exclusively to the construction of the Thames Tunnel. The account is much the same as that given in Clements's book (see above).

Noble, Lady Celia Brunel. *The Brunels: Father and Son.* London: Cobden Sanderson, 1938. The author was Isambard Brunel's granddaughter, and Marc Brunel's great-granddaughter. She provides information about their family life that is available no place else.

West, Graham. *Innovation and the Rise of the Tunnelling Industry*. New York: Cambridge University Press, 1988. Survey of technological innovations in the tunneling industry, from Brunel's invention of a shield for the Thames Tunnel in 1825 to construction of a tunnel under the English Channel.

SEE ALSO: William Fothergill Cooke and Charles Wheatstone; Benjamin Henry Latrobe; John Augustus Roebling; Thomas Telford.

RELATED ARTICLE in *Great Events from History: The Nineteenth Century, 1801-1900:* July 27, 1866: First Transatlantic Cable Is Completed.

WILLIAM CULLEN BRYANT

American poet and journalist

As a poet, Bryant is often regarded as a transitional figure because of his fluency in exploiting Romantic themes drawn from nature in conventional neoclassical verse forms. In his half-century as an editor for the New York Evening Post, *he was a vigorous spokesman for American liberal thought.*

BORN: November 3, 1794; Cummington, Massachusetts
DIED: June 12, 1878; New York, New York
AREAS OF ACHIEVEMENT: Literature, journalism

EARLY LIFE

William Cullen Bryant's father, Peter Bryant, was a physician who left Cummington, Massachusetts, to escape his debts soon after Bryant was born. When he returned two years later, the precocious child had already begun to read the Bible under the tutelage of his mother, née Sarah Snell, and her father, who was a noted deacon in the Congregationalist Church. The child was reared in an atmosphere of Calvinist piety and sober devotion to literature.

Bryant wrote his first notable poem when he was ten years old, a fifty-four-line celebration of American education composed for the commencement exercises at his school. In 1808, when the Embargo Act was creating a violent national controversy, he wrote a twelve-page poem, "The Embargo," attacking Thomas Jefferson—a piece of youthful invective that the mature Bryant, a Jeffersonian Democrat, came to regret. Bryant continued to write verses and to study under tutors, and, in 1810, he entered Williams College. By then, Bryant was already known as a poet, a reputation romantically enhanced by his tall, slender physique crowned with a shock of brown hair. He left Williams after two years, disappointed by the instruction and in the hope of attending Yale.

Family financial problems prevented Bryant from studying at Yale. Instead, in 1811, he went to Worthington to study law under Samuel Howe. In 1814, he moved again to Bridgewater to undertake his office training. In 1815, he was admitted to law practice. He continued to write verse, and, in 1817, five of his poems, including the first version of "Thanatopsis," appeared in the *North American Review*, to which they had been submitted by his father. Over the next few years, Bryant published more poems and essays in the *North American Review*. In 1821, firmly established in his legal practice in Great Barrington, Massachusetts, Bryant married Frances Fairchild, read "The Ages" as the Phi Beta Kappa poem at Harvard College's commencement ceremony, and published his first book of poetry. *Poems* was published through the efforts of three friends—Edward T. Channing, Richard Henry Dana, and Willard Phillips—and included such well-known works as "To a Waterfowl," "Inscription for the Entrance to a Wood," and the final version of "Thanatopsis." This successful year marked the beginning of his adult career as a stable husband and father and as a national man of letters.

LIFE'S WORK

The ambitious Bryant was not to be confined for long to the drudgery of practicing law in a small town, and, in 1825, he moved to New York City and assumed editorship of the *New York Review*. The new journal had circulation problems right from the beginning, however, and, in 1829, Bryant abandoned efforts to give it life and became part owner and editor-in-chief of the New York *Evening Post*. This crucial change shaped the remainder of his life, for he was able to turn the *Evening Post* into both a personal and a commercial success. Under his direction and often through his own editorials, the *Evening Post* became a major organ of democratic principles in American journalism.

The political quarrels in which Bryant involved the *Evening Post* became acrimonious at times. In one contretemps with the *Commercial Advertiser*, Bryant ended up beating William Stone, one of its editors, with a cowhide whip on Broadway. Although he was suspicious of

William Lloyd Garrison and the abolitionists, fearing that they would cause terrible harm to the Union, he defended eloquently the rights of antislavery writers. His outrage at the murder in Alton, Illinois, of the Reverend Elijah Lovejoy for his antislavery editorials produced a splendid defense of free speech:

> The right to discuss freely and openly, by speech, by the pen, by the press, all political questions, and to examine and animadvert upon all political institutions, is a right so clear and certain, so interwoven with our other liberties, so necessary, in fact to their existence, that without it we must fall at once into despotism or anarchy. To say that he who holds unpopular opinions must hold them at the peril of his life, and that, if he expresses them in public, he has only himself to blame if they who disagree with him should rise and put him to death, is to strike at all rights, all liberties, all protection of the laws, and to justify or extenuate all crimes.

Bryant expressed his humanitarianism in many ways. In 1857, he attacked the *Dred Scott* decision, fearing that it would make slavery a national institution. He was a fervent supporter of reform in the country's prisons and printed several editorials denouncing flogging and capital punishment. He was especially critical of the policy of imprisoning young people with veteran criminals, lamenting the corruption to which the practice led.

Bryant frequently wrote in the interest of civic reforms in New York City. He scrutinized both police and fire departments, urging that the police be given uniforms and that a paid fire department be organized. He editorialized in 1860 about the city's deplorable slum housing, demanding government regulation of tenement construction and rental. He conducted a long campaign to create a park in Manhattan, and when Central Park was planned, he fought the entrepreneurs who wanted to build apartments in the park. He was an enthusiastic friend of American dramatists and artists, lauding their efforts to produce truly American art. Aware of the lack of satisfactory copyright laws, Bryant sought the establishment of an international copyright law.

Over the years, Bryant had read such eighteenth century economists as Adam Smith, and their influence probably stood behind his swing from Federalism to Jacksonian democracy. However, Bryant was never a completely faithful adherent of party politics and could be independent when he believed that individual liberties were being threatened. Thus, in one editorial, he attacked the practice of burning abolitionist propaganda by southern justices of the peace. In 1839, he assailed the Democratic administration for ruling that a group of slaves who mutinied on the *Amistad* should be returned to their owners. Bryant described the mutineers as "heroes not malefactors."

As a result of the respect he commanded for his forthrightness, Bryant achieved some influence in politics. When the Civil War broke out, Bryant urged that the

William Cullen Bryant. (National Archives)

slaves be quickly freed and that the war be brought to an end. He supported Abraham Lincoln, apparently influenced him in his cabinet choices, and wrote to him concerning political issues.

The man of practical affairs continued to write poetry. A devoted traveler, Bryant visited Illinois in 1832 and wrote one of his most famous poems, "The Prairies," as a result. His later volumes of verse included *The Fountain, and Other Poems* (1842), *The White-Footed Deer* (1844), and *Thirty Poems* (1864). In 1870-1872, Bryant published his translations of Homer's *Iliad* (c. 800 B.C.E.) and *Odyssey* (c. 800 B.C.E.).

Bryant's poems of nature celebrate the opening up of the new nation: its topography and its flora and fauna. Famous poems such as "A Forest Hymn" and "Inscription for the Entrance to a Wood" are infused with a religious feeling that makes them confessions of personal faith. Although he did not embrace the Transcendentalism of Walt Whitman and Ralph Waldo Emerson, his poems often express a deep piety toward nature, an attitude that is essentially spiritual. Thus, in "A Forest Hymn" he sees in a "delicate forest flower . . . An emanation of the indwelling Life, A visible token of the upholding Love, That are the soul of this great universe."

SIGNIFICANCE

Bryant was certainly one of the giants of nineteenth century journalism. He has been praised for introducing culture to American newspapers, as well as for his important championing of free trade, civic consciousness, and the virtues of a rational liberalism. He was respected by his contemporaries as a man of high moral standards and varied literary accomplishments, and he proved to be a hardheaded businessperson who made a substantial success of the New York *Evening Post*. He was tireless in his role as a public figure, and his brief final illness was precipitated by his delivery, in Central Park, of an address honoring the Italian patriot Giuseppe Mazzini.

Although his poetry was extremely popular in his own day and was praised by Edgar Allan Poe and Emerson, he has not been accorded the highest honors by posterity. Such memorable poems as "Thanatopsis" and "To a Waterfowl" are moving dramatizations of universal emotions couched in simple language, but most of his works lack the complexity and richness associated with great poetry. Scholars have judged Bryant an able student of prosody, who influenced other poets both in his theory and in his practice, and he has been praised as the first American poet to respond sensitively to the literature of Latin America.

Bryant earned an honorable place in American history for his journalistic eloquence as an advocate of democratic principles, and he has given pleasure to many readers by his lyrical power in stating a true piety and idealism in smooth verse and assuring sentiments. He will be remembered for these accomplishments.

—*Frank Day*

FURTHER READING

Bigelow, John. *William Cullen Bryant*. Boston: Houghton Mifflin, 1890. Bigelow was a close friend and business partner of Bryant. His book lacks critical depth but is important for its firsthand account of Bryant's life and character.

Brown, Charles H. *William Cullen Bryant*. New York: Charles Scribner's Sons, 1971. A well-written, comprehensive, and reliable account of Bryant's life. The study of Bryant's long career at the New York *Evening Post* is excellent. Little literary analysis.

Bryant, William Cullen, II. "No Irish Need Apply: William Cullen Bryant Fights Nativism, 1836-1845." *New York History* 74, no. 1 (January, 1993): 29-46. Describes Cullen's campaign against the anti-immigration movement.

_____. "Painting and Poetry: A Love Affair of Long Ago." *American Quarterly* 22 (Winter, 1970): 859-882. Traces Bryant's involvement with painters such as Thomas Cole and his help in establishing the National Academy of the Arts.

Forshay, Ella M., and Barbara Novak. *Intimate Friends: Thomas Cole, Asher B. Durand, and William Cullen Bryant*. New York: New York Historical Society, 2000. Examines the close friendship of Bryant and the painters Cole and Durand.

Harrington, Joseph. "Re-Birthing 'America': Philip Frenaeu, William Cullen Bryant, and the Invention of Modern Poetics." In *Making America, Making American Literature: Franklin to Cooper*, edited by A. Robert Lee and W. M. Verhoeven. Atlanta, Ga.: Rodopi, 1996. Study of the two nineteenth century poets, comparing their work and examining their relation to America's national identity.

Krapf, Norbert, ed. *Under Open Sky: Poets on William Cullen Bryant*. New York: Fordham University Press, 1986. A tribute to Bryant, in the form of prose and poetry by twenty modern American poets. The writers provide an appraisal of Bryant's poetry.

McLean, Albert F., Jr. *William Cullen Bryant*. New York: Twayne, 1964. A thorough and sensitive study of Bryant's poetry, divided into three main sections:

"The Poems of Nature," "The Poems of Death," and "The Poems of Progress." Sees Bryant as a poet who "could never make the basic decision which Emerson was to formulate as the choice between self-reliance and conformity."

Nevins, Allan. *The Evening Post: A Century of Journalism*. New York: Russell & Russell, 1922. Includes a long account of Bryant's accomplishments as an editor, praising his business judgment, cultural influence, and liberal stance on social issues.

Parrington, Vernon L. "William Cullen Bryant: Puritan Liberal." In *Main Currents in American Thought*. Vol. 2. New York: Harcourt, Brace & World, 1930. Explicates Bryant's liberal politics and describes him as the "father of nineteenth century journalism."

Phair, Judith Turner. *A Bibliography of William Cullen Bryant and His Critics: 1808-1972*. Troy, N.Y.: Whitston, 1975. An extremely useful annotated bibliography of critical commentary on Bryant.

SEE ALSO: James Fenimore Cooper; Carolina Coronado.

RELATED ARTICLES in *Great Events from History: The Nineteenth Century, 1801-1900:* 1820's-1830's: Free Public School Movement; February 20, 1872: Metropolitan Museum of Art Opens.

JAMES BUCHANAN
President of the United States (1857-1861)

The last man to serve as president before the Civil War, Buchanan worked hard to preserve the Union. His presidency was devoted to trying to maintain the Democratic Party's North-South coalition.

BORN: April 23, 1791; Cove Gap, near Mercersburg, Pennsylvania
DIED: June 1, 1868; Lancaster, Pennsylvania
AREA OF ACHIEVEMENT: Government and politics

EARLY LIFE

James Buchanan was the second child of James and Mary Buchanan, both of whom were from strong northern Irish-Scottish Presbyterian families. The year James was born, his elder sister died, so, understandably, James received an unusual amount of attention and affection. After James, the Buchanans had nine more children: five girls followed by four boys. One of the girls and one of the boys did not live to be one year old. The arrival of so many brothers and sisters, however, did not diminish the special place James held in the Buchanan household.

James's formal education began at the Old Stone Academy in Mercersburg. In the autumn of 1807, he entered the junior class at Dickinson College. Although he was expelled once for disorderly conduct, he still managed to be graduated in 1809. James's personality was the source of most of his difficulties in college: He had a high opinion of himself and was quite obnoxious at times.

Buchanan's self-confidence was at least partially justified. He was an able student who became an extremely successful lawyer. Along with his intellectual ability, Buchanan was distinguished in appearance. He was tall with broad shoulders, had wavy blond hair, blue eyes, and fine features. He walked in a distinctive manner, with his head tilted slightly forward. His size, appearance, and mannerisms made him stand out, even in large crowds. After college, Buchanan studied law in the office of James Hopkins of Lancaster and was admitted to the Pennsylvania bar in 1812. He quickly established a successful law practice. The two main ingredients of his success were his knowledge of the law and his talent for oral presentation.

LIFE'S WORK

The political career of James Buchanan began with his election to the Pennsylvania House of Representatives in 1813. As a Federalist, he opposed the war with England, but once war was declared, he became a volunteer in a company of dragoons. In 1815, he was reelected. During this period, he spent considerable time and energy trying to delay the return of specie payment to protect the Bank of the United States.

Buchanan emerged on the national political scene in 1820, as a member of the U.S. House of Representatives. In 1824, with the demise of the Federalist Party, he found himself increasingly at odds with President John Quincy Adams. By 1826, Buchanan was working on a new Amalgamation Party in Pennsylvania, a mixture of Federalist Congressmen and old-line Democrats. What held the group together was its desire for a new political party and its support of Andrew Jackson. The main result of the creation of this new, vaguely defined party was that Buchanan became the primary dispenser of patronage in Pennsylvania.

After ten successful years in the House of Representatives, Buchanan was offered and accepted the ambassadorship to Russia. Before taking this post, he had been giving serious thought to leaving public life and returning to private law practice.

Buchanan stayed in St. Petersburg (now Leningrad) until August of 1833, returning home to run for the U.S. Senate. By that time, Buchanan was clearly identified with the Democratic Party, and he realized that this meant supporting President Jackson, which included following Vice President Martin Van Buren's lead in the Senate.

Buchanan was quickly recognized as a loyal and principled partisan. Although the Bank of the United States was located in his home state, Buchanan remained true to the Jackson administration's commitment to getting the federal government out of the banking business. Everyone knew that destroying the bank would move the financial center of the United States from Philadelphia to New York; still, Buchanan believed that the interests of the nation should come before the interests of his home state. Buchanan's ability to place the nation's interests above those of his state or region were motivated, at least in part, by his political ambitions. In 1838, many of his friends encouraged him to run for the office of governor of Pennsylvania; he chose instead to remain in the Senate and focus his attention on national issues.

James Buchanan. (Library of Congress)

President James K. Polk appointed Buchanan to serve as his secretary of state in 1844. Buchanan shared Polk's desire to expand the territory of the United States, but negotiating treaties for the rigid Polk was difficult at times. Buchanan's skills at settling disputes and striking compromises were perfected during his tour of duty at the State Department.

Buchanan's friends were surprised to learn that he was considering retirement as the 1848 presidential race approached. Whether it was the bitter division in the Democratic Party or the heightened concern over sectional rivalry, Buchanan sensed that 1848 would not be a good year for the Democratic Party. His instincts were correct. Buchanan's retirement from the State Department left him time to take care of some private affairs. He purchased his country estate, Wheatland, and began the groundwork for the 1852 presidential race. Buchanan's four years of retirement were some of the happiest he had known: He pursued the life of a gentleman farmer and spent time with the niece and nephew he was rearing. Unfortunately, his presidential ambitions were not well served by his temporary retirement.

The 1852 Democratic Convention was greatly divided. After some political maneuvering, much heated debate, and many caucuses, Franklin Pierce received the party's nomination. Pierce defeated Winfield Scott in the general election and then persuaded Buchanan to end his political retirement and serve as ambassador to Great Britain. Though Buchanan accepted this assignment reluctantly, it proved to be a good decision for him politically.

The Kansas-Nebraska Act was passed in 1854, repealing the Missouri Compromise and leaving both the nation and the Democratic Party bitterly divided. Buchanan's chief rivals for the 1856 Democratic presidential nomination were damaged by the sectional strife. When Buchanan returned home from London, many believed that he was the only candidate who could mend the Democratic Party's wounds and save the Union.

The 1856 party nomination did not come easily. Only after Stephen A. Douglas withdrew from the race was Buchanan able to acquire the 60 percent of the vote needed for the nomination. Fortunately for Buchanan, it was a transitional year for those who opposed the Democratic Party. Buchanan did not get a majority of the popular votes but was able to secure enough electoral college votes to win the presidency.

Buchanan's long journey to the White House was over. His quest for the presidency had been difficult, and so were his years in the White House. Buchanan's administration was haunted by the question of slavery in the United States territories. He hoped that the Supreme Court's *Dred Scott* decision would settle the issue once and for all, but his hopes were in vain. In many respects the Court's decision complicated the issue. Stephen Douglas found the Court's ruling to be a thorn in his side throughout the Lincoln-Douglas Debates of 1858. The battle raging within the Democratic Party was over the same issue. Douglas believed that "popular sovereignty" was the solution to the slavery controversy. Buchanan, like Abraham Lincoln, did not accept Douglas's solution. Unlike Lincoln, Buchanan believed that the *Dred Scott* decision denied the federal government authority over the institution of slavery in the territories and that only states had the authority to prohibit slavery within their boundaries. The end result was that Buchanan, the great compromiser and diplomat, could not settle the controversy.

Buchanan believed that the Democratic Party had held the Union together for the past decade; as president, he believed that it was his job to unite the party before 1860. However, Buchanan was unable to unify his party, and the Democrats lost the 1860 presidential campaign; then, as he expected, the Union came to face its greatest threat ever: civil war. Buchanan himself lived until June, 1868—long enough to observe the war and the beginnings of Reconstruction.

SIGNIFICANCE

Buchanan realized that the nation's strength was its ability to strike a compromise among conflicting interests. The Constitutional Convention of 1787 succeeded because it was able to forge a consensus among the different groups represented at the convention. The Democratic Party's success had been built upon its ability to rise above sectional disputes and focus on national issues. The United States, according to Buchanan, was a compromise republic that had succeeded in bending when necessary so that it would not break. Buchanan's unswerving commitment to the Union kept him from seeing that many Americans were tired of compromises. The old North-South coalition had been pushed to the breaking point, and the westward expansion had given the North a decided advantage. Those in the North knew this; those in the South knew this; but Buchanan seemed not to know.

What are often interpreted as Buchanan's southern sympathies were really little more than his sense of fair play coupled with his sincere desire to preserve the Union. One of the nation's great compromisers had the misfortune of being president at a time when compromise was no longer possible. Unfortunately, James Buchanan is remembered not for his thirty-eight successful years in politics but for his four unsuccessful years. Buchanan, like most other politicians in the United States, is remembered for what he did last.

—Donald V. Weatherman

FURTHER READING

Auchampaugh, Philip G. *James Buchanan and His Cabinet: On the Eve of Secession*. Lancaster, Pa.: Author, 1926. As the title indicates, this work deals with the Buchanan administration. Special emphasis is placed on Buchanan's handling of the slavery issue.

Baker, Jean H. *James Buchanan*. New York: Times Books, 2004. This book, one in a series on American presidents, offers a brief overview of Buchanan's life and an analysis of his presidency. Baker maintains that Buchanan's failed presidency illustrates the implications of weak leadership during a time of national crisis.

Binder, Frederick M. *James Buchanan and the American Empire*. Selinsgrove, Pa.: Susquehanna University Press, 1994. Examines Buchanan's influence on American foreign policy as president, secretary of state, U.S. senator, and minister to Russia and Great Britain. Concludes that Buchanan pursued an aggressive, but unsuccessful, foreign policy.

Birkner, Michael J., ed. *James Buchanan and the Political Crisis of the 1850's*. Selinsgrove, Pa.: Susquehanna University Press, 1996. Collection of essays providing a reassessment of Buchanan's presidency and a reexamination of American politics during the late 1850's.

Curtis, George Ticknor. *The Life of James Buchanan*. 2 vols. New York: Harper & Brothers, 1883. By far the most comprehensive work on the life of James Buchanan.

Jaffa, Harry. *Crisis of the House Divided*. New York: Doubleday, 1959. The best work on the theoretical issues involved in the Lincoln-Douglas Debates of 1858. Provides a good perspective for the issues that dominated American politics at that time.

Klein, Philip. *President James Buchanan: A Biography.* University Park: Pennsylvania State University Press, 1962. A comprehensive study that covers some secondary literature that was not available to Curtis (see above).

Moore, John Bassett, ed. *The Works of James Buchanan.* 12 vols. Philadelphia: J. B. Lippincott, 1908. A complete collection of Buchanan's public addresses and selected private papers. Includes a fine biographical essay by Moore.

Nichols, Roy F. *The Disruption of American Democracy.* New York: Macmillan, 1948. A careful examination of the Democratic Party from 1856 to 1861. Deals extensively with the differences between Douglas and Buchanan.

Reisman, David A. *The Political Economy of James Buchanan.* College Station: Texas A&M University Press, 1990. Focuses on President Buchanan's economic policies.

Smith, Elbert B. *The Presidency of James Buchanan.* Lawrence: University Press of Kansas, 1975. This work argues that Buchanan's actions were motivated by strong southern sympathies.

SEE ALSO: Stephen A. Douglas; Millard Fillmore; Abraham Lincoln; Edwin M. Stanton.

RELATED ARTICLES in *Great Events from History: The Nineteenth Century, 1801-1900:* February 2, 1848: Treaty of Guadalupe Hidalgo Ends Mexican War; July 6, 1854: Birth of the Republican Party; May, 1856-August, 1858: Bleeding Kansas; June 16-October 15, 1858: Lincoln-Douglas Debates; November 6, 1860: Lincoln Is Elected U.S. President.

CHARLES BULFINCH

American architect

One of the first American architects to have used drawings extensively for the construction of buildings, Bulfinch exercised a wide influence on the architecture of the early national period of American history, especially in his native New England.

BORN: August 8, 1763; Boston, Massachusetts
DIED: April 4, 1844; Boston, Massachusetts
AREA OF ACHIEVEMENT: Architecture

EARLY LIFE

The son of Thomas and Susan Apthorp Bulfinch, well-to-do and socially prominent Bostonians, Charles Bulfinch was born at the family home. He became one of the first American architects to complete a college education when he was graduated from Harvard in 1781, though not in architecture. His interest in architecture appears to have been awakened in 1785-1787, during a leisurely tour of England and the Continent.

In Paris, where Bulfinch lingered for a time, Thomas Jefferson, the American ambassador to the French court, took a friendly interest in him. It was at Jefferson's suggestion that Bulfinch continued his travels through southern France and Italy. After spending three weeks in Rome studying the city's ancient monuments, Bulfinch revisited Paris and London on his homeward journey. Upon his return to Boston, he took a position in the accounting office of a local merchant. In his spare time, he studied architectural works and, as did other gentleman-architects of the day, dabbled in design and construction.

Soon after his return from Europe, Bulfinch pointed toward his future dedication to architecture as a profession by submitting plans for a new Massachusetts statehouse, a project that eluded him until 1795, when he was chosen to design the building. Though he designed other important buildings during these early years, he continued to be only casually involved with architecture until he went bankrupt in 1796. On November 20, 1788, he married his cousin Hannah Apthorp, by whom he would have eleven children, including the author Thomas Bulfinch. In the spring of 1789, he visited Philadelphia and New York; his observations on this tour proved to be as influential in forming his style as those he had made while abroad.

Like most other early American architects, Bulfinch was self-taught. Nevertheless, he did not wish to design buildings simply by adapting various elements of architecture chosen from books. As did later architects, he tried to understand buildings, their materials and functions, and the methods by which they were built. He was concerned about how buildings related to their surroundings, about the connections between buildings and streets, walks, parks, other structures in the vicinity, and the city as a whole.

It has been said that between about 1790 and 1825, Bulfinch practically rebuilt Boston, transforming it from a provincial town with few buildings and meandering streets into a tasteful city of well-designed buildings set amid trees, plantings, and parks. One reason for his success was the excellence of his buildings. Another was his involvement in the affairs of Boston through his civic work. He would come to understand thoroughly the city and its needs by serving as a member, and chairman, of the board of selectmen.

Charles Bulfinch. (Library of Congress)

LIFE'S WORK

Though his later buildings are of the classical revival style, which came to be preferred by such architects as Benjamin Latrobe and Jefferson, Bulfinch's early work was Georgian in character, by way of the brothers Adam (Robert, John, James, and William) in England. In 1788, the Hollis Street Church in Boston was constructed from his plans. Representing Bulfinch's initial attempt at church design, it was followed by plans for churches in Taunton and Pittsfield, Massachusetts, and during a later period, others in Boston. His classical interests were exhibited in his triumphal arch, built in 1789 in Boston for George Washington's reception, and in his Beacon Hill Memorial Column, of Doric order, constructed in 1790-1791. More ambitious in scale than anything previously attempted in New England, the statehouse in Hartford, Connecticut, was begun from Bulfinch's plans in 1793. The same year, he provided the plans for the Boston Theatre. Erected at the corner of Franklin and Federal streets, it burned in 1798 and was rebuilt by Bulfinch in the same year.

Bulfinch was elected to Boston's board of selectmen in 1791; he would serve on the board, with only one break, for twenty-six years. He was active on the board committees that lighted Boston's streets for the first time in 1792 and admitted both male and female children to the city's public schools. For the last eighteen of these years, he chaired the board, a position similar to that of a mayor.

During the early 1790's, Bulfinch began a reformation of New England's architecture as he introduced the delicate detail of the Adam style. Many of his designs were built on or around Beacon Hill in Boston. It has been argued that their impact on the city was even stronger than that of his churches and public buildings because the houses and their settings established an atmosphere of beauty and charm long preserved in the Beacon Hill area. His first houses were for Joseph Coolidge, Sr. (1791-1792), and Joseph Barrell (1792-1793), both of which contained the first circular staircases in New England. The Barrell house in Somerville, Massachusetts, had an oval parlor projecting from the garden side beneath a semicircular portico with tall columns. Its layout was soon used in the Elias Hasket Derby mansion (1795-1799) in Salem, which was designed by Bulfinch, then modified and executed by Samuel McIntire.

Bulfinch joined with others during the mid-1790's in planning a block of sixteen houses in Boston known as the Tontine Crescent. Work on this project was partially completed when trouble with England brought unsettled business conditions to Boston. During the ensuing financial crisis, Bulfinch's partners withdrew, leaving him to assume the cost of completing the work. Losing both his own fortune and that of his wife, he was adjudged bankrupt in January of 1796. About the time of his bankruptcy, he resigned from the board of selectmen. Previously regarded as a scholar and gentleman of fortune but an amateur in architecture, Bulfinch was now faced with earning a livelihood. He turned his talent and full attention to the practice of architecture, with most successful results. In 1796, Bulfinch designed a house for the prominent and powerful Boston politician Harrison Gray Otis. He followed it with two others for Otis: the second in 1800, usually considered the finest of the three, and the third in 1805.

The Massachusetts statehouse (1795-1797) on Boston's Beacon Hill represents the crowning achievement of Bulfinch's early work. Though by the twentieth century it became only a part of a much larger complex—having been added onto a number of times—it has survived in good condition. A simple rectangular structure in plan and exterior, it is two stories high with a basement and a portico in front. The whole is crowned by a dome made of wooden planks, matched to fit tightly against one another. With its elegant proportions, the relationship of the dome to other elements, and its richly ornamented and spacious interiors, Bulfinch's Massachusetts statehouse was immediately hailed as a masterpiece.

In 1799, Bulfinch was returned to the Boston board of selectmen, serving as its chairman until his departure for Washington in 1817. He soon found himself deeply involved in all the financial, commercial, and governmental affairs of the city. The time of his chairmanship marked the years of the great development of old Boston. Its form would be attributable largely to Bulfinch in his dual capacity as city official and architect. During this period, his architecture and civic work complemented each other.

In addition to designing theaters, hospitals, churches, schools, government buildings, markets, prisons, wharves, warehouses, multifamily houses, and numerous single-family dwellings, Bulfinch planned several portions of Boston. The neglected Common was turned into a park; three sides were fronted with fine buildings of uniform character: Park Street, in 1803-1804; Colonade Row on Tremont Street, in 1810-1812; and Beacon Street, from about 1800. Bulfinch laid out plans for the lands on Boston Neck, in South Boston, and on the site of the Mill Pond. He also inaugurated the development of Franklin Street and certain changes in the city's street system.

Of Bulfinch's five churches in Boston, four were built after 1800. It is said that he followed the schemes of Christopher Wren's churches in London, paying great attention to the varieties of the type. Bulfinch designed the first Roman Catholic Church in Boston, the Church (later Cathedral) of the Holy Cross (1800-1803) at the corner of Franklin and Federal streets. Contemporary sources describe it as in the Italian Renaissance style. Completed in 1804, the New North Church (later St. Stephen's Catholic Church) is the only surviving example of Bulfinch's Boston churches. It has been much modified and is not considered one of his best designs. The Federal Street Church of 1809 represents Bulfinch's first and only Gothic work.

The New South Church was completed in 1814. Generally considered Bulfinch's most beautiful church, it was the first stone church erected in Boston since Bulfinch's grandfather, Charles Apthorp, got Peter Harrison to design King's Chapel. The distinctive features of the New South Church were an octagonal ground plan and a Doric portico of freestanding columns. One of the two surviving Bulfinch churches is the Church of Christ in Lancaster, Massachusetts, which was built in 1816. Its most prominent feature, the triple coeval arches in the portico, is an unexplained "improvement" by the master builder sent out from Boston to supervise the work.

Bulfinch's public buildings in Boston completed after 1800 include the almshouse (1799-1801); the admirable warehouses of India Wharf (1803-1807); the Boylston Hall and Market (1809), later occupied as the city's first public library; the Suffolk County Court House (1810-1812); and the first and central unit of the Massachusetts General Hospital (1818-1823). Among the public buildings built outside Boston from Bulfinch's plans, the best known are the state prison at Charlestown, Massachusetts (1804-1805), University Hall at Harvard (1813-1814), and the statehouse in Augusta, Maine (1829-1832). The private houses Bulfinch designed after 1800 were built mainly in Boston, typical examples being those at 85 Mount Vernon Street, 45 Beacon Street, and numbers 13, 15, and 17 on Chestnut Street.

In 1817, President James Monroe appointed Bulfinch to succeed Latrobe as architect in charge of rebuilding the United States Capitol, which had been burned by the British in 1814. Moving his family to Washington, Bulfinch remained in this position until 1830. Essentially, he was called upon to complete the wings and construct the central part along lines established by the Capitol's earlier architects. Bulfinch joined the two wings with a central dome. His principal contribution was the detailed form of the western front, a portico with steps and terrace forming an approach to it. Though his dome was later replaced by a larger and grander one, the west front remains. In addition to completing the Capitol, Bulfinch designed a church in Washington and acted as a consultant for several other government buildings. Returning to Boston at the age of sixty-seven, he lived in retirement, with occasional visits elsewhere, until his death in 1844.

SIGNIFICANCE

American architects during and before Bulfinch's day generally fell into one of two groups: amateur gentleman-architects who pursued some other career while designing buildings as an avocation, or architect-builders who were more concerned with construction than design. Though he began as one of the former, Bulfinch soon became totally involved with architecture. Unlike the architect-builders who actually worked on their buildings, Bulfinch saw his role—much in the same vein as later professionals—as that of supervising construction to ensure the proper implementation of designs and quality of workmanship.

Bulfinch's American practice of architecture combined his New England background with his European tastes. Appropriately, the site of his remains in Cambridge's Mount Auburn Cemetery is marked by the Franklin Urn, which Bulfinch placed in front of the Tontine Crescent in 1795 as a symbol of his plans to remake Boston in the image of neoclassical London. Early in his career, Bulfinch's city honored him for his architecture and his civic work, showing an appreciation which continued to grow. Over the years, his architecture came to belong not only to Boston and New England but also to the country as a whole.

—*L. Moody Simms, Jr.*

FURTHER READING

Brown, Glenn. *History of the United States Capitol.* 2 vols. Washington, D.C.: Government Printing Office, 1901-1904. Relates the story of Bulfinch's long and sometimes frustrating assignment in Washington.

Bulfinch, Ellen Susan. *The Life and Letters of Charles Bulfinch.* Boston: Houghton Mifflin, 1896. The major source for biographical information. Bulfinch's granddaughter provides a good treatment of the forces that shaped his ultimate professional commitment.

Kimball, Fiske. *Mr. Samuel McIntire, Carver: The Architect of Salem.* Salem, Mass.: Essex Institute, 1940. Details Bulfinch's work for the Derby family of Salem.

Kirker, Harold. *The Architecture of Charles Bulfinch.* Cambridge, Mass.: Harvard University Press, 1969. Concentrates on the works themselves. Bulfinch's commissions are arranged chronologically; each is treated separately. One of the appendixes deals with "minor commissions and attributions." Well illustrated.

Kirker, Harold, and James Kirker. *Bulfinch's Boston, 1787-1817.* New York: Oxford University Press, 1964. Deals largely with the social and cultural history of Boston during the period. Bulfinch's architectural work is subordinated to his public career.

Maurer, David. "Charles Bulfinch." *Classic American Homes* 27, no. 3 (July, 2001): 94. Profile of Bulfinch, with information about his family, career, architectural training, and the neoclassical designs of his buildings.

Morison, Samuel Eliot. *The Maritime History of Massachusetts, 1783-1860.* Boston: Houghton Mifflin, 1921. Provides a good summary treatment of Bulfinch's architecture as well as a picture of the Boston merchants who were his chief clients.

Place, Charles A. *Charles Bulfinch: Architect and Citizen.* Boston: Houghton Mifflin, 1925. A biographical treatment that focuses on Bulfinch as a citizen and Christian gentleman.

Shand-Tucci, Douglass. *Built in Boston: City and Suburb, 1800-2000.* Rev. and expanded ed. Amherst: University of Massachusetts Press, 1999. Part 1 of this architectural history contains information about Bulfinch and other nineteenth century architects.

SEE ALSO: Benjamin Henry Latrobe; James Monroe; Louis Sullivan.

RELATED ARTICLE in *Great Events from History: The Nineteenth Century, 1801-1900:* May, 1819: Unitarian Church Is Founded.

LUTHER BURBANK
American horticulturalist

The leading American plant breeder of his time, Burbank introduced more than eight hundred new plants and gave the world a lesson in the value of horticultural science by demonstrating how to make plants work for the benefit of human society.

BORN: March 7, 1849; Lancaster, Massachusetts
DIED: April 11, 1926; Santa Rosa, California
AREA OF ACHIEVEMENT: Agriculture

EARLY LIFE

Luther Burbank was the thirteenth child of Samuel Walton Burbank, a farmer and brickmaker and a descendant of seventeenth century English stock. Luther's mother, Olive Ross, a strong-featured and strong-willed woman of Scottish and French descent, was Samuel's third wife. He was a shy youngster seldom disciplined by his parents. His siblings included a brother and sister as well as three half-brothers and two half-sisters. He received an elementary school education near his home but was never comfortable with oral recitation.

At the age of fifteen, Burbank entered Lancaster Academy, a preparatory school for Harvard and Yale, and studied the basic curriculum of Latin, Greek, French, geometry, algebra, arithmetic, philosophy, drawing, and English. Burbank was apparently a good student, ranking eighth out of the top ten students in his class in 1867. He was an avid reader, as is evidenced by his early familiarity with the works of Charles Darwin, Alexander von Humboldt, and Henry David Thoreau. The writings of these naturalists were to have a lasting impact on young Burbank, but the most important influence in developing his scientific curiosity was his cousin Levi Sumner Burbank, the curator of geology at the Boston Society of Natural History.

As a young man, Burbank was five feet, eight inches tall, about 125 pounds, with sparkling blue eyes. After his school experience, he attempted two nonacademic careers. The first was a job in the Worcester branch factory of the Ames Plow Works. Burbank had gone to the factory for three or four summers to learn the trade of a mechanic. After high school, he worked at the Ames Plow Works turning plow rounds on a lathe at a wage of three dollars a week. He soon designed an improvement in his machine that increased productivity, and his piecework wages rose significantly. He was not able to keep this job very long, however, because his health suffered because of the sawdust in the air.

Burbank next studied medicine under a local doctor for several months. He gave this up when his father died, in 1868. Burbank was not interested in farming at this time, although as a young boy he had shown some interest in gardening. (To the dismay of his father, Burbank transplanted weeds into the family garden plot to see if they would grow.)

In 1870, the young Burbank, always afflicted with a frail constitution, decided to take a sea voyage to improve his health. The schooner was wrecked, and he almost lost his life.

LIFE'S WORK

In 1871, Burbank made a decision that would change his life dramatically: He resolved to try his hand at truck-gardening. At the age of twenty-one, he bought seventeen acres of land adjoining his mother's home in Lunenburg, Massachusetts. He pursued this profession for about five years, but he was more interested in experimenting with plants than in growing them for market. In 1872, Luther found a seed ball on the plant of a potato containing twenty-three seeds, a rare occurrence. He planted the seeds and discovered one good potato (later named the "Burbank") of attractive shape with a white skin. The tuber was destined later to become a huge commercial success. Burbank sold sixty bushels of the potatoes to James J. H. Gregory, a seedsman of Marblehead, Massachusetts, for $150.

With the money he made from the potatoes, Burbank left for California in October, 1875, as the climate there was better suited for the horticultural work that he had decided to pursue. (His mother packed him a nine-day box lunch for the long train trip.) He arrived in San Francisco on October 29, 1875. Burbank was shocked at the amount of liquor consumed in the city and he vowed never to drink liquor himself. On October 31, 1875, he reached Santa Rosa, a frontier town, north of San Francisco, that was blessed with a temperate climate. The plants he saw there grew larger than any he had ever seen, because the area had no frost.

Burbank lived for a short time with his brother Alfred and another bachelor in an eight-by-ten-foot cabin. To earn money, Burbank did carpentry work and odd jobs in the area. In the winter of 1876, Burbank went to work in Petaluma, California, at the large nursery of W. H. Pepper. He saved his money and soon returned to Santa Rosa.

In the summer of 1877, Burbank's mother and sister Emma came to Santa Rosa and bought a house with four acres of adjacent land. Burbank rented the land and started his own nursery. Within ten years, the quality of his fruit and shade trees was famous, and he was making sixteen thousand dollars annually with his plants. His skill in plant-breeding was to assure his commercial success. In the spring of 1881, he received an order for twenty thousand prune trees for delivery in the fall. According to other nurserymen, it would take eighteen months to fill such a large order, but Burbank used the technique of "force budding" to deliver the trees on schedule.

Burbank was interested in cross-breeding domestic plant stock with foreign material, so in 1885, he imported plum seedlings from Yokohama, Japan. One of these seedlings became the famous "Burbank plum" that is still popular today. That same year, Luther bought eighteen acres at Sebastopol near Santa Rosa to use for experimental growing. By 1888, he was committed to the development of new varieties of plants, so he sold part of his retail nursery business (the fruit and shade tree segment) to his partner, R. W. Bell. Burbank could now concentrate on the creation of new or unusual plant materials to sell at wholesale to other nurserymen.

Luther Burbank. (Library of Congress)

On September 23, 1890, the forty-one-year-old horticulturist married a domineering young widow, Helen A. Coleman, from Denver, Colorado. Almost immediately, conflicts developed between Helen and Burbank's mother and sister. The marriage, which lasted six years, caused Burbank much mental and physical aggravation, partly because of Helen's violent temper.

By 1893, Burbank had developed enough different varieties of walnuts, berries, plums, prunes, roses, lilies, potatoes, and quinces to list them in his nursery catalog, *New Creations in Fruits and Flowers* (1893). Stark Brothers' Nurseries of Missouri and several large eastern retail nurseries made significant purchases from this catalog, thereby assuring Burbank's future financial success. As the years passed, Burbank attracted a large clientele of professional nurserymen both in the United States and abroad.

On the threshold of the twentieth century, Burbank's products were being grown throughout the world, and his reputation as the "wizard of horticulture" was well established. There was no magical formula, however, to the Burbank success story, only hard work, perseverance, and a keen intuition as to what plants would prove a commercial success. At this time, Burbank developed the Shasta daisy, a perennial favorite of home gardeners. His breeding method consisted of choosing American wild daisies as breeding stock, introducing pollen from European daisies, and crossing the resultant hybrids with a Japanese species. Any plant in any part of the world was fair game in Burbank's search for marketable products.

Burbank was to come increasingly under the criticism of other horticulturists, particularly those attached to university experiment stations. (Burbank did not have the formal college education in the plant sciences that some university-trained experts thought necessary, although he did receive an honorary doctor of science degree from Tufts College in 1905.) It was true that he did not keep proper records of his experimental crossings or always guard against self-pollination in his work, but he was more interested in the results of experimentation, not the theory. He gave the impression at times of being a consummate egotist; he was the most famous plant breeder in America, and none too modest about this reputation. He allowed others to exaggerate the merits of his products, and because of the sheer volume of the materials he was turning out, he did not take as much time to prove the reliability of those creations as he had been able to earlier in his career.

The Carnegie Institute became interested in Burbank's techniques and plants and, between 1905 and 1909, awarded him a grant of ten thousand dollars annually with the stipulation that a representative from the institute would observe Burbank's methods and write a report on them. (The report on the observations was never compiled by the Institute, in part because of the difficulty of interpreting Burbank's experimental notes.)

Burbank had been working on the development of a spineless cactus for use as cattle food, and in 1906, he introduced this cactus to the nursery trade. It proved to be a disappointment because it was not completely spineless, and the resultant unfavorable publicity damaged Burbank's reputation. Other products that did not live up to the claims of his catalog included the "Winter rhubarb" and a hybrid berry that Burbank called the "Sunberry." These failures called into question his credibility, particularly among those horticulturists and breeders who may have felt resentful of his fame.

In 1912, the Luther Burbank Society and the Luther Burbank Press were formed for the purpose of promoting and selling a multivolume work on the man and his accomplishments, *Luther Burbank: His Methods and Discoveries and Their Practical Applications* (1915). Unfortunately, the promotional tactics and "hype" associated with marketing the twelve-volume set cast a further shadow upon his reputation, although the color photographs and illustrations in them were quite unusual for that time.

That same year, 1912, saw the organization of the Luther Burbank Company, another vehicle used by exploiters, with Burbank's unwitting consent, to promote his name in association with the marketing of his horticultural creations. Rollo J. Hough and W. Garner Smith received the exclusive rights to sell Burbank's products. These financiers, however, knew very little about the nursery business. Soon quality control grew lax, and Burbank's reputation suffered accordingly. By 1916, the Luther Burbank Press went out of business, and many investors lost their money in the enterprise. That same year the Luther Burbank Company declared bankruptcy and Burbank resumed control of his nursery and seed business. These failures suggest that Burbank was not a very good businessperson in his later years, but in spite of these failures, he still prospered financially.

In 1916, at the age of sixty-seven, Burbank married his young secretary, Elizabeth Jane Waters. International affairs were to involve the United States in World War I by the next year, and although Burbank was a pacifist, he was to support the American war effort. During the war he introduced a wheat, "Quality," which turned out to be a previously bred Australian variety. His credibility as a cereal breeder was called into question, although he initially believed that he had developed a new hybrid.

For all the criticisms arising from the professional horticultural ranks, Burbank's popular image remained intact. His health, however, never robust, grew worse. During the first few years of the 1920's, a series of illnesses beset him that were to undermine further his already failing constitution. On March 24, 1926, Burbank suffered a heart attack; on April 11, he died. He was buried in the yard of his old home in Santa Rosa, under a cedar of Lebanon that he had grown from a seed years before.

SIGNIFICANCE

In order to evaluate the work of Luther Burbank it is necessary to evaluate the man. Born into a strict New England Puritanical background, he changed his religion to that of the Baptist faith, then to Unitarianism. He believed that he had psychic powers, a conviction that may have contributed to his high-strung, nervous personality. Something of a hypochondriac and diet faddist, he ascribed in his latter years to the practice of yoga.

Burbank the man was always different from those around him, as is so often the case with those who might be labeled "creative." He saw things differently from the way most of his peers did, and because of his outspoken opinions, he often became the center of controversy, both in his professional and personal life. The maverick in Burbank dictated his unique approaches to horticulture. He dared to experiment, to attempt the new and untried, and sometimes to fail. These failures were difficult for a man who needed the approval and praise of his colleagues and adoring supporters.

It was among the general gardening public that Burbank was to have the greatest appeal. He popularized horticulture as a science among those amateur gardeners who wanted something new, something different, something unique. It is for this spirit of seeking the unknown that Burbank should best be remembered: He was a pioneer unafraid to reach for the unreachable. Burbank epitomized that spirit of discovery coupled with the hope of success that so characterized early twentieth century America.

—*Charles A. Dranguet, Jr.*

FURTHER READING

Burbank, Luther, with Wilbur Hall. *The Harvest of the Years*. Boston: Houghton Mifflin, 1927. This alleged autobiography was ghostwritten by Wilbur Hall and published the year after Burbank's death. An introductory biography gives no real background to his life. The volume in general is a laudatory account of Burbank's work. Not documented, but Burbank does attempt to dispel the aura of mystery surrounding his plant developments.

_____. *Partner of Nature*. Edited by Wilbur Hall. New York: D. Appleton-Century, 1939. This book, ghostwritten and published after Burbank's death, is a single-volume condensation of the twelve-volume work by Burbank, *Luther Burbank: His Methods and Discoveries and Their Practical Application*, which was edited by John Whitson, Robert John, and Henry Smith Williams and published in New York by the Luther Burbank Press between 1914 and 1915. The condensed volume is aimed at a general audience interested in gardening rather than in the technical aspects of plant breeding.

"Crazy for Shasta Daisies." *Martha Stewart Living* 124 (March, 2004): 62. Recounts Burbank's efforts to breed the ideal daisy, despite skepticism from some botanists.

Dreyer, Peter. *A Gardener Touched with Genius: The Life of Luther Burbank*. New York: Coward, McCann and Geoghegan, 1975. Rev. ed. Berkeley: University of California Press, 1985. This revised edition of the original 1975 work is still the definitive biography of Luther Burbank. Incorporating the correspondence of his friend Edward J. Wickson and the papers of the plant scientist George H. Shull, this book expands and refines the previous 1945 biography of Burbank by Walter L. Howard and the unpublished critical work of the plant geneticist Donald Jones. Well documented, but no separate bibliography is included.

Felciano, Renée, and Jean C. Fisher. *Gold Ridge Experiment Farm, Sebastopol, California: A History of the Property, 1884-1986*. Sebastopol, Calif.: Sonoma County Landmarks Commission, Sebastopol Area Housing Corporation, 2004. A history of Burbank's experimental farm, which is listed on the National Register of Historic Places. The book is available from the Western Sonoma County Historical Society, a Sebastopol-based organization that is restoring the farm's cottage.

Gould, Stephen Jay. "Does the Stoneless Plum Instruct the Thinking Reed?" *Natural History* 101, no. 4 (April, 1992): 16. Examines Burbank's vision of a genetically superior genetic race, a concept that was part of a wider eugenics movement.

Harwood, W. S. *New Creations in Plant Life: An Authoritative Account of the Life and Work of Luther Burbank*. New York: Macmillan, 1905. An exaggerated account of Burbank's achievements. Misleading statements abound in this work, giving Burbank the status of a miracle worker with almost supernatural powers. This was, however, the first complete account of Burbank's plant breeding techniques.

Howard, Walter L. "Luther Burbank: A Victim of Hero Worship." *Chronica Botanica* 9 (Winter, 1945): 299-506. Written by an emeritus professor of pomology at the University of California, this book-length article is a successful effort at portraying the real Burbank beneath the exaggerated facade that the general public knew. Points out the controversial episodes in Burbank's life and brings him "down to earth." Supplies the honest facts about Burbank's work without prejudice or judgmental rhetoric.

Kraft, Ken, and Pat Kraft. *Luther Burbank: The Wizard and the Man*. New York: Meredith Press, 1967. The first of the modern biographies of Burbank that dared to point out some of his faults and omissions. This well-written, readable work contains one particularly interesting chapter on Burbank's attitudes on diet and health. Generally informative, balanced account of the "plant wizard."

SEE ALSO: Johnny Appleseed; Ferdinand Julius Cohn.

RELATED ARTICLE in *Great Events from History: The Nineteenth Century, 1801-1900:* 1894-1895: Kellogg's Corn Flakes Launch the Dry Cereal Industry.

JACOB BURCKHARDT
Swiss historian

A uniquely gifted historian and literary artist, Burckhardt was a pioneer in the development of modern Kulturgeschichte, *the study of nonpolitical aspects of civilization. His lasting contribution was in Renaissance historiography, a field in which his work became a model for the treatment of culture in the study of civilization.*

BORN: May 25, 1818; Basel, Switzerland
DIED: August 8, 1897; Basel, Switzerland
ALSO KNOWN AS: Jacob Christopher Burckhardt (full name)
AREA OF ACHIEVEMENT: Historiography

EARLY LIFE

Part of an influential, aristocratic Swiss family, Jacob Burckhardt recalled his early childhood in Basel as being very happy. For three centuries, Jacob's ancestors utilized their financial abilities to amass a considerable fortune in the silk industry and international trade, which they parlayed into political power. The Burckhardts held one of the two burgomaster positions in the city for nearly two centuries, while other members of the family served the community as professors and clergymen. Jacob's own father, one of the less affluent Burckhardts, studied theology in Heidelberg and was pastor of the Basel ministry at the time of his son's birth. In 1838, the senior Burckhardt became the administrative head of the Reformed church in the Basel canton. Jacob recalled his father as being pleasant, a good scholar, and a capable artist. It was his father's artistic ability that first stimulated the youth's enduring love for art.

The joys of early childhood turned to sorrow with the unexpected death of his mother in 1830. This experience made a lasting impression on twelve-year-old Jacob, as he became painfully aware of the transitoriness of all living things. Throughout his adult life, Jacob experienced difficulty in establishing lasting relationships, and it may well have been memories of his mother's death that influenced his decision to remain a bachelor.

Burckhardt's patrician heritage instilled in him an aristocratic prejudice, a sensitivity to beauty and form, a deep, abiding respect for the dignity of humankind, and a Protestant morality, all of which would be reflected in his life as a teacher and scholar. As he matured into adulthood, however, his personal appearance seemed to belie his conservative nature. As a young man, he was notable for his uniquely stylish clothes, distinct coiffure, finger rings, and excessive taste for red wine and cigars. In later years, he dropped the foppish airs but retained his taste for wine and cigars.

The public school in Basel provided Burckhardt with an excellent primary education in the classics but left him undecided as to a vocation. After a brief stay in French-speaking Neuchâtel, where he wrote an essay on Gothic architecture, he entered the University of Basel in 1837 to study theology. Eighteen months later, he experienced a prolonged religious crisis that resulted in his abandoning his orthodox religious beliefs and rejecting the ministry. Because of the support and encouragement of his father, Burckhardt attended the University of Berlin from 1839 to 1843 to pursue his historical interests.

While he was at Berlin, Burckhardt was praised by the renowned classical scholars August Boeckh and Johann Gustav Droysen for his extensive knowledge of antiquity, but Burckhardt ultimately took his degree in 1843 under the eminent scientific historian Leopold von Ranke. Burckhardt greatly admired Ranke and his seminars, but the two never established a close relationship. Although master and student have been used to illustrate two diametrically different approaches to historiography, it should be noted that Ranke had praise for his student, and in 1872 Burckhardt was offered the chair of history at the University of Berlin as Ranke's successor—an offer that he refused because of his abhorrence of German politics.

Burckhardt's closest association in Berlin was with the pioneer art historian Franz Kugler, who encouraged Burckhardt to combine his love for history with his love for art and directed the attention of the fledgling student to Italy and the Renaissance.

LIFE'S WORK

In 1843, the University of Basel awarded Burckhardt a Ph.D. in absentia and the following year invited him to become a lecturer on history and art—a position he held with distinction for nearly fifty years. Because the university did not have an official vacancy until 1858, Burckhardt had to supplement his lecturing income with a variety of other jobs. For two years, he was the editor of the conservative *Basler Zeitung*, and he taught at the local grammar school for most of his career.

In 1846, Burckhardt was given permission by Kugler to revise the latter's text on art history, which brought in some revenue, and he was offered a lucrative position at the Academy of Art in Berlin. Burckhardt had no desire to return to Berlin but did so out of friendship to Kugler. Over the next twelve years, Burckhardt taught at Basel, Berlin, and Zurich, with lengthy visits to Italy in 1847, 1848, and 1853.

Despite his excessive workload and extensive travels, Burckhardt was able to publish two important works during this period. His first major work, *Die Zeit Konstantins des Grossen* (1853; *The Age of Constantine the Great*, 1949), attested his love for ancient civilization. Although the study showed the important role Christianity played in the cultural life of the Middle Ages, Burckhardt's sympathies lay clearly with the decaying ancient world. His second publication, *Der Cicerone* (1855; *The Cicerone*, 1873), was a detailed study of Italian art, and it became the most popular travel guide to Italy in Europe. In 1855, Burckhardt accepted a teaching position at the new polytechnical institute in Zurich, not only to increase his earnings but also to gain access to the rich collection of Renaissance materials housed there. Three years later, there was a vacancy at the University of Basel, and Burckhardt readily accepted that university's only chair of history.

Family influence, formal education, work experience, and foreign travel provided Burckhardt with the inspiration for his life's work. After observing at first hand the political turmoil in Germany, the quiet, freedom-loving Swiss was repulsed by those scholars who saw history as past politics or a chronology of state development. It was the nonpolitical past, more specifically, the moral and mental past, that fascinated Burckhardt. His objective was to undertake a meticulous study of thought and conduct, religion and art, scholarship and speculation in an attempt to penetrate the *Kultur* of the people and discover what he called "the spirit of the age." Thus, in 1842 he announced that it was to *Kulturgeschichte* that he intended to devote his life, and the fulfillment of this self-established goal is represented par excellence in *Die Kultur der Renaissance in Italien* (1860; *The Civilization of the Renaissance in Italy*, 1878).

Burkhardt divided his book on the Renaissance into six sections, each of which discussed a specific aspect of Italian *Kultur*. The section on the state as a work of art provided the political framework, as it emphasized the conflict between emperors and popes, but it was not political history in the traditional sense. His intent was to demonstrate how the state became free of outside control and, in the process, produced what Burckhardt called the modern "state-spirit."

Burckhardt's phenomenon of the state-spirit has its counterpart in the evolution of modern individualism, which was explained in the second section of the book. The development of the individual was characterized primarily by the rebirth of secularism and the perception of the Italian Humanists as independent entities, free of any corporate structure, such as the Church. While rebirth was the general theme of the entire work, it was of specific concern in the third section on the revival of antiquity. Here, Burckhardt argued that while the rebirth of Humanism complemented the newly emerging spirit of secular individualism, it was the result of what was happening in Italy and not the cause. Individualism and secularity would have evolved without the rebirth of antiquity. The last three sections of the work provided evidence of how the new secular individualism operated in society and how it influenced the culture and moral life of the age.

SIGNIFICANCE

After more than a century, Jacob Burckhardt's history of the Italian Renaissance remains one of the most controversial works ever published. With justification, critics have stated that the work is too static and that it exaggerates the creativeness of Italy. It is too sharply delimited in time and space, as it neglects the other European countries and fails to consider the creative forces at work during the late Middle Ages. Burckhardt overemphasizes individualism, immorality, and irreligion in Italy and exaggerates the rediscovery of the classical world. Furthermore, Burckhardt's work is limited to a study of the upper class, is devoid of any economic analysis, and is based on the debatable assumption that there was a common spirit of the age that characterized all Italy for two hundred years.

Even the most ardent critics regard Burckhardt's book as a penetrating analysis of history and civilization. Burckhardt's work was unique in that he was one of the first to interpret the psychology of an epoch with power and insight. His methodology was highly original, as he employed a topical approach that permitted him to study what he termed "cross sections in history" from a variety of directions. His work treated civilization as a unit in a series of parallel discussions, each approaching the central problem from a different point of view. Critics of Burckhardt should also remember that he approached history as an artist, not as a philosopher, and with regard to written history he always considered himself an "arch dilettante," whose vocation was teaching.

Although Burckhardt lived forty more years after completing his history of the Renaissance, he never again published. With his health waning, Burckhardt requested to be relieved of his position in art history in 1885, and in 1893, suffering from acute asthmatic troubles, he surrendered his chair of history. Four years later, in August, 1897, he died in his small two-room apartment over the local bakery in Basel. Although Burckhardt never published again, three of his major historical works were published posthumously: *Griechische Kulturgeschichte* (1898-1902; *History of Greek Culture*, abridged 1963), *Weltgeschichtliche Betrachtungen* (1905; *Force and Freedom: Reflections on History*, 1943), and *Historische Fragmente* (1929; translated in *Gesamtausgabe: Judgments on History and Historians*, 1958).

—*Wayne M. Bledsoe*

FURTHER READING

Burckhardt, Jacob. *The Civilization of the Renaissance in Italy*. Translated by S. G. C. Middlemore with an introduction by Benjamin Nelson and Charles Trinkaus. Vol. 1. New York: Harper & Row, 1958. The introduction contains an excellent summary and response to the critics of Burckhardt. Discusses what Burckhardt intended to do with his work as opposed to what others would have liked him to have done.

_____. *Letters*. Selected, edited, and translated by Alexander Dru. New York: Pantheon Books, 1955. With none of Burckhardt's biographies having been translated, this introduction contains the best biographical information available in English. Also included is a bibliography of all the principal editions of Burckhardt's letters.

Ferguson, Wallace K. *The Renaissance in Historical Thought*. Boston: Houghton Mifflin, 1948. The most scholarly coverage of Burckhardt in English. Contains little on his early life but gives detailed information on his place in Renaissance historiography. Good synopsis of his major works.

Gooch, G. P. *History and Historians in the Nineteenth Century*. New York: Longmans, Green, 1913. Rev. ed. Boston: Beacon Press, 1959. The best work on nineteenth century historiography. Attempts to establish Burckhardt's place among nineteenth century scholars. Apologetic in nature, containing little criticism of Burckhardt.

Gossman, Lionel. *Basel in the Age of Burckhardt: A Study in Unseasonable Ideas*. Chicago: University of Chicago Press, 2000. Describes intellectual life in nineteenth century Basel, focusing on four of the city's residents, including Burckhardt and Friedrich Nietzsche.

Hinde, John R. *Jacob Burckhardt and the Crisis of Modernity*. Montreal, Que.: McGill-Queen's University Press, 2000. Focuses on Burckhardt's lesser known writings and how they reflected his conservative view of nineteenth century society. Describes Burckhardt's concern about the rise of mass politics and industrial capitalism, and his fear that these developments would impede individual genius.

Howard, Thomas Albert. *Religion and the Rise of Historicism: W. M. L. de Wette, Jacob Burckhardt, and the Theological Origins of Nineteenth-Century Historical Consciousness*. New York: Cambridge University Press, 2000. Describes how nineteenth century secular historic thought rose out of Europe's religious heritage, focusing on the careers of Burckhardt and theologian de Wette.

Thompson, James Westfall. *A History of Historical Writing*. Vol. 2. New York: Macmillan, 1942. Reprint. Gloucester, Mass.: Peter Smith, 1967. A good first source for Burckhardt. Brief, chronological, and factual, with little attempt at analysis. Must be supplemented by one of the other sources, as Thompson's omissions can be misleading.

Weintraub, Karl Joachim. "Jacob Burckhardt: The Historian Among the Philologists." *The American Scholar* 57 (Spring, 1988): 273-282. A concise, readable discussion of Burckhardt's posthumously published history of Greek culture. Taking as his point of departure the harshly critical response to this work among scholars of Burckhardt's time, Weintraub illumines Burckhardt's conception of cultural history.

_____. *Visions of Culture*. Chicago: University of Chicago Press, 1966. Second only to Ferguson in scholarly analysis of Burckhardt's history of the Renaissance. Surpasses Ferguson in biographical information and concentrates on Burckhardt's contribution to *Kulturgeschichte*.

SEE ALSO: Barthold Georg Niebuhr; Leopold von Ranke.

RELATED ARTICLE in *Great Events from History: The Nineteenth Century, 1801-1900:* 1824: Ranke Develops Systematic History.

FRANCES HODGSON BURNETT

English-born American writer

Burnett's immensely popular stories and dramatizations brought pleasure and hope to many people and bridged divides between British and American audiences, the rich and the poor, and children and adults.

BORN: November 24, 1849; Manchester, England
DIED: October 29, 1924; Plandome, Long Island, New York
ALSO KNOWN AS: Frances Eliza Hodgson (birth name)
AREA OF ACHIEVEMENT: Literature

EARLY LIFE

Frances Eliza Hodgson was born into the family of a relatively prosperous hardware merchant who ran a store in Manchester, England, one of the foremost cities of the Industrial Revolution. Frances had two older brothers and two younger sisters. She had few memories of her father, Edwin, who died in 1853, leaving her mother, Eliza, to run the business. Financial constraints forced them to move to an inexpensive house in Islington Square, Salford, a little island of "respectable" houses in a sea of poor housing inhabited by cotton mill operatives. Frances was not encouraged to play with their children or speak the local Lancashire dialect. With a quick ear, however, she was able to precisely reproduce it.

Frances was an imaginative child, describing herself as having "a positively wolfish appetite for books," and from three years old began "a lifelong chase after the story." She also described how she discovered the delights of her father's library, especially a shelf of *Blackwood's Magazine* periodicals, which the Brontë sisters had also found influential in developing a taste for Romantic stories and poetry. Frances soon found an eager audience for her own first efforts at story telling at the small private school she attended.

Frances described her mother as a gentle person who instilled into her the moral priority of kindness and the need to be "always the little lady." Eliza continued to run the family business until the depression caused by the American Civil War and the slow drying up of the supply of raw cotton. Eliza's brother had previously emigrated to eastern Tennessee, and he wrote to Eliza about the opportunities available in the United States; in 1865, the nearly destitute Hodgsons decided to join him in the small township of New Market, Tennessee.

Postwar depression affected business in the United States as well, and there was little work available in Tennessee. Despite this, Frances described these as her "Dryad days," especially when they moved to the outskirts of Knoxville, Tennessee. For a city girl, the abundance of forests and mountains was overwhelming. However, the desperate need for income finally induced her to write a short story for one of the popular women's magazines of the day. After a request for a second story, she had them both accepted by *Gody's Lady's Book* for the sum of thirty-five dollars, with an invitation to write more. She was eighteen years old.

LIFE'S WORK

Frances had stated in the cover letter sent with her first story that "my object is remuneration." After Eliza's death in 1870, this became even more vital. Frances began writing five or six stories per month at ten or twelve dollars each. These early stories were stylized romances of the period. In 1871 she tried a realistic story written in the Lancashire dialect called "Surly Tim," which was accepted by *Scribner's Magazine*, a literary magazine. This began a long association with the Charles Scribner's Sons publishing house.

At this time Frances was being courted by Swan Burnett, the son of a doctor in New Market. He too was training to be a doctor. Frances was reluctant to marry, preferring to return to England for fifteen months in 1872, the second of her thirty-three transatlantic crossings. On her return, however, they did marry and lived in Knoxville, where their first son, Lionel, was born in 1874. Burnett wanted to further his medical studies in ophthalmology and also wanted Frances to get away from the South. A stay in Paris, France, was arranged with advances from Frances's publishers. While there, the couple's second son, Vivian, was born at the same time that Frances was writing her first novel, *That Lass o' Lowrie's*, a story of a Lancashire mining girl, in the style of Elizabeth Gaskell's *Mary Barton* (1848). Serialization began in 1876 and complete publication came in 1877, to much acclaim.

After some financial hardship upon their return to the United States, they managed to settle in Washington, D.C., still supported by Frances's writings. Frances became a society hostess and boasted President James Garfield among her acquaintances. Sales of *That Lass o' Lowrie's* soared, as did a collection of short stories, *Surly Tim, and Other Stories* (1877). *Haworth's*, also set in Lancashire, followed in 1879. Some twelve novels and

Frances Hodgson Burnett. (Library of Congress)

five collections of stories were published at this time, climaxing with her novel of Washington life, *Through One Administration* (1883). Signs of an unhappy marriage showed through, however: The book was one of her few novels without a happy ending.

In 1885, Frances wrote the novel that was to make her name, *Little Lord Fauntleroy* (1886), published with illustrations by Reginald Birch. The story was based on her own son Vivian, who never quite threw off the image constructed by the book throughout his life. It was one of the three best sellers of the year, and over one million copies sold in Great Britain alone. The novel was also dramatized, a process that involved a court case over the copyright laws of the day. Much of the later criticism that the book was sickly sentimental was misplaced: Compared to other popular late Victorian fiction, *Little Lord Fauntleroy* was filled with political and psychological insights, and the "lost heir" motif was used for moral purposes in a focused storyline. Sentimentalities arose out of Frances's self-projection as "Dearest," the ideal mother, and in the strange mix of childish and adult language given to the seven-year-old hero.

Now in her thirties, Frances was famous. She was described as being plump and short with a square, projecting forehead and possessing large, soulful eyes and luxurious hair. Some accounts depicted her as being animated in talk and affable in manners. She also enjoyed excellent health during this period. As the need to write lessened, the urge to travel grew. Leaving her boys behind, she stayed longer and longer in Europe. While in Rome, Italy, during the winter of 1889-1890, she heard that her son Lionel was ill. Frances returned to Washington, D.C., and found that the diagnosis was tuberculosis. She refused to tell him, and went everywhere looking for cures and nursing him devotedly. Lionel died in Paris in December, 1890.

Little Lord Fauntleroy had been her first book to have a child hero; thereafter followed a series of books about children, including *The Pretty Sister of José* (1889). In 1896 she returned to adult heroines, most notably in *In Connection with the De Willoughby Claim* (1899) and *The Making of a Marchioness* (1901). By now Frances was reunited with her sister Edith, was based in London, and was involved in the theater and philanthropic work. She moved in high society and adopted an increasingly expensive lifestyle. She met the novelist Henry James frequently. She had also met Stephen Townesend, a doctor ten years younger than herself and a would-be actor who became her personal assistant. In 1898 she officially divorced Swan and then, to everyone's surprise, married Townesend in 1900. He had a volatile temper and was often possessive and bullying. The marriage only lasted two years. Parts of this tempestuous marriage are reflected in her novel *The Shuttle* (1907).

Another autobiographical detail reflected in *The Shuttle* was Maytham Hall, an old country mansion in southern England that Frances leased from 1898 to 1907. During this time she took up her previous children's story *Sara Crewe* (1888) and dramatized it as *Little Princess* (1903). The extra material generated was then rewritten into an enlarged novel of the same name, which was published in 1905. Although not immediately as popular as *Little Lord Fauntleroy*, *Little Princess* has since become much more so. The heroine showed the same qualities of *gentillesse* as had the hero of *Little Lord Fauntleroy*, but she also demonstrated courage in adversity, a development of Frances's favorite Cinderella theme. A surge of other children's books followed, the most popular being *Racketty Packetty House* (1906).

My Robin (1912) recorded Frances's last visit to Maytham Hall and also provided a clue to the setting of her greatest novel, *The Secret Garden* (1910). *The Secret Garden*'s real genesis was probably an incident recorded in a memoir of finding an abandoned garden in a Manchester house and, by sheer force of imagination, seeing it as intensely alive. The development of her rose garden at Maytham Hall and her observation of a robin combined with this memory. The Cinderella motif was reversed, for neither the heroine nor the hero of *The Secret Garden* possessed any moral qualities. Both were neglected, unloved, and unlovely children. The novel avoided much of Frances's earlier sentimentality, and the psychological realism was completely convincing. Its structure and movement demonstrated her storytelling abilities at their best.

In 1905 Frances became a U.S. citizen and, after 1908, never leased an English property again. Instead, she bought land in Plandome, Long Island, New York, and built an ornate Italianate house and gardens. She continued to write popular works such as *The Dawn of a Tomorrow* (1906; dramatization, 1909), which contained elements of fashionable Christian Science thinking. Her final children's book was *The Lost Prince* (1915), based on a meeting with exiled Serbian aristocracy during her last visit to Europe early in 1914. By then, the cinema had begun to attract Frances, and she gained the interest of Mary Pickford, who starred in four films based on Frances's books, including *Little Lord Fauntleroy*. No less than three other motion picture versions of this book were made. After World War I, public taste turned against Frances's Victorian style, and her last books received poor reviews. In 1921 she became ill in Bermuda and then recovered. In constant ill health, she commuted between summers at Plandome and winters in New York hotels. She died in Plandome in October, 1924, and was buried in Roslyn, Long Island.

SIGNIFICANCE

The New York Times obituary suggesting that Frances's greatest successes were her work to bring about the 1911 Copyright Act and her book *Little Lord Fauntleroy* merely recorded the reaction against her at the time of her death. Biographer Ann Thwaite cites the claim that *Little Lord Fauntleroy* changed "relationships between America and Britain" as well as the dress styles and even the emotional health of countless young boys of the day. To this must be added Frances's own claim that she "tried to write more happiness into the world," especially with regard to the books that have now become classics of children's literature. Her understanding of childhood and her ability to re-create it have certainly helped develop modern children's literature. *The Secret Garden* still stands as a pinnacle of Romance literature that holds realism and fantasy in perfect tension.

As a career writer, Frances Hodgson Burnett was at the forefront of defining "the new woman" as she balanced traditional views of motherhood with those of emancipation and the liberty to develop her own career. The role of wife was the one role she could not fit into the equation, though she was an excellent breadwinner, combining this with a "fairy godmother" role of philanthropist. Thwaite suggests that what she cared for most was "the invincibility of the human spirit . . . the acceptance of all experience, courage born of adversity." This was precisely what Frances portrayed in her best fiction.

—David Barratt

FURTHER READING

Bixler, Phyllis. *Frances Hodgson Burnett*. Boston: Twayne, 1984. The first chapter surveys Burnett's life and writings. Successive chapters deal with the three main periods of her writing career. The final chapter seeks to define her achievement. Includes a selective bibliography and index.

_____. *The Secret Garden: Nature's Magic*. New York: Twayne, 1996. An analysis of the book many consider Hodgson's masterpiece. Bixler describes how Hodgson altered themes from other stories about children and adapted the literary pastoral to create the book.

Burnett, Frances Hodgson. *The One I Knew the Best of All*. London: Frederick Warne, 1974. Burnett's only attempt at autobiography. Written for children, the book follows her life as far as her first publication.

Burnett, Vivian. *The Romantick Lady: The Life Story of an Imagination*. New York: Charles Scribner's Sons, 1927. An invaluable memoir by Burnett's son Vivian and the only source for some of her correspondence.

Dusinberre, Juliet. *Alice to the Lighthouse*. New York: St. Martin's Press, 1987. An invaluable study of the link between children's and adult literature from Lewis Carroll to Virginia Woolf. Includes an excellent chapter on *The Secret Garden* and a bibliography.

Foster, Shirley, and Judy Simons. *What Katy Read: Feminist Re-readings of "Classic" Stories for Girls*. Iowa City: University of Iowa Press, 1995. Twentieth century feminist analysis of eight books written between

1850 and 1920, including *The Secret Garden*, *Little Women*, and *Anne of Green Gables*.

Gerzina, Gretchen Holbrook. *Frances Hodgson Burnett: The Unexpected Life of the Author of "The Secret Garden."* New Brunswick: N.J.: Rutgers University Press, 2004. Narrative biography, based in part on previously unpublished material.

Laski, Marghanita. *Mrs. Ewing, Mrs. Molesworth, and Mrs. Hodgson Burnett*. London: Arthur Baker, 1950. One of the earliest critical studies of Burnett's writings; Laski sets her in the context of late Victorian children's fiction, especially by women authors.

Thwaite, Ann. *Waiting for the Party: The Life of Frances Hodgson Burnett*. London: Secker & Warburg, 1974. This is the definitive biography even though its thesis that Burnett never quite succeeded in achieving her ideals or her need to be loved can be questioned. Includes a complete list of all her writings and dramatic pieces.

SEE ALSO: Horatio Alger; L. Frank Baum; Lewis Carroll; Robert Louis Stevenson.

RELATED ARTICLES in *Great Events from History: The Nineteenth Century, 1801-1900:* July, 1881-1883: Stevenson Publishes *Treasure Island*; December, 1884-February, 1885: Twain Publishes *Adventures of Huckleberry Finn*; December, 1887: Conan Doyle Introduces Sherlock Holmes.

DANIEL HUDSON BURNHAM

American architect

Energetic and practical, Burnham was a master of the utilitarian, technical, and financial aspects of architecture. He made important contributions to the development of the American skyscraper form, the organization of the modern architectural office, and the encouragement of comprehensive urban and regional planning.

BORN: September 4, 1846; Henderson, New York
DIED: June 1, 1912; Heidelberg, Germany
AREA OF ACHIEVEMENT: Architecture

EARLY LIFE

Daniel Hudson Burnham was the son of Edwin Burnham, later a wholesale merchant of drugs, and Elizabeth Weeks Burnham, the daughter of a Swedenborgian minister. Born in New York, he moved to Chicago with his family when he was nine years old. He was an indifferent student, receiving his education in the city schools and excelling only in freehand drawing. Burnham was then sent to Bridgewater, Massachusetts, to study with a private tutor. There, his interest in architecture and his talent for drawing became increasingly apparent.

After failing the entrance examinations of both Harvard and Yale, Burnham returned to Chicago in 1868. For short periods, he tried one thing after another—clerking in a Chicago retail store, mining for gold in Nevada, and running unsuccessfully for a seat in the Illinois senate. Burnham's dissatisfactions with these undertakings led his father to seek advice from William Le Baron Jenney (1832-1907), one of Chicago's leading architects. Shortly thereafter, Burnham became an apprentice in Jenney's architectural office. He gained further experience by working with John Val Osdel and Gustav Laureau.

In 1872, at the age of twenty-six, Burnham joined the firm of Carter, Drake and Wight. Working as a draftsman under Peter Bonnett Wight, he acquired a deeper appreciation of architectural scholarship and broadened the scope of his training. Among his fellow draftsmen was a young Georgian, John Wellborn Root (1850-1891). Their friendship led to a new partnership in an architectural office of their own in 1873. Root was inventive, romantic, and versatile; Burnham was businesslike and practical, bringing to the partnership a keen understanding of the points that make an office building a profitable enterprise. One of the firm's first draftsmen was William Holabird (1854-1923), who later established his own reputation as an architect. After a slow start, the partnership's practice grew rapidly; between 1873 and 1891, the firm designed 165 private homes and seventy-five buildings of various types.

LIFE'S WORK

In 1874, Burnham and Root completed a large and fashionable house for their first important client, John B. Sherman, a wealthy Chicago stockyard executive. Two years later, Burnham married Sherman's daughter, Margaret. Three sons and two daughters were born to Daniel and Margaret Burnham during the first decade of their marriage. Two of the sons—Hubert and Daniel, Jr.—

eventually became architects and joined their father's firm.

Burnham and Root concentrated on house design during the partnership's first few years. Their first big commission was the Montauk Building (1882, since demolished), followed by the Calumet Building (1884). Both in Chicago, they were constructed of masonry with cast-iron columns. The term "skyscraper" is said to have been applied first to the Montauk Building, which, at ten stories in height, was the first distinctly tall building in Chicago. Its commercial success made it the forerunner of tall, fireproof buildings throughout the country.

Other masonry buildings in Chicago followed, the most notable being the Rookery (1886) and the Monadnock Building (1891). Austere and subtly proportioned, the latter structure was sixteen stories high, with brick bearing walls. It demonstrated Burnham's belief that architecture should express the uses intended for a building. In 1890 came the Rand-McNally Building (since demolished), the first all-steel, skeleton-framed building. The firm did several other metal, skeleton-framed buildings that were designed before and constructed after Root's death. Among these were the Masonic Temple (1892, since demolished), with a steel frame, and the Great Northern Hotel (1892, since demolished), with a wrought-iron and steel skeleton. Twenty stories in height, the Masonic Temple was, at the time, the tallest building in the world.

The Reliance Building is considered by many to represent the partnership's finest design. Planning for the structure had begun before Root's death and was finished by the head of the firm's design department, Charles B. Atwood (1849-1895). The design of the Chicago skyscraper is said to have reached its logical conclusion in the Reliance Building, with its steel skeleton, its glass and terra-cotta walls (revealing the structure underneath), and its skillfully balanced proportions and details.

With Root and landscape architect Frederick Law Olmsted, Burnham worked out the master plan for the World's Columbian Exposition in Chicago. Jackson Park, then a sandy waste, was selected as the location; improvements were designed to fit the area ultimately for use as a city park. Five outside and five local firms of architects were selected to design the principal buildings. Root died during the first meeting of the architects in January, 1891. Burnham, as chief of construction and then chief consulting architect, assumed the responsibility of maintaining the teamwork necessary to accomplish an opening date for the exposition in 1893.

Daniel Hudson Burnham. (Library of Congress)

The eastern architects had already determined that the buildings surrounding the exposition's Court of Honor should be classical in design. Although no building of classical design had been erected previously in Chicago, their plan was adopted. It is commonly argued that things would have been different had Root lived. Supposedly, his authority and predilection for the romantic would have given the exposition an altogether different appearance. It should be noted, however, that the classical design of the Court of Honor had been decided upon before Root's death, with both his and Burnham's assent. Moreover, the minds of both men were already attuned to the classical notes struck in the East, especially those of the firm of McKim, Mead and White. In addition, Burnham found attractive the sense of orderliness and the largeness of conception in a series of related public buildings.

To Burnham, the World's Columbian Exposition not only represented an opportunity to express American prowess in invention, manufactures, and production, but also gave Americans a vehicle for demonstrating the capacity of the country in such areas as architecture, painting, and sculpture. Burnham found great satisfaction in the associations created and cultivated during the two years of the exposition's construction period. His management and leadership style allowed for an opportunity for individual creative activity, and his generous nature led him to give full credit to those who worked under him.

Immediate results of the exposition's success were honorary degrees bestowed on Burnham by Harvard and Yale, election to the presidency of the American Institute of Architects, and membership in New York's Century Club. Burnham was now the best-known architect in the United States. However, the exposition's conclusion also left him with an architectural practice broken by the death of Root and two years of interrupted work. He took on three new partners, Ernest R. Graham, Edward C. Shankland, and Charles B. Atwood, all associates at the exposition.

As early as 1897, Burnham had begun thinking about a plan for the development of the Chicago lakefront. Later, working with Jens Jensen (1860-1951) as the landscape architect, he would see this planning result in the construction of Grant Park and other Chicago parks, beginning in 1904. It would also lead to his widely acclaimed Chicago Plan of 1909.

Burnham was called to Washington, D.C., in 1901, to become chairman of a commission to plan the enlargement and extension of the L'Enfant plan for the District of Columbia. To assist him, Burnham chose Charles McKim, a leading New York architect, and Olmsted. He insisted that studies be made of those European capitols that had furnished precedents for L'Enfant's plan. The unity of the Mall was to be restored. Burnham obtained the consent of the Pennsylvania Railroad to remove its tracks from the Mall. The Union Station and the adjoining Post Office Building were planned to be subordinate to the Capitol. In this subordination and in the monumental nature of these buildings, Burnham secured results that marked his desire for teamwork and his sense of proportion.

Among Burnham's more notable later buildings are the Fisher Building (1896), the Field Museum of Natural History (1900), and the Railway Exchange Building (1904)—all in Chicago. In 1902, his Flatiron Building, New York's first skyscraper, became the tallest building in the world. Nevertheless, with the Washington project, Burnham embarked on a new phase of his career, city planning, which occupied much of his time and thought for the remainder of his life. A number of large city governments—San Francisco, Cleveland, Detroit, and Chicago—sought his aid in developing comprehensive city plans. He used these plans for civic development to express his own ideas of dignity, orderliness, and beauty. In 1904, at the request of William Howard Taft, the secretary of war, Burnham served as head of a commission to undertake the rebuilding and modernization of Manila in the Philippine Islands. There, the French idea of turning outgrown fortifications into boulevards was carried out successfully.

In 1910, President Taft appointed Burnham to head a newly organized National Commission of Fine Arts. One of the first important pieces of business for the commission was the location of the proposed Lincoln Memorial and the selection of an architect and sculptor. Early in 1912, Burnham's health began to fail. To the very end a keen student, he died during a trip to Europe in Heidelberg, Germany, on June 1, 1912.

After Burnham's death, Ernest Robert Graham (1868-1936), who had administered the company since 1900, continued the firm in partnership with Burnham's sons, Hubert and Daniel, Jr. The firm continued later as Graham, Anderson, Probst, and White.

SIGNIFICANCE

By the late 1920's and early 1930's, as Louis Sullivan's critical writings became more widely known and as European modernist architects spread their message, the derivative neoclassicism of Burnham's day came increasingly under attack in the architectural community. Recent historians and critics have tried to redress the fashionable practice of attacking the Burnham school—a revisionist movement long overdue.

Burnham was as important as his contemporaries believed, and as great as he knew himself to be. Above all others, Burnham made distinguished and original contributions in four areas: first, in the creation of the large, modern architectural office, a hierarchical system of specialists working together in various departments; second, in the development of the skyscraper form, in the perfection of the internal arrangement and layout of tall office-building systems; third, in his early call for comprehensive planning, which included entire urban and geographical regions; and, fourth, in his work as an architectural philanthropist and cultural entrepreneur who organized and encouraged the cultivation of both the public and the private arts in the United States.

—L. Moody Simms, Jr.

FURTHER READING

Condit, Carl W. *The Chicago School of Architecture: A History of Commercial and Public Building in the Chicago Area, 1875-1925*. Chicago: University of Chicago Press, 1964. A nearly definitive treatment of the Chicago School and its influence. Any recent work on Chicago architecture during the latter part of the nineteenth century and the early part of the twentieth century is in debt to Condit's study.

Hines, Thomas S. *Burnham of Chicago: Architect and Planner*. New York: Oxford University Press, 1974. The standard biography of Burnham. Solid on architectural criticism. "On Sources" is a particularly valuable section.

Hitchcock, Henry Russell. *Architecture: Nineteenth and Twentieth Centuries*. 4th ed. New York: Penguin Books, 1977. The classic one-volume history of modern architecture that deals with Burnham and his contemporaries judiciously and intelligently, if sometimes briefly.

Hoffmann, Donald. *The Architecture of John Wellborn Root*. Baltimore: Johns Hopkins University Press, 1973. The standard study of Root's work. Good on Root's relations with Burnham.

Larson, Erik. *The Devil in the White City: Murder, Magic, and Madness at the Fair That Changed America*. New York: Crown, 2003. Best-selling history of the World's Columbian Exposition of 1893. Larson tells his story by concentrating on the lives and careers of two men: Burnham and Henry H. Holmes, a serial killer who built a hotel near the fair to more easily find victims. Larson is a superb writer and he provides a richly detailed account of Burnham's life and career, focusing on the many challenges he faced in designing and building the fairgrounds.

Moore, Charles. *Daniel H. Burnham: Architect, Planner of Cities*. 2 vols. Boston: Houghton Mifflin, 1921. A valuable source of an almost primary nature. Moore knew Burnham well and had access to friends, relatives, and associates.

Reps, John W. *The Making of Urban America: A History of City Planning in the United States*. Princeton, N.J.: Princeton University Press, 1965. A helpful overview of American urban planning. Brief text but extensive illustrations.

Schaeffer, Kristen. *Daniel H. Burnham: Visionary, Architect, and Planner*. Edited by Scott J. Tilden, photographs by Paul Rocheleau. New York: Rizzoli, 2003. Schaeffer assesses Burnham's role in American architecture. Profusely and beautifully illustrated with large photographs.

Schuyler, Montgomery. *American Architecture and Other Writings*. Edited by William Jordy and Ralph Coe. Cambridge, Mass.: Belknap Press of Harvard University Press, 1961. Writings of the best contemporary architectural critic, who wrote extensively about Burnham and the Chicago School.

SEE ALSO: Andrew Carnegie; Henry Hobson Richardson; Louis Sullivan.

RELATED ARTICLES in *Great Events from History: The Nineteenth Century, 1801-1900:* 1883-1885: World's First Skyscraper Is Built; May 1-October 30, 1893: Chicago World's Fair.

AARON BURR

American politician

One of the most enigmatic political leaders in American history, Burr was considered a hero of the American Revolution and narrowly missed being elected president over Thomas Jefferson. His views on women's rights, African American education, and other subjects were far ahead of their time, and he was a driving force behind the liberalization of New York's penal codes and political process. However, his legacy was tainted by his killing of Alexander Hamilton in a duel and his role in several political scandals.

BORN: February 6, 1756; Newark, New Jersey
DIED: September 14, 1836; Port Richmond, Staten Island, New York
AREA OF ACHIEVEMENT: Government and politics

EARLY LIFE

Aaron Burr's mother, Esther Edwards Burr, was the daughter of the Reverend Jonathan and Sarah Edwards; his father, Aaron Burr, was pastor of the Newark Presbyterian Congregation and president of the College of New Jersey, which, within the year, moved to Princeton. When Burr was nineteen months old, his father died. Within the year, his mother and grandparents died as well, leaving Burr and his older sister Sarah wards of their twenty-year-old uncle, Timothy Edwards.

After graduation from Princeton at the age of seventeen, Burr completed his study for the ministry but decided to become a lawyer. His preparations were interrupted by the American Revolution. After he served with distinction at the battles of Quebec, New York, and

Monmouth and commanding American forces in Westchester, Burr's health forced him to resign, and he returned to the study of law. He was about five feet, two inches in height, thin, and always looked frail.

In 1782, after Burr was admitted to the New York Bar, he married Theodosia Bartow Prevost, ten years his senior and the widow of a British army officer. The Burrs moved to New York City as soon as the British evacuated it. Four children were born: two sons, who died at birth; a daughter, who died in 1789; and Theodosia, the firstborn, who disappeared at sea in 1812.

Burr became noted as a superior attorney; he won many cases "by default." The city's other lawyers, including Alexander Hamilton, sought Burr as co-counsel in arduous litigations. People reported other traits: Burr seldom ventured opinions on public issues, he had difficulty in expressing his wishes or seeking favors, and he seldom joined groups—though groups joined him. Observers noted his unusual interest in the well-being of children. Mental health professionals indicate that the trauma of early parental death can lead to such behavior.

LIFE'S WORK

As a military hero and the heir of the Reverend Edwards and the Reverend Burr, Colonel Burr would be an asset to any of the political groups forming in New York, but he refused to join the factions led by Senator Philip Schuyler, Governor George Clinton, or Chancellor Robert Livingston. In 1784, a radical group persuaded him to allow his name to be placed in nomination for the state assembly; he agreed and was elected.

In February, 1785, Burr sponsored a bill to emancipate all those of "Negro, Mulatto, Indian and Mustee blood born in New York." The measure failed, but Burr continued to seek legislative means to end slavery. Burr was reelected but seems not to have served; he declined further nomination. Refusing to join any faction, Burr nevertheless developed friendly relations with Schuyler's son-in-law, Hamilton, and Livingston's brother, Edward. The Schuyler and Livingston factions supported the new Constitution, while Clinton opposed ratification. In 1789, after New York joined the Union, Clinton attempted to placate Burr by appointing him attorney general. Burr was an efficient official and before resigning prepared a series of recommendations to liberalize the state's laws.

In 1791, the Livingstons, angered by Hamilton's use of his friendship with President George Washington to secure favors for the Schuyler group, combined with the Clintons to prevent the reelection of Senator Schuyler. Burr was elected in his place. Outwardly, Burr and Hamilton remained friends, but Hamilton was determined to "destroy" Burr.

As senator, Burr became identified with the Thomas Jefferson group led by James Monroe in the Senate and James Madison in the House. Burr supported measures to make Senate sessions public and liberalize laws. Because of his stand on slavery, however, he was not fully trusted by the Jeffersonians. He praised the French Republic and objected to the presence of British forts on American soil; he favored funds to the military to protect Americans from Indian raids. After Monroe left the Senate, Burr was acknowledged as Jeffersonian spokesperson in the Senate, and his name was unsuccessfully put forward for vice president during the 1796 campaign.

Following the death of his wife, Burr did not seek reelection. Returning to New York, he entered the legislature, where he was instrumental in passing a manumission law, securing the construction of public and private roads and canals, and in creating the Manhattan Company with its "notorious" bank. The Bank of the Manhattan Company, by providing venture capital, enabled New York City to replace Philadelphia and Boston as the

Aaron Burr. (Library of Congress)

preeminent American financial center. The bank also provided an alternative source of capital to the Bank of the United States, dominated by the Schuyler faction (or Federalists), which had used the bank to deny loans to Antifederalists.

As an attorney, Burr represented individuals being prosecuted under the Federalist-sponsored Alien and Sedition laws. Although never a member, he helped restructure the Tammany Society into a political organization. Despite his leadership role in the Antifederalist, or Democratic Republican, Party, Hamilton, in 1798, persuaded Federalist governor John Jay to appoint Burr overseer of the state's defenses to prepare for war with France.

Burr developed a plan that would have prevented a foreign fleet from entering New York Harbor. The legislature rejected most of the plan as too costly. Burr, however, was able to persuade many Federalists, most of whom had considered the Antifederalists as too pro-French, to switch parties. He gathered a slate of candidates that would ensure that pro-Jeffersonians would be selected as presidential electors for the election of 1801. When, for the first time, the state elected an Antifederalist slate, the Jeffersonians agreed that Burr would be their vice presidential candidate.

Burr and Jefferson received equal numbers of vote for president, so the House of Representatives had to decide the election. The balloting started on February 11, 1801. Burr received a majority of the votes, but, for him to be elected, nine states had to concur; Jefferson had a majority in eight states, Burr a majority in six, and two states split evenly. By February 16, the Federalists, having reached an understanding with Jefferson's spokesperson, Samuel Smith, abandoned their opposition to Jefferson, who was elected president while Burr became vice president.

With the Senate evenly split between Federalists and Republicans, Burr's role as president of the Senate became crucial in securing passage of Jeffersonian legislation. Only when the administration attempted to impose an embargo on trade with the black revolutionists of Haiti did Burr act in opposition. By 1804, however, Burr, realizing that Jefferson was grooming Madison as his successor, decided to seek the governorship of New York. Much to Hamilton's annoyance, the Federalists decided to support Burr. Tammany also endorsed Burr, but the Livingston and Clinton groups combined to nominate their own candidate. Burr carried New York City, Albany, and a few urban centers but was overwhelmed in rural areas.

After the defeat, Burr's supporters persuaded him to question Hamilton about some comments he allegedly had made. Despite the efforts of Hamilton's friends, Hamilton exacerbated the issue. He was fatally wounded in the resulting duel. Burr's enemies in New York and New Jersey (where the duel took place) attempted to arrest Burr, who fled to Philadelphia.

Burr returned to Washington, where as president of the Senate he frustrated another administration attempt to place an embargo on trade with Haiti and presided over the unsuccessful attempt to impeach Judge Samuel Chase. Following an emotional farewell speech, Burr left the Senate.

Unable to return to New York or New Jersey because of the illegal murder indictments—dueling was legal in New Jersey, and New York had no jurisdiction in the matter—Burr, having secured the temporary presidential appointment of several of his friends to important posts in Louisiana Territory, took a trip down the Ohio and Mississippi Rivers to New Orleans. He returned to Washington in the fall of 1805 and held a series of meetings with Jefferson, who, in January, 1806, sought and received Senate confirmation of the appointment of Burr's friends. Amid talk of war with Spain, Burr embarked on a second voyage down the rivers. Soon rumors began to circulate that Burr planned either to separate the Mississippi Valley from the rest of the country or to invade Spanish territory. All Burr would say was that he had purchased land along the Washita River and that he intended to populate the region with individuals capable of organizing a strike force in the event of war with Spain.

Burr's ally, General James Wilkinson, the highest-ranking officer in the Army, governor of Louisiana, and a paid Spanish agent, suddenly declared that Burr was a traitor. After a series of trials along the Mississippi in which he was found innocent, Burr was captured by troops and dragged to Richmond, Virginia, to stand trial for treason. Burr acted as his own attorney, although he was assisted by some of the best legal minds in the country. Chief Justice John Marshall acted as circuit judge. The trial became a landmark, because it defined the constitutional meaning of treason, clarified who had the right to declare martial law, and established the right of a defendant to subpoena the president. Burr was found not guilty. The government then charged him with committing a misdemeanor. He was found not guilty. When the government ordered that he stand trial on the same charges in Ohio, he fled to Europe.

In England Burr was welcomed by Jeremy Bentham and William Godwin, the widower of Mary Wollstonecraft, whose feminist views Burr shared. Burr attempted to persuade the British government to help liberate Latin America. He also tried to persuade those Spaniards who were resisting the French occupation of their country to adopt the liberal constitution developed by Bentham. He failed in both attempts. He left England for Germany, Sweden, and France. In Paris he sought the aid of Napoleon in removing all European colonies from the Western Hemisphere. Again he failed.

Burr returned to New York in 1812; he learned that his only grandchild had died and that his daughter's ship had disappeared at sea. Burr remained in New York—the murder indictments had been quashed, but the treason charges would not be dropped until 1816. He resumed his legal practice and maintained a low profile. His private and legal papers, however, indicate that he was still active in politics. He corresponded with South American revolutionists and was offered a post in their army. He maintained his friendship with Andrew Jackson and Martin Van Buren, the latter serving as cocounsel on several cases. Toward the end of his life, he became interested in bringing German settlers to Texas and attempted to establish contact with Texan revolutionists.

Burr suffered a minor stroke in June, 1830, but that did not prevent him from continuing his work or, on July 1, 1833, marrying Eliza Jumel, a wealthy widow twenty years his junior. A year later, however, his new wife sued for divorce, charging that Burr had taken some of her money for the Texas project. After a sordid trial—the legal grounds for divorce being adultery—the divorce was granted July 14, 1836, to become effective on September 14. Because Burr died on that same day, his wife decided that she did not want the divorce after all.

SIGNIFICANCE

In some ways, Burr represented the United States that was to be rather than the United States that was. He opposed slavery and favored the education of black people; he was a feminist who believed that women should be educated to the same degree as men and that women should be able to divorce men who abused them; he opposed property qualifications for voting and did everything possible to void or circumvent the laws. He encouraged government support for commerce and industry; to protect American commerce and independence, he favored the military and naval establishment. He advocated the annexation of Florida and Texas and U.S. support for the liberation of Latin America. In his legal work, he insisted that the burden of proof rested with the prosecution and challenged the validity of circumstantial evidence; he demanded that courts follow the rules of evidence.

The contested election of 1800, the killing of Hamilton, and the treason trials made Burr a political pariah. Many of his friends would publicly shun him but privately seek his advice. Most of the legislation he proposed as attorney general became law; Tammany Hall became a model for democratic urban political machines; the Bank of the Manhattan Company blueprinted a policy that was to become normal during the 1980's, and Martin Van Buren secretly called upon his expertise during the War of 1812. People would follow Burr's ideas as long as they could omit his name.

—J. Lee Shneidman

FURTHER READING

Burr, Aaron. *The Papers of Aaron Burr*. Edited by Mary-Jo Kline. 27 reels. New York: Microfilm Corporation of America, 1978. The basis for all current scholarly research. All known and available documents to and from Burr are included, as are all existing legal papers. Where the original document has disappeared, printed versions are included. At times a typed transcription of the manuscript is appended. Includes not only all archival documents but also documents from private collectors and family collections that have never been used.

_____. *Political Correspondence and Public Papers of Aaron Burr*. Edited by Mary-Jo Kline. 2 vols. Princeton, N.J.: Princeton University Press, 1983. Using selections from the microfilm edition of Burr's papers, the editor has grouped well-edited and well-annotated papers into topical sections that are introduced by superb long historical essays. While recognizing Burr's personality faults, it presents a positive view of his role.

Daniels, Jonathan. *Ordeal of Ambition: Jefferson, Hamilton, Burr*. Garden City, N.Y.: Doubleday, 1970. An excellent popular political biography of Burr, Jefferson, and Hamilton, in which the author is rather impartial.

Davis, Matthew Livingston, ed. *Memoirs of Aaron Burr*. 2 vols. New York: Harper and Brothers, 1836-1837. Reprint. New York: Da Capo Press, 1971. A political ally of Burr, Davis used Burr's papers to write a defense of his actions prior to 1809. Liberties were taken with the documents.

_____. *The Private Journal of Aaron Burr*. 2 vols. New York: Harper and Brothers, 1838. Reprint. Upper Saddle River, N.J.: Literature House, 1970. A continuation of the memoirs, covering the period 1809-1836. The basis of the work is the journal kept by Burr while in Europe, letters written to his daughter and son-in-law, and letters from various individuals interested in Latin American affairs. The journal, written in abbreviated English, French, German, Swedish, and Latin, is quite salacious and shocked Davis, who sanitized it for publication. The original manuscript was sold to William K. Bixby, who decoded and translated it as *The Private Journal* (published by The Genesse Press in 1903).

Fleming, Thomas J. *Duel: Alexander Hamilton, Aaron Burr, and the Future of America*. New York: Basic Books, 1999. Fleming set the rivalry of two men firmly within the chaotic political environment of the time.

Geissler, Suzanne. *Jonathan Edwards to Aaron Burr, Jr.: From the Great Awakening to Democratic Politics*. New York: Edwin Mellin Press, 1981. Using unpublished documents, the author traces the development of a democratic ideology. An excellent defense of Burr's position.

Hammond, Jabez D. *The History of Political Parties in the State of New York*. 2 vols. Cooperstown, N.Y.: H. and E. Phinney, 1845. Well written, this is still the best work describing the conflict among the supporters of Burr, Hamilton, Clinton, and Livingston.

Lomask, Milton. *Aaron Burr: The Years from Princeton to Vice President, 1756-1805*. New York: Farrar, Straus and Giroux, 1979.

_____. *Aaron Burr: The Conspiracy and Years of Exile, 1805-1836*. New York: Farrar, Straus and Giroux, 1983. A popular biography. The first volume repeats much that had been previously written. The second volume, however, benefited from the publication of the microfilm edition of the Burr papers and presents some positive new insights.

Melton, Buckner F., Jr. *Aaron Burr: Conspiracy to Treason*. New York: Wiley, 2002. Describes Burr's plot to set up an independent republic in the western United States or Mexico. Melton, a lawyer and constitutional law expert, provides a highly detailed account of Burr's subsequent treason trial.

Parmet, Herbert S., and Marie B. Hecht. *Aaron Burr: Portrait of an Ambitious Man*. New York: Macmillan, 1967. Making extensive use of documents in various archives, the authors have presented a well-written, scholarly, but unflattering biography.

Syrett, Harold C., and Jean G. Cooke, eds. *Interview in Weehawken: The Burr-Hamilton Duel as Told in Original Documents*. Middletown, Conn.: Wesleyan University Press, 1960. A complete collection of all the letters, memoranda, editorials, and testimony leading up to and following the Burr-Hamilton duel.

SEE ALSO: Henry Clay; DeWitt Clinton; John Marshall; Zebulon Pike.

RELATED ARTICLES in *Great Events from History: The Nineteenth Century, 1801-1900:* February 17, 1801: House of Representatives Elects Jefferson President; September 25, 1804: Twelfth Amendment Is Ratified; March, 1805-September 1, 1807: Burr's Conspiracy.

SIR RICHARD FRANCIS BURTON

English explorer and scholar

A British army officer and Orientalist, Burton led major explorations in Asia, Africa, and South America and became famous as the author of travel books and many literary translations, including The Arabian Nights' Entertainments.

BORN: March 19, 1821; Torquay, Devonshire, England
DIED: October 20, 1890; Trieste, Austro-Hungarian Empire (now in Italy)
AREAS OF ACHIEVEMENT: Exploration, scholarship, military

EARLY LIFE

Richard Francis Burton was the eldest son of Mary Baker and Colonel Joseph Netterton Burton, an Irish officer who retired from an undistinguished military career in 1821. His parents moved to Tours, France, where Burton acquired a fluency in European languages while accompanying his parents on their frequent travels on the Continent. After an inconsistent early education, including a brief stay at a private school in Richmond, Burton returned to the Continent, where his adolescence consisted of an unruly, undisciplined lifestyle. He attended Trinity College, Oxford, from 1840 to 1842, but he was dismissed for an ambivalent attitude and disobedience. Fellow students at Oxford called him "Ruffian Dick."

Having developed an interest in Oriental languages while at Trinity College, Burton enlisted in 1842 as an officer in the East India Company Army. He was sent to Gujarat and then to the Sind, where he lived among the Muslims for seven years while learning several Eastern languages, including Hindi and Arabic. Burton served briefly as an intelligence officer under Sir Charles Napier, the British Commander during the Indian wars (1842-1849).

Burton often performed intelligence missions that entailed going to local bazaars in disguise and bringing back reports, which were generally excellent. On Napier's orders in 1845, Burton, with his usual thoroughness, undertook an investigation of the influence of homosexual brothels on British soldiers, and his detailed study led to their destruction. Unfortunately, a jealous officer later used the report in an effort to destroy Burton's military career. Although exonerated, Burton, suffering from cholera, was sent back to England on extended sick leave in 1849.

Burton lived with his family in Boulogne for the next three years while writing three books about his Indian experiences. At the age of thirty, Burton was an imposing figure. Almost six feet tall, with piercing eyes and a dark complexion, he looked like an Arab. While in France, he continued his study of Asian languages (during a lifetime of travel, he would eventually master more than forty languages and dialects) and completed plans for his first great adventure, a visit to Arabia.

LIFE'S WORK

Burton had always wanted to visit the Muslim shrines in Mecca. In 1853, the Royal Geographical Society helped him obtain a leave from the army, and Burton traveled by caravan from Cairo to the sacred city of Mecca disguised as an Afghan doctor. Using four languages and performing all the ceremonies and rituals of a devout Muslim, he penetrated the holiest shrines of Islam. Instead of returning to England to write of his experiences, Burton traveled to the equally forbidden Muslim city of Harar in Abyssinia. In 1854, he became the first European to visit Harar without being executed. He later wrote *Personal Narrative of a Pilgrimage to El-Medinah and Meccah* (1855-1856), which was not only a great adventure story but also a commentary on Muslim culture, and *First Footsteps in Africa* (1856), which described his adventures in Harar.

While in Africa, Burton met John Hanning Speke, also an East India Company officer. After his visit to Harar, the two officers led an expedition into Somaliland. Their camp was unexpectedly attacked by Somali warriors near Berbera. One member of the expedition was killed, and Speke was seriously wounded. Burton suffered a spear-wound in the jaw and was forced to return to England to recover.

In July, 1855, Burton volunteered for the Crimean War and trained the Turkish Bashi-Bazouk Irregular Cavalry while serving as chief of staff to General William F. Beatson. Despite his efforts, Burton saw no action at the front, and when Beatson left the army, Burton also resigned and returned to England in October, 1855.

In London, Burton again met Speke, who had also served in the Crimea, and described his plan to form an expedition to find the source of the Nile River. Speke had for a long time shared this goal, and when Burton asked him to join the expedition, Speke readily agreed. Because Burton had secured a grant of a thousand pounds from the Foreign Office and had obtained the patronage of the Royal Geographical Society, he was the leader of the expedition, with Speke as second in command. Their charge was to ascertain the limits of the Sea of Ujiji, which had been described by East African missionaries, to determine the exportable goods of the interior and to study the ethnography of the tribes. They were also instructed to discover the source of the Nile and the location of the legendary, but nonexistent, Mountains of the Moon. Organizational ability was not one of Burton's great talents, and they wasted nearly six months planning and exploring the coastal areas near Zanzibar before hurriedly recruiting porters and moving into the interior.

On July 1, 1857, Burton and Speke departed from Bagamoyo and followed the traditional trade route to Kazeh, the site of modern Tabora. They reached Kazeh on November 7 and spent nearly a month reorganizing the expedition. They set out for Ujiji on December 5 with the knowledge gained from Swahili-speaking merchants that the Sea of Ujiji was actually three lakes—Nyasa, Tanganyika, and Victoria. Both Burton and Speke suffered remittent bouts of fever during this part of the journey. On February 13, 1858, Burton became the first European in modern times to see Lake Tanganyika. Speke was bitterly disappointed because he had contracted ophthalmia and could see nothing but a glare.

Sir Richard Francis Burton. (Library of Congress)

Frustrated because their health precluded an exploration of Lake Tanganyika and running low of supplies, the explorers started back to the coast on May 26. By this time, a growing strain in their relationship had turned to open animosity. While Burton recovered from malaria at Kazeh, Speke decided to examine the more northern Lake Victoria, which he reached on August 3. Although unable to explore the massive lake, he was convinced that Victoria was the source of the Nile. Burton, a much more literate geographer, refused to accept Speke's theory, which led to more quarrels and their eventual estrangement. Speke quickly returned to England, where he was feted and given command of a new expedition by Sir Roderick Impey Murchison, President of the Royal Geographical Society. Burton, when he finally arrived, was ignored and denied financing for a new expedition. He wrote *Lake Regions of Central Africa* (1860), a highly acclaimed book that attacked Speke's theory and exacerbated their public feud.

In 1860, Burton unexpectedly sailed for the United States, where he traveled by stagecoach to Salt Lake City to visit the Mormon capital. In *City of the Saints* (1861), he compassionately described the Mormon Church, its leadership, and its controversial practice of polygamy. After returning to England, Burton married Isabel Arundell on January 22, 1861. She was the daughter of an aristocratic Catholic family, and Burton had been courting her since 1856.

A turning point came in Burton's life in 1861, when he left the Indian army to accept a consular service appointment to Fernando Po on the unhealthy West African coast. During the next three years, he explored Dahomey, the Bight of Benin and Biafra, the Cameroons, and the Gold Coast. He used these experiences to write five anthropological books about the tribes of that region.

Burton returned to London in September, 1864, and was scheduled to debate Speke in a public meeting about his second expedition and the claim that Lake Victoria was truly the source of the Nile. After an introductory meeting, Speke died of an apparently self-inflicted shotgun wound in a questionable hunting accident. Although most scholars agreed with Burton's theory, the source of the Nile remained unknown until 1876, when Henry Morton Stanley proved that Speke's intuition had been correct. Shortly after Speke's death in 1864, a bitterly disappointed Burton was given a consulate position at Santos, Brazil, where he continued his writing and explored the interior of South America. He quickly developed an aversion to Santos and began drinking heavily.

In 1869, after several pleas from his wife, Burton was transferred to Damascus but was recalled in 1871 when he and Isabel became involved in local affairs that offended several Muslim leaders. Burton argued that his actions had been misrepresented, and his conduct was finally approved by a Foreign Office review. After some months, he reluctantly accepted the consulate appointment to Trieste, but he believed that his diplomatic career was ruined. Trieste was Burton's last appointment, and he used the position to travel and to write and translate an astounding number of books. In February, 1886, Burton was remembered for his service to the Crown when Queen Victoria made him a Knight Commander of St. Michael and St. George. Burton accepted the knighthood in the hope that it would lead to a better appointment, but he was never formally invested.

Burton's last years were spent in completing his monumental translation of *The Arabian Nights' Entertainments* (1885-1888), more correctly called *The Thousand Nights and a Night*. He had suffered from the gout since 1883, and his health began to deteriorate noticeably. After two minor heart seizures, Burton died of a heart attack in Trieste on October 20, 1890. His body was returned to England and buried at the Roman Catholic cemetery at Mortlake, Surrey, in a white marble mausoleum sculptured in the form of an Arabian tent. After his death, his wife destroyed his forty-year assemblage of diaries, notes, and journals, including the revised edition of *The Perfumed Garden of the Cheikh Nefzaoui* (1886), on which he was working when he died. The significance of that loss to biographers, historians, and anthropologists is immeasurable.

SIGNIFICANCE

Sir Richard Francis Burton's adventurousness, curiosity, linguistic skills, and writing talent make a summary of his contributions almost impossible to believe. He was a Renaissance man: soldier, diplomat, explorer, ethnologist, archaeologist, translator, and poet. He was also competent as a botanist, zoologist, geologist, swordsman, artist, and physician. His greatest claim to fame, however, was in the field of exploration. He possessed the same passion for geographical study that produced great British African explorers such as Speke, Stanley, David Livingstone, Samuel Baker, and others. Unlike his fellow explorers, Burton was a scholar, who described much more than his expeditions. In carefully footnoted and annotated books, he described tribes, customs, religions, climate, geography, and countless other topics. He wrote forty-three volumes on his explorations and travels, two volumes of poetry, and more than a hundred articles, and he translated twenty-eight volumes from other languages.

Burton's translations of Oriental erotica, including the *Kama Sutra of Vatsyayana* (1883), *The Perfumed Garden of Cheikh Nefzaoui*, and the unexpurgated "Arabian Nights" tales, earned for him greater literary fame and financial rewards than his heavily documented works on exploration, swordsmanship, falconry, religion, gorillas, and archaeological ruins.

In the field of human sexual behavior, Burton anticipated the psychological insights of Sigmund Freud and Havelock Ellis. Burton has been recognized by modern scholars as one of the pioneers in anthropology. Unfortunately, many of Burton's scientific achievements were overshadowed by his adventures in Mecca and Harar, his expeditions to Africa, and his public anger over the cant and hypocrisy of Victorian prudery. He approached all challenges with enthusiasm, earnestness, dedicated scholarship, and courage. Burton's adventurous life and difficult disposition dominated the books that he wrote, but he lived according to his personal creed that he preferred honor to honors.

—*Phillip E. Koerper*

FURTHER READING

Assad, Thomas J. *Three Victorian Travellers: Burton, Blunt, Doughty*. London: Routledge & Kegan Paul, 1964. An interpretive character study. Concentrates almost exclusively on Burton's preoccupation with Arabia and the Muslim world.

Brodie, Fawn M. *The Devil Drives: A Life of Sir Richard Burton*. New York: W. W. Norton, 1967. A highly respected psychoanalytic biography that argues that Burton was "devil-driven" as an explorer-adventurer.

Farwell, Byron. *Burton: A Biography of Sir Richard Francis Burton*. New York: Holt, Rinehart and Winston, 1964. One of the best biographies of Burton: objective, straightforward, and engagingly written.

Hastings, Michael. *Sir Richard Burton: A Biography*. New York: Coward, McCann and Geoghegan, 1978. A popular biography. While it lacks documentation, it does provide some information lacking in earlier biographies.

Lovell, Mary S. *A Rage to Live: A Biography of Richard and Isabel Burton*. New York: W. W. Norton, 1998. A dual biography of Burton and his wife, Isabel, who is depicted as Burton's collaborator, editor, and staunchest advocate.

McLynn, Frank. *Burton: Snow upon the Desert.* London: John Murray, 1990. Like Brodie (above), McLynn takes a psychoanalytical approach to his subject, explaining Burton's confused inner life. While crediting Burton's genius and unparalleled accomplishments, McLynn points out his subject's destructiveness, lack of a stable identity, racial bigotry, and sexism.

Moorehead, Alan. *The White Nile.* New York: Harper & Row, 1960. A marvelous and powerfully written account of the quest for the source of the Nile. Excellent integration of Burton's role in the exploration of East Africa.

Mountfield, David. *A History of African Exploration.* Northbrook, Ill.: Domus Books, 1976. A well-illustrated coverage of African exploration. The sections on East Africa and Burton's expeditions are excellent.

Rawling, Gerald. "Ruffian Dick." *British History Illustrated 5* (February/March, 1979): 6-18. Brief, colorful coverage of Burton's controversial life. Excellent description of Burton's African explorations.

Rice, Edward. *Captain Sir Richard Francis Burton: The Secret Agent Who Made the Pilgrimage to Mecca, Discovered the "Kama Sutra," and Brought the "Arabian Nights" to the West.* New York: Charles Scribner's Sons, 1990. Well-written and researched biography of Burton.

SEE ALSO: David Livingstone; John Hanning Speke; Henry Morton Stanley.

RELATED ARTICLE in *Great Events from History: The Nineteenth Century, 1801-1900:* September 12, 1853: Burton Enters Mecca in Disguise.

JOSEPHINE BUTLER

English feminist and social reformer

Butler was one of the major British feminist leaders of her time, but she often went against the mainstream of the feminist movement and is best known for her battles against British laws that compromised the rights of women in the name of eradicating prostitution.

BORN: April 13, 1828; Glendale, Northumberland, England

DIED: December 30, 1906; Wooler, Northumberland, England

ALSO KNOWN AS: Josephine Elizabeth Butler (full name); Josephine Elizabeth Grey (birth name)

AREAS OF ACHIEVEMENT: Women's rights, government and politics

EARLY LIFE

Born Josephine Elizabeth Grey, Josephine Butler was the seventh of ten children of John and Hannah Annett Grey. Her father's politics were exceptionally liberal by the standards of his time; he was linked by kinship with members of the government and was involved in the abolition of the English slave trade. Indeed, her father's hatred of injustice was a powerful influence on his children. Josephine heard abolitionist speakers as a child, and in 1847, when she was nineteen, she was taken to Ireland at the height of the great potato famine and saw starving peasants.

Josephine's father also believed in universal education and did not regard women as having inferior brains, as was commonly believed in his time. He provided for the education of all who worked for him. From her mother, Josephine gained the fervent religious faith that inspired her later activities. Her mother supervised her children's education and instilled in them the desire to excel. Josephine mastered music, painting, and horsemanship but was physically fragile and throughout her life suffered from bleeding from the lungs.

While visiting Durham University, where a brother studied, Josephine met classics master George Butler. Butler came from a less aristocratic but intellectually distinguished family. In 1850, he was named public examiner in the schools of Oxford University. Josephine married him on January 8, 1852. Like Josephine's father, George was unconventional in his hatred of social restrictions. He hesitated before joining the ministry because of his dislike of ministers, and he loathed the ritualism that then dominated much of the Church of England. His ideas about marriage were enlightened: He regarded the institution as the coming together of equals during an age when most wives were expected to be subservient. George supported his wife's political campaigns throughout his life and suffered professionally because he would not stop her.

LIFE'S WORK

When Josephine Butler settled in Oxford, she encountered a new and somewhat unpleasant way of life. Although she bore her first two sons in that town, she still expected to participate in Oxford intellectual life. However, she found that women's opinions were not welcomed there. Her later activities were influenced by prejudices against women she heard expressed. She was especially angered by the sexual double standard that regarded sexual activities of women as unforgivable while condoning promiscuity on the part of men, who were thought to need releases for their animal feelings. When she attempted to find help for young women who were in trouble, she was advised to keep quiet. In Oxford, she began the first of her rescue activities, taking into their home a woman who had been seduced and abandoned and had then killed her baby.

In 1857, Josephine's husband became vice principal of Cheltenham College, a private boys' school. At Cheltenham, Josephine gave birth to her last son and only daughter, and the most traumatic event in her life took place. On August 20, 1864, her beloved five-year-old daughter Eva fell over a banister at the top of the hall stairs while excitedly awaiting the return of her parents. The child died three hours later. Josephine's grief was so intense that her health broke down, and she sought the company of others who had suffered. With the assistance of a Baptist minister, she visited the Brownlow Hill Workhouse to share the unpleasant tasks of women who were being punished for various offenses and those who had voluntarily entered for food and shelter. She made friends, finding in the institution not the conventional figures of female vice but women who were the victims of social and economic forces beyond their control.

Afterward, Butler opened the first of a series of refuges for women, promising them love and help during an age when most refuges for indigent women generally offered only discipline and punishment. She also became involved in feminist causes. In 1846, she was one of the founders of the North of England Council for Promoting the Higher Education of Women. She also signed the first petition to Parliament in favor of woman suffrage. She was among the feminists who opposed the Factory Acts of 1874 and 1878—laws that were supposed to protect women but that have limited their income by restricting their working hours. She was also among those opposing the Infant Life Protection Act of 1872, considered by many feminists an attempt to blame the problem of infant mortality solely on women. Instead, feminists focused on the need to find employment for unmarried mothers and to force fathers to take financial responsibility for their children.

Butler left the feminist mainstream to oppose the Contagious Diseases Acts of 1864, 1866, and 1869, which passed without parliamentary debate. These laws first applied to towns with military installations, but medical and political authorities proposed to extend them to all of Great Britain. Under the laws, any woman could be arrested on mere suspicion of being a prostitute and then be subjected to a physical examination and, if found to be diseased, imprisoned for up to six (later nine) months.

The first organization to oppose the Disease Acts, the National Association for the Repeal of the Contagious Diseases Acts (1869), barred women from membership, so Butler founded a new organization, the Ladies' National Association. She argued that the government legislation deprived women of basic civil rights available to men. She also argued that the laws placed the rights of women entirely in the hands of police. (The laws were enforced by plainclothes policemen.) Women who were arrested were not allowed to respond to the complaints against them. Butler also protested the brutal way in which the physical examinations were conducted by police and male physicians and argued that it was unjust to force examinations upon women and not upon their sexual partners. The laws, she believed, treated women as commodities and were designed to protect a supply of healthy prostitutes for men who could afford them. Moreover, she argued, the laws could not be shown to reduce venereal disease.

Butler was deeply opposed to any system that allowed police the power of arrest and conviction without proper hearing. Many people, including some feminists, objected to her speaking on such topics in public, and she was threatened by mobs of men intent on her death. Increasingly, she saw parallels between the Contagious Diseases Acts and slavery.

To learn about countries that regulated prostitution, Butler visited the Continent and came to see the commercial marketing of prostitutes as an international problem. She was appalled by the political corruption born of the profits to be made from the regulation and marketing of prostitutes and was horrified by the trade in children as young as three years old.

After the Contagious Diseases Acts were repealed in 1883, Butler focused on raising the age of legal consent from age twelve and prohibiting women from being forced or defrauded into prostitution. London police minimized the problem, but Butler and her co-workers had seen evidence of the widespread use of children for the sexual gratification of adult males. Attempts to prosecute individual cases of girls who had been raped and discarded were thwarted when judges deemed the girls too young to give evidence. Butler gained an ally in *Pall Mall*

Gazette editor W. T. Stead, who formed a secret commission with her and members of the Salvation Army to prove that children could be purchased for sexual purposes. He revealed his finding in a series of articles beginning with "The Maiden Tribute of Modern Babylon." Afterward, Parliament quickly passed the Criminal Law Amendment Act, rising the age of consent to sixteen.

After long enduring failing health, George Butler died on March 14, 1890. By then, Josephine was out of touch with the times. She was still pushing for the eradication of the social and economic conditions that drove women into prostitution, but the public debate on prostitution was again focusing on its eradication. By the 1890's, Butler's own health was declining; she spent her last years adding to her formidable list of publications. She died on December 30, 1906.

SIGNIFICANCE

Among nineteenth century feminists, Butler was almost alone in addressing problems of the impoverished. Most feminist agitation of that era pushed for rights that benefited mostly middle- and upper-class women. She differed from other social reformers of her time in her insistence that prostitutes could be converted, not with punishment, but with affection and the promise of gainful employment outside prostitution. Because she was convinced that she was carrying out God's will, no criticism stopped her.

—*Betty Richardson*

FURTHER READING

Boyd, Nancy. *Three Victorian Women Who Changed Their World: Josephine Butler, Octavia Hill, Florence Nightingale*. New York: Oxford University Press, 1982. Discusses how the achievements of Butler, Hill, and Nightingale were inspired by their religious faith.

Caine, Barbara. *Victorian Feminists*. New York: Oxford University Press, 1992. Uses Josephine Butler, Emily Davies, Frances Power Cobbe, and Millicent Garrett Fawcett as examples of Victorian approaches to feminism.

Fisher, Trevor. *Prostitution and the Victorians*. Stroud, England: Sutton Publishing, 1997. Discusses controversies involving prostitution with extensive quotation from original sources.

Jordan, Jane. *Josephine Butler*. London: John Murray, 2001. This is the best full-length study to date of Butler's personal life and beliefs.

Petrie, Glen. *A Singular Iniquity: The Campaigns of Josephine Butler*. New York: Viking Press, 1971. This biography is less accurate in its biographical facts than Jordan's biography, but it offers a broad discussion of the Victorian attitudes and sexual beliefs that supported Butler's beliefs and those of her opponents.

Shanley, Mary Lyndon. *Feminism, Marriage, and the Law in Victorian England, 1850-1895*. London: I. B. Tauris, 1989. Discusses Butler's achievements in context of other legal reforms.

SEE ALSO: Annie Besant; William Booth; Dame Millicent Garrett Fawcett; Octavia Hill.

RELATED ARTICLE in *Great Events from History: The Nineteenth Century, 1801-1900:* July, 1865: Booth Establishes the Salvation Army.

SAMUEL BUTLER
English novelist

Butler is a nineteenth century example of what later came to be known as a Renaissance man. He trained in the classics but was more interested in the arts and wrote both an outstanding utopian novel and an important autobiographical novel, as well as four books about Darwinian theory, a travel book, translations of the classics, and an analysis of William Shakespeare's sonnets.

BORN: December 4, 1835; Langar Rectory, Nottinghamshire, England
DIED: June 18, 1902; London, England
AREAS OF ACHIEVEMENT: Literature, music, art, biology

EARLY LIFE

Samuel Butler's childhood, which he later fictionalized in *The Way of All Flesh* (1903), was an unhappy one. His father, the Reverend Thomas Butler, was a clergyman who instilled religion and learning through a liberal use of punishment, and his mother provided no relief. When Samuel was ten, he attended a private school near Coventry to prepare him for Shrewsbury School, where his grandfather and father had taught. Although Samuel's father had prepared him for Greek and Latin, his own chief interests at Shrewsbury were art and music. In 1853, before he completed his classical studies at Shrewsbury, he persuaded his father and his headmaster to let him interrupt his studies so he could go to Europe with his family. After his return to England, he won a scholarship to St. John's College at Cambridge.

In 1857, Butler did a walking tour of Switzerland and Italy, which he described in a piece written for *The Eagle*, a St. John's journal that he had helped found. The following year he took a first class in classical studies and then spent six months doing volunteer parish work in the London slums in preparation for a career in the ministry. During that time he realized that he was not suited for his intended vocation; however, his father wanted him either to be ordained or to become an educator. Butler knew that his father would not finance his studies in art or music, so he instead proposed emigrating to New Zealand and to become a farmer.

In September of 1859, Butler went to New Zealand, bought land, and stocked it with sheep. During the next four years he built a home he called Mesopotamia, prospered, and, leaving his property under the supervision of friends, moved to New Zealand's major city, Christchurch. There his reading of Charles Darwin prompted him to publish an essay in the *Press* on Darwinian ideas on evolution, which were the antithesis of what his father had taught him.

Without his approval or knowledge, his father used his letters and some pieces that he had written for *The Eagle* and published *A First Year in Canterbury Settlement* (1863), to which he added his own preface.

LIFE'S WORK

In 1864, Butler sold his New Zealand holdings at a considerable profit and returned to England. After settling in at Clifford's Inn in London, be pursued a painting career, studying at Heatherley's Art School. In 1874, his paintings *Mr. Heatherley's Holiday* and *A Child's Head* were exhibited at the Royal Academy. His real talent was writing, however, and in 1872 he published *Erewhon*, a kind of satiric utopian novel, which he had printed at his own expense.

Erewhon was Butler's only book that made a profit, and it went through nine editions during his lifetime. It is essentially an imaginative rendering of how his rebellion against his father, his New Zealand experience, and his reading of Darwin liberated him. The book is a journey to a land that is simultaneously utopian and satiric, in some ways similar to Jonathan Swift's *Gulliver's Travels* (1726). Butler's comments on the dangers posed by machines were at odds with the Industrial Revolution that brought so much prosperity to some Englishmen. Not surprisingly, the novel received a great deal of critical attention, most of it negative. In 1873, Butler published his second novel, *The Fair Haven*, which troubled readers because of its subtlety, caused in part by his use of two imaginary authors who may or may not reflect Butler's own views. The book is ostensibly a defense of Christ's Resurrection, and some people read it that way, but it also is an attack on the miraculous.

Butler began using the reading room of the British Museum in 1877 and continued his interest in Darwin by writing four books on evolution. In *Life and Habit* (1877) he modified Darwin's ideas about development occurring as the result of pure chance, affected by natural selection or the survival of the fittest. He introduced the idea of "unconscious memory," a mental process to complement the Darwinian mechanical process. In some ways he was on the same track as Sigmund Freud, the Austrian founder of psychoanalysis, but his work lacked the scientific apparatus of Freud's work.

In *Evolution Old and New* (1879), Butler asserted that Darwin's work was not as original as was generally thought and went on to use the works of the French naturalists Comte Georges Louis Leclerc de Buffon and Chevalier de Lamarck to buttress his ideas about "unconscious memory." His book *Unconscious Memory* (1880) continues the attack on Darwin, who, Butler claims, fails to explain why variations occur. In 1887, he published *Luck or Cunning*, which, in addition to covering old ground, comments on the attacks he has endured and the controversy over evolution.

Despite his forays into scientific speculation, Butler retained his early interest in music and art. With his friend Henry Festing Jones, also an admirer of George Frederik Handel's music, he published *Gavottes, Minuets, Fugues, and Other Short Pieces for the Piano* (1885). After the two men continued their study of harmony, he published *Narcissus: A Cantata in the Handelian Form* (1888). In 1904, after Butler's death, his collaboration with Jones, *Ulysses: An Oratorio*, was published.

Butler's interest in Handel is also reflected in his *Alps and Sanctuaries* (1882), which begins with a comparison of Handel and William Shakespeare, giving the nod to Handel. This book, which includes several of Butler's sketches, is also a travel book with commentaries on Italian art and Roman Catholicism. In this good-natured, insightful book there is a mellowing and a regret that his narrow religious upbringing may have made him unduly skeptical of religion.

Butler's work on the oratorio about Ulysses sparked a return to his interest in the classics, and his *Authoress of the Odyssey* (1897), in which he claims that the *Odyssey* was written by a woman, was the result. He followed this work with translations of Homer's *Odyssey* (1888) and *Iliad* (1890). These modern translations of the two epics received some favorable reviews but did not do well commercially.

Butler's last work on the classics was *Shakespeare's Sonnets Reconsidered and in Part Rearranged* (1899), in which he undertook to explore what he called the "more Greek than English" relationship between Shakespeare and "Mr. W. H." Before his death in 1902 he extensively revised his utopian novel as *Erewhon Revisited*, which satirizes Christianity and all similar religions. His posthumously published novel, *The Way of All Flesh* (1903), which he started writing in 1873 and modeled on his own life, is a *Bildungsroman*—a coming-of-age story—in which Butler uses his theory of the unconscious and his knowledge of Handel to show how his protagonist comes to develop and realize his own personality.

BUTLER ON "UNCONSCIOUS MEMORY"

Samuel Butler was a devoted follower of Charles Darwin's theory of evolution and wrote four books on the subject himself. However, he went beyond Darwinian theiry by adding his own twist, which he called "unconscious memory." This extract from one of his books reveals some of his ideas on that subject.

An organised being, therefore, stands before us a product of the unconscious memory of organised matter, which, ever increasing and ever dividing itself, ever assimilating new matter and returning it in changed shape to the inorganic world, ever receiving some new thing into its memory, and transmitting its acquisitions by the way of reproduction, grows continually richer and richer the longer it lives.

Thus regarded, the development of one of the more highly organised animals represents a continuous series of organised recollections concerning the past development of the great chain of living forms, the last link of which stands before us in the particular animal we may be considering. As a complicated perception may arise by means of a rapid and superficial reproduction of long and laboriously practised brain processes, so a germ in the course of its development hurries through a series of phases, hinting at them only. Often and long foreshadowed in theories of varied characters, this conception has only now found correct exposition from a naturalist of our own time. For Truth hides herself under many disguises from those who seek her, but in the end stands unveiled before the eyes of him whom she has chosen. . . .

Man's conscious memory comes to an end at death, but the unconscious memory of Nature is true and ineradicable: whoever succeeds in stamping upon her the impress of his work, she will remember him to the end of time.

Source: Samuel Butler, *Unconscious Memory* (London: D. Bogue, 1880), chapter 6.

SIGNIFICANCE

Butler had to finance the publication of most of his writings himself, and *Erewhon* was his only profitable work. Consequently, he did not have a significant impact on a mass audience during his lifetime. However, he did reach the intellectuals and scientists of the day, even if they often disagreed with him. *The Way of All Flesh* and *The Note-Books of Samuel Butler* (1912), which his friend Festing Jones edited after his death, did enhance his reputation. *The Shrewsbury Edition of the Works of Samuel Butler* (1923-1926) made his work available for the reading public. At the turn of the twenty-first century, editions of most of his books were still in print.

After World War I, in which Great Britain lost nearly a full generation of young men, Butler's *The Way of All Flesh*, with its theme of rebellion against the father—and by extension all father figures—appealed to a generation unhappy with the Victorian mores and religion in which they were raised. In his *History of the English Novel* (1934) critic Ernest A. Baker compared Butler's influence on novelists with that of the French writers Gustave Flaubert and Émile Zola. Moreover, time has shown that some of Butler's ideas about the unconscious are valid and are tied to what has become the field of social psychology.

Butler had the misfortune to be what is now popularly known as a Renaissance man, a person accomplished in many fields at a time when specialization was in vogue. In effect, he may be considered a bit of a dilettante. He also appeared to vacillate, to say, or seem to say, contradictory things. His ambiguity and complexity, however, are more suited to the twentieth than to the nineteenth century.

—Thomas L. Erskine

FURTHER READING

Holt, Lee E. *Samuel Butler*. Rev. ed. Boston: Twayne, 1989. This book has a brief biographical chapter followed by analyses of Butler's literary works. Also contains a chronology and a bibliography of works by and about Butler.

Jeffers, Thomas L. *Samuel Butler Revalued*. University Park: Pennsylvania University Press, 1981. Focuses on *The Way of All Flesh*, Butler's lifelong work, which involves his family, the Christianity of his father, and Darwinism.

Jones, Henry Festing. *Samuel Butler: A Memoir*. 2 vols. Whitefish, Mont.: Kessinger Publishing, 2004. Originally published in 1919. Biography written by Butler's Cambridge friend and fellow musicologist.

Muggeridge, Malcolm. *Earnest Atheist: A Study of Samuel Butler*. New York: Haskell House, 1971. Originally published in 1936. Vicious attack on Butler, whom Muggeridge sees, contrary to received opinion, as the epitome of a Victorian writer.

Raby, Peter. *Samuel Butler: A Biography*. Iowa City: University of Iowa Press, 1991. Well-illustrated biography that ties Butler's work and life together.

Stillman, Clara G. *Samuel Butler: A Mid-Victorian Modern*. Port Washington, N.Y.: Kennikat Press, 1932. Early work focusing more on biography than literary analysis. Some illustrations.

SEE ALSO: Charles Darwin; Charles Dickens; Gustave Flaubert; Thomas Hardy; Anthony Trollope; Émile Zola.

RELATED ARTICLES in *Great Events from History: The Nineteenth Century, 1801-1900:* 1830's-1840's: Scientists Study Remains of Giant Moas; November 24, 1859: Darwin Publishes *On the Origin of Species*; 1871: Darwin Publishes *The Descent of Man*.

SIR THOMAS FOWELL BUXTON

English social reformer

Buxton was long active in a variety of humanitarian causes, including prison reform and charitable relief, but he is best known for his sustained efforts to bring about the abolition of slavery.

BORN: April 1, 1786; Castle Hedingham, Essex, England

DIED: February 19, 1845; Northrepps Hall, Norfolk, England

AREA OF ACHIEVEMENT: Social reform

EARLY LIFE

Thomas Fowell Buxton was the eldest son of Thomas Fowell Buxton of Earl's Colne, Essex, and Anna, daughter of Osgood Hanbury of Holfield Grange, Essex. The Hanburys and their relations, the Gurneys, as well as many within their circle, were Quakers. Although the young Thomas was brought up in the Church of England, an affiliation he retained throughout his life, evangelical and Quaker influences upon him were strong. Because he was only six years old when his father died, his mother's role was accentuated.

Buxton was sent to school in Kingston when only four and a half years old, but sickness caused his removal to the school of Charles Burney of Greenwich. He left school at the age of fifteen without having distinguished himself academically. In 1801 he first visited the home of the Gurneys at Earlham Hall on the outskirts of Norwich. The eleven youngsters, children of John Gurney, were his distant cousins, owing to the marriage of his aunt, Rachel Hanbury, to Richard Gurney, their uncle. With one of them, Hannah, the young "Fowell," as he was now called, fell instantly in love.

Through the association with the Gurneys the Quaker influence upon Buxton was strengthened, and he also acquired a desire to give up what he now saw as idleness and to apply himself studiously to continuing his education. In 1802 he prepared himself for college, and in October, 1803, he entered Trinity College, Dublin. Upon passing his examinations, mostly with distinction, he received the university gold medal. On May 7, 1807, Buxton married Hannah Gurney.

At the age of twenty-one, Buxton cut an imposing figure. He was six feet, four inches tall and broad-chested, with the physique of an outdoor sportsman. His fondness for hunting and shooting remained with him longer than his splendid build. His first child, Priscilla, was born in February, 1808, and shortly after, through the good offices of his uncles, Sampson and Osgood Hanbury, he joined the brewery firm of Truman, Hanbury, and Company. In 1811 he became a partner and worked long hours to reform the company's methods and bookkeeping. These improvements ensured that he would throughout the rest of his life have a comfortable income, affording him the leisure to pursue those philanthropic causes that had already begun to interest him.

LIFE'S WORK

From the early years of his employment with the brewery firm, Buxton took an active part in charitable enterprises in the district of Spitalfields, where the brewery was. This district was a center for silk-weaving, a trade that suffered numerous vicissitudes, as during the depression of 1816, when starvation was widespread. Buxton's first important public speech, at the Mansion House in 1816, raised more than forty-three thousand pounds for the relief of the poor of the area. This speech first brought Buxton to the attention of the famous reformer William Wilberforce, who had been largely instrumental in outlawing the slave trade in Great Britain in 1807.

Although this connection would later be of the utmost importance in Buxton's career, for the time being a far greater influence upon him was his sister-in-law, Elizabeth (née Gurney) Fry and her circle, whose chief interest lay in prison reform. After his Mansion House speech, Buxton went through Newton jail, and this as well as other visitations resulted in his publication in 1818 of a volume titled *An Inquiry Whether Crime and Misery Are Produced or Prevented by Our Present System of Prison Discipline*. This work went through five editions within a year and led to the founding of the Society for the Reformation of Prison Discipline. Buxton's zeal for prison reform also seems to have brought him to political awareness. He decided that his best chance for effecting changes would be as a member of Parliament.

Buxton stood for election in 1818 as candidate for Weymouth. Against all odds, despite the fact that he would not stoop to the electioneering methods then in vogue, he won. Thus he began his long parliamentary career, representing Weymouth for almost two decades, until he lost the election of 1837. Early in this career he served on two parliamentary select committees inquiring into capital punishment, a penalty he opposed, except for murder. In 1820 he supported Sir James Mackintosh's motion to abolish the death penalty for forgery, which was then but one of the many offenses so punished.

That same year brought great personal tragedy, when Buxton's eldest son died, followed by three of his daughters. After this loss he moved from his Hampstead house to Cromer Hall in Norfolk, in the district of his wife's family. He soon returned to Parliament, however, and participated in bills concerning prisons and education, and inquiries into the Hindu practice of suttee and the slave trade. Increasingly, Wilberforce noticed Buxton with approval. Finally, on May 24, 1821, that great abolitionist wrote Buxton to ask for his help in the struggle to end slavery and, in the event that he himself should become unable to pursue the cause, to ask that Buxton would carry on the effort. Wilberforce's request for help was reinforced by the dying prayer of Buxton's sister-in-law, Priscilla Gurney, on behalf of the slaves.

So began a reorientation of Buxton's parliamentary efforts. He was an active member of the African Institution. Besides Wilberforce, he worked with figures such as Zachary Macaulay, Stephen Lushington, and the Third Baron Suffield. The Anti-Slavery Society was formed in 1823, with the purpose of collecting evidence and spreading information. On May 15, 1823, Buxton brought before the House of Commons a resolution for the gradual abolition of slavery throughout the British Empire, on the grounds that that institution violated the principles contained in the British constitution and the Christian faith. The foreign secretary, George Canning, moved amendments that vitiated the real thrust of Buxton's resolution by adopting a process of "amelioration" of the condition of slaves. Accordingly, the British government issued a circular to its colonial governors recommending certain reforms with regard to slaves. In essence, the West Indian planters denounced the advice to the governors as an attack upon their rights.

While Buxton thus did not meet with success in the House of Commons, it was clear that extraparliamentary opposition to slavery was growing, and that the popular if unenfranchised voice was becoming increasingly a factor in parliamentary politics. Reform was in the air. Although evangelicist and Quaker sections of the public may not have been beloved by members of Parliament, they usually were not disbelieved. Their petitions carried weight. One of them, said to have seventy-two thousand signatures, Buxton presented to Parliament in 1826, with a demand for better treatment for West Indian slaves. Parliament, he said, would have to enact reform measures, because the colonial governments would not. Furthermore, the petitioners wanted to end the system by which sugar produced by slave labor was subsidized by the British government. In other words, they raised the issue of free trade. Increasingly, the aims of the reformers were finding endorsement in the attitudes of the rank and file as well as the educated mind. Slavery was becoming abhorrent to the British conscience.

In 1829, Parliament voted to allow Catholic emancipation; in other words, Catholics could now hold civil and military office on equal terms with Anglicans. The death of King George IV in the following year required a general election, which in the existing climate of affairs almost ensured a movement in the general direction of reform. In April of 1831, Buxton, impatient with the government's failure to act on the slavery issue, brought forward in Parliament a resolution for the abolition of slavery. His initiative failed because the reforming efforts of Parliament were then devoted to the House of Commons itself. When the Reform Act of 1832 finally became law, he and his supporters could hope that abolition would become reality.

So as to forestall the motion Buxton intended, the government promised in 1833 that it would introduce a bill to abolish slavery. The legislation the government proposed was a compromise, allowing compensation to slave owners and an apprenticeship period before slaves would receive complete freedom. The bill passed Parliament just after the death of Wilberforce and received the king's assent on August 28, 1833. It would go into effect on August 1, 1834.

After his triumph on abolition of slavery, Buxton hoped to use that momentum to gain protection for the native Africans of the Cape Colony against "vagrancy" laws and other discriminatory acts. In 1835 he pressed for and obtained a select committee of the House of Commons to consider the state of the aborigines in the British Empire. His report on the aborigines, frequently referred to as the Buxton Report, became public in 1837. It called for sweeping protections for aboriginal rights, particularly with regard to native lands and customs. The spirit of this report animated the Treaty of Waitangi with the Maori of New Zealand in 1840, and there is little question that compliance with the treaty would have prevented the Maori Wars. In South Africa the report contributed to the Great Trek of the Afrikaners, or Boers (farmers), and the terrible divisiveness that ensued. The report was a high-flown idealistic statement that could not be made operational.

Buxton's attention was now riveted upon the slave issue. In 1839 and 1840 he published two volumes, *The African Slave Trade* and its sequel, *The Remedy*. He recommended a larger naval patrol in West African waters, treaties with native chiefs to stop the slave trade, the purchase of Fernando Po as a headquarters, an expedition up the Niger River to make more treaties with native chiefs and to establish a model farm, and the forming of a company for introducing agriculture and commerce into Africa. For these purposes the Society for the Extinction of the Slave Trade and the Civilisation of Africa was established. Buxton's influence induced the British government to dispatch a Niger expedition that proved a failure and cost many lives.

In 1839 Buxton was suffering from ill health, so he toured abroad as a change of pace. He could not resist, however, turning his journey to valuable advantage by investigating the crimes of banditti and the state of Roman jails.

Buxton had lost his parliamentary seat in 1837. After his return to England he resumed private life, broken only by the queen's granting him a baronetcy in 1840. He devoted himself to the cultivation of his estates and to land improvement. His essay on the management of his estates won the gold medal of the Royal Agricultural Society in 1845. Meanwhile, by the spring of 1843, his health was failing, and he died on February 19, 1845, at Northrepps Hall, Norfolk. Admirers raised a monument to him in Westminster Abbey.

SIGNIFICANCE

Sir Thomas Fowell Buxton's life was one of almost constant toil for humanitarian goals. He wanted to save life and improve conditions of life. To an unusual degree his idealistic efforts were crowned with success, for he saw in his lifetime penal and judicial reform and, above all, the abolition of slavery throughout the British dominions. His account of how to end the African slave trade was vague and unrealistic in its optimistic vision, and the Niger expedition to end the slave trade that those writings inspired ended in fiasco. Nevertheless, Buxton was in large measure responsible for bringing to an end an institution that had tyrannized an entire race. That his health was gravely affected by his emotional response to the failed expedition attests his identification with and fervent support of a lifelong cause.

—*Mary B. Wickwire*

FURTHER READING

Barclay, Oliver. *Thomas Fowell Buxton and the Liberation of Slaves*. York, England: Sessions, 2001. Recent biography of Buxton. Contains illustrations and bibliography.

Buxton, Sir Thomas Fowell. *The African Slave Trade and Its Remedy*. London: J. Murray, 1840. Reprint. London: Dawsons of Pall Mall, 1968. This volume contains the two books that Buxton first published in 1839 and 1840. The first part contains many statistics on the extent of the slave trade, and the second part demonstrates Buxton's vision of a civilized and Christianized Africa.

_____. *Memoirs of Sir Thomas Fowell Buxton*. Edited by Charles Buxton. London: John Murray, 1848. The principal source for knowledge of Buxton's private life as well as much of his public life.

Gallagher, John. "Fowell Buxton and the New African Policy." *Cambridge Historical Journal* 10 (1950): 36-58. Discusses the plans for the Niger expedition.

Great Britain, Parliament. *Report of the Select Committee on Aborigines (British Settlements) with Minutes of Evidence, Appendix, and Index*. 2 vols. Facsimile reprint. Cape Town, South Africa: G. Struik, 1966. This important document shows what Buxton considered the best ways to protect aboriginal rights.

Harlow, Vincent, and Frederick Madden, eds. *British Colonial Developments, 1774-1834*. Oxford, England: Clarendon Press, 1967. A series of important colonial documents, including a letter from Buxton.

Mottram, Ralph H. *Buxton the Liberator*. New York: Hutchinson, 1946. Dated and slim, but draws heavily from the published memoirs.

Pugh, Patricia M. *Calendar of the Papers of Sir Thomas Fowell Buxton, 1786-1845*. London: Swift, 1980. An important reference tool.

Walls, Andrew F. "The Legacy of Thomas Fowell Buxton." *International Bulletin of Missionary Research* 15, no. 2 (April, 1991): 74. Examination of Buxton's campaign against slavery in Sierra Leone, featuring information about his background and other missionary work.

SEE ALSO: George Canning; Samuel Ajayi Crowther; Elizabeth Fry.

LORD BYRON

English poet

Byron wrote satirical and lyrical poetry of the highest order, and his life seemed, to many of his contemporaries, to be the embodiment of the revolutionary spirit of Romanticism. His figure of the "Byronic hero" became vastly influential in nineteenth century European culture.

BORN: January 22, 1788; London, England
DIED: April 19, 1824; Missolonghi, Greece
ALSO KNOWN AS: George Gordon (birth name)
AREA OF ACHIEVEMENT: Literature

EARLY LIFE

Born George Gordon, Lord Byron had an aristocratic heritage on both sides of the family. On his father's side, the Byrons had long been known for their eccentricity, and Byron's father, Captain John Byron, led a wild and reckless life, squandering the family wealth. He died when the poet was three, having separated from his wife the previous year. The poet's mother, Catherine Gordon of Gight, was descended from one of the most notable families in Scotland.

Until 1798, the young Byron lived with his mother in Aberdeen, Scotland, but on the death of his great uncle, the notorious "Wicked Lord," he became the sixth Baron Byron of Rochdale, and he and his mother moved to Newstead Abbey in England, the traditional family seat. Byron was schooled at Harrow and Cambridge, where the personality that would entrance so many soon became apparent: generous and openhearted, ambitious and idealistic, self-willed, but with an almost feminine quality of softness and sentimentality.

Byron also had the advantage of being strikingly handsome; his fellow poet Samuel Taylor Coleridge remarked, "so beautiful a countenance I scarcely ever saw . . . his eyes the open portals of the sun—things of light, and for light." Byron's classic, almost Grecian beauty was flawed only by a deformed right foot, which embarrassed him throughout his life, and a tendency to become overweight, which he combated by strict dieting and exercise.

Byron's literary career was launched when, after privately printing two volumes of verse anonymously, he published *Hours of Idleness* (1807) and a highly successful satire about contemporary writers, *English Bards, and Scotch Reviewers* (1809), which went through four editions in three years. In 1809, he took his seat in the House of Lords, and for a number of years he anticipated a career as a statesman.

In spite of Byron's early success, however, his restless spirit was seeking to escape from the increasingly dissolute life he was living in London. He always sought new experiences and felt strongly the lure of foreign climes. In July, 1809, he embarked on a tour of Europe with his lifelong friend John Cam Hobhouse. They visited Portugal, Spain, Sardinia, Sicily, Malta, Albania, and Greece, which was then under Turkish rule, and later traveled to Ephesus and Constantinople. Athens in particular made a deep impression on Byron, and his two years of traveling gave him a cosmopolitan outlook that shaped his future life and attitudes. He always preferred the spontaneity and freedom of life in the Mediterranean lands to what he saw as the restraint and hypocrisy of English upper-class society.

Byron's travels also gave him a virtually inexhaustible supply of literary material. It was from his experiences on this first European tour that he wrote the first two cantos of *Childe Harold's Pilgrimage*, and it was the publication of this work in 1812 that first brought him widespread fame.

LIFE'S WORK

With the overwhelming success of *Childe Harold's Pilgrimage*, Byron became celebrated in the social circles of fashionable upper-class London. Women in particular were fascinated by the handsome, sensitive, and apparently melancholy poet of noble birth; his romantic wanderings in Greece made him mysteriously attractive. For his part, Byron was always ready to cultivate women friends and lovers. He could not, he said, exist without some object of attachment, and he always felt more at ease in the company of women. In particular, he became involved with the impulsive and unstable Lady Caroline Lamb, and for several months during 1812 they carried on an indiscreet, passionate, and tempestuous affair.

Lord Byron. (Library of Congress)

Byron's fame, popularity, and literary reputation continued to grow between the years of 1812 and 1815, following the publication of his "Oriental" verse tales: *The Giaour* (1813), *The Bride of Abydos* (1813), *The Corsair* (1814), which sold an unprecedented ten thousand copies on the day of publication, and *Lara* (1814). Each of these romances contained the famous figure of the "Byronic hero," a restless and moody wanderer, an outcast from society, who possessed a lofty disdain for conventional values and for the common run of humankind.

Byron's personal life during this period remained tempestuous. In part to free himself from the now unwelcome and frequently absurd and vindictive attentions of Caroline Lamb, he entered into a marriage with Annabella Millbanke, an intelligent, serious-minded young woman who was in every way the opposite of Caroline. The marriage, however, proved short-lived and disastrous. Byron, worried by financial difficulties, drank heavily and went into wild rages. Annabella, pregnant with their child, could not cope with his erratic behavior and was also deeply shocked by her discovery of Byron's incestuous relationship with Augusta, his half sister. The brother and sister had been brought up separately but had spent time together during 1813, and Byron always felt at ease in Augusta's supportive and undemanding company. Annabella convinced herself that Byron was insane, and they separated in January, 1816, exactly one year after their marriage.

During 1816, Byron's fortunes in England began to decline. Rumors regarding the nature of his liaison with Augusta were widespread, and he found himself a social outcast. In April he left England, never to return. Traveling to Switzerland, he met in Geneva another poet in exile, the young Percy Bysshe Shelley. It was the beginning of a famous friendship. Shelley was accompanied by his future wife Mary Godwin and Claire Claremont, a young girl who had forced her attentions on Byron in London and who was now pregnant with Byron's child.

During his four-month stay in Geneva, Byron wrote more stanzas of *Childe Harold's Pilgrimage* as well as two of his most popular and accomplished works, the dramatic monologue *The Prisoner of Chillon* (1816), which was inspired by his own visit to the castle at Chillon, and the drama *Manfred* (1817), Byron's version of the Faust legend.

By October, 1816, Byron and his friend Hobhouse had moved on to Italy, visiting Milan and Rome (his impressions of which formed the core of the fourth canto of *Childe Harold's Pilgrimage*) and settling in Venice. Italy was to be Byron's home for seven years. Having sold Newstead Abbey, he was able to clear his debts and enjoy a comfortable income, and his years in Italy were to be some of the most productive of his life.

In the fall of 1817, Byron wrote the light satire *Beppo: A Venetian Story* (1818), which in form and tone served as a prelude to his masterpiece, the mock-heroic epic *Don Juan* (1819-1824, 1826), which he began in July, 1818. He was to continue working on it intermittently for the next five years; the *ottava rima* verse form that he adopted was ideally suited to the easy, colloquial style that came naturally to him and in which he was best able to express himself. The poem had a controversial impact in England. Byron's publisher called it "outrageously shocking," and many readers were offended by its bawdiness. During this period Byron also wrote a masterful satire directed toward his fellow poet Robert Southey, *The Vision of Judgment* (1822).

In Italy Byron continued to indulge his sensual and romantic nature, entering into numerous love affairs with local women. In particular, he formed a liaison with the nineteen-year-old Countess Teresa Guiccioli, who had recently married a man forty years her senior. Byron became her *cavalier servante*, or sanctioned lover. It was to be his last passionate affair.

Through his involvement with Teresa's nationalistic family, the Gambas, Byron became involved in the movement to free northern Italy from Austrian rule. He became a member of the Carbonaria, a secret revolutionary society, and was regarded by the Austrian authorities as a dangerous subversive. When the Gambas were forced to move to Pisa in 1821, Byron went with them, where he was reunited with Shelley and his friends, and they were joined by the colorful adventurer Edward John Trelawny, and the writer Leigh Hunt and his family. The "Pisan circle" dissolved in 1822, when the Gambas were expelled from the state of Tuscany, and Shelley was drowned. Byron, still with Teresa, moved on to Genoa, his fourth and last residence in Italy.

Byron was becoming bored and dissatisfied with the directionless drift of his life and longed for active involvement in a great cause. By 1823 he had decided to travel once more to Greece, in order to aid the Greeks in their war of independence against the Turks. He made large amounts of money available to the Greeks, and on July 15, with his small group of friends and servants, he sailed to the island of Cephalonia, one of the Ionian islands under British protection. There he assessed the political situation, before sailing for Missolonghi on the Greek mainland in November, where he was greeted enthusiastically by the local population.

In Missolonghi, Byron kept five hundred Albanian warriors under his pay, and he planned to lead an assault on the Turkish garrison at Lepanto. The planned action never materialized, however, and as the months passed, Byron felt increasingly depressed at the apparent failure of his mission. He had not succeeded in bringing together the quarreling Greek factions; he could not even trust his own soldiers; and his health, already weakened by years of excessive dieting, was deteriorating. On April 10, he contracted a fever, and he died nine days later. There was mourning throughout Greece for the loss of the English lord who had embraced their cause as his own, and the news of his death, according to the *London Magazine* in August, 1824, "came upon London like an earthquake."

SIGNIFICANCE

Byron's name will forever be associated with the cause of Greek freedom. Not only his efforts in life but also the wave of feeling that swept through Greece at his death helped to galvanize and unite the Greek people. To this day, Byron is a national hero in Greece; almost every town has a street named for him, and his statue stands at Missolonghi.

Byron's literary achievements are many. Johann Wolfgang von Goethe called him "the greatest genius of our century," and the Italian nationalist leader Giuseppe Mazzini truly said that Byron "led the genius of Britain on a pilgrimage throughout all Europe." Byron's work, and the myth surrounding his name, became a pervasive influence throughout nineteenth century European culture. He has never belonged to England alone, nor did he ever wish to belong solely to the country of his birth. *Childe Harold's Pilgrimage*, for example, was translated forty-one times and appeared in ten different languages in the nineteenth century.

In France, novelist Honoré de Balzac, painter Eugène Delacroix, and composer Hector Berlioz were inspired by Byron's work. In Russia, novelist Fyodor Dostoevski, poet Alexander Pushkin, and composer Peter Ilich Tchaikovsky all felt Byron's spell. Throughout Europe, countless minor writers, now forgotten, took up Byronic attitudes and adopted Byronic themes. In his poetry and his life, Byron seemed to embody the restless and rebellious spirit of the Romantic age. The mysterious and aloof "Byronic hero," impatient of convention and scorning established authority, endorsed the kind of self-assertive individualism that the age found attractive.

Although Byron's standing as a poet has fallen lower than that of fellow Romantic poets such as William Wordsworth, Shelley, and John Keats, *Don Juan* stands untouched as the most amusing long poem in the English language, and many of Byron's short lyrics stand comparison with the best.

—*Bryan Aubrey*

FURTHER READING

Byron, George Gordon, Lord. *Byron*. Edited by Jerome J. McGann. New York: Oxford University Press, 1986. The most comprehensive one-volume edition of Byron's poetry and prose. Includes complete text of *Childe Harold's Pilgrimage* and *Don Juan*, as well as other poems and plays, and selections from Byron's incomparable letters.

_____. *Byron's Letters and Journals*. Edited by Leslie A. Marchand, 12 vols. Cambridge, Mass.: Belknap Press of Harvard University Press, 1973-1982. Byron's letters were always witty, irreverent, and highly entertaining, written quickly and without inhibitions. They mirror his many-sided personality and the charm of his conversation.

Crane, David. *The Kindness of Sisters*. New York: Alfred A. Knopf, 2003. A study of Byron's reputation after death, exploring bitter and conflicting accounts by the wife he divorced and the sister he seduced.

Eisler, Benita. *Byron: Child of Passion, Fool of Fame*. New York: Alfred A. Knopf, 1999. Eisler maintains Byron's poetry has been eclipsed by his oversized image as a literary bad boy, freedom fighter, and sexual adventurer. She seeks to present a more balanced view of her subject by analyzing his poetry in addition to recounting the events of his life.

Jump, John D. *Byron*. Boston: Routledge & Kegan Paul, 1972. Intelligent and circumspect introduction to Byron's life and works. Emphasizes the social and historical context of his work and the cultural and intellectual tradition in which he stands.

Longford, Elizabeth. *The Life of Byron*. Boston: Little, Brown, 1976. Concise, slightly romanticized, but factually accurate biography.

MacCarthy, Fiona. *Byron: Life and Legend*. New York: Farrar, Straus and Giroux, 2002. A biography that reexamines the life of the poet in the light of MacCarthy's assertion that Byron was bisexual, a victim of early abuse by his nurse.

Marchand, Leslie A. *Byron: A Portrait*. New York: Alfred A. Knopf, 1970. The best one-volume biography, condensed from Marchand's own three-volume biography of Byron (1957). Well documented, judicious, and highly readable.

Parker, Derek. *Byron and His World*. New York: Viking Press, 1969. Concise, attractively presented pictorial life, with illustrations of Byron, his associates, and the places associated with his name.

Peters, Catharine. *Byron*. Stroud, England: Sutton, 2000. A brief overview of Byron's life, one in a series of popular "pocket" biographies.

Quennell, Peter. *Byron in Italy*. New York: Viking Press, 1941. Detailed study of Byron's career in Italy, from 1816 to 1823. Also attempts to give an account of the Romantic movement, as a cultural force that exercised a major influence on the nineteenth century.

SEE ALSO: Ali Paşa Tepelenë; Honoré de Balzac; Hector Berlioz; Eugène Delacroix; Fyodor Dostoevski; Countess of Lovelace; Alexander Pushkin; Percy Bysshe Shelley; Peter Ilich Tchaikovsky.

RELATED ARTICLES in *Great Events from History: The Nineteenth Century, 1801-1900:* December, 1816: Rise of the Cockney School; March 7, 1821-September 29, 1829: Greeks Fight for Independence from the Ottoman Empire; June 16, 1855-May 1, 1857: Walker Invades Nicaragua.

FRANCES XAVIER CABRINI

American religious leader

The first American citizen to be canonized a saint in the Roman Catholic Church, Mother Cabrini was the founder of a religious community dedicated to helping the poor. She contributed to missions among Italian immigrants to America, eventually establishing convents, schools, and charitable orphanages all over the world.

BORN: July 15, 1850; Sant' Angelo Lodigiano, Lombardy (now in Italy)
DIED: December 22, 1917; Chicago, Illinois
ALSO KNOWN AS: Mother Cabrini; Saint Frances Xavier Cabrini
AREA OF ACHIEVEMENT: Social reform

EARLY LIFE

The last of thirteen children born of Augustino and Stella (Oldini) Cabrini, Frances Xavier Cabrini was baptized Maria Francesca, at which time miraculous evidence of her piety was said to have appeared in the form of white doves that flitted about the house on that day. Her family was well known for its dedication to the Roman Catholic Church, and one of her uncles, Luigi Oldini, was a priest and foreign missionary. Luigi taught her games associated with missionary work that helped to mold young Frances into a surprisingly serious and pious young girl.

By the time Frances was twelve, she began taking an annual oath of virginity, which she declared permanent at the age of eighteen. She attended a private normal school under the direction of the Daughters of the Sacred Heart of Arluno, where her sister Rosa was preceptress. Frances graduated in 1870. In September of that same year, the united Kingdom of Italy was established after the Papal States capitulated and acknowledged the sovereignty of Savoyard forces. The birth of a united Italy resulted in a severe curb on the traditional authority of the Roman Catholic Church over schools, hospitals, and charitable enterprises.

In 1872, Frances fell victim to a smallpox epidemic while caring for the sick. While she was still recovering, she began teaching at the school of Vidardo, where she found her ability to teach Christian doctrine firmly repressed by secularizing laws. Unsatisfied with her limited opportunities to serve the Roman Catholic Church in this role, she petitioned in 1874 to become one of the Daughters of the Sacred Heart. Her petition was denied on the basis of her fragile health, but her zeal was noted by Father Antonio Serrati, who appointed her to supervise an orphanage in Codogno.

Three years later, in 1877, Frances founded a new convent, called the Institute of the Missionary Sisters of the Sacred Heart. Her foundation grew rapidly; in 1888, her society received an official decree of commendation. Mother Frances Xavier, as she then became known, led the sisters in founding orphanages and schools all over Italy. Pope Leo XIII commended her work and called her "a woman of marvelous intuition and of great sanctity."

LIFE'S WORK

Mother Frances Cabrini also expressed a strong desire to begin a foreign mission, preferably in China. Pope Leo XIII instead decided to send her to the United States, an area that was becoming a great concern among Vatican leaders. More than one million Italian immigrants were flooding into the United States between 1880 and 1902. These new arrivals crowded into makeshift tenements located in teeming neighborhoods in large American cities. They worked long and grueling hours for pitiful wages under the control of Italian *padrones*, agents who organized labor gangs to work in exchange for paying for their passage across the Atlantic, and American sweatshop owners. Practically all of these Italian émigrés considered themselves to be Roman Catholics, but their religious practices, if they engaged in any at all, consisted of an informal jumbling of local traditions from back home and family superstitions that bore little resemblance to official Catholic teachings.

By the 1880's, the Vatican was beginning to take an intense interest in the plight of Italian Americans. With the support of Pope Leo XIII, Giovanni Battista Scalabrini began a concentrated endeavor to minister to the spiritual and physical needs of these uprooted people. A Scalabrinian mission was sent to New York. As part of this ministerial program, the Catholic Church would encourage female religious orders to assist Italian American communities by providing staff for local orphanages and schools.

Cabrini was sent to New York to fulfill plans for an Italian orphanage for girls proposed by Countess Mary Reid DiCesnola. The countess's proposal to fund a Catholic charity was common in a day when the intellectual and social elite were expected to engage in at least a token attempt to alleviate the suffering of the illiterate and unwashed masses. Consequently, the countess designed

Frances Xavier Cabrini. (Library of Congress)

an orphanage to provide young girls with basic schooling as well as training in fine needlework and fine laundrywork, all skills that would be useful to the countess's society friends, where the girls were expected to practice their crafts.

When Scalabrini and the pope suggested that Mother Cabrini go to New York, Cabrini was given the impression that her charitable work would be performed under the supervision of Archbishop Michael Corrigan of New York, and that preparations had already been made for the arrival of the sisters. Cabrini arrived in New York on March 31, 1889, only to find that her superiors in Italy had been gravely misinformed. No accommodations for the sisters had been secured; in fact, Corrigan had written to Cabrini shortly before her departure from Italy suggesting that she delay her journey, but the letter had arrived too late.

Corrigan greeted Cabrini coolly and suggested that the sisters return to Italy immediately. Cabrini stoutly refused. Corrigan finally agreed to allow the nuns to stay if they would establish an Italian school on the lower East Side of the city. He quickly came to loggerheads with the countess over this issue. The countess wanted the sisters to serve as inexpensive labor for her orphanage and suggested that they support themselves by seeking outside employment. In the end, the countess was forced to yield to the archbishop and turn control of the orphanage, along with all money previously collected, over to Mother Cabrini. The orphanage opened on April 21, 1889.

Growing tension between the countess and the archbishop convinced Cabrini of the necessity of acquiring another site for the orphanage. By June, 1890, she had raised sufficient funds to purchase a Jesuit novitiate that became the new site of Sacred Heart Orphan Asylum and a novitiate for the Missionary Sisters of the Sacred Heart. Cabrini also became more closely involved in the projects begun by the Scalabrinian missionaries in New York, including a proposal to build an Italian hospital, for which Cabrini and her sisters solicited the funds. Columbus Hospital was incorporated on May 18, 1891.

Not content to rest on her laurels, the dynamic Mother Cabrini left her New York projects in the hands of other sisters and traveled to Nicaragua in September, 1891, where she founded a house and school. From there she opened a school for Italian children in New Orleans, where she remained until recalled to New York to settle a dispute between the Scalabrinian priests and her nuns.

Cabrini returned to New York in April of 1892, where she found the Columbus Hospital in dire financial straits. The leader of the Scalabrinian mission, the Reverend Felice Morelli, had pushed the mission deeply into debt by borrowing money at exorbitant interest to purchase buildings and land. Morelli was unable to pay the debt on the hospital, which was threatened with public auction to satisfy his creditors. In Mother Cabrini's absence, Morelli had attempted to shift the debt onto the shoulders of the sisters. Cabrini decided to disassociate her order from the original hospital and, with a grant of $550 from Archbishop Corrigan and some wealthy Italians, she opened a new Columbus Hospital in two rented apartments. The new hospital was expanded in 1894.

The work of the Missionary Sisters of the Sacred Heart continued to grow after Corrigan's death in 1902 to include more schools and orphanages. The sisters also visited hospitals and almshouses, tombs and prisons. Quietly but persistently, the small and frail Frances Cabrini cultivated the support of bishop after bishop throughout the United States and around the world. She founded orphanages and schools in Denver, Los Angeles, Chicago, Seattle, and Philadelphia, as well as in such far-off locations as Buenos Aires, Paris, Madrid, London, and Brazil. She also founded several modern charitable hospitals in New York, Chicago, and Seattle.

Following a brief illness, Mother Cabrini died on December 22, 1917, at Columbus Hospital in Chicago. At her death, she was mother-general to some four thousand nuns and had founded seventy charitable institutions the world over. Her funeral was officiated by Archbishop (later Cardinal) Mundelein and her remains were laid to rest in New York. Soon after her death, her associates, led by Cardinal Mundelein, promoted her cause before the pope and the archdioceses of New York and Chicago. She was beatified by the Roman Catholic Church on November 13, 1938, after the rule that required fifty years to elapse before the beatification process could be initiated was waived for her case. She became the first American to achieve this honor.

SIGNIFICANCE

Frances Xavier Cabrini brought increased unity to the Italian community in New York through her charitable efforts. Her highest goal in her mission work was to strengthen the ties between the Italian immigrants and the Roman Catholic Church. Although she was often frustrated in her failure to wipe out "the worldly spirit" that she felt all around her, she contributed greatly to the growth of popular faith in the Italian community in New York City and in cities throughout the United States. Her worldwide missions also established charitable organizations to help those living in less affluent parts of the world.

Mother Cabrini achieved a worldwide reputation for her religious zeal, her diplomatic skill, and her talents as a businesswoman. She fought valiantly to create a role for Catholic women in foreign missionary work. When reminded by a male colleague that missionaries historically had always been men, Cabrini is said to have replied, "If the mission of announcing the Lord's resurrection to his apostles had been entrusted to Mary Magdalene, it would seem a very good thing to confide to other women an evangelizing mission." Contemporaries often referred to her as "a great man" or "a statesman" for want of a better term. Pope Pius XI considered her name "equal to a poem—a poem of activity, a poem of intelligence, a poem above all of wonderful charity." Through her zeal and her intrepid determination, Mother Cabrini helped to establish a vital role for Catholic women in the area of foreign missions and to increase their visibility within the Roman Catholic Church.

—*Kimberly K. Estep*

FURTHER READING

Border, Lucille Papin. *Francesca Cabrini: Without Staff or Script*. New York: Macmillan, 1945. An older biography meant for popular audiences, this work is extremely sympathetic to Cabrini and focuses primarily on her role as head of the Missionary Sisters of the Sacred Heart.

Di Donato, Pietro. *Immigrant Saint: The Life of Mother Cabrini*. Reprint. New York: St. Martin's Press, 1991. Originally published in 1960, this modern, scholarly biography of Cabrini gives the best background information on the period in which she lived. It uses archives of the Vatican opened to the public in 1978, as well as materials from the Congregation of Propaganda Fide that were opened by Pope John Paul II.

DiGiovanni, Stephen Michael. "Mother Cabrini: Early Years in New York." *Catholic Historical Review* 77, no. 1 (January 1, 1991): 56-77. This is the most comprehensive account of the circumstances that led to Mother Cabrini's dispatch to New York and of her early work with the Italian population there. DiGiovanni sets Cabrini's work in the context of political developments within the Roman Catholic leadership both in Rome and in New York during the 1880's.

Martindale, Cyril C. *Life of Mother Francesca Saverio Cabrini*. New York: Burns, 1931. Based on biographical materials collected by the Institute of the Missionary Sisters of the Sacred Heart, this brief treatment of Mother Cabrini was compiled as part of the campaign by her colleagues and friends to convene a hearing for Cabrini's beatification.

Maynard, Theodore. *Too Small a World: The Life of Francesca Cabrini*. Milwaukee, Wis.: Bruce Publishing, 1945. An uncritical and simple biography, this book concentrates on Mother Cabrini's role as a worldwide ambassador for the Roman Catholic Church. It is the best source for study of Cabrini's work outside the United States.

Sullivan, Mary Louise. *Mother Cabrini: "Italian Immigrant of the Century."* New York: Center for Migration Studies of New York, 1992. Biography placing Cabrini within the framework of the Italian immigrant experience.

Sultan, Timothy, and Alex Heard. "Cabrini at 50." *New York Times Magazine* 145, no. 50481 (July 7, 1996): 8. Brief history of Cabrini's canonization, including the miracles she performed and the display of her remains in New York City.

SEE ALSO: James Gibbons; Leo XIII.

RELATED ARTICLE in *Great Events from History: The Nineteenth Century, 1801-1900:* 1892: America's "New" Immigration Era Begins.

CALAMITY JANE

American frontier pioneer

Famous for being independent and determined to live as she chose in a man's world, Calamity Jane became a legendary exemplar of the mythic character of the American West.

BORN: May 1, 1852?; Princeton, Missouri?
DIED: August 1, 1903; Terry, South Dakota
ALSO KNOWN AS: Martha Jane Cannary (birth name); Martha Jane Burke; Martha Canary
AREA OF ACHIEVEMENT: Exploration

EARLY LIFE

Born in Missouri, Calamity Jane was christened Martha Cannary (or Canary). All the information about her birth comes from her seven-page autobiography. Although she wrote her life's story, was photographed many times, and had many witnesses to her activities, her early life, like her later life, is greatly lacking in valid documentation and is shrouded in tall tales and accounts of fictive deeds. Indeed, there is no official evidence that she was born in Missouri instead of Illinois or Iowa, that "Jane" was either a middle name or an early nickname, or that 1852 was her birth year, and not, as some biographical accounts have claimed, 1847, 1848, or 1853.

One biographer, Clarence Paine, cites an official census that places an Illinois-born M. J. Conarray—age sixteen and living with an Abigail Conarray—in Marion Township, Missouri, in 1860. If M. J. Conarray is M(artha) J(ane) Cannary, the birth date of Calamity Jane would have to be 1844. Her mother may have been Abigail Conarray or the Charlotte Canarry who was married to a young farm-bred idler named Bob. Also, her father may have been either a heavy drinker named John Cannary or a Baptist minister named B. W. Coombs. The written statements about her early life are so variable that one must consider her own statements, however ill-informed and exaggerated they may be, to be practicable.

In her autobiography, Calamity Jane claims to have had two brothers and three sisters. Again by her account, the family moved from Princeton, Missouri, to Virginia City, Montana, in 1865. She developed her skills as a horse rider and markswoman in her teens. Her mother, she writes, died in 1866, followed by her father in the following year, after having moved his family to Salt Lake City. From Utah, Calamity Jane and, presumably, her siblings, moved on to the Wyoming Territory.

The autobiography becomes demonstrably fanciful at this point. Flouting historical accuracy, Calamity Jane claims that she joined "General Custer as a scout at Fort Russell . . . in 1870, and started for Arizona for the Indian Campaign." Scholar Roberta Beed Sollid points out, however, that "Custer never was at Fort D. A. Russell" and that Custer "never in his lifetime set foot inside the bounds of Arizona, much less fought in the Indian campaigns there." Calamity Jane dates her donning the uniform of a soldier and getting "to be perfectly at home in men's clothes" to this period. During her year of activity in Arizona (1870-1871) at the age of nineteen, whatever the actual circumstances, Calamity Jane is seen to have perfected her skills with horses and firearms and to have matured.

LIFE'S WORK

Men's clothing was in accord with the masculine cast of Calamity Jane's physique and features. The photographs of her make this clear. Those that can be authenticated show her to be plain featured and stocky with a somewhat plump oval face, high cheekbones, and a long, prominent nose. Photographs of a trim, handsome, square-jawed younger woman, one in the buckskin trappings of an armed scout and one in full feminine finery, almost seem to be a different person but are generally accepted as the young Calamity Jane; at least they are consistent with verified photographs of Calamity Jane by the grave of James Butler "Wild Bill" Hickok and laid out in her coffin, in which her aged and gaunt face may recall a youthful angularity.

The striking photograph of the buckskin-clad female scout fits Calamity Jane's purported military activities in Wyoming from 1872 to 1876. This is the period during which, in her account, she was named Calamity Jane by a grateful Captain Egan, whom she, on horseback, had rescued from American Indians. There are numerous explanations of how she gained her epithetic name, most having to do with her being either the source or the carrier of calamity and many reflecting her hard-driving activities, coarse language, heavy drinking, rough attire, and constant gun wielding. The epithet is also associated with her devoted care of a little girl who was terminally ill with a contagious disease, against whose contagions she took no preventive measures for herself. The most that can be said about her acquisition of the epithet with any approximation to historical accuracy is that it occurred during the very early 1870's and that it was well known by the time she had moved to Deadwood City, South Dakota.

In 1876 she became a friend of James Butler "Wild Bill" Hickok at Fort Laramie, Wyoming, and accompanied him to Deadwood City, South Dakota, in June of that year. It was here, Hickok's death within two months of their arrival notwithstanding, that the legends of Wild Bill Hickok and Calamity Jane took root, the former as gambler and gunfighter, the latter as a gun-carrying virago. The personal relationship of the two cannot be established beyond mutual regard and possible friendship. It is certain that they were never joined in wedlock, although this became part of the legend.

There were other marriages attributed to Calamity Jane. She is said to have married a railroad man named Steers in Rawlins, Wyoming, in 1874 and, in the following year, a Sergeant Frank Siechrist, whom she supposedly accompanied in disguise on an infantry escort for mineralogists who were to determine the extent of a gold find in the Black Hills of South Dakota. Sollid lists a total of twelve variously reported husbands, with three of whom Calamity Jane was supposed to have had one child each; with Clinton Burke, her husband of actual record and the only one she acknowledges in her autobiography, she is said to have had one daughter, as she herself claims, and possibly a second.

Calamity Jane. (Library of Congress)

Calamity Jane's livelihood in Deadwood was gained chiefly by prostitution, although her claim, not without some basis, was that it was gained as a Pony Express rider "between Deadwood and Custer, a distance of fifty miles." Her distress when Wild Bill Hickok was shot in the back by Jack McCall in the Nuttall and Mann saloon on August 2, 1876, was very likely genuine, but not to the extent, as she claims, of her confronting McCall with a meat cleaver. McCall had, in fact, been arrested within an hour; a local court subsequently acquitted him, honoring the allegation that Hickok had murdered McCall's brother in Kansas and, as Duncan Aikman surmises, probably "relieved to be rid of the peril of Mr. Hickok's presence."

Continuing her involvement with construction crews and military units, Calamity Jane was active in South Dakota, Wyoming, and Montana after Hickok's death. In recounting her activities, she embellished them, as was the custom of miners, soldiers, and gamblers, and she came, perhaps, to believe some of the tales herself, as they ultimately found their way into her autobiography.

History accommodates her, however, in recording her noble ministrations to the smallpox victims of Deadwood during the plague of 1878. Heedless of contagion and sincerely devoted to attending and comforting those stricken, Calamity Jane lived through her finest hour. Oddly, she makes no mention of it in her autobiography. Sollid cites three reliable commentators on this episode—Estelline Bennett (*Old Deadwood Days*, 1935), William Elsey Connelley (*Wild Bill and His Era*, 1933), and Lewis Crawford (*Rekindling Camp Fires*, 1926). Each attests her humanitarian efforts, although Connelley dates the plague a year late and Crawford says that this was when "the people gave her the name 'Calamity Jane.'" Sollid cites two other sources who wrongly date the christening of "Calamity Jane" to this year (1878).

During the years after 1877, Calamity Jane became the subject of Wild West data and fiction. Horatio N. Maguire's book *The Coming of Empire* (1878) included an engraving of "Miss Martha Canary, the Female Scout." Pulp fiction, five-cent pocket library weeklies, and, later, dime novels were to follow as Calamity Jane became part of the colorful gallery that included Deadwood Dick, Wild Bill Hickok, Buffalo Bill, Belle Starr, Billy the Kid, and others. Her notoriety ranged from that of selfless nursing and charitable activism to prostitution, drunkenness, and imprisonment. That she did serve time in jail is documented: Cheyenne, Wyoming, in 1876; Miles City, Montana, in 1883; Rawlins, Wyoming, in 1885; Laramie, Wyoming, in 1890; and Livingston and Billings, Montana, in 1902 (the year before her death).

Capitalizing on her notoriety, Calamity Jane made public appearances on stage. She writes that her "first engagement began at the Palace Museum, Minneapolis, January 20, 1896, under Kohl and Middleton's management." She does not mention joining William Frederick Cody in his Buffalo Bill's Wild West Show, although in various of her letters she claims to have been part of his exposition (this would be during the years 1893-1895). Her itinerary in 1896 is said to have extended to Chicago and New York. Her appearance in the Pan-American Exposition at Buffalo, New York, in 1901 was not a success, owing primarily to her alcoholism. Buffalo Bill Cody himself nurtured the legend that he paid her fare as far as Chicago when she returned to the Midwest.

Calamity Jane's health failed after the terminus of her show-business efforts. Before she died in Terry, South Dakota, in August, 1903, she asked that she be buried next to Wild Bill Hickok. In accordance with her request, she was interred about eight miles northeast of Deadwood in Mount Moriah Cemetery, next to Hickok.

SIGNIFICANCE

There is evidence, varying in degree from slight to strong, that Calamity Jane was a markswoman, scout, soldier, Pony Express rider, prospector, layabout, prostitute, humanitarian, entertainer, author, and contributor in all of these contexts to the legends of the American Wild West.

Fictional accounts of her exploits have appeared in various printed narratives. Meanwhile, the factual biography of Calamity Jane is emerging in the scholarly research and writings of investigators such as Roberta Beed Sollid, Elizabeth Stevenson, and James D. McLaird. In film, Calamity Jane has been represented as an attractive, frequently glamorous heroine of the West, as played by Jean Arthur in *The Plainsman* (1936), Yvonne de Carlo in *Calamity Jane and Sam Bass* (1949), Doris Day in the musical *Calamity Jane* (1953), Jane Hamilton in the television movie *Calamity Jane* (1985), Anjelica Huston in the television miniseries *Buffalo Girls* (1994), and Ellen Barkin in *Wild Bill* (1995). Barkin's portrayal is closest to the Calamity Jane of fact and legend; dressed like the Calamity Jane photographed in the trappings of a scout, she achieves verisimilitude as a lean, attractive, coarse, sexually active, and capable virago.

—*Roy Arthur Swanson*

FURTHER READING

Aikman, Duncan. *Calamity Jane and the Lady Wildcats*. New York: Henry Holt, 1927. Reprint. Lincoln: University of Nebraska Press, 1987. This is a standard, entertaining story of the life and attributed deeds of Calamity Jane. Her short autobiography is included in the appendix.

Foote, Stella. *A History of Calamity Jane: Our Country's First Liberated Woman*. New York: Vantage Press, 1995. Biography based in part on Calamity Jane's autobiography and her letters to her daughter, Janey.

Lackman, Ron. *Women of the Western Frontier in Fact, Fiction, and Film*. Jefferson, N.C.: McFarland, 1997. This volume includes a brief but informative biography of Calamity Jane with a summary of fictional works and films based upon her character and legend. Also included are eight very good photographs.

McLaird, James D. *Calamity Jane: The Woman and the Legend*. Norman: University of Oklahoma Press,

2005. McLaird, a history professor at Dakota Wesleyan University, dispels many of the myths surrounding Calamity Jane's life.

Mumey, Nolie. *Calamity Jane: 1852-1903*. Denver: Range Press, 1950. This collection of documents and photographs includes a facsimile of her autobiography, newspaper reports, and a diary falsely ascribed to Calamity Jane.

Robinson, Gillian. *The Slow Reign of Calamity Jane*. Kingston, Ont.: Quarry Press, 1994. This is a long, free-verse poem in which Calamity Jane recounts paying Jack McCall to kill Wild Bill Hickok, her marriage to Charlie [Burke], and her status as a "free woman."

Sollid, Roberta Beed. *Calamity Jane: A Study in Historical Criticism*. 2d ed. Helena: Montana Historical Society Press, 1995. Sollid's accurate, well-researched study prunes the excesses of the legend. The book includes the autobiography, excellent photographs (including one of Calamity Jane in her coffin), and a good bibliography (added by John Hakola).

Stevenson, Elizabeth. "Who Was Calamity Jane? A Speculation." In *Figures in a Western Landscape: Men and Women of the Northern Rockies*. Baltimore: Johns Hopkins University Press, 1994. Stevenson outlines a factual approach to the life of Calamity Jane based on rejection of the romanticized legend. The book incorporates authentic information from the private papers of William Lull.

SEE ALSO: William Cody; Wild Bill Hickok; Jesse and Frank James.

RELATED ARTICLE in *Great Events from History: The Nineteenth Century, 1801-1900:* 1876-1877: Sioux War.

FANNY CALDERÓN DE LA BARCA

Scottish American travel writer

As the wife of Angel Calderón de la Barca, Spain's first diplomat to Mexico after Mexico's independence from Spain in 1821, Fanny was in a unique position to observe a New World nation in the making. Her book Life in Mexico During a Residence of Two Years in That Country *is considered the best book of the period on Mexico written by a foreigner.*

BORN: December 23, 1804; Edinburgh, Scotland
DIED: February 3, 1882; Madrid, Spain
ALSO KNOWN AS: Frances Erskine Inglis (birth name); Frances Calderón de la Barca; Marquessa Calderón de la Barca
AREAS OF ACHIEVEMENT: Literature, diplomacy

EARLY LIFE

Fanny Calderón de la Barca (cahl-deh-RON dee lah BAHR-kah) was born Frances Erskine Inglis (ihn-GALS) and was the fifth child of William Inglis and Jane Stein, who also had four sons and five other daughters. The well-born William Inglis was a Writer to the Signet, a special branch of the legal profession in Scotland. In 1828, when Fanny was twenty-four, the family moved to Normandy after her father was forced to declare bankruptcy. He died two years later and Fanny moved to Boston with her widowed mother, three of her sisters, and several nieces.

In Boston, Fanny and her family founded a school for girls. Though initially successful, the school foundered after the publication of an anonymous pamphlet satirizing prominent Bostonians that purportedly had been written by Fanny and a male admirer. Angry parents withdrew their children from the school and its enrollment fell. In 1835, the family moved again, to Staten Island, New York, where Fanny met her future husband, Angel Calderón de la Barca. He had been born in 1790 in Argentina when it was still a colony of Spain. He had been educated in Spain in science and entered the field of diplomacy. When he married Fanny on September 24, 1838, he was serving as Spanish minister to the United States during the administration of President Martin Van Buren. In October, 1839, the Calderóns sailed for Mexico, where Angel became Spain's first emissary to the former colony that had gained independence in 1821.

LIFE'S WORK

Fanny Calderón's fame comes from the book that she published based on letters that she wrote home to family and friends while living in Mexico as the wife of the Spanish envoy. *Life in Mexico During a Residence of Two Years in That Country* appeared in nearly simultaneous British and American editions in 1843. She wrote her first letter on October 27, 1839, the same day that

VERACRUZ

In 1843, a Mexican newspaper started serializing Life in Mexico. *However, readers reacted so negatively to Calderón's scathing description of the port city of Veracruz that the paper stopped the serialization, and her book about Mexico was not published in a Spanish-language edition until 1920. This extract recalls Calderón's first sight of Veracruz from the sea.*

At last [the city] appeared in view, faintly, certain spires beside the low sandy land, which for some time we had anxiously watched, and at length we could distinguish houses and churches, and the fort of San Juan de Ulua, of warlike memory. By slow but sure degrees, we neared the shore, until Vera Cruz, in all its ugliness, became visible to our much-wearied eyes. We had brought a pilot from Havana to guide us to these dangerous coasts, but though a native of these parts, it seemed that a lapse of years had blunted his memory, for we had nearly run upon the rocks. . . .

Anything more melancholy, *delabre* and forlorn, than the whole appearance of things as we drew near, cannot well be imagined. On one side, the fort, with its black and red walls: on the other, the miserable, black-looking city, with hordes of large black birds, called *sopilotes*, hovering over some dead carcass, or flying heavily along in search of carrion. Still, as the goal of our voyage, even its dreary aspect was welcome, and the very hills of red sand by which it is surrounded, and which look like the deserts of Arabia, appeared inviting. . . .

War and revolutions have no doubt done their work, yet I find difficulty in believing those who speak of Vera Cruz as having been a gay and delightful residence in former days, though even now, those who have resided here for any length of time, even foreigners, almost invariably become attached to it; and as for those born here, they are the truest of patriots, holding up Vera Cruz as superior to all other parts of the world.

Source: Fanny Calderón de la Barca, *Life in Mexico* (Boston: Charles C. Little and James Brown, 1843), chapter 4.

she sailed for Mexico with her husband. The last of her fifty-four letters is dated April 28, 1842. She wrote the letters without any thought of their later publication. It was only at the later urging of the noted historian William Hickling Prescott that she decided to publish the letters. Prescott, in turn, took full advantage of Fanny's sojourn in Mexico, availing himself of both the information gleaned from her letters and the couple's research on his behalf. Prescott published *History of the Conquest of Mexico* in 1843, one of the two major works on which his renown rests, without ever having visted Mexico. Four years later, he published *History of the Conquest of Peru*.

Fanny's book was well received in the United States. In Mexico, the *Siglo Diez y Nueve* newspaper planned to translate and serialize the entire volume. Four letters appeared in that newspaper in April and May of 1843. The fourth letter complained about pestilential conditions of the port city of Veracruz, offending some readers. The fifth letter would have dealt with General Antonio López de Santa Anna, who was the dictatorial president of Mexico at the time, but the newspaper did not publish any further letters. It was not until 1920 that the first Spanish-language edition of the book appeared.

A principal concern with Fanny's letters at the time of their publication was diplomatic. Some people feared that her husband had helped her in some way, and that her letters might, therefore, reveal secrets of the Mexican state. However, it was precisely because of her husband's political position that Fanny published *Life in Mexico* under the name "Mme. C—— De La B——." For similar reasons, she also used few names of real persons in her published letters. Instead, she typically substituted initial letters and dashes for names, such as "Señor A——." A massive new edition published in 1966 filled in such missing information.

Fanny was in Mexico at a time of intense political activity and change during which she witnessed two minor revolutions, a change of president, and a copper monetary crisis. She also traveled by stagecoach and horseback and experienced the fear of the nearly ubiquitous highway robbers. Her letters report on social and racial categories and on the wealthy and the poor. At the same time, her status as a diplomat's wife gave her entry to areas normally forbidden to outsiders, such as convents into which no outsider, foreign or native, was to enter and from which no insider, or nun, was ever to leave. Consequently her text reveals aspects of Mexico completely unknown to her audience.

After leaving Mexico, Fanny spent time in Scotland and Madrid, Spain, followed by nine years in Washington, where her husband was Spain's representative to the United States. They then returned to Madrid, where her husband was to be minister of foreign affairs. However, new political turmoil led to their exile from Spain from 1854 to 1856.

Fanny is believed to have written the anonymous *The Attaché in Madrid: Or, Sketches of the Court of Isabella II* (1856), purportedly a translation of the memoirs of a German diplomat to the Spanish court during the same period. After Angel died in 1861, Fanny stayed on as governess to the Princess Isabel. In 1876, she was rewarded with the title of marquesa de Calderón de la Barca for the long services of her and her husband to the crown. In early 1882, she died unexpectedly at the age of seventy-seven, probably from pneumonia.

SIGNIFICANCE

Life in Mexico remains in print and is still considered a rich source of information about the period of Mexican history that it covers. Fanny's portrait of Mexico is wide-ranging, from the broader political, historical, and social to the more intimate, the family, women's dress, gender customs, and behavior. The breadth and depth of detail undoes many stereotypes of the time.

With a rise of interest in travel writing and travel narratives in the late twentieth century, Fanny Calderón's work has again come under study. Recent research is mining the book for its contribution to social history and issues of gender in particular. *Life in Mexico* is one of the most important travel narratives by women of the period, and particularly by an American woman in a country of the Americas. As William Hickling Prescott said in his preface to the original edition, *Life in Mexico* contains "rich stores of instruction and amusement."

—*Linda Ledford-Miller*

FURTHER READING

Calderón de la Barca, Fanny. *Life in Mexico: The Letters of Fanny Calderón de la Barca, with New Material from the Author's Private Journals*. Edited and annotated by Howard T. Fisher and Marion Hall Fisher. Garden City, N.Y.: Doubleday, 1966. Using different typefaces to indicate original sources, the editors weave together the previously published text of *Life in Mexico* with correlating material from Fanny Calderón's journals. They also insert names where the original published text contained dashes. The edition is generously illustrated with drawings and photos of the period, and extensively annotated, providing a context not normally available to the modern reader. The introduction and short essay on "First Appearance of *Life in Mexico*; Early Comments; Subsequent History" complement the text. Bibliography.

Jagoe, Eva-Lynn Alicia. "'The Visible Horizon Bounds Their Wishes': Seclusion and Society in Fanny Calderón de la Barca's Postcolonial Mexico." In *Imperial Objects: Essays on Victorian Women's Emigration and the Unauthorized Imperial Experience*, edited by Rita S. Kranidis. New York: Twayne, 1998. An investigation of Calderón's views on nature, nation, race, and gender in writing during a period in which colonial perspectives were almost inevitable.

Ledford-Miller, Linda. "A Protestant Critique of Catholicism: Frances Calderón de la Barca in Nineteenth-Century Mexico." In *Gender, Genre, and Identity in Women's Travel Writing*, edited by Kristi Siegel. New York: Peter Lang, 2004. Analysis of the Protestant Calderón's often horrified reaction to Roman Catholic practices that she observed in Mexico, though ironically she herself converted to Catholicism several years later.

Méndez Rodenas, Adriana. "'The Cannon Are Roaring': Calderón de la Barca's *Life in Mexico* as Gendered History." In *Contesting the Master Narrative: Essays in Social History*, edited by Jeffrey Cox and Shelton Stromquist. Iowa City: University of Iowa, 1998. Discussion of Calderón's description and analysis of the series of revolutions and counterrevolutions during her two-year stay in Mexico.

SEE ALSO: Miguel Hidalgo y Costilla; Isabella II; William Hickling Prescott; Antonio López de Santa Anna; Martin Van Buren.

RELATED ARTICLES in *Great Events from History: The Nineteenth Century, 1801-1900:* September 16, 1810-September 28, 1821: Mexican War of Independence; May 13, 1846-February 2, 1848: Mexican War.

JOHN C. CALHOUN
American politician

In addition to wielding great influence in national politics for four decades, Calhoun wrote incisively on the problem of protecting minority rights against majority rule in a democracy and is remembered as one of the most innovative political theorists in American history.

BORN: March 18, 1782; near Calhoun Mills, Abbeville District (now Abbeville), South Carolina
DIED: March 31, 1850; Washington, D.C.
ALSO KNOWN AS: John Caldwell Calhoun (full name)
AREA OF ACHIEVEMENT: Government and politics

EARLY LIFE

John C. Calhoun's birthplace was a small settlement on the Savannah River in South Carolina, near the modern Abbeville. His Scotch-Irish forebears had made their way from Pennsylvania to Bath County, Virginia, then had been forced to migrate to South Carolina by the turmoil of the French and Indian War (1754-1760). The Up Country—as the western part of South Carolina is called—was a wild, untamed region, as evidenced by the murder of Calhoun's grandmother by marauding Cherokees in 1760. Calhoun's father, Patrick, was the youngest of four brothers who tenaciously carved out lives in the wilderness surrounding "Calhoun's Settlement." Patrick's first wife having died, he married Martha Caldwell, with whom he produced a daughter and four sons; the next-to-youngest child was named John Caldwell, after one of Martha's brothers.

Calhoun spent his youth on the family farm working in the fields with his father's slaves. Patrick's death in 1796 left John with a future seemingly bound by the needs of the farm and responsibilities to his family. However, upon the urging of an older brother, he enrolled in Yale College in 1802 and was graduated with honors in 1804.

After leaving Yale, Calhoun studied law at Tapping Reeve's Litchfield (Connecticut) Academy. During the two-year regimen at Litchfield, he developed habits in logic and discipline that would be his trademark in later years. However, he also discovered that the prospect of being an attorney bored him. A stint in Henry De Saussure's Charleston law office and, shortly thereafter, his opening a successful practice of his own near Abbeville did not enliven his interest. He soon left the profession to become a prosperous planter and to follow his consuming interest in politics.

This career change was made possible by Calhoun's marriage, in 1811, to his second cousin, Floride Bonneau Calhoun. The marriage brought Calhoun property that, when added to his, allowed him financial independence. Although Floride was ten years his junior, they were quite happy, and the marriage produced nine children. Calhoun would eventually establish residence at a plantation he built near his birthplace. He named it "Fort Hill" because the site once had been a garrison against Indian attack.

By the time of his marriage, Calhoun had developed those traits that would distinguish him for the remainder of his life. Physically imposing, standing over six feet tall, lanky, and with a rather hawklike face, he was craggily handsome. As the years wore away at him, ceaseless labor and care combined with checkered health to render the stern countenance fixed in the minds of students by the photograph taken by Mathew Brady around 1848. In it, Calhoun, nearing sixty, sits with a face that is lined, hollow, and unsmiling, yet lit by an arresting and wild stare. Perhaps this face was merely a mirror of his lifelong personality. Even as a boy, he was overly serious, and he seems to have always conducted relationships outside his family with the same cold logic he applied to his political theories. Anything but outgoing, Calhoun commanded respect but seldom inspired affection. Associates sometimes referred to him as the "cast iron man," describing a man who, while not unfriendly, nevertheless remained ever aloof and hence, on a personal level, essentially alone and friendless.

LIFE'S WORK

Calhoun entered state politics in 1807 and, after one term in the South Carolina legislature, won election to the U.S. House of Representatives in 1810. There he joined the ranks of the War Hawks, that group of influential congressmen (Speaker of the House Henry Clay was the most conspicuous of their number) who were intent upon war with Great Britain to protect American maritime rights.

During the War of 1812, Calhoun steadfastly supported all measures to bolster the nation's failing defenses. When the Treaty of Ghent ended the war in 1814, he remained convinced that it was only a truce before the renewal of the conflict. Beginning in 1816, he urged the adoption of a national program to prepare for another wave of British aggression. He supported a protective tariff, a national bank, an improved transportation system through federally financed internal improvements, and a large standing army. His nationalism won for him both praise and a place in James Monroe's cabinet as secretary of war in 1817.

Seeking to correct the many flaws made apparent by the poor showing of American forces in the recent war with Britain, Calhoun initiated numerous improvements for the Army. These included the establishment of new departments, especially those of commissary, quartermaster, and surgeon general. Well suited to the administrative demands of the War Department, he filled the post during Monroe's two terms with a flair for innovative management.

Calhoun adroitly remained aloof from the angry political turmoil that marked the end of the Era of Good Feelings and the beginning of the formation of a new national party system. Elected to the vice presidency in 1824 and 1828, he thus served in the administrations of both John Quincy Adams and Andrew Jackson, despite the bitter feud between the two. At the end of the 1820's, it appeared that he would succeed Andrew Jackson as president with Jackson's blessing, but the Nullification Controversy in South Carolina irrevocably estranged them and nearly ruined Calhoun's political career.

In spite of his earlier advocacy of the protective tariff, Calhoun became convinced that steadily increasing its duties financially victimized southern agriculturalists for the benefit of northern industrialists. When he wrote "South Carolina Exposition and Protest" in 1828, which stated his theory of nullification, it marked a significant turning point in his political career. Because he still hoped to attain the presidency, he kept secret his authorship of the doctrine. By turns, however, he was rapidly transformed from an American nationalist into a southern sectionalist. Elaborating upon Thomas Jefferson's ideas in the Kentucky Resolutions of 1798, Calhoun declared that a state could nullify a federal law it deemed unconstitutional or harmful to its interests by refusing to enforce the statute within its borders. Essentially then, nullification was a device whereby a minority could protect itself against the harmful will of the majority.

John C. Calhoun. (Courtesy of the University of Texas at Austin)

When South Carolina attempted to apply his theory by nullifying the Tariff of 1832, it brought the nation to the brink of civil war. Dismissing nullification as illegal, Jackson threatened to invade South Carolina to enforce federal law, and when it was revealed that Calhoun was the doctrine's father, Jackson branded him a subversive. In disgrace with the administration, Calhoun resigned the vice presidency, his national reputation in shambles. However, the governor of South Carolina promptly appointed him to the Senate, and there he worked feverishly with Henry Clay to draft a compromise tariff that helped to diminish the immediate crisis.

After the Nullification Controversy, Calhoun dropped all vestiges of his earlier nationalism and became the champion of southern planter interests in particular and southern rights in general. In the process, he earned the admiration of many southerners, and in South Carolina he came to exert virtually total control over a political system that only occasionally was not a reflection of his will. His towering reputation and talent made him a fixture in the Senate, wherein he increasingly focused his intellectual and political energies on combating what he perceived as northern assaults upon the southern way of life. Even his brief absence from the Senate—to serve as John Tyler's secretary of state from 1844 to 1845—was marked by his sectionalism: He successfully managed the annexation of Texas into the Union as a slave state.

As a strident antislavery movement grew in the North, Calhoun countered that slavery was a positive good. He opposed the Mexican War (which most of his southern colleagues supported) because he feared that northerners would try to exclude slavery from Western territories gained in the conflict. When his fears proved true, he was ultimately persuaded that northern restriction of slavery in the territories was a preliminary step toward the thorough abolition of the institution in the South as well. The result, he thought, would be economic and social chaos, avoidable only by the South's secession from the Union.

Calhoun's apprehension over both abolitionism and secession compelled him in his final months to attempt the unification of the South into an implacable front threatening secession. By so menacing the Union he hoped to frighten the North into concessions on the slavery question. Therein lay the safety of the South and the Union as well. His plan was unsuccessful, and as the nation reeled ominously toward disruption under the compounded sectional crises of 1850, he appeared before the Senate on March 4, 1850, almost for the last time. So ill that a colleague had to read his speech, Calhoun sat glowering from his chair as the chamber and crowded galleries heard his dire prediction that northern agitation over the slavery issue would inevitably destroy the Union. His warning, unhappily prophetic, went unheeded. As the nation strained toward yet another compromise, his shattered health forced him to his deathbed. He died on March 31, 1850, in his Washington quarters. His last words were "The South . . . the poor South."

SIGNIFICANCE

John C. Calhoun ranks as one of the most innovative political theorists in American history. Beginning with his complex arguments to justify nullification, he ever afterward sought legal and logical means whereby to protect minority rights against the overriding and insensible will of the majority. His fears over the diminishing influence of the South in national councils drove him, in 1843, to begin drafting proposals for significant innovations in American constitutional government. The notion of the concurrent majority became central to his thesis in both *A Disquisition on Government* (1851) and *A Discourse on the Constitution of the United States* (1851).

In these works, Calhoun declared that the nation comprised not only sections and states but also communities, each of these last possessing a unique character and interests different from the rest. The problem lay in the fact that any one community might be significantly smaller in relation to the others. The great danger in a democracy thoroughly wedded to majority rule, he insisted, was that a combination of larger communities could unjustly impose its will on any such minority through sheer force of numbers, ignoring the rights and privileges of the injured community. The resulting tyranny of the majority would be the very antithesis of the American ideal of government.

To avoid this result, Calhoun proposed that each unique community, regardless of its size, be given an equal voice in matters affecting the whole nation. A majority obtained under this arrangement would not reflect merely numerical strength, but would assure a general concurrence from all sectors of the society. In short, a concurrent majority would protect the rights of any minority. To reinforce the method further, he proposed instituting a dual presidency, one executive from each major section, each to have a veto on national measures.

Neither *A Discourse on the Constitution of the United States* nor *A Disquisition on Government* was completed when Calhoun died—indeed, his involvement in the sectional controversy of 1850 and his labors on these manuscripts combined to destroy his health—but they were published posthumously in 1851. They were lauded at the time by many southerners and scorned by many northerners. Calhoun's theories were complicated and made more so by the occasionally obscure prose of the former work. The latter work was often simply misunderstood. As the nation stumbled toward the disruption he had predicted, and after it had suffered the terrible Civil War, he was dismissed as both an ugly prophet of secession and a major cause of the catastrophe that followed.

Undoubtedly, before the Civil War Calhoun influenced in some degree the thinking of virtually every southerner and, it might be argued, a significant number of northerners. Nevertheless, subsequent scholarship has been unable to reach a consensus about Calhoun and the real meaning of the theories he produced. Cited as a major contributor to the outbreak of the Civil War, he also has been praised for tirelessly searching for ways to avoid it. Branded as little more than a sophisticated opportunist, always seeking his own advancement, he also has been eulogized as a careful statesman, aloof from the ordinary concerns of office and election. Labeled a stultifying obstructionist of the majority will, he also has been hailed as an innovative protector of minority rights.

In spite of the diversity of interpretation, one certainty emerges. For all of his imagination and mental agility, Calhoun never escaped the boundaries of his time and place. He bent his considerable talents to protecting and even extending the institution of slavery, a mockery of the ideals of liberty and, even in his time, disgraced by the considered judgment of humankind. Possessed of boundless vision, he yet remained blind to the fundamental evil of slavery and thus was at once a great man and a tragic figure.

—David S. Heidler

FURTHER READING

Bartlett, Irving H. *John C. Calhoun: A Biography*. New York: W. W. Norton, 1993. Scholarly biography, tracing Calhoun's evolution from ardent nationalist to advocate of sectionalism and nullification.

Calhoun, John C. *The Papers of John C. Calhoun*. Edited by Frank M. Merriwether, et al. 28 vols. Columbia: University of South Carolina Press, 1959-2003. An ambitious project, consisting of Calhoun's papers from 1801 to 1850, with skillful editorial comment integrated throughout.

_____. *Union and Liberty: The Political Philosophy of John C. Calhoun*. Edited by Ross M. Lence. Indianapolis: Liberty Fund, 1992. Includes Calhoun's two major political works, *A Disquisition on Government* and *A Discourse on the Government and Constitution of the United States*, printed in their entirety. Also contains some of Calhoun's speeches and papers.

Capers, Gerald M. *John C. Calhoun, Opportunist: A Reappraisal*. Gainesville: University of Florida Press, 1960. A revisionist biography that argues that self-interest was the primary motive for all of Calhoun's actions. Marred by a polemical tone, but valuable as a counterweight to uncritical biographers.

Coit, Margaret L. *John C. Calhoun: An American Portrait*. Boston: Houghton Mifflin, 1950. Pulitzer Prize-winning biography that offers an extraordinarily favorable view of its subject. Coit lauds the agrarian ideal and praises Calhoun as its defender who resisted the evils of an industrial society. The most humanized depiction of Calhoun, but frequently overly sympathetic.

_____, ed. *John C. Calhoun*. Englewood Cliffs, N.J.: Prentice-Hall, 1970. A brief compilation consisting of selections from Calhoun's writings, contemporary observations about him, and scholarly interpretations regarding his political theories. A good introductory survey of the diversity of modern scholarly opinion concerning those theories.

Freehling, William. *Prelude to Civil War: The Nullification Controversy in South Carolina, 1816-1836*. New York: Harper & Row, 1965. An excellent work on the great crisis that marked Calhoun's shift from nationalism to sectionalism. Includes a good description of his reluctant participation in the event and provides a penetrating analysis of the real significance of nullification.

Hamilton, Holman. *Prologue to Conflict: The Crisis and Compromise of 1850*. Lexington: University Press of Kentucky, 1964. An indispensable study of the complex problems afflicting the nation at the time of Calhoun's death. His significant part in the drama is competently portrayed and explained.

Lindsey, David. *Andrew Jackson and John C. Calhoun*. Woodbury, N.Y.: Barron's Educational Series, 1973. Dual biography of these major figures that is surprisingly thorough, given its brevity. Offers a good introduction to Jackson and Calhoun and is marked by measured judgments supported by broad research.

Wiltse, Charles M. *John C. Calhoun, Nationalist, 1782-1828*. Indianapolis: Bobbs-Merrill, 1944.

_____. *John C. Calhoun, Nullifier, 1829-1839*. Indianapolis: Bobbs-Merrill, 1949.

_____. *John C. Calhoun, Sectionalist, 1839-1850*. Indianapolis: Bobbs-Merrill, 1951. Grounded in decades of research and loaded with a wealth of detail, these three works make up an almost definitive biography. Especially good in placing Calhoun in perspective with the social, economic, and political forces of the early nineteenth century, but somewhat imbalanced by an overly sympathetic view of Calhoun and his ideas while hypercritical of his adversaries.

SEE ALSO: John Quincy Adams; Mathew B. Brady; James Gadsden; Andrew Jackson; John Tyler.

RELATED ARTICLES in *Great Events from History: The Nineteenth Century, 1801-1900:* December 1, 1824-

February 9, 1825: U.S. Election of 1824; c. 1830-1865: Southerners Advance Proslavery Arguments; January 19-27, 1830: Webster and Hayne Debate Slavery and Westward Expansion; November 24, 1832-January 21, 1833: Nullification Controversy; April 14, 1834: Clay Begins American Whig Party; January 29-September 20, 1850: Compromise of 1850.

JEAN-JACQUES-RÉGIS DE CAMBACÉRÈS

French politician and jurist

Cambacérès served France as a skilled jurist, an able legislator, and a prudent administrator during the revolutionary period. As second consul to Napoleon I, he effected a new civil code, controlled the media, and served as a moderating influence on the emperor. Without personal political ambitions, he dedicated himself to maintaining Napoleon's power and to serving his country.

BORN: October 18, 1753; Montpellier, France
DIED: March 8, 1824; Paris, France
AREAS OF ACHIEVEMENT: Law, government and politics

EARLY LIFE

Jean-Jacques-Régis de Cambacérès (kahn-bah-say-res) was one of eleven children of Jean-Antoine and Marie-Rose (née Vassal) Cambacérès. The Cambacérès family was a distinguished one, long active in politics. Cambacérès's father served as mayor of Montpellier, and Cambacérès was destined for a career in law. He attended the Collège d'Aix, rather than the one at Montpellier, which was judged not good enough for the young Cambacérès. A bright and diligent scholar, he excelled and developed a reputation for exactitude and a painstaking devotion to detail—these traits were to stand him in good stead later when he was helping draft the civil code for France.

By 1769, Cambacérès was practicing law in Montpellier, where he later (in 1774) became councillor of the local fiscal court (*Cour des comptes et des aides*). In 1771, he renounced his estate, a political move in keeping with the tenor of the times; Cambacérès was adept at gauging political barometers. His father had suffered some financial reverses, and Cambacérès had attempted to restore the family's financial position. He was ultimately to become a very rich man through his services to Napoleon. Because of his growing legal reputation, he was elected in 1789 president of the criminal tribunal at Hérault, and when the states-general were convened that year he was chosen as the nobility's second representative for the Montpellier district. When Montpellier was judged to be entitled to only one representative from the nobility, he returned from Paris. That political setback did not daunt Cambacérès, who in 1790 helped found the Société des Amis de la Constitution et de l'Égalité at Montpellier.

Because of his political activity and legal reputation, Cambacérès was elected in 1792 to the National Convention. A political moderate, he attempted to steer a middle course and avoid the impending excesses of the leftists, but the trial of King Louis XVI eventually forced him to take a stand, qualified as it was. After losing the fight to have the convention judged not competent to try the king, he did find the king guilty, but he recommended that the king's execution be effected only if France were invaded.

Cambacérès's "moderation" was politically dangerous, and he attempted to divert suspicion by absorbing himself in legislative and judicial matters. He submitted in 1793 a plan, containing 695 articles, for a civil code, but though the code reflected the politics of the times, it was not revolutionary enough for the convention; a shorter version, with only 297 articles, was rejected as well.

When the convention became more moderate, after Robespierre's downfall in 1794, Cambacérès emerged as one of its leaders, serving as president of the convention and later as president of the Committee for Public Safety. In that role, he helped conclude the peace treaties of 1795 with Prussia and Spain. He also called for a general amnesty and attempted to prevent vindictive behavior and new persecutions. When the convention was dissolved, he became a member of the Council of Five Hundred, but the Directory that came to power regarded his moderation with suspicion. His third draft of the civil code was also rejected, and he retired from his position as president of the Council and returned to practicing law.

LIFE'S WORK

Cambacérès returned to the government, serving as minister of justice, in June, 1799, just prior to the coup d'état of the Eighteenth Brumaire, which overthrew the Directory and established the consulate. Although he took no active part in the revolution, Cambacérès played a typically discreet role in assisting Napoleon and Emmanuel Sieyès with the coup. In recognition of his help and of his acknowledged legal prowess, Napoleon, who was named first consul in December, 1799, named Cambacérès second consul. (Charles François Lebrun, a sixty-year-old Norman with financial experience and more conservative views than Cambacérès, was named third consul.)

Although as second consul he was theoretically second in command to Napoleon, Cambacérès had no political ambitions of his own and directed his considerable abilities and energies to furthering Napoleon's interests. Cambacérès succeeded, through negotiating with selected ministers and reducing the size of the legislative body and the Tribunate, in reducing the number of influential opponents of Napoleon and engineered the assemblies' 1802 election of Napoleon as consul for life. Cambacérès's strategy effectively brought an end to representative government in France, and Napoleon was free to enact the long-desired civil code and to become emperor only two years later. Napoleon's ascension resulted in a promotion for the loyal Cambacérès, who became arch-chancellor of the empire, presiding in the emperor's frequent absence over the senate.

Although Napoleon held all the real power, Cambacérès was the emperor's trusted adviser and confidant, a bureaucrat who worked diligently to help him retain control of France. As his voluminous papers indicate, Cambacérès was in constant communication with Napoleon, even when the emperor was on one of his numerous military campaigns. One of Cambacérès's primary functions was to serve as an unofficial minister of propaganda for Napoleon, who recognized the value of the press. Cambacérès not only reviewed political articles and decided the fates of individual generals but also inserted articles in selected journals. He also was involved in ordering that books be written on selected topics, and in 1806 he printed the fictitious *Ms. trouvé dans le cabinet du roi de Prusse à Berlin*, a book about the partition of Poland.

Although Cambacérès was primarily concerned with domestic affairs, he did oversee the publication and distribution of maps of battles and campaigns. Even the discussions of the Council of State were edited by Cambacérès before they were subsequently printed in the *Moniteur*, the government's journal. This control was extended in 1811, when a special decree gave Cambacérès control over the telegraph linking Paris to major European cities—he effectively determined what messages would be transmitted.

In addition to managing the news, Cambacérès was active in the elaborate patronage system Napoleon and he devised in order to create a new supportive nobility to replace the old nobility. Because titles were not attached to land or to family but were granted by the state for service, people were encouraged to serve the state and to remain loyal to the new empire.

Cambacérès served not only as Napoleon's second in command but also as his personal legal adviser, though Napoleon's personal affairs certainly impinged upon his public political life. When the emperor wanted his marriage to Joséphine nullified, Cambacérès handled the intricate and delicate negotiations.

During his Napoleonic years, Cambacérès exercised considerable power over the media, the government, and the legal system, which he helped create. He also served as a moderating influence on Napoleon. However, his most important attempted interventions—to save the life of the Duc d'Enghien and to forestall the military campaigns of 1812-1813—were futile.

When Napoleon abdicated and the Bourbons were restored to power in 1814, Cambacérès survived and even endorsed the return of the monarchy, the current stabilizing force in France. When Napoleon returned to power the following year, Cambacérès was persuaded to resume his pre-Restoration duties, this time to direct the Ministry of Justice and preside over the Chamber of Peers, though he had undoubtedly had reservations about the likelihood of Napoleon's continued success. The Hundred Days did, indeed, end with Napoleon's defeat at Waterloo; upon Louis XVIII's final restoration to power, however, Cambacérès was not as fortunate as he had been before. He was exiled and moved to Belgium. Although he was permitted in 1818 to return to France and to regain his civil and political rights, he did not again hold public office. Six years later, in March, 1824, he died in Paris.

SIGNIFICANCE

As the titular head of the French government during Napoleon's frequent, extensive absences, Jean-Jacques-Régis de Cambacérès theoretically had a considerable amount of power. In fact, some historians have maintained that he governed France while Napoleon was away. As his own voluminous correspondence to the emperor indicates, Cambacérès was essentially an adviser and the administrator of Napoleon's policies, though he certainly had a hand in drafting key legislation and in coordinating and supervising the various codes that were implemented during Napoleon's reign.

Because Napoleon would not or could not delegate authority, the power to decide significant events was his alone; yet that centralized authority caused delays in dealing with governmental affairs and produced administrators unwilling to take the initiative and assume responsibility. Napoleon's grand schemes, including the reform of the codes, required implementation by an administrator who could handle detail, however trivial. Cambacérès, the legal technician, was the consummate lawyer, equally at home in administrative, legal, and financial matters. He also discharged some military tasks for Napoleon. Though he did not serve on the commission Napoleon appointed in 1800 to prepare a new draft of the civil code, Cambacérès's previous three drafts and his ideas found their way into the civil code adopted in 1804.

Cambacérès was a political survivor, an administrator, and a legislator who steered a middle course between extremes in the hope of serving in a stable, efficient French government. His moderation, his vacillation, and his desire to please all parties have made him as suspect to contemporary historians as he was to his political colleagues on the far Left. During his political career he was a Republican, an antiterrorist, a regicide, a Jacobin, an enthusiast, and a sometime supporter of Napoleon and the Bourbons—in short, whatever was expedient and consonant with his advocacy of a stable government.

Given his aversion to political chaos and corruption, which were rampant from 1795 to 1799, his support of Napoleon seems almost inevitable. He seems to have been attracted by Napoleon's authoritarianism and expediency and his desire to effect needed change. Although Cambacérès may have been more inclined to authoritarianism than Napoleon, his actions were as moderate as his views, and while he counseled Napoleon, he seems not to have urged his views with any vigor.

Richard Boulind, who has studied Cambacérès's ties to Napoleon, sees Cambacérès's homosexuality as the key to their productive working relationship. In a classic case of alter egos, Cambacérès, possessed with "feminine" tact, reflectiveness, and precaution, balances and is attracted to the "masculine" Napoleon, who is assertive and decisive. Regardless of how this working relationship is seen, there is no question about Cambacérès's having been the ideal statesman to complement Napoleon and his dreams for France.

—Thomas L. Erskine

FURTHER READING

Bergeron, Louis. *France Under Napoleon*. Princeton, N.J.: Princeton University Press, 1981. Part of Bergeron's book concerns the patronage system instituted under Napoleon's rule. Bergeron explains the system, examines Cambacérès's role, and shows how the system benefited both the recipients and Napoleon. Details of Cambacérès's social and financial ascent are provided.

Boulind, Richard. *Cambacérès and the Bonapartes*. New York: H. P. Kraus, 1976. Boulind includes the unpublished papers of Cambacérès, both letters to Napoleon and papers on the personal and dynastic interests of Napoleon. His introductions to both provide the most extensive discussion in English of Cambacérès. Boulind provides a brief biography and a psychological reading of the relationship between Cambacérès and Napoleon.

Cronin, Vincent. *Napoleon Bonaparte: An Intimate Biography*. New York: William Morrow, 1972. As the title suggests, Cronin's book mingles history with anecdotes and personal details. He is helpful in providing a comparison and contrast between Napoleon and Cambacérès and in detailing the degree to which Cambacérès advanced Napoleon's cause.

Holtman, Robert B. *Napoleon's Propaganda*. Baton Rouge: Louisiana State University Press, 1950. Holtman examines the means by which Napoleon and Cambacérès managed the news during Napoleon's rule. According to Holtman, Cambacérès was the primary agent of control, using such propaganda vehicles as news releases, the telegraph, and fabricated books.

Horne, Alistair. *The Age of Napoleon*. New York: Modern Library, 2004. This is not a conventional military or political biography of Napoleon, but an exploration of his character, lifestyle, and the social life of Paris during his years as emperor. The book includes information about Cambacérès's role in the reconstruction of Paris; his balls, parties and dinners; his fashions and self-image; and his loyalty to Napoleon.

Marquart, Robert. "The Fortunes of Cambacérès." *Revue de l'Institut Napoléon* 127 (1973): 43-52. Marquart provides a thorough discussion of Cambacérès's acquisition of an immense fortune through prudent management and imperial generosity. Marquart's findings attest the social and financial rise of a class that replaced the old nobility.

Thompson, J. M. *Napoleon Bonaparte: His Rise and Fall*. New York: Oxford University Press, 1952.

Thompson's book is particularly helpful in its discussion of Cambacérès's role in obtaining Napoleon's canonical divorce from Joséphine. Thompson details Cambacérès's painstaking preparation of the case and sees the divorce as evidence of the deterioration of Napoleon's character under stress.

SEE ALSO: Napoleon I.

RELATED ARTICLES in *Great Events from History: The Nineteenth Century, 1801-1900:* December 2, 1804: Bonaparte Is Crowned Napoleon I; April 11, 1814-July 29, 1830: France's Bourbon Monarchy Is Restored; June 18, 1815: Battle of Waterloo; November 20, 1815: Second Peace of Paris.

ALEXANDER CAMPBELL

Irish-born American religious leader

Campbell led a Protestant religious movement that attempted to restore the original structure of the Christian church of the first century, helping spawn both the Disciples of Christ and the Churches of Christ in the process.

BORN: September 12, 1788; Balleymena, County Antrim, Ireland

DIED: March 4, 1866; Bethany, West Virginia

AREA OF ACHIEVEMENT: Religion and theology

EARLY LIFE

The son of Thomas Campbell and Jane Corneigle Campbell, Alexander Campbell grew up in Ireland in a highly religious household that emphasized study of the Bible. When he was young, Campbell preferred the outdoors to academics and spiritual reflection but eventually developed a phenomenal memory and overcame his loathing of study. Around age sixteen, Campbell accepted the teaching of Christianity and began to fulfill his father's and his own dream of becoming a preacher. He read moral philosophy and church history. Although a Presbyterian, Campbell was especially impressed by the ideas of independent ministers such as John Walker and James Alexander Haldane, who suggested that creeds and denominational structures were made by humans.

These early encounters, augmented by his own reading of scripture and history, led Campbell to believe that the existing arrangement of Christian churches into various denominations was contrary to divine teaching and was the source of disunity. If the biblical principles of church membership, worship, and organization alone were the basis for church polity and practice, then a genuine unity among Christian people would be possible.

During this time, Thomas emigrated to the United States and eventually invited the rest of his large family to join him there. Circumstances permitted Campbell to attend the University of Glasgow for one year before moving to Pennsylvania in 1809. At Glasgow, Campbell was formally exposed to a set of assumptions called Scottish Common Sense Realism, according to which the human mind possessed the capacity to interpret right from wrong and could, therefore, determine which religious doctrines were true and which were false. Further, this approach to knowledge was inductive, so that one ascertained the great principles from religion by examining specific moral, ethical, and scriptural issues before drawing any general conclusions.

After joining his father in the United States, Campbell helped establish the Christian Association of Washington in 1809. The association was actually an independent church whose principles were articulated in a document called the Declaration and Address. Its purpose was to spread the Campbells' ideas about Christian Union and approaches to studying the Bible. The Campbells' creed and mode of divining appropriate Christian practices was "where the scriptures speak, we speak; where they are silent, we are silent." They hoped that these ideas would spread and that the divisive denominational labels of other Christian faiths would disappear and cause churches to restore the original organization and practice of Christianity of the first century, as depicted in the New Testament book of Acts. Campbell devoted the remainder of his long life to the realization of this cause.

LIFE'S WORK

Campbell's physical traits made him suitable to confront the labyrinth of Christian ideas in the moral landscape of the antebellum United States. He was tall, perhaps six feet, with powerful shoulders that he had developed by doing farm labor as a youth. He moved with vigor and grace. His face was of fair complexion and somewhat irregular in shape. A long, thin nose gave it some symmetry, but it was his cheerful expression that gave it order.

Alexander Campbell. (Library of Congress)

He possessed remarkable powers of concentration, great personal discipline, and skill as a speaker.

Campbell began to proclaim his ideas as a traveling preacher in 1810. He began to preach regularly at the Brush Run Church in Pennsylvania, which was organized along Campbell's principles. During this period, he became convinced that full immersion was the only appropriate mode of baptism, and he and his new wife, Margaret Brown, were baptized in 1811. He later came to conclude that baptism was not merely an ordinance or a symbol but actually part of the process of salvation and that immersion of the body was necessary for the remission of one's sins. This moved Campbell quite far from his Presbyterian roots and from the beliefs of many American Protestants and Catholics.

Campbell established the Buffalo Seminary at Bethany, Virginia (now in West Virginia), in 1818 to train young ministers and spread his own religious ideas. Students from the surrounding countryside boarded with Campbell, and he instructed them in the morning and evening, leaving much of the day free for farming, from which Campbell drew his living. He operated the seminary for several years.

In addition to teaching and preaching, Campbell spread his ideas in a series of well-attended debates with a variety of people. In the nineteenth century, debates were a form of outdoor theater that extended for hours in front of an always raucous and sometimes attentive audience. In 1820, he debated John Walker, a Presbyterian, on the subject of baptism. Campbell held that in New Testament times infants were not baptized, that immersion was the only mode for baptism, and that baptism was necessary for the forgiveness of sins.

In 1823, Campbell debated W. L. McCalla in Washington, Kentucky, again on the subject of baptism. Like many of the public exchanges and discourses of the nineteenth century, this one was eventually published. Campbell explained that salvation came through faith but baptism was a formal and necessary part of the process of faith. In 1829, Campbell debated Robert Dale Owen, a utopian socialist who had recently established a model community in Indiana. Owen was a skeptic who asserted that religion was a fruit of human ignorance. Campbell held forth for what he believed was the truth of religion as revealed in the Bible. At the conclusion of the debate, which about twelve hundred people attended, Campbell asked for all those who favored the spread of Christianity to move to one side. All but three in the audience did so. This debate elevated Campbell's standing from that of an obscure frontier preacher to that of a well-known controversialist.

In 1837, Campbell debated Bishop John B. Purcell. The real issues of debate pitted Roman Catholicism against American Protestantism, which was itself doctrinally divided. Unlike his other debates, Campbell did not emerge a clear winner, but both he and Purcell conducted themselves with equanimity so that the stature of both men was elevated in the public eye. In 1843, Campbell debated N. L. Rice, a Presbyterian. Henry Clay, an eminent politician, moderated the debate. Campbell and Rice argued about baptism, the Holy Spirit, and religious creeds, with Campbell holding that the scriptures plainly described and defined these terms. He believed that by looking at them in context, one could inductively arrive at the truth.

Campbell also busied himself for over forty years as an editor. In 1823, he founded the *Christian Baptist*, a religious periodical through which he attacked ideas and practices in American Christianity that he found contrary to scripture. In 1830, he ended the *Christian Baptist* and began a periodical called the *Millennial Harbinger*. Like many Americans, Campbell was fascinated with the idea of the Second Coming of Christ. Soon, however, the publication became the major medium for spreading Campbell's ideas about the Bible, baptism, and church organization. Campbell's list of subscribers for his publications was so large that the town of Bethany was given a post office and Campbell was made postmaster.

Although Campbell, like most ministers, typically eschewed formal involvement in politics and public issues, he did allow himself to be elected to serve as a delegate to the constitutional convention in Virginia in 1829-1830. The major issue confronting the convention involved political apportionment and whether all people—including slaves—should be counted while determining legislative districts. If slaves were included, the Tidewater region of Virginia would continue to have significantly greater political clout. Campbell and other upcountry constituents preferred to only count white people.

In the course of his service, Campbell debated John Randolph of Roanoke, Virginia, on the practical effects and morality of slavery. Campbell believed that slavery not only impoverished the slaves but also elevated the planter above the mass of laboring white people. Although he, like many white Christians, believed that the Bible did not condemn slavery per se, he believed that it specifically condemned many of the abuses of power and people perpetrated by white slave owners. Therefore, he worked for laws providing for the emancipation of slavery and spoke out against the abuses in the practice of the system. Although not an abolitionist in the manner of William Lloyd Garrison, he was increasingly antislavery in his opinions.

Ironically, however, Campbell's greatest achievement ran counter to his stated goal of effecting Christian unity. He, in the end, helped to found a sect called the Disciples of Christ. Initially a Presbyterian, Campbell broke with that denomination because he did not believe in infant baptism but in the immersion of those old enough to respond to the teachings of Jesus as contained in the New Testament. He then affiliated with the Baptists, but they did not find his emphasis on baptism for the remission of sins acceptable. Thus, he founded a loose association of like-minded people that he preferred to call the Disciples of Christ. Their goal was not to become a denomination—although that is what eventually happened—

MARK TWAIN REMEMBERS CAMPBELL

When Mark Twain was a boy, he and a free spirit named Wales McCormick apprenticed as printers in Hannibal, Missouri, One day, Alexander Campbell preached in their village and created a great stir. After delivering his sermon, local Campbellites raised money to have the sermon printed and took the job to the print shop where the boys worked. Twain recalls the incident in his autobiography.

We set up the great book in pages—eight pages to a form—and by help of a printer's manual we managed to get the pages in their apparently crazy but really sane places on the imposing-stone. We printed that form on a Thursday. Then we set up the remaining eight pages, locked them into a form, and struck a proof. Wales read the proof, and presently was aghast, for he had struck a snag. And it was a bad time to strike a snag, because it was Saturday; it was approaching noon; Saturday afternoon was our holiday, and we wanted to get away and go fishing. . . . Wales showed us what had happened. He had left out a couple of words in a thin-spaced page of solid matter and there wasn't another break-line for two or three pages ahead. What in the world was to be done? Overrun all those pages in order to get in the two missing words? Apparently there was no other way. It would take an hour to do it. Then a revise must be sent to the great minister; we must wait for him to read the revise; if he encountered any errors we must correct them. It looked as if we might lose half the afternoon before we could get away. Then Wales had one of his brilliant ideas. In the line in which the "out" had been made occurred the name Jesus Christ. Wales reduced it in the French way to J. C. It made room for the missing words, but it took 99 percent of the solemnity out of a particularly solemn sentence. We sent off the revise and waited. . . . Presently that great Alexander Campbell appeared . . . and his countenance cast a gloom over the whole place. . . . what he said was brief, but it was very stern, and it was to the point. He read Wales a lecture. He said, "So long as you live, don't you ever diminish the Saviour's name again. Put it *all* in." He repeated this admonition a couple of times to emphasize it, then he went away.

In that day the common swearers of the region had a way of their own of *emphasizing* the Saviour's name when they were using it profanely, and this fact intruded itself into Wales's incorrigible mind. It offered him an opportunity for a momentary entertainment which seemed to him to be more precious and more valuable than even fishing and swimming could afford. So he imposed upon himself the long and weary and dreary task of overrunning all those three pages in order to improve upon his former work and incidentally and thoughtfully improve upon the great preacher's admonition. He enlarged the offending J. C. into Jesus H. Christ. Wales knew that that would make a prodigious trouble, and it did. . . .

Source: Mark Twain's Autobiography, edited by Albert B. Paine (New York: Harper & Brothers, 1924), vol. 2, pp. 280-282.

but to work with other groups of other people who also hoped to reform American Christianity and improve American society by restoring the fundamentals of New Testament doctrine and practice. Some of these people used the term "Christians" to describe themselves, and the Christians and the Disciples of Christ worked closely together, especially in the upper Ohio River Valley.

The restoration movement—nineteenth century efforts to effect Christian unity by adhering to the primitive teachings of the Christians of the first century—did not achieve its goal. Campbell's Disciples of Christ became just another denomination, which itself fractured over issues raised by the American Civil War and questions of biblical interpretation. Many southern and literalist members termed themselves Churches of Christ, while more northern and less legalist brethren adhered to the name Disciples of Christ.

Campbell continued his labors to win adherents to his ideas and create a basis for Christian unity. In 1840, he established Bethany College in Bethany, which has been in continuous operation since that time. He traveled throughout the eastern half of the United States raising money for its endowment. His excursions even took him to Canada, France, and Great Britain. He also taught courses at the college in inductive biblical interpretation and moral philosophy.

In 1865, Campbell's health broke. He was bedridden for a time, after which he slowly regained the energy to continue his ministerial labors. He recovered enough in December, 1865, to deliver what is commonly called his "last discourse," which was based upon a fresh reading of Ephesians I. However, he caught a cold and was bedridden again through early 1866. He died in West Virginia on March 4 of that year.

SIGNIFICANCE

Despite his failure to effect Christian unity, Campbell nonetheless played a major role in the vigorous religious climate of antebellum America, which has been described as a "spiritual hothouse." His views on scriptural interpretation blended well with the democratic ethos prominent in the United States. By virtue of possessing a human brain, one could ferret out truth in both the Constitution and the Bible. Moreover, the Disciples of Christ continued to function more than one century after he founded the denomination.

—*E. R. Crowther*

FURTHER READING

Casey, Michael W., and Douglas A. Foster, eds. *The Stone-Campbell Movement: An International Religious Tradition*. Knoxville: University of Tennessee Press, 2002. Collection of twenty-six essays about the religious reform movement, including discussions of its origins, influence on the U.S. presidency, and multicultural aspects.

Garrett, Leroy. *The Stone-Campbell Movement*. Joplin, Mo.: College Press, 1981. An accessible history of the restoration movement, appraising Campbell's role in it.

Hughes, Richard T., ed. *The American Quest for the Primitive Church*. Urbana: University of Illinois Press, 1988. An excellent anthology of secular historical scholarship that places Campbell's restoration movement in historical context.

_____. *Reviving the Ancient Faith: The Story of Churches of Christ in America*. Grand Rapids, Mich.: W. B. Eerdmans, 1996. Describes the evolution of the nineteenth century restoration movement, from its origins in the theology of Campbell and Barton W. Stone to its current denominational status.

Imbler, John W. *Beyond Buffalo: Alexander Campbell on Education for Ministry*. Nashville, Tenn.: Disciples of Christ Historical Society, 1992. A thirty-four-page booklet examining Campbell's ideas for educating prospective ministers.

Richardson, Robert. *Memoirs of Alexander Campbell*. 2 vols. Cincinnati: Standard Publishing, 1897. The basic source of Campbell's life by a longtime ministerial associate. Includes some of Campbell's writings.

Seale, James M., ed. *Lectures in Honor of the Alexander Campbell Bicentennial, 1788-1988*. Nashville, Tenn.: Disciples of Christ Historical Society, 1988. Contains scholarly appraisals of Campbell's life and work and their meaning for subsequent U.S. history.

Webb, Henry E. *In Search of Christian Unity: A History of the Restoration Movement*. Abilene, Tex.: ACU Press, 2003. Examines the movement from its origins in the theology of Campbell and Barton W. Stone to its current incarnation.

West, Earl Irvin. *The Search for the Ancient Order*. 3 vols. Nashville, Tenn.: Gospel Advocate Company, 1974. This larger work looks at the successes and failures of Campbell's attempt to forge a truly national Christian unity movement.

SEE ALSO: Henry Ward Beecher; Henry Clay; James A. Garfield; William Holmes McGuffey; Carry Nation.

RELATED ARTICLE in *Great Events from History: The Nineteenth Century, 1801-1900:* May 8, 1816: American Bible Society Is Founded.

GEORGE CANNING
British politician

During a long and distinguished political career in which he rose to prime minister during the last year of his life, Canning performed his most notable service as foreign minister. He placed British power behind the national independence movements in Latin America and Greece and thereby helped further Great Britain's own economic and political interests and weakened the forces of reaction in Europe.

BORN: April 11, 1770; London, England
DIED: August 8, 1827; Chiswick, Devon, England
AREAS OF ACHIEVEMENT: Government and politics, diplomacy

EARLY LIFE

George Canning's father, who had the same name, came from an English family that had taken a manor in Londonderry, Ireland. The family had disinherited the elder George Canning, however, because of his misadventures, including his marriage to Mary Annie Costello, a beautiful but impoverished woman. The castoff son died on the first birthday of the younger George Canning. The widowed mother, desperate for a living, took up acting, a career then especially disdained by the more genteel. She married an actor named Reddish, who had a very unsavory reputation. Stratford Canning, a London banker and brother of the deceased father, ended the family's isolation from the outcast son's offspring. He took the young George Canning, then eight years old, into his home and provided for his education. The boy's grandfather provided him with an estate worth two hundred pounds annually.

At Eton and Oxford, Canning's knack for composition, prose, oratory, and witty expression soon became apparent. Along with other Etonians, he published the *Microcosm*, a journal that gave him an opportunity to develop further the witty style that he would later use to lampoon his political opponents. Canning would always be remembered as an acid-tongued rhetorician whose clever phrases could devastate an enemy. His opponents have so maligned his character that it is difficult to form a proper estimate of the man, but it is certainly true that self-effacing humility was not one of his virtues.

Early in his career, Canning displayed overweening ambition and arrogance. His obsession with seizing power so offended his contemporaries that sometimes his career would go into temporary eclipse. However, his rhetorical abilities were so impressive and his self-confidence so strong, that even with a legion of enemies he could not permanently be denied leadership. Canning had an abundance of energy and a capacity for hard work. Despite his flair for seeking the limelight, he was capable of spending long hours at work in government positions that brought him little attention or glamour. He also had a reputation for being a master of political intrigue. Portraits of Canning reveal a rather round face, a balding head with curly locks at each side, and eyes that suggest intensity and confidence.

In 1791, after completing three years at Christ Church, Oxford, Canning entered Lincoln Inn to begin the study of law. Politics quickly attracted the young scholar, and leading Whigs, such as Charles James Fox, saw in the oratorical skills of Canning a shining new star for the party. Canning's early dislike for the aristocracy and his initial inclination toward French revolutionary ideas drew him toward the Whigs at first.

Canning's Whig tendencies subsided quickly, however, as the revolution became a movement aiming to spread its excesses beyond France to the rest of the Continent. On the other hand, perhaps his perception that prospects for a rapid rise to political power were more favorable with the Tories motivated his decision to switch to that party. In 1793, it was as a Tory and a staunch supporter of Prime Minister William Pitt that Canning entered the House of Commons for Newton, Isle of Wight. His marriage to the wealthy Joan Scott on July 8, 1800, would give Canning the independence and financial security to pursue his political career without distraction. The marriage also produced four children.

LIFE'S WORK

Pitt gave Canning the post of undersecretary of foreign affairs in 1796, and Canning served in that post until 1799. During this time, he contributed to the *Anti-Jacobin*, a weekly journal dedicated to ridiculing English and French revolutionaries. From 1799 to 1800, Canning served as a member of the board of commissioners governing India. In 1800, he began a brief term as paymaster of the forces but left that office the next year, when Pitt resigned as prime minister. Canning spent the next few years as a member of the opposition, but in 1804, when Pitt returned to power, Canning became treasurer of the Royal Navy.

Canning did not receive a cabinet position until 1807, a year after Pitt died, when he received the important post of foreign secretary under the administration of the duke of Portland. Canning displayed an ability to act with decision in his new office. Aware of a secret French plan to seize the Danish navy, Canning dispatched a force of twenty-seven ships of the line to attack Copenhagen and seize the Danish navy. British sailors manned the captured Danish warships and sailed them back to England. Canning's decisiveness weakened the French effort, but because Copenhagen had not willingly surrendered its forces, Canning endured the abuse of foreign powers as well as the condemnation of the opposition party in England.

A dispute with Viscount Castlereagh, the secretary of war, produced even more suspicion of Canning. The foreign secretary had approved of the peninsular campaign against French power in Spain, but he disagreed with Castlereagh's manner of conducting the operation. Canning had no patience with those he considered inferior to himself, and he was restless in his quest for command. He tried without success to persuade the duke of Portland, the prime minister, to remove Castlereagh. Finally, Canning gave up his purge effort and resigned on September 9, 1809. Shortly afterward, the secretary of war learned of Canning's plot against him and challenged him to a duel. Canning suffered a slight injury to his thigh.

During the years from 1809 to 1822, Canning held no major office but continued to serve as a member of Parliament. Beginning in 1812, he represented Liverpool. In 1814, he became the ambassador to Portugal and two years later became a member of the board of control for India. Canning gave up his position in the government in 1820 because of his disapproval of the treatment of Queen Caroline, whose husband, George IV, had just become monarch. Caroline had been living in Europe for many years, and the new monarch tried to prevent her return to England or her recognition as queen. Failing this, George tried unsuccessfully to win his freedom in a divorce trial before the House of Lords. To protest his government's support of King George IV in the dispute, Canning resigned in December, 1820.

From 1822 to 1827, Canning finally achieved the pinnacle of power he had so long sought. He was nominated governor-general of India on March 27, 1822, but resigned this post before embarking for India. Castlereagh's suicide opened the path to be foreign secretary. Despite the king's hesitation, he approved Canning for both the secretaryship and the leadership of the House of Commons. Canning would be at the helm for the next five years.

The new foreign secretary continued and extended Castlereagh's policy of using England's influence to weaken the reactionary forces of the four major monarchies in Europe: Austria, Russia, France, and Spain. Since the Congress of Vienna (1815), these powers had concerted their efforts to repress liberal, constitutional, republican, and nationalistic movements in Europe. They had attained a measure of success under the leadership of Austrian prince Klemens von Metternich.

In 1823, French forces entered Spain to shore up the rule of Ferdinand VII against revolutionary challengers. The fear that France, with the encouragement of other reactionary countries, might undertake the restoration of the recently independent Latin American republics to a colonial status under Spain spurred Canning to propose to President James Monroe that the United States join England in supporting the independent republics.

Canning's suggestion intrigued Secretary of State John Quincy Adams, who encouraged the president to state unilaterally a policy that has come to be known as the Monroe Doctrine. Adams thought it would be unseemly for the United States to appear to be a cockboat following in the wake of the British man-of-war. The United States warned Europe to surrender any aspirations for recolonizing Latin America. It was George Canning who proposed the warning, however, and it was the power of the British Royal Navy that would enforce the prohibition. Great Britain hoped to protect its recently gained trading privileges with the former Spanish colonies. Thus, in 1825, Canning took the further step of granting recognition to the independent republics.

During the last years of his secretaryship, Canning put England's diplomatic power behind the Greek struggle for independence from Turkey. He also helped the Portuguese repel a threatened Spanish takeover (1826-1827). On February 17, 1827, Lord Liverpool's sudden paralysis removed him from office, and Canning became prime minister. Sir Robert Peel and other leading ministers resigned because of their disagreement with Canning's Roman Catholic policies. Canning supported removal of Catholic civil disabilities. The difficulty of forming a government without his former allies and the strain of keeping his beleaguered government in control took a heavy physical toll, and Canning died on August 8, 1827, having served less than half a year as prime minister.

SIGNIFICANCE

George Canning's famous remark, "I called the New World into existence to redress the balance of the Old," summarizes his most important achievement in foreign affairs. The position taken by England nullified in advance any dreams of reinstituting European monarchical control over Latin America. The defeat of the "Holy Alliance," a term used to describe the joint efforts to repress nationalistic efforts, can in part be attributed to Canning. No longer could Austria, Russia, Spain, and France hope by means of "congresses" to squelch revolutionary tendencies.

Canning's support of national movements in Europe itself was also significant. No other person outside Greece had more to do with Greek independence. Canning was not carried away with romantic mysticism in his support for Greece against Turkey; he said that he would not go into battle for "Aristides or Saint Paul." Nevertheless, public opinion in Great Britain strongly supported the Greek struggle for independence from the Turkish empire, and the death of Lord Byron in his attempt to aid the cause did stir the imagination of the English public. Canning's concern was more political. He did not wish to see Russia impose its own solution.

Czar Alexander I proposed establishing three separate partially independent Greek states. Supposedly, the Greeks would still have a tie to the Turkish empire, but the situation would provide Russia a chance to exert influence in the new states. Canning's negotiations with the Russians led to the Treaty of London of July, 1827. Russia, France, and England then undertook to make Greece autonomous, with only nominal control by Turkey. The three allies promised to take military action to force Turkish troops out of Greece. Canning did not live to see the Battle of Navarino in October of 1827, but his policies prepared the way for the destruction of Egyptian and Turkish naval forces at Navarino and the consummation of the Greek struggle for independence.

—Richard L. Niswonger

FURTHER READING

Bagot, Josceline. *George Canning and His Friends*. 2 vols. London: John Murray, 1909. Contains many letters not available to earlier biographers. Many of the letters display Canning's distinctive wit. Included are not only letters to and from Canning but also references to him in the letters of third parties.

Canning, George. *The Letter-Journal of George Canning: 1793-1795*. London: Offices of the Royal Historical Society, 1991. The Society has reprinted Canning's journal for this period, which includes his initial years in the House of Commons.

Hinde, Wendy. *George Canning*. London: Collins, 1973. A well-written, scholarly account that ably blends the political and the personal life. Hinde views Canning as a victim of his own arrogance and stubbornness, a man whose own actions kept him in the twilight for long periods yet who was one of the ablest and most brilliant political leaders of his time.

Johnston, Henry McKenzie. *Missions to Mexico: A Tale of British Diplomacy in the 1820's*. London: British Academic Press, 1992. Examines the diplomatic procedures Great Britain pursued to grant diplomatic recognition to Mexico, including Canning's role and influence in the process.

Marshall, Dorothy. *The Rise of George Canning*. New York: Longmans, Green, 1938. A carefully researched study of Canning's early career. It is concerned primarily with the formation of his character and views and does not cover the last decades of his life, when he held power.

Rolo, P. J. V. *George Canning*. London: Macmillan, 1965. Rolo's book contains three parts. In the first section, Rolo deals with the man himself. He believes that personality played an especially significant role in Canning's career. In the second section, Rolo provides a consecutive account of Canning's political record. In the third, he evaluates Canning as a statesman. He concludes that the man was not exceptional in dealing with domestic matters but argues that he ranks with Otto von Bismarck in his brilliant handling of foreign policy.

Stapleton, Augustus Grenville. *Political Life of Canning, 1822-1827*. 3 vols. London: Longman, Rees, Orme, Browne, and Green, 1831. The author was Canning's private secretary and wrote in part to clear the man's memory from "aspersions" of his enemies. Despite bias and lack of access to documents as yet unavailable, it is an important work.

Temperley, Harold. *The Foreign Policy of Canning, 1822-1827*. London: G. Bell and Sons, 1925. A very carefully researched and laudatory study of Canning's record as foreign secretary from 1822 to 1827, written by one of the early biographers of Canning. This book places Canning's later years in the context of European diplomacy.

SEE ALSO: John Quincy Adams; Viscount Castlereagh; George IV; Second Earl of Liverpool; Second Viscount Melbourne; James Monroe; Sir Robert Peel.

RELATED ARTICLES in *Great Events from History: The Nineteenth Century, 1801-1900:* June 18, 1812-December 24, 1814: War of 1812; October 20-30, 1822: Great Britain Withdraws from the Concert of Europe; December 2, 1823: President Monroe Articulates the Monroe Doctrine; August 28, 1833: Slavery Is Abolished Throughout the British Empire.

ANTONIO CANOVA
Italian sculptor

Canova fixed the ideal style in neoclassical sculpture for generations. His works were considered the standard of international artistic excellence in his day and his name and opinions held great authority.

BORN: November 1, 1757; Possagno, Republic of Venice (now in Italy)
DIED: October 13, 1822; Venice (now in Italy)
AREA OF ACHIEVEMENT: Art

EARLY LIFE

Antonio Canova (kah-NOH-vah) was the son of Angela and Pietro Canova. In 1761, his twenty-six-year-old father, a stonemason, died. The following year, his mother remarried and moved to a village west of Possagno, leaving young Antonio in the care of Pasino Canova, his paternal grandfather, who was also a stonemason. In 1768, Antonio was apprenticed to Giuseppe Bernardi, known as Torretti, in nearby Pagnano. He received his first formal lessons in this active studio that manufactured garden sculpture. There, Canova would have absorbed proficiency in handling stone, in efficient delegation to specialized assistants of the various mechanical steps in the production process, and in the administration of the technical and financial aspects of a studio.

In autumn of 1768, Torretti took the young Canova to his other studio in Venice. For the first time Canova was able to study Greco-Roman sculpture in private Venetian collections. He also studied the collections of plaster casts in the palace of Filippo Farsetti and frequented the academy. In 1770, Senator Giovanni Falier, who had shown an interest in Canova's work, commissioned two baskets of fruit in stone and two life-size figures.

Encouraged, Canova left Torretti's studio and in 1775 established his own studio in the cloister of Santo Stefano in Venice. At this time he won second place in a competition organized by the Venice Academy. Having achieved a reputation for portraiture, he carved the naturalistic life-size marble *Daedalus and Icarus* (1779), his first truly original work, for the procurator Pietro Vittor Pisani. Exhibited at the annual Venetian art fair of the Ascension, it was a great public and financial success. With this money Canova left for Rome October 9, 1779.

On November 4, 1779, via Bologna and Florence, Canova arrived in Rome. He was received by the Venetian ambassador Girolamo Zulian, who provided him with a studio in the embassy palace. There he was able to study private and public collections and the sculpture of Roman churches. The young Canova also benefited from his acquaintance with the most advanced artists and critics of the age.

LIFE'S WORK

In the winter of 1780, Canova visited Naples, where he saw great collections of antiquities. Back in Rome, he exhibited a plaster cast of his *Daedalus and Icarus* to the influential artist and archaeologist Gavin Hamilton, who recognized his talent. Hamilton advised Canova on the direction his style should take and was instrumental in turning him from the Baroque to the revolutionary neoclassical style first propagated by the German archaeologist and historian Johann Joachim Winckelmann. The young sculptor became determined to study antique style thoroughly.

Winckelmann's aesthetic revolution carried an enormous moral charge. He condemned the excesses of the Baroque as not only offensive to sensibility but also injurious to rationality, humankind's highest faculty. He favored the pure Greek art with its noble simplicity and calm grandeur over the corrupt Roman art.

In 1781, Ambassador Zulian commissioned the marble *Theseus and the Minotaur*. This gave Canova the chance of proving himself in the new style. He accepted the advice of men he had grown to respect, restrained his natural inclination toward liveliness, and altered his style in accordance with the new doctrine of tranquil grandeur.

In 1783, the Venetian Giovanni Volpato, to whose daughter Canova had been briefly engaged, attained for Canova the commission for the monumental *Tomb of Pope Clement XIV* (1783-1787). Here he purifies the Baroque elements represented by such funerary monuments as Gianlorenzo Bernini's *Tomb of Pope Urban VIII* by replacing Bernini's lavish allegorical approach with figures in noble, body-clinging draperies, their restraint and pose reinforcing the clean severity of the entire composition. The figures do not interact but appear to be juxtaposed, an arrangement that heightens the quiet solemnity. At the unveiling of this piece in 1787, Canova's international reputation was established. The immediate, enormous success made him the most celebrated sculptor of his time.

Canova's work on the tomb of Clement XIV was so intense that, as a result of his constant running of the drill that had to be pressed against the stone with his chest, he suffered severe deformation of the ribs. This injury was connected to the cause of his death in 1822. Canova's output would vary between two stylistic extremes: powerful, life-size monuments and intimate figures of an erotic nature. Works such as the tender *Cupid and Psyche* (1787-1793) were calculated to give greatest satisfaction when contemplated in a private manner.

Canova's sculpture combined the purity of white marble and the simplicity of antique forms with the softness of execution. His mature works were so successful because the references to the ancients were always clear. Their sensuality was often heightened by the working of the marble and by the definite sense of line and silhouette. Except for a few works, Canova's productions are of a translucent delicacy.

Canova's human figures display his knowledge of formalized anatomy. He did not try to portray the body realistically. Part of the appeal of such pieces as *Hebe* (1796) is the intricate, undulating lines that abstract the forms, aided by the unnatural whiteness of the marble, and thus negate realism. Canova's movement toward abstraction was evident by the ease with which his works translated into outline engraving without losing total effect.

Antonio Canova. (Library of Congress)

With the rise of Napoleon I, circumstances in France changed for sculpture. Neoclassicism, because it assumed a political position of patriotism and social progress, was the ideal style for propagandizing the very meaning of the empire. Canova's popularity generated commissions from Napoleon and his family. In most of these pieces he sought to depict the dynasty as successors to their imagined imperial Roman ancestors.

The period from 1800 to 1814 was extremely productive for Canova. Two of his greatest masterpieces, *Pauline Borghese as Venus Victorious* (1804-1808) and the *Tomb of Archduchess Maria Christina* (1805-1809), were produced during this period. The tomb deliberately detaches itself from the church, focuses the viewer's attention exclusively on itself, and remains stoically silent about the possible meaning or resolution of death. It is strangely lacking in both instruction and celebration. The participants do not face the observers; they simply participate in the endless procession to the grave. The portrait of Pauline Borghese is an ideal image where the elements of classicism, technical virtuosity, and a submerged sensuality are joined in a subtly evocative whole. This cool yet voluptuous figure shows the wide range of sexuality that Canova's outline style can express. With these two works, Canova reached the peak of his career; unlike most artists he managed to stay there for the rest of his life.

In his later life, Canova traveled extensively between Venice, Rome, Vienna, Paris, and London. His reputation for neutrality, for his dedication to basic ethical causes as well as his reputation as an artist, made Canova the ideal papal agent at the Congress of Paris in 1815. The Papal States won back most of their vast artistic treasures through Canova's shrewd diplomatic tactics. From Paris he traveled to London, where he saw the Elgin Marbles. There he quickly realized that most of the works on which he had based his style had been Roman copies, and he identified the copies as affected, exaggerated, and conventional. His advanced age, however, prevented any further change in his artistic direction.

Little is known about Canova's intimate life. Although he experienced enduring hurt over his father's early death and his mother's abandonment, there appeared to be a detachment from conventional personal affections or passions. However, throughout his life Canova was a modest, kind, and generous man, especially to young and struggling artists and to his half brother, who seemed not to deserve his generosity. In

1820, the first sharp symptoms of his fatal illness appeared and undermined his strength as he continued to work. Scarcely able to eat, suffering from severe abdominal pain, he died on October 13, 1822. He was buried in the new Tempio, the church that he built for Possagno, his native town.

SIGNIFICANCE

Antonio Canova's achievement was to remain the ideal exemplar for academic sculptors throughout most of the nineteenth century. He worked in enough genres to provide a variety of imitable forms. His superficially simple antique style was pure and graceful without overemphatic voluptuousness. It was repeated all over Europe and the United States but with an intensification of hardness and dryness that became too evident in the studio repetitions and other copies of his art.

Canova was the one man who actually made sculpture in accordance with Winckelmann's theories. The lack of high-quality sculpture in the classical manner after Canova's death resulted from following those theories that deadened more talents than they inspired because imitation soon became mechanical. Eventually it was the entire neoclassical style within which Canova worked, with all of its moral and political overtones, that was completely rejected.

Because of the highly polished purity of Canova's marble forms and their intentional connections with the masterpieces of antiquity, he has received negative criticism from modern critics who favored the sketch over the finished work and who condemned imitation as the enemy of spontaneity. Late nineteenth century criticism condemned his sensuality and his idealization of nature. The twentieth century turned against him for precisely opposite reasons: He was considered too blandly realistic and too lacking in sensual fervor.

During Canova's lifetime and well after his death, however, his excellence was not questioned. The success of his style entailed its spread in the form of originals, copies by assistants, and engravings that he himself commissioned.

The greatest following of Canova's style was in France. His own style was partly formed from French ideas as a result of his friendship with the antiquarian Quatremère de Quincy. Their exchange of letters over many years enlightened Canova with a program of classical aesthetics. The Frenchman made subject suggestions and gave encouragement and approval. Canova even tried tinting some of his statues according to ancient practice as suggested by Quatremère's researches.

Canova was highly influential among such contemporary French artists as the sculptors Antoine Chaudet and Joseph Chinard and the painters Anne-Louis Girodet, François Gérard, Pierre Guérin, and J. Jean-Auguste-Dominique Ingres. These painters were inspired by his delicately linear representations of the nude. Many of Girodet's works adapt Canova's figures to paint. Ingres's *Bather of Valpinçon* (1808) was influenced by Canova's *Venus Italica* (1804-1812). Canova's popularity in England is evidenced by the large number of his works in English collections. The sculptor and draftsman John Flaxman, who obtained at least one commission from Canova, was strongly influenced by his style.

Canova's significance, in part a result of his diplomatic activities, passed beyond the boundaries of the art world and made him a figure accessible to a broad public. With the exception of Peter Paul Rubens, no other artist had ever been able to ingratiate himself and his art to so many European courts during his lifetime.

—*John A. Calabrese*

FURTHER READING

Boime, Albert. *A Social History of Modern Art*. Vol. 1 in *Art in an Age of Revolution, 1750-1800*. Chicago: University of Chicago Press, 1987. A brief treatment of Canova's career and the significant political implications of his art in the light of events at the end of the eighteenth century.

Clark, Anthony M. *The Age of Canova*. Providence: Rhode Island School of Design, 1957. An appreciative evaluation of Canova's work in this brief catalog for the exposition of his work held in the Museum of Rhode Island School of Design, fall, 1957.

Clifford, Timothy, et al. *The "Three Graces": Antonio Canova*. Edinburgh: National Galleries of Scotland, 1995. Catalog, consisting primarily of illustrations, from an exhibition of *Three Graces*, the sculpture many critics consider Canova's masterpiece. The exhibition was held at the National Galleries of Scotland from August 9 through October 8, 1995.

Honour, Hugh. *Canova's Theseus and the Minotaur*. Reprint. London: Phaidon Press, 1969. An excellent scholarly essay explaining the complete evolution of this, the first neoclassical piece of sculpture by the artist. Bibliography, detailed notes, and black-and-white reproductions.

_____, et al. *The Age of Neoclassicism*. London: Arts Council of Great Britain, 1972. A comprehensive catalog for the fourteenth exhibition of the Council of Europe housed in the Royal Academy and Victoria and Albert Museum, fall, 1972. Includes eleven essays on seminal aspects of neoclassical culture, ideas, and specific art forms; bibliographical outlines and historical sketches of each artist; and plates.

Johns, Christopher M. S. *Antonio Canova and the Politics of Patronage in Revolutionary and Napoleonic Europe*. Berkeley: University of California Press, 1998. Examines how patrons, the patronage system, and politics affected Canova's choice of subjects and methods of working. Johns describes how Canova created sculpture and painting that allowed him to maintain his political and personal integrity, without using his art in the service of the state.

Licht, Fred. *Canova*. Photographs by David Finn. New York: Abbeville Press, 1983. This elaborate and handsome volume, the only major recent work in English, presents Canova's sculpture by means of photographic and textual interpretation. More than three hundred color and black-and-white photographs sensitively convey both the grandeur and delicacy of Canova's sculpture. Contains detailed analyses on individual works. Epilogue, notes, chronology, and an excellent bibliography.

Praz, Mario. *On Neoclassicism*. Translated by Angus Davidson. London: Thames and Hudson, 1969. Chapter 6 is an analytical review of the predominantly adverse criticism accompanied by reassessment of Canova's art within the larger context of the aesthetics of neoclassicism.

SEE ALSO: Jean-Auguste-Dominique Ingres; Auguste Rodin; Georges Seurat.

RELATED ARTICLES in *Great Events from History: The Nineteenth Century, 1801-1900:* 1803-1812: Elgin Ships Parthenon Marbles to England; 1888: Rodin Exhibits *The Thinker*.

WILLIAM CAREY

English missionary

As the first English-speaking Protestant missionary, Carey set a pattern for the modern missionary movement. A brilliant self-taught linguist, he spent his entire career as a missionary in India, where he translated the Bible into several languages and founded an important institute of higher learning and many schools and churches.

BORN: August 17, 1761; Paulerspury, Northamptonshire, England

DIED: June 9, 1834; Frederiksganar (now Serampore), India

AREAS OF ACHIEVEMENT: Religion and theology, linguistics, education

EARLY LIFE

William Carey (KAYR-ee) rose from humble origins to become a world-famous missionary and a professor of Bengali in Calcutta, India. He was born in a small village in the East Midlands area of England. His parents, adherents of the Church of England, apprenticed him to a shoemaker so that he could learn an indoor trade because of a skin allergy to sunlight that the young William developed. Under the influence of a fellow apprentice, John Warr, Carey underwent a religious conversion and became a Baptist. The East Midlands area was one of two centers of small Baptist denominations in England at the end of the eighteenth century. The famous Baptist preacher and writer John Bunyan lived in the same area during the previous century.

Carey began to preach in the local chapels and soon felt the call to become a pastor, but his preaching was so poor that his first church initially refused to ordain him. He was largely self-taught, learning Latin and Greek while working at his cobbler's bench. His workshop wall held a large world map, on to which he wrote as many details of each country's culture, religion and languages as he could discover. He eventually gave up cobbling to combine pastoring with teaching in the village school. There, famously, he constructed a leather-covered globe of the world, impressing on his students the needs and extent of "the heathen."

Until that time, Protestant missionary work had been confined to the British colonies of North America. Carey developed a far wider vision. In 1792 he published a pamphlet titled *An Enquiry into the Obligations of Christians to Use Means for the Conversion of the Heathen*. Its purpose was to counter the hyper-Calvinistic theology of some of his denominational colleagues, who believed God would convert the non-Christian world without human intervention at some moment in the future. The pamphlet was also a call to take worldwide missionary work seriously. Carey reinforced his pamphlet with a now-famous sermon before his fellow ministers, in which he took as his text: "Expect great things from God; attempt great things for God."

At a meeting in Kettering in 1792, the Northamptonshire Baptist Association resolved to set up a "Particular Baptist Missionary Society for propagating the gospel among the heathen." This organization later became known as the Baptist Missionary Society, the first English-speaking Protestant missionary society, shortly to be followed by the primarily Congregational London Missionary Society in 1795, and the Anglican Church Missionary Society in 1799. Andrew Fuller became the secretary and correspondent to the new society, working tirelessly for it in England until his death in 1815.

LIFE'S WORK

In June, 1793, Carey, with his wife Dorothy, her sister, and their five children, sailed for Calcutta, India, which was then under the rule of the chartered British East India Company. They were accompanied by Dr. John Thomas and his wife. Thomas was a former employee of the company and had put before Carey the needs of India. The party arrived in India on November 11, 1793.

Technically, Carey was not the first missionary to India. Roman Catholic missions to India dated back to the beginnings of the Portugese commercial empire in the sixteenth century, and before that, to the Mar Thoma church of South India, reputedly founded by the apostle Thomas. There had also been a small Danish Lutheran and Moravian mission during the first part of the eighteenth century centered on one of the two small Danish trading enclaves, Tranquebar, also in South India. The Danish missionaries had built a good reputation under Otto Ziegenbalg and Christian Schwarz, but without reinforcements to follow, their work made no lasting mark.

The East India Company's policy at that time was to oppose all missionary work for fear of upsetting the delicate status quo between British traders and the Indian peoples, who were mainly Hindu and Muslim. The missionaries were therefore technically illegal and were certainly unwelcome. Morever, the missionaries' funds evaporated under Thomas's mismanagement. Forced to move out of Calcutta, they had to resort to hunt for their food in the Sunderbans, a jungle area in the Ganges Delta, before Carey secured the managership of an indigo plantation in the Malda district of Bengal. There, Carey's son Peter died in 1796. The boy's death help to disorder the mind of Carey's wife, who died in 1807. Carey's second wife also died, and he married a third time.

While he managed the plantation, Carey taught himself Bengali, the local language, and struggled to translate the New Testament into that language. He was to have to make seven further attempts to achieve an acceptable version, but in the end he succeeded in establishing a prose literature for Bengali, which previously had only possessed a high-flown poetic literature. He also began studying the great classical Indian language, Sanskrit, and Persian, the lingua franca of the Indian subcontinent at that time.

In 1799, the small missionary party was reinforced by four recruits

THE ARGUMENT FOR FOREIGN MISSIONS

At the time William Carey started his mission work, many theologians believed that missionaries were unnecessary, as God would somehow eventually bring heathens to the Gospel. Carey objected to that and other arguments against mission work and essentially struck out on his own.

It has been objected that there are multitudes in our own nation, and within our immediate spheres of action, who are as ignorant as the South-Sea savages, and that therefore we have work enough at home, without going into other countries. That there are thousands in our own land as far from God as possible, I readily grant, and that this ought to excite us to ten-fold diligence in our work, and in attempts to spread divine knowledge amongst them is a certain fact; but that it ought to supersede all attempts to spread the gospel in foreign parts seems to want proof. Our own countrymen have the means of grace, and may attend on the word preached if they choose it. They have the means of knowing the truth, and faithful ministers are placed in almost every part of the land, whose spheres of action might be much extended if their congregations were but more hearty and active in the cause: but with them the case is widely different, who have no Bible, no written language, (which many of them have not,) no ministers, no good civil government, nor any of those advantages which we have. Pity therefore, humanity, and much more Christianity, call loudly for every possible exertion to introduce the gospel amongst them.

Source: William Carey, *An Enquiry Whether the Commission Given by Our Lord to His Disciples Be Not Still Binding on Us* (1792).

from England, and the decision was made to relocate to Frederiksganar (now Serampore), the other Danish enclave in India, some sixteen miles west of Calcutta. Although two of the recruits succumbed to the climate and disease, the remaining two, Joshua Marshman and William Ward, a printer and former newspaper editor, stayed with Carey, with whom they formed a noble trio in the translation and printing of the Bible. Ward eventually also produced a four-volume work on Hinduism and became the pastor of the first permanent church to be founded by the mission.

As the Danish pioneers had found a century earlier, Indian converts came slowly—from both Hinduism and Islam. Carey himself did not baptize his first convert till December, 1800—seven years after his arrival in India. However, by 1821 the missionaries had baptized more than 1,400 people. Meanwhile, they lived communally, pooling their resources.

In 1798, Carey secured a well-paid position as professor of Bengali at the newly opened College of Fort William in Calcutta and held that post for twenty years. His income helped the mission to be financially independent. Carey's interest in horticulture also helped the mission maintain self-sufficiency in its food supply.

One of the main goals of the missionaries was to provide the Bible to Indians in their own languages. In addition to the Bengali Bible that they completed in 1809, the three men printed at least portions of Christian scriptures in more than forty languages by 1837. Carey alone managed to translate the entire Bible into Sanskrit, Marathi, Oraya, Hindi, and Assamese. He also wrote a well-respected Sanskrit grammar, and with Marshman a translation of the Hindu epic *The Ramayana*.

The missionaries also did educational work; they opened their first school in 1798, and over the next twenty years they opened another 126 schools, which had some 10,000 students. They also opened a boarding school for expatriate children that saw a good profit. Finally, in 1819 Carey founded Serampore College as a training college for native pastors and a liberal arts college for others that included a medical faculty. The king of Denmark awarded the school degree status in 1827.

Carey's interest in horticulture led him to help found the Agricultural Society of India in 1820. He also campaigned against the Indian practices of infanticide and the Hindu practice of *suttee*, which required widows to be burned with their dead husbands. His campaigning helped lead to the outlawing of both practices during his lifetime. Carey never returned to England and died in Frederiksganar in 1834.

SIGNIFICANCE

When Carey and his missionary colleagues started their work, they had no prototype to follow to show them what Protestant mission activity should be. Their instincts were to form independent churches from among their converts, train native pastors and leaders, equip them educationally, and provide Bibles in the local languages. They also saw the importance of understanding local cultures and belief systems and sought to be financially independent. In fact, they were so successful financially controversy arose in England over their "wealth" that was fueled by previous incidents of quick fortunes acquired by unscrupulous Englishmen in India.

Carey's instincts were proved correct by the test of time. Later Protestant missions followed similar patterns over the next 150 years, not only in India but also in other areas of Asia and Africa, though local constraints often meant subsidies from the sending countries. In the modern neocolonialist controversy over mission work, Carey cannot be accused of any imperialistic designs. It was not until 1813 that the East India Company revised its charter to permit mission work. Carey's humble origins and his identification with India exempt him from any of the grander political strategies that went on around him that led eventually to the formation of the British Raj.

—*David Barratt*

FURTHER READING

Annett, E. A. *William Carey: Pioneer Missionary*. Belfast, Northern Ireland: Ambassador Productions, 2001. This biography is typical of the large number of popular biographies of William Carey, largely of a semi-inspirational nature, stressing his spiritual qualities and his fortitude and single-mindedness.

Carey, William. *An Enquiry into the Obligations of Christians to Use Means for the Conversion of the Heathen*. London: Lightning Source U.K., 2002. A reprint on a website of Carey's groundbreaking pamphlet on world mission.

Mangalwadi, Ruth, and Vishal Mangalwadi. *Carey, Christ and Cultural Transformation*. London: Authentic Lifestyle/Tyndale, 1997. Asks large sociological and missiological questions about Carey, especially in the context of postcolonial discourse.

Mangalwadi, Vishal, and Ruth Mangalwadi. *The Legacy of William Carey: A Model for the Transformation of a Culture*. Crossway Books, 1999. Looks to see how Carey's methods can still be applied today.

Neill, Stephen. *A History of the Christian Church in India*. 2 vols. Cambridge, England: Cambridge University Press, 1985. The most scholarly account of the Indian church by a former missionary in India, and helps put Carey's endeavors into a wider context.

SEE ALSO: Samuel Ajayi Crowther; Sir James Outram; Iswar Chandra Vidyasagar.

RELATED ARTICLE in *Great Events from History: The Nineteenth Century, 1801-1900:* May 8, 1816: American Bible Society Is Founded.

DON CARLOS

Spanish royal pretender

The first of the Carlist claimants to the throne of Spain, Don Carlos dedicated his life to disputing the right of his niece, Doña Isabel, to Spain's throne and upholding the principles, laws, and institutions of the Old Regime.

BORN: March 29, 1788; Aranjuez, Spain

DIED: March 10, 1855; Trieste, Austrian Empire (now in Italy)

ALSO KNOWN AS: Carlos María Isidro de Borbón (birth name)

AREA OF ACHIEVEMENT: Government and politics

EARLY LIFE

Carlos María Isidro de Borbón was the second surviving son of Charles IV and Louisa María Isidro, king and queen of Spain. In 1808, with the help of French troops, Don Carlos's older brother became Ferdinand VII, king of Spain. Later that year, however, the royal family was ordered to Bayonne where Don Carlos, his brother, and his uncle, Don Antonio, were held captive and conducted to Valençay in central France, where they lived under house arrest until 1814. Ferdinand was persuaded to abdicate the throne in favor of Napoleon's brother, Joseph Bonaparte; however, Don Carlos, who was supposed to succeed his brother to the throne if the latter left no male heirs, refused to renounce his right to the throne, saying that he would rather be dead than betray his obligation to the Spanish people.

After his return to Spain in 1814, Don Carlos lived as a prince in Madrid. In September, 1816, he married Princess María Francesca de Asís de Braganza, daughter of King John VI of Portugal and sister of the wife (Queen Isabel) of Ferdinand VII. A loving brother and a loyal subject of Ferdinand VII, Don Carlos was rewarded with a few formal offices but with no substantial role in government. In June, 1814, Ferdinand VII made him a colonel of the Carabineros Reales, Spain's royal cavalry corps, and two months later named him captain general and commander in chief of the army. Ferdinand VII also allowed him to preside over the Council of State and the Council of War.

Don Carlos was always known for his devout Catholicism and unswerving belief in a traditional Spain in which the monarch governed absolutely. In 1820, when soldiers supposed to go to America rioted in favor of reinstating the liberal constitution of 1812, Don Carlos, as head of the Council of State, declared that it was necessary to oppose their demand with all possible force.

A revolutionary government during the Liberal Triennium (1820-1823) expelled the royal family from Madrid and made them go to Seville, where they were deprived of their rights and accused of treason. The royal family was then garrisoned in Cádiz, only to be rescued by French intervention, which put down the revolution in 1823. Once the royal family was free, the royalists deliberately set out to destroy the liberals. The most extreme royalists were the *apostólicos* (Apostolics), who believed in the infallible righteousness of the Roman Catholic Church and the legitimacy of a monarchy that would represent its interest. When Ferdinand VII, under international pressure, refused to sanction the worst excesses in the persecution of liberals, the royalists began to look to Don Carlos as their true leader.

LIFE'S WORK

If Don Carlos had been inclined to lead an insurrection against Ferdinand VII, the *apostólicos* would have risen against the king. Don Carlos refused to betray his brother, but his Portuguese wife and her older sister, María Teresa, the princess of Beira, had fewer scruples and actively intrigued with the *apostólicos*. In March, 1833, the princess of Beira, who happened to be in Madrid for the wedding of her son, Don Sebastian, was advised to leave for Portugal, and Don Carlos and his wife were authorized to accompany her. In April, the king asked Don Carlos, still in Portugal, to swear allegiance to his daughter Isabel, who had been born on October 10, 1830. In his letter of reply, Don Carlos refused to give up his claim to the throne unless Ferdinand would also bear a son.

Legal complexities exacerbated the disagreement over the right to succession. In 1789, the Cortes, Spain's parliament, had approved the Pragmatic Sanction on the right to succession. Charles IV, not wishing to promulgate the new law, published a revised Spanish legal code in 1805 in which the 1789 law was not mentioned but the semi-Salic law of Philip V, dating back to 1713, was. The older law stated that succession to the throne was to consist of male children of the king and his male descendants; females could reign in their own right only when no such males existed. Each brother had solid arguments in his favor. Ferdinand VII could argue that the 1789 law only needed promulgation and that the right of female succession had been in force in Spain for centuries before 1713. Don Carlos could counter that the Pragmatic Sanction had lapsed during the long interval between its approval by the Cortes and its promulgation on March 29, 1830; moreover, Don Carlos was born in 1788 and thus could argue that the 1789 law, even if valid, did not apply to him.

The death of Ferdinand VII on September 29, 1833, unleashed the forces behind the First Carlist War, or the Seven Years' War (1833-1840). The queen regent, María Cristina of Bourbon-Two Sicilies, indicated that she would favor the liberals if they supported her daughter's claim to the throne. She also ordered Don Carlos to Italy, but he refused to leave the Iberian Peninsula and tried to slip back into Spain, where his supporters were uprising and proclaiming him Carlos V. Failing to cross the heavily patrolled border, he helped Dom Miguel, a pretender to the Portuguese throne, who promised to reciprocate later in Spain.

The dynastic quarrels and the struggle between absolutism and liberalism in the Iberian Peninsula could not fail to arouse the interest of the rest of Europe. The old Holy Alliance of Russia, Prussia, and Austria was sympathetic to Don Carlos but held back material assistance. On the other hand, the government of Isabel received the support of the Quadruple Alliance (England, France, Portugal, Spain), which was formed on April 22, 1834, to support liberal constitutional government in western Europe by driving Don Carlos and Dom Miguel out of the Iberian Peninsula.

Dom Miguel had to renounce his claim to the Portuguese throne and was expelled to Genoa. On June 1, 1834, Don Carlos was allowed to leave for England, where he refused to renounce his rights to the throne in exchange for an annual pension. He slipped away under disguise to France, which he crossed to finally join his loyal junta and troops in Navarre in July, 1834. His wife, Doña María Francesca, remained in England and died of fever on September 4.

Although the uprisings in favor of Don Carlos were scattered throughout Spain and he enjoyed considerable sympathy in rural areas, the heart of his support was the Basque provinces, Navarre, Catalonia, and the mountainous area of the Maestrazgo. The Carlists could win battles from one end of Spain to another, with the exceptions of all-important Madrid and the twice-sieged Bilbao, but they could maintain control only in the countryside and small towns of the northeast. One of Don Carlos's tactical problems was his hesitation to close decisively on strategic targets, especially Madrid, because he erroneously expected that the masses would take up arms and fight for his cause. Some historians believe that the princess of Beira unintentionally created more problems for

Don Carlos. (Library of Congress)

Don Carlos after their marriage in 1838. Very much in the camp of the *apostólicos*, this strong-willed woman alienated Don Carlos's more moderate supporters.

The end of Don Carlos's hopes to win the crown came with the signing of the Convention of Vergara on August 31, 1839, when General Rafael Maroto of the Carlist northern army agreed to accept the conditions for peace offered by Captain-General Baldomero Espartero, the leader of Spain's army. Don Carlos bitterly remarked that Maroto had sold out God, king, country, and *fueros* (rights and privileges of certain groups) for military rank and foreign gold. No longer able to hold out in the Basque provinces, Don Carlos and thousands of troops sought refuge in France on September 14.

Don Carlos was arrested attempting to slip back into Spain across the eastern Pyrenees to join Ramón Cabrera and his Carlist army, which continued to fight until July, 1840. Don Carlos and his family were sent to Bourges, France, where they lived under house arrest until he abdicated in favor of his oldest son, Carlos Luis, on May 18, 1845, and took on the title of the count of Molina. That year Don Carlos established residence in Trieste, where he and his wife established a Spanish royal court in exile that became a gathering place for European traditionalists. In his final years, Don Carlos was frail and semi-invalid; he died, after receiving his last rites, on March 10, 1855, comforted by his second wife, the princess of Beira, and his second son, Don Fernando. He is buried in the San Guisto Cathedral of Trieste.

SIGNIFICANCE

To the very end, Don Carlos refused to acknowledge Queen Isabella II or accept the new liberal order, which recognized the sovereignty and will of the people. Carlists defended the dynastic claims of Don Carlos and his descendants for well over one hundred years. Carlism never prevailed in restoring an absolutist monarchy, reestablishing a traditional Spain, or regaining all the privileges and properties that the Catholic Church once had in Spain. However, Carlism has had a decided impact on Spanish life. The Second Carlist War (1846-1848) was centered in Catalonia and was spurred on by Carlos Luis (Carlos VI). Carlos Luis's second son, Don Carlos (Carlos VII), led the Third Carlist War (1872-1876). Carlism was an important force on the nationalist side in Spain's Civil War of 1936-1939, although Franco's victorious Falange and the Carlists soon parted company.

In modern Spain, Carlists have no intention of starting a war to establish a Carlist monarchy. Spain's King Juan Carlos I (r. 1975-) is, on his father's side, a descendant of King Alfonso XIII of Spain and Queen Victoria of England. On his mother's side, he is related to Don Carlos de Borbón. The two dynastic branches—those of Isabel II and the Carlist pretenders—that were separated upon the death of Ferdinand VII in 1833 have come together again in Juan Carlos, who remains a popular monarch and a symbol of national unity. However, Carlists continue to argue for the reestablishment of a traditional Spain in which there would be Catholic unity, strong regional rights to counter centralism, and a corporative Cortes in which the traditional estates of the clergy, aristocrats, and other interest groups would be represented. They would prefer a monarch who would pledge to uphold the customs, principles, and laws of traditional Spain. Above all else, they remain implacable enemies of liberalism.

—Steven L. Driever

FURTHER READING

Barahona, Renato. *Vizcaya on the Eve of Carlism: Politics and Society, 1800-1833*. Reno: University of Nevada Press, 1989. A study of the political and social conditions in Vizcaya, a Basque province of Spain, and how these conditions led to Basque support for the Carlist movement.

Blinkhorn, Martin. *Carlism and Crisis in Spain, 1931-1939*. Cambridge, England: Cambridge University Press, 1975. The first chapter provides a review of Carlism up until 1931. The rest of the book is a study of Carlism's role in the fall of Spain's Second Republic and the rise of political extremism and Franco's Falange. Includes illustrations, maps, and bibliography.

Clarke, H. Butler. *Modern Spain: 1815-1898*. New York: Ames Press, 1969. Clarke treats all the major figures and critical turning points of Spain in the nineteenth century. The book contains many details forgotten in more recent studies of the period and includes a map and a bibliography.

Flynn, M. K. *Ideology, Mobilization, and the Nation: The Rise of Irish, Basque, and Carlist Nationalist Movements in the Nineteenth and Early Twentieth Centuries*. New York: St. Martin's Press, 2000. Flynn recounts the general evolution of nationalism in western Europe by the nineteenth century, then describes the rise of nationalism among the Carlists and Basques in Spain as examples of this movement.

Holt, Edgar. *The Carlist Wars in Spain*. London: G. P. Putnam's Sons, 1967. This even-handed analysis of the three Carlist Wars has an epilogue covering events up to 1965, and includes illustrations, a map, and a bibliography.

Wilhelmsen, Alexandra. "Antonio Aparisi y Guijarro: A Nineteenth-Century Carlist Apologist for a Sacral Society in Spain." In *Saints, Sovereigns, and Scholars*, edited by R. A. Herrera, James Lehrberger, and M. E. Bradford. New York: Peter Lang, 1993. This is a good review of what the *apostólicos* wanted and the effects they have had on Spanish life. Includes bibliography.

_____. "Maria Teresa of Braganza." In *Mediterranean Studies* 6. Kirksville, Mo.: Thomas Jefferson University Press, 1996. The Princess of Beira, Don Carlos's second wife, had a major influence over him even before their marriage. This article, which includes illustrations and a bibliography, is particularly good for details on Don Carlos's later life.

SEE ALSO: Isabella II.

RELATED ARTICLES in *Great Events from History: The Nineteenth Century, 1801-1900:* September 30, 1868: Spanish Revolution of 1868; 1876: Spanish Constitution of 1876.

THOMAS CARLYLE

British historian and essayist

As the most eminent man of letters in the Victorian age, Carlyle thundered against what he saw as the materialism and moral decadence of that age. The uniqueness of his vivid and emphatic style, and his ability to re-create the flavor and feeling of historical events, have earned for him a place among the masters of English prose.

BORN: December 4, 1795; Ecclefechan, Dumfriesshire, Scotland
DIED: February 5, 1881; London, England
AREA OF ACHIEVEMENT: Historiography

EARLY LIFE

Thomas Carlyle was the eldest child of a stonemason who later became a small farmer. He lived in a large, close-knit family, and the influence of his early upbringing, in an atmosphere of stern piety and moral rectitude, was to remain with him all of his life.

Carlyle was educated at the local Annan Academy, as a preparation for his entry into Edinburgh University in November, 1809, at the age of thirteen. He was an able student, reading widely in English literature and excelling in the study of mathematics. He also developed the habit of supplementing his formal studies with long periods of solitary reading. In 1814, he became a tutor of mathematics at Annan School, and in the following year accepted a teaching post at Kirkcaldy. Carlyle disliked teaching, however, and resigned his position in 1818. With no clear vocation (he rejected the career that was expected of him, in the Church), he faced an uncertain future. For several difficult and frustrating years, during which he often complained of ill health, he survived by private tutoring and translating.

In 1819, Carlyle began his study of German philosophy and literature, and in 1820 his first-published work, a series of anonymous biographical essays, appeared in the *Edinburgh Encyclopaedia*. These were followed by his biography of the German poet Johann von Schiller, which appeared in the *London Magazine* in 1823, and a translation of Johann Wolfgang von Goethe's *Wilhelm Meisters Wanderjahre* (1821). In 1826, he married Jane Welsh, an intelligent and talented young woman who came from a respected and fairly prosperous family in Haddington, which was a short distance from Edinburgh. They had first met five years previously; Carlyle, nearly six feet tall, with thick brown hair, intense blue eyes, and a strong jaw, had cut an impressive and unusual figure.

By 1827 Carlyle had become a regular contributor to the prestigious *Edinburgh Review*, and the groundwork for his major achievements of the next thirty years had been laid. The world would soon hear from this strong-willed, self-reliant, and hardworking Scotsman, a man who in his personal life could be sarcastic, irritable, and impatient, but who also possessed great kindness, loyalty, and a capacity for close and enduring friendships.

LIFE'S WORK

From 1828 to 1834, the Carlyles lived at the farm of Craigenputtoch in Dumfriesshire, Scotland. It was here that Carlyle wrote his first major work, *Sartor Resartus*. Although the manuscript was completed by 1831, Carlyle was initially unable to find a publisher. It was eventually published in magazine form in London in 1833-1834, and the first book edition appeared in the United States in 1836, through the help of Ralph Waldo Emerson.

Sartor Resartus remains the most widely read of Carlyle's works and contains the essence of the philosophy that he espoused throughout his life. It is an extraordinary combination of novel—including strong autobiographical elements—and essay, written in Carlyle's characteristic exclamatory, oratorical style, full of imagery and metaphor, a style so distinct that it came to be known as "Carlylese." The central idea of *Sartor Resartus* is that humans must learn to distinguish between external appearances and true reality. Because everything in the time and space world is an emblem, or reflection, of an internal, spiritual condition, it is necessary to perceive the workings of spiritual laws in material forms and events. Carlyle calls this "Natural Supernaturalism," and he develops the argument in terms of an extended metaphor of clothing. Outer appearances are like clothing; they obscure the essential reality that is hidden within them.

In 1834, the Carlyles moved to Chelsea, London, and in the following year Carlyle commenced work on his history of the French Revolution. Disaster struck when the entire manuscript of the first volume was inadvertently used by a maid to light the fire (an act for which Carlyle's friend John Stuart Mill, to whom Carlyle had lent the manuscript, accepted responsibility). Only a few fragments survived. However, Carlyle, undaunted, rewrote the entire manuscript, and *The French Revolution* was published in three volumes in 1837. The vivid and dramatic narrative, in which the description of events took on the quality of eyewitness reports, was an immediate success.

Now with an established reputation as a historian and man of letters, Carlyle began to accumulate a wide circle of friends and acquaintances drawn from the leading literary figures of the day. These included not only his contemporaries such as Robert Southey but also younger men such as Robert Browning; Alfred, Lord Tennyson; Charles Dickens; William Makepeace Thackeray; Edward Fitzgerald; and the philosopher John Stuart Mill. In later years John Ruskin became a close friend.

In the next few years, Carlyle wrote a number of influential essays on contemporary political and social issues, such as *Chartism* (1839); *Past and Present* (1843), which was his response to the crisis of high unemployment and the poverty of industrial workers; and the controversial *Latter-Day Pamphlets* (1850). In all these publications Carlyle sternly opposed what he saw as the rampant materialism of the age, which was leading people further and further into moral and spiritual decay. He did not support the growth of democracy and called for a strong leader, a hero, who would rule according to nature's laws, as a representative of the divine spirit that is immanent in all things. Individuals must also reform themselves and bring duty, work, order, and self-discipline into their lives, as well as an awareness of the spiritual dimension of their lives and actions. With this philosophy, vigorously espoused, Carlyle emerged as the great prophet of mid-Victorian England, at a time when many people feared that social unrest would soon lead to violent revolution.

Carlyle's standing as the most prominent man of letters in England well established, Carlyle continued to produce major works. His edition of the letters and speeches of Oliver Cromwell was published in 1845, and his biography of John Sterling in 1851—a book that remains one of his most readable and popular works. In 1854, Carlyle began his study of the eighteenth century Prussian leader Frederick the Great, a task that was to take him twelve years to complete. The first two volumes were ready by 1858, and volumes five and six by 1865. The effort involved had been prodigious and painful; Carlyle had never regarded writing as an easy or pleasurable task (although he tended to feel even more miserable

Thomas Carlyle. (Library of Congress)

when he was not working), and *History of Friedrich II of Prussia, Called Frederick the Great* turned out to be the hardest labor of all.

The compensations, however, were many. Carlyle was now the world-famous "Sage of Chelsea," at the center of the most brilliant literary circle of the day. Carlyle was a brilliant conversationalist. Although his talk was often a near monologue, the monologue was usually so compelling that others were happy to absorb it silently.

Carlyle's major achievements were now behind him, but honors continued to come his way. In 1865, he was appointed Lord Rector of Edinburgh University, and his public speech of acceptance early the following year was received with wild enthusiasm by the university students. Only three weeks later, however, his wife, Jane, died, following many years of ill-health. Although the marriage had not been a smooth one, it had endured for forty years, and Carlyle was plunged into deep grief over his loss. He immediately wrote out his memories of her early years, as well as reminiscences of other friends such as Edward Irving and Francis Jeffrey. These essays were published posthumously as *Reminiscences* (1881). With the reminiscences, Carlyle's literary work was virtually complete.

In 1874, Carlyle received the Prussian Order of Merit, but the following year he declined a baronetcy offered to him by Prime Minister Benjamin Disraeli. He died on February 5, 1881, two months after his eighty-fifth birthday. Immediately after his death, he was universally hailed as one of the great men of the Victorian age, the *Saturday Review* calling him "the greatest writer of his time . . . a living teacher . . . a prophet."

CARLYLE'S MAJOR WORKS

1822	*Essay on Goethe's Faust*
1823-1824	*Life of Schiller*
1827	*Essay on Richter*
1827	*State of German Literature*
1828	*Life and Writings of Werner*
1828	*Essay on Burns*
1829	*Voltaire*
1831	*Characteristics*
1833-1834	*Sartor Resartus*
1837	*The French Revolution*
1838	*Sir Walter Scott*
1838	*Critical and Miscellaneous Essays* (4 volumes)
1839	*Chartism*
1841	*On Heroes, Hero-Worship, and the Heroic in History*
1843	*Past and Present*
1845	*Oliver Cromwell's Letters and Speeches, with Elucidations*
1849	*Occasional Discourse on the Nigger Question*
1850	*Latter-Day Pamphlets*
1851	*Life of John Sterling*
1858-1865	*History of Friedrich II of Prussia* (6 volumes)
1881	*Reminiscences*
1882	*Reminiscences of My Irish Journey in 1849*
1882	*Last Words of Thomas Carlyle*

SIGNIFICANCE

Thomas Carlyle lived during a time of rapid and bewildering social change. Great Britain had yet to come to terms with the massive changes that were occurring as a result of industrialization. There had been a huge drift of the population from the land to the cities, resulting in the creation of a new working class, who lived in poverty, cut off from their former stable foundations of life.

Acutely aware of the crisis, Carlyle responded to the urgent problem of social organization with vigor, eloquence, and prophetic fire. He spoke out against the dehumanizing effects of the machine age, and against what he saw as increasing chaos and disorder. He did not share the fashionable belief in "progress" and "prosperity" ("Progress whither? . . . prosperity in what?"), and what others saw as the growth of "freedom" Carlyle viewed as the destruction of authority. However, he did not merely advocate a return to established traditions—traditions, like clothes, wear out and must be replaced. Authority, he believed, must be held by the wise, who understand nature's laws and the workings of the divine will. The hero-leader must achieve *entsagen* or *Selbsttodtung* (renunciation of self); otherwise, the power he holds is usurped, not genuine.

Carlyle's prophetic and inspirational message, as well as the power and force of his prose, is well conveyed by some of the final words of his essay "Characteristics" (1831):

behind each one of us, lie Six Thousand Years of human effort, human conquest: before us is the boundless Time, with its as yet uncreated and unconquered Continents and Eldorados, which we, even we, have to conquer, to create; and from the bosom of Eternity there shine for us celestial guiding stars.

—*Bryan Aubrey*

FURTHER READING

Campbell, Ian. *Thomas Carlyle*. New York: Charles Scribner's Sons, 1974. Fair-minded, and despite its brevity, illuminating on many issues concerning both the man and his thought.

Carlyle, Thomas. *A Carlyle Reader: Selections from the Writings of Thomas Carlyle*. Edited by G. B. Tennyson. Cambridge, England: Cambridge University Press, 1984. The best one-volume selection from Carlyle's voluminous works. Representative texts from all periods and types of his writing, including his letters and journal, and the complete text of *Sartor Resartus*.

Collis, John Stewart. *The Carlyles: A Biography of Thomas and Jane Carlyle*. New York: Dodd, Mead, 1971. Centers on the Carlyles' marriage.

Desaulniers, Mary. *Carlyle and the Economics of Terror: A Study of Revisionary Gothicism in "The French Revolution."* Montreal, Que.: McGill-Queen's University Press, 1995. Carlyle has often been criticized for his dense, complex writing style. Desaulniers analyzes his use of language in *The French Revolution*, and argues that he deliberately used a "revisionary Gothic" style to discuss economic and political issues.

Froude, James Anthony. *Froude's Life of Carlyle*. Abridged and edited by John Clubbe. Columbus: Ohio State University Press, 1979. Condensation (largely through the omission of Carlyle's letters) of Froude's superb four-volume biography *Thomas Carlyle* (1882-1884), which created a furious controversy when first published. Froude was Carlyle's close friend and appointed biographer. His biography contained revelations of Carlyle's stormy relations with his wife, which did not show Carlyle in the best light.

Heffer, Simon. *Moral Desperado: A Life of Thomas Carlyle*. London: Weidenfeld & Nicolson, 1995. Heffer portrays Carlyle as an unlikeable person—selfish, obsessive, cruel to his wife — and an inaccessible writer.

Kaplan, Fred. *Thomas Carlyle: A Biography*. Ithaca, N.Y.: Cornell University Press, 1983. The standard biography, replacing Froude. A mass of detail, including some previously unpublished material, welded into a comprehensive and readable study.

Rosenberg, Philip. *The Seventh Hero: Thomas Carlyle and the Theory of Radical Activism*. Cambridge, Mass.: Harvard University Press, 1974. Deals with Carlyle's writings during the fifteen productive years that ended with *Past and Present*. Shows Carlyle struggling with problems that still confront political and social thinkers today.

Waring, Walter W. *Thomas Carlyle*. Boston: Twayne, 1978. Concise and straightforward introduction to Carlyle's thought.

SEE ALSO: Ralph Waldo Emerson; Barthold Georg Niebuhr; Leopold von Ranke; James McNeill Whistler; Walt Whitman.

RELATED ARTICLES in *Great Events from History: The Nineteenth Century, 1801-1900:* January 12, 1837: Mazzini Begins London Exile; 1843: Carlyle Publishes *Past and Present*; Fall, 1848: Pre-Raphaelite Brotherhood Begins.

ANDREW CARNEGIE

American financier and philanthropist

One of the wealthiest men in the world at the time of his retirement, Carnegie achieved great fame for his business success and for his many benefactions, which became the chief interest of his later years.

BORN: November 25, 1835; Dunfermline, Scotland
DIED: August 11, 1919; Lenox, Massachusetts
AREAS OF ACHIEVEMENT: Business, patronage of the arts

EARLY LIFE

Andrew Carnegie was born in Scotland, where his father, William Carnegie, was a prosperous handloom weaver at the time of his birth. However, his father could not compete with the new technology of steam looms and fell into poverty as Andrew grew older. Andrew's mother, Margaret Morrison Carnegie, proved under these circumstances to be the bulwark of the family. Ambitious for her two sons, Andrew and younger brother Thomas, she organized a family move to the United States in 1848, when Andrew was thirteen.

The Carnegies settled in Allegheny, Pennsylvania, where they had relatives and attempted to rebuild the family's fortunes. Although William Carnegie was never again a success, the family got by through hard work and timely assistance from the Pittsburgh area's close-knit Scottish community. Working long, hard hours in factories, Andrew improved his skills, learning double-entry bookkeeping in night school, and in barely a year left factory work to become a telegraph messenger in 1849, an operator in 1851, and in 1853, secretary and personal telegrapher to Tom Scott, superintendent of the Pennsylvania Railroad's western division.

LIFE'S WORK

Carnegie remained with the Pennsylvania Railroad for a dozen years, acquiring managerial skills and a sharp insight into the economic principles of the capitalist economy, and forming close personal relationships with several entrepreneurs who were to prove instrumental in his own success. Scott, who delegated increasing responsibility to the resourceful Carnegie, became vice president in 1859; he then named Carnegie superintendent of the western division, perhaps the most challenging position of its kind with any railroad in the United States. The demands of the Civil War would vastly increase his responsibilities, but Carnegie proved equal to them. At Scott's behest, he organized the movement of Union troops into beleaguered Washington in April, 1861, restored regular rail service between Washington and the north, and stayed in the capital for some months as Scott's assistant in charge of railroads and telegraph services. (Scott had been appointed assistant secretary of war with special responsibility for railroads.) Carnegie then returned to Pittsburgh to resume his duties with the Pennsylvania Railroad.

Carnegie was already losing interest in a salaried position. On a tip from Scott, he had purchased six hundred dollars' worth of stock in the Adams Express Company in 1856. The first dividend check he received was a revelation, and legend has it that Carnegie, thrilled to realize that he could earn money without physical toil, exclaimed, "Here's the goose that lays the golden eggs." More investments followed: in the Woodruff Sleeping Car Company, the Columbia Oil Company, and the Keystone Bridge Company, in which Carnegie held a one-fifth interest, enough to make him the dominant shareholder.

By 1863, Carnegie was earning more than forty thousand dollars annually from his investments, several times his salary, and left the Pennsylvania Railroad at the end of the Civil War to devote more of his time to the management of Keystone and to the Union Iron Mills, which was a principal supplier of Keystone. Carnegie left the operating decisions to experts in bridge construction, while concentrating on sales and finances. With Keystone, he secured contracts to sell materials to such projects as the Eads Bridge at St. Louis, the Ohio River bridges at Cincinnati and Point Pleasant, West Virginia, and the Brooklyn Bridge.

Carnegie's involvement in finance required that he travel often to Europe, and his lifestyle changed. Always interested in the world of ideas, he never allowed his lack of formal education to keep him from broadening his knowledge. He read extensively and cultivated friendships in Europe and in New York City, to which he moved with his mother in 1867. A bachelor throughout these years, Carnegie enjoyed the companionship of women and led an active social life. He also actively sought the company of intellectuals and eventually would count among his friends the British statesman William Gladstone and literary figures such as Matthew Arnold, Richard Watson Gilder, John Morley, Herbert Spencer, and Mark Twain. A man of much personal charm, the small-statured Carnegie—he stood but five

Andrew Carnegie. (Library of Congress)

feet, three inches tall—was equally at ease discussing ideas with the learned and business with financiers or potential customers.

Carnegie was still not content with his lot in life, for he believed that he had become too involved in financial speculation and wished instead to turn to manufacturing, which he considered a more constructive and respectable pursuit. His familiarity with the needs of railroads made him believe that there were large profits to be made in steel, for improved rails would be needed in immense quantities. In 1872, he organized a partnership, drawing on Pittsburgh business acquaintances of long duration to establish Carnegie, McCandless and Company to manufacture steel by the Bessemer process. After several reorganizations involving many different combinations of partners over the years, this firm would become known as Carnegie Steel Company, Limited, in 1892.

By 1874, the gigantic new Edgar Thomson Works was under construction, its development supervised by Alexander Holley, the foremost American expert on the Bessemer process, and its operations turned over to Bill Jones, who brought in top-notch department heads from other companies. Characteristically, Carnegie turned over the day-to-day operations to experts such as Jones, while he concentrated on sales and finances, employing the efficient cost-based management techniques learned in the railroad business.

Always alert to technological improvements that would lower the cost of production and lead to increased sales and profits, within a decade, Carnegie introduced to his plants the open-hearth steel production process. Carnegie's business philosophy led him to expand and diversify. During the mid-1880's, his organization acquired the massive Homestead Works and developed a major new market by selling steel structural members to the elevated railways and skyscrapers that were beginning to appear in major American cities.

In 1880, Carnegie met Louise Whitfield, the twenty-three-year-old daughter of a prominent New York merchant. Louise endured the tribulations of a relationship troubled by Carnegie's frequent and extended business travel. Moreover, he initially refused to marry, out of deference to his mother's wishes. The two were finally married in 1887, less than a year after the death of Carnegie's mother. The couple had one daughter.

At the time of his marriage, Carnegie was a millionaire several times over. The 1890's brought more prosperity, as well as some of Carnegie's greatest disappointments. The prosperity came in substantial measure from Carnegie's faith in the continued growth of the American economy and the business acumen of Henry Clay Frick. Chairman of the company since 1889, Frick conducted an aggressive campaign of expansion and cost-cutting that led to one of the bitterest episodes in American labor history, the Homestead Strike of 1892. During this period, Carnegie remained in virtual seclusion in Scotland, giving Frick authority to handle negotiations with the Amalgamated Association of Iron and Steel Workers. The labor-management strife led to intense press criticism of Carnegie in both England and the United States and, along with other issues, precipitated a split between Carnegie and Frick.

Carnegie, who held an interest of more than 50 percent in the firm, resumed a more active role in company affairs, forcing Frick out as chief operating executive at the end of 1894 and leading the business to its most profitable years. The key was Carnegie's success in increasing the firm's share of the market during the depression of the 1890's, acquiring ownership of more of its basic raw materials, its own railroads and its fleet of ore-carrying ships, and its modernizing facilities. Carnegie Steel's annual profits grew 800 percent between 1895 and 1900.

In Charles Schwab, a brilliant executive totally loyal to Carnegie, the company at last had a worthy successor to Frick.

At the end of the 1890's, new troubles arose from competitors. On one hand, Carnegie relished a fight; on the other hand, he was willing to sell out, provided the price was right. It was—nearly $500 million, of which Carnegie's share was $300 million in 5 percent first-mortgage bonds in the successor company, United States Steel. The investment banker J. P. Morgan, who had handled the transaction, said that Carnegie was "the richest man in the world." While a similar claim has been made for Carnegie's contemporary, John D. Rockefeller, there is no doubt that Carnegie had built one of the most formidable business enterprises of the nineteenth century; Carnegie Steel produced more than the combined output of the entire steel industry of Great Britain.

Carnegie devoted his remaining years to philanthropy. It was, however, philanthropy with a difference. In Carnegie's hands, philanthropy, a term that he disliked, itself became big business. In two articles published in 1886, Carnegie, a widely published author, had called for an understanding of the needs of the working man and for the acceptance of unions. The bitterness of the Homestead Strike had inevitably made Carnegie appear a hypocrite, and Carnegie was determined to demonstrate to the world that he was not insensitive to the needs of the less privileged. In an essay entitled "Wealth," first published in 1889 and often reprinted as "The Gospel of Wealth," he had set forth the essentials of his views on charitable giving. He held that the man of means should spend his fortune during his own lifetime in ways that would advance society. The millionaire, he argued, was but a trustee who should approach philanthropy scientifically and endow institutions such as universities, public libraries, and recreational areas for the masses.

On a relatively small scale, he had begun to dispense grants at the end of the 1880's, increasing the number and size of his benefactions as the years passed. In retirement, Carnegie had the time to systematize his giving. While he did provide some money for medical facilities, his usual response to a request for support from a hospital or medical school was to say "That is Mr. Rockefeller's specialty." The great bulk of Carnegie's support went to libraries and the support of education. He ultimately provided more than fifty million dollars to establish twenty-eight hundred public libraries, the vast majority in the United States and Great Britain. Carnegie ordinarily provided funds for the buildings only, for he expected the communities concerned to provide the revenues needed for books and maintenance. Fond of the limelight, Carnegie often appeared at the dedication of his libraries.

Carnegie also gave large amounts of money to Edinburgh University and three other universities in Scotland, and he established the Carnegie Institute of Technology in Pittsburgh (later the Carnegie-Mellon University) and the Carnegie Institution in Washington, D.C., which subsidized basic research in several disciplines. Another substantial sum went to the Carnegie Foundation for the Advancement of Teaching. Ostensibly a pension plan for college faculty, in practice the foundation did much to set standards that raised the quality of higher education in the United States. The largest sum of all, $125 million, was used in 1911 to endow the Carnegie Corporation of New York, which had the mission of advancing knowledge through the promotion of schools, libraries, research, and publication.

Carnegie dispensed still more money to causes designed to promote international peace, while he spent various amounts on such diverse items as church organs; the Hero Fund, which recognizes valorous deeds performed in everyday life; New York City's Carnegie Hall; and pensions for the widows of United States presidents and for tenant farmers on his Scottish estate, Skibo Castle.

During his lifetime, Carnegie had succeeded in giving away slightly more than $350 million, utilizing the Carnegie Corporation as his principal means of organizing the distribution of his fortune. Its establishment indicated Carnegie's recognition that it was impossible for a single individual as wealthy as he to supervise personally the administration and meaningful use of his own fortune, the tenet he had advocated in "The Gospel of Wealth." After his death at his summer home in Lenox, Massachusetts, in 1919, his will revealed that there were but thirty million dollars left to distribute; he had already made provisions for his wife and daughter. Praise for his generosity in the press was widespread.

SIGNIFICANCE

Andrew Carnegie was a man of contradictions. Despite having little formal education himself, he had a great respect for knowledge, writing books and essays on several topics, reading widely, and making it possible for countless others to read through the thousands of libraries he established. A ruthless businessperson, he made platitudinous statements about the dignity of labor but denied many workers that dignity through the practices of his company, a denial that culminated in the Homestead

Strike. However, as a businessperson, he must be remembered as an outstanding success, for, in three separate fields, he showed mastery.

Carnegie's first triumph was with the Pennsylvania Railroad, in whose employ he rose from secretary to one of its most responsible executives at a time when railroads were at the forefront of establishing patterns of modern business management. His next and greatest triumph was in building the giant Carnegie Steel Company. Finally, the practices that had served him so well in the business world enabled him to organize philanthropy on an almost unprecedented scale, as he spent his fortune generously and, on the whole, wisely. To many, he symbolized widely shared values in American culture: generosity combined with the success ethic.

—*Lloyd J. Graybar*

FURTHER READING

Bridge, James Howard. *The Inside History of the Carnegie Steel Company*. New York: Aldine, 1903. Written by a man who assisted Carnegie in some of his writing endeavors. The author knew not only Carnegie but also most of his key associates. Tends to see the management controversies of the 1890's from Frick's perspective.

Carnegie, Andrew. *The Autobiography of Andrew Carnegie*. Boston: Houghton Mifflin, 1920. Published the year after Carnegie's death, this book contains a wealth of interesting information but tends to be self-serving.

_____. *Triumphant Democracy: Or, Fifty Years' March of the Republic*. New York: Charles Scribner's Sons, 1886. Carnegie wrote several books, even more essays, and still more letters that appeared in newspapers under his name. This book and "The Gospel of Wealth" are perhaps his best-known works. Makes clear his ardent faith in capitalism, democracy, and opportunity.

Hendrick, Burton J. *The Life of Andrew Carnegie*. 2 vols. Garden City, N.Y.: Doubleday, 1932. Written in a vigorous style by a man who had a chance to talk with Carnegie's widow and many of his business associates.

Hessen, Robert. *Steel Titan: The Life of Charles M. Schwab*. New York: Oxford University Press, 1975. The best study of any of the hard-driving executives who did so much to put Carnegie Steel at the top of American industry. The first half of this biography deals with Schwab's early life and his years with Carnegie. The latter part discusses Schwab's own considerable success after he left United States Steel.

Hogan, William T. *Economic History of the Iron and Steel Industry in the United States*. 5 vols. Lexington, Mass.: D.C. Heath, 1971. The first two volumes of this five-volume work provide invaluable information on the steel industry during the years in which Carnegie was its dominant personality.

Krass, Peter. *Carnegie*. New York: John Wiley & Sons, 2002. A well-reviewed, detailed and thorough examination of Carnegie's life, career, and personality.

Krooth, Richard. *A Century Passing: Carnegie, Steel, and the Fate of Homestead*. Lanham, Md.: University Press of America, 2002. Krooth said this study of the 1892 Homestead Strike "describes how greed devastated a nineteenth century town and a great steel mill. The conflict foretold the death of vibrant national industry, perhaps basic U.S. industry itself."

Livesay, Harold C. *Andrew Carnegie and the Rise of Big Business*. Edited by Oscar Handlin. Boston: Little, Brown, 1975. Brief but invaluable biography that places Carnegie's business accomplishments in the context of developments in nineteenth century business management.

McHugh, Jeanne. *Alexander Holley and the Makers of Steel*. Baltimore: Johns Hopkins University Press, 1980. Biography of the man generally considered to be the foremost American expert in the Bessemer process. Attempts to place its subject in the context of the late nineteenth century technological revolution in steelmaking.

Swetnam, George. *Andrew Carnegie*. Boston: Twayne, 1980. While Carnegie will always be remembered as an industrialist and philanthropist, he became an author even earlier. This valuable, brief book examines his interest in writing and his best-known works.

Wall, Joseph Frazier. *Andrew Carnegie*. New York: Oxford University Press, 1970. More than a thousand pages in length, this is the definitive biography of Carnegie and is likely to remain so for many years.

SEE ALSO: Melvil Dewey; J. P. Morgan; John D. Rockefeller; Louis Sullivan.

RELATED ARTICLES in *Great Events from History: The Nineteenth Century, 1801-1900:* May 31, 1889: Johnstown Flood; October, 1889-April, 1890: First Pan-American Congress.

LEWIS CARROLL

English writer and mathematician

The creator of the immortal fairy tale Alice in Wonderland, *Lewis Carroll wrote stories and poems that fundamentally changed and enlivened children's literature. He also pioneered children's photography and published books that advanced the fields of logic and mathematics.*

BORN: January 27, 1832; Daresbury, Cheshire, England

DIED: January 14, 1898; Guildford, Surrey, England

ALSO KNOWN AS: Charles Lutwidge Dodgson (birth name)

AREAS OF ACHIEVEMENT: Literature, mathematics, photography

EARLY LIFE

Lewis Carroll was the pen name of Charles Lutwidge Dodgson, who retained his real name throughout his life. His father, Charles Dodgson, had given up his fellowship and lectureship in mathematics at Christ Church, Oxford University, to marry Frances Jane Lutwidge in 1827. Carroll was the first son of their eleven children. The family lived in Daresbury, where Carroll's father was parish curate, until 1843. Carroll showed an early talent for mathematics, cultivated by his father, and comic verse. Growing up in a close-knit upper-middle-class family, living in a secluded village, and deeply influenced by a stern but doting father, Carroll found childhood a time of innocent exploration and wonder, a view that colored his later literary works.

In 1844 Carroll attended a grammar school in Yorkshire, and in 1846 he went on to Rugby, one of England's leading private schools. Instructors at both schools helped him develop his mathematical and literary talents, but he disliked boarding away from his family. At Rugby the often harsh discipline administered by older students especially repelled him. For the rest of his life he disliked boys. At home on vacations, he helped his father teach in the local school, was a leader in games (many of which he invented), and wrote poetry and stories for magazines that he issued to amuse family and friends. These early poems were usually parodies of moralistic verse common during the early nineteenth century, and he explored several themes that appeared in his mature writing: violence, dreams and nightmares, family relationships, and the child's view of a bewildering adult world.

Carroll was a brilliant student. He won a scholarship to Christ Church, his father's alma mater. Like his father, he won a first in mathematics, the highest scholastic distinction for an undergraduate, and was awarded a fellowship even before he earned his bachelor of arts degree in 1854. The fellowship provided him a yearly stipend and rooms at Christ Church for life. He was appointed a lecturer in mathematics in 1855 and took vows as an Anglican deacon in 1861, becoming the Reverend C. L. Dodgson. From then on he dressed in black clerical clothes almost exclusively. A stammer made him shy of public speaking, and his clean-shaven boyish features, thick dark hair, and retiring manner made him seem ethereal to some contemporaries.

Using his birth name, Dodgson began to attract attention as a comic poet soon after earning his degree by publishing in newspapers and magazines some of the poems that he later incorporated into his children's books. In 1856 he published his first work under the name Lewis Carroll, an anagram of the latinized form of his first two names. The same year, he met Alice Pleasance Liddell, the daughter of Christ Church's dean, and took up photography. These interests—literature, photography, and Alice—blended to produce the most creative period of his life during the next twenty years.

LIFE'S WORK

Carroll remained a fellow at Christ Church for the rest of his life. He never married; in fact, the terms of his fellowship forbade it. He devoted himself to tutoring, lecturing, and performing religious and administrative duties at the college, but such work could not use up his creative energy, and he also pursued social and cultural interests outside his academic work.

Carroll was fastidious and almost obsessive with details, and he loved gadgets. Photography was ideally suited to him. At the time he took it up in 1856, it was a cumbersome art with bulky equipment. The photographer had to smear a glass plate with a colloid and dip it into silver nitrate, insert the plate into the camera, expose it for as much as a minute, and then develop the plate in a darkroom. During the exposure the subject had to stay perfectly still. Carroll soon mastered the techniques and tested his skill on architectural subjects and celebrities. Among those he photographed were the poet laureate Alfred, Lord Tennyson; the poet-painter Dante Gabriel Rossetti; and Queen Victoria's youngest son, Prince Leopold.

Photography was a means for Carroll to enter intellectual society and make friends. He soon ingratiated himself with parents by photographing their children. Although he occasionally photographed boys, he preferred girls. He believed that girls of about ten to fourteen years of age epitomized innocent beauty. Carroll told the girls stories or posed riddles of his own invention to put them at ease, dressed them in romantic costumes, and carefully posed them. Sometimes he photographed them nude. In all cases he first obtained the mother's permission and arranged for chaperonage. As well as photographing girls, he regularly sought their company, taking them to plays and museums and entertaining them at dinner parties. Deeply religious, conservative, and rigidly correct in his Victorian-era manners, he behaved with propriety; nonetheless, modern literary critics have speculated that Carroll's interest in girls came from suppressed pedophilia.

Carroll's favorite was Alice Liddell. On July 4, 1862, Carroll and his friend Robinson Duckworth took Alice and two of her sisters on a boating trip up the Thames River for a picnic. To entertain them on the return journey, he told them a tale, making it up as he rowed the boat. This became the nucleus of *Alice's Adventures in Wonderland* (1865), which became an international best seller. In the story, the fictional Alice falls asleep and dreams of a bewildering array of eccentric characters in the form of animals such as the White Rabbit and March Hare, people such as the Mad Hatter, and playing cards. The blending of fantasy, puns, games, nonsense poetry, and adventure story appealed to both children and adults. Even if comically presented, its themes—violence and punishment, growth, obedience, education and games, correct behavior, and the development of identity—nevertheless addressed the world from a child's point of view.

Lewis Carroll. (Library of Congress)

The sequel, *Through the Looking-Glass and What Alice Found There*, followed in 1871. Again, Alice falls asleep. This time she dreams of crawling through a mirror and becoming a pawn in a mammoth chess game. As she advances across the chessboard countryside to be crowned a queen, she meets some of Carroll's most beloved characters, such as the twins Tweedledee and Tweedledum and the White Knight, and hears more nonsense verse, including his most celebrated poem, "Jabberwocky." Many of the same themes appear, and the narrative emphasizes logical absurdities as the basis of humor as well as wordplay and bizarre behavior. Though not as successful as the first book, *Through the Looking-Glass and What Alice Found There* still sold well and brought praise from reviewers.

In 1876 Carroll published *The Hunting of the Snark*, his last masterpiece of nonsense literature. The puns of the subtitle—*An Agony in Eight Fits* (a struggle in eight chapters)—hint that it parodies epic poetry. Indeed, the story's quest for a mythical beast, the snark, by a brave band is a typical epic plot, but little else in the poem makes rational sense. Narrative jumps, eerie illogic, and the tension of supernatural peril give it a nightmarish quality. The poem attracted dedicated fans, especially among intellectuals, but it was not a popular success.

Carroll wrote other books of poetry, short stories, and games, including *Phantasmagoria* (1869), *Rhyme? and Reason?* (1883), *A Tangled Tale* (1885), and *Three Sunsets and Other Poems* (published posthumously in 1898). His last book-length prose tale for children came out in two parts: *Silvie and Bruno* (1889) and *Silvie and Bruno Concluded* (1893). It contains some of his best comic verse, but the story is convoluted and at times sermonizing. It had few admirers. Additionally, Carroll wrote articles and pamphlets on social problems and university affairs and left behind more than ninety-two thousand letters.

As Dodgson, Carroll earned a modest reputation during his lifetime as a mathematician. He was best known for clarifying the works of the classical Greek geometer Euclid in *Euclid and His Modern Rivals* (1879) and *Curi-*

CARROLL'S WORKS FOR CHILDREN

1865 *Alice's Adventures in Wonderland*
1867 "Bruno's Revenge"
1869 *Phantasmagoria*
1871 *Through the Looking-Glass and What Alice Found There*
1876 *The Hunting of the Snark: An Agony in Eight Fits*
1883 *Rhyme? and Reason?*
1898 *Three Sunsets, and Other Poems*
1977 *The Wasp in a Wig: The "Suppressed" Episode of "Through the Looking-Glass and What Alice Found There"*

osa Mathematica, Part I (1888), and for expositions of logical analysis such as *The Game of Logic* (1887) and *Symbolic Logic* (1896). He also published writings on number theory, and his work on voting theory was pioneering.

Carroll died of complications from a bronchial infection while staying at his sisters' house in Guildford, Surrey, in 1898. Because his health had always been excellent, the sudden death surprised and saddened his readers, colleagues, and friends. Although Carroll could be prickly and prudish, he was famous for his kindness, having supported his sisters and helped friends through financial straits.

SIGNIFICANCE

Lewis Carroll's biographers claim that he is second only to William Shakespeare as the most quoted English author. Certainly, his Alice books were widely popular, supporting almost continuous republication in many media. A musical called *Alice in Wonderland*, based on *Alice's Adventures in Wonderland*, was staged in 1886 with Carroll's help, and the first of sixteen motion picture versions appeared in 1903. The story has been told in cartoons, coloring books, pop-up books, audio cassettes, and audio-visual teaching guides. It was translated into at least seventy languages.

Before the Alice books, children's literature aimed to teach correct behavior and practical knowledge rather than entertain. Carroll mocked the moralism of this style to the delight of his young readers and gave them a character who embodied their point of view. His approach was revolutionary, and it inspired many imitators. Moreover, Carroll was among the first children's authors to make a girl the main character.

Almost immediately, intellectuals and artists began adapting the skewed logic and naïveté in Carroll's stories, poems, and photographs for purposes that spanned the variety of modern culture. For example, scientists employed his logic to explain the theories of relativity and quantum mechanics, surrealist painters borrowed his images, politicians quoted him, songwriters echoed his phrasing, psychoanalysts found archetypes and pathology in his characters, and philosophers pondered his elusive remarks on existence and reality. Many features of the Alice stories entered popular culture as well and became familiar even to people who never read the books, including the image of Alice at the Mad Hatter's tea party, such coinages as "chortle" and "galumphing," and such phrases as "off with his head!" and "curiouser and curiouser."

—Roger Smith

FURTHER READING

Carroll, Lewis. *The Annotated Alice*. Introduction and notes by Martin Gardner. New York: Bramhall House, 1960.

_____. *The Annotated Snark*. Introduction and notes by Martin Gardner. New York: Simon & Schuster, 1962. These two books have abundant marginal notes that relate references in the Alice tales and *The Hunting of the Snark* to Carroll's life, events, controversies in Victorian England, and mathematics. They also reproduce the original illustrations.

Cohen, Morton N. *Lewis Carroll: A Biography*. New York: Alfred A. Knopf, 1995. Cohen argues that Carroll rigidly conformed to Victorian Christian morality but that beneath his conservatism raged a painful incompleteness in his life, which he palliated through chaste friendships with girls and young women. His attempts to amuse these friends inspired his most beloved books. Carroll's photographs and drawings accompany the text.

Collingwood, Stuart Dodgson. *The Life and Letters of Lewis Carroll*. New York: Century, 1899. As Carroll's nephew, Collingwood had firsthand knowledge of his uncle's life. The biography is accordingly full of anecdotes. The letters quoted in the text often exemplify Carroll's dexterity with humor.

Elwyn Jones, Jo, and J. Francis Gladstone. *The Alice Companion: A Guide to Lewis Carroll's Alice Books*. New York: New York University Press, 1998. Commentary on the people and places that made up Carroll's and Alice Liddell's worlds in mid-nineteenth century Oxford and a source to existing literature on this period of Carroll's life.

_____ *The Red King's Dream: Or, Lewis Carroll in Wonderland.* London: Jonathan Cape, 1995. By the authors of *The Alice Companion*, a study of Carroll's life and times, including his literary milieu, friends, and influences.

Guiliano, Edward. *Lewis Carroll Observed.* New York: Clarkson N. Potter, 1976. This handsome, large-format book contains many drawings and photographs by Carroll, illustrations of his tales, and clips from early films. The text comprises fifteen essays about the children's books, photography, Carroll's style of humor and reputation, logic, and film versions of the Alice stories.

Leach, Karoline. *In the Shadow of the Dreamchild: A New Understanding of Lewis Carroll.* Chester Springs, Pa.: Peter Owen, 1999. Using original research, Leach refutes the commonly accepted image of Lewis Carroll as a sexual deviant, obsessed with little girls like Alice Liddell. Her book describes Carroll's sexual relations with grown women and other aspects of his life to destroy what she claims are the fictionalized accounts of previous biographers.

Thomas, Donald. *Lewis Carroll: A Portrait with Background.* London: John Murray, 1996. Thomas surmises the formative influences on Carroll's personality and intellect as he describes Victorian England. An invaluable guide for readers who want to understand how manners and ideas changed during Carroll's lifetime.

SEE ALSO: Hans Christian Andersen; Mathew B. Brady; Richard Dedekind; Ellen Terry.

RELATED ARTICLES in *Great Events from History: The Nineteenth Century, 1801-1900:* 1807: Bowdler Publishes *The Family Shakespeare*; 1812-1815: Brothers Grimm Publish Fairy Tales; May 8, 1835: Andersen Publishes His First Fairy Tales.

KIT CARSON

American frontiersman

As trapper, guide, Indian agent, and soldier, Carson helped open the American West to settlement. His frontier adventures continue to impress those fascinated by the West's romantic era.

BORN: December 24, 1809; Madison County, Kentucky
DIED: May 23, 1868; Fort Lyon, Colorado
ALSO KNOWN AS: Christopher Carson (full name)
AREAS OF ACHIEVEMENT: Exploration, military

EARLY LIFE

Christopher "Kit" Carson was born into a large Kentucky family. His father, Lindsey Carson, of Scotch-Irish heritage, fought in the American Revolution and had five children before his first wife died in 1793. Three years later, he married Kit's mother, Rebecca Robinson. The second marriage yielded ten more children, of whom Christopher was the sixth. Before Christopher was two years old, the family moved to Missouri, settling in Howard County. A falling tree limb killed his father when Kit was only nine years old. At fourteen, he was apprenticed to a saddler in Franklin. Kit received little formal schooling and remained illiterate most of his life (many years later, he did learn to write his name). Instead, he earned an education in the American wilderness from men tutored in frontier ways.

Before long, the young apprentice found the saddle trade "distasteful" and vowed to flee his fate at the first chance. Longing to visit new lands, he decided to join the first party headed for the Rocky Mountains. With his master's apparent connivance, Carson ran away in August, 1826, following a wagon train bound for Santa Fe, New Mexico. Taos then became Carson's adopted home, where he always returned after his long journeys.

From 1827 to 1829, Carson served as a cook, drove a wagon to El Paso, Texas, interpreted Spanish, and worked for a copper mine near the Gila River. In August, 1829, he joined Ewing Young's trapping party bound for California. Although not the first trapping venture to cross the continent, the Young expedition provided Carson with invaluable experience and helped shape his life. After trapping beaver along several Arizona streams, the party moved on to California, trapped in the San Joaquin and Sacramento valleys, and finally returned to Taos in April, 1831. Carson once again joined an experienced trapper's expedition, this time that of Thomas Fitzpatrick, known to Indians as "Broken Hand." Fitzpatrick's men headed north to trap in the central Rockies. For the next ten years, Carson roamed the American interior, hunting and trapping in much of present-day Colorado, Wyoming, Utah, Idaho, and Montana.

Carson immediately established a reputation as a reliable trapper and a man useful in a fight. Although later known for his wise counsel, at this point in his life he craved action and adventure. Experience taught him the value of caution; though excitable, he remained firm and determined in dangerous situations. Carson admitted that his most fearful moment came when two angry grizzly bears forced him up a tree. In 1835, an insufferable French trapper goaded him into a celebrated duel at point-blank range—so close, in fact, that Carson's face received powder burns. Wounded in the arm, the Frenchman gave Carson no more trouble.

Carson and his fellow trappers often fought Indians, particularly the Blackfeet, who struggled with the whites over hunting grounds and supplies of valuable horses. In 1835, a Blackfoot warrior wounded Carson in the shoulder, his most serious injury. Early in life, Carson decided that Indians could not be trusted; subsequent clashes confirmed his view that wayward Indians must be severely chastised. Still, he had no special hatred for Native Americans; he respected and understood them well enough to take two native women as his wives (although the second union ended in divorce).

In the Rockies, Carson traveled with many noted mountain men, including Jim Bridger, "Old Bill" Williams, Richard Owens, and Alexis Godey. Trappers lived a rigorous yet unrestrained life, no sooner trading their beaver pelts than setting off again for the mountains. By 1840, overtrapping brought their days to an end, but not before they began to pacify the frontier. Just over thirty years of age, Carson was left with an uncertain future.

In 1836, Carson married an Arapaho woman, Waanibe (or Singing Grass). She bore him two daughters but died in 1840 or 1841. For a wandering trapper, Carson was considerate of his Indian wife; her death meant that he had to care for two young daughters. In 1842, he decided to leave one daughter with Missouri relatives. Returning westward, he met John C. Frémont on a Missouri River steamer. This chance meeting proved a turning point in Carson's life.

Despite his fame as a mountain man and Indian fighter, Carson was barely average in height and spoke in a soft, nearly feminine voice. He nevertheless immediately impressed army explorer John C. Frémont, who described the frontiersman in his memoirs as "broad-shouldered and deep-chested, with a clear steady blue eye and frank speech and address; quiet and unassuming." Others agreed that Carson was a man of rare character: honest, dependable, fierce under fire, and modest. Younger than many experienced trappers, he became their equal and then won greater fame as Frémont's guide.

Kit Carson. (Library of Congress)

LIFE'S WORK

In 1842, John C. Frémont was directed by the United States Army to survey the Oregon route as far as South Pass in Wyoming. Known to be reliable, Carson had traveled the mountains extensively, and thus Frémont hired him as guide and hunter at one hundred dollars a month. Eventually, the two men developed great respect for each other, and their friendship proved of lasting benefit to both. Frémont later swore that "Carson and truth are one."

Beginning in June, 1842, Carson guided the main party along the Platte River to Fort Laramie. There rumors of Indian reprisals against white travelers compelled Carson to make an oral last will, a trapper custom.

Frémont persisted, and the party safely crossed the Rockies. Carson assisted the explorer in planting the American flag atop one of the Wind River peaks, then accompanied him in a rubber raft down the Platte on the return trip. The party escaped injury in an otherwise costly accident, then Carson took his leave at Fort Laramie. In January, 1843, he returned to Taos to marry his third wife, Josefa Jaramillo, who eventually bore him seven children.

Carson again served as guide (along with Thomas Fitzpatrick) for Frémont's second expedition, in 1843-1844, to Oregon and California. Crossing the Rockies, Frémont and Carson examined the Great Salt Lake in a rubber boat, then continued to the British posts in the Oregon country. Frémont next struck southward to explore the Great Basin, finally deciding to enter California across the high Sierra Nevada in the dead of winter. From a Sierra pass, Carson caught a glimpse of the California Coastal Mountains that he had first seen as a member of the Young party fifteen years earlier. After much hardship, he helped guide Frémont to the familiar Sacramento Valley.

The party encountered further trouble returning on the old Spanish Trail. A band of Indians robbed a Mexican family of their horses and then killed most of the family. Carson and Alexis Godey volunteered to pursue the marauders, expecting others to do the same. When none did, the two guides tracked the offenders for fifty miles and alone attacked the camp of thirty braves. The Indians were caught off guard and fled. Carson and Godey returned with two scalps and most of the horses, earning Frémont's everlasting praise. Later, another man was killed by Indians, but the addition of famed trapper and guide Joseph R. Walker helped the party to reach Bent's Fort on the Arkansas River without further injury in July, 1844.

The publication of Frémont's reports of his first two expeditions in 1843 and 1845 brought Carson to the attention of an American nation eager to create heroes of its drive to the West. In his first report, for example, Frémont wrote that "mounted on a fine horse, without a saddle, and scouring bareheaded over the prairies, Kit was one of the finest pictures of a horseman I have ever seen." Such descriptions created a frontier legend that helped Carson earn further fame in the service of his nation.

Along with Richard Owens, Carson started a farm in New Mexico but gladly sold their assets at a loss in August, 1845, to serve on Frémont's third expedition. The party crossed the Rockies and again investigated the Great Salt Lake. Frémont decided to strike straight across the desert to the West, sending Carson and an advance party on a forced march to locate water and grass. Crossing the Great Basin and then the Sierra again in winter, the party arrived in California amid growing turmoil between Mexico and the United States.

In March, 1846, Mexican authorities ordered Frémont's army of American frontiersmen to leave the province. After a show of defiance, Frémont did pass northward into Oregon. On the route, Carson joined much of the party in attacking an Indian village, leaving more than a hundred dead in their wake. He believed this "butchery" was justified as a deterrent to attacks on American settlers. The same night, a messenger from Washington arrived; Klamath Indians surprised Frémont's camp, killing three of the party. Carson was angered at the death of his friends, and he led the men in exacting vengeance on a nearby Indian village. In a subsequent encounter with the Klamath, quick action by Frémont and James Sagundai, one of Frémont's Indian auxiliaries, spared Carson's life.

Frémont had received messages that induced him to return to California to lead a revolt of American settlers in June, 1846. Although not authorized by the U.S. government, Frémont's actions earned for him more national acclaim and raised his guide's renown as well. Carson served in the volunteer California Battalion, assisting in the occupation of San Diego and Los Angeles. Apparently at Frémont's direction, Carson's men executed three Mexican prisoners in retaliation for the killing of two Americans. Carson avoided mentioning this grim episode in his memoirs. With California apparently pacified, Frémont sent Carson east in September, carrying news of the conquest to Washington, D.C.

Crossing New Mexico, Carson encountered General Stephen Watts Kearny commanding a force of United States dragoons. With great reluctance, the famous guide agreed to lead the general to California. Arriving in December, 1846, the small American army clashed with determined Californians at San Pasqual. Riding in an advance party, Carson barely escaped death when his horse tumbled and his gun was broken. Many of the soldiers were killed, and Kearny was wounded. The command urgently needed help, so Carson, Navy Lieutenant Edward F. Beale, and a Delaware Indian crept away at night and ran barefoot to San Diego. Despite the hardship and heroism of their actions, a relief force had already been dispatched to rescue Kearny. Carson was again present to see Los Angeles occupied by American forces.

In 1847 and 1848, Carson traveled twice across the continent carrying government dispatches. In the spring of 1848, George Brewerton accompanied Carson from

California to New Mexico. The young lieutenant later wrote of his ride with the famous scout. Carson arrived in the East with early news of the California gold strike. At the capital, he and Jessie Benton Frémont urged President James K. Polk to assist her husband in a dispute over authority with General Kearny. Carson had another meeting with the president and was appointed first lieutenant in the United States Army. The Senate, however, refused to confirm the nomination, because of hostility toward the Frémont family. Informed of the rebuff, Carson nevertheless fulfilled his duty in carrying dispatches overland to California. Late in 1848, he returned to private life.

Carson did not accompany Frémont on his ill-fated final expeditions, but he did succor the exhausted explorer in Taos after his fourth expedition had ended in disaster in the San Juan Mountains. For the next several years, Carson engaged in various pursuits, often aiding government parties. In 1849, he guided soldiers seeking to rescue Mrs. James White and her child, who had been taken by Apache. Carson was saddened when the commander hesitated to follow his instructions; the Indians killed the mother and escaped with the child. In 1853, he took part in a great drive of sheep to California. Early in 1854, he began a new career as an Indian agent, primarily for the Ute.

From his office in Taos, Carson distributed government supplies to the Ute and took part in numerous efforts to pacify other tribes. In 1855, he helped government troops defeat hostile bands in battles at Saguache and Ponca Pass in Colorado. Despite the handicap of illiteracy, Carson proved an effective Indian agent. His facility with Spanish and many Indian languages offset his inability to read and write. Moreover, he knew and respected Indian customs. His hope was to see Indians removed from harmful contact with whites, where they could learn to provide their own support. Sometime in 1856, he dictated his memoirs, probably to his secretary. In 1860, a fall from his horse left Carson in declining health.

Until June, 1861, Carson continued in his post as Indian agent. Then the Civil War came to New Mexico Territory, bringing him a new career as military leader. Born a Kentuckian, Carson sided with the Union, helping to erect a United States flag in Taos after secession sympathizers raised the Confederate banner. He was commissioned a colonel in a New Mexico volunteer regiment. In February, 1862, his troops engaged invading Confederates at Valverde, New Mexico. Later action forced the rebels to withdraw.

For the remainder of the war, Carson sought to pacify several southwestern Indian tribes. Most notable was his 1863-1864 campaign against the Navajo, a large and proud nation. Following the orders of General James H. Carleton, he fought essentially a scorched-earth campaign, destroying crops and seizing livestock. His efforts to force the Navajo to surrender earned for him the name "Rope Thrower." In January, 1864, his troops drove the Navajo from their Canyon de Chelly stronghold. Relatively few were killed in the conflict; cold and starvation forced the defeated people to move to the Bosque Redondo, a remote reservation. Hundreds of Navajo died on the journey, however, because of inadequate provisions. Carson had not been responsible for the harsh policy and urged that more food be provided. His campaign helped settle the government reservation system, but in 1868 the Navajo were allowed to return to their tribal lands.

Carson's largest battle took place at Adobe Walls along the Canadian River in Texas. In November, 1864, he led more than three hundred troops (and seventy-five Ute and Apache) against a large force of Kiowa and Comanche. His troops destroyed an Indian village before perhaps as many as three thousand Indians forced him to withdraw. Carson was not beaten; his caution and experience prevented a potential disaster similar to General George A. Custer's defeat. Carson's foray inaugurated a long campaign to pacify the Kiowa and Comanche. In March, 1865, he was breveted brigadier general of United States Volunteers for his valuable service in New Mexico.

In 1866, Carson commanded Fort Garland in Colorado. The next year, he resigned his military position and was appointed superintendent of Indian affairs for the Colorado Territory. In poor health, he accompanied several Ute chiefs on a tour of eastern cities, hoping to negotiate a favorable treaty. He also visited his old friends the Frémonts and sought medical help. On his return to Fort Lyon, Colorado, his wife died after giving birth to another child. A month later, on May 23, 1868, the famous scout succumbed to death from an aortic aneurysm. Buried initially at Boggsville, Colorado, both Carsons were later moved to Taos, New Mexico, their beloved home. A river, a mountain pass, and the capital city of Nevada bear the Carson name.

SIGNIFICANCE

Kit Carson was an ideal representative of the American frontiersman. Unlettered but resourceful, he and his fellow mountain men lived a brief, romantic existence before decline of the beaver population brought their way of life to an end. Forced to become guides, traders, or Indian agents, former trappers continued to facilitate the

West's settlement, but in roles subordinate to the more powerful agents of American expansion. As Frémont's guide, Carson surpassed all the mountain men and emerged as a legendary figure of the American frontier. At the same time, his judgment and experience contributed to the success of Frémont's ventures. Through such former trappers as Carson, geographical knowledge of the West passed into the hands of army explorers such as Frémont. As an Indian agent, Carson sought to end Indian-white conflict, while his Civil War service helped protect the Southwest from Confederate attack and Indian unrest.

Carson's adventures require little embellishment, yet writers created a fictional Kit Carson, familiar to most Americans as a loyal army scout and Indian slayer. An early example of the Western hero, the Carson figure linked earlier eastern woodsmen (such as Daniel Boone) to the Indian fighter of the Western mountains and plains. Barely civilized himself in these fictional accounts, the famous scout assisted in the spread of American civilization to barren Western lands. More than most legendary heroes, however, the historical Kit Carson approaches his fictional reputation. Several brutal encounters with Indians and Mexicans mar his otherwise impressive career. Carson was nevertheless a man of simple courage and devotion to duty. He remains an American character deserving regard.

—*Vernon L. Volpe*

FURTHER READING

Brewerton, George Douglas. *Overland with Kit Carson: A Narrative of the Old Spanish Trail in '48*. Lincoln: University of Nebraska Press, 1993. A republication of one of the few accounts of Carson written by a man who knew and rode with the famous guide.

Carter, Harvey Lewis. *"Dear Old Kit": The Historical Christopher Carson*. Norman: University of Oklahoma Press, 1968. This authoritative work provides a richly annotated edition of Carson's memoirs, virtually the only source of information for his life to 1856. Includes a survey of works on Carson and assesses his character and later life.

Dunlay, Tom. *Kit Carson and the Indians*. Lincoln: University of Nebraska Press, 2000. In recent years, the old image of Carson as romantic hero has been replaced by the image of a brutal Indian slayer. Dunlay provides a balanced view of Carson's relations with the Indians, showing him capable of using violence but also able to denounce injustice against, and forge friendships with, Native Americans.

Estergreen, M. Morgan. *Kit Carson: A Portrait in Courage*. Norman: University of Oklahoma Press, 1962. Inaccurate in some respects, this helpful account is based partly on Carson family memories.

Guild, Thelma S., and Harvey L. Carter. *Kit Carson: A Pattern for Heroes*. Lincoln: University of Nebraska Press, 1984. Readable and generally reliable, this biography is based primarily on Carson's memoirs.

Jackson, Donald, and Mary Lee Spence, eds. *The Expeditions of John Charles Frémont*. 3 vols. Urbana: University of Illinois Press, 1970-1984. The widely read reports of John C. Frémont's first two expeditions (in volume 1) made Carson a national hero.

Kelly, Lawrence C., ed. *Navajo Roundup: Selected Correspondence of Kit Carson's Expedition Against the Navajo, 1863-1865*. Boulder, Colo.: Pruett, 1970. Generally favorable to Carson, this source contains many valuable documents covering his Navajo campaign.

Roberts, David. *A Newer World: Kit Carson, John C. Frémont, and the Claiming of the American West*. New York: Simon & Schuster, 2000. An account of Frémont's expeditions in the western United States from the early 1840's until the beginning of the Civil War. Describes Carson's role in the expeditions and the relationship of the two men.

Sabin, Edwin Legrand. *Kit Carson Days*. Chicago: A. C. McClurg, 1914. Rev. ed. New York: Press of the Pioneers, 1935. Dated and flawed in parts, this standard biography is still useful for Carson's later career. Includes his agent and military reports.

Simmons, Marc. *Kit Carson and His Three Wives*. Albuquerque: University of New Mexico Press, 2003. Simmons has spent four decades researching Carson's personal life, resulting in the publication of this book about Carson's relations with his family, wife, and children.

Trafzer, Clifford E. *The Kit Carson Campaign: The Last Great Navajo War*. Norman: University of Oklahoma Press, 1982. This work examines Carson's 1863-1864 campaign from the Navajo perspective.

SEE ALSO: William Cody; John C. Frémont; Wild Bill Hickok.

RELATED ARTICLES in *Great Events from History: The Nineteenth Century, 1801-1900:* May, 1842-1854: Frémont Explores the American West; June 30, 1846-January 13, 1847: United States Occupies California and the Southwest; April 30, 1860-1865: Apache and Navajo War; August, 1863-September, 1866: Long Walk of the Navajos.

MARY ANN SHADD CARY

American abolitionist and journalist

A pioneering educator and lifelong advocate of equality for African Americans, Cary wrote and lectured widely in support of abolition and black emigration to Canada, and after emancipation was achieved, she participated in the woman suffrage and temperance movements. She was also first African American woman newspaper publisher and the first black woman to enter Howard University Law School.

BORN: October 9, 1823; Wilmington, Delaware
DIED: June 5, 1893; Washington, D.C.
ALSO KNOWN AS: Mary Ann Shadd (birth name)
AREAS OF ACHIEVEMENT: Journalism, women's rights, law

EARLY LIFE

Mary Ann Shadd Cary was born Mary Ann Shadd, the first of thirteen children of Harriet Parnell, a mulatto woman born in North Carolina, and Abraham Shadd, a shoemaker descended from a German soldier named Hans Schad and a free black Pennsylvania woman named Elizabeth Jackson, who married in 1756. Like her father and paternal grandfather, Mary Ann was born free. The fact that her grandfather and great-grandfather had been butchers by trade secured the status of the Shadd family within the black middle class of Wilmington, Delaware, where she grew up. However, their comparative material prosperity did not spare free blacks, such as the Shadds, from the black codes that Delaware enacted during the 1830's to restrict the freedoms of former slaves.

At an early age, Mary Ann was exposed to the movements to abolish slavery and achieve political and social equality for free African Americans. Her father was active in local and national social protests throughout his life. He offered his homes in Wilmington and later in West Chester, Pennsylvania, as stations on the Underground Railroad, which was used by people escaping from southern slavery. He also solicited subscriptions for abolitionist newspapers such as William Lloyd Garrison's *Liberator*. In 1831, Abraham Shadd was one of three authors and signatories of a statement condemning the American Colonization Society, which worked to ship freed slaves to Africa. He was also among the first five African Americans on the board of managers of the American Anti-Slavery Society when that organization began in 1833.

During 1833, the Shadd family escaped from the increasing harshness of Delaware's black codes by moving to nearby West Chester, Pennsylvania. There, Mary Ann received six years of private instruction provided by local Quakers, under whom she studied Latin, French, literature, and mathematics. In 1840, when she was seventeen and her schooling was completed, she returned to Wilmington and opened a school for African American children. Throughout the 1840's, she taught not only in Wilmington but also in West Chester and Norristown, Pennsylvania, and in Trenton, New Jersey, where she failed in an effort to establish another school for African Americans in 1844.

LIFE'S WORK

In 1849, Mary Ann Shadd entered the public debate on obtaining black equality. During that year, she published a letter in Frederick Douglass's newspaper, *The North Star*, and also published a pamphlet, *Hints to the Colored People of the North*, in which she stressed education, morality, and economic self-help as the means through which African Americans could integrate themselves into American society. Passage of the Fugitive Slave Act by the U.S. Congress in 1850 permitted federal marshals to reclaim runaway slaves even after they reached free states. That law added new urgency to Mary Ann's emerging activism.

After attending an antislavery convention in Toronto, Canada, in September, 1851, Mary Ann decided to join the thousands of free and slave-born African Americans who were emigrating to Great Britain's Canadian colonies. After giving up her teaching job in New York City, she settled in the town of Windsor (now in Ontario). There she opened a school with the support of the American Missionary Association and became that organization's only black missionary in Canada West. In 1852, Mary Ann published *Notes of Canada West*, an essay extolling the benefits of life in Canada to potential African American migrants. By the end of the decade, Mary Ann's parents as well as several siblings had also moved to Canada.

Mary Ann's advocacy of Canadian immigration and racial uplift challenged the established leadership of Henry Bibb, another immigrant, who had established the newspaper *Voice of the Fugitive* in 1851. The friction between Mary Ann and Bibb came to a head in 1853, when the American Missionary Association responded to Bibb's criticisms of Mary Ann by withdrawing its support of her school. On March 24, 1853, the day after her

Windsor school closed, Mary Ann began publishing and editing her own newspaper, the *Provincial Freeman*, in Toronto. She was the first African American woman to do so, even though the conventions of the time required her to list a man as the newspaper's editor on its masthead.

The *Provincial Freeman* provided Mary Ann with a public voice with which to articulate her support of black immigration to Canada and racial integration and to critique other abolitionists. The newspaper also published letters and articles debating woman suffrage and women's participation in the public sphere. Mary Ann spread her message further and solicited subscriptions for her newspaper by lecturing in the United States. She was one of only a few black women who spoke publicly during that period. In 1855, she moved her newspaper from Toronto to Chatham.

On January 3, 1856, Mary Ann married Thomas Cary, a free-born African American and barber who relocated to Toronto during the early 1850's and had three children from an earlier marriage. Mary Ann's marriage to Cary was unusual, in that she and her husband traveled back and forth between the separate homes they maintained in Chatham and Toronto. They had two children together: Sara Elizabeth, born in 1857, and Linton, born in 1860.

Mary Ann continued editing the *Provincial Freeman* until it folded in 1860 because of insufficient funds. After her husband's death later that same year, Mary Ann taught briefly in Michigan, opened another school in Chatham with her sister, and continued to publish articles in the abolitionist press. At the urging of the black nationalist leader Martin Delaney, Mary Ann traveled throughout the United States in 1863 to encourage African American men to join the Union army during the Civil War. After the war ended, the promise of Reconstruction and diminishing employment opportunities for African Americans in Canada prompted Mary Ann's permanent return to the United States in 1867. She worked as a teacher in Detroit before moving to Washington, D.C., in 1869.

As Mary Ann settled into life as a teacher, and later as a school principal, in Washington, D.C., she began to pay more attention to women's issues in her social activism. She attended the yearly meetings of the National Women's Suffrage Association during the early part of the decade and wrote frequently for Frederick Douglass's newspaper *New National Era* in support of woman suffrage, a position that diverged from the African American community's primary goal of obtaining the vote for black men. After ratification of the Fifteenth Amendment gave black men the vote in 1870, Mary Ann herself attempted to register to vote several times. In 1880, she established the short-lived Colored Women's Progressive Franchise Association. She also advocated temperance as a means of promoting black self-sufficiency.

Meanwhile, Mary Ann became the first black woman to enter Howard University Law School. She began her legal studies there in 1869 and combined being a law student with being a teacher and school principal until she received her degree in 1883. Throughout the 1880's, she practiced law in Washington and continued to lecture and write on strategies of racial uplift. She died of stomach cancer in Washington, D.C., on June 5, 1893, during her seventieth year.

SIGNIFICANCE

Mary Ann Shadd Cary is remarkable, not only for her notable firsts in the fields of journalism and law, but also for the space that she carved out for herself as a woman activist during the long African American struggle to obtain racial equality. She defied the mainstream social convention that a woman's rightful place was in the home by inserting herself into public debate, first on the issue of abolition of slavery and extension of civil rights to free blacks, and later in her advocacy of woman suffrage. She also defied the assumptions of other African American activists who asserted that gender equality should be subordinate to racial uplift. Her career as an educator, lecturer, and newspaperwoman—which did not cease with marriage and motherhood—was its own protest against the twin sets of limitations that she faced as an African American and as a woman.

—Francesca Gamber

FURTHER READING

Cimbala, Paul A. "Mary Ann Shadd Cary and Black Abolitionism." In *Against the Tide: Women Reformers and American Society*, edited by Paul A. Cimbala and Randall M. Miller. Westport, Conn.: Praeger, 1997. This essay places Mary Ann Shadd Cary within the broader community of African American abolitionists and in relation to the particular concerns of black women activists.

Ferris, Jeri. *Demanding Justice: A Story About Mary Ann Shadd Cary*. Minneapolis: Carolrhoda Books, 2003. Illustrated children's book about Shadd Cary.

Rhodes, Jane. *Mary Ann Shadd Cary: The Black Press and Protest in the Nineteenth Century*. Bloomington: Indiana University Press, 1998. A thorough recent treatment of Shadd Cary's life, this book pays special attention to her years as a newspaper editor and publisher and the role she played in the antebellum black press.

Silverman, Jason H. *Unwelcome Guests: Canada West's Response to American Fugitive Slaves, 1800-1865.* Millwood, N.Y.: Associated Faculty Press, 1985. Contests the view that Canada provided a safe haven for African Americans by describing the obstacles and racism that immigrants such as the Shadds faced there.

SEE ALSO: Frederick Douglass; Abby Kelley Foster; William Lloyd Garrison; Sarah and Angelina Grimké; Lucretia Mott.

RELATED ARTICLES in *Great Events from History: The Nineteenth Century, 1801-1900:* December 3, 1847: Douglass Launches *The North Star*; October 16-18, 1859: Brown's Raid on Harpers Ferry; December 6, 1865: Thirteenth Amendment Is Ratified.

MARY CASSATT

American painter

Using Impressionist techniques to create vivid, unsentimental portraits, Cassatt became one of the foremost American painters at a time when the art world was regarded as an exclusively male domain.

BORN: May 22, 1844; Allegheny City (now Pittsburgh), Pennsylvania
DIED: June 14, 1926; Château de Beaufresne, France
ALSO KNOWN AS: Mary Stevenson Cassatt (full name)
AREA OF ACHIEVEMENT: Art

EARLY LIFE

Mary Stevenson Cassatt was the second daughter and fourth child of Robert and Katherine Johnson Cassatt. Robert Cassatt earned a comfortable income from stock trading and real estate. In 1849, the family moved to Philadelphia, but in 1851, they left for an extended stay in Europe. The Cassatts first lived in Paris, but in 1853 they moved to Germany, where the eldest son, Alexander, could study engineering, and another son, Robert, could receive medical attention. In 1855, Robert died and was buried in Darmstadt; many years later, Mary Cassatt would have his body moved to be interred with others of the family at her French château.

The family returned to the United States in 1855, settling first in the Pennsylvania countryside and then back in Philadelphia, where Mary enrolled, in 1861, at the Pennsylvania Academy of Fine Arts. During her four years at the academy she received a solid, if uninspiring, education in artistic fundamentals. Students began with drawings from casts of statues, progressed to live models, and completed their training by making oil copies of paintings. The faults of this process were that the instructors were competent but undistinguished, and the paintings available for students were mediocre. At this time there were no major collections of art in the United States. Cassatt realized that to become an artist she needed exposure to the best in art, so she decided she must go to Europe.

In 1865, it was unheard of for a young woman to become a professional artist, and shocking for her to leave family and embark alone on a tour of Europe. However, these were precisely the goals that Cassatt determined to achieve. There was considerable opposition from her family, to both her desire for an artistic career and the European visit, but she persuaded them to accept her plans. This determination was characteristic of Cassatt, and its lifelong nature could be seen in her appearance. She was tall, thin, with fine but strong features and blue-gray eyes. Direct and forceful, she expressed her beliefs and opinions without reserve or regard for the sensibilities of others. Extremely energetic, she could work from dawn until the light faded but was able to put her paintings aside to care for her family; she herself never married. Such was the young woman who sailed for Europe in 1866, anticipating the first steps in her real artistic apprenticeship.

LIFE'S WORK

In Paris, Cassatt enrolled in the École des Beaux Arts and studied briefly with a fashionable society painter. Soon she left to study independently, mainly visiting museums and galleries and copying their paintings. In 1867, the Paris World's Fair was held. Outside the official exhibitions, the painters Gustave Courbet and Édouard Manet held a private show. Unlike conventional painters, Courbet and Manet chose subjects that were contemporary rather than classical and portrayed them with vivid, unsparing realism, precise in observation and presentation. Cassatt was deeply influenced; Manet had the most important impact on her work prior to her association with Edgar Degas.

During the Franco-Prussian War of 1870, Cassatt returned to Philadelphia, but in 1871 she was back in Europe, spending eight months in Parma, Italy, where she made an extensive study of the painter Antonio Allegri da Correggio. The result can be seen in her work, chiefly in her depictions of children, which owed much to Correggio's paintings of Madonna and Child. She visited Spain, where she was particularly impressed by Diego Rodriguez de Silva Velázquez and El Greco. She also visited the Netherlands, where the paintings of Peter Paul Rubens, with his outstanding flesh tints and mastery of the human form, made a profound contribution to her style.

In 1873, Cassatt decided to settle permanently in Paris. Given the artistic ferment of the French capital and its central role in art, at the time it was the only natural place for a serious artist. In 1872, a painting of hers, signed "Mary Stevenson," had been accepted by the Paris Salon. She continued to submit work to the Salon for several years but grew increasingly disenchanted with the Salon's arbitrary and restrictive standards. One of her paintings was rejected because the background was too light; with a darkened background the painting was resubmitted and accepted.

Decisions such as this were one reason Cassatt ceased exhibiting in the Salon after 1877. The most important reason, however, was her discovery of the Impressionist movement and her association with Edgar Degas. The first Impressionist show was held in 1874, with works by such artists as Degas and Manet. The exhibition was fiercely attacked by traditional critics, but Cassatt perceived immediately the breakthrough that had been made. The Impressionist group contained widely diverse artists, who shared a common preoccupation with light—how to capture it, how to set it down on canvas. Their use of light and color was the key element in the movement, and after Cassatt viewed their work, light and color became essential in her work as well.

Degas had seen her work and admired it, and in 1877, they met. At forty-three, he was ten years older, an established artist known for his paintings and his sharp, often cutting remarks. The two had a stormy but productive relationship that lasted forty years. Although some have speculated on a romantic liaison between the two, it appears likely that their friendship, while close, was mainly professional. They had bitter arguments, over painting, politics, or personalities, but they always reconciled, usually at Cassatt's initiative. Degas was certainly the most important influence on Cassatt's artistic career.

Mary Cassatt. (The Granger Collection, New York)

Degas asked her to join the 1877 exhibition of the Impressionists. "I accepted with joy," she later said. "Now I could work with absolute independence without considering the opinion of a jury. I had already recognized who were my true masters. I admired Manet, Courbet, and Degas. I took leave of conventional art. I began to live."

Cassatt's relationship with Degas reinforced her natural strengths. They both chose contemporary subjects, preferring the human figure rather than landscapes, and both insisted on the importance of drawing and line. It was through Degas that Cassatt came to know the Japanese prints that had been introduced to France during the 1850's. From these she developed a simple, strong style that emphasized unusual angles of vision (from above, from the side, with the main figure only partially in view), a flattening of perspective, and the use of contrasting areas of pattern. Some of her best pieces were aquatints inspired by the Japanese prints.

By 1880, Cassatt was an acknowledged member of the Impressionist movement and exhibited regularly in its shows; she was the only American painter ever to do so. Urged on by Degas, she branched into pastels and prints, showing great promise in both.

Cassatt's father, mother, and sister Lydia joined her in Paris in 1877; nursing them through a series of illnesses often deprived her of painting time. In 1880, her brother Alexander and his family came to live with the Cassatts. Inspired by her nieces and nephews, Mary began her paintings of mother and child, the theme with which she is most popularly associated.

The 1890's were Mary Cassatt's most creative and productive period. In addition to her paintings and pastels, it was then that she produced the series of aquatints inspired by Japanese woodblock prints that she exhibited in her first one-woman show of 1891.

Back in the United States, Cassatt's fame grew slowly. An exhibit of the Impressionists in 1886 included three of her works, and her paintings were shown in Philadelphia, Boston, New York, and other cities. By 1891, she was well known enough to receive a commission for a mural on the theme of "modern woman" at the Chicago World's Fair. She painted the canvas, her largest work, at the Château de Beaufresne, which she had recently purchased.

Meanwhile, full recognition in Cassatt's homeland lagged. Her first one-woman show in New York (1895) had a lackluster reception, and she was not fully appreciated until after her death in 1926. In France, however, Cassatt was well known. Her second one-woman show, held in Paris in 1893, was a large one: ninety-eight works, consisting of oils, pastels, and graphics. Her exhibition was well received by the public and the critics. Other shows were equally acclaimed, and she was quickly recognized as a major artist. In 1904, she was awarded the Legion of Honor.

In addition to being a creative artist, Cassatt was extremely important in bringing artwork to the United States. In 1873, she met Louisine Elder, who shared her interest in art. In 1901, Cassatt went on an extended European purchasing tour with Elder and Elder's husband, the wealthy banker H. O. Havemeyer. Over the next decade Cassatt advised them on a large number of purchases. Thanks to her perceptive eye and knowledgeable advice, the Havemeyers bought many Impressionist works and many important earlier paintings, such as El Greco's *View of Toledo* and his *Assumption of the Virgin*—the two most notable works of that artist to be found outside Spain. In 1929, the Havemeyer Collection went to the New York Metropolitan Museum of Art, forming the foundation of a national treasure.

After 1900, Cassatt's work declined in quantity and, to some extent, in quality. Partly this was a result of her extensive work in collecting, but primarily her artistic decline was caused by family problems and failing eyesight. Her sister Lydia had died at an early age; in 1895, her mother died after a long illness, during which Cassatt was occupied as her nurse. The death of her favorite brother, Alexander, in 1906 was another severe blow, and five years later, after a tour of Egypt, her brother Gardner fell seriously ill and died in Paris. For a time, Mary Cassatt suffered from what she, and others, termed a "breakdown." It was not until 1912 that she began to work again.

When she did, it was in pastels, mainly because her failing eyesight did not allow the precision of prints or oils. Bothered by cataracts, she submitted to treatments and operations, none of which restored her sight; by 1913 her work was ended. She spent World War I removed from her beloved Château de Beaufresne because it was close to the battle lines.

In 1917, her friend and fellow professional, Degas, died. He had been the last link with the work and success of earlier years. She returned to her château in 1920 and remained there for the rest of her life. Nearly blind, she could not work but entertained young artists, mostly Americans, with her fiercely held, forcefully delivered views on art. She died at the Château de Beaufresne on June 14, 1926.

SIGNIFICANCE

"I am not willing to admit that a woman can draw that well," Degas said upon viewing a work by Cassatt. This remark of an exceptional artist, who was Cassatt's closest friend and influence, reveals the obstacles facing a woman artist in the latter half of the nineteenth century. It is proof of Cassatt's determination and talent that she was accepted during her lifetime as one of the premier artists of the day; significantly, Degas purchased the very picture that inspired his comment.

Cassatt's contributions to art came in two phases: her own creations and her work in collecting. As an adviser to wealthy Americans such as H. O. Havemeyer and the banker James Stillman, Cassatt helped build some of the truly outstanding art collections of the twentieth century and brought priceless treasures to American museums. Cassatt made certain that no American art student would again face her early dilemma of living in a country that possessed no great artistic works. Such collections were important to Cassatt, because she firmly believed that the only way of learning to paint was to see, and copy, great paintings.

The energy that went into building collections was energy lost to her own work. She was also burdened with caring for her family, and she was increasingly troubled with eye problems. Cassatt, therefore, had a relatively limited production as an artist: about 225 prints and 617 oils and pastels, many of them studies rather than finished works.

It is the excellence of her work, rather than its quantity, which signals Cassatt's undeniable achievement. In her chosen subjects, mothers and children, and the female form, she achieved a powerful, accurate, and original vision that rejected traditional sentiment and convention. She brought together the emphasis on light stressed by the Impressionists, the new angles of vision revealed by photography and Japanese prints, and the clarity and directness demanded by all great painters. Mary Cassatt blended these qualities together through her own honesty, efforts, and genius, producing a body of work that is among the most important in modern art.

—Michael Witkoski

FURTHER READING

Breeskin, Adelyn. *Mary Cassatt: A Catalogue Raissoné of the Oils, Pastels, Watercolors, and Drawings*. Washington, D.C.: Smithsonian Institution Press, 1970. Contains a short but highly informative biography of Cassatt's life and career. The notes that accompany the illustrations are excellent and provide the reader with a solid guide to Cassatt's development as an artist.

Bullard, E. John. *Mary Cassatt: Oils and Pastels*. New York: Watson-Guptill, 1976. The introductory sketch of Cassatt's life is excellent, and the commentary on the pictures is first-rate. Cassatt believed that the only way to learn painting was to copy great works; the best way to study her is to look at her works.

Carson, Julia. *Mary Cassatt*. New York: David McKay, 1966. A fine introductory biography, geared toward the younger reader.

Cassatt, Mary. *Cassatt and Her Circle: Selected Letters*. Edited by Nancy Mowll Mathews. New York: Abbeville Press, 1984. A generous collection of letters by Cassatt and her associates. More of interest to the specialist than to the general student.

Hale, Nancy. *Mary Cassatt*. Garden City, N.Y.: Doubleday, 1975. This biography is generally good on facts and relationships, but occasionally strays into confusing speculation about Cassatt's thoughts and motives.

McKown, Robin. *The World of Mary Cassatt*. New York: Thomas Y. Crowell, 1972. A wide-ranging view of Cassatt's development as an artist; the work assumes that the reader already has a fair understanding of the period under discussion. Contains an excellent bibliography.

Mancoff, Debra N. *Mary Cassatt: Reflections of Women's Lives*. New York: Stewart, Tabori & Chang, 1998. A good introduction to Cassatt's life and work. Excellent reproductions of her paintings, with detailed captions providing critical information that make the work more meaningful.

Mathews, Nancy Mowll. *Mary Cassatt: A Life*. New York: Villard Books, 1994. Reprint. New Haven, Conn.: Yale University Press, 1998. Mathews, an art historian who edited a collection of Cassatt's letters (see above), provides a multifaceted portrait of the artist, depicting her as sometimes difficult and always outspoken, single-minded, and independent.

Pollock, Griselda. *Mary Cassatt: Painter of Modern Women*. London: Thames and Hudson, 1998. Pollock, a feminist art critic, contradicts the image of Cassatt as a wimpy painter of babies. She maintains that Cassatt was a "painter of modern women," influenced by Degas, Manet, and other Impressionists, who brought a feminist perspective to the art world.

Sweet, Frederick. *Miss Mary Cassatt: Impressionist from Pennsylvania*. Norman: University of Oklahoma Press, 1966. This biography has good sources—Sweet was one of the first authors with wide access to letters of Cassatt and her associates—and excellent documentation. The approach, however, is neither critical nor analytical.

SEE ALSO: Gustave Courbet; Édouard Manet; James McNeill Whistler.

RELATED ARTICLES in *Great Events from History: The Nineteenth Century, 1801-1900:* April 15, 1874: First Impressionist Exhibition; Late 1870's: Post-Impressionist Movement Begins.

VISCOUNT CASTLEREAGH
Irish politician

Castlereagh's political skills helped create the Act of Union between Great Britain and Ireland that created the United Kingdom. His role in the peace negotiations following the Napoleonic Wars helped ensure a just and long-lasting peace.

BORN: June 18, 1769; Dublin, Ireland
DIED: August 12, 1822; Cray Farm, North Cray, Kent, England
ALSO KNOWN AS: Robert Stewart, Second Marquis of Londonderry (full name); Robert Stewart (birth name)
AREAS OF ACHIEVEMENT: Government and politics, diplomacy

EARLY LIFE

Viscount Castlereagh (KAHS-ahl-ray) was born Robert Stewart in his grandfather's house in Dublin. His mother, Lady Frances Seymour-Conway, was the daughter of the earl of Hertford, Lord Lieutenant of Ireland in 1765. She died in 1770. His father, Robert Stewart, came from a landed Presbyterian Ulster family. The little boy's elder brother died the year he was born. He was the only surviving son of his father's first marriage. Baptized a Presbyterian, Stewart was brought up as an Anglican so as to avoid any obstacles to a political career. At the time, not only Roman Catholics but also non-Anglican Protestants lacked first-class citizenship.

Until he was eight years old, Stewart lived with his paternal grandparents. Then he attended the Royal School at Armagh, from which an early letter (October 6, 1777) assured his family that he was still a loyal "American," by which he meant a supporter of the American revolutionaries, as both his father's and his stepmother's families were. He then joined his father's household at Mount Stewart, County Down, and transferred to a nearby school. His father's second wife was the daughter of the British Lord Chancellor Camden, a formidable figure in English Whig circles, who took a great interest in his step-grandson's future. Camden persuaded Stewart's father to send him to Cambridge, and he duly matriculated at St. John's College in 1786. Until then, he had taken pleasure in the usual pursuits of the gentry—riding, sailing, dancing—and had shown no particular academic aptitude. At Cambridge, he was not impressed by the intellectual life and never took his degree.

Meanwhile, with the general election of 1790 looming, Stewart's father was determined to reassert the family's political influence in Down and to avenge his own electoral defeat in 1784 by putting up his son for a county seat in the Irish House of Commons. At enormous expense (some said sixty thousand pounds), Stewart was successful. He had not been quite twenty-one when he declared his candidacy, standing as an Independent Reformer. His father had accepted an Irish peerage so that both father and son would attend the new Irish Parliament, one as peer, the other as a member of Parliament (M.P.).

Three points about Stewart's next few years are especially important. First, he went abroad, to Spa in 1791 and to Brussels in 1792. His acumen in assessing the impact of the French Revolution was quickly apparent. He told the refugees at Spa that there was no hope of restoring the France of 1789; at the same time, he foretold the collapse of the revolutionary paper currency, the assignats. Stewart's departure from the Whig principles of Charles James Fox dates from this time, as does Lord Camden's advice to him before his maiden speech in the Dublin Parliament. Camden explained that although his family tradition and election platform opposed the unreformed character of the Irish executive, which was responsible to the British cabinet, Stewart could all the same indicate his sympathy with William Pitt the Younger, prime minister in Great Britain. He could and did.

Second, in 1794, the tall, slim, and handsome M.P. married Lady Amelia (Emily) Hobart, daughter and only child of the earl of Buckinghamshire's second marriage. This match reinforced the aristocratic English connections already begun with his mother's family and continued with his stepmother's. Third, he combined the tenure of his seat in the Irish House of Commons with election to a seat in the House of Commons of Great Britain. He first sat for Tregony, Cornwall, and later for Orford, Suffolk, until, in 1797, his acceptance of office in Ireland obliged him to give up any British seat. When he returned to Westminster it would be as M.P. in that new entity, the United Kingdom of Great Britain and Ireland, which he did so much to create.

By this time, Stewart's admiration for Pitt and distrust of the French Revolution cut him off from his earliest political supporters in Ireland, many of whom continued to support the French Revolution and to hope that war between England and France would force England to make further concessions to Ireland, as had happened during the American Revolutionary War. Stewart, however (now Viscount Castlereagh), had already voted with Pitt to suspend habeas corpus in England. While shuttling between Dublin and Westminster, he supported the measures to limit civil liberties in both countries. He had moved away from his early Irish Whig reform principles and joined the Pittite supporters of an act of union, amalgamating the kingdoms of Great Britain and Ireland.

LIFE'S WORK

Castlereagh's appointment as Keeper of the Privy Seal in Ireland obliged him to resign his seat in the British Parliament, and at that time, 1797, he was reelected for his Irish seat at County Down. Already, Castlereagh had played a role as officer in the yeomanry, distinct from Pitt's militia, which had been raised as an alternative to the suspect Irish Volunteers.

Informers betrayed the leadership of the United Irishmen, which had begun to link Ulster Presbyterians with southern Roman Catholics in a revolutionary organization, and Castlereagh participated in a preemptive strike at its leadership in Ulster in 1797. This success undoubtedly limited the scale of the Ulster rebellion in 1798. By that time, Castlereagh had become acting chief secretary of Ireland, during the illness and absence of Thomas Pelham (Lord Pelham and later second Earl of Chichester). He was the right-hand man of the Lord Lieutenant, chief resident executive of Ireland. His calm resourcefulness during the rebellion recommended him to the new Lord Lieutenant, Lord Cornwallis, who arrived after the suppression of the rebellion in the south at the Battle of Vinegar Hill, June 21, 1798. Cornwallis strongly supported Castlereagh as permanent replacement to Pelham as chief secretary in November, 1798.

Meanwhile, the last French effort to intervene failed. In 1796, General Hoche had been unable to make a landing at Bantry Bay. Another force under General Humbert, ill-coordinated with the local Irish rebellion, landed in August and surrendered in September, 1798. Had Napoleon Bonaparte sailed for Ireland rather than for Egypt, the outcome might have been different. As it was, Castlereagh's problem was one of conciliation. He embraced Cornwallis's amnesty for past rebels, though it infuriated ardent Protestant members of Orange Societies, thirsting for revenge. Castlereagh began serious correspondence with Pitt about a union of Ireland with Great Britain as a long-term solution to the problem of the relations of the two kingdoms.

Castlereagh had no confidence in a policy of concessions to Roman Catholics in the narrow context of a quasi-autonomous Ireland. The religious problem could be addressed only after Ireland merged with the larger entity of a single united kingdom. For almost two years (1799-1800), Castlereagh devoted himself to the job of persuading the Irish Parliament to abolish itself and to accept representation by one hundred M.P.'s at a new House of Commons at Westminster. These means of persuasion harked back to those used at the unification of Scotland with England in 1707: bribery, compensation for the loss of "property" in control over boroughs, new peerages, and promotions within the peerage. The idea that a borough "owner" was entitled to monetary compensation was current. Pitt had used it in his own abortive plan to reform the British House of Commons. Castlereagh's task was to distribute some one and a quarter million pounds so as to guarantee majority votes in the Irish Parliament. Because most of the borough "owners" were Irish peers, they received most of the money.

Just as the whole Scottish peerage was not absorbed into the House of Lords of Great Britain, so the Irish peerage was to elect twenty-eight of its number to join the House of Lords of the United Kingdom. However, Scottish peers were elected at every general election; the Irish representative peers were to be elected for life.

Viscount Castlereagh. (Library of Congress)

Therefore, Irish peers not elected as representative peers were to be eligible for election to the new House of Commons. Castlereagh was not affected, as his courtesy title left him eligible anyway. He did not succeed his father as an Irish peer until 1821 (by then the title had become Marquis of Londonderry). Others, such as Viscount Palmerston, were to find an Irish peerage compatible with not being an elected Irish representative peer.

The Act of Union with Ireland went into effect January 1, 1801, and by the time Castlereagh attended the new House of Commons, he had resigned as chief secretary. George III obstinately refused to accept ending the barriers to Roman Catholics being elected to the House of Commons and to their holding office. No precise pledge had been made by Pitt or Castlereagh, but Pitt's cabinet had been favorable and Castlereagh hopeful.

Castlereagh hoped that with political union accomplished, the Roman Catholics would receive not only equal civil rights but also relief from tithes paid to support the Anglican Church in Ireland. He hoped that the state would increase funds for the education of both Roman Catholic and non-Anglican Protestant clergy in Ireland. None of these measures passed in his lifetime. The immediate result of the royal opposition was the resignation of Pitt with many cabinet colleagues and the departure of both Cornwallis and Castlereagh from their Irish posts. On arriving at Westminster, Castlereagh sat near Pitt on the government back benches, while Henry Addington succeeded Pitt as prime minister. Castlereagh believed that if Pitt had not been so tired and ill he might have dealt with the king more effectively.

Castlereagh had no intention of joining the opposition, however, and in fact accepted office as president of the Board of Control (India) under Addington in 1802. He had to mediate between East India Company directors in London and the governor-general in India, which required tactful management of prickly personalities. When Pitt returned as prime minister, he kept Castlereagh as president and made him secretary for war in July, 1805. Though Castlereagh lost both offices the next year, after Pitt's death, he alone of the cabinet had sat with Pitt in the House of Commons, sharing with him the negotiations with Czar Alexander I in 1805, the basis for Castlereagh's own foreign policy in 1815.

Back at the War Office in 1807, Castlereagh improved the recruitment procedure and developed the militia for home defense. The disastrous military failure at Walcheren led him to resign in 1809. Rivalry with George Canning preceded his resignation. Castlereagh challenged Canning, and their duel was fought September 21, 1809. On the second firing, he wounded Canning. Contemporaries thought the duel unnecessary as well as undesirable. Certainly it revealed the emotions churning behind Castlereagh's mask of cold indifference to public opinion. His view was that Canning's intrigues to oust him from office justified the duel and his insistence on a second shot. Castlereagh returned to office as foreign secretary in 1812 and, when Prime Minister Spencer Perceval was assassinated on May 11, 1812, as leader of the House of Commons under the premiership of Lord Liverpool. He held both positions until his death ten years later.

Castlereagh now revealed on a grander scale the qualities already exhibited as chief secretary in Ireland. Industry, method, and application won a greater acceptance if not acclaim. Castlereagh never equaled Pitt's Biscayan roll in oratory or Canning's memorable eloquence. Similarly, his French, while fluent, was so far from idiomatic as to reduce sophisticates such as the Princess Lieven to fits of laughter. The House of Commons listened to him carefully for his substance, not his style.

As Pitt's heir, Castlereagh promoted allied unity first of all. If he made little headway in 1813, he was eventually successful with the Treaty of Chaumont, March 9, 1814, which not only bound the allies to continue the war against Napoleon but also committed them to work together for twenty years afterward to secure the peace. Pitt's blueprint for postwar Europe had included an enlarged Netherlands, backed by Prussia, and an enlarged Piedmont, backed by Austria. The czar had agreed with Pitt that the war was against Napoleon, not against the French people. Therefore, a generous peace was most likely to stabilize postwar France. In 1805, neither Pitt nor Alexander I was committed to a restoration of the Bourbons, but both wished to establish something like a concert of Europe to avert future wars.

Castlereagh achieved most of the British objectives in the first Peace of Paris, May 30, 1814. France was left with its 1792 borders and no indemnity. Castlereagh was criticized for allowing France a five-year delay in abolishing the slave trade, though this was certainly congruent with the basic policy of a lenient peace, to assist the restored Bourbon monarchy as arranged by Talleyrand. At the Congress of Vienna, Castlereagh's most daring initiative came when he organized a secret alliance of Austria, France, and England against Prussian demands.

There was little that Castlereagh could do about the Russian occupation of Poland, but the Prussians were forced to back down and accept a compromise over Saxony. Napoleon's return, ousting Louis XVIII from his throne, brought a new crisis. Again, Castlereagh was calm and persevering. He defeated those in Parliament who were ready to patch up a peace with Napoleon and, after Waterloo, outmaneuvered those who were now determined to have a punitive peace.

France was reduced to the frontiers of 1790 and had to pay an indemnity and accept an occupation force. The Bourbons were restored, however, and Wellington supported Castlereagh for this comparatively lenient peace. Castlereagh's crowning diplomatic achievement was winning parliamentary support for the Quadruple Alliance, accepted in England as of February 20, 1816. The agreement bound the allies to maintain the peace and to meet together periodically: the concert of Europe, or congress system, idea.

The first of the congresses, held at Aix-la-Chapelle in 1818, saw the completion of arrangements for payment of the indemnity, an end to the occupation, and the acceptance of France as a peacekeeping partner in what now became the Quintuple Alliance. Thereafter, difficulties posed by revolutions in Spain and Italy made Castlereagh more reluctant than Prince Metternich to support a policy of military intervention. At Troppau in 1820, the English sent only an observer, and they did the same at Laibach in 1821. Castlereagh was drawing a distinction between deterring aggressors bent on destroying the international balance of power worked out in 1815 and intervening in the internal politics of states, as Metternich and the czar were more inclined to do. Castlereagh met Metternich for the last time in October, 1821, in Hanover. They understood that their main objective, peace, was the same, even if their tactics differed.

At home, Castlereagh suffered great unpopularity for the repressive measures that he was responsible for steering through the House of Commons. It is fair to say that, like his mentor Pitt, he continued to support repression long after the evidence of clear and present danger had passed away. It is curious that he was singled out far more than his colleagues Lord Liverpool and Lord Sidmouth (as Addington had become) for the ferocious attacks by critics. Perhaps he drew more fire because he was so visible as Leader of the House, perhaps because his lofty disdain enraged more opponents.

By 1822, Castlereagh's labors had worn him out. Observers feared for his sanity after the end of the parliamentary session. Wellington insisted that his doctor accompany him to his country retreat in Kent. There, on August 12, 1822, he committed suicide by cutting his throat. He was certainly deranged. It is less clear that his principal delusion was fear of blackmail for a homosexual offense in which he had been entrapped. Wellington dismissed this as sheer delusion. Psychohistorians might ask why that particular delusion. His widow insisted on burial in Westminster Abbey, and the hostile mob followed him there, jeering and hooting. Some obituaries were outright jubilant. Nevertheless, a dispassionate assessment would award Castlereagh high marks both for his farsighted views respecting the conciliation of Roman Catholics in Ireland and for his enlightened commitment to European peace through periodic conferences.

SIGNIFICANCE

There seems little doubt that without the blocking of Roman Catholic emancipation by the Crown, the history of the United Kingdom would have been happier; it is at least possible that the Irish problem in the form confronting Sir Robert Peel and later William Ewart Gladstone might have vanished. Viscount Castlereagh's vision at least offered that possibility. In foreign affairs, Castlereagh could not have hoped to hold the line precisely where he had drawn it in 1820, even if he had lived.

Castlereagh's death certainly accelerated the collapse of his policy as Metternich turned to reliance on Russia, and Canning, Castlereagh's successor, abandoned the commitment to Europe. Most contemporary English criticism was shortsighted or simply unfair. For example, Castlereagh never had anything to do with the "Holy Alliance," that strange vision of Czar Alexander. Castlereagh's vision of some means to anticipate and deter the menace of future Napoleons long survived the details of his diplomacy. Not surprisingly, in 1919, when another great peace conference was to be held, the Foreign Office went back to the records of Castlereagh's peacemaking to guide the English delegation at Versailles.

—*Barry McGill*

FURTHER READING

Bartlett, Christopher J. *Castlereagh*. New York: Charles Scribner's Sons, 1966. The author discounts the blackmail delusion as the proximate cause for Castlereagh's suicide. Contains a good bibliography.

_____. "Castlereagh, 1812-1822." In *The Makers of British Policy: From Pitt to Thatcher*, edited by T. G. Otte. New York: Palgrave, 2002. This essay about Castlereagh is included in a book about prominent British statesmen from the Glorious Revolution to 1991.

Hyde, H. Montgomery. *The Rise of Lord Castlereagh*. London: Macmillan, 1933. This is the fullest treatment of the early years. Hyde rejects the blackmail story out of hand.

_____. *The Strange Death of Lord Castlereagh*. London: Heinemann, 1959. Here Hyde reverses himself completely concerning the suicide without giving any cogent reasons for the reversal.

Leigh, Ione. *Castlereagh*. London: Collins, 1951. Until Bartlett's study (see above) this was the best short biography, and it is better organized.

Nicholson, Harold. *The Congress of Vienna: A Study in Allied Unity, 1812-1822*. New York: Grove Press, 2000. A reprint of the classic book originally published in 1947. Nicholson provides a comprehensive narrative of the negotiations at the Congress and the power struggle among Castlereagh and other participants.

Webster, Charles K. *The Congress of Vienna*. London: G. Bell and Sons, 1945. This is a reprint of the London Foreign Office booklet printed in 1919 and used by the British delegates at Versailles.

_____. *The Foreign Policy of Castlereagh, 1812-1815*. London: G. Bell and Sons, 1931. The first volume of a magisterial study that, while not uncritical, rescues Castlereagh from the more ridiculous charges made against him.

_____. *The Foreign Policy of Castlereagh, 1815-1822*. London: G. Bell and Sons, 1947. Sequel to the preceding volume.

SEE ALSO: George Canning; Second Earl of Liverpool; Metternich; Napoleon I.

RELATED ARTICLES in *Great Events from History: The Nineteenth Century, 1801-1900:* April 11, 1814-July 29, 1830: France's Bourbon Dynasty Is Restored; August 13, 1814: Britain Acquires the Cape Colony; September 15, 1814-June 11, 1815: Congress of Vienna; February 17, 1815: Treaty of Ghent Takes Effect; November 20, 1815: Second Peace of Paris; July 2, 1820-March, 1821: Neapolitan Revolution; October 20-30, 1822: Great Britain Withdraws from the Concert of Europe; December 2, 1823: President Monroe Articulates the Monroe Doctrine.

GEORGE CATLIN

American painter

Catlin painted some of the earliest depictions of the culture of the upper Missouri River Valley Indians, and his books include much significant ethnological material about tribal ceremonies.

BORN: July 26, 1796; Wilkes-Barre, Pennsylvania
DIED: December 23, 1872; Jersey City, New Jersey
AREAS OF ACHIEVEMENT: Art, scholarship

EARLY LIFE

George Catlin was the fifth of fourteen children born to Polly Sutton and Putnam Catlin, and he achieved the most fame. Polly, his mother, had been born on the Pennsylvania frontier and as a child had been captured by the Indians during the 1778 "Wyoming Massacre." His Connecticut-born father, Putnam Catlin, served as a fife major during the American Revolution. After the war, Putnam studied law, moved to Wilkes-Barre, and married Polly Sutton. The Catlins hoped that young George would become a lawyer also, and in 1817, they sent the twenty-one-year-old back to Connecticut to study.

After Catlin completed his training, in less than two years he returned home with reasonable skills but little enthusiasm for the law. Rather, he wanted to become a portrait painter, and even during court proceedings he sketched scenes and people in the room. Sometime between 1821 and 1823, he quit his law practice and moved to Philadelphia, where he set out on his life's work. A handsome young man of no more than five feet nine inches, he had a deep scar on his left cheek, black hair, blue eyes, and a medium complexion. He was a friendly, outgoing person who made friends easily and usually kept them for life. These attributes enabled him to penetrate the artistic society in Philadelphia, and by early 1824, he became a member of the Pennsylvania Academy, the literary and artistic group in that city.

Soon Catlin had enough commissions for miniatures and portraits, and financial security seemed at hand, yet he was restless and dissatisfied. A visiting group of Indian leaders who were in the East to negotiate with the government caught his attention. They seemed natural and dignified compared to his city acquaintances, and Catlin decided to paint them and record their customs. Before he could do so, he continued to do portraits and to make friends with wealthy and prominent people to finance his later western travels. While in Albany, New York, working on a portrait of Governor DeWitt Clinton, Catlin met Clara Bartless Gregory, and on

May 20, 1828, the two were married. Between portrait assignments, Catlin traveled to nearby reservations to paint Indian leaders, and he did several portraits of the noted Seneca leader Red Jacket. Despite his marriage, his continuing restlessness overcame him, and in early 1830, Catlin set out for St. Louis to begin what was to be his life's work: painting, observing, and describing the western Indians.

LIFE'S WORK

In St. Louis, Catlin met the famous explorer William Clark, who was then superintendent for Indian affairs for the tribes beyond the Mississippi. Clark knew the western tribes as well as anyone and proved to be very helpful. He answered Catlin's questions and invited him to paint portraits of the Indians who came to the city to confer with him. During the summer of 1830, Catlin accompanied Clark to Prairie du Chien, Wisconsin, to observe a treaty council meeting there, and later that same year, they visited Indians encamped along the Kansas River. In late 1830, Catlin traveled to Fort Leavenworth to observe and paint tribes there, while the next spring, he accompanied an Indian agent up the Missouri River to what is now Omaha, to visit other villages. By the end of 1831, the artist had observed, met, and painted Indians from perhaps fifteen distinct tribes, and he had acquired artifacts from many of them in addition to his sketches and portraits.

Still, Catlin wanted to observe villages and tribes that were farther removed from white society. His chance came in March, 1832, when he set off up the Missouri River on the American Fur Company steamboat *Yellowstone*, traveling upstream to Fort Union, at the mouth of the Yellowstone River in western North Dakota. Catlin worked as rapidly as possible, painting as many as five or six pictures a day. From Fort Union, Catlin and two trappers went back down the Missouri in a small skiff. Along the way, they halted at the Mandan villages in central North Dakota, where Catlin drew detailed pictures of the Mandan Okeepa Ceremony. Five years later, a smallpox epidemic virtually destroyed this tribe; his data, as a result, constitute almost the only information about the ceremony that survived.

Two years later, Catlin accompanied an army expedition west onto the southern plains. Catlin also traveled north to Fort Snelling at what is now Minneapolis-St. Paul to paint villagers there. In 1836, he decided to visit the famous Pipe Stone Quarry in southwestern Minnesota, the site from which the Lakota (Sioux) obtained the red stone that they used for their pipes. Despite the Indians' efforts to discourage them, Catlin and several companions traveled to the quarry, where he made sketches and gathered samples of the stone. A geologist later named the mineral Catlinite in his honor. By this time, Catlin had executed approximately six hundred paintings and sketches of Indians, as well as collecting artifacts that varied from a Crow tepee to beads and feather headdresses. He had taken copious notes that he would later transcribe and publish along with his drawings.

By 1837, Catlin had moved this collection east, and late that year, he began exhibiting his paintings and artifacts, or Indian Gallery, as he called the collection. The exhibit drew large crowds, and he soon took it to Washington, Philadelphia, and Boston. Catlin, however, proved to be an inept businessperson. He hoped to sell his material to the U.S. government and worked for some years to interest Congress in buying it. When it became apparent that the government had little serious interest in Indian materials, a disappointed Catlin set sail for England. He arrived there in 1839 and again exhibited before large and enthusiastic crowds. In 1841, he published the first of his several books about the Indians. Always short of money, by 1845 he moved to Paris, where he was asked to exhibit the paintings at the Louvre.

Catlin's years in France were among the most unhappy of his life. On the edge of bankruptcy, and with little chance of getting back to the United States, he became discouraged at the news that Congress voted repeatedly not to buy his paintings. Then, in July, 1845, his wife, Clara, died of pneumonia, and a year later his three-year-old son George died as well. His wife's family arranged for his three daughters to return to the United States, but Catlin remained mired in debt and unable to leave Paris. In 1852, Joseph Harrison, a wealthy American, bought Catlin's paintings and took them back to Philadelphia, leaving the artist more or less free from debt. With little more than determination, he began to paint new copies of his original Indian Gallery during the 1850's. He also made several trips to South America and to the West Coast of North America. In 1870, he returned to the United States and was reunited with his daughters. Catlin died in 1872, believing that his country had spurned his life's work.

Ironically, had Congress bought the paintings during the 1840's, they would not have survived the Smithsonian fire. As it was, when Catlin's exhibit of his cartoon collection failed in New York in 1870, Joseph Henry of the Smithsonian invited the artist to display them in Washington.

SIGNIFICANCE

George Catlin stands out as a man with single-minded purpose: to preserve knowledge of the western Indians, their dress and customs, for all Americans. This goal took him west, where he painted Indians from dozens of tribes. As art, his work does not rank as great. He was largely self-taught, and he often painted hurriedly and under crude conditions. When he had time, he used a style similar to that which he had employed as a Philadelphia portrait painter. Often he sketched quickly, focusing on a person's face and barely sketching in the remainder of the body. Regardless of the style, Catlin's work is considered among the most accurate and unadorned in depicting Native Americans. Hundreds of his paintings have survived, and he did succeed in preserving knowledge of Indian life.

In addition to his paintings, Catlin kept knowledge of the Indians alive in other ways. As a showman and exhibitor, he exposed thousands of Americans to Indian scenes and artifacts during the mid-nineteenth century. Of more significance, his writings provide valuable ethnological data for knowledge of the tribal societies that he visited. His more significant books include *Letters and Notes on the Manners, Customs, and Conditions of North American Indians* (1841), *Catlin's North American Indian Portfolio* (1844), *Life Amongst the Indians* (1861), and *Last Rambles Amongst the Indians of the Rocky Mountains and the Andes* (1867). In addition to these, Catlin published catalogs of his exhibits and many articles for newspapers in the United States. Throughout his career, he labored to bring knowledge of the Indians to white society. For artists and ethnologists, his legacy is rich.

—*Roger L. Nichols*

FURTHER READING

Catlin, George. *Episodes from Life Among the Indians and Last Rambles*. Edited by Marvin C. Ross. Norman: University of Oklahoma Press, 1959. Includes selections from Catlin's first and last books about his experiences with Indians. This well-edited collection includes more than 150 photographs of Catlin's paintings.

_____. *George Catlin and His Indian Gallery*. Edited by George Gurney and Therese Thau Heyman. Washington, D.C.: Smithsonian American Art Museum, 2002. Includes 275 reproductions of the Catlin paintings in the Smithsonian's collection. Also features essays about his life and work.

_____. *Letters and Notes on the Manners, Customs, and Conditions of North American Indians*. 2 vols. London: D. Bogue, 1841. Reprint. Mineola, N.Y.: Dover, 1973. A clearly reprinted edition of Catlin's most significant ethnological writing, done only a few years after he left the West.

Dippie, Brian W. *Catlin and His Contemporaries: The Politics of Patronage*. Lincoln: University of Nebraska Press, 1990. Examines Catlin's battle to seek patronage and make a living from his artwork, including his efforts to persuade the U.S. government to purchase his Indian Gallery.

Ewers, John C. *Artists of the Old West*. New York: Doubleday, 1965. Ewers is probably the most knowledgeable student of Catlin's contributions to ethnology, and he discusses those in his chapter on Catlin.

Haberly, Loyd. *Pursuit of the Horizon: A Life of George Catlin, Painter and Recorder of the American Indian*. New York: Macmillan, 1948. A full-length popular biography of Catlin that gives a balanced treatment of his long life, including his years in Europe. It has neither notes nor bibliography but is based on solid research.

Hassrick, Royal B. *The George Catlin Book of American Indians*. New York: Watson-Guptill, 1977. This volume, featuring both color and black-and-white plates, reproduces a generous selection of Catlin's paintings. It briefly discusses his life, art, and writings, but its value lies chiefly in the illustrations.

Haverstock, Mary Sayre. *Indian Gallery: The Story of George Catlin*. New York: Four Winds Press, 1973. This popular biography focuses primarily on Catlin's pre-1839 activities. The last four decades of his life are compressed into a mere fifty pages.

McCraken, Harold. *George Catlin and the Old Frontier*. New York: Dial Press, 1959. The result of thorough research, this well-written biography focuses almost entirely on Catlin's life to 1839; it devotes only two of twenty-two chapters to his career between 1839 and 1872.

Moore, Robert J., Jr. *Native Americans, a Portrait: The Art and Travels of Charles Bird King, George Catlin, and Karl Bodmer*. New York: Stewart, Tabori & Chang, 1997. Contains more than one thousand images of artwork by these three Native American artists, including more than three hundred works reproduced in color. Also features an essay by Moore, placing their art within the context of American politics during the 1830's, when the government was forcibly removing Native Americans from their homelands.

Roehm, Marjorie Catlin. *The Letters of George Catlin and His Family: A Chronicle of the American West.* Berkeley: University of California Press, 1966. Based on several hundred Catlin family letters used for the first time, this book combines the author's narrative with extensive selections from family correspondence. Half of the book considers Catlin's activities after he left the country. The use of family papers gives an immediacy to the story.

SEE ALSO: Albert Bierstadt; George Caleb Bingham.

RELATED ARTICLE in *Great Events from History: The Nineteenth Century, 1801-1900:* November 21, 1817-March 27, 1858: Seminole Wars.

COUNT CAVOUR

Italian politician

As prime minister between 1852 and 1861, Cavour gave Piedmont the economic and diplomatic leadership of Italy and played a key role in the country's political unification. He is generally regarded as the founder of modern Italy.

BORN: August 10, 1810; Turin, Piedmont, French Empire (now in Italy)

DIED: June 6, 1861; Turin, Italy

ALSO KNOWN AS: Camillo Benso di Cavour (birth name)

AREA OF ACHIEVEMENT: Government and politics

EARLY LIFE

Count Camillo Benso di Cavour (kah-VEWR) was the son of a woman, Adèle de Sellon, who had come from a line of wealthy Huguenots who had been expelled from France by Louis XIV and had settled in Geneva. His father, the Marquis Michele Benso di Cavour, was the head of an ancient noble family, a businessperson and administrator who rose to high office in the reactionary regime of Restoration Piedmont. Cavour soon rejected this world. As a second son, he was expected to make his living in the army, but, while attending Turin's Royal Military Academy, he was frequently punished for rebelling against military routines. He was graduated in 1826 and served in the army for five years, while formulating increasingly liberal political views. After the revolution of 1830, in which Charles X of France was overthrown, Cavour was put under surveillance by Piedmontese authorities as a dangerous radical. In November, 1831, he resigned his commission.

Cavour was eager for a political career, but his ambitions remained blocked by Piedmont's autocratic government for the next sixteen years. Instead, he engaged in various economic activities, such as supervising family estates; investing in new factories, banks, and railway companies; and speculating profitably in government securities and foreign exchange. He also devoted himself to the study of political and economic developments in Great Britain and France, visiting both countries periodically and acquiring a deep admiration for the ideas of Jeremy Bentham and the practices of François Guizot and Sir Robert Peel.

By the mid-1830's, he had become an advocate of the *juste milieu*, or middle way, which he thought would obviate the dangers posed by the extremes of reaction and revolution. Specifically, he recommended a parliamentary government controlled by an educated, wealthy elite that would promote social progress by means of gradual, rational reform. Thus, after briefly espousing radical opinions in his youth, Cavour adopted a liberal-conservative stance that he maintained for the rest of his life.

LIFE'S WORK

Cavour's political opportunity finally arrived as a result of King Charles Albert's reluctant reforms during the revolutionary atmosphere of the late 1840's. In 1847, Cavour was one of the founders and the editor of a moderate liberal newspaper, *Il Risorgimento*. In 1848, he served on the commission that established a restricted parliamentary franchise similar to his own ideal and, in June, was elected to the Chamber of Deputies.

Initially, Cavour's chances of rapid political advancement must have appeared slim, for he had neither parliamentary allies nor a commanding personal presence. He was short and stocky, with a round face, thinning, reddish hair, a scanty beard, and spectacles, and was more familiar with the French language than Italian, which he spoke imperfectly and unattractively. However, he proved an engaging character, self-confident, down-to-earth, humorous, and conscientious, with the somewhat racy image of an incorrigible gambler, a lifelong bachelor, and a womanizer.

More important, Cavour was a highly skilled politician, well versed in parliamentary practice, and an extremely penetrating, logical speaker. He quickly won the allegiance of conservatives by backing Massimo d'Azeglio's center-right government and of leftists by supporting the Siccardi laws against ecclesiastical privileges. It thus came as no surprise when he was appointed minister of marine, commerce, and agriculture in October, 1850, added the Finance Ministry six months later, and became the dominant figure in the government. He was able to seize complete power in 1852, when Azeglio resigned in protest at the senate's rejection of a civil-marriage bill. Cavour was a rationalist who generally sympathized with attempts to reduce the Church's authority, but on this occasion he agreed to King Victor Emmanuel II's demand that the bill be abandoned and was appointed prime minister on November 4.

Count Cavour. (Library of Congress)

During the early years of his premiership, Cavour concentrated on domestic affairs, attempting to convert backward Piedmont into the most progressive and powerful country in Italy. Accordingly, he resisted royal attempts to subvert parliament's constitutional supremacy, resumed the attack on the Church by dissolving half of the monasteries in 1855, and increased military expenditure. In addition, he terminated Piedmont's dependence on costly loans from the Rothschilds' Paris bank and promoted economic growth by expanding bank credit; financing the development of mines, railways, and utilities; and maintaining tariff agreements that he had negotiated earlier as finance minister. As a result, Piedmont became the only liberal, reforming state in the peninsula and the acknowledged leader of the Italian national cause.

Cavour's important contribution to that cause was a tribute to his remarkable flexibility and opportunism. At heart a Piedmontese nationalist, he was concerned to further the interests of his native state. To do so, he invariably opposed revolutionary efforts by republicans such as Giuseppe Garibaldi and Giuseppe Mazzini but otherwise was prepared to modify tactics and objectives in the light of experience and circumstances. During the 1840's, he expected the Italians themselves to expel Austria and create a Turin-based, northern kingdom to the exclusion of the central and southern parts of Italy. Austria's easy victories over Piedmont in 1849, however, convinced him that little could be achieved without foreign aid, and he carefully avoided hostilities until the Crimean War. Before its outbreak, Cavour was reluctant to meet British and French requests for help and did so in 1855 only in order to foil Victor Emmanuel's plan to replace him with a more warlike minister. Nevertheless, participation in the war proved a boon.

On the one hand, the army's creditable performance increased Piedmont's prestige in Italy. On the other, at the Congress of Paris in 1856 Cavour raised the Italian question in an international forum for the first time and learned that Napoleon III was sympathetic to the idea of a moderately powerful, independent kingdom in northern Italy. Subsequently, he maintained contact with the emperor and, in 1858, negotiated the secret Pact of Plombières, committing France to send military assistance in return for territorial concessions if Cavour engineered a crisis in which Austria appeared the aggressor. He was able to do so in April, 1859, largely because of Austria's foolish ultimatum demanding unilateral demobilization by Piedmont.

During the resultant war, stiff Austrian resistance led Napoleon to withdraw after two narrow victories and negotiate the Armistice of Villafranca with Emperor Francis Joseph. Cavour, who was not invited to the talks, was bitterly disappointed at the peace terms, which obliged Austria to cede only Lombardy and ordered the restoration to the central Italian duchies of absolutist rulers who had been ousted during the war and replaced by Piedmontese sympathizers. On learning that Victor Emmanuel had accepted the terms, he angrily resigned on July 11, 1859.

During the last two years of Cavour's life, a series of unexpected developments enabled him to achieve goals he had previously dismissed as impracticable. While he was out of office, the faltering alliance with the French was replaced by British support. Foreign Minister Lord John Russell criticized the Villafranca agreement as unworkable, insisting that Italians be allowed to determine their own future, and pressured Victor Emmanuel into reinstating Cavour in January, 1860. On his return, he was thus fully confident that Piedmont's control would soon be extended into central Italy.

In March, after Cavour had guaranteed Napoleon's acquiescence by ceding Nice and Savoy to France, plebiscites were held in Modena, Parma, Romagna, and Tuscany, whose subjects voted overwhelmingly for annexation. At this juncture, Cavour looked for a lengthy period of peace in which the new territories could be consolidated, but his hopes were rudely shattered by Garibaldi's startling conquest of Sicily and Naples between May and September, 1860. Desperate to prevent Italian leadership's falling into popular, democratic hands, he first convinced Napoleon that his purpose was to protect the pope from advancing revolutionaries and then boldly sent the army south. Having taken Umbria and the Marche, the central and eastern parts of the Papal States, it entered Naples, where Garibaldi relinquished authority to Victor Emmanuel in late October. Subsequently, the people of Naples, the Marche, and Umbria voted for annexation by Piedmont.

In January, 1861, elections were held for a national parliament that, on March 17, gave the Italian crown to Victor Emmanuel. Tragically, Cavour was unable to enjoy the fruits of his triumph, for soon afterward he contracted a fever, probably malaria, and died on June 6, 1861.

SIGNIFICANCE

Count Cavour's achievements fully justify his reputation as one of the most successful statesmen in modern European history. In a mere eight years, he made Piedmont the leading Italian state and, with a rare combination of diplomatic skill, opportunism, and military daring, unified most of the peninsula. When he died, the only remaining independent territories were Venetia and Rome, which were added in 1866 and 1870.

However, Cavour's legacy was by no means untarnished. Essentially, the process of unification entailed the imposition on all Italy of Piedmont's political system, which gave power to the largely anticlerical upper middle class. In conjunction with Cavour's seizure of papal territory, the extension of the political system contributed to the rift that was to divide church and state for the remainder of the century. It also aroused intense hostility among the thousands who had fought or voted for annexation expecting democracy, and aggravated the serious class and regional conflicts that racked Italian society. Equally detrimental were Cavour's methods of controlling parliament, such as tampering with elections, invalidating unfavorable returns, and disarming opposition by giving office to its moderate elements. The latter practice underlay the *connubio* (marriage), which united Cavour's moderate conservative deputies and Urbano Rattazzi's center-left group from 1852 to 1857, when leftist electoral losses facilitated a return to the Right.

Such expedients enabled Cavour to establish a virtual dictatorship, unfettered by king, cabinet, or parliament. Whether he viewed them as temporary, emergency measures is unclear because he died so soon after the prolonged national crisis ended. After 1861, the imitation of these measures by less talented politicians produced many of the features that characterized later Italian politics, including a tendency to tolerate autocratic power, the absence of cabinet responsibility, and reliance on fluctuating centrist coalitions that survived only by avoiding controversial issues. Thus, Cavour can be viewed as the founder not only of the Italian state but also of traditions responsible for its chronic political weakness.

—Ian Duffy

FURTHER READING

Blumberg, Arnold. *A Carefully Planned Accident: The Italian War of 1859*. Selinsgrove, Pa.: Susquehanna University Press, 1990. A history of the war against Austria, including Cavour's role in provoking the conflict.

Coppa, Frank J. *Camillo di Cavour*. Boston: Twayne, 1973. A brief, well-written biography by an American

Catholic scholar, focusing on aspects of Cavour's career not normally stressed. Particularly useful for church-state relations and diplomacy prior to Plombières. Contains a detailed bibliography with some omissions.

Di Scala, Spencer. *Italy from Revolution to Republic: 1700 to the Present*. 3d ed. Boulder, Colo.: Westview Press, 2004. Includes a section on the Risorgimento unification movement, with chapter 8 entitled "Cavour and the Piedmontese Solution."

Hearder, Harry. *Cavour*. 2d ed. London: Historical Association, 1985. An updated version of a 1972 pamphlet. Provides an excellent introduction, with sections on Cavour's life, opinions, and achievements, and a well-balanced assessment of his contribution to Italian history. Contains a useful, short bibliography.

Mack Smith, Denis. *Cavour*. New York: Alfred A. Knopf, 1985. A fully documented, lucid biography, containing much fresh information and new insights. Good on all aspects of Cavour's life, particularly on economic policies and the development of his character. Contains a useful bibliographical note. Essential reading.

_____. *Cavour and Garibaldi, 1860: A Study in Political Conflict*. Cambridge, England: Cambridge University Press, 1954. Reprint. Cambridge, England: Cambridge University Press, 1985. A seminal work based on newly released archival material. Brilliantly clarifies the complex events of 1860, demonstrating the conflicts between Italian leaders and undermining traditional myths about Cavour. The 1985 reissue includes the author's reflections on the controversy generated by the original edition.

Riall, Lucy. *The Italian Risorgimento: State, Society, and National Unification*. London: Routledge, 1994. A history of the Risorgimento unification movement and Cavour's participation in it.

Whyte, A. J. *The Early Life and Letters of Cavour, 1810-1848*. London: Oxford University Press, 1925. A scholarly account of Cavour's life before his entry into Parliament, making extensive use of his correspondence. Offers useful insights into his character and his preparations for a political career.

_____. *The Political Life and Letters of Cavour, 1848-1861*. London: Oxford University Press, 1930. The sequel to the above entry, with similar qualities. Deals with Cavour's political career, emphasizing his diplomatic activities.

SEE ALSO: Giuseppe Garibaldi; Napoleon III; Pius IX.

RELATED ARTICLES in *Great Events from History: The Nineteenth Century, 1801-1900:* 1831: Mazzini Founds Young Italy; October 4, 1853-March 30, 1856: Crimean War; July 11, 1859: Napoleon III and Francis Joseph I Meet at Villafranca; May-July, 1860: Garibaldi's Redshirts Land in Sicily; March 17, 1861: Italy Is Proclaimed a Kingdom.

GEORGE CAYLEY

English inventor

Cayley was the first inventor to publish a description of the essential components of airplanes—namely, the concept that an airplane should consist of one or more fixed wings, a fuselage, and a tail. Moreover, he was the first to carry out a serious program of aeronautical research.

BORN: December 27, 1773; Scarborough, Yorkshire, England

DIED: December 15, 1857; Brompton, Yorkshire, England

ALSO KNOWN AS: Sir George Cayley

AREA OF ACHIEVEMENT: Science and technology

EARLY LIFE

George Cayley was born in a Scarborough house named Paradise. His mother, Isabella Seton Cayley, was a member of a well-known Scottish family descended from Robert Bruce. His father, Sir Thomas Cayley, was descended from the eleventh century Norman invaders of England. Because of the chronic ill health of Cayley's father, Cayley's parents spent much time abroad, and Cayley's early days were spent at the family house at Helmsley, where he enjoyed much freedom. There, he acquired an early interest in mechanical devices, and he was frequently to be found at the village watchmaker.

After the death of Cayley's grandfather (also Sir George Cayley), the major and extensive family estate at Brompton passed quickly to Cayley's father, who lived for only another eighteen months, and then to George Cayley. By the year 1792, Sir George Cayley had become the sixth baronet at Brompton Hall—at the early age of eighteen. He was to spend the rest of his life as a moderately well-to-do Yorkshire country squire.

As was not unusual in the eighteenth century, Cayley had virtually no formal education. There is some evidence that he went to school briefly in York, but his main education stemmed from two powerful and influential tutors: George Walker, a mathematician of high reputation, a Fellow of the Royal Society, and a man of extensive intellect; and George Morgan, a Unitarian minister, scientist, and lecturer on electricity. Both tutors were freethinkers, and they had a major impact on the wide breadth of education and open-mindedness acquired by Cayley during the first twenty-five years of his life. Cayley never lost his enthusiasm for knowledge and invention; by the early nineteenth century he was recognized and sought after as one of England's leading scholars in matters of science, technology, and social ethics.

Struck by the beauty and intelligence of his first tutor's daughter, Sarah Walker, Cayley fell deeply in love in 1792, the same year in which he acquired the family estate at Brompton. Three years later they were married; their marriage was to last for sixty-two years, ended only by Cayley's death in 1857.

Cayley's contributions to aeronautics also began in his early life. At the age of nineteen, he designed and flew a simple helicopter-like model made of wood and feathers and powered by a string-and-bow mechanism. This was the leading edge of a virtual outpouring of aeronautical thought, research, and invention to follow for the next eighteen years.

LIFE'S WORK

The concept of the modern airplane—namely, that of a machine with fixed wings, fuselage, and horizontal and vertical tail—was first advanced by Cayley in 1799. This concept was a marked departure from all previous aeronautical thinking, which was focused on machines called ornithopters, characterized by flapping wings for both lift and propulsion—an idea fostered from the Greek and Roman ages in an attempt to emulate bird flight directly. Cayley's idea was ingenious. It involved the separation of the mechanisms for producing lift and thrust: A fixed wing, inclined to the airflow, would produce the lift, and a separate mechanism using either flappers or an airscrew driven by an internal combustion engine would provide the propulsion. In 1799, Cayley etched a picture of his airplane concept on a small silver disk (about the size of an American quarter); this disk is the first rendering of the modern airplane, and it is now displayed with distinction at the British Science Museum in South Kensington, London.

In 1804, Cayley designed and successfully flew a hand-launched glider made of wood and cloth, incorporating his fixed-wing, fuselage, and tail concept. It was the first modern-configuration airplane to fly in history. During the first decade of the nineteenth century, Cayley carried out numerous aeronautical experiments, the results of which were published in a momentous "triple paper" titled "On Aerial Navigation," which appeared in three issues of *Nicholson's Journal of Natural Philosophy, Chemistry, and the Arts* (November, 1809; February, 1810; and March, 1810).

Cayley's paper published many "firsts" in the technical development of aeronautics. Cayley was, for example, the first to use a whirling arm for obtaining aerodynamic data on the lift and drag force exerted on winglike shapes; the first to realize that lift is obtained from the combination of low pressure on the top surface of the wing and high pressure on the bottom surface; the first to recognize that a cambered (curved) airfoil shape produces more lift than a straight, flat surface; the first to realize that a dihedral angle (wings bent upward slightly from the center section) achieves lateral (rolling) stability for the airplane; and the first to obtain research results on aeronautical streamlining to reduce drag. This triple paper by Cayley is of such aeronautical and historical significance that it was reprinted by the Royal Aeronautical Society in 1876, 1910, and 1955; by the American journal *The Aeronautical Annual* in 1895; by two French journals in 1877 and 1912; and, as appendixes, in two definitive books on Cayley, one by J. Laurence Pritchard (1961) and the other by Charles H. Gibbs-Smith (1962).

In concert with his aeronautical interests, Cayley carried out extensive works on the design of internal combustion engines. He recognized that existing steam engines, with their huge external boilers, were much too heavy in relation to their power output to be of any practical application to airplanes. To improve on this situation, Cayley invented the hot-air engine in 1799 and spent the next fifty-eight years of his life trying to perfect the idea, along with a host of other mechanical designers of that day. The invention of the successful gas-fueled engine in France during the mid-nineteenth century finally superseded Cayley's hot-air engine.

For reasons not totally understood, Cayley directed his aeronautical interest to lighter-than-air balloons and airships during the period from 1810 to 1843, making contributions to the understanding of such devices and inventing several designs for steerable airships. Then, from 1843 until his death in 1857, he returned to the airplane, designing and testing several full-scale aircraft. One was a machine with triple wings (a triplane) and human-actuated flappers for propulsion; in 1849 this machine made a floating flight off the ground, carrying a ten-year-old boy for several yards down a hill at Brompton. Another was a single-wing (monoplane) glider, which in 1853 flew across a small valley (no longer than five hundred yards) with Cayley's coachman aboard as an unwilling passenger. (At the end of this flight, the coachman was quoted as saying, "Please, Sir George, I wish to give notice. I was hired to drive and not to fly.")

Although Cayley's standing in history is based on his aeronautical contributions, this broadly educated and liberal-thinking man accomplished much more during his long life of nearly eighty-four years. Of particular note is his invention in 1825 of the tracted land vehicle, a vehicle that was the forerunner of the Caterpillar tractor and the military tanks of the twentieth century. In 1847, he invented an artificial hand. This artificial limb was a breakthrough in such devices, replacing the simple hook that had been in use for centuries. Cayley's interests were purely humane; he expected and received virtually no financial compensation for this invention.

Among Cayley's main other nonaeronautical accomplishments were his contributions to parliamentary reform, leading to a publication on that subject in 1818; election to the chair of the powerful Whig Club at York in 1820; his work as a member of Parliament for Scarborough (starting in 1832); his founding of the Polytechnic Institution in Regent Street, London, in 1839, for scientific and technical exhibitions and education (now the Regent Street Polytechnic, an institution for continuing education); and his inventions to promote railway safety (again, he was driven by a genuine concern for improving the lot of humankind, especially that of the poor). His social conscience was never more in evidence than in his efforts to help unemployed laborers from the York area in 1842; he wrote an appeal for help in the newspapers and contributed a large sum of his own money (although he was not a rich man) to help relieve the social and economic distress in the area.

A portrait of Sir George Cayley hangs in the National Portrait Gallery in London; it was painted when he was sixty-eight years old. It shows a still-handsome man with a soft, kindly, and scholarly countenance. It is no surprise that Cayley was well liked and respected by his family as a father and husband, by his friends as a kind, thoughtful, and humorous country squire, and by his scientific and technical colleagues as one of the most innovative, knowledgeable, and well-read people in England at the time. When Cayley died, peacefully at Brompton Hall on December 15, 1857, many members of social and scientific England strongly felt his loss, as evidenced by numerous obituaries and statements at that time.

SIGNIFICANCE

It is well known that Orville and Wilbur Wright accomplished the first successful, heavier-than-air, powered, manned flight, on December 17, 1903. If Sir George Cayley had been alive at that moment, he would have been the first to applaud the accomplishment, because it is clear from his writings that he took for granted the eventual successful development of the airplane. Contrary to much popular belief, however, the Wright brothers did *not* invent the concept of the airplane; instead, they invented the world's first successful, working airplane. The concept of the modern airplane is Cayley's, and his alone. All modern historians of aviation agree to this, and indeed even the Wright brothers gave credit to Cayley in this regard.

It is interesting to note that credit to Cayley for his aeronautical contributions faded during the last half of the nineteenth century, in spite of his numerous publications in the field. Many would-be inventors in aviation either repeated some of Cayley's work or used his ideas without knowing the source, mainly because of their ignorance of the literature. Historical research in the twentieth century, however, clearly gives Cayley his rightful place in history as the grandparent of modern aviation. He established, in total, all the essential ideas of powered heavier-than-air flight, even including the invention of a lightweight, wire-braced wheel for an undercarriage—a wheel that was to be utilized as the bicycle wheel when that vehicle was invented, during the late 1880's.

—John D. Anderson, Jr.

FURTHER READING

Anderson, John D., Jr. *Introduction to Flight*. 5th ed. Boston: McGraw-Hill, 2005. Includes a lengthy discussion of Cayley's contributions to the development of aviation, entitled "Sir George Cayley: The True Inventor of the Airplane."

_____. *Inventing Flight: The Wright Brothers and Their Predecessors*. Baltimore: Johns Hopkins University Press, 2004. Anderson's history includes a chapter on Cayley's concept of flight and his proposal for the first modern design of a fixed-wing aircraft.

Gibbs-Smith, Charles H. *Aviation: An Historical Survey from Its Origins to the End of World War II*. London: Her Majesty's Stationery Office, 1970. A balanced survey of the historical development of aviation, including Cayley's work. This is a good book from which to obtain an overall perspective on Cayley's contributions in comparison with the complete picture of aeronautical development.

_____. *Sir George Cayley, 1773-1857.* London: Her Majesty's Stationery Office, 1968. An excellent pamphlet printed for the Science Museum, with a concise presentation of Cayley the man and the inventor.

_____. *Sir George Cayley's Aeronautics, 1796-1855.* London: Her Majesty's Stationery Office, 1962. A thorough and definitive historical presentation of Cayley's technical contributions, along with insightful commentary on Cayley's work. A must for any serious student of Cayley's life and contributions.

Hallion, Richard P. *Taking Flight: Inventing the Aerial Age from Antiquity Through the First World War.* New York: Oxford University Press, 2003. Chapter 6, "Sir George Cayley and the Birth of Aeronautics," describes Cayley's work and his influence on the development of aircraft.

Pritchard, J. Laurence. *Sir George Cayley: The Inventor of the Aeroplane.* London: Max Parrish, 1961. This is the definitive biography of Sir George Cayley, a must for any student of his life.

SEE ALSO: Alexander Graham Bell.

RELATED ARTICLE in *Great Events from History: The Nineteenth Century, 1801-1900:* July 2, 1900: Zeppelin Completes the First Flying Dirigible.

CETSHWAYO

Ruler of South Africa's Zulu kingdom (r. 1872-1879)

The last independent Zulu king and the only nineteenth century Zulu ruler to visit England, Cetshwayo delivered one of the most humiliating defeats ever administered to a British imperial force in history and rallied sympathy in Great Britain to the plight of colonized Africans.

BORN: c. 1826; near Eshowe, Zululand (now in South Africa)

DIED: February 8, 1884; Eshowe, Zululand

ALSO KNOWN AS: Cetewayo; Cetywayo; Ketshwayo

AREAS OF ACHIEVEMENT: Government and politics, warfare and conquest

EARLY LIFE

The first son of the Zulu king Mpande, Cetshwayo (keh-TSHWAY-oh) grew up under the shadow of his paternal uncle, the great Shaka, who founded the Zulu kingdom. However, although Cetshwayo was Mpande's oldest son, he was not guaranteed the right to inherit his father's kingship because his mother, Mgqumbhazi, did not rank as Mpande's "great wife." Mpande favored Mbulazi, Cetshwayo's younger brother, as his successor but never formally named him as such. To earn the kingship, Cetshwayo sought to gain popular support. When the Zulu fought a successful campaign against the Swazi people in 1854, Cetshwayo returned home as the hero. Soon many Zulu began comparing him to Shaka, commenting that his appearance, personality, eloquent speech, and singing and dancing skills resembled those of Shaka.

As Cetshwayo gained in popularity, tensions mounted between him and his brother until 1856, when a violent civil war broke out. Mbulazi's izi-Gqoza faction had seven thousand fighting men, and Cetshwayo's Usuthu (a word that became Cetshwayo's battle cry) faction had twenty thousand. Eventually the izi-Gqoza retreated to the Tugela River and were defeated at Ndondakasuka. The Izi-Gqoza were routed, and Cetshwayo became the undisputed heir to the kingship. He then took real control of the kingdom, even though his father was still alive.

Cetshwayo's control of the kingdom did not go uncontested. In an effort to legitimize his rule, Theophilus Shepstone, a British colonial official based in Natal, arrived in 1861 to show that England formally recognized Cetshwayo's rule. Cetshwayo's power was not absolute; warriors owed their primary loyalty to their districts and the chiefs that led them, not to the king. Cetshwayo therefore needed as much support as possible.

LIFE'S WORK

In 1872, when Cetshwayo was made king after his father died, Shepstone attended his coronation. To garner more support, Cetshwayo reinstated the militaristic policies of Shaka by keeping his military well prepared. He also restored Shaka's conscription system, which forbade young men from marrying until they had served in the military.

Despite his military strength and tactics to secure the kingdom, Cetshwayo was not as aggressive as Shaka and did not use Shaka's methods, such as executions, to maintain domestic peace. Rulers of individual districts could order executions, but Cetshwayo himself did not. The only instance when Cetshwayo showed aggression toward his neighbors after becoming king occurred during a cattle shortage in 1878. He asked permission from the colonial administration in Natal to raid the Swazi kingdom for cattle. When Natal denied his request, Cetshwayo did not pursue the matter.

Not everyone in Cetshwayo's kingdom agreed with his policies. In 1878, several hundred men and women defied the marriage ban by marrying without the necessary time in the military. In July of that same year, two adulterous wives of a Zulu chief fled to Natal to avoid execution. Under Zulu law, the women were apprehended and returned to Zululand. The Natal government interpreted the incident as an act of aggression and demanded that Cetshwayo surrender the Zulu men who had crossed into Natal, but Cetshwayo refused. A few months later, two Englishmen who wandered into Zulu territory were briefly detained, and the British regarded that incident as an act of aggression as well. The governor of the Cape Colony, British commissioner for South Africa, Sir Henry Bartle Frere, used the incident to support his claim that the Zulu kingdom needed to be suppressed by force.

On December 11, 1878, an ultimatum written by Frere was delivered to Cetshwayo. It demanded that the Zulu disband their army and abolish military conscription. It gave Cetshwayo only thirty days to complete a task that was impossible, even if he were willing to comply. Not wanting war, Cetshwayo met with his great council to find a means of preserving peace without accepting the British ultimatum. Cetshwayo offered to give the British cattle and to surrender the men who went after the women in Natal. However, the British ignored his offer, and the ultimatum expired.

On January 11, 1879, Frere declared war on the Zulu, thus beginning the brief Zulu War. The British general Lord Chelmsford marched an army into Zulu territory. While his force was camped at Isandlwana on January 22, the soldiers who remained at the camp were overwhelmed by a large Zulu army. In the slaughter that followed, the British lost about 52 officers—more than had died in the Battle of Waterloo in 1815—along with 806 regular soldiers and 500 African allies. Later that same day, another Zulu army, commanded by Cetshwayo's younger brother Dabulamanzi, attacked a small British detachment at Rorke's Drift. In a heroic defense of a mission station, the British repelled the Zulu attack, even though they were greatly outnumbered. However, Cetshwayo was not trying to fight a war and had no plans to attack British settlements in Natal.

After these opening battles, the British were more determined than ever to destroy Zulu military power, and they denied Cetshwayo's repeated requests for a truce. A large British army pushed onward to Ulundi, one of Cetshwayo's royal kraals. On March 29, 1879, the British managed to defeat a large Zulu army at Kambula. As Chelmsford continued the British advance on Ulundi, Cetshwayo continued his efforts to negotiate peace. However, his efforts failed, and he fled Ulundi before it fell to the British on July 4, 1879. The British occupation of Ulundi broke the Zulu power, but Cetshwayo himself evaded capture until August, when he was found in a kraal in the Ngome forest. Despite his defeat, observers noted that he still retained his regal dignity.

On September 1, 1879, Cetshwayo boarded the steamship *Natal* and sailed to Cape Town. Upon his arrival there, crowds gathered to see the famous Zulu king. Cetshwayo was housed in Cape Town's old castle during his first months in exile. Later he was moved to a farm called Oude Molen, where he received many visitors, including the prince of Wales, the future king of England. In 1881, Cetshwayo received two more visitors, Prince Louis of Battenberg and Lady Florence Dixie. The latter was enthralled with Cetshwayo and met with his longtime friend and ally, Anglican bishop John Colenso. In mid-1882, after Dixie had returned to England and pleaded Cetshwayo's case before the government, Cetshwayo was invited to go to England to meet with colonial officials. He arrived in England in August and became a major attraction for the public and reporters.

While he was in England, Cetshwayo met with many people, including the prince and princess of Wales and Queen Victoria, with whom he exchanged portraits. He also met with the secretary of state for the colonies, Lord Kimberley, with whom he discussed the conditions of his return to the Zulu kingship. The British government demanded that Cetshwayo disband his army, accept a British adviser, and recognize the borders of British territories. Cetshwayo accepted Kimberley's terms and returned to Zululand on January 10, 1883.

Cetshwayo returned home to find his people badly divided. The Usuthu were immersed in infighting and had become uncontrollable. Zibhebhu, a rival chief, was the Usuthu's main target. In March, 1883, Zibhebhu attacked the Usuthu, killing more than four thousand men. In July, he attacked Ulundi and burned the royal kraal. Cetshwayo himself suffered a leg wound and fled to the British-controlled Nkandla Forest. In October,

Cetshwayo's British adviser, Henry Francis Flynn, moved him to a Gqikazi village. Still fearing Zibhebhu, Cetshwayo refused to return to Zululand.

On February 8, 1884, Flynn was informed that Cetshwayo was very ill and took a doctor to Eshowe, where the king was staying. On his arrival there, he found Cetshwayo dead. Unable to perform an autopsy, the doctor ruled the king's death as due to heart failure. However, the Usuthu disagreed, claing that the king had become ill after eating meat that was not supplied by them. Cetshwayo had gone into convulsions and died quickly, prompting suspicions that he had been poisoned by Zibhebhu's followers.

SIGNIFICANCE

In an effort to secure British military support, High Commissioner Frere often described the Zulu as fierce, brutal, and inhumane—warriors who were completely uncivilized and devoid of humanity. He also portrayed Cetshwayo as being as fierce and brutal as Shaka had been. Frere treated minor conflicts with the Zulu as signs of aggression and impending war, and eventually forced an actual war. However, although Frere portrayed the Zulu as dangerous, he also assumed that the British could defeat them easily. It was an egregious error that led to the British disaster at Isandlwana—the most humiliating defeat in British colonial history. The Zulu War that followed Frere's declaration of war has become a well-studied area of history.

Cetshwayo became an iconic figure among British subjects who opposed imperialism. His victory at Isandlwana helped to illustrate the economic and human cost of British imperial desires. Moreover, although one of the justifications of imperialism was to civilize so-called "savages," Cetshwayo himself appeared to be anything but a savage. His calm and friendly manner defied Frere's description and helped to change the imperial view of the Africans.

—*Tina Powell*

FURTHER READING

Binns, C. T. *The Last Zulu King: The Life and Death of Cetshwayo*. London: Longmans, 1963. Sympathetic popular biography of Cetshwayo.

Cetshwayo, King of Zululand. *A Zulu King Speaks: Statements Made by Cetshwayo kaMpande on the History and Custom of His People*. Edited by Colin de B. Webb and John B. Wright. Pietermaritzburg: University of Natal Press, 1987. Posthumous collection of documents and testimonials in Cetshwayo's own words, edited by professional historians.

Edgerton, Robert B. *Like Lions They Fought*. London: Macmillan Press, 1988. Popular account of the battles of the Zulu War, with detailed discussions of Isandlwana and Rorke's Drift.

Guy, Jeff. *The Destruction of the Zulu Kingdom: The Civil War in Zululand, 1879-1884*. London: Longman, 1979. Scholarly study of Zulu politics during the fall of the Zulu kingdom.

Knight, Ian. *The Anatomy of the Zulu Army: From Shaka to Cetshwayo, 1818-1879*. Mechanicsburg, Pa.: Stackpole Books, 1999. Military history of the Zulu kingdom that considers Cetshwayo from a military perspective.

Lock, Ron, and Peter Quantrill. *Zulu Victory: The Epic of Isandhlwana and the Cover-Up*. London: Greenhill Books, 2002. Detailed study of the Zulu victory at Isandlwana and its ramifications in the British military.

Morris, Donald R. *The Washing of the Spears: The Rise and Fall of the Zulu Nation*. New York: Simon & Schuster, 1972. Popular history of the Zulu with detailed and well-written descriptions of events in the Zulu War. Many reprint editions.

Omer-Cooper, J. D. *History of Southern Africa*. 2d ed. London: James Currey, 1994. Comprehensive history of Southern Africa by a specialist in Zulu history who helps to put the Zulu in the broader context of regional history.

Robert, Brian. *The Zulu Kings: A Major Reassessment of Zulu History*. New York: Charles Scribner's Sons, 1974. Popular history of the Zulu and detailed discussion of the Zulu kings.

SEE ALSO: H. Rider Haggard; Paul Kruger; Lobengula; Menelik II; Samory Touré; Shaka; Tewodros II; Queen Victoria.

RELATED ARTICLES in *Great Events from History: The Nineteenth Century, 1801-1900:* c. 1817-1828: Zulu Expansion; January 22-23, 1879: Battles of Isandlwana and Rorke's Drift; 1884: Maxim Patents His Machine Gun.

PAUL CÉZANNE
French painter

One of the leading figures of post-Impressionist painting, Cézanne had an innovative and brilliant style that challenged the conventions of nineteenth century art and had a major influence on twentieth century cubists and abstract artists.

BORN: January 19, 1839; Aix-en-Provence, France
DIED: October 22, 1906; Aix-en-Provence, France
AREA OF ACHIEVEMENT: Art

EARLY LIFE

Paul Cézanne (say-zahn) was born in the south of France, not far from Marseilles and the Mediterranean. His father's family came from the Italian Alpine village Cesana (hence the surname) in the seventeenth century and had a history of minor business activities. Louis-Auguste, Paul's father, started out as a hat maker, at which he was a success, and eventually became a banker in Aix. He lived with Anne-Élisabeth-Honorine Aubert for several years before marrying her in 1844, and Paul was one of their children born before they were married. The family was financially secure, and Paul was educated locally. Interested in art, he took some instruction at the local École des Beaux Arts. One of his closest friends then, and in later life, was Émile Zola, who was to become one of France's greatest men of letters.

Cézanne's enthusiasm for art was tolerated by his father, but he was expected to make a career in the law. He was a good student and entered the University of Aix-en-Provence to study law, but after passing his first-year exams, he asked his father if he might join his friend Zola, who had gone to Paris to make his way as a journalist. Cézanne wanted to study at the prestigious Académie des Beaux-Arts in Paris. His father allowed him to quit school in late 1859, but he kept him in Aix until April, 1861, when he took him to Paris to study as an artist. Cézanne was refused entrance to the school and joined the Académie Suisse, a studio in which young artists banded together to work with live models. He was virtually untrained, and his work showed little promise. Often difficult and inclined to be morose and withdrawn, he was often unhappy with himself and his work. His father supported him, but not generously. In September he gave up, returned to Aix, and joined the family bank.

LIFE'S WORK

Cézanne's self-portraits reveal a thick-set, hard-mouthed peasant glaring out of the canvas, and if there is one thing that marks him as a man and as an artist it is his weighty, determined stubbornness that the paintings suggest. Once back in Aix, he began to draw again and to take some classes locally. In 1862, his father gave in once again and allowed him to return to Paris, and he began to associate with a group of young artists whose work had been rejected by the conservative power structure of artists, critics, and teachers who controlled the Académie des Beaux-Arts and the annual Salon, an exhibition of supposedly the best art being produced in France. Camille Pissarro became his closest friend, but he also came to know Édouard Manet, Pierre-Auguste Renoir, and Claude Monet, all, in one way or another, out of step with established standards of taste in the art world.

This group of painters would ultimately be called the "Impressionists," a name that was originally imposed on them with contempt because of their insistence on a new, looser, lighter style of painting in which they attempted to catch the transitory nature of visual experience. There was considerable difference in their individual contributions to the movement, and it can be argued that Manet, whose work was sometimes accepted by the Salon, was on the fringe of the group. The artist most clearly not quite an Impressionist was Cézanne. After attempting to get his work accepted by the Salon and being pointedly rejected, he joined the Impressionists in exhibitions outside official circles, and he continued to exhibit with them for several years; like them, he was to be ridiculed and neglected.

During the late 1860's, he established a relationship with the model Marie-Hortense Fiquet, who was often a subject of his paintings; they had a child, Paul, in 1872. Like his father, Cézanne did not wed his mistress for several years. He sold practically nothing, was still dependent upon his father, and often disappeared for months at a time. In 1877, he exhibited for the last time with the Impressionists and was so derided for his work that he simply gave up public exhibitions.

Cézanne's early work was often awkward, his colors muddy, his themes uninviting. Rape, murder, or other emotionally excessive subjects seemed to mirror personal problems with which he was attempting to deal in his art. There is much piling on of paint with the palette knife, and a sense of great power not quite successfully expressed. During the 1870's, he was closest to being something of an Impressionist. He spent a considerable amount of time with Pissarro, who was something of a teacher-father to him, and began to paint less morbid

Paul Cézanne. (The Granger Collection, New York)

subjects, his colors becoming brighter, and his draftsmanship more sophisticated. He was still tonally serious, and he never quite gave way to the looser, feathery style of the Impressionists. Where the Impressionists attempted to record the evanescence of experience, its constant change, he chose to seek its basic structures, painting the planes, the conjunctions, the solidity of objects.

By 1880, Cézanne had finally developed a style all his own, entirely different from that of any other painter, incorporating the "open air" freshness of Impressionism to the austere monumentality of painters such as Nicolas Poussin and Gustave Courbet. In a sense, he invented himself.

Cézanne went his own way, almost forgotten, spending most of his time around Aix, painting landscapes, still lifes, and portraits very slowly, painstakingly, in planes of color placed sometimes at seemingly perverse angles, eschewing line for mass, teasing volume, depth, and relationships out of small dabs of color, knowing that colors laid flatly side by side suggest depth or protrusion to the human eye. At close range such work resembles a jigsaw puzzle.

Cézanne seemed to reject the idea that a painting was supposed to be an accurate rendering of reality. His paintings start with reality but ultimately are independent of it: They are aesthetic experiences with their own internal logic. He often subverted the commonly held idea that paintings represent one point of view. He deliberately tipped one end of a table, while the other end was left perfectly flat. He represented his subjects from more than one point of view in ways that are often subtle shifts of perspective. What looks simply like bad draftsmanship was, in fact, deliberate distortion, which creates rhythms, associations, and patterns transcending normal representational painting.

This experimental urge is absorbed in a tender solemnity of tone that suggests that the paintings, however simple in subject, have a haunting metaphysical weight, often reminiscent of the same deep stillness in the work of Jean-Baptiste-Siméon Chardin. The subject, ultimately, is less important than the experience of its aesthetic presence. Cézanne painted more than sixty studies of Mont Sainte-Victoire, a rather unimposing mountain that can be seen on the horizon just across the road from his last studio on the Chemin des Lauves on the outskirts of Aix. The paintings are all quite magnificent, all disturbingly alike factually and different aesthetically, often quite clearly presaging the cubist attempt to turn reality into design.

During the late 1890's, Cézanne began to receive some public recognition, and a group of young artists became aware of the fact not only that he was a formidable painter, but also that he had broken new ground in how one might think about art.

Cézanne worked doggedly, never entirely satisfied, avoided by most because of his notorious irascibility, completely committed to his work. He was beginning to get the attention he had deserved, but seemed not to need it. Watercolors became more important than ever to him, proving his long-held theory that there was no such thing as line and modeling; there were only contrasts. His oils are gloriously rich in his later years, and his work kept exploring the old themes: a few apples, a jug, the old hill, bits and pieces that can still be seen on the tables in the studio as he left it. He suffered from diabetes but continued to work. He caught a cold while painting on October 15, 1906, but he was painting the next morning. However, he died on October 22, exactly one week later.

SIGNIFICANCE

It is generally accepted that Paul Cézanne is one of the greatest artists in the history of painting. His own work as a colorist and as an exponent of an entirely original style in both oils and watercolors might be sufficient proof of this judgment, but he was much more than simply a superlative practitioner. For all of his rough provincialism, he was a theorist who not only put his theories into practice but also showed the way for the entirely new art of the twentieth century. It is difficult to think how that art might have gone had Cézanne not provided it with three singularly important clues.

Cézanne's own work—beginning so unpromisingly, slowly accumulating form and individuality, absorbing the influences of the past and that of his contemporaries, especially the struggling Impressionists, blossoming into one of the most singularly distinctive styles in the history of painting—proved that there was always room for making art new if ambition, will, and talent could hold out against indifference, neglect, and derision.

Cézanne's decision not to become a follower of Impressionism but to use it to go forward into his own realm of expression allowed him to discover one of the most important secrets behind one of the major movements of twentieth century painting: that just as light is always on the move across the landscape, so is the eye. Therefore, the point of view need not be fixed in a painting but can express that movement in the single canvas. This insight was the key needed to trigger the cubist movement in modern art.

Perhaps even more important, Cézanne proved that art need not necessarily be an accurate representation of what the eye sees. Styles had changed through the centuries, as had theories about how the artist was to represent reality. Cézanne argued for the proposition (and put it into action in his art) that the work of art might start in nature but need not simply reflect it. It could transcend reality; it could be abstract.

Cézanne had said it best: "The eye is not enough, reflection is needed." Moreover, he had illustrated it best in paintings that at one and the same time could convey the aesthetic illusion of depth and the sense of flat design consistent with the nature of the medium. His one-man show of 1895, organized by his old friend Pissarro, started him on his way to the reputation he deserved. In 1907, a memorial showing of fifty-six paintings was displayed in Paris at the Salon which so long before had turned him away. From that moment onward, he was to be seen as the most influential painter of the century.

—Charles H. Pullen

FURTHER READING

Athanassoglou-Kallmyer, Nina Maria. *Cézanne and Provence: The Painter in His Culture*. Chicago: University of Chicago Press, 2003. Examines how Cézanne's alliance with the region of Provence affected his innovative painting style and critical reputation. Illustrated with 120 color plates and halftones.

Callen, Anthea. *Techniques of the Impressionists*. London: New Burlington Books, 1987. So much of understanding Cézanne is dependent upon a recognition of the central concern of the artist and his Impressionist friends for technique. This book analyzes individual paintings by artists prior to the Impressionist period and during the period of Impressionist activity. Two Cézanne paintings are carefully discussed.

Cézanne, Paul. *Paul Cézanne*. Edited by Ellen H. Johnson. Great Artists 18. New York: Funk & Wagnalls, 1978. Contains a short, informed article by Johnson, which is mindful of the general audience. Large reproductions of several paintings, accompanied by short but sensible notes.

Harris, Nathaniel. *The Art of Cézanne*. New York: Excalibur Books, 1982. A short, inexpensive, but generously illustrated discussion of the artist's life and painting.

Lewis, Wyndham. *Wyndham Lewis on Art: Collected Writings, 1914-1956*. New York: Funk & Wagnalls, 1969. Lewis was a great admirer of Cézanne, whom he speaks about with the cogency of a practitioner of the same trade.

Platzman, Steven. *Cézanne: The Self-Portraits*. Berkeley: University of California Press, 2001. Explores how Cézanne's many self-portraits reflect his emotions, his artistic development, and his view of himself and others. Includes reproductions of sixty paintings and drawings.

Rewald, John. *Paul Cézanne: A Biography*. New York: Schocken Books, 1968. Based on the correspondence of the painter and his friends, this biography has a homey intimacy and easy charm.

_____. *Paul Cézanne: The Watercolours—A Catalogue Raisonné*. New York: Graphic Society Books, 1984. The watercolors have often been ignored, but they not only are first-class art in their own right but also provide another way of understanding the artist's obsession with technique and the peculiar way he achieves dimensional effects by juxtaposing slabs of pure color.

SEE ALSO: Eugène Delacroix; Thomas Eakins; Vincent van Gogh; Hiroshige; Camille Pissarro; Pierre-Auguste Renoir; Georges Seurat.

RELATED ARTICLES in *Great Events from History: The Nineteenth Century, 1801-1900:* April 15, 1874: First Impressionist Exhibition; Late 1870's: Post-Impressionist Movement Begins.

EDWIN CHADWICK

English physician and social reformer

The most active and determined of Jeremy Bentham's disciples, Chadwick sought to reform British government with utilitarian rigor and efficiency, hoping to make it more responsive to the massive social problems created by industrialization and urbanization.

BORN: January 24, 1800; Longsight (now Manchester), England
DIED: July 6, 1890; East Sheen, Surrey, England
AREA OF ACHIEVEMENT: Social reform

EARLY LIFE

Edwin Chadwick was the grandson of Andrew Chadwick, a friend of John Wesley, and a major figure in the establishment of the first Methodist Sunday schools in Lancashire. Edwin's father, James Chadwick, was an unsuccessful businessperson who, inspired by the French Revolution and the ideas of Thomas Paine, became a radical journalist. Edwin's childhood was rendered difficult through his father's financial straits and his mother's early death. Nevertheless, he received a sound education at local schools and from private tutors. He moved to London in 1810 when his father assumed an editorial post there. In 1818, he embarked upon his legal education by entering an attorney's office as an apprentice. In 1823, having raised his sights to the more prestigious profession of barrister, he entered the Middle Temple to begin seven years of residence and study.

There was little formal structure to legal education in this period, leaving Chadwick with ample opportunity to explore the exciting and turbulent life of the capital. His residence, Lyon's Inn, was in the midst of London, close not only to the law courts and lawyers' offices but also to the medical schools, hospitals, and the very center of government itself—the Houses of Parliament. Eager, curious, and resolute, Chadwick explored every corner of his new world, from the corridors of power in Westminster to the most appalling and wretched slums of east London. He was also quick to strike up acquaintances, many of whom became lifelong friends and colleagues. The intersecting spheres in which he moved and studied during the late 1820's—law, medicine, politics, and administration—were to shape the course and define the content of his career as a reformer.

Among Chadwick's first and most enduring contacts from these years were medical men such as Thomas Southwood Smith and Neill Arnott, who belonged to the group of intellectuals and reformers known as the Philosophical Radicals. Followers of Jeremy Bentham, they shared his disdain for existing institutions and longed to reform political and legal structures along Utilitarian lines. Finding the tone and style of this iconoclastic set exactly to his taste, Chadwick quickly became a fixture of the Benthamite circle.

Chadwick began to attract the notice of the more eminent Philosophical Radicals such as Francis Place, Joseph Hume, and John Stuart Mill. In 1830, he was introduced to Bentham himself and was invited by the eccentric and reclusive old sage to become his private secretary. This was a signal honor and opened the prospect of Chadwick becoming Bentham's intellectual heir. Indeed, when Bentham died in 1832, he left his library to Chadwick, along with a promise of a comfortable annuity in return for Chadwick devoting his life to carrying out Bentham's literary projects. Chadwick declined this bequest, for he had already embarked on a more ambitious public career.

LIFE'S WORK

Although he was called to the bar in 1830, Chadwick never practiced law. Possessed of energy, wide-ranging interests, and considerable writing ability, he was at first inclined to pursue a career in journalism. His first article, on life insurance, appeared in 1828 in the major organ of the Philosophical Radicals, *The Westminster Review*. It was followed in 1829 and 1830 by articles on medical charities in France and on preventive police in the short-lived radical journal *The London Review*. These latter articles brought Chadwick to the attention not only of Bentham but also of certain influential political economists such as Nassau William Senior and reform-minded

Whigs such as Henry Brougham. It was through them that Chadwick was soon to be propelled into government service as an investigator and analyst of social problems and as a designer of new administrative structures to solve them.

The victory of the Whigs in the turbulent election of 1830 provided Chadwick with his opportunity. Beyond their commitment to parliamentary reform, many members of the aristocratic Whig cabinet believed that it was necessary to devise solutions to social and economic problems such as child labor in factories and the abuses of the poor law system. Because some cabinet ministers had been exposed to the principles of political economy as well as to Benthamism, they naturally turned to economists and Philosophical Radicals to undertake the inquiries and write the official reports that would serve as the basis for remedial legislation.

In 1832, Chadwick was brought in as an expert investigator on two new royal commissions—on the poor laws and on child labor in the factories. Shortly thereafter, he abandoned his journalistic career by resigning as subeditor of the radical newspaper *The Examiner*. For the next twenty-two years, with one brief but important foray into private enterprise, he was to be a hard-driving, innovative, and controversial civil servant.

With Chadwick taking a dominant part on both royal commissions, the Benthamite character of the inquiries was enhanced. However, Bentham's insistence that the superiority of expert investigation derived in part from its impartiality was not borne out. Far from being impartial, Chadwick commenced his inquiries with his mind largely made up as to the nature and extent of the abuses as well as the necessary remedial measures. He was quite willing to ignore or even suppress evidence contrary to his opinions. Furthermore, he crafted his reforms in terms of both political expediency and the advancement of his own career.

The clamor to reform the poor law system proceeded from a widespread perception that poor relief policies were overly indulgent, resulting in higher rates (local taxes), population growth, the breakdown of labor discipline, and the loss of social cohesion. Some followers of the gloomy doctrines of Thomas Malthus claimed that catastrophe could be averted only by the total abolition of the poor laws. Chadwick, however, followed Bentham in his insistence that a public relief system could be safely maintained if it was rigorously overhauled and infused with deterrent strategies.

The major recommendations of the report of the royal commission on the poor laws, written largely by Chadwick and issued in 1834, were the principle of less eligibility and the use of the workhouse test. The former embodied the concept that the condition of the pauper receiving public relief should be less eligible (less desirable) than that of the lowest paid independent laborer. The workhouse test was designed to put this concept into practice. The harsh regimen of the new workhouses would act as a test of destitution for the able-bodied and would ensure that any laborer who did subject himself to the discipline, hard work, and monotonous diet of the new workhouses would seize the first opportunity to take even the lowest-paid job on the outside. The spirit, if not the complete letter, of these recommendations was enacted by Parliament in 1834 as the Poor Law Amendment Act, or New Poor Law.

For his prominent part in forging the workhouse system, Chadwick provoked the wrath of the poor and their defenders. Simultaneously, he was incurring unpopularity for his part in the royal commission on child labor in the factories. The government had appointed this royal commission after a humanitarian-dominated parliamentary investigation (the Sadler Committee) had recommended abolition of all factory labor for children. Chadwick's commission was widely viewed in the factory districts as a device to negate the Sadler Committee, and its proceedings were picketed and disrupted. Nevertheless, the commission took much evidence, including medical testimony about the effects of factory labor on children. Chadwick's Factory Report of 1833 and the ensuing Factory Act abolished all labor for children under the age of nine and limited it to eight hours per day for those aged nine to thirteen.

Chadwick deeply resented the public abuse that was loaded on him because of his key role in these two measures. He also suspected, with some reason, that the government found it convenient to have him as the scapegoat for unpopular policies. Furthermore, he believed both the New Poor Law and the Factory Act to be in the best interest of the poor. The Poor Law restored the dividing line between honest, respectable labor and the condition of pauperism, a line that had become blurred before 1834, with consequent demoralization of the poor. The Factory Act, even if the protection afforded did not go as far as the misguided Sadler bill, had an all-important enforcement mechanism in the form of the factory inspectors. This Benthamite device of an inspectorate would ensure that protection of the young was real and enforceable, not a set of pious wishes.

Although Chadwick believed that the government had mangled both pieces of legislation, he looked forward eagerly to implementing the New Poor Law. Anticipating an appointment to the new Poor Law Commission, he was bitterly disappointed when the three positions were filled by time-honored methods of aristocratic patronage. He reluctantly accepted the post of secretary to the Commission, with the promise that he would be a virtual "fourth commissioner." His thirteen-year tenure in this post would be deeply frustrating. Resented by his superiors, whom he considered incompetent, he was unable to prevent what he considered a gross maladministration of the new law, characterized by a fitful and very partial application of the workhouse test.

In spite of these frustrations, Chadwick persuaded the cabinet to let him undertake investigations into other areas of needed reform such as police and public health. Both inquiries were in part an outgrowth of his poor law work. Attacks by angry laborers on the new workhouses had convinced him of the need for a rural constabulary, while the evidence of a close correlation between sickness and poverty pointed him toward sanitary reform. Named to a royal commission on rural police in 1836, he conducted lengthy investigations and published his report in 1839. The ensuing Rural Constabulary Act was a keen disappointment, however, because it did not embody his recommendation of a centralized police system along Benthamite lines. Instead, control of the new county forces was entrusted to the unpaid rural magistracy, dominated by peers, squires, and clergy—the same elements that controlled many of the local poor law boards of guardians.

The sanitary investigation was ostensibly conducted by the Poor Law Commission, but in fact it was done entirely by Chadwick. Published under his name in 1842 as *The Report on the Sanitary Condition of the Labouring Population*, it is Chadwick's greatest work. Deploying a formidable array of statistics and expert medical testimony, he made a compelling case for the connection between sickness and poverty. He also demonstrated that much if not most sickness was a result of the appalling overcrowding and lack of sanitation in the towns. Chadwick called for dramatic government action to provide fresh water and create radically new sewer systems using small-bore earthenware pipes so that urban refuse could be efficiently removed before a deadly "miasma" (believed to be the predisposing cause of most illness) could form.

The 1840's witnessed a major public health movement throughout England, and Chadwick was one of its most determined proponents. Believing himself to be the virtual inventor of the "sanitary idea," he was increasingly impatient with those reformers who refused to accept him as the movement's leader. Some of them in turn found Chadwick arrogant, irascible, and wedded to unproven engineering solutions to the public health crisis. He was further irritated by the unwillingness of the government (controlled by the Conservative party since the 1841 general election) to act. Cabinet ministers fobbed him off with vague promises and kept him occupied with further inquiries. The most notable of these was the investigation into the appalling state of the cemeteries of London, which resulted in Chadwick's notable *Interment Report* of 1843. However, once again the government refused to adopt the necessary remedial legislation.

Despairing of government action, Chadwick sought sanitary reform as well as riches by launching the Towns Improvement Company in 1844. The company was a joint stock enterprise designed to provide a range of urban services, including water supply, drainage, and sewers, on contract to municipalities at home and abroad. With typical Chadwickian thoroughness, it also included a plan to sell the "sewer manure" to nearby farms. Ingenious though it doubtless was and reflective of his peculiar passion for efficiency, it failed to attract sufficient investment and expired in 1846. During these two years Chadwick was obsessed by the scheme and bent every effort, including the manipulation of related official inquiries, to push enabling legislation through Parliament that would have conferred signal advantages on his own company.

Driven by the failure of his company back to a career of official service, he was heartened by the return of the Whigs to office in 1846. Because they were disposed to accept some kind of sanitary legislation, his prospect of securing a post in the new executive board seemed bright. He first had to contend with a crisis in the Poor Law Commission when a local case of abuse of paupers in a workhouse became a national scandal. The ensuing inquiry into the abuses at Andover (where the workhouse was located) pitted Chadwick against his superiors in a barrage of lurid charges and countercharges. Drawing fully upon his powerful combative instincts and skillfully mobilizing public opinion, he gained the upper hand. The case ended with the commissioners as well as Chadwick deprived of their posts in a major poor law reorganization. Chadwick, however, managed to force the government into promising him a public health post in return for his refraining from any further embarrassing disclosures on poor law administration.

With the passage of the Public Health Act of 1848, Chadwick at last tasted real executive authority. While he considered the statute defective in its coercive powers over recalcitrant local authorities, he set to work vigorously with his colleague on the General Board of Health, Lord Shaftesbury, to reform England's sanitary institutions. Between 1848 and 1854, Chadwick made the board as well as the Metropolitan Commission of Sewers powerful instruments of sanitary reform.

Using his limited coercive powers to the full, Chadwick compelled many reluctant municipalities to appoint local boards and begin the process of draining, sewering, and providing fresh water. He also made numerous enemies by his dictatorial and dogmatic manner, especially in London, where the powerful entrenched metropolitan vestries joined leading civil engineers in opposing Chadwick's nostrums. This proved to be the undoing of both Chadwick and the General Board of Health. The hue and cry against his overbearing manner and the flaws in some of his engineering nostrums finally reached Parliament. In 1854, Chadwick was stripped of his post, and the general board was reorganized and placed under the control of one of his leading critics. It was to be his last paid government position.

In spite of this repudiation by Parliament, Chadwick continued to be a dynamic force in the public health movement for the remaining thirty-six years of his life. Indeed, his many publications as well as his active participation in groups such as the Social Science Association made him a revered elder statesman of the sanitary movement. He also continued his interest in other reforms, including his pet scheme of "half-time education" (half the school day to academic subjects, the other half to military drill and physical exercise). He failed repeatedly to win a seat in Parliament, but another lifelong ambition was at last realized in 1889, when he received a knighthood. Sir Edwin Chadwick died a year later at his home in East Sheen, Surrey, leaving the considerable sum of forty-seven thousand pounds, most of it in trust to provide an annual prize to the local sanitary authority showing the greatest reduction of the death rate.

SIGNIFICANCE

Edwin Chadwick's influence on British government and society was considerable. He possessed, as John Stuart Mill put it, one of the great organizing and contriving minds of the time. His passion for efficiency and comprehensiveness knew no bounds. Building on the legacy of Jeremy Bentham's *Constitutional Code* (1830), he labored to create a rationally structured government providing an array of social services while it simultaneously deterred crime and pauperism through an efficient national police and a deterrent workhouse system. He hated waste in all of its forms and believed that all members of society could be rendered efficient and productive by a vigorous, enlightened government. He drove himself incredibly hard throughout his life, taking few holidays and little time off.

Chadwick considered the legislation that resulted from his inquiries to be a series of half measures, the result of the laziness and ignorance of government ministers and the opposition of vested interests. He seemed not to appreciate that part of the opposition was to his abrasive personality. His dictatorial manner and humorlessness, coupled with a tendency to deviousness, made him many enemies. Furthermore, the rigid ideology he embraced was hostile both to the aristocratic laxness of the established order and to the emerging democratic system. As *The Economist* put it after his fall from power in 1854: "He is essentially a despot and a bureaucrat. He thinks people ought to be well governed, but does not believe in the possibility of their governing themselves well." Clearly, what were sometimes described as his "Prussian" tendencies were out of step with the values of most Victorians, but this makes his many achievements all the more remarkable. His dogged persistence led to a number of key reforms, and he is rightly viewed as an intrepid early pioneer in the making of the British welfare state.

—Anthony Brundage

FURTHER READING

Brundage, Anthony. *England's "Prussian Minister:" Edwin Chadwick and the Politics of Government Growth, 1832-1854*. University Park: Pennsylvania State University Press, 1988. Examines Chadwick's reform policies and their impact on the role of English government.

_____. *The Making of the New Poor Law: The Politics of Inquiry, Enactment, and Implementation, 1832-1839*. New Brunswick, N.J.: Rutgers University Press, 1978. Detailed account of the politics of one of Chadwick's key reforms, showing how the act was shaped more by the aristocracy and gentry than by Benthamite principles, in spite of Chadwick's determination and sometimes devious methods.

Chadwick, Edwin. *Edwin Chadwick: Nineteenth Century Social Reform*. Edited by David Gladstone. 5 vols. London: Routledge/Thoemmes Press, 1997. Reprints of a wide range of Chadwick's writings, from his *Report on the Sanitary Condition of the Labouring Population*, to rare pamphlets and addresses to learned societies. Vol. 1 reprints Finer's *The Life and Times of Sir Edwin Chadwick* (see below). Each volume includes a specially prepared introduction.

Finer, S. E. *The Life and Times of Sir Edwin Chadwick.* London: Methuen, 1952. A full and very readable biography with a tendency to ignore some of Chadwick's more questionable tactics. While noting Chadwick's personality quirks and his punitive ideas on the poor laws, the book treats him as the embattled hero of an attempt to overcome vested interests and indifferent political leaders.

Hamlin, Christopher. *Public Health and Social Justice in the Age of Chadwick: Britain, 1800-1854.* Cambridge, England: Cambridge University Press, 1998. A thorough, well-researched account of Victorian Britain's efforts to improve public health through the construction of public works. Hamlin explains how Chadwick's advocacy of sanitation fit the political needs of the Poor Law Commission and the Whig and Tory governments.

Henriques, Ursula. *Before the Welfare State: Social Administration in Early Industrial Britain.* London: Longmans, Green, 1979. A judicious, well-balanced treatment of all aspects of governmental reform during Chadwick's ascendancy, noting his contributions but also stressing the complexities of each reform.

Lewis, R. A. *Edwin Chadwick and the Public Health Movement, 1832-1854.* London: Longmans, Green, 1952. Skillful analysis of Chadwick's active involvement in the public health movement and his emergence as one of the principal leaders of the sanitary movement. However, like Finer (see above), Lewis is inclined to turn a blind eye to some of Chadwick's less admirable methods.

MacDonagh, Oliver. *Early Victorian Government, 1830-1870.* London: Weidenfeld & Nicolson, 1977. A useful survey of the major areas of government growth and reform. Similar to the book by Henriques (see above) in its sense of balance and avoidance of ascribing too much influence to Chadwick or to Benthamism generally.

Roberts, David. *Victorian Origins of the British Welfare State.* New Haven, Conn.: Yale University Press, 1960. An important study of nineteenth century reforms in the poor laws, factory acts, public health, police, education, and other areas, noting the influence of paternalism on the reforms as well as the powerful opposition to centralization. Good biographical detail on Chadwick and the other key officials of the period.

SEE ALSO: James Mill; John Stuart Mill.

RELATED ARTICLE in *Great Events from History: The Nineteenth Century, 1801-1900:* August 14, 1834: British Parliament Passes New Poor Law.

JOSEPH CHAMBERLAIN

British politician

Perhaps the most important Victorian statesman who never became prime minister, Chamberlain was an influential politician who supported the British Empire and a strong economic union between its members.

BORN: July 8, 1836; London, England
DIED: July 2, 1914; Highbury, Birmingham, England
AREA OF ACHIEVEMENT: Government and politics

EARLY LIFE

The son of a Unitarian shoemaker, Joseph Chamberlain received his early education in London at one of the most famous of the dissenting academies, University College School. After graduation he planned to attend University College, but his father opposed "that godless school." In addition, his father refused to educate Chamberlain any more than he would be able to afford for his younger sons, and instead offered Chamberlain two hundred pounds to enter the ministry, which was refused.

At the age of eighteen Chamberlain was sent from London to Birmingham to represent his father's interests in a family woodscrew-manufacturing firm that had been influenced by an American invention for screw manufacturing displayed at the Crystal Palace Exhibit of 1851. In Birmingham, Chamberlain prospered, retiring with a comfortable income after twenty successful years in business. Machine technology had made him rich, and he now turned his attention to social engineering. Chamberlain's first foray into the political world involved his election to the Birmingham school board in 1870. Chamberlain strongly stressed the principle that education should be universal, compulsory, and free. His efforts on behalf of educational reform led him to higher office, first as city councillor, later as mayor.

LIFE'S WORK

While mayor of Birmingham, Chamberlain established a reputation as a radical; he endeavored in particular to improve housing conditions and public education. Encouraged by his local political successes, in 1876 he entered Parliament as a Liberal member from Birmingham. Birmingham, one of the large industrial towns to benefit from the Reform Bill of 1867, was allotted three seats in the House of Commons, and all three were dominated by the Liberal Party.

By close association in the House with Sir Charles Dilke, Chamberlain was able to rise in party prominence until the 1880 elections, when he was invited by Prime Minister William Gladstone to serve in his cabinet as president of the Board of Trade. Although still a virtual newcomer after only four years in the Commons, Chamberlain benefited from a disagreement between Gladstone and Dilke on the choice of a government post. Dilke had contacted Gladstone about cabinet posts for himself and his friend Chamberlain. "I also think that we are far more powerful together than separated," claimed Dilke; Gladstone's compromise was to give a minor cabinet job to Chamberlain and the undersecretaryship to Dilke.

Although Chamberlain held radical views on questions of social reform, he was traditional in his sense of maintaining and expanding the British Empire. When Gladstone introduced an Irish home rule (political autonomy) bill in 1886, Chamberlain chose to resign from the cabinet rather than support the government's policy. "I can never consent to regard Ireland as a separate people," he claimed, "with the inherent rights of an absolutely independent community." Chamberlain then founded the National Liberal Federation, which he hoped would become a national party in opposition to the Gladstonian Liberals; instead, his dissenting effort forged an influential role for himself in an ultimate union with the Conservative Party.

In 1895, the marquis of Salisbury formed a coalition government, a combination of traditional Conservatives and the followers of Chamberlain, called Liberal Unionists. Chamberlain could have named practically any cabinet position for himself but chose the Colonial Office as the agency with which to propel himself into national prominence for the next decade. For Chamberlain, the Colonial Office allowed him to fulfill an imperial vision he had long relished: "I said again I should prefer the Colonies—in the hope of furthering closer union between them and the United Kingdom." While colonial secretary he maintained two objectives: cementing the ties between Great Britain and the colonies, and increasing the trade within the empire. The passive imperialism of the 1870's had been replaced during the 1890's with pride in Great Britain's imperial possessions and a belief that Great Britain was becoming a world state, with its colonies an extension of itself. The word "imperialism" had come to defend proudly Great Britain's civilizing mission along with the British system of peace and good government.

Joseph Chamberlain. (Library of Congress)

To help spread the concept of good government and preservation of peace, Chamberlain favored an imperial *Zollverein*, a union of freely trading partners within the empire. He thought that a commercial union would give an opportunity to call together representatives from various parts of the empire—a gathering that could lead to the creation of an imperial council, one step along the way toward an imperial federal parliament. An opportunity arose in 1897, the year of Queen Victoria's Diamond Jubilee celebrating her sixty-year reign; representatives from throughout the empire had gathered in London to mark the occasion. An informal conference with the colonial representatives was arranged, with Chamberlain presiding, but sentiments were mixed as to whether there was a need for an imperial parliament. The best Chamberlain could solicit was an agreement for periodic conferences for the discussion of "matters of common interest." The subsequent colonial conferences became, therefore, the means by which colonial views came to be aired collectively. Those views, however, were never united.

Of all Chamberlain's imperial activities, he is most closely associated with those in Southern Africa, which was to serve as a proving ground for the Victorian mission of progress. Such lofty ideals, however, were quickly cast aside when gold and diamonds were discovered there during the 1870's. Chamberlain's policies in South Africa were influenced by the interests of Cecil Rhodes and his fellow mining magnates, who had practically overwhelmed the two small agrarian states of the Transvaal and the Orange Free State. Both were sparsely populated with Afrikaner (Boer) farmers descended from Dutch settlers, but had been inundated with outsiders (*uitlanders*) who poured into the mining areas during the gold and diamond rush.

Rhodes, having made a tremendous fortune, became convinced that all Southern Africa should come under British control. Resistance by the Afrikaners persuaded Rhodes and his friends that the only solution to this dilemma was a military one. As a result, they hatched a half-baked scheme for the invasion of the Afrikaner republics, which led to the ill-fated Jameson Raid of 1895-1896. Chamberlain seems to have had knowledge of the plan, as he informed the prime minister on December 26, 1895, that there would probably be an uprising in the Afrikaner republics within the next several days. During the subsequent debate in the Commons over responsibility for the raid, Chamberlain asserted that all parties other than Leander Starr Jameson were "equally ignorant" of the plans for the raid, and a parliamentary investigation cleared Chamberlain of any complicity. Following the raid, the Afrikaner republics began a frantic arms build-up that better prepared them for the war that began with Great Britain in 1899.

Scholars have debated the role of Chamberlain in fomenting the resultant South African (Boer) War of 1899-1902. Although he was exonerated by the House of Commons for complicity in the Jameson Raid, modern scholars have proved his strong interest in the need for British annexation of the Afrikaner republics and exposed his gift to Rhodes of a free hand in the attempted Jameson takeover. Before the war there was no strong public demand for war, but Chamberlain, increasingly influential in the Salisbury government, was able to win support from several members of the cabinet for strong ultimatums sent to the Afrikaner republics—ultimatums that could only be rejected by the Afrikaners.

Following the war, in 1903 Chamberlain resigned from the Conservative-Unionist government over the question of whether tariff barriers for the members of the empire should be reduced, thus creating an imperial customs union. He spent the remainder of his public life campaigning for his plan of "imperial preference," which would create a commercial union to solidify the empire. In a speech in Birmingham on May 15, 1903, he made his formal declaration for imperial preference. This speech has been described as a turning point in Edwardian politics. The issue threatened to divide not only the cabinet but also the country and the empire.

Chamberlain began a whistle-stop tour in the autumn of 1903 to take his imperial preference plan to the people. His speeches were tailored to meet the interest of each audience, discussing mining in Cardiff, agriculture in the provinces, and industry in Birmingham. In several by-elections in December, 1903, the success of his efforts was demonstrated. Even Chamberlain commented on how impressive were the effects of his speeches in winning over two opposition seats to the side of the government. A powerful Tariff Reform League was established and headquartered in his home bastion of Birmingham. In spite of the growing influence of Chamberlain within the Unionist cabinet and the increasing monies spent on his crusade, Chamberlain's hold on the country declined by early 1904, and he was never again able to ride such a political crest. The tariff reform campaign failed to persuade the British masses.

In addition to winning over the country, Chamberlain also had to deal with a deteriorating relationship with Lord Salisbury's successor as prime minister, his nephew Arthur James Balfour. Balfour, far more philosophically conservative than Chamberlain, had to be won over to preferential tariffs and active social reform. By 1905, however, elections had to be called, and the coalition government of Chamberlain and Balfour was voted out of office by the Liberal Party.

In the short term Chamberlain won a personal victory over Balfour. In the long run, however, Chamberlain failed entirely in his imperial and tariff schemes. On July 10, 1906, he delivered an exhausting speech at Bingly Hall, Birmingham. The next day, after returning to London for a Tariff Commission meeting, he felt "a wreck." On the evening of the eleventh he collapsed with a stroke that paralyzed his right side. Chamberlain would never again actively participate in politics. He was confined to a wheelchair until he died suddenly in Birmingham in July, 1914.

SIGNIFICANCE

Joseph Chamberlain possessed great gifts of personality, oratory, and intellect. During his career he was an overwhelming success as businessperson, mayor, House of Commons member, and cabinet member. At various times he almost captured the leadership of both the Liberal and Conservative parties. He also almost brought about a colonial policy that would unite the empire economically. Ultimately, however, he failed. His failures have been blamed on a variety of causes. He was known to be excessively impulsive. "Pushful Joe," as he was sometimes called, with his monocle in place, his orchid in his lapel, and his ostentatious home in Birmingham, was considered by a still strongly aristocratic political world to be "just a tradesman" overreaching his station.

On the other hand, there are perhaps more subtle accomplishments to the career of Joseph Chamberlain. Beginning with his political origins in Birmingham he was able to recognize the coming influence of the newly enfranchised masses. He was able to construct a political machine in Birmingham that expanded to a national scale during his early days in Parliament, and his organizational tactics were used by both Liberals and Conservatives, as well as much later, by the Labour Party. His business background also gave Chamberlain increased sensitivity to Great Britain's industrial decline toward the end of the nineteenth century; he was far more in touch with business realities, for example, than either Salisbury or Balfour. Perhaps one reason for the failure of his dream of imperial preference was the too favorable position it provided for Great Britain; the colonies would gain little while Great Britain would benefit greatly.

There was one additional significant gift for Great Britain left by Joseph Chamberlain. His two sons were major figures in British political affairs well into the twentieth century. The elder son, Austen (1863-1937), held high cabinet office, was offered the prime ministry twice, and, in 1925, was awarded the Nobel Peace Prize for his work on the Locarno peace pact. The younger son, Neville (1869-1940), held cabinet rank and was prime minister from 1937 to 1940. Joseph Chamberlain, therefore, founded a brief political dynasty unique in British history.

—*Newell D. Boyd*

FURTHER READING

Chamberlain, Joseph L. *Mr. Chamberlain's Speeches*. Edited by C. W. Boyd. 2 vols. London: Routledge & Kegan Paul, 1914. A collection of some of the most representative of Chamberlain's speeches.

_____. *A Political Memoir, 1880-1892*. Edited by C. H. D. Howard. London: Batchworth Press, 1953. An autobiographical fragment that unfortunately stops just at the climax of Chamberlain's career. This account deals primarily with the making of a politician.

Drus, Ethel. "A Report on the Papers of Joseph Chamberlain Relating to the Jameson Raid and the Inquiry." *Bulletin of the Institute of Historical Research* 25 (1952). One of several studies of Chamberlain's role in the Jameson Raid. Although a parliamentary commission exonerated Chamberlain of playing any part, scholars such as Drus have been far more critical.

Fraser, Peter. *Joseph Chamberlain*. London: Cassell, 1966. Until recently, this was the standard biography. Although it is still quite reliable for general information, it does not contain the most recent interpretations.

Garvin, J. L., and Julian Amery. *Life of Joseph Chamberlain*. 6 vols. London: Macmillan, 1934-1969. This massive "official" biography is quite sympathetic to Chamberlain and reproduces numerous letters and documents.

Jay, Richard. *Joseph Chamberlain: A Political Study*. Oxford, England: Clarendon Press, 1981. Perhaps the best interpretive study. This account incorporates the best scholarship then available and tries to set Chamberlain in his times.

Judd, Denis. *Radical Joe: A Life of Joseph Chamberlain*. London: Hamish Hamilton, 1977. One of the newer interpretive works. This biography provides a serviceable survey, although it fails to be entirely convincing in some of its attempts at breaking new ground.

Marsh, Peter T. *Joseph Chamberlain: Entrepreneur in Politics*. New Haven, Conn.: Yale University Press, 1994. More recent biography of Chamberlain, describing his initial career in private industry and dissecting his subsequent career in politics. The majority of the book focuses on his role as colonial secretary from 1895 through 1903.

Parsons, Neil. *King Khama, Emperor Joe, and the Great White Queen: Victorian Britain Through African Eyes*. Chicago: University of Chicago Press, 1998. In 1895, the Ngwato ruler Khama III and two other Tswana chiefs went to London to implore Queen Victoria not to cede Southern Africa's Bechuanaland Protectorate (modern Botswana) to Cecil Rhodes's British South Africa Company. Denied an audience with the queen, they pled their case directly to the public, gaining support for their cause and leading Chamberlain to draft a settlement allowing Bechuanaland to remain independent of Rhodesia (modern Zimbabwe). Parsons's book describes the chiefs' journey, providing an African perspective on British imperialism.

Tyler, J. E. *The Struggle for Imperial Unity*. London: Longmans, Green, 1938. A work that stresses the economic background of the imperial preference battle from the time before Chamberlain became involved until he was fully committed to the fray.

SEE ALSO: Sir Edmund Barton; William Edward Forster; William Ewart Gladstone; Paul Kruger; Cecil Rhodes.

RELATED ARTICLES in *Great Events from History: The Nineteenth Century, 1801-1900:* 1843: Carlyle Publishes *Past and Present*; December 6, 1884: British Parliament Passes the Franchise Act of 1884; June, 1886-September 9, 1893: Irish Home Rule Debate Dominates British Politics; October 11, 1899-May 31, 1902: South African War.

WILLIAM ELLERY CHANNING

American religious leader

Channing led the attack by Protestant clergy on New England Congregationalism and helped found the Unitarian movement that established the basis for modern liberal Christianity.

BORN: April 7, 1780; Newport, Rhode Island
DIED: October 2, 1842; Bennington, Vermont
AREA OF ACHIEVEMENT: Religion and theology

EARLY LIFE

William Ellery Channing was born in British-occupied Newport toward the end of the Revolutionary War, one of ten children of William and Lucy (née Ellery) Channing. Young Channing was the grandson of a signer of the Declaration of Independence on the paternal side, and of perhaps the richest merchant in Newport on the maternal side. The boy attended school in Newport until the age of twelve, at which point he was sent to New London, Connecticut, to prepare for Harvard. He began his collegiate studies at Harvard in 1794 and spent four happy years there. During his Harvard years, young Channing had an adolescent religious experience, and the event persuaded him to seek a career in the clergy. He was a popular student, and at the end of his stay at Harvard, the class of 1798 elected him as their graduating speaker.

Upon graduation, Channing went south to Richmond, Virginia, to take a post as a tutor to the socially prominent Randolph family. The young New Englander felt ill at ease in Richmond's heady atmosphere of dancing, drinking, and Deism, and for the most part he shunned society and read books. Alone in his study, Channing again had a conversion experience, and his letters of 1800 demonstrate the intensity of his encounter and his belief that faith alone provided the basis of Christian belief. He returned to Newport in 1800 and struck up a friendship with the local minister, Samuel Hopkins, who had once been a follower of the great Jonathan Edwards. Hopkins had shed some of his earlier adherence to the rigid Calvinist notions of predestination, and in turn his thinking influenced Channing. In December, 1801, Channing returned to Harvard as a divinity student, and upon his ordination in 1803, he was called to the ministry of the well-to-do Federal Street Church in Boston, a post he held until his death four decades later.

Channing postponed marriage until 1814, when he wed his cousin Ruth Gibbs. The couple had four children over the next six years, but only two survived infancy. Channing himself suffered from ill health throughout his adult life. He was a small man, only five feet tall, and weighed little more than a hundred pounds. Portraits painted of him each decade after his coming to Federal Street show a once handsome man with a face growing ever thinner and more pinched. However, if his frame was unprepossessing, his voice more than made up for any deficiency in stature. By all accounts, Channing was one of the finest religious speakers in nineteenth century America.

LIFE'S WORK

William Ellery Channing's name has come down in history in connection with the famous "Unitarian Controversy" in early nineteenth century New England. Few of his contemporaries at divinity school might have predicted that the quiet, intense Channing would someday lead a revolt of rationalist Christians against the remnants of the Congregational church established by the Puritans during the 1630's. The controversy first became public in 1805 when Harvard appointed a known Unitarian, Henry Ware, to a chair in theology. The name "Unitarian" implied a host of beliefs at the time, not simply the contention that the deity was single and unfragmented, as opposed to the more traditional "Trinitarian" concept of God as Father, Son, and Holy Ghost. Many clergymen opposed to Ware publicly protested the appointment, and after failing to get Ware dismissed, the recalcitrants in 1809 established their own rival school of theology at Andover.

The years between 1805 and 1820 saw bitter intellectual and personal struggles between the Harvard and Andover wings of New England Congregationalism. The vituperation of the controversy seems out of proportion to the actual differences between the two camps, but it is worth remembering that the split came at a time of general religious fervor in the nation, a period known as the Second Great Awakening, and a time when toleration was difficult to practice.

Beyond the nominal difference between Unitarianism and Trinitarianism over the nature of God, Unitarians differed from traditional New England Calvinists in disputing the total depravity of humankind. Men such as Channing believed that human beings were a mixture of good and bad and that part of the clergy's job was to encourage the former and discourage the latter. Unitarians also had doubts about the Calvinist doctrine of predestination, or the notion that God had already determined the fate of all human beings and that mortal actions on earth could have no influence on the divine. Moreover, Channing and other Unitarians refused to believe the old Congregationalist doctrine that humankind on earth could be divided into the "elect" (those who knew their salvation) and all the rest. Unitarians, under Channing's leadership, came to believe that salvation was within all people's power but that people needed careful religious instruction in order to avoid the many falsehoods and errors inherent in the various denominations of Christianity.

Channing kept a low profile during the most heated years of the Unitarian Controversy, between 1809 and 1815. He emerged as a Unitarian leader only in 1819 with a deliberately crafted public address that served as a counterblast to the Andover wing. Indeed, his address was so compelling and succinct that the split in Congregationalism became permanent. After Channing's 1819 "Baltimore Sermon," Unitarianism and Trinitarian Congregationalism went their separate ways.

The location for his grand theological pronouncement was a bit unusual. Instead of Boston, Channing chose the southern city of Baltimore as the setting, and the ordination of a Harvard-trained minister named Jared Sparks as the occasion. Sparks had been called to the pulpit of the newly established First Independent Church of Baltimore, an outpost as far south as any that Unitarianism had established.

Channing took as his text for his Baltimore Sermon a verse from 1 Thessalonians: "Prove all things; hold fast to that which is good." The audience was filled with a host of Unitarian ministers, and Channing sought to summarize for them his belief that rationalism should be the core of Unitarian religious practice. He told the ordination assembly that as Christians they needed to affirm that the Bible was, in part, God's revelation to humankind but also, in part, humankind's imperfect attempt to understand God. Channing emphasized that the Old Testament was full of errors and superstitions and that Christians should concentrate on the teachings of Jesus. The job of the Unitarian minister, he went on, was to separate the divine in the Bible from the mundane by use of reason

William Ellery Channing. (Library of Congress)

and scholarship, all for the benefit of the congregation. This required a sound education in many fields for the would-be clergyman, from knowledge of the ancient languages to a familiarity with modern science. More than any other Unitarian leader, Channing sought to push the clergy into seeing its role as primarily one of scholar-teacher.

Channing also used the occasion of Sparks's ordination in Baltimore to pull together the separately articulated but as yet uncollected strands of Unitarian doctrine. He insisted that the notion of a Trinity was a logical absurdity and maintained as well that the doctrine of Original Sin mocked God by ascribing base motives to him such as jealousy and rage. From these two assumptions, Channing went on to reason that the purpose of Christ was to perform an errand for the superior God by sending a message that humankind was forgiven its sins. Moreover, Channing proposed that Christ had only partly completed his mission, which, fully understood, involved transforming humankind into a species marked by complete love and goodness.

The Baltimore Sermon of 1819 circulated widely in print and made its author famous on both sides of the Atlantic. During the early 1820's, Channing and his family journeyed to England and the Continent, where he was received by many leading intellectuals, including William Wordsworth and Samuel Taylor Coleridge. He continued to speak out forcefully against the Trinitarian Congregationalists (many of whom called him an infidel), and in 1825, he helped establish the American Unitarian Association, thereby officially ratifying the schism in the Church that John Winthrop and John Cotton had created in 1630.

Though honored as a leader while still a comparatively young man, Channing had a less than happy tenure at Federal Street Church in the years after 1819, particularly in his last decade. He faced two great challenges, one moral and one intellectual, that troubled him until his death. The first was the problem of slavery in America. Channing knew of southern slavery from his Richmond days, but a visit to the West Indian island of St. Croix in 1831 upset him deeply. He saw directly the hard lot of black slaves on the sugar plantations, and he returned to Boston just as the abolitionist movement began organizing in that city.

American abolitionism during the 1830's was highly unpopular, in large part because its backers were thought to favor interracial marriage. Boston and other cities were wracked by antiabolitionist mob violence, and while Channing condemned the mob, he also earned the scorn of the abolitionists for not wholeheartedly endorsing their cause. Only in his "Duty of the Free States," written in 1842 just before his death, did he come to see slavery as a manifestation of evil so great that forceful means would be required to overcome it. Until that time, Channing had hoped that Christian appeals to the conscience of the southern slaveholder would work to end the institution without violence.

The other great challenge to Channing and the new Unitarian Association was from within: the intellectual challenge of the Transcendentalists. The sources of Transcendentalism are complex, found partly in European Romanticism, partly in the reflected enthusiasm of Jacksonian America, but in any event, its notions of the primacy of sensation, intuition, and nature posed a direct challenge to the rationalist approach to Christianity. Channing died in October, 1842—before his former student Ralph Waldo Emerson would call Boston Unitarianism "corpse-cold"—but even by 1842, Channing could see that Unitarianism was not satisfying the spiritual needs of many its adherents.

SIGNIFICANCE

By devising a rational Christianity still reliant on faith, Channing reached an optimistic end similar to that proposed by a contemporary New England "Universalist" preacher named Hosea Ballou, who interpreted the Crucifixion as the sign that all sinners everywhere and forever had been pardoned in advance and that salvation would be "universal." In their own ways, the rationalist Channing and the Universalist Ballou built the basis for an American liberal Christianity that offered hope without resorting to threats of hellfire and brimstone. Indeed, after the Civil War, Unitarians and Universalists saw their common interests and, after many fits and starts, eventually effected a merger in the twentieth century.

Channing also took liberal Christianity in the direction of social reform. His stress on the goodness of humanity and the possibility of moral instruction got him involved in many of the reform movements of Jacksonian America. He was an active temperance enthusiast, supported the emerging antiwar movement, and advocated an extensive system of public education. Channing communicated many of these concerns to the public, first in sermons at Federal Street and then in pamphlets written for a wider audience.

At the same time, Channing served as mentor to many of the young writers and thinkers in Boston, men such as Ralph Waldo Emerson, Henry Wadsworth Longfellow, and Robert Lowell. Channing's 1830 pamphlet *Remarks on American Literature* was a direct call for American writers to create a new, national, and republican literature that was divorced from the monarchical and antidemocratic British literature then in fashion. The call was taken up in the great flowering of New England culture in the last decades before the Civil War. Like any good teacher, then, Channing should be remembered as much for the students he helped tutor as for the ideas he advanced himself.

—*James W. Oberly*

FURTHER READING

Channing, William Ellery. *The Works of William E. Channing*. 6 vols. Boston: J. Munroe, 1848. The chief virtue of Channing's papers is that they allow one to gauge the breadth of his interests. Here is a clergyman involved in an extraordinary range of religious and secular matters.

Delbanco, Andrew. *William Ellery Channing: An Essay on the Liberal Spirit in America*. Cambridge, Mass.: Harvard University Press, 1981. This work is concerned mostly with placing Channing in the context of American thought during the early nineteenth century. Especially good at discussing the intellectual origins of Unitarianism as a reaction against Calvinism.

Edgell, David D. *William Ellery Channing: An Intellectual Portrait*. Boston: Beacon Press, 1955. The first modern biography of Channing. Seeks to understand him as the synthesizer of rational Christianity.

Mendelsohn, Jack. *Channing the Reluctant Radical: A Biography*. Boston: Little, Brown, 1971. Mendelsohn gives considerable detail about Channing's personal and family life. A sympathetic account of liberal Christianity then and now.

Robinson, David. *The Unitarians and the Universalists*. Westport, Conn.: Greenwood Press, 1985. Strong on the Unitarian Controversy and its aftermath, this work also considers Channing's response to the Transcendentalist challenge.

Toulouse, Teresa. *The Art of Prophesying: New England Sermons and the Shaping of Belief*. Athens: University of Georgia Press, 1987. A scholarly study of sermons by Channing, Ralph Waldo Emerson, John Cotton, and other New England preachers.

Wright, Conrad, ed. *A Stream of Light*. Boston: Unitarian Universalist Association, 1975. A series of essays commemorating the establishment of an official Unitarian church. The chapter by Charles Forman is helpful in giving Channing's place in the Unitarian Controversy.

_____. *Three Prophets of Religious Liberalism: Channing, Emerson, Parker*. Boston: Beacon Press, 1961. This handy volume contains Channing's Baltimore Sermon, as well as a helpful introduction to American Unitarianism.

_____. *The Unitarian Controversy: Essays on American Unitarian History*. Boston: Skinner House Books, 1994. Essays on the controversy by a leading Unitarian scholar. One essay is entitled "The Channing We Didn't Know."

SEE ALSO: Dorothea Dix; Nathaniel Hawthorne; Fanny Kemble; Emma Lazarus; Elizabeth Palmer Peabody; Rammohan Ray; Joseph Story.

RELATED ARTICLE in *Great Events from History: The Nineteenth Century, 1801-1900:* May, 1819: Unitarian Church Is Founded.

CHARLES XIV JOHN

French king of Sweden and Norway (r. 1818-1844)

Charles XIV lived two virtually distinct lives. First, he was a soldier in the French army with strong republican convictions; later, he became the conservative king of Sweden.

BORN: January 26, 1763; Pau, France
DIED: March 8, 1844; Stockholm, Sweden
ALSO KNOWN AS: Jean-Baptiste-Jules Bernadotte (birth name); Charles John
AREAS OF ACHIEVEMENT: Government and politics, military

EARLY LIFE

Charles XIV was born Jean-Baptiste-Jules Bernadotte in the southern French province of Gascony. The son of Henri, an attorney, and Jeanne, he was reared in a typical provincial bourgeois manner. He abandoned his law education after the death of his father in 1780 and joined the army. An intelligent young man, with a better education than the French army was accustomed to, he rose through the ranks. On the eve of the French Revolution, he held the rank of sergeant major, the highest noncommissioned position in the army. When the revolution opened the ranks of the officer corps to men of ability, Bernadotte was among the first to benefit. He was commissioned a second lieutenant in November, 1791.

Soon after France went to war with Russia and Austria in April, 1792, Bernadotte was promoted to captain. He first saw combat at the head of a company in 1793. Promotions came quickly for able officers in those crucial years of the French Republic, and Bernadotte was catapulted in one year, 1794, from captain to general of division. While campaigning in Belgium and on the Rhine, he earned the reputation of a competent and careful division commander.

Bernadotte took an active part in the campaigns of 1795 and 1796. Then in February, 1797, he was sent to Italy with reinforcements for Napoleon I. This was the first time that he served under the future emperor of the French. As was the case with the other generals of division in the army of Italy, Bernadotte was senior in time served but with the same rank as Napoleon and resented the fact that he had to serve under an officer who had never commanded a division in combat until he was given the army of Italy in 1796. Bernadotte was also six years older than the twenty-seven-year-old aristocrat from Corsica and had much more combat experience. However, Napoleon had already won stunning victories over the Austrians at Castiglione, Arcola, and Rivoli before Bernadotte had arrived and had established somewhat of a reputation. The newcomer from the Rhine had no choice but to take orders. He played a waiting game.

LIFE'S WORK

Bernadotte spent all of his adult life as a soldier until 1798. Duirng that year, he was appointed by the government of the Directory to be ambassador to Austria. His stay in Vienna was brief, as a lack of social graces combined with strong republican beliefs caused him to be quite unacceptable in the heart of aristocratic Europe. Returning to Paris after only a few months in Vienna, he met and quickly married Désirée Clary. In 1795, Napoleon had unsuccessfully sought her hand in marriage after his brother Joseph had married Désirée's sister Julie. As a result of his marriage, Bernadotte became a part of the extended Bonaparte family. Despite this relationship, he was seldom on good terms with the man who would rule France for fifteen years.

When Napoleon went to Egypt in 1798, Bernadotte remained in Paris, and in July of the following year he was appointed minister of war by the Directory. It was his strong republican views that won for him this position, but he did not work well with the directors, and within a few months he was relieved of the office. When Napoleon returned to France and took part in the coup d'état of Brumaire, Bernadotte refused to have any part in the overthrow of the government. He sat on the sidelines while Napoleon made himself master of France with the title of first consul.

To ingratiate the staunch republican, Napoleon named Bernadotte councillor of state in January, 1800. Despite the fact that he remained a republican, he accepted the prestigious position and gave tacit support to the new regime. He was also given a command in the army, and between 1800 and 1804 he served in the west of France and in northern Europe. It seems to have been during the first decade of the nineteenth century that Bernadotte was transformed from a republican into a monarchist. Napoleon showered him with wealth, titles, honors, and decorations, which he could never have gained under a republic. However, if the emperor was able to buy his loyalty and support, he was not able to purchase his affection. Bernadotte never came to like Napoleon.

In 1805, when war again broke out with Austria and Russia, Bernadotte commanded the I Corps of the Grand

Army. At the Battle of Austerlitz, he held the left flank and supported Marshal Nicolas Jean de Dieu Soult's decisive attack against the center of the Russian line. His corps fought well, and he contributed to this, perhaps Napoleon's finest, victory.

The following year, Bernadotte was made prince of Ponte-Corvo. By the end of the summer of 1806, France was again at war with a Continental power. This time it was Prussia and the campaign was in southeast Germany. Unlike at Austerlitz, however, Bernadotte and his I Corps sat idly in between the Battles of Jean and Auerstadt on October 16. He was strongly criticized by Napoleon and the army for not marching to the aid of Marshal Louis N. Davout, who fought and defeated a Prussian army at Auerstadt that was more than twice the size of his III Corps.

Although the emperor threatened to court-martial Bernadotte for his lack of initiative, no action was taken against him, and the I Corps, rested and unscarred, led the pursuit of the devastated Prussian army. Bernadotte received the surrender of the city of Lübeck and then marched east to support the main army. He was not at the Battle of the Eylau in February, 1807, but he was wounded in action at Spanden in June of the same year, shortly before the campaign came to a victorious conclusion with the defeat of the Russian army at Friedland. Upon his recovery from his wound, he was named governor of Hamburg, Bremen, and Lübeck.

During the two years Bernadotte spent in northern Germany he had various dealings with Serden, which had held territory on the south Baltic coast. The renewal of hostilities with Austria in the spring of 1809 brought Bernadotte back into Central Europe at the head of the IX Corps. Following the victory at Eckmuhl and a setback at Aspern-Essling, Napoleon engaged the Austrian army at Wagram on July 5. Bernadotte's Saxon Corps held the left center of the French line. When the Austrians attacked the French left, the Saxons broke and fled to the rear. Despite Bernadotte's efforts, it was necessary to fill the gap created by redeploying Marshal André Masséna's IV Corps. Napoleon was furious with Bernadotte. He accused him of losing the battle, which the French eventually won, and of cowardliness in the face of the enemy. Bernadotte was ordered to leave the army in disgrace and to retire to Paris.

The year 1810 was a pivotal one for Bernadotte. In 1809, the Swedish king, Gustavus IV Adolphus, was forced into exile, and his uncle was put on the throne with the title of Charles XIII. With the death of Charles XIII's adopted son, the Swedish Parliament elected Bernadotte crown prince. Having formally changed his name—he was now known as Charles John—and his religion, he left France with Napoleon's blessing, landing in Sweden on October 20, 1810. As crown prince, Charles John did not become involved with domestic affairs, but he did play an active role in foreign policy. He realized that Sweden's interests lay in cooperation with Russia and England, not France. Therefore, in 1813 he encouraged the Swedes to declare war on France in order to acquire Norway, owned by Denmark, as compensation for the loss of Finland, which had been taken by the Russians in 1809.

Charles John led a Swedish army of twenty thousand men into Germany to fight against France. He defeated Marshal Nicolas Charles Oudinot at Gross-Beeren on August 23, 1813, and arrived at Leipzig on the last day of the three-day battle to witness the defeat of Napoleon. He played a minor role in the campaign of 1814 that forced the French emperor to abdicate in April of that year. He seems to have grasped at the hope of becoming king of France but was never seriously considered by the French. Most Frenchmen, and in particular those in the army, considered him to be a traitor.

After returning to Sweden, Charles John played no part in the campaign of the Hundred Days when Napoleon returned in 1815. However, Sweden did receive Norway as a reward for having joined the grand alliance against France in 1813. When Charles XIII died in 1818, the once-strong republican was crowned Charles XIV, king of Sweden. His twenty-six-year reign was not particularly eventful. He had been put on the throne by the grace of Parliament, and he did not overstep the limitations placed on the Crown. He became progressively more conservative, and during the later years of his reign clashed with the reform-minded Parliament. Charles John died at Stockholm on March 8, 1844, and was succeeded by his son Oscar I.

SIGNIFICANCE

As Charles XIV John, king of Sweden, the man born Jean-Baptiste-Jules Bernadotte found an improbable fulfillment of his ambitions. If his story sounds like something out of the pages of Alexandre Dumas, *père*, the reality was considerably less romantic. The reign of Charles XIV John came at a time in Sweden's history when power was decisively shifting from the throne to Parliament; this period was the foundation of modern Swedish democracy. Still, if Charles's role was sharply circumscribed, his years on the throne were peaceful and prosperous ones for Sweden, and history has labeled him as a good king.

—John G. Gallaher

FURTHER READING

Barton, Dunbar Plunket. *Bernadotte: The First Phase, 1763-1799.* London: John Murray, 1914.

_____. *Bernadotte and Napoleon, 1799-1810.* London: John Murray, 1921.

_____. *Bernadotte, Prince and King, 1810-1844.* London: John Murray, 1925. Taken together, these three volumes still represent the definitive work on Charles John. They provide a detailed account of his long and active life with numerous quotations from his correspondence. See also the abridged one-volume edition of Barton's work entitled *The Amazing Career of Bernadotte* (1929), which is much more widely available then the multivolume study.

Dewes, Simon. *Sergent Belle-Jombs: The Life of Marshal Bernadotte.* London: Rich & Cowan, 1943. This readable account, favorable toward its central figure, concentrates on Charles John's military career during the Napoleonic years. Dewes is primarily concerned with military affairs and tends to minimize the political and administrative aspects of Bernadotte's life.

Heathcote, T. A. "'Serjent Belle-Jambe': Bernadotte." In *Napoleon's Marshals*, edited by David G. Chandler. New York: Macmillan, 1987. A very good twenty-two-page chapter in an excellent study of the marshals of the Napoleonic Empire. The emphasis is on Charles John's early years and his career in the French army. There is virtually nothing on him as king of Sweden.

Palmer, Alan. *Bernadotte: Napoleon's Marshall, Sweden's King.* London: John Murray, 1990. Most recent books about Charles are written in languages other than English; this popular biography is one of the rare English-language books, and it offers a nonscholarly overview of Charles's life.

Scott, Franklin D. *Bernadotte and the Fall of Napoleon.* Cambridge, Mass.: Harvard University Press, 1935. This is a scholarly study of Charles John's role in the removal of Napoleon from the throne of France in 1814. Although it covers only a brief period of the life of Charles John, it provides a good understanding of the man and his ambitions and motivations.

Wencker-Wildbery, Friedrich. *Bernadotte: A Biography.* London: Jarrolds, 1936. Written in a popular style with many undocumented quotes, this is a very readable account of the life of Charles John. It also contains a number of good pictures of him and his family into the twentieth century. Although it is reasonably accurate, it is not a scholarly work.

SEE ALSO: Alexandre Dumas, *père*; Napoleon I.

RELATED ARTICLES in *Great Events from History: The Nineteenth Century, 1801-1900:* December 2, 1805: Battle of Austerlitz; October 16-19, 1813: Battle of Leipzig.

SALMON P. CHASE

American politician and jurist

As an attorney, politician, and constitutional theorist, Chase contributed to the abolition of slavery. During the 1850's, he served as a U.S. senator and as governor of Ohio, and he participated in the formation of the Republican Party. He was later appointed secretary of the treasury and became chief justice of the United States.

BORN: January 13, 1808; Cornish, New Hampshire
DIED: May 7, 1873; New York, New York
ALSO KNOWN AS: Salmon Portland Chase (full name)
AREAS OF ACHIEVEMENT: Government and politics, law

EARLY LIFE

Salmon P. Chase's father, Ithamar Chase, whose family had come to North America during the 1640's, was a farmer who held minor local offices and occasionally served in the state legislature. Chase's mother, Janette Ralston, was the daughter of Scottish immigrants who became prominent landowners in Keene, New Hampshire. Ithamar died when the younger Chase was eight, so the boy spent his youth living with various friends and relatives, including his uncle, Philander Chase, the bishop of the Episcopal Church in Ohio.

In 1821, Chase entered Cincinnati College, where his uncle Philander was president. Philander's influence on his nephew was profound. For the rest of his life, Chase would be extremely pious. His later commitment to the abolition of slavery would be as much religious as political. By 1823, Chase had returned to New Hampshire, where he briefly taught school before entering Dartmouth College. In 1826 he was graduated eighth in his class, a member of Phi Beta Kappa. Chase then moved to Washington, D.C., where he taught school before beginning law studies under William Wirt in 1827. In December, 1829, he was admitted to the bar.

In 1830, the athletic, tall, vigorous, and ambitious Chase settled in Cincinnati, where he practiced law and took an active role in civic affairs. Between 1831 and 1833, he published historical essays in *The North American Review*, anonymous editorials in Ohio newspapers, and a three-volume, comprehensive compilation of Ohio's laws, *The Statutes of Ohio* (1833-1835). Chase was neither brilliant nor eloquent in court, but he was hardworking, careful, and scholarly. These traits brought him a comfortable and growing commercial practice that, by 1835, included such clients as the Bank of the United States and the Lafayette Bank of Ohio. By 1845, his firm of Chase and Ball earned an estimated ten thousand dollars a year—an extraordinarily large sum for the era. In 1834, Chase married his first wife, who died in 1835. Two other marriages (in 1839 and 1846) would also end with the death of his wives. Of his six daughters only two, Katherine Chase Sprauge and Jeanette Chase Hoyt, survived to adulthood.

LIFE'S WORK

Chase's national career had four phases: abolitionist lawyer, United States senator and governor of Ohio, secretary of the treasury, and chief justice of the United States.

From 1830 to 1849, Chase lived in Cincinnati, where his law firm flourished. In addition to this profitable practice, Chase offered free legal services to abolitionists, fugitive slaves, and free blacks. In 1836, mobs destroyed the office of Cincinnati's antislavery newspaper, the *Philanthropist*, and threatened the life of its editor, James G. Birney. Also threatened was Chase's brother-in-law, Dr. Isaac Colby. Through this incident, Chase became an attorney for the antislavery cause. Chase was initially attracted to the abolitionist movement because he abhorred the mob violence and disrespect for law directed against it. He evolved into a passionate and articulate supporter of the cause. In 1836, he won a damage suit against members of the mob, recovering some money for Birney to rebuild the office of the *Philanthropist*. A year later, Chase unsuccessfully defended the freedom of a fugitive slave, Matilda, who had been harbored by Birney. Birney was then convicted for helping Matilda, but Chase won a reversal on appeal.

By 1841, Chase was a leading antislavery attorney in Ohio. Chase rejected the anticonstitutionalism of William Lloyd Garrison and instead developed a constitutional theory consistent with opposition to slavery. In 1843 and 1848, he was the chief author of the platform of the national Free-Soil Party. Besides his Free-Soil political activities, Chase defended numerous fugitive slaves and their white and black allies. During the 1840's, Chase corresponded with antislavery lawyers throughout the Midwest, persuading them to take cases that he had no time to handle and advising them on legal strategies. Chase lost his most famous fugitive slave case, *Jones v. Van Zandt* (1847), but his printed Supreme Court brief, titled "Reclamation of Fugitives from Service," added to his growing national reputation as the "attorney general for fugitive slaves."

In 1849, a small group of Free-Soilers held the balance of power in the Ohio legislature. Guided in part by Chase, these political abolitionists secured two victories: They negotiated the repeal of most of Ohio's racially restrictive "black code," and they secured the election of Chase to the U.S. Senate.

In the Senate, Chase failed in his attempt to create a "Free Democracy" made up of antislavery Democrats such as himself. Effectively separated from all parties, he remained one of the most uncompromising Senate opponents of slavery, constantly challenging southerners and their northern allies. As a politician, Chase was somewhat ponderous, pompous, and self-righteous. While he was not a great debater, his carefully written speeches read well on the stump and in the Senate.

In 1850, Chase was one of the leading opponents of the Fugitive Slave Law and other proslavery aspects of the Compromise of that year. While in the Senate, Chase continued to develop his antislavery constitutional analysis, arguing that the Fifth Amendment made slavery unconstitutional wherever the federal government had jurisdiction. This led to his concept of "freedom national, slavery sectional," which became a rallying cry for the Republican Party, especially after the *Dred Scott* decision (1857). Chase also laid out the theoretical basis for the Republican Party's slogan of 1856: Free Soil, Free Labor, Free Speech, Free Men.

In 1854, Chase emerged as a leader of the opposition to the Kansas-Nebraska Act and in the process once again tried to organize a party of "Independent Democrats." No "Independent Democracy" emerged in 1854, but by 1855 a broader coalition of Free-Soilers, northern Democrats, and Whigs had united into an "Anti-Nebraska Party," which soon became the Republican Party. Chase was instrumental in the founding of this new political organization in Ohio. In 1855, he became one of the first Republican governors in the nation by defeating candidates from both the Whig and Democratic parties. In 1857, he was reelected governor of Ohio.

As Ohio's governor, Chase helped create the Republican Party in both the state and the nation. In part because of his cold personality, however, he was unable to unify the state party behind his own presidential ambitions; in both 1856 and 1860, he was unsuccessful in his efforts to gain the Republican nomination for that office.

While governor, Chase opposed the extradition of fugitive slaves but was unable to prevent the removal of the slave Margaret Garner, who killed her own daughter to prevent the child's return to slavery. After the rescue of an alleged fugitive slave near Oberlin, however, Chase gave support to the rescuers and appeared willing to confront federal authorities. In another case, Chase prevented the extradition of a free black accused of helping slaves to escape from Kentucky. This ultimately led to the Supreme Court decision in *Kentucky v. Dennison* (1861), in which Chief Justice Roger B. Taney chastised Ohio for its antislavery activities but refused actually to order the return of the accused fugitive.

Throughout his governorship, Chase tried to walk a fine line between actual defiance of federal law and the Constitution, and his thoroughgoing opposition to slavery and the Fugitive Slave Law. When not sparring with the federal government, Governor Chase directed his energies to reorganizing the Ohio militia, which would ultimately be a major asset to the Union during the Civil War.

In 1860, Governor Chase failed to obtain the Republican presidential nomination. He was, however, elected to the U.S. Senate in the fall of that year. During the secession crisis, he served as a "peace commissioner" from Ohio, where he opposed any extension of slavery into the territories but also disclaimed any intention of interfering with slavery where it already existed. In March, he had barely taken his seat in the Senate when President Abraham Lincoln appointed him secretary of the treasury.

In his new office, Chase faced the formidable task of financing the Civil War. With the aid of financier Jay Cooke, Chase was able to market government bonds, thus providing a constant flow of capital into the national treasury. Chase's initiatives led to the establishment of a national banking system in 1863 with a system of currency backed by federal bonds and securities. Because the Treasury Department was also responsible for confiscated and abandoned property from the Confederacy, Chase was able to take an active role in the dismantling of slavery.

Chase, the most radical abolitionist in Lincoln's original cabinet, used his office to chip away at slavery in the period before the Emancipation Proclamation (1862). He supported generals who used their power to undermine or destroy the institution, as long as they did not overtly go beyond administration policy. Under Chase's protégé, Edward L. Pierce, the first steps toward educating former slaves for life as free men and women took place in 1862 on the sea islands of South Carolina. Chase encouraged dedicated abolitionists to run this "rehearsal for reconstruction." In the cabinet, Chase argued for an early end to slavery itself. Chase strongly supported the Emancipation Proclamation, even though he believed that it did not go far enough. Chase's personal piety led him to persuade Lincoln to ask for the "gracious favor of Almighty God" at the end of the proclamation.

Throughout his tenure as secretary of the treasury, Chase's relationship with Lincoln was strained. He had serious policy disagreements with Lincoln, especially on such issues as emancipation and black rights. Chase was far ahead of his president on these matters. In addition, Chase wanted Lincoln's job: Chase had his eye on the White House in 1856 and 1860. He thought that after a single term Lincoln would step aside, and he could step forward. Chase's feuding with Secretary of State William H. Seward and his persistent campaigning for the Republican presidential nomination in 1864 made it increasingly difficult for him to remain in the cabinet. In June, 1864, a conflict over the appointment of a subordinate led Chase to offer his resignation. This was the fourth or fifth time he had done so. Much to his surprise, Lincoln accepted the resignation and Chase was out of the cabinet.

In spite of his disagreements with Lincoln, Chase ultimately campaigned actively for the Republican ticket throughout the fall of 1864. After his reelection, Lincoln appointed Chase to replace the late Roger B. Taney as chief justice of the United States. Chase was a logical choice. He had been an eminent attorney and had developed the most coherent antislavery legal-constitutional arguments of the antebellum period. He was sympathetic to emancipation and the other war policies of the Lincoln administration.

Rather than marking a fitting end to his lifetime of public service, however, Chase's years in the Supreme Court were an anticlimax if not an embarrassment. Chase joined a Court that was deeply divided between antislavery Lincoln appointees and proslavery holdovers from the prewar years. During Reconstruction, the court was asked to decide on questions that were at the heart of the political crisis of the period. The Court's answer, and Chase's leadership, were mixed.

Chase presided over the impeachment of Andrew Johnson with fairness and skill. He earned the respect of most of the Senate, and of much of the nation. This might have been the capstone of his career. Chase still had his eye on the presidency, however, and he used his newfound prestige to campaign for the office. Chase's hunger for the White House led him to repudiate his previous support for black suffrage, in hopes of getting the Democratic nomination. He failed in this effort and in the process lost support from moderates as well as former abolitionists.

When he appointed Chase, Lincoln told a friend "we wish for a Chief Justice who will sustain what has been done in regard to emancipation and the legal tenders." Had Lincoln lived, he would have been disappointed by Chase on the latter issue. In *Hepburn v. Griswold* (1870) and in the Legal Tender cases (1871), Chase voted to void the financial system that he had set up as the secretary of the treasury. The chief justice was severely criticized for this.

On black rights, Chase's record was more consistent. Despite his willingness to oppose black suffrage in order to gain the presidential nomination in 1868, Chase was a genuine supporter of black rights. In the Slaughterhouse cases (1873), Chase vigorously dissented, arguing that the majority opinion undermined the rights of the freedmen. In other Reconstruction decisions, Chase generally supported Congress over the president or the states. The one major exception was the loyalty oaths, which Chase opposed from the bench. In his most important Reconstruction decision, *Texas v. White* (1868), Chase upheld the basic theory of congressional Reconstruction in an opinion that was sensitive to the political realities of the era. Chase also upheld the power of Congress to limit Supreme Court jurisdiction in the postwar South in *Ex parte McCardle* (1868). In *Ex parte Milligan* (1866), however, he denied the right of the executive branch to abolish civilian courts in those states that remained within the Union.

SIGNIFICANCE

Few men in American history have held so many important governmental positions. Chase's contributions to the antislavery movement and the Republican Party were critical. His defense of fugitive slaves and abolitionists was unmatched by other lawyers of his age; his development of a coherent antislavery constitutional theory helped pave the way for Lincoln's victory in 1860 and the ultimate abolition of slavery. As secretary of the treasury, Chase was a valuable and hardworking member of Lincoln's cabinet. Besides organizing the financing of the war effort, Chase helped develop Reconstruction policy. During the early years of the war, he also helped Lincoln manage the War Department, which was being incompetently and corruptly run by Secretary of War Simon Cameron.

As chief justice, Chase was a disappointment. He was unable to assert the authority and leadership that he had displayed in his other public positions. His opinions were never as sharp as his prewar speeches had been. Moreover, his positions, so clear and consistent in the antebellum period, were sometimes vague on the bench. His grasping for the presidency reflected poorly on him and on the office he held. Nevertheless, Chase guided the Supreme Court through the impeachment crisis with dignity. He also avoided running afoul of Congress at a time when that branch might have seriously damaged the Supreme Court, had Chase and his brethren opposed congressional Reconstruction policies. Similarly, Chase left the bench on a high note, vigorously asserting the rights of the freedmen in the Slaughterhouse cases, at a time when a majority of the Supreme Court and the nation were rejecting any commitment to racial equality.

—Paul Finkelman

FURTHER READING

Chase, Salmon Portland. *Inside Lincoln's Cabinet: The Civil War Diaries of Salmon P. Chase*. Edited by David H. Donald. New York: Longmans, Green, 1954. Chase kept a detailed diary while in the cabinet. This carefully edited edition offers great insight into Chase and his role in the cabinet. Part of the diary is also available, along with many Chase letters, in volume 2 of the *Annual Report of the American Historical Association for the Year 1902*, published by the U.S. Government Printing Office in 1903.

Foner, Eric. *Free Soil, Free Labor, Free Men: The Ideology of the Republican Party Before the Civil War*. New York: Oxford University Press, 1970. Contains an important chapter on Chase's constitutional theory and its relationship to Republican ideology. Throughout this book, Chase is a major figure.

Hart, Albert Bushnell. *Salmon Portland Chase*. Boston: Houghton Mifflin, 1899. Although dated, this volume remains the best available biography of Chase. The book is relatively weak on his judicial career but is an excellent introduction to his abolitionist efforts and political career.

Hyman, Harold M. *The Reconstruction Justice of Salmon P. Chase: In Re Turner and Texas v. White*. Lawrence: University Press of Kansas, 1997. Hyman analyzes the U.S. Supreme Court's rulings in two Reconstruction era cases regarding the legal rights of slaves and the status of former Confederate states. After a brief sketch of Chase's life, he describes how Chase's decisions in these two cases reflected his abolitionist beliefs and activist judicial philosophy.

Hyman, Harold M., and William M. Wiecek. *Equal Justice Under Law: Constitutional Development, 1835-1875*. New York: Harper & Row, 1982. Covers the developments in constitutional and legal thought during Chase's career.

Kutler, Stanley I. *Judicial Power and Reconstruction Politics*. Chicago: University of Chicago Press, 1968. Best short introduction to the problems of the Supreme Court under Chase.

Niven, John. *Salmon P. Chase: A Biography*. New York: Oxford University Press, 1995. Niven portrays Chase as a complex mixture of idealism and ambition, whose pursuit of abolition was equaled by an ardent pursuit of power.

Niven, John, James P. McClure, and Leigh Johnsen, eds. *The Salmon P. Chase Papers*. 5 vols. Kent, Ohio: Kent State University Press, 1993-1998. One of the five volumes consists of entries from Chase's journal between 1829 and 1872; the remaining four volumes contain his correspondence from 1823 to 1873. These documents provide insight into Chase's role in the antislavery movement, his political career, and the legal issues he confronted as chief justice.

Schuckers, Jacob W. *The Life and Public Services of Salmon Portland Chase*. New York: Da Capo Press, 1970. Written by one of Chase's protégés (and originally published in 1874), this book presents an overly heroic portrait of its subject but is nevertheless useful, particularly for the many Chase letters and speeches that it reprints.

Warden, Robert. *An Account of the Private Life and Public Services of Salmon Portland Chase*. Cincinnati: Wilstach, Baldwin, 1874. Much like the Schuckers biography, this volume is useful but uncritical.

Wiecek, William M. *The Sources of Antislavery Constitutionalism in America, 1760-1848*. Ithaca, N.Y.: Cornell University Press, 1977. Places Chase's antislavery theories and legal arguments in the context of other abolitionist constitutional theorists.

SEE ALSO: Jay Cooke; Andrew Johnson; Abraham Lincoln; Roger Brooke Taney.

RELATED ARTICLES in *Great Events from History: The Nineteenth Century, 1801-1900:* September 18, 1850: Second Fugitive Slave Law; May 30, 1854: Congress Passes Kansas-Nebraska Act; July 6, 1854: Birth of the Republican Party; January 1, 1863: Lincoln Issues the Emancipation Proclamation; February 25, 1863-June 3, 1864: Congress Passes the National Bank Acts; February 24-May 26, 1868: Impeachment of Andrew Johnson.

FRANÇOIS-RENÉ DE CHATEAUBRIAND

French politician, diplomat, and writer

The founder of French Romanticism, Chateaubriand popularized the melancholy hero and deeply influenced many other nineteenth and twentieth century writers and was the first writer to appreciate the literary potential of the American frontier.

BORN: September 4, 1768; Saint-Malo, France
DIED: July 4, 1848; Paris, France
ALSO KNOWN AS: François-August-René de Chateaubriand (full name)
AREA OF ACHIEVEMENT: Literature

EARLY LIFE

François-August-René de Chateaubriand (shah-TOH-bree-ahn) was the youngest of ten children of René-Auguste de Chateaubriand. His father had become rich as a shipowner and merchant sailor; with his wealth, he had purchased the château of Combourg. There the young Chateaubriand spent a lonely childhood, wandering the woods with his sister Lucile, four years his senior, who early recognized and fostered her brother's genius. Already as an adolescent he revealed himself as a dreamer. He later recalled that when he spoke with Lucile about the world, "it was the world that we carried within us," that of the imagination.

Chateaubriand's father initially intended for him to pursue a naval career. To this end the youth attended the College of Dol, near Combourg, and then the Jesuit college of Rennes. Having rejected the sea, Chateaubriand next went to the College of Dinan to study for the priesthood but soon abandoned this field as well. An older brother, Jean-Baptiste, who was living in Paris and moving in court circles, then secured for him a military commission; Chateaubriand was to remark that both he and Napoleon I began their careers as sublieutenants. He was also to observe that he spent fifteen years as a soldier before devoting fifteen to writing and another fifteen to politics.

Actually, Chateaubriand's military career was considerably briefer. When his father died in September, 1786, Chateaubriand left the army, returned to Combourg, and, in 1789, joined his brother at the French capital. An unintentional witness to the fall of the Bastille and the increasingly violent French Revolution that ensued, in July, 1791, Chateaubriand sailed to America, hoping to find true liberty, fraternity, and equality. On the banks of the Ohio, Chateaubriand chanced upon a newspaper report of the flight of Louis XVI. He hastened back to France to fight for the monarchy. Lacking funds sufficient to join the émigré army, he married the rich and acerbic Céleste Buisson de la Vigne. Wounded and left for dead at the siege of Thionville, he managed to escape to England, where he made a living as a tutor and translator.

François-René de Chateaubriand. (Library of Congress)

LIFE'S WORK

In the evenings, Chateaubriand also began to produce original works. Among the earliest of these is his "Lettre sur l'art du dessin dans les paysages" (1795; letter on the art of landscape painting), a significant contribution to the Romantic movement. From the Renaissance through the eighteenth century, artistic theory emphasized the importance of learning technique through imitation of past masterpieces. Chateaubriand recognized the importance of technical skill, but he argued that the painter must first immerse himself in nature and respond to it emotionally, then attempt to recapture these feelings in his work. The artist should faithfully record what he has observed—Chateaubriand had studied botany before going to the United States so that he would recognize and understand what he was seeing—but landscape painting should seek not photographic realism but rather the ideal. One sees here a number of concepts that recur in writings on Romantic literary theory.

Just as Chateaubriand's observations on landscape painting challenged the neoclassical aesthetic, so his *Essai sur les révolutions* (1797; *An Historical, Political, Moral Essay on Revolutions*, 1815) rejected the political attitude of the Enlightenment. Intended as the first volume of a detailed study of revolutions, it devotes relatively little attention to the one then engulfing Europe. However, it does comment on events in France, denying the idea of progress and perfectibility, seeing the French Revolution as only one of an ongoing series of upheavals that left people no freer or happier than they were before.

The next year Chateaubriand apparently began to change his mind about religion, though he would never allow his devotion to Catholicism to interfere with his pleasures. He began work on *Le Génie du Christianisme* (1799, 1800, 1802; *The Genius of Christianity*, 1802), a spirited defense of traditional belief. Again he was rejecting the views of the eighteenth century philosophers, and, by couching his arguments in aesthetic and emotional terms, he was allying himself once more with the Romantics.

Some portions of this work were published in England, but Chateaubriand was still revising the manuscript when he returned to France in May, 1800. Seeking literary fame and needing money, he detached from *The Genius of Christianity* a novella intended to illustrate how religion improves literature; this piece he published separately in 1801. *Atala* (English translation, 1802), the first work by a European to use the American wilderness and the Indian as central features, told of the love of Atala for the Indian Chactas. Unwilling to betray the vow of chastity made to her dying mother, and unable to overcome her passion for her lover, Atala poisons herself. Here, as in *René* (1802; English translation, 1813), Chateaubriand portrayed the melancholy Byronic hero well before George Gordon, Lord Byron, himself, did so. The dreamlike landscapes that mirror the inhabitants' moods and at the same time seem to control their actions, the emphasis on emotion, the descriptions that use the senses (as when each blade of grass emits a different note) are devices that would influence succeeding generations of writers.

The popularity of *Atala* was matched, if not surpassed, by that of its parent work when it appeared in France the next year. The timing of its publication could not have been more fortunate for the author: On April 8, 1802, Napoleon concluded the Concordat, restoring Catholicism as the official religion of France; *The Genius of Christianity* appeared six days later.

Encouraged by the book's success and by recommendations from Chateaubriand's current mistress, Pauline de Beaumont, Napoleon appointed the author to the post of secretary to the French embassy in Rome (1803). Chateaubriand soon sought, and obtained, another assignment, that of chargé d'affaires to the puppet state of Valais. However, before he could settle his affairs in Paris, he learned of Napoleon's kidnapping and execution of the Bourbon Duc d'Enghien, an act meant to warn the Royalists against any attempted coup. Chateaubriand resigned his office and broke with the French ruler.

Using Royalist funds, Chateaubriand bought the newspaper *Mercure de France* and, on July 4, 1807, published a harsh attack on the dictator. Napoleon retaliated by forcing him to sell the paper, though at a profit sufficient to allow Chateaubriand to acquire a country house outside Paris, where he completed *Les Martyres* (1809; *The Martyrs*, 1812), another tale of doomed love. The heroine, Cymodocéa, is modeled on Natalie de Noailles, who had succeeded Pauline de Beaumont as Chateaubriand's mistress. Throughout his life, he would attract France's most beautiful and clever women, earning for himself the title "the enchanter." Short, stocky, broad-shouldered, and pale, he had a leonine head that compensated for any physical flaw, flashing gray eyes, and wild brown hair that gave him an aura of romance.

Set in the reign of Diocletian, *The Martyrs* presents a thinly veiled attack on Napoleon by comparing the French emperor to the Roman. Having arrested the pope and, therefore, having been excommunicated, Napoleon chose to ignore the criticism and sought to renew his friendship with the leading French Catholic author of the day. He arranged Chateaubriand's appointment to the prestigious Académie Française, but the latter's acceptance speech, so harsh that Napoleon censored it, showed that reconciliation was impossible.

In 1814, Chateaubriand wrote an even sterner indictment of the French ruler. "What have you done, not with a hundred thousand, but with five million Frenchmen . . . our relatives, our friends, our brothers?" he asked in *De Buonaparte et des Bourbons* (1814; *On Buonaparte and the Bourbons*, 1814). Again Chateaubriand's timing was perfect: The piece appeared on the day the allied troops entered Paris, and the newly crowned Louis XVIII claimed that the publication was worth 100,000 soldiers.

Chateaubriand's relationship with the Bourbons was uneasy. On June 4, 1814, Louis issued a charter that reaffirmed individual rights and sought to establish a constitutional monarchy along English lines, with ministerial responsibility to the legislative majority rather than to the king. Within two years, though, Chateaubriand was disillusioned. In his memoirs he was to write, "Descending from Bonaparte and the empire to those who followed them, is like falling from . . . the summit of a mountain into an abyss." While supporting the freedoms won since 1789, Chateaubriand claimed that the king's ministers did not share the views of the majority of Frenchmen and were thus betraying the Charter of 1814.

On February 13, 1820, the Duc de Berry, son of the future Charles X, was assassinated at the opera. In his newspaper *Le Conservateur*, Chateaubriand wrote,

> The hand that struck the blow does not bear the greatest guilt; they that have murdered the Duc de Berry are those that have been introducing democratic laws into the monarchy for the last four years.

The government of Elie Decazes fell, and its successor named Chateaubriand minister of state and envoy to Berlin. He did not remain in Prussia long before returning to Paris to devote himself to Juliette Récamier, Claire de Duras, and Delphine de Custine.

In January, 1822, Chateaubriand again went abroad, this time as ambassador to the Court of St. James, where his chef, Montmireil, immortalized his name among many who never would read *René* or *Atala* by naming a thickly cut beefsteak for the diplomat. Chateaubriand left London in September to represent France at the Congress of Verona, and on December 28, 1822, he was named minister of foreign affairs. He was to claim that in this office he succeeded in doing what Napoleon had not—conquering Spain. A popular revolution had dethroned Ferdinand VII, and Chateaubriand persuaded France to intervene and restore the king to his throne.

In June, 1824, Chateaubriand was himself deposed, losing his ministerial position, though in 1827 he returned to a government post as ambassador to Rome. When Charles X named the conservative Jules de Polignac as chief minister, Chateaubriand resigned. As Chateaubriand feared, Polignac proved to be the downfall of the Bourbon monarchy; in 1830, the Orléans Louis-Philippe assumed the throne after a short revolution. Despite his treatment by the Bourbons, Chateaubriand refused to take the oath of allegiance to the new king, preferring to renounce his titles of peer and minister of state together with the salary they carried.

By then, Chateaubriand no longer needed this stipend, for he had been paid 550,000 francs for the rights to the collected works, and he received another 156,000 francs and a life pension for his memoirs, which appeared posthumously. Chateaubriand's last years were dedicated to the completion of this autobiography and to Juliette Récamier, who was with him when he died in Paris on July 4, 1848. At his request, he was buried in a simple tomb on the rock of Grand Bé off the coast of Saint-Malo.

SIGNIFICANCE

In 1831, when the Gothic church of Saint-Germain l'Auxerrois faced demolition, Chateaubriand played an important role in its preservation, though he remarked that too many such buildings were appearing in the literature of the day. That writers were filling their pages with descriptions of Gothic cathedrals was, however, in large part attributable to Chateaubriand himself. Théophile Gautier claimed that *The Genius of Christianity* restored the popularity of Gothic architecture, just as *Les Natchez* (1826; *The Natchez*, 1827) unlocked the natural sublime and *René* invented the modern melancholy hero. Chateaubriand was an idol to a generation of French Romantics—the young Alphonse de Lamartine waited outside Chateaubriand's house for two days to catch a glimpse of the man—and later authors such as Gustave Flaubert and Charles Baudelaire were equally influenced by his works.

The first writer to appreciate the literary potential of the American frontier, Chateaubriand placed within that setting the brooding hero that Byron would popularize a decade later. The poet of sadness, night, suffering, and ennui, he gave the world the character who searches for a self he will never find. He also taught the French how to read their own classics. He was among the first to recognize the tragic sense that underlies much of Molière's comedy and the sadness and dreamlike qualities of Jean de La Fontaine, Blaise Pascal, and Jean Racine.

Honoré de Balzac wanted to be a literary Napoleon; Chateaubriand hoped to be a political Napoleon as well. He lacked the talent and temperament necessary to rival his fellow sublieutenant in the field or in the cabinet, but in the study he reigned supreme. As Bonaparte remarked, "Chateaubriand has received the sacred fire from Nature; his works bear witness to it. His style is not that of Racine but that of the prophet."

—*Joseph Rosenblum*

FURTHER READING

Bales, Richard. *Persuasion in the French Personal Novel: Studies of Chateaubriand, Constant, Balzac, Nerval, and Fromentin*. Birmingham, Ala.: Summa, 1997. Bales analyzes *René* and several other nineteenth century French romantic novels in which characters persuade themselves (and their readers) that their private failures are public successes.

Evans, Joan. *Chateaubriand: A Biography*. New York: Macmillan, 1939. Relies primarily on Chateaubriand's autobiography but corrects and supplements this work with other accounts. Readable, with many fine vignettes but little analysis.

Hilt, Douglas. "Chateaubriand and Napolean." *History Today* 23 (December, 1973): 831-837. Traces Chateaubriand's political career under Napoleon and the author's subsequent portrayal of Napoleon in his memoirs.

Maurois, André. *Chateaubriand: Poet, Statesman, Lover*. Translated by Vera Fraser. New York: Harper & Row, 1938. Drawing heavily on Chateaubriand's own writing, Maurois artfully weaves his subject's own words into a readable narrative.

Painter, George D. *Chateaubriand: A Biography*. London: Chatto & Windus, 1977. First volume of an apparently unfinished three-volume biography. It offers an extensively detailed account of Chateaubriand's life from 1768 to 1793. Painter has not written the other two volumes, but when he does it will be the definitive biography.

Porter, Charles Allan. *Chateaubriand: Composition, Imagination, and Poetry*. Saratoga, Calif.: Anma Libri, 1978. A stylistic analysis of Chateaubriand's major works. Like many of Chateaubriand's contemporaries, Porter sees discontinuities of time and space in the prose. Porter finds in these disjunctions a modern attempt to engage the reader in the creative process.

Schor, Naomi. *One Hundred Years of Melancholy*. New York: Clarendon Press, 1996. A 17-page reprint of a lecture delivered by Schor, a professor of French at Harvard University. Schor analyzed the sense of melancholy in Chateaubriand's book *Mémoires d'outre-tombe*.

Sieburg, Friedrich. *Chateaubriand*. Translated by Violet M. MacDonald. Winchester, Mass.: Allen & Unwin, 1961. Concentrates on biography rather than literary analysis. Argues that "Chateaubriand's ambition and his desire for action were . . . forever undermining the foundations of his existence" and that his life is a tissue of contradictions.

SEE ALSO: Napoleon I.

RELATED ARTICLES in *Great Events from History: The Nineteenth Century, 1801-1900:* October 20-30, 1822: Great Britain Withdraws from the Concert of Europe; March 3, 1830: Hugo's *Hernani* Incites Rioting; July 29, 1830: July Revolution Deposes Charles X.

ANTON CHEKHOV

Russian dramatist and writer

Although Chekhov had a significant impact on the creation of modern drama with his four major plays, his most important literary influence has been on the development of the modern short story. With his numerous lyrical stories, Chekhov liberated the short story in particular from its adherence to the parable form and fiction in general from the tedium of the realistic novel.

BORN: January 29, 1860; Taganrog, Russia
DIED: July 15, 1904; Badenweiler, Germany
ALSO KNOWN AS: Anton Tchekhov; Anton Pavlovich Chekhov (full name)
AREAS OF ACHIEVEMENT: Literature, theater

EARLY LIFE

Anton Chekhov (CHEHK-ahf) was born in a small port town in the Crimea. His grandfather was a former slave who bought his own freedom. In what is perhaps the best-known remark Chekhov ever made about his life, he said he felt the necessity to "squeeze the slave" out of himself. Chekhov's father, Pavel Egorovich, owned a small general store in which Chekhov worked as a child. When Chekhov was sixteen, however, his father had to declare bankruptcy and escape his creditors by going to Moscow. Chekhov's mother, along with the two youngest children, followed soon after. Chekhov stayed behind as a tutor to the son of one of his mother's former boarders.

After living in poverty and fending for himself for three years, Chekhov was graduated from high school in Taganrog and went to Moscow to enter medical school at Moscow University. Because his father had a low-paying job outside town and was home only on Sundays and holidays, Chekhov had to assume the role of head of his family's household and find work. Having shown an early interest in writing while he was a child in Taganrog, he sought to supplement his family's meager income by contributing anecdotes and stories to humorous magazines, especially at the urging of his elder brother Aleksander, who was already earning a small income by publishing in such magazines. At first Chekhov had little success with his writing efforts, but in March, 1880, his first story was published in the humor journal *Strekoza* (dragonfly). Chekhov later called this the beginning of his literary career.

LIFE'S WORK

In 1882, Chekhov became a regular contributor of jokes and anecdotes to a weekly St. Petersburg magazine, *Oskolki* (fragments), edited by Nikolai A. Leikin. He submitted a large number of short pieces to the journal, many under various pseudonyms. By 1884, he had published more than two hundred short pieces, but when his first collection, *Skazki Melpomeny* (1884; *Tales of Melpomene*, 1916-1923), was published, he included only twenty of them. Also in 1884, Chekhov finished his degree and began practicing medicine. By the following year, when he went to St. Petersburg, he found, much to his surprise (because he did not consider his work significant), that he was quite well known as a writer there.

Chekhov's increasing desire to write more serious fiction, however, made him chafe against the restrictions of the humor magazines, as well as against Leiken's insis-

Anton Chekhov. (Library of Congress)

tence that he stick to jokes. Thus, when Aleksey S. Suvorin, the owner of the influential newspaper *Novoye vremya* (new times), asked Chekhov to contribute more substantial stories to his newspaper, Chekhov was pleased to comply. During 1886 and 1887, Chekhov wrote a large number of stories and short pieces for Suvorin, including some of his best-known stories. His second collection, *Pystrye rasskazy* (motley stories), was published in 1886, and a third, *V sumerkakh* (in the twilight), was published in 1887.

Still, Chekhov was not personally satisfied with his work, believing it to be ephemeral. Moreover, in 1886, he began to suspect that he had tuberculosis, although he refused to have another doctor give him an examination. In this spirit of anxiety about his health and dissatisfaction with his work, Chekhov left on a trip to his hometown in the Crimea to visit friends and relatives. This trip seemed to rejuvenate him, for several important stories of the provincial life of the people he encountered resulted from it. Perhaps the most important result of the journey, however, was his lyrical story "Step" ("The Steppe," 1915), which was published in a highly reputable literary monthly in 1888. Following the story's publication, Chekhov was given the Pushkin Prize for literature by the Academy of Sciences. Even Chekhov himself could no longer doubt that his work had more than ephemeral value.

Also in 1888, Chekhov turned to writing plays, beginning with *Leshy* (1889; *The Wood Demon*, 1925), which was so poorly received that he quit writing serious drama until 1895. This failure, along with a general sense of malaise, what Chekhov called a stagnation in his soul, was the cause of his decision to take a most treacherous journey to the penal colony on Sakhalin Island in the Northern Pacific to learn about the living conditions of the prison inmates. Taking extraordinary means to study the geography and history of the island, he embarked on April 21, 1890, and arrived on July 11. Chekhov spent three months on the island and did enough research on the inmates, he said, for "three dissertations." Although *Ostrov Sakhalin* (1893; the island of Sakhalin) was the formal result of the trip, more lasting fictional results are such stories as "V sylke" (1892; "In Exile," 1912) and "V ovrage" (1900; in the ravine).

On his return to Moscow, Chekhov once again had the urge to travel, this time to Europe. He found Vienna, Venice, Rome, and Florence overwhelming in the beauty of their art and landscapes. On his return, Chekhov purchased a country estate about fifty miles outside Moscow in Melikhovo, where he became a country gentleman and landowner and wrote many of his most famous stories, such as "Chorny monakh" (1892; "The Black Monk," 1903), "Palata No. 6" (1892; ward no. six), "Student" (1894; the student), "Muzhiki" (1897; peasants), and "Dom s mezoninom" (1896; the house with an attic).

In 1895, Chekhov began writing plays again, working on *Chayka* (*The Seagull*, 1909), which was first staged at St. Petersburg in October, 1896, but, partly because of the nature of the production, was an abysmal failure. Once again, Chekhov swore never to write plays. Shortly thereafter, his health worsened and he began to hemorrhage from the lungs. After entering a clinic, he was officially diagnosed as having tuberculosis and was advised to spend the winter months in a warm climate; he soon left for Nice, France. While Chekhov was in France, the Moscow Art Theater asked for permission to stage *The Seagull*. Although Chekhov first refused, he later agreed and went to Moscow to meet the cast. Among them was Olga Knipper, whom Chekhov would marry a few years later.

Chekhov's ill health again forced him to leave Moscow, this time for Yalta, where he had a house built. On December 17, 1898, *The Seagull* opened and was a tre-

CHEKHOV'S MAXIMS

In notebooks and diaries that Anton Chekhov kept throughout his adult life, he jotted down ideas for stories and plays, observations on people he met, and random thoughts about life. Many of his brief entries are poignant maxims on literature and writing.

New literary forms always produce new forms of life and that is why they are so revolting to the conservative human mind.

The young do not go in for literature, because the best of them work on steam engines, in factories, in industrial undertakings. All of them have now gone into industry, and industry is making enormous progress.

A writer of no talent, who has been writing for a long time, with his air of importance reminds one of a high priest.

The wife writes; the husband does not like her writing, but out of delicacy says nothing and suffers all his life.

He married, furnished a house, bought a writing-table, got everything in order, but found he had nothing to write.

In former times a nice man, with principles, who wanted to be respected, would try to become a general or priest, but now he goes in for being a writer, professor. . . .

Source: Anton Chekhov, *Note-Book of Anton Chekhov*, translated by S. S. Koteliansky and Leonard Woolf (New York: B. W. Huebach, 1921).

mendous success. Thus encouraged, Chekhov rewrote his first failure, *The Wood Demon*, and renamed it *Dyadya Vanya* (*Uncle Vanya*, 1914), which the Moscow Art Theater staged in 1899. The following year, when the troupe began a tour of the Crimea with both *The Seagull* and *Uncle Vanya* among their repertoire, Chekhov was at last able to see his two plays on the stage. He was also able to spend more time with Olga Knipper. Soon after, Chekhov finished his third play, *Tri sestry* (1901; *Three Sisters*, 1920). He and Olga Knipper were married on May 25, 1901.

In 1902, Chekhov's health took another turn for the worse; it is a tribute to his determination and genius that during this year he worked on his final play, *Vishnyovy sad* (*The Cherry Orchard*, 1908), and completed it in October. It was scheduled to premier on January 29, 1904, on his forty-fourth birthday; it was also presented in celebration of his twenty-five years as a writer. When Chekhov arrived at the theater after the third act, much to his embarrassment, he was honored with speeches and applause.

Chekhov went back to Yalta for the rest of the winter; on his return trip to Moscow in the spring, his health became worse. On June 4, he and his wife went to Berlin to see a specialist; from there, they went to Badenweiler, a spa in Germany. Chekhov died early in the morning on July 15, 1904. His body was shipped back to Moscow, where he was buried by his father.

SIGNIFICANCE

Anton Chekhov was one of the most influential literary artists at the close of the nineteenth century to usher in the era of modernism in narrative fiction, particularly in short fiction. When his stories were first made widely available in English in the famous Constance Garnett translations between 1916 and 1923, they were termed sketches or slices of life, lacking in all the elements that constituted the short-story form. Critics soon began to realize, however, that Chekhov's freedom from the prevailing conventions of social realism and formalized plot indicated the beginnings of a modern kind of narrative, which combined the specific detail of realism with the poetic lyricism of Romanticism.

Chekhov's most significant contributions to the short-story form, contributions that have influenced modern writers such as Ernest Hemingway and Raymond Carver, include the following: the presentation of character as a lyrical or psychological mood rather than as a two-dimensional symbol or as a realistic personality, the conception of a story as a lyrical sketch rather than as a highly plotted tale, and the assumption of reality as basically impressionistic and as a function of narrative perspective or point of view. The final result of these innovations has been the modernist and postmodernist view of reality as a fictional construct.

With Chekhov, the short story took on a new respectability and began to be understood as the most appropriate narrative form to reflect the modern temperament. Today, most critics agree that there can be no understanding of the short story as a genre without an understanding of Chekhov's contribution to the form.

—*Charles E. May*

FURTHER READING

Callow, Philip. *Chekhov: The Hidden Ground—A Biography*. Chicago: Ivan R. Dee, 1998. Callow, a novelist and biographer, recounts the incidents in Chekhov's complex life and analyzes his drama and prose.

Clyman, Toby, ed. *A Chekhov Companion*. Westport, Conn.: Greenwood Press, 1985. A collection of critical essays, especially commissioned for this volume, on all aspects of Chekhov's life, art, and career. Some of the most important critics of Chekhov's work are represented here in essays on his major themes, his dramatic technique, his narrative technique, and his influence on modern drama and the modern short story.

Hahn, Beverly. *Chekhov: A Study of Major Stories and Plays*. New York: Cambridge University Press, 1977. Hahn focuses on *The Cherry Orchard* as the principal Chekhov play with which to introduce his dramatic technique, although she does discuss the earlier plays as well. This study is particularly notable for its study of Chekhov's relationship with Tolstoy and of his depiction of women in his plays.

Hingley, Ronald. *Chekhov: A Biographical and Critical Study*. London: T. Fisher Unwin, 1950. Rev. ed. London: Allen & Unwin, 1966. Hingley provides a general introduction to the life and work of Chekhov, focusing on both Chekhov's language and his relationship to the social issues significant in Russia during that time.

_____. *A New Life of Anton Chekhov*. New York: Alfred A. Knopf, 1976. A more detailed and more thoroughly biographical study than Hingley's earlier work, this biography makes use of many documentary materials not previously available, particularly eight volumes of Chekhov's letters. It also focuses more on the mysterious subject of Chekhov's relationships with women than do previous studies.

Kirk, Irina. *Anton Chekhov*. Boston: Twayne, 1981. A general introduction to the life and art of Chekhov, focusing primarily on Chekhov's stories as being the embodiment of the search for a philosophy of life. love, and home. Although most of the book focuses on his stories, one final chapter analyzes the plays.

Pitcher, Harvey. *The Chekhov Play: A New Interpretation*. London: Chatto & Windus, 1973. A detailed discussion of the four Chekhov plays in the light of several premises Pitcher establishes about their basic nature: for example, that they focus primarily on the emotional side of life, that they follow a certain structural formula, that they follow the ensemble approach of the Moscow Art Theater, and that the language of the characters is dominated by a feeling of informality.

Pritchett, V. S. *Chekhov: A Spirit Set Free*. New York: Random House, 1988. This study by a master of the short story is neither straight biography nor literary criticism but rather a leisurely mixture of the two, with an emphasis on the latter. Pritchett discusses many of Chekhov's stories in detail and attempts to distill the essential qualities of his art.

Rayfield, Donald. *Anton Chekhov: A Life*. New York: Henry Holt, 1998. Rayfield, a professor of Russian and noted Chekhov scholar, spent more than five years combing previously unexamined archives to research this biography. The result is an extensively detailed book that places Chekhov within the context of nineteenth century Russian society.

_____. *Understanding Chekhov: A Critical Study of Chekhov's Prose and Drama*. Madison: University of Wisconsin Press, 1997. A thorough examination of Chekhov's writings, describing how his work connects to European literature before and after his lifetime. Rayfield also places Chekhov's work within the context of Russian theater and literature during the late nineteenth century.

Winner, Thomas. *Chekhov and His Prose*. New York: Holt, Rinehart and Winston, 1966. A chronological study of Chekhov's development as a story writer, from his beginnings as a writer of humorous anecdotes, to his experimentation with his impressionistic style, through his final concern with the Russian social scene.

SEE ALSO: Fyodor Dostoevski; O. Henry; Guy de Maupassant; Ivan Turgenev.

RELATED ARTICLES in *Great Events from History: The Nineteenth Century, 1801-1900:* 1871-1885: Przhevalsky Explores Central Asia; 1886: Rise of the Symbolist Movement; October 14, 1898: Moscow Art Theater Is Founded.

LYDIA MARIA CHILD

American writer

One of the first successful American women writers and editors of her time, Child combined popular writing with a lifetime's dedication to the causes of racial equality and general public enlightenment.

BORN: February 11, 1802; Medford, Massachusetts
DIED: October 20, 1880; Wayland, Massachusetts
ALSO KNOWN AS: Lydia Maria Francis (birth name)
AREAS OF ACHIEVEMENT: Literature, social reform

EARLY LIFE

Lydia Maria Child was born Lydia Maria Francis. When she was young, she wished that her father would pay as much attention to her as he did to her older brother, Convers. Maria, as she preferred to be called, envied her brother's inquisitive spirit and her father's willingness to encourage it. Throughout her life, her choices would reflect the strength of mind and heart that she so early learned from having to act on her own.

Maria's father, David Convers Francis, a prosperous baker, had little time for his strong-minded daughter. When his wife, Susannah (Rand) Francis, died, he sent twelve-year-old Maria to live with a married sister in Norridgewock, Maine. By age fifteen, Maria was already reading the works of John Milton, Homer, and Sir Walter Scott and was beginning to show the literary interests that were soon to make her famous. At eighteen, she opened a private academy, which had become well established when next she decided to join her brother Convers, now a Unitarian minister, and his wife in Watertown, Massachusetts, just outside Boston. There, her literary career began to flower.

Francis's first novel, *Hobomok* (1824), was an instant success. This romance, involving an Indian male and a white female, reflected her childhood talks in Maine with local Abamake Indians and foreshadowed her lifelong opposition to the U.S. government's Indian policies. *Hobomok* also hinted at Maria's radical social views, because the plot featured an interracial marriage. A second work, *The Rebels: Or, Boston Before the Revolution* (1825), also sold well, and in 1826 she began publishing the *Juvenile Miscellany*, America's first periodical created exclusively for children. All the while, Francis continued to teach in the private academy that she had founded in Watertown. Her childhood dream of being as independent as her brother was rapidly becoming a reality.

Francis's popular writing soon brought her notice in Boston's aristocratic literary circles, where she became known for her charm and intelligence, though she was not regarded as a natural "beauty." By 1827, she had been successfully courted by David Lee Child, a dashing figure eight years her senior, who had diplomatic experience in Europe and who aspired to become a politician. They were married on October 19, 1828, and settled in Boston, where David, for a meager salary, edited a political newspaper.

To augment family income, Child published yet another successful book, *The American Frugal Housewife* (1829), which passed on to readers the methods she was learning for running a household at low cost. (One cake recipe, however, did call for twenty-eight eggs and three pounds of butter.) The volume, which sold widely in both Europe and the United States, brought the Childs much-needed income, for from the start David Child did poorly in his career. His newspaper attacks on Andrew Jackson for forcibly removing the Cherokee Indians from their land in Georgia after the discovery of gold there made him unpopular, as did his sudden decision to become a vigorous opponent of slavery.

Child, however, agreed with her husband's radical views. While he editorialized, she wrote a history of the Indians in her own region, *The First Settlers of New England* (1829); she soon became an abolitionist as well. In 1831, she encountered William Lloyd Garrison, the most militant of New England's antislavery leaders, and was immediately converted to his cause. However, after she embraced this controversial new reform, her popularity as a writer vanished. Patrons snubbed her, and publishers refused her work. Her lucrative career was at an end. "Hardly ever was there a costlier sacrifice," remarked Wendell Phillips, a close friend of Child and another leading Bostonian abolitionist. "Fame and social position [were] in her grasp. But confronted suddenly by the alternatives—gagged life or total wreck—she never hesitated." In 1832, Child had irrevocably committed herself to emancipating the slaves and to seeking social justice. From then on, her brief enjoyment of fame was transformed into a lifetime of struggle against the formidable challenges of poverty and unpopularity.

LIFE'S WORK

In 1833, Child published her views on slavery, *An Appeal in Favor of That Class of Americans Called Afri-*

cans, a highly influential work that guaranteed her banishment from Boston's literary circles and sealed her public commitment to a career as a social reformer. The work persuaded Charles Sumner, Wendell Phillips, Thomas Wentworth Higginson, and others to examine the slavery question, particularly because Child presented her case in such a logical fashion. (In all of her radical publications, Child seldom made use of overemotional rhetoric.) In calm tones, she denounced racial prejudice, called for equal education and employment opportunities for black people, demanded an immediate abolition of slavery, and called for the repeal of all segregation laws, including those prohibiting racial intermarriage. Several other abolitionist publications soon followed, and the sales of her other books dwindled in proportion. Even another romantic novel, *Philothea* (1836), set in ancient Greece, failed to sell.

In the place of popularity came mobs of enraged citizens, eager to purge the North of dangerous radicals such as Child. The famous Boston mob of 1835 specifically aimed at suppressing the Boston Female Anti-Slavery Society of which Child had become a leading member.

Lydia Maria Child. (Library of Congress)

By 1840, she had secured prominence in antislavery circles, becoming a close associate of Henry B. Chapman and Maria Weston Chapman and of Ellis Gilman Loring and Louise Gilman Loring, as well as of Phillips, Garrison, and other Bostonians who provided leadership for the American Anti-Slavery Society. In 1840, she was named to the executive committee of that society, and in 1841, she moved to New York City to edit its official weekly newspaper, *The National Anti-Slavery Standard.*

When Child left for New York, David Lee Child remained behind in Massachusetts, nearly destitute but committed to the goal of producing sugar from beets, hoping to develop free-labor alternatives to slave-grown cane sugar from the South. In 1837, he and Child purchased a ramshackle farm in Northampton, Massachusetts, where for three years they had struggled to eke out a living. The need for additional income explained much of Child's reason for assuming the editorship of *The National Anti-Slavery Standard* and for temporarily leaving her husband.

While the paper's readership grew substantially under Child's direction, Child herself found the day-to-day work demoralizing and the endless controversies with her abolitionist colleagues distracting. When she resigned in 1843, her husband (now disengaged from the sugar beet business) briefly replaced her before moving on to Washington, D.C., to lobby at an uncertain salary for antislavery causes. In the meanwhile, Child remained in New York. The patterns of extended separation between her and her husband that had been repeated over the years had now become established. Though each would always profess and show deep love for the other, David's inability to secure a rewarding career had caused their marriage to fracture partially. The couple would always remain childless.

Alone in New York City, Child succeeded somewhat in reestablishing her literary career. Her popular *Letters from New York* (1843) gave readers vivid pictures of all aspects of life in the nation's major metropolis. Some of her scenes depicted the grinding poverty of New York's slums, the injustices endured by the black community, and the degradation suffered by its unskilled workers. She also investigated prison conditions and the bistros and bawdy houses of the notorious Five Points District. She passed no smug judgments on the social outcasts she encountered, writing, "They excite in me more of compassion than dislike." God alone knew, in her opinion, "whether I should not have been as they are, with the same neglected childhood, the same vicious examples, the same overpowering temptation of want and misery."

Such insights soon led her to publish *Fact and Fiction: A Collection of Stories* (1846), a book describing the plight of New York's prostitutes.

Though *Letters from New York* proved a popular success, and though Child contributed frequently to other literary periodicals, by 1849 she and her husband continued to face destitution. Still lacking a stable income, David returned to his spouse, and in 1850 both moved to Weymouth, Massachusetts, to take up farming on land furnished at no cost by their Boston friends, the Lorings. By 1852, however, penniless and exhausted, they moved again, this time into a house in Wayland, Massachusetts, owned by Child's father (now in his eighties). There, Child tended to both her husband's and her father's needs, until the latter died, in 1856.

During this arduous period of domestic labor, Child somehow continued to write a history of Western religion, *The Progress of Religious Ideas* (1855), in three volumes, which few purchased. Her next work, *Autumnal Leaves* (1857), a set of inspirational selections for those facing old age, suggested that, at the age of fifty-five, Child, too, believed her career to be ending. Indeed, she had written little about social questions since leaving New York City, though she participated in antislavery gatherings in Boston during the 1850's.

John Brown's 1859 raid on Harpers Ferry changed this state of affairs. "Before this affair," she wrote, "I thought I was growing old and drowsy, but now I am as strong as an eagle." She defended Brown's effort at violent emancipation in numerous pamphlets and letters that circulated all over New England. Her offer to nurse the injured Brown as he awaited execution provoked a widely read exchange of letters between Child and the wife of Virginia senator James M. Mason. By mid-1863, as the Civil War raged, Child had moved fully into the forefront of the struggle against slavery, a struggle she continued by demanding full black equality once the war ended. In 1865, she published *The Freedmen's Book* at her own expense, a compilation of writings of successful free blacks for the instruction of newly emancipated slaves. In the immediate postwar period, she pressed the Republican Party to legislate racial equality through the Fourteenth and Fifteenth amendments and supported the impeachment of President Andrew Johnson.

TIPS ON HOUSEHOLD ECONOMIES

Lydia Maria Child's book The American Frugal Housewife, *which she dedicated to "those who are not ashamed of economy," is a mixture of culinary recipes, practical household hints, and philosophical observations on life and living. The household hints extracted below come from a section of the book titled "Odd Scraps for the Economical."*

If you would avoid waste in your family, attend to the following rules, and do not despise them because they appear so unimportant: "many a little makes a mickle."

Look frequently to the pails, to see that nothing is thrown to the pigs which should have been in the grease-pot.

Look to the grease-pot, and see that nothing is there which might have served to nourish your own family, or a poorer one.

See that the beef and pork are always *under* brine; and that the brine is sweet and clean.

Count towels, sheets, spoons, &c. occasionally; that those who use them may not become careless.

See that the vegetables are neither sprouting nor decaying: if they are so, remove them to a drier place, and spread them.

Examine preserves, to see that they are not contracting mould; and your pickles, to see that they are not growing soft and tasteless.

As far as it is possible, have bits of bread eaten up before they become hard. . . .

Attend to all the mending in the house, once a week, if possible. Never put out sewing. If it be impossible to do it in your own family, hire someone into the house, and work with them.

Make your own bread and cake. Some people think it is just as cheap to buy of the baker and confectioner; but it is not half as cheap. . . .

When ivory-handled knives turn yellow, rub them with nice sand paper, or emery; it will take off the spots, and restore their whiteness.

When a carpet is faded, I have been told that it may be restored, in a great measure, (provided there be no grease in it,) by being dipped into strong salt and water. . . .

An ounce of quicksilver, beat up with the white of two eggs, and put on with a feather, is the cleanest and surest bed-bug poison. What is left should be thrown away: it is dangerous to have it about the house. If the vermin are in your walls, fill up the cracks with *verdigris*-green paint.

Source: Lydia Maria Child, *The American Frugal Housewife* (Boston: American Stationers', 1832).

By 1868, however, Child was clearly feeling her age. She rarely traveled from Wayland, where she and her husband, now crippled from arthritis, began living in near seclusion. In that year, she published her last important reform statement, *An Appeal for the Indians*, recalling her first humanitarian efforts nearly forty years earlier. In 1874, when David Lee Child died, Child felt even less reason to engage the outside world. She became intensely reclusive, developing an interest in spiritualism. Few noticed when her last set of essays, *Aspirations of the World*, was published in 1878. When she died in Wayland two years later, at the age of seventy-eight, the few surviving abolitionist crusaders attended; John Greenleaf Whittier rendered a poem, "Within the Gate," and Wendell Phillips delivered the oration.

SIGNIFICANCE

Lydia Maria Child embodied the idealism and reform spirit that lay behind the great crusade against slavery. Her most enduring work, *An Appeal in Favor of That Class of Americans Called Africans*, is recognized as a classic expression of the abolitionist's version of a racially just and egalitarian society. Her many-sided interests, her noteworthy sense of humor, and her suspicion of self-righteous rhetoric, moreover, disproved the stereotype of the abolitionists as a collection of narrow-minded fanatics and eccentrics. Further, her long association with the cause of black equality illustrated the depth and sincerity of the abolitionist's commitment.

Child's literary career and her long struggle for self-sufficiency also suggest the limits and possibilities of female emancipation in the pre-Civil War years. Clearly, her novels and other writings mark her as a pathfinder in the area of women's literature; however, she wrote often about the virtues of housework and cheerful obedience to the demands of husband and children. Her lifelong struggle to maintain not only herself but also her husband testifies to the tremendous burdens faced in the nineteenth century by "independent-minded" women who still believed in the primary importance of these domestic roles.

—James Brewer Stewart

FURTHER READING

Baer, Helen G. *The Heart Is Like Heaven: The Life of Lydia Maria Child*. Philadelphia: University of Pennsylvania Press, 1964. A good modern biography of Child, based on primary research and a grasp of the scholarly literature then available on the antislavery movement.

Child, Lydia Maria. *An Appeal in Favor of That Class of Americans Called Africans*. Boston: Allen and Ticknor, 1833. Her classic abolitionist exposition of doctrines and arguments. Conveys the full range of Child's opinions on slavery, race equality, and racial prejudice, while standing as a fine example of her expository style as a reformer.

_____. *Letters from New-York*. New York: C. S. Francis, 1843.

_____. *Letters from New York: Second Series*. New York: C. S. Francis, 1845. Child's reports on poverty and luxury in America's largest city give vivid glimpses of her social convictions. Other portions of these letters show her facility as an art critic, theatergoer, and fashion commentator. The best introduction to Child's "popular" writings.

_____. *Philothea: A Romance*. Boston: Otis, Broaders, 1836. Typifies Child's literary romanticism. Set in ancient Greece, the plot features proslavery and antislavery themes but also incorporates a dramatic love story and much melodrama. Because it tried to appeal to both reformers and the general reading public, this romance reveals in one work most of Child's intentions as a fiction writer.

Clifford, Deborah Pickman. *Crusader for Freedom: A Life of Lydia Maria Child*. Boston: Beacon Press, 1992. Clifford provides new information on Child's literary career, portraying her subject as a free spirit, quick to speak and write against injustice.

Karcher, Carolyn L. *The First Woman in the Republic: A Cultural Biography of Lydia Maria Child*. Durham, N.C.: Duke University Press, 1994. Meticulously detailed biography. Karcher questions why Child's writings have disappeared from textbooks and argues her reputation was erased by a "backlash against Reconstruction."

Meltzer, Milton. *Tongues of Flame: The Life of Lydia Maria Child*. New York: Thomas Y. Crowell, 1965. The best popular biography of Child, written by an experienced historian and based on primary research. Presents Child's personality in especially vivid terms while giving a compact, readable summary of her public and private lives.

Mills, Bruce. *Cultural Reformation: Lydia Maria Child and the Literature of Reform*. Athens: University of Georgia Press, 1994. Mills analyzes Child's writings within the context of sermons, newspaper editorials, and other nineteenth century reformist literature. He describes how Child's writings aimed to redefine the boundaries of gender and race.

Stewart, James Brewer. *Holy Warriors: The Abolitionists and American Slavery*. New York: Hill & Wang,

1976. This brief synthesis of the history of the abolitionist crusade gives attention to principal figures and events that bore on Child's career. This work traces the development of antislavery from its origins in the eighteenth century until the end of Reconstruction.

Thomas, John L. *The Liberator: William Lloyd Garrison—A Biography*. Boston: Little, Brown, 1965. This major biography of Boston's leading abolitionist conveys an excellent sense of the culture, people, and movements with which Child was intimately associated. A major scholarly study of the person who most permanently influenced Child's views on social reform.

SEE ALSO: John Brown; William Lloyd Garrison; Thomas Wentworth Higginson; Wendell Phillips; Charles Sumner.

RELATED ARTICLES in *Great Events from History: The Nineteenth Century, 1801-1900:* December, 1833: American Anti-Slavery Society Is Founded; May 28-29, 1851: Akron Woman's Rights Convention.

FRÉDÉRIC CHOPIN

Austrian composer and musician

Chopin achieved musical eminence as both a performer and a composer. He was the foremost pianist of his time, although his delicate style and unwillingness to perform in public placed him outside contemporary fashion and practice. His eminence as a composer is equally startling, for unlike every other composer of comparable stature, Chopin devoted himself almost exclusively to keyboard music. Against what some have perceived as the narrowness of his interests, one may posit the brilliance and diversity of his compositions.

BORN: March 1, 1810; Zelazowa Wola, duchy of Warsaw (now in Poland)

DIED: October 17, 1849; Paris, France

ALSO KNOWN AS: Fryderyk Franciszek Szopen; Frédéric-François Chopin (full name)

AREA OF ACHIEVEMENT: Music

EARLY LIFE

Frédéric Chopin (shoh-PAHN) was born in a Polish village located thirty-four miles from the then-provincial city of Warsaw. His mother, Justyna, was the well-educated daughter of an impoverished, upper-class family. His father, Nicholas, a Frenchman by birth, was employed as a tutor by another and more well-to-do branch of that same family, the Skarbeks. Shortly after Frédéric's birth, the family moved to Warsaw, where Nicholas eventually secured a position as a teacher of French at the Lyceum. Impressed by the playing of his mother and older sister, Ludwika, Chopin began to play the piano at the age of four or five.

At the age of six, Chopin was already composing and taking lessons from Wojciech Zwyny. His first published work, the Polonaise in G Minor, appeared when he was only seven, and he made his first public appearance the following year (1818) at a charity concert. Soon afterward, he played before Poland's Grand Duke Konstantine and in 1825 was selected to demonstrate the aeolomelodicon before Czar Alexander I. While still a student at the Lyceum (1823-1826), Chopin began taking lessons from Josef Elsner, director of the Warsaw Conservatory. Elsner proved an especially fortunate choice; himself inclined toward the Romanticism that Chopin would perfect, he was willing to bend his own strict academic standards to accommodate his student's evident genius.

While under Elsner's tutelage, Chopin composed his first major work, a set of variations on Wolfgang Amadeus Mozart's "La ci darem" from *Don Giovanni* (1787), which evidenced a surprising originality and maturity. The trip he made to Berlin in 1828 seems to have whetted his appetite for travel and, more important, for a wider musical world than Warsaw could then provide, and so, after having their request for a travel scholarship rejected by the government, his parents financed his 1829 trip to Vienna themselves. There with the help of a letter of introduction from Elsner, Chopin secured a publisher for his Mozart variations and, as part of his agreement with the publisher, Tobias Haslinger, gave a free concert in order to advertise his work. In fact, Chopin gave two concerts while in Vienna, both of which were successful. His audience was surprised by the lightness of his touch and delighted by his technical skills and use of Polish materials.

Upon his return to Warsaw, Chopin fell in love with Konstantia Gladkowska and continued to be well received by Polish audiences. Chopin grew restive, however, and on November 2, 1830, he again journeyed to Vienna, this time accompanied by his close friend, Tytus Wojciechkowski. News of the Polish revolt against the Russians reached them later that month. Wojciechkowski immediately returned to Poland. Chopin, at the urging of his family, remained in Vienna, where he expected to repeat his earlier success. In this he was mistaken. The few concerts he gave attracted little attention and even less cash. After eight months he left Vienna for Paris, learning en route that the revolt had failed and Warsaw had fallen.

LIFE'S WORK

Until his death nineteen years later, Paris was to be Chopin's home. The city was then the center of European culture, and thanks to a Viennese friend, Chopin quickly gained entrance to its cultural life. Just as important, Paris was also home to a large number of Polish émigrés, including Adam Mickiewicz, an exile, a poet, and a patriot. Unlike Mickiewicz, Chopin could return to Poland but chose not to do so. Although sensitive to the plight of his countrymen and even supportive of many of them, Chopin was not an activist; nor are his works nationalist in the same sense or to the same degree that Mickiewicz's poems and plays clearly are. Himself half French, Chopin quickly adapted to his new home, largely because it received him so warmly.

Chopin's first concert, on February 26, 1832, attended by Franz Liszt and Felix Mendelssohn, was a decided success, and in the autumn of that year he was invited to play for the Rothschilds. Having gained entry into the highest level of Parisian society, Chopin quickly became the most fashionable and highest paid piano teacher in the city. Financially secure, he could afford to give up the public concert hall performances he disliked so much and that were so ill-suited to both the character of his music and the delicacy of his playing. His immense and financially rewarding success in the salons of Paris, however, extracted its own price.

By the 1830's, an important shift had occurred in the world of music. Aristocratic patrons of the arts, especially music, had begun to play a less significant role, while the mass audience was beginning to exert a far greater influence than ever before. Liszt's style of music and playing was well suited to this new audience; Chopin's was not. The aristocratic salons of Paris therefore played a most important role in nurturing Chopin's genius, but not without limiting or at least misunderstanding it as well, for what the Rothschilds and others prized was not Chopin's compositions but his playing, his imitations, and his improvisations in particular.

Three years after his introduction into this world, there began a sequence of events that was to have a profound effect on Chopin's life and art. Chopin met and fell in love with Maria Wodzinska in 1835, but when he proposed marriage, the family, having heard the rumors of Chopin's poor health, refused to give their consent. Disappointed, Chopin paid a short visit to England and within the year had begun his famous liaison with the author Amandine-Aurore-Lucile Dupin, or George Sand, as she is better known. It was Sand who made the first overtures (in 1836), and these Chopin refused, disturbed by her evident masculinity. However, in 1837 he became as passionately drawn to her as she was to him.

Over the next nine years, Chopin transformed his passion into some of his greatest music. (Over the same period, Sand's passion would undergo a quite different change in the direction of maternal devotion.) At Sand's suggestion, they spent the winter of 1838-1839 on the island of Majorca. Poor food and even worse weather,

Frédéric Chopin. (Library of Congress)

coupled with the islanders' fear of contagion caused by Chopin's tubercular condition as well as their distaste for this evidently immoral bohemian household, made composing difficult and the worsening of Chopin's health inevitable. They returned to the mainland in February, but the seriousness of Chopin's condition (he had begun to hemorrhage) forced them to delay their arrival at Sand's country home in Nohant until June.

Located 180 miles south of the French capital, Nohant was well suited to Chopin's needs. Sensitive to noise and other distractions, and physically weak, Chopin always found it difficult to write while in Paris, and so the summers he spent at Nohant (1839, 1841-1849) proved to be especially rewarding. Even as his art advanced, the relationship with Sand deteriorated into recriminations and finally separation, first as her passion cooled and then as the result of plots hatched by her two grown children.

Chopin's physical decline, which had begun on Majorca and that had worsened upon his learning of his father's death (May 3, 1844), advanced more precipitously following his estrangement from Sand. On February 16, 1848, he gave his first public concert in ten years; it was also the last one he would ever give in Paris. A second concert had been planned but had to be canceled when revolution broke out in the city's streets. The revolutions of 1848 put an end not only to the French monarchy but to Chopin's patronage as well. Out of necessity, he accepted an invitation from Jane Stirling, a wealthy former pupil, to visit Great Britain.

After spending much of the year traveling and performing in London and Scotland, Chopin returned to Paris in late 1848, too weak either to write or to teach. Generously supported by the Stirlings and comforted by his sister, he continued to decline. His death occurred on October 17, 1849, but preparations were so elaborate that the funeral had to be delayed nearly two weeks. Some three thousand mourners were in attendance as the funeral march from his Sonata in B Minor and (at Chopin's own request) Mozart's *Requiem* were played. Chopin was buried in Paris, and his heart was interred in Warsaw.

SIGNIFICANCE

For Frédéric Chopin, playing and composing were integrally related. A brilliant if unusual performer, he preferred to be judged chiefly as a composer, and it was to this end that he increasingly devoted himself from the late 1830's onward. Chopin gave no public concerts from 1838 until 1848; in fact, he gave only thirty public performances during his entire career. However, as Derek Melville has noted, "Curiously enough, the less he played in public, the more legendary he became." Unfortunately, the acclaim he received as early as 1837 as Europe's greatest pianist overshadowed his work as a composer. Even after his death, Chopin's compositions have rarely been given the credit they are due. That he wrote almost exclusively for the piano has been misunderstood as a major limitation, one that has barred him from the ranks of greatness. While his contribution to harmonic development has been acknowledged, critics have tended to slight his overall achievement.

The narrow range of Chopin's achievement is not a sign of weakness, however, but of a strength comparable to what his near contemporary, the novelist Jane Austen, managed to achieve on her "inch of ivory." To defend Chopin's breadth is impossible, and to defend his sense of musical structure along conventional lines is fruitless. This is not to say that he was, as often accused, inattentive to form or unable "to develop his materials on a large scale." Chopin's great strength lies not in his adherence to the conventions but in his innovations, including his use of a "departure and return pattern" in many of his works and his experimentation with organic form in a number of his later ones.

When Chopin felt the need to do so, he was more than willing to learn and to adopt traditional techniques, such as counterpoint, which he began to study in earnest only during the 1840's. The very real narrowness of range of Chopin's oeuvre needs, therefore, to be reevaluated. As a performer, Chopin was physically too frail to compete with his contemporaries in terms of virtuosity and dramatic effects, and as a result both as performer and as composer he chose, or was perhaps forced, to explore and exploit the subtleties of his playing, his music, and his medium, the piano, in compositions and performances far better suited to the intimacy of the salon than to the impersonal space of the concert hall.

Although Chopin wrote almost exclusively for the piano, he did so with incredible variety: waltzes, nocturnes, preludes, études, scherzos, polonaises, and mazurkas, with the emphasis clearly on the solo piano (139 of his 167 compositions). In his desire to make the piano imitate the human voice, Chopin utterly transformed keyboard music and keyboard technique. One needs to realize that in Chopin's age, the piano was essentially a new instrument. The introduction of leather-bound hammers, for example, made possible the production of much softer tones than in previous times. Although it was John Field and J. N. Hummel who first began to compose music adapted to this new instrument and sound, it was Chopin who came to exploit the piano so masterfully.

Legend often portrays Chopin as at best a melancholy Romantic and at worst a pampered high-society narcissist. Fact portrays a quite different figure, fashionable in his dress and fastidious in his conduct, sickly and shy, less proud than committed to his art, and not so much a recluse as an introvert. The facts are perhaps too few to draw as complete a portrait as one might like. For this reason one may turn to the music to distinguish more definitely the character of the man from the qualities of his music: passionate yet introspective, emotional but never sentimental, delicate and refined, expressive yet restrained, as much concerned with perfection as with originality.

In many respects, Chopin is the very embodiment of Romanticism, yet he is a strange avatar of the Romantic movement, for his music was clearly influenced by the classical style of Johann Sebastian Bach and Mozart at least as much as it was by the Italian opera of his own age. Chopin's influence on others has, however, been far greater than anyone else's influence on him: on the keyboard music of Liszt, Arnold Schönberg, and others, and on the use of national—especially folk—materials by Antonín Dvořák, Manuel de Falla, Pyotr Ilich Tchaikovsky, and others. Chopin stands as the first and perhaps the most important of the modern composers to become aware that the breadth, grandeur, and order that were both possible and inevitable in the classical period might no longer be advisable even if they were technically still possible. Narrowness, or specialization, Chopin proved, has its own possibilities and its own frontiers.

—*Robert A. Morace*

FURTHER READING

Abraham, Gerald. *Chopin's Musical Style*. London: Oxford University Press, 1939. A brief but important study of the "unfolding and maturing of Chopin's musical style," intended chiefly, but by no means exclusively, for performers and students of harmony. Abraham distinguishes three significant periods of development (1822-1831, 1831-1840, and 1841-1849) but fails to discuss the problems of chronology within each period and does not consider the origins of Chopin's style. Nevertheless, long considered the standard work on the subject.

Chopin, Fryderyk. *Chopin's Letters*. Edited by Henryk Opienski. Translated by E. L. Voynich. New York: Alfred A. Knopf, 1931. Although it has been largely superseded by later editions, Opienski's work is noteworthy both for its relative extensiveness (given the time it was published) and for the excellence of Voynich's translations from the original Polish and French. The dating of many items is, however, incorrect.

_____. *Selected Correspondence of Fryderyk Chopin*. Edited and translated by Arthur Hedley. New York: McGraw-Hill, 1963. This volume is abridged from Chopin's correspondence, collected and edited by Bronislaw Edward Sydow. Although less exhaustive than Sydow's volume of nearly eight hundred items, Hedley's book does add appreciably to the slimmer Opienski work. However, Hedley not only omits pieces included in Sydow but also abridges a number of items. Even so, this is an indispensable volume; the eleven-page appendix concerning the history and inauthenticity of the erotic "Chopin-Potocka Letters" is especially interesting.

Hedley, Arthur. *Chopin*. London: J. M. Dent & Sons, 1947. Especially noteworthy because Hedley's *Chopin* does not merely summarize previous scholarship. Recognizing the inadequacy of the standard English-language study, Frederick Niecks's *Fredrick Chopin* (1888), Hedley has examined materials at first hand, many for the first time. He devotes somewhat more than half of his authoritative study to Chopin's biography and the remainder to discussions of Chopin as performer, as teacher, and as composer and of Chopin's works according to type.

Huneker, James. *Chopin: The Man and His Music*. New York: Charles Scribner's Sons, 1900. Trained as a pianist, Huneker was the foremost American music critic at the time he wrote this study. Enthusiastic and knowledgeable, he devotes the first third of this book to biographical analysis, the import of which is clearly evident in his chapter titles "The Artist" and "Poet and Psychologist." The remaining chapters deal with each of the various kinds of musical compositions Chopin wrote.

Melville, Derek. *Chopin*. Hamden, Conn.: Linnet Books, 1977. Part of the Concertgoer's Companion series, Melville's book includes a surprising amount of material in its very few (108) pages. Despite going unnecessarily far in his efforts to undermine the credibility of George Sand's remarks about Chopin, Melville's writing is balanced and especially well informed. His lengthy annotated bibliography of works in English about Chopin and his music (pp. 62-78) is particularly useful.

Samson, Jim. *Chopin*. New York: Oxford University Press, 1996. Biography written by a Chopin scholar, containing musical analysis as well as information on Chopin's life.

_____, ed. *Chopin: The Four Ballades*. Cambridge, England: Cambridge University Press, 1992. Collection of essays providing a brief biography and more detailed descriptions of Chopin's music. Essays include analyses of nocturnes, sonatas, and etudes, and discussions of Chopin's reception in nineteenth century Poland and Victorian attitudes toward the composer.

Szulc, Tad. *Chopin in Paris: The Life and Times of the Romantic Composer*. New York: Charles Scribner's Sons, 1998. Biography focusing on the eighteen years Chopin spent in Paris. Szulc uses primary sources, such as diaries, memoirs, letters, and Chopin's journal, to provide information about Chopin's personality, relationship with George Sand, and the artistic and intellectual life in Paris.

SEE ALSO: Jane Austen; Franz Liszt; George Sand; Robert Shumann.

RELATED ARTICLE in *Great Events from History: The Nineteenth Century, 1801-1900:* April 7, 1805: Beethoven's *Eroica* Symphony Introduces the Romantic Age.

KATE CHOPIN

American novelist

The author of the early feminist novel The Awakening, *Chopin created works that showcased the Louisiana bayou country and often featured women struggling against society's restrictions. Her reputation faded quickly after she died but reached new heights after her work was rediscovered during the 1960's.*

BORN: February 8, 1851; St. Louis, Missouri
DIED: August 22, 1904; St. Louis, Missouri
ALSO KNOWN AS: Katherine O'Flaherty (birth name)
AREA OF ACHIEVEMENT: Literature

EARLY LIFE

Kate Chopin (shoh-PAHN) was born Katherine O'Flaherty in Missouri. Her father was an Irish merchant, and her mother was the daughter of an old French family. Chopin's early fluency with French and English, and her roots in two different cultures, were important throughout her life.

Kate's father, Thomas O'Flaherty, was killed in a train accident in 1855 (the imagined effect on her mother was later depicted in "The Story of an Hour"). Kate lived her preteen years in a female-centered household. Her sophisticated grandmother had a great impact on Kate, encouraging her to reject hypocrisy, to love music and storytelling, and to indulge in unconventional behavior. Kate's formal education began at Sacred Heart Academy, a Catholic school devoted to creating good wives and mothers, while also teaching independent thinking. Kate's readings included fairy tales, John Bunyan's *The Pilgrim's Progress* (1678), old-fashioned romances, and contemporary popular novels by women.

The Civil War meant that Kate spent much time at home; she saw the war's violence at first hand. After Kate returned to the academy, her English teacher encouraged her to write. Kate kept a "commonplace book" from 1867 to 1870, where she recorded observations on her reading and studies. At the age of eighteen, Kate was known as one of St. Louis's prettiest and most popular belles. Her diary, however, reveals that she was torn between social pressures—to attend dances, flirt, and be agreeable—and her passion for voracious reading of authors such as Victor Hugo, Dante, Molière, Jane Austen, and Henry Wadsworth Longfellow. In an age known for producing restless women, Kate also seemed to want something more.

When she was twenty, Kate married Oscar Chopin, a twenty-six-year-old businessperson of cosmopolitan background. In their first ten years of marriage, Kate gave birth to five sons and a daughter. Motherhood's joys and demands, as well as societal restraints on women, are important themes in her fiction. During these years, Kate and the children lived three seasons in New Orleans and spent long summers at the Creole resort Grande Isle.

In 1879, Oscar Chopin's money-lending business was in deep trouble. The family moved to Cloutierville, Louisiana, where Oscar ran a general store. Kate Chopin's sophisticated behavior and dress inspired gossip in the small, closely knit town. Her husband, worn down by financial worries, died in 1882, leaving Kate with debts of some $12,000 and six children to rear alone. She decided to manage Oscar's businesses herself. During this time she was romantically linked with Albert Sampite, a

Kate Chopin. (Missouri Historical Society)

handsome and unhappily married man. In 1884, Kate left Cloutierville and Sampite to return to St. Louis, where she lived with her mother.

The death of Kate's mother the following year left Kate devastated; a physician friend suggested that she write for solace—and for much-needed money. Kate's writings at the time indicate that she sometimes longed for the security of marriage, but also recognized that the deaths of the two people closest to her gave her independence unavailable to other women. She later characterized this period as a time of "growth."

LIFE'S WORK

These sudden deaths and her own unconventional ideas demanded that Kate Chopin make her own way. She started her first short story in 1888 and became a published author in 1889 when her poem "If It Might Be" appeared in the journal *America*. Her stories and sketches from this early period show that she questioned traditional romance. "Wiser than a God" depicts a woman who chooses a career as pianist over marriage. Other stories portray a suffragist and a professional woman who try to determine their own lives. Chopin's friends during this period included "New Women"—single working women, suffragists, and intellectuals—who doubtless influenced her previously private questioning of women's role in society.

At Fault (1890), Chopin's first novel, focuses on a woman who renounces her lover after she learns he is divorced. The conflict between morality and sexual attraction is a major theme, and the novel is ahead of its time in depicting an alcoholic woman, the lover's estranged wife. This novel suggests that environment is a greater influence on behavior than heredity—an unpopular idea during the 1890's. *At Fault* was praised for its local color and believable characters, but was attacked by literary moralists, who disliked its subject matter and language. Because one publisher had rejected the novel and Chopin was impatient for publication, she paid to have it printed and distributed.

Chopin also wrote children's stories that appeared in national magazines. Her stature as author began to grow. In her adult stories, she persisted in writing about taboo subjects: "Mrs. Mobry's Reason" (1893), repeatedly rejected, concerned venereal disease; "The Coming and Going of Liza Jane" (1892) focuses on a woman who, longing for a more glamorous life, leaves her husband. Chopin's output from this period is oddly split between formula writing of predictable morality tales and stories of individuals' conflicts with society.

Throughout her career, Chopin gained inspiration from her time in Louisiana. Much of her fiction was set there: she valued its dreamy, less structured, and more sensual atmosphere. Chopin was pigeonholed as a regional writer but badly wanted to reach a national audience. She tried hard to place her collection of Creole stories and finally succeeded. *Bayou Folk* (1894) collected mostly Cane River country stories. Praised for its exotic and bewitching subjects and atmosphere, the collection solidified Chopin's reputation as a local colorist.

The 1890's were a time of achievement for Chopin. *Bayou Folk*'s success led to more short-story publications in national magazines and to regional celebrity. "The Story of an Hour" (1894) recounts the ironic reversal in emotion—from grief to joy—of a woman who mistakenly believes she has been widowed. It is one of Chopin's most powerful—and controversial—stories, and it anticipates *The Awakening* in its depiction of a repressive marriage.

In St. Louis, Chopin held salons where the city's cultural elite could play cards, listen to music, and argue about philosophy and literature. Chopin translated contemporary French writer Guy de Maupassant's tales and was greatly influenced by his writing. Maupassant was thought to be immoral; his satires, like Chopin's mature fiction, focus on betrayal of ideals, questioning of traditional values, sex, and depression.

CHOPIN'S MAJOR WORKS

1890 *At Fault*
1894 *Bayou Folk*
1897 *A Night in Acadie*
1899 *The Awakening*

Through the mid-1890's, Chopin wrote mainstream fiction but continued to address more daring subjects such as aging, obsessive love, extrasensory perception, and gambling. *A Night in Acadie* (1897), Chopin's second short-story collection, focused on the Cane River country she knew so well. Women characters, some repressed and others rebelling, were prominent. This collection was generally well received, though some reviewers disliked its coarseness—a muted charge that would become a roar with the publication of *The Awakening* in 1899.

The Awakening features a strong female protagonist. After twenty-nine years "asleep" to life's possibilities, Edna Pontellier awakens to the need to find her identity. Like her creator, Edna sometimes feels as if she lives two lives: one that conforms and one that questions. Edna's attraction to both sides is illustrated in her friendships with the conventional "mother-woman" Adele Ratignolle and the eccentric pianist Mademoiselle Reisz.

Edna grows up desiring unattainable men. Believing that she is renouncing the world of illusion, she marries a man for whom she has only fondness and no passion, and settles into motherhood. In a series of small incidents at Grand Isle, however, Edna's rebellion against her rigid role is shown: her unexpected emotional response to Mlle Reisz's concert; her exultation on learning to swim; her desire for Robert Lebrun, a young man with whom she is in sympathy; and her defiance of her husband's wishes.

Edna disproves Victorian ideas about women's moral superiority through her open longing for Robert and her affair with the roguish Alcée Arobin; she moves into her own house and tries to attain fulfillment through painting and an unconventional social life. For a time she behaves solely in accordance with her desires. Eventually Adele summons Edna to her bedside and implores her to think of her children. Edna realizes that she cannot give her children honor and good reputation without sacrificing her independence, her sensuality, and her newfound enjoyment of life. Ironically, freedom means that a "solitary soul" (the novel's original title) will be isolated from society and from sensual experience. Because of her husband's death and her own strength, Chopin was able to escape rigid social convention to an extent. Edna, unable to compromise her desires with her duties, commits suicide.

The Awakening became Chopin's major literary achievement; it was also far in advance of its time as one of the earliest American novels to question marriage as an institution. Edna's discontent and her various attempts to find fulfillment caused a scandal. The novel was attacked as immoral and as unfit for reading. Critics praised the beauty and power of the novel's style and setting, its careful pacing, and its subtly drawn characters, but many questioned Edna's (and Chopin's) morality. Like Norwegian playwright Henrik Ibsen's *A Doll's House*, *The Awakening*'s realistic portrayal of a woman's desire to find her identity outraged many.

Chopin was hurt by the negative reaction to the novel, though she published a tongue-in-cheek "retraction" apologizing for Mrs. Pontellier making such a mess of things and ensuring her own damnation. Chopin's career slowed markedly after 1899. She continued to write poetry and reviews but published little until her death in 1904. At that time Chopin was eulogized chiefly as a regional writer of note; little was said of *The Awakening* until decades later.

SIGNIFICANCE

Kate Chopin's reputation as a writer faded soon after her death. After the initial sensation when *The Awakening* was first appeared in 1899 and in a 1906 reprinting, the novel remained out of print for half a century. During the 1960's, however, Norwegian writer Per Seyersted rediscovered Chopin and edited *The Complete Works* and a critical biography in 1969. Chopin's reputation blossomed, and her novel is now considered a classic, taught in university literature and women's studies courses. Largely through the attention of scholars and critics, Chopin's work has enjoyed a renaissance. Her writing beautifully illustrates a variety of feminist concerns: the clash between individual freedom and social duty, the stifling quality of unequal marriage, the hypocrisy of the sexual double standard, and women's desire for creativity and independence. Her characters are utterly believable: complex, thoughtful, and intelligent.

The Awakening is a fine example of the rehabilitation of a "disappeared" writer. Considered out of step with its times, it is a powerfully written novel by a writer whose work had been safely categorized as regional and domestic; these reasons explain its fading from public view. Like several other women's novels enjoying renewed attention as American classics (African American writer Zora Neale Hurston's *Their Eyes Were Watching God* and New Yorker writer Dorothy Parker's cynical comedies, for example), *The Awakening* is being reevaluated by critics and readers. It is a startlingly radical and honest book that deservedly stands as a classic.

—*Michelle L. Jones*

FURTHER READING

Chopin, Kate. *The Awakening: An Authoritative Text, Contexts, Criticism*. Edited by Margaret Culley. New York: W. W. Norton, 1976. The novel's complete text, including explanatory footnotes that help explain its context. Contains excerpts from writers contemporary with Chopin as well as a sampling of reviews from the novel's first publication to its rediscovery during the 1960's.

_____. *The Complete Works of Kate Chopin*. Edited by Per Seyersted. Baton Rouge: Louisiana State University Press, 1969. Reprints Chopin's work, including unpublished and uncollected stories, sketches, essays, and poetry. Valuable for the overview these writings give of Chopin's evolution as a writer.

Rankin, Daniel. *Kate Chopin and Her Creole Stories*. Philadelphia: University of Pennsylvania Press, 1932. An early biography that relies on interviews with Chopin's friends and relatives and Chopin's manuscripts and journals. Examines Chopin primarily as a writer of unique and rich Creole stories; reprints some stories and sketches.

Seyersted, Per. *Kate Chopin: A Critical Biography*. Baton Rouge: Louisiana State University Press, 1969. A reexamination of Chopin's life and career, using previously unavailable materials. Examines her importance as a writer of realism and her ambitious and assertive life; links Chopin's experience and her work.

Toth, Emily. *Kate Chopin*. New York: William Morrow, 1990. A detailed and fascinating critical biography; gives much valuable information on Chopin's childhood and passionate, secretive life. Shows relationships and influences in Chopin's life and their effects on her writing. Includes thorough bibliography of Chopin's writings and criticism of her work, a chronology, and exhaustive footnotes.

_____. *Unveiling Kate Chopin*. Jackson: University Press of Mississippi, 1999. Toth argues that Chopin's literature was unusual for her time because she led an unconventional life, not because she held strong feminist convictions.

Walker, Nancy A. *Kate Chopin: A Literary Life*. New York: Palgrave, 2001. Examines the work of Chopin and other nineteenth century American women writers to analyze how contemporary standards of literary propriety affected Chopin's work.

Wheeler, Otis. "The Five Awakenings of Edna Pontellier." *Southern Review* XI (January, 1975): 118-128. Focuses on Edna's rejection of "angel in the house" and "scarlet woman" roles; traces Edna's development through her awakenings about personhood, true love, sex, biology, and despair. A useful psychological study of Chopin's most complex character.

Ziff, Larzer. *The American 1890's: Life and Times of a Lost Generation*. New York: Viking Press, 1966. Examines the decade when Chopin flourished as a writer. Ziff puts in context the two impulses of American society—conformity versus individuality—and criticizes the literature of the decade as overly optimistic and unrealistic.

SEE ALSO: Sarah Orne Jewett; Olive Schreiner.

RELATED ARTICLE in *Great Events from History: The Nineteenth Century, 1801-1900:* December, 1884-February, 1885: Twain Publishes *Adventures of Huckleberry Finn*.

HENRI CHRISTOPHE

Haitian president (1806-1811) and king (r. 1811-1820)

Christophe was one of the three great black leaders of the Haitian revolution. After the removal of Toussaint-Louverture to France and the assassination of Jean-Jacques Dessalines, he was chosen president of the Haitian republic, but his rule proved to be disastrous.

BORN: October 6, 1767; island of Grenada, British West Indies
DIED: October 8, 1820; Sans Souci palace, Haiti
ALSO KNOWN AS: Henri I
AREA OF ACHIEVEMENT: Government and politics

EARLY LIFE

Henri Christophe (kree-stohf), who was known as the "Civilizer," was born on the island of Grenada four years after the island was ceded to Great Britain by France in accord with the Treaty of Paris. For political reasons, Christophe was always imprecise about his family background, but it seems probable that one of his parents was not of pure African descent (his own complexion was not black but a deep red-brown) and that he was born free. Even as a child it is said that he was flinty, argumentative, and unbendable. Before he was ten years old, his father sent him to sea as a cabin boy to the French skipper of a coasting vessel, who in turn found him too much of a handful and sold him to a Saint Dominican sugar planter named Badêche. Badêche set the small boy to work as a helper in his own kitchen and, after getting reports of his neatness and energy, decided to train him as a cook.

Badêche employed Christophe at the Couronne, a hostelry that he owned, but here again Christophe's initial stay was short. He went off at the age of eleven with a regiment that a French officer raised from mulattoes and free blacks to aid the insurgent American colonists. He was slightly wounded at the siege of Savannah and subsequently sailed back to Haiti. Within ten years of his return to the Couronne, he was in effect managing the hotel. For several years, Christophe apparently stayed clear of the violent turmoil that plagued Haiti after 1789. However, in 1794, at the age of 27, he joined Toussaint-Louverture's forces and began his fight for the independence of Haiti as a sergeant.

LIFE'S WORK

In 1796, having already ascended to the rank of major, Christophe distinguished himself in a campaign against mulatto commanders and became a colonel. In 1801, when civil war erupted between the mulattoes who held the south and the blacks under Toussaint-Louverture, Christophe again distinguished himself and was promoted to brigadier. After Toussaint-Louverture secured absolute domination over the island with the defeat of the Spanish in Santo Domingo, Christophe was given divisional jurisdiction in a system of military administration that divided the island into districts run by senior military personnel.

With a French attempt to restore dominion over Haiti in 1802, Toussaint-Louverture and his generals, Jean-Jacques Dessalines and Henry Christophe (his admiration for everything English prompted him to begin to sign his first name with a *y* rather than the French *i*), were beaten back. After running low on food supplies, Christophe suspended hostilities and was given a command in the French army with 1,500 of his regular troops. The surrender and imprisonment of Toussaint-Louverture followed soon after.

As the French forces became weakened with illness, French commander Charles Leclerc was increasingly forced to depend on the black and the mulatto generals, particularly in the face of a revolt as word spread of impending restoration of slavery. As French atrocities against blacks and mulattoes increased, Christophe joined the rebels. With the black and mulatto generals united under Dessalines, the French forces were finally defeated. Under Dessalines, Haiti was declared independent on January 1, 1804. The country was divided into four districts, and Christophe was appointed the general in command of the north. When Dessalines invaded Santo Domingo in 1804, Christophe led the invasion force in the north and quickly overcame French and Spanish troops.

Dessalines was killed in 1806 during an attempt to quell an uprising of generals in the south. Christophe was declared provisional leader, but a constitutional assembly, controlled by mulatto generals, drafted a republican constitution that provided President Christophe with very little power. In response, Christophe led his black forces from the north toward Port-au-Prince, the capital. After some initial success, Christophe was forced to retreat back to the north, where he set up a separate state. The country remained divided for thirteen years, and, in 1811, Christophe declared himself king.

Christophe had many reasons for turning Haiti into a kingdom. Vanity was not the least of them, but neither was it the greatest. A king was still a man of power and splendor, not yet an antique oddity. The title gave him an advantage over Alexandre Pétion—the president in the south—in the eyes of the people of both regions, who had been brought up to honor kings. Christophe also expected his declaration to raise Haiti in the estimation of the white world, where French emperor Napoleon Bonaparte was still setting up kingdoms for his relations. It was a valuable reinforcement of his authority in domestic affairs, now that he was about to turn to his long-contemplated but equally long-delayed reforms at home. As king of the blacks, he would have a greater chance to lead his people to equality with white people.

Because Christophe could neither read nor write more than his signature, he imported English teachers to staff the schools that he opened. His organization of the north rested on a combination of benevolent qualities (with certain military despotism) and a nobility that he created and cultivated. Under this system, estates, now in government hands, were given to loyal supporters and the wealthy on five-year leases. Labor was organized along militaristic lines, with a heavy emphasis on hard work and discipline. The workers got one-quarter of the income of the plantations and were also given small plots of land to provide for their personal needs. The system was economically successful, allowing Christophe to raise revenue equaling that of the immediate prerevolutionary period during which Saint Domingue was France's richest colony. However, the system was rooted—like all monarchies—in firm class divisions and rested on a labor force with few civil and political rights.

The laissez-faire system of the south under Pétion enticed many from the north. Hostilities with the south intensified Christophe's dislike and distrust of the mulatto population. He began to persecute them. His own people began to distrust him, and he in turn began to distrust everybody. He ordered the construction of the Citadelle, a fortress conceived in fear and built at an untold cost of toil, tears, and blood. The fortress characterized the tyrant into which Christophe had grown. The end came when Christophe, suffering from a paralytic stroke, was deserted by his army and most of his courtiers. In 1820, he is said to have shot himself at his palace of Sans Souci, after which the queen and one faithful courtier dragged his body up the precipitous trail to the Citadelle. Unable to find tools or sufficient men to dig a grave, they buried his body in a heap of quicklime.

SIGNIFICANCE

Under the triumphant republic, Henri Christophe's reputation was denigrated, his name and monuments erased. In 1847, however, he was at last lifted from the bed of lime and given a proper burial in a simple concrete tomb on the Citadelle's Place d'Armes. Even then he was not allowed to rest in peace. While seeking the treasure that legend said Christophe had hidden in the fortress, someone broke into the tomb; finding nothing, the thief took a finger bone as a souvenir. Others followed, until the walls of the Citadelle that had been constructed to protect the king continued to stand guard over nothing at all.

—Juana Goergen

FURTHER READING

Beard, John R. *The Life of Toussaint L'Overture*. Westport, Conn.: Negro University Press, 1970. Beard covers the history of the independence movement under Toussaint-Louverture's leadership. Contains a chapter on Christophe.

Cole, Herbert. *Christophe: King of Haiti*. London: Eyre and Spottiswoode, 1967. Cole's book remains the best biographical scholarship on Christophe. Contains photographs and illustrations of him and his kingdom.

Dubois, Laurent. *Avengers of the New World: The Story of the Haitian Revolution*. Cambridge, Mass.: Belknap Press of Harvard University Press, 2004. A thorough and well-researched history of the Haitian revolution. Dubois emphasizes the historical significance of the revolution—the only successful slave revolt in the Americas—and its subsequent impact on the Atlantic world.

James, C. L. R. *The Black Jacobins*. London: Allison and Busby, 1980. This book provides a very complete biography of Toussaint-Louverture, Dessalines, and Christophe and gives details of their personal relationship and political agendas. Includes an appendix with a table of events.

Moran, Charles. *Black Triumvirate*. New York: Exposition, 1957. This biography of Toussaint-Louverture, Dessalines, and Christophe focuses on the political aspect of their lives and work. Includes photographs, illustrations, and an appendix with a chronology of events.

Nicholls, David. *From Dessalines to Duvalier: Race, Colour, and National Independence in Haiti*. Cambridge, England: Cambridge University Press, 1979. Reprint. New Brunswick, N.J.: Rutgers University Press, 1996. An overview of Haitian history from 1804 until 1971, including information on Christophe and the other "fathers of independence," as Nicholls refers to them in his book.

Syme, Ronald. *Toussaint: The Black Liberator*. New York: William Morrow, 1971. Syme's book includes a section on Christophe and an extensive bibliography.

SEE ALSO: Simón Bolívar; Napoleon I; Pedro I.

RELATED ARTICLE in *Great Events from History: The Nineteenth Century, 1801-1900:* March 2, 1807: Congress Bans Importation of African Slaves.

CIXI

Chinese dowager empress (r. 1861-1908)

Cixi was one of the most powerful women in China's history. As empress dowager, she dominated imperial China for more than fifty years from "behind the curtain."

BORN: November 29, 1835; Beijing, China
DIED: November 15, 1908; Beijing, China
ALSO KNOWN AS: Tz'u-hsi; Hsiao-ch'in; Hsien Huang-hau (all Wade-Giles)
AREA OF ACHIEVEMENT: Government and politics

EARLY LIFE

Cixi (tsee-shee) may have been the daughter of a minor Manchu official; however, recent Chinese scholarship has suggested that she was ethnically Han Chinese. In 1851, when she was about sixteen, she became one of the many concubines of Emperor Xianfeng (r. 1851-1861). Fated to govern during the Taiping Rebellion that almost destroyed the Qing Dynasty, the weak and ineffective Xianfeng died at the age of thirty. His only significant accomplishment was to father a son, Tongzhi, by Cixi, who remained his favorite concubine after the son was born in 1856. On Xianfeng's death, Cixi placed the five-year-old Tongzhi on the Chinese throne. Cixi herself was only twenty-six years old at that time.

LIFE'S WORK

Because of Tongzhi's youth, Cixi served as regent for the young emperor, along with Prince Gong, the boy's uncle. In 1861, imperial China seemed on the verge of disintegration, but the Tongzhi Restoration, as it is known, reversed the process by attempting to emulate the West, particularly its technology, under the banner of "self-strengthening." Nevertheless, at the time of Tongzhi's early death in 1874 at the age of eighteen, China still lagged behind. Not only were nations such as Great Britain and France militarily stronger, but to some the increasing presence of Christian missionaries also was a threat to traditional Chinese culture.

Officially, Tongzhi died of smallpox, but according to some rumors, Cixi was responsible for his death because she believed that her son's young wife, Alute, would reduce her own influence. After Tongzhi died, his widow empress was made to commit suicide, and Cixi installed her four-year-old nephew, Guangxu, as emperor. When she did that, she ignored the laws of royal succession because the new emperor was of the same generation as Tongzhi and could not perform the filial or ancestral rituals. Guangxu's mother, Xiao Chen, was Cixi's sister, and the two dowager empresses controlled the government and the young emperor together. After Xiao Chen died in 1881, Cixi continued to rule as regent for Guangxu until 1889.

As the only woman to achieve significant power in China during the long Manchu reign that had begun in 1642, Cixi was extremely capable but also cruel and callous. Referred to as the Venerable Buddha, a term usually reserved for men, she was both literate and charismatic and was Machiavellian enough to manipulate government ministers and advisers despite her diminutive stature. She was five feet tall but wore five-inch heels to increase her height. Like most upper-class Manchu women, Cixi had long fingernails, and she was known to scratch the faces of servants when she was displeased. She also used a great amount of makeup, whitening her face and rouging her cheeks. Her power and perhaps her sexual charms attracted to her side ambitious young men, whom she often rewarded with political office.

Given her position and rank, it was to be expected that Cixi would be conservative in maintaining Manchu power and the status quo in Qing China. However, that was not easily accomplished while Western nations were making inroads into China during the nineteenth century. As a result of the 1839-1842 Opium War with Great Britain, Britain and then other nations obtained commercial and legal privileges in China. In 1860, Cixi and Emperor Xianfeng were forced to flee the capital of Beijing ahead of its capture by British and French troops.

China's situation improved somewhat as a result of the self-strengthening movement, which Cixi supported, but not sufficiently to resist Western and Japanese economic, political, and religious demands. By most accounts, Cixi diligently heard reports and made decisions, but from behind a screen to satisfy the needs of propriety in male-dominated China. However, in her royal isolation it is impossible to know if she truly understood the state of her country. Because of Prince Gong's suspected involvement in the execution of one of Cixi's favorite eunuchs, Cixi had him politically marginalized, and most of her other advisers were as conservative as she was.

France's defeat of China's weak navy in 1884 in a struggle over French ambitions in Indochina and China's defeat a decade later at the hands of a modernizing Japan emphasized China's continuing weakness. Cixi contributed to some of these problems. An example of her occasionally irresponsible use of authority occurred in 1893, when she spent money that was supposed to be employed in modernizing China's navy on the construction of a full-sized marble boat resembling a paddle-steamer.

Cixi. (Library of Congress)

The 1895 Treaty of Shimonoseki that ended the Sino-Japanese War forced China to abandon its long-term influence in Korea, making Korea a de facto Japanese protectorate. China also had to cede the island of Taiwan and other Chinese territories to Japan. Afterward, a new reform movement emerged in China. It was led by Kang Youwei, who claimed that the ancient philosopher Confucius—whose teachings remained the inspiration for Chinese government philosophy during the nineteenth century—was not the conservative so often claimed. Instead, the reformists argued, Confucius had believed in progress and reform.

By that time, Cixi had given up her day-to-day political involvement, which allowed her nephew, Emperor Guangxu, to assume more power. Sympathetic to Kang and other reformers, Guangxu, although often cowed by his fierce aunt, was well educated, spoke some English, and was aware of China's weakness and the need to modernize. The culmination of Guangxu's efforts culminated in the Hundred Days' Reform between June and September, 1898, during which the emperor issued edicts reforming the educational system, strengthening the army, and modernizing the economy.

The young emperor apparently believed that Cixi would support his reforms, but she did not, fearing foreign influence and the possible weakening of Qing rule. In mid-September, 1898, when rumors circulated that a coup was developing to remove Guangxu, Cixi returned to Beijing from her semiretirement. Two days after her return she issued a proclamation stating that Guangxu had asked her to assume power. Several reformers were executed, but Kang managed to escape, and the hapless Guangxu was restricted to royal palaces for the rest of his life.

Western nations and Japan continued to infringe upon China's sovereignty, carving out spheres of influence from Manchuria in the north to the island of Hainan in the south. Missionaries were also actively engaged in converting Chinese to Christianity. The response was the antiforeign Boxer movement, which began in 1898. Fueled by floods and droughts and eclectic religious beliefs, many of the so-called Boxers believed they were impervious to bullets. Most were peasants, and their targets were the missionaries and their Chinese converts as well as other Westerners.

By 1900, violence was reaching Beijing and other cities. The Western nations seized Chinese forts and attempted to send troops to relieve Beijing. On June 21, 1900, Cixi, believing she had to keep the support of the people—who were represented by the Boxers—issued a declaration of war against the foreigners. However, the weak Qing forces could not stop the Western and Japanese troops, who arrived in Beijing on August 16. Cixi and her nephew fled to Xi'an in the west, and a peace treaty, the Boxer Protocol, was signed in September. Leading Boxers and Qing officials who supported the Boxers were executed, and China was required to pay an indemnity of 333 million dollars to the invading powers.

Cixi and Guangxu returned to Beijing's Forbidden City in January 1902, but the emperor continued to play no political role. In a gesture of reconciliation, Cixi received the foreign ambassadors and held a reception for their wives. Meanwhile, Chinese opposition to the Qing increased. Some Chinese regarded the Manchus as foreigners, even though they had been ruling China for centuries. Others resented the weakness of the government in the face of Western and Japanese incursions. Cixi and her ministers grudgingly began to institute reforms, such as abolition of the examination system based upon the Confucius and other ancient sages. In 1908, Cixi announced constitutional reforms that would take nine years fully to implement. However, these reforms came too late. On November 15, 1908, Cixi died at the age of seventy-two.

SIGNIFICANCE

After Cixi died, it was announced that Emperor Guangxu had died the previous day. Before her death, Cixi named her three-year-old grandnephew, Puyi, as the new emperor. Two years later, the Revolution of 1911 swept Puyi and the Qing from power, and imperial China ended with the establishment of the Republic of China, under Sun Yatsen.

Cixi dominated China for almost fifty years. Historically, only Empress Wu rivaled her power and influence. Cixi was ruthless in dominating her ministers, destroying her enemies, and reducing the titular emperors to mere ciphers. She was a conservative in the desire to maintain her authority and Manchu rule in the face of the need to modernize and reform China. She was also an able politician. However, because she was a woman and perceived to be a foreigner—a Manchu—she became a scapegoat for many of China's problems that were beyond the capability of any single person to solve, as evidenced by the failure of republican China in the decades that followed.

—*Eugene S. Larson*

FURTHER READING

Laidler, Keith. *The Last Empress*. New York: John Wiley & Sons, 2003. A well-written biography of "The She Dragon of China," filled with anecdotes.

Paludan, Ann. *Chronicles of the Chinese Emperors*. New York: Thames and Hudson, 1998. An excellent account of China's emperors, including an acute portrayal of Cixi.

Seagrave, Sterling. *Dragon Lady*. New York: Alfred A. Knopf, 1992. This sympathetic biography is the classic account of Cixi's life and her legend.

SEE ALSO: Kang Youwei; Zeng Guofan; Zhang Zhidong.

RELATED ARTICLES in *Great Events from History: The Nineteenth Century, 1801-1900:* 1860's: China's Self-Strengthening Movement Arises; May, 1900-September 7, 1901: Boxer Rebellion.

CARL VON CLAUSEWITZ
Polish military theoretician

Clausewitz played an important role in Prussian military and political history during the Napoleonic Wars but is best known as a leading modern philosopher of war. His most famous work, On War, *has been characterized as "not simply the greatest, but the only great book about war."*

BORN: June 1, 1780; Burg, near Magdeburg, Prussia (now in Germany)
DIED: November 16, 1831; Breslau, Silesia (now Wrocław, Poland)
ALSO KNOWN AS: Carl Philipp Gottlieb von Clausewitz (full name)
AREA OF ACHIEVEMENT: Military

EARLY LIFE

Carl von Clausewitz (KLOHZ-vihtz) was born into a Prussian family that, despite its pretensions to nobility, was in fact of middle-class origins. The elder Clausewitz had obtained a commission in the army of Frederick the Great but was forcibly retired during Frederick's purge of nonnoble officers after the Seven Years' War. Clausewitz seems, however, to have believed in the family's claim to noble status; on the basis of his own achievements, Clausewitz had his claim confirmed by the king of Prussia in 1827.

The ambiguity of Clausewitz's social position may be a key to understanding his life and personality, although it does not appear to have blocked his advancement. He tended, as his correspondence and comments by contemporaries reveal, to feel and to be treated like an outsider. Sensitive, shy, and bookish by nature, he could also be passionate in his politics, his love for his wife, and his longing for military glory. Slim and rather handsome, he frequently displayed coolness and physical courage in battle. His keen analytical intelligence was accompanied by a certain intellectual arrogance. These qualities may account for the fact that, although he rose to high rank in the Prussian service, he served always as a staff officer rather than as a commander.

Clausewitz entered the Prussian army as a cadet at the age of twelve; he first saw combat, against revolutionary France, at thirteen. After 1795, he spent five years in the rather dreary garrison town of Neuruppin. There, he applied himself energetically to his own education, a project in which he was so successful that he was able to gain admission to the new War College in Berlin in 1801. With this appointment, his rise to prominence had begun.

LIFE'S WORK

The director of the War College was Gerhard Johann von Scharnhorst, who was to become Clausewitz's mentor and a key figure in the Prussian state during the upheavals of the Napoleonic Wars. Many of Clausewitz's basic historical, political, and military views derived from the influence of Scharnhorst and other Prussian military reformers.

Clausewitz was graduated first in his class in 1803 and was rewarded with the position of military adjutant to the young Prince August. The same year, he met and fell in love with his future wife, the Countess Marie von Brühl. However, the ambiguity of his social background and his poverty posed problems. Marie's family would resist this poor match for seven years, until Clausewitz's rapid promotion undermined their objections to a marriage.

Prussia had remained at peace with France since 1795 but, alarmed at the devastating French victories over Austria and Russia in 1805, mobilized for war in 1806. Clausewitz and most other Prussian officers anticipated the struggle with confidence, but the timing was poor and the nation was ill-prepared. The Prussian forces were shattered in humiliating defeats at Jena and Auerstedt. Both Clausewitz and Prince August were captured. The experience was both shocking and enlightening for Clausewitz.

When Clausewitz returned from internment in 1808, he joined Scharnhorst and the other members of the reform movement in helping to restructure both Prussian society and the army, in preparation for what Clausewitz believed to be an inevitable new struggle with the hated French. His enthusiasm was not, however, shared by the king, who was more concerned with maintaining his position in the much-reduced Prussian state. Clausewitz's disillusionment reached a peak when Prussia, allied with France, provided an army corps to Napoleon I to assist during the 1812 invasion of Russia. Along with about thirty other officers, Clausewitz resigned from Prussian service and accepted a commission in the Russian army. He fought at the bloody Battle of Borodino and witnessed the disastrous French retreat from Moscow. He then played a role, the importance of which is disputed, in negotiating the defection of the Prussian corps from the French army.

None of this won for Clausewitz any affection in the court at Berlin, where he was referred to on at least one occasion as "Louse-witz." The eventual entry of Prussia into the anti-Napoleon coalition nevertheless led, after some delay, to his reinstatement in the Prussian army. Clausewitz participated in many key events of the "War of Liberation," but bad luck and the lingering resentment of the king prevented him from obtaining any significant command.

In 1818, Clausewitz was promoted to general and became administrative head of the War College. This position offered him little scope to test his educational theories or to influence national policy. Perhaps because of the conservative reaction in Prussia after 1819, as a result of which many of the liberal reforms of the war years were weakened or rescinded, Clausewitz spent his abundant leisure time quietly, writing studies of Napoleonic campaigns and preparing the theoretical work that eventually became his magnum opus, *Vom Kriege* (1832-1834; *On War*, 1873).

Clausewitz saw war as essentially a creative activity: Victory goes not to the general who has learned the rules but to the general who makes them. Therefore, military theory must not attempt to prescribe a general's actions but should aim instead at educating his judgment so that, on the battlefield, he will be able to weigh all the factors that apply in his own unique situation. Clausewitz was scornful of military dilettantes such as Adam Heinrich Dietrich von Bülow, who tried to reduce the art of war to a mathematical equation. The strategist, like the artist, will make use of science, but the end result in both cases will be something quite different from the predictable, repeatable results of an experiment in physics. This outlook surely stemmed from Clausewitz's own experience of the overthrow of traditional armies by the radically new forces of the French Revolution.

Carl von Clausewitz. (Library of Congress)

Clausewitz's approach contrasts with that of his initially more influential contemporary, the Swiss theorist Antoine-Henri de Jomini. Where Jomini saw fixed values, Clausewitz looked for variable quantities. Where Jomini worried about physical forces, Clausewitz discussed the effects of morale and psychological factors. Where Jomini prescribed unilateral action, Clausewitz showed that war is the continuous interaction of opposites. Where Jomini sought to achieve certainty on the battlefield, Clausewitz stressed uncertainty, chance, suffering, confusion, exhaustion, and fear, factors that added to what he called the "friction" of war.

The most famous and often-quoted line from *On War*, possibly the only line ever read by most quoters of Clausewitz, is that "War is the continuation of politics by other means." His point was that war is not in any way a sphere separate from politics and that military operations must always serve a rational political end. The crux of the problem is that neither soldiers nor statesmen are infallible, even within their own areas of competence, and Clausewitz's dictum will work only if the generals and the politicians understand one another's limitations.

Clausewitz returned to active field duty in 1830, when revolutions in Paris and Poland seemed to presage a new general European war. Before leaving, he sealed his manuscripts with the warning, "Should the work be interrupted by my death, then what is found can only be called a mass of conceptions not brought into form . . . open to endless misconceptions." Although war was averted, Clausewitz remained in the east, organizing a sanitary cordon to stop the spread of a cholera epidemic from Poland. He returned home to Breslau in 1831, seemingly healthy, but contracted the deadly disease and died the same day. He was fifty-one years old. Despite his note of warning, his fiercely loyal wife continued his work. It was she who edited and published *On War*, the first volumes of which appeared in 1832.

ON WAR

One of Carl von Clausewitz's major contributions to military philosophy was his articulation of the interconnections between warfare and politics.

War is a mere continuation of policy by other means. We see, therefore, that War is not merely a political act, but also a real political instrument, a continuation of political commerce, a carrying out of the same by other means. All beyond this which is strictly peculiar to War relates merely to the peculiar nature of the means which it uses. That the tendencies and views of policy shall not be incompatible with these means, the Art of War in general and the Commander in each particular case may demand, and this claim is truly not a trifling one. But however powerfully this may react on political views in particular cases, still it must always be regarded as only a modification of them; for the political view is the object, War is the means, and the means must always include the object in our conception.

Source: Carl von Clausewitz, *On War*. Translated by J. J. Graham (1874. Reprint, London, 1909).

SIGNIFICANCE

Although Carl von Clausewitz wrote a considerable amount of history, particularly campaign studies, he is read almost exclusively for the military philosophy contained in *On War*. This book was received with the respect its famous author deserved but remained in obscurity until cited by Helmuth Karl Bernhard von Moltke as the key to his victories over Austria in 1866 and France in 1870-1871. It then became a virtual military cult object. *On War* has gradually assumed a status as the preeminent philosophical examination of war and military theory.

Unfortunately, many later interpreters have twisted Clausewitz's argument—and even altered the text—concerning the relationship of war and political policy, with the intent of winning greater independence for military leaders. Colmar von der Goltz, writing in 1883, reconciled these two seemingly irreconcilable ideas by saying that "war serves the ends of politics best by a complete defeat of the enemy," even though this formulation directly contradicted the lessons of Prussia's greatest military-political successes, that is, the victorious wars against Austria and France.

Although Clausewitz is often supposed to have been the "apostle of total war," in fact, this is merely the unfortunate by-product of his quasi-Hegelian analytical method, which led him to begin with a discussion of war as an "absolute," an ideal. Clausewitz was writing in the years before nuclear weapons, but his abstract discussion of absolute war seems now to be prophetic of today's balance of terror. There is even a group of modern strategic theorists who have been called the "neo-Clausewitzians," including such prominent nuclear strategists as Henry Kissinger and Herman Kahn. Clausewitz, however, recognized that war could be either total or limited and that in reality no war would be a perfect example of either.

That *On War* or its misinterpretation actually led to the debacle of World War I, as some have charged, is dubious. Few generals of this war ever read this notoriously difficult book. Furthermore, as Clausewitz himself recognized, war changes over time; societies fight the wars for which they are physically, socially, and psychologically equipped. The nature of war in any given environment is determined by Clausewitz's trinity of government policy, the capabilities of the army, and the attitudes of the population.

If Clausewitz's work is understood as descriptive in nature, it can be a useful tool for military analysis. If, instead, the reader tries to use it prescriptively, as Clausewitz feared might happen, he will constantly be misled by his own cultural preconceptions and by the tendency to see war in its ideal, absolute form, rather than in the disorderly form in which it actually exists. To see in Clausewitz's rather matter-of-fact description of war as "a continuation of policy" a justification for resorting to arms is to miss the point of his argument; no leader who truly grasps Clausewitz's description of the role of chance in war is likely to take the gamble lightly.

—Christopher Bassford

FURTHER READING

Aron, Raymond. *Clausewitz: Philosopher of War*. Translated by Christine Booker and Norman Stone. Englewood Cliffs, N.J.: Prentice-Hall, 1985. Although not a good translation from the French, this book contains a useful biography of Clausewitz, a subtle analysis of his ideas, and an account of the scholarly controversies that they have spawned.

Clausewitz, Carl von. *On War*. Edited and translated by Michael Howard and Peter Paret. Princeton, N.J.: Princeton University Press, 1976. The best of three English translations of Clausewitz's major theoretical work. The volume also contains essays on Clausewitz by each of the editors as well as a guide to reading by

Bernard Brodie, a prominent American strategic analyst.

Gallie, W. B. *Philosophers of Peace and War: Kant, Clausewitz, Marx, Engels, and Tolstoy*. Cambridge, England: Cambridge University Press, 1978. Treats Clausewitz's theories in their philosophical and military contexts.

Handel, Michael I., ed. *Clausewitz and Modern Strategy*. London: Frank Cass, 1986. A collection of essays discussing Clausewitz, his theories, and his influence on the military strategies followed by various nations, including Germany, France, and Italy.

Howard, Michael. *Clausewitz: A Very Short Introduction*. New York: Oxford University Press, 2002. A brief (84-page) explanation of Clausewitz's theories of warfare described within the context of his experience in the Napoleonic Wars and the intellectual background of his time.

Paret, Peter. "Clausewitz." In *Makers of Modern Strategy: From Machiavelli to the Nuclear Age*, edited by Peter Paret and Gordon A. Craig. Princeton, N.J.: Princeton University Press, 1986. A short essay on Clausewitz in an excellent anthology of essays on other strategic thinkers.

_____. *Clausewitz and the State: The Man, His Theories, and His Times*. Princeton, N.J.: Princeton University Press, 1976. The most sophisticated biography of Clausewitz.

_____. *Understanding War: Essays on Clausewitz and the History of Military Power*. Princeton, N.J.: Princeton University Press, 1992. A collection of Paret's essays about Clausewitz, examining his theories of warfare and how they relate to war as a general historical phenomenon.

SEE ALSO: August von Gneisenau; Napoleon I; Gerhard Johann David von Scharnhorst.

RELATED ARTICLES in *Great Events from History: The Nineteenth Century, 1801-1900:* June 23-December 14, 1812: Napoleon Invades Russia; September 7, 1812: Battle of Borodino.

HENRY CLAY
American politician

Clay was a dominant figure in American politics during the first half of the nineteenth century. His so-called American System and efforts to find a national compromise in the controversy over slavery helped ease the growing tensions within the Union.

BORN: April 12, 1777; Hanover County, Virginia
DIED: June 29, 1852; Washington, D.C.
ALSO KNOWN AS: Great Compromiser; Great Pacificator
AREA OF ACHIEVEMENT: Government and politics

EARLY LIFE

Henry Clay was born on a Virginia farm. His parents, the Reverend John Clay, a Baptist minister, and Elizabeth Hudson Clay, were of English descent and reasonably prosperous, though certainly not wealthy. His father died when Henry was four, but his mother was remarried within a year to Captain Henry Watkins, who maintained the family's financial status. Henry received a few years of schooling and developed remarkable penmanship, a skill that served him well when his stepfather moved the family in 1792.

At the age of fifteen, Clay stayed in Richmond to work for the Clerk of the High Court of Chancery. In 1793, Clay was hired by the famous lawyer George Wythe as a part-time secretary. Almost seventy, Wythe was a leader of Virginia's bar and had enjoyed a distinguished career as teacher of law and classics. Under Wythe's tutelage, Clay studied the law and, a few years later, left his clerk's position to study under Robert Brooke, former governor and later attorney general of Virginia. In November, 1797, Clay passed his bar examination.

Like other ambitious Virginians, the young attorney moved to Kentucky, where confusion over land claims created a lawyer's paradise. At twenty, Clay was over six feet tall, thin, and walked with a shambling gait. His face, capable of creating considerable impact with a change of expression, was capped by hair so light as to be almost prematurely white. His eyes were small, gray, and piercing, his nose prominent, and from his large mouth issued his most valuable asset: his voice. Coupled with an emotional temperament, this voice, suited for an actor, made him a formidable opponent in frontier courts, where persuasion was frequently more important than legal knowledge.

The stage for Clay's legal theatrics was Lexington, Kentucky, a village on its way to becoming the "Athens of the West." Though appearing in frail health, Clay demonstrated his skill in local debates and was admitted to the Kentucky bar on March 20, 1798. Before a successful legal career made him a local legend, the budding jurist married Lucretia Hart, daughter of the influential merchant Thomas Hart. The marriage not only connected Clay with an important local family but also provided him with a patient, loving wife who bore him eleven children. By 1800, Henry Clay was a member of Lexington's establishment.

LIFE'S WORK

Clay's debut as a radical Jeffersonian came when he spoke for a liberalization of the state's constitution and made speeches attacking the Alien and Sedition Acts. He supported Jefferson in 1800 and, in 1803, won election to the Kentucky legislature. There he demonstrated his talent as a parliamentary tactician and also flirted with disaster by becoming counsel for Aaron Burr, who was charged with an alleged conspiracy to invade Mexico. Unaware of the extent of Burr's activities, Clay successfully defended Burr in Kentucky's courts, but later, as the import of Burr's schemes became apparent, Clay repudiated his dangerous client.

While acting as counsel for Burr, Clay was selected to fill an unexpired term in the U.S. Senate. Apparently no one paid any attention to the fact that he was a few months short of the required age. This brief performance in Washington, D.C., began a lifelong crusade for a national program based on internal improvements at federal expense and a protective tariff. Such measures were joined by an expansionistic, anti-British foreign policy. Clay's jingoism increased when he moved to the House of Representatives and became its Speaker. There, along with other "war hawks," Clay helped push the nation into the War of 1812. When the struggle did not bring victory, Clay found himself a member of the American delegation sent to Ghent, Belgium, to negotiate an end to the war he had helped to create. In spite of the negative reaction of John Quincy Adams, head of the delegation, who objected to Clay's Western habits of drinking, swearing, and gambling, the Kentuckian proved an able diplomat.

In the postwar years, Clay became a chief proponent of American nationalism and envisioned a truly united country tied together by bonds of economic interest as well as a common ideology. The government's role in his American System was to promote harmony through economic development. Key to his system was a new national bank. Suspicious of the first Bank of the United States, Clay had helped to block its recharter in 1811, but financial confusion during the war convinced him that a centralized financial system was imperative. From this time until the end of his career, Clay's name would be associated with the idea of a national bank.

Clay's legislative success made it seem that Clay's elevation to the White House was only a matter of time. His successful solution to the slavery controversy further encouraged his supporters. In 1819, Missouri applied for admission as a slave state. Hostility on both sides of the question threatened to divide the Union. Though a slave owner himself, Clay had moral reservations about slavery and supported gradual emancipation coupled with colonization. In fact, Clay had been a founder of the American Colonization Society in 1816. In his mind, however, the abolition of slavery was of less importance than the preservation of the Union. In the House, he helped frame the famous Missouri Compromise, which brought in Maine as a free state to balance Missouri and divided the rest of the Louisiana Territory. Though many politicians were involved, the compromise was seen as Clay's handiwork.

Clay's popularity did not immediately convert into political success. Clay was unhappy with the Monroe administration. The president selected a New Englander, John Quincy Adams, as secretary of state, a post that Clay had expected. Sectional harmony had been purchased at the cost of alienating Kentucky's "Hotspur." Clay frequently criticized the administration's lack of support for the Latin American revolutions, a stand that made him popular in South America. His persistence was rewarded with Monroe's famous doctrine in 1823, but from Clay's perspective it was too little, too late. Most important, however, his quibbling with the Monroe administration obscured a serious threat to his political future: Jacksonian democracy.

Since 1800, the U.S. politics had been dominated by Jefferson's party, but, in 1824, four prominent leaders, Clay, Andrew Jackson, William H. Crawford, and John Quincy Adams, entered the contest for president. Almost everyone underestimated the military hero from the War of 1812, Jackson. When the final votes were in, no candidate had a majority, but Jackson won a plurality. Shocked and disappointed, Clay came in fourth and was thus eliminated from consideration by the House. When Clay announced his support for Adams, which in effect made Adams president, Jackson was furious.

Suspicions of underhanded dealing seemed confirmed when Adams appointed Clay secretary of state.

Henry Clay. (Library of Congress)

This supposedly "corrupt bargain" provided a rallying cry for Jacksonians in the next election. While there is no evidence of prior arrangement, Jackson's complaint reveals an important difference between him and his rivals. Adams, Crawford, and Clay were all part of the leadership in Washington. Jackson, while a national military hero, had never been part of the Washington establishment. There was simply not enough room at the top, and Jackson became a lightning rod attracting those in politics and society who felt left out. Moreover, Democrats, taking advantage of extended suffrage, directed their appeal toward the common person even though Jackson and his allies were hardly common men.

Clay's new role in foreign affairs turned out be of little political value. The real drama was taking place internally, where followers of Jackson made a wreck of Adams's administration. The president was no match for the new kind of politician. Adams's style of leadership suited an earlier age; politics now stressed personality. Cold, aloof, and even arrogant, the president introduced a program designed to improve his constituents. Jacksonians were content to direct their appeal to the lowest common denominator. In 1828, Jackson's presidential victory changed American politics forever.

With Jackson and his minions ensconced in the White House, the anti-Jacksonian opposition began to fall apart. By mid-1829, however, Clay's Kentucky estate had become the center of another presidential campaign, and, in late 1831, its master once again returned to the Senate and was quickly nominated for president by a national Republican convention. The ensuing struggle revolved around the second Bank of the United States. Motivated by partisan concerns, the bank's supporters pushed for recharter before it was necessary. Clay believed that the effort would place Jackson in an untenable position. He was wrong. Jackson reacted quickly by vetoing the recharter bill and destroying the bank by removing government deposits. Jackson's policies did cause defections among his supporters, but his enemies miscalculated the impact on the electorate. As ignorant of banking practices as their president, voters sympathized with Jackson's struggle, and the result was a smashing defeat of Clay's presidential aspirations.

There was no time for recriminations. As dust from the election settled, a South Carolina convention passed an Ordinance of Nullification against the tariffs of 1828 and 1832. The power to act rested with the president. Supposedly in favor of states' rights and less than enthusiastic about a tariff, Jackson, as usual, surprised everyone. Standing firmly for national supremacy, he asked Congress to pass the so-called Force Bill, granting the executive special authority in the crisis. Congress began to scramble for a compromise that would avert a military confrontation between South Carolina and the federal government. At center stage was Henry Clay. His compromise tariff gave South Carolina an excuse to back down without losing face. Once again, Clay had been instrumental in saving the Union.

In Jackson's second term, a new opposition party was created by a single idea: hatred of Andrew Jackson. It reached into British history for a name signifying resistance to tyranny: Whig. Its program was dominated by Clay's American System coupled with a bias against executive power, but it also adopted attitudes toward political opportunism pioneered by Jacksonians. To Clay's disappointment, the new party was too fragmented to unite around a single candidate in 1836.

Hoping to throw the election into the House, the Whigs selected three sectional candidates to face Jackson's successor, Martin Van Buren. The strategy failed; Van Buren won. Whig frustration vanished when, a few months into the new administration, the country was rocked by an economic depression. Clay, secure in the Senate, was in an excellent position for the election of 1840, but his fellow Whigs were unsure. With his legions of enemies, Clay's name could unite Jacksonians as nothing else could. As a result, the party's convention turned away from its real leader and chose William Henry Harrison. Inwardly furious, Clay publicly supported the Harrison ticket.

The Whigs won, at last, by turning the tables on their enemies. Harrison was a military hero, and the campaign that elected him avoided serious political discussion. Still, most Whigs viewed the victory as a chance to reverse the tide in favor of Clay's American System. They soon realized that they were mistaken. Harrison's death a few months after inauguration brought to the White House a man who did not share Whig ideals. John Tyler had been nominated for vice president to ensure the loyalty of southern Whigs. When Congress passed the Whig legislative agenda, Tyler promptly vetoed the most significant measure, a bill creating a national bank. The result was chaos. Most of the cabinet resigned, and Tyler governed without party backing.

Tyler's defection left Clay the unchallenged leader of his party, and the presidency, in 1844, seemed his. Once again, however, fate intervened. Pressure for annexation of Texas had been growing. Clay, like other established leaders, feared Texas would rekindle the slavery controversy. Though generally an expansionist, he came out against annexation, expecting that a similar stand by the likely Democratic nominee, Van Buren, would remove the touchy question. After Clay's nomination, the Democrats repudiated Van Buren and nominated the ardent annexationist James K. Polk of Tennessee. As the campaign progressed, Texas captured the public imagination, and Polk's narrow victory was probably the bitterest defeat of Clay's career.

In such circumstances most men would have welcomed retirement, but Clay's unquenchable love of political combat made it impossible. Moreover, the country needed him.

THE EXPUNGING RESOLUTION

One of President Andrew Jackson's most fervent political opponents, Henry Clay feared that Jackson was abusing the presidency by amassing too much power. In this extract from a speech that Clay delivered to the U.S. Senate in 1837, he expresses his scorn for the move to expunge from the official record a Senate resolution condemning Jackson for his position on the Bank of the United States.

What patriotic purpose is to be accomplished by this Expunging Resolution? What new honor or fresh laurels will it win for our common country? Is the power of the Senate so vast that it ought to be circumscribed, and that of the President so restricted that it ought to be extended? What power has the Senate? None, separately. It can only act jointly with the other House, or jointly with the Executive. And although the theory of the Constitution supposes, when consulted by him, it may freely give an affirmative or negative response, according to the practice, as it now exists, it has lost the faculty of pronouncing the negative monosyllable. When the Senate expresses its deliberate judgment, in the form of resolution, that resolution has no compulsory force, but appeals only to the dispassionate intelligence, the calm reason, and the sober judgment, of the community. The Senate has no army, no navy, no patronage, no lucrative offices, no glittering honors, to bestow. Around us there is no swarm of greedy expectants, rendering us homage, anticipating our wishes, and ready to execute our commands.

How is it with the President? Is he powerless? He is felt from one extremity to the other of this vast Republic. By means of principles which he has introduced, and innovations which he has made in our institutions, alas! but too much countenanced by Congress and a confiding people, he exercises, uncontrolled, the power of the State. In one hand he holds the purse, and in the other brandishes the sword of the country. Myriads of dependants and partisans, scattered over the land, are ever ready to sing hosannas to him, and to laud to the skies whatever he does. He has swept over the government, during the last eight years, like a tropical tornado. Every department exhibits traces of the ravages of the storm. Take as one example the Bank of the United States. No institution could have been more popular with the people, with Congress, and with State Legislatures. None ever better fulfilled the great purposes of its establishment. But it unfortunately incurred the displeasure of the President; he spoke, and the bank lies prostrate. And those who were loudest in its praise are now loudest in its condemnation. What object of his ambition is unsatisfied? When disabled from age any longer to hold the sceptre of power, he designates his successor, and transmits it to his favorite! What more does he want? Must we blot, deface, and mutilate the records of the country, to punish the presumptuousness of expressing an opinion contrary to his own? . . .

Source: Henry Clay, "On the Expunging Resolutions," speech in U.S. Senate, January 16, 1837.

As feared, Texas brought with it the Mexican War and reopened debate over slavery. Clay hoped for the Whig presidential nomination in 1848, but for the last time his party betrayed him. Concerned about his age and poor health, the Whigs nominated another military hero, Zachary Taylor.

Bitter but unbowed, Clay played one last role on the American political stage. Unsophisticated in politics, newly elected President Taylor only exacerbated the conflict over slavery. When California applied for admission as a free state with the administration's blessing, the country once again faced disunion. As always, the senator from Kentucky stood in the way of a complete rupture within the Union. In spite of frail health, he framed a series of measures that became the famous Compromise of 1850. Working in the brutally hot Washington, D.C., summer until his health broke, Clay turned over the leadership of the compromisers to a younger colleague, Stephen A. Douglas of Illinois, and watched from the sidelines as Douglas pushed through the final legislation. This desperate attempt at sectional peace had only a brief life, but Henry Clay did not live to see it collapse. He died in Washington, D.C., the scene of so many of his triumphs, on June 29, 1852, two years before his last compromise unraveled.

SIGNIFICANCE

Throughout his long career, Clay's programs and personality were always controversial. To supporters, he was the best that American politics had to offer, and they often regarded him with near adulation. To enemies, he represented the United States at its worst, and they hated him with unbridled passion. Like most politicians, some of his positions changed with time and circumstance, but one element remained consistent—his vision of national purpose. Clay saw his country as the hope of humankind. He genuinely believed the republican system to be superior and looked forward to its spread. In a sense, his American System was designed to further this aim by making the United States stronger. The Union could continue to exist, Clay believed, only if the states would work for mutual benefit. The cement that would glue the nation together was a cooperative economic system managed by the common government.

Clay's vision was a short-run failure. During his own time, the American System was submerged under the rising tide of Jacksonian democracy and the new style of politics it spawned. Only eight years after Clay's death the country he loved was embroiled in the civil war that his many compromises had sought to avert. Like so many of his generation, Clay had been unable to face the moral dilemma created by slavery, which could not be compromised away. In the long run, however, Clay's vision was a success. The country that emerged from the Civil War was much closer to Clay's America than to Jackson's.

—David Warren Bowen

FURTHER READING

Baxter, Maurice G. *Henry Clay and the American System*. Lexington: University Press of Kentucky, 1995. Detailed study of Clay, his views on economic development, and his impact upon American government.

Eaton, Clement. *Henry Clay and the Art of American Politics*. Boston: Little, Brown, 1957. A concise biographical treatment in The Library of American Biography, edited by Oscar Handlin. Concentrating on Clay's political career, it follows the evolution of Clay from an advocate of Western interests to a true nationalist.

Howe, Daniel Walker. *The Political Culture of American Whigs*. Chicago: University of Chicago Press, 1979. A thoughtful analysis of Whig ideology. Clay is a central figure, and the book contains valuable insights into the source of Whiggery.

Mayo, Benard. *Henry Clay: Spokesman of the New West*. Boston: Houghton Mifflin, 1937. The classic, scholarly biography of Clay. A colorful, well-written account that deals with Clay's private as well as public life. The treatment of Clay's early life in Kentucky is particularly valuable.

Poage, George Rawlings. *Henry Clay and the Whig Party*. Chapel Hill: University of North Carolina Press, 1936. A biographical treatment that concentrates on Clay's role in the founding and development of the Whig Party. The work is well documented but somewhat dated.

Remini, Robert Vincent. *Henry Clay: Statesman for the Union*. New York: W. W. Norton, 1991. Remini, who has written several books about Andrew Jackson, here provides a comprehensive and scholarly biography of Jackson's rival, Clay. Includes a chronology and a genealogy of Clay's family.

Sargent, Epes. *The Life and Public Services of Henry Clay Down to 1848*. Buffalo, N.Y.: Derby, Orton, and Mulligan, 1853. Completed soon after Clay's death as a memorial to the leader of American Whiggery. Biased and dated, but still an excellent example of the pro-Clay biographies written during his era.

Shankman, Kimberly Christner. *Compromise and the Constitution: The Political Thought of Henry Clay.* Lanham, Md.: Lexington Books, 1999. Examines Clay's political thinking and his approach to republican statecraft.

Van Deusen, Glyndon G. *The Life of Henry Clay.* Boston: Little, Brown, 1937. A somewhat critical biography of Clay. Well researched and well written, the study provides balance when compared with the usual attitude of Clay's biographers.

Watson, Harry L. *Andrew Jackson vs. Henry Clay: Democracy and Development in Antebellum America.* Boston: Bedford/St. Martin's, 1998. Dual biography, describing the two men's conflicting visions for the future of the United States. Includes reprints of twenty-five primary documents, including speeches and letters.

SEE ALSO: John Quincy Adams; Albert Gallatin; Andrew Jackson; Abraham Lincoln.

RELATED ARTICLES in *Great Events from History: The Nineteenth Century, 1801-1900:* March 3, 1820: Missouri Compromise; December 1, 1824-February 9, 1825: U.S. Election of 1824; December 3, 1828: U.S. Election of 1828; July 10, 1832: Jackson Vetoes Rechartering of the Bank of the United States; November 24, 1832-January 21, 1833: Nullification Controversy; April 14, 1834: Clay Begins American Whig Party; January 29-September 20, 1850: Compromise of 1850.

GROVER CLEVELAND

President of the United States (1885-1889, 1893-1897)

The only president in U.S. history to serve in split terms, Cleveland brought great strength of character and inestimable political courage to the nation during years of political turmoil and economic crisis.

BORN: March 18, 1837; Caldwell, New Jersey
DIED: June 24, 1908; Princeton, New Jersey
ALSO KNOWN AS: Steven Grover Cleveland (full name)
AREA OF ACHIEVEMENT: Government and politics

EARLY LIFE

Steven Grover Cleveland was the fifth of nine children of Richard Falley and Ann Neal Cleveland. His father, a graduate of Yale University, was a minister who moved his growing family from Caldwell, New Jersey, to Fayetteville, New York (where Grover spent most of his youth), Clinton, New York, and thence to Holland Patent, New York. The Cleveland family, staunchly middle class, was influenced by their Puritan heritage, their Presbyterian faith, and their belief in hard work. Young Grover had few intellectual, cultural, or academic interests, preferring instead the outdoor life and fishing. When his father died in 1853, Grover found it necessary to work and help support his family. After teaching for one year as an assistant at the New York Institute for the Blind, he decided that his fortune and future lay to the West.

Cleveland followed the westward path, however, no further than the booming town of Buffalo, New York. There, Cleveland worked for and lived with his uncle, Lewis P. Allen, a wealthy cattle farmer, helping to keep the record books for the farm. After a year, he decided to read law and joined the office of Henry W. Rogers, Dennis Bowen, and Sherman Rogers as a clerk. By 1856, young Cleveland was completely self-supporting. In that year, also, he determined to join the Democratic Party—not a typical choice but one that reflected the party affiliation of the law office in which he worked and his own opinion that the Republican presidential nominee, John C. Frémont, was too radical. Cleveland began to work for the Democratic Party, attending meetings and working in the wards. At the age of twenty-five, he was elected ward supervisor and the same year served a brief appointment as assistant district attorney.

Cleveland's years in Buffalo served as preparation for his meteoric rise to national fame. There he astounded his colleagues with his capacity for long hours, attention to tedious detail, powers of concentration, and phenomenal physical energy. He showed little flair or imagination or awareness of either a cultural world or a world much beyond the boundaries of Buffalo. Cleveland, a bachelor, associated in his spare time with the other young men of the town, hunting, fishing, and enjoying an occasional beer in the local saloons. He was a large, round-faced man, with sandy hair and brilliant blue eyes. His girth led his nieces and nephews to call him "Uncle Jumbo"; his size represented considerable strength, however, rather than excess fat.

Cleveland was a staunch Unionist, a war Democrat, but when the Civil War broke out, he felt no particular inclination to fight. He provided the major support for his mother and two sisters, and, when drafted in 1863, he hired a substitute soldier, as permitted by law. In 1870, Cleveland was elected sheriff of Erie County, a position attractive in part because of the regular income it provided. While sheriff, Cleveland himself pulled the lever to hang two convicts, believing that it was wrong to require of others that which he was not willing to do himself. This incident provided further evidence of the absolute integrity that was an integral part of Cleveland's character. After one term as sheriff, Cleveland resumed his practice of law.

For the next ten years, Cleveland was a diligent and respected member of the bar in the expanding city of Buffalo (its population grew from 42,000 in 1850 to 155,000 in 1880). He was a contented plodder, satisfied with his place in the world and admired for his common sense. With its larger size, however, Buffalo government and politics became more corrupt, and when the Republicans nominated a "ring" candidate for mayor in 1881, the Democrats looked for an honest alternative. Attracted to Cleveland by his integrity (though, as a political novice, he was not the party's first choice), the Democrats persuaded him to run. At the age of forty-four, Cleveland was sworn in as mayor of Buffalo in 1882. His attacks on corruption and his courage in defying political bosses quickly gained for him a statewide reputation.

Grover Cleveland. (Library of Congress)

LIFE'S WORK

Luck played a part in Cleveland's career. The New York Democratic Party was badly divided over the power of Tammany Hall. The same moral outrage of the people who had elected Cleveland mayor of Buffalo made him an attractive candidate for governor of New York. Once again, the Republicans nominated a machine politician and the Democrats looked for a reformer. The big, bluff man from Buffalo caught the party's attention, was nominated, and in 1882 was elected governor of New York. Cleveland's administration was notable for its honesty, openness, strong values, good appointments, and courage in quarreling with John Kelly, the leader of Tammany Hall.

Once again, luck played a role in Cleveland's career, for the national Democratic Party was seeking a reformer, especially after the Republicans nominated James G. Blaine, a politician tainted with corruption since the Ulysses S. Grant administration, for president of the United States. The opposition of Tammany Hall to Cleveland's nomination merely endeared his candidacy to other Democrats across the country, and in 1884 he received the Democratic nomination for president. As in his races for mayor and for governor, the major issue was corruption, and Cleveland's strength was his unquestioned honesty and integrity.

The campaign of 1884, however, soon collapsed into mudslinging. Blaine was increasingly identified with corruption in government, while the Republicans countercharged that Cleveland had fathered an illegitimate child. In reaction to the rhyme "Ma! Ma! Where's my pa? Gone to the White House, Ha! Ha! Ha!" Cleveland responded only, "Tell the truth." The truth appeared to be that Cleveland had acted honorably in a relationship with Mrs. Maria Halprin, and his courage and honesty once again impressed itself upon his countrymen. Cleveland made only four speeches during the campaign, while Blaine traveled more widely. A turning point came in the closing days of the campaign, when the Reverend Mr. Samuel D. Burchard, who accompanied Blaine, charged that the Democrats were the party of "Rum,

Romanism, and Rebellion." This influenced a heavy turnout among the Irish Catholic voters of New York City, and by a narrow margin Cleveland became the first Democratic president since 1856.

Cleveland was admirably suited to the needs of the United States in 1885. He headed a government that endeavored to correct the abuses of the past and establish honesty and efficiency in the administration of government. Cleveland appointed an excellent cabinet, including the southern wing of the party once again. The major issues of his first administration were civil service reform, the role of silver currency, and a reduction of the tariff. He successfully expanded the Civil Service Act and moved toward a more professional government bureaucracy. In connection with the many patronage bills that flowed through Congress, Cleveland vetoed more than 300 measures in his first administration (compared to 132 vetoes by the previous twenty-one presidents). He opposed the free-silver faction in the party, supporting instead a sound money policy based on gold. He was forced to retreat on the tariff issue in the face of congressional opposition.

Cleveland's administration was also noteworthy for the passage of the Dawes Act, which encouraged the "Americanization" of Native Americans. Additionally, the Interstate Commerce Act was adopted under and signed by Cleveland. There was a greater awareness of labor unrest as well, provoked by the Haymarket Square Riot in Chicago in 1886, which left several persons dead and reawakened a fear of organized labor. For the public, however, the most memorable part of Cleveland's first administration was his marriage in 1886 to Miss Frances Folsom, the twenty-two-year-old daughter of his former law partner (Cleveland was the first president to be married in a White House ceremony). The public was delighted with the romance, and, indeed, the marriage was a remarkably happy one.

As the election of 1888 approached, the Republicans began to gather funds and support to regain control of the national government. To oppose Cleveland, they nominated Benjamin Harrison, who vigorously campaigned against Cleveland and especially against tariff reform. Cleveland once again won a majority of the popular vote, but this time he narrowly lost the electoral vote to Harrison. Cleveland took his family to New York City, where he resumed the practice of law and where his first child (known to the country as "Baby Ruth") was born.

As discontent with the extravagant policies of Harrison grew, the Democrats turned once again to Cleveland in 1892. Again opposed by the New York Tammany Hall machine, Cleveland nevertheless was nominated on the first ballot. With his usual courage, he endorsed the gold standard in the face of strong party support for free silver.

THE CHINESE QUESTION

Grover Cleveland became president three years after the U.S. Congress enacted the Chinese Exclusion Act of 1882, which severely restricted Chinese immigration the United States. In his first state of the union address, Cleveland touched on U.S. relations with China and ongoing discrimination and acts of violence against Chinese immigrants within the United States—which he blamed on other foreign immigrants.

The harmony of our relations with China is fully sustained.

In the application of the acts lately passed to execute the treaty of 1880, restrictive of the immigration of Chinese laborers into the United States, individual cases of hardship have occurred beyond the power of the Executive to remedy, and calling for judicial determination.

The condition of the Chinese question in the Western States and Territories is, despite this restrictive legislation, far from being satisfactory. The recent outbreak in Wyoming Territory, where numbers of unoffending Chinamen, indisputably within the protection of the treaties and the law, were murdered by a mob, and the still more recent threatened outbreak of the same character in Washington Territory, are fresh in the minds of all, and there is apprehension lest the bitterness of feeling against the Mongolian race on the Pacific Slope may find vent in similar lawless demonstrations. All the power of this Government should be exerted to maintain the amplest good faith toward China in the treatment of these men, and the inflexible sternness of the law in bringing the wrongdoers to justice should be insisted upon.

Every effort has been made by this Government to prevent these violent outbreaks and to aid the representatives of China in their investigation of these outrages; and it is but just to say that they are traceable to the lawlessness of men not citizens of the United States engaged in competition with Chinese laborers.

Race prejudice is the chief factor in originating these disturbances, and it exists in a large part of our domain, jeopardizing our domestic peace and the good relationship we strive to maintain with China. . . .

Source: Grover Cleveland, "State of the Union Address," December 8, 1885.

He was reelected president and returned to Washington (where his daughter Esther became the first child born in the White House) on the eve of the great Panic of 1893. Once again, the country needed a man of courage and honesty and was fortunate to have the leadership of Cleveland—who possessed these qualities in great abundance, along with a certain stubbornness and a lack of vision.

Before attending to the economic problems of the nation, Cleveland had to attend to a problem of his own—a malignant growth was discovered in the roof of his mouth. Fearing that public knowledge of his illness would fuel the panic, Cleveland chose to undergo a secret operation on board a borrowed yacht. The operation was successful, and not for twenty-five years did the full truth of that cruise emerge. Meanwhile, the debate over free silver was spurred on by the economic crisis. Cleveland continued to stand firm for a solid currency. He called a successful special session of Congress to repeal the Sherman Silver Purchase Act, which Cleveland believed contributed to the continuing economic decline. Unable to obtain adequate tariff reform, Cleveland continued nevertheless to protest the high tariff as also contributing to the panic.

In an effort to avert the constant drain of gold from the United States Treasury, Cleveland agreed to a sale of government bonds handled by J. P. Morgan. Although a financial success, this apparent "sell-out" to the interests of big business hurt Cleveland and his party, already badly divided over the question of free silver. Similarly, his action in sending federal troops to help put down the Pullman workers' strike (1894) and his hostility to the unemployed workers who marched to Washington, D.C., as Coxey's Army convinced the working-class supporters of the Democratic Party that Cleveland had abandoned them in favor of the rich.

In the area of foreign policy, Cleveland opposed imperialism, refusing to bring the treaty for Hawaiian annexation before the Senate. He maintained strict neutrality in the Cuban revolt, though encouraging Spain to moderate its treatment of the Cuban people. In the border dispute between British Guiana and Venezuela, Cleveland encouraged arbitration. He supported the Monroe Doctrine and appeared ready to risk war with Great Britain if a peaceful settlement was not reached. Once again, Cleveland acted strongly and courageously and won both the respect of and stronger ties with Great Britain as a result.

Silver continued to be the simplistic, single answer for those in and out of the Democratic Party who sought relief from the panic. As the election of 1896 approached, it was clear that Cleveland had lost much of his party's support. Once again, Cleveland stood with courage for his principles and against free silver; this time, courage without compromise proved fatal. Although he had no desire for a third term, the Democratic convention repudiated him thoroughly in its platform. With William Jennings Bryan as their candidate and free silver as their issue, the Democrats' repudiation was silently returned by Cleveland, who privately sympathized with the Republicans in the election. He was satisfied with the election of William McKinley, though it must have hurt to notice that Bryan, in losing, received almost a million votes more than Cleveland had received in his 1892 victory.

After the inauguration of McKinley, Cleveland and his family planned to retire to private life. Because of the children, Cleveland and his wife preferred an area less crowded than New York City and chose to settle in Princeton, New Jersey. There, Cleveland mellowed and enjoyed to the fullest his children and his community. He became deeply involved in the life of Princeton University, where he received an honorary degree and in 1901 was named a trustee. There, the eldest of his five children (his daughter Ruth) died in 1904, leaving a great void in her father's life. There also Cleveland knew, liked, and quarreled with the next Democrat to be elected president, Woodrow Wilson. There, also, Cleveland died, in June, 1908.

SIGNIFICANCE

Grover Cleveland was admirably suited to his time. His disciplined life made him more comfortable as a supporter of the status quo than as a reformer, and his courage and conscience made him strong in actions he believed best for the interests of the United States. It was Cleveland's misfortune sometimes to be wrong in his judgment of what was best; the rigid strength of character that held him firm before the winds of pressure from special interests held him equally firm against compromise when it would, perhaps, have been wise. Nevertheless, Cleveland brought conscience, courage, and honesty to the White House at a time when those qualities had often been lacking. He provided an image—backed up by reality—of the integrity and leadership that the United States needed. He worked long hours, bringing his legal intellect to the consideration of all sides of a problem before making a rational decision about the wisest course to follow. Once that decision was made, he did not depart from it.

Though Cleveland was wildly unpopular in 1896, especially among the Bryan faction of Democrats, it was always his position and never his character that came under attack. In later years, he emerged with much greater popularity, and Americans, Democrats and Republicans alike, honored him for his courage and his honesty. The nation had come to realize the value of his leadership and to believe that the economic stability that had eventually prevailed would not have been possible without his strong opposition to free silver. Cleveland was a good man in an age in which goodness was not often cherished. The verse of James Russell Lowell perhaps best memorializes his contribution to America:

> We, who look on with critic eyes
> Exempt from action's crucial test,
> Human ourselves, at least are wise
> In honoring one who did his best.

—*Carlanna L. Hendrick*

FURTHER READING

Cleveland, Grover. *Letters of Grover Cleveland: 1850-1908*. Edited by Allan Nevins. Boston: Houghton Mifflin, 1933. Reprint. New York: Da Capo Press, 1970. Useful for insight into Cleveland's mind and the reasons for his decisions. Includes some delightful letters of a more personal nature as well.

_____. *Presidential Problems*. New York: Century, 1904. Writings of the president after leaving office. Clear and comprehensive but not particularly insightful, which is generally true of the many books and articles Cleveland wrote in his retirement.

Ford, Henry Jones. *The Cleveland Era: A Chronicle of the New Order in Politics*. New Haven, Conn.: Yale University Press, 1919. One of a series of books on American history. Concise, without much interpretation.

Graff, Henry F. *Grover Cleveland*. New York: Times Books, 2002. A brief but substantial biography, one in a series of presidential biographies. Graff depicts Cleveland as a decisive president, a man of action and uncompromising integrity.

Hollingsworth, Joseph Rogers. *The Whirligig of Politics: The Democracy of Cleveland and Bryan*. Chicago: University of Chicago Press, 1963. Excellent coverage of political events from 1892 to 1904. A readable account, especially helpful on the antagonisms within the Democratic Party and the silver issue. Strong analysis of the election of 1896.

Jeffers, H. Paul. *An Honest President: The Life and Presidencies of Grover Cleveland*. New York: William Morrow, 2000. Jeffers portrays Cleveland as a staunch reformer, a man of high moral character and courage who restored dignity to the presidency.

Merrill, Horace Samuel. *Bourbon Leader*. Boston: Little, Brown, 1957. Excellent analysis, again largely political, of Cleveland and the Democratic Party both nationally and in New York.

Nevins, Allan: *Grover Cleveland: A Study in Courage*. New York: Dodd, Mead, 1966. Indispensable Pulitzer Prize-winning biography. The definitive study of Cleveland and his political career, covering all the details as well as offering a broad analysis of Cleveland's career. Wonderfully readable style.

Welch, Richard E., Jr. *The Presidencies of Grover Cleveland*. Lawrence: University Press of Kansas, 1988. Welch portrays Cleveland as a complex, strong-willed executive who helped strengthen the role of the presidency.

SEE ALSO: John Peter Altgeld; James G. Blaine; Benjamin Harrison; Liliuokalani; William McKinley.

RELATED ARTICLES in *Great Events from History: The Nineteenth Century, 1801-1900:* November 4, 1884: U.S. Election of 1884; October 28, 1886: Statue of Liberty Is Dedicated; December 8, 1886: American Federation of Labor Is Founded; October, 1889-April, 1890: First Pan-American Congress; January 24, 1895: Hawaii's Last Monarch Abdicates; November 3, 1896: McKinley Is Elected President.

DEWITT CLINTON
American politician

Clinton controlled New York State for his faction of the Republican Party, advocating both social stability and an active role for government. He was an unsuccessful presidential candidate and fought the emerging power of Martin Van Buren. His best-known project was the Erie Canal, concrete and practical, like his approach to politics, and exemplifying a proper resolution of several types of problems in a growing nation.

BORN: March 2, 1769; Little Britain, New York
DIED: February 11, 1828; Albany, New York
AREA OF ACHIEVEMENT: Government and politics

EARLY LIFE

DeWitt Clinton was descended from English grandparents who had been transplanted to Ireland before immigrating to North America in 1729. In 1831, they settled in New York, where Clinton's father, James, was born. James, married to Mary DeWitt, of Dutch ancestry, had been a major general in the revolution; his brigade had received the British colors at Yorktown. DeWitt was educated at the grammar school of the Reverend Mr. John Moffat and then studied for two years at the Kingston Academy, the best in the state. Two years later, in 1786, having emphasized courses in natural philosophy and mathematics, he was graduated from Columbia College at the head of his class. After studying law with Samuel Jones, Jr., he was admitted to the bar in 1790 but did not often practice; his legal training aided him in land transactions and in his growing involvement in politics.

Clinton's uncle, George Clinton, was the first governor of New York and the creator of a powerful political machine; thus, Clinton was accustomed to a political environment. In the *New York Journal* in November, 1787, Clinton published a series of letters from "A Countryman," opposing ratification of the proposed constitution; he attended sessions of the New York ratifying convention at Poughkeepsie and wrote a report from the Antifederalist position. He became his uncle's private secretary and shortly thereafter also secretary of the board of regents and of the board of fortification. While involved in politics early, he did not engage in politicking at the lower levels of party workers; this fact may explain his inability to deal with the mechanics and compromises of factional and party maneuvering.

Clinton was an impressive man, six feet tall and often referred to as "Magnus Apollo." His high forehead, large square face and firm features, and dark eyes gave the impression of strength and determination. He married Maria Franklin, daughter of an important Quaker merchant, who brought him four thousand pounds and landed property, on February 13, 1796. They had ten children, of whom four sons and three daughters were still living when Maria Clinton died in 1818. At the time of his marriage, Clinton was not active in politics, as the Republicans had succumbed to the greater political strength of the Hamiltonians (Federalists); Governor George Clinton retired in 1795, and the Federalists elected John Jay to the office. Clinton would undoubtedly have become a scientist of note had not opportunity and environment joined to bring him back into politics. Defeated for the state assembly in 1796, he was elected in 1797, and in 1798 won a four-year term in the state senate.

In 1801, the assembly elected Clinton as one of the four senators who, with the governor, constituted the council of appointment. This body controlled nearly fifteen thousand civil and military appointments and was therefore deeply entwined with the complex politics of both state and nation, still in flux during the early constitutional period, and with a two-party system not yet fully developed. The policy and partisan balances of state and national governments were also still unclear, and the tensions between executives and legislatures stemming from revolutionary politics were institutionalized in the new constitution and exacerbated when different parties controlled the two branches.

With its large number of presidential electors, the state of New York was vital, under the influence of Aaron Burr, in the "Revolution of 1800," which brought the Republicans to national power. State politics, however, were characterized by factions among the Republicans; Burr did not attempt to control the state, and the influential Livingston family, politically neglected by the Federalists, gave its support to the popular Clinton group. Clinton emerged as the state's Republican political leader.

The relative powers of the governor and council had not been completely clarified in the 1777 constitution, and consequently a bitter argument developed, ending in an appointment stalemate. Clinton at that time was young, energetic, and ambitious; his integrity and self-confidence and his ability to attract political loyalty were major advantages, balancing his ineffectiveness in handling people and in developing compromises. He was not a political theorist, always preferring the concrete and the practical, but his ideas were clear concerning the proper approach of the victorious Republicans to the offices of government.

Opposing the Federalists' exclusion of Republicans from office, Clinton maintained that Republicans must be appointed in order that appointive positions might correspond to the verdict of the elections. To accomplish this, it was necessary to remove Federalists from most if not all major offices and from a sufficient number of minor ones to equalize the parties. As a dominant council member, Clinton took the lead in removing most of the governor's power over appointments and in implementing the appointment of Republicans. Rather than being the origin of the "spoils system," as many historians have suggested, this policy was simply more active in accommodating the appointive positions rather closely to the elective ones under the new political conditions of a developing national two-party system (rather than the older one of personal and local factions within the state alone).

On February 19, 1802, Clinton was appointed to a vacant seat in the U.S. Senate. During the next two sessions, he opposed a Federalist proposal to seize New Orleans from Spain over the issue of the right of deposit and supported the proposed Twelfth Amendment. The Senate at this time tended to be overshadowed by the House, however, and Clinton's personal and party interests were in New York. Late in 1803, Clinton resigned from the Senate to accept appointment (from Governor George Clinton and the council) as mayor of New York City. This was an important office, and its fifteen-thousand-dollar annual income was also welcome to Clinton, whose finances were frequently in disorder.

DeWitt Clinton. (Library of Congress)

LIFE'S WORK

For the remainder of his career, Clinton acted in the state, rather than in the national, political arena. From 1803 to 1815 (except for 1807-1808 and 1810-1811), he was mayor of New York. At the beginning of his political career, in the assembly, he had been concerned with sanitation laws, debt reform, abolition, and the encouragement of steam navigation and agriculture. As mayor, he organized the Public School Society and aided the New York Orphan Asylum and the New York Hospital. In 1806, he supported the removal of political disabilities from Roman Catholics. As required of a mayor, he attended fires, helped to calm mobs, and inspected markets and docks. With a $100,000 defense appropriation, he supervised construction of fortifications on Governor's Island and elsewhere in the city. He took a firm stand against British impressment and blockade attempts off New York City. He supported a plan for city development and presided in the mayor's court. During his tenure as mayor, he served also as state senator (1806-1811) and lieutenant governor (1811-1813).

Dominating New York politics, Clinton assured the nomination of Morgan Lewis as governor in 1804. Thereafter, the Burr wing lost power in the party and Clinton broke with the Livingstonians, succeeding in having his choice, Daniel D. Tompkins, elected governor. Although basically a Republican, Clinton not only often attracted the support of Federalists but also was frequently in opposition to the Virginia Dynasty and to New York's Tammany Society. The Tammany "Martling-Men" or "Bucktails" viewed him as a political heretic and a cunning dealer in political offices and influence.

Federalist leaders in 1812 strongly favored Clinton as a presidential candidate, and the New York Republican legislature nominated him; his position on the War of 1812 was, however, equivocal. Had he received Pennsylvania's twenty-five electoral votes, Clinton, rather than James Madison, would have been president. (Soon after the election, on December 22, 1812, Clinton's father died.) Following his defeat, Clinton turned his energies to the development of "Clintonianism," a political position rather than a party, opposed to party labels and organization, seeking a wide base of support in the state. Clintonian Republicans saw an intellectual and benevolent elite, opposing "Jacobinical" chance, factions, mobs, urban vice, and crime; yet they considered governmental power as derived from the people as a whole and to be used to meet their needs.

An urban politician, hoping to make New York a cultural center to rival Boston and Philadelphia, Clinton was sufficiently Jeffersonian to develop a strong rural bias in his programs; the canal project was designed to stimulate both commercial prosperity and a westward movement, thereby reducing poverty and violence and averting the development of an urban proletariat and demagoguery. Clinton was ambivalent about both urban centers and government itself; appealing to both Federalists and Republicans, operating outside the increasingly delimited national party boundaries, Clinton emphasized the work of private societies to accomplish the necessary expansion of knowledge and the provision of facilities for "the people" in general.

Clinton's involvement in voluntary societies was by no means merely a personal and private activity but was closely associated with his political life. He belonged to several dozen societies, was active in most, and held offices in many. He was a member of several agricultural societies, the New York Bible Society, the American Bible Society, foreign and domestic scientific societies (natural history, geology, biology), the American Antiquarian Society, the Western Museum Society, the American Academy of Arts and Sciences, the American Philosophical Society, the New York Military Society, the New York Historical Society, and the Education Society of the Presbyterian Church.

Clinton was also a prominent Mason; in 1814, he was cofounder and president of the Literary and Philosophical Society, presenting a book-length paper on American natural history; in 1816, he was able to get one large building to gather all the cultural societies in New York under one roof. His defeat in 1812 reduced his political power; he lost renomination for lieutenant governor and in 1815 lost the mayoralty as well. However, he was rebuilding his support: His brother-in-law, Ambrose Spencer, was influential in President James Monroe's administration, he continued to attract Federalist as well as Republican voters, and the canal project was very popular.

As early as 1810, Clinton had been one of the commissioners planning a state canal between the Hudson River and the Great Lakes. The War of 1812 delayed the project, but by 1816 Clinton was actively promoting it; he was on the commission responsible for planning the canals between the Hudson, Lake Erie, and Lake Champlain. When Governor Tompkins resigned in 1817 to become vice president, Clinton was nominated (by a state convention including both Federalists and Republicans) and won by a landslide over Tammany's Peter B. Porter. Thereafter, however, President Monroe directed the majority of the federal patronage in New York not to the Clintonians but to their minority opposition, Martin Van Buren's Tammany Bucktail faction.

Monroe's encouragement of intraparty strife was intended to avert a successful bid by Clinton during the 1820 presidential election; Monroe also believed that Clinton's associates in Congress were intensifying the Missouri crisis in order to reorganize national parties along sectional lines, a development that he considered a threat to the nation. Although Clinton won the gubernatorial election in 1820, the New York Republican Party schism was permanent: The Bucktails controlled the legislature and therefore the state patronage as well (through the council of appointment). At this point, Clinton attacked Monroe for having interfered in the state election process, a states' rights stand that could evoke support from both parties. In order to affect the 1821 state constitutional convention, Clinton had to prove his charges, which he did by submitting bulky documents, in a green cover, to the assembly. His "Green Bag Message" set off a debate over the permissible extent of political activity on the part of federal officials.

The administration's hostility having prevented him from consolidating his political position, Clinton decided not to seek a third gubernatorial term in 1822. Van Buren was therefore able to develop his control and establish the "Albany Regency," which controlled New York State politics for a long time thereafter. (Tammany Hall was to benefit also from the flood of Irish voters resulting from the constitutional amendment Clinton had supported, eliminating the property requirement for voting.) The regency's removal of Clinton from the canal commission in 1824 provoked a reaction which helped the "People's" party elect him governor in November of that year. It was therefore as the state's executive that he participated in the 1825 celebrations opening both the Erie and Champlain canals.

Clinton declined the post of minister to England offered to him by President John Quincy Adams. In 1827, an Ohio convention nominated him as a presidential candidate, but he would have had little chance: He had a states' rights stand, there was a strong Anti-Masonic movement, and the issues of patronage and party organization continued to alienate support from the Clintonian group. On February 11, 1828, Clinton died suddenly. He was survived by his second wife, Catharine Jones, daughter of a New York physician, whom he had married on May 8, 1819; the New York legislature voted to appropriate ten thousand dollars for his minor children, as Clinton had left debts. His chief association in the public mind was with one of his most cherished projects, the great Erie Canal.

SIGNIFICANCE

At the outset of his political career, DeWitt Clinton was associated with the great national political figures of the time, the young postrevolutionary leaders who were to dominate national politics until the Civil War. He was always to be involved in the complex and bitter partisanship of the early nineteenth century, pitting state, sectional, and national interests against one another, swirling in a confusion of intrastate and intraparty factions. In contrast to his political contemporaries such as James Monroe, John C. Calhoun, John Quincy Adams, Henry Clay, Martin Van Buren, and Andrew Jackson, Clinton's primary political service was to be in his state rather than at the national level. However, as a dominant politician in New York State, Clinton was necessarily a factor in national politics, and he shared the presidential aspirations of his colleagues: The electoral votes of only one state kept him from the presidency in 1812, and he remained a real political threat to the Virginia Dynasty.

As a politician, Clinton was a figure of ambiguities and contradictions. His preferences and policies placed him from time to time in all the varying political denominations; an elitist with a power base in one state only, he could never have developed a party organization around his own national leadership. He was never able in the mechanics of politics, and his personality, reserved and cold, did not attract supporters. Despite these shortcomings, he was usually admired and respected for his governmental abilities and positive programs. He supported states' rights yet viewed government as the necessary agency for developing programs to ensure general prosperity, balance and order in society, and economic expansion and opportunities.

Clinton's version of an earlier "country ideology" led him to numerous local agricultural societies, to the Society for the Promotion of Agriculture, Arts, and Manufactures, and to the canal project. At the same time, he was concerned with urban problems, advocating, for example, the inexpensive Lancasterian educational system and supporting the establishment of Emma Willard's academy at Troy; from 1805 until his death, he was president of the New York Free School Society. His concept of the role of government frequently gained for him Federalist support, yet he had begun in politics as a Republican. Conflicts with the Virginia Dynasty and Tammany Hall meant that he could never control the Democratic Republican Party, despite his support of Jackson, yet to play a prominent part among the National Republicans, he would have had to cooperate with John Quincy Adams, whom he disliked. A patrician elite providing leadership for the independent yeomanry was an idea belonging more to the eighteenth century than to the nineteenth, but Clinton was somewhat ahead of his time in his concept of government as a meliorative agency in society.

Closely connected to Clinton's emphasis on learned and benevolent societies was his own work in the sciences. In the undifferentiated field of early nineteenth century science, professionals and amateurs studied and worked over a wide range. Contemporaries (including the eminent scientists David Hosack, Samuel Latham Mitchill, and Constantine S. Rafinesque) considered Clinton a great naturalist, and he was responsible for the discovery of a type of American indigenous wheat and of the archaeological remains of prehistoric Indian tribes in New York. No theorist, he nevertheless agreed with the intellectual radicals of the day in accepting the concept of biological extinction as opposed to the consensus view of a static "chain of being." He played a major role as a patron and promoter of science, primarily through the voluntary societies and whatever governmental aid he could provide, as in the establishment of the New York Institution for the Promotion of the Arts and Sciences.

Not a Renaissance man, not a scientific theorist, not the founder of a new political alliance, long a state governor but never president, Clinton enjoyed a fruitful career of public service. Less of a national figure in historical perspective than his fellow senators were to be, he has been less well known than they, to later times. The Erie Canal, one of his favorite projects, has enjoyed greater publicity than the man who helped to develop it in the context of wide programs for public improvement. Although Clinton may have taken a narrower view of public policies than his contemporaries, he nevertheless worked to acquire political support for his programs from a wide range of intrastate interests and areas, a political condition that, if operating at the national level, might have helped avert the increasing political polarization obvious even before the Missouri crisis. Although he died at a relatively young age, he had probably already accomplished nearly all that would have been possible for him in the social and political conditions of his time.

—*Marsha Kass Marks*

FURTHER READING

Bobbé, Dorothie De Bear. *De Witt Clinton*. New York: Minton, Balch, 1933. Reprint. Port Washington, N.Y.: I. J. Friedman, 1962. Written during the early 1930's, this was the only full-length biography since James Renwick published his book during the early 1840's. A rather uncritical admiration.

Cornog, Evan. *The Birth of Empire: De Witt Clinton and the American Experience, 1769-1828*. New York: Oxford University Press, 1998. Comprehensive and well-reviewed biography, emphasizing Clinton's political accomplishments and how they impacted New York City and state.

Hanyan, Craig R. "De Witt Clinton and Partisanship: The Development of Clintonianism from 1811 to 1820." *New-York Historical Society Quarterly* 56, no. 2 (1972): 108-131. Clear analysis of the political developments and programs, and intraparty factionalism in the state. Based chiefly on primary sources.

Hanyan, Craig R., with Mary L. Hanyan. *De Witt Clinton and the Rise of the People's Men*. Buffalo, N.Y.: McGill-Queen's University Press, 1996. A detailed history of the "People's" party in early nineteenth century New York, describing the party's ideas and relationship to the emerging political culture.

Harris, Jonathan. "De Witt Clinton as Naturalist." *New-York Historical Society Quarterly* 56, no. 4 (1972): 264-284. Examines Clinton as a scientist and concludes that his contributions were more as a promoter of science. Includes 1825 portrait of Clinton by George Catlin.

Hopkins, Vivian C. "The Empire State—DeWitt Clinton's Laboratory." *New-York Historical Society Quarterly* 59, no. 1 (1975): 6-44. Has a higher opinion of Clinton as a scientist than the opinion expressed in Harris's article (see above).

McBain, Howard Lee. *De Witt Clinton and the Origin of the Spoils System in New York*. New York: Columbia University Press, 1907. Reprint. New York: AMS Press, 1967. Insightful study of developing party politics during the early national period and Clinton's role in that development.

Nadler, Solomon. "The Green Bag: James Monroe and the Fall of DeWitt Clinton." *New-York Historical Society Quarterly* 59, no. 3 (1975): 202-255. Good examination of national and state politics and issues of the 1810's and 1820's, and Clinton's position on these issues.

Siry, Steven E. *De Witt Clinton and the American Political Economy: Sectionalism, Politics, and Republican Ideology, 1787-1828*. New York: P. Lang, 1990. Examines Clinton's career, describing the "practical republicanism" that characterized his political philosophy.

SEE ALSO: John Quincy Adams; Andrew Jackson; James Monroe; Martin Van Buren; Emma Willard.

RELATED ARTICLES in *Great Events from History: The Nineteenth Century, 1801-1900:* 1820's-1830's: Free Public School Movement; October 26, 1825: Erie Canal Opens.

WILLIAM COBBETT

English journalist and social reformer

Known in his time as "the Poor Man's Friend," Cobbett was the leading radical journalist of his day and was among the most prolific writers in English history. Through more than three decades, his Political Register *led the popular attack on privilege and corruption in English government.*

BORN: March 9, 1763; Farnham, Surrey, England
DIED: June 18, 1835; Normandy Farm, near Guildford, Surrey, England
ALSO KNOWN AS: Peter Porcupine (pseudonym)
AREA OF ACHIEVEMENT: Journalism

EARLY LIFE

William Cobbett was born into the "Old England" of the picture books. His father, George Cobbett, was a farmer and publican in the quiet Surrey village of Farnham, forty miles southwest of London. His mother figures little in Cobbett's fragmentary memoirs. Apart from his father's tutelage, Cobbett had no formal education. His childhood was given completely to traditional rural pursuits: riding, hunting, visiting fairs, or working in the fields, gathering in crops that in his later recollection were always rich and bountiful. Over the whole scene of his remembered youth there hangs a golden glow that determined the peculiarly retrospective nature of his radicalism. Whatever else he became, Cobbett was first to last a farmer. To preserve the rural virtues in the new industrial age was his sustaining political purpose.

Despite all Cobbett's love of it, the English countryside could not long contain him. At the age of fourteen, he went on a whim to London, where he happened on a copy of Jonathan Swift's *A Tale of a Tub* (1704). Swift produced in him "a sort of birth of the intellect." He learned from *A Tale of a Tub* the power of prose satire and political common sense. After a few more restless years on the farm, Cobbett returned to London as a legal clerk in Gray's Inn. He "sighed for a sight of the world," however, and in 1784 enlisted in the army. His public career began five years later, when, upon return from his posting in Nova Scotia, he published his first pamphlet, *The Soldier's Friend* (1792), exposing the corruption of the officer class and expressing the grievances of the common infantryman.

After his marriage to Ann Reid in 1792 and a brief sojourn in revolutionary France, Cobbett went to America. From his father, he had "imbibed principles of republicanism" and was thus "ambitious to become a citizen of a free state." However, the United States brought out the English patriot in Cobbett. In a series of polemical pamphlets, he denounced Jeffersonian Democrats (he was only slightly more approving of the Anglophilic Federalists), French revolutionaries, Thomas Paine ("mad Tom"), Jean-Jacques Rousseau, and anyone else who indulged "this eternal cant about *virtue* and *liberty*."

Cobbett spent eight years in the United States, first in Wilmington, then in New York, teaching English, becoming a self-taught authority on English grammar, and acquiring a reputation on both sides of the Atlantic as a determined defender of the English government. Indeed, upon his return to London in 1800, Cobbett was offered control of one of the two government newspapers, but he declined it, preferring, he said, to remain independent. On January 16, 1802, he brought out the first issue of the *Political Register*, destined to make him, as Hazlitt later remarked, "a fourth estate in the politics of the country."

LIFE'S WORK

Initially in the *Political Register*, Cobbett simply carried on his patriotic diatribe against democratic reformers at home and abroad. With a subscription list headed by the Prince of Wales, he published in twelve volumes his American writings, dedicating the lot to the founder of a "Loyal Association against Republicans and Levellers." Slowly, however, he began to realize that the England he defended was not the England he had long imagined, was not the England of his idyllic youth. Living in London, he became aware of the extent of corruption in high places, of the essential injustice of England's system of taxation, of the whole body of pensioners and placemen that lived, so it soon seemed to him, at the crippling expense of the honest provincial laborer.

In 1803, Cobbett reread Paine, whose diagnosis of the English financial system he now found astute. When nothing came of his several proposals for fiscal and military reform, when in fact he found himself under the suspicious scrutiny of the very Tory government he had so long professed to support, Cobbett committed himself to the necessity of parliamentary reform. He undertook to publish verbatim transcripts of parliamentary debates (since 1812 known as *Hansards Parliamentary Debates*) in order to strengthen the principle of public accountability. He wrote a popular *Parliamentary History of En-*

William Cobbett. (Library of Congress)

gland (1804-1812), in which he traced the decline of democratic institutions since 1066. By 1806, this erstwhile anti-Jacobin had embraced the French and American revolutions and was intervening in constituency by-elections on behalf of "we, the people."

Physically, Cobbett was well suited to the life of public agitation that he now undertook. At six feet, one inch, he dwarfed most of his contemporaries. His voice was strong and deliberate, his countenance hale and portly. In dress, complexion, and manner, he was the perfect representation of what he always wished to be—an English gentleman farmer. He was supremely confident, even in the face of repeated disappointment, of his own ability to alter the course of his nation's history. Indeed, he was justified in his belief: By 1818, circulation of the *Political Register* had risen to more than fifty thousand copies a week. Avoiding theoretical abstraction, relying instead on perfected rhythms of everyday English and the powerfully distilled prejudices of ordinary people, Cobbett achieved a unique relationship with his readers. He became the voice of his own audience and thus represented a potentially explosive force in domestic politics.

Cobbett's first run-in with the government came in 1810, when he was convicted of sedition for having satirically exposed the practice of military flogging. For the next two years, he edited the *Political Register* from a comfortable cell in Newgate Prison, where he also wrote his well-known monetarist treatise, *Paper Against Gold* (1815); he was not alone in finding the innovation of paper currency responsible for much of England's economic distress.

Upon his release in 1812, Cobbett affirmed his radicalism by repudiating the war against France, which had been fought, he now thought, in the interests not of the people but of autocracy and corruption. At the same time, he began to interest himself in the plight of industrial workers. He blamed the cotton masters—seigneurs of the twist, he called them—for the social crises attendant upon industrialization, and he recommended working-class enfranchisement as the only remedy for the recent outbreak of industrial violence: the Luddite Riots. Indeed, in spite of all of his agrarian predilections, in the years after the war Cobbett became the leading public spokesman for the rights of industrial labor.

Cobbett advocated controlled agitation rather than sporadic violence, but the authorities could not appreciate the distinction. When in 1817 the government suspended habeas corpus as part of its ongoing suppression of popular discontent, Cobbett fled to the United States. There, he lost much of his direct influence over political events in England. He returned in 1819, having written three more books and bringing with him the now sanctified bones of Thomas Paine, to find a radical movement that had gone on without him and did not seem to need him. He regained prominence in 1820 as a champion of Queen Caroline, whose husband, the degenerate George IV, was attempting to renounce her.

Cobbett twice stood unsuccessfully for Parliament, first at Coventry and then at Preston, and wrote a series of highly personal radical advice books: *The Farmer's Friend* (1822), *The Poor Man's Friend* (1826), and *Advice to Young Men* (1829). In all these, and in the pages of the *Political Register* (which he had continued to produce even from the United States), Cobbett propounded upon his now familiar themes: agricultural distress, industrial exploitation, governmental corruption, and aristocratic profligacy. In 1830, in the midst of the rural "Swing Riots," he was again tried for sedition, but this time he acquitted himself to the government's grave discomfiture. After the reform of Parliament in 1832, he was finally returned, at the age of sixty-nine, for the industrial borough of Oldham. He spent three years in the Commons championing the cause of factory reform and resisting the introduction of the infamous Poor Law Amendment Act of 1834. He died on June 18, 1835, at home on his farm near Guildford.

SIGNIFICANCE

Much has been made of William Cobbett's "conversion" from Toryism to radicalism. Indeed, historians frequently resort to the awkward formula "Tory Radical" to describe the oddly nostalgic progressivism that Cobbett represented. However, if one thinks of him essentially as a populist, the conversion looms less large and the emotive consistency of his politics begins to emerge. In his youth, Cobbett defended an England of self-subsisting yeoman farmers that in fact existed only in his imagination. Once aware of that, he turned not so much radical as angry, in a desperate effort to restore what he perceived as lost democratic liberties. His enemies were the oligarchs, plutocrats, speculators, and sinecurists whose privileged grasp was strangling the decent, hardworking men and women of England. He was no political theorist, no socialist, no revolutionary. He was simply a journalist, inspired to political activism by a populist faith in the rightness of common people.

Cobbett's political influence passed quickly. Industrialization proceeded apace in England, independent farming went into precipitous decline, and universal manhood suffrage was, at his death, still the better part of a century away. Nevertheless, Cobbett's style lingered. Simplicity, truthfulness, and directness in writing was the creed he passed on to well-known masters of the political essay such as George Orwell. *Rural Rides* (1830), Cobbett's volume of ruminations on the state of the English countryside, and country, during the 1820's, is an acknowledged, though neglected, classic of English prose. Through the *Political Register*, Cobbett established the tradition in England of independent journalism. As an editorial critic of established elites, he has never been matched.

—*Stewart A. Weaver*

ADVICE TO YOUNG MEN

This extract from William Cobbett's Advice to Young Men *is typical of his popular advice books in stressing the importance of abstemious behavior.*

"Show me a man's *companions*" says the proverb, "and I will tell you *what the man* is;" and this is, and must be true; because all men seek the society of those who think and act somewhat like themselves: sober men will not associate with drunkards, frugal men will not like spendthrifts, and the orderly and decent shun the noisy, the disorderly, and the debauched. It is for the very vulgar to herd together as singers, ringers, and smokers; but, there is a class rather higher still more blamable; I mean the tavern-haunters, the gay companions, who herd together to do little but *talk*, and who are so fond of talk that they go from home to get at it. The conversation amongst such persons has nothing of instruction in it, and is generally of a vicious tendency. Young people naturally and commendably seek the society of those of their own age; but, be careful in choosing your companions; and lay this down as a rule never to be departed from, that no youth, nor man, ought to be called your *friend*, who is addicted to *indecent talk*, or who is fond of the *society of prostitutes*. Either of these argues a depraved taste, and even a depraved heart; an absence of all principle and of all trust-worthiness; and, I have remarked it all my life long, that young men, addicted to these vices, never succeed in the end, whatever advantages they may have, whether in fortune or in talent. Fond mothers and fathers are but too apt to be over-lenient to such offenders; and, as long as youth lasts and fortune smiles, the punishment is deferred; but, it comes at last; it is sure to come; and the gay and dissolute youth is a dejected and miserable man. After the early part of a life spent in illicit indulgences, a man is *unworthy* of being the husband of a virtuous woman; and, if he have anything like justice in him, how is he to reprove, in his children, vices in which he himself so long indulged? These vices of youth are varnished over by the saying, that there must be time for "sowing the *wild oats*," and that "*wildest colts* make the *best horses*." These figurative oats are, however, generally like the literal ones; they are *never to be eradicated from the soil*; and as to the *colts*, wildness in them is an indication of *high animal spirit*, having nothing at all to do with the *mind*, which is invariably debilitated and debased by profligate indulgences. Yet this miserable piece of sophistry, the offspring of parental weakness, is in constant use, to the incalculable injury of the rising generation. What so amiable as a steady, trustworthy boy? He is of *real use* at an early age: he can be trusted far out of the sight of parent or employer, while the "pickle," as the poor fond parents call the profligate, is a great deal worse than useless, because there must be some one to see that he does no harm. If you have to choose, choose companions of *your own rank in life* as nearly as may be; but, at any rate, none to whom you acknowledge *inferiority*; for, slavery is too soon learned; and, if the mind be bowed down in the youth, it will seldom rise up in the man. . . .

Source: William Cobbett, *Advice to Young Men* (London, 1829), section 36.

FURTHER READING

Burton, Anthony. *William Cobbett, Englishman: A Biography*. London: Aurum Press, 1997. Biography by a prolific author and BBC broadcaster.

Chesterton, G. K. *William Cobbett*. London: Hodder & Staughton, 1926. This book may be more revealing of Chesterton than Cobbett, but it is a pungent and brilliantly written testament to Cobbett's hold over the English political imagination during the early twentieth century.

Cobbett, William. *The Opinions of William Cobbett*. Edited by G. D. H. Cole and Margaret Cole. London: Cobbett, 1944. A useful and representative sample of Cobbett's writing, much of which is out of print.

Cole, G. D. H. *The Life of William Cobbett*. London: William Collins Sons, 1924. The once-definitive biography by a figure significant to British labor history in his own right. Still invaluable for a sense of what Cobbett meant to English socialists a century after his death.

Green, Daniel. *Great Cobbett: The Noblest Agitator*. London: Hodder & Staughton, 1983. A highly approving biography by a latter-day Cobbettite. Concentrates deliberately, and approvingly, on Cobbett's "Tory" phase, but prefers to stress the "populist" theme.

Sambrook, James. *William Cobbett*. Boston: Routledge & Kegan Paul, 1973. Part of the publisher's Authors Guides series, the book combines an alternative critical reading of Cobbett with rare literary appreciation.

Schweizer, Karl W., and John W. Osborne. *Cobbett in His Times*. Leicester, England: Leicester University Press, 1990. Examines Cobbett's writing and its influence on public opinion and the government, describing how he became the dominant voice of romantic reactionary Toryism.

Spater, George. *William Cobbett: The Poor Man's Friend*. 2 vols. Cambridge, England: Cambridge University Press, 1982. Authoritative, comprehensive biography. Great detail and able handling.

Thompson, E. P. *The Making of the English Working Class*. London: Gollancz, 1963. Only passingly about Cobbett, Thompson's work offers a broad sense of the popular movement in which he was involved. Contains an invaluable discussion of Cobbett's relationship to the emergent working-class consciousness in England.

Williams, Raymond. *Cobbett*. Oxford, England: Oxford University Press, 1983. A brief but dense volume in the Oxford Past Masters series by a highly learned literary and cultural critic. Passes quickly over Cobbett's life to a deft discussion of themes and issues.

SEE ALSO: Fourteenth Earl of Derby; George IV; James Mill.

RELATED ARTICLES in *Great Events from History: The Nineteenth Century, 1801-1900:* January, 1802: Cobbett Founds the *Political Register*; December 11-30, 1819: British Parliament Passes the Six Acts; February 23, 1820: London's Cato Street Conspirators Plot Assassinations; October 5, 1823: Wakley Introduces *The Lancet*; June 4, 1832: British Parliament Passes the Reform Act of 1832.

RICHARD COBDEN

English politician

Cobden was the undoubted champion of free trade in Victorian Britain and a well-known figure in the Manchester school of economic thought. With the Anti-Corn Law League, Cobden led the fight for repeal of the corn and provision laws in 1846. He also negotiated the Cobden-Chevalier Treaty with France in 1860.

BORN: June 3, 1804; Heyshott, near Midhurst, Sussex, England

DIED: April 2, 1865; London, England

AREA OF ACHIEVEMENT: Government and politics

EARLY LIFE

Born in a tiny hamlet in western Sussex, Richard Cobden was the fourth of eleven children of William Cobden and his wife, Millicent Amber. Cobden's father was descended from a long line of Sussex yeoman farmers, but he was forced to sell his land in the agricultural crisis at the conclusion of the Napoleonic Wars. This experience was undoubtedly traumatic for the young Richard Cobden, for he was unable to speak about it as an adult. Relatives took charge of the Cobden children, and Millicent Cobden's brother-in-law, a London merchant, sent the ten-year-old boy to an appallingly harsh school in Yorkshire that he was forced to endure for five years. In 1819, young Cobden became a clerk in his uncle's warehouse. He had an abiding desire to understand the affairs of the world and hoped that by self-education he could improve his situation. To the dismay of his guardians he taught himself French and devoted his spare time to "book learning."

The youthful Cobden was quite a romantic figure in appearance. His alert face was clean-shaven and dominated by his dark hair and eyes; it revealed the sincerity and curiosity that were the hallmarks of his character. Cobden was imbued with what he himself characterized as a "Bonapartian" feeling that any obstacle could be overcome if confronted with sufficient energy. His confidence was considerable. Contemporaries found Cobden to be intelligent, engaging, and above all practical. He showed interest in theoretical principles, such as the phrenological conceptions of George Combe or the political economy of Adam Smith, but his practical sense grounded him in the actualities of the present. Cobden preferred to deal with specific issues rather than with abstractions; perhaps that is why he was a superb organizer.

Beginning in 1825, Cobden worked as a commercial traveler for his uncle, taking orders on his route for muslins and calicoes and collecting accounts. He learned the workings of the calico trade, and with two friends Cobden determined to set up his own business in 1828. The three raised one thousand pounds, most of it borrowed, and made arrangements with a Manchester calico printer, Fort Brothers and Company, for selling goods on commission. By 1831, the partners were successful enough to lease their own factory at Sabden and expand their trade. Within a year, Cobden was a wealthy man and took up residence in Manchester, where he was soon a prominent citizen and active in the borough incorporation movement.

Financially secure for the moment, Cobden traveled extensively. He went to France and Switzerland. He visited the United States in 1835 and on a lengthy Mediterranean tour visited Greece, Egypt, and Turkey the following year. His visit to Germany in 1838 convinced him of the potential political and economic value of the recently organized customs union of German states, the Zollverein.

LIFE'S WORK

Travel played a considerable role in shaping Cobden's views. He entered public life with the publication of *England, Ireland, and America* (1835) under the pseudonym "A Manchester Manufacturer." The pamphlet advocated free trade, nonintervention in foreign affairs, and substantial domestic reforms, and recognized the potential of the United States as a formidable competitor. The following year, Cobden published *Russia and the Eastern Question* (1836), in which he urged Great Britain to abandon balance of power and foreign intervention as principles of its foreign policy and to recognize the primacy of commercial interests. Such views came to be called "Cobdenism" in foreign policy.

Cobden became involved in the Manchester Anti-Corn Law Association in late 1838 and was instrumental in transforming it into the National Anti-Corn Law League. The League agitated virtually without interruption for the next seven years for the total and immediate repeal of those laws that restricted, by high import duties, the importation of foreign cereal grains (corn) to Great Britain. With John Bright and others, Cobden organized local anti-Corn Law associations, stumped the country for free trade, lobbied Parliament, and helped the League organize its electoral activities. The League sent out lecturers, collected signatures on petitions, held mass meetings, and published its own newspapers, tracts, pamphlets, and books. Cobden was at the center of all this activity.

At first the League concentrated upon what Cobden called "enlightenment of the public mind" on the issue of free trade and upon petitioning, but after 1842 the League increasingly focused upon enrollment of new members, fund-raising by means of subscriptions, and registration of electors to take the campaign for repeal to the hustings. League agitations created the political climate that made repeal of the Corn Laws irresistible to Sir Robert Peel in early 1846, as the effects of the potato famine in Ireland made immediate relief imperative. The prime minister himself acknowledged in the House of Commons that no one had done more to achieve repeal of the Corn Laws than had Richard Cobden.

At Stockport in 1837, Cobden stood for election to Parliament on a broad radical platform that included free trade, suffrage extension, and the secret ballot. He narrowly lost that poll, but with League help he was successfully returned for that constituency in 1841. In Parliament Cobden was noted for his earnestness and command of factual detail, but it was at public meetings of the League that he was most effective. He was a very persuasive public speaker, invariably choosing apt illustrations and presenting his arguments in a fashion which carried the listener to the understanding that he intended. He was always certain of his facts and ready to meet any objection.

Between 1838 and 1846, Cobden devoted nearly all of his attention to League activity, though he married a Welsh schoolmate of his sister, Catherine Anne Williams, in May of 1840. His business, left in the less than capable hands of his brother Frederick, failed, and Cobden's League friends had to raise a subscription of eighty thousand pounds to relieve his embarrassment and provide him an income. His investments in the Illinois Central Railway showed little return, and a second subscription of forty thousand pounds was raised in 1860.

In 1847, Cobden was returned again for Stockport and by the numerous electors of the West Riding of Yorkshire. Cobden chose to sit for the county and represented that constituency in Parliament for a decade. While he was a member of Parliament for the West Riding, Cobden worked for international arbitration, financial reform, and arms reductions. He attended several Peace Congresses and carried on a lively correspondence with all manner of reformers and Radicals. He opposed the Ecclesiastical Titles Bill in 1851 and supported removal of Jewish disabilities.

Cobden was a consistent supporter of education; he believed that suffrage extension and national education must go hand in hand. Though an Anglican, he had supported the Maynooth Grant to supply public funds to a Roman Catholic seminary in Ireland in 1845 on the grounds that it would educate the teachers of millions of Irishmen. This was the only occasion on which Cobden and his friend and ally, John Bright, differed in the House of Commons in nearly a quarter of a century of public life.

Cobden resented what he perceived as aristocratic control of diplomacy and the military and believed that only landlords benefited from armed conflict and the preparations for it. In a series of pamphlets, *1793 and 1853, in Three Letters* (1853), *How Wars Are Got Up in India* (1854), and *What Next? and Next?* (1856), Cobden warned of the dangers of what he termed "Palmerstonism" in foreign policy. He opposed the conduct of the Crimean War and was among several proponents of "Cobdenism" to be defeated in the general elections of 1857. This defeat, combined with the recent loss of his son to scarlet fever, Mrs. Cobden's melancholia, and the temporary disability and exhaustion of his friend Bright caused him to retire from public life for a time. Cobden traveled to the United States once again, where he was astonished at the progress that had been made in two decades.

Cobden returned to Parliament in 1859 as a member of Parliament for Rochdale. He twice declined offers to join the cabinet, but in 1860 on a volunteer mission he successfully negotiated significant reciprocal tariff reductions with France for the Palmerston government. The Cobden-Chevalier Treaty stimulated trade and industry in both nations and improved the strained relations between them as well. For this effort Cobden was offered a baronetcy, but he declined the offer.

Cobden continued to differ with Viscount Palmerston over defense issues during the 1860's. As an opponent of slavery he expressed support for the federal government in the American Civil War. He differed with Palmerston on the issue of whether Great Britain should oppose Prussia and Austria in the Danish War, and on this occasion nonintervention carried the day.

Cobden fell ill in the autumn of 1864 and died in London from the complications of bronchitis on April 2, 1865. He was buried in the churchyard at Lavington in Sussex. Within a year of Cobden's death, some of his old Anti-Corn Law League friends founded the Cobden Club as a memorial to the "Apostle of Free Trade" and as a way to advance his principles. The club took Free Trade—Peace—Goodwill Among Nations as its motto and promoted Cobden's internationalism and economic principles into the next century.

SIGNIFICANCE

Richard Cobden was a middle-class manufacturer and a member of Parliament who advocated free trade, nonintervention in foreign affairs, and a variety of Radical political reforms, including suffrage extension and the secret ballot. He saw repeal of the Corn Laws as the keystone in the arch of "aristocratic misrule" and was the best-known lecturer and organizer of the Anti-Corn Law League. He opposed monopoly in all of its forms, economic and political, and advocated the laissez-faire doctrines associated with the Manchester school of economic thought and nineteenth century Liberalism. A free-trade Radical, Cobden believed that adoption of a new commercial policy would bring unprecedented economic growth and political progress.

—*Richard Francis Spall, Jr.*

FURTHER READING

Cobden, Richard. *The Political Writings of Richard Cobden*. 2 vols. London: William Ridgway, 1867. A complete collection of Cobden's pamphlets.

_____. *Speeches of Richard Cobden, Esq., M.P., Delivered During 1849*. London: James Gilbert, 1849. A series of speeches revised by Cobden himself for publication on the subjects of peace, retrenchment, colonial reform, and other subjects.

_____. *Speeches on Questions of Public Policy by Richard Cobden, M.P.* Edited by John Bright and J. E. T. Rogers. 2 vols. London: T. Fisher Unwin, 1870. A fine collection of Cobden's speeches in Parliament, on the hustings, for the League, and at public meetings. Topically organized.

Dawson, William Harbutt. *Richard Cobden and Foreign Policy*. New York: Frank-Maurice, 1927. An examination of Cobden's views on nonintervention, international peace and arbitration, and arms expenditure, with particular reference to the international problems of the 1920's. Makes considerable use of excerpts from Cobden's speeches and correspondence.

Edsall, Nicholas. *Richard Cobden: Independent Radical*. Cambridge, Mass.: Harvard University Press, 1986. Credits Cobden with a major role in defining radical Liberalism and reasserts the significance of his thought. Especially good for the post-repeal period.

Gowring, Richard. *Richard Cobden*. London: Cassell, 1890. A very brief popular biography in the World's Workers series. Concentrates on the period to 1846 and views Cobden's life as a watershed in modern history.

Hinde, Wendy. *Richard Cobden: A Victorian Outsider*. New Haven, Conn.: Yale University Press, 1987. A sympathetic biography that portrays Cobden the man as well as the public figure. Makes extensive use of Cobden's letters and papers. Illustrated.

McCord, Norman. *The Anti-Corn Law League, 1838-1846*. London: Allen & Unwin, 1958. An excellent and thoroughly scholarly study that concentrates upon the organizational structure and institutional activities of the League. Outlines the League's methods of proselytization and propaganda, its modes of fundraising, and its electoral and parliamentary tactics. Makes good use of League papers and those of its most prominent members.

Morley, John. *Life of Richard Cobden*. 2 vols. London: Chapman and Hall, 1879. A lengthy and rather detailed nineteenth century biography by a prominent Liberal quite sympathetic to Cobden. Still the place for the serious student to begin. Dated but quite readable and very useful for its lengthy extracts from Cobden's correspondence.

Pickering, Paul A., and Alex Tyrell. *The People's Bread: A History of the Anti-Corn Law League*. London: Leicester University Press, 2000. Supplements McCord's book (see above) with new information and a detailed analysis of the League's members and activities.

Read, Donald. *Cobden and Bright: A Victorian Political Partnership*. London: Arnold, 1967. An excellent comparative study of the two best-known free-trade Radicals. Drawn from a wide reading of manuscript sources. Read argues that Bright's Radicalism has been overplayed, that Cobden's views were not always identical with Bright's, and that it was Cobden, and not his Quaker friend, who was the more thoroughgoing democratic Radical.

Taylor, Miles, ed. *The European Diaries of Richard Cobden, 1846-1849*. Brookfield, Vt.: Ashgate, 1994. Includes previously unpublished diaries from Cobden's tour of the continent. The diaries record his observations of European conditions and are the basis for the development of his belief that peaceful economic cooperation is the only way to lasting international stability.

SEE ALSO: John Bright; Sir Henry Parkes; Sir Robert Peel.

RELATED ARTICLES in *Great Events from History: The Nineteenth Century, 1801-1900:* September 2, 1843: Wilson Launches *The Economist*; June 15, 1846: British Parliament Repeals the Corn Laws.

WILLIAM CODY

American frontiersman and showman

Capitalizing on the legends created about his prowess as a frontier plainsman, "Buffalo Bill" Cody popularized the American West through his Wild West Show, which brought the sights of the last frontier to the eastern United States and Europe.

BORN: February 26, 1846; Scott County, near LeClaire, Iowa
DIED: January 10, 1917; Denver, Colorado
ALSO KNOWN AS: William Frederick Cody (full name); Buffalo Bill
AREA OF ACHIEVEMENT: Entertainment

EARLY LIFE

William Cody was born in Iowa but grew up on the Kansas plains. His father, a staunch abolitionist, was pursued and attacked more than once by proslavery fanatics in the Kansas territory, and on several occasions only the young Cody's daring saved his father's life. When his father succumbed to illness in 1857, Cody sought work with what would become the firm of Russell, Majors, and Waddell, who hired him as a cattle driver and later as a Pony Express rider and stagecoach driver. By age twenty, the young man, grown to six feet and sporting shoulder-length, wavy hair and a goatee, had achieved his reputation among plainsmen as a daring scout and buffalo hunter, working for the Army and for the railroads. His brief stint in the Union Army during the Civil War brought him no distinction but did provide the opportunity for him to meet and woo Louisa Frederici in St. Louis. They were married in 1866, and Cody took his bride back to Kansas, to share his life on the plains.

Cody's work as a scout and buffalo hunter led to several important encounters that secured his future fame. A dime novelist, traveling the West in search of new material, was introduced to Cody and from that meeting took away ideas for future novels. During the next four decades, more than two hundred novels about "Buffalo Bill" appeared. The eastern United States soon was familiar with Cody's exploits as a buffalo hunter (extravagant claims put his total kill for a single day into the thousands) and as an Indian fighter, slayer of chiefs Tall Bull and Yellow Knife.

Cody's skill as a hunter for the railroads, the source of the legends that earned for him the sobriquet "Buffalo Bill," led to other career-enhancing engagements. He was called upon to lead several hunting expeditions for celebrities, including the Grand Duke Alexis of Russia, and a group of wealthy New York businesspeople. Some of the latter invited Cody to visit in New York, and from that visit his career as the premier American showman was launched.

LIFE'S WORK

When Cody went to New York City in 1872, he was merely accepting the invitation of the East Coast magnates whom he had entertained on a buffalo hunt. Once there, his reputation having preceded him, he found that he was a minor toast of the town. One evening's entertainment included a trip to the theater to see a play, *Buffalo Bill, the King of Border Men* (1871). Cody was captivated by the attention given to him by the audience in the theater, and to his stage character. E. Z. C. Judson, who as novelist Ned Buntline had done much to build Cody's legend, encouraged him to take up the stage part himself. Reluctant at first, Cody finally gave in, and Judson then quickly wrote and produced *The Scouts of the Plains* (1872).

While the show was extremely confusing and without dramatic merit, and Cody was stiff in his role, the play was a box-office success, and for several years, Cody appeared in a number of stage dramas. Through this endeavor, he met Nate Salsbury, who was to manage his later efforts with the Wild West Show. Salsbury, along with publicist and lifelong friend John Burke, would remain one of Cody's staunchest supporters when that show brought pressures to bear on the flamboyant and somewhat irresponsible Cody.

For several years, Cody alternated his acting career with real-life work as a scout and mediator in the last of the Indian Wars. Then, in 1883, he helped form a traveling troupe that would bring the western plains to the cities and towns of the East and Midwest. Buffalo Bill's Wild West Show toured for the next three decades, making stops in virtually every city of significance in the United States.

The troupe for Cody's show consisted of Indians whom Cody recruited from tribes that had been sent to reservations; plainsmen who had driven stagecoaches, herded cattle, or fought some of the same Indians with whom they now toured; and hundreds of horses, cattle, and buffalo. During the early years, Cody was the main attraction, performing feats with his rifle and introducing the cast in their grand parade at each location. He was joined at various times by other legendary figures such as

Chief Sitting Bull, the victor of Little Bighorn, and trick-shot artist Annie Oakley. Cody managed to secure for his show the original Deadwood Stage, and the exciting chase that led to its rescue from marauders became a highlight of the performance.

The show played at such diverse locations as the World Cotton Exposition in New Orleans in 1884 and the World's Columbian Exposition in Chicago in 1893. Cody and some of his cast were invited to the Vatican in 1889. Queen Victoria attended a performance in 1887, and the Prince of Wales, later Edward V, saw the show on more than one occasion. New Yorkers saw the show performed in Madison Square Garden; the residents of Paris and Barcelona also witnessed the feats of Cody's performers. Well into the new century, Cody moved with his collection of people, animals, and paraphernalia, collecting huge receipts from people whose appetite for the West seemed insatiable.

Showmanship took its toll on Cody, however, and brought out the worst as well as the best in his character. Always a hard drinker, he was sometimes so drunk while on tour that colleagues feared that he would not be able to perform. A generous man by nature, he often squandered huge sums of money on projects in which unscrupulous entrepreneurs or well-intentioned but ill-fated friends encouraged him to invest.

William Cody. (Library of Congress)

Cody found himself caught up in the fast life, and his relationship with his wife, never strong, deteriorated. For years, he had been accustomed to leave behind Louisa and his children, first for duty with the Army, then for his career onstage and with the Wild West Show. Other women pursued him; certainly he pursued some of them. His relationship with Louisa reached its low point in 1904, when Cody sued for divorce, claiming that Louisa had tried to poison him at Christmas in 1900, and that he could no longer live with her. At the divorce trial, Cody's affair with an actress and other improprieties were made public, Louisa was able to generate substantial public sympathy, and the suit was dismissed. After a period of estrangement, the two were reunited, and Cody managed to live amicably with Louisa in his later years.

The Wild West Show's prosperity, especially during the first decades of its life, allowed Cody to obtain significant real estate holdings in the West, most notably in the North Platte, Nebraska, area, and in Wyoming. He was also instrumental in founding the town in Wyoming that bears his name. Often, he would retire to one of these places during the off-season, to relax and renew ties with the land that he helped portray to the rest of the world.

Running a business such as the Wild West Show entailed certain risks. On one trip down the Mississippi River, a steamboat crash cost Cody half of his livestock. On one of the early tours in Europe, his Indians began to get homesick and to desert the show. Disease took a major portion of his livestock in another year. Competition became fierce at times, and especially after the death of Salsbury in 1902, Cody found himself going more and more in debt to keep the show running. Eventually, he found it necessary to accept offers from outsiders to finance his operation. In 1913, the show was seized by agents to pay creditors.

The last years of Cody's life were not pleasant. He tried his hand at the new motion-picture industry, persuading the aged General Nelson Miles to assist him in producing a documentary of the famous Battle of Wounded Knee. The film was not a commercial success. Other schemes, including a mining venture, were similarly unsuccessful. Meanwhile, Harry Tammen, an unscrupulous editor of the *Denver Post*, managed to loan Cody sufficient capital for his ventures so that Cody soon

CUSTER'S LAST STAND

William Cody knew George A. Custer from his own work as a scout for the U.S. Cavalry on the frontier and respected him as a gallant officer. Cody was doing scouting work at the time that Custer's Seventh Cavalry was annihilated at Little Bighorn. He comments on the event in one of his several autobiographies.

This massacre occurred June 25, 1876, and its details are known, or ought to be known, by every schoolboy. Custer was a brave, dashing, headlong soldier, whose only fault was recklessness.

He had been warned many times never to expose a small command to a superior force of Indians, and never to underestimate the ability and generalship of the Sioux. He had unbounded confidence, however, in himself and his men, and I believe that not until he was struck down did he ever doubt that he would be able to cut his way out of the wall of warriors about him and turn defeat into a glorious and conspicuous victory.

The news of the massacre, which was the most terrible that ever overtook a command of our soldiers, was a profound shock to all of us. We knew at once that we would all have work to do, and settled grimly into the preparations for it. . . .

Source: William Cody, *An Autobiography of Buffalo Bill* (New York, 1920), chapter 9.

found himself unable to reach a settlement and break his contract with Tammen. As a result, Tammen was able to force Cody to tour with the Sells-Floto Circus in 1914 and to restrict his activities further by limiting his salary and expense account.

By 1916, Cody was suffering the infirmities of old age. In the winter of 1916, he traveled to Denver to stay with his sister. There, on January 10, 1917, he died in her home. Despite his wishes to be buried in Wyoming, he was laid to rest atop Lookout Mountain, outside Denver.

SIGNIFICANCE

As a frontiersman, scout, and hunter, Cody would have achieved a place in American history without the fame that his Wild West Show provided him. Even when the exaggerations about his exploits are stripped away, his accomplishments in helping to settle the West were substantial: He helped bring to a successful close several skirmishes and one major uprising in the Indian Wars, he participated as the youngest member of the celebrated Pony Express team, and he kept the railroads moving across the country by providing meat for the construction crews.

Cody's Wild West Show did more than his real-life exploits on the frontier to bring to the civilized world of the eastern United States and to the countries of Europe a sense of the life of the American West. He was a symbol of that land: handsome, brash, generous, free-living, unafraid of any danger. Carrying on the tradition of the showman established by the legendary P. T. Barnum, Cody barnstormed across two continents, sharing the sense of excitement that had characterized the West in its infancy and adolescence. While he toured, the West matured, and the frontier that Cody dramatized in his shows was disappearing. Nevertheless, the thrills Cody and his fellow performers generated in countless youngsters lived on for years after his death. Cody's legacy continues in the games of "Cowboys and Indians" that endure, long after the West had become homogeneous with the rest of the United States.

—Laurence W. Mazzeno

FURTHER READING

Burke, John. *Buffalo Bill: The Noblest Whiteskin*. New York: G. P. Putnam's Sons, 1973. A popular biography, providing sufficient details about Cody's early life on the frontier but concentrating on the years Buffalo Bill spent as an actor and showman in the eastern United States and Europe. Informal style, highly readable.

Carter, Robert A. *Buffalo Bill Cody: The Man Behind the Legend*. New York: John Wiley & Sons, 2000. Popular biography, offering a narrative account of Cody's life. Carter argues that Cody's Wild West Show made him the first American media hero.

Cody, William F. *Story of the Wild West and Camp-Fire Chats*. Philadelphia: Historical Publishing, 1888. One of Cody's several autobiographies, containing accounts of various plainsmen. Because many details of Cody's early life are drawn from this autobiography, it is important for scholars; additionally, its informal style and tendency toward exaggeration mark it as typical of popular literature about the West written during the late nineteenth century.

Croft-Cooke, Rupert, and W. S. Meadmore. *Buffalo Bill: The Legend, the Man of Action, the Showman*. London: Sidgwick and Jackson, 1952. A brief account of Cody's life, relying heavily on Cody's autobiography for details of the early years. Contains an interesting introductory chapter on the impact of the Wild West Show in England.

Havighurst, Walter. *Annie Oakley of the Wild West*. New York: Macmillan, 1954. Life story of one of the star attractions in the Wild West Show; provides much information about Cody and others who traveled with her.

Hine, Robert V. *The American West: An Interpretive History*. Boston: Little, Brown, 1973. Provides excellent background about the American West; discusses Cody as the foremost American hero.

McMurtry, Larry. *The Colonel and Little Missie: Buffalo Bill, Annie Oakley, and the Beginnings of Superstardom in America*. New York: Simon & Schuster, 2005. A dual biography of Buffalo Bill and Annie Oakley, tracing Bill's career from his days as a scout and Indian fighter to his performances with the Wild West Show.

Russell, Don F. *The Lives and Legends of Buffalo Bill*. Norman: University of Oklahoma Press, 1960. A well-researched, scholarly biography that goes far in separating the legend from the facts about Cody's life.

Wetmore, Helen Cody, and Zane Grey. *Buffalo Bill: Last of the Great Scouts*. Commemorative ed. Lincoln: University of Nebraska Press, 2003. A new edition of a biography written by Cody's sister, originally published in 1899. Contains the original illustrations by Frederic Remington and other artists.

Yost, Nellie S. *Buffalo Bill: His Family, Friends, Fame, Failures, and Fortunes*. Chicago: Swallow Press, 1974. A carefully researched biography, relying heavily on records from the nineteenth century and on interviews with people who knew Cody or his family and friends. Debunks many legends and establishes a historical basis for many others.

SEE ALSO: P. T. Barnum; Calamity Jane; Kit Carson; Wild Bill Hickok; Annie Oakley; Sitting Bull.

RELATED ARTICLES in *Great Events from History: The Nineteenth Century, 1801-1900:* April 3, 1860-October 26, 1861: Pony Express Expedites Transcontinental Mail; c. 1871-1883: Great American Buffalo Slaughter; December 29, 1890: Wounded Knee Massacre.

FERDINAND JULIUS COHN

German botanist and bacteriologist

Cohn is considered one of the founders of modern bacteriology. As a botanist, he contributed to understanding the evolutionary position of many microscopic plantlike organisms by elucidating their life histories.

BORN: January 24, 1828; Breslau, Lower Silesia, Prussia (now Wrocław, Poland)

DIED: June 25, 1898; Breslau, Lower Silesia, Prussia

AREAS OF ACHIEVEMENT: Biology, science and technology

EARLY LIFE

The eldest of three sons of a poor Jewish merchant, Issak Cohn, Ferdinand Julius Cohn was born in Breslau's Jewish ghetto. He was a precocious child who, it is said, was able to read at the age of two and enter school at the age of four. At the age of seven he began higher school at the gymnasium of St. Maria Magdelina, and he began attending the University of Breslau at the age of fourteen. Influenced at the university by professors Heinrich Goeppert and Christian Nees von Esenbeck, he became interested in botany. Because of the rules against Jews receiving advanced degrees at Breslau, he could not be granted one there.

In 1846, Cohn moved to the more liberal University of Berlin, from which, a year later, he obtained a doctorate in botany. At Berlin, he was influenced by several professors, especially Christian Ehrenberg in microscopy and Johannes Müller in physiology. He was in Berlin during the uprisings of 1848, with which he sympathized but in which he did not actively participate. Returning the next year to Breslau at the age of twenty-one, he became a privatdocent at the university, working under Professor Jan Evangelista Purkinje in his Institute of Physiology.

At Breslau, Cohn began his work on the microscopic aspects of living organisms, at that time a new area of biological investigation, particularly because of the newly proposed cell theory of Theodor Schwann and Matthias Schleiden. In 1859, he became an extraordinary professor at the university, and in 1867, he married Pauline

Reichenbach. The remainder of his professional career was spent at the University of Breslau, where he became an ordinary professor in 1872.

LIFE'S WORK

Cohn's primary research interests were in microscopic organisms, both plant and animal, which he used to try to understand their relationships with higher groups of organisms and to understand their development and physiology. At first, he studied various microscopic algae, and, especially using the unicellular *Protococcus pluvialis*, he concluded that these organisms had a regular life cycle and various developmental phases including sexuality, and that the cellular substance was similar in all cells, both plant and animal. The latter conclusion led him to call the cell substance protoplasm, the name Hugo von Mohl had used for that in plant cells, rather than the term sarcode, which had been used by Felix Dujardin for animal cell substance.

Cohn is best known for his studies of bacteria. He believed that these organisms were more plantlike than animal-like. He showed that they had stable characteristics of form that varied within certain limits, allowing them to be given firm generic names and, at least, provisional specific names. His hesitation about specific names was based on his knowledge that sometimes those of the same form had different fermentative properties. He recognized six genera of bacteria based on their shapes: micrococcus (ball-shaped); bacterium (short rods); bacillus (straight threadlike); vibrio (wavy-shaped); and spirochete (long, flexible spirals). The genera were placed into four larger groups: spaerobacteria for the round ones, microbacteria for the rod-shaped ones, desmobacteria for the longer rod- and thread-shaped ones, and spirobacteria for the wavy or spiral-shaped ones. Because of his clear presentation of the information about the characteristics of bacteria, their cultivation, and their physiology, Cohn helped found the modern science of bacteriology.

Cohn was involved in some of the most important aspects of the developing field of microbiology. He undertook to understand why some bacteria in hay infusions were able to withstand high temperatures. He was able to show that certain bacilli were able to form heat-resistant endospores. This discovery came at a time to help Louis Pasteur, and later John Tyndall, substantiate the attack on the idea of spontaneous generation of microorganisms.

Because he was the major Germanic worker with bacteria, and because he had been trying to prove the importance of bacteria in causing diseases, the then-young Robert Koch wrote to Cohn asking if he could come and demonstrate his evidence for the bacterial cause of anthrax. Koch visited Breslau for three days and convinced Cohn and others at Breslau that he had definite proof that *Bacillus anthracis* was the sole cause of the disease. Cohn was very impressed with Koch's ability, supported his research program, and published his paper on anthrax in 1876, in the journal *Beitrage zur Biologie der Pflanzen* (contributions to the biology of plants), which Cohn had established in 1872 and used to publish many of his own findings.

Work in botany and the popularization of biology also occupied Cohn's time. From 1856 to 1886, he served as secretary of the botanical section of the Schlesiche Gesellschaft für Vaterländische Cultur (Silesian society for the culture of the fatherland), in which capacity he organized and edited a multivolume work on the cryptogamic flora of Silesia. Cohn wrote a popular work on bacteria, *Über Bacterien: Die kleinsten lebenden Wesen* (1872; *Bacteria: The Smallest of Living Organisms*, 1881), and one on plants, *Die Pflanze* (1882; the plants). In this way, and by articles and lectures, he helped to interest the general public and students in biological subjects. In 1866, he was able to establish an Institute of Plant Physiology at the University of Breslau, the first of its kind in the world, thus fulfilling a long-held dream. He made studies of tissues in plants that were involved with rapid movements that he believed to be similar to animal muscle tissue.

SIGNIFICANCE

Ferdinand Julius Cohn is historically important as a major figure in the foundation of modern microbiology, and as a sponsor of Robert Koch in his important studies of disease-causing bacteria. Cohn placed microscopic organisms, particularly algae, fungi, and bacteria, which he considered to be plants, into a Darwinian evolutionary framework. By elucidating their life cycles, and when possible their sexuality, he furthered biological understanding. He recognized the importance of protoplasm as the universal living substance of cells. An important educator, he popularized botany and bacteriology by his writings and lectures.

—*Emanuel D. Rudolph*

FURTHER READING

Brock, Thomas D., ed. *Milestones in Microbiology*. Englewood Cliffs, N.J.: Prentice-Hall, 1961. Contains English translations of two of Cohn's important papers, with some deletions. "Studies on the Biology of the Bacilli" is concerned with the survival of spores of some bacteria after boiling; "Studies on Bacteria" describes some of the problems in classifying bacteria, considering them best related to fungi. Comments accompany the papers indicating their historical importance.

Bulloch, William. *The History of Bacteriology*. New York: Oxford University Press, 1938. Reprint. Mineola, N.Y.: Dover, 1979. Cohn's work is considered within the context of the history of bacteriology. His studies on the survival of bacteria after sterilization of their media are considered, as are his ideas about bacterial classification.

Cohn, Ferdinand. *Bacteria: The Smallest of Living Organisms*. Translated by Charles S. Dolley, with an introduction by Morris C. Leikind. Rochester, N.Y.: F. D. Phinney, 1881. Reprint. Baltimore: Johns Hopkins University Press, 1939. Originally published in German by Cohn in 1872, and in a small English edition by the translator in Rochester, New York, in 1881, this introduction to bacteriology was written for the general reader. It gives a brief history of the knowledge of bacteria and presents a summary of what Cohn and others knew and thought about bacteria. The reprint in the Johns Hopkins University Press book contains a short biography and the original complete bibliography of Cohn's writings.

Geison, Gerald L. "Ferdinand Julius Cohn." In *Dictionary of Scientific Biography*. Vol. 3. Edited by Charles Coulston Gillispie. New York: Charles Scribner's Sons, 1971. This is the only scholarly, substantial biography of Cohn in English. In addition to providing basic biographical information, it stresses Cohn's importance in the development of microbiology and botany. Provides a detailed bibliography.

Lechevalier, Hubert A., and Morris Solotorovsky. *Three Centuries of Microbiology*. New York: McGraw-Hill, 1965. Reprint. Mineola, N.Y.: Dover, 1974. Cohn's place in the development of bacteriology is considered briefly. The authors stress Cohn's studies of spontaneous generation of microorganisms in relation to Pasteur's work and the relationship between his work and Koch's bacterial studies.

Talbott, John H. *A Biographical History of Medicine: Excerpts and Essays on the Men and Their Work*. New York: Grune & Stratton, 1970. A brief biographical sketch of Cohn, with a composite drawing, stresses his contributions to botany. It includes a long quotation from the English translation of his book, *Bacteria: The Smallest of Living Organisms*, which emphasizes the importance of bacteria as disease organisms and as possible extraterrestrial initiators of life on Earth.

SEE ALSO: Asa Gray; Robert Koch; Louis Pasteur.

RELATED ARTICLES in *Great Events from History: The Nineteenth Century, 1801-1900:* March 24, 1882: Koch Announces His Discovery of the Tuberculosis Bacillus; December 11, 1890: Behring Discovers the Diphtheria Antitoxin.

SAMUEL TAYLOR COLERIDGE

English poet and literary critic

Coleridge wrote several of the finest lyric poems in the English language and is considered one of the most brilliant of literary critics. As a speculative religious thinker, he had a seminal influence on many of the great minds of the nineteenth century.

BORN: October 21, 1772; Ottery St. Mary, Devonshire, England

DIED: July 25, 1834; Highgate, London, England

AREAS OF ACHIEVEMENT: Literature, religion and theology

EARLY LIFE

Samuel Taylor Coleridge was the youngest of ten children born to Ann Bowden, the second wife of Coleridge's father, John Coleridge, a clergyman and schoolmaster. Coleridge was an intellectually precocious child, with an early love of books and study. He was particularly enthralled by *The Arabian Nights' Entertainments* (c. 1450), which he read at the age of five.

In 1782, one year after the death of his father, Coleridge was enrolled in the Christ's Hospital Grammar School in London. He was a superior student and a voracious reader, devouring everything from classics to theology, philosophy, and medical books. In 1791, when he was almost twenty years old, this sometimes untidily dressed young man with dark penetrating eyes, a fine forehead, and long black, flowing hair, received a scholarship to Jesus College, Cambridge, where he continued to read extremely widely. He also gained a reputation as an enthusiastic and spellbinding talker, and his gregarious, generous, and sensitive nature won for him many friends. In spite of this, however, he tended to be dissatisfied with himself, annoyed by what he described as his own indolence. He was also beginning to experience the ill health that dogged him throughout his life.

In 1794, Coleridge became friends with fellow student Robert Southey, who was two years his junior and also destined to be a poet of distinction. Together they planned to emigrate to the United States and set up an ideal community in Pennsylvania on the banks of the Susquehanna. Coleridge was excited by the proposed venture, which he called "Pantisocracy" (meaning "equal government for all"). The plan came to nothing, but through it Coleridge became engaged to Sarah Fricker, one of several members of the Fricker family who were involved in the scheme. Coleridge married her in October, 1795; she was later to bear him four children.

Having left Cambridge without taking a degree, Coleridge and his new bride moved to the village of Nether Stowey, near Bristol, where they rented a small cottage. The marriage was not destined to be a happy one; nevertheless, Coleridge was on the threshold of several productive and creative years, in which he was to write all the poems that were to make him famous.

LIFE'S WORK

Coleridge's first major poem, "The Eolian Harp," dates from his period at Nether Stowey. During this time, he also gave public lectures on political topics, preached as a Unitarian, and started a short-lived journal called *The Watchman*.

In 1797, following a visit by William Wordsworth to Nether Stowey, one of the most famous friendships in literary history began. Coleridge relished the acceptance and encouragement he received from Wordsworth and his sister Dorothy, and he believed that he had discovered a receptive audience for his wide-ranging ideas and speculations. Wordsworth, for his part, found his conception of his own poetic task defined more clearly through his conversations with Coleridge. Coleridge, however, always generous in his admiration of others, felt inferior (although unjustifiably so) to a man of Wordsworth's talents.

In January, 1798, Coleridge's financial problems were eased when he received a lifetime annuity of £150 from his friends Josiah and Tom Wedgwood. The security this provided, together with his almost daily contact with the Wordsworths, who were now living at nearby Alfoxden, stimulated Coleridge to a year of brilliant achievement. In February, he wrote the fine lyric poem "Frost at Midnight" and completed *Christabel* (which would be published in 1816). The next month, he finished *The Rime of the Ancient Mariner*, probably the greatest of all of his poems. "Kubla Khan," a visionary dream-poem of extraordinary power and beauty, followed in May. In September, *The Rime of the Ancient Mariner* was published in a joint collection with Wordsworth entitled *Lyrical Ballads*.

In the same month, Coleridge and Wordsworth traveled to Germany. Coleridge remained there, learning the language and studying German metaphysics, until July, 1799. On his return, he met and fell in love with Sarah Hutchinson, the sister of Wordsworth's wife, Mary, and in 1800 he and his wife followed the Wordsworths to live in the Lake District in the northwest of England.

Coleridge was now to enter a dark period of his life, a decade of gloom, failure, guilt, and despair. He was to write only a few more outstanding poems, notably "Dejection: An Ode" and "To William Wordsworth." His physical health deteriorated alarmingly, aggravated by mental anxieties; his distress is readily apparent from his poem "The Pains of Sleep." He took to opium—a drug that was frequently prescribed for medical reasons at the time—and soon became dependent on it. He could not settle down to important work. Although he had many projects in mind, he was unable to persevere with them. The greater the task he set himself, the more paralyzed he became, and he constantly lamented his inability to concentrate on one project at a time.

In an attempt to improve his health, Coleridge left England in 1804 for a two-year stay in Malta, but on his return in 1806 his condition had not improved. He formally separated from his wife, and by 1808, after a nomadic year, he went to live with the Wordsworths in the Lake District village of Grasmere. There, he managed to launch a new periodical, *The Friend*, which kept going for twenty-seven issues. In 1810, however, came a serious, indirect quarrel with Wordsworth, when a friend passed on to Coleridge some critical remarks that Wordsworth had made regarding his self-destructive way of life. The breach took many years to heal.

The next few years of Coleridge's life were increasingly desperate. He was consuming larger quantities of opium than ever before (although he tried hard to break his addiction), and he wrote of his guilt and the complete paralysis of his will. At one point, he even wished to be admitted to a private lunatic asylum.

THE RIME OF THE ANCIENT MARINER

These verses constitute the first of the poem's seven parts.

It is an ancient Mariner,
And he stoppeth one of three.
"By thy long grey beard and glittering eye,
Now wherefore stopp'st thou me?

The bridegroom's doors are opened wide,
And I am next of kin;
The guests are met, the feast is set:
May'st hear the merry din."

He holds him with his skinny hand,
"There was a ship," quoth he.
"Hold off! unhand me, grey-beard loon!"
Eftsoons his hand dropt he.

He holds him with his glittering eye—
The Wedding-Guest stood still,
And listens like a three years' child:
The Mariner hath his will.

The Wedding-Guest sat on a stone:
He cannot choose but hear;
And thus spake on that ancient man,
The bright-eyed Mariner.

"The ship was cheered, the harbor cleared,
Merrily did we drop
Below the kirk, below the hill,
Below the lighthouse top.

The sun came up upon the left,
Out of the sea came he!
And he shone bright, and on the right
Went down into the sea.

Higher and higher every day,
Till over the mast at noon—"
The Wedding-Guest here beat his breast,
For he heard the loud bassoon.

The bride hath paced into the hall,
Red as a rose is she;
Nodding their heads before her goes
The merry minstrelsy.

The Wedding-Guest he beat his breast,
Yet he cannot choose but hear;
And thus spake on that ancient man,
The bright-eyed Mariner.

"And now the Storm-blast came, and he
Was tyrannous and strong:
He struck with his o'ertaking wings,
And chased us south along.

With sloping masts and dipping prow,
As who pursued with yell and blow
Still treads the shadow of his foe,
And forward bends his head,
The ship drove fast, loud roared the blast,
And southward aye we fled.

And now there came both mist and snow,
And it grew wondrous cold:
And ice, mast-high, came floating by,
As green as emerald.

And through the drifts the snowy clifts
Did send a dismal sheen:
Nor shapes of men nor beasts we ken—
The ice was all between.

The ice was here, the ice was there,
The ice was all around:
It cracked and growled, and roared and howled,
Like noises in a swound!

At length did cross an Albatross,
Through the fog it came;
As if it had been a Christian soul,
We hailed it in God's name.

It ate the food it ne'er had eat,
And round and round it flew.
The ice did split with a thunder-fit;
The helmsman steered us through!

And a good south wind sprung up behind;
The Albatross did follow,
And every day, for food or play,
Came to the mariners' hollo!

In mist or cloud, on mast or shroud,
It perched for vespers nine;
Whiles all the night, through fog-smoke white,
Glimmered the white moon-shine."

"God save thee, ancient Mariner!
From the fiends, that plague thee thus!—
Why look'st thou so?"—"With my cross-bow
I shot the Albatross."

Source: Samuel Taylor Coleridge, *Coleridge's Ancient Mariner and Select Poems*, edited by Frederick H. Sykes (New York, 1908).

In late 1811, however, Coleridge roused himself sufficiently to give a successful series of lectures on William Shakespeare and John Milton, which established his reputation as a literary critic of genius. During this period, he also produced three excellent short critical works, collectively titled "On the Principles of Genial Criticism Concerning the Fine Arts" (1814), as well as *Biographia Literaria: Or, Biographical Sketches of My Literary Life and Opinions*, written in 1815 and published in 1817. The latter is notable for Coleridge's assessment of Wordsworth's poetry and for his own critical theories, particularly those dealing with the creative function of the imagination.

In 1816 came a rescue. James Gillman, a physician from Highgate, London, who was captivated by the power of Coleridge's mind, took him into his house and cared for him. Initially it was intended as a temporary measure, but Coleridge was to live at Highgate with Gillman and his wife for the remaining eighteen years of his life. During these years, he gained a new lease on life. He gave more lectures on Shakespeare and other topics and also wrote the religious works that were to have such a strong impact on nineteenth century thought. These include the three lay sermons published as *The Statesman's Manual* (1816), *Aids to Reflection* (1825), *On the Constitution of the Church and State, According to the Idea of Each* (1830), and the posthumously published *Confessions of an Inquiring Spirit* (1840). His projected magnum opus, which was to synthesize all branches of existing knowledge into one coherent, all-embracing philosophy of nature, was never written.

During the later years, a social circle formed itself around the "Sage of Highgate"; many people were drawn to the compelling flow of Coleridge's conversation, which ran its course, as it had always done, like a mighty, meandering river.

When Coleridge died, on July 25, 1834, worn out at the age of sixty-one, his friends were quick to pay tribute to him. Wordsworth declared him to be the most "wonderful" man he had ever known, and Coleridge's lifelong friend Charles Lamb said, "never saw I his likeness, nor probably the world can see again."

SIGNIFICANCE

Samuel Taylor Coleridge's literary criticism and theory have remained influential for more than a century and a half, and although his greatness as a poet rests on only a handful of poems, his honored place in the history of English literature is unlikely ever to be challenged. His best poems are highly original; he had a marked gift, particularly noticeable in *The Rime of the Ancient Mariner* and *Christabel*, for evoking an atmosphere of the strange and the supernatural. In his "conversation poems," as they have come to be known (such as "Frost at Midnight" and "Dejection: An Ode"), he invented what is sometimes called the Greater Romantic lyric: a meditative lyric that features an isolated speaker interacting with his natural environment, resolving a problem or deepening an understanding, before the poem rounds back on itself to give a sense of resolution and wholeness.

Coleridge's philosophical thought was central to the English Romantic movement. Highly eclectic but rooted in Neoplatonism and German idealism, his mind was dominated by a search for unity. Coleridge opposed the mechanistic philosophy, with its tendency to fragment knowledge into separate compartments, with an organicism that viewed everything in connection with everything else, "the one life within us and abroad," as he put it in "The Eolian Harp." The "one life" could be realized through the power of the imagination, the creative aspect of the mind, which could overcome the ultimately false division between subject and object. Coleridge's later work is characterized by an attempt to reconcile this "dynamic philosophy" with orthodox Christianity.

Coleridge's later religious writings elaborated an unusual, subjective approach to Christian belief, analyzed the relation between reason (including the scientific method) and faith, and discussed the Bible's claim to authority and the role of the Church in national life. All these issues became central to Victorian religious inquiry.

Given the range of Coleridge's achievement, it is not surprising that the Victorian philosopher John Stuart Mill called him "one of the great seminal minds of England," to whom the Victorian age was indebted not only for "the greater part of the important ideas which have been thrown into circulation among its thinking men but for a revolution in its general modes of thought and investigation."

—*Bryan Aubrey*

FURTHER READING

Barfield, Owen. *What Coleridge Thought*. Middletown, Conn.: Wesleyan University Press, 1971. One of the clearest and most penetrating brief expositions of Coleridge's thought.

Bate, Walter Jackson. *Coleridge*. New York: Macmillan, 1968. Sound and balanced introduction to Coleridge's life and work by a leading literary critic and scholar.

Coburn, Kathleen, ed. *Coleridge: A Collection of Critical Essays*. Englewood Cliffs, N.J.: Prentice-Hall, 1967. Distinguished literary critics present the range and brilliance of Coleridge's achievement in poetry and literary criticism.

Coleridge, Samuel Taylor. *The Portable Coleridge*. Edited by I. A. Richards. New York: Penguin Books, 1977. One-volume selection from Coleridge's voluminous works. Includes poems, letters, notebooks, literary criticism (including long extracts from *Biographia Literaria*), and sections of *The Statesman's Manual* and *Aids to Reflection*.

_____. *Samuel Taylor Coleridge: Selected Letters*. Edited by H. J. Jackson. New York: Oxford University Press, 1987. Extensively annotated edition, which includes letters from every phase of Coleridge's career. Reveals his myriad-minded self as he ranges over everything from poetry to science and chronicles his tormented inner life.

Hanson, Lawrence. *The Life of Samuel Taylor Coleridge: The Early Years*. New York: Oxford University Press, 1938. Sympathetic, sometimes even rhapsodic, account of Coleridge's life up to June, 1800.

Holmes, Richard. *Coleridge: Early Visions*. New York: Viking Press, 1989.

_____. *Coleridge: Darker Reflections*. London: HarperCollins, 1991. An extensively researched, meticulously detailed two-volume biography. Holmes analyzes Coleridge's works and provides many quotations that demonstrate Coleridge's legendary conversational skills.

Newlyn, Lucy, ed. *The Cambridge Companion to Coleridge*. New York: Cambridge University Press, 2002. Essays on Coleridge's life, his poetry and notebooks, and his role as talker, journalist, critic, and political and religious thinker.

Perry, Seamus. *Samuel Taylor Coleridge*. London: British Library, 2003. Brief biography, intended as an introduction to Coleridge for students and general readers. Perry, who has written several other books about Coleridge, provides an overview of his life and work.

Willey, Basil. *Samuel Taylor Coleridge*. New York: W. W. Norton, 1972. Traces Coleridge's intellectual and spiritual development, from his early Unitarianism to the Christian orthodoxy of his later years.

SEE ALSO: Sir Humphry Davy; William Wordsworth.

RELATED ARTICLE in *Great Events from History: The Nineteenth Century, 1801-1900:* December, 1816: Rise of the Cockney School.

SAMUEL COLT

American inventor and manufacturer

Colt developed the revolving pistol and the revolving rifle and pioneered the large-scale production of guns with interchangeable parts. His mass-produced firearms played a significant role in nineteenth century U.S. history and also helped to transform the modern weapons of war.

BORN: July 19, 1814; Hartford, Connecticut
DIED: January 10, 1862; Hartford, Connecticut
AREAS OF ACHIEVEMENT: Engineering, business

EARLY LIFE

Samuel Colt was one of eight children of Christopher and Sarah Caldwell Colt. Christopher was in the manufacturing business in Connecticut and Massachusetts. Samuel's grandfather, Major Caldwell, was in the shipping and banking business and was one of the wealthiest men in Hartford. Major Caldwell, who had fought in the Revolutionary War, expressed strong opinions on military matters and weaponry and strongly influenced young Colt.

During his early school years, Colt performed poorly in subjects such as reading, writing, and arithmetic until his mother, to whom Colt was very close, impressed upon him that such disciplines were a means to better understand the workings of guns and the process of explosions. Colt's mother died when he was seven, but two years later his father married Olivia Sargent, who continued to support Colt's inquisitive nature.

Throughout those formative early years, Colt's increasing fascination with firearms and explosives led him to develop an interest in the natural sciences: physics, chemistry, and electricity. A series of experiments with firearms and gunpowder culminated in Colt's development of a way to ignite an underwater charge of gunpowder with an electrical spark. On July 4, 1829, at the age of fifteen, Colt successfully ignited an underwater mine with an electrical charge in a Ware, Massachusetts, pond in front of a crowd of people that included Elisha Root, a fellow inventor who would come to play a central role in Colt's future success in the manufacture of guns.

In August, 1830, at the age of sixteen, Colt signed on the brig *Carlo* as a seaman and headed for India. He occupied his off-duty hours whittling models of ships and firearms—most significantly, models of double-barreled handguns. Colt was intent on developing a more practical revolving handgun. However, he found that a revolving handgun with multiple barrels was impractical, so he concentrated on designing a more practical repeating handgun with a single barrel and a revolving spindle. The solution was a result of his observations of the workings of the ship's wheel. As the wheel was turned to navigate the ship, a clutch aligned the spokes and locked the wheel in position to maintain the ship's course; the clutch was then released to change course. In February, 1836, Colt secured the patent to a repeating handgun with a revolving and locking cylinder whose bullet chambers came in line with the single barrel by pulling the hammer back to the cocked position.

Samuel Colt. (Library of Congress)

LIFE'S WORK

Colt sought financial backing from his father to develop some working steel models of his handgun, but initial test firings of the models proved unsuccessful, and his father stopped financial support. Convinced that his repeating revolver was destined for success, Colt funded the enterprise by traveling around the United States and Canada using the stage name "Doctor Coult" and giving public demonstrations of nitrous oxide (laughing gas). The years Colt spent on the road raising capital also allowed him time to refine his design models and to have steel models produced and tested.

The manufacture of Colt firearms began in 1836 following Colt's travels abroad to secure patents in England, France, and Prussia; his first U.S. patent was granted on February 25. The Patent Arms Manufacturing Company of Paterson, New Jersey, produced five- and six-shot revolvers, revolving rifles, carbines, shotguns, and a few muskets—all referred to by the public as Colts—using the armory method of mass production, which was characterized by the use of a factory system, the specialization of labor, the use of precision tools and gauges, and the production of weapons with interchangeable parts that could be taken from one gun and used in another gun of the same model. Thus, damaged gun parts from one model could be replaced using spare parts from similar models. Prior to the introduction of the armory method of production, guns were laboriously crafted one at a time. Colt believed that the mass production of guns could best be accomplished by machinery.

Although the Patent Arms Manufacturing Company experienced financial failure in 1841, a number of significant events in the development and adoption of Colt firearms transpired during the six years of its existence. Colt guns manufactured in Paterson proved to be successful in tests and demonstrations for the government in Washington, D.C., but bureaucratic government officials were unable or unwilling to accept the advanced revolving design and dynamics of the weapons. In addition, the national financial climate was unsettled. Therefore, Colt was unable to land a government contract.

Undaunted, Colt believed that contracts for his weapons would come through increasing demonstrations, advertising, and placing his guns in the hands of active fighting men. During these financially lean years without the resources of an armory, Colt turned his attention away from guns and devoted his energies toward the successful development of waterproof ammunition and the successful development of underwater mines designed for harbor defenses. In addition, his association with Samuel F. B. Morse led to the development of the telegraph.

Colt's belief in himself and his revolving guns eventually paid off. He experienced his first success at placing his weapons in war conditions during the Second Seminole War, which raged in Florida from 1835 through 1842. Although the Seminole Indians had a tactical edge in fighting in the Florida Everglades and possessed rifles as good as the U.S. soldiers', Colt's repeating pistols and rifles were soon recognized as the weapons of choice by the Second Dragoons and played a key role in the conflict. The success of Colt's guns did not go unnoticed by military practitioners outside Florida. The ever-increasing influx of white settlers into Native American territory in Texas and the emerging conflict between the Republic of Texas and Mexico played significant roles in the evolution of Colt firearms and their adoption by men at war.

In 1844, U.S. dragoon forces and Texas Rangers armed with Colt firearms, some obtained from the Texas Navy, began confronting Native Americans as white settlers pushed west. In 1846, when the Mexican War began, Captain Samuel H. Walker of the U.S. Army met with Colt, and the two collaborated on the design of a new, more powerful revolver to replace the Paterson six-shooter. The newly designed "Walker" met with immediate success, and the U.S. Ordinance placed an order for one thousand of the new six-shooters. Colt suddenly found himself back in the gun business but without an armory. To meet the increasing demand for his weapons, Colt contracted with Eli Whitney, Jr. (son of the inventor of the cotton gin), to produce Colt guns at his Whitneyville, Connecticut, arms and cotton gin manufacturing facility.

In 1848, when Colts were no longer contracted for production at the Whitneyville armory, Colt built a small armory in Hartford, Connecticut, with the multitalented mechanic and inventor Elisha Root serving as its superintendent. The refinement of the armory production process and the continuing development of a wide range of sophisticated revolving guns produced at the Hartford armory led to the adoption of Colts for official use by Wells Fargo Express messengers and by the U.S. Navy during Matthew Perry's visit to Japan in 1852.

In response to an increasing demand for his pistols and rifles, Colt established an armory in London, England. Upon returning to the United States, he built the Armsmear factory located at South Meadows in Hartford, Connecticut, which was to become the largest private armory in the world upon its completion in 1855. The years of production of Colt guns at Whitneyville, the first Hartford armory, London, and Armsmear led to the continued development and refinement of pocket pistols, belt pistols, holster pistols, repeating rifles, sporting rifles, and shotguns for hunters, as well as special Colt models for military personnel and law-enforcement officers throughout the United States.

Colt was nearly forty-two when he married Elizabeth Hart Jarvis in 1856. Immediately following their wedding, they traveled to Europe and were entertained by European heads of state. They returned to the United States in 1857. As rumblings of an imminent civil war echoed throughout the country, Colt was burdened by the idea that the guns he had manufactured and sold to Texas would become instruments of war that fellow Americans from the North and South would use against each other. Colt showed sympathy toward the South prior to the Civil War; however, once the war between the states broke out, he devoted all of his arms manufacturing resources to production for Union forces. The Colt revolver was the revolver of choice by the North's Union Army, and it became the practice of many Northern cavalrymen to carry two Colts in their belts and two Colts on their saddles. Nearly 40,000 revolvers, 100,000 muskets, and 7,000 rifles were supplied to the Union troops by the Colt armories.

SIGNIFICANCE

Samuel Colt died on January 10, 1862, at the age of forty-seven. At his death, it was said of him that "Abe Lincoln may have freed all men, but Sam Colt made them equal." Colt will be remembered for his invention of the Colt revolver, which revolutionized methods of warfare and provided the critical link in the development of arms from the muzzle-loading musket to the magazine rifles and machine guns of the twentieth century. In addition, Colt developed and refined the armory method of weapons production, and the famed Colt revolver became one of the first products of American manufacture available around the world.

—Hugh J. Phillips

FURTHER READING

Boorman, Dean K. *The History of Colt Firearms*. New York: The Lyons Press, 2001. Like many books about Colt's products, this one may appeal more to the gun collector and enthusiast than to historians and students interested in biographical information. However, Boorman describes how Colt improved upon earlier designs for revolvers and set up factories that revolutionized gun manufacturing. Includes numerous photos of firearms and gun-making artifacts and copies of designers' drawings.

Edwards, William B. *The Story of Colt's Revolver*. Harrisburg, Pa.: Stackpole, 1953. Edwards's book provides a detailed biography of Colt. Includes illustrations.

Hosley, Walter. *Colt: The Making of an American Legend*. Amherst: University of Massachusetts Press, 1996. Hosley's voluminous, large-format biography places Colt in social and historical context. Contains numerous illustrations.

Hounshell, David A. *From the American System to Mass Production, 1800-1932: The Development of Manufacturing Technology in the United States*. Baltimore: Johns Hopkins University Press, 1983. An overview of the rise of mass production in the United States.

Mitchell, James L. *Colt: A Collection of Letters and Photographs About the Man, the Arms, the Company*. Harrisburg, Pa.: Stackpole, 1959. As the title implies, Mitchell uses personal correspondence and photographs to trace the development of Colt's inventions and company.

Reif, Rita. "The Man Behind the Guns That Won the West." *The New York Times*, December 1, 1996, p. H45. Provides biographical information about Colt and his role in the Industrial Revolution. Includes comments by Colt biographer Walter Hosley (see above).

SEE ALSO: Wild Bill Hickok; Annie Oakley.

RELATED ARTICLES in *Great Events from History: The Nineteenth Century, 1801-1900:* February 25, 1836: Colt Patents the Revolver; January 29, 1886: Benz Patents the First Practical Automobile.

AUGUSTE COMTE

French philosopher

One of the greatest systematic thinkers of nineteenth century France, Comte is considered the founder of positivism, a philosophy that saw the evolution of new ideas as the shaping force in history and regarded the empirical method of science as the only valid basis of knowledge. Comte sought to extend the method of science to the study of people, coining the word "sociology." His later thought took a Romantic swing, emphasizing the primacy of the feelings, glorifying religion in a secular guise, and proposing a highly regulated social order.

BORN: January 19, 1798; Montpellier, France
DIED: September 5, 1857; Paris, France
ALSO KNOWN AS: Isidore-Auguste-Marie-François-Xavier Comte (full name)
AREAS OF ACHIEVEMENT: Philosophy, historiography, religion and theology

EARLY LIFE

Isidore-Auguste-Marie-François-Xavier Comte (kahnt) was the eldest of his parents' four children. His father, Louis-Auguste Comte, was a tax official, a man of strict habits and narrow interests; his mother, Félicité-Rosalie Boyer, twelve years older than her husband, was a warm, emotional person who devoted her life to her children. Both parents were devout Roman Catholics and royalists.

Young Comte was nearsighted and small—his head and trunk seemed too large for his limbs. He had an extraordinary memory, however, and proved to be a brilliant student in the local lycée, winning prizes in Latin and mathematics, on occasion substituting for his teacher. At the age of fifteen, he was admitted to the prestigious École Polytechnique in Paris. There his diligence and acuteness led his awed classmates to nickname him "the philosopher."

Napoleon I had given this school, like Comte's lycée, a military tone and discipline. However, Comte, who at the age of fourteen had already rebelled against the religion of his parents by becoming an atheist, was one of the most unruly students at the school. Comte was a prominent spokesperson for the students when they supported Napoleon during his futile attempt to regain control of France in 1815. Later, Comte was judged by authorities a ringleader of a student effort to oust an unpopular professor, a conflict so heated that it served as a pretext for temporarily closing the school. He was sent home and was placed under police surveillance.

In 1817, Comte returned to Paris, studying independently and tutoring students in mathematics to support himself. The possibility of an offer to teach in a new American polytechnical school led Comte to immerse himself in the writings of Thomas Paine and Benjamin Franklin, but the project was not funded. Comte therefore became secretary to the exuberant social philosopher Henri Saint-Simon, borrowing the broad outlines of many of his own later doctrines while writing essays and articles that appeared under Saint-Simon's name. Comte served Saint-Simon for seven years but was uncomfortable with the religious bent of Saint-Simon's late writings and believed that his social theory needed a more systematic theoretical foundation. A critical preface by Saint-Simon to an essay Comte published under his own name precipitated the end of the relationship in 1824.

By then, the headstrong Comte had dropped his first name, Isidore, in favor of Auguste; had fathered an illegitimate daughter, who would die at the age of nine, by an Italian woman; and was living with Caroline Massin, herself the offspring of an unmarried provincial actress, whom he had known for three years and would marry in 1825. He praised her kindness, grace, wit, and cheerful disposition; she had been sold by her debauched mother to a young lawyer when in her mid-teens and was by this time a registered prostitute. It was partly to help her get her name off police rolls that he agreed to the marriage.

The marriage was marred by Comte's seeming indifference to their straitened economic circumstances and his wife's occasional disappearances. A final separation came in 1842. Nevertheless, his wife had provided needed support through the difficult period when Comte produced his most important work, the six-volume *Cours de philosophie positive* (1830-1842; course on positive philosophy). The most important part of this support came shortly after he had begun the series of seventy-two lectures out of which this book grew, when he had a nervous breakdown so severe that he was incapacitated for more than a year (1826-1827), was judged incurably insane by one physician, and attempted suicide.

LIFE'S WORK

Comte wanted to be a philosopher-prophet, like Francis Bacon, Nicolas Condorcet, or his mentor Saint-Simon. Living in an era scarred by deep social antagonisms and warring ideologies, he dreamed of creating a persuasive philosophical synthesis that could restore both spiritual and social order to European society. Such solid intellectual underpinning was lacking, he believed, in Saint-Simon's thought. Comte reasoned that if the method of science could be extended to every aspect of life, the intellectual unity that had characterized medieval Europe could be restored on a more lasting basis, and unity of thought would bring social order.

Auguste Comte. (Library of Congress)

Comte interpreted the rise of science and its extension to the study of humanity in the context of a general theory of human intellectual development he borrowed, via Saint-Simon, from the eighteenth century economist and statesman Jacques Turgot. The "law of the three stages" held that as positive knowledge of nature gradually replaces earlier tendencies to attribute much in life to unseen powers, thought moves from a theological to a metaphysical stage, replacing imagined divinities with nonobservable abstractions. However, they too fall to skepticism, and a scientific or positive outlook triumphs. For Comte, this concept constituted a general theory of history, accounting for institutional as well as intellectual development.

Comte held that theological societies have military political systems, metaphysical societies have a juristic social organization, and positivist societies will have an industrial polity. A positivist approach to phenomena came first in the simple sciences, such as astronomy and physics, while metaphysical or even theological modes of thought linger where phenomena are more complex. Because sciences dealing with the latter must rest on the foundation of more general, simpler ones, of necessity new positive sciences emerged in the following order: mathematics, astronomy, physics, chemistry, biology, and sociology. Although the later volumes of the book contain many prescriptive judgments about the future needs of society that now would not be termed scientific, *Cours de philosophie positive* was a tour de force, a landmark in both philosophy and the historical study of science.

With the publication of his philosophy and the growth of his reputation, Comte secured academic posts at the Institut Laville and the École Polytechnique. His outspoken criticisms of some academicians at the school led to the rejection of his candidacy for a chair there. He retaliated by appealing to European public opinion through a bitter attack on his opponents in the preface of the last volume of *Cours de philosophie positive*, an action that brought his final break with Caroline and cost him his positions. His financial difficulties led admirers in both France and England (including John Stuart Mill, later a critic) to raise funds on his behalf.

Comte lived modestly through his last years. The most significant episode in this period was a passionate emotional relationship with a beautiful but unhappy and ill young woman, Clotilde de Vaux. He had known her only a year and a half when she died in the spring of 1846 from tuberculosis. However, her memory absorbed him through his remaining years. He dedicated his late work to her, including a second monumental book, the four-volume *Système de politique positive* (1851-1854; *System of Positive Polity*, 1875-1877). He declared that it was she who had taught him the importance of feelings.

System of Positive Polity is a work that prophesies in great detail the future of Western society. Its vision is in part a realization of the plan of Comte's youth, but it reveals a remarkable shift in emphasis from reason and scientific understanding to the emotions. He had come to regard as futile his earlier dream of achieving intellectual unity through science. Now he made humankind's wants, that is, morality, the foundation for intellectual unity in positivism. The emphasis in this work had been presaged in his *Considerations sur le pouvoir spirituel* (1826; considerations on spiritual power), in which he wrote that the Roman Catholic Church, shorn of its supernaturalism, might provide an ideal structural model for positivist society. It was probably Comte's intense feelings for de Vaux that brought this hitherto inveterate rationalist to emphasize the heart above intelligence and knowledge, and to prescribe a cult of womanhood as the emotional center of his secular religion.

The object of worship in this system, which T. H. Huxley dubbed Catholicism minus Christianity, was humanity itself, past, present, and future. Scientist-priests were to control both religion and education, positivist in content, which would be the foundation of the new social order. Actual political power, Comte declared, would rest with bankers and industrialists, whom economic developments were already thrusting to the fore. They would, however, operate under the spiritual guidance of the priests. The new industrial working class, its morals strengthened by religion and examples of feminine virtue, would accept the dominion of the industrialists but also give full backing to the priests. The latter, as shapers of powerful public opinion, would ensure that the workers's interests were safeguarded.

Thus, Comte, who earlier had declared the intellect his lord, now saw the feelings, not reason, as the key to social unity. He contended that humans have a benevolent instinct—coining the word "altruism" to describe it—but that it is weak unless nurtured by good institutions. This need provided Comte a rationale for dictating the features of his positivist utopia in obsessive detail, from career paths to private devotions, from indissoluble marriage and perpetual widowhood to the particular heroes of human progress who were to be honored on each day of the (thirteen-month) positivist calendar.

SIGNIFICANCE

Like many in his age, including his German contemporary Georg Wilhelm Friedrich Hegel (whose complex philosophy paralleled Auguste Comte's in remarkable ways), Comte was a visionary, a self-proclaimed prophet for the ages who believed that he had unveiled profound truths with sweeping social implications. As was true of most other utopian visionaries, his concrete predictions were off the mark. Thus, while many were dazzled by the younger Comte's brilliance as an interpreter of the evolution of science and defender of its method in all realms of thought, the impact of his later writings was quite limited. Whereas a number of intellectuals, including Hippolyte-Adolphe Taine, Ernest Renan, and the logical positivists of the twentieth century, inherited his skepticism about nonempirical thinking, his religion of humanity was essentially stillborn, even though it championed the Humanism made popular by the Enlightenment.

In emphasizing the limits of reason and the importance of emotions, Comte was at one with the Romantic movement, as were many other major writers of the nineteenth century. His sympathy for medieval institutions, if not medieval belief, was also widely shared by other intellectuals of his time, particularly in literature and art—it was the period of Walter Scott and Gothic revival, the period when the works of Dante (whom Comte much admired) were finally translated into English.

Comte's humorless preoccupation with order and perfection was not well suited to winning for him a broad and enthusiastic following. He antagonized onetime supporters such as Mill with his obsession with ordering—down to the level of minute details of thought and feeling, artistic creation, and religious devotion—the life of positivist society, for which he planned to be the high priest.

Comte's indifference to democracy and individual freedom separated him from the liberals of his day. His interest in old forms without old content alienated conservatives, and he had no interest in the growing nationalism that was to provide yet another basis for ideology in the decades that followed him. Curiously, his thought had an affinity to a modern development for which he could have had little sympathy. In his obsession with uniformity and order, his vision of a society that sought to control every facet of humanity's intellectual and emotional life for social ends dictated by a small elite group, he was a precursor of the totalitarian movements of the twentieth century.

—*R. Craig Philips*

FURTHER READING

Comte, Auguste. *A General View of Positivism.* Translated by J. H. Bridges. London: Trubner, 1865. Reprint. New York: Speller, 1957. This book, written during the ferment of the revolutions of 1848 and published shortly after Comte founded the Positivist Society, is an excellent introduction to his later social philosophy. It relates his ideas to contemporaneous social developments.

Gould, F. J. *Auguste Comte.* London: Watts, 1920. This biography, though brief, provides a balanced survey of Comte's life and thought. It gives more attention than does the Sokoloff (see below) volume to those who made up his intellectual circle and treats his ideas more fully. The curious positivist calendar is published in the appendix.

Lévy-Bruhl, Lucien. *The Philosophy of Auguste Comte.* Translated by Kathleen de Beaumont-Klein. New York: G. P. Putnam's Sons, 1903. A thorough and sympathetic treatment of Comte's thought by a highly regarded French scholar. Takes issue with Mill's contention that there are serious discrepancies between Comte's early and later writings.

Manuel, Frank. *The Prophets of Paris.* Cambridge, Mass.: Harvard University Press, 1961. This survey of a number of important French social philosophers devotes an illuminating chapter to Comte. The study provides a good perspective from which to assess Comte in relation to his intellectual milieu. Seen in the company of other visionaries, his detailed prescriptions are somewhat less puzzling.

Mill, John Stuart. *Auguste Comte and Positivism.* Ann Arbor: University of Michigan Press, 1961. First published in 1865, this critical assessment of Comte's ideas remains one of the most important books by an English author on Comte. Highly critical of Comte's later writings, it slights the elements of continuity they share with the rest of his work.

Pickering, Mary. *Auguste Comte: An Intellectual Biography.* New York: Cambridge University Press, 1993. The first of a projected two-volume intellectual biography. This volume recounts the events of Comte's life from birth to 1842, when he completed the scientific foundation of his philosophy.

Scharff, Robert C. *Comte After Positivism.* New York: Cambridge University Press, 1995. A reconsideration of Comte's philosophy. In the first part of the book, Scharff analyzes Comte's philosophy and explains how it was misinterpreted by John Stuart Mill. The second part of the book places Comte within the history of Positivism, with Scharff arguing that Comte is the only positivist who remains relevant today.

Sokoloff, Boris. *The "Mad" Philosopher: Auguste Comte.* New York: Vantage Press, 1961. A brief, readable biography that summarizes Comte's chief ideas while treating more fully the biographical context within which they developed. Gives more attention to his youth and his relationship with women than to his ties to other intellectuals.

SEE ALSO: Claude Bernard; Sophie Germain; Frederic Harrison; Thomas Henry Huxley; Ernest Renan; Hippolyte Taine.

RELATED ARTICLE in *Great Events from History: The Nineteenth Century, 1801-1900:* 1851-1854: Comte Advances His Theory of Positivism.

JOHN CONSTABLE
English painter

Constable combined a passion for nature with his conception of an ideal rural England to paint some of the most evocative and poetic landscapes of all time. His paintings have a timeless and rugged beauty that are more impressive now than during his own time, because this ordered world exists only in his landscapes.

BORN: June 11, 1776; East Bergholt, Suffolk, England
DIED: March 31, 1837; London, England
AREA OF ACHIEVEMENT: Art

EARLY LIFE

John Constable was the fourth of the six children of Golding Constable and Ann Watts. Like Rembrandt's father, Golding Constable was a miller, owner of water mills at Flatford and Dedham and two windmills at East Bergholt. He also shipped grain, imported coal, and served on the commission that oversaw shipping on the River Stout. In 1774, he had moved from Flatford to East Bergholt, a mile away, to live the life of a country squire in a newly built mansion.

Young Constable went to schools in Lavenham and Dedham, but his preoccupation with painting from an early age made him an inattentive pupil. Golding Constable had originally intended his second son—John's older brother was mentally impaired—to become a clergyman, but when the boy proved to be no scholar, it was decided that he should go into milling. Although Constable eventually worked in his father's mills for only a year, he boasted, as an adult, of his broad, sensitive miller's thumb, which enabled him to judge a sample of flour by sifting it between his thumb and forefinger.

Constable's interest in art found considerable encouragement. He was friends with John Dunthorne, an East Bergholt plumber, glazier, and amateur painter. The two often went sketching together. Constable's mother approved of his ambitions and arranged for him to be introduced to Sir George Beaumont, an amateur painter, collector of paintings, and patron of the arts, whose mother lived at Dedham. Beaumont introduced the aspiring artist to landscapes by such painters as Lorrain Claude and Thomas Girtin, allowed Constable to copy his pictures, and kept him up to date on the latest aesthetic debates. In 1796, Constable, while visiting his uncle in Edmonton, met John Thomas Smith, who was working as a drawing master there. Smith encouraged Constable to find the subjects for his landscapes in domestic scenes and taught him to paint what actually appeared rather than invent figures.

When Golding Constable forced his son to work in his countinghouse in 1797, Constable wrote: "I see plainly that it will be my lot to walk through life in a path contrary to that in which my inclination would lead me." He continued painting, and in 1799 he met a final major influence, Joseph Farington, a pupil of landscape painter Richard Wilson. Farington had him copy the old masters, especially Jacob van Ruysdael, who had influenced Thomas Gainsborough, Constable's fellow painter of Suffolk landscapes.

That same year, Constable finally began devoting his full energies to art, enrolling in the Royal Academy Schools in London, where he was to study until 1811. His early landscapes were considered clumsy, and too often, under the pressure of criticism, he subverted his individuality to make his paintings resemble the work of other artists. He painted well enough, however, to receive his first considerable commission, *Old Hall, East Bergholt*, in 1801.

LIFE'S WORK

In 1802, Constable turned down the post of drawing master at a military academy in High Wycombe. He wrote John Dunthorne that if he had accepted the position, "it would have been a death blow to all my prospects of perfection in the Art I love." That same year, he exhibited his first painting at the Royal Academy and bought a studio in East Bergholt, near his parents' house. By 1803, he was convinced that he could produce paintings that "shall be valuable to posterity."

Because Constable felt compelled to prove to his family that he could make a living as an artist, he began producing life-size portraits in the mornings at East Bergholt, beginning in 1804, while devoting his afternoons to landscapes. The artist described landscape as his "mistress": "'tis to her I look for fame, and all that the warmth of imagination renders dear to man." He continued painting portraits for years, and the work he did for hire also included painting the altarpiece for Brantham Church, repairing and copying paintings for Lord Dysart of Helmingham Hall, and painting the background for a portrait by another artist. As late as 1828, he painted a mermaid for an inn sign in Warwickshire.

Constable was breaking new ground by devoting his serious art to the scenery of East Anglia. During this period, the Lake District, North Wales, Scotland, and the Peak District were fashionable for painters; the Stour Valley was not. Constable wanted to paint that into which he had insight, and he thoroughly understood the history, botany, and agriculture of the Stour Valley. Constable's family found his subjects to be too ordinary and suggested that he paint more dramatic scenery. Such pressure may have resulted in a tour of the Lake District in 1806 that produced six landscapes exhibited at the Royal Academy over the following two years. Golding Constable was unimpressed by his son's progress and considered him to be "pursuing a shadow." However, the painter's father continued to finance his career. Family income supported Constable throughout his life.

Constable, a plain man with a sloping forehead and a beak of a nose, fell in love with Maria Bicknell in 1810. Her father was solicitor to the Admiralty, and her grandfather, the Reverend Dr. Durand Rhudde, was rector of East Bergholt. The wealthy Rhudde opposed his granddaughter's marriage plans because Constable refused to abandon art and earn a respectable living, and perhaps because of the artist's friendship with Dunthorne, reputedly an atheist. The Bicknell family gave in to the rector's wishes because Maria was expected to inherit his fortune. Her parents forbade Maria to meet with Constable, but the two continued to correspond. In 1811, Constable failed to appease Rhudde with a watercolor of his church.

Constable discovered another important inspiration for his landscapes in 1811, when he first visited Salisbury. Constable had met the bishop of Salisbury in 1798, when John Fisher was rector of Langham, and now met the bishop's nephew, Archdeacon John Fisher, who was to become his closest friend. The younger Fisher was a substitute for the enlightened public Constable hoped for but never found. Through his friendship with Fisher, Constable came to feel the same affection for Salisbury as he had for the Stour Valley. He exhibited *Salisbury: Morning* at the Royal Academy in 1812.

Despite showing numerous paintings at the Academy, Constable displayed few signs of becoming a professional painter, though he sold paintings for the first time in 1814. His mother's death the next year was a blow, for she had always sympathized with his ambitions, even though she believed he would have more success as a portrait painter.

Golding Constable died in 1816, and because his son's share of the estate placed the artist in a better financial situation, the Bicknells agreed to allow their daughter's marriage. As the wedding day approached, however, Constable began worrying about having less time for his painting and wanted to postpone the ceremony. John Fisher soothed his friend's fears and married the couple at the church of St. Martin-in-the-Fields in London on October 2, 1816. The Constables spent part of their honeymoon with Fisher and his wife at their vicarage in Osmington, Dorsetshire. Maria's father eventually grew to approve of Constable, and her grandfather relented enough to leave her four thousand pounds. The Constables lived in Hampstead for most of their marriage, and the painter spent his last extended period in East Anglia in the summer of 1817. The first of the couple's seven children was born at the end of that year.

The White Horse, the first of Constable's large paintings of a canal scene on the Stour, was well received when exhibited at the Royal Academy in 1819. Though this success led to his election as an associate member of the Academy, Constable's full acceptance by this institution, which determined what was officially art in England, was not to come for several years. John Fisher purchased *The White Horse* and was to buy many more Constable paintings. The artist wrote his friend in 1820, "I should almost faint . . . when I am standing before my large canvases was I not cheered and encouraged by your friendship and approbation." He also confided to Fisher that he feared, for his family's sake, that he would never be a popular artist but must be reconciled to pleasing himself.

Living in Hampstead, Constable felt isolated from his aesthetic roots. "The Londoners with all their ingenuity as artists," he wrote in 1821, "know nothing of the feeling of a country life (the essence of Landscape)—any more than a hackney coach horse knows of pasture." This sense of isolation, together with the Royal Academy's indifference to a man it considered a pretentious amateur obsessed by rural scenery and the lack of economic rewards, led to Constable's seeing himself as an outsider in the art world. Regarding his failure to be elected to the Academy in 1822 he wrote, "I have nothing to help me but my stark naked merit, and although that (as I am told) far exceeds all the other candidates—it is not heavy enough."

Constable's best-known work, *The Hay Wain* (given its name by Fisher), was shown at the Royal Academy in 1821 and later at the British Institution. This painting, *View on the Stour near Dedham*, and *View on Hampstead Heath* were exhibited in Paris in 1824 and were immensely popular. They were acclaimed by French artists, especially Eugène Delacroix, and were awarded a gold medal by Charles X. This success encouraged French art students to show more interest in landscapes.

When Constable began selling his works to the Paris dealers John Arrowsmith and Claude Schroth in 1824, he was finally making money. A disagreement with Arrowsmith the next year, however, ended their relationship, and Schroth went out of business soon afterward. Constable's relative lack of success was as much the result of his personality as of his unfashionableness in English art circles. He had a reputation for being difficult with patrons and for being coarse and slanderous about his fellow artists. He is reported to have been a malicious gossip and was disliked by many for his sarcasm. In addition, he referred to his paintings as his "children" and was unwilling to part with art he considered successful. He wrote that he loved such paintings too well "to expose them to the taunts of the ignorant."

Constable's financial problems were solved unexpectedly in 1827 by the death of his father-in-law, who left a larger fortune than had been anticipated. This burden lifted, Constable wrote, "I shall stand before a 6 foot canvas with a mind at ease (thank God)."

This ease of mind, however, was short-lived. Worn out by childbearing—the last was born in January, 1828—Maria Constable, who had for years suffered from tuberculosis, died November 23, 1828, at forty-one. Constable was devastated by her death, and his landscapes began to become lonelier, more distanced; he increasingly saw nature as unstable. His mourning of Maria can be seen in *Hadleigh Castle. The Mouth of the Thames—morning after a stormy night* (1829). The aftermath of a storm, the ruined castle, and a lonely shepherd reflect his mental state, his sadness at the impermanence of human endeavor.

Constable was at last elected to the Royal Academy in 1829 but by only a single vote. Sir Thomas Lawrence, president of the Academy, told him that he was lucky to have been elected at all, because several painters of historical subjects—considered superior to landscape artists—had also been under consideration. Fisher called his friend's election "the triumph of real Art over spurious Art . . . of patient moral integrity over bare chicanery." The very next year, the Academy's hanging committee, of which Constable was a member, rejected his *Watermeadows at Salisbury* as a "nasty green thing."

After exhibiting the unusually large number of eight paintings at the Royal Academy in 1832, Constable began to work less because of rheumatism. He also experienced more sadness as both John Fisher and John Dunthorne, who had become his assistant, died. Constable called his friendship with Fisher "the pride—the honour—and grand stimulus of my life."

Constable died, probably of angina, on March 31, 1837. While working on *Arundel Mill and Castle* three days before, he is reported to have said, "It is neither too warm nor too cold, too light nor too dark, and this constitutes everything in a picture."

SIGNIFICANCE

John Constable's closest friend in his final years was the American painter C. R. Leslie, who published a biography of him in 1843, despite his belief that the English public would be indifferent to his subject. Although Constable labored under the shadows of his fellow landscapists Thomas Gainsborough and J. M. W. Turner, his genius was occasionally recognized during his lifetime. Critic Robert Hunt referred to him as the quintessentially English painter in 1823, and *The Times*, in 1827, called him "unquestionably the first landscape painter of the day."

Throughout his career, Constable was discouraged by his lack of recognition, though he occasionally agreed with critics that his landscapes were not as finished as they might have been. His work was not appreciated, according to Constable, because it "flatters nobody by *imitation*, it courts nobody by *smoothness*, it tickles nobody by *petiteness*, it is without either *fal de lal* or *fiddle de dee*, how then can I hope to be popular?" He was confident, however, that his art would eventually be recognized. While painting *Trees Near Hampstead Church* in 1821, he commented that the painting would one day be worth as much as the field it depicted.

Constable's reputation increased slowly after his death, but it did not begin to assume its present status until 1888, when one of his daughters gave nearly one hundred paintings and three hundred drawings to the Victoria and Albert Museum. These paintings, unseen by the public for half a century, could then be appreciated because of similar work done in the interim, especially by the French Impressionists. By this time, however, these artists had forgotten how Constable had influenced their mentors during the 1820's.

Constable's landscapes reflect what Leslie called a "peculiarly social" view of nature, because he painted scenes abounding in human associations. His paintings are full of cottages, farmhouses, churches, boats, wagons, and human figures, almost always in motion, engaged in some worthwhile activity. The interrelatedness of humans and nature reflects the artist's view of an ordered, moral world. The inseparability of humanity and nature in Constable's art has led many to see his work as the equivalent of the Romantic poetry of William Wordsworth. The power of his paintings comes in part from their being reminiscences of places to which Constable was emotionally attached. Such qualities help engender in his art a timeless, rugged beauty more impressive now than during his own time, because this ordered world exists only in his landscapes.

—*Michael Adams*

FURTHER READING

Constable, John. *John Constable's Correspondence*. 6 vols. Edited by R. B. Beckett. London: H. M. Stationery Office, 1962-1976. Main source of biographical information about the painter. These volumes include substantial explanatory material.

Cormack, Malcolm. *Constable*. Cambridge, England: Cambridge University Press, 1986. This critical biography emphasizes Constable's part in the Romantic movement and his scientific attitude toward landscape, particularly in relation to weather. Beautifully illustrated.

Fleming-Williams, Ian, and Leslie Parris. *The Discovery of Constable*. London: Holmes & Meier, 1984. Explains Constable's gradual rise to fame in the century following his death. Examines the role of his descendants in the reappraisal of his work. Also looks at his forgers and imitators.

Gadney, Reg. *Constable and His World*. New York: W. W. Norton, 1976. Brief overview of Constable's life and career; for general readers.

Lambert, Ray. *John Constable and the Theory of Landscape Painting*. New York: Cambridge University Press, 2004. Lambert studies Constable's landscapes and relevant writings to determine how the artist's aesthetic ideas led him to create landscape art.

Leslie, C. R. *Memoirs of the Life of John Constable, R.A.* London: J. Carpenter, 1843. 3d ed. London: Phaidon Press, 1995. Biography by the artist's close friend, first published in 1843. Based primarily upon Constable's substantial correspondence.

Parkinson, Ronald. *John Constable: The Man and His Art*. London: Victoria & Albert Museum, 1998. A series of essays about Constable, including an analysis of his paintings at the Victoria and Albert Museum, his way of working, and his influence on other artists.

Peacock, Carlos. *John Constable: The Man and His Work*. Greenwich: New York Graphic Society, 1965. Rev. ed. 1971. This three-part study looks at Constable's life, Romanticism, and the artist's relation to the sea. Discusses his influence on French painting.

Reynolds, Graham. *Constable: The Natural Painter*. New York: McGraw-Hill, 1965. Analysis of Constable's work interwoven with biographical information in study by the then-keeper of the Constable collection at the Victoria and Albert Museum.

Rosenthal, Michael. *Constable*. London: Thames and Hudson, 1987. Covers the highlights of Constable's life while providing an overview of his work. Emphasizes the social, political, and moral context of Constable's art.

Thornes, John E. *John Constable's Skies: A Fusion of Art and Science*. Birmingham, England: University of Birmingham Press, 1999. Thornes, a meteorologist, analyzes Constable's sky and weather paintings from a meterological perspective.

SEE ALSO: Eugène Delacroix; Vincent van Gogh; J. M. W. Turner.

RELATED ARTICLES in *Great Events from History: The Nineteenth Century, 1801-1900:* 1823-1831: Hokusai Produces *Thirty-Six Views of Mount Fuji*; Fall, 1848: Pre-Raphaelite Brotherhood Begins.

JAY COOKE
American financier

The foremost investment banker during the mid-nineteenth century, Cooke pioneered new ways of mobilizing the savings of Americans for productive ends. His banking innovations made possible many of the great financial undertakings of his time.

BORN: August 10, 1821; Sandusky, Ohio
DIED: February 18, 1905; Ogontz, Pennsylvania
AREAS OF ACHIEVEMENT: Government and politics, business

EARLY LIFE

Jay Cooke was the third son of Eleutheros and Martha Cooke, who had relocated in several moves from New England to the Lake Erie settlement of Sandusky. Eleutheros was an ardent Whig politician and served in Congress for a term when Jay was a young boy. The family atmosphere was devoutly Protestant. Jay attended public school in Sandusky until the age of fourteen, when he ended his formal education and took a job as a clerk in a general store.

After a year at work, Cooke left Ohio for St. Louis, staying there a year, until the commercial disruption following the Panic of 1837 caused him to return to Sandusky. Still only sixteen, Cooke left Sandusky in the spring of 1838 for Philadelphia, where he obtained work with his brother-in-law's canal transport company. The firm failed shortly after Cooke's arrival in the city, and he returned once more to Sandusky, staying only a few months, until he was lured back to Philadelphia with a job offer from the banker E. W. Clark. From 1839 to 1857, Cooke worked in the Clark banking house, first as an office boy; soon, because of his head for figures and nose for profits, he became a partner at the age of twenty-one.

An early photograph taken of Cooke during the 1840's shows a young man of modest stature, clear eyes, and somber nature. He looks as if he were trying to look older than he was. This fits the character of the man: earnest, sober, deeply religious, and a family man. Cooke took his older brothers, Henry and Pitt, into partnership when each needed money and supported them throughout numerous misadventures for most of their lives. He started his own family shortly after his 1844 marriage to Dorothea Allen, and the couple had eight children, though not all survived childhood. The Cookes did not entertain extensively, keeping the Episcopal Church at the center of their lives.

As a partner at E. W. Clark and Co., Cooke practiced mercantile banking as it existed before the Civil War. The profits of the firm came from dealing in "domestic exchange," that is, bank notes from various parts of the country that the firm discounted according to risk. The nation in those days had no official government currency except metallic money, so the paper medium of daily exchange was provided by private bankers. With the bank notes of so many banks in circulation, the banker had to judge shrewdly the worth of the paper that purported to be "good as gold." The firm also lent money for short periods of time to Philadelphia merchants and engaged in the commodity trade.

As Cooke prospered at E. W. Clark and Co. during the 1850's, he began to invest his own money in a number of outside ventures. These included a daring land speculation in Iowa and Minnesota that originated as a project to give work to his bankrupt brother Pitt. Cooke sent Pitt west to the Iowa prairies to obtain land from the government at prices below $1.25 an acre, with careful guidance about how to resell it to incoming farmers at three and four dollars an acre. The speculation made so much money that Pitt paid his debts and Cooke became even more wealthy. Growing restless as a junior partner at E. W. Clark and Co., he left the firm in 1857 and devoted his attention to private investing, particularly in railroads, for the next few years. He decided to reenter the banking business on the eve of the American Civil War and opened Jay Cooke and Co. on January 1, 1861.

LIFE'S WORK

President Abraham Lincoln took office to find the national treasury nearly empty, and with the firing on Fort Sumter, he faced a greater challenge in raising money than in raising volunteers to fight in the Civil War. Wars are expensive to fight, and governments can finance them either by taxation, borrowing, or printing paper money. The Confederate government in Richmond chose the last option and, by the end of the war, the Confederacy had an inflation rate of 5,000 percent. The Union government of Lincoln chose to borrow to pay for the war, a better strategy, but one that worked only because of the efforts of Jay Cooke.

The traditional method of government finance was to offer government bonds at competitive auction to private bankers. This practice worked well enough in peacetime, but in 1861, many bankers were unsure whether the

Union would survive to pay the debt. Secretary of the Treasury Salmon P. Chase insisted on selling the bonds at par (one hundred cents on the dollar), but most bankers considered them to be too risky at that price. The Treasury and the nation muddled through 1861, unable to raise enough money but uncertain of any other way of doing business. Cooke, however, had an idea about how to raise hundreds of millions for the war effort.

Through his older brother Henry, a Washington journalist, Cooke approached Secretary Chase and offered to be the government's sales agent for government bonds. For a small fee, Cooke promised to sell all the bonds that the government could issue. He based this confident assertion on his earlier experience as the fiscal agent for the state of Pennsylvania in selling a bond issue of three million dollars. He had simply marketed the bonds directly to the public at par, bypassing other investment bankers.

As the war turned against the Union during the summer of 1862, Chase became more receptive to Cooke's idea, if only out of desperation. In October, the secretary appointed Jay Cooke and Co. sole agent to sell fifty million dollars of government bonds at 6 percent interest. The bonds were due in twenty years, but the government could redeem them in five, hence the popular name of the debt was "5-20's." Cooke promised to sell a million dollars a day of 5-20's and took a fee of one half of 1 percent, on the first ten million dollars worth sold, and 0.375 percent on the remainder.

Cooke faced two challenges in selling the debt. First, he had to build a distribution network of retail sales agents to sell the bonds, and second, he had to persuade the public to buy them. In each case, he was spectacularly successful. Cooke appointed twenty-five hundred subagents to sell bonds throughout the Union and, by using the telegraph, effectively coordinated the efforts of this sales team. A heavy use of newspaper advertising and handbills worked to convince the public of the patriotic necessity of buying government bonds. Any Northern newspaper of 1863 was likely to carry a prominent ad placed by Cooke urging citizens to buy bonds.

The sales campaign began in earnest in February, 1863, and by the end of June, Cooke had marketed more than $175 million in 5-20's. Over the next seven months, until the loan was oversubscribed by late January, 1864, he sold more than $325 million. After paying advertising costs, office expenses, and commissions to the subagents, Cooke was left with a commission of perhaps one sixteenth of 1 percent of the sales. He did not get rich selling the bonds; rather, he earned something even greater, the title Financier of the Union.

The government bond business made Jay Cooke and Co. the best-known banking house in the United States, and this when Cooke was still in his early forties. In 1865, he repeated his earlier coup in helping the government to finance a new issue of bonds, the so-called 7-30's. This loan drive was even more extensive and more successful than the 1863 issue of 5-20's. From January, 1865, through the end of July of that year, Cooke managed to sell more than $800 million worth of new government bonds. The sales force was more than double that of the earlier sale, and for the 7-30's, Cooke even had itinerant salespeople follow the progress of the Union Army in the South to sell the Union public debt to the conquered rebels.

For several years after the war, Jay Cooke and Co. engaged in further government debt financings. By 1869, the government finance business had wound down and opportunities for profit appeared elsewhere. Cooke had some antebellum experience in railroad finance, and it was in this direction that he took his firm in 1869. That year, he agreed to be the banker and agent for the Northern Pacific Railway Company, a line projected to link Lake Superior with Puget Sound on the Pacific. The nation had just completed one transcontinental railroad in the Union Pacific-Central Pacific, linking Omaha to San Francisco, but the Northern Pacific promised to be the largest construction project in American history.

Cooke was attracted to the Northern Pacific for a number of reasons. He had speculated in Minnesota lands during the 1850's and believed in the future of the Northwest. He renewed his land speculation near the tiny settlement of Duluth in 1866, and when he visited the place in 1868, he saw it as the next Chicago, a mighty future metropolis handling the produce of the American West. Early in 1869, Cooke sold bonds for the Lake Superior and Mississippi Railroad, linking Duluth to St. Paul, and the success of that venture persuaded the investor to take on the Northern Pacific's tasks of raising capital to build the two-thousand-mile railroad.

The original financing plan intended for the Northern Pacific to build westward in anticipation of the traffic along the line. This, together with land sales from its magnificent fifty-million acre land grant from Congress, would finance further construction, operations, and debt service. This plan proved too optimistic, because there was almost no white settlement along the route. Cooke managed to raise five million dollars for construction in 1870, but only with great difficulty. His efforts to interest European bankers and investors failed, as they thought the Northern Pacific too risky.

In 1871, Cooke began a public campaign to sell $100 million in Northern Pacific bonds at 7.3 percent interest, the goal of the drive being to raise enough money from small investors to complete the road. Cooke used the same techniques he had learned in selling government bonds during the war: a nationwide network of subagents and hundreds of thousands of dollars spent on advertising. Indeed, Cooke made the Northern Pacific bond-selling slogan, "Safe! Profitable! Permanent!" ubiquitous in the country in 1871 and 1872. The results, however, were disappointing. Cooke only sold about sixteen million dollars worth of bonds in 1871 and 1872. The investing public judged the Northern Pacific too risky an enterprise, despite the high interest rate offered and the reputation for reliability that Cooke brought as the railroad's banker.

Gradually, Cooke crossed the line between banker and promoter of the Northern Pacific. The railroad repeatedly overdrew its account with Cooke's bank and showed signs of mismanagement. The road's problem was that in its first few years, it had substantial expenses and little revenue. The Cooke banking houses in Philadelphia, New York, Washington, and London became overextended in Northern Pacific affairs by 1872, and when a tightening of the money market in 1873 pressed banks in general, Jay Cooke and Co. was forced to close its doors: It no longer had sufficient reserves to pay the demands of its depositors. The shock of the failure of the leading private bank in the United States caused a panic on Wall Street and ushered in the worst business recession Americans had experienced to that date.

Cooke declared bankruptcy in 1873 and lost most of the multimillion-dollar fortune he had accumulated. He spent the next several years satisfying his creditors, and by 1880, he resumed business as an investor in Western mining ventures. He made a second fortune before his death but preferred to live a quiet life as an old man devoted to family and church. He died in Ogontz, Pennsylvania, in 1905.

SIGNIFICANCE

Jay Cooke performed three great services in his adult life as a banker. First, he earned the title Financier of the Union because he came to the rescue of an empty Treasury at a critical time in the Civil War. Had Cooke not successfully sold the 5-20's to the public in 1863, the Treasury would have probably had to resort to extensive printing of paper money, much as the Confederates did. The result would have been ruinous inflation and perhaps a different outcome to the war.

Second, even though Cooke failed in his endeavor to make the Northern Pacific a money-maker during the early 1870's, he did succeed in getting the road launched, and his vision of the Northwest as a great grain-, timber-, and coal-producing region of free and prosperous Americans did come true. Despite his 1873 bankruptcy, Cooke lived long enough to see his idea of the Northwest emerge as emigrants from the eastern United States and immigrants from Europe poured into the region. While Duluth never became the next Chicago, it developed into the greatest inland grain, coal, and iron port in North America, and the citizens of that city gratefully remembered Jay Cooke's part in their rise.

Third, Cooke helped change the nature of investment banking. Prior to his financing the Civil War debt, private banking consisted of discounting notes and short-term loans from bankers to merchants. The savings of average Americans were not tapped in any way except through a handful of small savings-and-loan associations. Cooke changed that by reaching out to hundreds of thousands of Americans in the war and appealing for their small holdings to support the cause. In the century following, Wall Street would devote increasing amounts of time and effort to attracting the savings of the individual investor. Without Cooke's innovation, the great financial undertakings of the day could not have taken place. Without the savings of millions of people, the government debt and the great industrial projects, such as the railroads, could not have been funded.

—*James W. Oberly*

FURTHER READING

Cooke, Jay, et al. "Guide to the Lands of the Northern Pacific Railroad in Minnesota." In *The Fruits of Land Speculation*, edited by Paul Wallace Gates. New York: Arno Press, 1979. This pamphlet amply demonstrates Cooke's talent as a promoter. It explains the route of the Northern Pacific and the advantages of moving to the country west of Duluth.

Hammond, Bray. *Sovereignty and an Empty Purse: Banks and Politics in the Civil War*. Princeton, N.J.: Princeton University Press, 1970. This book examines how the Treasury found itself in desperate condition in 1861, and how it mobilized itself to raise the necessary funds to prosecute the war. The author treats at length Cooke's relationship to the Treasury.

Harnsberger, John L. *Jay Cooke and Minnesota: The Formative Years of the Northern Pacific Railroad, 1868-1873*. New York: Arno Press, 1981. Recounts Cooke's role in financing and promoting the railroad.

Larson, Henrietta M. *Jay Cooke: Private Banker*. Cambridge, Mass.: Harvard University Press, 1936. This is the standard biography of Cooke, concentrating on his banking career from the 1840's through the 1873 failure. Among biographies of businesspeople, this is one of the most outstanding.

Minnigerode, Meade. *Certain Rich Men*. New York: G. P. Putnam's Sons, 1927. Reprint. Freeport, N.Y.: Books for Libraries Press, 1970. This book consists of biographies of wealthy Americans of the late nineteenth century. The contrast between Cooke and some of his less scrupulous colleagues is noteworthy.

Oberholtzer, Ellis Paxton. *Jay Cooke: Financier of the Civil War*. Philadelphia: George W. Jacobs, 1907. Oberholtzer was the first to make use of the magnificent Jay Cooke Papers manuscript collection at the Historical Society of Pennsylvania. There is considerable emphasis on the private side of Cooke's life.

Sinisi, Kyle S. *Sacred Debts: State Civil War Claims and American Federalism, 1861-1880*. New York: Fordham University Press, 2003. Innovate study of the post-Civil War struggle between the states and the federal government over payment of the $468 million debt left over after the war.

Trescott, Paul B. *Financing American Enterprise: The Story of Commercial Banking*. New York: Harper & Row, 1961. This book has a good chapter on American railroad finance and puts the Northern Pacific episode in perspective.

SEE ALSO: Salmon P. Chase; Abraham Lincoln.

RELATED ARTICLE in *Great Events from History: The Nineteenth Century, 1801-1900:* February 25, 1863-June 3, 1864: Congress Passes the National Bank Acts.

WILLIAM FOTHERGILL COOKE AND CHARLES WHEATSTONE

English inventor and English physicist

From the joining of Cooke's entrepreneurial skills and Wheatstone's scientific knowledge came the world's first commercial telegraph network. In addition to his pioneering telegraph work with Cooke, Wheatstone also made valuable contributions to later developments in telegraph as well as dynamo technology, electrical engineering, and the physics of sound, light, and electricity.

WILLIAM FOTHERGILL COOKE

BORN: May 4, 1806; Ealing, Middlesex, England
DIED: June 25, 1879; Farnham, Surrey, England
ALSO KNOWN AS: Sir William Fothergill Cooke

SIR CHARLES WHEATSTONE

BORN: February 6, 1802; Barnswood, Gloucester, England
DIED: October 19, 1875; Paris, France
AREAS OF ACHIEVEMENT: Engineering, science and technology

EARLY LIVES

William Fothergill Cooke was born near Ealing, Middlesex, England. His father, William Cooke, was a surgeon, then professor of anatomy at Durham College (later Durham University). After the customary classical studies at Durham, Cooke attended the University of Edinburgh, renowned for its medical school. The young man seemed destined to enter his father's profession, while his brother, the Reverend Thomas Fothergill Cooke of the Church of England, chose the cloth. At the age of twenty, though, Cooke quit his studies and entered the army of India as an ensign (January 8, 1826). However, army life, particularly in mutinous India, was capable of providing ample firsthand anatomical experience.

In 1836, after ten years of service, Cooke resigned his commission, hoping to return to medical studies in the classroom. He attended lectures on anatomy and physiology in Paris and learned to model anatomical sections in wax. He was rather skilled at wax modeling and prepared a number of models for his father's anatomy classes. Late in 1836, Cooke attended some lectures at the Anatomical Institute of Heidelberg, where he saw Professor Georg Wilhelm Muncke demonstrate an electric telegraph. Muncke had published numerous articles on electricity and had received the telegraph from another German scientist.

Excited by the idea of commercializing Muncke's demonstration apparatus, Cooke built a telegraph of his own during the next month, partly at Heidelberg and partly at Frankfurt. Upon returning to England, he obtained a conditional arrangement with the Liverpool and Manchester Railway Company to test his device in Liverpool's Lime Street tunnel. In early 1837, Cooke showed his telegraph to Peter Mark Roget, credited with discovering the persistence of vision, and Michael Faraday, perhaps the greatest English scientist of his day and the author of an important extended study of electrical phenomena. Upon their recommendation, he visited Professor Wheatstone.

Charles Wheatstone was born February 6, 1802, in Gloucester, England, the son of William Wheatstone, who made a living making and selling musical instruments. Charles was educated in a private school in Gloucester and early showed an aptitude for physics and mathematics. His family was of more modest means than that of Cooke, and Wheatstone had to learn a trade and earn a living. After an apprenticeship at an uncle's music shop, Wheatstone and his brother William began making and selling musical instruments in London in 1821.

Wheatstone was enthusiastic about the wave theory of light and believed that a wave model would also explain acoustical phenomena. While helping to run the music shop, he began experimenting in acoustics and cleverly combined his scientific interests with the commercial need to advertise the shop. Wheatstone exhibited his first invention, which he called an "enchanted lyre," at the music shop to attract public attention and business. He also wrote a paper that explained how the instrument worked and that used his wave theory of sound. The paper appeared in an English scientific journal in 1823 and was soon translated and republished in French and German. Wheatstone's scientific career had begun.

The ability to combine the scientific and the practical marked that career. For example, over the following decades, as he continued his work on acoustics, Wheatstone published several scientific articles and reaped practical financial reward from those studies with his invention of the concertina, which he patented in 1829. In 1834, in recognition of his important scientific work, he became professor of experimental physics at King's College, London. Wheatstone had become part of the London scientific establishment.

Wheatstone's scientific curiosity and interest in wave explanations of phenomena drew him deeper into the physics of light and electricity and into closer relationships with the prominent scientists of the day. On one occasion, he built an instrument for Faraday to measure the velocity of electricity. Wheatstone attempted to measure the velocity of light with it. As electricity fascinated him more and more, he began to wonder whether electricity could be used as a means of communication.

Charles Wheatstone. (Library of Congress)

Wheatstone obtained permission from the London and Birmingham Railway to conduct an experiment with an electric telegraph along their tracks. In a note appended to an account of a German telegraph, published in the *Magazine of Popular Science* on March 1, 1837, the editor mentioned that Wheatstone, the previous June, had given a lecture at King's College in which he proposed using the instrument he had built for Faraday as a kind of electric telegraph. At that point, William Cooke introduced himself to Wheatstone.

LIVES' WORK

The two men tested Cooke's telegraph in Wheatstone's laboratory over a wire some four and a half miles long: It failed. Instead of a signaling mechanism using electromagnets, Cooke suggested galvanometers, instruments that measured current by the deflection of a needle. That, however, had been Wheatstone's idea. The two men realized that each had something to contribute and decided on a partnership. In May, 1837, they jointly applied for a patent for a galvanometer, or, as it was called, a needle telegraph. The patent was granted on June 10, 1837, but only in November, 1837, did they formalize their partnership with an agreement. Cooke became their business manager, for which he received a certain percentage of the profits, and the remainder was to be divided equally between the two.

The first Cooke-Wheatstone telegraph began operating on July 25, 1837, between Euston Square (the terminus of the London and Birmingham railway) and Camden on a railroad line built on an inclined plane. The instruments required five needles and five line wires to transmit and receive, although the deflections of only two needles were required to form signals. As a result, for every mile of line, five miles of wire had to be strung.

Wheatstone largely returned to his scientific work. In 1837, he began publishing his "Contributions to the Physiology of Vision" and invented the stereoscope in 1838, which he described at a meeting of the British Association for the Advancement of Science. Meanwhile, Cooke sought to commercialize the Cooke-Wheatstone telegraph. In April, 1838, he signed an agreement with the Great Western Railway for a line between Paddington and West Drayton (completed on July 9, 1839). Full of confidence in the newly founded telegraph business, Cooke was married to Louisa Wheatley on June 5, 1838. Cooke's mother disapproved of the marriage, and Cooke received few letters from her afterward.

In early 1840, Cooke sold another line, this time to the London and Blackwall Railway (completed July, 1840). As telegraph sales increased, Cooke and Wheatstone sought to simplify their system, especially the number of line wires required. On the Blackwall line in 1841, Cooke and Wheatstone initiated the use of the earth return in their telegraph circuits, a practice invented by the Alsatian scientist Carl Auguste Steinheil. The earth return saved wire by having current pass through the ground. In 1842, they patented a version of their telegraph that had only two indicating needles and required a single line wire. An 1845 version operated with one needle that was deflected to the right or left. The Cooke-Wheatstone needle instruments were a great success; in 1885, there were about fifteen thousand in use in Great Britain.

As one railroad company after another bought a telegraph line, Cooke sought to expand the market for them. In 1842, he advertised in the *Railway Times* and invited engineers and "other parties" to look at their telegraph "adapted for mines, coal pits, docks, &c." One 1842 announcement even claimed the patronage of the queen and Prince Albert. Moreover, for one shilling, the public could see the telegraph function at either Paddington or Slough station. On September 1, 1846, the South Eastern Railway Company, which then had a telegraph line 132 miles long—the longest in the world at the time—permitted messages of twenty words to be sent for one and a half pence per mile with a five-shilling minimum charge. Despite the great expense, the era of public use of the telegraph had begun.

In 1845, Cooke and Wheatstone sold their telegraph business to the newly founded Electric Telegraph Company, whose head was John Lewis Ricardo, a member of Parliament and the nephew of the famed political economist David Ricardo. Cooke was one of the four other company directors. After obtaining an act of Parliament in 1846, the company greatly expanded the number of lines and, by 1847, had built 20 lines covering 1,250 miles and connecting 253 stations with nearly 400 instruments. An 1849 contract with the Post Office to run telegraph lines from the General Post Office to most of the large towns in England and Scotland further ensured the company's future. Messages of twenty words or less on these lines went for one pence the first fifty miles. In 1849, the company transmitted the first message directly between London and Manchester.

In contrast with the enormous success of the telegraph, relations between Cooke and Wheatstone were hardly friendly. Cooke wanted commercial success, as well as at least a part of the scientific glory. He objected to being seen as merely Wheatstone's sleeping partner. Their relationship became especially strained in 1840. The telegraph appeared bound for success, and Wheatstone, independent of Cooke, invented a large number of new instruments: a so-called dial telegraph, which received messages by pointing to letters arranged along the edge of a dial; a printing telegraph, which printed messages in alphabetical characters on a strip of paper; a magnetoelectric telegraph, which required no batteries; an electric clock; and a "chronoscope," an instrument for measuring durations of small intervals of time (one seventy-three thousandth of a second).

These inventions heaped press attention on Wheatstone as an inventor, without placing Cooke in the limelight. Angry letters were sent back and forth between Cooke and Wheatstone. Overtaken by jealousy, Cooke demanded, and Wheatstone insisted upon, arbitration of the question "Who invented the telegraph?" The arbitrators were Marc Isambard Brunel, engineer, acting for Cooke, and John Frederic Daniell, professor of chemistry at King's College, Wheatstone's colleague and friend. On April 27, 1841, they made their decision: Cooke had played the role of the entrepreneur and Wheatstone that of the scientist, leaving unanswered any question about the invention of the telegraph.

Cooke's discontent was not Wheatstone's only problem. On November 26, 1840, he read a paper before the Royal Society of London describing his electric clock. Alexander Bain, a mechanic employed by Wheatstone between August and December, 1840, accused Wheatstone of having stolen from him the idea of the electric clock and, in a later series of allegations, the printing telegraph as well. Wheatstone's electric clock, however, was an adaptation of his magnetoelectric telegraph, patented before Bain's tenure with Wheatstone.

After Cooke assumed his position on the board of the Electric Telegraph Company in 1845, telegraph business continued to consume his time and energy, and he stopped filing for telegraph patents. During the 1850's, Cooke's jealousy resurfaced and spilled out into a pamphlet war with Wheatstone. In 1865, emotionally and financially spent, he moved to the country, purchased a quarry, and obtained the first of several patents for inventions relating to stone mining. When Cooke was knighted in 1869, he was in such financial straits that he had to depend upon money raised by relatives and a Civil List pension.

In contrast, Wheatstone prospered. An April, 1843, agreement between Cooke and Wheatstone had paved the way for selling their joint patents to the Electric Telegraph Company, but also reserved solely to Wheatstone the rights to underwater and private telegraphy. Private telegraph lines were owned or leased by individuals or companies and usually connected distant offices or offices and warehouses. Created in 1860, the Universal Private Telegraph Company used Wheatstone's dial instrument and was worth more than £180,000 when purchased by the Post Office.

Wheatstone had planned a telegraph line across the English Channel to France as early as 1840 and played a role in the laying of the Atlantic telegraph cable. In 1859, the Board of Trade selected him as a committeeman to investigate underwater cables, and in 1864 he was a member of the scientific committee appointed to advise the Atlantic Telegraph Company as to the manufacture, laying, and working of the 1865 and 1866 cables.

In 1868, Wheatstone invented a form of automatic telegraph that used patterns of holes punched in paper tape to transmit. The Wheatstone automatic operated at a rate higher than most instruments then used in Great Britain or elsewhere and therefore saved money. It was particularly helpful on high traffic lines such as those carrying press reports. When the Post Office took over all domestic telegraphs starting in 1869-1870, it sought ways to bring down operating costs. Though only four circuits had been using the Wheatstone automatic in 1870, two years later fifteen additional lines were using it. When Wheatstone died in 1875, there were 140 automatics in use in Great Britain alone. Although Wheatstone had received twelve thousand pounds for his automatic patent in 1870, it was so useful that the government agreed, in 1872, to pay an additional nine thousand pounds in six annual installments.

In addition to his numerous telegraph inventions and research into optics, acoustics, and electricity, Wheatstone contributed in no little way to the invention of the dynamo. His lasting fame among electrical engineers rests upon a portion of a speech that he delivered in 1843 before the Royal Society of London, of which he became a member in 1836. The paper described various methods for determining electrical voltage, amperage, and resistance. His means for determining an unknown resistance has since become known as the Wheatstone bridge method and continues to be a standard practice in electrical engineering.

SIGNIFICANCE

After some early attempts with semaphore, the electric telegraph provided the Industrial Revolution with its communications revolution. Neither Cooke nor Wheatstone invented the electromagnetic telegraph. More important, however, they turned it into a practical technology and, of equal importance, were the first to understand and exploit the telegraph's commercial value. Consequently, and despite the bitterness and anger that marked the eight years (1837-1845) of their collaboration, Cooke and Wheatstone laid the foundation for the establishment of Great Britain's and the world's first telecommunications network.

Significantly, their major customers were railroad companies. As long as trains ran on a single set of rails, they would have to travel slowly so as not to collide. Canals would remain the major commercial transport. The Cooke-Wheatstone telegraph allowed trains to signal one another, thereby lessening the likelihood of accidents and providing a means for sending assistance to the scene of an accident in a timely fashion. This marriage of rail and telegraph meant that trains could move goods faster and more safely, resulting in larger profits for the railroad companies. This marriage also furnished the means for tying local producers and consumers together into regional economic units and, eventually, into national markets by the end of the nineteenth century.

—Andrew J. Butrica

FURTHER READING

Beauchamp, Ken. *History of Telegraphy*. London: Institution of Electrical Engineers, 2001. A history of telegraphy over the past two centuries, including information on Cooke and Wheatstone and their telegraph systems.

Clark, Latimer. "Sir William Fothergill Cooke." *Journal of the Society of Telegraph Engineers* 8 (1879): 361-397. Detailed, though incomplete, accounting of the early years of the Cooke-Wheatstone partnership. Although it favors Cooke and the materials published during the 1850's, it also draws upon family material that is no longer available.

Cooke, William Fothergill. *The Electric Telegraph: Was It Invented by Professor Wheatstone?* 2 vols. London: W. H. Smith and Son, 1857. This two-volume work contains Cooke's 1854 pamphlet of the same title (which sets forth his claim to being the true inventor of the telegraph while attacking Wheatstone for falsely making the same claim for himself), Wheatstone's reply of 1855, and Cooke's response to Wheatstone's counterattack (published separately in 1856). The second half is of more historical interest and is a reproduction of the 1841 arbitration papers and drawings.

_____. *Extracts from the Private Letters of the Late Sir William Fothergill Cooke, 1836-1839, Relating to the Invention and Development of the Electric Telegraph*. Edited by F. H. Webb. New York: E. & F. N. Spon, 1895. This collection is for those who cannot see the letters at London's Institution of Electrical Engineers, although the selections have been made to cast Cooke in a favorable light.

_____. *Telegraphic Railways*. London: Simpkin, Marshall, 1842. Sets forth Cooke's notions about the value of the telegraph for railroads: safety, economy, and efficiency. Contains the idea of using the telegraph for what has become known as the block system of railroad signaling.

Hubbard, Geoffrey. *Cooke and Wheatstone and the Invention of the Electric Telegraph*. London: Routledge & Kegan Paul, 1965. A careful attempt to determine what Cooke and Wheatstone accomplished during their eight-year partnership. Based upon the manuscript letters of Cooke in the collections of the Institution of Electrical Engineers and the manuscript papers of Wheatstone at King's College, London. In the light of the lack of any historically respectable accounting of the early history of the telegraph, this book is a must.

Jeans, William T. *Lives of the Electricians*. London: Whittaker, 1887. Pages 105-230 are an account of Wheatstone's various accomplishments that heavily favors the scientist over Cooke.

Standage, Tom. *The Victorian Internet: The Remarkable Story of the Telegraph and the Nineteenth Century On-Line Pioneers*. New York: Walker, 1998. A history of nineteenth century telegraphy, likening the telegraph to the Internet. Includes information on Cooke and Wheatstone's contributions to telegraph development.

Wheatstone, Charles. *A Reply to Mr. Cooke's Pamphlet*. London: R. Taylor and W. Francis, 1855. Wheatstone's point-by-point rebuttal of Cooke's pamphlet.

_____. *The Scientific Papers of Sir Charles Wheatstone*. London: Taylor and Francis, 1879. Available in microprint in the Landmarks of Science series. New York: Readex Microprint, 1973. Contains virtually all of Wheatstone's published scientific works.

SEE ALSO: Marc Isambard Brunel; Michael Faraday; Countess of Lovelace; Samuel F. B. Morse; David Ricardo; The Siemens Family.

RELATED ARTICLES in *Great Events from History: The Nineteenth Century, 1801-1900:* May 24, 1844: Morse Sends First Telegraph Message; October 24, 1861: Transcontinental Telegraph Is Completed; July 27, 1866: First Transatlantic Cable Is Completed; June, 1896: Marconi Patents the Wireless Telegraph.

JAMES FENIMORE COOPER
American novelist

The author of such classic frontier tales as The Last of the Mohicans, *Cooper pioneered historical novels based on American themes and characters and also wrote the first sea novel. In both his fiction and nonfiction, he proved himself an astute social critic of the excesses of democracy.*

BORN: September 15, 1789; Burlington, New Jersey
DIED: September 14, 1851; Cooperstown, New York
ALSO KNOWN AS: James Cooper (birth name)
AREA OF ACHIEVEMENT: Literature

EARLY LIFE

James Cooper was the eleventh child of William Cooper and Elizabeth Fenimore Cooper (he added Fenimore to his name in 1826). When he was thirteen months old, the family left the urban Burlington for the wilderness at the southern shore of Ostego Lake. Here William Cooper built Ostego Hall and developed the surrounding area as Cooperstown. This frontier village would serve as the model of Templeton in *The Pioneers* (1823), as the novelist's father would become the aristocratic Judge Temple in that novel and Ostego Lake turn into Lake Glimmerglass. By the time the Coopers settled in New York, the Indians had departed; Cooper's Indians derive from books, not personal knowledge. The wilderness remained, though, and figured prominently in many of his novels.

Cooperstown soon established a local academy, which Cooper attended before going to Albany to study under the Reverend William Ellison. In 1803, Cooper entered Yale. At the age of thirteen, he was more interested in pranks than studies. After blowing up a classmate's door with gunpowder, Cooper was expelled.

The following year, he was sent to sea aboard the *Stirling*, where he encountered a series of adventures he would later use in his nautical novels. Off the coast of Portugal, the ship was pursued by pirates. Entering British waters, they found themselves no safer. With the Napoleonic Wars raging, Great Britain was impressing American seamen into its navy; the *Stirling* was boarded and several sailors removed.

Cooper returned safely to the United States, where he was eligible for a commission as midshipman in the Navy. His first assignment was to a ship in dry dock in New York; his second was to a ship still under construction on Lake Ontario. Eager to see active service in open water, he maneuvered to secure a berth aboard the *Wasp*, an eighteen-gun sloop. Again, though, he was disappointed, for the commanding officer was so impressed with the midshipman that he made him his recruiting officer, a post that required Cooper to remain onshore. Despite this series of disappointments, Cooper had learned much about ships, and this knowledge found its way into both his fiction and his nonfiction.

In December, 1809, Cooper's father died; in May, 1810, Cooper therefore requested a twelve-month furlough to attend to family business. This business included wooing Susan Augusta DeLancey, daughter of a country squire. On January 1, 1811, the two were married.

Cooper had promised Susan that he would surrender his commission in the Navy, so he turned his attention to earning a living as a gentleman farmer and speculator. Between 1813 and 1819, his six siblings died, making him heir to his father's extensive landholdings but also leaving him responsible for his brothers' dependents and debts. As he struggled with these various financial difficulties, a happy accident changed the course of his life and of American letters as well.

LIFE'S WORK

In 1820, the Coopers were living in Scarsdale. Among the popular recreations of the family was reading aloud. One day, Cooper began Jane Austen's *Persuasion* (1818). After a few pages, Cooper threw the book down in disgust and announced, "I could write you a better book than that myself." Because Cooper disliked any writing, even letters, his wife expressed her incredulity and challenged him to make good his boast. The result was *Precaution* (1820).

In itself, this first book is not noteworthy, for the work is a novel of manners typical of female British writers of the period. *Precaution* is important, though, because it launched Cooper's literary career. He next turned his attention to an American theme, though he found the writing difficult. As he wrote to Andrew Thompson Goodrich, "The task of making American manners and American scenes interesting to an American reader is an arduous one—I am unable to say whether I shall succeed or not." The popular response to *The Spy* (1821) resolved any doubts. The book quickly went through three editions and was adapted for the New York stage; a French translation appeared within a year. Critical appraisals were equally favorable: The *North American Review* called Cooper "the first who deserved the appellation of a distinguished American novel writer."

The novel was based on the actual life of a spy who served under John Jay during the American Revolution. Harvey Birch's wanderings between the British and American lines in Westchester County allowed Cooper to depict the landscape and manners of New York. The book is American in more than setting, though. Unlike the heroes of British fiction, Birch is an outsider, who, despite heroism and integrity, is never integrated into society.

With his next novel, *The Pioneers*, Cooper struck an even more responsive chord. The book sold some three thousand copies on the day of publication and introduced a character as enduring as Robinson Crusoe. Natty Bumppo, the pioneer, is a mythic figure whose image was to descend through the dime novels of Erastus F. Beadle to the Lone Ranger (whose companionship with Tonto mirrors Bumppo's relationship with the Indian Chingachgook) and similar television and film heroes. In this self-reliant frontiersman, Cooper produced an archetypal American and a microcosm of the nation moving ever westward.

The Pioneers was the first of five novels collectively known as the Leatherstocking Tales, which together trace Bumppo's life from his youth (*The Deerslayer*, 1841) during the 1740's to his death on the Great Plains in 1804 (*The Prairie*, 1827). Not only did Cooper create the mythic pioneer in these works but he also painted a mythic frontier that was to reappear in the histories of Francis Parkman and Frederick Jackson Turner. This frontier is majestic and overwhelming. Armies enter the wilderness to emerge as tattered remnants. The small forts are dwarfed by their harsh, rugged surroundings.

James Fenimore Cooper. (The Granger Collection, New York)

In this setting, Cooper plays out the conflict between savage Indians and the forces of white civilization. Cooper's novels thus serve as an apology for the displacement of the American Indians, many of whom, like the Iroquois and Lakota (Sioux), are portrayed as too evil to deserve survival. Not all of Cooper's Indians are bad; he incorporates the myth of the noble savage into his descriptions of the Delaware and the Pawnee tribes. These good Indians, though, are doomed by their very virtues, which render them easy prey to less scrupulous members of both the white and red races. Further, despite their nobility, they remain savage.

Though Cooper's frontier novels justify the conquest of the West, they also recognize the tragic consequences. The Indians are displaced, but so are the pioneers. Natty Bumppo's life is a series of migrations westward, because he brings a civilization that cannot tolerate his ways. Meanwhile, Cooper is aware of the beauty of this wilderness vanishing beneath the ax of civilization. When Judith Hunter in *The Deerslayer* asks Bumppo where his love is, he replies

> She's in the forest, Judith—hanging from the boughs of the trees, in a soft rain—in the dew on the open grass . . . and in all the other glorious gifts that come from God's Providence.

Cooper's next novel also broke new ground. At a dinner party in New York City, Cooper's companions of the Bread and Cheese Club were praising Sir Walter Scott's *The Pirate* (1822) for its realism. Scott, unlike Cooper, had never been to sea; Cooper quickly demonstrated numerous flaws in the work. When challenged to do better, Cooper responded with *The Pilot* (1824). Though Cooper is best remembered as a writer of the frontier, he was to produce eleven nautical novels, all replete with precise detail; later writers of the sea, among them Herman Melville and Joseph Conrad, praised Cooper's efforts in this area. Set, like *The Spy*, during the American Revolution, *The Pilot* was also successful.

COOPER'S MAJOR WORKS

1821 *The Spy: A Tale of the Neutral Ground*
1823 *The Pioneers: Or, The Sources of the Susquehanna*
1823 *The Pilot: A Tale of the Sea*
1825 *Lionel Lincoln: Or, The Leaguer of Boston*
1826 *The Last of the Mohicans: A Narrative of 1757*
1827 *The Prairie: A Tale*
1827 *The Red Rover: A Tale*
1831 *The Bravo: A Tale*
1838 *Homeward Bound: Or, The Chase*
1838 *Home as Found*
1840 *The Pathfinder: Or, The Inland Sea*
1840 *Mercedes of Castile: Or, The Voyage to Cathay*
1841 *The Deerslayer: Or, The First War-Path*
1842 *The Two Admirals: A Tale*
1842 *The Wing-and-Wing: Or, Le Feu-Follet*
1843 *Wyandotté: Or, The Hutted Knoll*
1844 *Afloat and Ashore: A Sea Tale*
1844 *Miles Wallingford: Sequel to Afloat and Ashore*
1845 *The Chainbearer: Or, The Littlepage Manuscripts*
1847 *The Crater: Or, Vulcan's Peak, a Tale of the Pacific*
1848 *Jack Tier: Or, The Florida Reef*
1848 *The Oak Openings: Or, The Bee Hunter*
1849 *The Sea Lions: Or, The Lost Sealers*
1850 *The Ways of the Hour*

Cooper's popularity led to his appointment to the committee that welcomed the Marquis de Lafayette when he returned to the United States in 1824. In that year, too, Columbia University recognized his achievements by awarding him an honorary master of arts degree.

The Last of the Mohicans (1826), another of the Leatherstocking Tales, further enhanced his reputation. In 1826, on the eve of his departure for Europe, Cooper was feted by the Bread and Cheese Club. Among those present were DeWitt Clinton, governor of New York; General Winfield Scott; Charles King, later to be president of Columbia University; and James Kent, former chancellor and chief justice of New York. In one toast, King placed Cooper on the same level as Sir Walter Scott; in another, Kent called Cooper "the genius which has rendered our native soil classic ground, and given to our early history the enchantment of fiction."

Cooper went to Europe nominally as American consul to Lyon, but his real intent was to see Europe and to arrange for the publication of his novels abroad. While in Europe, Cooper was urged by Lafayette to dispel certain misconceptions about the United States. The result was *Notions of the Americans* (1828), a glowing account of his native land. At Lafayette's prompting, he also involved himself in a pamphlet war between French monarchists and republicans.

Despite his defense of democracy, Cooper's reputation was declining in the United States. He was criticized for intervening in the political affairs of France, and his European novels—*The Bravo* (1831), *The Heidenmauer* (1832), and *The Headsman* (1833)—were not well received back home. By the time he returned to the United States on November 5, 1833, he was no longer the hero he had been seven years earlier. At the same time, he was not pleased with what he regarded as the excesses of democracy that had accompanied the presidency of Andrew Jackson. In *A Letter to His Countrymen* (1834), Cooper began a series of criticisms of the United States, and he announced his retirement as a novelist.

Cooper was to return to fiction in 1838, but he was not idle during the intervening years, publishing a series of travel books and a social satire on both England and the United States, *The Monikins* (1835). In his European novels, Cooper had warned his countrymen to beware of oligarchies and not to sacrifice their freedoms to powerful commercial interests. Now that he was home, he saw greater danger to the republic from the lower, rather than the upper, classes. *The American Democrat* (1838) offers Cooper's clearest vision of the United States, where "acts of tyranny can only proceed from the publick. The publick, then, is to be watched in this country, as, in other countries, kings and aristocrats are to be watched." He still believed in democracy as the best form of government, but his ideal democracy was Jeffersonian, not Jacksonian. Merit should have the chance to succeed regardless of pedigree, but the natural aristocrat should govern. While people should enjoy equality under the law, social distinctions should remain.

The American Democrat aroused little controversy, but the two novels issued that year to incorporate its ideas received harsh treatment: *Homeward Bound* and *Home as Found* were sharply attacked in the press. Cooper's aristocratic appearance did not help his popularity, either. In Mathew Brady's photograph he looks like a stern autocrat, with high forehead, penetrating gaze, Roman nose, and firm chin.

As the new decade began, Cooper briefly regained his popularity when he produced the last two of the Leatherstocking Tales, *The Pathfinder* (1840) and *The Deerslayer*. His next two novels, *The Two Admirals* (1842) and *The Wing-and-Wing* (1842), also mark a return to his earliest writing, in this case the sea adventure.

Cooper could not keep away from controversy for very long, though. In 1839, the Antirent War began in New York, as tenants insisted on owning their land instead of renting it. Cooper's sympathies were with the landowners, and the Littlepage novels—*Satanstoe* (1845), *The Chainbearer* (1845), and *The Redskins* (1846)—justify their position. Cooper was as disgusted with the politicians as with the tenants, and in his preface to *The Redskins*, he wrote that if the government could not curb the antirent faction, the sooner that government was abolished, the better.

Cooper's next novel, *The Crater* (1847), allowed him to achieve that wish, at least in fiction. An island arises in the South Pacific, and at first its government is a perfect Jeffersonian democracy. With the arrival of lawyers, journalists, and Fundamentalist preachers—all of whom Cooper regarded as the bane of American life—this ideal is corrupted. As if in divine retribution, the island then sinks back into the ocean.

Despite Cooper's long-standing feud with his countrymen, after his death at Cooperstown on September 14, 1851, Washington Irving arranged a memorial tribute for him in New York City. William Cullen Bryant delivered the eulogy, Daniel Webster attended, and leading literary figures sent tributes. Whatever the editorialists and general public thought of him, these men recognized the great contribution that Cooper had made to American letters.

SIGNIFICANCE

In *Notions of the Americans*, Cooper complained that the United States did not offer material for a national literature. In his thirty-two novels, though, Cooper gave the lie to this statement. He proved that the United States did offer the fabric for the romancer and dramatist to create a truly American literature.

Cooper's novels are American not only because of their setting but also because of their characters: pioneers, Indians, slaves, and the hero who is an outsider, shunning and shunned by society. The themes, too, are native; even when they criticize contemporary society they do so from the perspective of the ideals of the nation's Founders.

Cooper, however, did not simply create American novels; he also created an audience for them. Early in the nineteenth century, Sidney Smith had asked in the *Edinburgh Review*, "Who reads an American book?" He might have asked, too, "Who publishes an American book?" Cooper's own publisher, Carey of Philadelphia, had issued only two American novels before 1820. Between 1830 and 1840, it published 142. Other publishers in this country followed suit, and abroad Cooper's novels were printed in more than thirty cities.

As such works as *The History of the Navy of the United States of America* (1839) demonstrate, Cooper knew history and could present it well. His historical novels are not so much history, though, as myth. They established the prevailing image of the Indian as treacherous foe or doomed noble savage. They created the fiction of the empty wilderness waiting for the white man to settle it and so fueled the imagination of those who sought to fulfill America's manifest destiny to rule from sea to sea. Drawing on the already existing stories about Daniel Boone, Cooper provided in Natty Bumppo the American hero, whom Henry Nash Smith in *Virgin Land* (1957) calls "the most important symbol of the national experience of adventure across the continent."

Quintessentially American, Cooper nevertheless saw the dangers of rampant democracy. His social criticism was not popular, but it established a literary mode that, like his frontier and nautical novels, influenced later writers. William Dean Howells, Frank Norris, and Sinclair Lewis are but three who followed in this mode. Like his most famous creation, then, Cooper was indeed a pathfinder and pioneer.

—Joseph Rosenblum

FURTHER READING

Barker, Martin, and Roger Sabin. *The Lasting of the Mohicans: History of an American Myth*. Jackson: University Press of Mississippi, 1995. The authors explain how *The Last of the Mohicans* describes the American dream of colonizing the frontier. They examine how Cooper's novel has been adapted for movies, television, comic books, and other media, with each new version providing a contemporary variation of the myth.

Boynton, Henry Walcott. *James Fenimore Cooper*. New York: Century, 1931. Focuses on Cooper the man rather than Cooper the writer. Boynton notes Cooper's faults but tends to gloss over them or explain them away.

Dennis, Ian. *Nationalism and Desire in Early Historical Fiction*. New York: St. Martin's Press, 1997. Dennis reassesses the works of Cooper and other nineteenth century historical novelists in which the depiction of the desiring "other" generates hopes for national identity.

Franklin, Wayne. *The New World of James Fenimore Cooper*. Chicago: University of Chicago Press, 1982. Through a close reading of five of Cooper's novels—*The Pioneers*, *The Wept of Wish-ton-Wish* (1829), *Wyandotté* (1843), *The Crater* (1847), and *The Last of the Mohicans*—Franklin examines Cooper's attitude toward the frontier. Maintains that for Cooper, the wilderness begins as a place of hope and promise but ends as the source of tragedy.

McWilliams, John P. *Political Justice in a Republic: James Fenimore Cooper's America*. Berkeley: University of California Press, 1972. Argues that Cooper remained a dedicated republican all of his life. McWilliams shows that while Cooper's views are consistent, American society changed dramatically between 1820 and 1850 and hence produced a darkening vision of fiction.

Railton, Stephen. *Fenimore Cooper: A Study in His Life and Imagination*. Princeton, N.J.: Princeton University Press, 1978. A psychological approach to Cooper's life. Railton sees Cooper as dominated by his father and reads the life and fiction in the light of an Oedipal complex.

Spiller, Robert Ernest. *Fenimore Cooper: Critic of His Times*. New York: Minton, Balch, 1931. Concentrates on Cooper's social views and sees him as a writer who sought to analyze and express as well as criticize the United States of his day.

Walker, Warren S. *James Fenimore Cooper: An Introduction and Interpretation*. New York: Barnes & Noble, 1962. A biography organized around the various themes in Cooper's writing—the frontier, the sea, and American democracy. A concluding chapter reviews critical response to Cooper from 1820 to the middle of the twentieth century.

Waples, Dorothy. *The Whig Myth of James Fenimore Cooper*. New Haven, Conn.: Yale University Press, 1938. Claims that many of the attacks on Cooper during his lifetime came from Whigs who distorted his character. Stresses Cooper's political views.

SEE ALSO: Helen Hunt Jackson; Francis Parkman; Sir Walter Scott.

RELATED ARTICLES in *Great Events from History: The Nineteenth Century, 1801-1900:* 1814: Scott Publishes *Waverley*; May 8, 1816: American Bible Society Is Founded.

CAROLINA CORONADO

Spanish poet

Three themes characterized the life of Carolina Coronado: politics, iconoclastic behavior, and literature. She was a popular Spanish writer, especially of Romantic poetry, and was prominent in social and diplomatic circles for her literary pursuits, reformist activities, and diplomatic interventions.

BORN: December 12, 1820; Almendralejo, Spain
DIED: January 15, 1911; Lisbon, Portugal
ALSO KNOWN AS: Carolina Coronado Perry
AREAS OF ACHIEVEMENT: Literature, diplomacy

EARLY LIFE

Carolina Coronado (kah-roh-LEE-nah koh-roh-NAH-doh) was the granddaughter of Fermín Coronado, a political opponent of Spain's King Fernando VII, who was secretly assassinated in the king's prison. When she was a child, her father, Nicolás Coronado, was also imprisoned and his property seized. Her mother, María Antonia Romero de Coronado, then moved the family to Badajoz so she could visit Carolina's father in prison and take him food.

Coronado received the domestic education considered appropriate for a young woman of early nineteenth century Spain that focused on how to run a home and entertain socially. She rebelled and educated herself through extensive reading, secretly by night. She started her writing career by composing by memory at night and wrote her first poem at the age of ten. Because social mores of the time held that formal education of young women fostered immorality, Coronado suffered social ostracism when her literary pursuits became known. Her mother forbade her to continue in order to protect her reputation, but her male friends and family members helped her to continue.

In her first public political gesture, Coronado embroidered a banner for a liberal anti-Carlista battalion. Shortly before she turned nineteen, she published her first poem, "A la palma," in the November 22, 1839, issue of *El Piloto*, a Madrid magazine. The poem attracted the attention of famous Spanish literary figures, such as José de Espronceda, who dedicated a poem to her. She also started a correspondence with Juan Eugenio Hartzenbusch, who wrote the prologue to her first published collection of poetry in 1843.

LIFE'S WORK

Coronado's reputation was boosted by a macabre incident when the daily Madrid newspaper *El Mundo* falsely reported her death on January 10, 1844. Although she suffered her whole life from what were described as catatonic attacks, the young Coronado remained very much alive. Meanwhile, the publicity from the premature obituary fed public opinion, and Coronado began to give academic presentations, do charitable works, explicate art, and collaborate on literary magazines. Her works were published in magazines and then reprinted in newspapers.

Already the darling of a public entranced by the Romantic movement, Coronado seemed to be a classic suffering beauty who pursued an unrequited or impossible but obsessive love of a mysterious young man known only as Alberto. From the age of seventeen, Coronado dedicated poems to Alberto; however, he left Badajoz and died in Seville in May of 1847—an event about which she wrote yet another poem. Afterward, a story arose that she declared perpetual chastity in the cathedral in Seville as a result of her grief. Whether this was true or a merely a romantic myth is unknown; however, it is well established that she suffered a paralytic illness in Cadiz and her family moved near Madrid on her physicians' recommendation.

The press followed Coronado everywhere, and famous writers lionized her. On September 27, 1848, she was honored in a special session at the Liceo de Madrid along with the Cuban-born poet Gertrudis Avellaneda. Even Queen Mother Cristina and her daughter, Queen Isabel II, admired Coronado. However, it took four years for Coronado to establish herself at the royal court. During that time she wrote the poems for a second book and traveled to Madrid, the province of Andalucía, France, and England. She wrote about French novelist Victor Hugo and his wife, who responded by offering to go with Coronado to London. She was courted by the well-known Spanish intellectuals Juan Donoso Cortés and Francisco Martínez de La Rosa.

In early 1852, Coronado met Horatio Justus Perry, secretary of the U.S. embassy at Madrid. Perry had something of a reputation himself because of his affairs with various Spanish girls, but he had vowed to marry a Protestant. He was planning to return to the United States to begin a political career and take care of his two orphaned sisters and reportedly intended to have a last fling with Coronado. However, after she convinced him that she would die without him, they went to Gibraltar together in March, 1852, unsuccessfully seeking dispensation to marry in a Roman Catholic ceremony. They did marry in a Protestant ceremony in April but were granted the desired dispensation and married again in a Roman Catholic mass in July at the Spanish embassy in Paris. Coronado published her second book during the same year and gave birth to a daughter during the following January.

After marrying Perry, Coronado embraced the role of diplomatic wife. She became known for literary salons, a social convention she had earlier rejected. Although she was writing less, William C. Bryant took her work to the United States and supported the Perrys' continued residence in Madrid as a buffer to a conflict between the United States and Spain that was developing over the status of Cuba. Coronado herself averted open conflict at the last minute in that crisis by involving the British ambassador. As a result, Perry lost his job, as some in the United States saw that intervention as a betrayal. Soon after, the couple lost their second child, Horacio, and Perry started a transatlantic telegraph company with the inventor Samuel F. B. Morse. Meanwhile, their third child, Matilde, was born in 1857.

Coronado wrote to President Abraham Lincoln about Perry's situation, and he was restored to the position of secretary of the embassy. Coronado began to lobby for various political criminals with Queen Isabel and the government. She physically protected soldiers involved in the San Gil military insurrection of 1866 in the U.S. embassy and arranged their escape when the American ambassador, John P. Hale, refused to allow fugitives in the embassy. Coronado also took an active part in the demonstrations during the Spanish Revolution of 1868. An avowed abolitionist, she touted Lincoln publicly for his role in freeing American slaves. In 1863, she congratulated the Catalán abolitionist movement, and in 1868 she and the Spanish feminist and writer Concepción Arenal became president and vice president of the Madrid Abolitionist Association, about which she wrote a poem.

Coronado's older daughter died of measles in June, 1873, while her husband was in London on business for his telegraph company. Described as crazy with grief, she had her daughter embalmed, dressed up, and placed in the sacristy of the Convent of the Nuns of Pascualas de Recoletos. Her mind was never the same afterward.

The Perrys moved to Lisbon, the capital of Portugal, where Coronado alternated between holding literary salons in the Bessone and Mitra palaces in Paco d'Arcos and Poco do Bispo. Perry's business failed in 1885 after years of fighting lawsuits in English courts, leaving the Perrys broke. Around this same time, Coronado refused a literary tribute offered by the citizens of her hometown of Badajoz. Financial pressure, Coronado's mental problems, and political dishonor so plagued Perry that he began composing his memoirs about the United States but died on January 15, 1891, before they were finished. Coronado persuaded the archbishop of Lisbon and the governments of Spain, the United States, and Portugal to embalm him and place his cadaver in Mitra palace until a state funeral could be arranged.

The family's financial troubles continued, but Coronado's daughter Matilde helped support the family by doing translations, and they got some assistance from other relatives. Meanwhile, Coronado continued sponsoring salons. She died in Lisbon in January, 1911, and her body was taken to Badajoz—a fact that has caused confusion in some sources about when and where she died.

SIGNIFICANCE

Coronado's principal works include two books of poetry, five dramas, eight novels, and at least two essays. Her poetry has been translated into English and German. She remains a well-known figure in Spain, and numerous works about her are available in Spanish. She is remembered particularly for her feminist poetry and for her work for social reform of civil rights, especially for women and slaves.

—Debra D. Andrist

FURTHER READING

Galerstein, Carolyn L., ed. *Women Writers of Spain.* Westport, Conn.: Greenwood Press, 1986. A brief chapter on Coronado provides a minimal overview of Coronado's life and synopses of four of her novels and two collections of her poetry.

Hara, F. "Lamartine's Influence in the Poems of Carolina Coronado." *Crítica Hispánica* 16 (1994): 297-306. This article compares the sentimental and religious content in works by the French writer of the Romantic school Alphonse de Lamartine and his younger contemporary, Coronado, noting similarities in their work.

Kaminsky, Amy Katz. "The Construction of Immortality: Sappho, Saint Theresa, and Carolina Coronado." *Letras Femeninas* 19 (1993): 1-13. Feminist critic Kaminsky traces the content and form that the three poets, widely distanced in time, share.

_____, ed. *Water Lilies.* St. Paul: University of Minnesota Press, 1995. An anthology of five centuries of Spanish women's writing, the text includes selections by Coronado and critical commentaries of her work.

SEE ALSO: Rubén Darío; Victor Hugo; Abraham Lincoln; Samuel F. B. Morse.

RELATED ARTICLES in *Great Events from History: The Nineteenth Century, 1801-1900:* c. 1820-1860: *Costumbrismo* Movement; September 30, 1868: Spanish Revolution of 1868; 1876: Spanish Constitution of 1876.

GUSTAVE COURBET
French painter

Courbet contributed to the formation of modern art by liberating subject matter and style from academic dogma. The most profound aspects of his contributions are the influences his works have had upon the subsequent analysis of realism.

BORN: June 10, 1819; Ornans, France
DIED: December 31, 1877; La Tour-de-Peilz, Switzerland
AREA OF ACHIEVEMENT: Art

EARLY LIFE

Gustave Courbet (kewr-bay) was born in a town in the scenic Loue River valley of Franche-Comté in eastern France. There, his father, Eléonor Régis Stanislaus Courbet, was a prosperous landowner, whose ancestral home was in the neighboring village of Flagey. Gustave's mother, Suzanne Sylvie Oudot, came from a similar economic background of landed proprietors in Ornans. It was in the Ornans home of his grandfather, Jean-Antoine Oudot, a veteran of the French Revolution, that Gustave was born.

Courbet's early life and studies prior to his 1839 arrival in Paris at the age of twenty had provided him with valuable skills. The young artist's tutelage under Père Beau at Ornans followed his first years of school in 1831 at the *petit seminaire*. It was there that Courbet began to paint from nature. Subsequently, while attending the Collège Royal at Besançon (after autumn, 1837), Maître Flajoulot's emphasis on painting from the live model added another aspect of current artistic training to Courbet's abilities.

During this period, Courbet acquired a deep and lasting appreciation for the cultural heritage and rugged beauty of his native Franche-Comté. This region did not formally become a part of France until 1678 because of a long and complex history of geographical and political factors. The tradition of independence emanating from his native province played an important role in the formation of Courbet's character and notably influenced his attitudes toward formal training and academies.

In Paris, Courbet studied briefly with a minor painter. A greater source of inspiration was discovered at the Louvre, where Courbet diligently copied Dutch, Flemish, Venetian, and Spanish masters. Also significant were the friends he established in Paris: Alexandre Schanne, who became a character in Henri Murger's *Scènes de la vie de bohème* (1847-1849), the painter François Bonvin, and later, the writers Charles Baudelaire and Champfleury.

The decade of the 1840's proved to be a very important one for Courbet, in which his prodigious talent and originality became recognized. His first salon successes were *Self-Portrait with a Black Dog* (1844) and *The Guitarist* (1845). The artist's handsome features and vigorous physicality are evident in other numerous self-portraits of this period. With *After Dinner at Ornans* (1849), for which he received a gold medal at the Salon of 1849, Courbet had developed an artistic formula for elevating and monumentalizing common subjects that led to his first truly revolutionary works: *The Stonebreakers* (1849) and *The Burial at Ornans* (1849).

LIFE'S WORK

The revolutions of 1848 had occurred during the first crucial decade of Courbet's mature formation. Growing discontent with the failure of Louis-Philippe's government to incorporate democratic reform or acknowledge socialist ideas had led to this uprising that had a direct impact on Courbet's art. Courbet emerged as a pictorial advocate of a new, more democratic aesthetic.

The Stonebreakers, which appeared at the Salon of 1850-1851, depicted a young boy and an old man laboring side by side to repair a road. Courbet was, in fact, depicting a form of public service (*corvée*) that was customary in rural France; yet the Parisian audience found his large-scale, unidealized figures to be offensive, and even threatening, as they harbored connotations of peasant uprising or violence. Courbet's realist manifesto, *The Burial at Ornans*, also exhibited at the Salon of 1850-1851, recorded a funeral in his native town. Again, Parisians were provoked by a scene that did not depict a known historical event or idealize its characters. Courbet had glorified the idea that the peasantry and rural bourgeoisie were worthy of the serious artistic treatment usually reserved for aristocratic subject matter and concerns. Courbet's works thus threatened established Parisian social and aesthetic values.

Courbet had entered the decade of the 1850's as an artist with strong political associations, which were subsequently incorporated into his total philosophy, as is evident in a statement from the period: "I am not only a socialist, but a democrat and a republican; in short, I am in favor of the whole revolution, and above all I am a realist."

The ability of an artwork to shock its viewers was used by Courbet in major salon submissions from this time onward to draw attention to his name and artistic message. Courbet was thus a subject of great controversy; yet, whether in praise or criticism, there was widespread acknowledgment of the impact of his style. Two works, *Young Ladies of the Village* (1851) and *The Bathers* (1853), demonstrate how Courbet's art had begun to interact with salon criticism. The first painting portrayed his three sisters in a rural setting bestowing a charitable gift upon a young shepherdess. Even Courbet was surprised when the honest depiction was mocked for its ugliness, as he had thought it dignified, even gracious. Courbet decidedly responded in the Salon of 1853 by creating a depiction of woman that was more truly a mockery of the sort his critics espoused. *The Bathers* depicted two very corpulent and egotistical women decadently bathing in the pool of a wooded glade. The very decadence of the women became his prime focus. Thus, a new aspect of Courbet's works developed, which may be termed the painted caricature.

Gustave Courbet. (Library of Congress)

By the mid-1850's, Courbet had entered into politics of a different kind that formalized his new conception of the artist's role as activist and showman. Partly in reaction to the amount of negative criticism that he inevitably generated, and partly out of his own entrepreneurial desire to make his painting more profitable, he established his own exhibition independent of the combined Salon and World Exhibition of 1855. For this occasion, he conceived of a large canvas, *The Painter's Studio: A Real Allegory of Seven Years of My Artistic Life* (1854-1855), in which Courbet depicts himself in the act of painting. He paints amid two groups, one made up of supportive patrons and the other a puzzling assemblage of diverse characters and types that Courbet claimed to have seen in his travels. This huge work has had numerous interpretations and remains problematic, yet quite clearly it is an essential revelation of Courbet, as he sees himself in the process of creating, which is quite necessarily an act and role that he revolutionized.

Also beginning around 1855, Courbet envisioned a serial approach for his art, thus incorporating past works with future endeavors to create entire cycles of related paintings that would compare and contrast different aspects of society. The idea is said to have come from the novels of Honoré de Balzac; its relevance is exemplified in Courbet's works between the years 1855 and 1866.

In 1861, Courbet began to experience a strange mixture of acclaim and adversity. His *Fighting Stags* (1861) was widely admired, and there was even rumor of an official state purchase and Courbet's decoration with the highest honors. However, in the end, he received only a second-class medal—a great affront to an artist who had painted what many considered to be the best work in the salon.

This blow caused Courbet to break forever with the praised and accepted aesthetics of his time, as dictated by the salon. His reaction was deliberately to insult taste and sensibility in his salon submissions of 1863, 1864, and 1868. However, in the intervening year 1866, he reversed this trend and awed the critics with a new and fantasy-inspired image, *Woman with a Parrot*. Again, there was rumor of governmental purchase and Courbet's decoration. It did not come and was clearly meant to reprimand Courbet's past condemnation of accepted taste. A final reconciliation with the salon came in 1870, when he submitted two beautiful seascapes painted at Étretat in 1869, *The Stormy Sea* and *Cliffs at Étretat After the Storm*. Finally, the critics were filled with enthusiasm. Courbet had become a popular and briefly unproblematic artist.

Courbet's subsequent nomination for the Legion of Honor in June, 1870, caused a sensation; however, the painter held firm to his socialist principles and declined the award. With the outbreak of the Franco-Prussian War in July, Courbet was elected chairman of the arts commission, responsible for the protection of artworks in and around Paris. The duties of this position ultimately cast political overtones upon Courbet as the leader of a large and active group.

Courbet was transformed into a political scapegoat and held responsible for the destruction of the Vendôme Column. The subsequent trials, imprisonment, and exorbitant fines threatened to ruin Courbet and ultimately forced his exile to Switzerland, where he died four years later, a celebrated, but saddened, artist.

SIGNIFICANCE

Throughout his life, Gustave Courbet maintained a spirit of Fourierist political optimism. Though his paintings were often conceived to provoke confrontation, he nevertheless believed that through a liberated artistic manifesto human beings could ultimately derive a philosophy of social harmony. These ideas had become formalized in Courbet's early maturity and were perpetuated by the artist's relations with his greatest patron, Alfred Bruyas, and with the social philosopher Pierre-Joseph Proudhon. Through their encouragement and support, Courbet was able to assess his role and the nature of his art: "To know in order to be able to create, that was my idea. To be in a position to translate the customs, the ideas, the appearance of my epoch, according to my own estimation; to be not only a painter, but a man as well; in short, to create living art—this is my goal." Courbet had set these ideas down in paint as early as 1849 with *The Burial at Ornans*. That the message of Courbet's art was clear to his contemporaries is demonstrated by the 1851 commentary of Paul Sabatier:

> Since the shipwreck of the *Medusa*, . . . nothing as original has been made among us. The clothes, the heads, have a solidity, a variety of tone and a firmness of drawing that is half Venetian, half Spanish; it is close to Zurbarán and to Titian. . . . It was not an easy thing to give dignity . . . to all these modern clothes. . . .

Courbet's late seascapes and somber still lifes are unique pictorial expressions. They represent his most poetic statements, in which the sheer physicality of paint invigorates the expressive power of the work. Courbet's influence on modern art is documented by subsequent generations of avant-garde artists who studied and even collected his works, notably Puvis de Chavannes, Henri Matisse, André Dunoyer de Segonzac, and Pablo Picasso.

—Claudette R. Mainzer

FURTHER READING

Chu, Petra ten Doesschate, ed. *Courbet in Perspective*. Englewood Cliffs, N.J.: Prentice-Hall, 1977. Part of the Artists in Perspective series, containing essays about art history from the nineteenth and twentieth centuries. A very useful gathering and translation of important contemporary accounts of Courbet's life and art, including contextual and stylistic essays.

Clark, Timothy J. *Image of the People: Gustave Courbet and the 1848 Revolution*. Princeton, N.J.: Princeton University Press, 1982. The most detailed analysis of Courbet's life and art between 1848 and 1851. Clark's approach, which is both Marxist and structuralist, illuminates the social and political situations of the Second Republic and the simultaneous developments in Courbet's art—which contained strikingly appropriate pictorial representations of these underlying social tensions.

Courbet, Gustave. *Letters of Gustave Courbet*. Edited and translated by Petra ten Doesschate Chu. Chicago: University of Chicago Press, 1992. Reprints six hundred of Courbet's letters to Baudelaire, Monet, Hugo, and others. The letters portray a man whose intelligence and sophistication belied his carefully constructed image of the naive provincial artist.

Faunce, Sarah, and Linda Nochlin. *Courbet Reconsidered*. New Haven, Conn.: Yale University Press, 1988. A comprehensive, well-illustrated exhibition catalog comprising six essays and 101 entries. Topics addressed are a critical and historical summary of Courbet's oeuvre, reinterpretation of *The Painter's Studio*, gender studies in Courbet, contextual art history, and the American response to Courbet.

Lindsay, Jack. *Gustave Courbet: His Life and Art*. New York: Harper & Row, 1973. A comprehensive biography that incorporates most of the literature available at the time of publication. Includes eighty-nine black-and-white illustrations and an extensive bibliography.

Mack, Gerstle. *Gustave Courbet*. New York: Alfred A. Knopf, 1951. Reprint. Westport, Conn.: Greenwood Press, 1970. The first monograph in English, which is primarily based on the first substantial French biography and its nineteenth century sources by Georges Riat, *Gustave Courbet peintre* (1906).

Nochlin, Linda. *Gustave Courbet: A Study of Style and Society*. New York: Garland, 1976. A sophisticated analysis of the origins of Courbet's style by one of the foremost authorities on the artist. Select bibliography and 121 black-and-white illustrations.

Rubin, James Henry. *Courbet*. London: Phaidon Press, 1997. Part of the Arts & Ideas series, this is a collection of essays about Courbet's life and artwork.

_____. *Realism and Social Vision in Courbet and Proudhon*. Princeton, N.J.: Princeton University Press, 1980. Rubin considers Courbet's art, particularly *The Painter's Studio*, in relation to the theories of Proudhon, a contemporary and acquaintance of Courbet, to compare and contrast the doctrines of both enigmatic figures.

Toussaint, Hélène, et al. *Gustave Courbet, 1819-1877: [Exhibition] at the Royal Academy of Arts, 19 January - 19 March, 1978*. London: Arts Council of Great Britain, 1978. The largest retrospective of Courbet's work in the twentieth century was originally displayed at the Musées Nationaux in Paris in 1977 and 1978, and later exhibited in London. This is a translation of the catalog from the Paris exhibition. The catalog is a well-illustrated and scholarly monograph, with new interpretive breakthroughs made possible by sophisticated laboratory analysis at the Louvre. Essays include an introduction by Alan Bowness, an authoritative biography by Marie-Thérèse de Forges, and catalog entries and reinterpretive analysis of *The Painter's Studio* by Hélène Toussaint.

SEE ALSO: Mary Cassatt; Paul Cézanne; Édouard Manet; Pierre-Auguste Renoir; James McNeill Whistler.

RELATED ARTICLE in *Great Events from History: The Nineteenth Century, 1801-1900:* March 18-May 28, 1871: Paris Commune.

STEPHEN CRANE

American novelist

During a life tragically cut short by tuberculosis, Crane wrote what is now regarded as one of the finest war novels of all time, The Red Badge of Courage, *as well as estimable poetry and more than a dozen other novels and collections of stories.*

BORN: November 1, 1871; Newark, New Jersey
DIED: June 5, 1900; Badenweiler, Germany
AREA OF ACHIEVEMENT: Literature

EARLY LIFE

The youngest son of a youngest son, Stephen Crane was the last of fourteen children born to the Reverend Jonathan Townley Crane and his wife, Mary Peck. Crane's father was a presiding elder of the Newark, New Jersey, district of the Methodist Church (1868-1872) when Stephen was born and served in a similar capacity in the Elizabeth, New Jersey, district of the church from 1872 until 1876. Because Methodist clergymen were subject to frequent transfer, the young Stephen was moved from Newark to Paterson, New Jersey, before he was old enough to attend school and to Port Jervis, New York, shortly before he began school. His *The Third Violet* (1897) and *Whilomville Stories* (1900) are set in villages modeled after Port Jervis.

Crane's father died in 1880, when the boy was eight years old, and, in 1883, Stephen and his mother moved to Asbury Park, New Jersey, a seaside resort some sixty miles from New York City, to be near the Methodist camp community of Ocean Grove, a town adjacent to Asbury Park, which Jonathan Crane had been instrumental in establishing. Stephen's brother Townley already ran a press bureau in Asbury Park, and soon their sister Agnes moved there to teach in the public schools.

As Stephen strayed from the religious teachings of the Methodist Church, his mother became concerned about his spiritual welfare, and, in 1885, she sent him to Pennington Seminary, some ten miles from both Trenton and Princeton, in the hope that he would receive a solid academic background and would simultaneously grow closer to the Church. Crane's father had been principal of Pennington Seminary for the decade from 1848 to 1858, and his mother had spent the first ten years of her marriage at Pennington.

Stephen, a handsome, dark-haired youth with a prominent nose, sensuous lips, and deep, dark eyes, rankled under Pennington's strong religious emphasis. In 1888, he enrolled in the Hudson River Institute in Claverack, New York, a coeducational institution with a military emphasis for its male students. It was perhaps during this period that Crane became extremely interested in war.

During the summers, Crane assisted his brother in his news bureau, learning something about journalism as he went about his work. He entered Lafayette College in 1890 to study engineering, but failed in his work there and left after the Christmas holiday to attend Syracuse University, where he played baseball, managed the baseball team, and worked on the school newspaper. He was not a strong student, and he left school in 1891 to seek his fortune in New York City. His mother died on December 7 of that year.

Stephen, who had met and established a friendship with Hamlin Garland in the summer of 1891, tried to make his living as a newspaperman, but he was not initially successful in this work. In 1892, however, the serial publication of seven of his "Sullivan County Sketches" gave him the encouragement he needed to pursue a literary career diligently.

LIFE'S WORK

Buoyed up by seeing his work in print, Crane, in 1893, paid for a private printing of *Maggie: A Girl of the Streets* (1893), a book gleaned from his experience of living in New York City's Bowery during the preceding two years. This early work, highly shocking in its time because it views with sympathy a girl who becomes pregnant out of wedlock and shows the hypocrisy of her lower-class family's morality, was first published under the pseudonym Johnston Smith.

Maggie was unabashedly naturalistic, somewhat in the tradition of Émile Zola. Despite William Dean Howells's attempts to get the book distributed, it sold hardly any copies in its original edition. In 1896, however, Crane revised it, cutting out much of its offensive profanity, omitting some of its graphic description, and regularizing the grammar and punctuation. His reputation had by this time been established with the publication, the preceding October, of *The Red Badge of Courage* (1895), a book that grew out of Crane's fascination with war, battles, and men in combat. *Maggie*, although it still was deemed shocking to delicate sensibilities, was more favorably received in 1896 than it had been three years earlier.

The Red Badge of Courage existed in some form in 1894, when it was published abridged in newspapers by the Bacheller Syndicate. *George's Mother* (1896) appeared two years later, and in its use of realistic detail it goes far beyond that of William Dean Howells, who had become Crane's friend.

Stephen Crane. (Library of Congress)

With the publication of both *The Black Riders and Other Lines* and *The Red Badge of Courage* in 1895, Crane became an overnight celebrity. In March of that year, he also went to Mexico for the first time, and the trip made a substantial impression upon him. With the appearance of *George's Mother, Maggie, The Little Regiment and Other Episodes of the American Civil War* (1896), and *The Third Violet*, it was quite apparent that Crane, still only twenty-five years old, was on the way to becoming one of the leading literary figures in the United States. If readers complained because he wrote about subjects that depressed them, they could not reasonably contend that the conditions about which he wrote did not exist or that he wrote badly about them.

Although Crane was fascinated by war and by 1896 had written much about the subject, he had never known the battlefield, and he was keenly aware of this lack in his experience. Therefore, when the Bacheller Syndicate offered to send him as a correspondent to join the insurgents who were fighting against Spanish rule in Cuba, Crane enthusiastically accepted the assignment. He went first to Jacksonville, Florida, to wait for a ship, the *Com-*

CRANE'S MAJOR WORKS

1893 *Maggie: A Girl of the Streets*
1895 *The Red Badge of Courage: An Episode of the American Civil War*
1896 *George's Mother*
1896 *The Little Regiment and Other Episodes of the American Civil War*
1897 *The Third Violet*
1898 *The Open Boat, and Other Tales of Adventure*
1899 *The Monster, and Other Stories*
1899 *Active Service*
1900 *Whilomville Stories*
1900 *Wounds in the Rain: War Stories*
1902 *Last Words*
1903 *The O'Ruddy: A Romance* (with Robert Barr)

modore, to be outfitted for the short trip to Cuba. Arriving in Jacksonville in November, he met Cora Stewart, who owned a brothel and nightclub, the Hotel de Dream.

It took until December 31 for the *Commodore* to be ready to sail, and by that time Crane and Stewart, who already had a husband, had fallen in love. Nevertheless, Crane sailed for Cuba as planned. The ship, however, got only several miles down the St. John's River before it ran aground. Crane and some of his shipmates were forced to put to sea in a small, flimsy lifeboat before the *Commodore* capsized with some loss of life.

It was fifty-four hours before Crane and his companions were able to ride the heavy surf to shore at Daytona. One of his companions was drowned as they came to shore. From his frightening experience in the lifeboat, Crane wrote what is probably his best known and most artistically confident short story, "The Open Boat." The shipwreck scuttled, for the time, Crane's plans to go to Cuba. Instead, he and Stewart sailed for Greece in late March, both of them to report on Greece's war with Turkey.

In mid-1897, Crane and Stewart, who was six years older than he, went to England, where he wrote some of his most memorable short stories, including "The Monster," "Death and the Child," and his much anthologized "The Bride Comes to Yellow Sky." He introduced Cora Stewart as his wife, although the two had never been married because she was not free to do so. It was at this time that Crane met Joseph Conrad and became his close friend.

After Crane's collection *The Open Boat and Other Tales of Adventure* (1898) was published, the author returned to the United States to join the armed forces in the Spanish-American War, which the United States had just entered. He was, however, rejected for military service and instead went to Cuba as a war correspondent for Joseph Pulitzer. He was fearless in combat situations, but his health began to fail. He did some work in Puerto Rico and in Cuba for the Hearst newspapers, but in 1899, the year in which *War Is Kind* (1899), *Active Service* (1899), and *The Monster and Other Stories* (1899) were published, he returned to England, this time to live in the stately Brede Place in Sussex. While celebrating Christmas, Crane had a massive hemorrhage brought on by tuberculosis.

In the spring of 1900, the year in which *Whilomville Stories* and *Wounds in the Rain* were published, Crane's health declined, and in May, he and Cora, accompanied by a retinue consisting of their butler, maids, nurses, and a doctor, went to Badenweiler in Germany's Black Forest, hoping that the climate would benefit his health. There Crane died on June 5. Three of his works, *Great Battles of the World* (1901), *Last Words* (1902), and *The O'Ruddy* (1903), were published shortly after his death.

SIGNIFICANCE

Dead at twenty-eight, Stephen Crane had just begun to come into his own as a writer. His early work, particularly the original version of *Maggie*, reflected his passionate interest in reform and his understanding of the problems of the poor, but much of this early book was seriously flawed, largely because Crane had not yet mastered the basic mechanics of expression.

With *The Red Badge of Courage*, which stands as an acknowledged American classic, Crane demonstrated that he was getting a firm grip on his art. The classic naturalism of *Maggie* and of *George's Mother*, the conventional realism of *The Red Badge of Courage* and of *The Little Regiment and Other Episodes of the American Civil War*, and the impressionistic symbolism of *The Black Riders* suggest the great versatility of which Crane was capable.

Both in his insistence on living an action-packed life, often quite close to the edge, and in his accuracy and economy of description, Crane reminds one of Ernest Hemingway, along whose lines he might have developed had he lived a normal life span.

—*R. Baird Shuman*

FURTHER READING

Benfey, Christopher. *The Double Life of Stephen Crane*. New York: Alfred A. Knopf, 1992. Benfey argues that Crane's short life was overshadowed by his fiction. For example, he wrote about war in *The Red Badge of Courage* before he experienced the Spanish-American War as a reporter; he wrote *Maggie: A Girl of the Streets* before his common-law marriage to a former madam. While this hypothesis is debatable, the book provides a detailed analysis of Crane's life and work, including his neglected poetry.

Bruccoli, Matthew J. *Stephen Crane, 1871-1971*. Columbia: Department of English, University of South Carolina, 1971. Extremely valuable bibliography, although not readily accessible.

Cady, Edwin H. *Stephen Crane*. Rev. ed. Boston: Twayne, 1980. This updating of Cady's 1962 edition is carefully researched and well reported. It is a standard critical biography of Crane. Its updated bibliography is useful.

Colvert, James B. *Stephen Crane*. New York: Harcourt Brace Jovanovich, 1984. This biography, aimed specifically at the nonspecialist, is highly readable and enhanced by numerous illustrations; the author's research is impeccable. Its bibliography is limited but well selected.

Davis, Linda H. *Badge of Courage: The Life of Stephen Crane*. Boston: Houghton Mifflin, 1998. Davis describes Crane as "an explosion of color in a gray age," and her perceptive biography provides information about his bohemian life and work.

Gibson, Donald B. *The Fiction of Stephen Crane*. Carbondale: Southern Illinois University Press, 1968. This study, although badly dated, is valuable in suggesting the sources of much of Crane's fiction and in establishing some of Crane's literary relationships.

Gullason, Thomas A., ed. *Stephen Crane's Career: Perspectives and Evaluations*. New York: New York University Press, 1972. The contributors to this book consider Crane in the light of his times and background. They trace sources of his stories, review Crane research, consider Crane's short fiction quite thoroughly, and present some of Cora Stewart's original writing.

Katz, Joseph, ed. *Stephen Crane in Transition: Centenary Essays*. DeKalb: Northern Illinois University Press, 1972. The nine essays in this centenary edition commemorating Crane's birth consider the novels, the stories, Crane's journalistic career, his literary style, and his radical use of language. The introduction is astute, and the afterword gives a fine overview of resources for study.

Nagel, James. *Stephen Crane and Literary Impressionism*. University Park: Pennsylvania State University Press, 1980. Nagel sees Crane in a new light that suggests his remarkable versatility. The book has especially strong insights into *The Black Riders*.

Solomon, Eric. *Stephen Crane: From Parody to Realism*. Cambridge, Mass.: Harvard University Press, 1966. A penetrating study that shows Stephen Crane's remarkably swift development as a writer who found his metier in realism despite his sallies into naturalism and impressionism.

Stallman, Robert W. *Stephen Crane: A Critical Bibliography*. Ames: Iowa State University Press, 1972. This book is now somewhat dated, but is still useful to scholars and is more readily available generally than Matthew J. Bruccoli's splendid bibliography, which was completed the year before Stallman's.

Walford, Chester L., Jr. *The Anger of Stephen Crane*. Lincoln: University of Nebraska Press, 1983. Walford considers Crane a semiliterate genius and presents his work as a repudiation of the epic tradition and of conventional religion. Although the book is not always convincing, it is engaging and original in its approach.

SEE ALSO: Ambrose Bierce; Henry James; Mark Twain.

RELATED ARTICLE in *Great Events from History: The Nineteenth Century, 1801-1900:* c. 1865: Naturalist Movement Begins.

CRAZY HORSE

Native American war leader

The greatest of the Lakota (Sioux) war chiefs, Crazy Horse led his people in a valiant but futile struggle against domination by the white Americans and white culture. He fought to the last to hold his native land for the Indian people.

BORN: 1842?; Black Hills (now in South Dakota)
DIED: September 5, 1877; Fort Robinson, Nebraska
ALSO KNOWN AS: Curly; Tashunca-uitko (birth name)
AREA OF ACHIEVEMENT: Warfare and conquest

EARLY LIFE

Crazy Horse's Lakota name was Tashunca-uitko. Little is known of his early life; even the date of his birth and the identity of his mother are uncertain. He was probably born in a Lakota camp along Rapid Creek in the Black Hills during the winter of 1841-1842. Most scholars believe that his mother was a Brule Lakota, the sister of Spotted Tail, a famous Brule chief. His father, also called Crazy Horse, was a highly respected Oglala Lakota holy man. Tashunca-uitko was apparently a curious and solitary child. His hair and his complexion were so fair that he was often mistaken for a captive white child by soldiers and settlers. He was first known as "Light-Haired Boy" and also as "Curly." At the age of ten, he became the protégé of Hump, a young Minneconjou Lakota warrior.

When he was about twelve years old, Curly killed his first buffalo and rode a newly captured wild horse; to honor his exploits, his people renamed him "His Horse Looking." One event in Crazy Horse's youth seems to have had a particularly powerful impact on the course of his life. When he was about fourteen, His Horse Looking witnessed the senseless murder of Chief Conquering Bear by the troops of Second Lieutenant J. L. Gratton and the subsequent slaughter of Gratton's command by the Lakota. Troubled by what he had seen, His Horse Looking went out alone, hobbled his horse, and lay down on a high hill to await a vision. On the third day, weakened by hunger, thirst, and exposure, the boy had a powerful mystical experience that revealed to him that the world in which men lived was only a shadow of the real world.

To enter the real world, one had to dream. When Curly was in that world, everything seemed to dance or float—his horse danced as if it were wild or crazy. In this first crucial vision, His Horse Looking had seen a warrior mounted on his (His Horse Looking's) horse; the warrior had no scalps, wore no paint, was naked except for a breech cloth; he had a small, smooth stone behind one ear. Bullets and arrows could not touch him; the rider's own people crowded around him, trying to stop his dancing horse, but he rode on. The people were lost in a storm; the rider became a part of the storm with a lightning bolt on his cheek and hail spots on his body. The storm faded, and a small red-tailed hawk flew close over the rider; again the people tried to hold the rider back, but still he rode on. By the time he revealed this vision a few years later, His Horse Looking had already gained a reputation for great bravery and daring. His father and Chips, another holy man, made him a medicine bundle and gave him a red-tailed hawk feather and a smooth stone to wear.

When Curly went into battle thereafter, he wore a small lightning streak on his cheek, hail spots on his body, a breech cloth, a small stone, and a single feather; he did not take scalps. He was never seriously wounded in battle. His Horse Looking's father, in order to honor his son's achievements, bestowed his own name, Crazy Horse, upon the young man (he then took the name Worm) and asserted to his people that the Lakota had a new Crazy Horse, a great warrior with powerful medicine.

The Gratton debacle had one immediate effect other than the vision: It resulted in brutal reprisals by the Bluecoats. On September 3, 1855, shortly after Crazy Horse had experienced the vision, General W. S. Harney attacked the Brule camp in which Crazy Horse was living with Spotted Tail's people. The soldiers killed more than one hundred Indians (most of them women and children), took many prisoners, and captured most of the Lakota horses. Crazy Horse escaped injury and capture but was left with an abiding hatred of the whites. Because the major white invasion of the West did not begin until after the Civil War, Crazy Horse spent his youth living in the traditional ways: moving with the seasons, hunting, and warring with the other plains Indians.

LIFE'S WORK

The solitary boy grew into a strange man who, according to Black Elk,

> would go about the village without noticing people or saying anything. . . . All the Lakotas (Sioux) liked to dance and sing; but he never joined a dance, and they say nobody heard him sing. . . . He was a small man among

> the Lakotas and he was slender and had a thin face and his eyes looked through things and he always seemed to be thinking hard about something. He never wanted many things for himself, and did not have many ponies like a chief. They say that when game was scarce and the people were hungry, he would not eat at all. He was a queer man. Maybe he was always part way into that world of his vision.

Crazy Horse and the Oglala north of the Platte River lived in relative freedom from the white man's interference until 1864. From the early 1860's, however, there was ever-increasing pressure from white settlers and traders on the U.S. government to guarantee the safety of people moving along the Oregon and Santa Fe trails and to open the Bozeman Road that ran through the Lakota country.

The military began preparations early in 1865 to invade the Powder River Indian country; General Patrick E. Connor announced that the Indians north of the Platte "must be hunted like wolves." Thus began what came to be known as Red Cloud's War, named for the Lakota chief who led the Lakota and Cheyenne warriors. General Connor's punitive expedition in 1865 was a failure, as were subsequent efforts to force the free Indians to sign a treaty. In 1866, General Henry B. Carrington fortified and opened the Bozeman Road through Lakota territory. By 1868, having been outsmarted, frustrated, and beaten again and again by Red Cloud's warriors, the United States forces conceded defeat, abandoned the forts, closed the Bozeman Road, and granted the Black Hills and the Powder River country to the Indians forever.

Crazy Horse rose to prominence as a daring and astute leader during the years of Red Cloud's War. He was chosen by the Oglala chiefs to be a "shirt-wearer" or protector of the people. All the other young men chosen were the sons of chiefs; he alone was selected solely on the basis of his accomplishments. Crazy Horse played a central role in the most famous encounter of this war. On December 21, 1866, exposing himself repeatedly to great danger, he decoyed a troop of eighty-one of Colonel Carrington's men, commanded by Captain William J. Fetterman, into a trap outside Fort Phil Kearny. All the soldiers were killed.

Red Cloud's War ended in November, 1868, when the chief signed a treaty that acknowledged that the Powder River and Big Horn country were Indian land into which the white man could not come without permission. The treaty also indicated that the Indians were to live on a reservation on the west side of the Missouri River. Red Cloud and his followers moved onto a reservation, but Crazy Horse and many others refused to sign or to leave their lands for a reservation; Crazy Horse never signed a treaty.

As early as 1870, many whites who were driven by reports of gold in the Black Hills began to venture illegally into Indian territory. Surveyors for the Northern Pacific Railroad protected by United States troops also invaded the Black Hills in order to chart the course of their railway through Indian land. Crazy Horse, who became the war chief of the Oglala after Red Cloud moved onto the reservation, led numerous successful raids against the survey parties and finally drove them from his lands. The surveyors returned in 1873; this time they were protected by a formidable body of troops commanded by Lieutenant Colonel George A. Custer.

In spite of a series of sharp attacks, Crazy Horse was unable to defeat Custer, and the surveyors finished their task. In 1874, Custer was back in Indian territory; he led an expedition of twelve hundred men purportedly to gather military and scientific information. He reported that the hills were filled with gold "from the roots on down"; the fate of the Indians and their sacred hills was sealed. Not even the military genius of their war chief, their skill and bravery, and their clear title to the land could save them from the greed and power of the white men.

During the years between the signing of the 1868 treaty and the full-scale invasion of Indian lands in 1876, Crazy Horse apparently fell in love with a Lakota woman named Black Buffalo Woman, but she was taken from him through deceit and married another man, No Water. Crazy Horse and Black Buffalo Woman maintained their attachment to each other over a period of years, causing some divisiveness among the Lakota and resulting in the near-fatal shooting of Crazy Horse by No Water. Crazy Horse eventually married an Oglala named Tasina Sapewin (Black Shawl) who bore him a daughter. He named the child They Are Afraid of Her, and when she died a few years later, he was stricken with grief.

Because of the reports concerning the great mineral wealth of the Black Hills, the U.S. government began to try to force all the Indians to move onto reservations. On February 7, 1876, the War Department ordered General Philip Sheridan to commence operations against the Lakota living off of reservations. The first conflict in this deadly campaign occurred March 17, when General George Crook's advance column under Colonel Joseph J. Reynolds attacked a peaceful camp of Northern Cheyennes and Oglala Lakota who were on their way from the Red Cloud Agency to their hunting grounds. The survivors fled to Crazy Horse's camp.

Crazy Horse took them in, gave them food and shelter, and promised them that "we are going to fight the white man again." Crazy Horse's chance came in June, when a Cheyenne hunting party sighted a column of Bluecoats camped in the valley of the Rosebud River. Crazy Horse had studied the soldiers' ways of fighting for years, and he was prepared for this battle. General Crook and his pony soldiers were no match for the Lakota and Cheyenne guided by Crazy Horse. Crook retreated under cover of darkness to his base camp on Goose Creek.

After the Battle of Rosebud (June 17), the Indians moved west to the valley of the Greasy Grass (Little Bighorn) River. Blackfoot, Hunkpapa, Sans Arc, Minneconjous, Brule, and Oglala Lakota were there, as well as the Cheyenne—perhaps as many as fifteen thousand Indians, including five thousand warriors. The soldiers had originally planned a three-pronged campaign to ensnare and destroy the Indians. Crook's withdrawal, however, forced General Alfred Terry to revise the plan. On June 22, he ordered Colonel John Gibbon to go back to the Bighorn River and to march south along it to the Little Bighorn River. Custer and the Seventh Cavalry were to go along the Rosebud parallel to Gibbon and catch the Indians in between. General Terry, with the remaining forces, would trail them and provide whatever support was necessary. General Terry expected that Gibbon and Custer would converge and engage the enemy on June 26.

General Custer and his troops arrived on June 25, and Custer elected to attack the Indian encampment without waiting for Gibbon's column. His rash decision was fatal to him and to the Seventh Cavalry. The Lakota and Cheyenne, led by Crazy Horse and Gall, Sitting Bull's lieutenant, crushed Custer; more than 250 soldiers died. Perhaps Crazy Horse and Gall could have defeated the troops of Gibbon and Terry as well, but they were not committed to an all-out war, as were the whites, and they had had enough killing, so they moved on, leaving the soldiers to bury their dead.

The Battle of the Little Bighorn is recognized as a great moment in the history of the Lakota nation, but it also proved to be a sad one, for it confirmed the U.S. government's conviction that in spite of the Treaty of 1868, the free Indians must be either confined to a reservation or annihilated. In the brutal days that were to follow, Crazy Horse clearly emerged as the single most important spiritual and military leader of the Lakota.

The federal government's response was swift: On August 15, Congress enacted a new law that required the Indians to give up all rights to the Powder River country and the Black Hills. Red Cloud and Spotted Tail succumbed to what they took to be inevitable and signed documents acknowledging that they accepted the new law. Sitting Bull and Gall fought against the forces of General Crook and Colonel Nelson Miles during the remainder of 1876 but decided to take their people to Canada in the spring of 1877. Crazy Horse alone resolved to stay on his own lands in the sacred Black Hills.

General Crook led an enormous army of infantry, cavalry, and artillery from the south through the Powder River country in pursuit of Crazy Horse, and Colonel Miles led his army from the north, looking for the Oglala war chief. Crazy Horse was forced to move his village from one place to another in order to avoid the Bluecoats. He had little ammunition or food, the winter was bitterly cold, and his people were weary. In December, he approached Colonel Miles's outpost and sent a small party of chiefs and warriors with a flag of truce to find out what the colonel's intentions were. The party was attacked as it approached the outpost; only three Lakota survived. Miles's brutal intentions were made quite clear, and Crazy Horse was forced to flee again.

Colonel Miles caught up with the Lakota on January 8, 1877, at Battle Butte; in spite of his lack of ammunition and the weakened condition of his warriors, Crazy Horse was able, through bravery and superior tactics, to defeat Miles. Crazy Horse and his band escaped through the Wolf Mountains to the familiar country of the Little Powder River. The soldiers decided to cease their military operations until spring, but they redoubled their efforts to persuade the Indians to surrender. Numerous emissaries were sent throughout the northern lands with pack trains of food and gifts to tempt the suffering Lakota and Cheyenne into coming in to the security of the agencies.

Many small bands yielded to these entreaties, but Crazy Horse only listened politely and sent the messengers home. His fame and his symbolic value to the Indians grew daily; the longer he resisted, the more important he became to the thousands of Indians now confined to reservations. When Spotted Tail himself came to entice them to give up, Crazy Horse went off alone into the deep snows of the mountains in order to give his people the freedom to decide their own fate. Most chose to stay with their leader, but Spotted Tail did persuade

Big Foot to bring his Minneconjous in when spring came.

In April, General Crook sent Red Cloud to plead with Crazy Horse and to promise him that if he surrendered, the Lakota would be given a reservation in the Powder River country, where they could live and hunt in peace. At last, Crazy Horse gave in; the suffering of his people was so great, the prospects of renewed conflict with Crook and Miles so grim, and the promise of a Powder River reservation so tempting that he led his band to the Red Cloud Agency, arriving in an almost triumphal procession witnessed by thousands on May 5, 1877.

Predictably, Crazy Horse did not like living at the agency, and General Crook did not make good on his promise of a Powder River reservation. Black Shawl died, and Crazy Horse married Nellie Larrabee, the daughter of a trader. The more restive Crazy Horse became, the more concerned the government became, and the more vulnerable the chief was to the plots of his enemies. Wild rumors that Crazy Horse planned to escape or to murder General Crook circulated.

The government officials decided that it would be best to arrest and confine the war chief. On September 4, 1877, eight companies of cavalry and four hundred Indians, led by Red Cloud, left Fort Robinson to arrest Crazy Horse and deliver him to the fort. Crazy Horse attempted to flee but was overtaken and agreed to go and talk with Crook. When it became clear to him that he was not being taken to a conference but to prison, Crazy Horse drew his knife and tried to escape. He was restrained by Little Big Man and other followers of Red Cloud, and Private William Gentles bayoneted him. He died during the early hours of September 5; his father, Worm, was at his side. Crazy Horse's parents were allowed to take the body; they rode into the hills and buried their son in a place known only to them.

Later that fall, the Lakota were forced to begin a journey eastward to the Missouri River and a new reservation/prison. Among the thousands of Indians were Crazy Horse's Oglala. After approximately seventy-five miles of travel, the Oglala, two thousand strong, broke from the line and raced for Canada and freedom. The small cavalry contingent could only watch as these Lakota fled to join Sitting Bull—manifesting, in their refusal to submit to the white man, the spirit of Crazy Horse.

SIGNIFICANCE

Crazy Horse, like numerous other Indian patriots, was a martyr to the westward expansion of the United States, to the unity and technological superiority of the white culture, to its assumed racial and cultural superiority, and to the greed of white Americans. He also seems to have been a truly exceptional and admirable man; he was the greatest warrior and general of a people to whom war was a way of life. He provided a powerful example of integrity and independence for the Indians during a very difficult period of their history; he never attended a peace council with the whites, never signed a treaty, never even considered giving up his lands: "One does not sell the earth upon which the people walk." Furthermore, he seems to have been a basically selfless man who was genuinely devoted to the greater good of his people, to protecting his native land and his traditional way of life. To quote Black Elk:

> He was brave and good and wise. He never wanted anything but to save his people, and he fought the Wasichus (the whites) only when they came to kill us in our own country.... They could not kill him in battle. They had to lie to him and kill him that way.

When Crazy Horse was born, the Lakota were a strong, proud, and free people; they were skilled horsemen and masters of war and hunting. The rhythms of their lives were the rhythms of the seasons and of the game they hunted. They venerated nature and cherished individual freedom and achievement. When Crazy Horse died, the Lakota were still proud, but they were no longer truly strong or free. Freedom, independence, and cultural integrity were realities for Crazy Horse in his youth, but particularly after the tragic battle at Wounded Knee in December, 1890, freedom and independence and integrity as a people have only been dreams for the Lakota—dreams in which the legend and spirit of Crazy Horse, fierce, intelligent, indomitable, continue to play a vital part, as is evidenced by Peter Matthiessen's choice of a title for his angry and eloquent 1983 study of the contemporary struggles of the Lakota: *In the Spirit of Crazy Horse*.

—*Hal Holladay*

FURTHER READING

Ambrose, Stephen E. *Crazy Horse and Custer: The Parallel Lives of Two American Warriors*. New York: Anchor Books, 1996. Ambrose, a historian who has written several popular biographies and military histories, examines the similarities between Crazy Horse and Custer.

Andrist, Ralph K. *The Long Death: The Last Days of the Plains Indians*. New York: Macmillan, 1964. The story of the military conquest of the plains Indians, the Lakota as well as others. A vivid, meticulous, and well-written survey. Excellent maps.

Brown, Dee. *Bury My Heart at Wounded Knee: An Indian History of the American West*. New York: Holt, Rinehart and Winston, 1971. A revisionist history of the West from 1860 to 1890 told from an Indian point of view. Crucial to a full understanding of American history and the destruction of the culture and civilization of the American Indian. Crazy Horse's story is one of many.

Connell, Evan S. *Son of the Morning Star: Custer and the Little Bighorn*. San Francisco: North Point Press, 1984. An intelligent and thorough reconstruction of what might have happened and why at the Little Bighorn on June 25, 1876. A fascinating study of the major participants in that historic battle, focusing on Custer.

Hinman, Eleanor. "Oglala Sources on the Life of Crazy Horse." *Nebraska History* 57, no. 1 (1976). Interviews with Oglala Indians who witnessed various events in the life of Crazy Horse. Provides particularly interesting insights into his conduct in battle, his feud with No Water, and his death.

Josephy, Alvin M., Jr. *The Patriot Chiefs: A Chronicle of American Indian Resistance*. New York: Viking Press, 1958. The life stories of outstanding Indian leaders, including Crazy Horse, Tecumseh, and Chief Joseph. A good brief biography. Places Crazy Horse's struggle in the context of the heroic and tragic resistance of Indians to the white man throughout North America.

Marshall, Joseph, III. *The Journey of Crazy Horse: A Lakota History*. New York: Viking Press, 2004. Marshall, a Lakota who was raised on the Rosebud Sioux Reservation, drew on the recollections of his grandfather and other oral histories to produce this biography.

Neihardt, John G. *Black Elk Speaks*. Lincoln: University of Nebraska Press, 1961. A fascinating document that contains the life story of an Oglala holy man as told by himself. Black Elk was a member of Crazy Horse's tribe and was present at the Little Bighorn, as well as at Fort Robinson when Crazy Horse was killed. Invaluable insights into the Lakota culture and way of life.

Olson, James C. *Red Cloud and the Sioux Problem*. Lincoln: University of Nebraska Press, 1965. Well-documented appraisal of Indian affairs in the Western plains during the 1860's and the 1870's. Thorough account of relations between the Lakota and the federal government. Judicious treatment of contending leaders.

Sajna, Mike. *Crazy Horse: The Life Behind the Legend*. New York: John Wiley & Sons 2000. Detailed biography, offering new perspectives on Crazy Horse's role in the battle at the Little Bighorn and his eventual surrender and murder.

Sandoz, Mari. *Crazy Horse: The Strange Man of the Oglalas*. New York: Alfred A. Knopf, 1941. A comprehensive and authoritative biography in which the author attempts to tell not only the chief's story but also that of his people and culture. Told from Crazy Horse's point of view.

Vaughn, Jesse W. *Indian Fights: New Facts on Seven Encounters*. Norman: University of Oklahoma Press, 1966. A flawed study of seven significant battles that occurred between 1864 and 1877 in Wyoming and Montana. Vaughn's accounts of the Fetterman Massacre and Major Reno's part in the Battle of the Little Bighorn are quite useful.

SEE ALSO: Black Hawk; George A. Custer; Red Cloud; Sitting Bull.

RELATED ARTICLES in *Great Events from History: The Nineteenth Century, 1801-1900:* June 13, 1866-November 6, 1868: Red Cloud's War; December 21, 1866: Fetterman Massacre; 1876-1877: Sioux War; June 25, 1876: Battle of the Little Bighorn.

DAVID CROCKETT
American frontiersman and politician

As a congressman from western Tennessee and the author of a best-selling autobiography, Crockett became the most celebrated backwoodsman in the United States. His heroic death at the Battle of the Alamo transformed him into a legendary frontier hero.

BORN: August 17, 1786; Greene County, Tennessee
DIED: March 6, 1836; The Alamo, San Antonio, Texas
ALSO KNOWN AS: Davy Crockett
AREAS OF ACHIEVEMENT: Exploration, government and politics

EARLY LIFE

David Crockett grew up in the poverty-stricken frontier regions of eastern Tennessee, where his father operated a tavern. His formal education was limited to a six-month period during which he worked two days per week for the village schoolmaster in return for board and four days of schooling. Crockett's manuscript letters prove that he learned basic literacy in the one hundred or so days he attended school, although his spelling was always erratic and his grasp of grammatical rules was uncertain. On August 14, 1806, shortly before his twentieth birthday, he married Mary Finley, with whom he had three children. Crockett moved to central and then west Tennessee in search of better land, supporting his family through subsistence farming and his skill as a hunter.

When the Creek Indian War broke out in 1813, Crockett enlisted and served as a scout until March of 1815, during which time he was promoted to sergeant. Crockett's duties took him south into Alabama and eventually to Pensacola, Florida. The army was poorly supplied and constantly short of food; Crockett spent much time hunting to help feed his companions. He observed with some bitterness the effect of his lack of social rank when the commander of his regiment ignored his warning that an Indian attack was imminent but acted immediately when an officer reported the same information the next day.

Shortly after Crockett's return from the war, his first wife died. Within one year he had remarried. His new wife, Elizabeth Patton, was a widow with two young children of her own, as well as a substantial inheritance of cash and slaves. Her funds enabled Crockett to move to Lawrence County and set up a gristmill and a distillery in the spring of 1817. For a while he seemed to prosper, but his businesses did not succeed. In 1831 he had to sell some slaves in order to reduce his debts. Crockett was appointed a justice of the peace by the state of Tennessee in November, 1817. The next year his neighbors elected him colonel of the fifty-seventh regiment of militia in Lawrence County. In 1821 he was elected to the state legislature and was reelected in 1823. He failed to win his bid for Congress in 1825, but in 1827 he went to Washington, D.C., for the first of his three terms in the House of Representatives.

LIFE'S WORK

Crockett's tall tales and backwoods humor entertained and attracted the press, which covered his activities, real or imaginary, in detail and spread his fame across the country. Many of the reports were intentional exaggerations, such as claiming that his reputation as a hunter had spread so wide among the animals that when he aimed his rifle at a treed raccoon the animal meekly climbed down and surrendered, or that while traveling to the 1829 session of Congress he had waded into the Ohio River and towed a disabled steamboat back to shore. He was reputed to have shot forty-seven bears in one month and was said to ride alligators for exercise. When Crockett supported President Andrew Jackson, the Whig papers sneered at him as an example of an uncivilized westerner and alleged that he drank the water from his finger bowl at a White House dinner. After Crockett broke with Jackson, the Whig papers began to compliment him while the Jacksonian press, which had praised his rustic wisdom and virtue, began to attack him.

As much as he enjoyed his celebrity status and was willing to perform the part of the ignorant but shrewd backwoodsman, Crockett took seriously his work as a congressman. He was frustrated by his lack of success in advancing the interests of his subsistence farming constituents. In the state legislature, he had championed the cause of the western Tennessee squatters against the eastern Tennessee landholding aristocrats. In Congress he broke with the Jackson forces when they failed to support his Tennessee Vacant Land Bill, which would have allowed those living on and improving federal lands in western Tennessee to secure title to the land. When Crockett opposed Jackson's Indian Removal Bill in 1830 and also proposed using federal funds to aid poor American Indians living in his district, the break with Jackson was complete. Jacksonian opposition led to Crockett's loss in the 1831 election; however, he succeeded in winning a third term in 1833.

After his break with the Jacksonians, Crockett wrote an autobiography with the assistance of Thomas Chilton,

David Crockett. (Library of Congress)

a Kentucky congressman who lived in the same Washington, D.C., boarding house as Crockett. Crockett freely acknowledged Chilton's help and informed his publisher that Chilton was entitled to half the royalties from the work. The book was a campaign autobiography intended to help Crockett's bid for reelection. Like Benjamin Franklin's autobiography, a copy of which Crockett owned, the work described the rise of a self-made man who overcame hardships to achieve greatness.

Crockett's own voice and language dominated the book, which was a fairly accurate account of his life, apart from some exaggerations about his military career in the Creek Indian War and his prowess as a hunter. Crockett described several battles during which he was not present. The work portrayed a humorous braggart and backwoods trickster who rose to national prominence as a congressman. The language of the autobiography faithfully reproduced southwestern frontier idioms, and the book included some of the first printed examples of frontier humor. For example, when Crockett returned from an extended hunting trip to discover that his companions had reported him dead, he remarked, "I know'd this was a whapper of a lie, as soon as I heard it."

Narrative of the Life of David Crockett of the State of Tennessee appeared in 1834 and was an immediate success. Within one year, it went through seven editions, including one in London, England, and twelve new printings were released in 1835. Encouraged by the success of the autobiography, Crockett permitted the Whigs to publish, under his name, two books attacking the Jacksonians. *An Account of Colonel Crockett's Tour to the North and Down East* (1835) described the reception of Crockett's speeches attacking Jackson during his tour of Whig cities in the North. *The Life of Martin Van Buren* (1835) was a vitriolic satire of the Jacksonian candidate for president in 1836. Crockett wrote neither book, and they failed to attract the public.

The autobiography's success as a literary work did little to advance Crockett's political career. He reacted bitterly when he lost a hotly contested election for his House seat in August, 1835. He told his constituents that they could go to hell and that he was going to Texas. On November 1, Crockett and several of his friends left for Texas, where American settlers had revolted against Mexico. He hoped to find fertile land where he and his family could rebuild their fortunes and perhaps revive his political career in the new republic. Crockett was welcomed wherever he went in Texas, and in January, 1836, he took an oath of allegiance to the provisional government of Texas that entitled him to vote and run for office during the pending constitutional convention. He then joined the rebel army and moved south to San Antonio in early February.

The president of Mexico, General Antonio López de Santa Anna, determined to crush the Texan rebellion, arrived at San Antonio with some 2,400 troops. The Texan defenders, numbering 183, barricaded themselves in an old mission building, the Alamo, where they held out from February 23 to March 6. Santa Anna had ordered his men to take no prisoners, and none of the defenders survived. Crockett's active role and bravery during the siege is attested in all authentic accounts. However, the legendary scene in which Crockett, out of ammunition and using his broken rifle as a club, dies surrounded by the bodies of a dozen Mexicans he has shot is mythical. Documentary evidence shows that Crockett, along with a half-dozen other defenders, was captured after resistance ceased and brought before Santa Anna, who angrily ordered him executed.

SIGNIFICANCE

The process of turning David Crockett, eccentric backwoods congressman, into Davy Crockett, legendary superhero, began while Crockett was still alive. His colorful personality had made him one of the best-known politicians of the 1830's. Even before his death, exaggerated stories about him, some based on tall tales he loved to tell to amused Washington reporters and congressmen, had begun to circulate. Many were included in a work that Crockett repudiated, although it was published under his name: *Sketches and Eccentricities of Colonel David Crockett of West Tennessee* (1833). The work contained incidents that appeared to be based on Crockett's anecdotes.

Crockett's heroic death elevated him to almost mythic status. Crockett's publisher immediately commissioned Richard Penn Smith to write a fictional diary of Crockett's activities in Texas called *Col. Crockett's Exploits and Adventures in Texas, Written by Himself* (1836). Only the first two chapters, which were based on letters Crockett wrote to his publishers, are authentic. The fifty Crockett almanacs printed between 1835 and 1856 completed the transformation of Crockett into an American legend. These pamphlets, along with the usual calendars, weather predictions, domestic hints, and farming suggestions, included improbable Crockett hunting stories and endowed him with superhuman powers. Crockett is credited with saving the earth one winter when the entire planet froze: Crockett thawed the earth's axis with hot bear grease and kicked it loose again. Another tale claimed that he deflected Halley's comet from a collision course by climbing the Allegheny Mountains and twisting the tail off the comet.

Davy Crockett also figured as a fantastically successful hunter in six nineteenth century dime novels. A play that ran for over two thousand performances between 1874 and 1896 portrayed him as a handsome frontiersman whose gentlemanly conduct won the love of a wealthy neighbor's daughter. The most influential presentation of the legendary figure was Walt Disney's 1955 television production and film, *Davy Crockett, King of the Wild Frontier*, which used many of the legends that had grown up over the years to portray him as an ideal frontiersman and martyr of the Alamo. The production set off an enormous fad: Every young boy seemed to need a coonskin hat and fringed Crockett-style jacket so he could copy his hero. Crockett had become an icon of American heroism, and historians who wrote about the factual Crockett were assailed for subverting the image of this truly American hero.

—*Milton Berman*

FURTHER READING

Crockett, David. *Narrative of the Life of David Crockett of the State of Tennessee*. A facsimile edition with annotations and an introduction by James A. Shackford and Stanley J. Folmsbee. Knoxville: University of Tennessee Press, 1973. The insightful annotations make this the most useful version of Crockett's autobiography.

Davis, William C. *Three Roads to the Alamo: The Lives and Fortunes of David Crockett, James Bowie, and William Barret Travis*. New York: HarperCollins, 1998. Davis examines the lives of these three disparate men, describing what brought them to Texas and how they died there.

Derr, Mark. *The Frontiersman: The Real Life and the Many Legends of Davy Crockett*. New York: William Morrow, 1993. Derr supplies an informative and entertaining narrative of Crockett's life.

Hauck, Richard Boyd. *Crockett: A Bio-Bibliography*. Westport, Conn.: Greenwood Press, 1982. This book contains an excellent biography of Crockett and an analysis of the style and content of his writings.

Kilgore, Dan. *How Did Davy Die?* College Station: Texas A&M University Press, 1978. Kilgore provides a careful analysis of the evidence concerning the way Crockett died.

Lalire, Gregory J. "David Crockett." *American History* 38, no. 6 (February, 2004): 16. A modern tribute to Crockett, the politician and soldier.

Lofaro, Michael A., ed. *Davy Crockett: The Man, The Legend, The Legacy, 1786-1986*. Knoxville: University of Tennessee Press, 1985. This volume deals mostly with the legends about Crockett, from the early almanacs through Disney's television series of the 1950's.

Lofaro, Michael A., and Joe Cummings, eds. *Crockett at Two Hundred: New Perspectives on the Man and the Myth*. Knoxville: University of Tennessee Press, 1989. This book contains ten scholarly articles on Crockett's life, death, and writings, along with an extensive bibliography.

Shackford, James Atkins. *David Crockett: The Man and the Legend*. Edited by John B. Shackford. Chapel Hill: University of North Carolina Press, 1956. This is the definitive scholarly biography of Crockett, although it needs to be brought up to date by Kilgore's book on Crockett's death.

SEE ALSO: Stephen Fuller Austin; Antonio López de Santa Anna.

RELATED ARTICLE in *Great Events from History: The Nineteenth Century, 1801-1900:* October 2, 1835-April 21, 1836: Texas Revolution.

SAMUEL AJAYI CROWTHER

West African cleric

The first African to be ordained an Anglican bishop, Crowther escaped from slave traders as a boy and used his educational opportunities to become the most prominent West African cleric of his time, as well as an important figure in the European exploration of West Africa.

BORN: c. 1806; Osogun, Yorubaland (now in Nigeria)
DIED: December 31, 1891; Lagos (now in Nigeria)
ALSO KNOWN AS: Samuel Adjai Crowther
AREAS OF ACHIEVEMENT: Religion and theology, exploration

EARLY LIFE

Samuel Ajayi Crowther (AH-jah-yee KROW-ther) was born in the Yoruba-speaking region of what is now southwestern Nigeria at a time when few written records were kept. The details of his youth are known primarily through his own accounts, which he published in 1837 at the request of the Church Missionary Society of London.

Crowther was born Ajayi, the second of four children of a Yoruba man named Aiyemi, whom he described as skilled in weaving a traditional type of cloth with elephant patterns. His mother, Afala, was descended from the rulers of the Oyo Kingdom of the Yoruba people and had served as a priestess of Obatala. Crowther's later memoirs suggest that his father also had other wives, and children by them as well. Crowther grew up in Osogun in the Ibarapa district of the Yorubaland.

During Ajayi's teenage years, his homeland was engulfed in civil warfare, in which prisoners were often taken to the coast to be sold as slaves. During the spring of 1821, Osogun was attacked and his family was sold into slavery. He described his captors as Muslims from Oyo. During his ensuing journey, he was resold several times and finally ended up on a Portuguese slave ship in April, 1822.

Great Britain had outlawed the slave trade in 1806, and ships of the Royal Navy patrolled the waters off the western coast of Africa. On Ajayi's first day at sea, two British ships attacked the Portuguese slave ship. Nearly one hundred captive Africans were killed, but others, including Ajayi, were freed and taken ashore in Sierra Leone, a new colony that Britain had established for freed slaves. Thus, at the age of about sixteen, Ajayi found himself alone in the world. His father had been killed during the fighting in Yorubaland, and his mother and sisters had been separated from him after being taken captive. Twenty-five years later, however, he returned to Nigeria and was reunited with his mother, who had similarly been rescued.

Meanwhile, in Bathurst, Sierra Leone, Ajayi lived with a family named Davey and was taught to read and write. On December 11, 1825, he was baptized a Christian by missionaries of the Anglican Church Missionary Society (CMS) and took the name Samuel Crowther, after the vicar of Christ Church in London who was a member of the CMS. Having proven himself a good student, he was taken to London for a year of schooling and was then returned to Sierra Leone to become one of the first graduates of Fourah Bay College. In 1829, he married Susan Asano Thompson, another freed slave. While he was teaching school for several years, he and his wife had six children: Samuel, Jr., Abigail, Susan, Josiah, Julianah, and Dandeson.

LIFE'S WORK

Samuel Ajayi Crowther's full potential became known during the British exploration of the Niger River in 1841. At that time, in spite of British opposition, slavery was still a major problem. In England, Sir Thomas Fowell Buxton had written *The African Slave Trade* (1839) and its sequel, *The Remedy* (1840), two books that proposed a more aggressive approach to introducing "Christianity, Commerce, and Civilization" to Africa. A philanthropic London group then proposed establishing a farming settlement on the banks of the lower Niger River that would have a transforming effect and sent an expedition to West Africa to explore the river. A major obstacle to the expedition's success was the fact that Europeans were not physically prepared for conditions in tropical West Africa. Nearly all the 145 European members of the expedition contracted malaria, and forty of them died. Only Crowther, working alongside a missionary named J. F. Schön, was able to thrive.

After the expedition, Henry Venn, who became the secretary of the CMS in 1841, recognized that strong African leaders would be the key to the success of the society's missionary work in Africa. He invited Crowther to return to London for seminary education and to be ordained an Anglican priest on Trinity Sunday—the eighth Sunday after Easter—in 1843.

Over the next two decades, Crowther played a central role in the CMS's Yorubaland mission. Despite Venn's philosophy of involving Africans in mission work, Crowther still took a back seat to European leaders, including Henry Townsend, who led a major expedition to Abeokuta in Yorubaland. However, it was Crowther's ability with the Yoruba language, his personal communication skills, and his daily preaching under a tree near the market that led to success. He gained the confidence of a Yoruba holy man among the local people and convinced local leaders that the British would support them against attacking armies from the north. He also worked on translating the Bible and liturgies into the Yoruba language.

In 1854, Crowther led a second expedition up the Niger River, and a third trip soon followed. Although these expeditions fared better with the health of their crews, they met misfortune when their ship was wrecked along the way. However, Crowther used the opportunity to begin mission work among the Nupe and Hausa peoples of the northern Nigerian region.

The confidence that Venn had placed in Crowther was clearly bearing fruit. His next step was to transfer leadership completely. On June 29, 1864, at England's Canterbury Cathedral, Crowther was consecrated the first African bishop in the Church of England. This led to excitement in England with the church filled to capacity. However, Crowther's advancement was not made without controversy, and European prejudices against Africans continued to show through.

As bishop, Crowther based his work in Lagos, on the southern coast of Nigeria. However, there was some ambiguity about the actual expanse of his overseeing activity. However, in 1868, when all European missionaries were expelled from Abeokuta, Crowther was still able to journey into the interior to supervise the ongoing work of the African church. Evidence of the success of his leadership can be seen from the town of Bonny on the Niger River, where local tribal chieftains invited him to educate their children. With his own son Dandeson leading the effort, the missionaries began with elementary schools and then established technical schools and eventually the first girls' secondary school in Africa. In other locations, Crowther was well respected as he acted as a mediator with trade companies and development. A network of African pastors under his supervision continued to establish congregations throughout the interior regions.

The last part of Crowther's life was a struggle. In London, CMS leaders began to retreat from the vision of Henry Venn, who served as secretary from 1841 to 1872. Venn's replacement began making decisions about the Nigerian missions without consulting Crowther. Then he named a commission of inquiry to investigate alleged abuses of Crowther's office, including charges that the evangelistic work of the mission was being neglected. A lay leader of Crowther's mission was accused of beating a housemaid to death. The report was sent to London without even allowing Crowther to read it. The London-based mission society responded by reprimanding Crowther and firing twelve of fifteen African pastors. Crowther was forced to resign from the finance committee.

During Crowther's many expeditions and travels, he had been forced to leave his wife for long periods of time. After fifty years of marriage, his wife died on October 19, 1880. During the following July, Crowther suffered a stroke. He died around midnight on the last day of 1881.

SIGNIFICANCE

The life of Samuel Ajayi Crowther is significant for several reasons. First, it is a fascinating story of a young slave escaping his captors to rise to prominence in Africa. It is also the story of the first African bishop, a man ahead of his time when many of his European counterparts were holding on to the colonial past. Although Africans responded well to his leadership, both missionaries and missionary society members in England seemed to feel threatened by the presence of a strong African leader in the society. In 1882, after Crowther died, he was replaced by an English bishop. Africa's Anglican Church would not see another African bishop until 1952.

One of Crowther's biographers referred to him as the "Patriotic Bishop." Crowther's strengths went beyond his resistance to West African malaria and his mastery of the African languages and environment; he also had the indigenous vision, shared by Henry Venn, that he understood what was good for Africa. Crowther's mission philosophy was holistic; he established schools and promoted economic development alongside his evangelical work. He also appreciated the need to preserve African cultures. In addition to translating European books, he was a prolific journalist, recording in detail information from his expeditions to the interior. During a time Europeans labeled traditional religions as "pagan" and African Islam as "false," Crowther set an example of patient and humble dialogue. His views would later find wide acceptance. The mission philosophy of many twenty-first century mainline churches can be traced back to Samuel Ajayi Crowther.

—Fred Strickert

FURTHER READING

Ade Ajayi, J. F. *Christian Missions in Nigeria, 1841-1891: The Making of a New Elite*. Evanston: Northwestern University Press, 1965. Analysis of early period of Nigerian mission work by the leading historian of Christianity in Nigeria.

_____. *A Patriot to the Core: Bishop Samuel Ajaji Crowther*. Lagos, Nigeria: Spectrum Books, 2001. Analyzes the power struggle between London missionaries and the African bishop and the significance of his contributions.

Apter, Andrew. *Black Critics and Kings: The Hermeneutics of Power in Yoruba Society*. Chicago: University of Chicago Press, 1992. Chapter 9 of this book analyzes Crowther's diaries as a resource for information on Yoruba culture.

Milsome, J. R. *Samuel Adjai Crowther: Bishop of Courage*. Oxford, England: Oxford University Press, 1968. Biography aimed at adolescent readers.

Olsen, Ted. "Bishop Before His Time." *Christian History* 22, no. 3 (August, 2003): 10-15. Discussion of Crowther in an issue of the journal that focuses on the African "apostles"—indigenous leaders who contributed to Christianity in Africa.

Page, Jesse. *The Black Bishop: Samuel Adjai Crowther*. Westport, Conn.: Greenwood Press, 1979. A reprint of the comprehensive, though uncritical, 1908 biography of Crowther.

SEE ALSO: William Carey; Paul Cuffe; Mary Kingsley; David Livingstone.

RELATED ARTICLE in *Great Events from History: The Nineteenth Century, 1801-1900:* c. 1830-1865: Southerners Advance Proslavery Arguments.

PAUL CUFFE

American shipbuilder, abolitionist, and black nationalist

The son of an African-born slave and a Native American woman, Cuffe overcame racial discrimination to become a successful shipbuilder and trader and helped initiate a black nationalist movement that advocated colonizing of Africa by free African Americans.

BORN: January 17, 1759; Cuttyhunk Island, Massachusetts
DIED: September 7, 1817; Westport, Massachusetts
ALSO KNOWN AS: Paul Cuffee; Cuffe Slocum
AREAS OF ACHIEVEMENT: Business, social reform

EARLY LIFE

Paul Cuffe (KAH-fee) was the son of a man named Kofi who had been born in Africa and brought to New England as a slave in 1728. Given the surname of his owner, his father was known as Cuffe Slocum. After he was freed in 1742, he married a Native American woman, Ruth Moses, of the Wampanoag tribe. They then settled on a farm on Cuttyhunk, a small island off the coast of Massachusetts. Many of the local residents were Quakers—members of the Society of Friends. Although Ruth and Cuffe Slocum were not Quakers, they shared many Quaker beliefs and gave their ten children Christian names.

In 1766 Cuffe Slocum moved his family to Westport, Massachusetts, where Paul, his youngest son, worked on the family farm. There was no public school, so young Paul taught himself to read and write. Slocum died when Paul was fourteen; afterward, Paul and his brother John worked the farm to support the family. However, Paul was ambitious for an adventurous life. He signed on as a seaman, first on a New England whaling ship and later on cargo vessels. During these international voyages he learned the navigational skills that would serve him throughout his maritime career.

With the money Paul earned as a sailor, he and his brother David went into the shipbuilding business. During the Revolutionary War he ran ships through Great Britain's blockade of New England ports to supply the settlers of the coastal towns and Nantucket with trading goods. He was once jailed by the British and later was several times attacked by pirates and robbed of his cargos.

Proud of his African heritage, Paul took his father's name, calling himself Paul Cuffe (or Cuffee). At that time, free African Americans were few in Massachusetts, and although no state law prohibited them from voting, the local government denied them this right. Taking a stand against this injustice, Paul and his brother John refused to pay their taxes and were briefly jailed. Eventually, they negotiated a settlement to pay only part of their assessments and were freed. In 1783, Paul married Alice Pequit, a Native American woman, and began the career that would eventually make him one of the wealthiest black men in America.

LIFE'S WORK

Cuffe began building ships in his own shipyard in Westport and went into business with his brother-in-law. His crews were made up of African Americans and Native Americans, several of whom were his nephews. At that time, white Americans generally regarded African Americans as inferior and treated them poorly. However, Cuffe was highly regarded by white men as a "Negro" who "knew his place" and managed to make his way in a racist society by exercising great personal charm, without sacrificing his dignity. As captain of a ship with a mixed black and Indian crew, he made trading voyages into southern U.S. ports, where the slave owners feared rebellions. Cuffe and his crew won the respect and admiration of the local citizens with their model behavior.

With the money earned from his trading voyages Cuffe established a home for his wife and seven children in Westport, Massachusetts. Although recognized as a successful businessperson and a civic-minded member of the community, Cuffe still faced discrimination in his public life. Determined to educate his children properly, he petitioned the citizens of Westport in 1797 for support to found a school but was rejected at every turn. Undaunted, he built a schoolhouse on his own property, hired a teacher, and opened the school to all the children of Westport. Cuff's School, as it was called, was probably the first integrated school in America.

Cuffe embraced Quaker beliefs and had a number of influential white friends who admired his personal integrity and his skill in business. Although Quakers were committed to abolishing slavery, they did not accept African Americans as social equals. However, Quakers had successfully "civilized" several groups of Native Americans and helped them to become economically self-sufficient. With this example in mind and increasingly distressed by the injustice of slavery, Cuffe began a lifelong crusade to help free blacks achieve economic independence and end slavery in America

Cuffe believed that free African Americans, many of whom were skilled craftspeople and artisans, could emigrate to Africa and help "civilize" native Africans. Slavery would end, he thought, if the Africans who had profited by the slave trade were to become economically successful in other endeavors. His plan for an exploratory voyage to Africa was supported by such prominent abolitionists as Dr. Benjamin Rush and U.S. president James Madison. Cuffe hoped to transform the economy of West Africa with his American immigrants and to establish trade among the United States, Sierra Leone, and Great Britain.

During 1810 to 1811, Cuffe made his first voyage to Sierra Leone, a West African colony that Great Britain had established as a refuge for liberated slaves. By the time that Cuffe arrived there, the colony had undergone several transitions in government. The African Institutes, an organization founded by English abolitionists, supported Cuffe's mission. He traveled to England, winning the friendship and admiration of these influential men, then returned to Africa before coming home. However, trade restrictions instituted during the War of 1812 between Great Britain and the United States obstructed Cuffe's plans. Moreover, British merchants in Sierra Leone were hostile to his mission, which threatened their own economic interests.

Undaunted by these setbacks, Cuffe returned to West Africa in 1815 with thirty-eight African American emigrants who intended to settle there. Although Cuffe was supported by both British and American abolitionists, he faced many problems. Beset by restrictive trade regulations, he suffered severe financial losses when he attempted to sell his cargo. The British colonists continued to oppose his efforts. Ultimately, the abolitionists of both countries who nominally supported his mission did not support him financially. He returned to America, his dream of a self-sufficient colony unrealized.

Although Cuffe never abandoned his vision, he was forced to face reality. Having personally experienced many instances of racial discrimination and discouraged by the increasing opposition to the abolition of slavery, he continued to believe that Africa offered the only hope for the true freedom of African Americans. He was encouraged by the support of a new organization, the American Colonization Society, which had formed in 1817. That body endorsed the emigration of free blacks to Africa; however, it soon became clear to Cuffe that its primary goal was simply to rid the United States of free blacks. However, the society did play a role in the settling of Liberia, which became an independent black-ruled country in West Africa in 1847.

Reconciled to the knowledge that his life's work was at an end, Cuffe died peacefully at his home in Westport in 1817. In 1808, he had been accepted as a member of the Westport Friends Meeting. He was buried in the Quaker cemetery, but his grave was segregated from those of the white Quakers. The New Bedford, Massachusetts, Free Library now holds his journals and letters.

SIGNIFICANCE

Although Paul Cuffe's dream of a homeland in Africa for free black Americans was never fully realized, he is remembered as a founder of the black nationalist movement advocating the emigration of African Americans to Africa. He also made significant contributions to the abolitionist movement within the United States, even though he did not live to see abolition achieved.

As the first African American to earn a considerable fortune though hard work and entrepreneurship, Cuffe led a life that contradicted the prejudiced views of white Americans who believed that black people were intellectually inferior and incapable of achievement. His generous capacity for interracial friendships and his strong support for the freedom and dignity of African Americans mark him as an extraordinary man of his times.

—*Marjorie J. Podolsky*

FURTHER READING

Atkin, Mary Gage. *Paul Cuffe and the African Promised Land.* Nashville, Tenn.: Thomas Nelson, 1977. Contains useful details about early whaling and shipping industries and a detailed description of the Freetown, Sierra Leone, settlement that also describes tribal life in the surrounding area.

Diamond, Arthur. *Paul Cuffe: Merchant and Abolitionist.* New York: Chelsea House, 1989. A biography written for young-adult readers, this book is a good introduction to Cuffe's life. It includes a wealth of historical background about race relations of his era. It is part of the inspirational series *Black Americans of Achievement*, which is introduced by Coretta Scott King.

Harris, Sheldon H. *Paul Cuffe: Black America and the African Return.* New York: Simon & Schuster, 1972. Focuses on Cuffe's missionary activities in his attempt to colonize Sierra Leone. Includes journals of his African visit in 1811-1812 and a selection of his letters.

Thomas, Lamont D. "Paul Cuffe." In *Encyclopedia of African American Culture and History*, edited by Jack Saleman, David Lionel Smith, and Cornel West. Vol. 2. New York: Simon & Schuster, 1996. Succinct biography of major events in Cuffe's life; useful for quick reference.

_____. *Rise to Be a People: A Biography of Paul Cuffe.* Urbana: University of Illinois Press, 1986. A detailed scholarly account of Cuffe's life and work that draws on contemporary records, newspapers, and periodicals to place his career in historical context.

SEE ALSO: Samuel Ajayi Crowther; Frederick Douglass.

RELATED ARTICLES in *Great Events from History: The Nineteenth Century, 1801-1900:* April 9, 1816: African Methodist Episcopal Church Is Founded; January 1, 1831: Garrison Begins Publishing *The Liberator*; December, 1833: American Anti-Slavery Society Is Founded.

CALEB CUSHING

American politician and diplomat

Cushing enhanced the power and status of the U.S. attorney general's office through his legal opinions, his writings on the historical development and function of that cabinet post, and his recommendations for reform of the federal judiciary.

BORN: January 17, 1800; Salisbury, Massachusetts
DIED: January 2, 1879; Newburyport, Massachusetts
AREAS OF ACHIEVEMENT: Government and politics, diplomacy

EARLY LIFE

Caleb Cushing was the firstborn and only surviving son of John Newmarch Cushing, a merchant and shipowner, and Lydia Dow. A duty to serve his country came from his grandfather namesake, Judge Caleb Cushing, a representative in the Massachusetts General Court for twenty-seven years, and his uncle, Benjamin Cushing, who had fought in the American Revolution. His father's shipping trade with India influenced Cushing's promotion of U.S. trade to Asian markets.

Cushing received a bachelor's degree from Harvard in 1817. He then entered Harvard Law School and served a three-year apprenticeship under Ebenezer Moseley in Newburyport before being admitted to the bar in 1822. In November, 1824, he advanced his legal career by marrying Caroline Elizabeth Wilder, the daughter of a Massachusetts Supreme Court justice. The couple had no children, and Cushing never remarried after his wife's death in August, 1832.

Ambitious, intelligent, and tireless, Cushing quickly became a prominent resident of Essex County, Massachusetts, through his legal and literary accomplishments. By 1826, he was arguing cases before the Supreme Judicial Court of Massachusetts and had been commissioned a justice of the peace. In addition, Cushing received much acclaim for his articles on law, nature, history, philosophy, and science that were published in the *North American Review*, *U.S. Literary Gazette*, *Annual Register*, *Boston Monthly Magazine*, and *Boston Lyceum*. He also gained notice for his translation of French jurist Robert-Joseph Pothier's *Supplément au Traité du contrat de louage: Ou, Traité des contrats de louage maritimes* (1764; *A Treatise on Maritime Contracts of Letting to Hire*, 1821), his discussion of the tariff in *A Summary of Practical Principles of Political Economy* (1826), and his historical scholarship in *The History and Present State of the Town of Newburyport* (1826).

Influenced by Federalism's strong roots in Essex County and modeling himself after statesmen-scholars Edward Everett and Daniel Webster, Cushing entered politics in 1824 as a supporter of John Quincy Adams. He won election as a representative to the Massachusetts General Court and two years later became a state senator. In 1826, Cushing sought the North Essex District congressional seat. He lost the contest to pro-Andrew Jackson candidate John Varnum in a campaign marked by excessive mudslinging, which influenced Cushing's opposition to abolitionism. After serving three more terms in the general court, Cushing was elected to the House of Representatives in 1834 as a member of the anti-Jackson Whig Party.

LIFE'S WORK

Cushing served four consecutive terms in Congress (1835-1843). A staunch Whig during the first three terms, Cushing supported his party's economic programs—a protective tariff, internal improvements, reestablishment of the national bank, and distribution of proceeds from the sale of public lands among the states. He distinguished himself by leading Whig opposition against the financial policies of presidents Jackson and Martin Van Buren, particularly the Independent Treasury Bill. Furthermore, he resisted southern efforts to suppress the reading of antislavery petitions in Congress (the "gag rule").

As a member of the House Committee on Foreign Affairs, Cushing exhibited an Anglophobia and ardent support for U.S. territorial and commercial expansion that became quite evident. He demanded Great Britain's withdrawal from the disputed Aroostook Valley in northern Maine and urged an end to the agreement with Britain to jointly occupy the Oregon territory. Cushing also supported the annexation of Texas to check British interests there. Finally, he promoted trade with China to challenge British supremacy in the Pacific.

Cushing's dislike of Senator Henry Clay and his preference for territorial expansion advocated by the Democratic Party led him to abandon the Whigs. He supported William Henry Harrison rather than Clay as the party's standard-bearer in the presidential election of 1840. Following Harrison's death in April, 1841, Clay pushed his economic program in an unsuccessful attempt to catapult himself into the White House in 1844. Cushing defended President John Tyler's vetoes of Clay's national bank and tariff bills as consistent with Tyler's southern states' rights principles. He thus became the leading member of the president's "Corporal's Guard," a small group of staunch Tyler Whigs in the House of Representatives.

Irate Whigs rejected Cushing's assertion that he had opposed Clay on patriotic grounds and ignored him throughout the remainder of the Twenty-seventh Congress. Cushing decided not to seek a fifth congressional term after learning that his support of Tyler had been unpopular with many of his constituents and that Massachusetts Whigs had already declared their intention to support Clay in the next presidential contest. Tyler repaid Cushing for his loyalty by nominating him for secretary of the treasury in March, 1843. The Senate, however, rejected the appointment three times in one evening as both Democrats and Whigs questioned Cushing's political convictions.

Despite this embarrassment, Tyler remained determined to reward Cushing for his loyalty. In May, 1843, Tyler took advantage of a congressional recess to appoint Cushing envoy extraordinary and minister plenipotentiary to China with instructions to negotiate a commercial treaty. In July, 1844, Cushing concluded the Treaty of Wanghia, the first Sino-American trade agreement. The treaty increased U.S. trade with China by opening Canton, Amoy, Fuzhou, Ningbo, and Shanghai to U.S. merchants. It also granted the United States most-favored-nation trade status with China, established commercial and tariff regulations, and included the principle of extraterritoriality.

After returning from China, Cushing associated himself with southern Democrats. He became more adamant in demanding the annexation of Texas and supported the acquisition of Cuba. His aversion to abolitionism increased as he accepted the states' rights defense of slavery. One of the few northern politicians to support the Mexican War, Cushing organized the First Massachusetts Volunteer Regiment with his own money. Known for his discipline and strict adherence to regulations, he attained the rank of brigadier general but did not participate in any battles.

Massachusetts Democrats nonetheless recognized Cushing's military service by nominating him for governor in 1847 and 1848, but he lost both elections. In 1851, Cushing became mayor of Newburyport. The following year he was appointed associate justice of the Supreme Judicial Court of Massachusetts. There Cushing won the respect of his colleagues with his fairness and legal brilliance. In 1852, Cushing, a delegate to the National Democratic Convention, helped manage the party's nomination of Franklin Pierce as a compromise candidate for president. After winning the election, Pierce appointed Cushing attorney general of the United States.

As the first full-time attorney general, Cushing enhanced the prestige and influence of the office. At the request of Secretary of State William L. Marcy, Cushing assumed responsibility for judicial appointments, extradition cases, pardons, and official correspondence between department heads. His study of the function of the attorney generalship became the standard description of the office. His official opinions clarified jurisdiction between federal and state power and defined the administration of executive power. Finally, despite his failed effort to reform the federal judiciary and organize a law department, his recommendations shaped the creation of the Department of Justice in 1870.

Cushing's advancement of the Pierce administration's pro-southern domestic and foreign policies, however, overshadowed his accomplishments as attorney general. He advocated the strict enforcement of the Fugitive Slave Law, discouraged any union between Democrats and Free-Soilers (a third party that advocated free homesteads, free speech, and a higher tariff), and favored the Kansas-Nebraska Act (1854) and proslavery territorial legislature in Kansas. Furthermore, Cushing aggravated the slavery debate by supporting the Gadsden Purchase (the 1853 purchase of a strip of Mexican land by the United States) and endorsing the Ostend Manifesto, which advocated the purchase of Cuba from Spain.

Cushing's love for the Union led him to join the Republican Party during the secession crisis of 1860-1861. While he expected the South to defend slavery at all costs and had supported southern extremists in nominating John Breckinridge for president in 1860, Cushing deemed secession illegal and deserted southern Democrats once South Carolina left the Union. He supported President Abraham Lincoln against General George B. McClellen in the presidential election of 1864. Cushing later strengthened his standing within the Republican Party by assisting Senator Charles Sumner and Congressman Thaddeus Stevens in writing the Fourteenth Amendment.

After the American Civil War, presidents Andrew Johnson and Ulysses S. Grant benefited from Cushing's legal and diplomatic reputation and skill. Under Johnson, Cushing chaired a commission that revised and codified the statutes of the United States. In 1868, Cushing continued a lifelong commitment to expanding U.S. commerce by negotiating a treaty with Colombia for a canal across the Isthmus of Panama. Three years later, Grant appointed Cushing counsel for the United States before the Geneva Tribunal of Arbitration on the Alabama Claims. Cushing's knowledge of international law, linguistic skill, persistence, and patriotism helped his government secure a $15,500,000 settlement.

Despite these achievements, Cushing's allegiance to the Republican Party continued to be questioned. When Grant nominated him as chief justice of the United States in 1873, Republicans uncovered a letter from Cushing to Jefferson Davis written in March, 1861, recommending a former clerk in the Ordinance Department in Washington, D.C., for a job in the Confederacy. This attack on Cushing's loyalty to the Union forced him to withdraw his name from consideration for the post. He then served as minister to Spain from 1874 to 1877.

SIGNIFICANCE

Cushing's tenure as attorney general and his diplomatic success in China, Colombia, Spain, and Geneva, Switzerland, would rank him as a prominent figure in nineteenth century U.S. politics had he not supported the states' rights defense of slavery during the 1840's and 1850's. Although Cushing was not an apologist for slavery, his blind attachment to rational, legalistic procedure prevented him from understanding the moral dilemma of slavery addressed by abolitionists.

Although Cushing recognized the political threat that slavery posed to the Union, his overemphasis in applying reason to politics led him to embrace policies (territorial expansion, states' rights, and enforcement of federal law) that exasperated the slavery debate. Cushing's support of these policies and the use of force to maintain the Union led to two major political shifts during his public career that left him vulnerable to charges of being a political opportunist. This criticism cost him the ultimate achievement of his legal training, the office of chief justice of the United States, and a place alongside his mentors Edward Everett and Daniel Webster as an eminent statesman-scholar in U.S. history.

—*Dean Fafoutis*

FURTHER READING

Belohlavek, John M. "Race, Progress, and Destiny: Caleb Cushing and the Quest for American Empire." In *Manifest Destiny and Empire: American Antebellum Expansionism*, edited by Sam W. Haynes and Christopher Morris. College Station: Texas A&M Press, 1977. Cushing's arrogant and aggressive application of social Darwinism in promoting U.S. expansion before the American Civil War is addressed through an examination of his writings and speeches on U.S. nationality. Contains valuable notes.

Dennett, Tyler. *Americans in Eastern Asia: A Critical Study of United States' Policy in the Far East in the Nineteenth Century*. New York: Macmillan, 1922. Reprint. New York: Barnes & Noble Books, 1963. Includes five chapters covering the foundations of U.S. policy in Asia during the first four decades of the nineteenth century, preparations for the Cushing mission to China, and the negotiation of the Treaty of Wanghia. Comprehensive bibliography.

Donahue, William J. "The Cushing Mission." *Modern Asian Studies* 16 (April, 1982): 193-216. Donahue praises Cushing as an "able diplomat" for the commercial success of his mission to China but recognizes that throughout the nineteenth century the United States followed Britain's lead in acquiring trade concessions from China. Includes extensive notes and an abbreviated version of the Treaty of Wanghia.

Fuess, Claude M. *The Life of Caleb Cushing*. 2 vols. New York: Harcourt, Brace & World, 1923. Reprint. Hamden, Conn.: Archon Books, 1965. Fuess defends Cushing's political shifts by presenting him as a man of honest convictions, moral courage, and principle who helped preserve the Union and defended the nation's honor as a member of Congress, attorney general, and diplomat. Based on exhaustive use of the Caleb Cushing Papers, it is the most complete biography of Cushing.

Gara, Larry. *The Presidency of Franklin Pierce*. Lawrence: University Press of Kansas, 1991. Gara's examination of Pierce's presidency includes information on Cushing's work as attorney general and minister to China.

Hodgson, M. Michael Catherine. *Caleb Cushing: Attorney General of the United States, 1853-1857*. Washington, D.C.: Catholic University of America Press, 1955. This study focuses on Cushing's efforts to strengthen the office of attorney general as well as his influence on the foreign policy of the Pierce administration. Includes appendixes and a bibliographical note.

Nichols, Roy Franklin. *Franklin Pierce: Young Hickory of the Granite Hills*. Rev. ed. Philadelphia: University of Pennsylvania Press, 1958. Nichols criticizes Cushing as Pierce's worst cabinet appointment because of his lack of political principles and common sense. Discusses Cushing's role in helping Pierce secure the Democratic party presidential nomination in 1852 and his strong voice in the cabinet on both domestic and foreign affairs. Extensive notes and bibliography.

SEE ALSO: Henry Clay; William Henry Harrison; John Tyler.

RELATED ARTICLE in *Great Events from History: The Nineteenth Century, 1801-1900:* July 28, 1868: Burlingame Treaty.

GEORGE A. CUSTER

American military leader

Although Custer's reputation is obscured by the events surrounding his legendary death at the Battle of the Little Bighorn, his illustrious Civil War exploits made him one of the nation's most respected military figures and a national idol. After the war, his expeditions into the Yellowstone region and the Black Hills earned for him renown as an explorer and compiler of scientific information.

BORN: December 5, 1839; New Rumley, Ohio
DIED: June 25, 1876; Little Bighorn River, Montana
ALSO KNOWN AS: Autie; George Armstrong Custer (full name)
AREA OF ACHIEVEMENT: Military

EARLY LIFE

George Armstrong Custer was born in Ohio. When he was ten, his father sent him to live with his married half sister, Lydia Reed, in Monroe, Michigan. The elder Custer wanted his favorite son to acquire the best possible education, and he had been assured by his daughter that the private "Young Men's Academy" in Monroe would benefit George. At the age of sixteen, "Autie," as Custer's family affectionately nicknamed him, returned to his parents' home and began a career as a schoolteacher. Always devoted to his family, Custer faithfully presented his mother his monthly salary of twenty dollars as a token of his appreciation of their sacrifices to enable him to become educated.

Like many young men who had been swept up in the thrilling accounts of the Mexican War, Custer nurtured his boyhood love for the military and was determined to make it his profession. In 1857, Custer entered West Point, but during his four years at the Academy his academic record and numerous demerits placed him near the bottom of his class. "My career as a cadet," he recounted in his "War Memoirs" (1876), "had but little to commend it to the study of those who came after me, unless as an example to be carefully avoided." What became known as "Custer's luck" prevailed, however, and in early summer, 1861, the Union Army, desperate for officers, took Custer's entire class, and three days before the first Battle of Bull Run, Second Lieutenant Custer reported to the Army of the Potomac.

LIFE'S WORK

While Custer was serving as aide-de-camp to Generals George Brinton McClellan, Philip Kearny, and Alfred Pleasonton, his enthusiasm, bravery, and dedication to duty earned for him rapid promotion to the rank of captain. While under Pleasonton, the chief of the Union cavalry, Custer gained a reputation for zeal, sound tactics, and active participation in combat. Consequently, upon Pleasonton's recommendation, on June 29, 1863, Custer, at the age of twenty-three, was made brevet brigadier general in command of the Michigan Cavalry Brigade.

As a general, Custer's initial distinction was his attire. In an attempt to achieve a look of maturity, the sad-eyed youth grew a mustache and allowed his sandy blond locks to drape nearly to his shoulders. To adorn his wiry five-foot, ten-inch, 165-pound frame, the Army's youngest general chose rather foppish clothing. Unlike his more conservative fellow officers, Custer wore a broad-billed hat, blue velvet coat with a wide sailor collar, red silk tie, gold insignia tie clasp, white gloves, and loose trousers tucked inside high riding boots.

Any doubts as to the well-dressed cavalier's leadership qualities vanished quickly, as Custer's junior officers marveled at his acts of bravado. Custer enjoyed the thrill of battle and led his men into the fray, waving either his hat or sword, and exhorting them to charge with a shrill "Come on, you Wolverines!" Unlike many Union commanders, Custer gave his troops all the credit for his victories, while shouldering all blame in defeat. This gave "Old Curly," as his men dubbed him, the reputation of being a "soldiers' general," and by the end of the war Custer ranked behind only Ulysses S. Grant, William Tecumseh Sherman, and Philip Sheridan as a beloved savior of the Union.

Custer's combat record was outstanding, and his victories over J. E. B. Stuart's forces at Gettysburg and Yellow Tavern were instrumental in the ultimate triumph of the North. To honor his achievements, Custer, who had risen to the rank of brevet major general in 1864 and had accepted Robert E. Lee's symbolic white towel of surrender, was permitted to witness Lee's official surrender in the McLean House at Appomattox Courthouse. General Sheridan then purchased the table upon which the document had been signed and presented it to Custer's wife, Elizabeth, with the notation: "There is scarcely an individual in our service who has contributed more to bring about this desirable result than your very gallant husband."

Custer's war record was sufficient to warrant his place as an American military hero. Custer differed from many of his fellow generals, however, in that he felt himself too young to retire on his laurels and had no desire to enter politics. Therefore, he remained in his chosen profession and was sent West. In May, 1865, he was dispatched to Texas to help destroy the remnants of General Edmund Kirby-Smith's rebel forces, and the following year he was ordered to Washington, D.C., to testify before a congressional committee on conditions in Texas and western Louisiana. In 1866, he reverted to his regular army rank of captain and returned to Monroe. The remainder of that year was spent writing his memoirs and accompanying President Andrew Johnson on his campaign "Swing Around the Circle."

In late 1866, Custer was promoted to lieutenant colonel and assigned to Fort Riley, Kansas, to head the newly formed Seventh Cavalry. The next year, he participated in General Winfield S. Hancock's campaign against the Lakota (Sioux) and Cheyenne. During this expedition, Custer and his men broke through a virtual siege of Fort Wallace and rescued the garrison. Finding the post ravaged by cholera, he took part of his command on a two-hundred-mile trek to Fort Harker to obtain medical supplies for Fort Wallace. He sent the medicine back with a junior officer, while he obtained permission from the commanding general at Fort Harker to return to Fort Riley to visit Elizabeth. Following the disastrous campaign, Hancock told Congress that he had been undermined by actions of his subordinates, especially Custer, and demanded that the offending junior officer be court-martialed for deserting his command. Despite saving Fort Wallace from attack and disease and having authorization for his absence, Custer was found guilty and suspended, without pay, for one year.

In September, 1868, Generals Sherman and Sheridan had Custer reinstated to lead the Seventh Cavalry on another campaign. Sheridan told Custer: "I rely on you in everything, and shall send you on this expedition without orders, leaving you to act entirely on your own judgment." This faith was rewarded, as a surprise dawn attack on an encampment of hostile Cheyenne along the Washita River resulted in one of the military's most successful Indian battles. Custer seized large quantities of ponies, blankets, weapons, and food, but found himself criticized in the eastern press because during the daylong fighting fifty-three Indian women and children were slain.

Four years of relative inactivity ended in 1873, when Custer was named second in command for General David Stanley's fifteen-hundred-man force assigned to guard the Northern Pacific Railroad Company survey party. During this service in the Yellowstone region, Custer enhanced his reputation as an Indian fighter by defeating a war party of three hundred Lakota, while sustaining only one casualty among his ninety men.

In July, 1874, Sheridan again called upon Custer, whom he said was "the only man who never failed me," this time to lead an expedition into the Black Hills of the Dakotas. Sheridan feared that if the Lakota went to war, they would use their sacred territory in that area as a refuge. Because the Black Hills had never been explored by whites, Custer was instructed to take more than one thousand men, including soldiers, geologists, paleontologists, zoologists, botanists, and photographers, to reconnoiter the region. Custer sent back voluminous data on scientific discoveries, but the public was most interested in his finding of gold and other precious minerals. Soon a rush of miners flooded onto land reserved by treaty for the Lakota.

Ironically, Custer's downfall was his successful Black Hills expedition. As the Lakota joined with the northern Cheyenne to repel the white trespassers, the federal government embarked upon a military campaign intended to celebrate the nation's centennial by ridding the plains of all Indian resistance to white expansion. A coordinated

George A. Custer. (The Granger Collection, New York)

three-prong attack, under the leadership of Generals Alfred Terry, George Crook, and John Gibbon, was to converge on the suspected main Indian encampment along the Little Bighorn River in the Montana Territory. Custer, commanding the only cavalry in the expedition, was sent ahead by Terry to scout the area, and he arrived at the Little Bighorn late on June 24, 1876, two days before the scheduled rendezvous.

On the morning of June 25, fearing that his force had been seen and that the enemy would flee before the vise could close around them, Custer decided to launch an attack. Splitting his forces for a pincer movement, as he had done successfully in the past, Custer found himself facing between three thousand and five thousand warriors, nearly three times the number Sheridan had predicted. Cut off from all assistance, Custer and the remainder of his 225 men staved off two charges before succumbing to the superior numbers and weaponry of the Indians.

SIGNIFICANCE

Articulate and intelligent, Custer exemplified the nineteenth century career officer by making the motto "duty, honor, country" a way of life. Although his best friends at West Point were southerners, Custer fought against them because he believed their cause was traitorous. Personally sympathetic to the plight of Indians being driven from their land, he fought against them because his government ordered him to do so. Insubordination was intolerable to Custer, and he believed that orders, no matter how personally offensive, had to be obeyed. Contrary to allegations, Custer did not attack a day early because he sought glory, but rather because his orders from Terry permitted him to act upon his own best judgment.

In death, Custer achieved the ultimate goal of the campaign. National outrage demanded vengeance, and, to avoid possible annihilation, the Indian forces disbanded. Even defeat could not dim Custer's fame in the eyes of his adoring country.

—*Bruce A. Rubenstein*

FURTHER READING

Ambrose, Stephen E. *Crazy Horse and Custer: The Parallel Lives of Two American Warriors*. New York: Anchor Books, 1996. Ambrose, a historian who has written several popular biographies and military histories, examines the similarities between Custer and Crazy Horse.

Carroll, John M. *Custer in the Civil War: His Unfinished Memoirs*. Edited by John M. Carroll. San Rafael, Calif.: Presidio Press, 1977. A compilation of documents relating to Custer's Civil War career, followed by a reprinting of the seven chapters of the general's unfinished "War Memoirs," first published in *Galaxy Magazine* in 1876. Although self-centered, these chapters are significant because they represent the final works in Custer's prolific literary career.

Connell, Evan S. *Son of the Morning Star: Custer and the Little Bighorn*. San Francisco: North Point Press, 1984. A thoroughly researched examination of the personalities of Custer, government officials, and Indian leaders. A skillful blend of biography and history of the Plains Indian Wars.

Custer, Elizabeth. *Boots and Saddles: Or, Life in Dakota with General Custer*. Reprint. Williamstown, Mass.: Corner House, 1974. This facsimile reprint, without introduction, of the original 1885 edition recounts the travels of "Libbie" with her husband from the spring of 1873 through what she calls "Our Life's Last Chapter." An adoring wife, Mrs. Custer dedicated her life to the glorification of her husband. This book, like her *Tenting on the Plains* and *Following the Guidon*, is in her husband's memory and, for that reason, must be read with scrutiny.

Custer, George A. *My Life on the Plains*. Edited by Milo Quaife. New York: Citadel Press, 1962. Originally written as a two-year series of articles for *Galaxy Magazine*, this first appeared in book form in 1874. It offers a self-serving account of Custer's activities from 1867 through 1869. This edition offers the best introductory material and a faithful reprinting of the original.

Frost, Lawrence A. *The Custer Album*. Seattle: Superior Publishing, 1964. Former curator of the Custer Room of the Monroe County (Michigan) Museum, Frost is one of the foremost experts on his hometown hero. The text is completely sympathetic to Custer, but even those who do not share that view will be fascinated by the wealth of photographs of Custer and his family.

Graham, William A. *The Custer Myth: A Source Book of Custerania*. Harrisburg, Pa.: Stackpole, 1953. An encyclopedia of events concerning Custer's last battle. Graham spent much of his life obtaining interviews with Indian and white participants of the Little Bighorn. Essential for anyone seriously interested in Custer.

Hatch, Thom. *The Custer Companion: A Comprehensive Guide to the Life of George Armstrong Custer and the Plains Indian Wars*. Mechanicsburg, Pa.: Stackpole Books, 2002. Hatch's book seeks to help readers sift through the many materials about Custer's life. Each chapter provides an overview of a specific phase of his life, followed by articles and biographies of people associated with Custer. Hatch focuses on Custer's post-Civil War career on the Plains, including the controversy surrounding the Battle of the Little Bighorn.

Jackson, Donald Dean. *Custer's Gold: The United States Cavalry Expedition of 1874*. New Haven, Conn.: Yale University Press, 1966. A brief, scholarly account of the Black Hills expedition and its impact on both Indians and westward expansion.

Monaghan, Jay. *Custer: The Life of General George Armstrong Custer*. Boston: Little, Brown, 1959. Perhaps the most balanced biography of Custer. Well-researched and written in a flowing narrative, the book is sympathetic to Custer, but Monaghan resists the temptation to gloss over the general's flaws.

Utley, Robert M. *Cavalier in Buckskin: George Armstrong Custer and the Western Military Frontier*. Norman: University of Oklahoma Press, 2001. A revised and expanded edition of the best-selling biography originally published in 1998. Utley disagrees with historians who maintain that Custer lost the Battle of the Little Bighorn because it was a vain attempt to achieve personal glory. Instead, Utley argues, the battle was lost because of bad intelligence and because Custer underestimated the ability and determination of his opponents.

Van de Water, Frederic F. *Glory Hunter: A Life of General Custer*. Indianapolis: Bobbs-Merrill, 1934. As the title indicates, this is a hostile biography, written to counter the image set forth by Mrs. Custer's works. Custer is portrayed as a selfish, vain glory-seeker, willing to risk his men's lives to achieve fame. Still considered by many "Custer haters" as a classic, this book should be read with Frost's or Monaghan's to gain a more accurate picture of Custer.

SEE ALSO: Calamity Jane; Crazy Horse; William Tecumseh Sherman; Sitting Bull.

RELATED ARTICLES in *Great Events from History: The Nineteenth Century, 1801-1900:* December 21, 1866: Fetterman Massacre; November 27, 1868: Washita River Massacre; c. 1871-1883: Great American Buffalo Slaughter; 1876-1877: Sioux War; June 25, 1876: Battle of the Little Bighorn.

GEORGES CUVIER

French naturalist

Cuvier was an anatomist who greatly extended the classification system of Linnaeus by dividing living organisms and the fossil record into phyla. He was also an antievolutionist who adapted the theory that organic changes in the world were shaped by series of catastrophes.

BORN: August 23, 1769; Montbéliard, Württemberg (now in France)

DIED: May 13, 1832; Paris, France

ALSO KNOWN AS: Baron Georges Cuvier; Georges Léopold Chrétien Frédéric Dagobert Cuvier (full name)

AREA OF ACHIEVEMENT: Biology

EARLY LIFE

Georges Léopold Chrétien Frédéric Dagobert Cuvier (kew-vee-ay) was the son of a retired French officer. His father had married late in life and had moved to Montbéliard. Montbéliard had been part of French Burgundy but came under the control of the duke of Württemberg. The region kept the French language but adopted Lutheranism. His family had originally wanted young Cuvier to become a Lutheran minister, but he was denied a scholarship to theology school. In 1784, he found a patron in the wife of the governor of the city and was able to attend Caroline University, near Stuttgart. Although his initial studies were in legal and administrative areas, Cuvier befriended the zoology lecturer Karl Kielmayer, who taught him comparative anatomy and the intricacies of dissection. Cuvier was a short man with bright blue eyes and thick red hair. His weight increased throughout his life, with the result that he eventually was given the nickname "Mammoth."

Cuvier completed his studies in 1788, and for the next six years he served as a private tutor to a noble Protestant family in Normandy. During this time, the French Revolution was occurring, and, while many dramatic and far-reaching events were taking place in Paris, Cuvier lived his life quietly in the countryside. There he continued

Georges Cuvier. (National Archives)

his dissection of various ocean organisms and recorded his work. An acquaintance suggested to Cuvier that he send his unpublished papers to Étienne Geoffroy Saint-Hilaire. Invited by Geoffroy to be his assistant at the Museum of Natural History, Cuvier went to Paris in 1795 and launched his career in science.

LIFE'S WORK

Once Cuvier settled in Paris, his career progressed rapidly through the combination of his scientific accomplishments, his teaching abilities, and his administrative acumen. As a result of the dissections he performed in Normandy, he presented a paper in which he demonstrated that the classification of invertebrate animals into insects and worms could be reclassified into mollusks, crustaceans, insects, worms, echinoderms, and zoophytes. With his keen eye for detail and his ability to classify organisms accurately, he was appointed both professor of zoology and assistant professor of animal anatomy.

Through the rest of his life, promotions and honors came to Cuvier almost without pause. In 1800, he succeeded the eminent anatomist Louis Daubenton as a professor at the Collège de France and was given the responsibility of organizing the science departments of several lower schools. In 1808, Napoleon I made him university counselor, and he provided leadership in organizing the new Sorbonne in Paris. With the restoration of the monarchy in 1814, Cuvier continued to offer his services. Beginning in 1819, he chaired the Council of State in the Interior Department. He was made a baron in that same year, was elevated to the Legion of Honor in 1824, and became a Peer of France in 1831.

Cuvier's scientific accomplishments were the direct result of his position at the Museum of Natural History. The French government was committed to the creation of an internationally recognized research institution. Upon Cuvier's arrival, he immediately arranged to increase the anatomy collection. By 1804, he had increased this collection to three thousand items and by 1832 to more than thirteen thousand items. Without leaving Paris, Cuvier could dissect and prepare the anatomy of his organisms and create his classification systems for birds and fish. In fact little progress had been made before Cuvier in the classification of invertebrates. They were all thrown into a single catchall group called worms. In 1795, when Cuvier first arrived in Paris, he divided these into six new classes. By 1812, he was able to classify all animals into four phyla: vertebrates, mollusks, articulates, and radiates. Within these phyla, Cuvier discovered a number of new classes, orders, and families. Some of these had been grouped with others, and many were simply overlooked.

Cuvier's method of classification was a departure from the earlier Linnaean system, in which an organism had a number of independent and arbitrary characteristics. Taking a cue from Comte de Buffon, who treated an organism as a whole entity, Cuvier expanded this idea into the correlation of parts. Because all the functions of an organism are dependent on one another, the anatomical parts are also integrated in the organism. Through one well-preserved bone, it is possible to determine the class, order, genus, and in many cases the species of the animal. The application of this method not only produced rapid advances in the study of comparative anatomy but also was expanded to fossil remains. As early as 1804, Cuvier had tried to reconstruct the shape of the muscles of an extinct animal from the imprint left on the bones. The final step was to imagine a skin on this extinct animal, and it was resurrected.

Cuvier's contributions to anatomy and paleontology could have placed him among the earliest of the evolutionists. He found that several geological strata contained organisms peculiar to them. He also possessed ample evidence of extinction, because he examined the remains of an extinct elephant that differed significantly from any known living species.

In addition, Cuvier's knowledge of comparative anatomy was unequaled until the publication of Charles Darwin's theory of evolution. Cuvier, however, rejected all evolutionary explanations of his discoveries. One possible explanation for this position can be found in his belief that nature was an immense network that had remained fixed in place since the Creation. After 1812, he admitted that creation must have taken place over several stages, and he adapted Charles Bonnet's theory of catastrophism, which postulated that the world was totally flooded on several occasions. After each flood, life was created again, hence the various strata and different organic remains.

Although Cuvier was a devout Christian, his opposition to evolution could have originated from his intellectual makeup rather than from his religious beliefs. A review of his extensive writings shows that religious doctrines rarely entered his scientific work. Possibly, Cuvier rejected the notion of evolution because he did not see a chain of organisms that evolved from simple to more complex functions. His network was not a continuous one moving from a series of related species, but rather a discontinuous one in which each species was complete in itself, and the parts worked in total harmony. Also, the geological record of his time was limited and supported the conclusion that organic forms from one stratum could not be found in a later one. Later, when Cuvier found a similar organic form in several strata, he modified his catastrophe theory toward local events such as earthquakes, volcanic action, and mountain building.

Whatever Cuvier's reasons were for rejecting a theory of evolution, he became engaged in a famous academic conflict, beginning in 1802, that was to last until his death in 1832. The conflict involved his former friends Geoffroy and Jean-Baptiste Lamarck. The conflict produced secret investigations on the religious beliefs of Lamarck and Geoffroy. Mummified animals were brought back from Egypt to demonstrate the transformation of species. In a further episode, Cuvier had erroneously classified an extinct crocodile, an event that brought Geoffroy to the attack. While this battle was vigorously fought among the combatants and their disciples, the press and political groups also entered the fray to champion their own views. Despite his power and prestige, Cuvier was unable to prevail in this dispute. As Cuvier lay dying, Sir Charles Lyell published his work on geology, which produced crucial evidence for Darwin's theory of evolution.

SIGNIFICANCE

Georges Cuvier lived and worked in a world that was undergoing rapid change. The French Revolution dramatically altered European society and culture. Cuvier moved adroitly through a dangerously revolutionary Paris, rose to prominence under the empire of Napoleon, and maintained his administrative positions through the restoration of the monarchy and its fall in the July revolution of 1830. He was a Protestant in a predominantly Catholic country, and he was a poor man who acquired wealth and titles. Even without his scientific contributions, his activities would rate a minor place in the history of France. He was a man who had extensive interests; indeed, his personal library included more than nineteen thousand books covering history, law, and natural sciences. He absorbed this material and committed it to memory. With this knowledge, he completed a vast amount of work as secretary of the National Institute, and under Napoleon he shaped and changed the university system of France.

It was not a narrowness of vision which kept Cuvier from arriving at a theory of evolution or considering the merits of such an idea. He possessed a grand and ordered view of nature, along with an intricate knowledge of the anatomical parts of hundreds of species. For him, each organic form was already perfect, with not one evolving into greater complexity. Perhaps he understood too much to see the simple mechanism of change built into the individuals of a species. Without his discoveries in anatomy, paleontology, and the theory of correlation of parts, however, many others would have had to duplicate this work before the theory of evolution could have been developed.

—*Victor W. Chen*

FURTHER READING

Bourdier, Franck. "Geoffroy Saint-Hilaire Versus Cuvier: The Campaign for Paleontological Evolution (1825-39)." In *Towards a History of Geology*, edited by Cecil J. Schneer. Cambridge, Mass.: MIT Press, 1969. Covers the acrimonious conflict between Cuvier and Geoffroy through the differences in their temperaments and careers. The author's sympathies lie with Geoffroy, and he cites him as one of the great precursors to Darwin. Reviews some new sources of information to make his case.

Coleman, William R. *Georges Cuvier, Zoologist: A Study in the History of Evolutionary Theory*. Cambridge, Mass.: Harvard University Press, 1964. Covers Cuvier's zoological and anatomical work in detail. Several sections are too complex for the general reader, but the information on Cuvier's methodology and classification is valuable. Suggests that Cuvier's rejection of evolution is less influenced by his religious attitudes than by his intellectual makeup.

Cuvier, Georges. *Cuvier's Animals: 867 Illustrations from the Classic Nineteenth Century Work*. Selected and arranged by Carol Belanger Grafton. Mineola, N.Y.: Dover, 1996. A collection of Cuvier's engraved illustrations of mammals, birds, reptiles, insects, mollusks, and other creatures.

Eisley, Loren. *Darwin's Century: Evolution and the Men Who Discovered It*. Garden City, N.Y.: Doubleday, 1958. Presents Cuvier as a crucial predecessor to Darwin in the story of evolution. The sections on Cuvier are scattered in several parts of the text. Written in a simple style with ample information on Cuvier. An excellent overview of the history of evolutionary theory.

Mayr, Ernst. *The Growth of Biological Thought: Diversity, Evolution, and Inheritance*. Cambridge, Mass.: Harvard University Press, 1982. Mayr is the recognized authority on Darwin and the history of biological evolution. In each of the major sections of this work there are sections on Cuvier and his contributions to the world of biological ideas. The material can be difficult at times, but the treatment is definitive.

Nordenskiöld, Eric. *The History of Biology*. New York: Tudor, 1928. Chapter 2 of part 3 covers Cuvier's life and career. The topics include comparative anatomy, correlation of parts theory, paleontology, catastrophe theory, and the controversy with Geoffroy. Dated but competent.

Outram, Dorinda. *Georges Cuvier: Vocation, Science, and Authority in Post-revolutionary France*. Manchester, England: Manchester University Press, 1984. Biography of Cuvier, placing him within the context of nineteenth century French science and politics.

Rudwick, Martin J. S. *George Cuvier: Fossil Bones and Geological Catastrophes—New Translations and Interpretations of the Primary Texts*. Chicago: University of Chicago Press, 1997. Rudwick has translated and interpreted many of Cuvier's writings on fossils and catastrophes. He advocates the importance of the ideas expressed in these works, which anticipated modern research into mass extinction and the use of fossils as a record of plant and animal life.

SEE ALSO: Louis Agassiz; Karl Ernst von Baer; Charles Darwin.

RELATED ARTICLES in *Great Events from History: The Nineteenth Century, 1801-1900:* 1809: Lamarck Publishes *Zoological Philosophy*; July, 1830: Lyell Publishes *Principles of Geology*.

JACQUES DAGUERRE
French inventor and photographer

Daguerre's renown rests largely on his contributions to the technology of photography. He achieved the earliest fixed-image photographs developed from latent images, and the process he discovered produced photographic plates that were named daguerreotypes after him.

BORN: November 18, 1787; Cormeilles, near Paris, France
DIED: July 10, 1851; Bry-sur-Marne, France
AREAS OF ACHIEVEMENT: Photography, science and technology

EARLY LIFE

The formal education of Jacques Daguerre (dah-gahr) in the schools of Orléans was brief and poor because of the distractions of the French Revolution. Fortunately, he revealed a gift for drawing early in his childhood, which, in some measure, offset the quality of his education. Daguerre was apprenticed by his father to a draftsman. Though the training in detailed exactitude was later to prove beneficial, it was Daguerre's wish to study painting. In 1804, his father allowed him to go to Paris for that purpose. He was apprenticed to the chief stage designer at the Paris Opera, with whom he lived and worked for three years.

At the end of this apprenticeship, Daguerre took employment with Pierre Prévost, a painter who had achieved a certain celebrity with his panoramas. These were representations akin to those currently called cycloramas. The viewer was situated at the center of a cylindrical painting of very large dimensions, comprising a single expansive view. Such paintings must be executed with scrupulous attention to accuracy of scale and fidelity to perspective. Once more, his experience in draftsmanship served him well. In 1810, one week before his twenty-third birthday, Daguerre married twenty-year-old Louise Georgina Smith, sister of a fellow employee at the Prévost studio. He continued his association with Prévost for six years after his marriage, starting an independent career only in 1816.

Daguerre quickly distinguished himself as a set designer, where an ability to achieve delightful illusions and exotic effects came fully into play. Until 1821, he was engaged in designing sets for some of the best-known theaters in Paris, and in 1819 the Académie Royale de Musique enlisted his widely acclaimed talents. For two years, he was one of the chief designers for the Académie.

LIFE'S WORK

During 1821 and 1822, Daguerre devoted much time and effort to the development of a new technique for creating scenes of very convincing realism that he called the "diorama." This new form of illusion was developed by Daguerre in conjunction with another former associate from Prévost's studio, Charles-Marie Bouton.

The diorama was clearly the product of a series of incremental advances on previous techniques for creating visual illusion. The most recent, the diaphanorama, was itself a departure from the panorama. Franz Niklaus König, the creator of the diaphanorama, was Swiss by birth and was also an experienced set designer.

König's effects were produced by painting with watercolors on transparent papers, the backs of which he subsequently oiled to increase their translucence. Displayed at a distance in darkened rooms, the paintings were illuminated by controlled, reflected light played on the back as well as the front, the relative intensity of the light being adjustable in minute transitions. It is a virtual certainty that Daguerre witnessed a display of König's ingenuity when the latter traveled to Paris in 1821 and that his own diorama was actually a refinement of the basic concept devised by König.

Daguerre and Bouton bought land and constructed a specially designed structure. An enormous building was necessary because of the very large paintings involved and the distance to be maintained between the paintings and the viewers. The "picture rooms"—there were two—lay at the end of corridors that were arranged like spokes radiating from the circular viewing salon, widening as they moved away from the audience. Viewers sat or stood in a darkened, circular, revolvable salon that was positioned in such a way that they could look down only one of the two corridors, at the end of which was the scene.

After all the effects of the first scene had been rehearsed, the gallery faded into darkness, and the salon was imperceptibly made to revolve to the position from which the second gallery could be brought into view by the gradual introduction of light upon the second scene. Illumination was achieved by light introduced through windows, controlled by shutterlike devices, sometimes colored by filters and conducted to the desired surfaces by reflection. The structure itself and the ingenious system of illumination were so central to the scheme that they were independently patented.

Jacques Daguerre. (Smithsonian Institution)

The paintings, which were periodically changed so that audiences could return to see a new set of scenes, were executed upon both sides of a white calico fabric, optimally translucent and prepared with sizing. The pigment was suspended in a turpentine vehicle and applied to the fabric in as thin a coat as would achieve the effect without causing complete opacity. The painting was then shaded with translucent colors. By illuminating the painting first on one side and then the other and by using lights of various colors, parts of the composition were made to disappear, while others seemed to advance. It was possible in this manner to present a before-and-after history of a scene, for example, a peaceful Swiss valley that fell victim to an enormous landslide. By using several painted cloths in echelon with the lighting such that the viewer could see through one, two, or more of them simultaneously, it was possible to achieve an astonishing degree of three-dimensional realism as well as to give the illusion of transitory atmospheric effects.

The diorama was received with enthusiasm, and Daguerre was made a Chevalier of the Legion of Honor in 1824; however, the enterprise appears never to have been much of a financial success. In March of 1839, a fire destroyed the Paris Diorama, which, because of the highly combustible materials it contained, was a constant danger.

By that time, Daguerre had brought to fruition his work on a means of fixing an image made upon a light-sensitive surface in a camera obscura. A man of his time, Daguerre was motivated not only by an interest in the accurate study of proportion and perspective but also by a desire for celebrity and wealth. Possibly this drive to distinguish himself explains why he periodically made claims to successes that proved to be false or that were only subsequently achieved.

Sometime during the year 1826, Daguerre learned of the work being done on heliography by Nicéphore Niépce. Niépce, in 1826, had produced the world's first photograph. Using a pewter plate coated with bitumen of Judea (asphaltum) and placed at the back of a camera obscura, he achieved an image of a scene from the second story of his country home. The process, however, required an exposure time of eight hours. Upon learning of this shortcoming in the exposure process, Daguerre at once approached Niépce by letter. By misrepresenting the extent of his own success, Daguerre drew a reluctant Niépce into a partnership. Having failed to secure any return on his own developments, Niépce on December 14, 1829, signed an agreement with Daguerre, who said that he had a strategy by which Niépce could profit from his discoveries.

The partnership was entitled "Niépce-Daguerre," and by its terms Daguerre was obliged to "improve" a process of which Niépce was named "inventor." Daguerre was also to contribute a camera of an improved design, which he claimed to have developed and that would substantially reduce the exposure time. The camera, in the form described by Daguerre, did not exist. Daguerre, however, was twenty-two years younger than the senior partner, and Niépce hoped to enjoy the fruits of the great capacity for hard work and the unflagging optimism that characterized his new partner.

Daguerre learned from Niépce that it was not necessary to expose a plate until the image became visible on its surface; a faint or even completely invisible image could be brought out (developed) by chemical processes. Daguerre also seems to have learned from his partner that iodine could be used as the photosensitive coating to receive the image.

Niépce died in great poverty in 1833, before the partnership yielded any advantage to him. His son and legatee, Isidore, succeeded him as Daguerre's partner. At that time, the original problems remained unsolved: Images using iodine were negative, the exposure time remained seven to eight hours, and no means had been found to prevent the image from deterioration in light.

Daguerre, however, began to make critical discoveries after the death of Niépce. First, he made the discovery (evidently by the purest chance) that iodized silvered plates could be used as the surface upon which to secure light images in the camera. Then, sometime in 1837, he found (also quite by chance) that mercury vapors would precipitate out on the light-affected portions of an iodized silver surface. These two critical discoveries are credited entirely to Daguerre in spite of his haphazard methods. The great advantage in them was the production of a positive image at a substantial reduction in the exposure time, though he had not as yet discovered any means of making the image thus obtained permanent.

On May 9, 1835, Daguerre secured a modification of the partnership agreement. Isidore reluctantly signed, and Daguerre soon announced publicly that he had discovered a means of fixing permanently the images that he was securing. In fact, it was not until two years later, in May of 1837, that he made such a discovery.

Over the strong objections of Isidore, terms of the partnership were again revised. The names in the partnership were reversed, and it was made clear that Daguerre had pressed beyond mere improvement of someone else's discovery. Isidore was told that the new process (mercury development) reduced exposure time to four minutes. In truth, it still required twenty to thirty minutes of exposure to secure an image, which was still too long to make portraiture a practical possibility.

An effort to finance further development of the process through a public subscription failed in 1839. In March, the diorama was consumed in a spectacular fire. Daguerre was fifty-one, and his fortunes seemed to have hit a low point. He and Niépce decided to realize what they could by offering the process to the French government. They revealed the method to François Arago, a member of the Chamber of Deputies as well as president of the Academy of Sciences. Arago then secured the government's acceptance. Daguerre was made an Officer of the Legion of Honor, and both he and Niépce were given comfortable life pensions. The French government at once donated the process to the world at large.

Within months, a flood of developments vastly improved the quality and practicality of daguerreotypy. Among the more important of these were the use of thiosulfate as a fixative; a lens that corrected Daguerre's original mirror image; the introduction of the tripod and leather bellows, which made the camera more easily portable; and the discovery of bromoiodide and iodine bromochloride to increase significantly the sensitivity of plates, which, coupled with improved cameras, reduced exposure time to between 90 and 120 seconds for good-quality results.

Daguerre, much lionized for his discoveries, retired to a country estate at Bry-sur-Marne, where he died quite suddenly on July 10, 1851, at the age of sixty-three. The surviving daguerreotypes taken of their eponymous creator reveal a gentleman of ample but not excessive girth, a very round face still crowned by a full complement of curly, salt-and-pepper hair, a full mustache, and a look of fixed determination about the hooded eyes.

SIGNIFICANCE

During an age when an individual's worth was considered to be the precise equivalent of his wealth and the self-made man was the social ideal, Jacques Daguerre, by hard work and seriousness of purpose, built upon native talents rather than education or social privilege to become both wealthy and famous. In the creation of the diorama, he produced not merely the most exciting optical illusion prior to motion pictures but also techniques that are still used in stage settings for the ballet and the opera to achieve mysterious or transitional effects.

Daguerre turned his attention to the emerging technology of photography when the diorama provided recognition but no appreciable wealth. Though the extent of his indebtedness to Niépce remains unresolved, it is certain that it was his own efforts that resulted in the first fixed-image photograph developed from a latent image. It is, therefore, equally certain that the foundation for the art in its present state was laid by Daguerre.

—*John Knox Stevens*

FURTHER READING

Barger, Susan, and William B. White. *The Daguerreotype: Nineteenth-Century Technology and Modern Science*. Washington, D.C.: Smithsonian Institution Press, 1991. Reprint. Baltimore: Johns Hopkins University Press, 2000. Describes the daguerreotype process and explains how nineteenth century photographers and scientists understood and used the new technology.

Bisbee, A. *The History and Practice of Daguerreo-Typing*. Dayton, Ohio: L. F. Clafting, 1853. Reprint. New York: Arno Press, 1973. An early and very clear description of the process used by Daguerre. This little book was written for the American public at the crest of the enthusiasm over the technology.

Buerger, Janet E. *French Daguerreotypes*. Chicago: University of Chicago Press, 1989. A catalog for the daguerreotype collection at the International Museum of Photography. Includes information on Daguerre's background, intentions, and competition, and describes the contemporary intellectuals who understood and developed the new photographic medium.

Cork, Richard. "The End of Art." *New Statesman* 130, no. 4546 (July 16, 2001): 44. Chronicles the rise of photography, including a description of Daguerre's invention. Discusses British society's response to the daguerreotype.

Eder, Josef Maria. *History of Photography*. Translated by Edward Epstean. New York: Columbia University Press, 1945. This book is annoyingly chauvinistic but sound in its scholarship. It is technically more informed than the Gernsheim work (see below). Eder always thought that the critical discoveries were those of Niépce and evidently thought Daguerre not above taking credit for discoveries not, in fact, his own.

Gernsheim, Helmut, and Alison Gernsheim. *L. J. M. Daguerre (1787-1851): The World's First Photographer*. Cleveland: World, 1956. Rev. ed. *L. J. M. Daguerre: The History of the Diorama and the Daguerreotype*. New York: Dover, 1968. The only biography devoted to Daguerre's life and work. This study includes plates of the earliest efforts at photography and the two best daguerreotypes of Daguerre.

Rinhart, Floyd, and Marion Rinhart. *The American Daguerreotype*. Athens: University of Georgia Press, 1981. This book, which includes a number of photographs of original daguerreotype equipment and some beautiful examples of the art, includes a brief account of its development.

Werge, John. *The Evolution of Photography*. London: Piper & Carter and J. Werge, 1890. Werge emphasizes the haphazard nature of Daguerre's research and recounts in detail stories that emphasize the utter happenstance by which the critical discoveries were made.

SEE ALSO: Mathew B. Brady; Williamina Paton Stevens Fleming; Sir William Robert Grove; Samuel F. B. Morse; Nicéphore Niépce.

RELATED ARTICLES in *Great Events from History: The Nineteenth Century, 1801-1900:* January, 1839: Invention of Daguerreotype Photography Is Announced; 1878: Muybridge Photographs a Galloping Horse.

GOTTLIEB DAIMLER

German inventor

As much as any one person, Daimler was the inventor of the first high-speed motor. A brilliant technician and industrial entrepreneur, he overcame the problems that had retarded the progress of automobile development. Thanks to his carburetion process and development of light engine weight, his motor became adaptable to driving both motor cars and aircraft.

BORN: March 17, 1834; Schorndorf (near Stuttgart), Württemberg (now in Germany)
DIED: March 6, 1900; Cannstatt, Germany
AREA OF ACHIEVEMENT: Engineering

EARLY LIFE

The second son of a master baker, Gottlieb Daimler (DIM-lahr) was relatively well educated. He attended public school, followed by two years of Latin school. One of his closest boyhood friends was the son of a master gunsmith, under whose tutelage he apprenticed himself for three years until he produced a piece of work that qualified him as a journeyman. His work entailed precise drawings, which Daimler particularly loved and carried into later life with his depictions of plants and animals.

Journeyman status meant further training en route to mastery. Gottlieb went to work in Alsace, designing machine tools. Recognizing his educational deficiencies, particularly in mathematics, he soon applied his earned savings for two additional years of formal training, this time at the Stuttgart Polytechnic. While in Stuttgart, he came in contact with some of developing Germany's leading engineers such as Ferdinand von Steinbus. Steinbus, who had been instrumental in the industrial development of Württemberg, subsidized Daimler's further training in France and England, where he worked variously as a mechanic, foreman, and manager before returning to Württemberg as the manager of Bruderhaus of Rentlingen's—a highly esteemed firm of machine builders.

While at Bruderhaus, Daimler met Wilhelm Maybach, whose career he helped to shape and with whom he would later collaborate. Maybach, a remarkable young man twelve years Daimler's junior, had already demonstrated his manual skills and his grasp of mathematics, physics, and mechanical drawing. In 1868, when Daimler assumed the management of one of Karlsruhe's leading machine shops, he brought Maybach into his drawing office.

As the by-then-unified Germany rapidly industrialized under Otto von Bismarck and opportunities for skilled men blossomed, Daimler accepted a position with the firm of Otto and Langen in Deutz. Nikolaus August Otto and Eugen Langen furthered the practical design and production of an internal combustion engine. Beginning during the 1860's, Étienne Lenoir made several hundred marketable gas (not gasoline) fired internal combustion engines employed in machine shops and for pumping water. To Lenoir's impressive, if commercially unsuccessful work, Otto and Langen added the development, largely because of Daimler, of the first four-cycle engine, which in its operations is still the basis of most gasoline engines.

Gottlieb Daimler. (The Granger Collection, New York)

LIFE'S WORK

When Daimler was in his late forties, he decided to leave his employers' Deutz plant and establish a plant for himself at Cannstatt in 1882. With him went Wilhelm Maybach, by then a masterful machine builder. Daimler's objective was to develop a practical, high-speed, gasoline-driven motor that would be adaptable to vehicle locomotion. By the beginning of the 1880's, Daimler's new four-stroke machines achieved between 150 and 180 revolutions per minute. At 250 revolutions per minute, however, there were problems with ignition and with the proper metering and timing of admixtures of gasoline and air. Daimler had resolved this problem in mechanical terms while working for Otto and Langen by introducing a flame carried in a special slide valve. This commercial result was Daimler's high-speed motor, capable of nine hundred revolutions per minute. Thirty thousand of these motors were sold internationally within the first decade of its development.

The problem that Daimler set out to resolve when he left Otto and Langen's remarkably inventive works had to do with the uses to which his inventions were put amid bitter international patent battles. Most of the Otto and Langen (or so-called Deutz) motors were sold to perform stationary functions. After years of losses and borrowing, Otto and Langen, to survive, addressed the available market for their product—customers who required stationary engines requisite to the needs of small workshops and mines. The production of moving vehicles, not only on the ground but also in the air, however, was what Daimler had in view.

At his Cannstatt workshop, Daimler had by 1884 developed a high-speed gasoline engine in which the fuel for the combustion chambers was metered by a wick carburetor and ignited by an electric spark. It was a vertical engine that would soon be built in sizes from one-half to twenty-five horsepower with one, two, and four cylinders and eventually ran at six hundred revolutions per minute. Daimler claimed that he had created the basis for an entirely new industry.

Daimler tested his new motor on a wooden cycle, which he drove in the garden of his Cannstatt home in November, 1885, and then on a boat, the first to be powered by a gasoline engine, both tests proving successful. By the following year, he had produced the four-wheeled Daimler carriage, which soon began making its appearance in Cannstatt and nearby Stuttgart. Its top speed was about six kilometers per hour. Daimler's motor, with improvements constantly insisted upon by Maybach, was swiftly patented. Maybach, meanwhile, urged Daimler to join his motor and chassis to form a single machine unit. Because Daimler was excited by prospects of mass-producing his vehicles as well as by turning a profit, he soon acquiesced and built a four-wheeled, gasoline-driven carriage that really was an automobile.

While late nineteenth century Germany furnished a marvelous environment for invention and technological innovation, and as a consequence had become one of the world's foremost industrial powers, Daimler's automobile did not become popular in that country. It remained for the French to lend the notoriety to Daimler's car that was essential to its popularity.

On July 1, 1894, the first international automobile race, along the one-hundred-kilometer Paris-Rouen road, was held. The winner was a Daimler machine that reached unprecedented speeds of up to sixty-five miles (110 kilometers) per hour. With world attention on the race, Daimler received eighty thousand francs in prize money. It was manifest at a practical level that the automobile was no longer a rich man's toy. The race had justified the previous formation of the Daimler Motoren-Gesellschaft in Cannstatt on January 28, 1890, a concern that became one of the world's great producers of automobiles.

Daimler and Maybach came to be driven less by pure technical considerations than by demands from prospective customers to increase the power of their automobiles from nine horsepower to thirty and forty horsepower. Under these immediate pressures, Daimler by 1900 developed and produced the first modern automobile, judged by power and appearance. Its name was "Mercédès."

Daimler did not live to enjoy the success of the first Mercedes after 1900. His health had been declining, and he was unable to bear the pressures under which he had worked for more than forty years. He died on March 6, 1900, in Cannstatt.

SIGNIFICANCE

A brilliant technician and industrial entrepreneur, Gottlieb Daimler resolved the major problems that had plagued, and had thus retarded, the progress of men who had sought to design and produce automotive vehicles. His competence and technical skill exercised in the development of an efficient carburetor and a lightweight, gasoline-driven engine were responsible for the emergence of the world's first true automobile, the ultimate expression of which was the Mercedes. His vision was extraordinary as was demonstrated in 1897 by his recommendations to German authorities that they entertain plans for the creation of a motor-driven airship.

Like so many nineteenth century men of achievement, Daimler combined an extraordinary capacity for hard work with keen powers of observation and exceptional farsightedness. Daimler had spoken to his ultimate objectives while still a young man, and he never deviated from them.

—Clifton K. Yearley

FURTHER READING

Burstall, Aubrey F. *A History of Mechanical Engineering*. Cambridge, Mass.: MIT Press, 1965. Chapters 7 and 8, although they spend little time on Daimler, place him in context. Excellent schematic illustrations of the Otto engine and Daimler's 1897 gasoline engine. Directed to intelligent lay readers, it is richly illustrated. Contains reference footnotes, bibliographies, and an index.

Clark, Dugald. *The Gas, Oil, and Petrol Engine*. 2 vols. London: Basil Blackwell, 1916. Few other works so extensively trace the evolution of these varied engines and the problems that had to be resolved to render them effective. Volume 2 is particularly pertinent in regard to Daimler's achievements. While the work is old, it remains authoritative and is quite readable. Contains illustrations, bibliographical notations, and a useful index.

Field, D. C. "Internal Combustion Engines." In *The Late Nineteenth Century, c. 1850 to c. 1920*. Vol. 5 in *A History of Technology*, edited by Charles Singer, E. J. Holmyard, A. R. Hall, and Trevor Williams. Oxford, England: Clarendon Press, 1958. Clearly and authoritatively written for a general readership, this essay places Daimler's major contributions in context. There are many precise illustrations. Good select bibliographies follow this (and other) chapters, and there is a useful index for the entire volume.

Hill, Frank Ernest. *The Automobile: How It Came, Grew, and Changed Our Lives*. New York: Dodd, Mead, 1967. Intended primarily for high school readers rather than for college or university students. The early chapters, while somewhat simplistic compared to works cited above, nevertheless afford a sound general picture of Daimler's work. Includes photographs and an index.

Kames, Beverly Rae. *The Star and the Laurel: The Centennial History of Daimler, Mercedes, and Benz, 1886-1986*. Montvale, N.J.: Mercedes-Benz of North America, 1986. The history of Daimler-Benz's first hundred years, including information on Daimler's and Benz's inventions before and after they joined forces.

"Maybach Worked, Succeeded in the Shadow of Daimler." *Automotive News* 78, no. 6077 (January 26, 2004): 92B. A profile of Wilhelm Maybach, describing his relationship with Daimler and his inventions.

Rae, John B. "The Internal Combustion Engine on Wheels." In *Technology in the Twentieth Century*. Vol. 2 in *Technology in Western Civilization*, edited by Melvin Kranzburg and Carroll Pursell. New York: Oxford University Press, 1967. Written by specialists for a general readership. Rae's chapter helps place the work of Daimler and other early automotive pioneers in an evolutionary context. Contains an extensive bibliography and an extensive index.

Rolt, Lionel Thomas C. *Great Engineers*. London: G. Bell and Sons, 1962. The only work in English that affords personal details on the life of Daimler and those with whom he worked and competed. Rolt, a British engineer, established himself as a fine, readable historian of engineers, precise and accurate without being pedantic. Contains a useful index.

Wernle, Bradford. "Industry Pioneer Didn't Even Like to Drive Cars." *Automotive News* 75, no. 5908 (December 18, 2000): 20F. A tribute to Daimler, describing how he invented the internal combustion engine, worked with Maybach, and founded his automobile manufacturing company.

SEE ALSO: Carl Benz; Rudolf Diesel; Étienne Lenoir; Nikolaus August Otto.

RELATED ARTICLE in *Great Events from History: The Nineteenth Century, 1801-1900:* January 29, 1886: Benz Patents the First Practical Automobile.

FIRST MARQUIS OF DALHOUSIE

British colonial administrator

In a long career as a colonial administrator, Dalhousie's greatest accomplishment was the development of a communications system linking all of India while he was governor-general there.

BORN: April 22, 1812; Dalhousie Castle, Midlothian, Scotland

DIED: December 19, 1860; Dalhousie Castle, Midlothian, Scotland

ALSO KNOWN AS: James Andrew Broun Ramsay (birth name)

AREA OF ACHIEVEMENT: Government and politics

EARLY LIFE

James Andrew Broun Ramsay was the youngest of three brothers. His father, George, the ninth earl of Dalhousie, served with distinction during the Peninsular War from 1812 to 1814, and from 1819 to 1828, he was captain-general and governor-in-chief of Canada. Christina, his mother, was the heir of Charles Broun of Colstoun. In 1816, the ninth earl became lieutenant-governor of Nova Scotia, and Ramsay accompanied his father and mother to their new home. In 1817, the Ramsays learned that James's middle brother, Charles, had died of the measles. Further sadness struck in 1832, when Ramsay's elder brother died of rheumatism. Ramsay now became the heir to the title.

Ramsay received his early education from a private tutor, but in 1825, he entered Harrow. For the next two years, Ramsay was an energetic if not devoted student, occupying his time in playing cards, smoking, and drinking. These activities led to his withdrawal from the school at the end of 1827. In 1829, he entered Oxford, from which he received his B.A. in 1833.

Early in his life, Ramsay showed a predilection for introspection. In 1824, at the age of twelve, he began a diary that he continued until the end of his official career. Already, the sensitivity on which his contemporaries were later to remark was evident, as was a hint of melancholy. His physical appearance, along with this sensitivity, at first suggested weakness, for he was both short and small. His profile showed his true strength, however, in the aquiline nose, straight brows, and firm mouth. Ramsay's melancholic temperament did show itself with time, spurred by the death of his two brothers, the paralytic stroke suffered by his father in 1832 and his death in 1838, the death the following year of his mother, and the untimely death of his wife in 1853.

During the mid-1830's, Ramsay entered public life, standing as a Conservative candidate for the city of Edinburgh, where he was defeated. In 1836, he married Lady Susan Hay, the daughter of the marquis of Tweeddale, a political ally. Standing for election again in 1837, this time in Haddingtonshire, he was successful, but he was forced to give up his seat on his accession to the earldom at his father's death in 1838.

LIFE'S WORK

In the House of Lords, Dalhousie gained confidence under the eye of the duke of Wellington, whose personal regard for the ninth earl was immense. Sir Robert Peel appointed him to his first government position, vice president of the Board of Trade, in 1843. In this capacity, Dalhousie concerned himself with the burgeoning railway system in Great Britain. His abilities were recognized by the leaders of both parties, and in 1847, Lord John Russell appointed him governor-general of the British possessions in India.

Dalhousie immediately faced the problems created by the Second Sikh War. The question of the annexation of the Punjab was instrumental in setting Dalhousie's policy of British expansionism for the rest of his term in office. Following the defeat of the Sikh army at Gujarat, Dalhousie decided that the British would rule the Punjab directly, rather than through a local prince, and on March 29, 1849, he declared the Punjab a British province. This move established a precedent, which was often invoked in subsequent years.

Dalhousie also took steps to abolish rituals and traditions fundamental to Indian society. The practice of suttee was suppressed and the right of Hindu widows to remarry established, as were the rights of converts from Hinduism. In addition, Dalhousie advanced a plan for a system of education that would extend throughout India, and he drew India together by erecting telegraph lines, building railroads, instituting a cheap postal service, and completing the Great Trunk Road that connected Peshawar, Bombay, Calcutta, and Delhi.

During the 1850's, Dalhousie's policy of outright annexation of territory proceeded apace. Upon the cessation of hostilities in the Second Burmese War in 1851, Dalhousie proclaimed Lower Burma a British province under the same guidelines as the Punjab. The province of Oudh also was annexed because of "misgovernment" on the part of its rulers. At the same time, Dalhousie declared that the traditional practice by which a childless rajah adopted an heir would no longer be recognized by the government. Any territory without a legitimate heir would automatically come under direct British rule. Nagpur, Jhansi, and Sattara fell to British control in this manner.

The annexation policies of Dalhousie contributed greatly to the general anti-British feeling in India. The suppression of both Hindu and Muslim traditions, especially his refusal to recognize the right of adopted sons to carry on royal lines, created a backlash against his policies. At the same time that Dalhousie was attempting to build what he considered a better society, Indians were preparing to reaffirm and, if necessary, reassert by force their age-old customs. The rumor that new cartridges for the use of the sepoys in the Indian Army in 1857 were greased with pig and cow fat was the trigger. The Indian Mutiny followed and Dalhousie was ordered back to Great Britain.

Dalhousie's health suffered greatly while he was in India. His wife had died unexpectedly in 1853, and his habit of overwork drained his energies. The disappointment and anguish of the mutiny diminished his strength further and he went directly to Dalhousie Castle on arrival in Great Britain. He died there on December 19, 1860. He was survived by his two daughters.

SIGNIFICANCE

The first marquis of Dalhousie's reputation has suffered much from studies blaming him for the onset of the Sepoy Mutiny. While these works are not wrong in assuming that Dalhousie was largely unaware of the tremendous tensions developing in India through the 1850's, many of the preconditions for rebellion existed prior to Dalhousie's regime.

Dalhousie must also be considered as the architect of modern geographical India. The building of roads and telegraph systems as well as the beginning of railroad construction date from his tenure as governor-general and rank among his most cherished accomplishments. Although subsequent rulers developed this web of communication and transportation further, Dalhousie set out its parameters and planned its expansion. Nevertheless, Dalhousie was also an archetype of the British colonial administrator. His educational reforms aimed not at creating schools in which Indians might become literate but rather institutions in which future clerks and minor officials could learn English and join in administering the empire.

Dalhousie's decision to put aside the inheritance rights of adopted sons of native princes spread direct rule by the British throughout India. In short, Dalhousie demonstrated his belief that Western, and specifically English, ways were inherently superior to those of India, and he set about, piece by piece, undermining all Indian customs he deemed either barbaric or detrimental to the proper workings of the empire.

Finally, Dalhousie was extraordinarily conscientious and hardworking. A day's work was not over until his desk was clear. While this heavy load almost certainly contributed to his early death, colonial affairs proceeded more smoothly during his tenure in India than they ever had before, primarily as a result of Dalhousie's intelligence and attention to detail. Dalhousie set an example for colonial administrators of every nation.

—*John Phillips*

FURTHER READING

Bayly, C. A. *Indian Society and the Making of the British Empire*. Cambridge, England: Cambridge University Press, 1987. Outlines British expansion and administration in India, including information on Dalhousie's policies and governance. One of the volumes in *The New Cambridge History of India*.

James, Lawrence. *Raj: The Making and Unmaking of British India*. New York: St. Martin's Press, 1998. A history of British rule in India, containing information on Dalhousie's administration and policies.

Lee-Warner, Sir William. *The Life of the Marquis of Dalhousie K.T.* 2 vols. New York: Macmillan, 1904. Although outdated in style and interpretation, Lee-Warner's work remains the most comprehensive biography of Dalhousie. Lee-Warner had access to all of Dalhousie's private papers and was himself stationed in India.

Lloyd, T. O. *The British Empire, 1558-1983*. Oxford, England: Oxford University Press, 1984. A general account of Great Britain's imperial expansion and decline. Allows comparison of Indian policies generally, and Dalhousie's specifically, with other territories and times.

Mason, Philip. *The Men Who Ruled India*. London: Jonathan Cope, 1985. A study covering the period from 1600 to 1947. Mason's work provides valuable material about the middle-level bureaucrats who carried out and often opposed Dalhousie's policies.

Moore, R. J. *Sir Charles Wood's Indian Policy, 1853-66*. Manchester, England: Manchester University Press, 1966. Provides an account of Indian policy from the point of view of the home government. Moore admits that Dalhousie must shoulder some of the blame for the Sepoy Mutiny but argues that his later years in office more than made up for his early stumbles. Valuable for its perspective of Dalhousie's policies.

SEE ALSO: John Laird Mair Lawrence; Sir James Outram; Duke of Wellington.

RELATED ARTICLE in *Great Events from History: The Nineteenth Century, 1801-1900:* May 10, 1857-July 8, 1858: Sepoy Mutiny Against British Rule.

JOHN DALTON

English chemist and physicist

Dalton's work with gases led him to develop modern atomic theory, and for his contributions he is considered one of the founders of the modern physical sciences.

BORN: September 6, 1766; Eaglesfield, Cumberland, England
DIED: July 27, 1844; Manchester, England
AREAS OF ACHIEVEMENT: Physics, chemistry

EARLY LIFE

John Dalton, born September 6, 1766, in Eaglesfield, Cumberland, was the second son of Joseph Dalton, a poor weaver, and Deborah Greenup, a woman of vigor and intelligence. His parents came from old Quaker stock, and they had six children, three of whom, Jonathan, John, and Mary, lived to maturity. John was deeply influenced by his mother's tenacity and frugality. The Society of Friends, which formed a strong social fabric in west Cumberland, was another powerful influence. The Cumberland Quakers emphasized both general education and particular training in natural philosophy, and this provided a favorableF environment for John's development as a scientist.

Dalton made rapid progress under John Fletcher in the village school, and he quickly attracted the attention of Elihu Robinson, a prominent Quaker naturalist who became Dalton's patron and lifelong friend. Because of the poverty of his family, Dalton was forced to work for a time as a farm laborer, but in 1781 he was liberated from this way of life by an invitation to replace his elder brother as assistant at Kendal, a boarding school some forty miles from Eaglesfield. The school, newly built by Quakers, had a well-stocked library that contained Sir Isaac Newton's *Philosophiae Naturalis Principia Mathematica* (1687; *Mathematical Principals of Natu-*

ral Philosophy, 1729) as well as works of both British and Continental natural philosophers. As at Eaglesfield, so at Kendal, Dalton was fortunate in forming an important friendship. In this case, his patron and friend was the blind natural philosopher John Gough. Under Gough's tutelage, Dalton made rapid progress in mathematics, meteorology, and botany. In imitation of his master, Dalton started in 1787 keeping a daily meteorological record, a practice he continued until the day of his death.

At Kendal, Dalton began giving a series of public lectures in physics and astronomy. As a teacher, he was clear and orderly, though rather colorless. In physical appearance, he was a tall, gaunt, and awkward man with a prominent chin and nose, and he dressed in the Quaker fashion: knee breeches, gray stockings, and buckled shoes. Though modestly successful at Kendal, he became restless and sought a different profession. He made inquiries about studying medicine at Edinburgh, but he met with discouraging replies. Eventually, Dalton accepted a position as professor of mathematics and natural philosophy in Manchester. He was pleased with this appointment because, in addition to mathematics and natural philosophy, he was allowed to teach chemistry.

In 1800, encouraged by his success in Manchester, Dalton decided to resign his position and open his own "mathematical academy," where he would offer courses in mathematics, experimental philosophy, and chemistry. This endeavor prospered, and within two years Dalton had enough students to provide him with a modest income. Private teaching on this scale would occupy and support him for the rest of his days.

John Dalton. (Library of Congress)

LIFE'S WORK

Dalton was deeply influenced by the British tradition of popular Newtonianism, a way of visualizing the world through the internal makeup of matter and the operation of short-range forces. As shown so well by Newton, these forces could be described mathematically. Besides his interest in theoretical Newtonian physics, Dalton was involved with more practical concerns—constructing barometers, thermometers, rain gauges, and hygrometers. Dalton produced essays on trade winds, proposed a theory of the aurora borealis, and advanced a theory of rain.

Dalton's meteorological investigations led him to question how the gases of the air were held together: Were they chemically united or were they physically mixed together in the air just as sand and stones were in the earth? He concluded that gases, composed of particles, were physically mixed together, and this led him to deduce that in a mixture of gases at the same temperature, every gas acts independently (Dalton's law of partial pressures). It is ironic that in trying to provide a proof for his physical ideas, Dalton discovered the chemical atomic theory. What started as an interest in meteorology ended up as a new approach to chemistry.

To support his theory of mixed gases, Dalton experimented on the proportions of the different gases in the atmosphere. It was this investigation which accidentally raised the whole question of the solubility of gases in water. In 1802, he read a paper to the Manchester Literary and Philosophical Society in which he proposed that carbon dioxide gas (which he called "carbonic acid" gas) was held in water, not by chemical attractive forces but by the pressure of the gas on the surface, forcing it into the pores of the water.

This explanation provoked William Henry, Dalton's close friend, to begin a series of experiments to discover the order of attractions of gases for water. He eventually found that, at a certain temperature, the volume of a gas taken up by a given volume of water is directly proportional to the pressure of the gas (Henry's law). Dalton was quick to see the relevance of Henry's results to his own ideas. He saw the absorption of gases by water as a purely mechanical effect. He realized that the greatest difficulty with the mechanical theory of gas-water solubility came from different gases obeying different laws. Why does water not admit into its bulk every kind of gas in the same way? Dalton answered this question by saying that gases whose particles were lightest were least absorbable and those with greater weight were more absorbable. Therefore it is clear that Dalton's important decision to investigate the relative weights of atoms arose from his attempt to find experimental support for his theory of mixed gases. The paper that he wrote on this subject in 1803 closed with the very first list of what would come to be called atomic weights.

Dalton's method of calculating the relative weights of atoms was quite simple. Following the postulates of his theory of mixed gases, he assumed that when two elements come together in a chemical reaction, they do so in the simplest possible way (the rule of greatest simplicity). For example, Dalton knew that water was a compound of oxygen and hydrogen. He reasoned that if water was the only compound of these two elements that could be obtained (and it was at the time), then water must be a binary combination of one hydrogen atom and one oxygen atom (HO). Dalton also gave rules for deciding on formulas when there were two or more compounds of two elements. Armed with this mechanical view of combining atoms, it was easy for Dalton to argue from the experimental knowledge that, in forming nine ounces of water, eight ounces of oxygen combined with one ounce of hydrogen to the statement that the relative weights of their atoms were as eight to one.

When Dalton published his table of atomic weights in a Manchester journal, his theory, for the most part, provoked little reaction. It is true that Humphry Davy at the Royal Institution rejected Dalton's ideas as speculations that were more ingenious than important. Despite this lack of enthusiasm, Dalton continued to develop his theory, and in 1804 he worked out the formulas for different hydrocarbons. By 1807, he was spreading the news of his system of chemical philosophy (the first part of which was published in 1808, the second part in 1810). With this publication, the chemical atomic theory was launched. Unfortunately, the theory was the climax of Dalton's scientific creativity, and although he did much work in several scientific fields for the next twenty-five years, the main thrust of his work was in providing atomic weights for known chemical compounds, a problem that would plague chemists for the next fifty years.

Dalton's scientific studies were nourished by the Manchester Literary and Philosophical Society. This group gave him encouragement, an audience, and recognition. In contrast, the Royal Society was dilatory in making him a member, which they did in 1822 at the urging of some of Dalton's friends. In 1831, Dalton helped to found the British Association for the Advancement of Science, and he chaired several of its committees. His activity in these scientific societies was halted in 1837 by two severe paralytic attacks, which left him an invalid for the remaining years of his life.

Dalton lived according to regular and rigid habits. He never married, but he was deeply attached to several relatives and associates, in particular, Jonathan, his brother, and Peter Clare, his closest friend. In his later years, Dalton was admired by his countrymen, and after he died on July 27, 1844, he was given a civic funeral with full honors. His body lay in state in the Manchester Town Hall for four days while more than forty thousand people filed past his coffin. This response to his death was an indication of his scientific achievements and a manifestation of the love for him felt by the inhabitants of the city where he spent his happiest years.

SIGNIFICANCE

John Dalton sometimes used the word "atom" in the sense of the smallest particle with a particular nature. If the atom were divided any further, it would lose its distinguishing chemical characteristics. Dalton also began, however, to think of atoms in the more radical sense of indivisible particles. With this usage, he provided a new and enormously fruitful model of matter for chemistry, because he was able to develop a way of determining atomic weights.

In his *New System of Chemical Philosophy* (1808, 1810), Dalton emphasized that chemical analysis is only the separating of ultimate particles, and synthesis is only the uniting of these particles. God created these elementary particles, and they cannot be changed. All the atoms of a particular element are alike, but the atoms of different elements differ. Though the atoms cannot be changed, they can be combined. Water, Dalton wrote, is composed of molecules formed by the union of a single particle of oxygen to a single ultimate particle of hydrogen.

Many chemists were unwilling to adopt Dalton's chemical atoms. Others used the atomic theory in a pragmatic way, for it helped to make sense of their observations in the laboratory, but they could not grasp its philosophical basis. Some scientists continued to object to atoms well into the twentieth century. They were a minority, however, and a characteristic theme of nineteenth century chemistry was the triumphant march of Dalton's ideas.

—*Robert J. Paradowski*

FURTHER READING

Cardwell, D. S. L., ed. *John Dalton and the Progress of Science*. Manchester, England: Manchester University Press, 1968. A valuable record of the conference held in Manchester in 1966 to celebrate the bicentennial of Dalton's birth. It contains articles by scholars on various aspects of Dalton's achievement. The focus is on the intellectual background to the chemical atomic theory.

Dickinson, Christine, Ian Murray, and David Carden. *John Dalton's Colour Vision Legacy: Selected Proceedings of the International Conference*. London: Taylor & Francis, 1997. The proceedings of a conference commemorating the two-hundredth anniversary of Dalton's description of a newly discovered congenital color vision defect. The text is written by experts in the field and the book is most useful for readers with some knowledge of color vision.

Greenaway, Frank. *John Dalton and the Atom*. Ithaca, N.Y.: Cornell University Press, 1966. This book, intended for general audiences, explores the reasons that Dalton's atomic theory had greater impact on the scientific world than other similar theories produced before his time. Greenaway also investigates Dalton's work in other fields, such as his discovery of color blindness.

McDonnell, John J. *The Concept of an Atom from Democritus to John Dalton*. Lewiston, N.Y.: Edwin Mellen Press, 1991. Chronicles how scientists throughout the ages have sought to determine if a primary indivisible body exists. Traces these scientific attempts from Democritus in the fifth century B.C.E. through Dalton's proposed atomic theory of 1802.

Patterson, Elizabeth C. *John Dalton and the Atomic Theory: The Biography of a Natural Philosopher*. Garden City, N.Y.: Doubleday, 1970. Patterson's study developed out of a fusion of two of her interests: early nineteenth century science and autodidacts, or self-taught persons. The book was part of the Science Study series for high school students, and it provides an analysis of Dalton and his work for the young student or layman.

Roscoe, H. E., and A. Harden. *New View of the Origin of Dalton's Atomic Theory: A Contribution to Chemical History, Together with Letters and Documents Concerning the Life and Labour of John Dalton, Now for the First Time Published from the Manuscript*. London, 1896. Reprint. New York: Johnson Reprint, 1970. Most of Dalton's manuscripts were destroyed in World War II, but important extracts from Dalton's notebooks have been preserved in this book. For example, it contains selections from Dalton's notebooks during the crucial years from 1802 to 1808. The reprint includes an introduction by Arnold Thackray.

Smyth, A. L. *John Dalton: A Bibliography of Works by and About Him*. Manchester, England: Manchester University Press, 1966. Rev. ed. Brookfield, Vt.: Manchester Library and Philosophical Publications in Association with Ashgate, 1998. This book, more than a bibliography, describes Dalton's portraits and illustrations and many of his surviving manuscripts. Smyth also provides a useful guide to the enormous secondary literature on Dalton.

Thackray, Arnold. *Atoms and Powers: An Essay on Newtonian Matter-Theory and the Development of Chemistry*. Cambridge, Mass.: Harvard University Press, 1970. This book provides an excellent treatment of the background by means of which Dalton's ideas were developed. It traces the development of chemistry from Newton to the radical break with Newtonian chemistry engineered by Dalton.

_____. *John Dalton: Critical Assessments of His Life and Science*. Cambridge, Mass.: Harvard University Press, 1972. Thackray is a leading scholar on Dalton, and in this book, which relies on new documentation, he situates Dalton in the social and cultural context of the Industrial Revolution. He also uses Dalton to exemplify certain aspects of scientific change.

SEE ALSO: Amedeo Avogadro; Karl Ernst von Baer; Sir Humphry Davy; Joseph-Louis Gay-Lussac.

RELATED ARTICLE in *Great Events from History: The Nineteenth Century, 1801-1900:* 1803-1808: Dalton Formulates the Atomic Theory of Matter.

RUBÉN DARÍO

Nicaraguan poet

Darío was the most influential writer of the movement in Spanish American literature known as Modernismo *and was also one of the greatest poets in the Spanish language. His strikingly original poetry, which includes stylistic experiments in meter and imagery, reinvigorated literature in both the Americas and Europe. His poetic vision, in which he sought to craft an aesthetic world as wondrous as the world itself, changed the direction of poetry in Spanish.*

BORN: January 18, 1867; Metapa (now Ciudad Darío), Nicaragua

DIED: February 6, 1916; León, Nicaragua

ALSO KNOWN AS: Félix Rubén García Sarmiento (birth name)

AREA OF ACHIEVEMENT: Literature

EARLY LIFE

Rubén Darío (rew-BEHN dah-REE-oh) was the well-known pseudonym of the Nicaraguan writer Félix Rubén García Sarmiento. When Rubén was three, his young mother, Rosa Sarmiento—who was separated from her middle-aged husband—permanently turned him over to her great uncle and aunt, Félix Ramírez and Bernarda Sarmiento in León. Some biographers speculate that Darío's future restlessness, lifelong traveling, and stormy relationships may be explained in part by this early experience of abandonment.

A child prodigy, Rubén quickly learned to read and write poetry. By the time he was fifteen, he had worked as a journalist for several employers and was studying Greek and Latin classics under the tutelage of Jesuit priests in León. In January of 1882, he recited one of his poems before Nicaraguan president Joaquín Zavala and also received a short-lived appointment from the president of El Salvador to teach at a secondary school in that country. Later, he had a job in the Nicaraguan national library that enabled him to read widely and compose poems. He completed the promising but amateurish *Epístolas y poemas: Primeras notas* (epistles and poems: first notes) in 1884.

According to Darío's 1915 autobiography and other accounts, he was already drinking heavily at the age of nineteen. Drinking and womanizing became habits that he would never renounce. After separating for a second time from love interest Rosario Murillo, he left Nicaragua for Chile and took a job there as a customs officer, a post he split with his duties as editor for *La Época*. His poem *Canto épico a las glorias de Chile* (epic song to the glories of Chile) won first prize in a Chilean competition, and his *Rimas*, named after the famous work by poet Gustavo Adolfo Bécquer of Spain, received an honorable mention.

LIFE'S WORK

Although the sway of the Iberian Romantics such as Bécquer was clear in Darío's early work, French Parnassianism, with its anti-Romantic insistence on objective description, and the related movement, Symbolism, with its experiments in poetic musicality, would prove key influences on Darío's developing writing style. His 1888 publication of *Azul* (blue) inaugurated a new direction for poetry in Spanish, infusing it with a directness that discarded the ornate and less precise style of much Romantic poetry.

Darío's experimental and genre-breaking collection of intermixed prose and poetry was revised and republished two more times, culminating in the 1905 edition, which Darío considered definitive. The second and third versions included a prologue by the established Spanish novelist Juan Valera, who championed Darío's work widely, ensuring Darío considerable fame as a powerful new voice in both Spanish American and European letters.

For four years, Rubén traveled tirelessly throughout Central America, editing and writing for several newspapers, including *La Prensa Libre* in Costa Rica. In 1890, he married Rafaela Contreras. His first son, Rubén Darío Contreras, was born the following year. Although he was to have more children with his Spanish companion, Francisca Sanchez, his first son was the only child who would outlive him.

In 1892, when Darío was developing notoriety in Spain, he met several leading Spanish writers and critics in Madrid, where he had been called to serve as Nicaraguan representative for festivities commemorating the four-hundredth anniversary of Christopher Columbus's discovery of America. In addition to Valera, he became acquainted with Menendez y Pelayo and established a lasting friendship with the poet Salvador Rueda. His stay was cut short when his wife died in January of the following year, prompting his return to Nicaragua.

Although Darío claims to have been forced to do so, he married Rosario Murillo in May of 1893 at the insistence of her brother. He then fled from her for the remainder of his life, beginning with trips to New York and

Rubén Darío.

Paris two months after the marriage. During that same year, he served as a consul for Colombia in the cosmopolitan Argentine city of Buenos Aires, where he enjoyed a remarkable following as the leader of the modernist movement. His position as consul was disbanded in 1895, forcing him to live solely from journalism until he accepted an appointment as secretary to the postal director one year later.

In 1896, he published his second major work, *Prosas profanas, y otros poemas* (*Prosas Profanas, and Other Poems*, 1922). This verse collection exhibited the sort of experimentation that Darío had begun in *Azul*. However, in a fashion that was similar to the poetry written by French Parnassians who had become Symbolists, the verses in *Prosas profanas* are less objectively descriptive. Rather, they experiment with rhythm, meter, and sound in an attempt to evoke the spiritual through the physical, wherein highly charged eroticism is conjured in concert with an aestheticized spiritual vision.

Although Darío's art was in many respects removed from the everyday and the political, he promoted a new *hispanidad*, which was a feeling of solidarity among all Spanish-speaking peoples in reaction to the growing Anglo-American dominance of the Western Hemisphere. In response to the Spanish-American War in 1898, he wrote "A Roosevelt" (to [Theodore] Roosevelt), an indictment against the United States. However, as one who keenly sensed the plight of humanity as universally tragic, he also encouraged all human potential to take flight, and he could still admire the laudable aspects of the vaunting new nation: an 1890 sonnet to Walt Whitman heralds him as the great prophet and leader of a rising nation, and the 1906 poem "Salutación al águila" (salutation to the eagle) praises the democratic and enterprising spirit of the United States.

While continuing to work for Buenos Aires newspapers, including *La Nación*, Darío set off to Spain in 1899 and then began a series of travels throughout Europe, stopping often in Madrid, Majorca, and Paris. He worked in Paris as a Nicaraguan consul until 1907. While he was there, he fostered a collaboration and friendship with Spanish poet Juan Ramón Jiménez, who encouraged him to refine his drafts of old and new work in preparation for his 1905 masterpiece, which compiles over a dozen years of compositions: *Cantos de vida y esperanza: Los cisnes, y otros poemas* (songs of life and hope: "The Swans," and other poems).

After a brief trip to Nicaragua in 1907 in a failed attempt to secure a divorce from his wife, Darío returned to Europe. Although he had been appointed a Nicaraguan consul to Spain, he never got paid. Desperate for funds, he hastily published *El canto errante* (the wandering song). Over the next few years, he traveled through Europe and wrote for newspapers and magazines but was constantly on the brink of poverty. By 1914, he was living on the Spanish island of Majorca, where he began to embrace Roman Catholicism passionately while still struggling with his own drinking and womanizing. One of his last works, *Canto a la Argentina, oda a Mitre, y otros poemas* ("Song to Argentina," "Ode to Mitre," and other poems), swings back and forth between religious salvation and erotic dissipation and perdition. These poems are true to his sense that art must embrace as much of life as possible, even if death, which he feared intensely, is inevitable.

Darío's death did approach quickly. Diagnosed with incurable cirrhosis of the liver, he returned home to Nicaragua where, too weak to refuse, he was delivered to his lifelong pursuer, Rosario Murillo, who took care of him until he died on February 6, 1916.

SIGNIFICANCE

Although Darío's modernism became *passé* in the eyes of many following the dawn of the surrealists and the avante-garde in Spain and France, and even though his somewhat apolitical stance seemed inappropriate for artists living after the world wars, his poetry is among the best in the language, and later writers from both sides of the Atlantic, including Frederico Garcia Lorca, Pablo Neruda, Jorge Luis Borges, and Octavio Paz, acknowledged his work as foundational, affirming that he changed literature forever.

—*William Gahan*

FURTHER READING

Acereda, Alberto, and Rigoberto Guevara. *Modernism, Rubén Darío, and the Poetics of Despair*. New York: University Press of America, 2004. This indexed work is a penetrating study of Darío's work as a specific expression of despair in context with his life and the modernist movement.

Darío, Rubén. *Songs of Life and Hope: Cantos de Vida y Esperanza—A Bilingual Edition*, translated and edited by Will Derusha and Alberto Acereda. Durham, N.C.: Duke University Press, 2004. This collection of Darío's poems includes a concise and useful English introduction to Darío's life and works, a brief glossary, and English translations of the poems.

Derusha, Will, and Alberto Acereda, eds. *Selected Poems of Rubén Darío: A Bilingual Anthology*. Lewisburg, Pa.: Bucknell University Press, 2001. Includes a useful English introduction and a broad selection of more than sixty of Darío's poems.

Jrade, Cathy Login. *Rubén Darío and the Romantic Search for Unity: The Modernist Recourse to Esoteric Tradition*. Austin: University of Texas Press, 1983. An accessible critical study of Darío's works and the movement he inaugurated in the context of his time.

Watland, Charles D. *Poet-Errant: A Biography of Rubén Darío*. New York: Philosophical Library, 1965. This biography makes extensive use of Dario's autobiography to narrate a tragic tale of a poet whose experiences and poetry, whose beauty were worthwhile in themselves, never quite served to overcome Darío's initial abandonment by his mother.

SEE ALSO: José Martí; Clorinda Matto de Turner; Walt Whitman.

RELATED ARTICLES in *Great Events from History: The Nineteenth Century, 1801-1900:* c. 1820-1860: *Costumbrismo* Movement; June 16, 1855-May 1, 1857: Walker Invades Nicaragua.

CHARLES DARWIN

English naturalist

A towering figure in natural history, Darwin developed a theory of evolution through natural selection that revolutionized biology by providing a scientific explanation for the origin and development of living forms.

BORN: February 12, 1809; Shrewsbury, Shropshire, England
DIED: April 19, 1882; Downe, Kent, England
ALSO KNOWN AS: Charles Robert Darwin (full name)
AREA OF ACHIEVEMENT: Biology

EARLY LIFE

Charles Robert Darwin was born on February 12, 1809, in Shrewsbury, the fifth of six children. His mother, Susannah, the daughter of famed potter Josiah Wedgwood, died when he was eight, leaving him in the care of his elder sisters. His father, Robert Waring Darwin, was a robust and genial country doctor with a wide practice. In 1818, young Darwin entered Dr. Butler's Shrewsbury School, where he learned some classics but little else. At home he was a quiet, docile child, with an interest in solitary walks and collecting coins and minerals.

In 1825, Darwin was sent to Edinburgh to study medicine, because his family hoped he would enter his father's profession. He proved to be a poor student, showing little interest in anatomy and disliking the crude operations performed without anesthetics. When he left Shrewsbury, his father rebuked him, saying, "You care for nothing but shooting, dogs, and rat-catching, and you will be a disgrace to yourself and all your family."

As a last resort, the young Darwin was sent to Christ's College, Cambridge, to prepare for the ministry, a profession for which he felt no more enthusiasm than he did for medicine, and he soon fell in among the sporting set. Though not a distinguished student, Darwin took an interest in natural science and was influenced by Alexander von Humboldt's *Personal Narrative of Travels to the Equinoctial Regions of the New Continent During the Years 1799-1804* (1814-1829) and Charles Lyell's *Prin-*

ciples of Geology (1830-1833). He met John Stevens Henslow, a botany professor who encouraged his interest in natural history and helped to secure for him a position as naturalist aboard HMS *Beagle*, soon to depart on a five-year scientific expedition around the world. The *Beagle* sailed from Devonport on December 31, 1831. Darwin's experiences during the voyage from 1831 to 1836 were instrumental in shaping his theory of evolution.

The voyage of the *Beagle* took Darwin along the coast of South America, where twenty-nine months were spent charting the waters off the Pacific coast. Darwin explored the Andes and the pampas and kept detailed journals in which he carefully observed differences among the South American flora and fauna, particularly on the Galapagos Islands, where he found a remarkable divergence among the same species from different islands. Before he began his voyage, he had no reason to doubt the immutability of species, but from his firsthand experiences he gradually began to doubt the creationist view of life. He would later draw upon these extensive field observations to formulate his theory of natural selection. Darwin was able to draw together from his travels vast amounts of scientific evidence to buttress his arguments against scientific and religious challenges. When he returned to England on October 2, 1836, he was an accomplished naturalist, collector, and geologist with a new view of the natural history of life.

After his return to London, Darwin settled in an apartment and began a detailed study of coral reefs. He became secretary to the Geological Society and a member of the Royal Society. He married his first cousin, Emma Wedgwood, in January, 1839. Because his health was poor, the couple settled outside London, in Kent. Here, despite his infirmities, Darwin did his most important work. A thin man, about six feet tall, Darwin walked with a stoop that made him appear shorter, especially as his illness worsened later in life.

Charles Darwin. (Courtesy of the University of Texas at Austin)

LIFE'S WORK

At Downe House in Kent, Darwin worked for the next twenty years on his journals from the *Beagle* trip, gathering information to support his theory of evolution through natural selection. In 1837, Darwin had begun his first notebook on the "species question."

A chance reading of Thomas Robert Malthus's *An Essay on the Principle of Population as It Affects the Future Improvement of Society* (1798) in 1838 introduced Darwin to the idea of the struggle for existence, which Darwin thought applied better to plants and animals than to humans, who can expand their food supply artificially. Darwin had returned from his voyage with many unanswered questions. Why were the finches and tortoises different on each of the Galapagos Islands, even though the habitats were not that different? Why were similar creatures, such as the ostrich and the rhea, found on separate continents? Why did some of the South American fossils of extinct mammals resemble the skeletons of some living creatures? The species question fascinated him, and gradually Darwin formulated a theory of the mutability and descent of living forms, although he was still unsure about the mechanisms of adaptation and change.

Two preliminary sketches of 1842 and 1844 presented Darwin's theory of evolution in rudimentary form, but he was determined to amass as much detail as possible to support his deductions. He turned to the work of animal breeders and horticulturalists for evidence of artificial selection among domesticated species. His preliminary work might have continued indefinitely if he had not received on June 18, 1854, an essay from Alfred Russel Wallace, a field naturalist in the Malay archipelago, outlining a theory of evolution and natural selection similar to his own. Darwin immediately wrote to his friends, Sir Charles Lyell and Joseph Hooker, explaining his dilemma and including an abstract of his own theory of evolution. Lyell and Hooker proposed that in order to avoid the question of precedence, the two papers should be presented simultaneously. Both were read before a meeting of the Linnean Society in Dublin on July 1, 1858, and were published together in the society's journal that year.

Darwin then began writing an abstract of his theory, which he entitled *On the Origin of Species by Means of Natural Selection*. All 1,250 copies sold out on the first day of publication in London on November 24, 1859. Darwin argued that because all species produce more offspring than can possibly survive, and because species populations remain relatively constant, there must be some mechanism working in nature to eliminate the unfit. Variations are randomly introduced in nature, some of which will permit a species to adapt better to its environment. These advantageous adaptations are passed on to the offspring, giving them an advantage for survival. Darwin did not understand the genetic mechanism by which offspring inherit adaptations. It would take another seventy years before the forgotten work of the Austrian geneticist Gregor Mendel was rediscovered and Sir Ronald Fisher integrated the theories of Darwinian selection and Mendelian genetics.

A quiet and retiring man, Darwin was surrounded by a storm of controversy after the publication of *On the Origin of Species*. Objection came both from orthodox clergy and unconvinced scientists. At Oxford in 1860, there was a famous debate on evolution between Thomas H. Huxley and Bishop Samuel Wilberforce, in which Huxley answered the creationist arguments against evolution and silenced the religious critics.

For the rest of his life, Darwin himself worked at home on orchid- and pigeon-breeding experiments and successive editions of *On the Origin of Species*, as well as further studies on plant and animal domestication, climbing plants, cross-fertilization, orchids, the expression of emotions, and his famous *The Descent of Man*

DARWIN'S BOYHOOD INTERESTS

In 1876, Charles Darwin wrote a brief autobiography. He had no intention of publishing it but instead wished to use it merely to explain to his own children how his mind and character had developed. In this passage, he discusses his interests during his schooldays.

Looking back as well as I can at my character during my school life, the only qualities which at this period promised well for the future, were, that I had strong and diversified tastes, much zeal for whatever interested me, and a keen pleasure in understanding any complex subject or thing. I was taught Euclid by a private tutor, and I distinctly remember the intense satisfaction which the clear geometrical proofs gave me. I remember, with equal distinctness, the delight which my uncle gave me (the father of Francis Galton) by explaining the principle of the vernier of a barometer. With respect to diversified tastes, independently of science, I was fond of reading various books, and I used to sit for hours reading the historical plays of Shakespeare, generally in an old window in the thick walls of the school. I read also other poetry, such as Thomson's *Seasons*, and the recently published poems of Byron and Scott. I mention this because later in life I wholly lost, to my great regret, all pleasure from poetry of any kind, including Shakespeare. In connection with pleasure from poetry, I may add that in 1822 a vivid delight in scenery was first awakened in my mind, during a riding tour on the borders of Wales, and this has lasted longer than any other aesthetic pleasure.

Early in my school days a boy had a copy of the *Wonders of the World*, which I often read, and disputed with other boys about the veracity of some of the statements; and I believe that this book first gave me a wish to travel in remote countries, which was ultimately fulfilled by the voyage of the *Beagle*. In the latter part of my school life I became passionately fond of shooting; I do not believe that any one could have shown more zeal for the most holy cause than I did for shooting birds. How well I remember killing my first snipe, and my excitement was so great that I had much difficulty in reloading my gun from the trembling of my hands. This taste long continued, and I became a very good shot. When at Cambridge I used to practise throwing up my gun to my shoulder before a looking-glass to see that I threw it up straight. Another and better plan was to get a friend to wave about a lighted candle, and then to fire at it with a cap on the nipple, and if the aim was accurate the little puff of air would blow out the candle. The explosion of the cap caused a sharp crack, and I was told that the tutor of the college remarked, "What an extraordinary thing it is, Mr. Darwin seems to spend hours in cracking a horse-whip in his room, for I often hear the crack when I pass under his windows."

Source: Charles Darwin, *The Life and Letters of Charles Darwin, Including an Autobiographical Chapter*, edited by Francis Darwin (New York: D. Appleton, 1888).

and Selection in Relation to Sex (1871). His wife, Emma, nursed him during his bouts of illness, whose origin is uncertain. She also reared their ten children, seven of whom survived to adulthood, three to become distinguished scientists and members of the Royal Society. In his later years, Darwin regretted the loss of his appreciation for poetry and music, complaining that his mind had become a "machine for grinding general laws out of large collections of facts." Still, he maintained a wide correspondence and enjoyed entertaining close friends and occasional visitors at home. He died on April 19, 1882, at Downe House in Kent, and was buried with full honors in the scientists' corner at Westminster Abbey, next to Sir Isaac Newton.

SIGNIFICANCE

Perhaps more profoundly than any other single work, Charles Darwin's *On the Origin of Species by Means of Natural Selection* shaped the development of modern biology and, more broadly, the modern view of human nature. No longer was it possible to accept uncritically the biblical view of creation, with the implied special place of humanity in the divine order. Man became a creature among creatures, with a traceable evolution and descent from earlier hominoid forms. Darwin's ideas exerted a wide cultural influence, with a popular version of "the survival of the fittest" diffusing into the politics, literature, and sociology of the age, especially through Herbert Spencer's "social Darwinism."

Darwin's ideas were often mistakenly used to justify racism, discrimination , and repressive laissez-faire economic practices. Though Darwin drifted toward agnosticism and did not believe in a divinely sanctioned morality, neither did he condone a world of amoral violence and brute struggle for domination. He believed that human morality was the product of humanity's social and cultural evolution and that it did confer survival benefits. A gentle man who abhorred violence and cruelty, he would have been horrified at the political and social misapplications of Darwinian principles. Nevertheless, Darwin was not a Victorian liberal and accepted many of the unenlightened views of his age concerning "primitive" cultures.

During his lifetime, Darwin faced formidable challenges to his evolutionary theory, first from the scientist Fleeming Jenkin, who argued that fortuitous adaptations would be "swamped" and disappear in larger populations, and later from Lord Kelvin, who mistakenly questioned Darwin's estimate of the geological age of the earth on the basis of the laws of thermodynamics. These challenges led Darwin to revise *On the Origin of Species* extensively in successive editions and to back away from some of his earlier claims about the long timespan needed for slow, evolutionary changes to take place. In order to accommodate Lord Kelvin's shortened estimate of the earth's age, Darwin moved toward a neo-Lamarckian position concerning the inheritance of acquired characteristics. Darwin had no way of knowing that Mendel's discoveries in genetics would have answered many of his doubts about the sources of variation and the mechanisms of inheritance.

Darwin has had an immeasurable influence on the development of modern biology, ecology, morphology, embryology, and paleontology. His theory of evolution established a natural history of the earth and enabled humans to see themselves for the first time as part of the natural order of life. A lively debate continues among scientists about revisionist theories of evolution, including Stephen Jay Gould's notion of "punctuated equilibria," or sudden and dramatic evolutionary changes followed by long periods of relative stability. While they disagree about details, however, modern biologists agree that neoevolutionary theory remains the only persuasive scientific explanation for the diversity of life on earth.

—*Andrew J. Angyal*

FURTHER READING

Aydon, Cyril. *Charles Darwin: The Naturalist Who Started a Scientific Revolution*. New York: Carroll & Graf, 2002. Explains the theories described in *On the Origin of the Species*, and the subsequent debate over those ideas. Outlines the changing fortunes of Darwinian theories over the last two centuries.

Brachman, Arnold. *A Delicate Arrangement: The Strange Case of Charles Darwin and Charles Russel Wallace*. New York: Times Books, 1980. Brachman argues that Darwin and his friends conspired to deny Wallace credit for having first discovered the theory of biological evolution.

Clark, Ronald W. *The Survival of Charles Darwin: A Biography of a Man and an Idea*. New York: Random House, 1984. A study of Darwin's life and work, concentrating on the genesis of evolutionary theory and its development after Darwin's death.

Colp, Ralph, Jr. *To Be an Invalid: The Illness of Charles Darwin*. Chicago: University of Chicago Press, 1977. A detailed study of the various theories about what caused Darwin's chronic, debilitating illness after the *Beagle* voyage.

Darwin, Charles. *The Autobiography of Charles Darwin, 1809-1882*. Edited by Nora Barlow. New York: W. W. Norton, 1969. A new edition of Darwin's autobiography, edited by his granddaughter, with the original omissions restored.

De Beer, Sir Gavin. *Charles Darwin: A Scientific Biography*. New York: Doubleday, 1965. The standard authorized biography of Darwin by an English scientist who enjoyed full access to the Darwin Papers at Cambridge University.

Eiseley, Loren. *Darwin's Century: Evolution and the Men Who Discovered It*. New York: Doubleday, 1958. A rigorous intellectual history of the concept of evolution and its antecedents, from Darwin's precursors through the publication of *On the Origin of Species* and its reception.

Hodge, Jonathan, and Gregory Radick, eds. *The Cambridge Companion to Darwin*. New York: Cambridge University Press, 2003. Collection of essays examining Darwin's major theories, the development of his thinking, and how his thought has influenced philosophical, religious, and social debate. Includes an essay placing Darwin's work within the context of Victorian science.

Irvine, William. *Apes, Angels, and Victorians: The Story of Darwin, Huxley, and Evolution*. New York: McGraw-Hill, 1955. A detailed cultural study of Darwinism and its impact on the Victorian mind.

SEE ALSO: Louis Agassiz; Samuel Butler; Asa Gray; Ernst Haeckel; Thomas Henry Huxley; Sir Charles Lyell; Herbert Spencer.

RELATED ARTICLES in *Great Events from History: The Nineteenth Century, 1801-1900:* 1809: Lamarck Publishes *Zoological Philosophy*; July, 1830: Lyell Publishes *Principles of Geology*; 1854-1862: Wallace's Expeditions Give Rise to Biogeography; November 24, 1859: Darwin Publishes *On the Origin of Species*; 1861: *Archaeopteryx Lithographica* Is Discovered; 1871: Darwin Publishes *The Descent of Man*; 1883: Galton Defines "Eugenics."

JACQUES-LOUIS DAVID

French painter

David was the founder of nineteenth century neoclassicism. His participation in the political events of his time directed not only the course of his own art but that of European painting as well.

BORN: August 30, 1748; Paris, France
DIED: December 29, 1825; Brussels, Belgium
AREA OF ACHIEVEMENT: Art

EARLY LIFE

Jacques-Louis David's birth on August 30, 1748, coincided with the beginning of many profound political, social, and aesthetic changes in France. He was born in Paris into the merchant-and-artisan middle class, although his grandmother was the cousin of François Boucher, first painter to the king. During his early schooling, David was by all accounts an indifferent student who preferred drawing to any of his other studies. In 1764, at the age of sixteen, having declared his firm resolve to become a painter, David sought the help of Boucher.

Although no longer accepting students himself, Boucher saw promise in the young David and advised that he study with Joseph Vien, a professor at the Royal Academy of Painting and Sculpture. Vien was, according to Boucher, a good painter and teacher, but somewhat cold. He advocated a return to classical antiquity as a source of moral as well as artistic inspiration; his own work, however, consisted mostly of superficial borrowings of classical motifs that lacked understanding of the true meaning of the classical spirit.

After two years in Vien's studio, David entered the academy as a student. In the light of his subsequent actions against the academy, it is important to note that at this time David did not question the academy's control over the arts in France. Accepting the academy's hierarchy of categories in painting, he aspired to the highest—that of history painting—and was determined to win the coveted Prix de Rome, which would allow him three years of study at the academy's branch in Rome and almost certainly guarantee his eventual membership in the academy. As an academician, eligible for the best royal commissions and allowed to exhibit his work at the Salon, he would be assured of a successful career.

After three unsuccessful attempts to win the Prix de Rome, David contemplated suicide. Even though he finally won the competition in 1774 with his *Antiochus and Stratonice*, he now harbored a bitter resentment of the academy's earlier rejections of his work, never forgiving the academicians for their failure to recognize the talent he was certain he possessed. In fact, his style at this time was fragmented, reflecting the many currents in French painting during the early 1770's—he painted classical themes with something of Vien's sense of theatricality and exaggerated dramatic effect, while his use of light and brushwork came from the rococo tradition.

While studying in Italy from 1778 to 1780, David was influenced by Greco-Roman classicism, the masters of the High Renaissance, and the early Baroque works of Caravaggio and the Carracci family. He went to Rome determined not to be seduced by classical antiquity, believing it to be lifeless and static. After studying classical sculpture and the Pompeian frescoes, however, he realized that he had based his work on a false principle. He sensed that he would have to repudiate everything he had once thought about art. The qualities of virtue, austerity, and moral strength that he saw in ancient classical art reinforced his own desires for simplicity and strength. His work soon began to evidence the characteristics that would mark his mature style: solidity of drawing, clarity of form and narrative structure, and a Caravaggesque realism of light and texture.

Jacques-Louis David. (Library of Congress)

LIFE'S WORK

David's first public acclaim came with the exhibition of twelve paintings in the Salon of 1781, the most popular of which was *Belisarius*—the story of false accusation and unjust punishment in a past age, which viewers equated with a contemporary general falsely accused and executed for treason. In the next few years, David's reputation increased—he was praised by the encyclopedist Denis Diderot for his creation of a noble, didactic art, and he attained academy membership.

David's involvement with the political events of his day began with *The Oath of the Horatii* of 1785. This painting, with its theme of self-sacrifice for a noble cause, was perceived by viewers as a pictorial call to arms for the revolutionary sentiments rapidly gaining momentum in France. Just as he had done in *Belisarius*, David created a parallel between contemporary events and ancient history with this theme of the three Horatii who, united by a strict patriotic discipline of body and soul, swear an oath to fight to the death for their country, while the tragic personal loss that always accompanies heroic military feats is evidenced by the group of mourning wives and children who witness the oath. Then, with the exhibition of *The Death of Socrates* in 1787 and *Brutus Receiving the Bodies of His Sons* in 1789—both of which portray the same message of self-sacrifice for a greater good—David's reputation as a prophet of the revolution was firmly established in the minds of the French public.

Now a fervent Jacobin and friend of Robespierre, David took a more active role in revolutionary events after the fall of the Bastille. He became the director of all revolutionary festivals. He was elected as a deputy to the National Convention, during which time he voted for the execution of the king in 1793, signed hundreds of arrest warrants during the Reign of Terror, and proposed the creation of national museums that he also helped to organize. In 1790, he had avenged himself upon the academicians by organizing other dissident artists into the Commune des Arts, and, in 1793, he persuaded the convention to abolish the academy, replacing it with a jury to supervise the awarding of Salon prizes. As the principal juror, David had become the virtual dictator of the arts in France. Always a reformer, he freed French art from some of the old academic constraints while he led the way toward a new academicism.

David's political activities continued to give direction to his painting. The prophet of the revolution became the chronicler of the historic events of the present. His works of this period range from *The Oath of the Tennis Court* (1791)—commemorating the deputies of the Third Estate's writing of a new constitution—to his apotheosis of such slain republican heroes as Jean-Paul Marat, Vicomte Paul François Barras, and Paul Michel Lepeletier.

Political involvement, however, almost cost David his life. After the execution of Robespierre in 1794, David was arrested and, although his enemies demanded his death, he was imprisoned instead. An amnesty in 1795 set him free. While in prison, David—having vowed at his trial that he would henceforth attach himself to principles and not to men—began planning his next great classical painting, *The Battle of the Romans and Sabines* (1794-1799), a work that restored his artistic reputation.

David's determination to avoid political involvements was quickly forgotten when, in 1797, he acquired a new patron and hero, Napoleon Bonaparte—then first consul and later emperor of France. David became his court painter, documenting all the military splendor and pageantry of Napoleon's reign in portraits, in depictions of Napoleon leading his armies to victory, and finally in the coronation itself. David, who had earlier used history and mythology to refer to contemporary events, now turned contemporary events into new historical myths. His neoclassicism influenced everything from painting and sculpture to fashion and furniture design, and some of his most important works date from this period.

Unfortunately, David's political activities again proved to be his undoing. Napoleon's abdication and the First Bourbon Restoration of 1814 found David stubbornly maintaining his allegiance to the emperor, believing perhaps that his international reputation as an artist would protect him. During the Hundred Days, in fact, he met with Napoleon, who made him a Commander of the Legion of Honor, and he rashly signed the *Acte additionnel* (1815), again repudiating the rule of the Bourbon kings of France. The Second Restoration, however, saw the enactment of a law banishing all who had signed the *Acte additionnel*, and David, at the age of sixty-seven, went into exile in Brussels.

Despite some attempts at reprisal by his enemies in France, David's last years in Brussels were happy and productive. Sale of his works brought him financial security, and he enjoyed a position of prominence within the artistic community. He painted continually, concentrating on portraits and mythological subjects such as *Cupid and Psyche* (1817) and *Telemachus and Eucharis* (1818)—themes that were less dangerous, perhaps, than the real or legendary histories of Greece and Rome that had served him so well during the politically active years of the revolution, the republic, and the empire. He died peacefully at his home in Brussels on December 29, 1825, at the age of seventy-seven.

SIGNIFICANCE

Jacques-Louis David's art, like his personality, was extremely complex. Friends described him as intense and dogmatic, sensitive and spartan—an assessment of character substantiated by the severe, doctrinaire classicism of his prerevolutionary works, all of which are remarkable for their stoicism and their sense of emotion held in check by icy control. David eventually realized that the success of these heroically ethical creations—which had proclaimed a new aesthetic and moral order—could not be repeated indefinitely, even by him. In 1808, he declared that the direction he had set for art was too severe to please for very long in France.

A different facet of David's personality was reflected in his attempt to separate artistic activity from the demands of morality by concentrating on purely aesthetic problems in *The Battle of the Romans and Sabines*—a work in which he modified the severity of his Roman classicism for a more Greek and abstract refinement. In his paintings of contemporary events during the Napoleonic era and in many of his portraits, David proved himself an acute observer of nature and a realist.

As the different goals and interests embodied in later nineteenth century movements such as Romanticism and Impressionism led artists to turn away from classicism, David's principles and his art were shunned, and his reputation went into an eclipse that lasted until 1913. At that time, an exhibition in Paris prompted an interest in his work that has continued to grow, and today he is acknowledged as the true founder of nineteenth century European neoclassicism.

—*LouAnn Faris Culley*

FURTHER READING

Brookner, Anita. *Jacques-Louis David*. New York: Harper & Row, 1980. One of the most complete biographies, this book contains important documentation, never before published in English, of David's artistic sources and his political activities. Also contains an extensive catalog of paintings and drawings, although most plates are monochrome.

French Painting, 1774-1830: The Age of Revolution. Detroit: Wayne State University Press, 1975. Catalog of a French-American exhibition of paintings from the age of revolution. Excellent essays by foremost

Davidian scholars discuss the artistic disunity of the era and analyze David's contribution to mainstream trends. Includes brief biographies of all exhibitors.

Friedlaender, Walter. *David to Delacroix*. Translated by Robert Goldwater. Cambridge, Mass.: Harvard University Press, 1952. Emphasizes the historical structure of French painting by studying the sources of various stylistic and intellectual currents of the period. Discusses classicism and other trends in David's art and the transformation of his principles by his followers.

Lee, Simon. *David*. London: Phaidon Press, 1999. Comprehensive biography. Lee argues that David was the most important European painter of his age, creating a dramatic and noble style that matched the contemporary desire for heroic and morally elevating images.

Nanteuil, Luc de. *Jacques-Louis David*. New York: Harry N. Abrams, 1985. Detailed account of David's development from early through mature styles. Clear, concise discussion of political events that shaped his thinking. Excellent color plates of most significant works, with analysis of the formalistic elements of each.

Roberts, Warren. *Jacques-Louis David and Jean-Louis Prieur: Revolutionary Artists—The Public, the Populace, and Images of the French Revolution*. Albany: State University of New York Press, 2000. Compares the careers of David and Prieur, a popular illustrator of his times. Tracks the political careers of both artists, describing the relationship between their art and the politics of the French Revolution.

_____. *Jacques-Louis David, Revolutionary Artist: Art, Politics, and the French Revolution*. Chapel Hill: University of North Carolina Press, 1989. Popular biography, accessible to general readers with no prior knowledge of art or French history. Roberts describes the relationship of David's art to his personality and participation in the French Revolution.

Rosenblum, Robert, and H. W. Janson. *Nineteenth Century Art*. New York: Harry N. Abrams, 1984. A perceptive analysis of David's style through the Napoleonic era, contrasting his use of classical sources to that of his contemporaries. Provides detailed accounts of David's followers and their efforts to maintain the neoclassical style in spite of the growth of Romanticism.

SEE ALSO: Eugène Delacroix; Georges Seurat; Henri de Toulouse-Lautrec.

RELATED ARTICLE in *Great Events from History: The Nineteenth Century, 1801-1900:* October-December, 1830: Delacroix Paints *Liberty Leading the People*.

JEFFERSON DAVIS

President of the Confederate States of America (1861-1865)

Davis served the U.S. government ably as a senator and as secretary of war; however, his commitment to Southern secession led him to accept the presidency of the Confederacy and attempt to preserve Southern independence against bitter opposition and overwhelming odds. Both reviled and idealized as a symbol of the Confederacy, Davis maintained a consistency of principle and perseverance that balance out the fact that he was not well fitted for the demands of the times and the position he held.

BORN: June 3, 1808; Christian County (now Fairview, Todd County), Kentucky
DIED: December 6, 1889; New Orleans, Louisiana
AREA OF ACHIEVEMENT: Government and politics

EARLY LIFE

During the turbulent decades of the early eighteenth century, a son of Welsh immigrants moved his family from Philadelphia to the Georgia area; Evan Davis's son Samuel, as reward for his services as a Revolutionary War guerrilla captain, was granted land near Augusta. He was chosen county clerk and in 1783 married Jane Cook. Continuing the family pattern, Samuel migrated often; in 1792 he moved to Kentucky, where his tenth and last child, Jefferson (Finis) Davis, was born at Fairview in Christian (later Todd) County, on June 3, 1808. By 1811, the family was living in Louisiana but later moved to Wilkinson County, Mississippi Territory. In these frontier areas, owners worked in the fields with their slaves; Samuel Davis was able to give only a single slave to each of his children when they married. His eldest son, however, Joseph Emory Davis, demonstrated in his life the "flush times" and upward mobility of the lower South: He became a lawyer, the wealthy owner of a great plantation, and a "father" to his youngest brother.

In his youth, Jefferson Davis spent two years at the Roman Catholic St. Thomas's College in Kentucky and then attended local schools near home; in 1821, he studied classics at Transylvania University in Lexington, Kentucky. Just after his father's death, late in 1824, he entered West Point Military Academy. He was over six feet tall, slender, an active, high-spirited young man, with brown hair and deep-set gray-blue eyes, a high forehead and cheekbones, and an aquiline nose and square jaw. In 1828, twenty-third out of a class of thirty-three, he was graduated as a second lieutenant. For the next seven years he was on frontier duty at the dangerous and lonely posts in Wisconsin and Illinois, acquitting himself well and with initiative; in 1832, he briefly guarded the captive chief Black Hawk. In 1833, at Fort Crawford, Wisconsin, he met Sarah Knox Taylor, daughter of the commandant, Colonel Zachary Taylor; despite the latter's objections, they were married June 17, 1835, at her aunt's home in Kentucky.

Despite Davis's belief that he had an aptitude for the military, he resigned his commission; Joseph gave the young couple an adjoining new plantation, Brierfield, and fourteen slaves on credit. As neither was acclimatized, they left for the Louisiana plantation of a Davis sister, but they both contracted malaria, and Knox Davis died on September 15, 1835. A grieving Jefferson Davis, convalescing in Havana and New York, spent some time also in a senatorial boardinghouse in Washington, D.C., but soon returned to Brierfield.

For the next eight years, Davis led a solitary and reclusive life, reading extensively in literature, history, and the classics and associating primarily with his brother. During this period he developed the basic system of Brierfield, which was almost an ideal plantation: benevolent master, slaves trained and working according to their abilities and making many decisions concerning their labor and earnings, and Davis's personal slave James Pemberton as overseer with a practically free hand. During these years Davis developed his attachments, both theoretical and personal, to the soil, the South, and the new aristocratic society of the lower South.

Davis's identification was completed and symbolized by his marriage on February 26, 1845, to Varina Anne Banks Howell; she was half his age, a black-haired beauty of Natchez high society, with a classical education and a vivacious temperament. Throughout her life, "Winnie" Davis was high-strung, demonstrative, and emotionally turbulent, a determined woman who fought fiercely for those she loved and who was not always either tactful or forgiving.

By this stage of his life, Davis's personality had been formed. Despite his military experience and life as a planter, he had never really had to fight for place and position; he was more of a theoretician than a realist. He was affectionate with family and friends, essentially humorless, coldly logical, with a deep-rooted egotism and a sense of his own merit; he was never able to believe that others' criticism or disagreement could be sincere or impersonal. Committed firmly to aristocracy and slavery, state sovereignty and states' rights (under the Constitution and within the American nation), always a Democrat, Davis moved into politics. In 1843, he lost an election for the state legislature to a well-known Whig; in 1844 he was a Polk elector. In 1845, he was elected to the U.S. House of Representatives.

Jefferson Davis. (Library of Congress)

Davis entered into marriage in February, 1845, and entered Congress in December; in June, 1846, on the outbreak of the Mexican War, he resigned from the House to become colonel of the volunteer mounted First Mississippi Rifles. He trained his regiment and equipped his men with the new percussion rifles, and under Major General Zachary Taylor it participated creditably in the victory at Monterrey. When, in the following February,

General Antonio López de Santa Anna led fifteen thousand men across two hundred miles of desert to confront Taylor's five thousand at Buena Vista, Davis's Mississippi Rifles fought off a Mexican division in an action (the famous V-formation) that may have been decisive for the American victory. Davis led the regiment despite a wound in the foot that kept him on crutches for two years and in intermittent pain for the next decade. This episode gained for Davis a popular reputation as a military hero and reinforced his already ineradicable conviction of his own military capability.

After Buena Vista, with Taylor's influence waning and the regiment's enlistment expiring, Davis again resigned a military commission, and in December, 1847, was appointed to a vacancy in the Senate. An expansionist, he supported President James K. Polk on the Mexican Cession, even suggesting American acquisition of Yucatan; although he acquiesced in extending the Missouri Compromise line to the Pacific, he asserted that there was no constitutional power to prohibit slave property in any territory. The complex politics associated with the Compromise of 1850 included several southern groupings: Unionists, radical states' righters (in favor of immediate secession), southern "nationalists" (or "cooperationists," anticipating possible later secession by the South as a whole).

When his fellow Mississippi senator Henry S. Foote ran for governor on a Union ticket (a coalition of Whigs and some Democrats), Davis was persuaded to resign from the Senate (in September, 1851) and oppose him on the Democratic ticket; Davis lost by a thousand votes. Political defeat was offset by the birth of the Davis's first child, Samuel Emerson, on July 30, 1852.

Having aided in the campaign to elect Franklin Pierce, Davis was appointed secretary of war in March of 1853. Ironically, these four years were to be the most congenial and productive of his life. He was in good health and spirits; "Winnie" Davis was a charming and vivacious hostess and the Davis house was the social center of official Washington circles. There was a growing family: Although Samuel died on June 30, 1854, Margaret Howell (Maggie or Pollie) was born on February 25, 1855, and Jefferson, Jr., on January 16, 1857.

As secretary of war, Davis supported the concept (developed by John C. Calhoun during his tenure of the office) of an expansible army; infantry units were issued the new percussion-cap muzzle-loading rifles and Minié balls; infantry tactics were made somewhat more flexible; West Point officers were encouraged to study in Europe and to develop military theory; and the regrettable system of army departments was strengthened. Davis urged the use of camels in the Southwest, but the experiment failed. Davis was unable to influence the administration on the issues of the *Black Warrior* seizure and the Ostend Manifesto, but as a southern expansionist he enthusiastically organized a research expedition to the Southwest to provide data that led to the Gadsden Purchase.

The end of Davis's term in the cabinet was soon followed by his election to the Senate; he took his seat in March, 1857. Another son, Joseph Evan, was born on April 18, 1859. Davis's time as senator would have been the peak and epilogue of his political career, had it not been prologue to suffering and defeat. Nearly fifty, he was gaunt and neurotic; he suffered from dyspepsia and neuralgia and lost the sight of his left eye. He was an effective orator, aided by the obvious intensity of his convictions, and he strongly supported the South's interests in the increasingly bitter sectional confrontations of the 1850's. Within the Democratic Party, he fought the popular sovereignty position of Stephen A. Douglas and worked to prevent the latter's nomination as Democratic candidate in 1860.

Abraham Lincoln's election and nonnegotiable stand against expansion of slavery into the territories convinced Davis of the necessity and inevitability of secession; on January 21, 1861, upon learning of Mississippi's secession, he resigned from the Senate. Like few others at the time, Davis expected war, probably anticipating a command position; he was indeed appointed major general of Mississippi's troops. The Montgomery convention, which established a provisional government, however, needed a president more acceptable to the moderates (or earlier "cooperationists") and early in February, 1861, elected Jefferson Davis.

LIFE'S WORK

On October 6, 1861, Jefferson Davis was elected president of the Confederate States of America, for the constitutional six-year term. On December 16, William (Billy) Howell was born. Davis was inaugurated in the official Confederate capital of Richmond, Virginia, on February 22, 1862. On March 6, 1861, the Confederate Congress had authorized a hundred thousand volunteers for a twelve-month enlistment, but even after Fort Sumter, Davis did not move to ensure an adequate munitions supply or a financial base (for example, the use of cotton supplies to secure paper currency).

The emphasis on protecting the capital at Richmond effectively divided the eastern and western Confederacy; Davis retained the system of military departments, their heads responsible directly to him, and therefore eliminated the possibility of unified strategy or well-coordinated action. His military strategy was only to defend, meeting Union forces wherever they might move. He failed to understand that the military situation, as well as the political situation, was a revolutionary one; he could not come to grips with the conditions and concepts of this first modern war. It is true that few at that time fully comprehended its implications; Lincoln, Ulysses S. Grant, and William Sherman were probably the only ones who realized its necessities.

Davis's long-standing quarrel with Joseph E. Johnston stemmed from the latter's failure to be ranked highest of the five Confederate full generals. Late in the war, Davis removed Johnston from command in Georgia at a critical point: General John Bell Hood's loss of Atlanta aided in Lincoln's reelection and continued Northern support of the war. Public and congressional opinion did not influence Davis: He refused to remove General Braxton Bragg despite that officer's ineffectiveness in battle, and when forced to remove Judah P. Benjamin as secretary of war, he "promoted" him to secretary of state. Davis spent too much time in battle areas; he neglected the West and refused to authorize the transfer of troops across the boundaries of military departments to areas where they were needed. Even after Antietam, he could not see that only a major offensive held any hope of victory and independence; instead, he insisted on scattering garrisons and attempting to hold every inch of territory. Robert E. Lee's offensive into Pennsylvania came too late and could not thereafter be repeated.

Close control of military policy overshadowed all other considerations in Davis's administration, although all policy in fact concerned the pursuit of the war. Davis's commitment to a "southern nation" provoked opposition, from "fire-eaters" such as Robert Barnwell Rhett and William L. Yancey, states' righters such as Governors Joseph E. Brown of Georgia and Zebulon B. Vance of North Carolina, and Vice President Alexander H. Stephens.

The influential *Richmond Examiner* and *Charleston Mercury* regularly opposed Davis's policies; his imperious approach and inability to handle the political situation gave rise to vague but frightening rumors that he was a despot who at any moment might take over the entire government and even use the army to control the people. The tension between sovereign states and an embryo national government in wartime can be seen in most of the controversial issues: general conscription was denounced as unconstitutional, attempts to suspend the writ of habeas corpus were deemed tyrannical. The "rich man's war and poor man's fight" continued with increasing military setbacks and declining supplies and morale.

During the last winter of the war, Davis remained strangely optimistic. He had always had strong faith; in May of 1862 he had joined St. Paul's (Episcopal) Church. Although devastated by the death of Joseph, who fell from a balcony on April 30, 1864, he was consoled by the birth of Varina Anne (Winnie) on June 27, 1864. He urged a draft of forty thousand slaves (to be freed after victory); he sent an agent to offer Great Britain an emancipation program in return for recognition and military alliance. Peace movements, projects to remove the French-imposed Emperor Maximilian from Mexico, the Hampton Roads conference: Davis would consider no compromising of Southern independence (just as Lincoln was committed absolutely to the Union). He seemed to believe that at

THE COMPROMISE OF 1850

Jefferson Davis was among the many southern politicians who were dissatisfied with the congressional Compromise of 1850. In this speech before the U.S. Senate, he hinted at the secessionist movement that was to come ten years later.

It is my opinion that justice will not be done to the South, unless from other promptings than are about us here—that we shall have no substantial consideration offered to us for the surrender of an equal claim to California. No security against future harassment by Congress will probably be given. The rain-bow which some have seen, I fear was set before the termination of the storm. If this be so, those who have been first to hope, to relax their energies, to trust in compromise promises, will often be the first to sound the alarm when danger again approaches. Therefore I say, if a reckless and self-sustaining majority shall trample upon her rights, if the Constitutional equality of the States is to be overthrown by force, private and political rights to be borne down by force of numbers, then, sir, when that victory over Constitutional rights is achieved, the shout of triumph which announces it, before it is half uttered, will be checked by the united, the determined action of the South, and every breeze will bring to the marauding destroyers of those rights, the warning: woe, woe to the riders who trample them down! I submit the report and resolutions, and ask that they may be read and printed for the use of the Senate.

Source: Jefferson Davis, speech to the U.S. Senate, May 8, 1850.

the last moment the South might yet be saved, perhaps by one great battle led by General Lee and by himself that would sweep the Union armies from the field.

Having evacuated his family, Davis, along with several associates, left Richmond on April 3, 1865, still committed to continuing the war. News of Appomattox persuaded the party to head southward; a cabinet meeting in Greensboro, North Carolina, agreed that General Johnston should ask for terms. At Charlotte, twelve days later, the group recognized Confederate defeat and dispersed, Davis moving south into Georgia to rejoin his family and attempt to leave the country. On May 10, the Fourth Michigan Cavalry came upon them at Irwinville, Georgia; Davis's brief attempt to slip away in a hastily snatched-up rain cape belonging to his wife gave rise to the story that he had tried to disguise himself as a woman to evade capture.

Over the next two years, Davis remained a state prisoner in a damp casemate cell in Fortress Monroe. He was once put forcibly in irons for five days, with a lamp burning continually and the guard marching regularly outside, without adequate clothing or books, and suffering from erysipelas. His fortitude, faith, and kindliness impressed the doctors assigned to him, and finally he was placed in more comfortable quarters in the fortress, his family (which had been kept in Savannah) permitted to join him and friends permitted to visit him.

On May 4, 1867, Davis was arraigned on a charge of treason in the federal district court in Richmond and released on bail supplied by ten men, among them Horace Greeley and abolitionist Gerrit Smith. Thereafter, he and his family traveled at various times to Canada, Cuba, New Orleans, Vicksburg, and Davis Bend, as well as to Europe. He was never brought to trial, as the complex constitutional issues surrounding secession remained too controversial and politically incendiary (especially during the Reconstruction period) to be aired in connection with the former president of the defeated Confederacy. His case was dropped on December 5, 1868.

During the remaining years of his life, Davis experienced a series of business failures, several unprofitable European trips, and a gradual recovery of his health. Maggie became Mrs. J. Addison Hayes and settled in Memphis, but Billy died of diphtheria in 1872, and the remaining son, Jefferson, Jr., having failed at Virginia Military Institute, died of yellow fever in 1878. Davis was able to salvage only part of the value of his old plantation in 1878. A friend of Varina, the widowed Mrs. Sarah A. E. Dorsey, gave him a cottage in which to work, on her plantation "Beauvoir," near Biloxi, on the Mississippi Gulf coast.

Varina was finally reconciled to this cooperation, and to Davis's inheritance of the estate in 1879, and aided him in his writing of the two-volume *Rise and Fall of the Confederate Government* (1881), primarily a justification of the constitutionality of secession. In the South, Davis was largely "rehabilitated," being often invited to make speeches and dedicate memorials (including one near his birthplace). His youngest, Winnie, the "Daughter of the Confederacy," was assailed for wishing to marry a New York lawyer, grandson of an abolitionist, and died in 1898 at thirty-three, still single and grieving.

Despite financial problems, Davis, as he had done previously, continued to support both Howell and Davis relatives and several poor children and to entertain a variety of visitors. In 1889, he fell ill with bronchitis in New Orleans, Louisiana, and died there on December 6. He was buried there but, on May 31, 1893, his remains were reinterred in Richmond. Davis had steadfastly refused to ask for a federal pardon, even in order to be elected senator from Mississippi, averring that he had committed no legal offense. The year after Davis's death, his widow wrote her two-volume *Memoir* (1890); living in New York, she kept his reputation alive, with the help of Joseph Pulitzer and the Confederate "expatriates" in the North. She died in New York on October 16, 1906, at the age of eighty, and was given a military funeral in Richmond.

SIGNIFICANCE

Jefferson Davis was poorly suited for the task of political leadership of the Confederacy at its birth. He had a strong will and iron self-discipline, willing to drive himself relentlessly despite failing health and personal troubles, but he could neither deal effectively with political personalities nor catch the public imagination and gain popular support. In a revolutionary situation he was a conservative and a legalist. Satisfied as to the right of secession and the constitutional basis of state sovereignty, he regarded Northern opposition as motivated only by jealousy, greed, and aggression; yet committed to the ideal of the Southern nation, he could not tolerate independent action by state governments or opposition to policies (such as drafting slaves) that the Confederate government believed were necessary to the war effort.

Davis shared with many other southerners the delusion that cotton was king and that economic pressures would lead quickly to European aid and victory; he therefore agreed to policies that resulted in the Confederacy's economic isolation. Free to act out his lifelong perception of himself as master strategist and commanding general, Davis kept tight control over all military aspects, never freeing even Lee from it completely, and refusing sound advice at crucial moments. Up to the end of the war, Davis never believed that defeat was possible; he thought that one more major campaign would turn the tide.

Davis's policy was passive-defensive; he always expected European aid even though he was informed of the actual situation. Politically naive, he apportioned cabinet appointments evenly among the states, thereby making bad choices and alienating the powerful radical secessionists. He dominated his cabinet, so that its able members could not act effectively, yet did not urge his cautious treasury secretary, C. G. Memminger, to be as financially audacious as necessary for real accomplishment. He himself frequently functioned as secretary of war, a position he would have preferred to the presidency or to any other except that of commanding general. He understood neither the proper role of the executive nor the exigencies of strategy, and in attempting to be both president and general, he failed to fulfill either function well.

A nationalist facing sovereign states, a logical theoretician dealing with volatile personalities and political realities, an egotist who could see only the goal but who could not believe that his political opponents also strove for ideals, a leader in revolutionary times who could not rally popular support for great sacrifices: Davis was more of a debit than a credit entry in the Confederacy's account. However, his dedication was total and his efforts unrelenting, and in the aftermath of defeat, Davis enjoyed more popular admiration than at any other time in his life. He had been a great senator and a great secretary of war. He had never sought public office, but accepted it as a duty.

Davis attracted intense loyalty and admiration as well as provoking bitter enmity, and with all his failings, it is difficult to imagine any other man in the Confederacy doing better in those circumstances. Surviving personal tragedies and the loss of an independent South, Davis died unshaken in his beliefs and conscious of his own rectitude and unswerving loyalties, in his own mind fully justified and fulfilled. On October 17, 1978, a unanimous joint resolution of Congress restored Davis's citizenship.

—Marsha Kass Marks

FURTHER READING

Cooper, William J., Jr. *Jefferson Davis: American*. New York: Alfred A. Knopf, 2000. A balanced, comprehensive biography. Despite Davis's support of the secessionist Confederacy, Cooper argues that Davis continued to see himself as a patriotic and faithful American.

Davis, Jefferson. *Jefferson Davis: Private Letters, 1823-1889*. Edited by Hudson Strode. New York: Harcourt, Brace & World, 1966. Very effectively edited, providing practically a condensed biography. As with the three-volume biography, strongly biased, placing even more emphasis than Strode's work on personalities.

Davis, Varina. *Jefferson Davis, Ex-President of the Confederate States of America: A Memoir by His Wife*. 2 vols. New York: Belford, 1890. A laudatory account, more than sixteen hundred pages; includes long quotations from Davis's speeches and correspondence as well as biographical information dictated by Davis shortly before his death and valuable information from participants in events. Apart from Davis's obvious bias, the book is detailed and usually reliable.

Davis, William C. *An Honorable Defeat: The Last Days of the Confederate Government*. New York: Harcourt Brace Jovanovich, 2001. Recounts the fall of the Confederacy during the four months before the surrender of the South and the assassination of Lincoln. Focuses on the activities and personalities of Davis and Confederate Secretary of War John C. Breckinridge.

_____. *Jefferson Davis: The Man and His Hour*. New York: HarperCollins, 1991. Biography focusing on the public career of Davis. The author describes how Davis developed his lifelong values at West Point and during the Mexican War. President Davis is depicted as a poor administrator, who lacked managerial skill and was unable to admit mistakes or delegate authority.

Dodd, William Edward. *Jefferson Davis*. Philadelphia: G. W. Jacobs, 1907. Reprint. New York: Russell & Russell, 1966. Written by a professor at Randolph-Macon College, the book reflects nineteenth century biases of time and place: contented slaves, good masters, Anglo-Saxon civilization. Dodd attempts to balance his own commitment to the United States with strong attachment to the rightness of Davis and the South on the constitutional issues and the "War Between the States."

Hathaway, Herman, and Richard E. Beringer. *Jefferson Davis: Confederate President*. Lawrence: University Press of Kansas, 2002. An analysis of Davis's presidency and the administration of the Confederate government, written by two Civil War historians. The authors analyze the Confederate government's institutions, constitution, and administrators, and discuss Davis's selection of generals and military strategy.

Strode, Hudson. *Jefferson Davis: American Patriot, 1808-1861*. New York: Harcourt, Brace & World, 1955.

_____. *Jefferson Davis: Confederate President*. New York: Harcourt, Brace & World, 1959.

_____. *Jefferson Davis: Tragic Hero—The Last Twenty-five Years, 1864-1889*. New York: Harcourt, Brace & World, 1964. This detailed, three-volume biography by a professor of creative writing is the result of painstaking research, based on both secondary sources and primary documents including a thousand previously unavailable personal letters. Neither scholarly nor analytical; detailed narrative and quotations replace the historian's generalizations. Pro-Davis with a pro-Southern, secessionist bias; often reads more as special pleading than as careful interpretation.

Tate, Allen. *Jefferson Davis*. New York: G. P. Putnam's Sons, 1969. A very brief account by one of the Nashville "Agrarians." Emotional and often contradictory defense of Davis as representative of the stable agrarian Southern society facing the aggression of the new industrial North; simultaneously blames Davis for the Confederate defeat.

Warren, Robert Penn. *Jefferson Davis Gets His Citizenship Back*. Lexington: University Press of Kentucky, 1980. Very brief, almost a memoir of the author's boyhood during the early twentieth century South, by a master writer. Effective evocation of the war and the man.

SEE ALSO: Black Hawk; Robert E. Lee; Abraham Lincoln; Franklin Pierce; Alexander H. Stephens; Zachary Taylor.

RELATED ARTICLES in *Great Events from History: The Nineteenth Century, 1801-1900:* March 2, 1853-1857: Pacific Railroad Surveys; December 31, 1853: Gadsden Purchase Completes the U.S.-Mexican Border; February 8, 1861: Establishment of the Confederate States of America; April 9 and 14, 1865: Surrender at Appomattox and Assassination of Lincoln.

SIR HUMPHRY DAVY

English chemist

As a philosopher of science, brilliant chemist, and president of the Royal Society, Davy advanced the cause of science as few men had before him. He identified the chemical elements barium, chlorine, magnesium, potassium, sodium, and strontium; pioneered anesthesiology with his experiments with nitrous oxide; invented the Davy lamp that protected miners from explosions; made significant contributions to the application of science for the betterment of society in fields such as agricultural chemistry and tanning; and wrote widely read books on philosophy, fly-fishing, and travel.

BORN: December 17, 1778; Penzance, Cornwall, England
DIED: May 29, 1829; Geneva, Switzerland
AREAS OF ACHIEVEMENT: Chemistry, philosophy

EARLY LIFE

Humphry Davy, born on December 17, 1778, in the remote town of Penzance in Cornwall, England, was the eldest of five children. Grace Millet Davy, his mother, was an orphaned child of a middle-class family. Robert Davy, his father, was a woodcarver who was of yeoman stock. He was an industrious, though not very successful, businessperson, who tried farming and who speculated in tin mining.

For the eighteenth century an unusual amount of detail is available on the future scientist's childhood. He was an active, healthy, and precocious child, who walked at nine months and spoke fluently at two years of age. This sweet, affectionate child was the family favorite. Even before he could read, which was at the age of five, he was reciting from *The Pilgrim's Progress*. At six, he went to school, which was a disappointment. Years later, he wrote that "learning is naturally a true pleasure," but that even the best school he went to made it painful. Davy considered it fortunate that his teachers generally left him alone and declared that "what I am I made myself." Though he left a grant to the school in his will, it was on the condition that the children be given a day off every year.

Robert Davy died in 1794, saddling his widow with a large debt as a result of his mining adventures. She supported her family by opening a millinery store until she received a small inheritance in 1799.

The twin crises of Humphry's childhood were the move of his family to a farm when he was six and the death of his father when he was fifteen. For the sake of his education, young Humphry lived in Penzance with the old surgeon and apothecary (pharmacist) who had reared his orphaned mother, and only saw his family on weekends. The lonely boy suffered from nightmares and sleepwalking and was terrified by ghost stories and tales of the French Revolution. He learned to amuse and frighten other boys by telling stories of faraway places based mainly on *The Arabian Nights' Entertainments*. He also loved to hunt and to fish and became passionately devoted to nature.

The death of his father changed Davy's life. He was determined to help his mother, by making something of himself. He set himself an extraordinarily ambitious program of self-study and actually accomplished much of his plan. Though soon apprenticed to a surgeon and apothecary, he was determined to prove his genius. Shortly after reading his first chemistry book, he wrote an article on heat and light that so impressed Dr. Thomas Beddoes of Clifton that nineteen-year-old Davy was invited to become superintendent to the Pneumatic Institution, where Beddoes was experimenting with the use of gases in medical treatment. Typically, the remainder of his five-year indentureship was waived as he took a crucial step toward scientific fame.

In his several years in Clifton, Davy carried out some extremely dangerous and important experiments with nitrous oxide (laughing gas). His friends William Coleridge, Peter Mark Roget, and Robert Southey were among the guinea pigs for his experiments. The most dangerous ones he saved for himself. The laughing gas experiments almost killed him and may have caused long-term damage to his health. He recommended that the gas be applied as an anesthesia for certain surgical procedures. Unfortunately, it would be half a century before nitrous oxide would be used to save lives in that way.

Davy's attention turned to the area of electrochemistry, which was made possible by the invention of the voltaic pile. He used electrical power to conduct experiments, isolate elements, and invent the carbon arc. In 1801, Davy was appointed lecturer at the Royal Institution and was made professor of chemistry the following year. This "boy wonder" had achieved the amazing feat of gaining a professorship five years after reading his first chemistry book. His previous plan of studying medicine at the University of Edinburgh and the idea of becoming a physician seem to have gradually fallen by the wayside.

Portraits and descriptions of Davy reveal that he was of medium height with a slight build, hazel eyes, and an aquiline nose. He had a lifelong boyish quality that caused him to appear younger than his years. He was lively and enthusiastic in manner and sometimes careless in his dress. The intensity of his eyes and the power of his intellect were remarked upon by his contemporaries.

Davy brought an amazing amount of energy to his scientific endeavors and typically made most of his discoveries in a short period of time as he sought proof for his intuitive flashes of insight. He was not the stereotypical prodding type of scientist who generalized only after examining all the facts. He was a passionate and poetic man. As he aged, however, his tendency toward irritability, mood swings, and vanity increased. Coleridge's fear, expressed when Davy was age twenty-five, that he would succumb to the vice of "ambition into vanity" was justified by both the snobbery and the narcissistic self-involvement that became apparent after his knighthood and marriage in 1812.

LIFE'S WORK

Davy's life was devoted to the understanding and popularization of nature. At the Royal Institution, he threw himself into laboratory research, lecturing, and editing. He gave courses on subjects such as applied chemistry, galvinism, "pneumatic chemistry," and tanning. Unlike many scientists, he considered his public lectures to be of great importance and carefully rehearsed them.

Davy attained celebrity status, because as many as a thousand people flocked to hear his extraordinary mixture of chemistry, latest research findings, poetry, and philosophy. They listened raptly to subjects as mundane as the chemical composition of organic fertilizers. His yearly Bakerian Lecturers to the Royal Society, from 1807 to 1812, brought him international fame. The Napoleon Prize was awarded to him by the Institute of France. In 1813, while England was still at war with France, he traveled to Paris to receive this award.

Davy, who was always eager to tackle the problems of applied science, almost had his career cut short in 1807 when he contracted a severe case of malaria while trying to save the inmates of Newgate Prison, who were being devastasted by this dreaded disease. His popularity was reflected in the public issuance of hourly bulletins as to his health. His close scrape with death and slow recovery did not cure him of risk-taking for the sake of science. Years later, he was almost blinded by an explosive that he knew to be extraordinarily dangerous. He also took some risks by going down into the coal mines to find a safe way of lighting those dangerous shafts.

The result was the Davy lamp, on which Davy refused to take a patent, that made possible a great increase in coal production. Though pride of invention was also claimed for George Stephenson and Dr. William Clanny, much to Davy's chagrin, the coal mine owners recognized the priority of his invention by giving him an extremely expensive gift. The outcomes of some other projects, specifically, unrolling the ancient Herculaneum papyri in Italy, protecting the copper sheathing on the Admiralty's ships, and ventilating the House of Lords, were not as successful. One of his greatest discoveries was of the chemist Michael Faraday.

Davy was knighted in 1812, and immediately thereafter he married a rich, intellectual widow named Jane (Kerr) Apneece. The marriage that began with high hopes soon became unhappy. The couple fought publicly and were informally separated as much as they were together. There were no children.

Davy was elected to the presidency of the Royal Society in 1820. He began his tenure with great expectations of major scientific achievements. He hoped to achieve the conversion of the British Museum into a research institution and hoped, too, to obtain far more financial support from the government for his projects. He was unsuccessful in these endeavors, as well as in inspiring most of his fellow scientists to greater efforts. Before long, Davy would be caricatured as one of the "humbugs of the age." In fact, he was uncomfortable in his administrative role and thought to escape it by foreign travel. Though his health deteriorated severely in 1825, Davy continued to travel, experiment, and write—his emphasis being on philosophical books such as *Salmonia: Or, Days of Fly Fishing* (1828) and *Consolations in Travel: Or, The Last Days of a Philosopher* (1830). He died on May 29, 1829, in Geneva.

SIGNIFICANCE

Sir Humphry Davy was a scientist of considerable achievement whose reputation was greater in his own lifetime than subsequently. His nitrous oxide experiments, invention of the safety lamp, isolation of a half dozen chemical elements, and improvements in tanning earned for him his reputation. In addition, he wrote the textbook on agricultural chemistry that would be used for more than a generation. His poetry, which does not read well to the twentieth century ear, was of sufficient quality to warrant the praise of Coleridge and Southey.

Davy's greatest achievement was as an advocate and popularizer of the scientific investigation of nature. The British, first in competition with and then in victory over the French, were eager to know the composition of the world that they dominated. Davy is an example par excellence of the self-made men who built the institutions of British greatness.

—*Paul H. Elovitz*

FURTHER READING

Davy, Sir Humphry. *The Collected Works of Sir Humphry Davy*. Edited by John Davy. 9 vols. London: Smith, Elder, 1839-1840. Volume 1 of this nine-volume set is a biography of Davy's famous brother. This very useful collection is far from definitive, because many sources were ignored and others were selected from rather than printed in their entirety.

Elovitz, Paul H. "The Childhood Origins of Sir Humphry Davy's Preoccupation with Science, Magic, and Death." In *Psychology and History*, edited by Jerrold Atlas. New York: Long Island University Press, 1986. The author draws on his dual training in history and psychoanalysis to offer an explanation for Davy's total devotion to the service of "Mother Nature." He provides psychological explanations for Davy's failure as president of the Royal Society, his physical collapse in 1825, and his disquieting belief in extraterrestrial communication and magic.

_____. "Psychohistorical Dreamwork: A New Methodology Applied to a Dream of Sir Humphry Davy." In *The Variety of Dream Experience*, edited by Montague Ullman and Claire Limmer. New York: Continuum, 1987. Davy was an unusually active dreamer who relied on dreams for insight and inspiration. He wrote an entire book on the basis of one of his dreams. Elovitz created a new method for biographers to use dreams to better understand their subjects.

Forgin, Sophie, ed. *Science and the Sons of Genius: Studies on Humphry Davy*. London: Science Reviews, 1980. These seven papers are the results of the Davy Bicentenary Symposium held in honor of the famous chemist at the Royal Institution. The authors examined his scientific procedures, policies, personality, and literary productions.

Fullmer, June Z. "Davy's Priority in the Iodine Dispute: Further Documentary Evidence." *Ambix*, March, 1975, 39-51. The author was trained as a chemist before devoting herself to the history of science and becoming the most outstanding authority on Davy. This is one of more than a dozen articles she published on many different aspects of his career and life. In this case she examines his goals during the period he was traveling in France in 1813. Though Napoleon had given this Englishman a guarantee of safe passage and prize, he was still under intellectual assault in the land of the enemy. An informative and interesting article.

_____. *Young Humphry Davy: The Making of an Experimental Chemist*. Philadelphia: American Philosophical Society, 2000. Fullmer was planning to write a multi-volume biography of Davy, but she died in 2000, just before she completed the manuscript for this book. The book recounts Davy's life from birth through age twenty-three, when he was a new member of the Royal Institution and was looking for a job.

Knight, David M. *Humphry Davy: Science and Power.* Oxford, England: Blackwell, 1992. Reprint. New York: Cambridge University Press, 1996. Standard biography, featuring information about Davy's scientific discoveries, poetry, and friendships with Coleridge, Wordsworth, and Byron.

Treneer, Anne. *The Mecurial Chemist: A Life of Sir Humphry Davy.* London: Methuen, 1963. This excellent life of Davy stresses his Cornish origins, affiliation with the Romantic poets, and nonscientific activities. It is well written and recommended for the nonscientific reader.

SEE ALSO: Michael Faraday; Joseph-Louis Gay-Lussac; William Thomas Green Morton.

RELATED ARTICLES in *Great Events from History: The Nineteenth Century, 1801-1900:* c. 1801-1810: Davy Develops the Arc Lamp; October, 1831: Faraday Converts Magnetic Force into Electricity.

FERENC DEÁK

Hungarian politician

Deák's abiding goal throughout his political career was to bring true self-government for Hungary and to enact liberal laws. His persuasive and undaunting efforts brought about Hungary's most important compromise, the Ausgleich. *He also led the liberals in the passage of much needed social reforms and was one of Hungary's greatest codifiers of progressive laws that brought Hungary out of feudalism.*

BORN: October 17, 1803; Söjtör, Austrian Empire (now in Hungary)

DIED: January 28, 1876; Pest, Austro-Hungarian Empire (now Budapest, Hungary)

ALSO KNOWN AS: Ferenc Deák, Jr. (full name)

AREA OF ACHIEVEMENT: Government and politics

EARLY LIFE

Ferenc Deák, Jr., was the son of a third-generation nobleman, Ferenc Deák, Sr. (deh-ahk), who followed the family tradition of increasing wealth and power through marriage. During the 1780's, the senior Deák married Erzsébet Sibrik of Szarvaskend, the daughter of the deputy sheriff of Győr County. In 1803, she gave birth to the youngest of their six children, Ferenc Deák, Jr. Several days later, she died of complications from childbirth. Consequently, her husband rejected his infant son and sent him to an uncle, József Deák. The family soon moved to Kehida, where Ferenc Deák, Sr., died on January 25, 1808. At that time, young Ferenc's elder brother, Antal, became his legal guardian.

Ferenc was tutored by a Franciscan until 1808. At that time, he started his formal education by attending elementary school at church schools in Köszeg, Keszthely, and Pápa. In 1817, Ferenc was graduated from the gymnasium in Nagykanizsa and then began his studies at the Royal Law Academy in Győr, where he excelled in German, Latin, and constitutional law and history.

Ferenc's future career and his thought processes were influenced by two major factors. First, he witnessed legislative resistance to royal decrees by local assemblies. Ferenc was maturing in an intense atmosphere of revolution and opposition to the Habsburg regime. In 1821, he attended, against royal mandate, the Assembly of Győr and witnessed its refusal to execute what it considered to be an unconstitutional royal decree. Then, he saw similar defiance in Zala County, when that assembly resisted the absolutism of the Metternich system. Zala County led the opposition against Austrian absolutism and Antal Deák led Zala County. The second major factor influencing Ferenc was the leadership of his brother. Antal advocated that loyalty to the dynasty should not prevent resistance to despotism and that local assemblies had a responsibility to resist any unconstitutional ordinances. He was well known throughout Hungary, and Ferenc was inspired by him.

In December, 1821, Ferenc was graduated from the Academy, and Zala County declared him legally of age. His first act was to emancipate his former wet nurse, symbolic of his future work in abolishing feudalism and in obtaining rights for all Hungarians. In November, 1822, Ferenc arrived in Pest and passed the bar examination with distinction on December 19, 1823. While in Pest, Hungary's cultural center, he came into contact with numerous cultural organizations. The most important of these was the *Auróra* circle, through which he developed lasting friendships with several liberal statesmen, politicians, and poets, many of whom greatly contributed to his intellectual development.

Ferenc began his public service at the county level by holding several unpaid positions. His first was given to him as a gesture of recognition for Antal's hard work. On December 13, 1824, Ferenc was elected notary to the County Commission for Orphans. He also held the position of county magistrate and was elected deputy high sheriff surrogate; however, he never took the latter post. When the national legislative body, the Diet, convened in Pozsony in 1832, Antal represented Zala County as deputy. In January, 1833, he resigned and recommended Ferenc to replace him. On April 15, 1833, Ferenc was subsequently elected to a seat in the lower house. With this position, his county service ended. His career as a national political figure began at this time and would influence Hungarian and Austrian history for the next forty-three years.

LIFE'S WORK

The 1830's and 1840's were critical years for Hungary. Plague, peasant revolts, and economic depression were widespread, and Hungary had a feudal constitution. Deák's experience at the county level enabled him to understand legal procedure and alerted him to Hungary's social, economic, and political problems. Thus, he joined the reform-minded liberals, led by Baron Miklós Wesselényi.

Ferenc Deák. (Library of Congress)

In 1836, Deák introduced his first legislative measure, calling for the emancipation of the serfs. When Ferdinand I vetoed the measure, Deák called an unofficial session of the Diet. As a result of this episode, Deák was acknowledged as the leader of the liberals in the lower house.

On May 2, 1836, Deák returned to Zala County to report on the proceedings of the Diet. He also proposed a program of reforms, which was printed and published by the assembly and sent to other counties without royal approval. The Crown reprimanded the assembly and ordered all copies to be collected. The assembly rejected the reprimand, and Deák became the symbol of Hungarian progressive ideas. In appreciation for his legislative leadership, he was elected an honorary member of the Academy of Sciences on November 21, 1839.

Deák successfully concluded his first compromise during the Diet of 1839-1840. Many liberal leaders had been arrested in 1836, and Deák had offered his services as mediator; however, the Crown was unwilling to compromise. He then warned that if the Crown did not respect Hungarian laws and rights, Hungary would employ passive resistance and defiance. Thus, on June 6, 1839, when Ferdinand summoned the Diet, Deák recommended that they not discuss any royal proposals until all grievances were resolved. He met privately with an agent of the Crown in March, 1840, and achieved a compromise to the satisfaction of the liberals.

Deák entered the 1840's with hopes for a legal revolution that would transform Hungary from a feudal to a modern state through peaceful legislation. At the 1841 Diet, he proposed drastic changes in the judiciary, but his legislative attempts all met with failure. Deák became apathetic and inactive; his aloofness began to compromise his influence. At this time, Lajos Kossuth assumed the leadership of the liberals. In 1846, Deák reluctantly helped write the Liberal Party platform, which called for universal reforms. This work promoted the unification of Hungary's first opposition party.

By August, 1847, Deák temporarily left Hungary, allegedly under doctor's orders. He was short and stocky, with great physical strength, but he was prone to sickness. In reality, however, he did not believe the liberals could achieve their goals at this time because of the stubbornness of the Crown. He realized the only course for Hungary was violence and revolution—actions that were against his values.

When the last feudal Diet (1847-1848) was summoned, Kossuth sent a list of grievances (written by Deák) to Ferdinand I. By 1848, much of the empire was in revolt. Faced with chaos, Ferdinand consented to the list of demands and granted Hungary independence. The first elected parliament met in July, 1848, and passed a series of reforms known as the April Laws, ending feudalism and introducing a liberal form of government. Deák led the new lower house and achieved the greatest social reforms of his legislative career. He was named Minister of Justice and succeeded in having his earlier judicial reform measures (of 1841) passed as the Press Act in 1848.

On September 11, 1848, Austria invaded Hungary. Deák abandoned his office, the ministry was in chaos, and counterrevolution began. On December 2, 1848, Ferdinand abdicated in favor of his nephew Francis Joseph I. Hungary considered the new ruler a usurper because he did not swear the required oath of loyalty to the Hungarian constitution. On April 14, 1849, the parliament deposed the Habsburg dynasty. Consequently, Francis Joseph ordered a massive assault on Hungary.

By August, 1849, the Hungarian revolution ended. Hungary was partitioned and placed under a repressive regime for many years. Most of the revolutionary leaders were either executed or exiled. Deák appeared before a military tribunal on December 14, 1849, and was interrogated for five months. Finally, he was released, as he had not supported the deposition of the royal dynasty.

From 1850 to 1859, Deák offered passive resistance to the Crown. In 1854, he sold the family estate and permanently moved to the Hotel Angol Királyné in Pest. At this time, he became the director of the Hungarian Academy of Sciences. His passive resistance ended in December, 1860, when he was granted an audience with Francis Joseph. The two men immediately developed a mutual trust and respect for each other. Deák was honest, always spoke frankly, and was open-minded. He accepted Francis Joseph's offer to participate in the Lord Chief Justice's Conference (January 23 to March 3, 1861) aimed at reconciling Hungary's civil and criminal court procedures with Austria's system. On February 27, however, the Crown announced its intention to reduce Hungary to a province. Deák left the conference angrily, believing that revolution was Hungary's only hope of remaining autonomous.

Deák again became inflexible in his attitude toward the empire. In 1861, the Crown summoned the first Diet in twelve years. This time, Deák represented Pest. Dissension among the liberals gave rise to two new political parties: the Party of Petition led by Deák and the Party of Resolution led by Count László Teleki. After Teleki committed suicide, Deák assumed the position of the leading statesman in Hungary.

With hostilities again developing, the Crown adopted more oppressive measures. Deák recommended a policy of passive defense to parliament, which was adjourned by the Crown on August 22, 1861. On November 5, 1861, Hungary became a province of the empire. From this position, Deák enjoyed his greatest level of prestige. He began to lay the foundations for a compromise. He anonymously wrote an article in *Pesti Naplo* entitled "Easter Article," followed by a series of similar articles. Through this vehicle he offered a solution to the volatile situation between Hungary and the dynasty. Deák knew that the time was right for compromise; Austria was nearly bankrupt and the empire's collapse was imminent.

Negotiations began and a new parliament was summoned in September, 1865. Deák's party won a majority of the seats. Deák began to shape Hungary's history and proved himself to be a practitioner of realpolitik. He did not create movements or ideas; he merely took advantage of situations, planned the right strategies, and knew how to manipulate the political forces that existed. For the first time in his long career, Deák exercised his very forceful and persuasive leadership ability. On December 20, 1865, the Deák Party Club was established to organize campaign strategies. Deák developed goals to be achieved and principles to be followed. He demanded discipline but never used force or humiliation to obtain his objectives.

On June 17, 1867, Austria went to war with Prussia. Deák now pushed for compromise. He met for a second time with Francis Joseph, and they agreed upon the *Ausgleich*, the Compromise of 1867. It provided for the following: the creation of the state of Austria-Hungary with a dual monarchy in the person of the emperor; the restoration of the Hungarian constitution of 1848; the separation of parliamentary bodies—the Hungarian parliament would meet in Budapest and the Austrian parliament in Vienna; the joint administration of military and foreign affairs by delegates from the two parliaments and three joint ministers (foreign affairs, war, and finance); and the renewal of terms of the *Ausgleich* every ten years. There was some opposition to the *Ausgleich*, especially from Kossuth. However, most Austrians and Hungarians rejoiced in the settlement, as it resolved a thirty-year-old conflict and provided stability for the empire (which lasted until World War I).

Deák also proposed a series of acts that created a new Hungary. The two most important were the Croatian-Hungarian Compromise and the Equality of the Nationalities Act. He finally saw fulfilled a lifetime of efforts to obtain and protect the rights of all people. Furthermore, Deák wanted Hungary to become a true democracy. After the *Ausgleich*, however, his party began to splinter, and his health deteriorated.

By 1871, Deák's era was coming to an end. His influence also began to wane, and he experienced legislative defeats. His last political act created the Parliamentary Liberal Party in 1873, with Kálmán Tisza as head, but liberalism was also beginning to decline. Deák's last speech was delivered to parliament on June 28, 1873. It was very reflective of his first presentation made forty years earlier in that his main emphasis was placed on the need for progressive legislation and liberalism.

In 1875, Deák was elected for the last time to parliament, but he was never seated. On January 28, 1876, he died in his hotel suite in Pest. The parliament, in his memory, commissioned a statue of him to be placed in front of the Academy of Sciences building in Budapest.

SIGNIFICANCE

Ironically, while Ferenc Deák was the author of the greatest compromise in Hungarian history, he was uncompromising on moral, constitutional, and social issues. He believed firmly in the Christian ideals of the brotherhood of all men and the stern morality of the ancient Hebrews. He emulated the Romans in their respect for the law and admired the Hellenistic culture for its love of beauty. These ideals were the basis for his moral standards and behavior. His commitment to certain values became apparent when, on his second day as a freshman member of the Diet, he broke with tradition and asked for the floor. It was here that he demonstrated for the first time his excellent oratorical skills and took the first step in his long journey toward making laws more humane and liberal.

Deák gained almost immediate recognition as a reformer. He spent the greater part of his life working toward creating a more liberal government in Hungary. He strove to remove the last remnants of feudalism and to achieve equality for all citizens through peaceful legislation. He strongly believed that law was the backbone of society. He therefore advocated changing unjust laws—not violating them. He worked earnestly at strengthening and modernizing the judiciary.

Deák was a man before his time. This was proved in his first legal case, which illustrated his basic philosophy. The case involved József Babics, a man charged with highway robbery, murder, and several lesser offenses. Deák admitted his client's guilt but not his fault. The defense rested on the premise that society was responsible for Babics's actions because it had not provided him with an education and values. Deák lost the case, but he argued against capital punishment and for societal responsibility.

Deák's life's ambition was to achieve a true self-government for Hungary and to obtain the passage of liberal laws. He did not consider the *Ausgleich* the climax of his career. Instead, he viewed it as a necessary interruption to his real task, the completion of the work that the liberals had begun in Hungary during the Reform Era of the 1830's and 1840's. He attempted to create a truly democratic government and society; he sincerely cared about the deprived masses and sought reform in their name.

—*Victoria Reynolds*

FURTHER READING

Freifeld, Alice. *Nationalism and the Crowd in Liberal Hungary, 1848-1914*. Washington, D.C.: Woodrow Wilson Center Press, 2000. Information about Deák is included in this history of Hungarian nationalism after the failed revolutions of 1848 until the start of World War I. The "crowd" cited in the title refers to the Hungarian people who created their own nation inside the Austro-Hungarian Empire.

Jászi, Oscar. *The Dissolution of the Habsburg Monarchy*. Chicago: University of Chicago Press, 1929. Describes Deák's political career from the 1830's through 1867 and his role in the Compromise of 1867. Contains an excellent bibliographical section for research on the Habsburgs, Austria, and eastern Europe, although many of the materials are in German.

Kann, Robert A. *The Multinational Empire: Nationalism and National Reform in the Habsburg Monarchy, 1848-1918*. 2 vols. New York: Columbia University Press, 1950. Addresses Deák's leadership ability and his drive for fair treatment of minorities. Volume 1 has somewhat more emphasis on Deák's role in the government than volume 2. Each volume contains an introduction and notes section, and volume 2 has a selected bibliography and index.

Király, Béla K. *Ferenc Deák*. Boston: Twayne, 1975. An excellent although somewhat biased biography containing a chronology of the Deák family from 1665, when the family was ennobled, to Ferenc's death in 1876. Stresses Ferenc's devotion to his political career and contains a thorough discussion of his private life. Includes notes, references, bibliographical sections, and an index.

May, Arthur J. *The Hapsburg Monarchy, 1867-1914.* Cambridge, Mass.: Harvard University Press, 1951. Focuses on Deák's work on the Compromise of 1867, his role as the leader of the moderates, and his other political contributions. Emphasizes Deák's great negotiating skills, needed to placate the various minority groups in Hungary. Contains quotes taken from Deák's correspondences and speeches.

Murad, Anatol. *Franz Joseph I of Austria and His Empire.* Boston: Twayne, 1968. A standard biography of Franz Joseph. Contains information about the circumstances under which the Compromise of 1867 was agreed upon, Deák's role in obtaining Franz Joseph's approval, and he relationship between Deák and such important revolutionaries as Count Gyula Andrássy.

Ormos, Maria, and Béla K. Király. *Hungary: Governments and Politics, 1848-2000.* Highland Lakes, N.J.: Social Science Monographs, 2001. A detailed account of the evolution of Hungarian politics and government activities from the revolutions of 1848 to the end of the twentieth century. Provides context and background for understanding the political situation in which Deák worked.

SEE ALSO: Friedrich von Beust; Francis Joseph I.

RELATED ARTICLE in *Great Events from History: The Nineteenth Century, 1801-1900:* May 29, 1867: Austrian Ausgleich.

ALFRED DEAKIN

Prime minister of Australia (1903-1904, 1905-1908, 1909-1910)

After serving a ten-year apprenticeship in Victoria's legislative assembly, Deakin spent the last decade of the nineteenth century working toward the federation of the Australian colonies. One of the primary founders of the Commonwealth of Australia, he served three times as prime minister, dominating the government during its first, formative decade.

BORN: August 3, 1856; Melbourne, Victoria, Australia
DIED: October 7, 1919; Melbourne, Victoria, Australia
AREA OF ACHIEVEMENT: Government and politics

EARLY LIFE

Alfred Deakin (dee-kihn) was born when Australia was still a collection of autonomous British colonies. His Welsh-born mother, née Sarah Bill, and his father, William Deakin, an English salesclerk, arrived in South Australia from England in December, 1849. After following the gold rush to Victoria (1851), they eventually settled in the Melbourne suburb of Collingwood, where their second child, Alfred, was born.

Educated primarily at Melbourne's Church of England Grammar School, as a young adult Alfred Deakin attended lectures in law at the University of Melbourne at night. His father's income as accountant with a big coaching company being modest, Deakin supported himself, partly by teaching, while qualifying for the bar and pursuing a deep and continuing interest in mysticism, religion, and psychic phenomena (in 1878 serving as president of the Victorian Association of Spiritualists) and a love of literature and writing. These interests introduced him to his true vocation and to his future wife.

Through David Syme, the powerful proprietor of the Melbourne *Age*, to whose newspaper he became a regular contributor, Deakin entered a political career, almost by chance. When the incumbent of the seat of West Bourke died during a constitutional crisis, Syme pushed Deakin forward, and in July, 1880, he took his place in Victoria's legislative assembly with the governing Liberal Party, an alliance of farming, manufacturing, and labor interests. His talents as a conciliator soon became evident: He helped to secure the Council Reform Act of 1881 and by 1883 was minister in a coalition government of Liberals and Conservatives.

Deakin was a tall, handsome man, fully bearded with dark hair and eyes and a rich voice that he used effectively as an outstanding orator and debater. On April 3, 1882, he married Pattie (christened Elizabeth Martha Anne) Browne, the daughter of a wealthy distiller and spiritualist; she had once been Deakin's pupil at the Progressive Lyceum, a spiritualist Sunday school conducted on American lines. The first of their three children, all girls, was born the following year.

At thirty, Deakin became leader of the Liberal Party and so, with Conservative Duncan Gillies, joint leader of the government. He headed the Victorian delegation to the Colonial Conference of 1887 in London, making his mark in an outspoken attack on the Colonial Office. His speech foreshadowed the federation of the Australian colonies, an objective to which he was to devote much of his time after the fall of the coalition government in October, 1890.

LIFE'S WORK

Alfred Deakin's experience as a conciliator and a leader in the Victorian parliament served him well from the time he supported the proposal put by Sir Henry Parkes, the great federationist from New South Wales, that a national Australian convention be held in Sydney in 1891, until the inauguration of the Commonwealth of Australia ten years later, and beyond.

After the drafting at the 1891 convention of a constitution modeled chiefly on the British North America Act and the U.S. Constitution, nothing much happened for a time. Deakin resumed the practice of law and attended parliamentary sessions, resisting suggestions that he again take a leadership role. During 1897 and 1898, however, the Federal Convention met at Adelaide, Sydney, and Melbourne under the leadership of Edmund Barton of New South Wales (Parkes having died).

The only member of the Victorian delegation who had also taken part in the 1891 convention, Deakin again took on the role of arbitrator while a new constitution bill was being framed. The next step was to present it to the people in referenda to be held in all the colonies. Determined to gain its adoption in Victoria, where strong forces appeared to be rallying in opposition, Deakin campaigned vigorously. His historic speech at Bendigo on March 15, 1898, at the annual conference of the influential Australian Natives Association, is regarded as one of his greatest, winning over Syme and impressing reluctant members of government. Victoria voted overwhelmingly (100,520 to 21,099) for the bill.

In 1900, Deakin went to London as part of an Australian delegation headed by Barton. Agreement on the constitution finally having been reached in Victoria, Tasmania, New South Wales, South Australia, and Queensland (Western Australia had not yet held a referendum), the Australian colonies had been requested to be represented while the act constituting the Commonwealth of Australia was being passed by the British parliament.

Barton became the first prime minister of Australia the following year, with Deakin's full support. The cabinet, established on lines proposed by Deakin, included his friend and ally as attorney general. Early legislation included a uniform tariff and the exclusion of non-European immigrants (the "white Australia" policy). On the passing of the Judiciary Act of 1903, setting up the High Court of Australia, Barton retired and was appointed one of the three justices. At forty-seven, "Affable" Alfred, the member for Ballarat (Victoria), became prime minister and minister for external affairs on September 24, 1903.

Alfred Deakin. (Library of Congress)

At this time, three parties were represented in the parliament: Deakin and the Liberal-Protectionists; Labor, led by John C. Watson; and the Free Traders, whose leader was Sir George Reid, former premier of New South Wales and a reluctant federationist. Barton had received Labor's support, and Deakin also felt more comfortable working with Watson than with Reid.

In April, 1904, a dispute over an arbitration bill started a game of musical chairs. Deakin went out of office and Watson came in, with William M. Hughes as his minister for external affairs. Within a matter of months it was Reid's turn. Deakin started his second term, which was considered a productive ministry, on July 15, 1905, although after the 1906 elections his party was the smallest of the three. Usually, therefore, only measures supported by all—such as the introduction of old-age pensions—were likely to be accepted.

Foreign affairs and defense were areas of great concern to Deakin from the time of the 1887 Colonial Conference—at which he raised the issue of French involvement in the New Hebrides. The Naval Agreement made then did not please him, nor did the revised agreement of 1902, under which Australia paid a subsidy to the imperial government toward the cost of maintaining the Australian Station of the Royal Navy. He foresaw Australian seamen becoming members of a squadron under local control, manning Australian-owned ships and with their wages being paid by Australia. His defense bill foreshadowed this, as well as universal military service and a military college, but in November, 1908, his government fell before the bill could become law.

Labor's second term (under Andrew Fisher) was almost as brief as its first. On June 2, 1909, Deakin was sworn in for his third term, this time as head of what was called the Fusion Ministry, an alliance of groups opposed to Labor. Deakin's personal reputation suffered from this decision to work with some of his hitherto political opponents, however, and in April, 1910, Labor won a decisive victory in both houses. His domination of Parliament had ended.

Deakin had no personal fortune. His income came mainly from what he earned as lawyer, journalist, and parliamentarian. From the 1890's onward, the family spent the summer holidays at Point Lonsdale, a small settlement near Melbourne on Port Phillip Bay, where Deakin would read, write, and swim. Abstemious and family-minded, Deakin was accompanied by his wife and baby daughter to California in 1884, and in 1900 his wife Pattie, his beloved sister Kate, and his three daughters (Ivy, Stella, and Vera) went with him to London. Pattie also (rather reluctantly) traveled with him to London for the Colonial Conference of 1907.

Like many brilliant, hardworking men, Deakin found relaxing difficult; he also suffered from insomnia. His health began to deteriorate after he entered the Commonwealth parliament, and from 1907 on, memory lapses caused him increasing distress. Deakin was a very private person, and his innermost thoughts were revealed only to his diary and notebooks, in which he also recorded hundreds of prayers. He retired from Parliament in January, 1913, broken in health, which was never restored despite visits to medical specialists in London and New York. He died on October 7, 1919.

SIGNIFICANCE

Of his time in the Victorian parliament, Alfred Deakin liked to recall that he introduced pioneering social legislation (the Factories and Shop Act of 1885) regulating factory working conditions. A greater and more personal achievement, however, when he was the minister of water supply, was the Irrigation Act (1886). This came out of a commission on droughts that he chaired and that resulted in water rights being transferred to the Crown to avoid ownership disputes similar to those prevalent in the United States. *Irrigation in Western America* (1885) reports the findings of a visit to the United States during which he met the Canadian-born Chaffey brothers, irrigation experts whom he later enticed to Victoria to establish a settlement at Mildura modeled on theirs at Ontario, California.

A consummate politician, Deakin's support was sought by men of all political factions, yet when he acted independently he took full responsibility and was even, at times, ruthless. As the minister in charge, in 1890 he called out the police and troops during a time of strikes and industrial unrest in Victoria. He did not hesitate when Labor was no longer prepared to give him unconditional support to make an arrangement with the Free Traders and then to drop them if they did not fulfill their commitments. Many of his policies were endorsed or adopted because they were appropriate for the times. One of his last official acts as prime minister was to place an order for three vessels for the Australian Navy, thus contributing greatly to Australia's readiness in 1914 when World War I began.

Alfred Deakin was also a sensitive man, more interested in intellectual and philosophical pursuits than many of his countrymen. He saw Australia, Canada, New Zealand, and South Africa remaining in the British Empire as equal partners with Great Britain, their interests being one and the same. More than once he referred to himself as an "Independent Australian Briton." Although an imperialist, Deakin declined offers of honors and knighthoods and lived simply, preferring to walk or ride a bicycle from his house in South Yarra to Parliament House, which until 1927 was in Melbourne. His fine intellect and political achievements won respect at home and abroad. Theodore Roosevelt, who ordered the "Great White Fleet" (sixteen American battleships showing the flag around the world) to call at Australian ports in 1908 at Deakin's personal request, wrote in 1912, "He is one of the statesmen for whom I have long cherished a very sincere and real admiration." A university in Victoria bears his name.

—Annette Potts

FURTHER READING

Deakin, Alfred. *The Federal Story: The Inner History of the Federal Cause*. Melbourne, Vic.: Melbourne University Press, 1963. First published with some omissions in 1944, this is a valuable primary document on events leading to federation. Includes an introduction by J. A. La Nauze.

_____. *Federated Australia: Selections from Letters to the "Morning Post," 1900-1910*. Edited by J. A. La Nauze. Melbourne, Vic.: Melbourne University Press, 1968. From 1900 until 1914, Deakin, identified only as "Australian Correspondent," wrote regularly on Australian affairs for the London *Morning Post*. His letters provide an excellent firsthand account of events during the Commonwealth's first decade.

Gabay, Al. *The Mystic Life of Alfred Deakin*. New York: Cambridge University Press, 1992. Deakin was convinced his political life had a divine mandate and he turned to mysticism and the occult to help him understand his duty. Gabay describes Deakin's intense spiritual life and how it related to his public career.

La Nauze, J. A. *Alfred Deakin: A Biography*. 2 vols. Melbourne, Vic.: Melbourne University Press, 1965. A scholarly study, with references and bibliography, written by a protégé of biographer Sir Walter Murdoch (see below).

Murdoch, Walter. *Alfred Deakin: A Sketch*. London: Constable, 1923. Written with complete family cooperation, this is an affectionate but still relevant biography by a university professor who knew him.

Rickard, John. *A Family Romance: The Deakins at Home*. Carlton, Vic.: Melbourne University Press, 1996. Examines Deakin's family life, focusing on his relationship with his wife, Pattie, and his sister, Catherine. Rickard describes the important influence of mysticism in Deakin's life, explaining how spiritualism brought Deakin and his wife together and haunted their marriage.

Souter, Gavin. *Lion and Kangaroo: Australia, 1901-1919, The Rise of a Nation*. Sydney, N.S.W.: William Collins, 1976. A well-written and entertaining account of the early years of the Commonwealth of Australia and the milieu that Deakin adorned.

SEE ALSO: Sir Edmund Barton; Sir Henry Parkes.

RELATED ARTICLE in *Great Events from History: The Nineteenth Century, 1801-1900:* 1868: Last Convicts Land in Western Australia.

STEPHEN DECATUR

American naval commander

The most colorful and successful open-sea naval commander of his time, Decatur was a national hero of the Barbary Wars and the War of 1812. However, despite his military accomplishments, his career had made little impact on naval policy and strategy.

BORN: January 5, 1779; Sinepuxent, Maryland
DIED: March 22, 1820; Bladensburg, Maryland
AREA OF ACHIEVEMENT: Military

EARLY LIFE

Stephen Decatur's father, Stephen, was a seafaring man who earned his living as a merchant ship captain and, during the American Revolution, as a privateer. Decatur was a sickly child during his early years. At the age of eight, suffering from a prolonged and severe cough, he accompanied his father on a voyage to the French port of Bordeaux. His malady, probably whooping cough, disappeared.

Because his father was at sea much of the time, Decatur was raised in Philadelphia, Pennsylvania, by his mother, Ann, who sent him to the Episcopal Academy and later to the University of Pennsylvania in the hope that he would become either a clergyman or a scholar. However, despite his health problems and his mother's wishes, Decatur craved the active over the contemplative life. As a young man, he was 5 feet 10 inches in height, possessed a muscular build, and had a handsome countenance with an aquiline nose.

Decatur first worked as a clerk in 1796 for Gurney and Smith, a Philadelphia shipping company, but after the United States Navy was established on April 30, 1798, and a naval war had commenced with France, Decatur, through his father's influence, secured a midshipman place on the newly constructed ship, the *United States*. Built in Philadelphia, this forty-four gun frigate was familiar to Decatur. Its captain, John Barry, was both a friend and professional colleague of Decatur's father.

The reasons for Decatur's determination to join the Navy are unclear. Perhaps it was the lure of adventure presented by the new United States Navy and the war with France, or perhaps he wanted to follow his father's nautical footsteps. A more murky reason was the apparent result of Decatur's attack upon a prostitute who had solicited him. He struck her with a blow that was powerful enough to kill her. To avoid a prison sentence for their client, Decatur's lawyers assured the court that Decatur would join the Navy.

LIFE'S WORK

Decatur's first real taste of glory occurred in 1804 during the Barbary Wars, when, as captain of the schooner *Enterprise* in Commodore Edward Preble's Mediterranean squadron, he captured a Barbary slave ship, the *Mastico*. Renamed the *Intrepid*, it was 60 feet in length with a 12-foot beam. A scheme was devised to burn the former U.S. frigate *Philadelphia*, which had run aground and been captured by the Tripolitans. Decatur chose a crew of seventy-four volunteers who would sail the *Intrepid* into Tripoli Harbor under the guise of a Barbary ship seeking repairs from a recent storm. The Americans were to board, burn, and escape, leaving the *Philadelphia* in ashes. It was a daring plan well suited to Decatur's adventuresome temperament.

Although delayed for one week because of severe weather, the attack, when executed at dusk on February 16, 1804, was a huge success. Decatur's crew sailed within a few yards of the *Philadelphia* before they were found out. They quickly overcame the defenders, many of whom feared for their lives and jumped overboard. During the next thirty minutes, twenty Tripolitans were killed, combustibles were laid and ignited, the attackers returned to the *Intrepid*, and the *Philadelphia* was engulfed in flames. During all of this, only one of Decatur's sailors was wounded. Burning the *Philadelphia* assured Decatur's role as a hero. He was promoted to captain at the age of twenty-five, the youngest American naval officer to attain that rank. Lord Horatio Nelson called the attack "the most bold and daring act of the age." President Thomas Jefferson presented Decatur with a sword and words of praise.

Later that same year, Decatur's brother, James, was killed by the commander of a Tripolitan gunboat, who shot James when he was boarding the already surrendered vessel. Along with ten others, Decatur tracked down the commander and killed him after some brutal hand-to-hand fighting. During the melee, Decatur's life was saved by a sailor who intentionally absorbed a blow that would have killed Decatur.

At the conclusion of the Tripolitan phase of the Barbary Wars, Decatur returned home, where he broke with his former fiancé and met and married Susan Wheeler, the daughter of the mayor of Norfolk, Virginia. She was a popular and beautiful young woman who had already rejected advances made by Vice President Aaron Burr and Jerome Bonaparte.

Decatur served in various naval positions during the six years from 1806 to 1812. In 1807 he served on the court martial panel that suspended Captain James Barron, Decatur's erstwhile friend and former tutor, from the Navy for five years because of his behavior as captain of the *Chesapeake*. Barron was found guilty for failing to adequately prepare his ship for action against the British ship the *Leopard* and thereby humiliating the United States Navy by demonstrating its inability to prevent the seizure of four British Royal Navy deserters, three of whom were Americans impressed earlier by the British. Another more personal reason for the deterioration and ultimately fatal culmination of Decatur's and Barron's relationship was the latter's implied criticism of Decatur's attraction to Susan Wheeler when Decatur already had a fiancé in Philadelphia. Decatur thought that it was none of Barron's concern.

When Great Britain and the United States went to war in 1812, the still young United States Navy consisted of just sixteen warships. Decatur was captain of one of them, the familiar *United States*. Sailing alone between the Azores and Madeira, he sighted the *Macedonian*, a British frigate. The U.S. ship was larger and now carried fifty-four 24-pound guns, compared to the *Macedonian*'s forty-nine 18 pounders. Ironically, this very encounter had been discussed prior to the war by Decatur and Captain John Carden, commander of the *Macedonian*. Despite the heavier gun advantage of the *United States*, Carden had argued that his ship would prevail because its crew was more experienced and because the *Macedonian* was a more maneuverable vessel.

As it turned out, even though Carden had the wind advantage, he failed to recognize the *United States* and instead assumed it was a smaller frigate with guns of lesser range and shot than his own. Carden's tactics played into Decatur's hands by allowing Decatur to press his advantage of more guns and greater destructive shot. Carden surrendered the *Macedonian* after losing one-third of his three-hundred-man crew in a two-hour fight, while seven were killed and five wounded aboard the *United States*. Decatur's reputation as a hero reached its summit. The government also awarded him thirty thousand dollars in prize money. Decatur's achievements during the remainder of the war were a good deal less dramatic, although his status as a genuine American hero remained high.

By tightening their blockade along the Atlantic coast, the British were able to prevent most ships from entering and sailing from U.S. ports. On January 14-15, 1815, unaware that the war had ended three weeks earlier, Decatur attempted to liberate his ship, the *President*, by escaping from New York Harbor. Heavy winds caused the ship to run aground for two hours and compelled Decatur to make a fifty-mile run along the Long Island coast. Four British warships chased him, and, although the frigate *Endymion* had to retire because of battle damage, the remaining British ships forced his surrender. British losses were less than half of the twenty-four Americans killed and the fifty-five who were wounded. Despite the defeat, Decatur maintained his status as a hero. A naval court of inquiry not only exonerated him but also determined that the surrender of the *President* was an American victory.

Two months after the Treaty of Ghent, which ended the War of 1812, the United States was at war again, this time with Algiers. Decatur, now a commodore (at that time the highest rank in the United States Navy), assembled a squadron of ten ships, including three frigates, one of which was the *Macedonian*. After capturing the Algerine flagship and killing the grand admiral of the Algerine fleet, Decatur's entire squadron sailed into Algiers Harbor. A treaty favorable to the United States was the result. Additional concessions were later made by Tunis as well. Decatur was the principal negotiator in both cases.

After returning home, Decatur was appointed to the three-member Board of Naval Commissioners. The Decaturs (they had no children) moved to Washington, D.C., where Decatur continued to contribute to naval affairs.

Decatur died as he had lived: defending his honor. The cashiered Barron returned to the United States from Denmark in 1818 and unsuccessfully applied for reinstatement in the U.S. Navy. Barron blamed the Board of Naval Commissioners and Decatur in particular. He initiated a correspondence with Decatur that ended when Barron challenged Decatur to a duel. They met at Bladensburg, Maryland, on March 22, 1820. Although Decatur, an excellent pistol marksman, aimed to wound his opponent, Barron aimed to kill—and succeeded. Shot in the groin, Decatur died twelve hours later. Congress adjourned to attend Decatur's funeral, naval officers wore crepe for thirty days, guns on ships at Washington and Norfolk fired at thirty-minute intervals, and numerous eulogies were presented by people of all ranks and classes. President James Monroe and his cabinet marched in the funeral procession.

Barron was finally reinstated in 1824. He was given command of the Philadelphia Navy Yard and later the Norfolk Navy Yard. He died in 1851 at the age of eighty-three.

SIGNIFICANCE

Decatur's contributions to the United States were revered a great deal more during his lifetime than by subsequent generations of Americans. Although no naval history of the post-Revolutionary War period would be complete without devoting considerable attention to Decatur, his heroic accomplishments, impressive as they were, made a limited impact on naval policy and strategy. Early nineteenth century Americans needed a hero to help represent and justify their nation's brief history and its full membership among contemporary nations. Decatur was the right person at the right place at the right time. Perhaps his dedication to his country was best expressed by a toast he made at a dinner held in his honor in 1816: "Our Country! In her intercourse with foreign nations, may she always be in the right, but our country right or wrong."

—*John Quinn Imholte*

FURTHER READING

Anthony, Irvin. *Decatur*. New York: Charles Scribner's Sons, 1931. Anthony's book is subjective but remains one of the few book-length biographies of Decatur. Includes much personal detail.

Blassingame, Wyatt. *Stephen Decatur: Fighting Sailor*. Champaign, Ill.: Garrard, 1964. This volume is suitable for early elementary students.

De Kay, James Tertius. *A Rage for Glory: The Life of Commodore Stephen Decatur, U.S.N.* New York: Free Press, 2004. A comprehensive, popular biography. De Kay, a naval historian, recounts the origins of Decatur's fierce patriotism and provides new details about his death.

Guttridge, Leonard F., and Jay D. Smith. *The Commodores*. New York: Harper & Row, 1969. This volume includes pithy accounts of Decatur and Barron, along with other high-ranking naval officers. Especially valuable for the Bladensburg duel.

Lewis, Charles Lee. *The Romantic Decatur*. Philadelphia: University of Pennsylvania Press, 1937. This is the standard book-length biography of Decatur. For the most part, Lewis remains objective throughout the book.

Schroeder, John H. "Stephen Decatur: Heroic Ideal of the Young Navy." In *Command Under Sail: Makers of the American Naval Tradition*, edited by James C. Bradford. Annapolis, Md.: Naval Institute Press, 1985. Most of this overview of Decatur's naval career is supported by primary sources.

Tucher, Glenn. *Dawn Like Thunder: The Barbary Wars and the Birth of the U.S. Navy*. Indianapolis: Bobbs-Merrill, 1963. Tucher details Decatur's participation in the Barbary Wars.

Tucker, Spencer. *Stephen Decatur: A Life Most Bold and Daring*. Annapolis, Md.: Naval Institute Press, 2005. A biography, in which Tucker relates Decatur's military achievements to the rise of the United States Navy in the nineteenth century. In his description of Decatur's raid at Tripoli Harbor, Tucker explains how Decatur's heroism set a new standard of courage for future naval officers.

SEE ALSO: David G. Farragut; Oliver Hazard Perry.

RELATED ARTICLE in *Great Events from History: The Nineteenth Century, 1801-1900:* Summer, 1801-Summer, 1805: Tripolitan War.

RICHARD DEDEKIND

German mathematician

Dedekind gave a new definition to the mathematical concept of irrational numbers, based exclusively on arithmetic principles. He helped clarify the notions of infinity and continuity and contributed to the establishment of rigorous theoretical foundations for mathematics.

BORN: October 6, 1831; Brunswick, Duchy of Brunswick (now in Germany)

DIED: February 12, 1916; Brunswick, Duchy of Brunswick

ALSO KNOWN AS: Julius Wilhelm Richard Dedekind (full name)

AREA OF ACHIEVEMENT: Mathematics

EARLY LIFE

Julius Wilhelm Richard Dedekind (DAY-dih-kihnd) was one of four children born to a well-established professional family in the Germanic duchy of Brunswick. His father was a professor of jurisprudence at the local Collegium Carolinum, and his mother was a professor's daughter. In school, Dedekind was primarily interested in physics and chemistry, but when he enrolled in the Collegium Carolinum, it was as a student of mathematics. From a résumé, written somewhat later and in Latin, it is clear that this change was based on his dissatisfaction with the lack of rigor in the natural sciences.

In 1850, Dedekind was matriculated at the University of Göttingen, where he followed various courses in mathematics (studying under Carl Friedrich Gauss), astronomy, and experimental physics. In 1852, Dedekind presented his doctoral dissertation, which, in the opinion of Gauss, showed promise. At that time, the standard of mathematics at Göttingen was not very high, and Dedekind spent the following two years studying privately and preparing himself to become a first-class mathematician. No doubt his friendship with the brilliant Georg Friedrich Bernhard Riemann, at Göttingen at the same time, was also a positive influence. In fact, Dedekind attended Riemann's lectures even after he himself qualified as a university lecturer in 1854. When Gauss died in 1855, Peter Gustav Lejeune Dirichlet, previously professor in Berlin, succeeded him. Dedekind described Dirichlet's arrival in Göttingen as a life-changing event. Dedekind not only attended Dirichlet's lectures but also became a personal friend of the new professor.

LIFE'S WORK

In 1858, the Federal Institute of Technology in Zurich, Switzerland, appointed Dedekind as professor of mathematics on Dirichlet's recommendation. Riemann also applied for the post but his work was considered too abstract. Dedekind stayed in Zurich until 1862 and then accepted an invitation from his old college in Brunswick, which had become a polytechnic by then.

While in Zurich, Dedekind taught differential and integral calculus and was disturbed by having to use concepts that had never been properly defined. In particular, he wrote: "Differential calculus deals with continuous magnitude, and yet an explanation of this continuity is nowhere given." He also deplored accepting without proof the belief that an increasing infinite sequence with an upper bound converges to a limit. He was dissatisfied that the notions of limit and continuity were based solely on geometrical intuition. On November 24, 1858, Dedekind succeeded in securing "a real definition of the essence of continuity." He waited until 1872 to publish this definition in book form, with the title *Stetigkeit und Irrationale Zahlen* ("Continuity and Irrational Numbers," translated in *Essays on the Theory of Numbers*, 1901).

Dedekind's problem was essentially that of irrational numbers, known already to the ancient Greeks. Rational numbers are dense in the sense that between any two rational numbers there is always another rational number, although there are infinitely many gaps between them. These gaps can be thought of as irrational numbers, and, before Dedekind began his work, they were characterized by infinite, nonrecurring decimal fractions. Dedekind devised a method, using "cuts," to define irrational numbers in terms of the rationals. If rational numbers are divided into two sets such that every number in the first set is smaller than every number in the second set, this partition defines one and only one real number. Should there be a largest or smallest number in one of the sets, the Dedekind cut corresponds to that rational number, while an irrational number is defined if neither set has a smallest or largest member.

A Dedekind cut can be imagined as severing a straight line composed of only rational numbers into two parts. Rational and irrational numbers together form the set of real numbers, and this set can now be made to correspond to all the points of a straight line. With this method, Dedekind not only managed to define irrational numbers in terms of rationals without recourse to geometry but also showed that a line, and by implication three-dimensional space, is complete, containing no holes. Furthermore, Dedekind upheld his philosophical principles, according to which numbers do not exist in a Platonic sense but are free creations of the human mind.

Closely connected to this work was the introduction of the concept of "ideals." Dedekind edited and published Dirichlet's lectures on number theory after the death of the latter. Dedekind can, in fact, be considered the author of the book, because Dirichlet left only an outline plan for publication, and that was already based on Dedekind's notes. In the tenth supplement to the second edition of this influential book, Dedekind developed the theory of ideals, following to a certain extent a line Ernst Eduard Kummer had already taken. Dedekind, however, went far beyond Kummer, avoided his mistakes, and made the theory more exact.

Ideals are an extension and generalization of the common number concept. According to the fundamental theory of arithmetic, ordinary integers either are prime numbers or can be uniquely factorized into primes. Unique factorization is a useful feature but does not generally apply to all algebraic integers in a given algebraic number field, algebraic numbers being defined as the roots of polynominal equations with integer coefficients. With the introduction of ideals, unique factorization can be restored. Dedekind subsequently revised and further developed this theory. In an important paper coauthored by Heinrich Weber, the analogy between algebraic numbers and algebraic functions was demonstrated with the help of ideals.

In *Was sind und was sollen die Zahlen?* (1888; "The Nature and Meaning of Numbers," translated in *Essays on the Theory of Numbers*, 1901), Dedekind utilized the concept of what he called systems, which later became known as sets, and developed logical theories of original and cardinal numbers and of mathematical induction. In addition to contributing papers to mathematical journals, Dedekind coedited Riemann's collected works and supplied a biography of Riemann.

Dedekind stayed at Brunswick until his death and became a director of the polytechnic between 1872 and 1875. It seems that Dedekind was not offered the posts he would have accepted, while he refused the posts, most notably the one at Halle, that he was offered. Dedekind never married but lived with one of his sisters until her death in 1914. Although he lived in relative isolation, he was never a recluse. He was an excellent musician: He played the cello as a young man and the piano in later life. His portraits show a fine-featured man with thoughtful eyes; his character was described as modest, mild, and somewhat shy.

SIGNIFICANCE

Although Richard Dedekind was a corresponding member of several academies and an honorary doctor of several universities, he never received the recognition he so fully deserved. It can be seen that his work was one of the most influential in shaping twentieth century mathematics. He is one of only thirty-one mathematicians meriting an individual entry in *Iwanami Sugaku Ziten* (1954; *Encyclopedic Dictionary of Mathematics*, 1977), in which he is described as a pioneer of abstract algebra. Transcending pure calculation, Dedekind made an attempt to find theoretical foundations to concepts used in algebraic number theory and in infinitesimal calculus. He defined and thereby created new mathematical structures that generalize the notions of number and serve as examples for further generalization.

Dedekind met Georg Cantor on a holiday in Switzerland and became his friend and also, at times, his frequent correspondent. Cantor submitted his theories to Dedekind for comment and criticism, and Dedekind was one of the first to support set theory in the face of hostility by other mathematicians. Independently of Cantor, he also utilized the concept of the actual, or concrete, infinite—a concept that was then regarded as taboo because there existed no theoretical foundation for its existence. Dedekind's work assisted in finding just such a foundation.

—*Judit Brody*

FURTHER READING

Bashmakova, I. G., and G. S. Smirnova. *The Beginnings and Evolution of Algebra*. Translated from the Russian by Abe Schneitzer. Washington, D.C.: Mathematical Association of America, 2000. Chapter 8 in this history of algebra includes information about Dedekind and the birth of numbers theory.

Bell, Eric T. "Arithmetic the Second." In *Men of Mathematics*. New York: Simon & Schuster, 1937. Reprint. New York: Penguin Books, 1965. This short chapter in a well-known collective biography of mathematicians discusses the life and work of Kummer and Dedekind. Bell makes a good attempt to explain the abstract and often difficult concepts that are necessary for the understanding and appreciation of Dedekind's work.

Corry, Leo. *Modern Algebra and the Rise of Mathematical Structures*. 2d rev. ed. Boston: Birkhäuser, 2004. Traces the development of algebra from the mid-nineteenth century to the present, focusing on ideas concerning algebraic structures. This revised edition includes a revised chapter on Dedekind.

Dauben, J. W. *Georg Cantor: His Mathematics and Philosophy of the Infinite*. Cambridge, Mass.: Harvard University Press, 1979. Not a biography of Cantor, but a study of the emergence of a new mathematical theory. Dedekind's life, work, and influence on Cantor are featured extensively, but these references are dispersed throughout the book. Readers whose main interest is in Dedekind can rely on the well-constructed index and the twenty-four-page bibliography.

Dedekind, Richard. *Theory of Algebraic Integers*. Translated by John Stillwell. New York: Cambridge University Press, 1996. Dedekind's theory, first published in French in 1877, was the genesis of modern algebraic numbers theory. Stillwell provides a detailed introduction offering historical background and outlining the challenges Dedekind faced in devising his theory.

Edwards, Harold M. "Dedekind's Invention of Ideals." *The Bulletin of the London Mathematical Society* 15 (1983): 8-17. Traces the influences on Dedekind's set theoretic approach mainly to Dirichlet but also to Kummer and Riemann. Évariste Galois's influence was limited and resulted in steering Dedekind toward conceptual thinking as opposed to mere calculating. Dedekind went beyond Dirichlet, and against the accepted classical doctrine, by using completed infinites. The author stresses the innovative nature of Dedekind's theories and the analogy between cuts and ideals.

_____. "The Genesis of Ideal Theory." *Archive for History of Exact Sciences* 23 (1980): 321-378. Analyzes Kummer's, Leopold Kronecker's, and Dedekind's versions of the theory of ideal factorization of algebraic integers. The author advances the thesis that as Dedekind revised the theory several times to match his philosophical principles, it did not improve from the mathematical point of view, and the first formulation remained the best.

Gillies, D. A. *Frege, Dedekind, and Peano on the Foundations of Arithmetic*. Assen, the Netherlands: Van Gorcum, 1982. A short paperback with an adequate index and a list of references. Investigates the relationship between logic and arithmetic in the work of the three men. Gillies regards Dedekind as fundamentally a logician and compares him to Gottlob Frege, who denied that a set was a logical notion, and to Giuseppe Peano, who thought that arithmetic could not be reduced to logic.

SEE ALSO: Henri Poincaré; Jakob Steiner.

RELATED ARTICLES in *Great Events from History: The Nineteenth Century, 1801-1900:* 1899: Hilbert Publishes *The Foundations of Geometry*; 1900: Lebesgue Develops New Integration Theory.

EDGAR DEGAS
French painter

Degas was one of the great figural painters and draftsmen of the nineteenth century. His work combined a deep understanding of tradition with a commitment to innovative portrayals of modern life. His artistic independence was asserted in his role as one of the leading figures of the Impressionistic exhibitions of 1874-1886.

BORN: July 19, 1834; Paris, France
DIED: September 27, 1917; Paris, France
ALSO KNOWN AS: Hilaire-Germain-Edgar Degas (full name)
AREA OF ACHIEVEMENT: Art

EARLY LIFE

Edgar Degas (day-gah) was born into a comfortable, upper-bourgeois Parisian family. His father managed the local branch of the family bank, headquartered in Naples, and his mother was the daughter of a cotton broker in New Orleans. The family's social connections in France, Italy, and the United States would play an important role in shaping Edgar's life and character. Frequent visits to the Louvre, as well as to the homes of friends who had substantial private collections, were regarded as an essential part of the boy's upbringing. Edgar attended the prestigious Lycée Louis-le-Grand in Paris, where he received his first instruction in drawing. Upon graduation in 1853, he briefly studied law but soon turned his attention wholeheartedly to a career in art.

Degas's early artistic training consisted of two stages: the period 1853-1856, spent mostly in Paris, and the period 1856-1859, dominated by two lengthy sojourns in Italy. In Paris, Degas studied under Louis Lamothe, a follower of the disciplined classicism of Jean-Auguste-Dominique Ingres. Working independently, Degas devoted much time to copying paintings in the Louvre and prints in the Bibliothèque Nationale. In 1855, he enrolled in the École des Beaux Arts. Instead of completing his formal studies and competing for the coveted Prix de Rome, however, he decided to go to Italy on his own. In Naples and Florence, where he visited relatives, and in Rome, where he stayed at the French Academy, Degas's devotion to the art of the past was expanded and deepened. At the same time, his contact with other young French artists studying in Italy, such as Gustave Moreau, helped turn his attention to the more recent achievements of artists such as Eugène Delacroix.

Apart from many copies and sketches, the most important works produced by Degas during these early years were portraits of family members. The crowning achievement of these early portraits was *The Bellelli Family*, a large painting of his Florentine relatives begun in Italy in 1858 and completed several years later in Paris. In its technical mastery and psychological sensitivity, this painting announced the beginning of a major career.

LIFE'S WORK

The emergence of Degas's artistic personality during the 1860's was characteristically complex. Soon after his return from Italy, he established a studio in Paris and began to work on a series of large history paintings. Although inspired in part by the classical tradition, Degas's historical scenes tended to recast tradition through a disarming straightforwardness of treatment. The last of this group of pictures, *Scene of War in the Middle Ages*, was shown at the Salon of 1865 as Degas's first major publicly exhibited work. Ironically, that marked the beginning of Degas's public career and the end of his interest in history painting. The following year, he exhibited *The Steeplechase*, and in 1868 he showed *Mlle Fiocre in the Ballet "La Source."* The themes of the racetrack and the ballet proclaimed the artist's new commitment to the subject matter of contemporary life. This commitment would be a decisive factor in determining the subsequent course of his career.

Degas's interest in contemporary subjects was inspired and shared by a growing circle of progressive artists and writers with whom he began associating during these years. By around 1862, he had met Édouard Manet, leader of a new generation of artists devoted to painting modern life, and Edmund Duranty, a naturalist writer and critic who would become a champion of Degas's art during the 1870's. Through the frequent gatherings of artists at the Café Guerbois, Degas became familiar with Claude Monet, Pierre-Auguste Renoir, and other young artists who would eventually form the core of the Impressionist group. His keen, perceptive intellect and brusque humor soon established Degas's prominence within the group. Although his role would develop into one of dedicated leadership, he would always maintain a degree of the aloofness of an outsider. An intriguing glimpse of this complex personality is provided in the *Self-Portrait* of about 1863, in which confidence, irony, and self-consciousness seem to coexist behind a facade of bourgeois elegance.

The 1870's were both a climax and a turning point in Degas's career. His paintings of familiar urban entertainments such as the ballet achieved full maturity, and his circle of colleagues finally banded together and organized a series of independent exhibitions. At the same time, however, he experienced some unexpected setbacks. The Franco-Prussian War of 1870-1871 found him serving in the artillery, and at this time he began to have problems with his eyesight. His financial security was seriously compromised as a result of the failure of the family bank following his father's death in 1874. Degas's commitment to the risky venture of the independent exhibitions from the first show in 1874 until the last one in 1886 is all the more impressive in the face of these circumstances.

Degas's accomplishments as an artist during the 1870's were an extraordinary combination of fully realized maturity and restless experimentation. The ballet scenes were a dominant theme, beginning with such works as *The Orchestra of the Opera* (c. 1870) and *The Dance Class* (1871), which established the performance hall and the rehearsal studio as the two realms of Degas's exploration of the dance. His portraits achieved new complexity and psychological depth, as exemplified by the group of paintings of his New Orleans relatives, done when the artist visited them in 1872-1873, and by various portrayals of friends and colleagues such as the portrait of Duranty of 1879. Several new themes were introduced or given greater prominence during the years of the Impressionist exhibitions, including the café and the café-concert, milliners, laundresses, and prostitutes. Along with these diverse themes, an increasing attention to varied techniques such as pastel, lithography, monotype, and sculpture contributed to the rich complexity of Degas's mature art.

The most decisive changes in Degas's later work were introduced in the years around 1880. The interest in sculpture was bold, experimental, and largely private. The subjects of the sculptures, especially dancers and bathers, paralleled the themes of his paintings at a time when pastel was increasingly replacing oil as his principal pictorial medium. The rich textures and glowing colors of the pastel bathers of the 1880's and 1890's represent the grand culmination of Degas's career. Seven such pictures were shown at the last Impressionist exhibit in 1886, including the famous *Woman Bathing in a Shallow Tub*. By presenting the nude in unconventionally natural poses seen from unexpected angles in realistic surroundings, these works revitalized tradition through an emphasis on the immediacy of experience and the ingenuity of artistic innovation.

Degas's late work was hampered by failing eyesight, although flashes of brilliance continued to appear until he finally had to stop painting entirely around 1908. He was able to turn his attention to collecting because of the rising prices he was receiving for his works, but for the most part the last years leading up to his death in 1917 were characterized by a frustrating inactivity and isolation.

SIGNIFICANCE

Edgar Degas's artistic contribution can be summarized in terms of his complex relation to Impressionism. As a leading figure behind the Impressionist exhibitions, Degas made a historic commitment to artistic independence that would help set the stage for the development of modern art. His dedication to subjects drawn from modern life and to bold technical and stylistic innovation are aspects of his art that played an integral role within the group. On the other hand, he was persistently somewhat of an outsider whose attitudes and alliances increasingly factionalized the group. He particularly opposed the label Impressionist (he preferred "Independents") and its associations with a spontaneous, directly naturalistic art.

Although Degas's art was committed to contemporary subjects and steeped in observation and experience, Degas was never entirely a naturalist. In contrast to Monet, who rejected tradition and painted directly before his subjects in nature, Degas executed his works in the studio and relied heavily on calculation, imagination, and memory of earlier works of art. His artistic repertoire expanded from an early love of Ingres and the classics to include such nontraditional sources as Japanese prints and photography, but throughout his career Degas's art remained informed by other art as much as by nature.

Even Degas's favorite themes, such as the theater and the ballet, reveal an antinaturalistic orientation in which the artificiality of costume, pose, and stage set are celebrated. By studying the richness of life in a variety of such artificial contexts, Degas was creating an art dedicated to the modern city. By advancing the importance of direct experience and innovation in art without discarding the lessons of tradition, he was both contributing to the emergence of modernism and transcending it.

—Dennis Costanzo

FURTHER READING

Adriani, Götz. *Degas: Pastels, Oil Sketches, Drawings.* Translated by Alexander Lieven. New York: Abbeville, 1985. The English translation of the catalog was produced in conjunction with the 1984 exhibition in Tübingen and Berlin. Includes a scholarly introductory essay, a well-documented catalog, and excellent illustrations.

Benfey, Christopher. *Degas in New Orleans: Encounters in the Creole World of Kate Chopin and George Washington Cable*. New York: Random House, 1997. Degas visited New Orleans in the autumn of 1872 to visit his relatives; he had both white and black relatives living there. Benfey describes the social turmoil in New Orleans during the Reconstruction era, and how this atmosphere and the city inspired Degas's art.

Boggs, Jean Sutherland. *Degas at the Races*. Washington, D.C.: National Gallery of Arts, 1998. Study of Degas's consuming interest in horses, jockeys, and racing and its place in his work. More than 120 paintings, drawings, sculptures, and pastels. Catalogs the 1998 exhibit of Degas's work at the National Gallery of Art in Washington, D.C.

Degas, Hilaire Germain Edgar. *Degas: The Complete Etchings, Lithographs, and Monotypes*. Text by Jean Adhémar and François Cachin. Translated by Jane Brenton. New York: Viking Press, 1974. A thoroughly illustrated and documented catalog of Degas's prints, with brief, informative introductory essays.

_____. *Letters*. Edited by Marcel Guérin. Translated by Marguerite Kay. Oxford, England: B. Cassirer, 1947. The English translation of the standard edition of the artist's letters. Provides important personal insights into his art, thought, and character.

_____. *The Notebooks of Edgar Degas*. Edited by Theodore Reff. 2 vols. Oxford, England: Clarendon Press, 1976. A carefully documented and annotated catalog of Degas's thirty-seven notebooks in the Bibliothèque Nationale in Paris. An indispensable publication on the artist's sources, development, and creative processes.

De Vonyar, Jill, and Richard Kendall. *Degas and the Dance*. New York: Harry N. Abrams, 2002. Degas painted and drew ballet dancers and other aspects of the ballet more frequently than any other subject. This catalog, which accompanied an exhibition of Degas's ballet-related artwork, reproduces some of these works and describes the artist's relationship to the ballet.

Growe, Bernd. *Degas*. New York: Taschen, 2001. A brief (96-page) analysis of Degas's art, part of the Basic Art Series. Although Degas is considered to be an Impressionist, Growe maintains he never fully adopted that style, but was far more influenced by classical painting techniques.

Halévy, Daniel. *My Friend Degas*. Translated by Mina Curtiss. Middletown, Conn.: Wesleyan University Press, 1964. A personal account of Degas during his later years, based on the journal Halévy began keeping in 1888 and continuing through the artist's death.

McMullen, Roy. *Degas: His Life, Times, and Work*. Boston: Houghton Mifflin, 1984. A comprehensive biography that is both scholarly and readable. Although considerable attention is given to major works, the emphasis throughout is on the artist's life and character. The best general biography in English.

Reff, Theodore, ed. *Degas: The Artist's Mind*. New York: Harper & Row, 1976. A collection of essays on various aspects of Degas's art. Most of the essays are revised versions of articles originally published in scholarly journals. A selection of important motifs, sources, and techniques are considered with a goal of better understanding Degas's artistic thought.

SEE ALSO: Mary Cassatt; Paul Gauguin; Henri de Toulouse-Lautrec.

RELATED ARTICLES in *Great Events from History: The Nineteenth Century, 1801-1900:* April 15, 1874: First Impressionist Exhibition; 1892-1895: Toulouse-Lautrec Paints *At the Moulin Rouge*.

EUGÈNE DELACROIX

French painter

A powerful colorist, Delacroix became the most important figure in the development of the Romantic painting movement in France in the nineteenth century. He was a prolific artist and sought to stir viewers deeply by appealing to their senses even though he chose to explore the dark side of their human emotions.

BORN: April 26, 1798; Charenton-Saint-Maurice, France
DIED: August 13, 1863; Paris, France
ALSO KNOWN AS: Ferdinand-Eugène-Victor Delacroix (full name)
AREA OF ACHIEVEMENT: Art

EARLY LIFE

Eugène Delacroix (dah-lah-krwah) was the son of a schoolteacher, Charles Delacroix, who rose to become minister of foreign affairs in 1795 under the revolutionary regime and French ambassador to the Netherlands some eighteen months later. Delacroix's mother, Victoire Oeben, descended from a distinguished family of royal cabinetmakers. Controversy surrounds Eugène's paternity. Some scholars maintain that his biological father was Talleyrand, one of Europe's most brilliant statesmen, to whom the artist is said to have borne a striking resemblance.

While in Marseilles as a result of an administrative appointment for his father, Charles, the young Eugène exhibited a precocious talent for piano and violin. His legal father died in late 1805, and Eugène's mother moved the family back to Paris and enrolled Eugène at the Lycée Imperial, one of the best schools in the capital. There Delacroix excelled in Latin, Greek, and drawing. He also furthered his drawing skills by copying prints in the manner of the English caricaturist James Gillray, a practice that shaped a career-long habit of seeking expressions of character and animated gestures. When not yet eleven, Eugène had a fateful experience—a visit to the Louvre on one of his free days. The sight of such pictorial variety, scale, and technical mastery caused him to decide upon a painting career.

When Delacroix was seventeen, his career goal was aided by an introduction to Pierre-Narcisse Guérin, a successful painter and follower of Jacques-Louis David, head of the neoclassical movement in art and practically an art dictator under Napoleon I. In Guérin's atelier, Delacroix drew rigorously, learning human anatomy from classical references. He enjoyed working on large historical compositions involving faraway battles. While there he met Théodore Géricault, once a Guérin pupil. The young Delacroix felt an immediate kinship with Géricault's ideas of infusing French art with sensuousness plus an insistence upon spontaneity. Unfortunately, Delacroix was forced to withdraw from Guérin's atelier after only six months, probably because he could not afford the cost of tuition.

In 1816, Delacroix enrolled at the École des Beaux Arts. Orthodoxy ruled at this government-patronized school where all students progressed in basically the same manner. The primary methodology, like that for Guérin's classroom, was the study of classical form through seemingly endless copying of antique imagery from plaster casts, sculpture busts, coins, and, finally, male and female models. Delacroix was responsive to such instruction, but concurrently he searched for flexibility of expression and, on his own, explored the printmaking mediums of etching and engraving as well as the new print form lithography.

Delacroix's growing need for emotional release was soon met by the emergence of a friendship with Géricault. The timing could not have been more propitious, as the slightly older Géricault was embarking on a sensational large work, *The Raft of the Medusa* (1819). Its subject, chosen to embarrass the restored monarchy of France with the hope of possibly becoming a success by scandal, depicts the moment of the initial sighting of the above-mentioned raft by a passing ship on the Atlantic horizon. The raft contained a dozen or so men who had survived twelve days adrift, their two ropes connected to lifeboats having been mysteriously cut within a day of abandoning the stranded and broken frigate *Medusa*.

The ship had been on its way to Senegal with about four hundred passengers before running aground off the West African coast, thanks to an incompetent captain. Delacroix posed for the seminude figure lying face down near the edge of the raft in the central foreground. Though *The Raft of the Medusa* was overpoweringly raw, it proved to be the emotional elixir Delacroix was seeking. He may have been marked by its example, for his best paintings subsequently dealt with cruelty and death.

As with other artists falling under the perplexing umbrella of Romanticism, Delacroix's appearance and manner could be misleading. By age twenty, his aristocratic lineage was evident in his stiff posture and finely etched features. Fashion-conscious, he was one of the first to introduce the English-cut suit to Parisians, and to many people Delacroix was a pretentious dandy. However, some historians suggest that the artist's elegant attire and fine manners were used to mock France's increasingly industrialized society, which he thought was crassly hopeful in its newfound material prosperity.

Delacroix also had a withdrawn and pessimistic nature, which he cultivated further by emulating the melancholic pathos in Dante's poetry and the works of George Gordon, Lord Byron. By contrast, the painter's work Delacroix most admired from the past was that of Peter Paul Rubens, whose high-keyed colors and dramatic action enthralled him. However, it was Lord Byron who became a personal hero with a personality profile containing passion, bravery, elegance, melancholy, a love of freedom, and pessimism.

LIFE'S WORK

Desiring a successful career in painting, which in his day meant salon acceptance, Delacroix began a salon entry in 1821, one that would ideally attract critical reviews but not a storm of controversy. Touched by reading *The Inferno* from Dante's *The Divine Comedy*, he selected an episode from Canto VIII. Known by various titles, for example, *Dante and Virgil Crossing the Styx* and *The Bark of Dante*, the 1822 painting simulated the emotional potential and large scale of Géricault's *The Raft of the Medusa*, still fresh in Delacroix's memory. Unfortunately, polite taste, long accustomed to contained forms, polished technique, and clarity of color and values, was not ready for the ambiguous spaces and murky tones of Delacroix's painting.

Something more troublesome than salon taste marked Delacroix's subsequent career, namely the fact that many of his best paintings depicted injury, frenzy, and killing. He did not need to wait long for those types of thematic opportunities. In 1822, as many as twenty thousand Greeks on the island of Chios in the eastern Mediterranean were killed by invading Turks. Delacroix seized the chance to compose a potentially sensational work riding the crest of public interest in the war. Called *The Massacre at Chios* ("and the massacre of painting" by some of his contemporaries), it would seem to have been intended as a history set piece, except that the artist was basically apolitical.

A chance encounter with three landscape paintings by English Romantic painter John Constable at a Paris picture gallery may ultimately have been as important to Delacroix's subject and stylistic development as the gruesome massacre imagery. The artist noticed the application of color in bright flecks and dabs. Then he tested Constable's choppy, unblended color strokes and found, as did Constable, that a viewer's eyes mix the colors. The effects are not as crucial as Delacroix's intentions, which was not fidelity to atmospheric conditions but a contribution to a depressing mood combining murder and eroticism. From that point onward, color and a more vigorous painting method played a larger role in his art.

The Massacre at Chios shocked conservatives but enraptured youthful artists. It also stimulated Delacroix to explore more themes of death with erotic overtones. In fact, an immediate exploration of that sort was his entry for the 1827 Salon. Known as *The Death of Sardanapolus*, it was inspired by a Lord Byron play based upon the suicide of an Assyrian prince whom Byron named Sardanapolus. That world-weary aesthete choreographed his own conflagration as a final work of art. Through Byron, Delacroix illustrated the sickening preparations for the prince's funerary pyre, during which Sardanapolus watches without remorse as his favorite wives, horses, and dogs are killed in front of him by his officers.

The Death of Sardanapolus suffered disapproval by the press, and the French government refused to purchase it. Delacroix was warned by the head of the Academy of Fine Arts to refrain from painting any more like it

Eugène Delacroix. (Library of Congress)

for a long time lest he become ineligible for state commissions. Luckily for the artist, new officials, eager to overthrow the tastes of their predecessors, came to power in the aftermath of the July revolution of 1830. Delacroix was soon in their good graces, and one of his few political paintings, *Liberty Leading the People*, was finished by late 1830. This painting became a much-copied icon of revolutionary propaganda, with versions appearing often as posters well into the twentieth century. It was born of a public uprising in Paris that Delacroix witnessed but in which he did not participate because, even here, he had little faith in the proletariat.

In *Liberty Leading the People*, a ragged army surges forward, stumbling over a barricade of paving stones, debris, and fallen comrades. They are led by a solidly built, resolute, young bare-breasted woman (Liberty), who holds a musket in her left hand and raises the flag of France with her right hand. The conflict stemmed from unresolved grievances of the revolution in 1789 plus retrogressive decrees in July of 1830 by King Charles X, which dissolved the Chamber of Deputies, suspended freedom of the press, and overturned the voting rights of the merchant class and the new industrialists. Delacroix seemed to express perfectly the collective sentiment of the Parisians in revolt, perhaps even the universal will of ordinary citizens to revolt against intolerable conditions. However, those were not his intentions. Nevertheless, the artist valued most the French flag defiantly raised by the spirit of Liberty, which was returned to the north tower of Notre Dame on July 28, 1832, and is visible at the extreme right of the composition.

The year 1832 was a turning point in Delacroix's development, for at that time he accepted an invitation to accompany Count Charles de Mornay on a goodwill trip to Morocco. The artist was asked to record picturesque events of a treaty-exploring journey that followed the recent French takeover of neighboring Algeria. In North Africa, Delacroix hoped to find brilliant colors, sensuality, and ferocity. Instead, he observed civility, dignity, simple lifestyles, and a sense of unbroken traditions. From the first day ashore, he began to fill sketchbooks with drawings, watercolor vignettes, written notes on color, and descriptive details of his discoveries such as bright robes, exotic women, and non-European types of buildings. A short trip to Algiers was just as fruitful, for, once there, he realized a fantasy of long standing—entry into a harem. Two years after completing his North African trip, Delacroix produced an enchanting work drawn from that rare experience, *Algerian Women in Their Quarters*. In it, reverie and sensuality are fused and suspended.

The diaries and sketchbooks Delacroix filled sustained his art until his death in 1863. Equally remarkable is the fact that, despite the time lapse between the 1834 watercolor studies and the paintings derived from them, the latter did not lack freshness. The most popular works best typify Delacroix's taste for violence and cruelty: *The Lion Hunt* (1861) and *Arabs Skirmishing in the Mountains* (1862). For almost three decades, beginning during the 1830's, Delacroix was also involved with commissions sponsored by the government for major public buildings. There were church commissions, too. Altogether, they were exactly the type of employment to which most artists aspired at the time. Noteworthy contracts included wall and ceiling compositions at the National Assembly-Paris, the Luxembourg Palace (1845-1846), the Apollo Gallery at the Louvre (1850-1851), and the Church of Saint-Sulpice (1856-1861). Delacroix's last years were marked by failing health while he worked on these large projects. He died in 1863 in Paris after willing nearly six thousand works to public sale.

SIGNIFICANCE

Eugène Delacroix became the leading figure of the Romantic movement of painting in France and did so without trying. Actually, he may not have seen himself as a leader of anything. Like a number of major figures in art during his life, he was an enigma fraught with contradictions. For example, his thematic preferences ran quickly to scenes of high drama on the seas and depictions of fierce animal combat. Ironically, it was the gentle *Algerian Women in Their Quarters* that was later much admired, copied, and assimilated by artists of such stature as Pierre-Auguste Renoir, Paul Cézanne, Henri Matisse, and Pablo Picasso.

Delacroix's output was phenomenal, including 850 paintings, hundreds of watercolors, about sixty sketchbooks, many lithographs, thousands of drawings, a three-volume journal, and the beginnings of a dictionary of the fine arts. Furthermore, Delacroix, so full of energy, so prolific in his career, so strong-willed, seemingly had little faith in civilization. His pessimism, which was at first cultivated as a badge of distinction, eventually enveloped him like an unwelcomed, unshakable cloak. He is remembered as a rich colorist who painted dark themes. Delacroix died in 1863. By then Romanticism had been eclipsed by Édouard Manet's unvarnished naturalism in the 1863 Salon, which would lead to the emergence of the next major painting movement, Impressionism.

—Tom Dewey II

FURTHER READING

Delacroix, Eugène. *The Journal of Eugène Delacroix.* Translated by Walter Pach. New York: Crown, 1948. The first English translation of the artist's thoughts recorded intermittently from 1822 to 1832 and from 1847 to 1863. Perhaps the most relished entries are his impressions of a six-month trip to North Africa in 1832. Delacroix's intentions toward his own art will be appreciated by those seeking to understand his state of mind when he worked on key paintings.

Fraser, Elisabeth A. *Delecroix, Art, and Patrimony in Post-Revolutionary France.* New York: Cambridge University Press, 2004. Focuses on the paintings Delacroix created during the Bourbon Restoration. Fraser maintains these paintings were an attempt to reconcile the political turmoil of the French Revolution with subsequent events occurring during the Restoration. Delacroix's art, she argues, was as much influenced by the monarchy as it was by his earlier resistance to it.

Grigsby, Darcy Grimaldo. *Extremities: Painting Empire in Post-Revolutionary France.* New Haven, Conn.: Yale University Press, 2002. Analyzes six paintings by four artists, including Delacroix's *The Massacre at Chios* and *Greece on the Ruins of Missolonghi.* Grigsby argues these paintings depict the history and politics of the French colonial empire, an empire that forced painters who previously advocated freedom to depict slavery and cultural and racial differences.

Huyghe, René. *Delacroix.* New York: Harry N. Abrams, 1963. One of the best books on Delacroix to appear in English. Huyghe skillfully weaves quotations from the artist's journal and statements from Delacroix's contemporaries with his own observations. Illustrations of key paintings are analyzed diagrammatically, stressing the compositional structure in Delacroix's aesthetics. Important themes or works in series are suitably illustrated in black and white as preparatory drawings, multiple painted versions, and lithographs.

Johnson, Lee. *The Paintings of Eugène Delacroix: A Critical Catalogue, 1816-1831.* 2 vols. Oxford, England: Clarendon Press, 1981. A publication of major importance. The first attempt at a complete compilation of Delacroix's paintings since the basic effort by Alfred Robaut in 1885. Johnson covers the artist's formative period and his early salon successes. He airs new data regarding problems of dating paintings, presents paintings absent in Robaut's books, offers new biographical information on several of Delacroix's portrait subjects, and relates pertinent drawings to their respective paintings.

Le Bris, Michel. *Romantics and Romanticism.* New York: Rizzoli, 1981. An intriguing and well-illustrated study of Romanticism as an international movement with roots in literature and folklore. By stressing themes and contextual tendencies, the book separates itself from watered-down profiles and superficial catalogs. Nineteenth century Romantic tendencies aptly explored include the appetite for death and pessimism, the desire to experience non-Western cultures, the yearning for lost worlds, and phantoms and the deadly sublime.

Néret, Gilles. *Eugène Delacroix, 1798-1863: The Prince of Romanticism.* Cologne, Germany: Taschen, 1999. A concise overview of Delacroix's life and an analysis of his art. One of the volumes in the Basic Art Series.

Prideaux, Tom. *The World of Delacroix.* Alexandria, Va.: Time-Life Books, 1966. A cultural-historical approach is used in this book, placing Delacroix's art within the artistic and historical currents of his time. Prideaux weaves biography, politics and revolution, the painter's craft, and pedagogical issues into an engaging and lively text.

Trapp, Frank A. *The Attainment of Delacroix.* Baltimore: Johns Hopkins University Press, 1970. An ambitious book that addresses the artist's major works in dutiful fashion. The author's primary interests lie in Delacroix's paintings from literary sources and in themes from past history and current events. The last two chapters, which are entitled "Theory and Practice" and "Delacroix and His Critics," are perhaps the most welcome.

Wright, Beth S., ed. *The Cambridge Companion to Delacroix.* New York: Cambridge University Press, 2001. Collection of essays aimed at providing students with an introduction to Delacroix's life and work. Some of the essays examine Delacroix's artistic technique, his aesthetics, his writing, his relationship to the Romantic movement, and his impact on art and culture in the nineteenth century.

SEE ALSO: Hector Berlioz; Edgar Degas; Paul Gauguin; Théodore Géricault.

RELATED ARTICLES in *Great Events from History: The Nineteenth Century, 1801-1900:* October-December, 1830: Delacroix Paints *Liberty Leading the People*; October 28, 1886: Statue of Liberty Is Dedicated.

LÉO DELIBES
French composer

As a composer, Delibes contributed significantly to the French ballet and opera of the nineteenth century. He is particularly noted for raising the quality of the music composed for ballets.

BORN: February 21, 1836; Saint-Germain-du-Val, France
DIED: January 16, 1891; Paris, France
ALSO KNOWN AS: Clément-Philibert-Léo Delibes (full name)
AREA OF ACHIEVEMENT: Music

EARLY LIFE

Clément-Philibert-Léo Delibes (duh-leeb) was born into a family that, on the maternal side, evinced musical talent. His grandmother was an opera singer, and his uncle, Antoine Édouard Batiste, was a noted organist and held important posts at the churches of Saint-Nicholas-des-Champs and at Saint Eustache. Clémence, Delibes's mother, was herself a musician, while his father, Philibert, worked as a civil servant in the postal service.

When Léo was eleven years old, his father died. His mother, who had provided her son with the fundamentals of music, moved the household to Paris. At this point, young Léo entered the Paris Conservatory and, in 1850, was awarded a *premier prix* in solfège. This skill in sight singing stood the future composer in good stead when he later turned his attention to opera. During his tenure at the conservatory, Delibes acquired skill as an organist through his study with François Benoist, a winner of the Prix de Rome in 1815 and a composer of ballets and operas, the two genres in which his pupil was eventually to make his mark. More important, Delibes studied composition with Adolphe-Charles Adam, a master of the opéra-comique (that is, *Le Postillon de Longjumeau*, 1836) and creator of such popular ballets as *Giselle* (1841) and *Le Corsaire* (1856). Adam, a pupil of François-Adrien Boïeldieu, became not only a mentor but also a partial father figure to his student.

Delibes's other musical enterprise as a youth included experience as a chorister at the Madeleine Cathedral and, on April 16, 1849, in the premiere of Giacomo Meyerbeer's *Le Prophète* at the Opéra. With the help of Adam, several professional positions were proffered him in 1853, and he thus found himself toiling as an accompanist at the Théâtre-Lyrique and as an organist at the Church of Saint Pierre de Chaillot. Despite his affinity for the organ (he worked as an organist steadily until 1871), Delibes developed an attraction for the theater. With the exception of a brief interlude as a critic (1858) for the *Gaulois hebdomadaire*, for which he wrote under the pen name Eloi Delbès, this attraction was cemented as early as 1856. In that year, his first stage work, *Deux Sous de charbon*, was produced at Hervé's Folies-Nouvelles and received a favorable reception.

LIFE'S WORK

Delibes found the light opera, or operetta, to be a genre well suited to his talent and inclination. Over the next fourteen years, he provided some dozen such entertainments, a few of which were staged at Jacques Offenbach's theater, the Bouffes-Parisiens. Among them was the enormously popular *Deux Vieilles Gardes*.

In his role as chorus master at the Théâtre-Lyrique, the young creator arranged the vocal score of Charles Gounod's *Faust* (1859) and worked also on two other major staples of the French operatic repertory, *Les Pêcheurs de perles* (1863) by Georges Bizet and *Les Troyens à Carthage* (1863) by Hector Berlioz. By 1864, in his role as chorus master at the Opéra, Delibes capitalized on the opportunities that presented themselves to him. His early successes were enlarged upon and solidified with the performance on November 12, 1866, at the Opéra, of the ballet *La Source: Ou, Naila*, on which he collaborated with the established Austrian-born composer Ludwig Minkus. Delibes's contribution to the music for scenes 2 and 3 has been adjudged superior to Minkus's contribution to scenes 1 and 4. A year later, with a divertissement for a revival of *Le Corsaire* by Adam, *Valse: Ou, Pas des Fleurs*, Delibes had created for himself a considerable following. An opera bouffe entitled *La Cour du roi Pétaud*, produced on April 24, 1869, at Variétés, proved to be his final work in this genre.

The single most acclaimed composition by Delibes, the ballet *Coppélia: Ou, La Fille aux yeux d'émail*, was mounted on May 2, 1870, at the Opéra. The first ballet to use symphonic music throughout and to unify the dance and music into a homogeneity heretofore absent in this art form, *Coppélia* is based on Ernst Theodor Hoffman's story "Der Sandmann" (1816; "The Sandman," 1844). Set in two acts and three scenes, the work opens with a prelude; after the atmosphere has been created, there follow twenty musical numbers, the last of which comprises eight individual sections.

The opera's story line, which is familiar to those who know Jacques Offenbach's *Les Contes d'Hoffmann* (1880), centers on the mechanical doll Coppélia, whose lifelike presence impels Franz, a young man who has become infatuated with her, to pursue her to the consternation of his fiancé, Swanhilda. Dr. Coppelius, the eccentric toymaker and magician who created the automaton, loves her as a daughter. When "the girl with the enamel eyes" is proved to be merely a toy, the lovers unite in marriage. It is at this juncture that number 20 of the score, "Festival of the Bell," with its eight sumptuous pieces featuring various uses of the bell, brings the ballet to a scintillating close. Assorted national dances, such as the mazurka number 3, *Thème slave varié* number 6, the czardas number 7, and the bolero number 16, coupled with orchestral brilliance and coloration, contribute to the opulence of the composition.

In 1871, Delibes made the decisions to marry Léontine Estelle Denain and to devote himself entirely to composition; the latter determination caused him to refrain from time-consuming activity as an organist and chorus master. *Le Roi l'a dit*, Delibes's first major operatic opus, was produced on May 24, 1873, at the Opéra-Comique. Its immediate success in Paris resulted in a performance in Antwerp (August 18, 1873) and, during the next year, performances in Vienna, Karlsruhe, and Prague.

Returning to the ballet, Delibes produced a second masterpiece in this genre with *Sylvia: Ou, La Nymphe de Diane*; it was premiered on June 14, 1876, at the Opéra. The story, based on Torquato Tasso's *Aminta* (1573), deals with Sylvia, a nymph of Diana, and her love affair with the shepherd Aminta. Interest and contrast are created by the involvement in the story of Diana, Eros, and Orion. Stylistically, this work differs from *Coppélia*; indeed, the political climate in France was also different. *Coppélia* was a creature of the Second Empire, a period in which Paris was the pleasure capital of the world.

Sylvia, on the other hand, with its stylized mythology, came at a time when France, now a republic, retained strong memories of the Franco-Prussian War and the internal upheavals of the commune. The orchestral scoring in *Sylvia* reveals immediately a more serious emotionality of expression; there are, in addition, traces of Wagnerian influence. Distinguished musicians, among them Peter Ilich Tchaikovsky, who probably heard *Coppélia* during his several trips to Paris during the 1870's, were exposed to *Sylvia* in Vienna.

Now riding the crest of a triumphant wave, Delibes produced his three-act *drame lyrique*, *Jean de Nivelle*, on March 8, 1880, at the Opéra-Comique. It was very successful and received one hundred performances until January 6, 1881, at this theater. During the period 1880-1882, it was also performed in Stockholm, Budapest, Copenhagen, Vienna, Geneva, St. Petersburg, and Brussels. Oddly, after its revival at the Gaîté-Lyrique on October 5, 1908, it has fallen into oblivion.

Perhaps feeling a need to supplement his reputation as a composer with academic respectability, Delibes took a position as professor of composition at the Paris Conservatory in 1881, this despite admitted weaknesses in fugal and contrapuntal technique. Yet another side of this artist's talent emerges in the *Le Roi s'amuse: Six airs de danse dans le style ancien*, written for a revival of Victor Hugo's *Le Roi s'amuse* (1832; *The King's Fool*, 1842), performed on November 22, 1882, at the Comédie-Française. Here, he reveals a distinct rapport for seventeenth century French classicism.

The three-act opera *Lakmé* premiered on April 14, 1883, at the Opéra-Comique. The exoticism of this work (the setting is India) in which the female lead, Lakmé, is the daughter of the Brahmin priest Nilakantha, has attracted audiences up to modern times, and the lilting strains of its famous love duet are frequently used in modern advertising commercials. In this nineteenth century story, the British officer Gérald is in love with the heroine, much to her father's displeasure; indeed, the priest vows to kill the English suitor. When, however, Lakmé realizes that Gérald is torn between his duty and his love for her, she eases his burden by committing suicide.

Of all the opera's many excellences, the coloratura showstopper, the "Bell Song," remains a tour de force. From 1883 until Delibes's death, he completed no other major work, but an incomplete opera, *Kassya*, was produced on March 24, 1893, at the Opéra-Comique. Jules Massenet provided the orchestration but did not add the overture that Delibes did not live to compose.

SIGNIFICANCE

Léo Delibes was described by French composer Henri-Charles Merechal as "restless, fidgety, slightly befuddled, correcting and excusing himself, lavishing praise, careful not to hurt anyone's feelings, shrewd, adroit, very lively, a sharp critic." This characterization aptly depicts those traits that most strongly affected the ballet master's creative path. The early works, notably the operettas, are always cited for their facile technique, their light and airy manner, and their elegance and wit. There is no plumbing of depths, no attempt at profundity. Delibes's operettas

Léo Delibes. (The Granger Collection, New York)

represent skillful treatment of a genre then in vogue and one that reached an apex of popularity in the hands of Offenbach, who, as a matter of interest, collaborated with Delibes on *Les Musiciens de l'orchèstre* (1861) and at whose theater Delibes produced nine of his light operas. Even at the height of his own fame, Delibes took time to complete Offenbach's *Belle Lurette* (1880) and *Mamzelle Moucheron* (1881).

As he matured, Delibes absorbed a variety of influences. Eclecticism as a modus operandi seems to have enabled the musician to create strikingly appealing dance numbers in *Coppélia* and *Sylvia*. In addition to the graceful turns of phrase, the orchestration reveals a genuine gift for originality. The use of alto saxophone in the barcarolle of *Sylvia* is a masterful stroke and one of the earliest efforts to make this instrument a practical member of the orchestra. The "Pizzicati" from the same ballet has been emulated by later composers. The oriental atmosphere in *Kassya* is skillfully wrought and is a portent of the direction in which Delibes was moving at his death.

Because his reputation had been solidified as a consequence of his stage works, there is a tendency to pay little heed to Delibes's many choruses, songs, piano pieces, and religious music, such as the *Messe brève* for two equal voices with organ and string quartet, the *Ave maris stelle* for two voices, and the *Ave verum* for two voices. There is no uniformity of opinion with regard to Delibes's historical place. It is significant, however, that in his own lifetime he was elected a member of the Institut de France (1884). Delibes was viewed by the establishment as one worthy to carry on the French traditions deemed meritorious.

Because as a genre ballet has not attained the status of symphonic music, chamber music, or piano music, Delibes's position in the pantheon of musical celebrities has suffered, and because he was not a prolific composer, the total number of his works that survive in today's repertory is less than one dozen. Those who have seen or heard his best creations, however, have experienced an enchantment that lives long in the memory.

—David Z. Kushner

FURTHER READING

Curtiss, Mina. *Bizet and His World.* New York: Alfred A. Knopf, 1958. Contains useful and insightful information about the relationship between Delibes and Bizet.

Downes, Olin. *The Lure of Music: Depicting the Human Side of Great Composers, with Stories of Their Inspired Creations.* New York: Harper & Brothers, 1918. Contains an excellent essay on Delibes and his music, and takes the position that Delibes's ballets are far more than a potpourri of uninspired dance pieces.

Macdonald, Hugh. "(Clément Philibert) Léo Delibes." In *The New Grove Dictionary of Music and Musicians*, edited by Stanley Sadie. Vol. 5. London: Macmillan, 1980. Probably the finest English-language reference article on Delibes. Includes a comprehensive list of works.

Studwell, William E. *Adolphe Adam and Léo Delibes: A Guide to Research.* New York: Garland, 1987. The heart of the section dealing with Delibes is a comprehensive annotated bibliography arranged topically and alphabetically. There is a valuable summary of Delibes's life and work, a discussion of the composer's relationship to his more illustrious contemporaries, and a commentary on the historical role of Delibes and his music's place in history. The bibliography includes four published writings of Delibes.

Van Vechten, Carl. *Excavations: A Book of Advocacies*. New York: A. A. Knopf, 1926. Van Vechten, a prominent cultural critic during the 1920's, includes an essay about Delibes in this collection of essays. Van Vechten credited Delibes with revolutionizing the ballet by introducing a symphonic approach to orchestration and by infusing his scores with melodic grace.

SEE ALSO: Charles Gounod; Gioacchino Rossini; Peter Ilich Tchaikovsky; Giuseppe Verdi.

RELATED ARTICLES in *Great Events from History: The Nineteenth Century, 1801-1900:* March 3, 1875: Bizet's *Carmen* Premieres in Paris; January 14, 1900: Puccini's *Tosca* Premieres in Rome.

FOURTEENTH EARL OF DERBY

Prime minister of Great Britain (February 21-December 17, 1852; 1858-1859; 1866-1868)

One of the leading British politicians at a time when Great Britain was at the height of its economic and political power, Derby oversaw the relatively peaceful democratic reform of his country.

BORN: March 29, 1799; Knowsley Park, Lancashire, England

DIED: October 23, 1869; Knowsley Park, Lancashire, England

ALSO KNOWN AS: Edward George Geoffrey Smith Stanley (birth name)

AREA OF ACHIEVEMENT: Government and politics

EARLY LIFE

The fourteenth earl of Derby (DAR-bee) was born Edward George Geoffrey Smith Stanley into one of the greatest and oldest aristocratic families in Great Britain. The Stanleys had been ennobled in the fifteenth century and the first earl of Derby was created by Henry VII as a reward for abandoning Richard III. This was not the last time that the Stanleys would change their political allegiance dramatically. So great was their preeminence in the north of England that the earls of Derby were virtually uncrowned kings of Lancashire.

Young Edward Stanley was educated at Eton and Christ Church, Oxford. He was the Stanley family heir, and a brilliant political future was predicted for him. In March, 1822, he was first elected to the House of Commons as a moderate Whig for Stockport, in his native Lancashire, a borough that his father had represented. His first session in Parliament established his reputation as a fine speaker.

Over the years, Stanley's brilliance as a slashing parliamentary debater was of major importance in bringing him political leadership, which even wealth and title could not guarantee. Perhaps the most significant development during his maiden session was personal. He was married in May, 1825, to Emma, the second daughter of Edward Wilbraham, later Lord Skelmerdale. In July, 1826, she gave birth to a son, Edward Henry Stanley, who would carry on the family tradition of political leadership as the fifteenth earl. Just before his son's birth, in June, Stanley was elected for Preston, which, unlike Stockbridge, was a popular borough, with a substantial electorate. One of the borough's two seats was usually held by a nominee of the Stanleys, and Stanley easily defeated the popular Tory journalist William Cobbett. In April, 1827, he accepted his first ministerial position, undersecretary for the colonies in George Canning's moderate Tory government, only leaving office when an ultra-Tory government came in (January, 1828).

LIFE'S WORK

Stanley's rise to the highest ranks of politics began when, after a long period of Tory dominance, the Whigs returned to power in July, 1830, under the second Earl Grey. Stanley was offered the post of secretary for Ireland, a thankless but important task because, following Daniel O'Connell's leadership, a revived Irish nationalism was stirring. Stanley's satisfaction at being offered this challenging post was chastened by an electoral setback. Ministers at this time, on appointment, were obliged to resign their seats and stand for reelection. When Stanley did so in August, 1830, a time of enthusiasm for reform, he was defeated by the radical candidate Henry "Orator" Hunt, and a safe seat had to be found for him before he could take up his responsibilities in July. A seat was found in Windsor in February, 1831. While Stanley generally acquitted himself well as Irish secretary, his personal relationship with O'Connell was extremely bitter. At one point he challenged the Irish leader to a duel, though nothing came of it.

The principal business of the Grey ministry was to deal with the demands for electoral reform. There had been virtually no redrawing of the boundaries of election districts for two centuries, though there had been much population growth and, more recently, movement of people as industrialization began to urbanize the country. As a result, virtually unpopulated areas had representation—"pocket" or "rotten" boroughs, such as Stanley's own first seat—while the newly grown cities were underrepresented or completely unrepresented.

Property qualifications for voting also excluded from political participation substantial numbers of prosperous literate citizens. The remedy for these complaints was electoral reform, which finally passed into law after some grave difficulties, in June, 1832. Stanley had a leading role as one of the managers of the legislation's successful passage through the house, though he had begun as a rather skeptical supporter of reform. He was hardly a believer in pure democracy, and his personal attitude is best exemplified by his suspicion that the secret ballot (not yet adopted at this time) would be used principally to conceal electoral fraud.

In December, 1832, following the elevation of his father to the peerage in his own right, as Lord Stanley of Bickerstaffe, he was elected to his father's seat as member for North Lancashire, which he held for the balance of his service in Commons. Then, in October, 1834, on the death of Stanley's grandfather (the twelfth earl), Edward Stanley became known by the courtesy title Lord Stanley, though still a commoner.

In March, 1833, Stanley changed office and became secretary for war and the colonies, and it became his responsibility to steer through the Commons a bill for the abolition of slavery in the British Empire. Despite his success, and the growth of his reputation, Stanley was displeased with his colleagues on the Irish issue, most particularly with Lord John Russell. Stanley was adamant that nothing should be done that might lead to depriving the Irish church of its privileged position. The state church in Ireland had more income than it could employ for ecclesiastical purposes. Russell pressed for the government to appropriate these funds for secular purposes. In protest, in May, 1834, Stanley led his followers, including three other cabinet ministers, out of the Whig Party and into opposition. O'Connell promptly dubbed them sarcastically "the Derby Dillies."

While reluctant, at first, to make more than a tactical alliance with the Tories under Sir Robert Peel, and declining to enter the first Peel ministry, eventually, in July, 1835, Stanley cast his lot with them. He was quickly accepted as one of the principal Tory leaders, second only to Peel. By 1841, Stanley had joined the Carleton Club, making permanent his adherence to the Tories. Peel, forming his second ministry, that year offered Stanley the Colonial Office, which he accepted. As a result of Stanley's objections, a relatively new Tory member, Benjamin Disraeli, was kept from a place. Stanley thought him a scoundrel.

In October, 1844, accepting a peerage as Lord Stanley of Bickerstaffe, probably because of growing differences with Peel, Stanley gave up his place in the Commons. At the time, Peel's ministry was confronted with a growing demand for free trade, ending the protection of British agriculture by the Corn Laws. While many Tory landlords believed that this would ruin them, the rest of the Tory Party, and about a third of the Tory M.P.'s, following Peel, conceded that free trade was necessary.

The party split sharply, and Stanley, though not an ardent protectionist, led the Tory backbenchers out of the government and into opposition. Together with his sporting friend Lord George Bentinck, who was as passionately devoted to horse racing and breeding as Stanley himself, Stanley provided the natural leadership of the anti-Peelite Tories. Bentinck brought in his train the unlikely figure of Disraeli, hardly a rural Tory but useful in the Commons as an effective speaker. When Bentinck died unexpectedly in 1848, Stanley found himself linked with Disraeli in an enduring political partnership that, not many years before, would have been thought impossible.

Peel died suddenly in 1850, which added to the continuing political instability. Leaderless, his followers gradually drifted toward the emerging Liberal group within the Whig Party. Liberalism was beginning to divide the Whigs as free trade had split the Tories, but the process was a slower and less dramatic one. In the meantime, Stanley's protectionist Tory Party, though the largest group in Parliament, was not numerous enough to form a ministry on its own. Despite Disraeli's urgings, Stanley declined to abandon protectionism, at least until public opinion had been tested on the issue by a general election. The Tory rejection of free trade isolated them, making it difficult, if not impossible, to join any governing coalition.

In February, 1851, when the government fell, Stanley failed to organize a ministry. In June of that year, his father died, and he succeeded to the earldom. The following February, Lord Derby, as he now was, finally became prime minister, with Disraeli as his Chancellor of the Exchequer. The rest of the government (which included his son at the Foreign Office) was so young, inexperienced, or insignificant that it was dubbed contemptuously the "who, who ministry."

The government was crippled from the start and never possessed the strength to carry on effectively. Derby clung to power, without a majority, until the end of the year. The succeeding government, Lord Aberdeen's coalition of Whigs and Peelites, lasted until it blundered unprepared into the Crimean War. Once again, in 1855, Derby was offered the opportunity to form a government. Despite much grumbling from his followers, again, he was reluctant to accept responsibility without any prospect of success. When he finally managed to form his second ministry in February, 1858, on the fall of Lord Palmerston's ministry, he had little success and was succeeded by Palmerston's returning to office in June, 1859.

A central difficulty for Derby was that, in addition to his own antipathy to the Whig leader Russell, Palmerston declined service in any government that included Derby. Palmerston's breezy popularity, in Parliament and the country, made him virtually indispensable in all the coalitions of the midcentury. Derby's problems with forming a government were thus nearly impossible to surmount, despite the impatience of his party to enter a government coalition.

When the American Civil War interrupted the supply of raw cotton to British mills (many of which were in Lancashire), Derby played a leading role in organizing voluntary relief. Eventually supplies of cotton from the empire ended the "cotton famine" and its devastating unemployment.

After Palmerston's death in 1865, the way was open, and Derby succeeded, in June, 1866, in organizing his third ministry with Disraeli as his chancellor and Leader of the House. Derby found widespread demand for electoral reform and a larger measure of democracy. Rather than leave the issue to the Whigs and Liberals, the Tories stole their program and passed the Reform Bill of 1867, which dramatically enlarged the electorate. Derby, carrying the bill through the Lords, conceded frankly that the new course, however necessary, was a leap in the dark. Derby's last ministry, like its predecessors, was too weakly based to survive for long. Derby, now close to seventy, in poor health, much troubled by gout, resigned in February, 1868. He went home to Lancashire in the summer of 1869 and died, after a lingering illness, on October 23, 1869.

SIGNIFICANCE

The fourteenth earl of Derby's career in politics spanned half a century. Though almost from the first he was near the pinnacle of power and a brilliant success was expected for him, it was thirty years before he led a government. In the end, his record was one of disappointment and frustration. All three of his ministries were relatively short-lived; the first two accomplished little and in the third the lion's share of the credit for its singular accomplishment, the passage of the Reform Bill, went to Disraeli.

Derby played a leading role in passing three of the century's most important pieces of legislation: the abolition of slavery and the two reform acts. It is a curious achievement and legacy for a highly aristocratic and intensely conservative politician that he had a central role in laying the foundation of modern democracy in Great Britain. Derby was not a democrat, or even a political reformer, as a matter of conviction. His goal was to preserve the existing social order, church, and empire. The concessions made to democracy were, in his own eyes, a statesmanlike gamble, which he had the necessary self-assurance to make, in order to preserve as much as possible of the world he knew.

Despite his important achievements, Derby has been seen essentially as a failure. Peel and Disraeli have overshadowed him in the annals of his party. His contemporaries feared his sharp tongue and regarded him as unstable because he had twice broken with his leadership. He had the bad luck to lead the Tories at the nadir of their fortunes, when they were politically isolated and impotent, for which he received much of the blame. Even his frustrated Tory followers, though they respected him, tended to view him as an aloof, remote figure, not as much interested in political success as in horse racing, shooting partridges, and winning at whist.

It is undeniable that Derby was, in his personal habits, a country squire, though on a vast scale. The pose of the amateur politician, indifferent to power, however, masked, in classic Victorian fashion, a more complicated figure, a classical scholar who translated Homer and, above all, a shrewd lifelong professional politician who tried to cope with a society changing in unprecedented fashion and with extraordinary velocity. Modern historians, whether fairly or not, have tended to follow the Victorian judgment. On the crowded stage of Victorian statemanship, despite his accomplishments, he is seen as a supporting player.

—*S. J. Stearns*

FURTHER READING

Conacher, J. B. *The Peelites and the Party System*. Newton Abbott, England: David and Charles, 1972. A careful political study of 1846-1852. Together with his work on the Aberdeen government and Gash's work, Conacher's book contains a detailed study of the critical decade following the repeal of the Corn Laws when both parties, Whig and Tory, were deconstructed and new ones created out of their pieces.

Disraeli, Benjamin. *Benjamin Disraeli Letters: 1862-1856*. Vol. 6 in *Benjamin Disraeli Letters*. Edited by J. A. W. Gunn, et al. Toronto: University of Toronto Press, 1982-2004. This volume of Disraeli's letters contains sixty-three letters to Derby, including thirty-four previously unpublished letters, written when Disraeli was Chancellor of the Exchequer and attempting to unify the Conservative Party.

Gash, Norman. *Sir Robert Peel: The Life of Sir Robert Peel After 1830*. London: Longman, 1972. The second of two volumes covering the whole of Peel's career. Whether as Derby's collaborator or antagonist, he was the dominant figure in British politics from the first reform bill to his death.

Hall, Catherine, Keith McClelland, and Jane Rendall. *Victorian Nation: Class, Race, Gender, and the British Reform Act of 1867*. New York: Cambridge University Press, 2000. A new interpretation of the second Reform Act. The authors maintain its passage was marked by controversy about the extension of the vote, concepts of masculinity, and the beginnings of the woman suffrage movement. Includes several references to Derby and an explanation of his reform proposals.

Harrison, Brian, and H. C. G. Matthew. *Oxford Dictionary of National Biography in Association with the British Academy: From the Earliest Times to the Year 2000*. New York: Oxford University Press, 2004. This standard reference work contains a biography of Derby. In addition to the print version, the dictionary is available in an on-line format that can be purchased by libraries and accessed by patrons.

Jones, Wilbur D. *Lord Derby and Victorian Conservatism*. Athens: University of Georgia Press, 1956. The standard modern work on Derby. Covers the whole career but the value is limited because its author did not have access to the Derby papers.

Prest, John. *Lord John Russell*. London: Macmillan, 1972. The political career of Derby's contemporary and lifelong rival.

Stewart, Robert McKenzie. *The Politics of Protectionism: Lord Derby and the Protectionist Party, 1841-1852*. London: Cambridge University Press, 1971. A sympathetic treatment of the critical political decade, based on the Derby manuscripts. Stewart's later work, *The Foundations of the Conservative Party, 1830-1867* (New York: Longman, 1978), is a careful and well-documented overview of party politics.

SEE ALSO: Benjamin Disraeli; Charles Grey; Lord Palmerston; Sir Robert Peel; Baron John Russell; Third Marquis of Salisbury.

RELATED ARTICLE in *Great Events from History: The Nineteenth Century, 1801-1900:* August, 1867: British Parliament Passes the Reform Act of 1867.

GEORGE DEWEY

American admiral

While commanding the American fleet in the Pacific theater of the Spanish-American War, Dewey destroyed the Spanish fleet in the Battle of Manila Bay. His triumph in what may have been the most one-sided victory in world naval history made him a national hero. He was afterward considered a serious contender for the presidency but served as senior officer of the Navy until his death.

BORN: December 26, 1837; Montpelier, Vermont
DIED: January 16, 1917; Washington, D.C.
AREA OF ACHIEVEMENT: Military

EARLY LIFE

George Dewey was the son of Julius Y. Dewey, a physician, and Mary Perrin Dewey. His mother died when he was five, but he seems to have had a happy childhood anyway, full of high spirits and practical jokes. He enjoyed a very close relationship with his father. After attending a military school in Norwich, Vermont, Dewey sought appointment to the United States Military Academy; because there were no vacancies at West Point, however, he went to the United States Naval Academy instead, graduating in 1858, fifth in a class of fifteen.

Promoted to lieutenant just as the Civil War began, Dewey served with distinction in the blockading fleet and especially on the Mississippi, where his courage and resourcefulness earned for him positions of considerable responsibility, despite his youth. It was also on the Mississippi that he came to admire the daring Admiral David G. Farragut, later famous for the immortal, although perhaps apocryphal, words "Damn the torpedoes! Full speed ahead!" More than thirty years later, Dewey would have reason to ponder these words.

Dewey reached the rank of lieutenant commander by the war's end; then, like other career officers, he had to settle down to the dull circumstances of the peacetime navy. On October 27, 1867, he married Susan B. Goodwin, daughter of a New Hampshire governor. She died in 1872, after the birth of their son, George Goodwin Dewey. The bereaved husband remained a bachelor for the next twenty-seven years—and a very eligible one he was: trim, sporting a glorious mustache, and handsome even into advanced middle age. He was also fairly well-to-do by virtue of his holding shares in his father's life insurance company.

LIFE'S WORK

The post-Civil War U.S. Navy had too many officers for its shrinking and obsolete fleet, yet Dewey managed by seniority and competence to gain his share of promotions and even more: commander in 1872, captain in 1884, and commodore in 1896. He spent fewer of these years at sea than is the norm, preferring duty in Washington, D.C. There he became head of the Bureau of Equipment in 1889 and president of the Board of Inspection and Survey in 1895. He sometimes used these positions to encourage naval progress, but he was too senior—and too devoted to intraservice harmony—to identify fully with the younger, reform-minded officers of that era. Like many other senior officers, he cultivated political connections instead. One of his friends, Assistant Secretary of the Navy Theodore Roosevelt, along with a Vermont senator, arranged for his appointment as commodore of the United States Asiatic Squadron in 1897.

Dewey was not an advocate of imperialism, but he knew that the Philippines in general, and the Spanish fleet in Manila Bay in particular, would be likely American targets should there be war with Spain. When that war began in April of 1898, his squadron was already well advanced in its preparations for combat. With the declarations of war, Dewey's ships were suddenly deprived of the services of Hong Kong and all other neutral ports, and they had none of their own. He could perhaps have violated Chinese neutrality by using a port on her coast—and the impotent Chinese government would not have been able to stop him—but that would have been no more than a temporary expedient.

Dewey's squadron either had to steam out of the Far East or conquer a base for itself in Manila Bay. Leaving was unthinkable: Apart from the psychological and diplomatic consequences of departing without a fight, the United States could hardly abandon its interests in Asia; nor could it allow Spain to keep the Philippines, valuable as they would be as bargaining chips at the peace table—or as the site of a permanent American base in the Far East to assist in the expansion of American interests there.

Flying his flag in the magnificent light cruiser *Olympia*, Dewey led five other ships out of Hong Kong on his way to battle. Spain's Admiral Patricio Montojo awaited him in Manila Bay with seven ships, but they were smaller and less well armed than Dewey's, and with fewer well-trained crews. Some of his ships were in wretched condition. Spanish weakness afloat could in theory be offset by some other factors: If Montojo could disperse his ships, he might be able to harass American commercial shipping indefinitely, or the Spanish could shelter their ships under the guns of Manila and sow mines in Dewey's path. However, none of these options came to anything: The Spanish ships could not scatter without exposing Manila to bombardment; Manila's coast artillery was inadequate; and the Spaniards lacked insulated wire with which to arm their mines. Thus, the gloomy Montojo fully expected to go down fighting for honor's sake alone, even giving up the slight protection of Manila's guns so as to spare the civil population an enemy bombardment.

The Americans could not have been fully aware of the extent of Spanish weakness. Although the United States consul in Manila had indicated Montojo's dilemma, his information might not have been complete; it was, in any case, many days old by the time Dewey set sail. The Spaniards might yet score heavily with lucky hits from their guns or with the few makeshift mines they had managed to sow, thereby making an American victory, if it could be achieved, either incomplete or dreadfully Pyrrhic.

Dewey himself had nothing but contempt for the Spanish defenses. He was more than willing to "damn the torpedoes," that is, the mines. His final words on the subject were perhaps not as stirring as Admiral Farragut's, but just as decisive: "Mines or no mines, I'm leading the squadron in myself." When his ships got in range of Montojo's, he gave his soon-to-be famous order to the captain of the *Olympia:* "You may fire when you are ready, Gridley." The result was the total destruction of Montojo's squadron in the Battle of Manila Bay, May 1, 1898; there were no American combat fatalities. Dewey subsequently maintained a blockade of Manila and cooperated with the newly arrived United States Army so as to force the city's surrender.

Two long-term international problems arose during the Manila Bay campaign. One was the American relationship with the anti-Spanish Filipino insurrectionists. Their leader, Emilio Aguinaldo, claimed that Dewey had promised freedom for the Philippines in return for the insurgents' help in defeating the Spaniards on land. Dewey denied agreeing to anything but a purely military alliance, with no commitments regarding the future of the islands. Given his—and Aguinaldo's—political naïveté, it is perhaps likely that they had genuinely misunderstood each other. In any case, their disagreement was a minor milestone on the road to war between the United States and the Filipino rebels.

Dewey's other political problem during the blockade concerned the attitude of Germany. The kaiser's Asiatic fleet visited Manila Bay and openly displayed its sympathy for the Spaniards. Americans wondered if the Germans wanted the islands for themselves. It is true that the Germans sometimes behaved as if the rules of blockade simply did not apply to them, and their ships far outclassed Dewey's. Fortunately, the matter was resolved, but Dewey, and many other Americans, carried away from this experience a lingering suspicion of Germany's intentions all over the world.

In 1899, Dewey returned to the United States, where he was lionized to an incredible degree. There were Dewey hats, cigarettes, canes, songs, and even paperweights. Congress elevated him to the rank of admiral of the Navy, making him the senior officer of the two armed services, with the right to remain on active duty for life. In 1900, he was appointed head of the Navy Department's General Board, and in 1903, he became the chairman of the Joint Army-Navy Board.

Meanwhile, there had been a Dewey-for-president boom, looking toward the election of 1900. Disliking public adulation, Dewey nevertheless allowed himself to be talked into running; his candidacy soon fell flat, however, mostly because of his own political ineptitude. For one thing, his cause was damaged by his comment about how easy the job of president would be. For another, his political ideas were few and ill-considered: He declared himself a Democrat, yet he despised the radical wing of that party; although he had originally wanted nothing in the Philippines but a coaling station, he nevertheless officially associated himself with the Republican president's decision to seek the annexation of the entire archipelago.

Dewey's second marriage, on November 9, 1899, also worked to his political disadvantage. He was the nation's darling, and for him to marry at all was bound to arouse popular jealousy; his choice of bride made the situation all the worse: She was Mildred McLean Hazen, a wealthy widow with the image of a snob. Worse yet, she was a Protestant who had turned Roman Catholic, apparently for no better reason than to please the best social circles in Austria, where she had once happened to live. Anti-Catholics in the United States therefore claimed that she might someday donate Admiral Dewey's house to the Roman Catholic Church—a house that had been purchased for him by subscription by the people of a grateful nation. It was all very silly, but the fuss engendered by his marriage nevertheless contributed to the collapse of Dewey's political hopes, such as they were, and he eventually withdrew from the presidential race. (His wife later turned Protestant again.)

Dewey's service as senior officer of the Navy showed him to be a conscientious but uninspired leader. He sought compromise, no matter what the cost, to prevent arguments within his beloved navy. He tried to please both sides in the controversy between the partisans of Admiral William T. Sampson and those of Admiral Winfield S. Schley concerning the latter's role in the Caribbean phase of the Spanish-American War; but his efforts along these lines led only to an obvious self-contradiction.

In another matter, Dewey supported the young reformers who wanted to establish a general staff within the Navy Department, yet he turned against them when their tactics offended his sense of propriety. He wanted the Navy to have modern battleships, yet he refused to make full public use of his prestige in order to acquire them because he disliked arguing with naval conservatives. Like many others, he suspected that the next war for the United States would be with Germany, but in this case he carelessly allowed his opinion to become public knowledge, thereby embarrassing his country.

Old age and arteriosclerosis finally took their toll on him, especially after a slight stroke in 1913. He died in Washington, D.C., on January 16, 1917.

SIGNIFICANCE

Dewey's career from 1865 to 1897 was only somewhat more lustrous than those of many other officers. He was resourceful and courageous enough, in 1898, to make his ships ready and then to seize the opportunity for glory in Manila Bay, yet the praises and promotion that followed were all out of proportion to his achievement. Sampson and Schley, after all, had commanded more and more heavily armed ships than Dewey had ever possessed, and in a more important theater of war, the Caribbean; moreover, they defeated a Spanish fleet that was stronger than

Montojo's. Dewey, it is true, had displayed a certain phlegmatic panache; clearly, however, what made him so much greater than Sampson and Schley in the public's eye was the mere fact that his triumph came at the very beginning of the war, before anyone else's victory could claim the headlines.

Dewey's postwar career did not provide much justification for his elevation to the highest of ranks. His judgments in the realm of politics were often ludicrous, and even in strictly naval matters they were sometimes flawed, largely because of his obsession with intraservice harmony. Perhaps Dewey's most important contribution after 1898 was his support for the modernization of the battle fleet, but even in this case he was simply on the side of an irresistible trend, and halfheartedly at that. Avoiding conflict within the Navy came at the cost of a more forceful and forward-looking role as his department's most senior admiral.

—*Karl G. Larew*

FURTHER READING

Cosmas, Graham A. *An Army for Empire: The United States Army in the Spanish-American War*. Columbia: University of Missouri Press, 1971. Despite its title, this book sheds much light on all aspects of the Spanish-American War. It is very scholarly, but also readable.

Herrick, Walter R., Jr. *The American Naval Revolution*. Baton Rouge: Louisiana State University Press, 1966. Another scholarly and well-written book. Herrick covers the political events that led to the building of the modern U.S. fleet during the 1890's; this was the program that gave Dewey the qualitative edge he enjoyed in Manila Bay.

Honan, William H., ed. *"Fire When Ready, Gridley!" Great Naval Stories from Manila Bay to Vietnam*. New York: St. Martin's Press, 1993. A collection of journalistic accounts of significant naval battles compiled and edited by a reporter for the *New York Times*. Joseph L. Stickney, a reporter for the *New York Herald*, was standing next to Dewey when the admiral ordered the command to fire, and the book includes Stickney's eyewitness account of the Battle of Manila Bay.

Karsten, Peter. *The Naval Aristocracy: The Golden Age of Annapolis and the Emergence of Modern American Navalism*. New York: Free Press, 1972. This is an important book that reexamines the naval officer corps of the late nineteenth century, including the generation of reformers whose projects Dewey sometimes endorsed.

O'Toole, G. J. A. *The Spanish War: An American Epic, 1898*. New York: W. W. Norton, 1984. A very enjoyable popular account.

Potter, E. B., and Chester W. Nimitz, eds. *Sea Power: A Naval History*. Englewood Cliffs, N.J.: Prentice-Hall, 1960. This is the standard textbook on all naval history, used, for example, at the United States Naval Academy. The editors are, respectively, an eminent naval historian and a great World War II admiral.

Spector, Ronald. *Admiral of the New Empire*. Baton Rouge: Louisiana State University Press, 1974. This is the only modern biography of Dewey; fortunately it is a magnificent, albeit brief, account. The author is a very prominent scholar as well as a good stylist. The brevity of his book is a result in part of a lack of existing source material.

Sprout, Harold M., and Margaret Sprout. *The Rise of American Naval Power*. Princeton, N.J.: Princeton University Press, 1946. An older but highly respected survey of American naval history.

Traxel, David. *1898: The Birth of the American Century*. New York: A. A. Knopf, 1998. An analysis of the significant events occurring in 1898, focusing on the Spanish-American War. Traxel describes how the events of that year transformed the United States from a rural, isolationist society to a major world power. The book includes an account of the Battle of Manila Bay and Dewey's heroic reception after his victory.

SEE ALSO: David G. Farragut; William McKinley.

RELATED ARTICLES in *Great Events from History: The Nineteenth Century, 1801-1900:* 1895: Rise of Yellow Journalism; April 24-December 10, 1898: Spanish-American War; February 4, 1899-July 4, 1902: Philippine Insurrection.

MELVIL DEWEY

American librarian

The creator of what has come to be known as the Dewey decimal system of library classification, Dewey was the most original and effective American educator in developing modern library organization and the professional training of librarians.

BORN: December 10, 1851; Adams Center, New York
DIED: December 26, 1931; Lake Placid Club South, Florida
ALSO KNOWN AS: Melville Louis Kossuth Dewey (birth name)
AREA OF ACHIEVEMENT: Education

EARLY LIFE

Melvil Dewey (he changed the spelling of his given name, Melville) grew up in rural upstate New York. Descended from one of the original English settlers in America, Dewey's family was comfortable but not wealthy; their income was based on small properties and business operations. During the first half of the nineteenth century, upstate New York was a center of intense Protestant evangelical zeal and movements for social reform. Reflecting this fervor, Dewey's youthful diaries recorded the beginning of his dedication to reform and concentrated work.

In 1870 Dewey chose to enroll in Amherst College in Massachusetts because it had an innovative curriculum that included physical education. Because of a life-threatening sickness during his youth, Dewey was concerned about maintaining his physical health. Another concern became the use of his time with maximum efficiency. The young man was tall and dark-haired with strong features, especially a prominent chin. Although only an average student, he did nonetheless distinguish himself in mathematics.

It was as a student employee in the Amherst College library that Dewey accomplished the first of a series of historic contributions he would make to librarianship. At that time, books in libraries were arranged by fixed location on shelves. The books were not arranged in relation to each other based on their contents but rather by their placement on a particular shelf in a bookcase. Dewey considered such a system ineffective. In 1873, as a junior, he devised a method for arranging books and other library materials based on subject matter using a system of whole and decimal numbers.

LIFE'S WORK

Upon graduation in 1874, Dewey became head of the Amherst library. He proceeded to apply and refine his decimal classification system, which, in its fundamental principles, is much the same today as it was then. In 1876 he published the first edition of his book on classifying library materials. It became the bible for library cataloging and is now known as the decimal classification and relative index. It was in its twenty-first edition as of 1996. The classification method became known as the Dewey decimal classification (DDC) system and was adopted in later decades by libraries in the United States and throughout the world.

Also in 1876, after meeting and corresponding with some of the leading librarians of the time, Dewey was the key person in organizing the American Library Association (ALA). Its first meeting occurred in Philadelphia, Pennsylvania, and Dewey was elected secretary. He also became managing editor of the association's official publication, the *Library Journal*. In 1878 Dewey married Annie Godfrey, librarian of Wellesley College. They had one son, Godfrey, born in 1887.

Improvements in libraries were only one of several reform movements that engaged Dewey. He was also instrumental in organizing associations for the use of the metric system in the United States and the reform of English spelling. After resigning from Amherst College in 1875, he began a series of businesses for selling supplies, equipment, and publications related to his reform interests. All of these interests had the common goal of using time more efficiently.

In 1883 Dewey was appointed head of the library of Columbia College (now University) in New York City. He quickly moved to reorganize and consolidate its library collection and supervised the construction of a new building. Because of the need for trained personnel for his expanding library work, Dewey established the first library school for the professional training of librarians in 1887, thereby establishing the modern profession of librarianship. This school, however, proved to be a bone of contention to the college administration. Dewey believed that librarianship was a field highly appropriate for "college-bred" women. Columbia, however, did not at the time admit women students. In opposition to this policy, Dewey enrolled women in the inaugural classes of his School of Library Economy. The ensuing controversy caused him to leave the college the following year.

In 1889, Dewey became the state librarian of New York and moved to Albany. In addition, he was made secretary to the board of regents for the University of the State of New York. The latter was not an educational institution but a government agency that supervised educational institutions. He moved his library school with him, renaming it the New York State Library School. As state librarian, Dewey initiated many innovations and presided over extensive growth. He determined that the library should collect not only books but also visual and audio materials. To expand access to materials, he established traveling libraries in book wagons (modern bookmobiles) and began statewide extension services. In addition, he established special services and collections for the blind, for women, for children, and for medicine.

Dewey's position as secretary to the regents had a political dimension that often led him to display a confrontational manner. He entered into conflict with other state officials concerning increased funding for public libraries, extension education, and certification of educational institutions. The bitterness of one of these conflicts forced him to resign as secretary in 1899. He nevertheless remained state librarian.

Dewey and his wife had long dreamed of establishing a recreational club in an area of natural beauty that would foster healthy recreation and cultural improvement. They selected Lake Placid, just north of Albany in the Adirondack Mountains, as the site of this club. The club, formulated in 1893, was meant to congregate the social peers of the Deweys, that is, upper-middle-class Protestant white people of Anglo-Saxon descent. To foster a wholesome atmosphere, the club prohibited or regulated smoking, drinking, gambling, and certain dancing. Furthermore, it prohibited the admission of African Americans and Jews. The latter, a growing ethnic group of rising influence in New York, challenged this prohibition in 1904. They questioned why a state official being paid by taxpayers that included Jews should be allowed to conduct such an exclusionary policy. Because of mounting criticism and controversy, Dewey presented his resignation as state librarian the following year.

Melvil Dewey. (Library of Congress)

Beginning in 1906, Dewey concentrated his attention almost exclusively on development of the Lake Placid Club. Transferring his residence there, Dewey expanded and elaborated its comforts and offerings so that in the following decades it became one of the largest and most famous resorts in the world and the pioneer for winter sports activities. The club hosted the Winter Olympics in 1932.

In 1922 Dewey's wife died; he remarried in 1924. During this decade, comments about intimate relations that Dewey attempted to impose on female colleagues and employees became increasingly open. A former stenographer threatened a lawsuit. In 1926 Dewey began spending his winters in Florida, where he devised the idea of establishing a club resort similar to the one in New York and created Lake Placid South. In 1931, he died in the midst of this endeavor just after his eightieth birthday.

SIGNIFICANCE

With exceptional energy and commitment to a range of educational reforms, Dewey was the single most important influence on the development of the profession of librarianship and the modern organization of libraries. Through his library schools, he created the core of professionals who developed and managed the exceptional infrastructure of libraries in the United States and who influenced the development of librarianship throughout the world.

Dewey's reforming efforts for metric measure and English spelling were not as successful as those for improved libraries. The nonlibrary movements had to struggle against deeply ingrained patterns of behavior and longstanding interests. The library movement, however, was an innovation without entrenched interests to oppose it. Moreover, it had the winds of time behind its sails. There was intense public interest in and support for improved

THE DEWEY DECIMAL SYSTEM

This brief extract from Melvil Dewey's introduction to his first book on the classification of library materials explains part of the rationale behind his complex system.

The selection and arrangement of the thousand headings of the classification cannot be explained in detail for want of space. In all the work, philosophical theory and accuracy have been made to yield to practical usefulness. The impossibility of making a satisfactory classification of all knowledge as preserved in books, has been appreciated from the first, and nothing of the kind attempted. Theoretical harmony and exactness has been repeatedly sacrificed to the practical requirements of the library or to the convenience of the department in the college. As in every scheme, many minor subjects have been put under general heads to which they do not strictly belong. In some cases these headings have been printed in a distinctive type, *e.g.*, 429 = Anglo-Saxon = , under = ENGLISH PHILOLOGY = . The rule has been to assign these subjects to the most nearly allied heads, or where it was thought they would be most useful. The only alternative was to omit them altogether. If any such omission occurs, it is unintentional and will be supplied as soon as discovered. Wherever practicable the heads have been so arranged that each subject is preceded and followed by the most nearly allied subjects and thus the greatest convenience is secured both in the catalogues and on the shelves. Theoretically, the division of every subject into just nine heads is absurd. Practically, it is desirable that the classification be as minute as possible without the use of additional figures, and the decimal principle on which our scheme hinges allows nine divisions as readily as a less number. This principle has proved wholly satisfactory in practice though it appears to destroy proper co-ordination in some places. It has seemed best in our library to use uniformly three figures in the class number. This enables us to classify certain subjects very minutely, giving, for example, an entire section to Chess. But the History of England has only one section, as our scheme is developed, and thus the two might be said to be co-ordinated. The apparent difficulty in such cases is entirely obviated by the use of a fourth figure, giving nine sub-sections to any subject of sufficient importance to warrant closer classification. In history where the classification is made wholly by countries, a fourth figure is added to give a division into *periods*. As the addition of each figure gives a ten-fold division, any desired degree of minuteness may be secured in the classing of special subjects. The apparent lack of co-ordination arises from the fact that only the first three figures of these more important heads are as yet printed, the fourth figure and the sub-sections being supplied on the catalogues in manuscript. Should the growth of any of these sub-sections warrant it, a fifth figure will be added, for the scheme admits of expansion without limit.

Source: Melvil Dewey, *A Classification and Subject Index for Cataloguing and Arranging the Books and Pamphlets of a Library* (Amherst, Mass., 1876).

and expanded educational opportunities, which offered the chance for the rapidly increasing U.S. population to obtain access to the goods and services of an expanding American economy and society. Libraries and librarians were considered vital elements in the educational process.

During Dewey's lifetime, public and college libraries in the United States increased rapidly in number. Steel magnate and philanthropist Andrew Carnegie was responsible at this time for building more than one thousand public libraries throughout the small towns and big cities of the United States. The energy and resolution of Dewey's commitments, however, frequently found him conflicted and overextended. Although known for his efficiency and for having accumulated a small personal fortune, he became mired in situations beyond his limits in terms of time and money. Moreover, in contradiction to the moral and cultural ideals he preached, he would later be judged for serious racist and sexist behavior.

—*Edward A. Riedinger*

FURTHER READING

Beck, Clare. "A 'Private' Grievance Against Dewey." *American Libraries* 27, no. 1 (January, 1996): 62. Based upon her reading of archival letters, Beck learned that a woman librarian at the New York Public Library charged Dewey with making improper advances. The article discusses these allegations and examines what Dewey did for women in library management positions. This is one of three articles about Dewey featured in this issue of *American Libraries*, the journal of the American Library Association. The issue also contains an excerpt from Wayne Wiegand's biography of Dewey (see below) and the recollections of a woman student at Dewey's New York State Library School.

Dawe, Grosvenor. *Melvil Dewey: Seer, Inspirer, Doer, 1851-1931*. Lake Placid, N.Y.: Lake Placid Club, 1932. This biography was published immediately after Dewey's death by the winter sports resort center that he founded and nurtured to world renown. Uncritical and full of high praise, the work is divided into three parts: early development, professional achievements, and a compilation of important writings. The work is extensively illustrated with photographs.

Rider, Fremont. *Melvil Dewey*. Chicago: American Library Association, 1944. The chapters of this slender volume each outline the contributions Dewey made in his various fields of endeavor. While highly praiseworthy of the founder of the ALA, it frankly confronts some of his personality difficulties.

Stevenson, Gordon, and Judith Kramer-Greene, eds. *Melvil Dewey: The Man and the Classification*. Albany, N.Y.: Forest Press, 1983. This work, published by a press founded by Dewey, is a compilation of presentations from a seminar in 1981 sponsored by the New York State Library commemorating the fiftieth anniversary of Dewey's death. Examining Dewey and his legacy from various perspectives, the articles deal with reminiscences about him, his evangelical zeal and ideals, and his work for the development and organizing of the library profession.

Vann, Sarah K., ed. *Melvil Dewey: His Enduring Presence in Librarianship*. Littleton, Colo.: Libraries Unlimited, 1978. The first fifty pages of this work provide a capsule life of Dewey. The remaining two hundred pages are a selection of Dewey's writings on librarianship, libraries, the ALA, education, cataloging, classification, and the future. It also includes a list of his publications.

Wiegand, Wayne A. *A Biography of Melvil Dewey: Irrepressible Reformer*. Chicago: American Library Association, 1996. This book by a noted library history scholar is among the most detailed, frank, and readable works on the life of Dewey. Through extensive archival research, Wiegand demonstrates the origins and methods of Dewey's thought and activities. Because of its candor and thoroughness, the book escapes an older mold among librarians of canonizing Dewey and stands as a singular contribution to understanding the complexities and contradictions of the man.

SEE ALSO: Andrew Carnegie.

RELATED ARTICLE in *Great Events from History: The Nineteenth Century, 1801-1900:* May 10-November 10, 1876: Philadelphia Hosts the Centennial Exposition.

PORFIRIO DÍAZ

President of Mexico (1876-1880, 1884-1911)

During more than three decades as president of Mexico, Díaz developed his nation's economy by encouraging foreign investment that brought major railroad construction and expanded the mining industry and oil production, but this success came at a great cost to the average citizen. Corruption was rampant during his administration and the extent of foreign control of Mexican land and resources was unprecedented.

BORN: September 15, 1830; Oaxaca, Mexico

DIED: July 2, 1915; Paris, France

ALSO KNOWN AS: José de la Cruz Porfirio Díaz (full name)

AREA OF ACHIEVEMENT: Government and politics

EARLY LIFE

José de la Cruz Porfirio Díaz (DEE-as) was born into a Mexican family of modest means. His parents operated a small inn, while his father worked as blacksmith to supplement their income. Díaz's father died while he was still young, and his mother was forced to sell the inn. The young Díaz and his siblings were forced to work at whatever jobs they could find. His mother wanted him to become a priest, but he left his seminary to study law. However, his public criticisms of government policies and accusations of corrupt electoral politics were resented by President Antonio López de Santa Anna, and he was not allowed to practice law upon completing his studies.

Fearing imprisonment for his continued criticism of Santa Anna, Díaz became a guerrilla fighter on the side of the Liberal Party faction that was trying to overthrow the government. When the Liberals captured Oaxaca in 1855, Díaz was rewarded with a minor government post. He used the position to create a political base that would later support him in his own political and military endeavors. Meanwhile, as the civil war progressed, Díaz rose in the military ranks, serving as a governor and eventually as a brigadier general. When it appeared that the Liberals had won the civil war, members of the Conservative Party invited the French government to establish a monarchy in Mexico. Díaz and his army temporarily stopped the French army at the Battle of Puebla on May 5, 1862—a date still celebrated as Cinco de Mayo—but the French regrouped and eventually took Mexico City.

Díaz passionately fought against the armies of France until he was captured in 1865. No prison could hold him, however, and he escaped. After he rebuilt his army, Díaz marched victoriously into Mexico City, effectively ending any possibility of a French empire in the country. Now a national hero and a frontrunner for the presidency, Díaz retired from the military to campaign for the 1871 presidential election.

Díaz's presidential hopes were dashed in what turned out to be another corrupt election, this time by his former friend President Benito Juárez. Angry and outraged by what he called "the forced, and violent reelection" of Juárez, Díaz began organizing to overthrow the government. Over the next four years, he quietly organized a private army, consolidated his strong position with leaders of the Roman Catholic Church in Mexico, and reassured anti-Juárez Conservatives that he would serve their interests. When Sebastian Lerdo de Tejada, Juárez's former vice president, declared victory in the presidential election of 1876, Díaz overthrew the government and declared himself president.

Porfirio Díaz. (Library of Congress)

LIFE'S WORK

Except for a single four-year term during which his friend Manuel Gonzalez held the title of president, Díaz served as president of Mexico from 1876 until 1911. After campaigning in favor of term limits in 1876, he decided it was probably a politically wise move to seek election in 1880. However, after he was again elected in 1884, he began to reveal his own corrupt nature and amended the national constitution so he could remain in office.

Díaz ruled by rewarding his friends and killing his enemies. Those who supported him were rewarded with bribes, appointments to public office, promotions, and pensions. Through the Liberal Party organization in each state, Díaz controlled government at every level. In an effort to maintain control of the army he divided Mexico into military zones, rotating generals among the zones to prevent them from building independent power bases that might threaten his hold on the central government. The army, which he reduced in size considerably after 1876, was led by men personally loyal to him. Taking kickbacks from gambling, prostitution, and other lucrative criminal endeavors allowed Díaz and his supports to acquire massive wealth while most of the poor of the country lived in squalor. The national army suppressed riots and rebellions led by opponents who demanded reforms.

Although Díaz ruled by force, he could not have remained in power as long as he did had he failed to expand Mexico's economy. The United States and European nations turned a blind eye to the excesses of his dictatorship, so long as he protected and encouraged entrepreneurs from their countries. By encouraging foreign investment, which brought considerable capital into the country, he paid off Mexico's national debt and balanced the national budget for the first time in Mexican history. He revised real estate, banking, and labor laws to make the country more attractive to foreign investors. He also amended the constitution to allow foreigners to own mineral and oil rights, thus opening mines and oil fields to foreign ownership.

During Díaz's presidency, foreign investors owned much of the nation's resources. New railroad construction increased the total mileage of tracks from fewer than four hundred to more than twelve thousand miles between 1876 and 1910. Foreign investors also built telephone and telegraph companies throughout Mexico, expanded the mining industry, built entirely new factories, and established Mexico as an exporter of oil. Foreigners made vast fortunes, but resentment against their wealth and increasing influence fostered political unrest and led to the eventual downfall of Díaz.

The Mexican Revolution of 1910, which brought an end to the corrupt Díaz regime, was led by presidential candidate Francisco I. Madero, a member of one of Mexico's most prominent families. Just as Díaz had done many years earlier, Madero called on voters to rid Mexico of electoral fraud and demand limits on years in office for politicians. However, Díaz controlled the electoral process, the military, and almost everything else in Mexico. When his government announced the results of the 1910 presidential election, Díaz claimed that he had received one million votes and that Madero had received only 196 votes. The electoral fraud was so obvious that even international observers questioned the validity of the election returns. Meanwhile, Madero and his supporters feared for their lives and fled to the United States, where Madero issued the Plan de San Luis Potosí, which declared him the legitimate president of Mexico.

Within a few months, Emiliano Zapata, Pascual Orozco, and Pancho Villa were leading armies in open revolt against Díaz. The national militia found itself unable to suppress the rebellions springing up throughout the countryside. Díaz desperately tried to negotiate with Madero, promising reforms if he were allowed to remain in office, but this attempt only encouraged his opponents and intensified the political crisis. Finally, fearing for his own life, Díaz resigned in May, 1911, and fled to France, where he died five years later.

SIGNIFICANCE

Porfirio Díaz is now considered by historians to have been one of the most ruthless and corrupt dictators in modern history. Although he was admired by other Latin American dictators of his time for his ability to hold power for more than thirty years, his legacy of cruelty, corruption, and selling the resources of his nation to foreigners places him among the ranks of the most despised men in the history of Latin America. Nevertheless, he is also in large part responsible for developing Mexico's modern economy and helping to bring that nation into the twentieth century.

—Donald C. Simmons, Jr.

FURTHER READING

Beals, Carleton. *Porfirio Díaz: Dictator of Mexico*. Philadelphia: J. B. Lippincott, 1932. This book contains almost endless amounts of information but it is painfully difficult to read. However, its 126 illustrations make the book worth consulting.

Garner, Paul. *Porfirio Díaz*. London: Longman, 2001. The text is an excellent political biography that deals primarily with the economic development of Mexico under Díaz. The chapter on Díaz's approach to foreign policy is especially insightful. Includes an excellent glossary, bibliographical essay, chronology, and map of Mexico in the Díaz era.

Gil, Carlos B., ed. *The Age of Porfirio Díaz: Selected Readings*. Albuquerque: University of New Mexico Press, 1977. Primarily concerned with the economic and political development of Mexico during the reign of Díaz, this collection of essays focuses on labor and social reforms of Díaz's era.

Gonzales, Michael J. *The Mexican Revolution, 1910-1940*. Albuquerque: University of New Mexico Press, 2002. Broad history of the Mexican Revolution that opens with a discussion of the forces leading to Díaz's overthrow.

Magner, James A. *Men of Mexico*. Freeport, N.Y.: Books for Libraries Press, 1968. The chapter on the life of Díaz is one of the best brief overviews of Díaz's life in print.

Tischendorf, Alfred. *Great Britain and Mexico in the Era of Porfirio Díaz*. Durham, N.C.: Duke University Press, 1961. Study focusing on economic and diplomatic relations between Mexico and Great Britain during the age of Díaz.

Villegas, Daniel Cosio. *The United States Versus Porfirio Díaz*. Translated by Nettie Lee Benson. Lincoln: University of Nebraska Press, 1963. Study of American-Mexican relations that exposes Díaz's contradictory positions on foreign investment in Mexico.

Zayas Enriquez, Raphael de. *Porfirio Díaz*. Translated by T. Quincy Browne, Jr. New York: D. Appleton, 1908. Written by a longtime friend of Díaz and member of the Mexican congress while Díaz was still in power, this book does an exceptional job of objectively analyzing the life of the dictator and providing striking contemporary insights into the final days of Díaz's reign. Contains wonderful period photos of the president and his wife.

SEE ALSO: Fanny Calderón de la Barca; Benito Juárez; Maximilian; Antonio López de Santa Anna.

RELATED ARTICLE in *Great Events from History: The Nineteenth Century, 1801-1900:* October 31, 1861-June 19, 1867: France Occupies Mexico.